Time Period	Important Philosophers (placed in period of main contribution)	Political, Cultural, and [...]
1000 A.D.	Anselm (1033–1109) Abelard (1079–1142) Averroes (1125–1198) Maimonides (1125–1204) Albert the Great (1206–1280) Roger Bacon (1214–1292) Thomas Aquinas (1225–1274) Duns Scotus (c. 1266–1308) William of Ockham (c. 1285–1349) Nicholas of Cusa (c. 1400–1464)	Sung Dynasty (960–1279[...] replaced by Mongol Dynasty (12[...]) Genghis Khan (Mongol) invades Russia (1222) Crusades (1096–1204) drive Muslims from Palestine Renaissance begins in Italy (1215) Dante (1265–1321) writes *Divine Comedy* (1307–1321) Black Death ravages Europe (1347) Chaucer (1340–1400) writes *Canterbury Tales* (c. 1390) Gutenberg prints *Bible* (1453) Turks capture Constantinople (1453) Columbus sails to New World (1492)
1500 A.D.	D. Erasmus (1465–1536) N. Machiavelli (1469–1527) Thomas More (1478–1535) M. E. Montaigne (1516–1592) Francisco Suarez (1548–1607)	da Vinci (1452–1519) paints *Mona Lisa* Michelangelo (1475–1564) sculpts *Pieta* and *David* Copernicus (1473–1543) puts sun at center of universe Luther (1483–1546) begins Protestant Reformation Elizabeth I crowned Queen of England (1558) Spanish Conquistadores defeat Aztecs of Mexico (1519–1524)
1600 A.D.	Francis Bacon (1561–1626) Thomas Hobbes (1588–1679) René Descartes (1596–1650) Anne Conway (1631–1679) Baruch Spinoza (1632–1677) Nicolas de Malebranche (1638–1715) Gottfried Leibniz (1646–1716) William Paley (1743–1805)	Shakespeare (1564–1616) writes plays and poems Kepler (1571–1630) discovers laws of planetary motion Galileo (1564–1642) condemned by Inquisition (1633) Age of Enlightenment begins in Europe (c. 1641) Civil War in England (1642) Leibniz invents the calculus (1675) Witchcraft trials in Salem, Massachusetts (1692) Manchu Dynasty (1644–1911) rules in China
1700 A.D.	John Locke (1632–1704) George Berkeley (1685–1753) Voltaire (1694–1778) Julien de La Mettrie (1709–1751) David Hume (1711–1776) Paul d'Holbach (1723–1789) Immanuel Kant (1724–1804) Edmund Burke (1729–1797) Jeremy Bentham (1748–1832) Mary Wollstonecraft (1759–1797) William Whewell (1794–1866)	Newton (1642–1727) publishes *Principia* (1687) Mendel (1822–1884) develops laws of heredity Laplace (1749–1827) writes *Celestial Mechanics* (1799) Swift (1667–1745) publishes *Gulliver's Travels* (1726) Bach (1685–1750), Handel (1685–1759) compose music American Revolution (1775–1783) Smith (1723–1790) writes *Wealth of Nations* (1776) Industrial Revolution in England (1780) French Revolution (1789–1791) Mozart (1756–1791), Beethoven (1770–1827) compose symphonies

Philosophy
A Text with Readings

SEVENTH EDITION

MANUEL VELASQUEZ

The Charles Dirksen Professor
Santa Clara University

Wadsworth Publishing Company

I(T)P® An International Thomson Publishing Company

Belmont, CA • Albany, NY • Bonn • Boston • Cincinnati • Detroit • Johannesburg
London • Madrid • Melbourne • Mexico City • New York • Paris
Singapore • Tokyo • Toronto • Washington

For my wife and children
Maryanne, Brian, Kevin, and Daniel

PHILOSOPHY EDITOR: *Peter Adams*
ASSISTANT EDITOR: *Kerri Abdinoor*
MARKETING MANAGER: *Dave Garrison*
PRINT BUYER: *Stacey Weinberger*
PERMISSIONS EDITOR: *Susan Walters*
PRODUCTION: *The Book Company*

COPY EDITOR: *Donald Pharr*
ILLUSTRATOR: *Impact*
COVER DESIGN: *Carolyn Deacy*
COVER IMAGE: *Waterfalls, Brenda Tharp, Photo Researchers, Inc.*
COMPOSITOR: *G & S Typesetters, Inc.*
PRINTER: *R. R. Donnelley & Sons, Crawfordsville, IN*

Printed in the United States of America
6 7 8 9 10

Art Acknowledgments are on page 699.

For more information, contact Wadsworth Publishing Company, 10 Davis Drive, Belmont, CA 94002, or electronically
at http://www.wadsworth.com

International Thomson Publishing Europe
Berkshire House
168-173 High Holborn
London, WC1V 7AA, United Kingdom

International Thomson Editores
Seneca, 53
Colonia Polanco
11560 México D.F. México

Nelson ITP, Australia
102 Dodds Street
South Melbourne
Victoria 3205 Australia

International Thomson Publishing Asia
60 Albert Street #15-01
Albert Complex
Singapore 189969

Nelson Canada
1120 Birchmount Road
Scarborough, Ontario
Canada M1K 5G4

International Thomson Publishing Japan
Hirakawa-cho Kyowa Building, 3F
2-2-1 Hirakawa-cho, Chiyoda-ku
Tokyo 102 Japan

International Thomson Publishing Southern Africa
Building 18, Constantia Square
138 Sixteenth Road, P.O. Box 2459
Halfway House, 1685 South Africa

Library of Congress Cataloging-in-Publication Data

Velasquez, Manuel G.
    Philosophy, a text with readings / Manuel Velasquez.— 7th ed.
      p.   cm.
    Includes bibliographical references and index.
    ISBN 0-534-55211-0
     1. Philosophy—Introductions.   I. Title.
BD21.V4 1999
100—dc21

98-28138

♺ *This book is printed on acid-free recycled paper.*

100   Donation
Vel $41.98

Contents

Preface to the Seventh Edition

NEW VIDEO SERIES: "THE EXAMINED LIFE"

A new series of videos for television has been produced to accompany the seventh edition of *Philosophy: A Text with Readings*. Entitled "The Examined Life," the 26 half-hour videos cover most (but not all) of the topics treated in this edition and move in sequence through each section of each chapter. Each video consists of interviews with contemporary philosophers, dramatizations, historical footage of well-known philosophers, discussions of classical philosophical texts, and visual interpretations of key philosophical concepts. Among the more than 100 philosophers newly interviewed for this video series are: W. V. O. Quine, Hilary Putnam, John Searle, James Rachels, Martha Nussbaum, Marilyn Friedman, Hans Gadamer, Gary Watson, Susan Wolf, Peter Singer, Michael Sandel, Daniel Dennet, Ronald Dworkin, and many others.

Instructors, universities, and colleges interested in previewing, renting, licensing, or acquiring these videos should contact the producer of the video series: INTELECOM, Intelligent Telecommunication; 150 East Colorado Blvd, Suite 300; Pasadena, CA 91105-1937. INTELECOM may also be reached by telephone at (626) 796-7300; by FAX at (626) 577-4282; and through its web site at http://www.intelecom.org

I have heard philosophers suggest that the very nature of time as a human experience is undergoing radical change as the social processes that constitute our cultural world move through their cycles with accelerating rapidity. Trends, fashions, fads, styles, technologies, political movements, and, yes, philosophies, are born, grow, flourish, wither, and are quickly succeeded by their novel replacements in ever shorter calendar periods, generating a sense that time is speeding up. Some claim that the increasing pace of change has profound implications for philosophy. Whether or not this is so, rapid change forces revisions of a more mundane sort in textbooks on philosophy such as this. So although *Philosophy: A Text with Readings* continues to get students excited about philosophy without sacrificing depth or rigor, the swift changes in the world our students inhabit necessitated revising the text once again. I have tried to enhance what users say they like best: that this book is easy to read, fun to use, and manages to cover all the traditional issues with a unique combination of attention to the history of philosophy, a regard for interesting contemporary concerns, and substantial selections from classic and contemporary texts. But I have made numerous revisions and introduced changes to ensure the text remains up-to-date, continues to meet teachers' needs, and provides a substantive yet delightful experience of philosophy for the reader who wonders what we and our rapidly changing world are all about.

CHANGES IN THE SEVENTH EDITION

Every chapter of this edition incorporates new material or extensively rewritten material. The main changes are as follows.

Chapter 1 has been rewritten to simplify its style and enhance its readability; Section 1.3 on

Socrates has been expanded to include a discussion of a new passage from *The Republic*.

Chapter 2 has been extensively revised, rewritten, and reorganized. The introduction to Chapter 2 is considerably shorter. Section 2.2 has been retitled and expanded to include new passages from Plato's *Phaedrus*, from Aristotle's *Nicomachean Ethics*, from Augustine's *Confessions*, and from Aquinas's *Summa Contra Gentiles*. A key new concept introduced is the teleological features of the traditional concepts of human nature. Section 2.2 also includes an entirely new discussion of Darwinian evolution (which particularly challenges the teleological conception of human nature) while the previous edition's discussion of Skinner's now somewhat dated behaviorism has been dropped and the materials on Hume and Buddhist "no-self" views have been moved into a new section 2.4 later in the chapter. Section 2.3 is a new section on the mind–body problem that brings together materials that were scattered throughout Chapters 2 and 4 of the previous edition. This new section 2.3 discusses dualism, identity theory, behaviorism, functionalism, and computer theories of mind, ending with a discussion of the Turing test and Searle's "Chinese Room" counter example. Section 2.4 is a new section on personal identity that discusses the views of Descartes, Locke, and the "no-self" views of Hume and Buddhism. Section 2.5 is also a new section on what some call the "atomistic" notion of the self, but that is here characterized as the notion of the "independent and self-sufficient individual." This section discusses Hegel's opposing views on "recognition" and some of the ideas of the Canadian philosopher Charles Taylor. The readings by Evans and Searle that were at the end of Chapter 2 have been dropped since their subject matter is now incorporated into the main text.

The previous edition's Chapter 3 on God and Chapter 4 on metaphysics have been switched in this new edition. Chapter 3 is now on metaphysics and Chapter 4 is now the Chapter on God. This sequence seemed to make more sense since the discussions on dualism and human nature in Chapter 2 seemed to flow more naturally into the metaphysical discussions of materialism and idealism now in Chapter 3.

This newly-positioned **Chapter 3** on metaphysics has been considerably revised and simplified. Section 3.1 is largely unchanged. The materials on identity theory and teleology in 3.2 have been moved into Chapter 2 and new passages from Berkeley have been added. The discussion of pragmatism in section 3.3 has been shortened and simplified, and the discussion of analytic philosophy in 3.4 has also been shortened and simplified. The discussions of phenomenology and existentialism, formerly in section 3.5, have been moved to section 3.6, and simplified, primarily by omitting a discussion of Nietzsche (whose views are still covered in the "Historical Showcase" at the end of Chapter 7). Section 3.7 is a new section on determinism, indeterminism, and compatibalism that brings together materials that had been scattered throughout Chapter 2 in the previous edition. Section 3.8 is a completely new discussion of the reality of time.

Chapter 4, on God and religion, remains largely unchanged, apart from a new discussion of the "big bang" and its relation to the cosmological argument in section 4.2 and the addition of Freud and Kant's views on God at the end of section 4.3. The readings by Cone and Christ have been dropped from the end-of-chapter readings in Chapter 4.

Chapter 5 has been rewritten to improve its readability. Section 5.2 includes a completely new discussion of innate ideas. Section 5.4, on Kant, has been completely rewritten and expanded to include discussion of constructivist theories after Kant. The discussion of Locke has been dropped from the "Historical Showcase" in section 5.7 since his views seem to be adequately covered in the main text of this chapter and of Chapter 8.

Chapter 6 also has been extensively rewritten. Section 6.2 has a new introduction that better motivates the discussion of theories of truth that follows. The discussion of instrumentalism in section 6.3 has been expanded. Section 6.4 is an entirely new section discussing truth in the humanities, with a particular focus on hermeneutics.

Chapter 7, while covering essentially the same material, has been reorganized. Introductory section 7.1 has been extensively rewritten, shortened, and simplified. Section 7.2 has been simplified and focuses solely on the issue of ethical relativism. Section 7.3, which is devoted to nonconsequentialist theories of ethics, now includes a discussion of Kant, which the previous edition had positioned as separate section 7.5, and a discussion of Buddhist ethics, which in the previous edition was separate section 7.6. The discussion of Mill has been dropped from the "Historical Showcase" in section 7.9 since his views are adequately covered in the main text of this and the following chapter.

Chapter 8 has been considerably reorganized. After an introductory section, the chapter now begins with a discussion of social contract theory in section 8.2. This section includes new discussions of Rawls's social contract ideas and of communitarianism. Section 8.3 is a completely rewritten and greatly expanded discussion of justice. The section on "government control" from the previous edition has been dropped since much (but not all) of this material is now incorporated into sections 8.2 and 8.3. The discussions on King and Gandhi have been dropped from the "Historical Showcase" at the end of the chapter since the essentials of their views are covered in the main text.

Chapter 9 is a completely new concluding chapter on two topics that are loosely related to each other: art and the meaning of life. While presenting all new material, this chapter is intended to recapitulate some of the discussions in earlier chapters.

ORGANIZATION

Self-discovery and autonomy remain the central notions around which this edition is organized (although these notions are criticized in Chapter 2). Each chapter repeatedly returns to these notions and links the materials discussed to the reader's growth in self-knowledge and intellectual autonomy. Each chapter, however, is sufficiently self-contained that instructors can assign chapters in whatever order they choose and may omit whatever chapters they wish.

Although the text is organized by topics, the chapters still have been arranged in a roughly historical order. The book opens with a lively introductory chapter on the nature of philosophy that focuses on Socrates as exemplar of philosophy and includes substantial selections from the Socratic

dialogues. Because of the book's focus on the self, the intrinsic importance of the topic, and because human nature was an important concern from the earliest time of philosophy, we turn immediately in Chapter 2 to the discussion of human nature, a discussion that raises several issues more fully treated in later chapters. Then, because Chapter 2 raises many metaphysical and religious issues, we turn to metaphysical issues in Chapter 3 and then to discussions of God and religion in Chapter 4. These issues, of course, were of passionate concern during the medieval and early modern periods of philosophy. Chapters 5 and 6 focus on questions of epistemology, which historically followed on the heels of the early modern interest in metaphysical issues. Chapters 7 and 8 are devoted respectively to ethics and social philosophy, topics that have preoccupied many philosophers during the late modern and contemporary periods. Chapter 9, the final chapter, focuses on art and the meaning of life, issues that have become particularly prominent during the contemporary period.

But no historical period has a monopoly on any of these topics. Consequently, each chapter moves back and forth from classic historical discussions of issues to contemporary discussions of the same or related issues. The chapter on metaphysics, for example, moves from the early modern controversy between materialism and idealism, to current discussions of antirealism that harken back to idealism.

SPECIAL FEATURES

This text is unique in many ways and includes the following special features:

1. **Historical Showcases.** Substantial summaries of the life and thought of major philosophers, including female and non-Western philosophers, are placed near the end of each chapter. These historical discussions feature large selections from the works of philosophers who have addressed the issues treated in the chapter. Arranged in chronological order, the Historical Showcases provide a clear and readable overview of the history of philosophy and enables students to see philosophy as a "great conversation" across centuries.

2. Philosophical readings by twentieth-century philosophers. Every chapter contains highly accessible readings examining a philosophical question raised in the text. These questions are as diverse as "Should actual events affect religious belief?" "Do we have moral obligations toward animals?" and "Is the use of force ever justified?"

3. Literature readings. At the end of every chapter is a short selection of literature that raises the issues discussed in the chapter. These readings provide a friendly entry into philosophy for readers who are unaccustomed to traditional philosophical style.

4. Many "Philosophy and Life" discussions scattered throughout the text. These inserts show the impact of philosophy on everyday life or its interesting connections to current issues, such as animal rights, medical dilemmas, sociobiology, psychology, and science.

5. Marginal "Critical Thinking" boxes. These boxes help the reader identify and criticize the underlying assumptions on which the arguments in the text depend.

6. Extended selections from primary sources. Primary source material is included not only in all the Historical Showcases but is liberally introduced into the main text, where it is always carefully explained. To make these materials accessible to beginning undergraduates, new, simplified translations of several texts (Plato, Aristotle, Aquinas, and others) have been prepared and several standard translations (such as Max Mueller's translation of Kant) have been simplified and edited.

7. Section on logic. The major aspects of formal and informal logic are introduced in an appendix to Chapter 1. This appendix includes a step-by-step method of analyzing philosophical arguments.

8. Chapter bibliographies. At the end of each chapter is an annotated list of works that expand on the themes of the chapter.

9. End-of-section questions. To encourage students to think philosophically, questions and ex- ercises are provided at the end of every section within a chapter.

10. Main points. Each chapter ends with a summary of the main points that have been covered, which is helpful as a review.

11. Modular organization. To ease understanding, each chapter is divided into numbered sections organized as modules that can be assigned for single class meetings.

12. Marginal definitions and glossary of terms. Unfamiliar philosophical terminology is explained in the text and defined in the margin; the definitions are collected in an alphabetized glossary at the end of the book for easy reference.

13. Historical time line. On the inside of the front and back of the cover is a time line that locates each philosopher in his or her historical context.

I have always found that working to revise this text is an enormously satisfying and exciting experience because of the new perspectives and ideas it leads me to confront. I hope that readers will be just as excited by their explorations and journeys into these many visions of what it is to be a human being in today's changing world.

ACKNOWLEDGMENTS

For their helpful comments and suggestions on the revision of this and earlier editions of the text, I offer sincere thanks to Ronald Barnette, Valdosta State University; David Crawford, University of Detroit Mercy; Timothy Davis, Essex Community College; Anis Deeb, Truckee Meadow Community College; Anne DeWindt, Wayne County Community College; Emily Dial-Driver, Rogers State College; Garth Gillan, Southern Illinois University at Carbondale; Cynthia Kirchoff, Pennsylvania State University, Harrisburg; Achim Koddermann, State University of New York College at Oneonta; Isabel Luengo, Mira Costa College; Jennifer McErlean, Siena College; Thomas R. Ryckman, Lawrence University; and Wanda Teays, Mount Saint Mary's College.

PART I

Introduction

The word *philosophy* comes from the Greek words *philein*, meaning "to love," and *sophia*, meaning "wisdom." Philosophy is the love of wisdom. It is the pursuit of wisdom about what it means to be a human being, what the fundamental nature of God and reality is, what the sources and limits of our knowledge are, and what is good and right in our lives and in our societies.

This book is divided into four parts. In this first part we devote the initial chapter to looking more closely at what philosophy is and the second chapter to discussing what it is to be a human being. We begin with these topics because they raise fundamental issues that affect our overall approach to the study of philosophy. Part II contains chapters examining our basic beliefs about reality and God. The third part is composed of a chapter on knowledge and a chapter on truth. The fourth part contains a chapter on ethics and one on the normative issues raised by life in society. We close with a chapter on art and the meaning of life.

CHAPTER 1

The Nature of Philosophy

The feeling of wonder is the mark of the philosopher, for all philosophy has its origins in wonder.

PLATO

Philosophy traditionally has been nothing less than the attempt to ask and answer, in a formal and disciplined way, the great questions of life that ordinary men put to themselves in reflective moments.

TIME MAGAZINE, 7 JANUARY 1966

1.1 Introduction: What Is Philosophy?

Philosophy begins with wonder. Although many of us know very little about the jargon and history of philosophy, we have all been touched by the feeling of wonder with which philosophy begins. We wonder about why we are here; about who we really are; about whether God exists and what She or He is like; why pain, evil, sorrow, and separation exist; why a close friend was killed; whether science tells us all there really is to know about the universe, or whether intuition and feeling open us to realms of experience and reality that science cannot grasp; whether there is life after death; what true love and friendship are; what the proper balance is between serving others and serving ourselves; whether moral right and wrong are based merely on personal opinion; and whether suicide, abortion, or euthanasia is ever justified.

This wondering and questioning begin early in our lives. Almost as soon as children learn to talk, they ask questions: Where did I come from? Where do people go when they die? What's beyond the sky? How did the world start? Who made God? Why are one and one two and not three? From the very beginning of our lives, we start to ask the questions that make up philosophy.

Although philosophy begins with wonder and questions, it does not end there. Philosophy tries to go beyond the standard answers to these questions that we may have received when we were too young to seek our own answers. The goal of philosophy is to get us to answer these questions for ourselves—to make up our own minds about our self, life, knowledge, art, religion, and morality without simply depending on the authority of parents, peers, television, teachers, or society.

Many of our religious, political, and moral beliefs are beliefs that we accepted as children long before we could question them or understand the reasons behind them. Philosophy examines these beliefs. The aim is not to reject them but to learn why we hold them and to ask whether there are good reasons to continue holding them. In this way our basic beliefs about reality and life become our own: We accept them because we have thought them through on our own, not because our parents, peers, and society have conditioned us to believe them. In this way we gain a kind of independence and freedom, or what some modern philosophers call autonomy. The goal of philosophy, then, is

The unexamined life is not worth living.
SOCRATES

We can help one another to find out the meaning of life, no doubt. But in the last analysis the individual person is responsible for living his own life and for "finding himself." Others can give you a name or a number, but they can never tell you who you really are. That is something you yourself can only discover from within.
THOMAS MERTON

It was philosophical reflection that brought me to the conclusion that our evidence for what we have been told in a religious way—of creation and salvation and all that— needed more evidence.
W. V. O. QUINE

Plato: **"And the climb upward out of the cave into the upper world is the ascent of the mind into the domain of true knowledge."**

autonomy: the freedom of being able to decide for yourself what you will believe in by using your own reasoning abilities.

Plato, one of the earliest and greatest Western philosophers, illustrated how philosophy aims at freedom with his famous parable the Myth of the Cave. The Myth of the Cave is a story Plato tells in *The Republic*, his classic philosophical work on justice. Here is an edited and simplified translation of the Myth of the Cave, which Plato wrote in his native Greek:

> Now let me describe the human situation in a parable about ignorance and learning. Imagine there are men living at the bottom of an underground cave whose entrance is a long passageway that rises through the ground to the light outside. They have been there since childhood and have their legs and necks chained so that they cannot move. The chains hold their heads so that they must sit facing the back wall of the cave and cannot turn their heads to look up through the entrance behind them. At some distance behind them, up nearer the entrance to the cave, a fire is burning. Objects pass in front of the fire so that they cast their shadows on the back wall where the prisoners see the moving shadows projected as if on a screen. All kinds of objects parade before the fire, including statues of men and animals whose shadows dance on the wall in front of the prisoners.
>
> Those prisoners are like ourselves. The prisoners see nothing of themselves or each other except the shadows each one's body casts on the back wall of the cave. Similarly, they see nothing of the objects behind them, except their shadows moving on the wall.
>
> Now imagine the prisoners could talk with each other. Suppose their voices echoed off the wall so that the voices seem to come from their own shadows. Then wouldn't they talk about these shadows as if the shadows were real? For the prisoners, reality would consist of nothing but the shadows.

autonomy the freedom of being able to decide for oneself by using one's own rationality

Plato is philosophy and philosophy Plato.
RALPH WALDO EMERSON

Next imagine that one prisoner was freed from his chains. Suppose he was suddenly forced to stand up and turn toward the entrance of the cave. Suppose he was forced to walk up toward the burning fire. The movement would be painful, and the glare from the fire would blind him so that he would not see clearly the real objects whose shadows he used to watch. What would he think if someone explained that everything he had seen before was an illusion, that now he was nearer to reality and that his vision was actually clearer?

Imagine he was then shown the objects that had cast their shadows on the wall and he was asked to name each one—wouldn't he be at a complete loss? Wouldn't he think the shadows he saw before were more true than these objects?

Next imagine he was forced to look straight at the burning light. His eyes would hurt. The pain would make him turn away and try to return to things he could see more easily. He would think that those things were more real than the new things they were showing him.

But suppose that once more someone takes him and drags him up the steep and rugged ascent from the cave. Suppose someone forces him out into the full light of the sun. Won't he suffer greatly and be furious at being dragged upward? As he approaches the light his eyes will be dazzled and he won't be able to see any of this world we ourselves call reality. Little by little he will have to get used to looking at the upper world. At first he will see shadows on the ground best, next perhaps the reflections of men and other objects in water, and then maybe the objects themselves. After this he would find it easier to gaze at the light of the moon and the stars in the night sky than to look at the daylight sun and its light. Last of all he will be able to look at the sun and contemplate its nature. He will not just look at its reflection in water but will see it as it is in itself and in its own domain. He will come to the conclusion that the sun produces the seasons and the years and that it controls everything in the visible world. He will understand that it is in a way the cause of everything that he and his fellow prisoners used to see.

Suppose the released prisoner now recalled the cave and what passed for wisdom among his fellows there. Wouldn't he be happy about his new situation and feel sorry for them? They might have been in the habit of honoring those among themselves who were quickest to make out the shadows and those who could remember which usually came before others so that they were best at predicting the course of the shadows. Would he care about such honors and glories or would he envy those who won them? Wouldn't he rather endure anything than go back to thinking and living like they did?

Finally, imagine that the released prisoner was taken from the light and brought back into the cave to his old seat. His eyes would be full of darkness. Now he would have to compete in discerning the shadows with the prisoners who had never left the cave while his own eyes were still dim. Wouldn't he appear ridiculous? Men would say of him that he had gone up and had come back down with his eyesight ruined and that it was better not even to think of ascending. In fact, if they caught anyone trying to free them and lead them up to the light, they would try to kill him.

I say, now, that the prison is the world we see with our eyes; the light of the fire is like the power of our sun. The climb upward out of the cave into the upper world is the ascent of the mind into the domain of true knowledge.[1]

> **CRITICAL THINKING**
> Does Plato assume that it is better to know the truth and be unhappy than to be happy but ignorant? Would this assumption be correct?

---

[1] Plato, *The Republic*, from bk. 7. This translation copyright © 1987 by Manuel Velasquez.

Plato wrote this intriguing parable more than two thousand years ago. The parable is important for us because it explains much about what philosophy is. First, in the parable, philosophy is the activity of journeying upward from the dark cave to the light. That is, philosophy is an activity. In this respect it differs from other academic subjects. Unlike some other subjects, philosophy does not consist of a lot of information or theories. True, philosophers have developed many theories and views. However, philosophical theories are the products of philosophy, not philosophy itself. While studying philosophy, of course, you will be asked to study the theories of several important philosophers. But the point of studying them is not just to memorize them. You will study them, instead, as an aid to help you learn how to "do" philosophy. By seeing how the best philosophers have "done" philosophy and by considering their views and theories, you can better understand what philosophizing is. More important, you can use their insights to shed light on your own philosophical journey. It's the journey—the activity—that's important, though, not the products you bring back from your journey.

Philosophy is not a theory but an activity.
LUDWIG WITTGENSTEIN

In philosophy there are no facts. It is all just arguing, thinking, reasoning.
W. D. HART

PHILOSOPHY AND LIFE

Groupthink

The psychologist Irving Janis has coined the term *groupthink* to refer to the tendency of cohesive groups to get increasingly out of touch with reality. Janis studied how numerous political leaders and their close advisors made decisions that were spectacularly out of touch with reality, including (1) the Japanese decision to attack the United States at Pearl Harbor; (2) President Truman's decision to escalate the Korean War; (3) President Kennedy's decision to invade Cuba at the Bay of Pigs; (4) President Johnson's decision to escalate the Vietnam War; and (5) President Nixon's decision to launch a cover-up of the Watergate break-in. Janis found that "the social pressures that develop in cohesive groups," particularly the desire "to preserve friendly intragroup relations," lead

such groups to develop an "us-versus-them" mentality that gradually distorts their ability to evaluate their situation realistically. Symptoms of such groupthink include an "illusion of the group's invulnerability"; a "belief in the inherent morality of the group" and its activities; "collective rationalization" that discounts any outside information that might conflict with the group's assumptions; "stereotypes" of outsiders and critics as weak, stupid, or evil; "direct pressure on dissenters" within the group; "self-censorship" that leads each member to discount his or her own doubts about the group's beliefs and assumptions; the "illusion of unanimity" within the group; and the emergence of "self-appointed mind-guards" who protect the group from any contrary outside information

that might shatter their comfortable assumptions.

QUESTIONS

1. What aspects of Plato's Myth of the Cave can be interpreted as groupthink?

2. Do you see any of the symptoms of groupthink in any groups within our society? In any of the groups to which you yourself belong?

3. Is it possible for an entire nation or society to suffer from groupthink? For the entire human race? Explain your answers.

4. What are the cures, if any, for groupthink? Can such cures work in "the Cave"?

SOURCE: I. L. Janis, *Victims of Groupthink* (Boston: Houghton Mifflin, 1972).

Second, as Plato made clear in the parable, philosophy is a difficult activity. The journey upward is hard because it involves questioning the most basic beliefs that each of us accepts about ourself and the universe. This means, as the parable suggests, that your philosophical journey may sometimes lead you in directions that society does not support. It may lead you toward views that others around you reject. Philosophy is also hard because it requires us to think critically, consistently, and carefully about our fundamental beliefs. We may rebel against being asked to systematically and logically question and criticize views that we have always accepted. Yet the journey out of the darkness of the cave requires intellectual discipline and the hard work of thinking things through as carefully and precisely as we can. That is why someone taking the first steps in philosophy can be helped by a teacher who, as Plato says, "drags him up the steep and rugged ascent from the cave and forces him out into the full light of the sun." The teacher does this by getting the learner to ask himself the hard questions he is reluctant to ask on his own.

Going from being in the dark to finding the light is not an easy process.
NICHOLAS SMITH

Third, as Plato indicates and as we have already suggested, the aim of philosophy is freedom. Philosophy breaks the chains that imprison and hold us down, the chains that we often do not even know we are wearing. Like the prisoners in the cave, we uncritically accept the beliefs and opinions of those around us, and this leads us to see the world in narrow, rigid ways. Philosophy aims at breaking us free of the prejudices and unthinking habits we have long absorbed from those around us and move toward more reflective views that are truly our own.

Philosophy means liberation from the two dimensions of routine, soaring above the well known, seeing it in new perspectives, arousing wonder and the wish to fly.
WALTER KAUFMANN

Fourth, Plato's parable suggests that the beliefs that philosophy examines are the most basic concerns of human existence. Like the prisoner who is led to look at the real objects whose shadows he always thought were real, the person who does philosophy examines the most basic assumptions we have about the world around us. The word *philosophy* itself suggests this, since it means "the love of wisdom." To do philosophy is to love wisdom. Since wisdom is an understanding of the most fundamental aspects of human living, to love wisdom (to do philosophy) is to grapple with and seek to understand the most basic issues in our lives.

This view of philosophy as the activity of examining our beliefs about the most fundamental and significant aspects of our lives was perhaps most clearly expressed not by Plato, but by Perictione, a woman philosopher who we think lived around the time of Plato:

CRITICAL THINKING
Do definitions of philosophy assume humans have certain abilities? Do they assume we can understand ourselves and the universe? If definitions of philosophy make such assumptions, can philosophy really question everything?

> Humanity came into being and exists in order to contemplate the principle of the nature of the whole. The function of wisdom is to gain possession of this very thing, and to contemplate the purpose of the things that are. Geometry, of course, and arithmetic, and the other theoretical studies and sciences are also concerned with the things that are, but wisdom is concerned with the most basic of these. Wisdom is concerned with all that is, just as sight is concerned with all that is visible and hearing with all that is audible. . . . Therefore, whoever is able to analyze all the kinds of being by reference to one and the same basic principle, and, in turn, from this principle to synthesize and enumerate the different kinds, this person seems to be the wisest and most true and, moreover, to have discovered a

noble height from which he will be able to catch sight of God and all the things separated from God in serial rank and order.[2]

Perictione is here suggesting that philosophy, the search for wisdom, is ultimately a search for an understanding of why we and our universe are here. It is a search for a kind of understanding that goes beyond mathematics and the other sciences. These—mathematics and the other sciences—look only at particular aspects of our world. Philosophy, on the other hand, is the attempt to understand the most basic and general aspects of ourselves, our place in the universe, and our relationship to the divine.

For example, philosophy examines the basic ideas that underlie religion when it asks: Is there a God? Is there an afterlife? What truth is there in religious experience? It examines the basic ideas that underlie science when it asks: Are there limits to what science can tell us about reality? Are scientific theories merely useful approximations, or do they impart real truths about the universe? What is truth? Philosophy examines the basic values that underlie our relations with each other when it asks: What is justice? What do we owe each other? What is love? And it examines the basic notions that underlie our views about reality when it asks: Is human freedom possible, or is everything determined by outside forces? Do things operate by chance, or is there some purpose to the universe? Are the ordinary objects we experience all that reality contains, or do other kinds of objects exist beyond the world that appears around us? To do philosophy, then, is to examine the basic and most important assumptions that underlie everything we do and believe. We can, in fact, define *philosophy*—the love and pursuit of wisdom—as the activity of critically and carefully examining the reasons behind the most fundamental assumptions of our human lives.

The search for wisdom is a concern of people of both sexes and of all races and cultures. Yet here in the United States, at least, philosophy often proceeded as if only Caucasian males did philosophy. In fact, college philosophy courses often paid attention only to those male philosophers who belong to Western culture. Western culture is the cultural tradition that began in ancient Greece and Rome (where it united with Christianity) and then spread to Europe, England, and the United States.

How can this be? Are there no important women philosophers? Have only white men philosophized? Have no other cultures—such as Indian, African, and Asian cultures—made important contributions to philosophy? Are the philosophical views of nonwhites insignificant?

It is clearly a mistake to assume that only the views of Western males are important enough to study. Women make up half of humanity, so looking at philosophical issues from the perspectives of women as well as men is important. The tradition of Western culture is important, of course, because of its

The scientist will ask, "What is the cause of cancer?" The philosopher will ask, "What's a cause? What is it for something to be a cause?"

JOHN SEARLE

Philosophy is the thoughts of men about human thinking, reasoning and imagining, and the real values in human existence.

CHARLES W. ELIOT

Philosophy is man's quest for the unity of knowledge: it consists in a perpetual struggle to create the concepts in which the universe can be conceived as a universe and not a multiverse.

WILLIAM HALVERSON

---

[2]Quoted in *A History of Women Philosophers,* ed. Mary Ellen Waithe (Boston: Martinus Nijhoff, 1987), 56.

profound influence on the social institutions that surround us. Yet other cultural traditions have had equally profound effects on the planet's civilizations and populations. As we enter the twenty-first century, it is becoming ever more impossible to ignore non-Western cultures. The cultural traditions of many Americans—Asian Americans and African Americans, for example—include elements from non-Western traditions. Examining these is vital. Moreover, because the nations of the world are now so interdependent, other cultures and other traditions now profoundly affect our social, political, and economic institutions. It is foolish to remain ignorant of the philosophical traditions of other nations and of people of color that are now having a significant effect on our lives.

Therefore, this book includes two approaches to philosophy that focus on ideas that are not always included in introductions to philosophy. One of these approaches is feminist philosophy. Feminist philosophy looks at philosophical issues from the perspectives of women. The other approach is that of multiculturalism, an approach to learning that takes in the perspectives of many different cultures.

Living in the United States, we need to understand the traditional Western philosophy that has shaped this country's institutions and its dominant culture. This traditional Western philosophy continues to influence and shape the thinking of each of us today. For a number of historical reasons (including both subtle and overt racism and sexism), the major contributors to this philosophy have been white males. Consequently, we will spend a good deal of time examining their views. Nevertheless, we will not ignore the contributions of women and members of other cultures and races. Looking at their contributions will enable you to expand your horizons. It will allow you to see more clearly and by contrast the ways in which traditional Western philosophy has shaped you. It will provide new ways of looking at yourself and reality, and new ways of shaping the institutions and cultures that will emerge in your future. By looking at worlds that are different from the one in which you live, you may come to see more clearly what your world is really like. More important, perhaps, you will envision ways of making it better.

QUESTIONS

1. Ask six friends what they think philosophy is. Is there any agreement?

2. Would it be true to say that every profession has its own philosophy? What does this mean? How would you describe the educational philosophy of the school that you attend or have attended?

3. The text suggests that in Plato's Myth of the Cave, the climb from the cave represents the climb "from the dark cave of ignorance up into the light of knowledge." Can you suggest other reasonable interpretations of Plato's parable?

4. Suppose someone objected, "If philosophy is an ongoing process, what's the point of engaging in it? You'll never get any certain answers; your search will never end. Such a prospect is thoroughly depressing." How would you respond to this criticism?

1.2 The Traditional Divisions of Philosophy

Another approach to understanding what philosophy means is looking at the kinds of questions it has traditionally asked. What are its main questions and major issues? Traditionally, philosophy has sought an organized understanding of reality and our place in it: an understanding of how we ought to live, including the bases for our personal and social moral values, and an understanding of what knowledge and truth are. Of course, philosophers approach these general concerns in many ways, each emphasizing some particular aspect of our human concerns.

The variety of approaches aside, philosophy overall has been concerned with three broad questions: What is knowledge? What is real? What is right and good? Although these questions cannot be considered in isolation and although the distinction among them is sometimes blurred, philosophers have traditionally seen most philosophical questions in terms of these three inquiries.

These traditional concerns suggest the three categories under which philosophical topics are usually grouped: knowledge, reality, and value. Philosophers generally term the fields of philosophy that explore these topics epistemology, metaphysics, and ethics.

Epistemology literally means "the study of knowledge." Among the problems usually discussed as parts of epistemology are the structure, reliability, extent, and kinds of knowledge we have; the meaning of truth (including definitions of truth and validity); logic and a variety of strictly linguistic concerns; and the foundation of all knowledge, including the question of whether real knowledge is even possible.

epistemology the branch of philosophy that investigates the nature, sources, limitations, and validity of knowledge

To get a fuller idea of what epistemology is, and its importance, consider the interesting views of Gail Stenstad, a contemporary feminist philosopher. Stenstad argues that male approaches to knowledge assume there is only one truth—one correct theory—and that all other conflicting insights must be wrong. She contrasts this approach to knowledge, which she calls theoretical thinking, with feminist "anarchic thinking." Feminist thinking, she says, recognizes that there is not just one "objective" truth but that there are many conflicting truths:

> In some ways the difference between theoretical thinking and anarchic thinking is analogous to the difference between monotheism [belief in one God] and polytheism [belief in many gods]. Theoretical thinking and monotheism both tend toward "the one." Monotheism, obviously, is oriented toward one god; historically, many monotheistic religions have also been very concerned with oneness in doctrine, with arriving at doctrine that can be taken to be the only true or correct one. "One lord, one faith, one baptism." This sort of focus creates an in-group and an out-group: the saved and the damned. While none but the most rigid theorists would go so far in demarcating an in-group and an out-group, accusations of "incorrectness" have

been used to silence disagreement. Further, in its very structure, any claim to possess *the* truth, or *the* correct account of reality or the good, creates an out-group, whether we like it or not. The out-group is all those whose truth or reality or values are different from those posited in the theory. . . . [But] polytheism has room to include a monotheistic perspective (though the reverse is not the case). A belief in many gods, or in many possibilities or sacred manifestations, can allow for an individual's preference for any one (or more) of those manifestations. Likewise, anarchic thinking does not abandon or exclude or negate the insights achieved by theoretical thinking, but rather demotes "the theory" to a situational analysis, useful and accurate within limits clearly demarcated in each case. Other, very different analyses, based on other women's situations and experiences, are not ruled out.[3]

In this passage, Stenstad is comparing male or theoretical thinking with monotheism. Monotheism is the belief that there is just one God and that any beliefs in other gods should be rejected. In a similar way, she says, male thinking assumes that there is only one true view of reality and that any contrary views must be rejected as false. Theoretical thinking, the male view of truth, assumes that if several views of reality conflict (are inconsistent), then only one can be true. We must turn away from such male approaches to knowledge and truth, she says. Instead, we should embrace the "feminist" view that truth is many and that several opposing insights can be equally valid and equally true. This new feminist approach to truth and knowledge will give us the power to break free of male theories that deny the equal validity of opposing views; it will also enable us to build communities that include individuals from different backgrounds and with different experiences, offering different insights and different truths.

Is truth many or one? Is there a male approach to knowledge and truth that is intolerant and exclusive? Should we embrace the view that truth is many and that there is no single correct truth about what the world is like? Are all truth and all knowledge relative? Out of these puzzling questions arises the field of epistemology, the attempt to determine what knowledge and truth are. As this short discussion of Stenstad's ideas shows, the answers to these questions influence even how we relate to each other as male and female.

Metaphysics, the second major area of philosophy, is the study of the most general or ultimate characteristics of reality or existence. Some issues that fall under metaphysics are the place of humans in the universe, the purpose and nature of reality, and the nature of mind, self, and consciousness. Also included are issues related to religion, such as the existence of God, the destiny of the universe, and the immortality of the soul.

metaphysics the branch of philosophy that studies the nature of reality

One of the core questions of metaphysics—one that gives us an idea of what metaphysics is about—is this: Is everything in the universe determined by outside causes, or are humans, at least, freely able to choose for themselves? Again, looking at how some philosophers have treated this issue will give us a better understanding of what metaphysics is about.

The first step towards philosophy is incredulity.
DENIS DIDEROT

---

[3] Gail Stenstad, "Anarchic Thinking: Breaking the Hold of Monotheistic Ideology on Feminist Philosophy," in *Women, Knowledge, and Reality: Explorations in Feminist Philosophy*, ed. Ann Garry and Marilyn Pearsall (Boston: Unwin Hyman, 1989), 333.

One important theory in metaphysics is determinism, the view that all things and all human beings are unfree. Paul Henri d'Holbach, who wrote in the eighteenth century, held such a view:

> In whatever manner man is considered, he is connected to universal nature, and submitted to the necessary and immutable laws that she imposes on all beings she contains. . . . He is born without his own consent; his [physical and mental]

PHILOSOPHY AND LIFE

Philosophical Issues

Virtually every activity and every profession raises philosophical issues. Science, theology, psychology, the practice of law and medicine, and even taxation all involve questions that more or less directly force us to address philosophical issues. Mark Woodhouse invites us to consider the following examples:

1. A neurophysiologist, while establishing correlations between certain brain functions and the feeling of pain, begins to wonder whether the "mind" is distinct from the brain.

2. A nuclear physicist, having determined that matter is mostly empty space containing colorless energy transformations, begins to wonder to what extent the solid, extended, colored world we perceive corresponds to what actually exists and which world is more "real."

3. A behavioral psychologist, having increasing success in predicting human behavior, questions whether any human actions can be called "free."

4. Supreme Court justices, when framing a law to distinguish obscene and nonobscene art forms, are drawn into questions about the nature and function of art.

5. A theologian in a losing battle with science over literal descriptions of the universe (or "reality") is forced to

redefine the whole purpose and scope of traditional theology.

6. An anthropologist, noting that all societies have some conception of a moral code, begins to wonder just what distinguishes a moral from a nonmoral point of view.

7. A linguist, in examining the various ways language shapes our view of the world, declares that there is no one "true reality" because all views of reality are conditioned and qualified by the language in which they are expressed.

8. A perennial skeptic, accustomed to demanding and not receiving absolute proof for every view encountered, declares that it is impossible to know anything.

9. A county commissioner, while developing new zoning ordinances, begins to wonder whether the effect or the intent (or both) of zoning laws makes them discriminatory.

10. An IRS director, in determining which (religious) organizations should be exempted from tax, is forced to define what counts as a "religion" or "religious group."

11. A concerned mother, having decided to convert her Communist son, is forced to read the Communist Manifesto and to do some thinking about Marxist and capitalist ideologies.

And, as Woodhouse also suggests, philosophical questions are continually raised in our everyday life and conversations. Consider, for example, the following statements, which all involve philosophical issues: Sociology is not a science. Drugs reveal new levels of reality. History never repeats itself. Every religion has the same core of truth. We should all be left free to do our own thing, as long as we don't hurt anyone else. All truth depends on your point of view. The most important thing you can do is find out who you are. This could all be a dream.

QUESTIONS

1. Are there any areas of life that do not involve philosophical issues?

2. What are your views on the issues Woodhouse lists?

3. How would the issues that Woodhouse lists be resolved?

4. What kinds of reasons would count for or against a given position on these issues?

5. Can these issues be resolved?

SOURCE: Mark D. Woodhouse, *A Preface to Philosophy* (Belmont, CA: Wadsworth, 1984), 1–2, 26–27. Used by permission.

organization does in no way depend on himself; his ideas come to him involuntarily; and his habits are in the power of those who cause him to have them. He is unceasingly modified by causes, whether visible or concealed, over which he has no control and which necessarily regulate his existence, color his way of thinking, and determine his manner of acting. . . .

His will is necessarily determined by the qualities, good or bad, agreeable or painful, of the object or the motive that acts upon his senses or which he retains in his memory. In consequence, he acts necessarily, his action is the result of the impulse he receives either from the motive, from the object, or from the idea which has modified his brain or disposed his will. When he does not act according to this impulse, it is because there comes some new cause, some new motive, some new idea, which modified his brain in a different manner, gives him a new impulse, and determines his will in another way. . . . In all this he always acts according to necessary laws from which he has no means of emancipating himself. . . .

In short, the actions of man are never free; they are always the necessary consequence of his temperament, of the ideas he has received, including his true or false notions of happiness, and of those opinions that are strengthened by example, by education, and by daily experience. . . . Man is not a free agent in any instant of his life.[4]

Yet many contemporary philosophers deny this deterministic picture of reality. One of them is Viktor Frankl, a Jewish psychologist and existentialist philosopher. Frankl suffered terrible degradations while imprisoned by the Nazis after they murdered his entire family. There, in the terror-filled hellholes of the German prison camps, he was struck by how often people responded to their situation with generosity and selflessness. His experience proved to him, he claims, that human beings are ultimately free and that each of us has the freedom to make of ourselves whatever kind of person we choose to be:

Man is *not* fully conditioned and determined; he determines himself whether to give in to conditions or stand up to them. In other words, man is ultimately self-determining. Man does not simply exist, but always decides what his existence will be, what he will become in the next moment. By the same token, every human being has the freedom to change at any instant. . . .

A human being is not one thing among others. *Things* determine each other, but *man* is ultimately self-determining. What he becomes—within the limits of endowment and environment—he has made out of himself. In the concentration camps, for example, in this living laboratory and on this testing ground, we watched and witnessed some of our comrades behave like swine while others behaved like saints. Man has both potentialities within himself. Which one is actualized depends on decisions but not on conditions.[5]

Some Eastern philosophers have turned to the Hindu idea of karma to argue that humans can be both free and determined. *Karma*, which literally means "action" or "deed," consists of the accumulation of a person's past deeds. For the Hindu, everything we have done in our past (possibly including past lives) determines our present situation—who and what we now are. Some Hindu philosophers have argued that although this seems to imply that we are not

---

[4] Baron Paul Henri d'Holbach, *System of Nature* (London: Dearsley, 1797).
[5] Viktor Frankl, *Man's Search for Meaning* (New York: Washington Square Press, 1963), 206, 213.

Gandhi: "The highest love is wherein man lays down his life for his fellow-men. That highest love is thus *Ahimsa*."

free, the idea of karma allows us to combine both determinism and freedom. Our past actions—our karma—they claim, determine the kind of being we have become, but we are still free to choose within the limits of what we have become. Freedom is choosing now within a situation that is determined by our past. As the Hindu philosopher Sarvepalli Radhakrishnan, for example, writes,

> Freedom is not caprice, nor is Karma necessity. . . . Freedom is not caprice since we carry our past with us. Our character, at any given point, is the condensation of our previous history. What we have been enters into the "me" which is now active and choosing. The range of one's natural freedom of action is limited. No man has the universal field of possibilities for himself. . . . Only the possible is the sphere of freedom. We have a good deal of present constraint and previous necessity in human life. But necessity is not to be mistaken for destiny which we can neither defy nor elude. Though the self is not free from the bonds of determination, it can subjugate the past to a certain extent and turn it into a new course. Choice is the assertion of freedom over necessity by which it converts necessity to its own use and thus frees itself from it.[6]

Which of these views is supported by the strongest reasons—the view that all reality (including ourselves) is causally determined, the view that we are completely free to choose what we will be, or the view that we are determined but free to choose within the constraints set by our past? This is but one example of the fundamental questions that metaphysics asks.

---

[6]Sarvepalli Radhakrishnan, *An Idealist View of Life* (London: George Allen & Unwin, 1932), 220–221.

Ethics, the third major area of philosophy, refers to the study of our values and moral principles and how these relate to our conduct and to our social institutions. Ethics includes questions about the nature of moral obligation, what basic moral principles we should follow and what is good for human beings, the nature and justification of social structures and political systems, and the morality of various kinds of behavior and social policies that involve crucial human interests.

ethics the branch of philosophy that tries to determine the good and right thing to do

The specific issues discussed in ethics vary widely and include questions such as these: Are abortion, suicide, and euthanasia ever morally right? Is capitalism or communism a better form of life? Should the law permit or prohibit adultery, pornography, capital punishment, or homosexuality? Again, some examples may make these inquiries a bit clearer. Consider the statement of Mahatma Gandhi, the great twentieth-century Indian statesman who successfully practiced nonviolent political resistance against the British rulers of India. Gandhi devoted his life to breaking down racial and religious forms of discrimination. He campaigned for equality of respect for all human beings. In doing this he advocated and practiced *ahimsa,* or nonviolence. In Gandhi's view, we should harm no living thing. Nevertheless, we should resist evil. In his struggles against the British, therefore, he would simply stand in the path of their violence, letting their blows fall on him, and passively resist their oppressive policies. Gandhi lived the philosophy that service toward others is our primary moral duty:

> To proceed a little further, sacrifice means laying down one's life so that others may live. Let us suffer so that others may be happy, and the highest service and the highest love is wherein man lays down his life for his fellow-men. That highest love is thus *Ahimsa* which is the highest service. . . . Learn to be generous towards each other. To be generous means having no hatred for those whom we consider to be at fault, and loving and serving them. It is not generosity or love, if we have goodwill for others only as long as they and we are united in thought and action. That should be called merely friendship or mutual affection. The application of the term "love" is wrong in such cases. "Love" means feeling friendship for the enemy.[7]

Yet not everyone agrees with such lofty sentiments. Many philosophers, in fact, have reasoned that ethics is a sham. For example, Harry Browne concludes that morality is really a kind of trap if we take it to mean that people should put the happiness of others ahead of their own. Selfishness, he holds, is and should be everyone's policy:

> Everyone is selfish; everyone is doing what he believes will make himself happier. The recognition of that can take most of the sting out of accusations that you're being "selfish." Why should you feel guilty for seeking your own happiness when that's what everyone else is doing, too? . . .
>
> To find constant, profound happiness requires that you be free to seek the gratification of your own desires. It means making positive choices.

---

[7] Mahatma Gandhi, *Gita—My Mother,* quoted in *Beyond the Western Tradition,* ed. Daniel Bonevac, William Boon, and Stephen Phillips (Mountain View, CA: Mayfield, 1992), 243.

If you slip into the Unselfishness Trap, you'll spend a good part of your time making negative choices—trying to avoid the censure of those who tell you not to think of yourself. . . .

If someone finds happiness by doing "good works" for others, let him. That doesn't mean that's the best way for you to find happiness.

And when someone accuses you of being selfish, just remember that he's only upset because you aren't doing what he selfishly wants you to do.[8]

Browne's view that morality is a sham because humans always try to satisfy themselves—therefore their actions are always selfish—is called *egoism*. The contemporary philosopher James Rachels strongly questions this view in the following passage:

Why should we think that merely because someone derives satisfaction from helping others this makes him selfish? Isn't the unselfish man precisely the one who *does* derive satisfaction from helping others, while the selfish man does not? Similarly, it is nothing more than shabby sophistry to say, because Smith takes satisfaction in helping his friend, that he is behaving selfishly. If we say this rapidly, while thinking about something else, perhaps it will sound all right; but if we speak slowly, and pay attention to what we are saying, it sounds plain silly.[9]

Which of these views is correct—that morality is a sham or that we have a duty to love and serve even our enemies? These kinds of inquiries form the subject matter of ethics, the third major area of philosophy.

Finally, there is a wide range of philosophical inquiries that are usually referred to as "the philosophy of . . ." or, simply, "philosophy and. . . ." For example, these include the philosophy of science, the philosophy of art, and philosophy and the meaning of life. Each of these areas of philosophy attempts to question and analyze the basic or fundamental assumptions of the subject. For example, the philosophy of science asks what the scientific method is, whether it is valid, and whether the theories it produces are merely useful mental constructs or objective descriptions of reality. The philosophy of art asks what art is, what its meaning is and what its point is, and whether we can judge art against objective standards or whether it is merely a matter of fads and personal tastes. An inquiry into philosophy and the meaning of life is an attempt to look carefully at the question of whether life has meaning and, if so, what that meaning might be.

> *Philosophy wrestles with problems that are still in a state of too much confusion for any self-respecting science to try to grapple with them. It's the junkyard of the sciences.*
>
> PAUL CHURCHLAND

QUESTIONS

1. Read through the various passages quoted as examples of philosophical writings in epistemology, metaphysics, and ethics. What makes these philosophical writings? What reasons are provided in support of a philosophical position? How does philosophy differ from the natural sciences? The social sciences? Literature?

---

[8] Harry Browne, *How I Found Freedom in an Unfree World* (New York: Macmillan, 1937).
[9] James Rachels, "Egoism and Moral Skepticism," in *A New Introduction to Philosophy*, ed. Steven M. Cahn (New York: Harper & Row, 1971).

2.   Think of as many philosophical questions as you can, and then place each in one or more of the three major philosophical categories.

3.   List the philosophical concerns you wish to learn about during your introductory philosophy course. Try to be specific. For example, suppose you'd like to learn something about religion. Exactly what would you like to learn? Try to formulate a question that will direct your study, such as "Is there any reason to believe that God exists?" or "If God is all good and all powerful, how can evil exist?"

1.3 An Example of Philosophy: Socrates

The best way to understand the nature of philosophy is to consider a philosopher in action. And the best place to begin is with the Greek thinker Socrates, who is sometimes called the father of Western philosophy. However, we should note that Socrates was not the first Western philosopher. A group of philosophers preceded him called the pre-Socratics. The **pre-Socratics** were the first thinkers in the West who questioned religious authority and tried to provide nonreligious explanations of nature. (For more information, see the showcase about the first philosophers at the end of this chapter.) Nevertheless, Socrates' life and views exemplify the meaning of philosophy, so we will look at his work.

pre-Socratics the Greek philosophers before Socrates

Socrates was born in 469 B.C. in Athens, Greece, a flourishing and remarkably vigorous city-state. The Greek theater had already produced the noted dramatist Aeschylus and would soon see the comedies of Aristophanes and tragedies of Sophocles and Euripedes. The Greek armies had defeated those of the much larger nation of Persia, and Athens was on the verge of attaining naval control of the Aegean Sea.

As he grew older, Socrates began to question the conventional beliefs held by his fellow Athenians. He would haunt the streets of Athens, buttonholing powerful men and asking them irreverent questions about their opinions. To those who pretended to know about justice, for example, he would ask: "What is justice? What does it mean? What do all just acts have in common?" Similarly, he would probe ideas about virtue, knowledge, morality, and religion. By continual questioning, Socrates would plumb a person's system of beliefs, deflating cherished certainties and exposing their emptiness. Although Socrates' persistent questioning of traditional habits of thought left many people puzzled, many more reacted with anger.

The adjusted American lacks self-approval; that is to say, he has not developed a self-image that he can believe is both accurate and acceptable. The culture abounds with misdirections, which the adjusted American acquires. . . . Perhaps above all he learns to seek self-acceptance indirectly, by seeking to substitute the good opinions of others for self-approval. It is thus that he becomes "other directed."

GAIL AND SNELL PUTNEY

Socrates saw Athens rise to glory under the great leader Pericles. Under Pericles, Athens enjoyed a splendid golden age of democracy, an age of great

Socrates: "The unexamined life is not worth living."

architectural, artistic, and literary advances. The golden age of Athens depended on the powerful military and economic forces that Athens commanded. But all this ended when Athens was defeated in war and became embroiled in a disastrous thirty-year civil war. Plague broke out, inflation struck the economy, and intense class struggles erupted between the rich, old aristocratic families and their poorer fellow citizens. In the end, the defeated, desperate, and frustrated Athenians searched for scapegoats to blame. Socrates and his habit of questioning everything, they said, had weakened the traditional values and beliefs that had once made Athens strong. So they sentenced Socrates to death.

Since Socrates left no writing, most of what we know about him comes from the *Dialogues*, written by Socrates' disciple Plato. The *Dialogues* are short dramas in which the character of Socrates plays a major role. There is some controversy over how accurately Plato's *Dialogues* reflect the real conversations of Socrates. Nevertheless, most experts today agree that the first dialogues Plato wrote (for example, *Euthyphro*, *The Apology*, and *Crito*) are faithful to Socrates' views although they may not contain Socrates' actual words.

One of these early dialogues, *Euthyphro*, presents a marvelous example of how Socrates questioned almost to the point of irritation. In fact, as you read through the dialogue, you will probably start feeling irritated and asking why Socrates doesn't get past the questions and start giving answers. He gives no answers because he wants you to realize that you, too, do not have any good answers to his questions.

The dialogue takes place at the court of the king. Socrates is there to learn more about an indictment for "unholiness" that has been brought against him for questioning traditional beliefs. He sees an old friend arrive, a priest named Euthyphro. Here, in a simplified and edited translation, is their dialogue as Plato wrote it:

EUTHYPHRO: Socrates! What are you doing here at the court of the King?

SOCRATES: I am being impeached, Euthyphro, by a young man I hardly know named Meletus. He accuses me of making up new gods and denying the existence of the old ones.

EUTHYPHRO: I am sure you will win your case, Socrates, just like I expect to win mine.

SOCRATES: But what is your suit, Euthyphro?

EUTHYPHRO: I am charging my father with murder, Socrates. One of my slaves in a drunken fit killed a fellow slave. My father chained up the culprit and left him in a ditch unattended several days to wait the judgment of a priest. But the cold, the hunger, and the chains killed him. So now I am charging my father with murder, against the ignorant wishes of my family who do not know what true holiness requires of a priest like me.

SOCRATES: Good heavens, Euthyphro! Do you have such a clear knowledge of what holiness is that you are not afraid you might be doing something unholy in charging your own father with murder?

EUTHYPHRO: My most valued possession, Socrates, is the exact knowledge I have of these matters.

SOCRATES: You are a rare friend, Euthyphro. I can do no better than take you as my teacher so that I can defend myself against Meletus who is accusing me of being unholy. Tell me, then, what is holiness and what is unholiness?

EUTHYPHRO: Holiness is doing what I am doing: prosecuting anyone who is guilty of murder, sacrilege, or of any similar crime—whether he is your father or mother, or whoever, it makes no difference—and not to prosecute them is unholiness.

SOCRATES: But wouldn't you say, Euthyphro, that there are many other holy acts?

EUTHYPHRO: There are.

SOCRATES: I was not asking you to give me *examples* of holiness, Euthyphro, but to identify the characteristic which makes all holy things holy. There must be some characteristic that all holy things have in common, and one which makes unholy things unholy. Tell me what this characteristic itself is, so that I can tell which actions are holy, and which unholy.

EUTHYPHRO: Well, then, holiness is what is loved by the gods and what is not loved by them is unholy.

SOCRATES: Very good, Euthyphro! Now you have given me the sort of answer I wanted. Let us examine it. A thing or a person that is loved by the gods is holy, and a thing or a person that the gods hate is unholy. And the holy is the opposite of the unholy. Does that summarize what you said?

EUTHYPHRO: It does.

SOCRATES: But you admit, Euthyphro, that the gods have disagreements. So some things are hated by some gods and loved by other gods.

EUTHYPHRO: True.

SOCRATES: Then upon your view the same things, Euthyphro, will be both holy and unholy.

EUTHYPHRO: Well, I suppose so.

SOCRATES: Then, my friend, you have not really answered my question. I did not ask you to tell me which actions were both holy and unholy; yet that is the outcome of your view. In punishing your father, Euthyphro, you might be doing what is loved by the god Zeus, but hateful to the god Cronos.

EUTHYPHRO: But Socrates, surely none of the gods would disagree about the rightness of punishing an injustice.

SOCRATES: Both men and gods would certainly agree on the general point that unjust acts should be punished. But men and gods might disagree about whether this particular act is unjust. Is that not true?

EUTHYPHRO: Quite true.

SOCRATES: So tell me, my friend: How do you know that all the gods agree on this particular act: that it is just for a son to prosecute his father for chaining a slave who was guilty of murder and who died in chains before the religious authorities said what should be done with him? How do you know that all the gods love this act?

EUTHYPHRO: I could make the matter quite clear to you, Socrates, although it would take me some time.

SOCRATES: Euthyphro, I will not insist on it. I will assume, if you like, that all the gods here agree. The point I really want to understand is this: Do the gods love what is holy because it is holy, or is it holy because they love it? What do you say, Euthyphro? On your definition whatever is holy is loved by all the gods, is it not?

EUTHYPHRO: Yes.

SOCRATES: Because it is holy? Or for some other reason?

EUTHYPHRO: No, that is the reason.

SOCRATES: Then what is holy is loved by the gods because it is holy? It is not holy because it is loved?

EUTHYPHRO: Yes.

SOCRATES: Then, Euthyphro, to be loved by the gods cannot be the same as to be holy. And to be holy cannot be the same as to be loved by the gods.

EUTHYPHRO: But why, Socrates?

SOCRATES: Because, Euthyphro, when I asked you for the essence of holiness, you gave me only a quality that accompanies holiness: the quality of being loved by the gods. But you have not yet told me what holiness itself is [the quality because of which the gods love what is holy]. So please, Euthyphro, do not hide your treasure from me. Start again from the beginning and tell me what holiness itself is.

EUTHYPHRO: I really do not know, Socrates, how to express what I mean. Somehow or other our arguments seem to turn around in circles and walk away from us.

SOCRATES: Then I will help you instruct me, Euthyphro. Tell me—Is it not true that everything that is holy is also just?

EUTHYPHRO: Yes.

Many talk like philosophers and live like fools.

H. G. BOHN

SOCRATES: Does it follow that everything that is just is also holy? Or is it rather the case that whatever is holy is just, but only some just things are holy while others are not? For justice is the larger notion of which holiness is only a part. Do you agree in that?

EUTHYPHRO: Yes; that, I think, is correct.

SOCRATES: Then, since holiness is a part of justice, let us ask what part.

EUTHYPHRO: I know, Socrates! Holiness is that part of justice which involves service to the gods, while the other part of justice involves service to our fellow men.

SOCRATES: Very good, Euthyphro. But there is still one small point on which I need your help: What do you mean by "service"? Is not service always designed to benefit or improve those who are served?

EUTHYPHRO: True.

SOCRATES: So does holiness, which is a kind of service, benefit or improve the gods? Would you say that when you do a holy act you make the gods better?

EUTHYPHRO: Good heavens, no!

SOCRATES: Then what is this service to the gods that is called holiness?

EUTHYPHRO: It is the kind that slaves show their masters.

SOCRATES: I understand. A sort of ministering to the gods.

EUTHYPHRO: Exactly.

SOCRATES: And now tell me, my good friend, about this ministering to the gods: What activities does it involve?

EUTHYPHRO: It would be difficult to learn them all, Socrates. Let me simply say that holiness is learning how to please the gods by prayers and sacrifices.

SOCRATES: And sacrificing is giving to the gods, while prayer is asking of the gods?

EUTHYPHRO: Exactly, Socrates.

SOCRATES: But real giving involves giving them something they want from us, does it not? For surely it would be pointless to give someone what they do not want.

EUTHYPHRO: Very true, Socrates.

SOCRATES: But then tell me, what benefit comes to the gods from our gifts? Clearly they are the givers of every good thing we have. So how we can give any good thing to them in return is puzzling.

EUTHYPHRO: But Socrates, you do not imagine that any benefits come to the gods from the gifts we give them?

SOCRATES: If not, Euthyphro, then what sort of gifts can these be?

EUTHYPHRO: What else but praise and honor and whatever is pleasing to them.

SOCRATES: Holiness, then, is doing what is pleasing to the gods and not what is beneficial to them?

EUTHYPHRO: I would say that holiness, above all, is doing what is loved by the gods.

SOCRATES: Does it surprise you our arguments go in circles? Surely you must remember that a few moments ago we concluded that to be holy is not the same as to be loved by the gods?

EUTHYPHRO: I do.

SOCRATES: Then either we were wrong in that admission or we are wrong now.

EUTHYPHRO: Hmm. I suppose that is the case.

SOCRATES: Then we must begin again and ask, "What is holiness?" If any man knows, you must. For if you did not know the nature of holiness and unholiness I am sure you would never have charged your aged father with murder and run the risk of doing wrong in the sight of the gods. Speak, then, my dear Euthyphro, and do not hide your knowledge from me.

EUTHYPHRO: Perhaps some other time, Socrates. Right now I am in a hurry to be off somewhere.

SOCRATES: My friend! Will you leave me in despair? And here I had hoped that you could teach me what holiness itself is.[10]

You get deeper and deeper into a question and finally you're into these really fundamental questions that we usually take for granted. And that's philosophy.

CHARLES TAYLOR

In this dialogue, Socrates is doing the kind of critical questioning that characterizes philosophy. With careful, logical reasoning, and in a systematic manner, he probes the religious beliefs on which Euthyphro bases his life and actions. Socrates brings logic and reason to bear on those issues that are most important both to Euthyphro and to himself, since he himself is being accused of acting against religion.

Moreover, Socrates' method reveals that Euthyphro—and we ourselves—do not really understand the basic things we take for granted. Socrates questions Euthyphro's easy assumption that he knows what his religious duty is, that he knows what it means for something to be religiously just, and that he knows what it is to serve the gods and why the gods want to be served through certain acts and not others. At every turn, Euthyphro finds that he does not really understand the conventional religious beliefs he has been brought up to hold. He does not even know what makes an action pleasing to the gods. All he can say is that he believes that the gods approve of certain acts, but he has no idea why they approve of those acts and not others.

Euthyphro might be you or I. Are you so sure about your own most basic religious beliefs? Do those of us who believe in God really know why God approves and commands certain acts and not others? What makes an act right? As Socrates might ask, do you believe that actions are right because God (or society) approves of them, or do you believe that God (or society) approves of certain acts because they are right? Do you really know what right action itself is, or do you merely know one of its accompanying characteristics? If Socrates' method of questioning without arriving at answers seems frustrating, it is so partly because it exposes our own lack of wisdom.

Perhaps it is not suprising to learn that Socrates' habit of showing people that they are ignorant of what they thought they knew angered many of them. In fact, Socrates quickly got a reputation for being a "gadfly," an irritating personality who picked away at people's confident assertions and who left them with nothing more than the embarrassing realization of their ignorance. Here, for example, in a selection from *The Republic*, we see Socrates using his questioning methods to show Thrasymachus, a teacher, that he does not know what he is talking about. We see, also, how Socrates used irony to poke fun at pretentiousness and how Socrates never pretended to know something he didn't. In

---

[10] Plato, *Euthyphro*. This edited translation copyright © 1987 by Manuel Velasquez.

this dialogue, Socrates has been asking people if they know what justice is. No one seems to have a good answer. Then Thrasymachus, who prides himself on his own knowledge as a teacher, and who is fed up with Socrates' methods, gets into the discussion:

> THRASYMACHUS: What nonsense are you talking about, Socrates? Why does everyone always give in to you? If you really want to know what justice is, Socrates, then don't just keep asking your questions and showing that everyone else's answers are wrong. As you know, of course, it's easier to ask a lot of questions than to provide answers. So why don't you try giving us some answers yourself? Tell us what you think justice is, Socrates. And don't give us a simple-minded answer like "justice is what ought to be," or "justice is what benefits us," or "justice is what profits us," or "justice is what is useful to us." Tell us clearly and in detail what you think, and don't just give us some simplistic stupidity.

> SOCRATES: Don't be so hard on us, Thrasymachus. If my friends and I have made a mistake in our discussions, I assure you we didn't do it on purpose. . . . We are searching for justice and that is more precious than gold. We don't want to spoil our chances of finding it by being easy on each other and not giving it our best efforts. As you see, we haven't been able to discover what it is. So a clever man like you shouldn't be angry with us. You should feel sorry for us.

> THRASYMACHUS: Oh, God! That's a great example of your well-known irony, Socrates. I knew you would do this. In fact, I warned everyone here before you came that you wouldn't answer any questions yourself, but would pretend to be ignorant. I told them you'd do anything rather than answer someone else's questions.

> SOCRATES: So you are very wise, Thrasymachus. . . .

> THRASYMACHUS: Well, what if I said that I'm willing to answer your question about justice anyway and that I can give you a better answer than anyone else has given?

> SOCRATES: Well, then, it would be best if an ignorant man like myself tried to learn from someone like you who has knowledge.

> THRASYMACHUS: Oh, yes, of course! That way Socrates can again avoid giving any answers and can cross-examine others and refute them.

> SOCRATES: But look, my friend, how can someone answer a question if, to begin with, he doesn't know the answer and doesn't claim to know it? . . . Isn't it more reasonable for you to answer since you say you know and can tell us? Don't be so stubborn. Do us a favor by giving us your answer and stop being so selfish with your wisdom. . . .

> THRASYMACHUS: Listen up, then. I say that justice is nothing more than whatever is advantageous to the stronger. Well, why don't you praise me? But no, you'd never do that!

> SOCRATES: Well, first I have to understand what you mean, for I don't quite get your point yet. You say justice is whatever is advantageous to the stronger. What exactly do you mean by this?

> THRASYMACHUS: As you must know, Socrates, some nations are ruled by tyrants, others are ruled by a democratic majority, and still others are ruled by a small aristocracy. . . . Whoever rules — the ruling party — is the stronger in each nation. . . . And in each nation, whoever rules passes laws that are to their own — the rulers' — advantage. After they pass these laws, they say that justice is obeying the law. Who-

The best philosophers I know are like Socrates: the talkativeness, the aggressiveness, the loving to just be with people, argue with people, talk to people. That's something special.

ROBERT SOLOMON

ever fails to keep the law is punished as unjust and a lawbreaker. So that, my good man, is what I say justice is. It is the same in all nations: whatever is to the advantage of the ruling group. The ruling group, you must admit, is the stronger. So if one reasons correctly, one will conclude that everywhere justice is the same: it is whatever is advantageous to the stronger.

SOCRATES: Now I think I know what you mean. But now we have to figure out whether you are right or not. You say that justice is something advantageous, but you add that it is what is advantageous to the stronger.

THRASYMACHUS: Perhaps you think that's only a small point?

SOCRATES: That's not clear yet. We need to see whether what you say is true. For I too think that justice is something advantageous. But you say that it is what is advantageous to the stronger, while I don't claim to know this. So we need to inquire.

THRASYMACHUS: Inquire away.

SOCRATES: First tell me, do you admit that it is just for citizens to obey their rulers?

THRASYMACHUS: I do.

SOCRATES: But are the rulers of a nation absolutely infallible, or do they sometimes make mistakes?

THRASYMACHUS: Of course, they sometimes make mistakes.

SOCRATES: So when they pass laws, they sometimes pass the right laws, and sometimes they mistakenly pass the wrong laws?

THRASYMACHUS: True.

SOCRATES: When they pass the right laws, they pass laws that are advantageous to their own interests, but when they make mistakes they pass laws that are contrary to their own interests. Is this your view?

THRASYMACHUS: Yes.

SOCRATES: But whatever laws they pass must be obeyed by their subjects, and that is what you say justice is.

THRASYMACHUS: Of course.

SOCRATES: Then justice, according to you, is sometimes what is not in the interests of the stronger, but something contrary to their interests?

THRASYMACHUS: What's that you just said?

SOCRATES: Didn't you just admit that the rulers might mistakenly pass laws that are not in their own interests, but that obeying such laws is still justice?

THRASYMACHUS: Why, yes, I think so.

SOCRATES: Then you must acknowledge that justice is not what is in the interests of the stronger when the rulers unintentionally pass laws that are contrary to their own interests! . . .

THRASYMACHUS: Well, I hope that you have been completely entertained, Socrates, since today is a holiday for feasting.

SOCRATES: And it is you who furnished the feast for us, Thrasymachus.[11]

---

[11] From *Republic*, bk. 1, lines 336c–339e, translated by Manuel Velasquez, © 1998 by Manuel Velasquez.

Thrasymachus has a cynical philosophy. His view is that might makes right. Justice is obeying the rules of society, and these rules, he claims, always favor the interests of whatever group happens to hold power in that society. For example, Thrasymachus might have said that in a society ruled by white people, right and wrong will be defined in terms of what benefits white people. In any society, Thrasymachus holds, the rules of justice are designed to benefit those in power. But is this cynical view of justice true? Socrates shows easily that it is simplistic and naive, and in doing so, he makes Thrasymachus look foolish.

Socrates' relentless and, to some people, infuriating questioning of his fellow citizens eventually led to his death. Shortly after the scene described in *Euthyphro*, Meletus and others indicted Socrates and brought him to trial. In his brilliant work *The Apology*, Plato summarized the speech that Socrates delivered in his defense. The speech is especially fascinating because it provides a summary of Socrates' life and of his devotion to philosophical questioning. Socrates is standing in court, facing the jury composed of five hundred Athenian citizens that has just heard the testimony of his accusers, who charge him with corrupting the youth of Athens and with not believing in the gods of the state:

> I do not know, my fellow Athenians, how you were affected by my accusers whom you just heard. But they spoke so persuasively they almost made me forget who I was. Yet they hardly uttered a word of truth.
>
> But many of you are thinking, "Then what is the origin of these accusations, Socrates?" That is a fair question. Let me explain their origins.
>
> Some of you know my good friend Chaerephon. Before he died he went to Delphi and asked the religious oracle there to tell him who the wisest man in the world was. The oracle answered that there was no man wiser than Socrates.
>
> When I learned this, I asked myself, "What can the god's oracle mean?" For I knew I had no wisdom. After thinking it over for a long time, I decided that I had to find a man wiser than myself so I could go back to the god with this evidence. So I went to see a politician who was famous for his wisdom. But when I questioned him, I realized he really was not wise, although many people—he especially—thought he was. So I tried to explain to him that although he thought himself wise, he really was not. But all that happened was that he came to hate me. And so did many of his supporters who overheard us. So I left him, thinking to myself as I left that although neither of us really knew anything about what is noble and good, still I was better off. For he knows nothing, and thinks that he knows, while I neither know nor think that I know. And in this I think I have a slight advantage.
>
> Then I went to another person who had even greater pretensions to wisdom. The result was exactly the same: I made another enemy. In this way I went to one man after another and made more and more enemies. I felt bad about this and it frightened me. But I was compelled to do it because I felt that investigating god's oracle came first. I said to myself, I must go to everyone who seems to be wise so I can find out what the oracle means.
>
> My hearers imagine that I myself possess the wisdom which I find wanting in others. But the truth is, Men of Athens, that only god is wise. And by his oracle he wanted to show us that the wisdom of men is worth little or nothing. It is as if he was telling us, "The wisest man is the one who, like Socrates, knows that his wisdom is in truth worth nothing." And so I go about the world obedient to god. I search and question the wisdom of anyone who seems to be wise. And if he is not wise, then to

Philosophy is at once the most sublime and the most trivial of human pursuits.

WILLIAM JAMES

clarify the meaning of the oracle I show him that he is not wise. My occupation completely absorbs me and I have no time for anything else. My devotion to the god has reduced me to utter poverty.

There is something more. Young men of the richer classes, who do not have much to do, follow me around of their own accord. They like to hear pretenders exposed. And sometimes they imitate me by examining others themselves. They quickly discover that there are plenty of people who think they know something but who really know nothing at all. Then those people also get angry at me. "This damnable Socrates is misleading our youth!" they say. And if somebody asks them, "How? What evil things does he do or teach them?" they cannot say. But in order not to appear at a loss, these people repeat the charges used against all philosophers: that we teach obscure things up in the clouds, that we teach atheism, and that we make the worst views appear to be the best. For people do not like to admit that their pretensions to knowledge have been exposed. And that, fellow Athenians, is the origin of the prejudices against me.

But some of you will ask, "Don't you regret what you did since now it might mean your death?" To these I answer, "You are mistaken. A good man should not calculate his chances of living or dying. He should only ask himself whether he is doing right or wrong—whether his inner self is that of a good man or of an evil one."

And if you say to me, "Socrates, we will let you go free but only on condition that you stop your questioning," then I will reply, "Men of Athens, I honor and love you. But I must obey god rather than you, and while I have life and strength I will never stop doing philosophy." For my aim is to persuade you all, young and old alike, not to think about your lives or your properties, but first and foremost to care about your inner self. I tell you that wealth does not make you good within, but that from inner goodness comes wealth and every other benefit to man. This is my teaching, and if it corrupts youth, then I suppose I am their corrupter.

Well, my fellow Athenians, you must now decide whether to acquit me or not. But whichever you do, understand that I will never change my ways, not even if I have to die many times. To talk daily about what makes us good, and to question myself and others, is the greatest thing man can do. For the unexamined life is not worth living.

[At this point Socrates rested his case. The jury debated among themselves; then, in a split vote, they reached their final verdict.]

Men of Athens, you have condemned me to death. To those of you who are my friends and who voted to acquit me let me say that death may be a good thing. Either it is a state of nothingness and utter unconsciousness, or, as men say, it is merely a migration from this world to another. If it is complete unconsciousness—like a sleep undisturbed even by dreams—then death will be an unspeakable gain. And if it is a journey to another world where all the dead live, then it will also be a great good. For then I can continue my search into true and false knowledge: In the next world, as in this one, I can continue questioning the great people of the past to find out who is wise and who merely pretends to be. So do not be saddened by death. No evil can happen to a good man either in this life or in death.

Well, the hour of departure has arrived, and we must each go our ways. I to die, and you to live. Which is better only god knows.[12]

> **CRITICAL THINKING**
>
> Socrates says that death is either complete unconsciousness or a journey to another world, and that both would be great goods. Are there other possibilities? Is it necessarily true that both would be great goods?

Again, Socrates' speech provides a remarkable example of what philosophy is. Philosophy is the quest for wisdom: an unrelenting devotion to uncover the

---

[12] Plato, *The Apology*. This edited translation copyright © 1987 by Manuel Velasquez.

truth about what matters most in one's life. This quest is undertaken in the conviction that a life based on an easy, uncritical acceptance of conventional beliefs is an empty life. As Socrates puts it, "The unexamined life is not worth living." Philosophy is a quest that is difficult not only because it requires hard thinking but also because it sometimes requires taking positions that are unpopular and not shared by others.

laws?

Socrates was jailed immediately after his trial. While awaiting his execution, he continued his avid questioning. But his questions then focused more on his own beliefs about right and wrong, good and evil. In one of his final conversations, recorded in the dialogue *Crito*, Socrates considered whether he had the courage to face death for his beliefs. The day before his execution he awoke to find his close friend Crito sitting in his jail cell next to him:

SOCRATES: Crito! What are you doing here at this hour? It must be quite early.

CRITO: Yes, it is.

SOCRATES: What time is it?

CRITO: The dawn is breaking.

SOCRATES: I am surprised the jailer let you in. Did you just get here?

CRITO: No, I came some time ago.

SOCRATES: Then why did you sit and say nothing? Why have you come here so early?

CRITO: Oh my dear friend, Socrates! Let me beg you once again to take my advice and escape from here. If you die I will not only lose a friend who can never be replaced, but people who do not know us will think that I could have saved you but was not willing to pay the necessary bribes. And you would be betraying your children since they surely will meet the unhappy fate of orphans.

SOCRATES: Dear Crito, your zeal is invaluable, if it is right. But if wrong, the greater the zeal, the greater the evil. I have always been guided by reason. I cannot turn away now from the principles I have always tried to honor. So let us look carefully at the issues before us. Shall we begin with your views about what people will think? Tell me, were we right long ago when we said that not all the opinions of men should be valued? Consider the athlete: Should he follow the advice and opinions of every man? Or should he listen to one man only—his doctor or trainer?

CRITO: He should follow the one man's advice.

SOCRATES: He should train in the way that seems good to the one man who has understanding rather than listen to the opinions of the many?

CRITO: True.

SOCRATES: Doesn't the same principle hold, Crito, in the matter we are discussing: which course of action is right and good and which is wrong and evil? In this matter should we follow the opinions of the many or of the one who has understanding? If the athlete follows the advice of men who have no understanding, he will destroy his body, won't he?

CRITO: Yes.

SOCRATES: And is the body better than that inner part of ourselves—the soul— that is concerned with right and wrong, good and evil?

CRITICAL THINKING

What does Socrates assume when he suggests that the body is less valuable than the soul? Are these assumptions correct?

CRITO: Certainly not.

SOCRATES: Then, Crito, you are wrong to suggest that we should listen to the opinions of the many about right and wrong or good and evil. The values you bring up—money, loss of reputation, and educating children—are based on the opinions of the many. They do not concern the only real issue before us: Is it right or wrong for me to escape against the wishes of the Athenians? So follow me now in my questioning.

PHILOSOPHY AND LIFE

Sanctuary and the Law

In January 1985, sixteen people, including two Roman Catholic priests, a Presbyterian minister, and three nuns, were charged with illegally smuggling and sheltering Central American refugees in the United States. The refugees were people fleeing from torture and virtually certain death in their own war-torn countries. The sixteen people charged with illegally helping the refugees argued that giving sanctuary to the refugees was a matter of conscience and that they were obligated to obey their conscience rather than the law. Several newspapers carried the story.

Tucson, Arizona—In direct defiance of immigration statutes, the Rev. John Fife and his compatriots in the sanctuary movement help transport Central American refugees across the Mexican border into the United States. They find food and shelter for them, often in churches, and then transport their wards through relays to cities such as Chicago, Los Angeles, Cincinnati and Seattle.

Two hundred churches publicly have declared their status as sanctuaries, and the pastors, priests, rabbis and lay workers who have joined the movement speak freely about their work. . . .

"When you hear about the fear and

the violence and the torture these people face at home, you have little choice but to help," said Jill Levis of Christ Church Presbyterian in Burlington, Vt. "The Bible says that God takes sides and he tells us to take the side of the needy."

"We are acting out our faith," said Peggy Hutchison, who was charged in the same federal indictment as Fife and fourteen other sanctuary workers. "We believe very strongly in what we are doing."

Fife said, "You have to help the refugees or else you lose your soul."

Ruth Anne Myers, district director in Arizona for the Immigration and Naturalization Service, insists that "the government's position is simply that it is against the law to smuggle, harbor or transport aliens into the United States.

"The law doesn't say if good people are doing it, it's OK, or if the people doing it think the law is wrong, it's OK," Myers added. "It's like the bombing of abortion clinics. These are people who take the law into their own hands for religious reasons."

Sanctuary activists argue that it is too difficult for most Central Americans to prove to the satisfaction of the INS that they will be murdered or tortured if they return home.

All of the Arizona activists facing trial have said they will not suspend

their sanctuary activity as long as they are free. Twenty-five unindicted co-conspirators, from places such as Seattle, Germantown, Pa., and Rochester, N.Y., have said they will continue their work and plan to refuse to testify against their indicted friends.

Even if all the charged activists are jailed, Fife said, the movement will not stop. "They can put Jim and I away for years, and sanctuary will go like gang busters," he said. "No one runs this movement. It runs by itself, on faith."

QUESTIONS

1. Is it wrong for the workers in the sanctuary movement to break the law? Is it wrong to refuse to testify against sanctuary workers who have broken the law? Is it wrong to continue to break the law once the courts have reached a decision on the sanctuary cases?

2. How would Socrates respond to the sanctuary movement workers? Would you agree with Socrates?

3. Is civil disobedience ever justified?

SOURCE: "Answering to a Higher Obligation," *San Jose Mercury News*, 1 January 1985, p. 1. Used by permission.

CRITO: I will do my best, Socrates.

SOCRATES: Is it true that we should never intentionally do wrong?

CRITO: It certainly is.

SOCRATES: And what about returning evil for evil—which is the morality of the many—is that right or not?

CRITO: It is not right.

SOCRATES: But in leaving this prison against the will of the Athenians, am I doing evil to anyone?

CRITO: I am not sure, Socrates.

SOCRATES: Well, imagine that just as I was about to escape, the laws of society arrived and asked me, "Socrates, what are you trying to do? Do you want to destroy us? Won't society fall if its law has no power and if private citizens can set the law aside whenever they want?" How will I answer them, Crito? Perhaps I could respond, "Yes, but society injured me: It sentenced me unjustly." Is that what I should say?

CRITO: Definitely, Socrates!

SOCRATES: Then what if the laws reply, "But didn't you agree to obey our judgments, Socrates?"

And if I show astonishment at this reply, the laws might add, "Do not be surprised, Socrates. You, who are always asking questions, answer us now. Long ago we gave you birth when your father married your mother by our aid and conceived you. Do you object to our marriage laws?"

"No," I would have to reply.

"Then do you object to the laws under which you were raised and which provided for your education?"

"They were fine," I would say.

"Well, then," they would conclude, "We gave you birth. And we raised and educated you. Can you deny then that you are like our son and should obey us? Is it right to strike back at your father when he strikes you?

"Moreover, after we brought you into the world, and after we educated and provided you with many benefits, we proclaimed that you and all Athenians were free to leave us with all your goods when you came of age. But he who had experienced how we administer our society and freely chose to stay, entered into an implied contract that he would obey us.

"So he who disobeys us, we maintain, wrongs us in three ways: First, because in disobeying us he is disobeying his parents; second, because in disobeying us he is disobeying those who gave him the benefits of an education; third, because he agreed to obey us and now he neither obeys nor does he show us where we were wrong. But are we right in saying that you agreed to be governed by us?"

How shall I answer that question, Crito? Must I not agree?

CRITO: There is no other way, Socrates.

SOCRATES: Then the laws will say, "Then, Socrates, in escaping you are breaking the agreement you made with us. So listen to us and not to Crito. Think not of life and children first and of justice afterwards. Put justice first."

This, Crito, is the voice I seem to hear quietly murmuring nearby, like a mystic who thinks he hears a flute playing in his ears. That voice is humming in my ears,

> **CRITICAL THINKING**
>
> Socrates assumes that by remaining in a society one enters into an "implied contract" to obey the law. Is this assumption correct?

The Death of Socrates, Jacques-Louis David.

and it prevents me from hearing any other. Still, if you have anything more to add, Crito, speak up.

CRITO: I have nothing more to say, Socrates.

SOCRATES: Then, Crito, let me do what I must, since it is the will of god.[13]

The next morning, after saying farewell to his family and friends, Socrates drank the poison hemlock and died.

Here again, then, on the eve of his death, we find Socrates doing philosophy. However, now he aims his philosophical questions at his own assumptions and his own life. He reasons that where morality is concerned, he should disregard the "opinions of the many"—that is, moral right and wrong do not depend on what most in our society believe. Instead, moral right and wrong depend on reasoning correctly about whether one is inflicting evil on others. Socrates says that if he escaped he would inflict evil on society because he has an obligation to obey its laws. He has this obligation because

---

[13] Plato, *Crito.* This translation copyright © 1987 by Manuel Velasquez.

society, like a parent, deserves obedience, because it has bestowed important benefits on him, and because he has tacitly agreed to obey. Other considerations, he claims, are irrelevant. And so he concludes that it is wrong for him to escape.

At this point you might well question Socrates' own beliefs. Is it true that moral right and wrong do not depend on what our society believes? Do we really have an obligation to obey the laws of society even to the death? If we do have such an obligation, do we have it because we must "repay" society through our unwavering obedience? Have we really entered an agreement to obey society? Must we obey any command of the law no matter how terrible?

We have not settled the answers to these questions, although they are obviously important to our lives. We must each decide for ourselves what morality is and which moral principles we choose to live by. We must each decide for ourselves whether we have an obligation to obey the law or whether there are some laws that we are free to disobey. We must each decide what, if anything, we owe society for what it has done for us. We should ponder these questions. Although we will not spend any more time on them now, we will return to them later. At this point what is important is the realization that answering such questions is what philosophy is all about. Socrates' own willingness to struggle with these questions even in the face of death gives us a priceless and still powerful example of what philosophy means.

In the philosopher's mind Plato is alive. The philosopher is taking part in a conversation where Plato's speech is there, Aristotle's reply, then Augustine, Thomas, Descartes, Leibniz, Spinoza, Locke, Berkeley, Hume, and Kant. And the philosopher is trying to tack on the next bit of the conversation.

W. D. HART

QUESTIONS

1. Have you known bright people who weren't wise? Why weren't they wise? Make two lists, one containing the characteristics of intelligent people, the other the characteristics of wise people. How much overlap is there? What kind of wisdom would you like to possess?

2. Are actions right because God or society says they are right? When you are unsure whether an action is right, do you try to determine its rightness or wrongness by trying to find out what God or society holds? Choose some action that you believe is clearly right or clearly wrong, and show that it is right or wrong. How is the rightness or wrongness of an action established?

3. It is sometimes said that the admission of ignorance is the beginning of wisdom. Why? Does Socrates' self-defense indicate this belief?

4. Do you have an obligation to obey the law? What is the basis of this obligation? How far does it extend? Could you ever have an obligation to disobey the law? What makes these questions philosophical questions?

5. What exactly is the meaning of Socrates' maxim "The unexamined life is not worth living"? How does it relate to philosophy?

6. Construct a dialogue between two people discussing the nature of beauty. One person insists that beauty lies in the eye of the beholder. The other person attempts to get the first person to analyze this claim, to clarify and crystallize the concept.

1.4 The Value of Philosophy

A person studying philosophy for the first time might ask: Why devote all this time and effort to study philosophy? We have seen that Plato, in the Myth of the Cave, suggested an answer: The value of philosophy is that through it we achieve freedom—freedom from assumptions we have unquestioningly accepted from others, and freedom to decide for ourselves what we believe about ourselves and our place in the universe.

Other philosophical traditions have suggested that philosophical wisdom is the key to a different, more profound kind of freedom. For example, Buddhism holds that when we have dispelled our philosophical ignorance and have understood our true place in the universe, we will be freed from the otherwise unending wheel of birth, suffering, death, and rebirth to which all living creatures are bound. In this view, each living thing, when it dies, is reincarnated in another living thing, its new condition determined by its past action, or karma. Yet by dispelling ignorance and acquiring wisdom we are each able to break out of the wheel. For example, Buddhist writings of the second century A.D. describe a vision experienced by the great Eastern sage Buddha:

> In the first watch of the night he recollected the successive series of his former births. "There was I so and so; that was my name; deceased from there I came here"—in this way he remembered thousands of births, as though living them over again. When he had recalled his own births and deaths in all these various lives of his, the Sage, full of pity, turned his compassionate mind towards other living things, and he thought to himself: "Again and again they must leave the people they regard as their own, and must go on elsewhere, and that without ever stopping. Surely this world is unprotected and helpless, and like a wheel it turns round and round." As he continued steadily to recollect the past thus, he came to the definite conviction that this world of suffering [samsara] is as unsubstantial as the pith of a plantain tree. . . . [I]n the second watch of the night, . . . he saw that the decease and rebirth of beings depend on whether they have done superior or inferior deeds. . . . Then, as the third watch of that night drew on, the supreme master of trance turned his meditation to the real and essential nature of this world: "Alas, living beings wear themselves out in vain! Over and over again they are born, they age, die, pass on to a new life, and are reborn! What is more, greed and dark delusion obscure their sight and they are blind from birth. Greatly apprehensive, they yet do not know how to get out of this great mass of ill." He then surveyed the twelve links of conditioned causes, and saw that, beginning with ignorance, they lead to old age and death, and, beginning with the cessation of ignorance, they lead to the cessation of birth, old age, death and all kinds of ill. Then the great seer had comprehended that where there is no ignorance whatever, there also the karma-formations are stopped—then he had achieved a correct knowledge of all there is to be known, and he stood out in the world as a Buddha. . . . For seven days he dwelt there. . . . He thought, "Here I have found freedom."[14]

---

[14] From *Sacred Texts of the World,* ed. Ninian Smart and Richard D. Hecht (New York: Crossroad, 1982), 234–235.

In the Buddhist perspective, then, philosophy is a search for the ultimate freedom: an escape from the endless cycles of birth, suffering, death, and rebirth to which we are condemned by our past. The value of philosophical wisdom is great indeed!

Still, the value that Plato and the Buddha attribute to philosophical wisdom may leave you unmoved. Today, mundane tasks and activities crowd our lives and leave us little time for anything else. Why should we spend the time and effort to study philosophy when so many more practical needs are pressing in on us? For example, it is clear why we should spend time studying those subjects that will provide the knowledge and skills needed to get a job or succeed in a career. We each need a job or a career to get along, to earn our living and meet our basic needs. But what needs does philosophy satisfy?

When people talk about getting along, they generally mean satisfying what psychologists often term "maintenance needs." These needs are the physical and psychological needs that people must satisfy to maintain themselves as human beings: food, shelter, security, social interaction, and so on. Little wonder, then, that most of us have no trouble understanding the need for job-preparation courses: They clearly help in satisfying maintenance needs.

Some modern psychologists, Abraham Maslow among them, point out that humans have needs other than maintenance needs, which they term "actualizing needs." Although more difficult to describe than maintenance needs, actualizing needs are associated with self-fulfillment, creativity, self-expression, and realization of our potential—that is, with being everything we can be. Why mention these? Because to evaluate the worth of courses and disciplines in terms of their job-preparation value is to take a narrow view of what human beings need. It completely overlooks higher-level needs. This doesn't mean, of course, that studying philosophy will necessarily lead to self-actualization. Nevertheless, philosophy helps by promoting the ideal of self-actualization, or what psychotherapist Carl Rogers terms "the fully functioning person."

Consider some characteristics of the self-actualized or fully functioning person. One is the ability to form one's own opinions and beliefs. Self-actualized people don't automatically go along with what's "in" or what's expected of them. Not that they are necessarily rebels; they just make up their own minds. They think, evaluate, and decide for themselves. What could better capture the spirit of philosophy than such intellectual and behavioral independence?

A second characteristic is profound self-awareness. Self-actualized people harbor few illusions about themselves and rarely resort to easy rationalizations to justify their beliefs and actions. If anything, philosophy deepens self-awareness by inviting us to examine the basic intellectual foundations of our lives.

A third characteristic is flexibility. Change and uncertainty don't devastate self-actualized people. They exhibit resilience in the face of disorder, doubt, uncertainty, indefiniteness, even chaos. Yet they are not indifferent or uncaring. Quite the opposite. They are much involved in their experiences. Because of their resilience, they not only recognize the essential ambiguity of human affairs but also develop a high tolerance for ambiguity. A lack of definite answers or concrete solutions does not overwhelm them. When seriously undertaken, the study of philosophy promotes what some have termed a "philosophical calm," the capacity to persevere in the face of upheaval. This stems in part from an ability to put things into perspective, to see the "big picture," to make neither too much nor too little of events.

A fourth characteristic of self-actualized or fully functioning people is that they are generally creative. They are not necessarily writers, painters, or musicians, for creativity can function in many ways and at various levels. Instead, such people exhibit creativity in all they do. Whether spending leisure time or conversing, they seem to leave their own distinctive mark. Philosophy can help in this process by getting us to develop a philosophical perspective on issues, problems, and events. This means, in part, that we no longer see or experience life on the surface. We engage it on deeper levels, and we interact with it so that we help fashion our world. In another way, because philosophy exercises our imaginations, it invites a personal expression that is unique.

Finally, self-actualized people have clearer, well-thought-out value systems in morality, the arts, politics, and so on. Values are a fundamental concern of philosophy. Philosophy often deals directly with morals, art, politics, and other value areas. So it offers us an opportunity to formulate our values in these areas and to find meaning in our lives. For some psychologists, the search for meaning and values is the human's primary interest.

Some philosophers have shared this psychological insight, although they have expressed it differently. Perhaps the best example is Aristotle. Aristotle developed his view of self-realization by distinguishing among bodily goods (such as health), external goods (such as wealth), and moral goods (such as virtue).

In his masterly analysis of happiness, Aristotle says that happiness is the end or goal of all human beings.[15] However, happiness does not consist in any action of the body or senses. In the language of Maslow, happiness consists in satisfying higher-level needs rather than maintenance needs. Aristotle holds that happiness is an activity of what is noblest and best in us: our reason. Yet happiness is not the activity of practical reason, for this is full of care and trouble in meeting basic needs. In contrast, happiness is the activity of speculative and theoretical reason; it is the life of the intellectual virtues, the chief of which is philosophic wisdom, which equips us for contemplating the highest truth and good. In brief, for Aristotle, health, maturity, education, friends, and worldly goods (all of which serve to satisfy maintenance needs) should be subordinate aids to living happily. And the happy life consists in a self-realization that takes root in philosophic wisdom.

So it seems safe to say that philosophy has value partly because it helps us satisfy higher-level needs, which arise when maintenance needs are met. Yet philosophy also contributes to the satisfaction of some maintenance needs. We mentioned previously the need for security. People often get insurance policies and go to extreme measures to avoid anxiety-inducing situations. Nevertheless, security needs show up on other levels. People seek to make sense of their world

CRITICAL THINKING

Philosophers assume that expanding our personal freedom, autonomy, and the alternatives open to us are all good, and that to the extent that philosophy expands these it must also be good. Is this assumption necessarily true?

I think that philosophy—from Socrates on—has been concerned with thinking carefully about how to live.

HILARY PUTNAM

Philosophers play a strange game. They know very well that one thing alone counts: Why are we born on this earth? And they also know that they will never be able to answer it. Nevertheless, they continue sedately to amuse themselves.

JACQUES MARITAIN

---

[15] See his *Nicomachean Ethics*, bk. 1, chs. 4–13; bk. 10, chs. 6–9.

in a variety of ways: through allegiance to religious beliefs, adherence to political systems, commitment to causes. In part, such loyalties and behaviors reveal the human need for putting order in our universe, for making sense of things. Can philosophy help?

In fact, it's hard to imagine a better place to begin this ordering process than with the study of philosophy. One goal of philosophy is the integration of experience into a unified, coherent, systematic world view. Studying philosophy will expose you to different ways of looking at the world. It will also show you how various philosophers have ordered the universe for themselves. Stated another way, philosophy aims to integrate at the personal level, thought, feeling, and action in a meaningful way. As a result, philosophy extends the range of

PHILOSOPHY AND LIFE

Viktor Frankl's Logotherapy

Dr. Viktor E. Frankl is one psychologist who believes that the search for meaning is the human's primary interest. Frankl, professor of psychiatry and neurology, spent three years at Auschwitz and other Nazi concentration camps. He then gained his freedom, only to learn that almost all his family had been wiped out. During those years of incredible suffering and degradation, which he in part describes in his *Man's Search for Meaning*, Frankl developed a theory of psychotherapy termed *logotherapy*.

Logotherapy is derived from the Greek word *logos*, for "meaning." Logotherapy focuses on the meaning of human existence as well as on humans' search for such meaning. According to Dr. Frankl and other logotherapists, the striving to find meaning in their lives is the primary motivational force in humans. He writes:

Man's search for meaning is a primary force in his life and not a "secondary rationalization" of instinctual drives. This meaning is unique and specific in

that it must and can be fulfilled by him alone; only then does it achieve a significance that will satisfy his own will to meaning. There are some authors who contend that meaning and values are "nothing but defense mechanisms, reaction formation and sublimation." But as for myself, I would not be willing to live merely for the sake of my "defense mechanisms," nor would I be ready to die merely for the sake of my "reaction formations." Man, however, is able to live and even to die for the sake of his ideals and values!

Logotherapy, therefore, considers humans as beings whose primary concerns are fulfilling a meaning and actualizing values, rather than merely gratifying and satisfying drives and instincts.

Dr. Frankl contends that the human search for meaning and value may arouse inner tensions rather than inner equilibrium. But he feels that these tensions are an indispensable prerequisite to mental health. There is nothing else that would so effectively help one survive even the worst conditions than the

knowledge that there is a meaning in one's life. As evidence, he recalls his prison experiences, in which he witnessed that those who believed that there was a task waiting for them, a meaning, were the most likely to survive. For Dr. Frankl, mental health is based in part on the tension that's inherent in humans who recognize the gap between what they are and what they should become.

QUESTIONS

1. Can the study of philosophy be related to the principles of logotherapy?

2. Is there any wisdom in the following words of the German philosopher Friedrich Nietzsche (1844–1900): "He who has a *why* to live for can bear almost any *how*"?

3. What, if any, meaning do you currently find in your life?

SOURCE: Frankl, *Man's Search for Meaning*, 154–155.

personal alternatives. Perhaps we believe things or have a particular outlook primarily because of our acculturation. We've never really thought about these beliefs or perspectives, having adopted them as an intellectual backdrop. We all have such taken-for-granted beliefs, but a different set of beliefs may exist that is more suitable for us. Or we may not fully understand and appreciate the worth of our own taken-for-granted ideas. Either way, philosophy offers the opportunity to test various beliefs, outlooks, and lifestyles.

Other things make philosophy worthwhile. For example, consider the importance of awareness. In part, personal freedom depends on awareness of self and the world. To a large degree, we are only as free as we are aware of the significant influences on our lives. In helping us deepen our awareness, philosophy gives us the ability to deal with and perhaps to slough off encumbrances to freedom.

What's more, philosophy exposes us to the history of thought. By portraying the evolutionary nature of intellectual achievement, it provides a perspective on the continuing development of human thought. As we confront the thought of various philosophers, we realize that one outlook is not necessarily true and another false; the value of any attitude lies chiefly in its usefulness within a given context. A merit of this exposure is that it breeds humility. We realize that if today's view has proved yesterday's inadequate, then tomorrow's may so prove today's. As a result, we become more tolerant, more receptive, and more sympathetic to views that compete or conflict with our own. We're less biased, provincial, ingrown; we're more open-minded and cosmopolitan.

Also, the study of philosophy helps us refine our powers of analysis, our abilities to think critically, to reason, to evaluate, to theorize, and to justify. As we said earlier, these skills are the tools of philosophy. Exposure to the great ideas of extraordinary thinkers can hone our own powers of analysis enough to apply them constructively to our own affairs.

This is, perhaps, the place to consider an important objection to the value of philosophy. Recently, some feminist philosophers have questioned whether philosophy has any value to women. Philosophy, they have argued, is essentially a male activity because the basic ideas and methods of philosophy are biased against women and in favor of men.

The feminist philosopher Janice Moulton, for example, has pointed out that most philosophers use an "adversarial method" of inquiry. That is, most philosophers approach other philosophers as adversaries whose views they must attack and prove wrong. The primary tool that philosophers use in attacking one another's theories are "counterexamples," examples that the other philosopher's theory cannot account for. The adversarial method, she suggests, seems to leave no room for the kind of nonadversarial search for the truth that women favor. Instead, it may be rooted in male aggression.[16]

Genevieve Lloyd, also a feminist philosopher, in an insightful and masterful analysis of the history of philosophy has pointed out that males have dominated

---

[16]Janice Moulton, "A Paradigm of Philosophy: The Adversarial Method," in *Women, Knowledge, and Reality*, 5–20.

philosophy from the beginning. These male philosophers have associated favorable traits with men and unfavorable ones with women. Lloyd notes that this has given philosophy a male bias that is unattractive to women:

> The equation of maleness with superiority goes back at least as far as the Pythagoreans. What is valued—whether it be odd as against even numbers, "aggressive" as against "nurturing" skills and capacities, or Reason as against emotion—has been readily identified with maleness. Within the context of this association of maleness with preferred traits, it is not just incidental to the feminine that female traits have been construed as inferior . . . to male norms of human excellence. The denigration of the "feminine" is to feminists, understandably, the most salient aspect of the maleness of the philosophical tradition.[17]

If Moulton and Lloyd are correct, if philosophy is at bottom a male activity with a male bias, it seems that women have little reason to consider philosophizing. Why engage in an activity that has produced such sexist views? Why should a woman engage in a man's game played by men's rules? Why should women philosophize? Lloyd answers these questions herself:

> Understanding the contribution of past thought to "male" and "female" consciousnesses, as we now have them, can help make available a diversity of intellectual styles and characters to men and women alike. It need not involve a denial of all difference. Contemporary consciousness, male or female, reflects past philosophical ideals as well as past differences in the social organization of the lives of men and women. Such differences do not have to be taken as norms; and understanding them can be a source of richness and diversity in a human life whose full range of possibilities and experience is freely accessible to both men and women.[18]

Lloyd is suggesting that the most important task—for women and men—is to understand and change the mistaken philosophical assumptions about men and women that past male philosophers have given us. Our world, our families, our friends, our music, our magazines, and our televisions all now repeat these assumptions. Yet these assumptions have been shaped by a philosophy that has excluded women. If we are to change these mistaken philosophical assumptions about our most basic sexual selves, women must enter philosophy with new philosophical ideas and new philosophical methods.

If feminists like Moulton and Lloyd are correct—and there is good reason to believe that they are—then philosophy has left us with sexist and distorted philosophical views of ourselves. We must all work together to change these. Women, no less than men, must engage in philosophical thought to correct these distortions. Women, especially, must create a new way of thinking about what it is to be a woman or a man in today's world. Moreover, unless women enter into philosophy, male philosophers will continue to use methods of inquiry that are unpalatable to women and that result in distorted ideas. Women must philosophize, then, to reshape the philosophical assumptions that influence our thinking, and to create more cooperative and inclusive methods of

---

[17] Genevieve Lloyd, *The Man of Reason: "Male" and "Female" in Western Philosophy* (Minneapolis: University of Minnesota Press, 1984), 103–104.
[18] Ibid., 107.

philosophizing. In short, if philosophy is the central problem, it is also the fundamental solution.

There are no free lunches, not even in philosophy. If you want what philosophy offers, you must pay a price. Part of the price is long, painstaking study and careful examination and reexamination of ideas, outlooks, and assertions. Another part is the realization that this process is endless; we will not reach a point at which we have resolved all our questions and removed all our doubts. Potentially the highest price to be paid for the rewards of philosophical study is the risk that philosophy creates, for in subjecting beliefs to the critical questioning that makes up an important part of the philosophical enterprise, we risk unmasking personal and cultural assumptions. Doubtless, the collapse of a cherished belief, like the loss of a loved one, can deeply wound and pain. Not surprisingly, we resist challenges to those ideas that we take for granted. So, as we begin our adventure into the exciting, though disturbing, worlds of great philosophical ideas, it's important to ponder this question: Can individuals or societies progress without intellectual suffering?

It seems not, though it might take many pages and volumes to illustrate and prove this belief. It is enough here to suggest that in many ways, if not all ways, we are better off today than our primitive ancestors were. Still, so-called civilization and all that it includes have not come easily. Many people along the way have suffered enormous intellectual agony. We met one such person in this chapter, Socrates, who ultimately paid with his life for what he believed. Consider how profoundly impoverished we would be, personally and collectively, had Socrates been unwilling to pay the price. He, like countless others, paid his intellectual dues and, in a way, ours as well.

Nevertheless, a considerable debt is still outstanding, for neither as individuals nor as a species do we have all the answers, the whole truth, the full meaning. Isn't that, after all, what we seek? Isn't it what we've always sought? If so, then let's press on, convinced that the goal that we seek is well worth the risks.

In the pages ahead, as we consider many enduring philosophical questions, uppermost in each of our minds will be this question: Who and what am I? We could call this the unifying theme that draws together what may seem disparate philosophical concerns. We'll see that the study of philosophy can help us in answering this question, for ultimately a human being is many things: a moral being, a social and political animal, an appreciator of art and beauty, a perceiver and knower, a scientist, a religionist. As we now know, all these aspects of humanity and self are areas of intense philosophical concern and speculation. Therefore, our adventure into the world of philosophy is more than an encounter with great ideas, thinkers, systems, and movements. It's a voyage into ourselves. It's a quest for self-definition and understanding.

> *When a speculative philosopher believes he has comprehended the world once and for all in his system, he is deceiving himself; he has merely comprehended himself and then naively projected that view upon the world.*
>
> CARL G. JUNG

> *The philosopher forces us to deepen our examination of public issues. In an age where powerful forces are trying to turn reasoning about public issues into manipulation by the media, serious, reflective thinking is terribly important.*
>
> HILARY PUTNAM

QUESTIONS

1. What indications of actualizing needs do you currently see in your life?

2. What evidence suggests that your college curriculum was devised in part with something like actualizing needs in mind?

3. It's not uncommon for "successful" people to be bored. Indeed, many academically successful students express profound boredom with school. What, in your mind, is the nature of boredom? Can it be related to actualizing needs? Can philosophy in any way combat boredom?

4. Can you think of any people whom you consider self-actualized? What traits do they show?

5. Give an example of how increasing your awareness has made you freer.

6. Exactly what is the difference, if any, between approaching reality through poetry and approaching reality philosophically?

7. What is the difference, if any, between approaching reality through the methods of the natural sciences and approaching reality philosophically?

8. Is there anything that women can bring to philosophy that men cannot? Explain. Do you think that women philosophize in a different way or about different things than men do? Explain.

1.5 Chapter Summary and Conclusions

In this opening chapter we have tried to communicate some of the interest and importance of philosophy and to show that philosophy is not to be feared but rather to be cultivated and relished. We began by observing that everyone philosophizes in daily life, and we saw how Plato pictured philosophy as a climb from darkness to light in the pursuit of wisdom. We cited the three main fields of philosophy and then turned to watch the philosopher Socrates at work. Finally, we saw the value of studying philosophy: It satisfies our higher-level needs, and it liberates us by intensifying our awareness, deepening our tolerance, and broadening our capacity to deal with the uncertainties of living. The main points of this chapter are as follows:

1. Philosophy, which literally means the love of wisdom, begins with wonder about our most basic beliefs. Its goal is to help us achieve autonomy by making us more aware of our own beliefs and encouraging us to reason and think through issues for ourselves (1.1).

2. The Myth of the Cave is one of the best-known passages in *The Republic*, a work of the Greek philosopher Plato. The myth describes the philosopher's climb from the dark cave of ignorance up into the light of philosophical wisdom (1.1).

3. Philosophy is the critical and rational examination of the most fundamental assumptions that underlie our lives, an activity of concern to men and women of all cultures and races (1.1).

4. The three main fields of philosophy are epistemology, metaphysics, and ethics (1.2).

5. Epistemology deals with questions of knowledge (including the structure, reliability, extent, and kinds of knowledge); truth, validity, and logic; and a variety of linguistic concerns. An example is the question of whether truth is relative (1.2).

6. Metaphysics addresses questions of reality (including the meaning and nature of being); the nature of mind, self, and human freedom; and some topics that overlap with religion, such as the existence of God, the destiny of the universe, and the immortality of the soul. An example is the question of whether human behavior is free or determined (1.2).

7. Ethics is the study of our values and moral principles and how they relate to human conduct and to our social and political institutions. For example, do we have a moral obligation to love and serve others, or is our only obligation to ourselves (1.2)?

8. Philosophy also includes several fields usually referred to as "the philosophy of . . . ," including the philosophy of science, the philosophy of art, and the philosophical meaning of life. These fields of philosophy examine the basic assumptions underlying particular areas of human knowledge or activity (1.2).

9. Socrates is usually considered the father of Western philosophy, although he was preceded by a group of earlier Greek philosophers, the pre-Socratics. Socrates was put to death for persistently examining the unquestioned assumptions of his fellow Athenians. The views of Socrates were preserved by his disciple, Plato, in his early dialogues, including *Euthyphro*, *The Republic*, *The Apology*, and *Crito* (1.3).

10. *Euthyphro* shows Socrates questioning traditional religious beliefs; *The Republic* shows Socrates inquiring into the meaning of justice; *The Apology* shows Socrates at his trial explaining his lifelong commitment to philosophy; *Crito* shows Socrates awaiting death and questioning his own beliefs about the authority of the state (1.3).

11. Philosophy can help satisfy actualizing needs (the need for self-fulfillment, realization of one's potential) by helping us develop our own opinions and beliefs, increasing our self-awareness, equipping us to deal with uncertainty, eliciting creativity, and aiding us in clearly conceptualizing our value systems (1.4).

12. In studying philosophy we risk having the weaknesses of our personal and cultural beliefs and assumptions exposed, but this risk is worth taking, considering the value of philosophy. Because philosophy has had many male tendencies, it is especially important now for women to philosophize (1.4).

Before concluding this chapter, let us point out a recurring problem in any introduction to philosophy. Because so much material is, and must be, covered, the overall treatment may lack focus and leave the student confused or with only a most superficial understanding. Although there is no easy solution to this problem, one useful device is to take a more in-depth look at important figures in the material being covered. This book will use this strategy. Because the purpose of this technique is to exhibit the writings and thoughts of philosophers, an appropriate term for it is *showcase*. Each showcase includes both an overview of the philosophy of important figures and edited selections from their writings so that you can read each philosopher's own words. Moreover, taken together, the showcases are intended to provide a feeling for the history of philosophy. Consequently, for the most part they are in historical order.

Because we are beginning philosophy, our first showcase spotlights the earliest Western and Eastern philosophers. Examining these will give us a better idea of the historical significance of philosophy. These first philosophers had a remarkable impact on how we view reality and ourselves today, an impact that philosophy continues to have through the ages.

1.6 HISTORICAL SHOWCASE

The First Philosophers

Western philosophy began with a question the Greek thinker Thales asked around 585 B.C.: What is the ultimate reality of which everything is made? Thales' answer will strike you as a bit funny and prosaic. He answered, "Everything ultimately is made of water!"

But the factual correctness of Thales' answer isn't really important. What is significant is that he was the first to take a radically new, "philosophical" approach to reality. Thinkers before Thales were content to explain reality as the whimsical work of mythical gods. For example, the Greek poet Hesiod (ca. 776 B.C.) explains how the sky came to rain on the earth by describing the sky as a male god who was castrated by his son while sleeping with goddess Earth:

Great Heaven came at night longing for love.
He lay on Earth spreading himself full on her.

Then from an ambush, his own son stretched out
  his left hand.
And wielding a long sharp sickle in his right,
He swiftly sliced and cut his father's genitals.
Earth received the bloody drops that all gushed forth.
And she gave birth to the great Furies and mighty
  giants.
Now when chaste Heaven desires to penetrate the
  Earth,
And Earth is filled with longing for this union,
Rain falling from her lover, Heaven, impregnates
  her,
And she brings forth wheat for men and pastures for
  their flocks.[1]

Thales departed in three ways from this mythological and poetic approach to reality. First, he had the idea that although reality is complex, it should be explainable in terms of one or a few basic elements. Second, he decided that reality should be explained in terms of natural, observable things (like water) and not by poetic appeals to unobservable gods. Third, he rejected the idea that reality

----
[1] Hesiod, *The Theogony*, pt. 11, lines 177–185. This translation copyright © 1987 by Manuel Velasquez.

should be explained through the authority of religious myths from the past, which could neither be proved nor disproved. Instead, he tried to provide a literal and factual explanation that others could evaluate for themselves through reasoning and observation.

Thus, although Thales' theory—that water is the basic stuff out of which everything is made—seems naive, he was the first to break away from religious myth and strike out on a path that uses human reason and observation to explore the universe. His having taken this momentous and daring step marks him as a genius. In fact, today we continue to travel the road Thales showed us. Much of our basic scientific research is still devoted to finding the simplest elemental forces out of which everything in the universe is made, and we still proceed by proposing theories or *hypotheses* that can be proved or disproved through reason and observation. It took the genius of Thales to set Western civilization on this amazingly fruitful path of discovery.

But two other early Greek philosophers, Heraclitus (ca. 554–484 B.C.) and Parmenides (ca. 480–430 B.C.), proposed the most interesting and radical of the early philosophical views of reality. Both philosophers left the question of what things are made of and turned their attention to the problem of *change*—whether change is a basic reality or a mere illusion, real or merely appearance.

Heraclitus, in a remarkable series of sayings, proposed that change is the fundamental reality. He asserted that like a fire's flame, "All reality is changing." Like a flowing river, everything in the universe changes from moment to moment, so we can never touch or perceive the same thing in two different moments. The only enduring realities are the recurring patterns (like the seasons) of change itself:

> In the same rivers we step and yet we do not step; we ourselves are the same and yet we are not. You cannot step in the same river twice, for other waters are ever flowing on. The sun is new every day. The living and the dead, the waking and sleeping, the young and the old, these are changing into each other; the former are moved about and become the latter, the latter in turn become the former. Neither god nor man shaped this universe, but it ever was and ever

shall be a living Fire that flames up and dies in measured patterns. There is a continual exchange: all things are exchanged for Fire and Fire for all things. Fire steers the universe. God changes like Fire.[2]

Parmenides, convinced that Heraclitus was completely mistaken, proposed a theory that was the exact opposite. Parmenides held that change is an illusion and that the universe in reality is a frozen, unchanging object: "We can speak and think only of what exists. And what exists is uncreated and imperishable, for it is whole and unchanging and complete. It was not nor shall be different since it is now, all at once, one and continuous."[3] How was Parmenides led to this view? He argued that nothingness or "nonbeing" cannot be real because we cannot even think of nothingness. Yet change requires nonbeing or nothingness. For if something changes, it must change into something that did not exist before: something must come into being out of nonbeing. But nonbeing does not exist. So nothing can come from nonbeing. Therefore, change cannot exist; the universe has no beginning, and nothing in it changes:

> For what beginning of the universe could you search for? From what could it come? I will not let you say or think "From what was not" because you cannot even conceive of "what is not." Nor will true thinking allow that, besides what exists, new things could also arise from something that does not exist. How could what exists pass into what does not exist? And how can what does not exist come into existence? For if it came into existence, then it earlier was nothingness. And nothingness is unthinkable and unreal.[4]

Parmenides' strange view received support from one of his students, Zeno. Zeno argued that "a runner cannot move from one point to another. For to do so, he must first get to a point half-way across, and to do this, he must get half-way to the half-way point, and to do this he must get half-way to that point, and so on for an infinite number of spaces."[5]

---

[2] Diels-Kranz, *Fragments of the Presocratics*, Heraclitus, fragments 49, 12, 6, 88, 30, 90, 64, 67, trans. Manuel Velasquez.
[3] Ibid., Parmenides, 7.
[4] Ibid., 8.
[5] Aristotle, *Physics*, 239b11, trans. Manuel Velasquez.

Because an infinite number of spaces cannot be crossed (at least not in a finite length of time), Zeno concluded that no object moves: motion is an illusion of our senses!

In spite of—or perhaps because of—their unusual views, the pre-Socratic philosophers made several crucial contributions to our thinking. They got us to rely on our reason and to search for new ways of looking at reality instead of relying on the authority of the past. They introduced us to the problem of the one and the many: Can the many things of our experience be explained in terms of one or a few fundamental constituents? They introduced the problem of appearance and reality: Does a more basic reality underlie the changing world that appears before us? Moreover, the views they proposed continue even today to have followers. Twentieth-century "process philosophers," for example, hold that change or "process" is the fundamental reality, and some twentieth-century British philosophers have held that change is an illusion.

But even before Thales, Parmenides, and Heraclitus had developed their fresh, nonmythical approach to reality, the great visionaries of India had put Eastern philosophy (those systems of thought, belief, and action espoused by many peoples in the Near and Far East) on a similar road to reality. However, this road would take Eastern philosophy in a very different direction.

Between 1500 B.C. and 700 B.C., the first of a long line of Indian thinkers composed the Vedas, poetic hymns that contain the beginnings of Indian wisdom and that were meant to be chanted in religious ceremonies. The authors of many of these hymns are unknown, and many of the hymns describe "visions" of "seers." These writings, steeped in myth and symbolism, nevertheless also contain early attempts to find a new, nonmythical understanding of the universe. Here is how one of the greatest of these hymns, the Rig Veda, describes the origin of the universe in the mythical terms of the seers, while at the same time wondering whether the seers' myths are adequate:

> In the beginning there was neither existence nor
> nonexistence;
> Neither the world nor the sky beyond.

> What was covered over? Where? Who gave it
> protection?
> Was there water, deep and unfathomable?

> Then was neither death nor immortality,
> Nor any sign of night or day.
> THAT ONE breathed, without breath, by its own
> impulse;
> Other than that was nothing at all.

> There was darkness, concealed in darkness,
> And all this was undifferentiated energy.
> THAT ONE, which had been concealed by the
> void,
> Through the power of heat-energy was manifested.

> In the beginning was love,
> Which was the primal germ of the mind.
> The seers, searching in their hearts with wisdom,
> Discovered the connection between existence and
> nonexistence.

> They were divided by a crosswise line.
> What was below and what was above?
> There were bearers of seed and mighty forces,
> Impulse from below and forward movement from
> above.

> Who really knows? Who here can say?
> When it was born and from where it came—this
> creation?
> The Gods are later than this world's creation—
> Therefore who knows from where it came?

> That out of which creation came,
> Whether it held it together or did not,
> He who sees it in the highest heaven,
> Only He knows—or perhaps even He does not
> know![6]

Although the author of this hymn is still groping for a nonmythical way of understanding the universe, he nevertheless succeeds in expressing a great insight: There is a fundamental reality beyond all the distinctions and concepts we make in our language, and this reality is the ultimate source of the universe. This reality, which can only be

---

[6]Rig Veda, 10.129, in *Oriental Philosophies*, 2d ed., ed. and trans. John M. Koller (New York: Scribner's, 1985), 23–24. © 1970, 1985 Charles Scribner's Sons. Reprinted with permission of Prentice-Hall, Inc., Upper Saddle River, NJ.

pointed to as "That One," is neither "existence nor nonexistence," it is "neither the world nor the sky beyond," it is "undifferentiated," and it was there before even God or the gods existed. This great idea of the Vedas posed a basic question for Eastern philosophy: What is the nature of this ultimate reality?

In the Upanishads, writings later added to the Vedas, we find the first attempts of Indian thinkers to understand this ultimate reality in philosophical terms. The Upanishads refer to the ultimate reality as Brahman and describe it in negative terms:

> Invisible, incomprehensible, without genealogy, colorless, without eye or ear, without hands or feet, unending, pervading all and omnipresent, that is the unchangeable one whom the wise regard as the source of beings.[7]

Thus, Brahman cannot be seen, smelled, felt, or heard. It cannot be imagined, and words cannot describe it. But it is the ultimate reality that must be present behind everything in the universe, causing everything to be, while itself being unlimited and greater than any specific knowable thing.

At this point the philosophers of the Upanishads took a momentous step that was destined to forever change the course of Eastern philosophy. Seeking to understand Brahman, the deepest reality that underlies the universe, they thought to ask, "What am I?" The self, after all, is part of reality. By understanding the self, one could perhaps also understand ultimate reality. The Upanishad philosophers thus turned to understand Atman, or the deepest self.

The Upanishad philosophers argued that Atman is the *me* that lies behind all my living, sensing, and thinking activities; it is the *me* that lies behind my waking experiences, my dreaming experiences, and my deep-sleeping experiences; it is the *me* that directs everything I do but that is not seen or heard or imagined. This deepest self, which can be known only by enlightened inner self-consciousness, the philosophers of the Upanishad concluded, is identical with Brahman, ultimate re-

ality. This profound idea is the foundation of Indian philosophy.

These ideas—that one ultimate reality underlies everything in the universe and that the self is identical with this reality—are beautifully expressed in an Upanishad parable. The parable is about a proud young man, Svetaketu, who returns from the Hindu equivalent of college only to find that his father is wiser than all his teachers:

> Now, there was Svetaketu Aruneya. To him his father said: "Live the life of a student of sacred knowledge. Truly, my dear, from our family there is no one unlearned. . . . "
>
> He then, having become a pupil at the age of twelve, having studied all the Vedas, returned at the age of twenty-four, conceited, thinking himself learned, proud.
>
> Then his father said to him: "Svetaketu, my dear, since now you are conceited, think yourself learned, and are proud, did you also ask for that teaching whereby what has not been heard of becomes heard of, what has not been thought of becomes thought of, what has not been understood becomes understood?"
>
> "What, pray, sir, is that teaching?"
>
> "Just as, my dear, by one piece of clay everything made of clay may be known—the modification is merely a verbal distinction, a name; the reality is just 'clay'—
>
> "Just as, my dear, by one copper ornament everything made of copper may be known—the modification is merely a verbal distinction, a name; the reality is just 'copper'—
>
> "Just as, my dear, by one nail-scissors everything made of iron may be known—the modification is merely a verbal distinction, a name; the reality is just 'iron'—so, my dear, is that teaching."
>
> "Truly, those honored men did not know this; for if they had known it, why would they not have told me? But do you, sir, tell me it."
>
> "So be it, my dear," said he. . . .
>
> "Understand that this [body] is a sprout which has sprung up. It cannot be without a root.
>
> "Where else could its root be than in water? With water, my dear, as a sprout, look for heat as the root. With heat, my dear, as a sprout, look for Being as the root. All creatures here, my dear, have Being as their root, have Being as their abode, have Being as their support. . . .

---

[7]Mundaka Upanishad, 1.1.6, in *Oriental Philosophies*, 28.

"When a person here is deceasing, my dear, his voice goes into his mind; his mind, into his breath; his breath into heat; the heat into the highest divinity. That which is the finest essence — this whole world has that as its soul. That is Reality. That is Atman. That art thou, Svetaketu."[8]

Svetaketu's father is here explaining that everything in the universe arises out of the same ultimate reality. We say there are many different things in the universe, but the differences we see are of our own making: They are mere "verbal distinctions." Underlying the variety of objects is a single unified reality, Brahman. And Brahman is identical with Atman—your deepest self. In short, you are the ultimate reality behind the universe!

The Upanishad philosophers did for the East what the pre-Socratics did for the West. Like the pre-Socratics, the Upanishad philosophers taught the need to inquire carefully into the nature of reality instead of merely accepting the authority of the past. And like the pre-Socratics, the Upanishad philosophers showed the need to look behind appearances to the one ultimate reality.

But the Upanishad philosophers took a further step that would forever distinguish the thought of the East from that of the West. The pre-Socratics taught the West that to find the ultimate constituents of reality, one must analyze the outer, physical world. The Upanishad philosophers, on the other hand, taught us that the way to discover the ultimate reality of the universe is to look within ourselves.

QUESTIONS

1.   Explain why Thales is so important to Western philosophy.

2.   How would Heraclitus have responded to someone who said: "Heraclitus is wrong because the objects we see around us continue to endure through time; although a person, an animal, or a plant may change its superficial qualities, it still remains essentially the same person, animal, or plant throughout these changes. In fact, we recognize change only by contrasting it to the underlying permanence of things. So permanence, not change, is the essential reality"?

3.   How would you answer Zeno's proof that no object moves?

4.   Are there any similarities between the views of Parmenides and those of the Upanishads? Are there essential differences? Explain.

5.   In the Upanishads, Svetaketu's father says, "That art thou, Svetaketu." What does "that" refer to? What does "thou" refer to? Do you see any problem with saying that these two (what "that" refers to and what "thou" refers to) are identical— that is, that they are exactly one and the same thing? Explain.

---

[8]Chandogya Upanishad, in *Beyond the Western Tradition*, 151.

1.7 Readings

Why study philosophy? In his short story, the eighteenth-century French philosopher Voltaire points out that even though an ignorant person may be much happier than a learned philosopher, we nevertheless "madly" prefer the despair of philosophy to the contentment of ignorance. In the second reading, Krishnamurti, a twentieth-century Indian philosopher, suggests that a philosophical understanding of life and self is the key to freedom and the purpose of education. As you read Voltaire and Krishnamurti, ask yourself whether they agree on the value of philosophy or whether they ultimately see philosophy as valuable for radically different reasons. And ask yourself whether you agree with either.

VOLTAIRE

Story of a Good Brahman

I met on my travels an old Brahman, a very wise man, full of wit and very learned; moreover he was rich, and consequently even wiser; for, lacking nothing, he had no need to deceive anyone. His family was very well governed by three beautiful wives who schooled themselves to please him; and when he was not entertaining himself with his wives, he was busy philosophizing.

Near his house, which was beautiful, well decorated, and surrounded by charming gardens, lived an old Indian woman, bigoted, imbecilic, and rather poor.

The Brahman said to me one day: "I wish I had never been born."

I asked him why. He replied:

"I have been studying for forty years, which is forty years wasted; I teach others, and I know

"Story of a Good Brahman," from *Candide, Zadig and Selected Stories by Voltaire* by Francoise Voltaire, translated by Donald M. Frame. Translation copyright © 1961 by Donald M. Frame. Used by permission of Dutton Signet, a division of Penguin Putnam Inc.

nothing; this situation brings into my soul so much humiliation and disgust that life is unbearable to me. I was born, I live in time, and I do not know what time is; I find myself in a point between two eternities, as our sages say, and I have no idea of eternity. I am composed of matter; I think, and I have never been able to find out what produces thought; I do not know whether my understanding is a simple faculty in me like that of walking or of digesting, and whether I think with my head, as I take with my hands. Not only is the principle of my thinking unknown to me, but the principle of my movements is equally hidden from me. I do not know why I exist. However, people every day ask me questions on all these points; I have to answer; I have nothing any good to say; I talk much, and I remain confounded and ashamed of myself after talking.

"It is much worse yet when they ask me whether Brahma was produced by Vishnu or whether they are both eternal. God is my witness that I don't know a thing about it, and it certainly shows in my answers. 'Ah! Reverend Father,' they say to me, 'teach us how it is that evil inundates the whole world.' I am as much at a loss as those who ask me that question; I sometimes tell them that all is for the very best, but those who have been ruined and mutilated at war believe nothing of it, and neither do I; I retreat to my house over-whelmed with my curiosity and my ignorance. I read our ancient books, and they redouble the darkness I am in. I talk to my companions: some answer that we must enjoy life and laugh at men; the others think they know something, and lose themselves in ab-surd ideas; everything increases the painful feeling I endure. I am sometimes ready to fall into despair, when I think that after all my seeking I know nei-ther where I come from, nor what I am, nor where I shall go, nor what shall become of me."

The state of this good man caused me real pain; no one was either more reasonable or more honest than he. I perceived that the greater the lights of his understanding and the sensibility of his heart, the more unhappy he was.

That same day I saw the old woman who lived in his vicinity: I asked her whether she had ever been distressed not to know how her soul was made. She did not even understand my question: she had never reflected a single moment of her life over a single one of the points that tormented the Brahman; she believed with all her heart in the metamorphoses of Vishnu, and, provided she could sometimes have some water from the Ganges to wash in, she thought herself the happiest of women.

Struck by the happiness of this indigent crea-ture, I returned to my philosopher and said to him:

"Aren't you ashamed to be unhappy at a time when right at your door there is an old automaton who thinks of nothing and who lives happily?"

"You are right," he answered; "I have told my-self a hundred times that I would be happy if I was as stupid as my neighbor, and yet I would want no part of such a happiness."

This answer of my Brahman made a greater im-pression on me than all the rest. I examined myself and saw that indeed I would not have wanted to be happy on condition of being imbecilic.

I put the matter up to some philosophers, and they were of my opinion.

"There is, however," I said, "a stupendous con-tradiction in this way of thinking."

For after all, what is at issue? Being happy. What matters being witty or being stupid? What is

more, those who are content with their being are quite sure of being content; those who reason are not so sure of reasoning well.

"So it is clear," I said, "that we should choose not to have common sense, if ever that common sense contributes to our ill-being."

Everyone was of my opinion, and yet I found no one who wanted to accept the bargain of be-coming imbecilic in order to become content. From this I concluded that if we set store by hap-piness, we set even greater store by reason.

But, upon reflection, it appears that to prefer reason to felicity is to be very mad. Then how can this contradiction be explained? Like all the others. There is much to be said about it.

JIDDU KRISHNAMURTI

The Function of Education

I wonder if we have ever asked ourselves what education means. Why do we go to school, why do we learn various subjects, why do we pass exami-nations and compete with each other for better grades? What does this so-called education mean, and what is it all about? This is really a very impor-tant question, not only for the students, but also for the parents, for the teachers, and for everyone who loves this earth. Why do we go through the struggle to be educated? Is it merely in order to pass some examinations and get a job? Or is it the function of education to prepare us while we are young to understand the whole process of life? Having a job and earning one's livelihood is necessary—but is that all? Are we being educated only for that? Surely, life is not merely a job, an occupation; life is some-thing extraordinarily wide and profound, it is a

From *Think on These Things* by J. Krishnamurti. Copyright © 1964 by the Krishnamurti Foundation of America. Re-printed by permission of HarperCollins, Publishers, Inc.

great mystery, a vast realm in which we function as human beings. If we merely prepare ourselves to earn a livelihood, we shall miss the whole point of life; and to understand life is much more important than merely to prepare for examinations and become very proficient in mathematics, physics, or what you will.

So, whether we are teachers or students, is it not important to ask ourselves why we are educating or being educated? And what does life mean? Is not life an extraordinary thing? The birds, the flowers, the flourishing trees, the heavens, the stars, the rivers and the fish therein—all this is life. Life is the poor and the rich; life is the constant battle between groups, races and nations; life is meditation; life is what we call religion, and it is also the subtle, hidden things of the mind—the envies, the ambitions, the passions, the fears, fulfillments and anxieties. All this and much more is life. But we generally prepare ourselves to understand only one small corner of it. We pass certain examinations, find a job, get married, have children, and then become more and more like machines. We remain fearful, anxious, frightened of life. So, is it the function of education to help us understand the whole process of life, or is it merely to prepare us for a vocation, for the best job we can get?

What is going to happen to all of us when we grow to be men and women? Have you ever asked yourselves what you are going to do when you grow up? In all likelihood you will get married, and before you know where you are you will be mothers and fathers; and you will then be tied to a job, or to the kitchen, in which you will gradually wither away. Is that all that *your* life is going to be? Have you ever asked yourselves this question? Should you not ask it? If your family is wealthy you may have a fairly good position already assured, your father may give you a comfortable job, or you may get richly married; but there also you will decay, deteriorate. Do you see?

Surely, education has no meaning unless it helps you to understand the vast expanse of life with all its subtleties, with its extraordinary beauty, its sorrows and joys. You may earn degrees, you may have a series of letters after your name and land a very good job; but then what? What is the point of it all if in the process your mind becomes dull, weary, stupid? So, while you are young, must you not seek to find out what life is all about? And is it not the true function of education to cultivate in you the intelligence which will try to find the answer to all these problems? Do you know what intelligence is? It is the capacity, surely, to think freely, without fear, without a formula, so that you begin to discover for yourself what is real, what is true; but if you are frightened you will never be intelligent. Any form of ambition, spiritual or mundane, breeds anxiety, fear; therefore ambition does not help to bring about a mind that is clear, simple, direct, and hence intelligent.

You know, it is really very important while you are young to live in an environment in which there is no fear. Most of us, as we grow older, become frightened; we are afraid of living, afraid of losing a job, afraid of tradition, afraid of what the neighbours, or what the wife or husband would say, afraid of death. Most of us have fear in one form or another; and where there is fear there is no intelligence. And is it not possible for all of us, while we are young, to be in an environment where there is no fear but rather an atmosphere of freedom—freedom, not just to do what we like, but to understand the whole process of living? Life is really very beautiful, it is not this ugly thing that we have made of it; and you can appreciate its richness, its depth, its extraordinary loveliness only when you revolt against everything—against organized religion, against tradition, against the present rotten society—so that you as a human being find out for yourself what is true. Not to imitate but to discover—*that* is education, is it not? It is very easy to conform to what your society or your parents and teachers tell you. That is a safe and easy way of existing; but that is not living, because in it there is fear, decay, death. To live is to find out for yourself what is true, and you can do this only when there is freedom, when there is continuous revolution inwardly, within yourself.

But you are not encouraged to do this; no one tells you to question, to find out for yourself . . . , because if you were to rebel you would become a danger to all that is false. Your parents and society want you to live safely, and you also want to live safely. Living safely generally means living in imitation and therefore in fear. Surely, the function of education is to help each one of us to live freely and without fear, is it not? And to create an atmosphere in which there is no fear requires a great deal of thinking on your part as well as on the part of the teacher, the educator.

Do you know what this means—what an extraordinary thing it would be to create an atmosphere in which there is no fear? And we *must* create it, because we see that the world is caught up in endless wars; it is guided by politicians who are always seeking power; it is a world of lawyers, policemen and soldiers, of ambitious men and women all wanting position and all fighting each other to get it. Then there are the so-called saints, the religious *gurus* with their followers; they also want power, position, here or in the next life. It is a mad world, completely confused, in which the communist is fighting the capitalist, the socialist is resisting both, and everybody is against somebody, struggling to arrive at a safe place, a position of power or comfort. The world is torn by conflicting beliefs, by caste and class distinctions, by separative nationalities, by every form of stupidity and cruelty—and this is the world you are being educated to fit into. You are encouraged to fit into the framework of this disastrous society; your parents want you to do that, and you also want to fit in.

Now, is it the function of education merely to help you to conform to the pattern of this rotten social order, or is it to give you freedom—complete freedom to grow and create a different society, a new world? We want to have this freedom, not in the future, but now, otherwise we may all be destroyed. We must create immediately an atmosphere of freedom so that you can live and find out for yourselves what is true, so that you become intelligent, so that you are able to face the world and understand it, not just conform to it, so that inwardly, deeply, psychologically you are in constant revolt; because it is only those who are in constant revolt that discover what is true, not the man who conforms, who follows some tradition. . . .

The question is: if all individuals were in revolt, would not the world be in chaos? But is the present society in such perfect order that chaos would result if everyone revolted against it? Is there not chaos now? Is everything beautiful, uncorrupted? Is everyone living happily, fully, richly? Is man not against man? Is there not ambition, ruthless competition? So the world is already in chaos, that is the first thing to realize. Don't take it for granted that this is an orderly society; don't mesmerize yourself with words. Whether here, in Europe, in America, or Russia, the world is in a process of decay. If you see the decay, you have a challenge: you are challenged to find a way of solving this urgent problem. And how you respond to the challenge is important, is it not? If you respond as a Hindu or a Buddhist, a Christian or a communist, then your response is very limited—which is no response at all. You can respond fully, adequately only if there is no fear in you, only if you don't think as a Hindu a communist or a capitalist, but as a total human being who is trying to solve this problem; and you cannot solve it unless you yourself are in revolt against the whole thing, against the ambitious acquisitiveness on which society is based. When you yourself are not ambitious, not acquisitive, not clinging to your own security—only then can you respond to the challenge and create a new world. . . .

When you are doing something with your whole being, not because you want to get somewhere, or have more profit, or greater results, but simply because you love to do it—in that there is no ambition, is there? In that there is no competition; you are not struggling with anyone for first place. And should not education help you to find out what you really love to do so that from the beginning to the end of your life you are working at something which you feel is worth while and which for you has deep significance? Otherwise, for the rest of your days, you will be miserable. Not knowing what you really want to do, your mind falls into a routine in which there is only boredom, decay and death. That is why it is very important to find out while you are young what it is you really *love* to do; and this is the only way to create a new society. . . .

1.8 Appendix: A Look at Logic

Philosophy is not mere speculation. When we merely speculate, we dream up grand ideas and visions about how things might be. We might speculate, for example, that "Everything might be a dream!" Philosophy is more than speculation: By philosophizing, we attempt to *prove* or show that certain ideas or visions are true. That is, philosophers *give reasons* for the views and positions they propose. Philosophizing, therefore, requires that you try to reach the truth through logical reasoning. Without logical reasoning, there is no philosophy, only speculation.

Logic is the study of the methods and principles of correct reasoning. Correct reasoning is reasoning in which the evidence or reasons offered in support of a statement really show that the statement is true. That is, in a piece of correct reasoning, the conclusion that one wants to prove or establish follows from the evidence or the reasons offered in its support, in this sense: If the evidence or reasons are themselves true statements, then the conclusion also has to be true or probably true.

Because philosophizing requires logical reasoning, it is crucial that you have some idea of what logical reasoning is when you start to do philosophy. Moreover, in the pages of this book you will encounter many philosophers trying to prove their views through reasoning. Some of this reasoning will be valid and logical; some of it will be poor or invalid. Therefore, it is important for you to learn how to distinguish valid from invalid reasoning. So we provide here some basic ideas about what logical reasoning is and how to tell when someone's reasoning is poor and when it is valid and logical. As we go along, we contrast good reasoning with instances of incorrect reasoning, or fallacies. A **fallacy** is a piece of reasoning in which the conclusion or claim that a person is trying to establish does not logically follow from the reasons or evidence given in its support.

> **fallacy** an incorrect way of reasoning; an argument that tries to persuade psychologically but not logically

Perhaps a good place to begin is with the principle or law that is considered the foundation of logical reasoning. This is the **law of noncontradiction** or, expressed more positively, the **principle of consistency:**

> **law of noncontradiction** or **principle of consistency** nothing can be said both to be and not be something at the same time and in the same respect

> Nothing can be said both to be and not be something at the same time and in the same respect.

The law of noncontradiction reminds us that if what we are saying is to be logical, then it must be consistent. We cannot say "The sky is blue, but the sky is not blue." To be inconsistent is to speak nonsense.

Sometimes people try to show that we can get along without consistency. For example, Ralph Waldo Emerson once wrote that "a foolish consistency is the hobgoblin of little minds," and some people have claimed that he thereby showed that only narrow thinkers try to be logical. But in fact, a moment's reflection will suffice to show that you cannot make sense unless you are consistent. Even Emerson had to be consistent. Suppose he really held that you don't have to be consistent. Then he would have to agree that it is perfectly acceptable to hold also that you do have to be consistent. After all, if consistency isn't required, then it is fine to be inconsistent, and so it is fine to hold both (1) "You don't have to be consistent" and (2) "You have to be consistent." But this, of course, is meaningless. Logical reasoning, then, is consistent reasoning. If you are reasoning logically, then you are reasoning consistently.

Not surprisingly, because you probably reason consistently at least some of the time, you already know something about logical reasoning. Suppose you are told that if you get a grade of 95 percent on the final examination, then you will get a grade of "A" for the course. And suppose that you get a grade of 95 percent on the final exam. You will no doubt soon be celebrating because you can conclude by logical reasoning that you will receive an "A" for the course. You put together two **premises:**

> (a) If you get a grade of 95 percent on the final exam, then you will get a grade of "A" for the course.

> (b) You got a grade of 95 percent on the final exam.

And you used logical reasoning to draw the **conclusion:**

> (c) Therefore, you will get a grade of "A" for the course.

This is an example of good or valid reasoning. But not all of our reasoning is as good as this. Suppose that instead of getting a grade of 95 percent on the final exam, you get a lower grade. Many people will conclude that since you did *not* get a grade of 95 percent, you will *not* get an "A" for the course. But then they would be engaging in bad or invalid reasoning. They would have put together two premises:

> (d) If you get a grade of 95 percent on the final exam, then you will get a grade of "A" for the course.

> (e) You did not get a grade of 95 percent on the final exam.

And they used invalid reasoning to conclude:

> (f) Therefore, you will not get a grade of "A" for the course.

You can probably see already why this is an example of poor or invalid reasoning. In this example, (f) does not logically follow from (d) and (e). That is, even if both (d) and (e) are true, you might still get a grade of "A" for the course. For example, you might get a grade of 93 percent, which might be high enough to qualify you for an "A," or perhaps other work you did for the course might qualify you for an "A." So it is a mistake to conclude from (d) and (e) that (f) has to be true.

There are, then, good or valid ways of reasoning and bad or invalid ways of reasoning. In **valid** reasoning, the conclusion follows from the evidence by logical necessity, whereas in invalid reasoning it does not. How do you tell the difference? How do you analyze someone's reasoning to determine whether the person is reasoning logically or not?

The first step in analyzing someone's reasoning is to figure out exactly what the person's argument is. An argument in philosophy is not a quarrel or a heated

premises the statements presented in an argument as reasons for accepting the conclusion

conclusion the statement that an argument is intended to demonstrate or prove

valid in logic, having a conclusion that follows from the premises by logical necessity

disagreement accompanied by shouting. Instead, an **argument** consists of a group of reasons or premises that are supposed to prove or establish a person's conclusion. Every argument has two parts: (1) a group of premises, which provide reasons or evidence for a conclusion, and (2) a conclusion, which expresses what a person is trying to prove with these premises. We have seen two arguments, one with premises (a) and (b) and the conclusion (c), the other with premises (d) and (e) and the conclusion (f).

argument a group of statements consisting of premises and conclusions of such a type that the premises are intended to prove or demonstrate the conclusion

Typically, when people are trying to set out an argument in support of a particular conclusion, they tend to use one set of words to identify their premises and another set to introduce their conclusion. For example, people often (but not always) use the following words to indicate their premises: *because, inasmuch as, since, for, otherwise, in view of the fact that, for the reason that, on account of, in view of, considering that*. And people often (but not always) use the following words to indicate their conclusions: *which shows that, as a result, therefore, we may infer that, we may conclude that, thus, hence, so, accordingly, consequently*.

Consider the following argument, for example:

We may conclude that a good God certainly does not exist. Because it is clear that there is evil in the world. And if a good God existed, there would be no evil.

Here the author has begun by stating his conclusion first ("A good God does not exist"). He then states one of his premises ("There is evil in the world") and follows this immediately with a second premise ("If a good God existed, then there would be no evil"). If we arrange this argument in traditional fashion by first listing the premises and then the conclusion, we have:

If a good God exists, then there is no evil in the world.

But there is evil in the world.

_____

Therefore, a good God does not exist.

The first step in analyzing any reasoning is what we have just done: Identify the premises and the conclusion of the reasoning, and then put all the premises together in a list with the conclusion at the end. The result is the person's argument.

Philosophers sometimes divide arguments into two groups: deductive and inductive. **Deductive arguments** are those in which the premises are intended to show that the conclusion must necessarily be true. That is, in a valid deductive argument, the conclusion has to be true if the premises are true. Take this argument as an example:

deductive argument an argument in which the premises are intended to show that the conclusion must necessarily be true

(a) All men are mortal.

(b) Socrates is a man.

_____

(c) Therefore, Socrates is mortal.

Here, if the premises (a) and (b) are true, then we can be sure that the conclusion (c) also has to be true. The truth of the premises guarantees the truth of the conclusion.

Inductive arguments are those in which the premises show only that the conclusion is *probably* true. The most familiar kind of inductive argument is one that is often used in surveys. For example, a sociologist interviews several hundred Americans and finds that they all profess to believe in a strong family life. She then reasons that because everyone she interviewed said they believe in a strong family life, she can conclude that *all* Americans believe in a strong family life. But, of course, this conclusion may be false; it is possible that some Americans that she did not interview do not believe in a strong family life.

We begin our examination of arguments by discussing how to tell valid from invalid deductive arguments; then we examine inductive arguments.

inductive argument an argument in which the premises are intended to show that the conclusion is probably true

DEDUCTIVE ARGUMENTS

After you have figured out a person's argument and determined that it is a deductive argument, how do you tell whether it is valid or invalid? One way of testing the validity of an argument is by discovering what *form* the argument has, and then figuring out whether arguments with that *form* are valid. To see what this means, we look at three kinds of deductive arguments: categorical arguments, hypothetical arguments, and disjunctive arguments; that is, we look at several *forms* of categorical arguments, several *forms* of hypothetical arguments, and several *forms* of disjunctive arguments. Then we discuss how to figure out whether these forms are valid—that is, whether the premises of arguments with these forms guarantee their conclusions. Finally, we contrast these valid forms of arguments with formal fallacies. A **formal fallacy** is a form of argument in which the premises do not guarantee the conclusion.

formal fallacy an argument whose form is such that the premises do not guarantee the conclusion

Before we do this, however, it is essential that you be clear about what it means to say that a deductive argument is valid. The difference between saying that a deductive argument states the *truth* and saying that it is *valid* is very great and very important. A valid deductive argument is merely an argument in which

if the premises are true, then the conclusion must be true.

But the premises of a valid deductive argument may be false! Knowing that a deductive argument is valid does not tell us whether its premises or its conclusion are true.

Let us look as some examples. Here is a valid deductive argument with true premises and a true conclusion:

(a) If the North won the Civil War, then the slaves were freed.

(b) The North won the Civil War.

_____

(c) Therefore, the slaves were freed.

In this valid argument, both the premises and the conclusion are true. But that is not what makes this a valid argument. This argument is valid because we know that if (a) and (b) are true, then (c) has to be true, too. Next, consider this valid argument:

(a) If the South won the Civil War, then the slaves were freed.

(b) The South won the Civil War.

(c) Therefore, the slaves were freed.

This argument is also valid, even though the premises (a) and (b) are both false. What makes it valid anyway is the fact that *if* (a) and (b) *were true*, then (c) would also *have to be true*. Last, consider this invalid argument:

(a) If it is raining, then the sky is cloudy.

(b) The sky is cloudy.

(c) Therefore, it is raining.

In this argument, even if (a) and (b) were both true, the conclusion (c) might still be false (sometimes the sky is cloudy, and it is not raining!). This argument is *invalid*, then, because *even if its premises were both true, its conclusion would not necessarily be true*.

Obviously, being able to tell whether an argument is valid is of great value. We can put together statements that we already know are true (premises), and by using valid reasoning we can reach new conclusions that we can also be sure are true. Valid arguments enable us to go from the truth we already have to a new truth.

When, then, are arguments valid? Let us begin by discussing categorical arguments.

Categorical Arguments

Categorical arguments are made up of categorical statements. A **categorical statement** is a statement that says that part or all of a category or class of things is included in another category or class of things, or that part or all of a class of things is *not* included in another class of things. The following examples are all categorical statements:

> All Americans are free. (The whole of the class of Americans is included in the class of free persons.)
>
> Some mammals are apes. (Part of the class of mammals is included in the class of apes.)
>
> No presidents are women. (The whole of the class of presidents is not included in the class of women.)
>
> Some politicians are not liars. (Part of the class of politicians is not included in the class of liars.)

categorical statement a statement that asserts or denies that part or all of one category of things is included in part or all of another category of things

We call the words that refer to a class of things the **terms** of the statement. In the preceding examples, *Americans, free persons, mammals, apes,* and so on are all terms. Categorical statements always have two terms, a subject and a predicate.

As you can quickly figure out for yourself, there are only four basic forms of categorical statements. Any simple statement consisting of two terms, a subject

terms in a categorical statement, the words that refer to the categories asserted or denied to be included in each other

and a predicate, has one of these forms. If we use letters in place of the terms of categorical statements, we can quickly see that the four main kinds of categorical statements are as follows:

All X are Y.

No X are Y.

Some X are Y.

Some X are not Y.

A group of categorical statements makes up a categorical argument. The most important kind of categorical argument is called the **categorical syllogism.** The categorical syllogism is an argument that contains exactly *two premises* and *one conclusion*, all of which are categorical statements. In addition, a categorical syllogism contains only *three terms*. For example, here is a categorical syllogism:

> **categorical syllogism** an argument that consists of two premises and a conclusion, which are all categorical statements, and that contains exactly three terms

All ideas exist only in minds.

All things we perceive are ideas.

_____

Therefore, all things we perceive exist only in minds.

Suppose we use the following symbols for the terms of this syllogism:

I = ideas

M = things that exist only in minds

P = things we perceive

Then this syllogism has the following form:

All I are M.

All P are I.

_____

Therefore, all P are M.

Notice that there are exactly *two premises* and *one conclusion*, together containing exactly *three terms*. Notice also that the term I occurs in each of the premises but not in the conclusion. In fact, in every categorical syllogism, one of the terms occurs in both premises but not in the conclusion. This term is usually called the middle term because it links the other two. Each premise relates one of the other two terms to the middle term, and the conclusion asserts that these two terms must therefore be related to each other.

Now for the point of all this: How can we figure out whether a categorical syllogism is valid? One method is to follow these three steps: (1) Find the form of the syllogism by replacing its terms with letters. (2) See if you can find an example of another syllogism that has the same form but in which the conclusion is false even though the premises are true. (3) If it is not possible for any syllogism with that form to have true premises and a false conclusion, then you know that any syllogism with that form must be valid.

What is the idea behind this method? We already saw that a categorical syllogism is valid when it has a form in which the truth of the premises guarantees the truth of the conclusion. This means that it is not possible for a syllogism with that form to have true premises and a false conclusion. So if you find a syllogism with the same form that has true premises and a false conclusion, you can be sure that syllogisms with that form are not valid and that arguments with that form are fallacies.

Let us see how this method works. Take the following syllogism:

All unmarried mothers are on welfare.

Some people on welfare are cheats.

Therefore, some unmarried mothers are cheats.

This syllogism has the following form:

All U are W.

Some W are C.

Therefore, some U are C.

Is this syllogism valid? Well, consider the following argument, which has the same form:

All men are human.

Some humans are women.

Therefore, some men are women.

Even though this argument has the same form, it is clear that the premises are true, but the conclusion is false. So syllogisms with this form are not valid. Consequently, the first argument is not valid.

Next, take this example:

All cows are mammals.

All cows have horns.

Therefore, some mammals have horns.

This syllogism has the following form:

All C are M.

All C are H.

Therefore, some M are H.

Try as you might, you will not be able to find an example of a syllogism with this form that has true premises and a false conclusion. This syllogism is valid, and any syllogism with the same form is valid.

As you might guess, applying this method is tedious. Moreover, it does not always work. Suppose that you don't find an example of a syllogism with true premises and a false conclusion. Does this mean that the syllogism is valid? Not necessarily—it may only mean that you did not look hard enough.

Fortunately, there is a shortcut. Philosophers have developed four rules for determining whether or not a categorical syllogism is valid. The way to use these rules is simple: A categorical syllogism is valid if it follows all of the rules; it is invalid if it breaks one or more of the rules.

To understand the rules, you should note two things about categorical statements. First, categorical statements can be affirmative or negative; that is, they can say that one class *is* included in another, or that it is *not*. For example: "All A are B" (all abortions are bad) is affirmative, and "No A are B" (no abortions are bad) is negative. Second, the terms in a categorical statement can refer to all the members of a class or only to some members of the class. For example, "All A" refers to all of the A's, whereas "Some A" refers only to some of the A's.

Here, then, are the rules for a valid categorical syllogism:

1. The middle term (the term that is present in both premises but absent from the conclusion) must refer to all members of the class in at least one premise.

2. If either term in the conclusion refers to all members of the class, it must also refer to all members of the class in the premises.

3. Both premises must not be negative.

4. If one of the premises is negative, then the conclusion must be negative.

You can see more clearly why syllogisms that break these rules are invalid by testing each rule. Simply find a form that breaks the rule and then find a syllogism with the same form that has true premises and a false conclusion. Here, for example, is a form that breaks rule 1:

Some X are Y.

Some X are Z.

_____

Therefore, some Y are Z.

And here is an example of a syllogism with this form that has true premises and a false conclusion:

Some mammals are apes.

Some mammals are whales.

_____

Therefore, some apes are whales.

Many of the syllogisms that you will encounter in philosophy are made up of categorical statements. Here, for example, is a moral argument that several philosophers have advanced:

It is clear that abortion is immoral, because abortion is the murder of innocent human beings, and the murder of innocent human beings is immoral.

If we sort this syllogism out into premises and conclusion and use the following symbols for the terms of the syllogism:

A = abortion

M = murder of innocent human beings

I = immoral

we can see that the argument has this form:

All *A* is *M*.

All *M* is *I*.

_____

Therefore, all *A* is *I*.

Is this argument valid or invalid? If you check it out, you will see that it does not break any of the four rules. It is therefore valid. So we know that *if* the premises are true (but they might not be true), then the conclusion must also be true.

Here is a second philosophical argument, this one proposed by a medieval philosopher whom we now know as Saint Anselm:

> By definition, God is a being than which nothing greater can be thought. But a being than which nothing greater can be thought is a being that has to exist. Hence, God is a being that has to exist.

If we sort this argument out into premises and conclusions and use the symbols

G = God

N = beings than which nothing greater can be thought

E = beings that have to exist

we can see that this argument has the form:

All *G* is *N*.

All *N* is *E*.

_____

Therefore, all *G* is *E*.

Is this argument valid? You should use the tests we have described to determine whether or not it is.

Hypothetical Arguments

A second important kind of argument is the **hypothetical argument.** Hypothetical arguments contain hypothetical or conditional statements. A hypothetical statement is made up of two simpler statements that are conditioned with the words *if—then*. For example:

> If it's raining, then the ground is wet.

> If you study, then you'll get a good grade.

> If Sue is late, then she must be sick.

> If we keep building bombs, then we'll use them someday.

The first simple sentence in a hypothetical statement is called the **antecedent,** and the second simple sentence is called the **consequent.** The antecedents in our examples are "it's raining," "you study," "Sue is late," and "we keep building bombs." The consequents are "the ground is wet," "you'll get a good grade," "she must be sick," and "we'll use them someday." If we use letters to symbolize

hypothetical argument an argument containing hypothetical or conditional statements

antecedent in a hypothetical statement, the first simple sentence, usually preceded by the word *if*

consequent in a hypothetical statement, the second simple sentence, usually preceded by the word *then*

the antecedents and consequents of hypothetical statements, we can say that they have this form:

If X, then Y.

The most common kind of hypothetical argument is the **hypothetical syllogism.** This kind of argument consists of two premises and a conclusion; one of the premises is a hypothetical statement, whereas the other premise and the conclusion consist of either the antecedent or the consequent of the hypothetical statement, or their denials. Here is one example and its form:

(a) If it's raining, then the ground is wet.   If R, then W.

(b) It's raining.   R.

_____

(c) Therefore, the ground is wet.   Therefore, W.

Notice that premise (a) is a hypothetical statement; premise (b) *affirms* the antecedent of this hypothetical statement, and the conclusion (c) *affirms* its consequent. Consider a second example and its form:

(a) If it's raining, then the ground is wet.   If R, then W.

(b) The ground is not wet.   Not W.

_____

(c) Therefore, it's not raining.   Therefore, not R.

In this example, premise (a) is once again a hypothetical statement, premise (b) now *denies* the consequent of this hypothetical statement, and the conclusion (c) *denies* the antecedent.

How do you figure out whether a hypothetical syllogism is valid or invalid? One way is to follow the same three-step method we outlined earlier, which involves trying to find an example of another hypothetical syllogism with the same form, but in which the conclusion is false even though the premises are true.

Take the following hypothetical syllogism as an example:

If interest rates rise, then the price of stocks will decline.

Interest rates are not rising.

_____

Therefore, the price of stocks will not decline.

If we use letters to symbolize the antecedents and consequents of this syllogism, we can say that it has this form:

If R, then D.

Not R.

_____

Therefore, not D.

Is this argument valid? No, because we can find an argument with the same form but with true premises and a false conclusion:

If ducks were human, then ducks would have two legs.

Ducks are not human.

_____

Therefore, ducks do not have two legs.

As we have already seen, this method is time-consuming and inconclusive, because the fact that we are unable to find an argument with the proper premises and conclusions does not prove that none exists. Fortunately, the number of important forms of hypothetical syllogisms is very limited, so the valid and invalid forms can be easily listed. The two important forms of *valid* hypothetical syllogisms are as follows:

If P, then Q.	If P, then Q.
P.	Not Q.
_____	_____
Therefore, Q.	Therefore, not P.

And the two important *invalid* or *fallacious* forms are as follows:

If P, then Q.	If P, then Q.
Not P.	Q.
_____	_____
Therefore, not Q.	Therefore, P.

If you examine these four examples, you can see that there is a simple rule for determining whether a hypothetical syllogism is valid:

A hypothetical syllogism is valid if and only if (1) one of its premises is a hypothetical statement and (2) the other premise affirms the antecedent, and the conclusion affirms the consequent; or the other premise denies the consequent, and the conclusion denies the antecedent.

Another important kind of hypothetical argument is the hypothetical chain argument. In hypothetical chain arguments, which can contain more than two premises, all the premises and the conclusion are hypothetical statements. Here is an example of a valid hypothetical chain argument:

If you study hard, then you will pass the exam.	If S, then P.
If you pass the exam, then you will get an A.	If P, then A.
If you get an A, then you will graduate.	If A, then G.
If you graduate, then you will be happy.	If G, then H.
_____	_____
So, if you study hard, then you will be happy.	So, if S, then H.

You can guess the rule for determining the validity of a hypothetical chain argument:

A hypothetical chain argument is valid if the consequent of one premise is the antecedent of a second premise, the consequent of the second premise is the antecedent of the third, and so on, and the antecedent of the conclusion is the antecedent of the first premise and the consequent of the conclusion is the consequent of the last premise.

Hypothetical arguments are perhaps even more important than categorical arguments because virtually any argument can be read as a hypothetical argument. Moreover, philosophers often use hypothetical arguments. Here, for example, is an argument proposed by the pre-Socratic Greek philosopher Zeno:

> If something moves from one point to another, then it must cross an infinite number of infinitely small intervals in a finite length of time. But nothing can cross an infinite number of infinitely small intervals in a finite length of time. Therefore, nothing moves.

In 1950, the philosopher Alan Turing advanced this argument:

> If each man had a definite set of rules of conduct by which he regulated his life, he would be no better than a machine. But there are no such rules, so men cannot be machines.

And Socrates advanced the following example, which we already have seen:

> If you freely consent to live in a country, then you have made an agreement to obey its laws. If you have made an agreement to obey a country's laws, then it is wrong for you to disobey its laws. If it is wrong for you to disobey a country's laws, then you should accept any punishments imposed by those laws. So if you freely consent to live in a country, then you should accept any punishments imposed by its laws.

Whether these philosophical arguments are valid or invalid is something that you can determine for yourself by using the rules and methods we have been discussing.

Disjunctive Arguments

A third important kind of argument is the disjunctive argument. A disjunctive argument is one that contains a **disjunctive statement.** A disjunctive statement is a statement that poses alternatives of the form

disjunctive statement a statement that poses alternatives of the form *either X or Y (or both)*

Either X or Y (or both).

A disjunctive statement, in other words, states that either one thing is true or another is true (or perhaps even both things are true). For example:

Either I will study or I will watch television.

Either Buddha was right or Christ was right.

Either it is raining or the sprinklers are on.

The two simpler parts of a disjunctive statement are called **disjuncts.** In the first example, the first disjunct is "I will study" and the second is "I will watch television"; in the second example, the disjuncts are "Buddha was right" and "Christ was right"; in the third, "it is raining" and "the sprinklers are on." Notice that a disjunctive statement does not assert that either of the disjuncts is true; it only asserts that *at least one* is true. Thus, a disjunctive statement leaves open the possibility that both disjuncts might be true.

disjunct one of the alternatives of a disjunctive statement

The most common kind of disjunctive argument is the **disjunctive syllogism.** It contains two premises and a conclusion; one of the premises is a disjunctive statement, the other premise affirms or denies one of the disjuncts, and the conclusion affirms or denies the other disjunct. Here is an example:

disjunctive syllogism an argument containing two premises and a conclusion, in which one premise is a disjunctive statement, one premise affirms or denies one of the disjuncts, and the conclusion affirms or denies the other disjunct

Either it is raining or the sprinklers are on.

It is not raining.

_____

Therefore, the sprinklers must be on.

If we use letters to symbolize the disjuncts of this argument, we can see that it has the form

Either *R* or *S*.

Not *R*.

_____

Therefore, *S*.

If you think about it a moment, you will see that only four forms of disjunctive syllogisms exist. Two of these are valid, and two are invalid. The two valid forms of disjunctive syllogisms are

Either *P* or *Q*.   *P* or *Q*.

Not *P*.   Not *Q*.

_____   _____

Therefore, *Q*.   Therefore, *P*.

These are valid forms because a disjunctive statement asserts that *at least one* of the disjuncts has to be true. Consequently, if one of them is not true, then the other *has* to be true.

The two invalid or fallacious forms of disjunctive syllogisms are

Either *P* or *Q*.   Either *P* or *Q*.

P.   *Q*.

_____   _____

Therefore, not *Q*.   Therefore, not *P*.

These two forms are invalid because disjunctive statements *leave open the possibility that both disjuncts are true*. Consequently, even though one is true, the other also might be true.

If you scan these two valid and two invalid forms of disjunctive syllogisms, you can formulate the rule for determining whether a disjunctive syllogism is valid. The rule goes like this:

> A disjunctive syllogism is valid if one premise denies one disjunct and the conclusion affirms the other; otherwise, it is invalid.

Chain Arguments

We have now looked at the most important kinds of deductive arguments: categorical, hypothetical, and disjunctive syllogisms. Before we leave them, we should note that these arguments are often found in combinations or chains, a bit like the hypothetical chain argument we discussed earlier. Sometimes, for example, one argument is used to prove a certain conclusion, and then this conclusion is used as a premise in a second argument that proves a further conclusion. To see what this means, consider a philosophical argument about the nature of morality:

> If morality depended on our personal feelings, then "this act is morally wrong" would mean "I personally feel bad about this act." But if "this act is morally wrong" means "I personally feel bad about this act," then I could find out whether an act is morally wrong by merely examining my own feelings. So if morality depended on our personal feelings, then I could find out whether an act is morally wrong by examining my feelings. But to find out whether an act is morally wrong I have to find out whether the act harms people. If to find out whether an act is morally wrong I have to find out whether the act harms people, then I cannot find out whether an act is wrong by examining my own feelings. So I cannot find out whether an act is morally wrong by examining my own feelings. Therefore, morality does not depend on our personal feelings.

At first sight this looks like a very complicated argument, but you will see how simple its form is if you use letters to symbolize the various antecedents and consequents of the argument.

P = Morality depends on our personal feelings.

M = "This act is morally wrong" means "I personally feel bad about this act."

E = I can find out whether an act is morally wrong by examining my own feelings.

H = To find out whether an act is morally wrong, I have to find out whether the act harms people.

Then we have:

(a) If P, then M.

(b) If M, then E.

(c) So, if P, then E.

(d) H.

(e) If H, then not E.

(f) So, not E.

_____

(g) Therefore, not P.

As you can see, premises (a) and (b) are used to prove conclusion (c). Then premises (d) and (e) are used to prove conclusion (f). Finally, (c) and (f) are used as premises to prove conclusion (g). Is the whole argument valid? It is valid if each of its parts is valid. You will have to figure this out for yourself by using the rules and methods we have discussed.

Chain arguments can occur in virtually any combination. Sometimes categorical arguments are combined with hypothetical arguments; sometimes hypothetical arguments are combined with disjunctive arguments. When analyzing any argument, you have to see what the various parts of the total argument are and how these parts fit together.

We said earlier that there are two main kinds of arguments: deductive and inductive. Having discussed deductive arguments, we now look at inductive arguments.

INDUCTIVE ARGUMENTS

Unlike deductive arguments, inductive arguments do not guarantee that the conclusion *must* be true if the premises are true. Instead, they show merely that the conclusion is probably true or that it is reasonable to accept the conclusion on the basis of the evidence. Court trials in which the court's final decision is based on circumstantial evidence usually use inductive arguments. Suppose, for example, that hair of the accused was found at the scene of the crime, that the accused earlier had boasted he would commit the crime, and that the accused was seen in the vicinity of the crime shortly before it was committed. Then the jurors might conclude that the accused committed the crime. Their reasoning would be based on an inductive argument: an argument that supports the conclusion by making it *probable* but not certain.

Most of our reasoning is inductive. When you hear a buzzing sound in the morning, for example, and conclude that your alarm clock is going off and that it's time to get up, you are using inductive reasoning. Having heard your clock make that buzzing sound before, you reason (in somewhat of a daze, perhaps) that the sound is coming from your clock. Of course, it is possible that something else is making that noise, so you cannot be absolutely certain that it is your clock. The evidence (the buzzing sound and your past experience) makes your conclusion (that the alarm clock is going off) highly probable but not certain.

Most generalizations are based on inductive reasoning. For example, you see that all of a certain group of people that you meet have a particular quality, and you conclude that *every* member of that group (even those you have not met) must have that quality. Or you may notice that the four or five of your friends who are the oldest in their families are all assertive people, and so you conclude that elder siblings are always assertive. Yet it may be a coincidence that the four or five elder siblings you happen to know are assertive. The evidence here (the fact that all of the elder siblings you have met are assertive and none are unassertive) makes your generalization probable but not certain.

Arguments that generalize from several observed instances also play an important role in science. When biologists notice that all the members they have observed of a species display a certain kind of behavior, they may conclude that all members of that species are characterized by that behavior. Or physicists may notice that certain atomic particles they have observed all have a certain feature, so they conclude that atomic particles of that type all have that feature. Because they are aware of the limitations of inductive arguments, however, they try to be alert for instances that do not fit their generalization.

Although inductive reasoning plays a central role in our lives, we have no simple rules for defining valid inductive reasoning as we have for defining valid deductive reasoning. However, all good inductive reasoning has several important qualities. We can put these qualities in the form of rules and contrast them with the fallacy that results when a rule is ignored:

1. In good inductive reasoning, the conclusion is based on a sufficient number of observations of a representative sample. Otherwise, the reasoning is said to commit the fallacy of **hasty generalization.** Take the following argument, for example:

> The person on welfare I saw at the local supermarket was cheating by using his welfare coupons to buy liquor instead of food.
>
> Another person on welfare I saw at the local store was cheating by using her welfare coupons to buy liquor instead of food.
>
> ───────────────────────────
>
> Therefore, all persons on welfare cheat by using their welfare coupons to buy liquor instead of food.

This argument is based on too few observations. The two people I happen to have seen are not a large enough sample to justify a generalization about tens of thousands of other people. Moreover, my sample is not representative. Two people at local stores do not necessarily represent all the different kinds of people throughout the country who are on welfare.

2.   Good inductive reasoning takes into account all the relevant data that might affect the conclusion. Otherwise, the reasoning is said to have committed the fallacy of **forgetful induction.** Suppose, for example, that I knew that the two persons whom I saw using their welfare coupons to buy liquor were both alcoholics. This would suggest that their behavior may be attributable to their alcoholism rather than to the fact that they are on welfare. But my reasoning would have failed to take this into account.

3.   Good inductive reasoning does not jump to the conclusion that because one event or condition was present *before* the other, the first must be the *cause* of the second. This would be the fallacy of **false cause.** For example, a person is falling into a false cause fallacy when he says that because a black cat crossed his path before he had an accident, the black cat must have caused the accident. Similarly, in the earlier argument, I am concluding that because the condition of being on welfare was present before the cheating incident, it must be the explanation of the cheating.

Of course, an inductive argument can be wrong even though the reasoning commits no fallacies. Inductive arguments, as we noted, have only a probable conclusion; it is always possible that the conclusion of a careful and well-founded inductive argument is false.

INFORMAL FALLACIES

We have seen several examples of formal fallacies—mistakes that involve the use of an invalid *form* of argument. There are two other important kinds of fallacies, called **informal fallacies.** These also are mistakes in arguments, but they are mistakes that are not based on the use of incorrect form. These are either fallacies of relevance or fallacies of ambiguity.

Fallacies of Relevance

Fallacies of relevance are mistakes that result from appealing to something that is not relevant to the argument. Some important fallacies of relevance are the following:

hasty generalization the fallacy of basing an inductive argument on insufficient observations or an unrepresentative sample

forgetful induction the fallacy of failing to take into account all the relevant evidence bearing on a conclusion

false cause the fallacy of arguing that since one event or condition was present *before* another, the earlier event or condition must be the *cause* of the later one

informal fallacy an argument in which the premises fail to guarantee the conclusion but in which the failure is not due to the use of an invalid form; often an argument that attempts to persuade emotionally or psychologically but not logically

fallacies of relevance fallacies of appealing to something that is not relevant to the argument

Appeal to emotion. This common fallacy is the attempt to establish a claim not by providing good reasons for the claim but by appealing to the passions and prejudices of the audience. Emotional appeals may persuade people to accept a conclusion, but they do not prove the conclusion.

Appeal to authority. Another common fallacy is the attempt to establish a claim by appealing to an unqualified expert or an irrelevant authority. We are perhaps justified in appealing to an authority to establish a point when the authority is qualified in the field under discussion. But even then, an appeal to authority does not prove the point but, at most, shows that the authority *could* prove the point.

Ad hominem argument. This is an argument that attacks the person making a claim instead of addressing the issue. I use an ad hominem argument, for example, when someone argues that God does not exist, and I reject his argument on the grounds that he's an evil person. The character of the person presenting an argument is irrelevant to the validity or truth of the argument.

Argument from ignorance. This kind of argument claims that because there is no evidence that something is false, it must be true. For example, I am arguing from ignorance if I say that because you cannot prove that God does not exist, God must exist.

Begging the question. This fallacy is also called a circular argument. It is an argument in which the premises used to prove a conclusion already assume that the conclusion is true. For example, if I say, "What she claims must be true because she always speaks the truth," then I am begging the question.

Fallacies of Ambiguity

Fallacies of ambiguity result from using words unclearly or ambiguously. Some important fallacies of ambiguity are the following:

fallacies of ambiguity fallacies that result from using words unclearly or ambiguously

Equivocation. An argument is based on equivocation when a word or expression changes its meaning in the course of the argument. For example: "Since I saw nobody in the room and you saw nobody in the room, we both saw the same person: nobody!"

Amphiboly. An argument is based on amphiboly when it uses a grammatical construction that is ambiguous because it can be understood in two ways.

Misplaced accent. An argument based on misplaced accent is misleading because it emphasizes a word or expression that is designed to mislead or because it omits relevant information. An automobile advertisement, for example, states in large letters, "ABSOLUTELY ALL REPAIRS COVERED FOR FIVE YEARS," and then notes in fine print, "except for tires, hoses, filters, and other parts subject to wear."

Composition. The fallacy of composition attributes the characteristics of the parts of a thing to the whole thing itself. Here is an example: "Since every book in the library is good, it must be a good library."

Division. The fallacy of division attributes the characteristics of a whole thing to one or more of its parts. For example: "Since it is a good library, every book in it must be good."

EVALUATING ARGUMENTS

You have seen how to put an argument together, and you have seen the main kinds of deductive and inductive arguments and several important fallacies. It is time now to integrate all of this.

You are going to meet a lot of reasoning in the pages that follow, which of course is why we have spent so much time looking at what logical reasoning is. But to use the ideas we have discussed, you should have a more or less systematic way of evaluating the arguments you encounter. The following four steps will help:

1. Begin by figuring out what the argument is. This means that you first have to figure out the main point the philosopher is trying to make; this is his or her conclusion. Then you have to figure out the reasons he or she is giving for this point; these are the premises. We saw some of the words that often signal a person's conclusions and premises.

This first step sounds easier than it often turns out to be. Sometimes a philosopher has several points to make and supports them with many different sets of reasons. You then have several conclusions and a lot of premises to line up. Even more often, an author constructs a chain of several related arguments. He or she may use several arguments to prove the same conclusion or may link arguments so that the conclusion of one argument becomes the premise of another. For example:

> God clearly exists, because everything in the universe obeys the laws of mathematics. And if everything obeys the laws of mathematics, then everything is orderly. Everything in the universe, then, is orderly. Now if everything is orderly, then that order must have been imposed on everything by some great being. So the order in everything must have been imposed on it by some great being. And if so, then there is a God.

This is really a chain of three related arguments: the conclusion of the first argument is a premise of the second, and the conclusion of the second argument is a premise of the third. We can put the argument as follows:

Everything obeys the laws of mathematics.

If everything obeys the laws of mathematics, then everything is orderly.

_____

Therefore, everything is orderly.

Everything is orderly.

If everything is orderly, then that order must have been imposed by some great being.

_____

Therefore, that order must have been imposed by some great being.

The order in everything was imposed by some great being.

If the order in everything was imposed by some great being, then God exists.

_____

Therefore, God exists.

In the chapters that follow, it will be important for you to read the materials carefully and then try to figure out the basic conclusion that a particular philosopher is trying to prove. Once you have done this, then figure out the main premises by which he or she hopes to prove this conclusion. Sort out the various premises and conclusions used on the way to the main conclusion, making clear any connections between them.

2.   Figure out whether the argument is inductive or deductive. If it is deductive, put the argument into proper form and figure out whether or not it is valid by using the rules we discussed earlier. If it is an inductive argument, then see whether it is based on the fallacies of hasty generalization, forgetful induction, or false cause.

At this stage, you will often find that the author of a deductive argument has not explicitly stated all of his or her premises, and you will have to supply the missing premises. For example:

> Wars are always morally unjustified because mass killing is always morally unjustified.

If we try to set out this argument as a categorical syllogism, we seem to have a conclusion supported by a single premise:

> All mass killings are morally unjustified.
>
> Therefore, all wars are morally unjustified.

Clearly, this conclusion does not follow from the premise. But it is easy to see what the missing premise is:

> *All wars are mass killings.*
>
> All mass killings are morally unjustified.
>
> ——————————————————————
>
> Therefore, all wars are morally unjustified.

By adding the premise in italics, we see the complete argument that the author had in mind, and we are better able to evaluate it.

Adding the missing premises in someone's argument is not always this easy, and no precise formula can tell you what a person's missing premises are. But we can say the following: First, try to add premises that make the author's argument *valid*. Second, try to add premises that you think the author probably believes in and that seem to make some sense.

3.   Weed out the informal fallacies. First, check to make sure that the author is not guilty of any fallacies of relevance; then make sure that he or she is not guilty of any fallacies of ambiguity.

Often, an author mixes a great deal of irrelevant material into an argument. Some of this material might be intended to appeal to your emotions. Watch out for this.

4.   Examine the truth of the premises. After you have laid out the argument, figured out whether it is valid, and eliminated all informal fallacies, you have to decide whether the premises of the argument are true. We have already noted that in a valid argument, if the premises are true, then the conclusion has to be true. So if the premises are true and the argument is valid, then you are stuck with the conclusion. Therefore, it is critical for you to determine whether the premises in any given argument are true.

Unfortunately, at this stage, many people simply give up. They say something like "The author's argument is all very logical, and I think his premises are true, but still I don't believe his conclusion." This approach is highly irrational. If you really do not believe the conclusion of an argument, then you *have* to believe that the premises are mistaken. If you want to reject the conclusion, you should figure out why the premises are mistaken. This means thinking very hard about what the author is saying, and that takes work.

Moreover, there is no formula for figuring out whether or not someone's statements are true. You have to use your head. Ask yourself what the author's premises mean. Ask yourself whether there are any reasons to think that they are true. Ask yourself whether all of the hidden premises you have supplied are true.

Many arguments contain premises that are generalizations. These are premises with words such as *all, always, every, whatever, any, none,* and *no.* Categorical arguments almost always have such premises. Often, you will find that when you examine such premises carefully, they turn out to be unacceptable. There are several techniques for showing that a generalization is unacceptable:

1. Find a counterexample, a case in which the generalization does not hold. Take, for example, the following generalization:

> All politicians are liars.

As a matter of fact, many politicians are not liars. Any of them will serve as a counterexample disproving the generalization.

2. Examine the inductive evidence that is offered for the generalization. Generalizations are often based on inductive reasoning. The person proposing the generalization bases it on a few observations he or she has made, or someone else has made. When generalizations are based on inductive reasoning, you should ask whether (a) the generalization is based on a sufficiently large and adequately representative sample and (b) whether all other explanations for the evidence were ruled out. If the answer to either of these questions is no, then there is no reason to accept the generalization as true.

3. Show that the assumptions on which the generalization is based are unacceptable. Generalizations are often based on assumptions that have not been made explicit. Consider the following argument, for example:

> The killing of a fetus is always the killing of a person.
>
> The killing of a person is always an immoral act.
> _____
> Therefore, the killing of a fetus is always an immoral act.

Here the first premise makes the assumption that a fetus is a human being. Is this assumption acceptable? Philosophers who favor abortion will probably say that it is not, whereas those who oppose abortion will probably say that it is. Underlying both positions are some other assumptions about what makes something a person. One side assumes that a person is something that has qualities that a fetus does not share, and the other side assumes that a person is something that includes the fetus. Whatever your position, the best way of dealing with this generalization is by looking closely at the assumptions and trying to determine whether or not they are correct. If they are not correct, then the generalization is also not acceptable.

CONCLUSION

After you have set out a philosophical argument, checked it for validity, and turned to figuring out whether its premises are true, you are really philosophizing. We said at the beginning of this chapter that philosophy is an activity. It should be much clearer now what this activity involves.

EXERCISES

Examine the following arguments and determine whether they are deductive or inductive, valid or invalid. For the invalid arguments, determine whether they make one or more of the fallacies identified earlier.

1. If there were a God, then there would be an afterlife, but since there is no God, there must be no afterlife.

2. None of the students we talked to has taken philosophy, so there must be no philosophy offered at this school.

3. Since we know that Plato was a homosexual, his arguments and claims about morality cannot be correct.

4. Surely anyone who has ever held a newborn baby must realize that the fetus is human and therefore that abortion is murder.

5. "'I'm all for women having equal rights,' said Bullfight Association president Paco Camino. 'But I repeat, women shouldn't fight bulls because a bullfighter is and should be a man.' "[1]

6. "Mysticism is one of the great forces of the world's history. For religion is nearly the most important thing in the world, and religion never remains for long altogether untouched by mysticism"—John and Ellis McTaggart.

7. If there is no single correct moral stand, then different societies will have different moral beliefs. Obviously, different societies have different moral beliefs, so there is no single correct moral standard.

8. If violence is never morally justified, then wars are always unjust. But wars are not always unjust, so violence is sometimes morally justified.

9. Sampras and Agassi are the two best tennis players in the world, so they'd make the best doubles team.

---

[1] *San Francisco Chronicle*, 28 March 1972.

1.9 Suggestions for Further Reading

Adler, Mortimer, J. *The Conditions of Philosophy*. New York: Dell, 1967. One of the great human-istic thinkers of our time provides a clear, readable account of the nature of philosophy. Adler's paperback contains several suggestions about what's needed to make philosophy more applicable to the modern world.

Allen, E. L. *From Plato to Nietzsche*. New York: Ballantine, 1983. A paperback presenting a simple overview of the thoughts of the great philosophers.

Angeles, Peter A. *The HarperCollins Dictionary of Philosophy*, 2d ed. New York: HarperCollins, 1992. An excellent short paperback book that provides understandable definitions of most philosophical terms.

Bontempo, Charles I., and S. Jack Odell, eds. *The Owl of Minerva*. New York: McGraw-Hill, 1975. This collection of original articles by eighteen leading contemporary philosophers explains what the authors find attractive and fulfilling about their work.

Bunnin, Nicholas, and E. P. Tsui-James, eds. *The Blackwell Companion to Philosophy*. Cambridge, MA: Blackwell Publishers, 1996. A very fine one-volume student reference that contains thirty-two articles, each covering a major division of philosophy (epistemology, metaphysics, ethics, etc.) or a major philosopher (Hobbes, Locke, etc.).

Chan, Wing-tsit. *A Source Book in Chinese Philosophy*. Princeton, NJ: Princeton University Press, 1963. A good collection of writings by the philosophers of China.

Cohen, Eliot D. *Philosophers at Work*. New York: Holt, Rinehart & Winston, 1989. A wonderful collection of informal and very readable essays by nonacademic philosophers who explain how they use philosophy in their professions. Includes accounts by a business manager, a physician, a social worker, a corrections officer, a historian, a dancer, a health care consultant, a clergyman, and many others.

Copleston, F. C. *History of Philosophy*. 8 vols. Garden City, NY: Doubleday, 1965. This series of paperbacks (also available combined into two fat volumes) provides the most comprehensive and authoritative treatment of Western philosophers in the English language.

DeGeorge, Richard T. *The Philosopher's Guide to Sources, Research Tools, Professional Life, and Related Fields*. Lawrence: The Regents Press of Kansas, 1980. Although somewhat dated, this reference work provides a complete guide to books, journals, and other sources of information about philosophy and particular philosophers.

Edwards, Paul, ed. *The Encyclopedia of Philosophy*. 8 vols. New York: Macmillan and Free Press, 1967. A basic source of information on virtually every conceivable subject in philosophy. Some of the articles are heavy going, but all are excellent.

Gaarder, Jostein. *Sophie's World*, trans. Paulette Moller. New York: Farrar, Straus & Giroux, 1994. This remarkable novel—a "must read" for anyone embarking on a study of philosophy—is the story of a fourteen-year-old girl who finds a piece of paper on which two questions are written: "Who are you?" and "Where did the world come from?" The search for answers takes her through a tour of the central issues in Western philosophy.

Gatens, Moira. *Feminism and Philosophy*. Bloomington: Indiana University Press, 1991. A very readable book on how philosophy has viewed women and why it is important for women.

Grimshaw, Jean. *Philosophy and Feminist Thinking*. Minneapolis: University of Minnesota Press, 1986. Perhaps the best discussion of the relevance of philosophy for feminism.

Honderich, Ted, ed. *The Oxford Companion to Philosophy*. New York: Oxford University Press, 1995. An outstanding one-volume encyclopedia of philosophy containing short and acces-sible articles on major philosophers and philosophical concepts.

Jacobson, Nolan Pliny. *The Heart of Buddhist Philosophy*. Carbondale: Southern Illinois University Press, 1988. A very readable introduction to this influential world view.

Kahane, Howard. *Logic and Philosophy*. Belmont, CA: Wadsworth, 1990. A very good and clear introduction to logic.

Klemke, E. D., ed. *The Meaning of Life*. New York: Oxford University Press, 1981. An outstanding anthology that includes a useful bibliography of additional materials.

Kolak, Daniel, and Raymond Martin. *Wisdom Without Answers*. Belmont, CA: Wadsworth, 1989. A very stimulating introduction to the art of philosophizing.

Koller, John M. *Oriental Philosophies*, 2d ed. New York: Scribner's, 1985. Undoubtedly the best single introduction to Hindu, Buddhist, and Chinese philosophy.

Lavine, T. Z. *From Socrates to Sartre: The Philosophic Quest*. New York: Bantam, 1984. The very readable paperback text of an extremely interesting PBS television series on the great philosophers.

Magill, Frank N., ed. *Masterpieces of World Philosophy*. New York: HarperCollins, 1990. A collection of essays on the major works of Eastern and Western philosophy, each of which first outlines the main ideas in the work and then describes the major commentaries on the work.

Mahowald, Mary Briody. *Philosophy of Women: Classical to Current Concepts*. Indianapolis: Hackett, 1978. An outstanding anthology of classical and contemporary philosophical writings on the nature of women.

Martin, Robert M. *There Are Two Errors in the Title of This Book*. Lewiston, NY: Broadview Press, 1992. A delightfully interesting introduction to philosophy through the use of puzzles, paradoxes, and problems.

Matson, Wallace. *A New History of Philosophy*. 2 vols. New York: Harcourt Brace, 1987. A very readable account of the major (male) Western philosophers.

McGreal, Ian P., ed. *Great Thinkers of the Western World*. New York: HarperCollins, 1992. A collection of articles on the principal ideas of one hundred of the greatest Western thinkers, including philosophers, theologians, and scientists.

McGreal, Ian P., ed. *Great Thinkers of the Eastern World*. New York: HarperCollins, 1995. A collection of articles on the principal ideas of one hundred of the greatest Eastern thinkers, including philosophers, theologians, and scientists.

Nozick, Robert. *The Examined Life*. New York: Simon & Schuster, 1989. A terrific, provocative, and easily readable introduction to philosophy by one of the foremost living philosophers.

Persig, Robert. *Zen and the Art of Motorcycle Maintenance*. New York: Bantam, 1980. This enjoyable novel raises interesting philosophical questions about the nature of reality and our way of looking at reality.

Philips, Michael, ed. *Philosophy and Science Fiction*. Buffalo, NY: Prometheus, 1984. A stimulating examination of philosophical themes in science fiction. This paperback contains seventeen science fiction stories that raise important philosophical questions.

Radhakrishnan, Sarvepalli, ed. *A Source Book in Indian Philosophy*. Princeton, NJ: Princeton University Press, 1973. An excellent anthology of selections from the writings of the major philosophies of India.

Russell, Bertrand. *The Problems of Philosophy*. New York: Oxford University Press, 1959. This short and simple paperback that seems to always stay in print is a fascinating introduction to the main problems of philosophy. Intended for nonexperts, it will be perfectly clear to the beginner.

Stone, I. F. *The Trial of Socrates*. New York: Doubleday, 1988. An excellent account of Socrates that reads like an intellectual thriller.

Stumpf, Samuel Enoch. *Socrates to Sartre: A History of Philosophy*, 3d ed. New York: McGraw-Hill, 1982. Stumpf provides an easy but accurate synopsis of the central views of the major Western philosophers.

Thomas, Edmund J., and Eugene G. Miller. *Writers and Philosophers: A Sourcebook of Philosophical Influences on Literature*. New York: Greenwood, 1990. This terrific resource provides short summaries of the philosophical influences on every major literary figure of the past and present. Each author has an entry that describes the author's philosophy and how this philosophy was articulated in his or her work.

Urmson, J. O., and Jonathan Ree, eds. *The Concise Encyclopedia of Western Philosophy and Philosophers*. Boston: Unwin Hyman, 1989. A short and useful dictionary summarizing many of the important concepts and thinkers of Western philosophy.

Waithe, Mary Ellen, ed. *A History of Women Philosophers*. 2 vols. Dordrecht: Kluwer Academic Publishers, 1991. The best (almost the only) existing work on the lives and views of the most significant women philosophers in the Western tradition, from 600 B.C. to 1900 A.D.

Woodhouse, Mark B. *A Preface to Philosophy*, 5th ed. Belmont, CA: Wadsworth, 1993. A good introduction to the nature of philosophy and to methods of philosophical reasoning.

CHAPTER 2

Human Nature

Indeed it is of the essence of man . . . that he can lose himself in the jungle of his existence, within himself, and thanks to his sensation of being lost can react by setting energetically to work to find himself again.

JOSÉ ORTEGA Y GASSET

2.1 Introduction: Why Study Human Nature?

The most basic question in philosophy is this: Who and what am I? Your answer to this question about **human nature**—what a human being is—will profoundly affect how you see yourself, how you see others, and how you live. To see how a view of human nature can affect us, let's look at what some psychologists and philosophers have said about human beings.

Imagine walking down the streets of a city on a wintry day and seeing an old, unshaven man in ragged clothes sitting cross-legged on the sidewalk. In front of him is a sign that reads "I am blind and deaf. Please help me." Almost immediately you reach into your pocket for a couple of dollar bills, which you put into his cardboard box. Then, feeling good, you walk on.

Why did you help him? You might respond with the easy answer that you helped because you wanted to do something for this unfortunate person: You wanted to relieve his obvious need. Yet was this your real motive for helping? Might it not be possible that your actual motive was self-interest? That you wanted the good feeling you knew you would get from helping him? Are human beings, yourself included, moved ultimately by self-interested desires? Are all your actions, even those that seem to arise out of love for others, ultimately motivated by a desire for self-gratification? Is self-interest an inescapable part of being human? Or are we at least sometimes unselfish?

Psychologists have long pondered the question of whether human nature is essentially self-interested or whether unselfish considerations can also motivate human beings. Some psychologists have championed the view that humans are essentially cruel and selfish. As an illustration, consider the conclusion that the father of modern psychology, Sigmund Freud (1856–1939), presented in his work *Civilization and Its Discontents:*

> Men are not gentle, friendly creatures wishing for love, who simply defend themselves if they are attacked, but . . . a powerful measure of desire for aggressiveness has to be reckoned as part of their instinctual endowment. The result is that their neighbor is to them not only a possible helper or sexual object, but also a temptation to them to gratify their aggressiveness . . . to seize his possessions, to humiliate him, to cause him pain, to torture and to kill him. . . .

human nature what it essentially means to be a human being; what makes us different from anything else

Philosophy is doubt.
MONTAIGNE

Every man has a wild beast within him.
FREDERICK THE GREAT

Sigmund Freud: "Men are not gentle, friendly creatures wishing for love, but [possess] a powerful measure of desire for aggressiveness."

Anyone who calls to mind the atrocities of the early migrations, of the invasion of the Hun or the so-called Mongols under Genghis Khan and Tamerlane, of the sacks of Jerusalem by the pious crusaders, even indeed the horrors of the last world-war, will have to bow his head humbly before the truth of this view of man.[1]

Many philosophers have agreed with Freud that human beings are essentially selfish and aggressive. Long before Freud, for example, the British philosopher Thomas Hobbes (1588–1679) argued for a similar view. Hobbes was a materialist who held that everything in "the Universe, that is the whole mass of things that are, is corporeal, that is to say body."[2] Humans, too, are material bodies, and we can explain their activities much like those of a biological mechanism. The mechanism of desire moves human beings to act. Consequently, whenever human beings do something, they are seeking satisfaction of their own mechanistic desires. In fact, Hobbes claimed, the antisocial desire for power over others is what mainly motivates human beings. "In the first place," he wrote, "I put for a general inclination of all mankind, a perpetual and restless desire of power after power, that ceaseth only in death."[3]

The European philosopher Moritz Schlick (1882–1936), also a materialist, suggested that we do not have to look at extreme instances of aggression to see self-interest at work. Schlick argued for the view called **psychological**

psychological egoism the belief that human beings are so constituted that they must always act out of self-interest

---

[1] Sigmund Freud, *Civilization and Its Discontents* (London: Hogarth, 1930), 85–86.
[2] Thomas Hobbes, *Hobbes's Leviathan* (Oxford: Clarendon Press, 1909; original work published 1651), 524.
[3] Ibid., 86.

egoism. This theory says that human beings are made so that they can act only out of self-interest. Self-interest is present in even the most apparently unselfish behaviors.[4] When people choose between any two options, they always choose the option that gives them the most pleasure. If we examine our own behavior and that of others, he held, we will see that this self-interested pursuit of pleasure is always present. We can explain even the apparent exceptions as the self-

---

[4]See Moritz Schlick, *Problems of Ethics*, trans. David Rynin (New York: Dover, 1939).

PHILOSOPHY AND LIFE

Koestler and James

Does it really matter which view of human nature you believe? Sure, they carry different implications. Some hold we're free, others that we're not; some say that we have a divine destiny, others that we don't. But in the last analysis, such claims raise unanswerable philosophical questions. So what difference does it make which view you hold?

Author and outspoken opponent of behaviorism Arthur Koestler (1905–1983) thinks it does make a difference. In his autobiography, *Arrow in the Blue*, Koestler recalls how his own belief in free will significantly affected his decision to abandon his studies in engineering for the uncertain career of an author:

I had no plans except "to lead my own life." In order to do that I had to "get off the track." This metaphorical track I visualized very precisely as an endless stretch of steel rails on rotting sleepers. You were born onto a certain track, as a train is put on its run according to the timetable; and once on the track, you no longer had free will. Your life was determined . . . by outside forces; the

rail of steel, stations, shunting points. If you accepted that condition, running on rails became a habit which you could no longer break. The point was to jump off the track before the habit was formed, before you became encased in a rattling prison. To change the metaphor: reason and routine kept people in a straitjacket which made their living flesh rot beneath it.

For Koestler, then, the belief in his own personal freedom led him to the conviction that he could "jump off the track" chosen for him by others, that he could lead his own life.

Koestler's account is reminiscent of the crisis that the American philosopher and psychologist William James (1842–1910) once faced. James had suffered throughout his life from a variety of emotional disorders that left him feeling profoundly alienated. Then, like Koestler, James seemingly took a giant step toward resolving his problems when he was able to satisfy himself that he was free. James captures the moment in a letter to his father:

I think that yesterday was a crisis in my life. I finished the first part of Renouvier's second "Essais" and see no reason why his definition of Free Will— "the sustaining of a thought because I choose to when I might have other thoughts"—need be the definition of an illusion. At any rate, I will assume for the present—until next year—that it is no illusion. My first act of free will shall be to believe in free will.

QUESTIONS

1. Illustrate how the belief in one or more of the views of human nature is concretely expressed in your life.

2. Have you ever felt or found yourself "blocked" because of how you saw yourself or what you believed you were or were capable of being?

Sources: Arthur Koestler, *Arrow in the Blue* (New York: Macmillan, 1952), 32. Henry James, ed., *The Letters of William James* (Boston: Atlantic Monthly Press, 1920), 148.

interested pursuit of pleasure. When a child "sacrifices" by giving up the larger slice of cake to a friend, Schlick claimed, it is because the child associates more pleasurable consequences with giving up the piece of cake. The pleasure of giving up the cake is greater than the pleasure of eating it. So the child gives away the larger slice of cake because doing so gives her the larger pleasure. Similarly, heroes risk their lives for others because they associate pleasurable emotions with the thought of being heroic and consequently choose the more pleasurable act. Even when no egoistic motive is obvious, self-interested motivations are always operating in human beings.

The views that we have just briefly described, then, say that human nature is selfish and material. Apart from their intrinsic interest, these views have profound and highly personal implications for each of us. For example, your views about these aspects of human nature will shape your relationships with other people. If a person thinks that human beings are basically unselfish, then won't that person instinctively relate to other people with trust and openness? Won't such a person accept the kind gestures of strangers as natural and not feel

Of all created creatures man is the most detestable. Of the entire brood he is the only one that possesses malice. Also he is the only creature that has a nasty mind.

MARK TWAIN

PHILOSOPHY AND LIFE

Is Selflessness Real?

Several contemporary biologists have argued that apparently selfless human behavior is actually a kind of selfish activity that our genes impel us to carry out. For example, Desmond Morris suggests that when a man rushes into a burning house to save his daughter—or if an old friend or even a complete stranger rescues the child—he is actually saving an organism that contains or, in the case of the friend or stranger, may contain his own genes. We have developed these protective behaviors so that our genes can survive and be passed on to future generations. Thus, helping behaviors are genetically selfish: They are mechanisms that our genes have evolved to ensure *their own* survival.

The man who risks death to save his small daughter from a fire is in reality saving his own genes in their new body-package. And in saving his genes, his act becomes biologically selfish, rather than altruistic.

But supposing the man leaping into the fire is trying to save, not his daughter, but an old friend? How can this be selfish? The answer here lies in the ancient history of mankind. For more than a million years, man was a simple tribal being. . . . [T]he chances were that every member of your own tribe was a relative of some kind. . . . [In saving your old friend] you would be helping copies of your own genes. . . . Again . . . genetic selfishness.

[Moreover, when man] was tribal, . . . any inborn urge to help his fellow men would have meant automatically that he was helping gene-sharing relatives. . . . But with the urban explosion, man rapidly found himself in huge communities, surrounded by strangers,

and with no time for his genetic constitution to alter to fit the startlingly new circumstances. So his altruism inevitably spread to include [complete strangers].

QUESTIONS

1. What do theories of evolution such as that proposed by Desmond Morris imply about our human nature?

2. Could all human behavior be explained in terms of genes?

3. If Morris is right, does it make sense to say that humans are or are not selfish?

SOURCE: Desmond Morris, *Manwatching, A Field Guide to Human Behavior* (New York: Harry N. Abrams, 1977), 153–154.

surprised that others help simply because they want to? But if a person believes that human beings are basically self-interested, then won't that person mistrust others? Won't she be suspicious of kindness and continually wonder what people are trying to get from her? Won't she feel that the only way to get help from others is by offering them something in return?

Your views about human nature also influence your relationship to the universe. If a person believes that human beings are spiritual as well as material, then won't that person be open to religious experience? Won't such a person see himself as having a spiritual aspect that makes him different from the purely material and biological universe? Won't such a person be willing to see his life in this material universe as a kind of preparation for a spiritual life in another world and universe? On the other hand, a person may feel that a human being is a purely physical creature. The person may feel that a human is a creature with a highly developed brain, to be sure, but not fundamentally different from other animals. For such a person, doesn't death have to be the end of existence? Won't such a person be convinced that this material universe is all there is and all that anyone can have?

Your view of human nature will determine even how you think we should set up our society. Ask yourself this, for example: Should our society be based on capitalism or socialism? Well, suppose humans are essentially self-interested. Then wouldn't the best way to get people to work be to allow every individual to keep whatever benefits he or she produces, and to not support those who don't work? Won't self-interest then lead every person to work hard and to produce as much as he or she can? Isn't this the fundamental idea behind capitalist societies, with their free enterprise systems and ideas about individualism? If all people are basically self-interested, then shouldn't we spend more on police, prisons, the military, and other institutions we use to protect people from one another? On the other hand, what if humans are not basically self-interested, but cooperative and unselfish? Then wouldn't it make sense to inspire people to work for one another's good and to share whatever each produces? Aren't socialist institutions, such as welfare programs and redistributive taxes, based on the idea that human nature is basically social and that humans can and should share with one another? Isn't the huge sum of money that we spend on prisons, police, and military a big waste that could be put to better use in helping meet human needs? Which of these two options is more realistic? How far should our society go in pursuing either one? Doesn't your answer depend on how you view human nature?

It is clear, then, that a lot hangs on how you answer the question "What is a human being?" In this chapter, you will begin your philosophical journey by looking at how several philosophers have tried to answer this question. By examining what they say in support of their views, you will be in a better position to form your own answer and to make up your own mind about the extent to which we are unselfish and spiritual beings, or self-interested and material beings. Our aim is not to convince you to accept any of the views of human nature presented here. Our aim is to help you decide for yourself what it means to be a human being.

QUESTIONS

1. Make a list of the fundamental properties that you think define a human being. Your list should enable you to distinguish humans from other kinds of creatures. How would you prove that these properties are essential to human beings?

2. Are there basic emotional and psychological differences between men and women? Are any such differences the result of their nature, or does society instill such differences through early training, education, and child-rearing practices?

3. Suppose that the emotional and psychological differences between men and women are the result of the way they were raised. What do you think this would imply about how we should arrange our society (e.g., our family life, our political life, our economic life)? Suppose that these differences are the result of the inherent natures of men and women. What would this imply about how we should arrange our society?

4. In your judgment, are humans basically selfless or selfish? If there were no social restraints—such as laws and police—would humans tend to take advantage of one another, or would they tend to help one another? In your judgment, do our social institutions tend to corrupt a fundamentally good human nature, or do they tame a fundamentally evil human nature? Explain your answers.

2.2 What Is Human Nature?

What happens when you die? Several years ago, a man who was revived after his heart stopped while he was in a hospital operating room described his experience as follows:

> I knew I was dying and that there was nothing I could do about it, because no one could hear me. . . . I was out of my body, there's no doubt about it, because I could see my own body there on the operating room table. My soul was out! All this made me feel very bad at first, but then, this really bright light came. It did seem that it was a little dim at first, but then it was this huge beam. It was just a tremendous amount of light, nothing like a big bright flashlight, it was just too much light. . . . It seemed that it covered everything, yet it didn't prevent me from seeing everything around me—the operating room, the doctors and nurses, everything. . . . The love which came from it is just unimaginable, indescribable.[5]

---

[5] Raymond Moody, Jr., M.D., *Life After Life* (New York: Bantam, 1979), 63–64.

This startling account is one of many similar stories told by people who have suffered near-death experiences. People whose hearts have stopped and then started again frequently report that at the moment of their "death" they left their body, hovered over the scene of their death, and encountered an "unimaginable, indescribable" bright white light that came for them. Convinced that they have experienced life after death, such people then lose all fear of death. They never again doubt that they have a soul that will survive. They are convinced that human life has a purpose: that humans have a destiny related to life after death.

Notice that all these accounts of life after death ask us to make some fundamental assumptions about human nature. First, and most obviously, they ask us to believe that all human beings have a **self:** the ego or "I" that exists in a physical body and that is conscious and rational. That is, this self can think, reason, and perceive. Tied to this is the idea that this thinking self can have a purpose: Its life can have a destiny. Second, they ask us to believe that this self is different from, but related to, the body. The body is a physical or material entity, whereas the self is a spiritual or immaterial entity (sometimes called a soul) that can survive the death of its body. Third, they ask us to believe that this self has continuity: The self during life can continue to be the same self after death. Finally, they ask us to believe that the self is an independent individual: It exists separate from other things and people, with an independent identity.

> **self** the individual person; the ego; the knower; that which persists through changes in a person

This view about human beings is prevalent among many of us today. It is also a view that many Western philosophers and thinkers have espoused. As we will see, it is a view with ancient roots. We will call this view the Traditional Western view of human nature because it has influenced Western thinkers since ancient times. The Traditional view holds, then, that all humans have an enduring spiritual self that is rational, has a purpose, and is a separate individual.

Not everyone accepts the Traditional view. As we will see, many thinkers have rejected the view that humans have a rational nature that has a purpose. Others deny that the self is separate from its body. Still others have rejected the assumption that humans have an enduring self. Still others quarrel with the idea that the self is an independent individual.

We begin our journey of self-exploration by considering two of the most influential versions of the Traditional view: the rationalist view of human nature and the religious view. We will look, also, at several challenges to the Traditional view. We next turn to examine the view that the self can exist separate from its body. Then we look at the view that the self endures through time. Finally, we discuss the assumption that the self can and should be an independent, self-sufficient individual. By examining these views of ourselves, we will understand how the doctrines they espouse affect how we see ourselves, how we interact with others, and how we live our lives.

THE TRADITIONAL RATIONALIST VIEW

The most influential version of the Traditional theory of human nature views the human primarily as a thinker capable of reasoning. This view is well illustrated in the thought and writings of a man considered by some to be the greatest philosopher—Plato. Although Plato did not think that reason is the sole constituent of human nature, he did hold that it was the highest part of human nature. Conversing in *The Republic*, Socrates and Glaucon present Plato's view by discussing a question: What is the self? Notice in the following passage the use of the word *soul*, a common translation of Plato's term *psyche*. Since Plato did not intend all the theological meanings that we give the word *soul*, it would be wiser to substitute *inner self* for *soul*.

> *Man is a rational animal who always loses his temper when he is called upon to act in accordance with the dictates of reason.*
>
> OSCAR WILDE

SOCRATES: Isn't it sometimes true that the thirsty person also, for some reason, may want not to drink?

GLAUCON: Yes, often.

SOCRATES: What can we say, then, if not that in his soul there is a part that desires drink and another part that restrains him? This latter part is distinct from desire and usually can control desire.

GLAUCON: I agree.

SOCRATES: And isn't it true in such cases that such control originates in reason, while the urge to drink originates in something else?

GLAUCON: So it seems.

SOCRATES: Then we can conclude that there are in us two distinct parts. One is what we call "reason," and the other we call the nonrational "appetites." The latter hungers, thirsts, desires sex, and is subject to other desires.

GLAUCON: Yes, that is the logical conclusion.

SOCRATES: But what about our emotional or spirited element: the part in us that feels anger and indignation? . . . Anger sometimes opposes our appetites as if it is something distinct from them. . . . Yet this emotional part of ourselves is [also] distinct from reason.[6]

> **CRITICAL THINKING**
>
> Plato assumes that the presence of two contrary desires in a person shows that there are at least two distinct parts in the person. Is this assumption correct?

To understand Plato's view, consider this illustration. Suppose that you are very thirsty. Before you is a glass of poisoned water. One part of yourself, what Plato called appetite (located in the abdomen), invites you to drink. By *appetite*, he meant thirst and hunger, as well as sexual and other physical desires. Yet a second part of yourself, reason, forbids you to drink. By *reason*, Plato meant the uniquely human capacity for thinking reflectively and drawing conclusions—the ability to follow relationships from one thought to another in an orderly and correct way. This rational part of the self, said Plato, has its center in the brain. In this illustration a conflict arises between appetite and reason.

But Plato claimed that conflict could arise in another way, as when our aggressive emotions flare up. Suppose that someone cuts you off on the highway. You become enraged; you begin to blow your horn and shake your fist at the other driver. You are even tempted to tailgate for a few miles just to vent your spleen. Yet your head tells you that would do no good. Besides, it would be dangerous. Plato would say that the conflict here is not between reason and appetite. The conflict is between reason and what he variously calls anger,

---

[6]Plato, *The Republic*, from bk. 4. This edited translation copyright © 1987 by Manuel Velasquez.

"spirit," or the "spirited element." The spirited element is what we would probably call our aggressiveness or self-assertiveness. According to Plato, it resides
in the chest and is displayed in war and anger. Whereas reason seeks what is
good and right, aggression seeks to overcome others and assert itself. Plato described these conflicts among reason, appetite, and aggression in a striking image in which he compares reason to a charioteer pulled by the horses of desire
and aggression:

> Let me speak briefly about the nature of the soul by using an image. Let the image
> have three parts: two winged horses and a charioteer. . . . One of the horses is of
> noble breed, the other ignoble. The charioteer controls them with great diffi-
> culty. . . . The vicious steed—when it has not been thoroughly trained—goes
> heavily, weighing down the charioteer to the earth. . . .
>
> Above them, in the heaven above the heaven, . . . there abides the true reality
> with which real knowledge is concerned: the Forms which are visible only to the
> mind and have no color, shape, or hardness. The souls that are most like gods are
> carried up there by their charioteer, although troubled by their steeds and only with
> great difficulty beholding true being. . . . Other souls rise only to fall again, barely
> glimpsing it and then altogether failing to see because their steeds are too unruly.[7]

Notice Plato's use of the word *Forms*. For Plato, the forms are eternal and perfect ideals that exist in an unchanging perfect heaven. Things here on earth are
but imperfect reflections of these ideals. The purpose or destiny of the soul is to
be free of its body and ascend to heaven, where it will be united with these
perfect forms. The soul can do this only if it controls its bodily desires and trains
its aggressive impulses so that both obey reason.

Thus, in Plato's view, reason, aggression, and appetite are the three defining
parts of human nature. Depending on which part dominates, we get three kinds
of people, whose main desires are knowledge, power, and wealth, respectively.
Yet Plato leaves no doubt about which element can and should dominate: reason. True, each element plays a part, but aggression and appetite have no
knowledge with which to order themselves and must be brought under the control of reason. Through reason we can discover the truth about how we ought
to live, and when aggression and appetite are subordinate to reason, we will live
according to this truth. This truth, according to Plato, involves knowledge of
ideals that exist in another dimension of reality that only reason can apprehend. After death, the person whose desires and aggressions are under the control of reason will be freed of his body and can ascend to this dimension. (For a
fuller discussion of Plato's view of human nature, see the showcase on Plato at
the end of this chapter.)

For Plato, then, humans can control their appetites and their aggressive
impulses by the use of their reason. They are not ruled by self-interested desires,
as Freud and Hobbes claim. However, Plato holds that reason's ability to control
appetite and aggression depends on one's past choices. If a person continually
gives in to his aggressive impulses and appetites, he will lose the ability to control his appetites and aggressions. Such people become slaves of their appetites

---

[7] Plato, *Phaedrus*, selections from 246a–247e. This translation by Manuel Velasquez.

and aggressive impulses. When something arouses their anger, they give in to this impulse. When something arouses their desires, they cannot control themselves. But if a person has learned to restrain and control his or her appetites and aggressive impulses, the person will gain the ability to do what reason says is best.

For Plato's student Aristotle (384–322 B.C.), reason is also the human's highest power. Although in many ways Aristotle's views differed from Plato's, he, too, held that human reason can discover the truth about human nature and how we ought to live. Still, Plato held that the truth about human nature involved knowledge of another world of reality. Aristotle held that the truth about human nature required only knowledge of our own world. (For a fuller discussion of Aristotle's views, see the showcase on Aristotle at the end of this chapter.) Anyway, Aristotle agreed that our ability to reason is the characteristic that sets the human self apart from all other creatures of nature.

Aristotle emphasized even more than Plato the idea that humans have a purpose. According to Aristotle all living things have a purpose. For example, it is clear that the purpose of the eye is to see, and of the ears to hear. As he puts it,

> Surely, just as each part of man—the eye, the hand, the foot—has a purpose, so also man as a whole must have a purpose. What is this purpose? Our biological functions we share in common even with plants. So these cannot be the purpose of man, since we are looking for something specific to man. The activities of our senses we also plainly share with other things: horses, cattle, and other animals. So there remain only the activities that belong to the rational part of man. . . . The specific purpose or function of man must involve the activities of that part of his soul that belongs to reason.[8]

Both Plato and Aristotle, then, stress reason as the most important feature of our human nature, certainly as more important than our desires and aggressiveness. Reason is what is unique in humans—what makes us unique and different from all other animals. In addition, both see the use of reason as the purpose of human nature. That is, the purpose of human beings is to be rational: to use their reason. To achieve this, reason must control its desires and aggressions.

Plato also emphasized the spiritual aspect of human nature. In one of his dialogues, *Phaedo,* Plato has Socrates argue that the self—the soul—is immaterial and so is immortal and survives our bodily death. Plato argues that our mental activities provide the clearest evidence of the immaterial nature of the soul. That is, our ability to think is evidence of our immaterial nature. When we think and reason, Plato held, we are engaged in activities that a physical body cannot carry on. In particular, the activity of thinking about ideals that do not exist in this material world provides evidence that we have an immaterial self—a soul. Notice in the following passage how Plato contrasts the changing physical objects around us with the unchanging nature of ideal concepts. He argues that the soul must be like these ideal immaterial concepts:

---

[8] Aristotle, *Nicomachean Ethics,* bk. 1, ch. 7. This translation by Manuel Velasquez.

SOCRATES: Consider perfect equality or perfect beauty or any other ideal. Does each of these always remain the same perfect form, unchanging and not varying from moment to moment?

CEBES: They always have to be the same, Socrates.

SOCRATES: And what about the many individual [material] objects around us— people or horses or dresses or what have you. . . . Do these always remain the same or are they changing constantly and becoming something else?

CEBES: They are continually changing, Socrates.

SOCRATES: These changing [material] objects can be seen and touched and perceived with the senses [of the body]. But the unchanging Ideals can be known only with the mind and are not visible to the [body's] senses. . . . So there are two kinds of existing things: those which are visible and those which are not. . . . The visible are changing and the invisible are unchanging.

CEBES: That seems to be the case. . . .

SOCRATES: Now which of these two kinds of things is our body like?

CEBES: Clearly it is like the visible things. . . .

SOCRATES: And what do we say of the soul? Is it visible or not?

CEBES: It is not visible.

SOCRATES: Then the soul is more like the invisible and the body like the visible?

CEBES: That is most certain, Socrates.

SOCRATES: . . . [W]hen the soul turns within and reflects upon what lies in herself [knowledge of Ideals], she finds there the perfect, eternal, immortal, and unchanging realm that is most like herself.[9]

> **CRITICAL THINKING**
> What is Plato assuming when he says that since the mind can think about immaterial objects, it must be immaterial? Is this assumption correct?

In the rationalist view of human nature, then, we are creatures with rational minds that can control our appetites and aggressions. We can see ourselves as distinct from the matter of the world because our mind enables us to stand apart from our material environment. With our mind we find meaning and sense in the events around us. We gain self-mastery through reason, by learning self-control, and by becoming conscious of the forces that have shaped us and the influences that make us what we are. Such self-mastery through reason is the purpose of human beings.

This view of human nature looks innocent and optimistic in the role it gives to reason. Yet is it? Consider one way that Aristotle used this theory. He claimed that if a group of people was less rational than the Greek people, they would be less human: They would be barbarians. Such "barbarians" could justifiably be enslaved by more rational, and therefore more human, people like the Greeks. As Aristotle wrote, "The lower sort are by nature slaves, and it is better for them as for all inferiors that they should be under the rule of a master." But if slavery can be justified by a view of human nature that says that real humans are only those who live up to its standards, then can't any form of exploitation be justified by such a view? In fact, aren't all forms of racism ultimately justified by views that define what "human nature" really is? Doesn't racism always claim

---

[9] Plato, *Phaedo*. This edited translation copyright © 1987 by Manuel Velasquez.

Adam and Eve. In his idealized figures of the first man and woman being tempted by Satan, the fifteenth-century Christian artist Albrecht Dürer (1471–1528) attempted to portray humans as rational, loving beings made in the image of God but capable of great good and evil.

that other races are not quite as human or as highly developed humans as one's own race?

So the implications of the rationalist view for our own image of what we are loom large. In the rationalist view, we see ourselves as reasoning beings, imbued with an immaterial soul, with a purpose in life. Our reason can and should control our appetites and aggressive impulses. Indeed, it is the possession of reason itself that gives us the power to rise above our desires and self-interest and that defines our purpose. This classical view is one of the most influential theories in Western civilization. Many people still accept parts of it, and it has deeply influenced a second important version of the Traditional view: the Judeo-Christian religious view of human nature.

If the world consisted only of beings without reason, the existence of such a world would have no worth whatever, because there would exist in it no being with the least conception of what worth is.

KANT

TRADITIONAL WESTERN RELIGIOUS VIEWS OF HUMAN NATURE

According to the Judeo-Christian tradition, humans are made in the image of God. They are like divine beings, because they contain something of the ability to love and know that characterizes their Creator. For example, the Judeo-Christian scriptures portray God as saying "And God said, let us make man in our image, after our likeness."

The abilities to love and know—will and intellect—are the distinguishing characteristics of human beings in the Judeo-Christian view. So unique, and

Nature tells me I am the image of God.

THOMAS BROWNE

wonderful, are these abilities that the Judeo-Christian tradition holds that these make human beings "like" God.

The Greeks believed that only those who can exercise their reason can realize the purpose of living. But the Judeo-Christian view contends that the two purposes of life—loving God and serving God—are open to all, whatever their level of intelligence. As Saint Paul writes, "If I understand all mysteries and all knowledge . . . but have not love, I am nothing" (1 Cor. 13:2). Since God gives this love, it is divine, and so allows humans to share in divinity.

However, the Judeo-Christian view is hardly a denial of the rationalist view. On the contrary, Plato strongly influenced Christian thought through philosophers such as the Roman Plotinus (205?–270?) and the early Christian Saint Augustine (354–430). Augustine, in particular, adapted many of Plato's doc-

PHILOSOPHY AND LIFE

Evidence of the Soul

For several years the American Society for Psychical Research has been carefully conducting the research called for in the will of an obscure seventy-year-old Arizona miner named James Kidd, who died in 1946. The old miner left a will that read:

Phoenix Arizona
Jan 2nd 1946
this is my first and only will and is dated the second day in January 1946. I have no heir's, have not been married in my life, an after all my funeral expenses have been paid and $100. one hundred dollars to some preacher of the gospital to say farewell at my grave sell all my property which is all in cash and stocks with E. F. Hutton Co. Phoenix some in safety box, and have this balance money to go in a research or some scientific proof of a soul of the human body which leaves at death I think in time their can be a Photograph of soul leaving the human at death,
     James Kidd

The stocks held by E. F. Hutton were worth more than $200,000. Several groups came forward to claim the money, asserting that they would carry out the research stipulated in Kidd's will. Superior Court Judge Robert Myers, before whom the will was read, was faced with the task of trying to determine which group should get the money. After ten years of deliberations, the estate was awarded to the American Society for Psychical Research. A few years later the ASPR announced early results of its search for the soul:

Six out-of-body (OBE) projects have been conducted. An OBE "fly-in" and an attempt to correlate OBE's and apparitions both supported the OBE hypothesis, but other interpretations (e.g. ESP) are possible. Perceptual experiments with OBEs and psychophysiological studies of subjects gave similar results: evidence in harmony with OBE hypothesis but other explanations possible. Instrumental recordings (i.e.

photos) and a test of mediums gave negative results.

Deathbed studies of apparitions, visions, hallucinations, etc. (reported by attending doctors and nurses) supported the conclusion that "some of the dying patients indeed appeared to be already experiencing glimpses of ecsomatic existence." But again, other interpretations can't be ruled out; so these results "should not be taken as a final balance of evidence for or against survival." Masses of data are still being processed.

QUESTIONS

1. What kind of evidence could disprove the existence of a nonmaterial soul? What kind could prove the existence of a soul?

2. How would you have decided who was to receive the money if you were in the position of Judge Robert Myers?

———

SOURCE: ASPR Newsletter, July 1976.

trines to Christianity. For example, from Plato, Augustine took the doctrine that the human self is a rational self: an immaterial soul that is conscious and that can think. The self, Augustine held, can with the help of God control its desires and has the power to allow reason to rule over passion.

Augustine also borrowed Plato's view that humans have an immaterial and immortal soul. Augustine used this idea to justify the Christian notion of an afterlife. Plato had said that after death the souls of those who love "perfect, eternal" ideals would rise to heaven. Augustine modified this, arguing that the souls of those who love the perfect, eternal *God* will rise to heaven.

For the Christian, the way to union with God is by emulating the life of Jesus of Nazareth. In the life of Jesus, we find an expression of the highest virtue: love. We love when we perform selfless acts as Jesus did, developing a keen sense of social-mindedness and realizing that people are creatures of God and are thereby worthwhile. Thus, Jesus said, "Love one another as I have loved you."

For the Jew, we serve and love God primarily through expressions of justice and righteousness. We also develop a sense of honor that we derive from a commitment to the ideals of truth, humility, fidelity, and kindness. This commitment also produces a sharp sense of responsibility to family and community.

The religious view fosters the idea of a moral self: Each of us is capable of great good, but also of great evil. Refusing to serve and love God is the greatest evil. This refusal is expressed in various ways: injustice, vanity, pride, and dishonesty. Whenever we commit these offenses against God, we lose touch with ourselves by retreating from our alliance with God. In contrast to the Greek belief that we must develop our rational powers to perceive the moral order in the universe, the Judeo-Christian view holds that high intelligence is no prerequisite for a moral sense. We do good when we make God the center of our lives; we do wrong when we retreat from this commitment.

Besides reason, then, Augustine emphasized the notion of a will. The will, Augustine held, is our ability to choose between good and evil, and this ability is the seat of the most significant Christian virtue: love. For the Christian, as for the Jew, the fundamental religious duty is that of freely choosing to love and serve God. The human will, the power of choice over desire, allows human beings to make this choice. Still, the will is a two-edged sword. Whereas it enables us to choose the good, it also enables us to choose evil. We humans, Augustine held, are constantly attracted to evil and away from God. He describes an event in his boyhood that illustrates this:

> Near our vineyard there was a pear tree, loaded with fruit. . . . I and some other wretched youths conceived the idea of shaking the pears off this tree and carrying them away. We set out late at night . . . and stole all the fruit we could carry. And this was not to feed ourselves. We may have tasted a few, but then we threw the rest to the pigs. Our real pleasure was simply in doing something that was forbidden. . . . I did evil for nothing, with no reason for the wrongdoing except the wrongdoing itself. . . . I loved the sin, not the thing for which I had committed the sin, but the sin itself.[10]

What a piece of work is a man! How noble in reason! how infinite in faculty! in form, in moving, how express and admirable! in action how like an angel! in apprehension how like a god! The beauty of the world, the paragon of animals! And yet, to me, what is this quintessence of dust?

SHAKESPEARE

---

[10] Augustine, *The Confessions of St. Augustine*, trans. Rex Warner (New York: New American Library of World Literature, 1963), 45.

Here, Augustine is echoing Plato. Like Plato, Augustine held that humans have within them powerful desires that, like an unruly "steed," constantly "weigh" us down to the earth and away from "heaven above." Nevertheless, Augustine held, with God's help, we humans can overcome "lust" and allow reason to rule over our lower desires. The human being, then, has both reason and will: the ability to know the truth about God and the ability to choose and love that God. Thus, the Judeo-Christian view agrees with the rationalist view, that human nature is not basically self-interested. In this respect, both differ from the views of Hobbes and Freud that we saw above. Humans are, instead, capable of rising above their self-interested desires and turning to God.

The Judeo-Christian tradition modified another key part of the rationalist tradition. Aristotle argues that like all living things, human beings have a purpose. The purpose of humans is to achieve happiness by using their reason. The Christian thinker Thomas Aquinas agreed that humans and everything in nature have a purpose. However, he said, the purpose of humans is to achieve happiness by using their reason to *know God:*

> The heavenly bodies cause the generation of all things here below. So the purpose of their motion is the generation of things below. Now [here below] . . . the simplest elements exist for the sake of compound minerals; these latter exist for the sake of living bodies, among which plants exist for animals, and animals for humans. So humans are the purpose of the whole order of generation. . . . Now humans naturally desire, as their ultimate purpose, to know the first cause of things. But the first cause of all things is God. So the ultimate purpose of humans is to know God.[11]

Man is absolutely not the crown of creation: every creature stands beside him at the same stage of perfection.

NIETZSCHE

In many ways, the rationalist and Judeo-Christian view of human nature is appealing. It seems to describe something that we all experience: the conflict between what our reason wants and what our desires pull us toward. It seems to provide an uplifting picture of human beings. Reason and will set us off from all other creatures, making us "like" God and capable of choosing between good and evil, between a course that will bring us closer to or take us further from our Creator. The rationalist and Judeo-Christian view argues for a self that is spiritual and so can survive the death of its body.

All these are familiar ideas about ourselves: the idea that it is possible for us to survive bodily death or that the self might leave its body, the idea that we humans are special and different from other animals, the idea that it is reason that makes us different and that reason should rule over our passions, the idea that human beings have a purpose and that this purpose may be related to the spiritual dimension of the universe.

Yet are these optimistic views of the Judeo-Christian tradition tenable? Is the assumption of a spiritual dimension supported by what modern science teaches us? If, as materialists claim, there is no immaterial element in human nature, then must we abandon the Judeo-Christian view? Are humans really able to choose between good and evil and the Judeo-Christian view suggest? Or

---

[11] Aquinas, *Summa Contra Gentiles*, bk. III, ch. 22, para. 5, 7, 8; ch. 25, para. 11. Translated by Manuel Velasquez.

are our choices ultimately determined by our upbringing, our society, our home, and our history? These are important questions that we must explore further in the chapters to come.

Perhaps more disturbing are the iimplications of cultural superiority that may lurk beneath this view. For if the Judeo-Christian view of human nature is the true one, then wouldn't we be justified in dismantling cultures that are inconsistent with this view? Has the Judeo-Christian view of human nature been in any way responsible for the destruction of cultures that has taken place when Christian societies have explored and colonized other lands?

As noted, the views of the human as a rational and loving being have been the most influential in Western civilization. In them we find the intellectual emphasis of the Greeks and the religious emphasis of the Jews and Christians. From them we inherit the view that all human beings share a nature that is rational and that has a purpose. Many of us today continue to look at ourselves in this way. Yet some philosophers have challenged these ideas. Perhaps the most serious challenge to these ideas has come from science. Of the many ways in which science has challenged our understandings of ourselves, the most important challenge has been the challenge posed by the theory of evolution. As we will see, the theory of evolution challenges key aspects of the traditional Western concept of who and what we are.

We will look closely at this challenge by looking at the ideas of Charles Darwin. Darwin, more than anyone else, forced us to take the theory of evolution seriously. He is also the man who saw more clearly than anyone else that the theory of evolution is a threat to our traditional Western ideas of who and what we are.

THE DARWINIAN CHALLENGE

Darwin proposed two key ideas. The first is the idea that animals and plants are sometimes born with features that are different from those of their parents but that they can pass on to their own offspring. Darwin called these differences "variations." For example, a giraffe may be born with a longer neck than its parents. The giraffe can then pass on this "variation" to its own offspring. Variations like these, Darwin argued, happen randomly. That is, each happens completely by chance.

The second key idea Darwin advanced is that all animals are caught in a great "struggle for existence"—that is, they are continuously competing with others to stay alive:

> A struggle for existence inevitably follows from the high rate at which all organic beings tend to increase. Every being, which during its natural lifetime produces several eggs or seeds, must suffer destruction during some period of its life, and during some season or occasional year, otherwise, on the principle of geometrical increase, its numbers would quickly become so inordinately great that no country could support the product. Hence, as more individuals are produced than can possibly survive, there must in every case be a struggle for existence, either one individual

Charles Darwin: "Natural selection is daily and hourly scrutinising, throughout the world, the slightest variations; rejecting those that are bad, preserving and adding up all that are good, silently and insensibly working at the improvement of each organic being."

with another of the same species, or with the individuals of distinct species, or with the physical conditions of life.[12]

A newborn cat, for example, starts life having to compete with its many brothers and sisters as they all struggle to suck from their mother's few nipples. Later, the cat has to compete with other cats for mates and food. Throughout its life, it struggles to keep away from wolves and other predators. Always it must struggle against head and cold, sun and snow, droughts and storms. This is a life-or-death struggle for every animal, and most fall by the wayside and die.

Darwin pointed out that the random variations an animal is born with can sometimes give it an advantage in this great struggle for existence. A giraffe with a longer neck can reach leaves that other giraffes can't. When an animal has a variation that gives it an advantage over other animals of the same kind (the same species), it will have a better chance of surviving. It is then more likely to pass the variation to its own offspring. A giraffe with a longer neck can feed itself better and so live longer, mate more often, and leave more offspring with long necks than other giraffes. The great struggle for existence, then, "selects" those animals with advantageous variations and lets them survive and multiply. At the same, the struggle for existence weeds out animals and plants that have less advantageous variations and lets them die. After many generations, all the surviving members of the species have the new variation:

---

[12] Charles Darwin, *The Origin of Species*, ch. 4.

[C]an we doubt (remembering that many more individuals are born than can possibly survive) that individuals having any advantage, however slight, over others, would have the best chance of surviving and of procreating their kind? On the other hand, we may feel sure that any variation in the least degree injurious would be rigidly destroyed. This preservation of favourable individual differences and variations, and the destruction of those which are injurious, I have called Natural Selection, or the Survival of the Fittest. . . .

Let us take the case of a wolf, which preys on various animals, securing some by craft, some by strength, and some by fleetness; and let us suppose that the fleetest prey, a deer for instance, had from any change in the country increased in numbers, or that other prey had decreased in numbers, during that season of the year when the wolf was hardest pressed for food. Under such circumstances the swiftest and slimmest wolves would have the best chance of surviving and so be preserved or selected.[13]

Over many thousands of years, the inexorable "weeding" process of natural selection can make a species (a kind of animal) change into wholly new species. A species of fish over millions of years may evolve into a species of frog-like amphibians, the amphibians may evolve into dinosaurs, and the dinosaurs may evolve into birds:

It may metaphorically be said that natural selection is daily and hourly scrutinising, throughout the world, the slightest variations; rejecting those that are bad, preserving and adding up all that are good; silently and insensibly working, whenever and wherever opportunity offers, at the improvement of each organic being in relation to its organic and inorganic conditions of life. We see nothing of these slow changes in progress, until the hand of time has marked the lapse of ages, and then so imperfect is our view into long-past geological ages, that we see only that the forms of life are now different from what they formerly were.[14]

We are so used to the idea of evolution that it is hard for us to understand how incredible Darwin's theory was to people of his time. The idea that one kind of animal might gradually evolve into an entirely new species, and that the new species might eventually give rise to yet another even more different species, was a disturbing new thought for many people. It meant that the world around us is not fixed, but is caught up in a dizzying and unsettling continual change.

Yet as disturbing as Darwin's ideas about animal species were, his ideas were even more disturbing when applied to human beings. For humans are animals, and if Darwin's theory applied to animals, it also applied to humans. Humans also must have evolved! Darwin himself made the point in *The Descent of Man*, a book that aroused a flurry of angry controversy:

Thus we can understand how it has come to pass that man and all other vertebrate animals have been constructed on the same general model, why they pass through the same early stages of development, and why they retain certain rudiments in common. Consequently we ought frankly to admit their community of descent: to take

The main argument which convinces us that animals have no reason is that no animal can make use of a true language so as to indicate to us by signs anything that could be referred to thought alone, rather than a movement of mere nature.

DESCARTES

---

[13] Ibid.
[14] Ibid.

any other view, is to admit that our own structure, and that of all the animals around us, is a mere snare laid to entrap our judgment. . . . It is only our natural prejudice, and that arrogance which made our forefathers declare that they were descended from demigods, which leads us to demur to this conclusion.[15]

Think of the implications of Darwin's theory for the Traditional view of human nature. Take, first, what the Traditional view says about the differences between humans and animals. The Traditional view says that although humans are animals, they have a characteristic that makes them unique. This is the ability to reason. Humans are rational animals, and our ability to reason and think goes beyond anything animals can do. Reason is not just a more developed and more powerful version of the same kinds of abilities that animals have. Instead, the Traditional view says that our ability to reason is a completely different kind of ability than any of the abilities that animals have.

Darwin's theory denied this. If humans evolved from lower animals, then all human abilities evolved from the abilities that animals have. If so, then all human abilities are merely more developed variations of the same kinds of abilities that animals have. According to Darwin, "[T]here is no fundamental difference between man and the higher mammals in their mental faculties."[16] The Traditional view held that the human power to reason is so unique, so different in kind from the powers of animals, that it could only have come from God. It is, in fact, what makes us like God. Yet if Darwin is right, then the human power to reason is not unique, and so it is no more "God-like" than any other developed animal ability. Humans are made not in the image of God, but in the image of the ape.

Second, and even more important, the Traditional view holds that, like all living things, human beings have a purpose. Aristotle and Plato held that the purpose of humans is to exercise their reason. Christian philosophers such as Augustine and Aquinas added to this that the purpose of humans is to exercise their reason to love God and neighbor.

Darwin's theory of evolution directly contradicted the idea that living things are designed for a purpose. The eye, the hand, the foot, and the whole human body were not made to serve a specific purpose but developed by random variations and the blind process of natural selection. Evolution happens by chance, not by purposeful design. Humans are the products not of a purposeful plan, but of chance "variations" and blind mechanical forces. Humans have no purpose.

Still, does this mean that the Traditional view of human nature is dead? Hardly. Many thinkers have attempted to respond to Darwin, some by pointing to problems with his theory and others by arguing that his theory does not disprove the unique and purposive nature of humans.

First, and most controversially, many have argued that Darwin's theory still lacks definitive proof. The main evidence for evolution is fossils. Fossils are preserved skeletons (or other remains) of ancient animals found in layers of rocks under the earth. If these fossils are placed in rows, with the oldest ones

Most of the more complex emotions are common to the higher animals and ourselves.
DARWIN

Our reverence for the nobility of manhood will not be lessened by the knowledge that man is, in substance and in structure, one with the animals.
T. H. HUXLEY

---

[15]Charles Darwin, *The Descent of Man*, ch. 1.
[16]Ibid., ch. 3.

first, and the most recent ones last, there is a progression among them: The oldest animals seem step by step to become more like the animals that are still living today. Darwin argued that this fossil progression shows that the animals living today evolved slowly from ancient animals. He claimed that only his theory of random variations and natural selection can explain how this evolution took place.

Nevertheless, many scientists have argued that fossils do not support Darwin's view that species gradually evolve into other species. When we examine the fossils buried in rocks, they claim, we find that most new species seem to appear suddenly, without earlier slightly different species leading up to them. It is as if there were sudden jumps from one complete species to another. Missing are the gradual changes and many intermediate steps that should be there if new species evolve by gradual steps through natural selection. As the contemporary biologist Stephen Jay Gould writes,

> The history of most fossil species includes two features inconsistent with [Darwinian] gradualism: 1. Stasis. Most species exhibit no directional change during their tenure on earth. They appear in the fossil record looking much the same as when they disappear. . . . 2. Sudden Appearance. In any local area, a species does not arise gradually by the steady transformation of its ancestors; it appears all at once and "fully formed."[17]

However, Gould does not think that the large gaps in the fossil record completely disprove evolution. Gould suggests that the gaps show only that evolution occurs by "jumps" or "saltations." However, others insist that the gaps "prove" that Darwin was wrong.

Does this debate mean that Darwin was wrong and that we should reject his theory? Not at all. Perhaps the "gaps" are simply the result of the fact that we have not yet found all the fossils or that we have not yet discovered exactly how evolution works. The debate merely shows, then, that we must not be dogmatic about Darwin's theory of evolution. It provides some powerful and profound ideas for understanding ourselves: how we are related to the rest of the animal kingdom and how chance and randomness may have created us. Nevertheless, the theory might be wrong, at least in its details, if not in major ways. We should remain open to this possibility.

Still, even if Darwin's theory is correct, opponents have argued, it is a mistake to think that evolution proves that humans were not designed for a purpose. For example, the contemporary philosopher George Mavrodes suggests that there are two ways of understanding evolution. A "naturalistic" understanding of evolution holds that evolution is "explicable entirely in terms of natural law without reference to a divine intention or intervention." But a "theistic" understanding of evolution holds that "there was a divine teleology in this process, a divine direction at each crucial stage in accordance with divine plan or intention."[18] In order words, a theistic understanding of evolution

In many respects man is the most ruthlessly ferocious of beasts.

WILLIAM JAMES

What a chimera, then, is man! What a novelty! What a monster, what a chaos, what a contradiction, what a prodigy!

PASCAL

---

[17] Stephen Jay Gould, *The Panda's Thumb* (New York: Norton, 1980), 182.
[18] George Mavrodes, "'Creation Science' and Evolution," *Chronicle of Higher Education*, January 7, 1987, 43.

holds that God directs evolution. Evolution is merely the tool of God's design. Evolution, and even the great struggle for existence that "selects" some animals to survive and others to die, is the instrument with which God designs human beings and other animals. Other philosophers, such as Henri Bergson (1859–1941) and Pierre Teilhard de Chardin (1881–1955), have also argued that the process of evolution is not blind and random, but directed.

But not all evolutionists agree that the theory of evolution is compatible with the idea that humans are designed for a purpose. As Stephen Jay Gould writes,

> Humans are not the end result of predictable evolutionary progress, but rather a fortuitous cosmic afterthought, a tiny little twig on the enormously aborescent bush of life, which, if replanted from seed, would almost surely not grow this twig again, or perhaps any twig with any property that we would care to call consciousness. . . . The course of evolution is only the summation of fortuitous contingencies, not a pathway with predictable directions.[19]

Is Darwin correct? Does his theory of evolution disprove the Traditional Western view of human nature? Is evolution incompatible with purpose and the uniqueness of the human species? You must decide the answers to these questions yourself. However they are answered, it is clear that a great deal hangs on them. Your view of yourself depends on the answer.

THE EXISTENTIALIST CHALLENGE

In the middle of the twentieth century, another, very different view of human beings arose to challenge the Traditional Western view of human nature. This view, called **existentialism,** holds that humans are whatever they make themselves. Existentialism denies any essential human nature in the traditional sense, insisting that individuals create their own nature through free, responsible choices and actions. We cannot say that humans have a fixed rational nature and a fixed purpose.

Although existentialism is also popular among religious thinkers, we'll confine our remarks to atheistic existentialism. The chief exponent of atheistic existentialism was Jean-Paul Sartre (1905–1980), who saw humans as "condemned to be free." We are free because we can rely neither on a God (who doesn't exist) nor on society to justify our actions or to tell us what we essentially are. We are condemned because without a fixed purpose or a guideline we must suffer the agony of our own decision making and the anguish of its consequences.

Although he believed that there are no true, universal statements about what humans ought to be, Sartre did make at least one general statement about the human condition: We are free. This freedom consists chiefly of our ability to envision additional possibilities for our condition, to conceive of what is not the case, to suspend judgment, and to alter our condition. Therefore, we should

existentialism a twentieth-century philosophpy that denies any essential human nature; each of us creates our own essence through free action

---

[19] Stephen Jay Gould, *Dinosaur in a Haystack* (New York: Crown Trade Paperbacks, 1995), 329, 332.

make individual choices, fully aware that we are doing so. We must take full responsibility not only for our actions but also for our beliefs, feelings, and attitudes.

To illustrate, many people believe that we have little control over our emotions. If we feel depressed, we feel depressed, and there's little we can do about it. Sartre argued that if we're depressed, we've often chosen to be. Emotions, he said, are not moods that come over us but are often ways in which we freely choose to perceive the world, to participate in it.

It is the consciousness of this freedom and its accompanying responsibilities that causes our anguish. The most anguishing thought of all is that we are responsible for ourselves. Sometimes we escape this anguish by pretending we are not free. For example, we pretend that our genes or our environment is the cause of what we are, or that we are spectators rather than participants, passive rather than active. When we so pretend, said Sartre, we act in "bad faith."

Self-deception or bad faith is the attempt to avoid anguish by pretending to ourselves that we are not free. We have many ways to do this. We try to convince ourselves that outside influences have shaped our nature. Or that forces beyond our control or unconscious mental states have shaped us. One graphic example of self-deception provided by Sartre involves a young woman sitting with a man who, she knows, is bent on seduction. He takes her hand. To avoid the painful necessity of making a decision to accept or reject the man, the woman pretends not to notice, leaving her hand in his. Isn't there bad faith in the woman's pretending to be a passive object, a being-in-itself, rather than what she really is, conscious and, therefore, a free being? Here's Sartre's account of the incident, as he develops it in *Being and Nothingness*:

> Take the example of a woman who has consented to go out with a particular man for the first time. She knows very well the intentions which the man who is speaking to her cherishes regarding her. She knows also that it will be necessary sooner or later for her to make a decision. But she does not want to realize the urgency; she concerns herself only with what is respectful and discreet in the attitude of her companion. She does not apprehend this conduct as an attempt to achieve what we call "the first approach"; that is, she does not want to see possibilities of temporal development which his conduct presents. She restricts this behavior to what is in the present; she does not wish to read in the phrases which he addresses to her anything other than their explicit meaning. If he says to her, "I find you so attractive!" she disarms this phrase of its sexual background; she attaches to the conversation and to the behavior of the speaker, the immediate meanings, which she imagines as objective qualities. The man who is speaking to her appears to her sincere and respectful as the table is round or square, as the wall coloring is blue or gray. The qualities thus attached to the person she is listening to are in this way fixed in a permanence like that of things, which is no other than the projection of the strict present of the qualities into the temporal flux. This is because she does not quite know what she wants. She is profoundly aware of the desire which she inspires, but the desire cruel and naked would humiliate and horrify her. Yet she would find no charm in a respect which would be only respect. In order to satisfy her, there must be a feeling which is addressed wholly to her personality—i.e., to her full freedom—and which would be a recognition of her freedom. But at the same time this feeling must be wholly desire; that is, it must

Man is but a reed, the most feeble thing in nature; but he is a thinking reed.

PASCAL

Man is a biodegradable but nonrecyclable animal blessed with opposable thumbs capable of grasping at straws.

BERNARD ROSENBERG

CRITICAL THINKING

Does Sartre assume that we can discover the truth about our inner motivations by examining our own consciousness? Would this assumption be correct? Is self-deception possible for Sartre?

address itself to her body as object. This time then she refuses to apprehend the desire for what it is; she does not even give it a name; she recognizes it only to the extent that it transcends itself toward admiration, esteem, respect and that it is wholly absorbed in the more refined forms which it produces, to the extent of no longer figuring anymore as a sort of warmth and density. But then suppose he takes her hand. This act of her companion risks changing the situation by calling for an immediate decision. To leave the hand there is to consent in herself to flirt, to engage herself. To withdraw it is to break the troubled and unstable harmony which gives the hour its charm. The aim is to postpone the moment of decision as long as possible. We know what happens next; the young woman leaves her hand there, but she does not notice that she is leaving it. She does not notice because it happens by chance that she is at this moment all intellect. She draws her companion up to the most lofty regions of sentimental speculation; she speaks of Life, of her life, she shows herself in her essential aspect—a personality, a consciousness. And during this time the divorce of the body from the soul is accomplished; the hand rests inert between the warm hands of her companion—neither consenting nor resisting—a thing.

  We shall say that this woman is in bad faith, but we see immediately that she uses various procedures in order to maintain herself in this bad faith. She has disarmed the actions of her companion by reducing them to being only what they are.[20]

Existentialism obviously emphasizes the free and conscious individual. However, the self in this view is not necessarily rational, or mechanical, or a creature of God. It is instead a project that possesses a subjective life; it is the sum, not of everything that happens to it, but of everything it ever does. In the end, we are what our choices make us; to be human means to create oneself.

  Yet can we have the kind of self-knowledge and control over ourselves that Sartre assumes people always have in situations like those facing the woman in the passage above? Doesn't our unconscious mind—the unconscious motivations and desires that psychologists say operate without our knowledge—control much of what we do? For example, doesn't that unconscious mind heavily influence how a woman reacts to the touch of a man or how a man responds to that of a woman? Doesn't the kind of conditioning we have received in the past shape our external behavior in the present moment?

  In *Existentialism and Humanism*, Sartre vigorously expresses the existential view of human nature. Notice in the selection that follows the primacy that Sartre gives to existence. Existence is prior to essence, he believes; humans exist first, and then they make something of themselves. In this fact lies the human condition:

> Atheistic existentialism, of which I am a representative, declares . . . that if God does not exist there is at least one being whose existence comes before its essence, a being which exists before it can be defined by any conception of it. That being is man. . . . What do we mean by saying that existence precedes essence? We mean that man first of all exists, encounters himself, surges up in the world—and defines himself afterwards. If man as the existentialist sees him is not definable, it is because to begin with he is nothing. He will not be anything until later, and then he will be what he makes of himself. Thus, there is no human nature, because there is no God to have

Man will do nothing unless he has first understood that he must count on no one but himself; that he is alone, abandoned on earth in the midst of his infinite responsibilities; without help, with no other aim than the one he sets himself, with no other destiny than the one he forges for himself on this earth.

JEAN-PAUL SARTRE

---

[20]Jean-Paul Sartre, *Being and Nothingness*, trans. Hazel E. Barnes (New York: Philosophical Library, 1956), 55–56. Copyright © 1956 by Philosophical Library. Reprinted by permission.

a conception of it. Man simply is. Not that he is simply what he conceives himself to be, but he is what he wills.[21]

Clearly, existentialism provides a profound challenge to the Traditional view of human nature. If existentialism is correct, then there is no such thing as a universal human nature shared by all people. Instead, we each create our own nature. If Sartre is right, we also cannot say that humans are defined by their rationality. Ahead of time, we cannot say what will define a person: Only his or her future choices can determine this. Moreover, if Sartre is right, we cannot say that humans have a purpose. Humans are not made for anything. We simply exist, and each of us must decide for ourselves what purpose our existence will serve. There is no way to say ahead of time that one purpose is right for everyone or that there is some purpose that is meant for everyone.

We are, therefore, ultimately responsible for our own nature and purposes. This radical responsibility—our inability to blame anyone else for what we are—is the basis for our feelings of despair, fear, guilt, and isolation. It is also the basis for our uncertainties and anxieties about death. There we confront the meaninglessness that is at the core of existence and thus discover a truth that enables us to live fully conscious of what being human means.

Yet do we have the kind of absolute freedom to create our nature that Sartre attributes to us? Are we fully responsible for the nature we have? Are you wholly to blame for who and what you are today? If you deny that you are free and responsible, are you in fact using this very denial as an excuse to escape your responsibility? Is the denial of freedom always a form of bad faith?

THE FEMINIST CHALLENGE

The most disturbing challenge to the Traditional picture of human nature is the criticism that it is fundamentally sexist—that is, it discriminates against women. This feminist objection strikes at the very center of the Traditional picture, and to examine it, we must go back to Plato and Aristotle.

To understand the feminist criticism, recall that in the Traditional view of human nature, humans are rational beings whose reason should rule over the body and its desires and emotions. In the part of his dialogue *Phaedo* that follows the portion excerpted earlier in this chapter, Plato, putting his own views into the mouth of Socrates, described the rationalist view like this:

SOCRATES: Yet once more consider the matter in another light: When the soul and the body are united, then nature orders the soul to rule and govern, and the body to obey and serve. Now, which of these two functions is akin to the divine and which to the mortal? Does not the divine appear to you to be that which naturally orders and rules, and the mortal to be that which is subject and servant?

CEBES: True.

SOCRATES: And which does the soul resemble?

CEBES: The soul resembles the divine, and the body the mortal—there can be no doubt of that, Socrates.

---

[21] Jean-Paul Sartre, *Existentialism and Humanism*, trans. Philip Mairet (London: Methuen, 1949), 85.

SOCRATES: Then reflect, Cebes: of all which has been said is not this the conclusion?—that the soul is in the very likeness of the divine, and immortal, and intellectual, and uniform, and indissoluble, and unchangeable; and that the body is in the very likeness of the human, and mortal, and unintellectual, and multiform, and dissoluble, and changeable. Can this, my dear Cebes, be denied?

CEBES: It cannot.

SOCRATES: But if it be true, then is not the body liable to speedy dissolution and is not the soul almost or altogether indissoluble?

CEBES: Certainly. . . .

SOCRATES: That soul, I say, itself invisible, departs [at death] to the invisible world—to the divine and immortal and rational: thither arriving, the soul is secure of bliss and is released from the error and folly of men, their fears and wild passions and all other human ills, and forever dwells, as they say of the initiated, in company with the gods. Is not this true, Cebes?

CEBES: Yes, beyond a doubt.

SOCRATES: But the soul which has been polluted, and is impure at the time of death, and is the companion and servant of the body always, and is in love with and fascinated by the body and by the desires and pleasures of the body, until it is led to believe that the truth only exists in a bodily form, which a man may touch and see and taste, and use for the purposes of his lusts,—the soul, I mean, accustomed to hate and fear and avoid the intellectual principle, which to the bodily eye is dark and invisible, and can be attained only by philosophy;—do you suppose that such a soul will depart pure and unalloyed?

CEBES: Impossible.

SOCRATES: Such a soul is held fast by the corporeal, which the continual association and constant care of the body have wrought into its nature.

CEBES: Very true.

SOCRATES: And this corporeal element, my friend, is heavy and weighty and earthy, and is that element of sight by which a soul is depressed and dragged down again into the visible world, because it is afraid of the invisible and of the world below—prowling about tombs and sepulchres . . . and these must be the souls, not of the good, but of the evil, which are compelled to wander about such places in payment of the penalty of their former evil way of life.[22]

Plato associates the soul with reason, and opposes these two to the body and its earthy desires. The "pure" soul is supposed to rule over the "impure" body and to turn away from the "desires and pleasures of the body." If the soul dominates the body and turns away from its desires and "wild passions" or emotions, it will be "good." At death, such a pure soul will rise to join the gods. But if the soul becomes the "companion and servant" of its body and bodily desires and pleasures, it will become "polluted" and "evil" and will be punished by being dragged down to wander among "tombs and sepulchres."

---

[22] Plato, *Phaedo*, in *Dialogues of Plato*, trans. Benjamin Jowett and ed. Justin D. Kaplan (New York: Simon & Schuster, 1950), 103–106.

Feminists have argued that here Plato inserted a critical assumption into the rationalist view of human nature: The soul and reason are superior and should rule, whereas the body and its desires and emotions are inferior and should obey. Aristotle, Plato's student, next made a move that would forever give this rationalist view of human nature a sexist bias. Aristotle associated men with reason and claimed that women do not share fully in reason. Consequently, men should rule over women:

> There are three elements of household rule, the first being the rule of the master over slaves, . . . the second that of the father over his children, and the third that of the husband over his wife. . . . His rule over his wife is like that of a magistrate in a free state, while his rule over his children is like that of a king. For the male is naturally more qualified to lead than the female, unless something unnatural happens, and the older and more complete adult is more qualified to rule than the younger and incomplete child. . . . For in the soul there is by nature an element that rules and also an element that is ruled; and in these elements we recognize different virtues, the virtue, to wit, of that which possesses reason, and the virtue of that which lacks reason [but which should obey reason]. It is clear, then that the same rule holds good in other cases also, so that most things in the world by nature are rulers or are ruled. But it is in different ways that the free man rules the slave, the male rules the female, and the adult rules the child. Although in each of these there is present an appropriate share of soul, it is present in each in a different manner. For the slave, speaking generally, does not have a reasoning faculty; the woman has it but without the power to be effective; and the child has it, but in an incomplete degree.[23]

Aristotle is claiming that the reason that characterizes the essential nature of humans is fully operational only in males. Women, like children, do not have a full share of reason, so, like our bodily appetites and emotions, they should obey the full reason of males.

From the very beginning, feminists have argued, the rationalist view of human nature has associated males with the superior traits that are supposed to set humans apart from all other beings. The rationalist view associates men with rationality and mind. It associates women with the bodily appetites and emotions that must be controlled. Reason is male and must rule, whereas feelings are female and must be ruled.

Centuries later, feminists charge, the religious version of the rationalist view of human nature adopted this association of reason with men and of appetites and emotions with women. For example, in the *Confessions*, the Christian philosopher Saint Augustine wrote the following in a prayer to God:

> Then you took man's mind, which is subject to none but you and needs to imitate no human authority, and renewed it in your own image and likeness. You made rational action subject to the rule of the intellect, as woman is subject to man.[24]

---

[23] Aristotle, *Politics*, quoted in *Philosophy of Woman: Classical to Current Concepts*, ed. Mary Briody Mahowald (Indianapolis: Hackett, 1978), 68.
[24] Augustine, *Confessions*, quoted in Genevieve Lloyd, "The Man of Reason," in *Women, Knowledge, and Reality: Explorations in Feminist Philosophy*, ed. Ann Garry and Marilyn Pearsall (Boston: Unwin Hyman, 1989), 111–128.

Somewhat earlier, the Jewish philosopher Philo also accepted the rationalist view of human nature and brought it into Judaic thinking:

> The male is more complete, more dominant than the female, closer akin to causal activity, for the female is incomplete and in subjection and belongs to the category of the passive rather than the active. So too with the two ingredients which constitute our life-principle, the rational and the irrational; the rational which belongs to mind and reason is of the masculine gender, the irrational, the province of sense, is of the feminine. Mind belongs to a genus wholly superior to sense as man is to woman.[25]

This brief look at the historical development of the rationalist view of human nature clarifies the fundamental issue: the rationalist view, and the Judeo-Christian religious view based on it, are sexist—they are biased against women. The rationalist view holds that reason is the essential characteristic that sets humans off from the rest of creation. Yet, as feminists point out, the rationalist view attributes full reason only to adult males: Reason and rationality are "male" whereas desire and feeling are "female." As a result, the rationalist view allows only men to be fully human because only men are fully rational, and women are incomplete and driven by their emotions.

Moreover, feminists argue, the rationalist view defines male rationality as superior to the bodily appetites and emotions, which it associates with women. This view asserts that reason must rule. Consequently, the rationalist view and the religious views that accept it imply that men should rule over women. The rationalist view thus justifies the oppression of women.

And finally, feminists argue, the rationalist view implies that rationality—the supposedly male quality—is good and should be cultivated. Our bodily desires and emotions—the supposedly female qualities—are bad and should be restrained. Male rationality is the key to attaining truth, knowledge, and even eternal salvation. But our bodily appetites and emotions "pollute" us and prevent us from thinking clearly and from attaining truth, knowledge, and eternal salvation. The result is a profound lack of respect for basic aspects of human nature: the body, the appetites, and the emotions.

The feminist objection to the rationalist and Judeo-Christian views of human nature is that they are fundamentally sexist. Yet is this objection correct? Are sexist views that assume the inferiority of women to men essential to the Traditional view of human nature? Can we talk about reason and emotion, body and spirit, truth and desire without covertly assuming sexist views? Although many people continue to think of rationality as a "male" trait and emotion as a "female" trait, can't we start to think differently? Granted, many people still feel that emotion is an obstacle to the attainment of the truth and knowledge that reason seeks. But can't we create new ways of thinking about truth, science, and knowledge? Granted, many people still believe that if we are to be moral and righteous, we should restrain our bodily appetites. But can't we start to think differently about the value of our body and its appetites? Finally,

---

[25] Philo, *Special Laws*, in *Philo*, vol. 1, trans. F. H. Colson and G. H. Whitaker, Loeb Classical Library (London: Heinemann, 1929), 125.

many religious people still feel that our bodily desires "pollute" us and prevent us from attaining eternal salvation. But can't we create new forms of religion and spirituality that look at our bodily desires from a different perspective? Is the rationalist picture of human nature such a deep part of our everyday way of thinking about ourselves that we can't change?

Consider a more radical proposal. Why don't we simply throw out the rationalist view of human nature if it is sexist? Genevieve Lloyd, herself a feminist philosopher, argues that this is not as easy to do as it may first appear:

> It is a natural response to the discovery of unfair discrimination to affirm the positive value of what has been downgraded. But with the kind of bias we are confronting here the situation is complicated by the fact that femininity, as we have it, has been partly formed by relation to, and differentiation from, a male norm. We may, for example, want to insist against past philosophers that the sexes are equal in possession of Reason; and that women must now be admitted to full participation in its cultural manifestations. But . . . this approach is fraught with difficulty. . . . For it seems implicitly to accept the downgrading of the excluded character traits traditionally associated with femininity, and to endorse the assumption that the only human excellences and virtues which deserve to be taken seriously are those exemplified in the range of activities and concerns that have been associated with maleness.
>
> However, alternative responses are no less beset by conceptual complexities. For example, it may seem easy to affirm the value and strengths of distinctively "feminine" traits. . . . Thus, it is an understandable reaction . . . to stress . . . the warmth of feeling as against the chillingly abstract character of Reason. But . . . subtle accommodations have been incorporated into the social organization of sexual division which allow "feminine" traits and activities to be both preserved and downgraded. There has been no lack of male affirmation of the importance and attractiveness of "feminine" traits—in women—or of gallant acknowledgement of the impoverishment of male Reason. Making good the lacks in male consciousness, providing it with a necessary complementation by the "feminine," is a large part of what the suppression . . . of "womankind" has been all about.[26]

Lloyd may be saying that one way of rejecting the rationalist view is to simply insist that women have as much reason as men. Yet, as she points out, why would we insist on this unless we agree that reason—the "male" trait—is really as superior as the rationalist view says it is? A second way of rejecting the rationalist view, she suggests, is to insist that the "female" traits of feeling and emotion are as valuable as the "male" trait of reason. But males have always "gallantly" said that these "female" traits are valuable, Lloyd says. This implies that women should be content with their place in society: to serve as the companions of males who unfortunately are stuck with cold (but ruling!) reason.

Are the very notions used by the rationalist view—reason and desire, body and mind, rationality and emotion—such an integral part of a centuries-old way of thinking that we can no longer rid ourselves of them? Do the very meanings of these words assume that women are inferior to men? When we use these notions, are we forced into seeing women as inferior to men? Is it possible for

---

[26] Genevieve Lloyd, *The Man of Reason: "Male" and "Female" in Western Philosophy* (Minneapolis: University of Minnesota Press, 1984), 104.

us to stop using the notions of reason and desire, body and mind, and rationality and emotion? In fact, is it possible for us to reject the rationalist view of human nature, which seems to be built into our very notions of what men and women are?

QUESTIONS

1. Some people argue that because nonhuman animals can think, humans are not unique at all. What is the difference between thinking and reasoning? What mental states indicate a thinking process? Would you say that reasoning presumes thinking but that thinking does not presume reasoning?

2. What historical evidence indicates that we are rational animals? What evidence indicates that we are not?

3. How do the rationalist and religious views foster a concept of the human as being at odds with nature? Does history indicate that Westerners have lived up to this concept? Does contemporary experience confirm or challenge the wisdom of this concept?

4. Suppose that the concept of evolution is valid. What implications would evolution have for how our societies should be arranged? What implications would evolution have for religion?

5. Sartre's existentialism leaves us with no moral rules or behavioral guidelines, yet it ultimately holds us responsible for all our choices. Do you find such a view appealing? Contradictory? Unsettling? Liberating?

6. To what degree and in what ways, if any, do you experience your life as free, as Sartre describes freedom?

7. In your view, are there ways of looking at women that ordinarily are not seen as sexist but that when examined more closely turn out to be sexist? What are the consequences of sexist ways of looking at women and men?

2.3 How Do Mind and Body Relate?

To most of us, it's obvious that we have minds and bodies. We spend much of our time fretting and fussing over our bodies. We exercise to keep our body healthy, diet to keep its weight down, comb its hair and paint its face to make it more alluring, life weights to inflate its muscles, jog to keep its stamina up, adorn it with clothes and jewelry to make it aesthetically pleasing, hire doctors to cure its illnesses. We know our body has weight and mass and is spread out in space. It has color, size, shape. It can be seen and touched and measured. It is, in short, a material entity.

Your mind, too, gets its share of attention. We study and learn to increase its knowledge, we travel to expand its experiences, we read to keep it entertained, we spend many hours daydreaming to while its time away, we hire psychiatrists to cure it of its illnesses, and we sleep to keep it rested. The mind is the source of our creativity and deepest feelings. It is with the mind that we experience the ordinary and the unusual, feel desires and emotions, believe or doubt. It is with our mind that we feel hope, fear, love, hate, disgust, shame, pride, amusement. Unlike the body, the mind seems to have no observable color, size, or shape. Its most characteristic feature is its consciousness. What is consciousness? Suppose you are sleeping, or sleepwalking, or anesthetized, or knocked out. Then you are unconscious and have no consciousness. As you wake up in the morning, and as you gradually become aware of yourself and the world around you, as you become aware that you see your bedroom, become aware that you feel the wrinkled sheets beneath you, become aware that you smell the musty odors of your closed room, and become aware of the dry stale taste in your mouth, you are becoming conscious. Consciousness is this awareness you have of yourself and your sensing when you are awake. Consciousness is subjective: I am directly in touch with and am directly aware of my own consciousness, and you with yours. But you are not directly aware of my consciousness, nor can I be directly in touch with yours. Strangely, consciousness seems not to be physical. It seems to have no weight, color, taste, mass, or physical dimensions. The conscious mind seems to be an immaterial substance.

To most of us, then, it seems obvious that we have both a mind and a body. Human beings—human nature—seem to be both mental and physical, seem to consist of both mind and body. Moreover, to most of us, it is also obvious that our immaterial mind interacts with its material body. The thoughts and desires in the mind have an effect on how the body behaves. When I decide to go for a walk, it is a simple matter for me to move my body's legs. When I injure my body, my mind is aware of the pain. Thus, the mind seems to be able to control the body, and the body is able to affect the mind.

But although this all seems obvious and commonsensical, the view of human nature as consisting of both mind and body has given rise to profound problems. Philosophers, like each of us, have long pondered our nature. And the feature of human nature that has most troubled them is this apparent dual identity of human beings. Some have simply accepted the commonsense view and have agreed that humans consist of two kinds of things: bodies and minds. Others, influenced by science, have recoiled from accepting this duality. We have only bodies, they have argued, and somehow the mind must be understood as a part of or a property of the body and its brain.

THE DUALIST VIEW OF HUMAN NATURE

The view that human beings are immaterial minds within material bodies is an ancient one. It is a view that many adherents of the Traditional view of human nature have adopted, including Plato and St. Augustine. Still, the view was

— dreaming?

most clearly expressed in the seventeenth century by the first philosophical figure of the modern European age, René Descartes (1596–1650). Notice that Descartes leaves no question that the human being is an immaterial mind. The essential nature of the mind is its conscious ability to think. This mind is very different from the body it inhabits:

> And then, examining attentively that which I was, I saw that I could conceive that I had no body, and that there was no world nor place where I might be; but yet that I could not for all that conceive that I was not. On the contrary, I saw from the very fact that I thought of doubting the truth of other things, it very evidently and certainly followed that I was. On the other hand, if I had only ceased from thinking, even if all the rest of what I had ever imagined had really existed, I should have no reason for thinking that I had existed. From that I knew that I was a substance [a thing] the whole essence or nature of which is to think and that for its existence there is no need of any place, nor does it depend on any material thing; so that this "me," that is to say, the soul by which I am what I am, is entirely distinct from body, and is even more easy to know than is the latter; and even if body were not, the soul would not cease to be what it is.[27]

CRITICAL THINKING

Descartes assumes that if it is possible to conceive of one thing without the other, then those two things are not identical. Is this assumption correct?

Descartes is pointing out here that we can conceive of ourselves as existing without a body. He then makes a crucial assumption: If we can conceive of one thing without the other, then those two things are different. Because we can conceive of the self as not having a body, he claims, the self is not a body—that is, it is not a physical thing. On the other hand, I cannot think of myself without thinking. So thinking is necessary for the self; it is part of the **essence** (the defining characteristic that makes something what it is) of my self. All humans, then, are selves that are immaterial, that are essentially conscious, and that can exist without the body, which is material and essentially unconscious. But what is the body? Descartes describes the body thus:

essence that which makes an entity what it is; that defining characteristic in whose absence a thing would not be itself

> By the body I understand all that which can be defined by a specific shape: something which can be confined in a certain place, and which can fill a given space in such a way that every other body will be excluded from it; which can be perceived either by touch, or by sight, or by hearing, or by taste, or by smell: which can be moved in many ways not, in truth, by itself, but by something different, by which it is touched.[28]

The Traditional view of human nature, as Descartes explained it, says that a human is composed of two kinds of things: a material body and an immaterial mind, or "soul." Philosophers call this view *dualism* because it claims that humans are made up of dual (meaning "two") substances. To many people, traditional dualism seems obvious. Don't our bodies have physical characteristics (like color, size, and shape) that our minds do not have? When people's bodies weaken, can't their minds remain strong? And can't the mind deteriorate even as the body remains vigorous? Don't these differences imply that the mind and the body are distinct entities? Isn't the separation of the mind from the body

Humans are the boundary line of spiritual and corporeal nature, and intermediate between the two, sharing in both corporeal and spiritual perfections.

AQUINAS

---

[27] René Descartes, *Discourse on Method*, in *The Philosophical Works of Descartes*, vol. 1, trans. and ed. Elizabeth S. Haldane and G. R. T. Ross (Cambridge: Cambridge University Press, 1911), 101.
[28] René Descartes, *Meditations*, meditation ii, ibid., 151.

important for religions that say that after the body dies the mind or soul can survive and live on in an afterlife?

Nevertheless, this dualist view—that the mind and body are two entities each made of a different kind of stuff—raises a hard problem. How can an immaterial mind move a physical body, and how can a body that consists of heavy, dense, spatial matter affect an immaterial mind? If the mind is immaterial, it is not part of the physical world. How can something like the mind reach into the physical world and affect it? If it did so, then the mind would somehow

PHILOSOPHY AND LIFE

Lana, Seeker of Truth

Sara of USC, Washoe and Lucy of Oklahoma, Nim of Columbia, Lana of Yerkes—all are names well-known to those who study human language. They're all chimpanzees.

Separately and together, these chimps have demonstrated the ability to converse with humans, to combine acquired words in order to describe new objects or situations, to distinguish difference and sameness, to understand "if-then" concepts, to describe their moods, to lie, to choose and use words in syntactical order, to express desires, to anticipate future events, to seek signed communications with others of their species, and, at least in one instance, to extract the truth from a lying human. This last remarkable occurrence is recorded by Duane Rumbaugh of the Yerkes Primate Center in Atlanta in *Language Learning by a Chimpanzee: The Lana Project.*

Human Tim, Rumbaugh recalls, had entered chimp Lana's room with a bowl of monkey chow, which Lana had requested be loaded into her food machine. But instead of honoring her request, Tim loaded the machine with cabbage, then told Lana that chow was in the machine. Rather than asking the machine for her chow, as was her custom, Lana asked Tim, "You put chow in machine?" Tim lied that he had.

LANA: Chow in machine?

TIM: [still lying] Yes.

LANA: No chow in machine [which was true].

TIM: What in machine [repeated once]?

LANA: Cabbage in machine [which was true].

TIM: Yes, cabbage in machine.

LANA: You move cabbage out of machine.

TIM: Yes [whereupon he removed the cabbage and put in the monkey chow].

LANA: Please machine give piece of chow [repeatedly until all was obtained].

In 1637 René Descartes wrote: "There are no men so dull and stupid that they cannot put words together in a manner to convey their thoughts. And this proves not merely that animals have less reason than man, but they have none at all, for we see that very little is needed to talk." Experiences with chimps like Lana and gorillas like Koko at Stanford, who has exhibited a learned vocabulary of 300 words and an IQ of around 85, would strongly call such an easy distinction between human and beast into question.

QUESTIONS

1. If chimps and apes have access to language, can they be expected to reason?

2. Primatologists currently suspect that there's no significant distinction between the ape's capacity for language and our own. Would this in any way affect our concept of human nature? Our responsibilities to animals?

3. Might Descartes counter that what matters is not so much whether chimps can use language, but whether they mean what they say, know what they mean, and have self-awareness—as indicated by language?

have to introduce new energy and force into the physical world. But scientists tell us that this is impossible, that it would violate the principle of the conservation of matter and energy.

Descartes recognized the problems created by saying that we have an immaterial mind that somehow interacts with a material body. Nevertheless, he held that the mind and body obviously interact, so there must be some point of contact between the two. He suggested that perhaps the mind interacts with the body through the pineal gland, a tiny gland near the brain. Descartes apparently felt that this gland is so tiny and so sensitive that even the immaterial mind could move it. Yet Descartes's own contemporaries ridiculed the idea that the immaterial mind and the material body interact at the pineal gland. The philosopher Gottfried Leibniz (1646–1716) suggested that the mind and body don't really interact at all, but just seem to. Suppose, Leibniz said, that the mind and body run in parallel order, like two clocks that are synchronized so that they seem to be connected yet operate independently. Then, whenever something happens to the body, it also seems to affect the mind, and vice versa. Nevertheless, the two never really interact. Other philosophers said that this was as ridiculous as Descartes's pineal gland theory. For example, the philosopher Nicolas Malebranche (1683–1715) agreed that the immaterial mind could not interact with a material body. Still, he refused to believe that by some incredible coincidence the mind and body were perfectly synchronized. What happens instead, he said, is that God steps in to synchronize the body and the mind. When something affects the body, God obligingly comes forward to cause a corresponding feeling in the mind. When the mind commands the body to move, God again obligingly steps forward to move the body for the mind.

Yet don't the contorted explanations of Descartes, Leibniz, and Malebranche show that dualism has gone wrong somewhere? Wouldn't it make more sense to reject dualism? This was the approach the philosopher Thomas Hobbes took.

THE MATERIALIST VIEW OF HUMAN NATURE

The problem with Descartes's dualism, Hobbes said, is that it says that there are two things in human nature. Instead, let us say there is only one: the material body that we observe with our senses. Let us agree that the activities we attribute to the mind are really activities of the material body. Thomas Hobbes was a *materialist* who felt that we can explain human activities as working much like those of a machine:

> For seeing life is but a motion of limbs, the beginning whereof is in some principal part within; why may we not say, that all *automata* (engines that move themselves by springs and wheels as does a watch) have an artificial life? For what is the *heart*, but a *spring*; and the *nerves*, but so many *strings*; and the *joints*, but so many *wheels*, giving motion to the whole body, such as was intended by the artificer?[29]

---

[29] Thomas Hobbes, *Hobbes's Leviathan* (Oxford: Clarendon Press, 1909; original work published 1651), 23.

This kind of view—that processes like thought and life are really nothing more than physical and chemical processes—is often called **reductionism.** Reductionism is the idea that we can completely understand one kind of reality in terms of another kind. Reductionists take what seems to be one thing and argue that it is really something else. Hobbes, in particular, claimed that although the mind seems to be an immaterial entity, it is really nothing more than a physical, material thing. He was, in short, a materialist.

What led Hobbes to embrace materialism and reject the traditional idea that the mind is an immaterial entity? In part, Hobbes was led to reject the immaterial mind because he could not see how an immaterial mind could affect a material body. But Hobbes was also motivataed by the many advances that science was making at his time. Through careful observations and measurements of nature, Copernicus, Galileo, Kepler, and others had made gigantic strides in understanding the universe. Their scientific advances seemed to be based on what they could observe with their senses and measure quantitatively. Hobbes decided that a scientific view of the universe required accepting as real only what we can observe and measure. Since we can observe and measure only material or physical bodies, Hobbes came to his famous conclusion: "The Universe, that is the whole mass of things that are, is corporeal, that is to say body; and has the dimensions of magnitude, namely length, breadth, and depth . . . and that which is not body is no part of the Universe." Since only material bodies exist, the mind must also be a material body.

Science has played an ever-increasing role in our lives since the fifteenth century. The success of the natural sciences has continued to encourage us to view human beings in the way that the natural sciences view the physical world. For example, one view of science claims that the methods and theories that the natural sciences use to study physical phenomena can also study and explain everything about human beings. True, people are more complex than some other entities, but we can completely explain them in terms of observable physical and chemical phenomena. Like Hobbes, this view holds that science reaches no further than observable facts, and these observable facts can explain human nature, including the mind. We can reduce human nature to the observable world of matter and its physical, chemical, and biological processes. In particular, we can reduce consciousness, the most characteristic feature of the mind, to observable bodily facts.

If materialists' views are to be acceptable, then they must somehow reduce our supposedly unique human qualities, such as consciousness, to the material. One kind of contemporary materialist view is what we now call "the identity theory" of the mind. The identity theory claims that states of consciousness are identical with states of the brain, which is a physical or material organ. When we have a mental experience such as a thought, this experience is nothing more than the material brain working. The same is true of any other conscious experience, such as dreaming, hoping, and feeling. Philosophers who accept the identity theory don't think that their theory is just a matter of definitions. That is, they do not hold that words for mental states *mean the same* as words for brain states. Instead, they say, science will someday *discover* which mental states are

reductionism the idea that one kind of thing is, or can be defined as, another kind of thing

CRITICAL THINKING

Suppose that by restricting ourselves to studying only physical entities we were able to make great scientific strides. Would this show that only physical entities exist? Would it show that only the study of physical entities is worthwhile?

One of the gross deficiencies of science is that it has not yet defined what sets man apart from other animals.

RENÉ DUBOS

identical with which brain states. The identity of mental states and brain states is thus a "contingent" relationship. For example, we know now that water and H_2O are identical. But science had to discover this. In the same way, we will someday know what brain states are identical with the mental states of desiring, seeing, feeling pains, being happy, being sad, etc. But science must discover this. We cannot know, just by thinking about the meanings of the words, what brain states are identical with "desiring," "seeing," "feeling pain," "being happy," and "being sad."

Yet won't the attempt to identify conscious experiences with brain states quickly run into problems? Consider, for example, that whereas brain states are publicly observable, our conscious experiences are not. If a surgeon exposes the brain, she can observe its brain states, such as the reaction of a ganglion; she could pinpoint the brain state's precise location, describe its color and shape, and truthfully say that anyone can literally *see* it. On the other hand, because only you can have your conscious experiences, no one else can literally see your experiences. Moreover, an experience such as thinking has no precise location, no color, and no shape. So doesn't it seem that a brain state and a conscious experience are two different things, with very different qualities? How can the strict materialist account for this fact? Does the distinct nature of consciousness suggest the presence of a nonmaterial reality? Is there something at the core of our mind that we cannot measure, pinpoint, or see?

A prime proponent of identity theory, the Australian philosopher J. J. C. Smart (1920–), thinks not. Smart contends that future scientific discovery will show that all conscious experiences are identical with processes taking place in the brain. He justifies his claim by arguing that a nonphysical property couldn't possibly develop during animal evolution:

> But what about consciousness? Can we interpret the having of an after-image or of a painful sensation as something material, namely, a brain state or brain process? We seem to be immediately aware of pains and after-images, and we seem to be immediately aware of them as something different from a neurophysiological state or process. For example, the after-image may be green speckled with red, whereas the neurophysiologist looking into our brains would be unlikely to see something green speckled with red. However, if we object to materialism in this way we are victims of a confusion which U. T. Place has called "the phenomenological fallacy." To say that an image or sense datum is green is not to say that the conscious experience of having the image or sense datum is green. It is to say that it is the sort of experience we have when in normal conditions we look at a green apple, for example. Apples and unripe bananas can be green, but not the experiences of seeing them. An image or a sense datum can be green in a derivative sense, but this need not cause any worry, because, on the view I am defending, images and sense data are not constituents of the world, though the processes of having an image or a sense datum are actual processes in the world. The experience of having a green sense datum is not itself green; it is a process occurring in grey matter. The world contains plumbers, but does not contain the average plumber: it also contains the having of a sense datum, but does not contain the sense datum. . . .

It may be asked why I should demand of a tenable philosophy of mind that it should be compatible with materialism, in the sense in which I have defined it. One reason is as follows. How could a nonphysical property or entity suddenly arise in the course of animal evolution? A change in a gene is a change in a complex molecule which causes a change in the biochemistry of the cell. This may lead to changes in the shape or organization of the developing embryo. But what sort of chemical process could lead to the springing into existence of something nonphysical? No enzyme can catalyze the production of a spook! Perhaps it will be said that the nonphysical comes into existence as a by-product: that whenever there is a certain complex physical structure, then, by an irreducible extraphysical law, there is also a nonphysical entity. Such laws would be quite outside normal scientific conceptions and quite inexplicable: they would be, in Herbert Feigl's phrase, "nomological danglers." To say the very least, we can vastly simplify our cosmological outlook if we can defend a materialistic philosophy of mind.[30]

In essence, Smart is defending the position that states of consciousness are identical with states of the brain. Smart asserts that science will discover which particular brain states will turn out to be identical with a particular mental state like feeling a pain. As Smart puts it, the identity between mental states and brain states is "contingent" and not "necessary." If the identity were "necessary," we could deduce it from the meanings of the words. But since science will discover it, it is "contingent."

Do all philosophers agree with Smart's analysis? Consider what the American philosopher Norman Malcolm (1911–), for one, says:

> I wish to go into Smart's theory that there is a contingent identity between mental phenomena and brain phenomena. If such an identity exists, then brain phenomena must have all the properties that mental phenomena have. . . . I shall argue that this condition cannot be fulfilled.
>
> a. First, it is not meaningful to assign spatial locations to some kinds of mental phenomena, e.g., thoughts. Brain phenomena have spatial location. Thus, brain phenomena have a property that thoughts do not have. Therefore, thoughts are not identical with any brain phenomena.
>
> b. Second, any thought requires a background of circumstances ("surroundings"), e.g., practices, agreements, assumptions. If a brain event were identical with a thought, it would require the same. The circumstances necessary for a thought cannot be described in terms of the entities and laws of physics. According to Smart's scientific materialism, everything in the world is "explicable in terms of physics." But if the identity theory were true, not even those brain events which are identical with thoughts would be "explicable in terms of physics." Therefore, the identity theory and scientific materialism are incompatible. . . .[31]

However, objections like these have not led materialists to abandon materialism. Many remain firmly convinced that dualism has to be wrong. Objections to one form of materialism have therefore spurred greater efforts to find other, more plausible kinds of materialism.

---

[30] J. J. C. Smart, "Materialism," *Journal of Philosophy* (24 October 1963). Reprinted by permission.
[31] Norman Malcolm, "Scientific Materialism and the Identity Theory," *Journal of Philosophy* (24 October 1963): 662–663. Reprinted by permission.

THE BEHAVIORIST VIEW OF HUMAN NATURE

One alternative kind of materialist view of human nature is behaviorism. **Behaviorism** began as a school of psychology that restricted the study of humans to what can be observed—namely, human behavior. Psychological behaviorists argued that they could not observe states of consciousness, so psychology should not be concerned with them. Some philosophers have agreed with this view. They have argued that when explaining human nature, we should restrict ourselves to what is publicly observable: the outward physical behavior of human beings. How, then, do we explain interior mental processes that are not physically observable, such as thinking, feeling, knowing, loving, hating, desiring, and imagining?

Behaviorist philosophers have argued that we can easily explain mental activities in terms of people's behaviors. For example, the British philosopher Gilbert Ryle claimed that we can explain mental activities and mental states in terms of the externally observable behaviors with which they are associated.[32] Ryle would argue, for example, that "John knows what chairs are" should be taken as meaning something like "When a chair is present, and given certain other conditions, John will engage in certain specific behaviors with the chair." In other words, to say that a person knows what a chair is, is to say that the person does certain things when a chair is near (sits on it, for example). Similarly, to say that a person loves someone is to say that she is disposed to behave in certain ways toward that person. For the behaviorist, then, the mind is just bodily behavior and dispositions to bodily behavior.

Still, are all interior thoughts reducible to exterior observable behavior? Can't you keep a certain very personal idea in your mind without ever betraying it in your exterior behavior? The contemporary philosopher Hilary Putnam has argued that it is very easy to come up with examples that show behaviorism is wrong. Imagine a "superactor" who is giving a perfect imitation of the behavior of someone in pain. Behaviorism says such a "superactor" is feeling pain, even if in fact the superactor is conscious of no pain whatsoever. Or imagine a "superspartan" who can endure pain without giving any external sign in his behavior of the pain he feels. Behaviorism says such a "superspartan" feels no pain even if the superspartan is conscious of excruciating pain.

In behaviorism our consciousness seems to have disappeared. But there is something odd here. We seem to be directly aware of what is in our consciousness. We seem to know directly, in a way that others cannot observe, what we are thinking, feeling, sensing. I know if something feels good to me in a way that you cannot know. Yet behaviorism says that all feelings are external behaviors that others can observe. So others who observe our behavior know just like I do—perhaps before I do—when something feels good to me. This seems wrong. In fact, behaviorism inspired a famous joke. Two behaviorist philosophers have just finished making love. So the first behaviorist says to the second: "It was great for you. How was it for me?"

> **behaviorism** a school of psychology that restricts the study of human nature to what can be observed rather than to states of consciousness

> *O man, strange composite of Heaven and earth!*
> CARDINAL NEWMAN

---

[32] See Gilbert Ryle, *The Concept of Mind* (London: Hutchineson, 1949).

Thomas Hobbes: "For seeing Life is but a motion of limbs, why may we not say that all automata (engines that move themselves by springs and wheels as does a watch) have an artificial life? For what is the heart, but a spring, and the nerves, but so many strings; and the joints, but so many wheels, giving motion to the whole body?"

The problem, then, is that behaviorism restricts itself to outer behaviors. In doing this, it seems to leave out the interior conscious states that cause behavior.

THE FUNCTIONALIST VIEW OF HUMAN NATURE

A recent view, which does not try to reduce all mental activities to external behavior but which research in computers has inspired, is called *functionalism*. Functionalism claims that humans should be thought of as complicated computers. During the middle part of the twentieth century, scientists made great strides in devising powerful machines that could calculate and manipulate bits of information at an amazing rate. When we give a computer certain "inputs," such as a mathematical problem, the computer will calculate and provide an "output," such as the answer to the problem. Many philosophers began to think that perhaps the computer provided a model of how the mind works.

Proposed by several philosophers, such as D. M. Armstrong,[33] functionalism holds that we should explain mental activities and mental states in terms of inputs and outputs. The inputs of the human mind are the stimulations that affect the nervous system—what we see, hear, taste, and feel. The outputs are the behaviors that result: running, walking, sitting, standing. We can think of a mental concept such as *belief* as a connnection the body makes between certain inputs and certain outputs. For example, suppose that when a certain

[33] See D. M. Armstrong, *A Materialist Theory of the Mind* (London: routledge & Kegan Paul, 1968).

person sees a dog (the input), he runs off (the output), and we explain this behavior by saying that he ran "because he believes that dogs bite people." Then we can say that the person's *belief that dogs bite people* is just something in the body's brain that links his sensory input (seeing a dog) to his behavior (running away). Functionalists claim that all conscious mental states and activities are shorthand terms for the complex connections that the body's brain makes between sense inputs and behavioral outputs.

Unlike earlier forms of behaviorism, functionalism allows that mental states can explain other mental states; thus, it gives a greater role to mental states than did earlier forms of behaviorism. For example, functionalists might agree that a person's intention (a mental state) can be explained in terms of the person's desires and beliefs (other mental states). For instance, when we see a person running to a bus stop after he sees a bus coming, we might say that he is doing so because he intends to catch the bus. We might then say that his intention to catch the bus is simply something that plays the role of linking his sensory stimulation (seeing the bus) to his desire to catch the bus and to his belief that by running he will catch the bus (mental states), and these to his behavior (running to the bus stop). Thus, some mental states (like intentions) are to be explained in terms of other mental states (desires and beliefs). Yet, according to the functionalist, all mental states ultimately are to be explained in terms of the roles they play (sometimes through other mental states) in linking our sensory stimulation to our external behavior.

But functionalism, too, seems to leave something out. Opponents argue that functionalism leaves out the inner conscious states we are directly aware of. They argue as follows: Imagine two people who experience colors differently. When one sees a red object, he has the kind of visual experience that the other person has when the other person sees a green object. The color red has the appearance to him that green has to the other person. And the color green has the appearance to him that red has to the other person. Otherwise, the two people are exactly the same. In fact, they don't even know that colors appear differently to them. How could they, since each can't get into the other's mind to see how colors appear? Now, suppose we ask them to look at some colored objects (the "input") and sort them into different piles (the "output"). Each person will sort colors exactly like the other: Green objects will go into one pile, red ones into another. Now, functionalism says that if two people have exactly the same inputs and give exactly the same outputs, those two people have exactly the same inner mental state. So functionalism says that the inner conscious states of the two people must be exactly the same. But clearly this is wrong. Inside, what one person consciously experiences is different from what the other person consciously experiences. So functionalism is mistaken. The problem is that functionalism wants to reduce mental states to inputs and outputs. But this seems to leave out what is most characteristic of our minds: our inner consciousness.

However, other philosophers still remain loyal to materialism. Some have adopted a view called "eliminative materialism." They grant that one of the biggest objections to materialism is the existence of consciousness. Somewhat strangely, they have concluded that we must therefore eliminate our belief in the existence of consciousness. People *think* they feel pains, desires, emotions, beliefs, longings, etc. But this belief is deceptive. It is based on "folk psychology." It is like people's earlier belief that the sun rises and goes around the earth. The advances of science showed that in fact what seemed to be there—the rising and setting sun—was merely an appearance. In reality, the sun does not rise and set on the earth; instead, the earth spins on its axis and spins around the sun. In the same way, the advances of science will show us that we do not have consciousness. We use the word because we don't know any better. But eventually science will show us that we do not feel, believe, desire. We have no consciousness at all.

Eliminative materialism seems a bit extreme. It denies what is there for all to experience. Moreover, it seems to misinterpret how science works. Science does not work by saying that people don't have the experiences they have. Instead, science works by giving new explanations for what people experience. For example, science did not show that we do not see the sun rising and setting. Instead, it explained why we see the sun rising and setting. Science offered a new explanation of our experience; it did not eliminate the experience. In the same way, scientific advances may someday give us new explanations of consciousness—perhaps materialistic explanations. But such new explanations will not eliminate the consciousness they explain.

THE COMPUTER VIEW OF HUMAN NATURE

In spite of the difficulties of functionalism, it led some philosophers to the view that the human brain is a kind of computer that processes inputs (our sense observations) and generates outputs (our behaviors). Some functionalists, in fact, believe that very soon computers will be able to imitate the input–output processing of the human brain. Some have argued that when computers can process inputs and outputs like the human brain does, they will have minds and be able to think. For example, Alan Turing suggested what we now call the "Turing Test."[34] Imagine that you are in a room where there are two computer keyboards and two printers. One keyboard and a printer are connected to a computer somewhere outside the room. The other keyboard and printer are connected to a human being who is also somewhere outside the room. You do not know which keyboard and printer are connected to the computer and which to the human being. You can type questions on the keyboards, which the computer or human on the other end will respond to by printing out the answer on the printer. Your job is to figure out which answers are coming from the computer and which are coming from the human being. According to Turing, when a computer is so powerful that we cannot tell the difference between its answers and the answers of a human being, that computer has a mind. That is, if the outputs a computer generates in response to the inputs it receives are the

---

[34] A. M. Turing, "Computing Machinery and Intelligence," *Mind* (1950), vol. LIX, no. 236.

Alan Turing. According to Turing, if we cannot distinguish between the answers a computer gives to questions and the answers a human being gives, then the computer has a mind.

same as the outputs a human mind would generate in response to the same inputs, the computer is the equivalent of the human mind.

Many computer experts, including Turing himself, predict that it is only a matter of time before computers will match the abilities of the human mind and pass the Turing Test. Then we can say that the computers think and have minds. We will then know that materialism is right. For if a machine, which is completely material, can have a mind, then the mind is not something immaterial. It is a chunk of physical machinery.

Several philosophers hotly contest this computer theory of the human mind. One of the most vociferous opponents of the theory is the American philosopher John Searle. Searle has pointed out that a computer is nothing more than a machine that follows the instructions in its program. But the instructions that a computer follows can also be followed by a human being. So if following a program can produce mental states in a machine, then when a human being follows the same software program, the same mental states should be produced in the human being. However, says Searle, when a person follows a program that is supposed to let a computer have certain mental states, the person will not have those states.

Searle gives a simple example of what he means. Suppose a computer had a program that let it pass the Turing Test in Chinese. Then, supposedly, the computer can think in Chinese. Now suppose a human being, like yourself, follows the same program. Then you should be able to think in Chinese. But, says Searle, following a program will not put Chinese thoughts into your head:

Suppose that we write a computer program to simulate the understanding of Chinese so that, for example, if the computer is asked questions in Chinese the program enables it to give answers in Chinese; if asked to summarize stories in Chinese it can give such summaries; if asked questions about the stories it has been given it will answer such questions.

Now suppose that I, who understand no Chinese at all and can't even distinguish Chinese symbols from some other kinds of symbols, am locked in a room with a number of cardboard boxes full of Chinese symbols. Suppose that I am given a book of rules in English that instruct me how to match these Chinese symbols with each other. The rules say such things as that the "squiggle-squiggle" sign is to be followed by the "squoggle-squoggle" sign. Suppose that people outside the room pass in more Chinese symbols and that following the instructions in the book I pass Chinese symbols back to them. Suppose that unknown to me the people who pass me the symbols call them "questions" and the book of instructions that I work from they call "the program." The symbols I give back to them they call "answers to the questions" and me they call "the computer." Suppose that after a while the programmers get so good at writing the programs and I get so good at manipulating the symbols that my answers are indistinguishable from those of native Chinese speakers. I can pass the Turing test for understanding Chinese. But all the same I still don't understand a word of Chinese. And neither does any other digital computer because all the computer has is what I have: a formal program that attaches no meaning, interpretation, or content to any of the symbols.[35]

Searle claims that this argument shows there is something that human minds have that a computer following a program does not have. What does the computer lack? Consciousness. Consciousness, argues Searle, is essential to the human mind, and a computer following a program does not have consciousness.

Nevertheless, Searle is not a dualist. Searle claims that humans are purely physical creatures in whom physical, chemical, and biological processes take place. These processes, he claims, cause or produce all our mental states or activities. These mental states of activities are not reducible to physical things, but a physical thing produces them—namely, our brain. Someday, Searle argues, science will succeed in explaining how the brain produces consciousness. However, consciousness is a unique kind of human quality, one that is not reducible to something else. Someday we will be able to explain consciousness, but we will not do this by reducing it to some other kind of familiar physical quality.

The failures of materialist views of human nature have prompted some philosophers to return to dualism. For example, the American philosopher David J. Chalmers is a kind of dualist. In his 1996 book *The Conscious Mind*, he writes the following:

[M]aterialism is false: there are features of the world over and above the physical features. . . . The character of our world is not exhausted by the character supplied by the physical facts; there is an extra character due to the presence of consciousness. This failure of materialism leads to a kind of dualism. . . . The arguments do not lead us to a dualism such as that of Descartes, with a separate realm of mental substance

---

[35] John Searle, "The Myth of the Computer," *The New York Review of Books*, 1982.

that exerts its own influence on physical processes. . . . The dualism implied here is instead a kind of property dualism: conscious experience involves properties of an individual that are not entailed by the physical properties of that individual, although they may depend lawfully on those properties.[36]

Chalmers argues that there could be a world that is physically identical to ours except that it has no conscious beings in it. Such a world could contain "zombies" that look and act exactly like human beings except that these zombies are not conscious. Chalmers concludes that consciousness is not a physical feature of the world. Instead, consciousness is a nonmaterial property of the world.

In a way, we have come full circle. Most philosophers are not willing to return to Descartes's idea that the mind is a special kind of thing that is different from the physical body. Yet the various materialist views of human nature all seem to leave out what is so familiar to all of us: our consciousness. This has now led philosophers like Chalmers to believe that mental states are special kinds of features that are different from physical features.

So is the mind reducible to any other kind of physical thing? Clearly, this question has tremendous implications for us. If the mind is a physical thing, or a physical feature of the world, then it is not immaterial. We are not unique. There is no spiritual realm. We do not have souls. We die with our bodies. Are these consequences acceptable?

Yet if we humans are both immaterial minds and material bodies, then how do the two relate? How can my ineffable, intangible, unobservable consciousness affect my heavy, solid, physical body?

QUESTIONS

1. What are some examples of "reductionism" that you think are true? What are some examples that you think are mistaken? What is the difference between them?

2. Behaviorists claim that the human can be measured experimentally. Are there any human characteristics that contradict this claim? What human qualities cannot be measured?

3. Behaviorists also argue that techniques and engineering practices can be used to shape behavior so that people will function harmoniously for everyone's benefit. What questions would you raise about such a proposal?

4. How would you determine whether a robot had a conscious mind? What tests would you use?

5. Read over Darwin's theory again. Suppose that consciousness is real. From an evolutionary viewpoint, do you think consciousness would give humans an advantage in the struggle for existence? Suppose that humans could think and act, like sleepwalkers do, but they were not aware of their thinking and acting.

---

[36] David Chalmers, *The Conscious Mind* (New York: Oxford University Press, 1996), 123, 124, 125.

Would this lack of consciousness put them at a disadvantage in the struggle for existence? What good is consciousness? What survival benefits does it have?

6.   Do you think it is possible for you to continue to exist after your body dies? Why or why not?

2.4 Is There an Enduring Self?

The Traditional Western view of human nature makes an assumption that may seem so obvious to you that you feel it would be foolhardy to question it. This view assumes that you are today the same person you were earlier in your life. In other words, it assumes that we humans are selves that endure through time. This simple, little, and obvious "fact" has enormous and profound consequences for you. Yet, as we will see when we explore this assumption, it will not seem as obvious as it initially appears.

Consider, first, how obvious it seems that you are now the same self you were yesterday. Of course you have changed a bit: You're a day older, maybe you weigh a bit more than you did yesterday, maybe you're a bit more tanned, your hair might be combed differently, maybe you're more tired or more sleepy, and, no doubt, you're not wearing the same clothes. Yet though you've changed in these ways, you can't say you're not basically the same person you were yesterday. In fact, you're going to admit or even insist that you are the same person today that you were yesterday. For example, suppose that yesterday you promised a friend that today you'd go to the movies with her. Then it wouldn't make sense for you to say, "It wasn't *me* who made that promise; it was the person I was yesterday who made the promise, but today *I'm* not *that* person, so *I'm* not the one who has to keep that promise!" Or suppose that yesterday someone promised that today he would help you with your schoolwork. Then you'd get pretty angry if today he said to you, "Hey, I didn't promise to help *you!* Yesterday I made a promise to the person you were then, but I never made any promises to the person you are today! So I don't have to help the person you are today." In both cases, won't you admit and even insist that you are today the same person you were yesterday? You'll insist that you're the same self not just from one day to the next: You'll insist that you're the same self from one week to the next, from one month to the next, from one year to the next, from one decade to the next.

We each carry with us, then, this belief that we remain the same person— one and the same self—throughout our lives. We believe that we remain the same person as we go through our lives though we may change in many small and many large and dramatic ways. When you were born, for example, you were only one-and-a-half-feet tall, weighed only eight pounds, and had no hair. Now you are five-and-a-half-feet tall, weigh one hundred and sixty pounds, and have hair over many parts of your body. When you were born, you knew nothing. Now you are a brilliant brain surgeon. Yet for all these changes, you are still the same person.

This belief about yourself, that you are a being who continues to be the same being as time passes, is a basic part of who you are. In fact, maybe it is the most important part of yourself. Think of how our lives would fall apart if we did not remain the same person from one moment to the next. No job or task or project would ever be completed, because the person who began it yesterday would not be here today to complete it. You could not have any personal relationships, because the person you liked and loved yesterday would not be here for you today; nor would you be here today for the person who loved you yesterday. There could be no personal commitments, because the person who committed herself yesterday would not be the same person today. So the person today would not have to keep the commitment that the other person made yesterday. There would be no personal history, no story of your life. Your life would not be the life of one continuing person, but would consist of many different lives of many different persons, each succeeding the other for a brief moment. Almost everything about yourself, everything about what you think you are, everything about who you think you are, everything you are trying to do, everything you plan or have planned for yourself, everything you have planned or wanted to do with your friends, your lovers, your family, all your projects and undertakings and commitments, all your hopes, your regrets, your sense of what you've done, what you've acomplished, what you've achieved—all these depend on your belief that you are a being who endures and remains the same through time.

Yet sometimes people say that this or that person has not remained the same person through time, and we accept it. For example, suppose that Susan, a good friend of yours, was in a very serious accident that produced some minor brain damage. As a result, her personality changed: She used to like going for walks, but now she doesn't; she used to talk rapidly, but now she talks slowly; she used to joke a lot, but now she tends to be serious. Suppose, further, that she has total amnesia and no longer remembers anything before the accident: who she was, who you or her other friends or family members are, what her life was like, where she lived, what her name was, etc. Then you might want to say "Susan isn't the same person she used to be." Or suppose that doctors diagnosed your great-grandmother with Alzheimer's disease a couple of years ago. Suppose that, as a result, she now doesn't remember anything that happened more than five minutes ago. When you tell her something or she tells you something, she has no memory of it five minutes later. She doesn't remember who you are; she doesn't remember where she is; she doesn't remember who the people around her are; she doesn't remember what she planned on doing a few minutes ago; she can't remember why she opened the refrigerator or why she turned on the CD player. Then you would certainly be willing to say that she "isn't the same person she used to be."

Still, these are unusual cases. There are some more normal situations where we are still willing to take someone's word that they are not the same person they used to be. For example, take situations where people have changed so much that we are willing to say that they are no longer the same people they used to be. Suppose that your parents, John and Susan, had been married for twenty years and had two teenage children—you and your sister. Then one day you hear your mom talking to your dad: "John, I'm leaving you and the kids. I just don't love you anymore, and I don't think I have any feelings for the children. When we got married, I probably loved you, and maybe wanted to be a mother. But now I want out." To this, your dad responds in anguish that your mother can't leave him: When she married him, he begs, she promised she would stay with him "till death do us part." But to all this, your mother answers: "John, you aren't the person I married. And I'm not the person you married. I was young and naive and dumb when we married. But since then I've come to realize what I really want, and figured out who I really am. I've grown up and changed. You've changed, too. You used to like to do new things all the time; you used to like to go out dancing with me; you used to be energetic, young, and exciting. Now look at you! You've gotten a fat beer-belly; you sit around all evening watching television, and we never go anywhere. I'm not the person who married you, and you're not the person I married. So I don't feel I have to stay tied down by a commitment two other younger people made." True to her word, your mom abandons the three of you and starts a new life as the new person she's become. When we feel that someone has changed so much that she is no longer the same person she used to be, we think that this can have enormous consequences for her and for everyone else around her.

Still, the fact that we change raises another interesting qustion: Do we ever truly remain the same person? Obviously, we change enormously as we go through life. In fact, doesn't everything about us eventually change completely? How, then, can we say that most of us most of the time remain the same person?

The ancient Greek philosopher Plato was also puzzled by how we remain the same person although everything about us seems to change. In his dialogue *The Symposium* he gives a sympathetic account of the views of the philosopher Diotima. She argued, he says, that people do not remain the same person as time passes, and so they "long for immortality":

> Although we speak of an individual as being the same so long as he continues to exist in the same form, and therefore assume that a man is the same person in his old age as in his infancy, yet although we call him the same, every bit of him is different, and every day he is becoming a new man, while the old man is ceasing to exist, as you can see from his hair, his flesh, his bones, his blood, and all the rest of his body. And not only his body, for the same thing happens to his soul. And neither his manners, nor his dispositions, nor his thoughts, nor his desires, nor his pleasures, nor his sufferings, nor his fears are the same thoughout his life, for some of them grow, while others disappear. . . . Thus, unlike the gods, a mortal creature cannot remain the same throughout eternity; it can only leave behind new life to fill the vacancy that is left as it passes away. . . . And so it is no wonder that every creature prizes its own offspring, since everything is inspired by this love, this passion for immortality.[37]

---

[37] Plato, *Symposium*, trans. Michael Joyce, in *The Collected Dialogues of Plato*, ed. Edith Hamilton and Huntington Cairns (Princeton, NJ: Princeton University Press, 1961), 559–560.

Obviously, we do change substantially as we go through our lives. How, then, can anyone ever say that he or she has remained the same person? In what sense am I today the same person I was when I was born? Philosophers call this the "problem of personal identity." What is it that makes a person be the same person from one moment to the next? And, indeed, can we be sure that a person remains the same from one moment to the next?

Perhaps what makes you the same person today that you were ten years ago is your body. Many philosophers have suggested as much. Even the ancient philosopher Diotima suggests in the passage above that "we speak of an individual as being the same as long as he continues to exist in the same form." It is true that the body changes dramatically as we grow older. Yet it never changes completely from one day to the next. Each day, most of the body continues to be what it was the previous day. Perhaps what makes us the same person today that we were ten years ago, then, is this bodily continuity between each succeeding period of our life: I am the person I was when I was born because during each day of my life, most of my body continues the same as it was the previous day, and most of it continues the same into the next succeeding day. Our body is like a ship sailing on the ocean, a ship made up of hundreds of wooden boards. If each day we remove one or two of the boards and replace them with new ones; eventually we will change all of the boards that make up the ship. Still, because most of the boards remain the same from one day to the next, we say it is the same ship from the beginning to the end of its voyage.

Moreover, think about how often we use a person's body to establish that a certain person today is the same as a person who did something earlier. For example, suppose that some person committed a crime. Suppose that at the scene of the crime the person's body left fingerprints, blood, and hair; suppose also that a hidden camera took pictures and someone witnessed the crime from a distance. Afterward, the authorities link this evidence to your body: The fingerprints match those of your body, the blood and hair match those of your body, the pictures are of your body, and the witness points to your body as that of the criminal. Wouldn't we decide that you and the person who earlier committed the crime are one and the same? Doesn't this show that bodily continuity is what makes you now the same person you were earlier?

However, there are many problems with the view that bodily continuity is what makes us remain the same person from one day to the next. First, if bodily continuity makes us the same person throughout our lives, then we could never become totally new persons during our lives. We would have to say that the people with total amnesia or Alzheimer's disease are "really" still the same persons they always were. We would have to say that the spouse who wants to abandon his or her marriage and family commitments because he or she feels that he or she is no longer the same person is also mistaken: The spouse is "really" still the same person he or she always was. Yet in at least some of these cases we are willing to say that a person may no longer be the person she used to be, though she continues to have the same body. So perhaps bodily continuity is not what makes a person remain the same person from one moment to the next.

Consider, second, that if bodily continuity makes us remain the same person from one moment to the next, then our ideas about a life after death should not make any sense. For example, some religions claim that persons are immortal and that after the death of the body, the person will continue to live in some kind of "afterlife." Such claims may be false. Nevertheless, even if they are false, they seem to make sense—that is, we seem able to understand the possibility they describe, even if we do not think that it will really happen. Yet if bodily continuity is what makes us remain the same persons, such claims should not make sense. We should not even be able to understand the possibility they describe. For if bodily continuity makes us remain the same person, how could we even understand what it means to say that a person remains the same after there is no bodily continuity? Since such claims at least make sense, bodily continuity is not what makes us remain the same person from one moment to the next.

Consider, third, a kind of "thought experiment." Imagine a brilliant but mad brain surgeon who kidnaps Manny, a man, and his best female friend, Maryann. In his secret laboratory the mad surgeon succeeds in extracting Manny's brain and implanting it inside Maryann's skull, while implanting her brain into Manny's skull. When Manny awakes from the operation, he finds himself "in" Maryann's body. He looks at the body lying on the bed next to him and is horrified to discover himself looking at what was previously his own body. Yet when that body—or the person "in" that body—speaks, he/she identifies himself/herself as Maryann and is just as horrified to find himself/herself with this new body.

This thought experiment, of couse, is totally fictional. Nevertheless, the question we need to ask is this: Given the ideas that you and I have about what makes a person at one time the same as a person at another time, what would we say about this fictional example? Wouldn't we say that the person Manny used to be is now the person in Maryann's body? Wouldn't we say that the person Maryann used to be is now in Manny's body? But if so, then bodily continuity is not what makes a person at one time the same as a person at another time. For in this imaginary case, Manny and Maryann's bodies continue the same, yet we say the person "in" the body is not the same. There is something else, something "in" the body, that makes a person continue to be the same person even if his or her body changes completely.

Such considerations have led some philosophers to conclude that what makes a person remain the same person over time is not the body. Instead, there is something "in" the body—an immaterial "soul" or "mind"—that remains the same even as the body changes.

I am a little world made cunningly of Elements and an Angelike spirit.

JOHN DONNE

THE SOUL AS THE ENDURING SELF

The Traditional Western view says that in each living human body is a soul. This soul is not made out of physical stuff like the body. Instead, the soul is "immaterial" or spiritual. This soul, in fact, is the self: the "me" who lives inside my body. This soul remains the same as the body changes. Yet as long as the soul remains in my body, I remain the same person.

René Descartes characterized this view of the enduring self. He wrote that the self is a "thinking thing" and that if "I should wholly cease to think, then I should at the same time altogether cease to be." For Descartes, it is the continuity of the thinking mind or soul that makes a person endure as the same person over time. Here is how he puts it in the *Meditations*:

> Thinking is another attribute of the soul; and here I discover what properly belongs to myself. This alone is inseparable from me. I am—I exist: this is certain; but how often? As often as I think; for perhaps it would even happen, if I should wholly cease to think, that I should at the same time altogether cease to be.[38]

Here, Descartes is implying that it is the continuity of his thinking mind that makes him remain the same person "as often as" as he exists. If his thinking mind or thinking soul did not continue to be the same, then "he" would no longer continue even to exist.

This Traditional view—that the soul or mind is the self and the thing that makes a person continue to be the same person through time—renders life after death very understandable. Since a person is a nonmaterial mind or soul, the person can continue to exist after the body dies. The Traditional view also accounts for the fact that we can imagine someone waking up with a different body, as in our "mad surgeon" mind experiment. In such cases, the mind has been transferred to a different body, and since the person is the mind, the person merely has a different body.

Yet there are also many problems with Descartes's view. For example, how are we supposed to know that a person's mind continues to be the same over time? For instance, I may know that you today are the same person you were when I talked with you yesterday. Nevertheless, I certainly do not see or perceive your mind or soul. So I know you are the same person today that you were yesterday without observing your mind or soul. This seems to suggest that it is not your soul or mind that makes you the same.

MEMORY AS THE SOURCE OF THE ENDURING SELF

The philosopher John Locke also objected to Descartes's view that it is people's immaterial souls or spirits that make them the same person over time:

> Let anyone reflect upon himself, and conclude that he has in himself an immaterial spirit, which is that which thinks in him, and, in the constant change of his body keeps him the same, and is that which he calls himself. Let him also suppose it to be the same soul that was in Nestor or Thersites at the siege of Troy. (For souls being as far as we know anything of them, in their nature indifferent to any parcel of matter, the supposition has no apparent absurdity in it.) . . . But [suppose] he now . . . [has] no consciousness of any of the actions of Nestor or Thersites. Does or can he conceive himself the same person with either of them? Can he be concerned in either of their actions? Attribute them to himself or think them his own?[39]

---

[38] René Descartes, *Meditations*, in *The Philosophical Works of Descartes*, vol. 1, trans. and ed. Elizabeth S. Haldane and G. R. T. Ross (Cambridge: Cambridge University Press, 1911), 151–152.
[39] Locke, *An Essay Concerning Human Understanding*, book 2, chap. 27, sec. 14.

Locke is here suggesting another "thought experiment." Suppose that people do have immaterial souls. And suppose that the soul of someone who lived a long time ago named "Nestor" (or "Thersites") somehow got into the body of someone living today. Then that person living today should be the same as the person Nestor who lived long ago. But suppose that the person living today has none of Nestor's memories. Then, claims Locke, the person would not think he was the same person as Nestor, even if he has the same soul that Nestor had.

Locke concludes that what makes a person at one time the same person later is not that the person has the same immaterial spirit. Instead, suggests Locke, what makes a person at one time the same as a person at another time is *memory*. Locke thinks that it is the continuity of "consciousness" (by which he means memory) that makes me today the same person I was yesterday. Here is what he says in *An Essay Concerning Human Understanding*:

> Since consciousness always accompanies thinking, and it is that which makes every one to be what he calls "self," in this alone consists personal identity, i.e. the sameness of a rational being. And as far as this consciousness can be extended backwards to any past action or thought, so far reaches the identity of that person; it is the same self now it was then. . . . If the same Socartes waking and sleeping do not partake of the same consciousness, Socrates waking and sleeping is not the same person. And to punish Socrates waking for what sleeping Socrates thought, and waking Socrates was never conscious of, would be no more right, than to punish one twin for what his brother-twin did.[40]

Locke's view is simple. What makes me be the same person I was ten years ago is that I remember being that person ten years ago. My memory of what happened to me in the past or of what I did in the past is what makes me today the same person I was then.

Locke's view has seemed correct to many people. Consider the example of a woman who has a serious automobile accident. Years later a friend finds her living in a town somewhere. She has no memory at all of her life before the accident. A man who says he is her husband shows up at her door. He has many pictures and witnesses to prove that this woman's body, at least, is the same as the body of the woman to whom he used to be married. After talking with her, the man comes to feel that her very soul is exactly the same as that of the woman he once married: She has the same mannerisms, the same voice, the same character traits, the same desires, preferences, values, and attitudes. Because he is now convinced that he was once married to this woman, he says she must return with him now and live with him as his wife. But must she go with him? Wouldn't we want to say that this woman is no longer the same person as the one who was once married to this man? Wouldn't we say this even if she has the same body and even if, somehow, we know she has the same soul? Wouldn't we want to say that if she has no memory of being the man's wife, then she is now simply no longer that same person?

Or take the case of a man whom police accuse of robbing a bank. Suppose that he honestly has no memory at all of ever having done so. He remembers

---

[40]Ibid.

all events on the day of the robbery, but has no memory of robbing a bank, or of planning to rob a bank, or of ever even considering robbing a bank. Then should police hold him responsible for robbing the bank? Most of us would say no: A person who has no memory whatsoever of having done something cannot be responsible for doing that thing.

Yet there are some troubling objections to Locke's view. For example, the British philosopher Thomas Reid (1710–1796) suggested that Locke's view produces contradictions.[41] Suppose that Tom is now twenty. Suppose that when Tom was ten, he used to remember many things that happened to him when he was five. So in Locke's view, Tom at age five is the same person as Tom at age ten. Suppose also that Tom, now in his twenties, remembers many things that happened to him when he was ten. So in Locke's view, Tom at age ten is the same person as Tom at age twenty. But then in Locke's view, since Tom at age five is the same person as Tom at age ten, and Tom at age ten is the same person as Tom at age twenty, it follows that Tom at age five is the same person as Tom at age twenty. Yet suppose, finally, that Tom at age twenty no longer remembers anything about himself when he was five. Then by Locke's view, Tom at age five is not the same person as Tom at age twenty. So we have a contradiction! In Locke's view, Tom at age five is the same person as Tom at age twenty. At the same time, in Locke's view, Tom at age five is not the same person as Tom at age twenty—a contradiction.

There are other problems with Locke's idea. For example, what about the fact that I cannot remember everything that I ever did? There are many things about my earlier life that I have just forgotten. Does this mean that some "other" person did those things? And what about the insane person who "remembers" that he was once Napoleon? Does this mean that he must be the same person as Napoleon because he has a "memory" of once being Napoleon?

Yet if the body, the soul, and the memory do not make a person be the same person he or she always was, what does? Some philosophers have suggested that there is a mistaken assumption in this question. The mistaken assumption is the assumption with which we began: the assumption that there is something called the "self" or the "person" that endures through time. Perhaps humans have no self. Could it be that there is no such thing as a "person" who stays the same throughout a human life?

THE NO-SELF VIEW

Perhaps the most radical views of human nature are those that completely deny the existence of an enduring self. With few exceptions, most Western thinkers have assumed that even if nothing else exists, I can be assured that at least I— my individual self—exist. The existence and significance of the individual self is, in fact, the foundation of most Western thought. Westerners tend to believe that the private self is all-important and that individuality should be exalted. We are each taught that it is terribly important to become aware of "who we

Every rational being exists as an end in itself, not merely as a means.

IMMANUEL KANT

---

[41] See Thomas Reid, "Mr. Locke's Account of Our Personal Identity," in *Personal Identity*, ed. John Perry (Berkeley: University of California Press, 1975).

Buddha: "It is simply the mind clouded over by impure desires and impervious to wisdom, that obstinately persists in thinking of 'me' and 'mine.'"

really are," and we each feel that our inner self is a unique being with immeasurable dignity and worth.

Yet not all people are convinced of the significance, or even the existence, of the self. Much of Eastern philosophy, in fact, is based on the notion that the individual self does not exist. Eastern philosophy holds that the delusion that the self exists is the source of all pain and suffering. When we speak of Eastern philosophy, we refer to those systems of thought, belief, and action espoused by many peoples in the Near and Far East. Because Eastern thought offers many views of human nature, it is impossible to mention them all. Here we briefly examine one Eastern philosophy, Buddhism, and its view of human nature. The treatment of Buddhism may prove too cursory for most readers. Still our intention is not to exhaust the subject but to provide a vital transcultural perspective as well as evidence of the global reach of philosophy.

Siddhartha Gautama (ca. 563–483 B.C.), the founder of Buddhism, was the son of a chief of a hill tribe in India. At the age of twenty-nine, Prince Siddhartha gave up his family life to be an ascetic. He eventually became the leader of a small group of followers who practiced a "middle way" between extreme asceticism and an indulgent worldly life. He is said to have gained enlightenment and thus become the Buddha under a pipal tree at Bihar and to have devoted his life to teaching his followers. He died at the age of eighty in the fifth century B.C.

About a century after his death, the Buddha's growing group of followers split into two groups: a group of dissenters named the Mahasanghikas and the Theravada, who claimed to remain true to the original teachings of the Buddha's first followers. It is uncertain how many of the legends and sermons attributed to the Buddha by the Theravada are really his and how many are the later work of his followers. But for our purposes we can accept the doctrines of the Theravada as the core doctrines of Buddhism.

Central to Buddhist thought is the belief that all things are composite and transient. All things are aggregates composed of elements that inevitably change over time. Therefore, nothing abides permanently as an individual. Constant movement and change characterize everything, including the gods and all living things.

The self, like everything else, is in a state of constant flux. It too is nothing more than a composite of constantly changing elements: our form and matter, our sensations, our perceptions, our psychic dispositions, and our conscious thought. But these are never the same from moment to moment. What we call the self, then, either considered as the body or considered as the mind, is utterly transient. It is a new aggregate from one moment to the next that cannot even control its own dissolving changes. As a permanently abiding individual entity, then, the self does not exist. According to the Buddha, the idea of self is an illusory belief that is the source of suffering and produces harmful thoughts of "me," "mine," desire, vanity, egoism, and ill will:

> If the body were an ego-personality, it could do this and that as it would determine. [But] a king . . . becomes ill despite his intent and desire, he comes to old age unwillingly, and his fortune and his wishes often have little to do with each other.
>
> If the mind were an ego-personality it could do this and that as it would determine, but the mind often flies from what it knows is right and chases after evil unwillingly.
>
> If a man believes that such an impermanent thing [as the body], so changeable and replete with suffering, is the ego-personality, it is a serious mistake. The human mind is also impermanent and suffering; it has nothing that can be called an ego-personality.
>
> Therefore, both body and mind . . . are far apart from both the conceptions of "me" and "mine." It is simply the mind clouded over by impure desires and impervious to wisdom, that obstinately persists in thinking of "me" and "mine."[42]

The supreme ideal of Greece is to save the ego from anarchy and chaos. The supreme ideal of the Orient is to dissolve the ego into the infininte and to become one with it.

KIMON FRIAR

Unless one grasps that everything, including the self, is transient, one cannot find salvation. If one resists the pervasive flux of phenomena and desires permanence when none exists, the inevitable result is the suffering that we suggested above.

Although the view that humans have no self is characteristic of Buddhist thought, some Western philosophers have put forward a very similar view. The Scottish philosopher David Hume (1711–1776) offered some strong reasons for rejecting the Traditional assumption that human beings have a self. In his book *A Treatise of Human Nature*, Hume argues that all real knowledge is based on what we can actually perceive with our senses: what we can see, hear, touch,

---

[42] *The Teachings of Buddha* (Tokyo: Bukkyo Deudo Kyokai, 1976).

smell, taste, and feel. Because genuine knowledge depends on prior sense experience, assertions that are not based on sense experience cannot be genuine knowledge. He then points out that we never actually perceive the self. Consequently, there is no such thing as a self; the notion of a self is a fiction made up by Traditional philosophers:

> There are some philosophers who imagine we are every moment intimately conscious of what we call our SELF; that we feel its existence and its continuance in existence; and are certain, beyond the evidence of a demonstration, both of its perfect identity and simplicity. . . .
>
> Unluckily all these positive assertions are contrary to that very experience which is pleaded for them, nor have we any idea of *self*. . . . For from what impression could this idea be derived? . . . If any impression gives rise to the idea of self, that impression must continue invariably the same, through the whole course of our lives; since self is supposed to exist after that manner. But there is no impression constant and invariable. Pain and pleasure, grief and joy, passions and sensations succeed each other, and never all exist at the same time. It cannot, therefore, be from any of these impressions, or from any other, that the idea of self is derived; and consequently there is no such idea.
>
> For my part, when I enter most intimately into what I call *myself*, I always stumble on some particular perception or other, of heat or cold, light or shade, love or hatred, pain or pleasure. I never can catch *myself* at any time without a perception, and never can observe anything but the perception. . . .
>
> [S]etting aside some metaphysicians . . . , I may venture to affirm of the rest of mankind, that they are nothing but a bundle or collection of different perceptions, which succeed each other with an inconceivable rapidity, and are in a perpetual flux and movement. . . . The mind is a kind of theatre, where several perceptions successively make their appearance, pass, re-pass, glide away, and mingle in an infinite variety of postures and situations.[43]

CRITICAL THINKING

Does Hume assume that all our ideas must be derived from impressions? Are there other possible sources from which our idea of the self could be derived? If there are other alternatives, would this show that Hume's view of the self is mistaken?

According to Hume, then, we cannot claim that there is an inner self, because all we experience is a constant flow of sensations; we never perceive among these sensations an object called an inner self. All we can say, Hume claims, is that we are "a bundle or collection of different perceptions." Not only is there no fixed nature in the Humean and Buddhist conceptions, but also, because everything is in flux, there is not even an enduring self.

Many similarities exist between Hume's views on the self and those of the Buddhist that distinguish them from other views we have seen. For both Hume and the Buddhist, our inner experience is one of pervasive flux and change without permanence. So for both Hume and the Buddhist, the self has no fixed existence.

In spite of their similarities, Hume's view about how we should deal with the absence of the self differs in important ways from the Buddhist's. Buddhism believes that we can give up the idea that we have an individual self. Buddhism suggests, in fact, that salvation is achievable only by giving up the craving for self-identity and the striving for personal success and self-fulfillment. However,

---

[43] David Hume, *A Treatise of Human Nature*, ed. L. A. Selby-Bigge (Oxford: Clarendon Press, 1896), 6.

Hume did not believe that we can give up the idea of the self and its importance. Hume believed that in the end, we will find it impossible to face the fact that there is no self.

But doesn't this Humean/Buddhist conception of the self conflict with the Traditional Western view that we humans are selves who endure through time? More important, perhaps, doesn't the Humean and Buddhist conception of the self conflict with the prevalent Western assumption that the self has individuality? Doesn't it conflict with the view that we should protect the interests of this individual self in its struggle against the world? Doesn't the assumption that the self has individuality underlie our belief in the primacy and importance of the individual? Doesn't it underlie the popular idea that individuals should have the liberty to pursue their legitimate self-interest because striving for personal success and individual fulfillment is intrinsically valuable? Don't the views of both Hume and Buddhism suggest that you should reject the delusion that your individuality is a reality worthy of protection, support, and enhancement? Is this possible for us?

To see the profound difficulties that the no-self view involves, consider how we continually look after our future interests. As children, we attend school to prepare for our future; we study in college to prepare for our future; we save money now for our future needs; we exercise now so we will be healthy in our future; we buy things so we can enjoy them in our future life. In short, we are continually looking after the interests of the person we will be in the future. But if there is no enduring self, then all this activity makes no sense. If there is no enduring self, then I will not be around in the future. Why then prepare for a future I myself will never see? Why not just enjoy myself as much as I can in this moment and forget about preparing for the future?

We are left, then, with a mystery. We assume in virtually everything we do that we have an enduring self—i.e., that we remain the same person from day to day. So does everyone else. Every day, every hour, every moment we are engaged in making preparations for this individual self. Yet when we probe this ordinary assumption, it seems that there is little to support it. Neither the body, nor the soul, nor even memory seem to provide a sound basis for our belief that we endure through time. Yet giving up the idea of an enduring self is also profoundly unsatisfying. Perhaps we should look more closely at the idea of individuality.

The familiar lament, "I don't know who I am," once thought to belong only to the crisis of adolescence, to be resolved by the adult stage, is heard not only from teenagers but from adults of all ages. Education, status, "success," material security or lack of it, seem to have little bearing upon the unhappiness and loneliness in the life of those who have found no focus of identity or pattern of meaning in their existence.

AARON UNGERSMA

QUESTIONS

1. Suppose that your soul could survive death. But suppose that at death your soul loses all memory of its past life, and all memories of who and what you were are completely erased from your soul. Suppose, also, that all personality traits, beliefs, desires, preferences, and all other conscious qualities are erased. Will you still exist after death? Explain why or why not.

2. Review the identity theory of human nature in the last section. Suppose that identity theory is true. Can you think of some ways that you could still survive the death of your body even if the identity theory is true?

3. Suppose that the computer theory of human nature discussed in the last section is true. Can you think of some ways that you could still survive the death of your body even if the computer theory is true?

4. How do we decide whether, say, a song, a novel, a television show, a nation, or a corporation continues to endure through time? That is, how do we decide that a song, novel, etc. that exists at one time is the same individual song, novel, television show, etc. as one that exists at a later time?

5. Tom Jones shot his girlfriend, Virginia Compton, in the head. Doctors declared she was "brain dead." Tom was tried and convicted of attempted murder. The jury sentenced him to twenty years in prison. Meanwhile, Virginia was kept alive in a hospital. After a year, her family asked the hospital to remove her life-support system, since she was "brain dead" and no longer existed. The hospital agreed, and Virginia's heart soon stopped beating. Now the district attorney indicted Tom Jones for murder. However, Tom and his lawyer claimed that he didn't kill Virginia. She died, they said, when the hospital removed her life-support system. Which side is correct? Why?

6. Contrast the Buddhist approach to human nature with the rational Western religious, scientific, and existentialist views.

7. Does the view of no self have anything to offer? What?

2.5 Are We Independent and Self-Sufficient Individuals?

Isn't it obvious that parents should help their children achieve independence and self-sufficiency? Isn't it obvious that one of the worst things parents can do is to raise their children to become and remain dependent on others all of their lives? To ensure that children become independent individuals, parents teach them to value and cultivate self-reliance. Parents also try to teach their children how to think on their own, how to make judgments on their own, how to choose and explore on their own. They try to teach children independence of thought and action.

Or consider some things parents teach children to avoid. One is conformity. Most parents don't feel that it is good to teach a child to like to conform. They advise children not to follow their friends or peer groups blindly. They teach children that it is not good to always submit to the expectations of others. Parents advise children, instead, to think for themselves, to learn to judge and evaluate for themselves whether what others tell them is true.

Parents also teach their children to try to be true to themselves. Parents teach their children the importance of being in touch with their real individual nature and inner feelings and needs. They should not try to change themselves to please others.

Finally, think about some things we value that support these parental ideas. Take privacy, for example. Don't we feel that we should allow people to live their own lives? Don't we feel that something is wrong when society forces its values on private individuals? Or consider how we value creativity in people, or how we enjoy novelty, excitement, and challenge in life. Consider how much we prize freedom, being able to "do your own thing." How we praise individual achievement and ambition. How we cherish individual freedom. How we believe that choosing a path that is his own is all-important for a person, rather than choosing one that others impose on him.

All these views about how we should raise children, and assumptions about what we should value, are part of a pattern. They are based on a certain view of the self: the view that the self is and should be independent of others, and self-sufficient. This view has deep roots in our culture and in our ways of thinking and feeling. It is a view that some philosophers call the atomistic view of the self. On this view, the self is, like the atom, self-contained and independent of other atoms. The self is an autonomous individual with its own unique inner qualities. The things I go through, the people I meet, and the things I witness can touch me and move me. They can injure and hurt me. Yet the real me, the core of my self, can always rise above these and remain independent and different from all that it meets. The great American poet Walt Whitman perhaps expressed this idea best in his well-known poem "Song of Myself."

> I celebrate myself, and sing myself. . . .
> Trippers and askers surround me,
> People I meet, the effect upon me of my early life or the ward and city
>   I live in, or the nation,
> The latest dates, discoveries, inventions, societies, authors old and new,
> My dinner, dress, associates, looks, compliments, dues,
> The real or fancied indifference of some man or woman I love,
> The sickness of one of my folks or of myself, or ill-doing or loss or lack of
>   money, or depressions or exaltations,
> Battles, the horrors of fratricidal war, the fever of doubtful news, the fitful
>   events;
> These come to me days and nights and go from me again,
> But they are not the Me myself.
>
> Apart from the pulling and hauling stands what I am,
> Stands amused, complacent, compassionating, idle, unitary,
> Looks down, is erect, or bends an arm on an impalpable certain rest,
> Looking with side-curved head curious what will come next,
> Both in and out of the game and watching and wondering at it.[44]

To see how powerful this view of the self is, think for a moment about your "real self." How do you get at the "real" you? Not the "you" that tries to live up to

---

[44]Walt Whitman, "Song of Myself," in *The American Tradition in Literature*, 3d ed., vol. 2, ed. S. Bradley, L. C. Beatty, and E. H. Long (New York: Grosset and Dunlap, 1967), 37, 39.

the expectations of others, not the facade that the world sees, but the real and genuine "you." Don't you find this real you by withdrawing into yourself and contemplating the you that lies within?

This is what many philosophers have also thought. Consider the example of Descartes. He tells us that one day he resolved to understand himself better, so he withdrew from the company of others to discover within himself the truth about himself:

> After I had employed several years studying the book of the world and trying to acquire some experience, I one day formed the resolution of also making myself an object of study. . . . Winter detained me in a place where I found no society to divert me and no cares or passions to trouble me. I remained there the whole day shut up alone in a stove-heated room, where I had complete leisure to occupy myself with my own thoughts.[45]

Alone, apart from others, Descartes could search for his inner real self and could decide for himself what is true and what is false:

> I shall now close my eyes, I shall stop my ears, I shall call away all my senses, I shall efface even from my thoughts all the images of corporeal things, or at least (for that is hardly possible) I shall esteem them as vain and false; and thus holding converse only with myself and considering my own nature, I shall try little by little to reach a better knowledge of and a more familiar acquaintanceship with myself. I am a thing that thinks, that is to say, that doubts, affirms, denies, that knows a few things, that is ignorant of many, that loves, that hates, that wills, that desires, that also imagines and perceives. . . .
>
> In order to try to extend my knowledge further, I shall now look around more carefully and see whether I cannot still discover in myself some other things which I have not hitherto perceived. I am certain that I am a thing which thinks; but do I not then likewise know what is requisite to render me certain of a truth? Certainly in this first knowledge there is nothing that assures me of its truth, excepting the clear and distinct perception of that which I state. . . . And accordingly it seems to me that already I can establish as a general rule that all things which I perceive very clearly and very distinctly are true.[46]

Notice what Descartes is saying. First, he is saying that the real me lies within myself. Second, he is claiming that the qualities of this real me—my desires, fears, hopes, loves, hatreds—are there inside me and are independent of others. Third, he claims that I, by myself, can discover this real me by withdrawing from others. Fourth, he claims that only I can be the judge of what the truth about myself is.

In short, Descartes gives us a picture of the independent and self-sufficient individual. I do not need others to be who I really am. Of course, I may need others to help me live. I depend on others, for example, for food, housing, and the many other material things I need. Still, I do not need others to have the qualities that make me who I myself am: My desires, fears, hopes, loves, and

---

[45] Descartes, *Discourse on the Method*, in Haldane, 87.
[46] Descartes, *Meditations*, in Haldane, 157–158.

hatreds are all there inside me, whether or not anyone is around to see them. These do not depend on others but come from within me: They are me. My real self is there, and it is independent of others. Moreover, a key aspect of the real me is my ability to decide for myself—i.e., the ability to judge the truth of things for myself without relying on others.

Some philosophers have gone even further than Descartes in emphasizing the importance of this ability to judge things for oneself. For example, the German philosopher Immanuel Kant argued that the core of the real self is the ability to choose for oneself the laws and principles by which one will live one's life:

> The laws to which man is subject are only those that he himself makes. . . . [This is] the principle of autonomy of the will, that is, the principle of self-imposed law. . . . The will's autonomy consists in its capacity to be its own law, without being influenced by the objects it chooses. . . . The will is a causal power that living beings have if they are rational. We say such a causal power has freedom if its acts are not determined by causal influences other than itself.[47]

Notice here how Kant is claiming that the real me is a being who can choose or will for himself. The real me can choose without having to conform to what external forces impose on him.

We see, then, in Descartes and in Kant some sources of a view of the individual self that is very familiar to us: the view that who I am is there inside me, independent of others and able to freely choose independently of others. As we suggested above, we value this view of self. We try to raise our children to become independent individuals in this sense: persons who will be true to their inner self, who will not merely conform to what external society demands, and who will exercise independent and free choice.

Still, now let us ask ourselves this: Is there such a thing as the independent and self-sufficient individual we have been discussing? Is it possible for children, or adults, to be independent and self-sufficient? The twentieth-century Canadian philosopher Charles Taylor does not believe so:

> In the twentieth century, we may no longer believe, like Descartes, in the soul or mind as an inner space open to transparent introspection . . . but we retain the idea that self-understanding is getting a clear view of the desires, aversions, fears, hopes, aspirations that are within us. To know oneself is to get clear on what is within.
>
> This seems so normal and inescapable to us, that we can hardly imagine an alternative. But let us try. If I can only understand myself as part of a larger order; indeed, if man as the rational animal is just the one who is rationally aware of this order; then I only am really aware of myself, and understand myself, when I see myself against this background, fitting into this whole. I must acknowledge my belonging before I can understand myself. Engaged in an attempt to cut myself off, to consider myself quite on my own, autonomously, I should be in confusion, self-delusion, in the dark.[48]

---

[47] Immanuel Kant, *Foundations of the Metaphysics of Reason*, quoted in M. Velasquez and C. Rostankowski, *Ethics: Theory and Practice* (Englewood Cliffs, NJ: Prentice-Hall, 1985), 90–91.

[48] Charles Taylor, "Legitimation Crisis?" in Charles Taylor, *Philosophy and the Human Sciences*, vol. 2 (New York: Cambridge University Press, 1985), 257.

W. F. Hegel: "Each self is in a struggle to convince the other that he is a free being worthy of the other's respect and recognition. This struggle is the basis of the rise of masters and slaves. The slave gives up his attempt to be recognized as free. The master sees in the slave the very sign of his freedom."

Taylor is suggesting that there is another way of understanding who the real me is besides that of getting in touch with what is within me apart from others. This other way is to see that who I am depends on my relationships to others.

We saw above that we depend on others for the material things we need to survive. Still, this is not what Taylor has in mind. Taylor is suggesting that we also depend on others for our very self: I need others to define for me who the real me is. Philosophers sometimes express this by saying that the self is "constituted" by its relations to others.

Yet, surprisingly, the Traditional view of the self that most of us share says that you are who you are independently of your relationships with other people. We feel that you can know yourself by withdrawing from others and looking deep within yourself to find the real you or your real "self."

Not all traditional views of the self assume that the self is independent of others. For example, Aristotle declared that humans are "social animals" who are not self-sufficient:

> The individual, when isolated, is not self-sufficing; and therefore he is like a part in relation to the whole. But he who is unable to live in society, or who has no need because he is sufficient for himself, must be either a beast or a god. . . . A social instinct is implanted in all men by nature.[49]

Aristotle is not just saying that we need others to survive. He is arguing that what a human being is, the person I am and the qualities I have, arise from my

No one would choose the whole world on condition of being alone.

ARISTOTLE

---

[49] Aristotle, *Politics*, bk. 1, ch. 2. This translation by Manuel Velasquez.

relationships with others. Without these relationships, which make me the human that I am, I would be an animal, or a god.

But it was the philosopher Hegel who most forcefully challenged the idea of the independent, self-sufficient individual. Hegel argued that my own identity—who I really am—depends on my relationships with others and that I cannot be who I am apart from my relationships with others:

> Every self wants to be united with and recognized by another self [as a free being]. Yet at the same time, each self remains an independent individual and so an alien object to the other. The life of the self thus becomes a struggle for recognition. . . . Each self is in a struggle to convince the other that he is [a free being] worthy of the other's respect and recognition. This mutual struggle for recognition by the other is mixed with feelings of mistrust and uncertainty. The struggle carries with it all the dangers and risks that the self faces when it dares to lay itself open to the other. This life-and-death struggle can degenerate into a bloody fight in which one of the combatants is killed. But then the whole issue of recognition will be missed. Recognition requires the survival of the other as a condition and sign of one's freedom.
>
> The struggle of the self is essentially a struggle for freedom. Historically, this struggle is the basis of the rise of masters and slaves. . . . Preferring survival to freedom, the slave gives up his attempt to be recognized as free. The master, on the other hand, is recognized as free. The master sees in the slave the very sign of his freedom.
>
> Independent masters and dependent slaves together form a community. To preserve and protect the life of his workers becomes the concern of the master. . . . The slave learns to work. He acquires habits and skills. At the same time he disciplines himself. In making objects [for the master] he also makes himself. In working together with others he overcomes his isolation and is recognized for his excellence. In this process, the relation of dependence and independence is reversed. The independent master becomes dependent on the skills and virtues of the servant.[50]

Hegel is here claiming that each of us can know we have certain human qualities only when others recongize those qualities in us. In particular, each of us can know that we are free and independent persons only if we see that others recognize us as free and independent persons. A free and independent person is one who is not a slave to his desires or to some external force. A free and independent person is one who is able to choose for himself what course his life will take. So Hegel is saying that we will not develop the capacity to choose for ourselves unless others develop this capacity in us by recognizing and affirming our freedom and self-mastery.

An analogy may clarify what Hegel has in mind. Consider how children come to feel that they are lovable and valuable. A child will not feel or believe that he is lovable and valuable if he sees that no one around him loves him or values him. In fact, if a child fails to experience himself as loved and valued by others, he will grow up to feel that he is unlovable and worthless. In a similar way, Hegel is arguing, a person cannot be nor become an independent, free person unless others respect him as a free and independent person. When people do not respect me as competent and able to direct my own life, when

Man comes into the world naked and unarmed, as if Nature had destined him for a social creature.

WILLIAM HARVEY

---

[50] Wilhelm Hegel, *Encyclopedia of Philosophy*, trans. Gustav E. Mueller (New York: Philosophical Library, 1959), 215–217.

they see me as the helpless slave of my own desires, when they denigrate me as weak, dependent, inept, and powerless, I come to believe that I am weak, inept, incapable, and powerless. Believing that I am incompetent and dependent, I become incompetent and dependent, unable and unwilling to choose and act on my own. On the other hand, when people recognize a person's independence and self-mastery, he will find the confidence and capacity to choose for himself what he will be. Thus, Hegel is arguing that even the core feature of the independent and self-sufficient self—its ability to choose for itself—depends completely on others.

Moreover, Hegel is claiming that each of us is continually involved in a struggle to get the recognition from others that we need to be truly independent, free persons. We realize that to be free and competent, we need others to acknowledge that we are worthy of being respected as free and competent persons. So we try to force others to respect us, even as they struggle to force us to respect them. In this struggle—a life-and-death struggle—some people emerge as dominant and others as submissive. The dominant ones are those who get the respect they demanded, whereas the submissive ones are those who give up the struggle for respect and settle for merely being allowed to live. Thus are formed the two great social classes: slaves and masters—those who command and those who obey. Yet though the slave appears to have lost the battle to the master, eventually the tables are slowly turned. For as the slave serves the master, the master recognizes the capability of the slave. The slave then becomes more confident of himself. He sees himself as a capable, competent supporter of the master. Meanwhile, the master gradually becomes dependent on the slave, and both recognize the master as incapable and incompetent.

Man is not only a social animal, but an animal which can develop into an individual only in society.

KARL MARX

The key idea, then, is that who you are ultimately depends on your relationships to others. The slave who identifies himself as a slave is such because he defines himself through his relationship to the master. The master who sees himself as free and independent is such only to the extent that others will recognize him as such.

The implications of Hegel's idea are profound. For in every society there are powerless and powerful people, strong and weak, dominant and submissive. Hegel is suggesting that these classifications are not there ahead of time. Instead, we create them by the qualities we are willing to recognize in others. The same is true of social classes. Some groups in society, perhaps some minority groups, for example, may exhibit submissive characteristics. Yet, to a large extent, we make them submissive by our failure to accord them the respect and recognition that alone can empower them to be assertive and independent. Charles Taylor is a leading authority on Hegel. He explains the importance of recognition:

> The thesis is that our identity is partly shaped by recognition or its absence, [or] by the misrecognition of others, and so a person or a group of people can suffer real damage, real distortion, if the people or society around them mirror back to them a confining or demeaning or contemptible picture of themselves. . . .
>
> Thus some feminists have argued that women in patriarchal societies have been induced to adopt a depreciatory image of themselves. They have internalized a picture of their own inferiority. . . . An analogous point has been made in relation

to blacks: that white society has for generations projected a demeaning image of them, which some of them have been unable to resist adopting. Their own self-depreciation, on this view, becomes one of the most potent instruments of their own oppression. . . . Recently, a similar point has been made in relation to indigenous and colonized people in general. It is held that since 1492 Europeans have projected an image of such people as somehow inferior, "uncivilized," and through the force of conquest have often been able to impose this image on the conquered.[51]

There is another important implication of Hegel's view. Consider that every person has a culture. A culture consists of the traditions and language, the arts, ideas, and outlooks, the practices and beliefs of a group of people. Hegel argues that a person's culture is the mirror through which society shows the person who and what he is. It is, in fact, through his culture that a person gets the recognition that makes him a free person. Recognition comes through culture.

What this means is that who I am, the qualities that define me, depends on my culture and on my relationships to the important people in my life. There is, then, no "real me" that I can find inside apart from others. Instead, I am who others tell me I am. Again, Taylor expresses the idea best:

> In order to understand the close connection between identity and recognition, we have to take into account a crucial feature of the human condition. . . . This crucial feature of human life is its fundamentally dialogical character. We become full human agents, capable of understanding ourselves, and hence of defining our identity, through our acquisition of rich human languages of expression. For my purposes here, I want to take language in a broad sense, covering not only the words we speak, but also other modes of expression whereby we define ourselves, including the "languages" of art, of gesture, of love, and the like. But we learn these modes of expression through exchanges with others. People do not acquire the languages needed for self-definition on their own. Rather, we are introduced to them through interaction with others who matter to us. . . .
>
> Moreover, this is not just a fact about genesis, which can be ignored later on. We don't just learn the languages in dialogue and then go on to use them for our own purposes. . . . We define our identity always in dialogue with, sometimes in struggle against, the things our significant others want to see in us. Even after we outgrow some of these others — our parents, for instance — and they disappear from our lives, the conversation with them continues within us as long as we live. Thus, the contribution of significant others, even when it is provided at the beginning of our lives, continues indefinitely.[52]

To understand what Taylor means, consider how you think of yourself. Don't you identify who you are by your relationships to others, particularly to the groups to which you belong? You identify yourself as the son or daughter of your parents. Your name identifies you in terms of the family to which you belong. You identify yourself as an American, a Canadian, a German, or a Mexican. You are a member of a racial or ethnic group: white or black, Indian or Asian. Consider the wants that make you who you are. The culture you were raised in

---

[51] Charles Taylor, "The Politics of Recognition," in *Multiculturalism and the Politics of Recognition*, ed. Amy Gutman (Princeton, NJ: Princeton University Press, 1992), 25.
[52] Ibid., 32–33.

determines the foods, the clothes, and the music you prefer. In short, all your wants are defined in terms of what your culture teaches you to want. From your culture you also draw all your ideas about the kind of person you can be. You use these ideas to understand yourself: lover, loner, kindly, coward, punk, rocker, beautiful, ugly, popular, unpopular, nerd, queen, thug, jogger, athlete, fox, beauty queen, selfish, compassionate, animal, chick, cold fish, rocket scientist, mother, father, son, daughter. Consider the most basic things you know: Each of them is the product of the investigations of all the humans who labored at discovering the nature of our world before you came along. Your religious ideas all come from the traditions of a church into which you have been socialized. The language you use to express your thoughts to yourself and others is a gift of your culture. Thus, not only do we depend on the recognition of others to be who we are; we depend also on our culture to give us all the ideas we use to define who we are.

Who is right, then? Is Descartes right when he claims that the real you is discovered within yourself and is independent of others? Or are Hegel and Taylor right when they claim that the real you is found only in relationship to others?

Think about it. From childhood and from every side we hear the constant refrains: "Be true to yourself and not to what others expect you to be," "Think for yourself and don't just follow the crowd around you," and "Take responsibility for yourself and don't blame others for what you are." Yet, if Hegel and Taylor are right, then all these ideas are radically and deeply false. The real me is not there inside, independent of others and waiting to be discovered. The real me is something that is created from my relationships with others and with my culture. The people I love and care for, the people who are important to me, the people whose opinions I trust, and the ideas and beliefs of my culture all make me who I am. It is to them I must turn to find myself. I cannot be true to myself unless I am what they and my culture make me. I cannot think for myself without using the ideas that they and my culture give me. I do not have responsibility for myself because in a very real way they have made me what I am.

Yet are Hegel and Taylor right? Perhaps not. If who and what you are depends on others, then you are not responsible for what you are. Nor are you responsible for what you do. But surely that is not right. Surely, in some way and to some extent you are responsible for who you have become and what you do. As Sartre and others have argued, to some extent you make yourself who you are.

Yet there is a deeper problem with the idea that who I am depends on my relationships with others. For my relationships with others are many. Are there many me's, one me for each person with whom I am related? Hegel says that what I am depends on what others recognize in me. Still, suppose that different people recognize different things in me. This person recognizes me as loving, that one as mean, that other one as wise, and this one as stupid. Which is the real me? Which of these different things go into making the real me? Are there many me's? The philosopher William James was not afraid to accept this conclusion:

Intelligence cannot be fully actualized in a single person nor in any single community. It requires the multitude of humanity.

DANTE

> Properly speaking, a man has as many social selves as there are individuals who rec-
> ognize him . . . [but] we may practically say that he has as many social selves as there
> are distinct groups of persons about whose opinion he cares.[53]

Yet this seems an odd conclusion. How can I be many me's? Are we, without realizing it, multiple personalities? Do we turn a different face to each person depending on what that person sees in us? Perhaps we do. But then, which of these many faces would really be me?

Moreover, isn't it true that many of the qualities you have do not depend on others? Take, for example, your basic physical qualities: your height, your weight, your hair color, your skin color, your facial features, your musculature, your health. Surely, these are a basic part of who you are and do not depend on your relationships with others. Or take your basic mental qualities, such as your I.Q. and your ability to feel pain, to hate, to love, to think. Even if *what* you feel, hate, love, or think depends on others, surely your *ability* to feel, hate, love, and think does not depend on others. Or take your basic personality traits, such as your tendency to feel cheerful or depressed, your willingness to take risks, and your dispositon. We inherit many of these kinds of qualities, scientists tell us; they depend on the genes we are born with. And surely these personality traits are part of who you are.

We have, then, a dilemma. On the one hand, we seem to be only what others make us: what the significant people in our lives make us and what society through its culture makes us. On the other hand, we seem to be indepen-dent selves with basic qualities that we are born with, including the ability to freely choose the path our lives will take. Which are we? The choice between these is important. Clearly, if others make us, then we, in turn, make others. The way we raise our children, the money we spend on schools, the kinds of social environments we create, the respect or lack of respect we give others, the way our culture talks about different races—all these become tremendously im-portant. For all these will ultimately make the young members of our society the kind of people they turn out to be: powerful or powerless, free or slave, capable or incapable, submissive or assertive. On the other hand, if we are in-dependent selves with the ability to freely choose, then these externals are not so important. More important is that we hold persons responsible for their choices, that people learn to look into themselves for their own inner power and resources, that people learn to rely on themselves and find in themselves who they really are.

The challenge for each of us, perhaps, is to find what comes from within and what comes from without: what comes from others and what comes from me. A great deal hangs on this.

QUESTIONS

1. Can you think of any qualities that you see in yourself that you do not need for others to have?

---

[53] William James, *Psychology (Briefer Course)* (New York: Collier, 1962), 192.

2. If each self in society is what it is because other selves have made it that way, then is all responsibility ultimately group responsibility? That is, when an individual does something evil, must we say that everyone in society is responsible for the evil?

3. Can you think of some of the implications that Hegel's views on the master–slave relationship have for workers in our society? Would Hegel explain the employer–employee or the boss–worker relationship as the outcome of the same processes of recognition that create the master–slave relationship? Explain your answer.

4. Compare the Buddhist–Hume no-self view with the view that the self is constituted by its relationships with others.

2.6 Chapter Summary and Conclusions

We opened the chapter by raising the issue of human nature: Who and what am I? How we see ourselves has been profoundly influenced by Traditional theories of human nature: the rationalist view and the Western religious view. These Traditional views have been challenged on a number of fronts. Darwinian evolution has challenged the ideas of uniqueness and purpose. Existentialism has challenged the idea of a universal human nature. Feminists have raised questions about the role of gender in forming our identities. The Traditional view has also favored dualism. Dualism has in turn been challenged by various forms of materialism. The Traditional view has also assumed that humans are enduring selves and that humans can and should be independent and self-sufficient.

Although it is impossible to say which of these views is most accurate, it is clear that we frequently interpret aspects of our lives from these viewpoints. They do not exist in isolation, but often overlap one another. We seldom find ourselves acting exclusively according to one school of thought; more often we must act under the influences of several. Hopefully, they should provoke some personal reflections about what you believe and why.

The main points of this chapter are the following:

1. *Human nature* refers to what it means to be a member of our species, what makes us different from anything else. Some important issues raised by our views of human nature are questions concerning whether humans have a spiritual aspect or are purely material and whether humans are aggressive and self-interested or cooperative and benevolent (2.1).

To be a philosopher is not merely to have subtle thoughts, nor even to found a school, but so to love wisdom as to live according to its dictates, a life of simplicity, independence, magnanimity, and trust.

HENRY DAVID THOREAU

2. Traditional Western views of human nature assume that all humans have the same human nature: They are conscious, rational selves who have a purpose. Some Traditional views refer to this immaterially defined self as the "soul" (2.2).

3. One important version of the Traditional Western view of human nature is the ancient Greek view that sees humans as uniquely rational beings with a purpose. This view contends that reason can and should rule over human desire and aggressiveness. The Judeo-Christian religious view claims that humans are made in the image of God, who has endowed them with rational self-consciousness and an ability to love. In the Christian version the self is immaterial and distinct from the body (2.2).

4. Some scientific views challenge the Traditional view of human nature. Darwin argued that humans evolved from earlier animal species through random variations and a natural selection that is the result of a struggle for existence. Darwin's view has been taken to imply that human nature has no purpose and is not unique (2.2).

5. Existentialist views deny that all humans have the same fixed nature. Instead, existentialists claim that each human creates his or her own nature. Existentialism asserts that although there is no fixed human nature, there is still a self that is a freely choosing, self-creating, active agent (2.2).

6. Feminists have argued that our concepts of reason, appetites, emotions, mind, and body are all biased in favor of men and against women, yet the rationalist and Judeo-Christian view is framed in terms of these sexist concepts. Reason, rationality, and mind are seen as superior "male" traits that must rule over the inferior "female" traits of emotion and bodily appetites, and this idea appears to be fundamentally sexist (2.2).

7. Descartes's dualist view of human nature says that humans are immaterial minds with material bodies. The material body is observable and has color, size, shape, and weight. The mind has no observable color, size, or shape, but it has consciousness. It is unclear how immaterial entities can interact with material ones (2.3).

8. Materialist views say that humans are solely material bodies. Identity theory holds that conscious states are identical with the body's brain states. Behaviorism says that conscious mental states are bodily behaviors or dispositions. Functionalism says that *conscious mental states* is a shorthand term for connections the body makes between sensory inputs and behavioral outputs. The computer view of human nature says that computers running programs can have minds and so the human mind is a computer (2.3).

9. The Traditional view of human nature and our ordinary thinking assume that humans have a self that endures through time. Descartes claimed that the enduring self is a soul. Locke argued that memory produces the enduring self. Buddhism and Hume suggest that there is no enduring self (2.4).

10. Many support the view that the human self can and should be independent of others, self-sufficient, and capable of thinking for itself. Hegel argued that who we are depends on the recognition of others and on our culture (2.5).

In examining any one of these views, we tend to see it as excluding others. Yet these theories rarely do that. For example, the rationalist, religious, and existentialist views all agree on the human's individuality. Buddhism and Hegel agree that the self does not exist in the way that Traditional Western thought would have it. So these traditions do overlap, and combined views are not only common but seemingly necessary to account for the full range of human experience. Differences in views are sometimes more differences of emphasis than of content.

In the last analysis, perhaps, no one theory can fully describe and explain human nature. The most reasonable position seems to be one that does not distort and ignore aspects of human experience beyond its own focus and that can accommodate additional data about the human condition. The most plausible view of human nature is one that is sufficiently rich in categories and concepts to allow theorists to formulate a variety of theories. This position accords significance to all phenomena, particularly subjectivity.

Although no one can decide for you which view best fulfills these requirements, it is clear that the acceptance or rejection of a particular view will have a tremendous influence on your life and how you live it. The issue of the enduring self is a good example. Whether we consider ourselves capable of being independent, self-sufficent selves depends to a large extent on what our view of human nature is. In turn, the attitude toward the self influences how we live and how we think our society should be arranged.

Also, our experiences affect our views of human nature because of the intimacy between our experiences and our self-concepts. Obviously, we can sail along smoothly in life buoyed up by unexamined assumptions, such as that we are unselfish. Then something happens; we run aground. A crisis forces us to evaluate what we take for granted, and we wonder whether we are really selfish. Our inquiry, if pursued with philosophical zest, leads to far-reaching questions about what kind of beings we are. In the last analysis, then, the question "What is a human?" is one of the most important that we can ask, and much hinges on its answer. Life's meaning and purpose, what we ought to do, what we can hope to accomplish—all are profoundly affected by how we view human nature.

Over two thousand years ago Socrates claimed that "the unexamined life is not worth living." When humans begin to examine their lives and themselves, they begin to philosophize. Philosophers are persons who perceive to some degree how the many experiences and insights of their existence form a pattern of meaning. Philosophy, as we saw in Chapter 1, is a journey undertaken by those who are deeply concerned with who and what they are and what everything means. We have taken the first steps on that journey by reflecting on the most basic question of philosophy. Although we now leave our direct reflections on this question, it will stay with us indirectly throughout the rest of this book.

Philosophy is the highest music.

PLATO

Girl Before a Mirror, Pablo Picasso. In the last analysis, the question "What is a human?" is one of the most important that we can ask. Life's meaning and purpose, what we ought to do, what we can hope to accomplish—all are profoundly affected by what we consider human nature.

Before we close, we should note that Socrates' own philosophical journey began with an oracle from the god at Delphi in Greece. History tells us that at the entrance to the temple at Delphi was the inscription "Know thyself!" Socrates' philosophical journey is thus often interpreted as a quest for self-knowledge. Our own philosophical journey can likewise be seen as a journey toward self-knowledge.

Plato, Aristotle, and Confucius

The preceding discussion was intended to provide an array of overviews of human nature and thus has certain pitfalls. One might conclude from the discussion that philosophy is merely a catalogue of diverse opinions, that when engaging an issue such as human nature, philosophy ultimately does little more than serve up a smorgasbord of opinions. Moreover, focusing on a single issue as we have just done inevitably dislodges the portion from the mosaic of interrelated pieces that, taken together, make up a full-scale philosophy. In fact, one cannot fully appreciate a position on an issue without understanding how it fits in with an entire outlook. To avoid these pitfalls and give the preceding material a sharper focus, we will now take a more in-depth look at three philosophers: Plato, Aristotle, and Confucius.

PLATO

Plato was born in 427 B.C. into a wealthy family of the nobility of Athens, Greece. As a teenager he met and became well acquainted with Socrates, eventually adopting him as an informal teacher. Plato admired Socrates deeply, feeling that Socrates' reliance on reason was the key to the solution of the many political and cultural problems that then plagued Athens. Since the death of the great Athenian statesman Pericles, Athens had been engaged in an unending series of wars that Pericles himself had initiated and that ended with the defeat of Athens at the hands of the city-state of Sparta. After peace was restored, the Athenians condemned Socrates to death, accusing him of undermining Athenian culture and thus being responsible for its many troubles. Shocked and disillusioned by Socrates' execution, Plato withdrew from public life and devoted himself to philosophy until his death in 347 B.C.

Plato: "If, as we say, perfect beauty and goodness and every ideal exist, then it is a necessary inference that just as these ideals exist, so our souls existed before we were born."

In his philosophical theories, Plato fashioned a distinctive view of human nature, a view that has had a crucial formative influence on all subsequent theories of human nature. In fact, an important twentieth-century philosopher, Alfred North Whitehead, asserted that "all philosophy is nothing more than a footnote to Plato." Whitehead was referring to the fact that Plato was the first philosopher to develop philosophical notions of human nature, human knowledge, and metaphysics. He was also the first to pose the basic questions about these topics that all subsequent philosophers have continued to ask. Plato's views on human nature are important, then, not only for themselves but also because of their enduring influence.

Most of what we know about Plato's philosophy is based on the many dialogues he wrote in which the character of Socrates is the major speaker. In his early dialogues, Plato more or less faithfully reported Socrates' views. But as Plato grew older and his own theories began to develop, the character of Socrates increasingly became the mouthpiece for Plato's own views. In what are called the middle and late dialogues, in fact, the views expressed by the character Socrates are entirely those of Plato.

Plato's most fundamental contribution to philosophy was the distinction he drew between the changing physical objects we perceive with our senses and the unchanging ideals we can know with our minds. One of his clearest examples of this distinction is drawn from the science of geometry. Plato pointed out that we use our minds in geometry to discover unchanging truths about ideally perfect lines, squares, and circles. Yet the physical objects in the visible world are never perfectly straight, square, or circular, and they are continually changing. At best, physical objects are imperfect replicas of the ideal objects we contemplate in geometry. As Plato put it, "Those who study geometry use visible figures and reason about them. But they are not thinking of these, but of the ideals which they resemble. They are thinking of a perfect square or a perfect line, and so on, and not of the imperfect figures they draw. . . . The visible figures they draw are merely replicas and what they are seeking is to understand the ideals which can be known only by the mind."[1]

Plato pointed out that this distinction between a perfect ideal and its imperfect replicas also applies to art and morality. With our minds we are able to think about the ideal of perfect beauty and perfect goodness. But the many physical objects we see with our senses are only imperfectly beautiful and imperfectly good. The following dialogue, in which Plato put his own ideas into the mouth of Socrates, expressed the matter in this way:

SOCRATES: We say there are many objects that are beautiful and many objects that are good and simi-larly many objects that are instances of something specific.

GLAUCON: Yes, indeed.

SOCRATES: And, in addition, we say there is perfect beauty itself and perfect goodness itself. And a similar thing may be said about any definite ideal which has many instances. Each of the many instances is related to its perfect ideal insofar as each shares in that ideal and each gets its name from that ideal.

GLAUCON: Very true.

SOCRATES: The many objects are visible but they are not the objects we know [with our minds], while the ideals are the objects we know [with our minds] but they are not visible to the eye.[2]

As this passage suggests, Plato realized that his distinction between a perfect ideal and its many imperfect physical replicas actually extended to every class of things "of which there are many instances." The many human beings we see, the many oak trees, and the many tables are more or less imperfect replicas of what we think of as the ideal human being, the ideal oak tree, and the ideal table. Again, in Plato's words as expressed by Socrates in dialogue,

SOCRATES: Don't we usually assume that when there are many things that have the same name, there is also an ideal that corresponds to them? You understand, don't you?

GLAUCON: I do.

SOCRATES: Consider any such group of many things. For example, there are many things we call beds and many tables.

GLAUCON: Yes, there are.

SOCRATES: And these have ideals corresponding to them. Two, in fact: one of the bed and one of the table.[3]

To these ideals Plato gave the name *forms*. He came eventually to hold that a separate form exists

---

[1] Plato, *The Republic*, from bk. 6. This translation copyright © 1987 by Manuel Velasquez.

[2] Ibid.
[3] Ibid., from bk. 10.

for each kind of thing. For example, for things that are good, there is the form of goodness; for things that are human, there is the form of humanness; for things that are triangular, there is the form of triangle. The form of a certain class of objects consists of those characteristics that make those objects the kind of objects they are. For example, the form of horse consists of those characteristics that make each horse a horse.

The visible objects in our world never perfectly embody their forms: Visible objects are only imperfect and changing reflections of the invisible, perfect, and unchanging forms. For example, each of the many horses in our world is an imperfect duplicate or copy of the one perfect form of horse, just as each human is a replica of the one perfect form of human being.

To a large extent, Plato's theory of forms was inspired by the questioning of his teacher Socrates. Socrates, you may recall, would often ask his hearers for the characteristic that makes a thing what it is. For example, in the dialogue *Euthyphro* Socrates says, "I was not asking you to give me *examples* of holiness, Euthyphro, but to identify the characteristic that makes all holy things holy. There must be some characteristic that all holy things have in common, and one which makes unholy things unholy. Tell me what this characteristic itself is." In a similar manner, Socrates searched for the characteristic that makes a thing just and the characteristic that makes a thing beautiful. Plato believed that his forms were the characteristics for which Socrates had been searching, since the form of a thing is what makes it what it is. Thus, Plato felt that in discovering the forms he had discovered the objects for which Socrates had searched all his life.

All sciences, Plato said, must be based on these ideals we know with our minds and not on their visible, changing, and imperfect replicas. As geometry is about ideal figures and morality is about ideal goodness, so also each science is about the ideal forms that pertain to a certain class of things. For example, the science of medicine is based on the doctor's knowledge of the ideally perfect human body. Because visible objects are continually changing and imperfect, they cannot be what a science studies, for science, like geometry, tries to state laws and truths that are exact and do not change from moment to moment.

However, Plato's discovery that the mind knows perfect ideals that are not found in the visible world created a problem. Since they do not exist in the visible world, are those perfect ideals merely arbitrary creations of the mind? Are they mental figments that have no reality outside the mind? Plato saw that if the ideals that make up geometry, morality, and the sciences had no reality, then all of these sciences would be worthless, because they would be about unreal objects.

Plato had a passionate faith that our scientific and moral knowledge is concerned with reality, so he drew the only conclusion possible: The perfect ideals with which geometry, morality, and the sciences are concerned must be real. That is, these perfect ideals, or forms, really exist outside the mind. Since they do not exist in the visible world, they must exist in a world that is not visible to us. Plato concluded that there are two real worlds: the nonvisible world of unchanging perfect forms and the visible world that contains their many changing replicas. In fact, Plato held, the forms are *more* real than their replicas, since somehow (Plato suggested that God was responsible) the forms are the basic models according to which their imperfect replicas are made. As he put it, "These ideals are like patterns that are fixed into the nature of things. Each of the many things is made in the image of its ideal and is a likeness to it. The many replicas share in the ideal insofar as they are made in its image."[4]

But how do we acquire our knowledge of the perfect ideals if they do not exist in the visible world? Plato's solution to this problem was ingenious. He argued that since we do not see the perfect ideals in our present world and since we obviously have knowledge of these ideals and investigate them in the sciences, we must have acquired this knowledge in a previous life. This shows, he held, that we have souls and that our souls must be immortal. Thus Plato's theory of forms directly

---

[4] Plato, *Parmenides*. This translation copyright © 1987 by Manuel Velasquez.

influenced his views on human nature, as Plato's own words, expressed by the character Socrates, reveal:

SOCRATES: Tell me, Simmias, do we think that there is such a thing as perfect justice?

SIMMIAS: We certainly do.

SOCRATES: And perfect beauty as well as perfect goodness?

SIMMIAS: Of course.

SOCRATES: Well, did you ever see these with your eyes?

SIMMIAS: Certainly not. . . .

SOCRATES: And do we say there is such a thing as perfect equality? I do not mean the imperfect equality of two lengths of wood or two stones, but something more than that: absolute equality.

SIMMIAS: We most certainly say there is. . . .

SOCRATES: But when did we come to think about perfect equality? Didn't we do so when we saw the imperfect equality of stones and pieces of wood and this brought to mind something else, namely perfect equality?

SIMMIAS: Certainly.

SOCRATES: Now when we see one thing and it brings to mind something else, that is what we call remembering, is it not?

SIMMIAS: Surely. . . .

SOCRATES: Do we agree, then, that when someone sees something that he recognizes as an imperfect instance of some other thing he must have had previous knowledge of that other thing? . . .

SIMMIAS: We must agree. . . .

SOCRATES: Then we must have had a previous knowledge of perfect equality before we first saw the imperfect equality of physical objects and recognized it fell short of perfect equality. . . .

SIMMIAS: Yes.

SOCRATES: Then before we began to see or hear or use the other senses, we must somewhere have gained a knowledge of perfect equality. . . .

SIMMIAS: That follows necessarily from what we have said before, Socrates.

SOCRATES: And we saw and heard and had the other senses as soon as we were born?

SIMMIAS: Certainly.

SOCRATES: Then it appears that we must have acquired our knowledge of perfect equality before we were born.

SIMMIAS: It does.

SOCRATES: Now if we acquired that knowledge before we were born, and . . . lost it at birth, but afterwards by the use of our senses regained the knowledge which we had previously possessed, would not the process which we call learning really be recovering knowledge which we had? And shouldn't we call this recollection?

SIMMIAS: Assuredly.

SOCRATES: Then, Simmias, the soul existed previously, before it was in a human body. It existed apart from the body and had knowledge. . . . If, as we say, perfect beauty and goodness and every ideal exists, and if we compare to these whatever objects we see, then it is a necessary inference that just as these ideals exist, so our souls existed before we were born. . . .

SIMMIAS: Yes, Socrates. You have convinced me that the soul existed before birth. . . . But perhaps Cebes here still has doubts. . . .

SOCRATES: Well, these ideals of Forms, which are true reality, are they always the same? Consider perfect equality or perfect beauty or any other ideal. Does each of these always remain the same perfect form, unchanging and not varying from moment to moment?

CEBES: They always have to be the same, Socrates.

SOCRATES: And what about the many individual objects around us—people or horses or dresses or what have you—which we say are equal to each other or are beautiful? Do these always remain the same or are they changing constantly and becoming something else?

CEBES: They are continually changing, Socrates.

SOCRATES: These changing objects can be seen and touched and perceived with the senses. But the unchanging Forms can be known only with the mind and are not visible to the senses. . . . So there are two kinds of existing things: those which are visible and those which are not. . . . The visible are changing and the invisible are unchanging.

CEBES: That seems to be the case. . . .

SOCRATES: Now which of these two kinds of things is our body like?

CEBES: Clearly it is like visible things. . . .

SOCRATES: And what do we say of the soul? Is it visible or not?

CEBES: It is not visible.

SOCRATES: Then the soul is more like the invisible and the body like the visible?

CEBES: That is most certain, Socrates.

SOCRATES: Recall that we said long ago that when the soul relies on its bodily senses—like sight or hearing or the other senses—it is dragged by the body toward what is always changing. Then the soul goes astray and is confused as it staggers around drunkenly among these changing things.

CEBES: Very true.

SOCRATES: But when the soul turns within and reflects upon what lies in herself [knowledge of the Forms], she finds there the perfect, eternal, immortal, and unchanging realm that is most like herself. She would stay there forever if it were possible, resting from her confused wanderings. So long as she continues to reflect upon the unchanging [Forms], she herself is unchanging and has what we call wisdom.

CEBES: That is well and truly said, Socrates.

SOCRATES: So which kind of thing is the soul most like?

CEBES: The soul is infinitely more like what is unchanging. . . .

SOCRATES: And the body is more like the changing?

CEBES: Yes.

SOCRATES: One more thing: When soul and body are united, it is the nature of the soul to rule and govern and of the body to obey and serve. Which of these two functions is like god and which is like a mortal? Is it not true that what rules is like god and what is ruled is like a mortal?

CEBES: True. . . .

SOCRATES: Then, Cebes, does it not follow that the soul is most akin to what is divine, immortal, intellectual, perfect, indissoluble, and unchanging, while the body is most like what is mortal, unintellectual, indissoluble, and ever changing?

CEBES: That cannot be denied.[5]

Plato's view of human nature, then, is a direct consequence of his theory of forms. Because we know the forms, it follows that we have souls and that our souls existed apart from our bodies before we were born into this world. Whereas our bodies are visible, changing, and subject to decay, our souls are like the forms and so they are invisible, eternal, immortal, and godlike.

Having come to the conclusion that our souls—our inner selves—existed before we were born and will continue to exist after our deaths, Plato felt that it is imperative to care for our souls. He held that the soul consists of three parts that sometimes struggle against each other:

SOCRATES: But does our soul contain . . . three elements or not? . . . Do we gain knowledge with one part, feel anger with another, and with yet a third desire food, sex, drink, and so on? This is a difficult question.

GLAUCON: I quite agree.

SOCRATES: Let us approach the question in this way. It is clear that the same parts of a single thing cannot move in two opposing directions. So if we find that these three elements oppose each other, we shall know that they are distinct parts of ourselves.

GLAUCON: Very well. . . .

SOCRATES: Now consider a thirsty man. Insofar as he is thirsty, his soul craves drink and seeks it.

GLAUCON: That is clear. . . .

SOCRATES: Yet isn't it sometimes true that the thirsty person [who wants to drink] also, for some reason, may *not* want to drink?

---

[5]Plato, *Phaedo*. This edited translation copyright © 1987 by Manuel Velasquez.

GLAUCON: Yes, often.

SOCRATES: In his soul there is a part that desires drink and another part that restrains him. This latter part then is distinct from desire and usually can control desire. . . . Doesn't such control originate in reason, while the urge to drink originates in something else? . . .

GLAUCON: So it seems.

SOCRATES: Then we can conclude that there are in us two distinct parts. One is what we call "reason," and the other we call the nonrational "appetites." The latter hungers, thirsts, desires sex, and is subject to other desires. . . .

GLAUCON: Yes, that is the logical conclusion.

SOCRATES: So there are at least two distinct elements in us. But what about our emotional or spirited part: the part in us that feels anger and indignation?

GLAUCON: Perhaps we should say that it is part of our appetites.

SOCRATES: Maybe. But think about this story which I think is true. Leontius was walking up from Piraeus one day when he noticed the bodies of some executed criminals on the ground. Part of him was overcome with a desire to run over and look at the bodies, while another part felt angry at himself and tried to turn away. He struggled with himself and shut his eyes, but at last the desire was too much for him. Running up to the bodies, he opened his eyes wide and cried, "There, damn you! Feast yourselves on that lovely sight!"

GLAUCON: I'm familiar with that story.

SOCRATES: The point of the story is that anger sometimes opposes our appetites as if it is something distinct from them. And we often find that when our appetites oppose our reason, we become angry at our appetites. In the struggle between appetite and reason, our anger sides with reason. . . .

GLAUCON: That is true. . . .

SOCRATES: Yet this emotional part of ourselves is distinct from reason. The poet Homer, for example, . . . describes people whose reason inclines them to choose the better course, contrary to the impulses of anger.

GLAUCON: I entirely agree.

SOCRATES: So . . . the soul has three distinct parts.[6]

Plato thought that his discovery of the three-part soul provided us with the key to happiness and virtue. Personal happiness and virtue, Plato held, can be achieved only when the three parts of our soul are in harmony with one another and are properly subordinated to one another. Happiness is possible only if reason rules the emotions and desires and both the emotions and desires have been trained to be led harmoniously by reason.

We become unhappy when the three parts of ourselves are constantly fighting against one another so that we lack inner harmony, and we fall victim to vice when we are ruled by our emotions or desires:

SOCRATES: A man is just when . . . each part within him does what is proper for it to do. . . .

GLAUCON: Indeed.

SOCRATES: Isn't it proper for reason to rule since it can acquire knowledge and so can know how to care for the whole soul; and isn't it proper that the emotions should obey and support reason?

GLAUCON: Certainly. . . .

SOCRATES: When reason and the emotions have been trained and each has learned its proper function, they should stand guard over the appetites . . . lest the appetites grow so strong that they try to enslave and overthrow them.

GLAUCON: Very true. . . .

SOCRATES: In truth, justice is present in a man . . . when each part in him plays its proper role. The just man does not allow one part of his soul to usurp the function proper to another. Indeed, the just man is one who sets his house in order, by self-mastery and discipline coming to be at peace with himself, and bringing these three parts into tune like the tones in a musical scale. . . . Only when he has linked these parts together in well-tempered

[6]Plato, *Republic*. This translation copyright © 1987 by Manuel Velasquez.

harmony and has made himself one man instead of many will he be ready to go about whatever he may have to do, whether it be making money, satisfying his bodily needs, or engaging in affairs of state. . . .

GLAUCON: That is perfectly true, Socrates. . . .

SOCRATES: Next we must consider injustice. That must surely be a kind of war among the three elements, whereby they usurp and encroach upon one another's functions. . . . Such turmoil and aberration we shall, I think, identify with injustice, intemperance, cowardliness, or the other vices.

GLAUCON: Exactly. . . .

SOCRATES: Virtue, then, seems to be a kind of health and beauty and strength of the soul, while vice is like a kind of disease and ugliness and weakness in the soul.[7]

To train the emotions and appetites so that they will readily obey reason was crucial for Plato. He likened our emotions and appetites to two winged steeds that can either drag our reason downward into the confusions and illusions of the visible changing world or can help carry our reason upward to contemplate the world of unchanging perfect forms through the study of the sciences and the acquisition of wisdom. In a beautiful image Plato compared the three-part soul to a chariot, with the charioteer driving a white-winged horse and a black-winged horse:

> Let me speak briefly about the nature of the soul by using an image. And let the image have three parts: a pair of winged horses and a charioteer. . . . One of the horses is of a noble breed, the other ignoble and the charioteer controls them with great difficulty. . . . The vicious steed goes heavily, weighing down the charioteer to the earth when it has not been thoroughly trained. . . . Above them . . . in the heaven above heaven . . . there abides the true reality with which real knowledge is concerned: the Forms which are visible only to the mind and have no color, shape, or hardness. . . . It is the place of true knowledge . . . where every soul which is rightly nourished feeds upon pure knowledge, rejoicing at once again beholding true reality. . . . There souls can

behold perfect justice and temperance . . . not in things which change, but in themselves. The souls that are most like god are carried up there by their charioteer . . ., although troubled by their steeds and only with difficulty beholding true being. Other souls rise only to fall again, barely glimpsing it and then altogether failing to see because their two steeds are too unruly.[8]

As this passage suggests, Plato held that we can be completely virtuous only if our reason knows the forms. In particular, our reason must know the form of the good, since only by grasping what goodness is can we know what the three parts of the soul must do to be good. Thus, for Plato, complete virtue can be achieved only by coming to have knowledge of the form of the good, which exists unchanging in a world of forms separate from ours.

Plato held that the best ruler, the perfect king, would be a person—male or female—whose soul was self-disciplined enough to enable him or her to contemplate true being in the perfect forms. Such a person, Plato wrote, would be a true *philosopher*, which in Greek means "lover of wisdom":

SOCRATES: If a man believes there are many things which are beautiful but does not know beauty itself . . . is he awake or is his life nothing but a dream?

GLAUCON: I would say he is dreaming.

SOCRATES: And if a man knows beauty itself and can distinguish it from its many replicas, and does not confuse beautiful things with beauty itself . . . is he dreaming or awake?

GLAUCON: He is awake. . . .

SOCRATES: If people look at the many visible things which are beautiful, but do not know beauty itself, . . . and similarly see things which are just but do not know justice itself, then they merely have opinions and do not have real knowledge of these things. . . . While those who know the real unchanging [Forms] have true knowledge . . . and are philosophers. . . .

---

[7] Ibid.

[8] Plato, *Phaedrus*. This edited translation copyright © 1987 by Manuel Velasquez.

GLAUCON: By all means.

SOCRATES: Well, are those who have no knowledge of true being any better than blind men? They have no true models in their souls to illuminate things. They cannot fix their eyes on true reality nor can they refer to it when they lay down their laws regarding what is beautiful, just and good. . . . So should we make them rulers? Or should we establish as rulers those who know true reality and who are virtuous?

GLAUCON: Obviously the latter.[9]

Rulers, even more than ordinary citizens, then, must keep their minds fixed on the unchanging ideals or forms—especially the form of the good—and their emotions and appetites under the control of reason. Only in this way will they rule states in such a way that, like the virtuous individual, they will have harmony and happiness.

Plato's theory of forms, which he developed under the influence of Socrates' teaching, was the basis for his influential view of human nature. All future philosophers would struggle with Plato's problem: How can we account for the fact that our mind comprehends perfect ideals that this world only imperfectly duplicates? Many twentieth-century philosophers (such as Kurt Gödel, John McTaggart, Alfred North Whitehead, and Bertrand Russell) have agreed that only Plato's theory of forms can adequately account for our knowledge of certain ideals, especially mathematical ideals. And many philosophers who have rejected Plato's theory of forms have agreed, nevertheless, with Plato's claims concerning the soul and the body. Plato's philosophy remains very much alive today.

ARISTOTLE

Although Aristotle was a student of Plato, his approach to human nature was very different from Plato's. Son of a physician of a Macedonian king, Aristotle was born in 384 B.C. at Stagira in northern Greece. When he was seventeen, his father sent him to Athens to study in Plato's Academy,

the ancient equivalent of a modern-day university. There he found in Plato an inspiring teacher whom he later described as a man "whom bad men have not even the right to praise, and who showed in his life and teachings how to be happy and good at the same time." Aristotle stayed on as a teacher at the academy until Plato's death twenty years later. After leaving the academy, Aristotle was asked by King Philip II of Macedonia, the new conqueror of the Greeks, to tutor his young son, the future Alexander the Great. Three years later, when his pupil ascended the throne, Aristotle returned to Athens to set up his own school, the Lyceum. There he taught and wrote for twelve years until the death of Alexander, his protector, released a wave of pent-up anger the Greeks had long harbored toward their Macedonian conquerors and their friends. Under threat of death, Aristotle fled Athens and took refuge in a Macedonian fort, saying that he did not want the Athenians to "sin twice against philosophy" by killing him as they had killed Socrates. He died there one year later.

As a young man Aristotle seems to have been a close follower of Plato, but as he grew older, he came to have increasing doubts about Plato's views. Aristotle agreed that each class of things has certain essential characteristics—its form. But unlike Plato, Aristotle did not believe that forms exist in some separate world apart from the visible things around us. Instead, he held, the forms of visible things exist in the visible things themselves. How is this possible?

According to Aristotle, those characteristics that make a thing what it is and that all things of that kind have in common are the form of a thing. For example, the form of roundness consists of those characteristics that all round things have in common and that make a thing round. The form of a horse consists of those characteristics that all horses have in common and that make a thing a horse and not, say, a cow. Although we can distinguish *in our minds* between roundness and visible round things, this does not mean that, besides the visible round things around us, there also exists *in reality* a *separate* ideal object called roundness. Roundness exists only in round things, and horseness exists only in actual horses.

---

[9] Plato, *Republic*.

Aristotle: "In all our activities there is an end which we seek for its own sake, and everything else is a means to this end. . . . Happiness is [this] ultimate end. It is the end we seek in all that we do."

Once Aristotle realized that the world could be explained without a separate world of ideal forms, he began to develop a new view of reality that was much closer to common sense than Plato's. Aristotle explained the changing world by using his new concept of form together with three other kinds of causes: the material cause, or the stuff out of which things are made; the efficient cause, or the agent who brings about a change; and the final cause, or the purpose of the change.

Consider, for example, how a lump of marble can be changed into a statue of Socrates by a sculptor. If we ask *why* the marble changed as it did, we can give four kinds of explanations. First, we can explain why the marble statue came to have some of its characteristics by identifying its form, or *formal cause:* Because it has the form of a statue of Socrates, it came to be shaped like Socrates. Second, we can explain why the statue has other characteristics by identifying the matter out of which it

is made, or the *material cause:* Because it is made out of marble, it is hard and white. Third, we can explain why the marble changed as it did by identifying the agent who made the statue, or the *efficient cause:* Because the artist chiseled the marble, it gradually came to be shaped like Socrates. And fourth, we can explain why the statue came to be by identifying the purpose for which it was made, or the *final cause:* The artist made the statue because he was trying to please a patron. Thus, things can be explained completely in terms of their causes in this world without having to theorize forms from some other world, as Plato did.

Aristotle explained his four causes in these words:

Next we must examine explanations or "causes," and state clearly the number and kinds of explanations there are. For we are seeking knowledge of things and we know a thing only when we can explain why it is as it is. And we explain something by identifying its basic causes. So, obviously, if our aim is to know the changing and perishing objects of nature, we will have to know their basic causes and use them to explain things.

One kind of explanation [the material cause] is provided by identifying the material of which a thing is made and which remains present in the thing. For example, the bronze of which a statue is made or the silver of a bowl. . . .

A second kind of explanation [the formal cause] is provided by identifying the form or plan of a thing, that is, by stating the essential characteristics that define a thing. . . .

A third kind of explanation [the efficient cause] is provided by identifying the agent who produced or changed something. For example, an advisor is the efficient cause of the changes he advises, a father is the efficient cause of the children he produced, and generally whatever produces or changes anything is the efficient cause of what is produced or changed.

Finally, a kind of explanation [the final cause] is also provided when we give the end or purpose of a thing. For example, health can explain taking a walk, as when we ask, "Why is he taking a walk?" and reply, "For the sake of his health" and thereby feel that we have given an explanation.[10]

---

[10] Aristotle, *Physics*, bk. 2, ch. 3. This edited translation copyright © 1987 by Manuel Velasquez.

Aristotle held, then, that everything in the universe has a certain form, is made out of a certain matter, is produced by certain efficient causes, and is made to serve a certain purpose or function. The purpose of science is to explain the many things in the universe by identifying their four causes. Science should study the individual things in *this* world to identify their various causes, Aristotle held, instead of spending time thinking about an invisible world of forms.

Besides rejecting Plato's views on a separate world of unchanging forms, Aristotle also rejected his views on the soul. Plato had argued that the soul can exist apart from the body and that in an earlier existence it had acquired knowledge of the forms, which it remembered in this life. Aristotle thought that here, too, we must adhere to the four causes, which involve our experience in this world only. Therefore, he noted, to say that something has a soul is to say that it is alive. Consequently, the human soul is nothing more than those characteristics that distinguish a living human from a dead one. This means that the soul cannot exist apart from the body and cannot survive death.[11] The soul is merely the form of a living human— those essential characteristics that make each of us a living human being—and like other forms, it cannot exist apart from the visible things in this world:

> Let us leave behind, then, the theories of the soul that have come down to us from our predecessors and let us make a fresh start by trying to define what the soul is. . . .
>
> As I have said, the individual things in the world are composed in part of the matter [out of which they are made] . . . , and in part of a form which makes them be the kind of thing that they are. . . .
>
> The most common individual things are physical bodies, especially the natural physical bodies from which everything else is made. Now some physical bodies have life, and some do not. . . . Every natural physical body that has life is an individual thing and

so it, too, must be composed of matter and form. . . . Now a physical body itself, when it has life, cannot be a soul. For the body is what *has* attributes [such as life or soul] and is not itself an attribute. The body is rather the matter [of which the living being is made]. The soul, therefore, must be the form of a physical body that has the power of living. . . .

It is pointless, therefore, to ask whether the body and the soul are identical, as to ask whether the wax and its shape are identical, or, in general, to ask whether the matter of a thing is identical with its form. . . .

So we now have the definition of the soul. The soul is the form or the essential characteristics of a body that has the power of living. . . . Clearly, then, the soul is not separable from the body.[12]

But if the soul does not preexist (as Plato had suggested), how then do we come to have knowledge of the forms of things? Aristotle's answer to this question was straightforward. We know the forms of things—their essential characteristics— because through repeated experience, our minds come to know the essential characteristics of physical things and can consider them apart from these physical things. For example, after seeing many round things, we become capable of thinking about the characteristic of roundness itself, and after studying many horses, we become capable of thinking about horseness. In this way our minds are able to abstract or mentally separate the form of a thing from the thing itself. Through this process of abstraction, the mind forms the ideal concepts with which the sciences deal. For instance, by considering many imperfect circles, lines, and squares, we abstract the idea of the perfect circle, the perfect line, and the perfect square and reason about these in the science of geometry. The sciences deal with these ideal essences of things. Thus, Aristotle concluded, although the sciences deal with ideal forms, this does not require us to posit a separate world where these ideal forms exist. The forms of things are real enough because the real objects in our visible world embody these forms. And the sciences

---

[11] However, Aristotle may have thought that *part* of the soul— what he called the active intellect—survived death. In some passages he seems to hint at this, but scholars still debate his meaning.

[12] Aristotle, *De Anima*, bk. 2, ch. 1. This edited translation copyright © 1987 by Manuel Velasquez.

deal with these forms when our minds abstract them and consider them as ideals separate from the visible objects in our world. But although we *think* of them as separate, they do not *exist* as separate.

Aristotle also departed from Plato's views on happiness and virtue. Plato held that we could achieve full happiness and virtue only by coming to know the perfect forms that exist in another world. Aristotle rejected this view and held, instead, that happiness and goodness had to be found in *this* world: "Even if there were a perfect Good that existed apart from the many things in our world which are good, it is evident that this good would not be anything that we humans can realize or attain. But it is an attainable good that we are now seeking."[13]

To discover what kind of goodness is attainable in this life, Aristotle examined the various pursuits and activities in which we actually engage. In doing this, he was following the method required by his theory of the four causes: Everything is to be explained in terms of its cause in *this* world. Aristotle began by pointing out that when we do something, we are usually trying to achieve some other aim or good. Our "highest good" or "highest end," then, would be whatever we are ultimately seeking in everything we do:

> Every art and every inquiry, and likewise every activity, seems to aim at some good. This is why the good is defined as that at which everything aims.
>
> But sometimes the end at which we are aiming is the activity itself while other times the end is something else that we are trying to achieve by means of that activity. When we are aiming at some end to which the activity is a means, the end is clearly a higher good than the activity. . . .
>
> Now if in all our activities there is some end which we seek for its own sake, and if everything else is a means to this same end, it obviously will be our highest and best end. Clearly there must be some such end since everything cannot be a means to something else since then there would be nothing for which we ultimately do anything and everything would be pointless. Surely from a practical point of

view it is important for us to know what this ultimate end is so that, like archers shooting at a definite mark, we will be more likely to attain what we are seeking [in all our actions].[14]

Since human beings are in continual search of something, it is obviously important for us to be clear about what this "something" is. This "something," of course, would be the "final cause" that explains *why* we humans do what we do. Aristotle tries to identify this "highest end," or "final cause," in the following passage, in which he remains true to his view that we must look for the causes of things by examining what happens in *this* world:

> Some people think our highest end is something material and obvious, like pleasure or money or fame. One thinks it is this, and another thinks it is that. Often the same person changes his mind: When he is sick, it is health; when he is poor, it is wealth. And realizing they are really ignorant, such men express great admiration for anyone who says deep-sounding things that are beyond their comprehension. . . .
>
> Most people think the highest end is pleasure and so they seek nothing higher than a life of pleasure. . . . They reveal their utter slavishness in this for they prefer [as their highest end] a life that is attainable by any animal. . . . Capable and practical men think the highest end is fame, which is the goal of a public life. But this is too superficial to be the good we are seeking since fame depends on those who give it. . . . Moreover, men who pursue fame do so in order to be assured of their own value. . . . Finally, some men devote their lives to making money in a way that is quite unnatural. But wealth clearly is not the good we are seeking since it is merely useful as a means to something else. . . . What, then, is our highest end?
>
> As we have seen, there are many ends. But some of them are chosen only as a means to other things, for example, wealth, musical instruments, and tools [are ends we choose only because they are means to other things]. So it is clear that not all ends are ultimate ends. But our highest and best end would have to be something ultimate. . . .
>
> Notice that an end that we desire for itself is more ultimate than something we want only as a means to

---

[13] Aristotle, *Nicomachean Ethics*, bk. 1, ch. 6. This translation by Manuel Velasquez.

[14] Ibid., bk. 1, chs. 1–2.

something else. And an end that is never a means to something else is more ultimate than an end that is sometimes a means. And the most ultimate end would be something that we always choose for itself and never as a means to something else.

Now happiness seems more than anything else to answer to this description. For happiness is something we always choose for its own sake and never as a means to something else. But fame, pleasure, . . . and so on, are chosen partly for themselves but partly also as a means to happiness, since we believe that they will bring us happiness. Only happiness, then, is never chosen for the sake of these things or as a means to any other thing.

We will be led to the same conclusion if we start from the fact that our ultimate end would have to be completely sufficient by itself. . . . By this I mean that by itself it must make life worth living and lacking in nothing. But happiness by itself answers this description. It is what we most desire even apart from all other things. . . .

So, it appears that happiness is the ultimate end and completely sufficient by itself. It is the end we seek in all that we do.[15]

Having concluded that in everything we do we are seeking happiness, Aristotle then turned to this question: What must we do to achieve happiness? Plato had said that we will be happy only if we achieve knowledge of those forms that exist in another world. Aristotle rejected this suggestion. Human happiness must be achievable in this life, through our activities in this world. Aristotle felt that before we can discover the path to happiness, we must first know what the specific purpose of humanity is: What is it that human nature is meant to do and that nothing else can do? Here is Aristotle's answer:

The reader may think that in saying that happiness is our ultimate end we are merely stating a platitude. So we must be more precise about what happiness involves.

Perhaps the best approach is to ask what the specific purpose or function of man is. For the good and the excellence of all beings that have a purpose— such as musicians, sculptors, or craftsmen—depend on their purpose. So if man has a purpose, his good will be related to this purpose. And how could man not have a natural purpose when even cobblers and carpenters have a purpose? Surely, just as each part of man—the eye, the hand, the foot—has a purpose, so also man as a whole must have a purpose. What is this purpose?

Our biological activities we share in common even with plants. So these cannot be the purpose or function of man since we are looking for something specific to man. The activities of our senses we also plainly share with other things: horses, cattle, and other animals. So there remain only the activities that belong to the rational part of man. . . . So the specific purpose or function of man involves the activities of that part of his soul that belongs to reason, or that at least is obedient to reason. . . .

Now the function of a thing is basic, and its good is something added to this function. For example, the function of a musician is to play music, and the good musician is one who also plays music but who in addition does it well. So, the good for man would have to be something added to his function of carrying on the activities of reason; it would be carrying on the activities of reason but doing so well or with excellence. But a thing carries out its proper functions well when it has the proper virtues. So the good for man is carrying out those activities of his soul [which belong to reason] and doing so with the proper virtue or excellence.[16]

Human happiness, then, is to be found by doing well what humans are best able to do: live their lives with reason. And to do something well is to act with virtue. So human happiness is achieved by acquiring the virtues that will enable us to use our reason well in living our lives. But what is human virtue? What does it mean to have the "virtue" of using our reason well in living our lives? Aristotle replies that human virtue requires learning to achieve "the mean" in our feelings and actions, learning to avoid both excess and deficiency. We have virtue when our reason knows what the mean is and when we live according to this knowledge:

Since our happiness, then, is to be found in carrying out the activities of the soul [that belong to reason],

---

[15] Ibid., bk. 1, chs. 4–5, 7.

[16] Ibid., bk. 1, ch. 7.

and doing so with virtue or excellence, we will now have to inquire into virtue, for this will help us in our inquiry into happiness. . . .

To have virtue or excellence, a thing (1) must be good and (2) must be able to carry out its function well. For example, if the eye has virtue, then it must be a good eye and must be able to see well. Similarly, if a horse has its virtue, then it must be all that it should be and must be good at running, carrying a rider, and charging. Consequently, the proper virtue or excellence of man will consist of those habits or acquired abilities that (1) make him a good man and (2) enable him to carry out his activities well. . . .

Now the expert in any field is the one who avoids what is excessive as well as what is deficient. Instead he seeks to hit the mean and chooses it. . . . Acting well in every field is achieved by looking to the mean and bringing one's actions into line with this standard of moderation. For example, people say of a good work of art that nothing could be taken from it or added to it, implying that excellence is destroyed through excess or deficiency but achieved by observing the mean. The good artist, in fact, keeps his eyes fixed on the mean in everything he does. . . .

Virtue, therefore, must also aim at the mean. For human virtue deals with our feelings and actions, and in these we can go to excess or we fall short or we can hit the mean. For example, it is possible to feel fear, confidence, desire, anger, pity, pleasure, . . . and so on, either too much or too little — both of which extremes are bad. But to feel these at the right times, and on the right occasions, and towards the right persons, and with the right object, and in the right fashion, is the mean between the extremes and is the best state, and is the mark of virtue. In the same way, our actions can also be excessive or can fall short or can hit the mean.

Virtue, then, deals with those feelings and actions in which it is wrong to go too far and wrong to fall short but in which hitting the mean is praiseworthy and good. . . . It is a habit or acquired ability to choose . . . what is moderate or what hits the mean as determined by reason.[17]

The path to human happiness, then, is by living according to the moderation that our reason discovers. By using our reason, Aristotle is saying, we can know what it means not to go to excess in our feelings and actions. To the extent that we live according to his knowledge, we have virtue and will be happy in this world. Aristotle provides several specific examples of what virtue is:

> But it is not enough to speak in generalities. We must apply this to particular virtues and vices. Consider, then, the following examples.
>
> Take the feelings of fear and confidence. To be able to hit the mean [by having just enough fear and just enough confidence] is to have the virtue of courage. . . . But he who exceeds in confidence has the vice of rashness, while he who has too much fear and not enough confidence has the vice of cowardliness.
>
> The mean where pleasure . . . is concerned is achieved by the virtue of temperance. But to go to excess is to have the vice of profligacy, while to fall short is to have the vice of insensitivity. . . .
>
> Or take the action of giving or receiving money. Here the mean is the virtue of generosity. . . . But the man who gives to excess and is deficient in receiving has the vice of prodigality, while the man who is deficient in giving and excessive in taking has the vice of stinginess. . . .
>
> Or take one's feelings about the opinion of others. Here the mean is the virtue of proper self-respect, while the excess is the vice of vanity, and the deficiency is the vice of small-mindedness. . . .
>
> The feeling of anger can also be excessive, deficient, or moderate. The man who occupies the middle state is said to have the virtue of gentleness, while the one who exceeds in anger has the vice of irascibility, while the one who is deficient in anger has the vice of apathy.[18]

Our human nature, then, is capable of achieving happiness in this world. Although we do not have an immortal soul as Plato argued, nevertheless we do have reason and can use our reason to control our feelings and actions. To live according to reason by being moderate in our feelings and actions is to acquire human virtue. And this kind of virtue will produce the happiness that our human nature seeks in everything we do.

Thus, although Aristotle's views of human nature grew from the views of his teacher Plato (much as Plato's views grew from those of his teacher Socrates), Aristotle's final theories were quite different

---

[17] Ibid., bk. 1, ch. 13; bk. 2, ch. 6.

[18] Ibid., bk. 2, ch. 7.

from Plato's (as different as Plato's were from Socrates'). Where Plato looked to another world of unchanging forms to explain human nature, Aristotle looked for the "four causes" of things completely within this world. As a result, Aristotle looked only to this world to explain how our human nature can achieve knowledge and happiness. Where Plato said that human knowledge was acquired in some earlier life when the soul existed without the body, Aristotle held that we acquire all our knowledge in this life and that the soul cannot exist apart from the body. And where Plato believed that happiness is acquired by coming to know the forms that exist in another world, Aristotle held that happiness is acquired by being moderate in our feelings and actions in this world.

CONFUCIUS

About a century before Plato and Aristotle set the path for Western philosophy by their reasoned inquiries into the nature of reality and the soul, a very different approach to philosophy was being developed in China. Confucius, who was destined to become the most influential thinker in the history of China, fashioned a philosophy the method and concerns of which were quite unlike those of Plato and Aristotle.

Confucius was born about 551 B.C. and died about 479 B.C. China at the time was a feudal nation ruled by the Chou dynasty and characterized by war, violence, intrigue, and a general breakdown of morality. The Chou kings were often mere puppets of whatever group of feudal lords managed to take power through force or trickery. Political upheavals, poverty, strife, suffering, and the constant threat of death were the order of the day. Confucius emerged in this context as a reformer who believed that the problems of China derived from the immorality of its rulers and its citizens. Throughout his life he argued that China would emerge from its crisis only when both rulers and subjects lived up to the highest standards of moral integrity.

Although a member of the nobility, Confucius lost his father when he was three and grew up in poverty, learning firsthand about the hardships to which the ordinary people of China were being subjected. Self-educated, Confucius entered government service in his early twenties, where he gained some experience in practical politics and a keen interest in contributing something to his afflicted society. The central question he soon set himself was this: How can the happiness of society be achieved? His answer was simple: through widespread adherence to humanistic principles of morality.

Confucius's views are expressed in his main work, *The Analects*, a collection of sayings recorded by his disciples and students. Although it is unclear to what extent *The Analects* are exact renditions of the words of Confucius, they have for centuries been accepted as more or less faithful expressions of his key ideas.

Unlike the lengthy reasonings that became characteristic of Western philosophy in general and of Plato and Aristotle in particular, the method of philosophizing that Confucius used was epigrammatic. *The Analects*, in fact, contains virtually no passages of lengthy, sustained reasoning. Instead, it sets forth pithy sayings that summarize Confucius's views in a highly compressed and intuitive manner.

The philosophy of Confucius in *The Analects* also contrasts starkly with that of Plato and Aristotle in the issues it discusses. Plato and Aristotle were keenly interested in metaphysical issues, including, for example, questions relating to the nature of the gods, the immortality of the soul, and the nature of humankind. However, Confucius counseled his followers to turn away from such inquiries. For Confucius, the only significant questions related to how one ought to behave. *The Analects* recounts the following sayings of Confucius:

2:16—The Master said, "The study of strange doctrines is injurious indeed!"
5:12—Tsze-kung said, "The Master's personal displays of his principles and ordinary descriptions of them may be heard. His discourses about man's nature and the way of Heaven cannot be heard."
6:20—Fan Ch'ih asked what constituted wisdom. The Master said, "To give one's self earnestly to the duties due to men, and, while respecting spiritual beings, to keep aloof from them, may be called wisdom."

Confucius: "To subdue one's self and return to propriety, is perfect virtue.... The superior man does not, even for the space of a single meal, act contrary to virtue."

11:11—Chi Lu asked about serving the spirits of the dead. The Master said, "While you are not able to serve men, how can you serve their spirits?" Chi Lu added, "I venture to ask about death?" He was answered, "While you do not know life, how can you know about death?"[19]

Confucius's philosophy, then, turned away from supernatural matters and focused entirely on ethics and humanity. His philosophy, in fact, is often characterized as an "ethical humanism." That is, his ethics is not based on religion but on human nature. This basic idea is the unifying principle behind all his philosophy:

4:15—The Master said, "Shan, my doctrine is that of an all-pervading unity." The disciple Tsang replied, "Yes."

The Master went out, and the other disciples asked, saying, "What do his words mean?" Tsang said, "The doctrine of our master is to be true to the principles of our nature and the benevolent exercise of them to others,—this and nothing more."[20]

What are these "principles of our nature"? Confucius insisted that to develop our human nature, we must develop *jen*, or virtue. By virtue, Confucius meant those uniquely human qualities of benevolence and humanity that form the foundation for all human relationships. This sense of love for humanity is, Confucius claimed, the basis of all morality and the quality that distinguishes humans from animals. Without it, life is not worth living. Virtue, according to Confucius, should be our ultimate value, and we should forsake even riches or honor rather than act contrary to virtue:

4:5—The Master said, "Riches and honors are what men desire. If they cannot be obtained in the proper way, they should not be held. Poverty and meanness are what men dislike. If they cannot be obtained in the proper way, they should not be avoided.

"The superior man does not, even for the space of a single meal, act contrary to virtue. In moments of haste, he cleaves to it. In seasons of danger, he cleaves to it."[21]

But what, exactly, is virtue? For Confucius the heart of virtue is reciprocity: the firm resolve to treat others as you would like others to treat you:

12:2—Chung-kung asked about perfect virtue. The Master said, "It is, when you go abroad, to behave to everyone as if you were receiving a great guest; to employ the people as if you were assisting at a great sacrifice; not to do to others as you would not wish done to yourself; to have no murmuring against you in the country and none in the family." Chung-kung said, "Though I am deficient in intelligence and vigor, I will make it my business to practice this lesson."

15:23—Tsze-kung asked, saying, "Is there one word which may serve as a rule of practice for all one's life?" The Master said, "Is not RECIPROCITY such

[19] From Confucius, *The Analects*, in *The Chinese Classics*, vol. 1, ed. and trans. James Legge (Oxford: Clarendon, 1893), reprinted in Daniel Bonevac, William Boon, and Stephen Phillips, *Beyond the Western Tradition* (Mountain View, CA: Mayfield, 1992), 256, 257, 259. The numbers preceding the excerpts refer to the numbering of the paragraphs in the Oxford edition.

[20] Ibid., 257.
[21] Ibid., 256.

a word? What you do not want done to yourself, do not do to others."[22]

Such virtue, Confucius held, is the key to inner peace and tranquillity. It is also the basis of true feelings toward others and the source of right behavior:

> 4:2 — The Master said, "Those who are without virtue cannot abide long either in a condition of poverty and hardship, or in a condition of enjoyment. The virtuous rest in virtue; the wise desire virtue."
> 4:3 — The Master said, "It is only the truly virtuous man who can love or who can hate others."
> 4:4 — The Master said, "If the will be set on virtue, there will be no practice of wickedness."[23]

Achieving virtue is not an easy matter. Virtue requires self-restraint in the use of one's senses and in one's conduct. It requires that we channel our selfish impulses into civilized behavior. Such self-control, Confucius warned, is something that each individual must achieve for himself or herself; it is not something that others can do for one:

> 1:14 — The Master said, "He who aims to be a man of complete virtue in his food does not seek to gratify his appetite, nor in his dwelling place does he seek the appliances of ease."
> 12:1 — Yen Yuan asked about perfect virtue. The Master said, "To subdue one's self and return to propriety, is perfect virtue. If a man can for one day subdue himself and return to propriety, all under heaven will ascribe perfect virtue to him. Is the practice of perfect virtue then from a man himself or is it from others?"
> Yen Yuan said, "I beg to ask the steps of that process." The Master replied, "Look not at what is contrary to propriety; listen not to what is contrary to propriety; speak not what is contrary to propriety; make no movement which is contrary to propriety." Yen Yuan then said, "Though I am deficient in intelligence and vigor, I will make it my business to practice this lesson."[24]

Although reciprocity in general should guide our actions, we need to know just what reciprocity requires in specific circumstances. Confucius held that *li*, the "rules of propriety" or the moral customs of one's society, provide this specific and concrete guidance. Reciprocity is attained, then, by restraining oneself in accordance with the moral customs of one's society, which spell out the proper behavior for specific situations:

> 2:5 — The Master said, "Mang-sun asked me what filial piety was, and I answered him, 'Not being disobedient.'"
> Fan Ch'ih said, "What did you mean?" The Master replied, "That parents, when alive, should be served according to propriety; that, when dead, they should be buried according to propriety; and that they should be sacrificed to according to propriety."
> 6:25 — The Master said, "The superior man, extensively studying all learning and keeping himself under the restraint of the rules of propriety, may thus likewise not overstep what is right."[25]

Confucius held that virtue should serve not only as the basis of personal behavior but also as the foundation of political authority. If the ruler exercised virtue, Confucius claimed, then citizens would eagerly follow his leadership. Moreover, if the ruler appointed virtuous ministers, social unrest would end. Thus, virtue is the foundation of a well-ordered society and the key to peace within the state:

> 2:1 — The Master said, "He who exercises government by means of his virtue may be compared to the north polar star, which keeps its place and all the stars turn towards it."
> 2:19 — The duke Ai asked, saying, "What should be done in order to secure the submission of the people?" Confucius replied, "Advance the upright and set aside the crooked, then the people will submit. Advance the crooked and set aside the upright, then the people will not submit."[26]

Confucius also believed that one of the functions of the ruler was to help make people virtuous. Government is not established merely to keep the peace nor to raise taxes and fund public enterprises. The virtue of the ruler, Confucius held, affects the

---

[22] Ibid., 259.
[23] Ibid., 256.
[24] Ibid., 255, 259.

[25] Ibid., 255, 258.
[26] Ibid., 255, 256.

virtue of his subjects. For example, the ruler who attempted to instill order through laws and punishments would find that his subjects would be dependent upon external motivations and would not become virtuous. But the ruler who attempted to rule by setting a virtuous example and by enacting laws that were consistent with the rules of propriety would find that his subjects would be motivated by their own internal desire to do what is right and would in time become virtuous:

> 2:3—The Master said, "If the people be led by laws, and uniformity sought to be given them by punishments, they will try to avoid the punishment, but have no sense of shame.
>
> "If they be led by virtue, and uniformity sought to be given them by the rules of propriety, they will have the sense of shame, and moreover will become good."
>
> 12:17—Chi K'ang asked Confucius about government. Confucius replied, "To govern means to rectify. If you lead on the people with correctness, who will dare not to be correct?"
>
> 13:6—The Master said, "When a prince's personal conduct is correct, his government is effective without the issuing of orders. If his personal conduct is not correct, he may issue orders, but they will not be followed."
>
> 13:13—The Master said, "If a minister make his own conduct correct, what difficulty will he have in assisting in government? If he cannot rectify himself, what has he to do with rectifying others?"[27]

Thus, for Confucius the key to overcoming the political strife and unrest that had held China in their grip for so many centuries was personal virtue. Virtue should not only be the primary concern of the individual; it should also be the basic concern of the ruler. When rulers and citizens behave virtuously in all their social relationships, political strife will end. These ideas are succinctly stated in *The Great Learning*, another work attributed to Confucius:

> 3. Things have their root and their branches. Affairs have their end and their beginning. To know what is first and what is last will lead near to what is taught in the Great Learning.
>
> 4. The ancients who wished to illustrate illustrious virtue throughout the kingdom, first ordered well their own states. Wishing to order well their states, they first regulated their families. Wishing to regulate their families, they first cultivated their persons. Wishing to cultivate their persons, they first rectified their hearts. Wishing to rectify their hearts, they first sought to be sincere in their thoughts. Wishing to be sincere in their thoughts, they first extended to the utmost their knowledge. Such extension of knowledge lay in the investigation of things.
>
> 5. Things being investigated, knowledge became complete. Their knowledge being complete, their thoughts were sincere. Their thoughts being sincere, their hearts were then rectified. Their hearts being rectified, their persons were cultivated. Their persons being cultivated, their families were regulated. Their families being regulated, their states were rightly governed. Their states being rightly governed, the whole kingdom was made tranquil and happy.
>
> 6. From the Son of Heaven [the ruler] down to the mass of the people, all must consider the cultivation of the person the root of everything besides.[28]

Confucius devoted his life to living and propagating these views. He spent numerous years traveling through China, teaching his views to more than three thousand disciples and students. Although during his lifetime most political rulers were uninterested in his views, his teachings eventually became part of the official philosophy of China.

QUESTIONS

1. Why is Plato's philosophy sometimes said to be poetic? Is this a good or bad quality for philosophy?

2. Mathematicians often make statements such as "There exist two primes between x and y." What kind of existence are they talking about? How does Plato explain this kind of existence?

---

[27] Ibid., 255, 259, 260.

[28] From Confucius, *The Great Learning,* in *The Chinese Classics,* vol. 1, ed. and trans. James Legge (Oxford: Clarendon, 1893), reprinted in Daniel Bonevac, William Boon, and Stephen Phillips, *Beyond the Western Tradition* (Mountain View, CA: Mayfield, 1992), 263.

3. What is the source of the ideas we have about ideals that are not encountered in our physical world (such as beauty, justice, goodness)?

4. "If each person derived her ideas of mathematics by generalizing from her personal experience, then the laws of mathematics would differ from person to person: for one person, 2 plus 2 would equal 4, and for another, it would not. If mathematical ideas were constructed by society, then the laws of mathematics would differ from society to society: In America, 2 plus 2 would equal 4, but in other societies, it might not. The fact that the laws of mathematics must be the same for every person and every society proves that numbers and their laws exist independently of any person or society. And this shows that Plato was right." Evaluate this argument.

5. Compare Plato's theory of the soul to Freud's view that the human psyche contains three parts—an irrational id, a conscious ego, and an unconscious superego, each of which can be distinguished from the others by the psychological conflicts that arise among them.

6. Do you agree with Plato's view that appetite and emotion (at least anger) must be subject to reason? Why or why not?

7. Does Aristotle's theory of abstraction account for the knowledge we have of mathematical laws, which must be the same for all persons and all societies? (See question 4.) Does Plato or Aristotle best account for our knowledge of mathematics and our knowledge of ideals such as beauty, goodness, and justice?

8. Do you agree with Aristotle's view that all moral virtue is a mean between the extremes of excess and deficiency? What about the virtues of honesty and love?

9. Does Aristotle's theory imply that only a virtuous person can be happy? Do you agree that happiness without virtue is impossible? Explain.

10. Is there any difference between doing what is morally right and doing what will make one happy?

11. Compare how Aristotle and Confucius each deal with virtue. In what ways are they similar, and in what ways do they differ?

12. What is reciprocity for Confucius? What role does reciprocity play in his philosophy?

13. Do you agree with Confucius's view that government should make people good? Explain your answer.

2.8 Readings

Many people believe that the *Confessions*, from which the selections in our first reading are taken, is the greatest autobiography ever written. In it, Saint Augustine (354 A.D.–430 A.D.) describes his life—and by implication the life of every man and woman—as a tempestuous journey toward or away from God. He writes that his early years were spent in a journey indulging the pleasures lusted after by his bodily desires, pursuing a prideful supremacy over others, and satisfying a morbid curiosity, a journey that ultimately left his soul dissatisfied and miserable. At last, his soul found peace and freedom when he turned away from lust, curiosity, and pride and instead humbly turned to God by obeying the voice of a child. As you read Augustine's story, notice that he has a very definite idea of human nature. We humans are spirits who are enchained by the lower desires of our bodies, which keep us from God, in whom alone our spirits can find rest and true fulfillment. Clearly, this view of human nature has had a profound influence on our culture, on religion, and on the way many people today continue to think about sex and bodily desires. But is it true?

Philosopher C. E. M. Joad, in the reading that follows, supports Augustine's view that we are spirits distinct from our bodies. Joad argues that our mental abilities imply that we are in fact spirits—immaterial minds—who are distinct from our bodies. Joad does not think that this claim can be definitively proved. Yet he does think that there are a number of considerations that argue against the materialist view that the mind is a feature of a physical brain. In the tradition of Descartes, Joad believes that "mind is distinct from both body and brain." Joad argues, first, that the mind's ability to comprehend the meanings of written words indicates that the mind is not material because meaning is "immaterial and can be grasped . . . only by a mind." He next argues that the mind has an "active" ability to "synthesize" so that, for example, it can put sound sensations together into a coherent symphony. This indicates that the mind is an active, dynamic force and so is more than a physical organ. In the final reading, feminist philosopher Elizabeth Spelman argues that the mind/body distinction serves mainly to oppress and denigrate women and minorities. The view, she says, that "there are minds (or souls) and bodies," is almost always associated with the view that "woman is body," and man is mind, and that mind is supposed to rule over body. The mind/body distinction, therefore, should be rejected by feminists. As we set out on our philosophical journey, then, these readings ask us to think more deeply about who and what we are. Are we, as Augustine and Joad suggest, immaterial spirits or minds living in bodies that continually tempt us to desire what can only take us further from our true destiny? Or, as Spelman suggests, is this way of thinking about ourselves profoundly mistaken? Is the mind really distinct from the body? Should we reject the mind/body distinction as sexist in the way that Spelman argues? Or is the distinction both valid and useful?

SAINT AUGUSTINE

From *The Confessions*

FROM BOOK ONE

What have I to say to Thee, God, save that I know not where I came from, when I came into this life-in-death — or should I call it death-in-life? I do not know. I only know that the gifts Your mercy had provided sustained me from the first moment: not that I remember it but so I have heard from the parents of my flesh, the father from whom, and the mother in whom, You fashioned me in time.

Thus for my sustenance and my delight I had woman's milk: yet it was not my mother or my nurses who stored their breasts for me: it was Yourself, using them to give me the food of my infancy, according to Your ordinance and the riches set by You at every level of creation. . . .

From infancy I came to boyhood, or rather it came to me, taking the place of infancy. Yet infancy did not go: for where was it to go to? Simply it was no longer there. For now I was not an infant, without speech, but a boy, speaking. . . .

O God, my God, what emptiness and mockeries did I now experience: for it was impressed upon me as right and proper in a boy to obey those who taught me, that I might get on in the world and excel in the handling of words to gain honor among men and deceitful riches. I, poor wretch, could not see the use of the things I was sent to school to learn; but if I proved idle in learning, I was soundly beaten. For this procedure seemed wise to our ancestors: and many, passing the same way in days past, had built a sorrowful road by which we too must go, with multiplication of grief and toil upon the sons of Adam. . . .

From *The Confessions of St. Augustine*, trans. F. J. Sheed (Kansas City, MO: Sheed & Ward, 1943). Copyright 1943 by Sheed & Ward. Reprinted by permission. Selections taken from pages 6, 7, 10, 11, 12, 13, 27, 28, 41, 44, 45, 61, 62, 105, 112, 113, 114, 124, 125, 126, 157, 158, 170, 175, 176, 177, 178, 179, and 183.

Yet my parents seemed to be amused at the torments inflicted upon me as a boy by my masters, though I was no less afraid of my punishments or zealous in my prayers to You for deliverance. But in spite of my terrors I still did wrong, by writing or reading or studying less than my set tasks. It was not, Lord, that I lacked mind or memory, for You had given me as much of these as my age required; but the one thing I revelled in was play; and for this I was punished by men who after all were doing exactly the same things themselves. But the idling of men is called business; the idling of boys, though exactly like, is punished by those same men: and no one pities either boys or men. . . . And what difference was there between me and the master who flogged me? For if on some trifling point he had the worst of the argument with some fellow-master, he was more torn with angry vanity than I when I was beaten in a game of ball. . . .

But in this lay my sin: that I sought pleasure, supremacy, and truth not in God but in the beings He had created, myself and others. Thus I fell into sorrow and confusion and error. . . .

FROM BOOK TWO

I propose now to set down my past wickedness and the carnal corruptions of my soul, not for love of them but that I may love Thee, O my God. I do it for love of Thy love, passing again in the bitterness of remembrance over my most evil ways that Thou mayest thereby grow ever lovelier to me, O Loveliness that dost not deceive, Loveliness happy and abiding: and I collect my self out of that broken state in which my very being was torn asunder because I was turned away from Three, the One, and wasted myself upon the many.

Arrived now at adolescence I burned for all the satisfactions of hell, and I sank to the animal in a succession of dark lusts: *my beauty consumed away*, and I stank in Thine eyes, yet was pleasing in my own and anxious to please the eyes of men. . . .

My one delight was to love and to be loved. But in this I did not keep the measure of mind to mind, which is the luminous line of friendship; but from the muddy concupiscence of the flesh and the hot imagination of puberty mists steamed up to becloud and darken my heart so that I could not distinguish the white light of love from the fog of lust. Both love and lust boiled within me, and swept my youthful immaturity over the precipice of evil desires to leave me half drowned in a whirlpool of abominable sins. Your wrath had grown mighty against me and I knew it not. I had grown deaf from the clanking of the chain of my mortality, the punishment for the pride of my soul: and I departed further from You, and You left me to myself: and I was tossed about and wasted and poured out and boiling over in my fornications: and You were silent, O my late-won Joy. You were silent, and I, arrogant and depressed, weary and restless, wandered further and further from You into more and more sins which could bear no fruit save sorrows. . . .

Where then was I, and how far from the delights of Your house, in that sixteenth year of my life in this world, when the madness of lust—needing no licence from human shamelessness, receiving no licence from Your laws—took complete control of me, and I surrendered wholly to it?

FROM BOOK THREE

I came to Carthage, where a cauldron of illicit loves leapt and boiled about me. I was not yet in love, but I was in love with love, and from the very depth of my need hated myself for not more keenly feeling the need. I sought some object to love, since I was thus in love with loving; and I hated security and a life with no snares for my feet. For within I was hungry, all for the want of that spiritual food which is Thyself, my God; yet [though I was hungry for want of it] I did not hunger for it: I had no desire whatever for incorruptible food, not because I had it in abundance but the emptier I was, the more I hated the thought of it. Because of all this my soul was sick, and broke out in sores, whose itch I agonized to scratch with the rub of carnal things—carnal, yet if there were no soul in them, they would not be objects of love. My longing then was to love and to be loved, but most when I obtained the enjoyment of the body of the person who loved me.

Thus I polluted the stream of friendship with the filth of unclean desire and sullied its limpidity with the hell of lust. And vile and unclean as I was, so great was my vanity that I was bent upon passing for clean and courtly. And I did fall in love, simply from wanting to. O my God, my Mercy, with how much bitterness didst Thou in Thy goodness sprinkle the delights of that time! I was loved, and our love came to the bond of consummation: I wore my chains with bliss but with torment too, for I was scourged with the red hot rods of jealousy, with suspicions and fears and tempers and quarrels. . . .

Those of my occupations at that time which were held as reputable were directed towards the study of the law, in which I meant to excel—and the less honest I was, the more famous I should be. The very limit of human blindness is to glory in being blind. By this time I was a leader in the School of Rhetoric and I enjoyed this high station and was arrogant and swollen with importance: though You know, O Lord, that I was far quieter in my behaviour and had no share in the riotousness of the *eversores*—the Overturners—for this blackguardly diabolical name they wore as the very badge of sophistication. Yet I was much in their company and much ashamed of the sense of shame that kept me from being like them. I was with them and I did for the most part enjoy their companionship, though I abominated the acts that were their specialty—as when they made a butt of some hapless newcomer, assailing him with really cruel mockery for no reason whatever, save the malicious pleasure they got from it. . . .

With these men as companions of my immaturity, I was studying the books of eloquence; for in eloquence it was my ambition to shine, all from a damnable vaingloriousness and for the satisfaction of human vanity. Following the normal order of study I had come to a book of one Cicero, whose tongue practically everyone admires, though not his heart. That particular book is called *Hortensius* and contains an exhortation to philosophy. Quite definitely it changed the direction of my mind, altered my prayers to You, O Lord, and gave me a new purpose and ambition. Suddenly all the vanity I had hoped in I saw as worthless, and with an incredible intensity of desire I longed after immortal wisdom. I had begun that journey upwards by which I was to return to You. My father was now dead two years; I was eighteen and was receiving money from my mother for the continuance of my study of eloquence. . . .

FROM BOOK FOUR

Throughout that nine-year period, from my nineteenth year to my twenty-eighth, I was astray myself and led others astray, was deceived and deceived others in various forms of self-assertion, publicly by the teaching of what are called the liberal arts, privately under the false name of religion; in the one proud, in the other superstitious, in both vain. . . .

In those years I took one woman, not joined to me in lawful marriage, but one whom wandering lust and no particular judgement had brought my way. Yet I had but that one woman, and I was faithful to her. And with her I learnt by my own experience what a gulf there is between the restraint of the marriage-covenant entered into for the sake of children and the mere bargain of a lustful love, where if children come they come unwanted—though when they are born, they compel our love. . . .

FROM BOOK SIX

O God, my hope from my youth, where were You all this time, where had You gone? For was it not You who created me and distinguished me from the beasts of the field and made me wiser than the birds of the air? Yet I walked through dark and slippery places, and I went out of myself in the search for You and did not find the God of my heart. I had come into the depths of the sea and I had lost faith and all hope of discovering the truth. . . .

I was all hot for honours, money, marriage: and You made mock of my hotness. In my pursuit of these, I sufffered most bitter disappointments, but in this You were good to me since I was thus prevented from taking delight in anything not Yourself. Look now into my heart, Lord, by whose will I remember all this and confess it to You. Let my soul cleave to You now that You have freed it from the tenacious hold of death. At that time my soul was in misery, and You pricked the soreness of its wound, that leaving all things it might turn to You, who are over all and without whom all would return to nothing, that it might turn to You and be healed. I was in utter misery and there was one day especially on which You acted to bring home to me the realisation of my misery. I was preparing an oration in praise of the Emperor in which I was to utter any number of lies to win the applause of people who knew they were lies. My heart was much wrought upon by the shame of this and inflamed with the fever of the thoughts that consumed it. I was passing along a certain street in Milan when I noticed a beggar. He was jesting and laughing and I imagine more than a little drunk. I fell into gloom and spoke to the friends who were with me about the endless sorrows that our own insanity brings us: for here was I striving away, dragging the load of my unhappiness under the spurring of my desires, and making it worse by dragging it: and with all our striving, our one aim was to arrive at some sort of happiness without care: the beggar had reached the same goal before us, and we might quite well never reach it at all. The very thing that he had attained by means of a few pennies begged from passers-by—namely the pleasure of a temporary happiness—I was plotting for with so many a weary twist and turn.

Certainly his joy was no true joy; but the joy I sought in my ambition was emptier still. In any event he was cheerful and I worried, he had no cares and I nothing but cares. Now if anyone had asked me whether I would rather be cheerful or fearful, I would answer: "Cheerful": but if he had gone on to ask whether I would rather be like that beggar or as I actually was, I would certainly have chosen my own state though so troubled and anxious. Now this was surely absurd. It could not be for any true reason. I ought not to have preferred my own state rather than his merely because I was the more learned, since I got no joy from my learning, but sought only to please men by it—not even to teach them, only to please them. Therefore did You break my bones with the rod of Your discipline. . . .

Great effort was made to get me married. I proposed, the girl was promised me. My mother played a great part in the matter for she wanted to have me married and then cleansed with the saving waters of baptism, rejoicing to see me grow every day more fitted for baptism and feeling that her prayers and Your promises were to be fulfilled in my faith. . . . Still she pushed on with the matter of my marriage, and the girl was asked for. She was still two years short of the age for marriage but I liked her and agreed to wait. . . .

Meanwhile my sins were multiplied. She with whom I had lived so long was torn from my side as a hindrance to my forthcoming marriage. My heart which had held her very dear was broken and wounded and shed blood. She went back to Africa, swearing that she would never know another man, and left with me the natural son I had had of her. But I in my unhappiness could not, for all my manhood, imitate her resolve. I was unable to bear the delay of two years which must pass before I was to get the girl I had asked for in marriage. In fact it was not really marriage that I wanted. I was simply a slave to lust. So I took another woman, not of course as a wife; and thus my soul's disease was nourished and kept alive as vigorously as ever, indeed worse than ever, that it might reach the realm of matrimony in the company of its ancient habit. Nor was the wound healed that had been made by the cutting off of my former mistress. For there was first burning and bitter grief; and after that it festered, and as the pain grew duller it only grew more hopeless.

FROM BOOK EIGHT

But I was unhappy at the life I led in the world, and it was indeed a heavy burden, for the hope of honour and profit no longer inflamed my desire, as formerly, to help me bear so exacting a servitude. These things delighted me no longer in comparison with Your sweetness and the beauty of Your house which I loved. But what still held me tight bound was my need of woman. . . .

I in my great worthlessness—for it was greater thus early—had begged You for chastity, saying: "Grant me chastity and continence, but not yet." For I was afraid that You would hear my prayer too soon, and too soon would heal me from the dis-

ease of lust which I wanted satisfied rather than extinguished. . . .

Thus I was sick at heart and in torment, accusing myself with a new intensity of bitterness, twisting and turning in my chain in the hope that it might be utterly broken, for what held me was so small a thing! But it still held me. And You stood in the secret places of my soul, O Lord, in the harshness of Your mercy redoubling the scourges of fear and shame lest I should give way again and that small slight tie which remained should not be broken but should grow again to full strength and bind me closer even than before. For I kept saying within myself: "Let it be now, let it be now," and by the mere words I had begun to move towards the resolution. I almost made it, yet I did not quite make it. But I did not fall back into my original state, but as it were stood near to get my breath. And I tried again and I was almost there, and now I could all but touch it and hold it: yet I was not quite there, I did not touch it or hold it. I still shrank from dying unto death and living unto life. The lower condition which had grown habitual was more powerful than the better condition which I had not tried. The nearer the point of time came in which I was to become different, the more it struck me with horror; but it did not force me utterly back nor turn me utterly away, but held me there between the two.

Those trifles of all trifles, and vanities of vanities, my onetime mistresses, held me back, plucking at my garment of flesh and murmuring softly: "Are you sending us away?" And "From this moment shall we not be with you, now or forever?" And "From this moment shall this or that not be allowed you, now or forever?" . . . And now I began to hear them not half so loud; they no longer stood against me face to face, but were softly muttering behind my back and, as I tried to depart, plucking stealthily at me to make me look behind. Yet even that was enough, so hesitating was I, to keep me from snatching myself free, from shaking them off and leaping upwards on the way I was called: for the strong force of habit said to me: "Do you think you can live without them?"

But by this time its voice was growing fainter. In the direction towards which I had turned my face and was quivering in fear of going, I could see the austere beauty of Continence, serene and indeed joyous but not evilly, honourably soliciting me to come to her and not linger, stretching forth loving hands to receive and embrace me, hands full of multitudes of good examples. . . .

Yet I was still ashamed, for I could still hear the murmuring of those vanities, and I still hung hesitant. And again it was as if she said: "Stop your ears against your unclean members, that they may be mortified. They tell you of delights, but not of such delights as the law of the Lord your God tells." This was the controversy raging in my heart, a controversy about myself against myself. . . .

When my most searching scrutiny had drawn up all my vileness from the secret depths of my soul and heaped it in my heart's sight, a mighty storm arose in me, bringing a mighty rain of tears. . . . I flung myself down somehow under a certain fig tree and no longer tried to check my tears, which poured forth from my eyes in a flood, *an acceptable sacrifice to Thee.* And much I said not in these words but to this effect: *"And Thou, O, Lord, how long? How long, Lord; wilt Thou be angry forever? Remember not our former iniquities."* For I felt that I was still bound by them. And I continued my miserable complaining: "How long, how long shall I go on saying tomorrow and again tomorrow? Why not now, why not have an end to my uncleanness this very hour?"

Such things I said, weeping in the most bitter sorrow of my heart. And suddenly I heard a voice from some nearby house, a boy's voice or a girl's voice, I do not know: but it was a sort of sing-song, repeated again and again, "Take and read, take and read." I ceased weeping and immediately began to search my mind most carefully as to whether children were accustomed to chant these words in any kind of game, and I could not remember that I had ever heard any such thing. Damming back the flood of my tears I arose, interpreting the incident as quite certainly a divine command to open my book of Scripture and read the passage at which I should open. . . . I snatched it up, opened it and in silence read the passage upon which my eyes first fell: *Not in rioting and drunkeness, not in chambering and impurities, not in contention and envy, but put ye*

on the Lord Jesus Christ and make not provision for the flesh in its concupiscences. [Romans xiii, 13]. I had no wish to read further, and no need. For in that instant, with the very ending of the sentence, it was as though a light of utter confidence shone in all my heart, and all the darkness of uncertainty vanished away. . . .

For You converted me to Yourself so that I no longer sought a wife nor any of this world's promises. . . .

FROM BOOK NINE

How lovely I suddenly found it to be free from the loveliness of those vanities, so that now it was a joy to renounce what I had been so afraid to lose. For You cast them out of me, O true and supreme Loveliness, You cast them out of me and took their place in me, You who are sweeter than all pleasure, yet not to flesh and blood; brighter than all light, yet deeper within than any secret; loftier than all honour, but not to those who are lofty to themselves. Now my mind was free from the cares that had gnawed it, from aspiring and getting and weltering in filth and rubbing the scab of lust. And I talked with You as friends talk, my glory and my riches and my salvation, my Lord God. . . .

C. E. M. JOAD

The Mind as Distinct from the Body

The issue between those who endeavor to interpret mind action in terms of body action, and those who contend for the unique, distinct, and in some sense independent status of mind, is not capable of definite settlement. . . . The most that can be done is to suggest certain objections that can be

From *How Our Minds Work* by C. E. M. Joad. Published by Philosophical Library. Reprinted by permission.

and have been brought against the materialist position, . . . and at the same time to indicate a number of independent considerations which seem to demand a different kind of approach to psychology, and a different interpretation of its problems. This interpretation, to put it briefly, insists that a living organism is something over and above the matter of which its body is composed; that it is, in short, an expression of a principle of life, and that life is a force, stream, entity, spirit, call it what you will, that cannot be described or accounted for in material terms; that in human beings this principle of life expresses itself at the level of what is called mind, that this mind is distinct from both body and brain, and, so far from being a mere register of bodily occurrences, is able, acting on its own volition, to produce such occurrences, and that no account of mind action which is given in terms of brain action, gland activity or bodily responses to external stimuli can, therefore, be completely satisfactory. This is the view which in some form or other is held by those who find a materialist explanation of psychology unsatisfactory, and in this chapter we shall be concerned with the reasons for it.

THE APPREHENSION OF MEANING

An important fact about our mental life is that we are capable of appreciating meaning. A statement of fact written on a piece of paper is, so far as its material content is concerned, merely a number of black marks inscribed on a white background. Considered, then, as a collection of visual, physical stimuli, it is comparatively unimportant; what is important is the meaning which is attached to these marks. If they inform us, for example, that we have received a legacy of ten thousand pounds it is not the black marks on the white background but the meaning they convey that effects a disturbance in our emotional life, sufficiently profound to keep us awake all night. Now the meaning of the marks is obviously not a physical stimulus; it is something immaterial. How, then, is its effect to be explained in terms of bodily responses to physical stimuli which the mind merely registers? Let us take one or two further examples in order to present the difficulty in a concrete form.

Let us suppose that I am a geometrician and am thinking about the properties of a triangle. As I do not wish at this point to enter into the vexed question of whether *some* physical stimulus is or is not necessary to initiate every chain of reasoning, we will assume that in this case there was a physical stimulus—it may have been a chance remark about Euclid, or the appearance of a red triangular road signpost while I am driving a car—a stimulus which we will call X, which prompted me to embark upon the train of speculations about the triangle. My reasoning proceeds until I arrive at a conclusion, which takes the form of a geometrical proposition expressed in a formula. I carry this formula in my head for a number of days and presently write it down. In due course I write a book, setting forth my formula and giving an account of the reasoning which led me to it. The book is read and understood by A. Presently it is translated into French, and is read and understood by B. Later still I deliver a lecture on the subject which is heard and understood by C. As A, B, and C have each of them understood my formula and the reasoning upon which it is based, we may say that the reasoning process has had for them the same meaning throughout. If it had not, they would not all have reached the same conclusion and understood the same thing by it. Yet in each of the four cases the sensory stimulus was different; for myself it was X, for A it was a number of black marks on a white background, for B a number of different black marks on a white background, and for C a number of vibrations in the atmosphere impinging upon his eardrums. It seems incredible that all these different stimuli should have been able to produce a consciousness of the same meaning, if our respective reactions to them were confined to physical responses (which must in each case have been different) which were subsequently reflected in our minds by a process of mental registration of the different responses. The stimuli being different, the intervention of something possessed of the capacity to grasp the *common* element among these physically different entities alone seems able to account for the facts, but the common element is the meaning, which is immaterial and can be grasped, therefore, only by a mind.

Let us take another example instanced by Professor McDougall:

A man receives a telegram which says "Your son is dead." The visual physical stimulus here is, as before, a collection of black marks on an orange field. The reaction experienced in terms of his bodily behaviour may take the form of a complete cessation of all those symptoms usually associated with life—that is to say, he may faint. When he recovers consciousness his thoughts and actions throughout the whole of the remainder of his life may be completely changed. Now that all these complicated reactions are not constituted by and do not even spring from a response to the *physical* stimulus, may be seen by comparing the reactions of an acquaintance who reads the telegram, and so subjects himself to the same stimulus. Moreover, the omission of a single letter, converting the telegram into "Our son is dead." would cause none of the reactions just described, but might result at most in the writing of a polite letter of condolence.

The independence of the bodily reactions of the physical stimuli actually presented is in these cases very marked, and, unless we are to introduce conceptions such as the intellectual apprehension of the *meaning* of the marks, it seems impossible to explain their effect. Yet such a conception again involves the active intervention of mind.

Synthesizing Power of Mind. This conclusion is reinforced by what we may call the synthesizing power of mind. Synthesizing means putting together, and one of the most remarkable powers that we possess is that of taking a number of isolated sensations and forming them into a whole. We shall have occasion to return to this point at greater length in connection with our account of sensation in the next chapter. For the present we will content ourselves with giving one or two examples of mental synthesis.

Let us consider for a moment the case of aesthetic appreciation. The notes of a symphony considered separately consist merely of vibrations in the atmosphere. Each note may, when sounded in isolation produce a pleasant sensation, and as one note is struck after another we get a sequence of pleasant sensations. But although this is a sufficient description of the symphony considered as a collection of material events, and of our reactions to these events considered merely in terms of sensations, it is quite clear that we normally think of a symphony as being something more than this. We think of it in fact as a whole, and it is as a whole that it gives what is called aesthetic pleasure. Now in thinking of the symphony in this way our mind is going beyond the mere sequence of pleasant sensations which its individual notes produce, and putting them together into some sort of pattern. If the notes were arranged in a different order, although the actual vibrations which impinged upon our sense would be the same, the pleasurable aesthetic effect would be destroyed.

It seems to follow that our pleasure in a symphony cannot be wholly accounted for, although it may depend upon our physical responses to the stimuli of the individual notes; in order to obtain aesthetic pleasure we must somehow be able to perceive it as more than the sum total of the individual notes—that is, as a whole pattern or arrangement. The pleasure ceases when the *wholeness* of the object perceived is destroyed, as it is, for example, by the transportation of certain notes. We may compare the difference between the physical sensations which are our responses to the visual stimuli of the colours and canvas of which a picture is composed, with our synthesized perception of a picture as a work of art.

We must conclude, then, that we possess the power of realizing external objects not merely as collections of physical stimuli, which of course they are, but as wholes in which the actual sensory elements are combined to form a single object of a higher order. This faculty of combining or putting together seems to involve the existence not only of a mind, but of a mind of an active, creative type which is able to go out beyond the raw material afforded by our bodily sensations, and to apprehend ideal objects as wholes which are more than the collection of physical events which compose their constituent parts.

SUMMARY OF ARGUMENT

The conclusion to which the arguments of this chapter appear to point is that, in addition to the body and brain, the composition of the living organism includes an immaterial element which we call mind; that this element, although it is in very close association with the brain, is more than a mere glow or halo surrounding the cerebral structure, the function of which is confined to reflecting the events occurring in that structure; that, on the contrary, it is in some sense independent of the brain, and in virtue of its independence is able in part to direct and control the material constituents of the body, using them to carry out its purpose in relation to the external world of objects, much as a driver will make use of the mechanism of his motorcar. Mind so conceived is an active, dynamic, synthesizing force; it goes out beyond the sensations provided by external stimuli and arranges them into patterns, and it seems to be capable on occasion of acting without the provocation of bodily stimuli to set it in motion. It is, in other words, creative, that is, it carries on activities which even the greatest conceivable extension of our physiological knowledge would not enable us to infer from observing the brain.

ELIZABETH V. SPELMAN

Woman as Body

(*Author's Postscript, 1993:* The early part of this essay relies on a distinction between women and other subordinate groups—for example, between women and slaves—which has a pernicious effect: it obscures or erases the fact, for example, that some women are (or were) slaves and some slaves are (or were) women. In light of this, the reader is asked to pay special attention to the "Final Note" section of the excerpt.)

From *Feminist Studies*, vol. 8, no. 1 (1982): 109–131. Feminist Studies, Inc., c/o Women's Studies Program, University of Maryland, College Park, MD 20742.

There are a number of reasons why feminists should be aware of the legacy of the soul/body distinction. . . .

First of all, as the soul or mind or reason is extolled, and the body or passion is denounced by comparison, it is not just women who are both relegated to the bodily or passionate sphere of existence and then chastised for belonging to that sphere. Slaves, free laborers, children, and animals are put in "their place" on almost the same grounds as women are. The images of women, slaves, laborers, children, and animals are almost interchangeable. For example, we find Plato holding that the best born and best educated should have control over "children, women and slaves . . . and the base rabble of those who are free in name," because it is in these groups that we find "the mob of motley appetites and pleasures and pains." . . . Plato lumps together women, children, and animals as ignoramuses. (For Aristotle, there is little difference between a slave and an animal, because both "with their bodies attend to the needs of life.") A common way of denigrating a member of any one of these groups is to compare that member to a member of one of the other groups—women are thought to have slavish or childish appetites, slaves are said to be brutish. Recall too, that Plato's way of ridiculing male homosexuals was to say that they imitated women. It is no wonder that the images and insults are almost interchangeable, for there is a central descriptive thread holding together the images of all these groups. The members of these groups lack, for all intents and purposes, mind or the power of reason; even the humans among them are not considered fully human.

It is important for feminists to see to what extent the images and arguments used to denigrate women are similar to those used to denigrate one group of men vis-à-vis another, children vis-à-vis adults, animals vis-à-vis humans, and even—though I have not discussed it here—the natural world vis-à-vis man's will (yes, man's will). For to see this is part of understanding how the oppression of women occurs in the context of, and is related to, other forms of oppression or exploitation.

There is a second reason why feminists should be aware of the legacy of the soul/body distinction.

Some feminists have quite happily adopted both the soul/body distinction and relative value attached to soul and to body. But in doing so, they may be adopting a position inimical to what on a more conscious level they are arguing for. . . .

In *The Feminist Mystique*, [Betty] Friedan remarks on the absence, in women's lives, of "the world of thought and ideas, the life of the mind and spirit." She wants women to be "culturally" as well as "biologically" creative—she wants us to think about spending our lives "mastering the secrets of the atoms, or the stars, composing symphonies, pioneering a new concept in government or society." And she associates "mental activity" with the "professions of highest value to society." Friedan thus seems to believe that men have done the more important things, the mental things; women have been relegated in the past to the less important human tasks involving bodily functions, and their liberation will come when they are allowed and encouraged to do the more important things in life.

Friedan's analysis relies on our old friend, the mind/body distinction, and Friedan, no less than Plato . . . quite happily assumes that mental activities are more valuable than bodily ones. Her solution to what she referred to as the "problem that has no name" is for women to leave (though not entirely) women's sphere and "ascend" into man's. Certainly there is much pleasure and value in the "mental activities" she extolls. But we can see the residue of her own negative attitude about tasks associated with the body: the bodily aspects of our existence must be attended to, but the "liberated" woman, who is on the ascendant, can't be bothered with them. There is yet another group of people to whom these tasks will devolve: servants. Woman's liberation—and of course it is no secret that by "woman," Friedan could only have meant middle-class white women—seems to require woman's dissociation and separation from those who will perform the bodily tasks which the liberated woman has left behind in pursuit of "higher," mental activity. So we find Friedan quoting, without comment, Elizabeth Cady Stanton:

I now understood the practical difficulties most women had to contend with in the isolated house-hold and the impossibility of women's best development if in contact the chief part of her life with servants and children . . . .

Friedan at times seems to chide those women who could afford to have servants but don't: the women pretend there's a "servant problem" when there isn't, or insist on doing their own menial work. The implication is that women could find servants to do the "menial work," if they wanted to, and that it would be desirable for them to do so. But what difference is there between the place assigned to women by men and the place assigned to some women (or men) by Friedan herself? . . .

What I have tried to do here is bring attention to the fact that various versions of women's liberation may themselves rest on the very same assumptions that have informed the deprecation and degradation of women, and other groups which, of course, include women. Those assumptions are that we must distinguish between soul and body, and that the physical part of our existence is to be devalued in comparison to the mental. Of course, these two assumptions alone don't mean that women or other groups have to be degraded; it's these two assumptions, along with the further assumption that woman is body, or is bound to her body, or is meant to take care of the bodily aspects of life, that have so deeply contributed to the degradation and oppression of women. . . . There is nothing intrinsically sexist or otherwise oppressive about dualism, that is, about the belief that there are minds and there are bodies and that they are distinct kinds of things. But historically, the story dualists tell often ends up being a highly politicized one: although the story may be different at different historical moments, often it is said not only that there are minds (or souls) and bodies, but also that one is meant to rule and control the other. And the stage is thereby set for the soul/body distinction, now highly politicized and hierarchically ordered, to be used in a variety of ways in connection with repressive theories of the self, as well as oppressive theories of social and political relations. Among the tasks facing feminists is to think about the criteria for an adequate theory of self. Part of the value of Adrienne Rich's work is that it points to the necessity of such an undertaking, and it is no criticism of her to say that she does no more than remind us of some of the questions that need to be raised.

A FINAL NOTE ABOUT THE SIGNIFICANCE OF SOMATOPHOBIA IN FEMINIST THEORY

In the history of political philosophy, the grounds given for the inferiority of women to men often are quite similar to those given for the inferiority of slaves to masters, children to fathers, animals to humans. In Plato, for example, all such subordinate groups are guilty by association with one another and each group is guilty by association with the bodily. In their eagerness to end the stereotypical association of woman and body, feminists such as de Beauvoir, Friedan, Firestone, and Daly have overlooked the significance of the connections—in theory and in practice—between the derogation and oppression of women on the basis of our sexual identity and the derogation and oppression of other groups on the basis of, for example, skin color and class membership. It is as if in their eagerness to assign women a new place in the scheme of things, these feminist theorists have by implication wanted to dissociate women from other subordinate groups. One problem with this, of course, is that those other subordinate groups include women.

2.9 Suggestions for Further Reading

Adler, Mortimer. *Aristotle for Everybody*. New York: Macmillan, 1980. In this short paperback, Adler explains Aristotle's basic ideas for the beginning reader of philosophy.

Barret, William. *Death of the Soul: From Descartes to the Computer*. Garden City, NY: Doubleday, 1987. An interesting discussion of how philosophy has affected and been affected by our cultural views of human nature.

Churchland, Paul. *Matter and Consciousness*, rev. ed. Cambridge: MIT Press, 1988. A well-written defense of a materialist view of the mind.

Erickson, Erik. *Identity, Youth and Crisis*. New York: Norton, 1968. In this classic on the quest for self-identity, psychoanalyst Erickson relates issues of individual identity to the historically changing patterns of social organization.

Green, Marjorie. *Introduction to Existentialism*. Chicago: Chicago University Press, 1976. This is an excellent introduction to existentialist thought.

Hofstadter, Douglas. *Gödel, Escher, and Bach*. New York: Basic Books, 1979. A highly stimulating and readable discussion of the nature of the mind.

Hofstadter, Douglas, and Daniel Dennet, eds. *The Mind's I*. New York: Basic Books, 1981. A terrific anthology of interdisciplinary writings on the nature of the human mind. Includes some great short stories.

Kohn, Alfie. *The Brighter Side of Human Nature*. New York: Basic Books, 1990. A very readable overview and discussion of current research on whether humans are altruistic by nature.

Lloyd, Genevieve. *The Man of Reason: "Male" and "Female" in Western Philosophy*. London: Methuen, 1984. A very brief but extremely important account of how Western philosophers have developed views of human nature that are biased against women.

McGinn, Colin. *The Character of Mind*. New York: Oxford University Press, 1982. A very good short introduction to the philosophy of human nature.

Nozick, Robert. *Philosophical Explanations*. Cambridge: Harvard University Press, 1981. A contemporary philosopher explores questions of identity.

Organ, Troy Wilson. *The Self in Indian Philosophy*. London: Mouton, 1964. A short work on how Indian philosophy has looked at human nature.

Penrose, Roger. *The Emperor's New Mind*. New York: Penguin Books, 1989. A breathtaking account of what contemporary physics has to tell us about the nature of the human mind.

Robinson, William S. *Computers, Minds, and Robots*. Philadelphia: Temple University Press, 1992. A discussion of the implications that current research on artificial intelligence has for human nature.

Sacks, Oliver. *The Man Who Mistook His Wife for a Hat*. New York: Harper & Row, 1987. A very interesting collection of real-life stories of people who have suffered brain traumas that have affected their identity. Sacks writes with simplicity, warmth, and sympathy.

Sanders, Steven, and David R. Cheney, eds. *The Meaning of Life*. Englewood Cliffs, NJ: Prentice-Hall, 1980. An anthology of writings discussing the value of life.

Sartre, Jean-Paul. *Nausea*. New York: New Directions, 1964. In this novel Sartre illustrates his views on freedom, ambiguity, anxiety, and nothingness.

Searle, John. *The Rediscovery of the Mind*. Cambridge, MA: MIT Press, 1992. This lively and well-written book provides a good summary of the major issues in contemporary philosophical discussions of human nature.

Shoemaker, Sydney, and Richard Swinburne. *Personal Identity*. Oxford: Basil Blackwell, 1984. A stimulating debate on personal identity and immortality between two opponents.

Skinner, B. F. *Walden II*. New York: Macmillan, 1962. Psychologist Skinner presents his behaviorist utopia, governed by principles of stimulus and response, positive reinforcement, and aversive conditioning. The novel is a good introduction to the ideas spelled out in Skinner's *Beyond Freedom and Dignity*.

Stevenson, Leslie. *Seven Theories of Human Nature*. London: Clarendon, 1974. This fine short book examines the views of seven philosophers (Plato, Jesus, Marx, Freud, Sartre, Skinner, and Lorenz) on human nature.

PART II

Metaphysics

Metaphysics is the branch of philosophy that studies the nature of reality. The term encompasses a number of problems whose implications are so broad that they affect just about every other field of philosophy. Specifically, metaphysics is an inquiry into the first principles of being—that is, the attempt to discover the most pervasive characteristics that underlie all our knowledge of, and reasoning about, existence. Metaphysics also refers to subjects that are nonempirical and nonscientific.

Among the problems that traditionally fall under metaphysics are the structure and development of reality viewed in its totality; the meaning and nature of being; the nature of mind, self, and consciousness; the existence of God; the destiny of the universe; and the immortality of the soul. The next two chapters, titled "Reality and Being" and "Philosophy and God," engage a number of these issues.

The term *metaphysics* (literally "after or beyond physics") has a curious origin. It arises with Aristotle, who wrote a series of essays on fundamental problems about the classifications or categories of being. In catalogues, early librarians listed these essays after Aristotle's works on physics. Later philosophers began to call them (in Greek) *ta meta ta physika biblia*—that is, the books that come after the physics. Subsequently, this was shortened to *The Metaphysics*, and the topics dealt with in these essays were called metaphysics. Eventually, metaphysics came to be associated with subjects that transcend physics, including the supernatural and the mysterious.

CHAPTER 3

Reality and Being

The true lover of knowledge is always striving after being. . . . He will not rest at those multitudinous phenomena whose existence is appearance only.

PLATO

3.1 Introduction: What Is Real?

One night you're awakened by a frightened scream. Even though you're groggy with sleep, you recognize your little brother's cry and you quickly stumble out of bed. Apparently, your brother's cry did not awaken anyone else. You make your way through the darkness to his bedroom, where you find him shivering with his head hidden under his blanket. "What's the matter?" you ask.

"I'm scared."

"Of what?"

"I don't know. Something's here in my room."

"There's nothing here," you tell him, as you flip on a small night-light: "See for yourself."

Your brother looks around the empty room but isn't convinced. "I *saw* them," he insists. "They're here. They're big, with big mouths and staring eyes. They were coming to get me."

"You were only dreaming," you assure him. "It wasn't real. What you saw was only a dream, and dreams aren't real."

"They're real!" he persists.

"No," you say. "If they were real, then why can't you see them now? Where did they go?"

"Sometimes you can see them and sometimes you can't," he replies. "They're here right now in the house, but you can't see them. They're spirits! They're waiting for the dark. They're waiting to get me alone again."

"Shush!" you say. "You're just scaring yourself. I'm going back to bed."

"Don't leave me alone!" he wails. "They'll get me!"

"Just tell yourself that they aren't real," you say as you turn off the light. You don't tell him, but for some reason you feel a little uneasy as you make your way back to your bed through the dark. You hear small creaking noises and faint rustling sounds behind you. So you tell yourself, "They aren't real. Spirits aren't real!" But how do you know? Recall the line in Shakespeare's *Hamlet*: "There are more things in heaven and earth, Horatio, Than are dreamed of in your philosophy." Why can't spirits be real? Why does your philosophy reject the reality of spirits?

> *Let us settle ourselves, and work and wedge our feet downward through the mud and slush of opinion, and prejudice and tradition, and delusion, and appearance, that alluvion which covers the globe . . . till we come to a hard bottom of rocks in place, which we call reality.*
>
> JAMES THOMSON

> *Reality, however, has a sliding floor.*
>
> RALPH WALDO EMERSON

The Persistence of Memory, Salvador Dali. **The critical study of the nature of reality is called metaphysics. But perhaps we can never say what reality ultimately is; perhaps the question and any subsequent theories are meaningless.**

What is reality? A child trembling in the dark may be fearful because he believes that reality is more than the hard material objects around him: Reality for him also includes an unseen spiritual realm. You may defend yourself against these fears by insisting that such a realm cannot be a part of reality. Reality consists only of the hard, enduring objects around you that can be seen, heard, touched, and smelled. But what grounds do you have for this belief? In fact, many intelligent and thoughtful people have concluded that reality includes more than material objects. And many people—perhaps even you—have suspected that spirits are very real. What reasons can you give for saying that they are wrong? Don't virtually all religions declare that reality is more than the material world around us? Can a person even claim to be religious without believing that there is more to reality than the material world around us? Doesn't God or "the gods" have to constitute a kind of reality that is utterly different from material reality?

But it is not just spirits and gods that raise troubling questions about what we admit to be real. For example, what are we to say about most of the things for which people are willing to live and die? Consider justice, or goodness, or liberty, or truth, or beauty, or love. Are these material? Can they be seen, touched, smelled, or heard? Do they have a size, a shape, or even a place? Are these real? Haven't millions of people died for these ideals? Don't millions of people devote their entire lives to the pursuit of ideals such as these? Does such devotion imply that they are real?

But perhaps to a practical person these notions seem too soft-minded to be real. So consider some tougher notions. Economists regularly discuss "inflationary pressures" and the "forces" of supply and demand. Has anyone ever heard, seen, or physically felt these pressures and forces? Yet surely they are real; indeed, their reality creates the wealth of the rich and the impoverishment of the poor. But in what sense are these pressures and forces real? What does it mean to say that these are real? And if these unseen entities are real, then why can't spirits be admitted into the realm of reality? Or consider the physicist's force fields, electrons, protons, neutrons, quarks, and other subatomic particles; the mathematician's numbers, formulas, roots, and equations; and the astronomer's laws, curved spaces, black holes, and compressed or stretched intervals of time. Do we admit these odd entities into our notion of "reality"? Yet none of these are like the hard, visible, colored objects that make up our material world. What, then, is reality? What does it include?

These questions are puzzling. But are they important? Let us see. Think about what you imply when you say that something is not part of reality. For example, consider what you imply when you tell your little brother that "spirits aren't real." Isn't the point of saying this to convince him that he should pay no attention to so-called spirits? Aren't you telling him that spirits can exert no causal influence on him? That they cannot act on him or on anything else and so can neither hurt nor harm (nor even help) him? That they do not matter and cannot matter? Are you saying that they have no importance, no power, no actuality, no significance? That they should be disregarded, paid no attention, dismissed?

If these are some of the implications of saying something is unreal, then the implications of saying something is part of reality are great indeed. For in saying that something is part of reality, are we not saying that it has importance, significance, actuality, power? Are we not saying that it is something that should not be dismissed, something that can make a difference to our lives, something to which we need to be attentive? As the contemporary philosopher Robert Nozick has said, to say something is real is to say it has "value, meaning, importance, and weight."

Metaphysical questions about what reality is, then, are among the most significant questions we can ask, since they are intimately linked to questions about what is important for us, what we need to pay attention to, what has significance, what matters. If ghosts are not real, then ghosts don't matter. If God is not real, then God doesn't matter. If the spiritual realm is not real, then it is something that can make no difference in our lives. If only the material exists, then only the material is important. Clearly, our beliefs about reality will profoundly affect what we do with our lives and what we strive for, what we respect and what we ridicule, what we dismiss and what we are willing to live and die for. Only what is real (in some sense) can matter.

In Chapter 2 we raised the question of whether human nature is material or spiritual. But we did not directly examine the most fundamental issue underlying this question: Is all reality matter, or is there another kind of reality besides matter? In this chapter we focus directly on this question of what is ultimately real, what the essence of all being, including our own, is. In philosophy, the critical study of the nature of reality is called *metaphysics*.

Perhaps, however, we can never say definitely what reality is; perhaps the question and the theoretical answers are meaningless. Perhaps the search for reality is meaningless. As we will see, some people believe that it is. If so, perhaps we cannot say with certainty what aspects of ourselves and of the universe around us are real. Perhaps we cannot say with certainty what must ultimately matter to us. We must wait and see.

We begin this chapter with what many still see as the most fundamental question in metaphysics: Is reality purely material, or does reality also include a nonmaterial element? We will look first at the case for materialism and next consider its opposite, idealism. However, many twentieth-century philosophers have responded with disdain to the debate between materialism and idealism. We therefore turn next to look at two important twentieth-century philosophical movements that reject the significance of this debate: pragmatism and logical positivism. Pragmatists reject the debate between materialism and idealism because, they say, it has no experiential consequences. Logical positivism argues that the debate is a meaningless one that arises out of a misuse of language. Next we turn to examine an approach to philosophy that focuses on how we experience being. This is the school of phenomenology and existentialism. The school of phenomenology and existentialism also ignores the debate between materialism and idealism on the grounds that this debate is focused on abstractions that have little to do with reality as it is revealed to human consciousness. Then we look at a very new approach—sometimes labeled "postmodernism"—which holds that there are many realities, an approach that is of some significance to feminists. Finally, we end by looking at two metaphysical questions that interest many people: Is freedom real? Is time real? As we look at each of these approaches to reality, keep in mind that each is telling us what ultimately matters.

QUESTIONS

1. In his 1989 book *The Examined Life*, the Harvard philosopher Robert Nozick writes the following: "The notion of reality has various aspects or dimensions. To be more intense and vivid is to be more real (holding other things equal), to be more valuable is to be more real, and so on. To have a higher score along any one of the various dimensions [value, meaning, importance, and weight] that make up the notion of reality (holding everything else constant) is to be more real" (p. 162). Can you provide examples of what he means? Do you agree? What are the implications of the claim that reality has these aspects?

2. Is it possible that nothing else exists in the universe besides you? Is it possible that the people and things you see around you are all products of your own mind, much like a dream? How could you show that other things exist in the universe besides you and your ideas?

3.2 Reality: Material or Nonmaterial?

Saint Augustine (354–430), one of the greatest of the early Christian theologians, did not find it difficult to believe that spirits are real. In fact, Augustine held that reality—the real existing universe—contains within itself every possible kind of being, from the "lowest" kind of inert matter to the "highest" kind of spirit. Since God is all-powerful and wanted to fill reality with goodness, Augustine reasoned, God placed in the universe every possible kind of creature that had within itself some degree of goodness:

> So great is the variety of earthly things that we can conceive of nothing which belongs to the form of the earth in its full extent which God, the Creator of all things,

PHILOSOPHY AND LIFE

The Reality of Corporations

Several years ago the Department of Defense charged that a corporation had sold it computer parts without testing them properly and then had falsified records to cover up the fraud. The computer parts are now installed in ships, planes, weapons, and nuclear bombs around the world and cannot be tracked down. A government official commented that if a component malfunctioned, "We're talking about lives. You could have a missile that would end up in Cleveland instead of the intended target."

Although the corporation was indicted on criminal charges, no individuals were ever charged. The Department of Defense objected that since "a corporation acts only through its employees and officers," the individuals who make up the company should have been held responsible for the crimes. The company's president felt differently: "We

totally disagree with the Defense Department's proposal. We have repeatedly stated that we accept responsibility as a company [only] and we steadfastly continue to stand by that statement." According to the company president, corporations and not their members should be held responsible for such criminal acts.

The position of the Department of Defense was defended by metaphysical individualists. Metaphysical individualism says that only individuals are real and that corporations are fictitious mental constructs; consequently, only individuals can be responsible for crimes. The position of the company's president was supported by metaphysical collectivists, who hold that corporations are as real as individual human beings. Metaphysical collectivism says that corporations are like living organisms that think, act, and direct

the activities of their members and that, consequently, the corporation and not its members must be held responsible for its criminal acts. Legal experts are divided on this issue, some siding with individualism, others with collectivism.

QUESTIONS

1. What kind of reality does an organized group like a corporation have? Is a corporate group nothing more than the sum of its members, or is it more like a living organism?

2. Which theory should our legal system use when determining punishments for corporate crimes: the individualist theory or the collectivist theory? Why?

SOURCE: *San Jose Mercury News*, 31 May 1984, p. 1, and 4 June 1984, p. 7.

has not already created. . . . There can exist in nature things which your reason is incapable of conceiving. It cannot be, however, that what you conceive with true reasoning cannot exist. You cannot conceive of anything better in creation which has escaped the Maker of the creation.[1]

Where are human beings in the order of Augustine's universe? Augustine placed us somewhere in the middle of his hierarchy of reality: Humans have material bodies, so we belong to the lower material world; but we also have spirits, or souls, making us part of the higher spiritual world. Humans are both matter and spirit: We straddle two realms of reality.

But can Augustine's view of reality make sense to a person in the modern world? Has modern science's success in explaining the universe in material terms made such belief impossible for us? Although much of the world continues to believe that spiritual beings inhabit the universe and that humans are partly spirit, does it make more sense now for us to believe that matter is all that exists in the universe? Many people today are in fact materialists, who deny that spirit can be real.

REALITY AS MATTER

Materialism, the view that matter is the ultimate constituent of reality, is at least as old as the ancient Greeks. At various times, philosopher-scientists viewed water, fire, air, or earth as the fundamental substance of reality. Others believed that reality could best be explained in terms of constant change.

> **materialism** the metaphysical position that reality is ultimately composed of matter

The philosopher Democritus (460–360 B.C.) believed that reality could be explained in terms of matter. The smallest pieces of matter he called *atoms;* he described them as solid, indivisible, indestructible, eternal, and uncreated. Atoms were not qualitatively distinguishable from one another, and they constantly moved through space, where they combined to form the recognizable physical objects of the universe. According to Democritus, the universe consisted of atoms and empty space. He believed that even the soul, which he equated with reason, consisted of atoms. In this atomic universe "all things happen by virtue of necessity, the vortex being the cause of the creation of all things."[2]

> **CRITICAL THINKING**
>
> **Suppose that all reality can be explained in terms of matter. Does it follow that only matter exists?**

But Democritus's theory never became popular, because by that time people were becoming disenchanted with the many attempts to explain the cosmos. Their interest turned to more personal concerns, such as how to lead a good and contented life. This interest was sparked by classical philosophy.

Although their interests reached much further than such questions, the Greek philosophers Socrates, Plato, and Aristotle saw the moral life as the road to knowledge and truth. The rise of Christianity fanned this interest in personal

---

[1] Saint Augustine, On *Free Choice of the Will,* trans. Anna S. Benjamin and L. H. Hackstaff (New York: Bobbs-Merrill, 1964), 96–97.
[2] Quoted in Diogenes Laërtius, *Lives and Opinions of Eminent Philosophers,* vol. 2, trans. R. D. Hicks (Cambridge, MA: Harvard University Press, 1925), 455.

conduct, which predominated throughout the Middle Ages. In particular, the idea of a soul, which included the concept of personal immortality, gave the view of reality a distinctly nonmaterial bias.

In the seventeenth century, however, a growing interest in the world and the rise of scientific method and scientific discovery turned minds once again to materialism. Awakened by the discoveries of Copernicus, Kepler, Galileo, and Newton, people watched science cultivate a full-blown materialism. Committed to the belief that the world could be quantified, scientists made the materialistic claim that all is matter.

In the philosophy of Thomas Hobbes (1588–1679), for example, we see the Democritean belief that everything can be explained in terms of matter in motion now presented as the view that everything can be explained in terms of measurable matter:

> Every object is either a part of the whole world, or an aggregate of parts. The greatest of all bodies, or sensible objects, is the world itself; which we behold when we look round about us from this point of the same which we call the earth. Concerning the world, as it is one aggregate of many parts, the things that fall under inquiry are but few; and those we can determine, none. Of the whole world we may inquire what is its magnitude, what its duration, and how many there be, but nothing else.[3]

Hobbes concluded that measurable matter is all there is in the universe. Only matter is real:

> The universe, that is the whole mass of things that are, is corporeal, that is to say body; and has the dimensions of magnitude, namely, length, breadth, and depth. Also every part of body is likewise body, and has the like dimensions. And, consequently, every part of the Universe is body, and that which is not body is no part of the Universe. And because the Universe is all, that which is no part of it is nothing, and, consequently, nowhere.[4]

Anticipating many contemporary psychological theories, Hobbes postulated that mental states are brain states and that a "general inclination of all mankind" is "a perpetual and restless desire of power after power." (For a fuller discussion of Hobbes's views, see the showcase at the end of this chapter.) In 1748, Julien Offroy de La Mettrie carried Hobbesian psychology further when he published *Man a Machine*, a book that argues that humans are nothing more than complex machines. In de La Mettrie, materialism reached its logical conclusion.

What had happened to the religious doctrine of the soul? What remained of the creature supposedly made in the image of God and possessed of an eternal destiny? So much medieval superstition! declared the materialists. Even Newton's mechanical universe was rapidly growing obsolete, because Newton had proposed a God who regulated things.

There exists no kind of spiritual substance or entity of a different nature from that of which matter is composed.

HUGH ELLIOT

---

[3] Thomas Hobbes, "Elements of Philosophy," in *The English Works of Thomas Hobbes*, vol. 1, ed. Sir W. Molesworth (London: J. Bohn, 1839), chap. 1, sec. 8.
[4] Thomas Hobbes, *Hobbes's Leviathan* (Oxford: Clarendon Press, 1909; original work published 1651), 524.

In contrast, astronomer-mathematician Pierre Laplace proposed that the universe is self-regulating. In 1812, Laplace formulated the idea of the "Divine Calculator," which knew the velocities and positions of all the particles in the world at a particular instant and could calculate all that had happened and all that would happen. Laplace's universe needed not a God but a supercomputer as regulator. Bertrand Russell describes the situation nicely:

> When Laplace suggested that the same forces which are now operative (according to Newton's laws) might have caused the planets to grow out of the sun, God's share in the course of nature was pushed still further back. He might remain as Creator, but even that was doubtful, since it was not clear the world has a beginning in time.[5]

There is an interesting footnote to this historical development: It is said that when Napoleon asked Laplace why his theory omitted God, Laplace simply replied that God was an unnecessary hypothesis. God did not matter.

But these early materialists' optimistic faith that humans could eventually explain the universe and themselves has become tarnished over the last century, as we shall see. Nevertheless, just as a culture generally lags behind its science, so today we frequently find ourselves as enthusiastically materialistic as our nineteenth-century counterparts.

Today, philosophical materialism takes many forms, but all have at least four characteristics that survive from the past. First, materialism seeks answers through objective methodology. Specifically, it is committed to the method of sense observation, analysis, and tentative conclusions. What cannot be found out by this method cannot be known. Second, materialism is deterministic; in other words, it believes that every event has a cause. Some materialists attribute these causes to physicochemical processes. Others would add biological causes. Still others introduce psychological, sociological, and anthropological causes. We may not know the causes, they say, but these causes exist nevertheless. Third, materialism denies any form of supernatural belief, including belief in spirit, soul, mind, or any other nonmaterial substance. Reality is composed of matter and only of matter. Finally, materialism is reductionistic; it attempts to explain the whole exclusively in terms of its parts or units.

OBJECTIONS TO MATERIALISM

The fundamental objection to materialism is its difficulty in accounting for human consciousness—that is, for our conscious mental activities such as thinking, wishing, experiencing, hoping, dreaming, loving, and hating. Many people believe that these kinds of activities can be generated only by some kind of nonmaterial or spiritual entity: the human soul or spirit. But haven't many beliefs that once were widely held later turned out to be false, such as the belief that the earth is at the center of the universe? We must look more closely at why materialism is thought to have a difficult time accounting for human consciousness.

---

[5] Bertrand Russell, *A History of Western Philosophy* (New York: Simon & Schuster, 1945), 537.

Materialism holds that everything is material. A material thing is simply a physical object that takes up space, that has length, width, mass, and volume. Typically, material things have a color, a taste, a weight, and a set of measurements; they exist in a specific location. So materialists hold that human consciousness can be explained in terms of things that have these qualities. What do we mean by "consciousness"? First, to say that something has consciousness is to say that it has an awareness of things. For example, when I think, I am aware of the thoughts I am thinking; when I perceive, I am aware of what I

An age of science is necessarily an age of materialism. Ours is a scientific age, and it may be said with truth that we are all materialists now.

HUGH ELLIOT

PHILOSOPHY AND LIFE

Our Knowledge of the World

What kind of world do we live in? Physicists today generally describe it as a flux of energy that exists in different forms at different levels. Due to the limitations of our sense organs, our brains cannot know directly about all of the world's energy. Indeed, a relatively small part of the electromagnetic spectrum—that is, of the entire range of radiation—can stimulate our eyes. In other words, although we can hear or feel parts of it, we can't see a large portion of the spectrum. Electromagnetic energy covers a wide range of wavelengths, from extremely short gamma rays, having wavelengths of about a billionth of an inch, to the extremely long radio waves, which have wavelengths that are miles long. In fact, we can see very little of the electromagnetic spectrum.

Our ears also sense a limited range of the mechanical vibrations transmitted through the air. Similarly, although we can smell and taste certain chemical substances and feel the presence of some objects in contact with our skin surface, most of what occurs in our environment cannot be perceived by these senses either. In effect, the

great flux of energy that physicists say exists is largely lost to our senses. We know about it only indirectly, through specially devised instruments that can detect radio waves, X rays, infrared rays, and other energy forms that we can't directly experience.

What implications do these facts hold for our view of reality? If nothing else, they should make us wonder just how complete a picture of reality we have and how accurate our interpretation of it is. In *New Pathways in Science*, Sir Arthur Eddington addresses this issue:

As a conscious being I am involved in a story. The perceiving part of my mind tells me a story of a world around me. The story tells of familiar objects. It tells of colors, sounds, scents belonging to these objects; of boundless space in which they have their existence, and of an ever-rolling stream of time bringing change and incident. It tells of other life than mine busy about its own purposes.

As a scientist I have become mistrustful of this story. In many instances it has become clear that things are not what they seem to be. According to the

storyteller I have now in front of me a substantial desk; but I have learned from physics that the desk is not at all the continuous substance that it is supposed to be in the story. It is a host of tiny electric charges darting hither and thither with inconceivable velocity. Instead of being solid substance my desk is more like a swarm of gnats.

So I have come to realize that I must not put overmuch confidence in the storyteller who lives in my mind.

QUESTIONS

1. Undoubtedly, things are often not what they appear to be. But to say that is to imply another experience of things. Can we be sure that alternative experiences are any closer to how things are?

2. If a desk is indeed more like "a swarm of gnats" than a solid substance, what practical difference does that make in the way you live? Or is such a question irrelevant?

SOURCE: Sir Arthur Eddington, *New Pathways in Science* (Ann Arbor: University of Michigan Press, 1959), 11. Reprinted by permission.

am perceiving; when I experience, I am aware of what I am experiencing. Second, to say that something has consciousness is to say that the objects of which it is aware need not exist. For example, I can think of a golden mountain or a unicorn, even though they do not exist. I can feel fear of things that don't exist. I can hallucinate and see or hear things that aren't there. And when I am dreaming I can experience things that don't exist. Modern philosophers call this feature of consciousness its *intensionality*. Many philosophers have felt that the qualities of consciousness are so different from those of matter that they must indicate the existence in the universe of two irreducibly different kinds of entities: material entities and conscious, nonmaterial entities.

If materialists' views are to be acceptable, then mustn't they somehow reduce our supposedly unique human qualities, such as consciousness, to the material? For example, some materialists claim that states of consciousness are states of the brain, which is a physical or material organ. When we have a mental experience such as a thought, this experience is nothing more than the material brain functioning in a certain way. The same is true of any other conscious experience, such as dreaming, hoping, and feeling.

But doesn't the attempt to reduce conscious experience to brain states run into an almost insurmountable obstacle? Brain states can be seen, felt, and touched, whereas our conscious experiences cannot. For example, a biologist and his students can together observe the state or condition of a ganglion in the brain and identify its location, color, and shape. Yet no one can know what your inner conscious experience is like. No one can know what it is like to consciously see and experience the world from your point of view. And your conscious experience has no location, color, or shape. Because they have such different qualities, mustn't we conclude that a brain state and a state of consciousness are two different things? The materialist does not seem to be able to account for these differences. The unique qualities that conscious experiences have, in fact, seem to imply that consciousness is a nonmaterial reality.

The debate about the nature of consciousness has arisen in the midst of some startling discoveries in atomic physics. For a long time we have known that matter consists of molecules, of which there are a tremendous number of types. But there are only a few more than one hundred types of atoms of which all the molecules are made. Before the twentieth century, no one believed that atoms could be split. Today we know that several particles make up the atom: the electron, proton, and neutron. Yet not everything in existence can be explained in terms of these three particles.

Physicists have discovered more than two hundred so-called elementary particles. Some believe that they are made up of still more elementary particles, called quarks. The point is that modern scientists are showing reality to be ever more complex.

But, even more important, these elementary particles do not seem to be matter. They are more likely energy forces. True, matter may depend on interactions of elementary particles, but the particles themselves seem to be composed of energy, not matter. And what is energy? Nobody knows for sure. Whatever it is, it is in motion and exerts force, but it does not appear to be matter as matter is traditionally understood.

Ever since the early 1930s, when Werner Heisenberg discovered that the activity of individual electrons cannot be completely measured, materialism has been losing credibility. Heisenberg formulated his principle of indeterminacy on a startling premise: that there is no orderly causation. Because electrons change their positions at random, rational prediction is not possible. In his article "The Dematerialization of Matter," philosopher-scientist N. R. Hanson states the full implications of Heisenberg's discovery:

> Matter has been dematerialized, not just as a concept of the philosophically real, but now as an idea of modern physics. Matter can be analyzed down to the level of fundamental particles. But at that depth the direction of analysis changes, and this constitutes a major conceptual surprise in the history of science. The things which for Newton typified matter—e.g., an exactly determinable state, a point shape, absolute solidity—these are now the properties electrons do not, because theoretically they cannot, have. . . .
>
> The dematerialization of matter . . . has rocked mechanics at its foundations. . . . The 20th century's dematerialization of matter has made it conceptually impossible to accept a Newtonian picture of the properties of matter and still do a consistent physics.[6]

As a result, many scientists, including Heisenberg, believe that we may live in an idealistic universe, one whose reality depends on the mind. Their view finds some support in the unified field theories of contemporary scientists such as Kip Thorne. When electromagnetic and gravitational theories are synthesized, matter disappears entirely, leaving only "field." To understand better what is meant by an idealistic universe, in the next section we will consider idealism as an explanation of ultimate reality.

QUESTIONS

1.   Look up the meaning of *materialism* as it is ordinarily used. Do you detect any connection between its ordinary and its philosophical meanings?

2.   Some people claim that the persistence of a belief in the soul removes this belief from the realm of superstition or ignorance. Do you agree? Can you think of any beliefs that have so persisted? What about beliefs that lasted an extremely long time but are no longer widely held?

3.   Our discussion so far has focused almost exclusively on the problem of self. How is this question relevant to the question of what is real?

4.   The eighteenth-century English poet Alexander Pope, exuding the enthusiasm of his age for scientific discovery, wrote an "Epitaph Intended for Sir Isaac Newton, in Westminster Abbey."

Nature and Nature's laws lay hid in night;
God said, "*Let* Newton *be*!" and all was Light.

---

[6]N. R. Hanson, "The Dematerialization of Matter," in *The Concept of Matter,* ed. Ernan McMillin (Notre Dame, IN: University of Notre Dame Press, 1963), 556–557.

What view of human nature does Pope suggest? Do you think that Heisenberg's indeterminacy principle advances, sets back, or has no effect on the belief that all can be explained in terms of cosmic laws?

5. Does research into the causes of human thought, consciousness, and behavior indicate a growing simplicity or a growing complexity of understanding?

6. Do you see the workings of the universe as orderly? Why or why not? (You might first define *orderliness* in terms of predictability.)

7. Suppose in the year 2020 you pick up a telephone and hear a voice at the other end. You are not sure whether the voice belongs to a human being or to a computer that is programmed to fool you into thinking it is a human being. What questions would you ask it that might enable you to determine whether the voice is human? If there is no way to distinguish the computer from a human, does this show that a human being is really nothing more than a complicated material machine?

REALITY AS NONMATTER

Modern atomic theory has led some philosophers to claim that reality consists of more than matter. If we push the question of reality far enough, matter alone does not seem to account for everything; things are not just what they appear to be. In fact, some philosophers have held that if we push our investigation of nature far enough, we end up with only a mental world, a world of ideas, not matter. Such philosophers are called *idealists*. Idealists hold that ideas and mind are concepts foreign to matter and materialism. They hold that a mental or spiritual force is needed to account for the order they perceive in nature. But they go beyond this to conclude that everything must be mental: The universe is not matter, but only idea.

> *The great majority of mankind are satisfied with appearances, as though they were realities, and are often more influenced by the things that seem than by those that are.*
>
> NICCOLÒ MACHIAVELLI

THE DEVELOPMENT OF IDEALISM

Although idealists differ, let us define **idealism** as the belief that reality is essentially idea and mind rather than matter. Whether idealists believe that there is a single, absolute mind or many minds, they invariably emphasize the mental or spiritual, not the material, presenting it as the creative force or active agent behind all things. This is the view that the great English playwright William Shakespeare expressed toward the end of his life in his final play, *The Tempest*, when he characterized the universe around us as "this vision" that exists only in our minds:

idealism in metaphysics, the position that reality is ultimately nonmatter; in epistemology, the position that all we know are our ideas

> Our revels now are ended. These our actors,
> As I foretold you, were all spirits and
> Are melted into air, into thin air:
> And, like the baseless fabric of this vision,
> The cloud-capp'd towers, the gorgeous palaces,
> The solemn temples, that great globe itself,
> Yea, all which it inherit, shall dissolve

And, like this insubstantial pageant [play] faded,
Leave not a rack behind. We are such stuff
As dreams are made on, and our little life
Is rounded with a sleep.

The belief that reality is ultimately idea is at least as old as the ancient Greek Pythagoras (about 600 B.C.). However, Plato first formalized this belief. He held that individual entities are merely shadows of reality, that behind each entity in our experience is a perfect form or ideal. This form or ideal is what makes the entity understandable to the human mind. Individual entities come and go, but the forms are immortal and indestructible.

Such thinking fit in well with the Christian thought developed by Saint Augustine. In *The City of God*, Augustine warned us to beware of the world and the flesh, because they are temporary. What is real is the spiritual world, the world without matter. Although we are citizens of the physical world, we are ultimately destined to be citizens of the spiritual world of God. For Augustine and fellow Christians, Jesus Christ is the embodiment of all perfection, of all forms; he is the meaning of all that is. As Saint John wrote, "In the beginning was the Word and the Word was with God and the Word was God. He was in the beginning with all things" (John 1:1–2). By the way, the Greek *logos* means "law" as well as "word." In the nineteenth century, the German romantic poet Goethe expressed a similar idealistic notion in *Faust*: "In the beginning was the meaning."

But the founder of modern idealism is George Berkeley, who reacted against materialist philosophies like Hobbes's. Berkeley claimed that the conscious mind and its ideas or perceptions are the only reality. He did not deny the reality of the world; he denied only that the world is independent of mind. For Berkeley, only mind—only spirit—can ultimately matter.

> **CRITICAL THINKING**
> "We have no evidence for saying that reality is something other than our sensations and perceptions; so reality is not something other than our sensations and perceptions." Evaluate this argument.

Berkeley claimed that all our acquaintance with the external world consists of the sensations and perceptions of our senses. We have no evidence for saying that reality is anything other than these sensations and perceptions. So, Berkeley concluded, we have no reason to postulate the existence of any external physical reality. All that exists are the mental sensations and ideas that we experience and the minds in which we experience them.

The external world is that collection of perceptions we mistakenly call physical reality. But where does that collection of perceptions derive its uniformity, consistency, and continuity? This can only be explained as the work of the supreme mind: the mind of God. God produces in our minds the display of perceptions that we call the external world, and it is God that gives this display its order and stability. Berkeley attributed the orderly succession of events that we perceive in everything to the will of God. (For a fuller explanation of Berkeley's views, see the showcase at the end of this chapter.)

> **CRITICAL THINKING**
> "We have no evidence for the existence of anything other than our sensations and perceptions; so only sensations, perceptions, and minds exist." Evaluate this argument.

To appreciate idealism, it's helpful to distinguish between two varieties of idealism, subjective and objective. Berkeley's version of idealism includes elements of both.[7]

---

[7]See Elmer Sprague, *Metaphysical Thinking* (New York: Oxford University Press, 1978), 93–103.

Berkeley claimed that things are ultimately mental, or mind-dependent. This mind-dependency can be viewed as either "me-dependent" or "other-dependent." At least in its initial stages, Berkeley's idealism is me-dependent.

Berkeley said that we find out about the things of the world through experience. That is, we learn of trees, rocks, houses, cats, and dogs by using our senses of sight, touch, taste, smell, and hearing. When we use our senses, we see light or color; feel hardness or softness, smoothness or roughness; smell sweetness or decay. So, for Berkeley, all things are bundles of one's own perceptions:

> By sight I have the ideas of light and colors. . . . By touch I perceive hard and soft, heat and cold, motion and resistance. . . . Smelling furnishes me with odors, the palate with tastes, and hearing conveys sounds. . . . As several of these are observed to accompany each other, they come to be marked by one name and so to be reputed as one thing. Thus, for example, a certain color, taste, smell, figure and consistency having been observed to go together, are accounted one distinct thing, signified by the name *apple*. Other collections of ideas constitute a stone, a tree, a book, and the like sensible things. . . .
>
> But besides all that endless variety of ideas or objects of knowledge, there is likewise something which knows or perceives them. . . . This perceiving, active being is what I call *mind, spirit, soul* or *myself*.
>
> It seems . . . evident that the various sensations or ideas imprinted on the sense, however blended or combined together (that is, whatever objects they compose) cannot exist otherwise than in a mind perceiving them. Their *esse* [being] is *percipi* [to be perceived]. Nor is it possible they should have any existence out of the minds or thinking things which perceive them.
>
> It is indeed an opinion strangely prevailing among men that houses, mountains, rivers, and, in a word, all sensible objects have an existence, natural or real, distinct from their being perceived by the understanding. But with how great an assurance and acquiescence soever this principle may be entertained in the world, yet whoever shall find in his heart to call it in question may, if I mistake not, perceive it to involve a manifest contradiction. For what are the forementioned objects but the things we perceive by sense? And what do we perceive besides our own ideas or sensations? And is it not plainly repugnant [contradictory] that any one of these or any combination of them should exist unperceived? . . .
>
> All of the choir of heaven and furniture of the earth, in a word all those bodies which compose the mighty frame of the world, have no substance without a mind. Their being is to be perceived. Consequently so long as they are not actually perceived by me or other created spirits, they must either have no existence at all or else exist in the mind of some eternal spirit.[8]

Thus, any object that I experience is the sum of my perceptions of that thing. Since these perceptions are my own, everything I perceive is me-dependent. This me-dependency translates into mind-dependency, since Berkeley assumed that perception is a mental act and that all perceptions are located in some part of the mind. If we stop Berkeley's analysis right here, we're left with **subjective idealism,** or *subjective immaterialism*, the position that the world consists of my

subjective idealism in epistemology, the position that all we ever know are our own ideas

---

[8] George Berkeley, *Principles of Human Knowledge* (1710), part I, para. 1–4, 6. Spelling and punctuation have been modernized.

The Solar System, Helmut Wimmer. According to Hobbes, "The Universe, that is the whole mass of things that are, is corporeal, that is to say, body." But according to Berkeley, "All the Choir of Heaven and the furniture of the world, in a word all those bodies which compose the mighty frame of the world, have no substance without a mind; so long as they are not actually perceived, . . . they have no existence at all."

own mind and things that are dependent on it. But Berkeley went further and introduced an objective dimension.

Berkeley pointed out that not all the contents of my mind are the same. Ideas vary. Some are short-lived, even changeable at my will. Others occur regularly and seem constant. For instance, if you choose to, you can imagine that you are now basking in the warm sun on a South Sea island. The air is balmy, the vegetation lush, and the sounds mellow and serene. In contrast, consider your usual route to class; you experience the same landmarks repeatedly—perhaps the library, the gym, and the old clock tower—and when you get to class, you experience a comparable regularity, a steadiness about your perceptions. This latter collection of perceptions is clearly different from the imaginings that transported you to the South Sea island. The difference seems to be that your perceptions of the way to class are more than me-dependent.

If your classroom is a collection of perceptions, it must be dependent on mind—if not your own mind, then some other mind. For Berkeley, this other mind was ultimately the mind of God. This second stage of idealism, or immaterialism, is termed *objective* because it is independent of certain perceptions that I have. The advantages of **objective idealism** are that it accounts for the steadiness or regularity of our experiences and that it allows the world to be viewed as an ultimately intelligible system because it is the product of mind.[9]

> **objective idealism** the position that ideas exist in an objective state, associated originally with Plato

The varieties of idealism all appear to share several characteristics. First, they all believe in mind, spirit, or thought as what is ultimately real. Second, they perceive purpose, order, and meaning in the workings of things. Third, they see some kind of purpose acting in our lives. As there are laws governing the operations of the physical universe, so there are laws governing the operations of our own lives: moral laws. Finally, all forms of idealism are as reductionistic as materialism.

> **CRITICAL THINKING**
> Does Berkeley assume that if a perception is not under my voluntary control it must be controlled by a divine mind? Is this assumption correct?

The tension between idealism and materialism is in the kind of reductions that each proposes. Both speak of trees and rocks and houses as having "parts"; a tree has bark and pulp, and a house has a roof and a foundation, but the bark, pulp, roofs, and foundations also have parts. Both materialism and idealism agree that trees and houses are complexes of simples, but they disagree on what kind of complexes such entities are and how they are to be analyzed. Of course, if you reject the idea that things are complexes, then neither materialism nor idealism has any basis. In other words, both assume that things are analyzable into simples.[10]

OBJECTIONS TO IDEALISM

As we have seen, idealists often rely on the assumption that the universe has order and purpose. But aren't the terms *order* and *purpose* too vague to be useful? Doesn't the reality we experience include such seemingly chaotic and purposeless events as natural disasters (the so-called acts of God), the human catastrophes of disease and war, and the personal and national tragedies of senseless deaths? The French writer Voltaire perhaps best summed up this criticism in *Candide*, in which he uses ironic wit to question the belief of philosopher Gottfried Leibniz (1646–1716) that everything happens for the best in this "best of all possible worlds." At one point in that philosophical tale, Candide points out to his traveling companion, Martin, the merits of a shipwreck: "You see that crime is sometimes punished; that scoundrel of a Dutch shipowner has had the fate he deserved." Martin responds, "Yes, but did the passengers who were on the ship have to perish too?"[11]

---

[9] Sprague, *Metaphysical Thinking*, 97.
[10] Ibid., 93–94.
[11] Voltaire, *Candide*, trans. Tobias George Smollet (New York: Washington Square Press, 1962), 77.

A more important problem is this: Don't idealists commit the fallacy of **anthropomorphism?** That is, don't they attribute human characteristics to the universe as a whole? It is one thing to speak of people as having minds, but can we speak of the universe as having one? Is the leap from ideas to Idea really warranted?

Consider, also, whether you or anyone else has ever experienced mind, idea, or spirit independent of a matter-energy system. Is it necessary to posit a nonmaterial reality to account for what we observe? These thoughts suggest further problems, which require a closer look at subjective and objective idealism.

Isn't subjective idealism's claim that whatever I perceive is merely one of my perceptions or a collection of my perceptions at least puzzling? If I'm looking at a tree, for example, isn't there a difference between my seeing and the tree that I see? Can subjective idealism make such a distinction? Yet, if I say that there is more to the tree than my perceivings, can't subjective idealists ask me

> **anthropomorphism** the attributing of human qualities to nonhuman entities, especially to God

PHILOSOPHY AND LIFE

The Neutrino

The neutrino is perhaps the most bewildering of all the elementary particles known to physics, and among the most philosophically provocative. It has no physical properties—no mass, no electric charge, and no magnetic field. It is neither attracted nor repelled by the electric and magnetic fields of passing particles. Thus, a neutrino originating in the Milky Way or in some other galaxy and traveling at the speed of light can pass through the earth as if it were so much empty space. Can it be stopped? Only by a direct, head-on collision with another elementary particle. The chances of that are infinitesimally small. Fortunately, there are so many neutrinos that collisions do occur. Otherwise, physicists would never have detected them. Just think, even as you read this sentence, billions of neutrinos com-

ing from the sun and other stars are passing through your skull and brain. And how would the universe appear to a neutrino? Eminent astronomer V. A. Firsoff provides a picture:

The universe as seen by a neutrino eye would wear a very unfamiliar look. Our earth and other planets simply would not be there, or might at best appear as thin patches of mist. The sun and other stars may be dimly visible, in as much as they emit some neutrinos. . . . A neutrino brain might suspect our existence from certain secondary effects, but would find it very difficult to prove, as we would elude the neutrino instruments at his disposal.

Our universe is no truer than that of the neutrinos—they exist, but they exist in a different kind of space, governed by different laws. . . . The neutrino . . . is subject neither to gravita-

tional nor to electromagnetic field. . . . It might be able to travel faster than light, which would make it relativistically recede in our time scale.

QUESTIONS

1. What impact does the presence of neutrinos have on your view of reality?

2. Arthur Koestler writes: "To the unprejudiced mind, neutrinos have indeed a certain affinity with ghosts—which does not prevent them from existing." What does this mean?

Sources: V. A. Firsoff, *Life, Mind and Galaxies* (New York: W. A. Benjamin, 1967).
Arthur Koestler, *The Roots of Coincidence* (New York: Random House, 1972), 63.

how this "more" is to be found out? Can't the subjective idealist say that there is no other way to find out about trees than to use our senses? Thus, if I claim that there's more to the tree than my perceivings, I am postulating the existence of something that I cannot know. But can I have solid grounds for claiming that something is real when I can't even know it?

"But," as philosopher Elmer Sprague points out, "it still seems odd to say that I perceive my perceptions, and not that I perceive something out there to be perceived. It seems odd to say that to perceive the [tree] is but to perceive my own mind. It is all very well for the Subjective Immaterialist to say 'That's just the way it is.' Less hardy mortals still wonder if we might not say something else instead."[12] Sprague concedes that what subjective idealists say cannot be disproved experimentally because their theories cannot be falsified. But we can still ask them how they know that their claim is true. Ultimately, the claim seems to hinge on the assumption that perceptible *things* are mere collections of perceptible *qualities*. But why this assumption? Why not the more common-sensical distinction between perceptions and the objects of perceptions?

Related to this assumption is subjective idealism's insistence that things are collections of perceptible qualities. This belief follows only if we don't make a sharp distinction between perceptible things and our perceptions. But can we really say how things are without making such a distinction? Subjective idealism does not really seem to answer the question of what things are — rather, it seems to dissolve it. Things are as I perceive them. But doesn't this rule out the possibility of objective knowledge?

As for objective idealism, we observed two apparent strengths: It explains why perceptible things persist in the mind, and it offers an intelligible world system. However, Sprague believes that neither of these aspects is as strong as it may appear.

Recall your classroom experience. You perceive the classroom because some other mind, call it God, perceives it all the time, thus holding the classroom in place each time you happen to perceive it. But do we really need such an explanation? Won't a materialistic explanation account for the composition of the classroom and of the things that you pass en route to it? And should they one day disappear, can't materialism also account for that eventuality — they fell down, were torn down, or were blown up? Why do you need to involve the mind of God?

Objective idealists are seeking some ultimate explanation. Thus, "God minds it." But what does that tell us? While the classroom stands, God minds it. When it lies in ruins, it does so because God minds it. What does "God minds it" add to a commonsensical account of the classroom?

Objective idealists also claim that the world is intelligible because it's a product of God's mind or of some sort of cosmic intelligence. But simply because our own mind may be intelligible, does that mean God's is? How are we to know God's mind? How can we distinguish between our own perceptions,

Laws of Nature are God's thoughts thinking themselves out in the orbits and the tides.

C. H. PARKHURST

---

[12] Sprague, *Metaphysical Thinking*, 98.

which by strict idealistic principles we can never get beyond, and God's perceptions? It seems that idealism must answer these questions before it can be considered as the most compelling explanation of ultimate reality.

But what is the alternative to idealism? Many philosophers believe that materialsm is just as inadequate. Is perhaps the most viable option to admit that the universe contains both nonmaterial spirit and physical matter? As we saw in Chapter 2, this is the view of dualism. Dualism holds that reality contains two irreducibly different kinds of things: immaterial spirits and material objects. Yet as we saw in our earlier discussion of dualism, this view raises an almost insoluble question: How can an immaterial spirit interact with a material universe? If a nonphysical entity moved or affected an object in the physical universe, it would violate the most basic law of science. Science is based on the law of the conservation of energy (sometimes called the first law of thermodynamics) discovered by James Joule and Lord Kelvin in the nineteenth century. This law states that the total energy contained in a closed physical system can change its forms, but can neither increase nor decrease in total quantity. For example, energy in the form of motion may be changed into heat, which is another form of energy (for example, when you rub your hands together quickly to heat them). But the total amount of energy in the physical universe can neither increase nor decrease. Yet if an immaterial spirit somehow changed or altered some physical object in the slightest way, this would introduce additional energy into the physical universe. This would violate the basic law of the conservation of energy. Similarly, if a physical object somehow moved or changed an immaterial spirit, this would in effect dissipate energy out of the physical universe, again violating the law of the conservation of energy. If nonmaterial spirits coexist with material objects, then, neither should be able to affect each other in the slightest way. Neither should even be able to perceive the existence of the other!

Dualism, then, seems as improbable as materialism and idealism. What, then, is left? For Voltaire's Candide, the answer is to reject both extreme materialism, which he sees as leading to nothingness, and extreme idealism, which leads to blind optimism. Yes, disorder, chaos, even evil exist. But Candide does not succumb to them. He decides that he can cultivate virtue and justice, although he probably will not find them in the universe. Thus, Candide attempts to avoid what he considers the false dilemma of all or nothing. His attitude uses the practical consequences of a belief. In this sense, it is pragmatic. Pragmatism offers another approach to reality, one which rejects the materialism/idealism debate.

Great men are they who see that spiritual is stronger than any material force, that thoughts rule the world.

RALPH WALDO EMERSON

QUESTIONS

1. Some people argue that a universal law is at work in the universe, giving everything design and purpose and ordering our experiences. Do you see such a principle or law?

2. Can there be a principle or law at work without a purpose or goal? If not, must the idealist account for the purpose of things?

3.   In what sense is it true that the relationships among things are the only meaningful reality? Can you think of anything that you can understand without reference to something else?

4.   It has often been said that idealism encourages a withdrawal from the world, a retreat from secular problems, and an immersion in otherworldly concerns. As a result, the idealist neglects real and pressing social concerns. Explain why you think this charge is justified or not justified.

5.   Read Alexander Pope's "Essay on Man." What is his metaphysical position? What would be Candide's reaction to it?

3.3 Reality in Pragmatism

To many people, the debate between materialism and idealism seems to be a pointless philosophical exercise. Nothing will change, they claim, if we decide that all reality is ultimately matter. For example, people who believe in an after-life will continue to believe in an afterlife, but the afterlife will be in a material world. And similarly, they insist, nothing will change if we decide that all reality is ultimately immaterial. The things around us will still feel hard, will still smell, will still have shapes, colors, positions, and motions, even if we decide that they are made up of something we term "immaterial reality." Because the outcome of the debate between materialism and idealism seems to have no important con-sequences, such people have concluded that it is pointless to debate whether reality is material or spiritual.

Underlying their conclusion is the assumption that our beliefs about reality are meaningful only to the extent that they have important consequences. This assumption is the cornerstone of a particularly American approach to reality called *pragmatism*.

Pragmatism as a philosophical movement has grown up in the United States during the last hundred years through the writings of Charles S. Peirce (1839–1914), William James (1842–1910), and John Dewey (1859–1952). James de-fines **pragmatism** as "the attitude of looking away from first things, principles, 'categories,' supposed necessities; and of looking towards last things, fruits, con-sequences, facts."[13] Pragmatism is also a reaction to traditional systems of phi-losophy, such as materialism and idealism. These systems, claim the pragmatists,

pragmatism the philosophical school of thought, associated with Dewey, James, and Peirce, that tries to mediate between idealism and materialism by re-jecting all absolute first prin-ciples, tests truth through work-ability, and views the universe as pluralistic

---

[13] William James, *Pragmatism: A New Name for Some Old Ways of Thinking* (New York: Longmans, Green, 1907), 54–55.

William James: "Pragmatism is the attitude of looking away from first things, principles, 'categories,' supposed necessities; and of looking towards last things, fruits, consequences, facts."

have erred in looking for absolutes. Reality is hardly a single thing: It is pluralistic. And we are part of it. Using intelligence and reason, we can understand and exercise some control over nature; we can help create it.

To grasp the metaphysical content of pragmatism, it is essential to understand its general approach to philosophy and the social climate out of which it arose.[14]

PRAGMATISM'S APPROACH TO PHILOSOPHY

Pragmatism is decidedly humanistic. Peirce, James, and Dewey tried to understand philosophy and reformulate its problems in the light of psychology, sociology, scientific method, and the insights provided by the arts. They opposed the insularity of philosophy, its failure to view problems in a larger human and social context. "In a subject like philosophy," wrote James, "it is really fatal to lose connection with the open air of human nature, and to think in terms of shop-tradition only."[15] Philosophy is not just a self-contained discipline with its own cluster of problems; it is an instrument used by living individuals who are wrestling with personal and social problems and struggling to clarify their standards, directions, and goals. Such impulses are not novel to philosophy, but pragmatism took this position deliberately, systematically, and vigorously.

---

[14] The following discussion is indebted to Charles Frankel, *The Golden Age of American Philosophy* (New York: George Braziller, 1960), 1–17.
[15] Quoted in Frankel, *The Golden Age*, 3.

John Dewey: "Philosophy originated not out of intellectual material, but out of social and emotional material."

John Dewey, writing in *Reconstruction in Philosophy*, argued that all philosophy arises out of people's continual struggles to deal with social and moral problems. Two important observations follow from this fact. First, we cannot understand a philosophy without an awareness of the social forces that have produced it. Second, and more important here, any philosophy or doctrine has worth only to the degree that it helps people resolve their problems. Notice especially this second point in the following passage from *Reconstruction in Philosophy*:

This is the trait which, in my opinion, has affected most deeply the classic notion about the nature of philosophy. Philosophy has arrogated to itself the office of demonstrating the existence of a transcendent, absolute or inner reality and of revealing to man the nature and features of this ultimate and higher reality. It has therefore claimed that it was in possession of a higher organ of knowledge than is employed by positive science and ordinary practical experience, and that it is marked by a superior dignity and importance—a claim which is undeniable *if* philosophy leads man to proof and intuition of a Reality beyond that open to day-by-day life and the special sciences.

This claim has, of course, been denied by various philosophers at various times. But for the most part these denials have been agnostic and skeptical. They have contented themselves with asserting that absolute and ultimate reality is beyond human ken. But they have not ventured to deny that such Reality would be the appropriate sphere for the exercise of philosophic knowledge provided only it were within the reach of human intelligence. Only comparatively recently has another conception of the proper office of philosophy arisen. This course of lectures will be devoted to setting forth this different conception of philosophy in some of its main contrasts to what this lecture has termed the classic conception. At this point, it can be referred to only by anticipation and in cursory fashion. It is implied in the account

CRITICAL THINKING

Suppose it is proven that a philosophical view originated out of the social and emotional influences operating on a philosopher. Does it follow the view should be rejected?

which has been given of the origin of philosophy out of the background of an authoritative tradition; a tradition originally dictated by man's imagination working under the influence of love and hate and in the interest of emotional excitement and satisfaction. Common frankness requires that it be stated that this account of the origin of philosophies claiming to deal with absolute Being in a systematic way has been given with malice prepense. It seems to me that this genetic method of approach is a more effective way of undermining this type of philosophic theorizing than any attempt at logical refutation could be.

If this lecture succeeds in leaving in your minds as a reasonable hypothesis the idea that philosophy originated not out of intellectual material, but out of social and emotional material, it will also succeed in leaving with you a changed attitude toward traditional philosophies. They will be viewed from a new angle and placed in a new light. New questions about them will be aroused and new standards for judging them will be suggested.[16]

We should note that pragmatism evidences a confidence in the ability and power of the mind to make the world over. The universe is plastic and unfinished; the human intellect can make its ideals a reality. Peirce, James, and Dewey believed that ideas can actually lead the way in human life. This ideal underlay their insistence that the truth of an idea lies in its capacity to get us through life in a desirable way.

Corollary to this is the view that all thinking exists to defend personal interests and unconscious wishes that thinking cannot change. All thinking strengthens or secures some human interest. Rather than compromising human ideals, this notion shows that ideals have a natural home in the world. We discover new ways of thinking in order to realize these ideals more effectively.

Understandably, pragmatism damns any belief that limits what the human mind and will can accomplish. "Damn the absolute," James once wrote to a fellow philosopher. And more than once he penned, "Pragmatism looks to the future." The future is limited only by human aspiration, and that is limited by the human capacity to slough off inherited beliefs in eternal truths. Philosophy must recognize this.

Pragmatism denies sharp distintions between matter and mind, science and morals, and experience and reason. For pragmatists, we must examine human ideas and ideals from the biological and social points of view and treat them as instruments for making sense of experience. We must judge any idea or ideal in terms of its context. Its value depends on its problem-solving capacity. The heart of pragmatism is the pragmatic method.

> **CRITICAL THINKING**
>
> Suppose that no one feels that materialism and idealism are meaningful, stimulating, or interesting views. Does it follow that they are false?

THE PRAGMATIC METHOD

The pragmatic method is a way to discover what our ideas mean by studying their consequences in actual experience. Any inferences about the world drawn from metaphysical inquiries must have premises that refer to facts in the world and not to human reasoning alone. We cannot base judgments on their con-

---

[16]John Dewey, *Reconstruction in Philosophy* (New York: Henry Holt, 1920), 406–407.

nectedness to some presupposed transcendent or ultimate reality. Any judgment must be rooted in the things of experience that are meaningful to humans. Thus, any view of reality is tied to the values inherent in social traditions. In effect, there are no ultimate principles, no self-evident values, and no irreducible sense data. In fact, pragmatism allows no certainties. Ultimately, the test of an idea or ideal is its capacity to solve the particular problems that it addresses. Both materialism and idealism fail this test. Here is how William James expresses the point in his important work, *Pragmatism* (1907):

> The pragmatic method is primarily a method of settling metaphysical disputes that otherwise might be interminable. Is the world one or many? Fated or free? Material or spiritual? Here are notions either of which may or may not hold good of the world; and disputes over such notions are unending. The pragmatic method in such cases is to try to interpret each notion by tracing its respective practical consequences. What difference would it practically make to anyone if this notion rather than that notion were true? If no practical difference whatever can be traced, then the alternatives mean practically the same thing, and all dispute is idle. Whenever a dispute is serious, we ought to be able to show some practical difference that must follow from one side or the other's being right.[17]

Pragmatists differ in their practice—understandably, since pragmatism is not a monolithic system of thought. For example, Peirce was concerned with the logical implications of ideas, not their psychological effects. He focused on the scientific function of ideas—their role in fostering reasoned consensus. In contrast, James, a physiologist and psychologist, was interested in ideas as events in personal experience, as instruments of will and desire. Dewey was neither a student of logic and science nor a psychologist. His main interest was social criticism. He used the pragmatic method to reassess the functions of education, logic, the arts, and philosophy in human civilization. Nonetheless, the observations about pragmatism presented here underlay the thought of each of these highly influential American philosophers, and the pragmatic method guided their thoughts.

Applied to metaphysical questions, the pragmatic method indicates certain criteria for determining what's real. Many materialists rely on sense observation and scientific method; some idealists (although not Berkeley) rely primarily on reason. In contrast, James accepted neither of these as the final determinant of reality. In fact, he argued that people recognize a number of realities. Among them are the worlds of sense experience; of scientific knowledge; of belief and opinion; and of the transcendent, religious, or the supernatural. According to James, each of us selects the reality that is most personally meaningful. In effect, we choose our own ultimate reality by the criterion of meaningful usefulness. While metaphysicians speak of one world as having more reality than another, James interpreted their view as expressing a relation to our emotional and active life. Simply put, reality is what stimulates and interests us, and our interests will ultimately determine what our reality is.

There are people for whom even the reality of the external world constitutes a grave problem. I do not address them; I presuppose a minimum of reason in my readers.

PAUL FEYERABEND

Materialists and madmen never have doubts.

G. K. CHESTERTON

---

[17] William James, *Pragmatism* (1907), 46.

Although rejecting scientific method as the exclusive determinant of reality, pragmatists nonetheless employ it in order to learn the secrets of reality and self. But they do not look for cosmic mind or reason; the fact that we have minds does not mean that the universe does, as some idealists would contend. Pragmatism asserts that mind is real but only as a function of behavior. We develop this function when we learn about the things around us. For pragmatists, thinking is coming to understand the connection between action and consequence.

OBJECTIONS TO PRAGMATISM

Is pragmatism an acceptable middle ground between materialism and idealism? Or is it muddled thinking? Does pragmatism give us a clear notion of what it understands to be real? Some pragmatists claimed to know only their experiences, which critics argue is a claim of idealism. Peirce, in fact, opted for a version of idealism. But if we know only our experiences, how can we maintain the pragmatic belief in an objective physical reality?

We only think when we are confronted with a problem.
JOHN DEWEY

Are pragmatists correct, also, in holding that mind is just a function of behavior, that it is only an instrument of biological survival? People meditate, contemplate, and use the mind to compose great symphonies and to ask philosophical questions. Are these activities necessary for biological survival? Mind, say the pragmatists, exists to fulfill desires. Then why the commitment to scientific inquiry? Why such a stress on impartiality when seeking truth and not more reliance on the subjective impulses of the mind?

Consider, finally, whether pragmatism erases the distinction between the structure of the mind and the structure of the universe, between the knowledge of facts and the existence of facts apart from our knowledge.[18] When pragmatism emphasizes the mind's capacity to impose order on an open, unlimited world, does this imply that there is no antecedent order in the world? Does it mean that there is no configuration of things aside from what we may think or desire? This seems to be the version of pragmatism proposed by James and Dewey. Of course, pragmatists do not deny the existence of a world independent of the presence of human beings, but they do deny that anything in the world is settled or finished.

QUESTIONS

1.   What are the assumptions of materialism and idealism that pragmatism ignores?

2.   In what respects does pragmatism incorporate materialism and idealism?

3.   If you were a pragmatist, how would you reconcile your belief that you can know only your experiences with your belief that an objective reality exists?

4.   Compare and contrast the everyday and philosophical meanings of *pragmatist*.

---

[18] See Frankel, *The Golden Age*, 7.

3.4 Reality and Logical Positivism

We saw that pragmatism attempts to understand reality in terms of pragmatic consequences. However, another influential twentieth-century philosophy ends by rejecting all metaphysical attempts to understand reality. This is the outlook of **logical positivism,** which concentrates on language and meaning.

Like pragmatism, logical positivism is a reaction to the disputes between idealists and materialists. Pragmatism reacts by objecting that these disputes are pointless because they do not focus on "fruits, consequences, facts." Logical positivists react by objecting that idealists and materialists never stop to look carefully at the meaning of the language they use. In fact, positivist philosophers have claimed, the trouble with all metaphysical approaches to reality, including those of the pragmatists, is that the language they use is essentially meaningless. All metaphysics, logical positivists have claimed, is literally nonsense.

One of the most influential of the logical positivists was Alfred J. Ayer (1910–1989), a British philosopher. According to Ayer, philosophers have to be extremely careful to ensure that they are not speaking nonsense, and almost all metaphysics is mere nonsense. To clarify his point, Ayer offered "a criterion by which it can be determined whether or not a sentence is literally meaningful":

> I divide all genuine [meaningful] propositions into two classes: those which, in this terminology, concern "relations of ideas," and those which concern "matters of fact." The former class comprises the *a priori* propositions of logic and pure mathematics, and these I allow to be necessary and certain only because they are analytic. That is, I maintain that the reason why these propositions cannot be confuted in experience is that they do not make any assertion about the empirical world, but simply record our determination to use symbols in a certain fashion. Propositions concerning empirical matters of fact, on the other hand, I hold to be hypotheses, which can be probable but never certain. . . . I require of an empirical hypothesis . . . that some possible sense-experience should be relevant to the determination of its truth or falsehood. If a putative proposition fails to satisfy this principle, and is not a tautology, then I hold that it . . . is neither true nor false, but literally senseless.[19]

Ayer's point is that there can only be two kinds of meaningful statements: (1) tautologies, or "relations of ideas," and (2) empirical hypotheses, or "statements of fact." Tautologies are statements that are true by definition, such as "All bachelors are unmarried," "His sister is a female," and "Triangles have three sides." Tautologies, sometimes called *analytic propositions*, are propositions in which the meaning of the predicate is part of the meaning of the subject. Tautologies do not give us any real information about the world but only about the meanings of words. Statements of fact, on the other hand, are those that can, at least in theory, be verified by some imaginable observation. Examples are "It's raining," "California is about three thousand miles from New York," and "A

logical positivism the philosophical school of thought associated with Carnap and Ayer that claims that only analytic and synthetic statements are meaningful and that because metaphysical and ethical statements are neither, the latter are meaningless

---

CRITICAL THINKING

Is Ayer's assumption that all meaningful statements are tautologies or statements of fact correct? Are there other possibilities?

Consider this table in front of us. It is not what it seems. Leibniz tells us it is a community of souls. Bishop Berkeley tells us it is an idea in the mind of God. Sober science, scarcely less wonderful, tells us it is a vast collection of electric charges in violent motion.

BERTRAND RUSSELL

---

[19] Alfred J. Ayer, *Language, Truth, and Logic*, 2d ed. (New York: Dover, 1952), 31.

spirochete causes syphilis." Statements of fact, which are sometimes called *synthetic* or *empirical statements*, do give us information about the world. They tell us that the world is one way rather than another. We cannot know whether such statements are true without making some observations.

If a statement is neither a tautology nor a statement of fact, Ayer argued, then it is meaningless; it is nonsensical. Because metaphysical statements are neither tautologies nor statements of fact, he concluded, they are meaningless. Look at how he argues for this point:

> The traditional disputes of philosophers are, for the most part, as unwarranted as they are unfruitful. The surest way to end them is to establish beyond question what should be the purpose and method of philosophical inquiry. And this is by no means so difficult a task as the history of philosophy would lead one to suppose. For if there are any questions which science leaves it to philosophy to answer, a straightforward process of elimination must lead to their discovery.
>
> We may begin by criticizing the metaphysical thesis that philosophy affords us knowledge of a reality transcending the world of science and common sense. . . . [I]t is convenient for us to take the case of those who believe that it is possible to have knowledge of a transcendent reality as a starting point for our discussion. The argument which we use to refute them will subsequently be found to apply to the whole of metaphysics.
>
> One way of attacking a metaphysician who claimed to have knowledge of a reality which transcended the phenomenal [observable] world would be to inquire from what premises his propositions were deduced. Must he not begin, as other men do, with the evidence of his senses? And if so, what valid process of reasoning can possibly lead him to the conception of a transcendent reality? Surely from empirical premises nothing whatsoever concerning the properties, or even the existence, of anything superempirical can legitimately be inferred. But this objection would be met by a denial on the part of the metaphysician that his assertions were ultimately based on the evidence of his senses. He would say that he was endowed with a faculty of intellectual intuition which enabled him to know facts that could not be known through sense-experience. And even if it could be shown that he was relying on empirical premises, and that his venture into a nonempirical world was therefore logically unjustified, it would not follow that the assertions concerning this nonempirical world could not be true. For the fact that a conclusion does not follow from its putative premise is not sufficient to show that it is false. Consequently one cannot overthrow a system of transcendent metaphysics merely by criticizing the way in which it comes into being. What is required is rather a criticism of the nature of the actual statements which comprise it. And this is the line of argument which we shall, in fact, pursue. For we shall maintain that no statement which refers to a "reality" transcending the limits of all possible sense-experience can possibly have any literal significance; from which it must follow that the labors of those who have striven to describe such a reality have all been devoted to the production of nonsense. . . .
>
> The criterion which we [will] use to test the genuineness of apparent statements of fact [such as those of metaphysics] is the criterion of verifiability. We say that a sentence is factually significant to any given person if, and only if, he knows how to verify the proposition which it purports to express—that is, if he knows what observations would lead him, under certain conditions, to accept the proposition as being true, or reject it as being false. If, on the other hand, the putative proposition is of such a character that the assumption of its truth, or falsehood, is consistent

CRITICAL THINKING

Does Ayer assume that statements of fact—that is, statements about what the real universe around us is like—must be based on what we observe? Is this assumption correct? What else might statements of fact be based on?

CRITICAL THINKING

"Surely from empirical premises nothing concerning the properties or even the existence of anything superempirical can legitimately be inferred." Is this true? Are empirical statements the only basis for believing in superempirical things?

CRITICAL THINKING

Suppose I didn't know what observations would lead me to accept a proposition as true or reject it as false. Would it necessarily follow that I do not understand it?

with any assumption whatsoever concerning the nature of his future experience, then, as far as he is concerned, it is, if not a tautology, a mere pseudoproposition. The sentence expressing it may be emotionally significant to him; but it is not literally significant. . . .

In the first place, it is necessary to draw a distinction between practical verifiability and verifiability in principle. Plainly we all understand, in many cases believe, propositions which we have not in fact taken steps to verify. Many of these are propositions which we could verify if we took enough trouble. But there remain a number of significant propositions concerning matters of fact which we could not verify even if we chose, simply because we lack the practical means of placing ourselves in the situation where the relevant observations could be made. A simple and familiar example of such a proposition is the proposition that there are mountains on the further side of the moon. No rocket has yet [in 1936] been invented which would enable me to go and look at the further side of the moon, so that I am unable to decide the matter by actual observation. But I do know what observations would decide it for me, if, as is theoretically conceivable, I were once in a position to make them. And therefore I say that the proposition is verifiable in principle, if not in practice, and is accordingly significant. On the other hand, such a metaphysical pseudoproposition as "the Absolute enters into, but is itself incapable of, evolution and progress," is not even in principle verifiable. For one cannot conceive of an observation which would enable one to determine whether the Absolute did, or did not, enter into evolution and progress. Of course it is possible that the author of such a remark is using English words in a way in which they are not commonly used by English-speaking people, and that he does, in fact, intend to assert something which could be empirically verified. But until he makes us understand how the proposition that he wishes to express would be verified, he fails to communicate anything to us. And if he admits, as I think the author of the remark in question would have admitted, that his words were not intended to express either a tautology or a proposition which was capable, at least in principle, of being verified, then it follows that he has made an utterance which has no literal significance even for himself.[20]

Logical positivists like Ayer would view not only metaphysical statements as meaningless but most ethical, aesthetic, and theological ones as well, because most of them are neither tautologies nor statements of fact that can be verified by observation. Thus, they would consider the following statements nonsensical: "God exists," "God doesn't exist," "Lying is wrong," "Lying is right," "A moral law operates in the universe," and "The best form of government is the one that governs least." The fact that very few people consider such statements meaningless raises a question: How can such statements be rejected as meaningless when so many people believe that they are filled with meaning?

Logical positivists have replied that although metaphysical statements are not literally meaningful, they nevertheless carry another, nonliteral kind of meaning: They express emotion. Much as lyrical poets use words to express feelings, metaphysicians—and philosophers in general—use words to express feelings and not to represent facts about the world. Here is how the point is put by Rudolph Carnap (1891–1970), another analyst of the logical positivist school:

---

[20] Ibid., 33, 34, 35, 36.

Now many linguistic utterances are analogous to laughing in that they have only an expressive function, no representative function. Examples of this are cries like "Oh, Oh" or, on a higher level, lyrical verses. The aim of a lyrical poem in which occur the words "sunshine" and "clouds" is not to inform us of certain meteorological facts, but to express certain feelings of the poet and to excite similar feelings in us. A lyrical poem has no assertive sense, no theoretical sense, it does not contain knowledge.

The meaning of our anti-metaphysical thesis may now be more clearly explained. This thesis asserts that the metaphysical statements—like lyrical verses—have only an expressive function, but no representative function. Metaphysical statements are neither true nor false, because they assert nothing, they contain neither knowledge nor error, they lie completely outside the field of knowledge, of theory, outside the discussion of truth or falsehood. But they are like laughing, lyrics, and music, expressive. They express not so much temporary feelings as permanent emotional or volitional dispositions. Thus, for instance, a metaphysical system of monism [the view that reality is only one kind of thing—either matter or spirit, but not both] may be an expression of an even and harmonious mode of life, a dualistic system [the view that reality is made up of two kinds of things, matter and spirit] may be an expression of the emotional state of someone who takes life as an eternal struggle. . . . Realism [materialism] is often a symptom of the type of constitution called by psychologists extroverted, which is characterized by easily forming connections with men and things; idealism, of an opposite constitution, the so-called introverted type, which has a tendency to withdraw from the unfriendly world and to live within its own thoughts and fancies.

Thus we find a great similarity between metaphysics and lyrics. But there is one decisive difference between them. Both have no representative function, no theoretical content. A metaphysical statement, however—as distinguished from a lyrical verse—seems to have such a content, and by this not only is the reader deceived, but the metaphysician himself. He believes that in his metaphysical treatise he has asserted something, and is led by this into argument and polemics against the statements of some other metaphysician. A poet, however, does not assert that the verses of another are wrong or erroneous; he usually contents himself with calling them bad.

The non-theoretical character of metaphysics would not be in itself a defect; all arts have this non-theoretical character without thereby losing their high value for personal as well as for social life. The danger lies in the *deceptive* character of metaphysics; it gives the illusion of knowledge without actually giving any knowledge. This is the reason why we reject it.[21]

Metaphysical statements about reality, then, are meaningless. They serve only to express our feelings about reality.

OBJECTIONS TO LOGICAL POSITIVISM

Although many contemporary philosophers, especially in the United States and England, have embraced the views of the positivists, others continue to feel that they are mistaken. One of the fundamental objections to the views of the logical positivists in particular is that their basic "criterion of meaning" is an unproved assumption. Critics claim that logical positivists argue in this way:

---

[21] Rudolph Carnap, "The Rejection of Metaphysics," [1935], in *Twentieth-Century Philosophy: The Analytic Tradition*, ed. Morris Weitz (New York: Free Press, 1966), 215–216.

All meaningful statements are either analytic or synthetic (the basic criterion of meaning).

Metaphysical, religious, ethical, and aesthetic statements are neither analytic nor synthetic.

Therefore, metaphysical, religious, ethical, and aesthetic statements are meaningless.

But, say critics, the first statement in this argument is an assumption; it is not proved by the analysts and can never be proved. Perhaps utterances other than analytic and synthetic ones *can* transmit meaning and truth. Moreover, critics contend, if we apply the logical positivists' criterion of meaning to itself, it would turn out to be meaningless. The criterion of meaning states "All meaningful statements must be either tautologies or empirically verifiable." But this statement is not a tautology because the dictionary does not define *meaningful statements* as "either tautologies or empirically verifiable." Nor is this statement empirically verifiable: How would you ever verify the statement "True statements must be either tautologies or empirically verifiable"? So, critics say, the criterion of meaning is itself meaningless. The criterion of meaning would have to be nothing more than the analysts' own "expression of emotion." Maybe the logical positivists are merely expressing their uncomfortable feelings about other philosophers and choose to express their feelings by shouting "Meaningless!"

Finally, other critics have argued, in refusing to discuss metaphysical questions about reality merely because they do not meet their own unproved assumptions about meaning, the analysts have in effect pretended that our real human questions and problems do not exist. True, by taking this approach logical positivists have avoided the many hard questions raised by materialists, idealists, pragmatists, phenomenologists, and existentialists. But that is playing ostrich. The problems, critics contend, are still there, and people still continue to think about them. But in failing to deal with these problems, logical positivists have turned away from dealing with some of the most profound and significant issues that human beings face. This, critics claim, is one of the most disappointing aspects of logical positivism: its failure to discuss the questions that really matter.

Many philosophers who were once sympathetic to logical positivism have noticed this failure and have come to recognize as legitimate not just one or two but many modes of meaning, including those dealing with the questions posed by metaphysics. Ultimately, they may agree with the critics of logical positivism, who defend the philosopher's right and need to discuss questions not only of language but also of metaphysics, morality, religion, politics, and education. Certainly, any inquiry into ourselves, any search for what we are, that ignores these aspects of human experience seems incomplete.

QUESTIONS

1. In what sense do the logical positivists apply the adjective *meaningless* to nonsensical statements? Can something be intellectually meaningless but emotionally meaningful? Can you give an example?

2. What is your reaction to the following evaluation by Alfred J. Ayer?

> It is impossible to find a criterion for determining the validity of ethical judgment . . . because they [ethical judgments] have no objective validity whatsoever. If a sentence makes no statement at all, there is obviously no sense in asking whether what it says is true or false. . . . They are pure expressions of feeling . . . unverifiable for the same reason as a cry of pain or a word of command is unverifiable — because they do not express genuine propositions.[22]

3. Which of the following statements would a logical positivist consider meaningful? Meaningless?

    a. She wore a blue dress.

    b. Her blue dress was green.

    c. At the bottom of the ocean there's a shiny new penny lying in the belly of a dead carp.

    d. The zite dwart oilated twarily near an ach grul.

    e. The action in the preceding sentence takes place near an ach grul.

    f. Tooth fairies never appear to bad children.

    g. The good go to heaven, the bad to hell.

    h. Killing orphans without reason is an evil thing to do.

    i. Oxygen is necessary for combustion.

    j. Love makes the world go 'round.

4. How valid do you consider the criticism that the logical positivist's definition of what is meaningful makes a sham of the things that we take seriously?

5. Some people charge that the logical positivist's position is inconsistent and self-contradictory. Why do they say this? Do you agree?

6. What would you say is the primary contribution of logical positivism to philosophy?

3.5 Antirealism: The New Idealists

Throughout much of the twentieth century, the "new" philosophies of pragmatism and logical positivism overshadowed the earlier debates between idealists and materialists. Recently, however, some philosophers, including a number of feminists, have begun to espouse views that are in many ways a return to traditional idealism and its rejection of the existence of an external reality. These views, as we will see, are "postmodern" in the sense that they reject the

---

[22] Ayer, *Language, Truth, and Logic*, 107–109.

"modern" belief in a single reality. We must examine these "new" views about reality because, as we will see, they have critically important implications about the relations between men and women. These new approaches to reality have been labeled *antirealist* to indicate that like Berkeley, they reject realism, the view that an external reality exists independent of our minds.

More precisely, **realism** is the view that a real world exists independent of our language, our thoughts, our perceptions, and our beliefs.[23] The realist holds that the features of this world would have been exactly the same as they are now even if no one had ever existed who could perceive them, think about them, or describe them with language. And these features will continue the same long after each of us is gone. Take, for example, the object in our sky that we refer to as the moon and describe as the largest satellite orbiting the earth. The realist holds that the moon would exist and continue to be the largest object orbiting the earth whether or not we or anyone else ever described it, perceived it, or thought of it in this or any other way.

> **realism** the doctrine that the objects of our senses exist independently of their being experienced

The realist holds, then, that an external world exists, a world whose existence and features don't depend on how, or even whether, anyone describes it, perceives it, or thinks about it. The antirealist, on the other hand, denies that such a world exists. **Antirealism** claims that the world or worlds we inhabit and everything in them depend completely on how they are described, perceived, and thought about.

> **antirealism** the doctrine that the objects of our senses do not exist independently of our perceptions, beliefs, concepts, and language

Unlike Berkeley, modern antirealists do not argue that all we know are our own sensations or ideas. Instead, the new antirealists base their views on language, arguing, in effect, that all we know are our own linguistic creations. These antirealists argue that when we think about or talk about reality we must use a particular language with its own special way of describing things. Different languages describe the same reality in very different ways. So, antirealists conclude, we cannot say that reality has features independent of our language. The features of reality depend on the language or system of concepts we use to describe or think about reality. For us, as an example, the moon exists because our language and way of thinking mark off a part of the sky as the moon, and in our language it is the largest satellite orbiting the earth. But our language did not have to mark off the sky in this particular way. In fact, if our language had partitioned the sky in a different way, we might not have counted the moon as the largest satellite orbiting the earth.

For the antirealist, then, there is no reality independent of the particular language or system of concepts we use and the particular world or worlds we create with them. Many contemporary philosophers have held this antirealist view, including Paul Feyerabend, Richard Rorty, Jacques Derrida, Liz Stanley, Sue Wise, Ruth Hubbard, Nelson Goodman, Hilary Putnam, and Dale Spender. We will concentrate on the arguments of Goodman, Putnam, and Spender.

Nelson Goodman was one of the first contemporary philosophers to argue that there is no independent real world. Goodman asserts that we "make" reality

---

[23] My account here follows the discussion of realism by philosopher John Searle in his unpublished paper "Is There a Problem About Realism?" presented on February 28, 1992, at Santa Clara University.

or "worlds" by choosing a particular way of describing, seeing, or drawing boundaries around things:

> Now as we thus make constellations by picking out and putting together certain stars rather than others, so we make stars by drawing certain boundaries rather than others. Nothing dictates whether the sky shall be marked off into constellations or other objects. We have to make what we find, be it the Great Dipper, Sirius, food, fuel, or a stereo system.[24]

Goodman suggests, further, that we humans in fact construct and live in a multitude of different real worlds, each created by different and overlapping languages and systems of thought. Not only do artists, poets, and novelists create new and pleasing worlds by fashioning new languages and ways of thinking, but many others of us also create our own more or less pleasing, more or less successful worlds, each of them as "real" as the others.

Hilary Putnam, another prominent antirealist, makes a similar argument. Consider, he suggested, the objects in Figure 1. Our ordinary system of counting would say there are three objects in Figure 1. But certain nonstandard systems of counting would say there are seven objects. In addition to the three objects A, B, and C, these nonstandard systems would "see" the object that consists of A and B together, the object that consists of B and C together, the object that consists of A and C together, and the object that consists of A, B, and C together. There is, Putnam concludes, no single correct answer to this question: How many objects are there in the reality of the figure? What reality is depends on the system we use to describe it.

The antirealist position has been especially important to several feminist philosophers. For example, Dale Spender has also argued that there is no reality independent of our language:

> Language is not neutral. It is not merely a vehicle which carries ideas. It is itself a shaper of ideas, it is the programme for mental activity. In this context it is nothing short of ludicrous to conceive of human beings as capable of grasping things as they really are, of being impartial recorders of their world. For they themselves, or some of them, at least, have created or constructed that world and they have reflected themselves within it.
>
> Human beings cannot impartially describe the universe because in order to describe it they must first have a classification system. But, paradoxically, once they have that classification system, once they have a language, *they can see only certain arbitrary things*.[25]

The importance of the antirealist view for feminists such as Dale Spender is that it explains why the world that women ordinarily are forced to accept is so sexist. Often the words we use to describe women are demeaning; male experiences are taken as the norm for thinking about and describing the experiences of women; women are referred to by the supposedly generic word *man*. If lan-

---

[24] Nelson Goodman, *Of Mind and Other Matters* (Cambridge, MA: Harvard University Press, 1984), 36.

[25] Dale Spender, *Man Made Language*, 2d ed. (Boston: Routledge & Kegan Paul, 1985), 139.

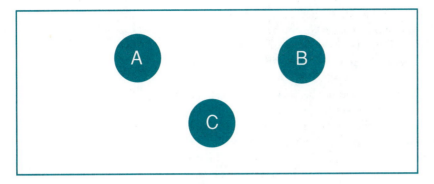

Figure 1. Hilary Putnam's circles—how many things do *you* count?

guage creates reality, then it is not surprising that our common reality is focused on males:

> Given that language is such an influential force in shaping our world, it is obvious that those who have the power to make the symbols and their meanings are in a privileged and highly advantageous position. They have, at least, the potential to order the world to suit their own ends, the potential to construct a language, a reality, a body of knowledge in which they are the central figures, the potential to legitimate their own primacy and to create a system of beliefs which is beyond challenge. . . .
>
> In the patriarchal order this potential has been realized.
>
> Males, as the dominant group, have produced language, thought and reality. Historically it has been the structures, the categories and the meanings which have been invented by males—though not of course by all males—and they have been validated by reference to other males. In this process women have played little or no part.[26]

Like Nelson Goodman, Dale Spender suggests that we must recognize that there are different female worlds or realities that are just as real as the male world that women are usually forced to inhabit:

> Most women within the women's movement are developing their skills at handling more than one reality. The pluralism of the movement is itself both a source and a manifestation of the ability to function in a multidimensional frame of reference. There are numerous "truths" available within feminism and it is falling into male defined (and false) patterns to try and insist that only one is correct. Accepting the validity of multidimensional reality predisposes women to accept multiple meanings and explanations without feeling that something is fundamentally wrong. . . .
>
> The concept of multidimensional reality is necessary, for it allows sufficient flexibility to accommodate the concept of equality. Multiple reality is a necessary condition for the acceptance of the experience of all individuals as equally valuable and viable. Only within a multidimensional framework is it possible for the analysis and explanation of everyone to avoid the pitfalls of being rejected, of being classified as wrong.[27]

---

[26] Ibid., 142–143.
[27] Ibid., 102–103.

The new antirealists, then, do more than deny that there is one external real world independent of our thought and language. For the new antirealists, there are many different real worlds, each created by different, but perhaps overlapping, languages and ways of thinking. Moreover, each of these worlds is as real and valid as the others.

The views of such antirealists have sometimes been said to be "postmodern" views. Postmodernism is a late-twentieth-century movement that rejects the view — popular from the eighteenth to the early twentieth century — that there is only one reality and that through rational inquiry we are progressing toward an ever fuller unified scientific understanding of that one reality. Whereas the "modern" world of the eighteenth to the early twentieth century believed in this unified account of a single reality, our own "postmodern" world recognizes a Babel of different and contradictory accounts of many distinct and equally valid realities created by people from many different cultures and subcultures and from many different times and places. Postmodernism, then, is the view that there are many realities and that these realities are constructed by the many languages of the cultures and subcultures that now swirl around us.

OBJECTIONS TO ANTIREALISM

Not everyone has been convinced by the postmodern arguments of the antirealists. In particular, several feminists have voiced concern over the implications of some antirealist claims, and we must consider their objections.

The antirealist claims that the worlds created by different languages and ways of thinking are equally real and valid and that there is no reality apart from our language and thought. But if all worlds are equally valid, then isn't the oppressive world created by sexist male language as valid a reality as any other? Moreover, if most men do not see women as oppressed so that in most men's reality women are not oppressed, don't we have to admit that this reality is entirely valid? And if men's reality is every bit as valid as women's reality, then shouldn't we stop criticizing men? As the feminist philosopher Jean Grimshaw writes,

> This highlights what is perhaps the most central problem of all in the theory of "multiple realities," all of which are equally "valid." Theories, ideas and ideologies are not only ways of "making sense" of the world. They may also be means by which one group of people may dominate or exercise control over another. And the fact that one group has power over or exploits another, cannot be reduced to anyone's belief that this is so; nor does the fact that someone does not understand their own experience in terms of oppression or exploitation necessarily mean that they are *not* oppressed or exploited. . . . [T]he assumption of multiple female "realities," all of which are "valid" and none of which have any claim to be regarded as more adequate than any other, cannot provide a way of conceptualizing things such as oppression, exploitation, the domination of one social group by another.[28]

Grimshaw is pointing to a fundamental problem in antirealism. For the antirealist, something is real if and only if it is part of someone's language or way of

---

[28] Jean Grimshaw, *Philosophy and Feminist Thinking* (Minneapolis: University of Minnesota Press, 1986), 100, 102.

thinking; otherwise, it is not real. But this means that if women do not believe they are being exploited, oppressed, or dominated, then in reality they are not being exploited, oppressed, or dominated. And if women speak and think in a male language that sees them as inferior, weak, and contemptible, then in reality they are inferior, weak, and contemptible. And if men think and speak as if nothing they do is domineering and oppressive, then this too is as real and as valid as the view that some male actions are oppressive and domineering.

Antirealism seems to imply, then, that sexism or oppression cannot be an objective reality because there is no objective reality. Sexism and the oppression of women cannot be real if men think otherwise in their world. And if men or women believe there is no sexism, then this belief is as valid and real as the feminist belief that sexism exists, and this is the end of the matter. Antirealism, then, does not allow the feminist to say that sexism is objectively real or that in reality all women suffer oppression, as long as men or women think and speak otherwise. It allows the feminist to say merely that sexism and oppression exist in her own world. Thus, antirealism seems to counter some of the basic claims of feminism.

Many other contemporary philosophers have argued that antirealism is mistaken. Philosopher John Searle is an example. He agrees that there are many different languages or systems for describing or "seeing" reality. But he claims that although the descriptions we give of reality depend on our language, the reality we are describing does not. Searle argues that Putnam and Goodman confuse our descriptions of reality (which depend on language) with the reality we are describing (which does not depend on language):

> From the fact that the *description* of any fact can only be made relative to a set of categories, it does not follow that the facts themselves only *exist* relative to a set of categories. . . . What counts as a correct application of the term "cat" . . . is up to us to decide and is to that extent arbitrary. But once we have fixed the meaning of such terms in our vocabulary by arbitrary definitions, it is no longer a matter of any kind of relativism or arbitrariness whether actual features of the world satisfy those definitions. We arbitrarily define the word "cat" in such and such a way; and only relative to such definitions can we say, "That's a cat." But once we have made the definitions and once we have applied the concepts relative to the system of definitions, whether or not something satisfies our definition is no longer arbitrary or relative.[29]

To understand Searle's point, let us return to Putnam's example of the three objects. In our ordinary system of counting objects, Figure 1 must be described as showing three objects. And in the proposed nonstandard system of counting objects, the figure must be described as seven objects. But in either case the objects—the reality—in the figure remain the same and do not change. Thus, our *description* of the figure depends on the system of concepts we use, but the *reality* of the figure does not depend on either system since it remains unchanged whichever system we use.

Is it possible to *prove* that the real world exists, as the realist says it does? Searle believes that a kind of proof is possible. To understand his argument, it

[29] Searle, "Is There a Problem About Realism?" 10.

will help if we first consider a point that Searle makes about Berkeley's idealism. Searle points out that "Berkeley saw that it was a problem for his account that if each person refers only to his own ideas when he speaks, then there is a question about how we succeed in communicating with other people." Searle's point is this: If idealists like Berkeley were correct, then each of us would know only his or her own particular ideas. If so, people could never talk to one another about the same thing; each of us could know and talk only about our own personal ideas, which no one else could know! Since people would never be talking about the same thing, they could never really communicate with and understand one another. But we do sometimes succeed in communicating with and understanding one another. So Berkeley's idealism must be wrong: Sometimes, at least, we must be talking about the same external reality.

Searle makes a similar argument against the new antirealism of Putnam, Goodman, and Spender. If we believe that people at least sometimes understand one another's language, Searle claims, then we must believe that they are referring to an independent reality. In order for two people to understand each other's statements, their statements must mean the same thing to both of them. But in order for a statement to mean the same thing to two people, both must see their statements as having the same "conditions of satisfaction." That is, both people must take the same facts as making their statement true. This means that the two people must take their statements as expressing the same facts about the same reality. Thus, if people understand each other, they must assume the existence of an independent reality—an external world—that they are all talking about:

> The person who denies metaphysical realism presupposes the existence of a public language, a language in which he or she communicates with other people. But what are the conditions of possibility of communication in a public language? What do I have to assume when I ask a question or make a claim that is supposed to be understood by others? At least this much: if we are using words to talk about something, in a way that we expect to be understood by others, then there must be at least the possibility of something those words can be used to talk about. Consider any claim, from particular statements such as "my dog has fleas," to theoretical claims such as "water is made of hydrogen and oxygen," to grand theories such as evolution or relativity, and you will see that they presuppose for their intelligibility that we are taking metaphysical realism for granted.
>
> I am not claiming that one can prove metaphysical realism to be true from some standpoint that exists apart from our human linguistic practices. What I am arguing, rather, is that those practices themselves presuppose metaphysical realism. So one cannot within those practices intelligibly deny metaphysical realism, because the meaningfulness of our public utterances already presupposes an independently existing reality to which expressions in those utterances can refer.[30]

Notice that Searle assumes that, sometimes at least, we understand and communicate with each other. But is it possible that we never really succeed in understanding each other? That we never really know what each other is talk-

---

[30] John Searle, "The Storm Over the University," *The New York Review of Books*, December 6, 1990, 40.

ing about because we live in different worlds created by our different ways of thinking and speaking? For example, do men and women live in different worlds and therefore always misunderstand each other? Are all worlds equally real and valid, even those that deny the reality of sexism and oppression? Or is there only one real world in which we all live and about which we all talk and think? Is it possible to say that sexism, for example, is an objective reality for all women, even those who believe otherwise?

The debate between the realists and the antirealists has intensified during these last few years and has not yet been resolved. However, it is clear that a great deal hangs on this debate's resolution.

QUESTIONS

1. Compare the views of the new antirealists with the views of Berkeley. On what points do they agree? On what points do they differ?

2. Some people have claimed that if you are an antirealist, you cannot really care about changing or reforming the world. Can you explain what this claim means and how people who have made this claim would probably argue for it? Do you agree with their claim?

3. Putnam says that the same reality can be described as three objects or as seven objects. Is he assuming that reality is there to be described even before we describe it? If he is, then is he also assuming that reality exists independently of our descriptions and our language, just as the realist says it does?

4. Is it possible that each of us lives in a different world, as some antirealists have suggested? If so, can we ever really understand each other? Is each of us ultimately alone, locked in a private world that no one else can ever know or understand?

3.6 Encountering Reality: Phenomenology and Existentialism

Many people feel that the approaches to reality that we have examined are too distant from human reality. In trying to understand existence, traditional philosophies have reduced it to abstractions having little to do with our concrete existence and concerns. But there is nothing abstract about existing. Existence is what is real. And existence involves the human individual who exists. We find this emphasis on human existence in existentialism and its predecessor, phenomenology.

Phenomenology and existentialism share a number of outlooks on reality. For example, many phenomenologists and existentialists focus on the human condition as a key to what reality is. In particular, existentialists point out that we endure all kinds of pain: physical, emotional, and psychological. We feel anxious, uncertain, and indecisive. We know what it is to dread, to feel despair, and to suffer. Daily, we face the reality of death. True, we are not always conscious of death's imminence, but it is always with us. Anxiety, uncertainty, dread, suffering, and death all reveal something about reality, such as how contingent, fortuitous, and limited it is.

Building on this insight into the human condition, phenomenologists and existentialists claim that we shall never understand reality as long as we attempt to explain life and people merely objectively—from the outside, as it were. Materialism in particular has been guilty of this failure. In reducing individuals to scientific explanations, materialism in effect turns people into objects. Nor can we understand reality by relying on presuppositions that force us into "nothing-but" views. The idealism of philosophers like Berkeley has been guilty of this. Berkeley decided that reality was nothing but ideas, not because he carefully examined the nature of reality but because of his psychological presupposition that we perceive only our own ideas.

The phenomenologist and the existentialist try to approach reality from the inside, by focusing on reality as it is subjectively revealed by our human condition and human consciousness. And they attempt to approach reality not by relying on theoretical presuppositions but by trying to examine and describe reality as it presents itself to our unprejudiced view. Truth about our human existence cannot be grasped and repeated by means of neat, objective statements. We experience truth, like everything else, through living; the truth is within, not without. Despite these general similarities, various points distinguish phenomenology and existentialism.

PHENOMENOLOGY

To understand phenomenology, look at the term itself. *Phenomenology* consists of the Greek root *phenomenon,* meaning "what appears," and the suffix *logy,* meaning "the study of what appears." Without becoming enmeshed in the historical development of the term, we can say that in contemporary philosophy *phenomenology* means the study of what appears to consciousness.

In his *Phenomenology of Perception,* Maurice Merleau-Ponty (1907–1961) says that "The aim of phenomenology is described as the study of experiences with a view to bringing out their 'essences,' their underlying reason."[31] **Phenomenology** is the philosophical school that contends that being is the underlying reality that appears to our consciousness, which itself is being.

phenomenology the philosophical school founded by Edmund Husserl which contends that being is the underlying reality, that what is ultimately real is our consciousness, which itself is being

---

[31] Quoted in Edo Pivcevic, *Husserl and Phenomenology* (London: Hutchinson University Library, 1970), 11.

Husserl

For the founder of phenomenology, Edmund Husserl (1859–1938), the overriding issue is the reality that discloses itself to consciousness. You can think away everything, but you cannot think away thought. Reality, to the extent that it means anything to us, must be what is revealed to pure consciousness.

To understand what Husserl is saying, it's helpful to know more about him. An entry in his diary from 1906 provides a good look at what concerned him:[32] "I have been through enough torment from lack of clarity and from doubt that goes back and forth. Only one need absorbs me: I must win clarity else I cannot live; I cannot bear life unless I can believe that I shall achieve it."[33] His intense desire for certainty was intensified by the relativism of the age, a relativism he saw as encouraged by the belief that scientific method is the only reliable way of knowing anything. In Husserl's view, relativism was self-contradictory. Anyone who denied the possibility of absolute certainty was involved in a contradiction, for to deny that possibility was to logically allow the existence of "an objectively valid science."

Of course, this argument wouldn't budge pragmatists. They would likely have viewed Husserl's insistence on an objectively valid science as indicating more about his fear of uncertainty than about the actual existence of such a science. Nonetheless, Husserl attacked relativism, not only because he viewed it as inconsistent but also because he felt that it generated undesirable social consequences. Writing in 1935, when the Nazis held power in Germany, Husserl viewed the European crisis as fundamentally attributable to the gradual erosion of the belief in rational certainty.

In Husserl's view, Europe had inherited rational certainty from the Greeks. Recall that the attitude of Plato and Aristotle was that of the disinterested spectator, the overseer of the world. With this attitude, they were led to a distinction between the presented and the real world, and ultimately to a universally valid truth — to truth in itself. Dewey, and pragmatism generally, had condemned the Greek attitude for locking people into ultimate principles, self-evident views, and a hierarchy of absolute values. Dewey wanted philosophy to adopt the methods of natural science instead and to turn to the practical problems that beset individuals and society. In contrast, Husserl attributed the "crisis of European man" to a blind allegiance to the methods of natural science. His prescription was to revive the disinterested attitude and to return to rationality in the original Greek sense.

Specifically, Husserl objected to the application of the methods of natural science to the mental life, to treating mental phenomena as if they were material objects. Such thinking leads to a caricature of reality. What's more, he saw psychology as compounding this error. Having distinguished between minds

---

[32] See W. T. Jones, *From Kant to Wittgenstein and Sartre* (New York: Harcourt Brace, 1969), 385–399.

[33] Quoted in H. S. Spiegelberg, *The Phenomenological Movement* (The Hague: Martinus Nijhoff, 1965), 82.

and bodies, psychologists treated minds as if they were like bodies. Husserl proposed a radically different investigative method to avoid these errors, a method, he believed, that could ultimately be applied to all the sciences. The perfection of phenomenology would demonstrate that the quest for certainty was not futile or frivolous. It would accomplish this by establishing a firm foundation for the sciences.

Vital to understanding Husserl's method is understanding his phenomenological stance, as opposed to what he called "the natural standpoint":

> Our first outlook upon life is that of natural human beings, imagining, judging, feeling, willing, *"from the natural standpoint."* Let us make clear to ourselves what this means in the form of simple meditations which we can best carry on in the first person.
>
> I am aware of a world, spread out in space endlessly, and in time becoming and become, without end. I am aware of it, that means, first of all, I discover it immediately, intuitively, I experience it. Through sight, touch, hearing, etc., in the different ways of sensory perception, corporeal things somehow spatially distributed are *for me simply there*, in verbal or figurative sense "present," whether or not I pay them special attention by busying myself with them, considering, thinking, feeling, willing. . . .
>
> [Further,] what is actually perceived, and what is more or less clearly copresent and determinate (to some extent at least), is partly pervaded, partly girt about with a *dimly apprehended depth or fringe of indeterminate reality*. I can pierce it with rays from the illuminating focus of attention with varying success. . . .
>
> As it is with the world in its ordered being as a spatial present—the aspect I have so far been considering—so likewise it is with the world in respect to its *ordered being in the succession of time*. This world now present to me, and in every waking "now" obviously so, has its temporal horizon, infinite in both directions. . . .
>
> [Moreover,] this world is not there for me as a mere *world of facts and affairs*, but, with the same immediacy, as a *world of values*, a *world of goods*, a *practical world*. . . . I find the things before me furnished not only with the qualities that befit their positive nature, but with value-characters such as beautiful or ugly, agreeable or disagreeable, pleasant or unpleasant, and so forth. . . .
>
> We emphasize a most important point once again in the sentences that follow: I find continually present and standing over against me the one spatio-temporal fact-world to which I myself belong, as do all other men found in it. . . . This "fact-world," as the word already tells us, I find to *be out there*, and also *take it just as it gives itself to me as something that exists out there*. All doubting and rejecting of the data of the natural world leaves standing the *general thesis of the natural standpoint*. "The" world is as fact-world always there; at the most it is at odd points "other" than I supposed, this or that under such names as "illusion," "hallucination," and the like, must be struck *out of it*, so to speak; but the "it" remains ever . . . a world that has its being out there. To know it more comprehensively, more trustworthily, more perfectly than the naive lore of experience is able to do . . . is the goal of the *sciences of the natural standpoint*.[34]

People usually assume the natural standpoint toward the world. This consists of being aware of a world that is "simply there," whether or not we pay any

---

[34]Edmund Husserl, *Ideas: General Introduction to Pure Phenomenology*, trans. W. R. Boyce-Gibson (New York: Macmillan, 1962), sec. 27, 30. Reprinted by permission of Simon & Schuster, Inc., and George Allen & Unwin Ltd.

special attention to it. This "fact-world," as Husserl calls it, we find to be "out there," and we take it just as it gives itself to us. Occasionally, this fact-world differs from what we supposed: We experience illusions or hallucinations. But a world that has its being out there remains. Thus, although we may suspect or even reject parts of our experience, we most often unquestioningly accept the world as a whole. Indeed, this natural standpoint seems a most reasonable position. Yet Husserl asks us to question it—to suspend judgment about the world as a whole.

Husserl does not want us to abandon the thesis of the natural standpoint—that the fact-world has its being out there—but to set it aside. He asks us to "set it as it were out of action," to "disconnect it, bracket it." The natural standpoint remains, but we simply make no use of it. We reserve judgments based on the natural standpoint. Although we continue to be conscious of the entire natural world, we phenomenologically bracket it, an act that "completely bars us from using any judgment that concerns spatio-temporal existence."

CRITICAL THINKING

Does Husserl assume that people have the ability to bracket? Is this assumption correct?

Suppose you are looking at a die in the palm of your hand. What do you experience? From the natural standpoint, the die is a cube of a certain color and size. There are dots on each side, from one to six of them. When you bracket this experience, as Husserl suggests, you do not doubt the experience of having the die in hand, but you do not assume that you actually have a die in hand. After all, you may be dreaming, hallucinating, or imagining, and your hand may actually be empty. Husserl asks you not to assume that the die has being in the mode of existence. This is what he means by the phenomenological stance, which he would prescribe for all our experience.

Husserl is suggesting that we suspend the truth claims of our everyday cognitive processes. Because we assume the natural standpoint, this suspension seems unnatural for most of us. Why should I not assume that I actually have a die in my hand when I can feel and see it? Husserl insists that bracketing, far from leaving us in a state of ignorance and skepticism, will present important truths that would otherwise elude us. He believes that these truths are important because whatever remains after bracketing is absolutely certain.

CRITICAL THINKING

Does Husserl assume that if something remains after you make yourself think that nothing around you has existence, that thing is part of "ultimate reality"? Is this assumption correct?

The obvious question is this: What survives bracketing? In general, Husserl believes that what survives is consciousness; ultimate reality consists of consciousness: "For what can remain over when the whole world is bracketed, including ourselves and our thinking? . . . Consciousness in itself has a being of its own which in its absolute uniqueness of nature remains unaffected by the phenomenologic disconnection."[35]

By consciousness, Husserl means that which involves both an act of intending (the experience of being conscious of something) and the intended object (that of which one is conscious). For example, when you look at the palm of your hand, you may be conscious of a white die, on one of whose faces is a black dot. Husserl points out that from the natural standpoint we hardly ever doubt this kind of fact. But, says Husserl, you can doubt that there was in fact a white die on your palm. However, you cannot doubt the experience of having seen and

---

[35] Ibid., sec. 33.

felt the die in the palm of your hand. Moreover, within this experience, it is possible to distinguish the die (the intentional object) from your act of intending it. When you bracket, what you experience is both your experiencing (that is, intending) of the die in the palm of your hand and the die as experienced (that is, intended) by you.

Further thought about how objects are present to consciousness persuaded Husserl to emphasize acts of intending more than the objects themselves. Bracketing revealed to him deeper and deeper levels of ego activity that are impossible to understand without profound phenomenological training. Suffice it to say that when all is bracketed, including ourselves, Husserl contends that consciousness remains. When we bracket our whole world, we tap our essence and realize that something precedes our experiences — namely, being: "It therefore remains as a region of Being which is in principle unique and can become in fact the field of a new science — the science of phenomenology." [36]

For Husserl, phenomenology is a new science of being. It reveals a sphere of being that is ultimate, in the sense that it presents itself with certainty within our experience. Studying being is not, for Husserl, investigating another reality. It is delving deeper and deeper into the reality that is consciousness.

Heidegger

Profoundly influenced by phenomenology, Martin Heidegger (1889–1976) made this question of being his primary concern. The problem with traditional thinking, claimed Heidegger, is that it is confused over the question of being. Being is the very act of existing. Being does not consist of all the characteristics of the individual, for that is to speak of the individual as *a* being. To speak of the individual's being is to acknowledge that when all qualities and properties not necessary to being as being are stripped away, being remains as *this* being, as individual.

Being is a difficult concept to communicate, because it is not a thing, although we may identify it with things. But this identification makes it all the more elusive, for we end up identifying the thing with being. You may have heard someone say, "Love me for what I am." Heidegger might have said, "Don't love me for *what* I am; love my *am*. Love my being, not what you may see as an expression of it: matter, mind, or soul." If we are to understand reality, says Heidegger, we must abandon our mad commitment to the world of things. By becoming conscious of our own being, we may better understand the being that underlies everything. At that point we may establish a meaningful relationship with another person.

This emphasis on reality as being underlies the view of the human as an existential being. But it is also curious to note its connection with Buddhist thought, even though, as we have previously seen, Buddhism seems to share some outlooks with the Western view of Hume, especially in its denial of the self.

---

[36] Quoted in Pivcevic, *Husserl and Phenomenology*, 11.

Although Heidegger is undoubtedly a Western thinker, his thought has enough Oriental flavor to lead him to remark, on reading the work of Zen scholar D. T. Suzuki, "If I understand this man correctly, this is what I have been trying to say in all my writings."[37] The Oriental thinker is generally more concerned with the inner nature of the self than with an objective, empirically verifiable reality. The world of the senses is short-lived and illusory. As a result, Eastern thought is preoccupied not with what is real but with *being* real. It distinguishes between the idea of ourselves and the immediate concrete feeling of ourselves. As Zen scholar Alan Watts puts it, "Zen points out that our precious 'self' is just an idea. . . . When we are no longer identified with the idea of ourselves, the entire relationship between subject and object, knower and known undergoes a sudden and revolutionary change. It becomes a real relationship, a mutuality in which the subject creates the object just as much as the object creates the subject. The knower no longer feels himself to be independent of the known; the experiencer no longer feels himself to stand apart from the experience."[38] If we are looking for a concrete reality, we shall find it *between* the individual and the world, "as the concrete coin is 'between' the abstract, Euclidean surfaces of its two sides."[39]

Eastern thought rejects the polarities of knower and known, experiencer and experience, and subject and object, because they are artificial and preclude true knowledge of self and being. Heidegger also seems to consider this Western penchant for dividing as a great error that began with Plato, who located truth in the intellect. Against the intellect Plato set nature—a realm of objects to be studied, manipulated, and quantified. Today we find ourselves inheritors of this tradition, as technological "masters" of the planet. Along with this dubious distinction, we have suffered, as Heidegger and Eastern thinkers have also observed, an estrangement from being and from ourselves, which the will to power and dominance only intensifies.

EXISTENTIALISM

The emphasis that phenomenology, particularly in the hands of Heidegger, has given to consciousness and being takes a more concrete form in the philosophy of existentialism. Along with phenomenology, existentialism can be viewed partially as a reaction to the idea that an objective knowledge of the human can be attained by applying the scientific method to sociology and psychology. Like phenomenology, existentialism is unsympathetic to science as a cognitive enterprise, suspicious of scientism, and wary of applying the scientific method to the solution of economic and political problems. What interests existentialists is the subjective flow of experience. But whereas phenomenologists might suggest that we become truly a self in the classical contemplation of a truth,

---

[37] D. T. Suzuki, *Zen Buddhism*, ed. William Barrett (Garden City, NY: Doubleday Anchor Books, 1956), xi–xii.
[38] Alan Watts, *The Way of Zen* (New York: Pantheon, 1957), 120–121. Reprinted by permission.
[39] Ibid., 122.

existentialists find self-definition in the passionate commitment to act and deed. This fact must be remembered to understand existentialism's metaphysical leanings.

Kierkegaard

In sketching the thought of Husserl, we began by quoting from his diary. We glimpsed the energizing force behind his philosophy: the need for certainty. It's useful to contrast this with an entry from *The Journals* of the founder of modern existentialism, Søren Kierkegaard (1813–1855):

> What I really lack is to be clear in my mind what I am to do, not what I am to know, except insofar as a certain understanding must precede every action. The thing is to understand myself, to see what God really wishes me to do; the thing is to find a truth which is true *for me*, to find *the idea for which I can live and die*. What would be the use of discovering so-called objective truth, of working through all the systems of philosophy and of being able if required, to review them all and show up the inconsistencies within each system;—what good would it do me to be able to develop a theory of the state and combine all the details into a single whole, and so construct a world in which I did not live, but only held up to the view of others;—what good would it do me to be able to explain the meaning of Christianity if it had no deeper significance *for me and for my life;*—what good would it do me if truth stood before me, cold and naked, not caring whether I recognized her or not, and producing in me a shudder of fear rather than a trusting devotion? I certainly do not deny that I still recognize an *imperative of understanding* and that through it one can work upon men, *but it must be taken up into my life*, and that is what I now recognize as the most important thing.[40]

Several themes are worth noting in this entry. First, Kierkegaard, like Husserl, is concerned with clarity—not the clarity of some absolute truth but the clarity of what he is to do. This emphasis on action and doing recurs in all existentialist thinking. It constitutes a lens through which existentialists view all philosophical questions, including metaphysical ones. Second, notice the emphasis Kierkegaard gives to the subjective—to "I," "me," and "my life." This is also a recurring theme in existential philosophy and literature. Third, observe Kierkegaard's religiosity. He wants to know what God expects of him. Kierkegaard was deeply religious, and the central issue of his life and thought was what it means to be a Christian. How can an individual bridge the gap between himself and his Maker, between creation and Creator?

For Kierkegaard, reality cannot be separated from existence. To exist is to struggle, to face opposition, and to experience passion; to exist is to make decisions, not to flounder. What's more, existence and selfhood are identical. To exist is *to become* a self, not just to be a self. It follows, then, that things that are not selves do not have an independent status. They exist only insomuch as they are "for" selves, for things that truly exist.

---

[40] Søren Kierkegaard, *The Journals of Kierkegaard*, trans. A. Dru (London: Collins, 1958), 44. Reprinted by permission of Oxford University Press.

Even this crude sketch of Kierkegaard's thought shows the self as the focus of reality—not the self as thinker, but as doer and actor, as decision maker. Kierkegaard's metaphysical concerns focus on the inner reality of what it is to be human; consequently, he is preoccupied with the predicament of decision making: What is *really* real? Kierkegaard wants people to take decisions seriously. More important, he wants people to relate this decision predicament to religion, specifically to Christianity, which he sees as the only cure for the agony of decision making.

Sartre

Although Kierkegaard first propounded existentialism, its chief exponent has been Jean-Paul Sartre (1905–1980), whom you first encountered in Chapter 2. Kierkegaard believed in God, though he felt that belief required a "leap of faith." However, Sartre felt that belief in God was no longer possible. Sartre found the idea that God does not exist a deeply disturbing thought. In his essay "Existentialism and Human Decision," he wrote the following: "The existentialist thinks it very distressing that God does not exist." In Sartre's view, there is no fixed human nature, so we are free to be what we choose. If God existed, then he could have conceived a nature for humans, and his conception of human nature might have fixed what humans are. But without a fixed human nature, all the responsibility for what we are rests with ourselves. There is nothing we ought to do, since there is nothing we ought to be. There are no absolutes, no norms of right behavior; we are on our own. We exist; whatever is uniquely ours, whatever explains each of us as an individual—our **essence**—is ours for the making. We do not discover who we are so much as we *make* ourselves.

> **essence** that which makes an entity what it is; that defining characteristic in whose absence a thing would not be itself

What kind of creatures are we who have no fixed nature? What are we to do who find ourselves living in a world without a compass? What kind of universe has no God? These are some of Sartre's central concerns that cannot be answered by Kierkegaard's leap of faith. Indeed, for Sartre the leap of faith is a cowardly act because it pushes people further into a world of illusion and false hope.

In contrast, Sartre's prescription for some of these dilemmas is related to his view of reality. Like phenomenologists, Sartre believes that reality exists in phenomena—that is, in "consciousness of." Furthermore, he accepts the phenomenological claim that "consciousness of" consists not only of intentions but also of intentional objects. Under intentional objects Sartre would include everything short of pure consciousness. Intention, then, is the pure, impersonal nothingness of consciousness. This is the departure point for both phenomenology and Sartre's existentialism.

Although both phenomenology and existentialism reject the distinction between appearance and reality, Sartre introduces a dichotomy between appearance and consciousness. For Sartre, reality consists of two kinds of being: the being of consciousness and the being of what appears to consciousness, phenomena. He terms the former (consciousness) *being-for-itself* and the latter (phenomena) *being-in-itself*.

Jean-Paul Sartre: "Thus human reality does not exist first in order to act later; but for human reality, to be is to act, and to cease to act is to cease to be."

To grasp this distinction, consider a table that stands across the room from you. Clearly, there are innumerable ways in which you can "intend" the table—that is, in which you can think about, remember, and imagine it. The table, of course, cannot perform any of these operations. It has no consciousness. Sartre calls such an intentional object being-in-itself. On the other hand, consciousness—that is, being-for-itself—can conceive of things as they are not. Consciousness involves such unique human activities as imagining, lying, negating, and questioning. Most important, being-for-itself makes meaning. In other words, being-for-itself exists in a world of its own making; it is its own God. It is also responsible for the world that it makes.

This distinction between being-in-itself and being-for-itself leads Sartre to conclude that humans *are* only insofar as they act. Our action may be trivial or momentous. We may move to a new town, or we may risk our lives for a cause. This is of no matter to Sartre. What counts is that we act—in other words, that we freely adopt a "project." When we do, we are truly human beings because we are in the mode of being-for-itself. Failing to act, we are in the mode of being-in-itself. Sartre expresses this point in *Being and Nothingness*, a definitive statement of his philosophy:

> A first glance at human reality informs us that for it being is reduced to doing. . . .
> Thus we find no *given* in human reality in the sense that temperament, character,
> passions, principles of reason would be acquired or innate *data* existing in the manner

of things. . . . Thus human reality does not exist first in order to act later; but for human reality, to be is to act, and to cease to act is to cease to be. . . .

Furthermore, . . . the act . . . must be defined by an *intention*. No matter how this intention is considered, it can be only a surpassing of the given toward a result to be obtained. This given . . . cannot provide the reason for a phenomenon which derives all its meaning from a result to be attained; that is, from a non-existent.

Since the intention is a choice of the end and since the world reveals itself across our conduct, it is the intentional choice of the end which reveals the world, and the world is revealed as this or that (in this or that order) according to the end chosen. The end, illuminating the world, is a state *of* the world to be obtained and not yet existing. . . . Thus my *end* can be a good meal if I am hungry. . . . This meal which [is] beyond the dusty road on which I am travelling is projected as the *meaning* of this road. . . .

Thus the intention by a single unitary upsurge posits the end, chooses itself, and appreciates the given in terms of something which does not yet exist; it is in the light of non-being that being-in-itself is illuminated. . . .

This characteristic of the for-itself implies that it is the being which finds *no help, no pillar of support* in what it *was*. But on the other hand, the for-itself is free and can cause there to be a world because the for-itself is *the being which has to be what it was in the light of what it will be*. Therefore the freedom of the for-itself appears as its *being*. . . . We shall never apprehend ourselves except as a choice in the making. But freedom is simply the fact that this choice is always unconditioned.

Such a choice made without base of support and dictating its own causes to itself . . . is absurd.[41]

CRITICAL THINKING

Does Sartre assume that we can act or choose without reliance on our past, our temperament, our character, or our learning? Is it true that this kind of freedom is possible?

Sartre suggests a rather unconventional view of human behavior here. Because of the influence of social science, specifically psychological behaviorism, many people assume that we are who we are because of our experiences. We might say that a man cheats and robs because he's a thief, and he's a thief because of the conditions under which he grew up. Sartre rejects this notion. He would argue that if a man is a thief, he chooses to be one, and he chooses all that this decision entails. He could choose to be an honest man. He could choose, in effect, a new project rather than the one he has adopted. Furthermore, he may do this whenever he chooses. In other words, nothing about a thief's past makes his future inevitable. In fact, there's no telling how many different projects he could undertake in defining who he will be.

For Sartre, then, first we exist. Our uniqueness, our essence, is not predetermined. Rather, it depends on whether we act. Sartre succinctly expresses this seminal insight of his philosophy in his statement "Existence precedes essence."

Simone de Beauvoir (1908–1986), perhaps the greatest female existentialist philosopher and a companion of Sartre, agreed that humans are not determined and must accept ultimate responsibility for what they are. Women in particular, de Beauvoir argued, are subject to social influences that attempt to rob them of an awareness of their own freedom, and they must overcome these constraints through courageous self-assertion. In *The Second Sex*, de Beauvoir

---

[41] Jean-Paul Sartre, *Being and Nothingness*, trans. Hazel E. Barnes (New York: Philosophical Library, 1956), 476–479. Copyright © 1956 by Philosophical Library. Reprinted by permission.

argues that in our male-dominated society, men define women wholly in terms of men's own nature: A woman is simply "the other," the nonmale one who relates to the male. Moreover, women accept this role and thereby forego their freedom to define and make themselves: They become mere things for men. Women must reject the male myths that define what they are; they must instead collectively create woman as a free and independent being. This will require, she suggests, overcoming the social and economic institutions through which men keep women effectively enslaved. Social and economic liberation is the key to freedom and self-determination for women.

Even this brief exposition should indicate that existentialists are extremely diverse. Among the best-known existentialists are Kierkegaard, the Jewish scholar Martin Buber (1878–1965), the Protestant theologian Paul Tillich (1886–1965), the atheists Friedrich Nietzsche (1844–1900) and Sartre, the novelist Albert Camus (1913–1960), and many other thinkers, writers, and artists. Although their views often differ radically, they share a concern for subjective experience, for the importance of personal freedom, and for the reality of personal responsibility. In our treatment of phenomenology and existentialism, we have attempted to touch only on those areas of metaphysical importance. Even here we have had to be sketchy. These important thinkers have had many ideas of merit that the serious student of philosophy will want to explore.

OBJECTIONS TO PHENOMENOLOGY AND EXISTENTIALISM

Since phenomenological thought and existential thought have so many nuances, let's confine our critical remarks to Husserl and Sartre. As Husserl became more skilled in bracketing, he uncovered more and more activities of the ego at increasingly deeper levels. For Husserl these activities do not underlie experience but are within it, waiting to be disclosed by bracketing. But, critics have asked, what of those less adept at bracketing than Husserl? What about people who are unable to uncover these activities? It seems that if such people are not to doubt the entire method, they must view these activities as lying entirely outside of the field of phenomenon.

Critics have also asked if things are "self-given" when we bracket. To illustrate, suppose that you had bracketed and reported that you did not find anything that was self-given, anything that presented itself with absolute certainty within experience. Husserl might accuse you of having bracketed unsuccessfully, but you could reply that bracketing itself is a frame within which Husserl insists on viewing things. In other words, you could argue that all seeing is relative to the frame through which one chooses to view things—relative, that is, to our assumptions, presuppositions, and values. If you were of a different philosophical bent from Husserl, you could go on and associate these frames with language. Husserl would counter that his is a special kind of seeing that's free of language when we bracket correctly. Thus, we see what is the case, and then we hunt around for the right words to describe it. But is this so? Much of twentieth-century philosophy argues that all philosophy, including phenomenology, is linguistic. In other words, all thinking and seeing are related to certain preconceptions that are inherent in language. Thus, bracketing is also a kind of frame, though admittedly subtler than most. Thus, what for Husserl seems certain might be better described as his own projection of the quest for certainty.

Turning to Sartre, recall that he insists that to be human is to make a world by adopting a project. For example, suppose that you find that you are a Christian. You didn't *choose* to become one; you simply followed a script or line or direction that, for a number of reasons, was laid out for you. Sartre would say that you're caught in a logical contradiction: You're a person who is not a person, a for-itself whose being is in the mode of an in-itself. For Sartre this evaluation is not just a bias or even a value judgment. It's an assertion of an ontological truth. But is it?

Even if you were a Christian who did not *choose* Christianity, you wouldn't be a Christian in the way that a desk is a desk or a rock is a rock. You wouldn't have being in the mode of the in-itself in the way that those things do. In fact, Sartre would agree that, as humans, we can't have being simply in the mode of the in-itself. Like it or not, we're condemned to be free.

If we can't be simply in the mode of the in-itself, then we're always in the mode of the for-itself. But is it any more possible to be in the mode of the for-itself? Suppose that you don't drift or slip into being a Christian, but you *choose* it. This fact doesn't seem to make any real difference to Sartre, because once you become a Christian, you accept a set of values, ways of looking at things, and a course of conduct. Christianity becomes your "taken-for-granted," and, evidently, you now have being in the mode of the for-itself.

Obviously, this problem doesn't exist only for Christians. People who adopt nihilism as their project slip just as easily from freedom to playing the role of nihilist. Even those who adopt existential freedom as their project can slide from freedom while playing the role of existentialist. True, some projects are more likely to invite slippage into bad faith than others. But is any project immune? Professor of philosophy W. T. Jones captures this paradox:

> One of the difficulties for a man who is committed to "commitment" is that in order to get things done in this world he must combine forces with other men—not only join a movement but institutionalize (even bureaucratize) it. And this, it would seem, means surrendering one's freedom and hence becoming a thing. This is the paradox Sartre encountered in his own life; it helps to explain his on-again, off-again relationship with the Communist Party.[42]

Sartre's account of the for-itself, then, seems to commit him to holding freedom as an all-or-nothing proposition. But many people see it as one of degree. The same is true of responsibility. In the Holocaust, for example, the attempt by the German Nazi regime to exterminate the Jewish race by murdering them in prison camps during the Second World War, who was responsible?

Man is the being through whom nothingness comes to the world. This nothing is human reality itself as the radical negation by means of which the world is revealed.

JEAN-PAUL SARTRE

---

[42] Jones, *From Kant*, 444.

Some people might reply that the individual Nazi soldiers who committed the murders were responsible. But those individuals all claimed that they were merely "following orders." Were the military officers who ordered the murders responsible? What about Nazi politicians who designed the plans that the military followed? Or the German citizens who supported the Nazi regime, or those who knew about the camps and did nothing to stop them? What about the English and Americans who were aware of the camps and also did nothing? Are these parties each responsible but to different degrees?

The idea of degrees of responsibility doesn't seem to fit with Sartre's view of morality. Sartre says humans are totally responsible because they are totally free. Since all of us could have made a world that excluded the Nazi massacre, we are all equally responsible. It's true that in *Being and Nothingness* Sartre relaxes this view by speaking of the social restraints on individual freedom, but then one wonders whether this modification is consistent, or even needs to be, with his existential phenomenology.

Despite their differences, existentialists, phenomenologists, and many of their critics agree at least on one point: Statements about ultimate reality and being are meaningful. Whether reality is matter, idea, a combination, being, or consciousness, all the views we have discussed so far—except for the logical positivists—agree that we can sensibly talk about metaphysical issues.

QUESTIONS

1.   What would an existentialist mean if he said, "It's clear that, for you, *what or who* I am is more important than *that* I am"? Why would this matter to him?

2.   What is the difference between being and being human?

3.   In what sense are you both being and a being?

4.   Show how a failure to distinguish between being as a thing and the being of a thing leads to "thingifying" everything, including people.

5.   Do existentialism, phenomenology, and pragmatism share any beliefs?

6.   In what sense would you call Kierkegaard a rationalist?

7.   Sartre claims that Kierkegaard's leap of faith to God is cowardly and not in the true existential spirit. Why would he say this? Do you agree?

8.   What does Sartre mean when he says, "Existence precedes essence"?

9.   How would you describe what Heidegger calls your being?

10.   If someone said, "If everything is being, then everything is nothing," what would she mean?

11.   Is it possible to maintain a concept of individual difference if everything has being in common?

12.   Sartre claims that in making a choice for self, we are really making a choice for other. Is this statement consistent with a denial of any kind of universal human nature? If it is, why did Sartre make such a claim?

3.7 Is Freedom Real?

No other metaphysical issue is as debated as the question of freedom. It has given rise to a controversy that still rages in our society. Consider the case of Leopold and Loeb.

Nathan Leopold and Richard Loeb, both eighteen-year-olds, were wealthy and brilliant. They had just graduated from college when they brutally murdered a fourteen-year-old boy in a rented automobile in Chicago's south side on May 21, 1924. During college the two had been addicted to reading crime magazines and novels. They had experimented in petty theft and arson. Then together they came up with the idea of committing the "perfect crime." The challenge of planning, executing, and getting away with a murder intrigued and fascinated them. For what they later described as the "intellectual thrill" of it, they kidnapped the young Bobbie Franks. They beat him on the head with a chisel, suffocated him by stuffing a gag in his mouth, and then phoned his wealthy parents to demand $10,000 in ransom. The family alerted police investigators, who soon found the boy's bloody body half-buried in a railway culvert. Lying next to the body were Leopold's eyeglasses. When confronted, the two quickly confessed and were subsequently tried for murder, punishable by death.

Their lawyer was the famous defense attorney Clarence Darrow. At trial before Judge John R. Caverly, for thirty-three days in July–August 1924, Darrow argued that the boys, who had already pleaded guilty, should not be executed. Science has proved, Darrow suggested, that everything in the universe is governed by rigid laws of causality. These laws ensure that everything that happens has to happen. Therefore, no one is responsible for his or her actions. The real causes of our actions lie outside us, in the events and conditions that caused us to act as we did and in the laws that govern our acts. In particular, Darrow claimed, Leopold and Loeb's murderous act was caused by their heredity and the way they were raised. Speaking in defense of "Dickie" Loeb, Darrow said this at the trial:

> I do not claim to know how it happened. I know that something or some combination of things is responsible for this mad act. I know that there are not accidents in nature. I know that effect follows cause. What had this boy to do with it? He was not his own father. All this was handed to him. He did not make himself. . . . Do you mean to tell me that Dickie Loeb had any more to do with his making than any other product of heredity that is born upon the earth? . . . And yet there are men who seriously say that for what nature has done, for what life has done, for what training has done, you should hang these boys. . . . [But] to believe that any boy is responsible for himself or his early training is an absurdity that no lawyer or judge should be guilty of today. . . . I know that if this boy had been understood and properly trained . . . he would not be in this courtroom today with the noose above his head. If there is responsibility anywhere, it is back of him; somewhere in the infinite number of his ancestors, or in his surroundings, or in both. And I submit, your

Honor, that under every principle of natural justice, under every principle of conscience, of right, and of law, he should not be made responsible for the acts of someone else. . . .[43]

In the end, Judge Caverly agreed with Darrow and refused to impose the death penalty. Instead, he sentenced the two boys to life in prison, the only other option available to him. His decision raised a public outcry. Darrow was simply wrong, the public claimed. Leopold and Loeb acted freely and deliberately. They were fully responsible for what they did and deserved the maximum penalty.

Although the case of Leopold and Loeb is an old one, the issues it raised are still argued in courtrooms everywhere. On April 21, 1992, for example, Robert Alton Harris was executed in California for the casual and callous murder of two young boys. But newspaper editorials everywhere urged the courts to grant clemency to Harris because of the brutal upbringing to which his parents had subjected him. According to one newspaper account,

> His father was an alcoholic who was twice convicted of sexually molesting his daughters. He frequently beat his children . . . and often caused serious injury. . . . All of the children had monstrous childhoods. But even in the Harris family . . . the abuse Robert was subjected to was unusual. The constant abuse [his mother] was subjected to by her husband, turned her against her son. Money was tight, she was overworked and he was her fifth child in just a few years. She began to blame all her problems on Robert, and she grew to hate the child.
>
> [His sister said of him:] "He wanted love so bad he would beg for any kind of physical contact. He'd come up to my mother and just try to rub his little hands on her leg or her arm. He just never got touched at all. She'd just push him away or kick him. One time she bloodied his nose when he was trying to get close to her. . . ."[44]

Numerous editorials argued that what Harris did was the predictable outcome of the violent life that preceded it. No one could legitimately hold such a man morally responsible for his acts. Therefore, the governor or the courts should set aside the death penalty and commute Harris's sentence to life imprisonment without possibility of parole. Understandably, people everywhere objected. People are morally responsible for what they do, many claimed. No matter how we are brought up, we have the power to choose what we will do. Harris freely chose to kill the boys. Now he must receive a fitting punishment.

DETERMINISM

There is, perhaps, no more controversial question in metaphysics than the one Darrow raised: Is everything that happens in the universe determined by earlier causes and the laws of nature? Many philosophers have thought so. Everything that happens, including every human action, is determined by previous events and the laws of nature. There can be no freedom.

---

[43] Clarence Darrow, "Leopold and Loeb," quoted in G. L. Bowie, M. W. Michaels, and R. C. Solomon, *Twenty Questions: An Introduction to Philosophy* (New York: Harcourt Brace, 1988), 688, 691.

[44] Miles Corwin, "Icy Killer's Life Steeped in Violence," *Los Angeles Times*, May 16, 1982.

The view that human actions are completely determined by prior events is called *determinism*. Stated in another and perhaps more accurate way, **determinism** is the view that every event has prior conditions that cause it, so each event is at least theoretically predictable if we know all its prior conditions and the laws governing those conditions. Determinists argue that human actions are part of this causal chain of nature and so are also determined. Stated in another way, determinists hold that there is only one path leading from the past through the present and into the future. It is not possible for the future to take any path other than the one that prior events and the laws of nature force it to take.

determinism the theory that everything that occurs happens in accordance with some regular pattern or law

Materialism and determinism have been close allies. Materialism holds that mental events—our decisions and choices—are caused by the brain or are events in the brain. But these brain processes are physical processes. As such, they have to be caused by antecedent physical events, like any other physical process.

This materialist view received important support in the seventeenth century from the theories of the great British scientist Sir Isaac Newton (1642–1727). Newton argued that all material bodies in the universe, from the smallest atoms to the largest planets and stars, move in accordance with the universal laws of nature that he described in *Principia Mathematica Philosophia Naturalis*. These laws included, for example, the law of inertia, which states that all bodies continue moving in a straight line unless acted on by an external force, and the law of universal gravitation, which states that all bodies in the universe attract all other bodies with a force proportional to their masses and their distances from one another. If the locations, masses, and velocities of any set of bodies are known for any moment in the past, then one can determine their exact locations and velocities at any moment in the future by using Newton's laws. Materialists quickly saw that if the brain is made up of small bodies such as atoms, then the motions and activities of the atoms that make up the brain must also follow Newton's universal laws. The activities of the human brain, then, are as enmeshed in the mechanical workings of the universe as are atoms, clocks, and planets. Since human actions and choices are the outcome of the activities of the brain, they too are subject to the universal laws of nature.

These ideas were brilliantly expressed by the French mathematician Pierre Simon, Marquis de LaPlace, who wrote the following in 1812:

> Present events have a connection with previous ones that is based on the self-evident principle that a thing cannot come into existence without a cause that produces it. This axiom . . . extends even to actions which people regard as [free]. . . . We must regard the present state of the universe as the effect of its preceding state and as the cause of the one which is to follow. An intelligence which in a single instant could know all the forces which animate the natural world, and the respective situations of all the beings that made it up, could, provided it was vast enough to make an analysis of all the data so supplied, be able to produce a single formula which specified all the movements in the universe from those of the largest bodies in the universe to those of the lightest atom.[45]

---

[45] Pierre Simon de LaPlace, *Essaie Philosophique sur les Probabilities* [1812]. Trans. John Cottingham. Quoted in *Western Philosophy, An Anthology*, ed. John Cottingham (Oxford, UK: Blackwell, 1996), 227.

It may seem to us that we are free. But, in actuality, this freedom is just a result of our ignorance of the laws that govern us. Eventually, LaPlace thought, we will discover the laws that govern human actions. Then we will see clearly that freedom is nothing but an illusion.

In our own century, determinism has been encouraged by psychological theories, such as those of Sigmund Freud. Although Freud himself did not espouse a determinist position, some of his followers used his theories to argue that unconscious psychological desires are the real causes of actions that people think they have freely chosen. Psychological mechanisms place human actions squarely within the casual chain of nature. For example, the contemporary philosopher John Hospers holds that "the unconscious is the master of every fate and the captain of every soul":

> A man is faced by a choice: shall he kill another person or not? Moralists would say, here is a "free" choice—the result of deliberation, an action consciously entered into. And yet, though the agent himself does not know it, and has no awareness of the forces that are at work within him, his choice is already determined for him: his conscious will is only an instrument, a slave, in the hands of a deep unconscious motivation which determines his action. If he has a great deal of what the analyst calls "free-floating guilt," he will not; but if the guilt is such as to demand immediate absorption in the form of self-damaging behavior, this accumulated guilt will have to be discharged in some criminal action. The man himself does not know what the inner clockwork is; he is like the hands on the clock, thinking they move freely over the face of the clock.[46]

Determinists don't just hold that everything is determined. They also assume that determinism rules out human freedom and responsibility. Freedom is the ability to choose among alternatives. If humans cannot help but do what they do, then they are not free to act otherwise. In this sense, they lack freedom. They also lack responsibility. We are responsible for an action only if we are in control of the action or its causes. But we do not control our actions if determinism is right. Instead, the events and forces that led us to act control what we do. Determinism is therefore inconsistent with the idea that we are each personally responsible for our actions. The determinist view of reality, then, is summarized in the following argument:

1. All events and actions are causally determined by previous events and the laws of nature.

2. Causal determinism rules out human freedom and personal responsibility.

3. So humans are not free, nor are they personally responsible for what they do.

The implications of determinism are disturbing. If determinism is true, then punishment, at least in the traditional sense, makes little sense. More broadly, if determinism is true, then it makes no sense to hold individuals responsible for their actions, whether for good or evil. The saint should no more be praised

---

[46]John Hospers, "What Means This Freedom?" in *Determinism and Freedom in the Age of Modern Science*, ed. Sidney Hook (New York: New York University Press, 1958).

than the criminal should be punished. For neither is ultimately responsible for what he did. Regret would also become incomprehensible, since one cannot regret doing what one could not help but do.

But is determinism correct? Perhaps events in the natural world are determined, but should human actions be assimilated to natural events? When we act, don't we directly experience our freedom? Aren't we sometimes directly aware that we have control over our actions and so are morally responsible at that moment for the actions we choose? Some philosophers have argued that unlike objects in nature, which are determined, human beings are free.

LIBERTARIANISM

Many people have argued that determinism is wrong because it denies the freedom that we all directly experience when we choose. But how can we be outside the causal chain of nature? No philosopher has argued so vigorously in favor of freedom as Jean-Paul Sartre. We have seen how Sartre's existentialism analyzes our consciousness of reality. Based on this experience of ourselves as conscious, Sartre argues that we are indeed free.

Sartre's argument for freedom depends on an interesting view he has of how humans choose. Humans, he argues, project from a present that exists to a future that does not yet exist. In this way, argues Sartre, humans can stand apart from the world as it is, and can conceive and be moved by what does not yet exist. Sartre calls this ability to conceive and be moved by what is not, the ability to apprehend "negativity" or "non-being." Past or present existence, says Sartre, cannot determine a person's conception of what does not exist. In this power to conceive what is not lies our freedom:

> It is strange that philosophers have been able to argue endlessly about determinism and free-will, to cite examples in favor of one or the other thesis without ever attempting first to make explicit the structures contained in the very idea of action. We should first observe that an action is on principle intentional. . . . But if this is the case, we establish that an action necessarily implies as its condition the recognition of a "desideratum" [something desired], that is, of an objective lack or negativity. The [emperor Constantine's] intention of [building a Christian city to] rival Rome could come to him only through the apprehension of an objective lack: . . . a Christian city at the moment is missing.
>
> This means that from the moment of the first conception of the act, consciousness has been able to withdraw itself from the full world of which it is conscious and leave the level of being [i.e., what exists] to approach that of non-being [i.e., what does not yet exist]. Consciousness . . . cannot find in being any motive for revealing non-being.
>
> Two important consequences result. (1) No factual state whatever it may be (the political and economic structure of society, the psychological state, etc.) is capable by itself of motivating any act whatsoever. For an act is a projection of the for-itself [i.e., of the human being] toward what is not, and what is can in no way determine by itself what is not. (2) No factual state can determine consciousness to apprehend it as a negativity or as a lack. . . .
>
> Human-reality is free because . . . it is perpetually wrenched away from itself and because it has been separated by a nothingness from what it is and from what it will

be. . . . Freedom is precisely the nothingness which is made to be at the heart of man and which forces human reality to make itself instead of to simply be.[47]

Sartre utterly rejects determinism. Instead, Sartre holds a form of what is sometimes called **libertarianism** or *indeterminism*. A libertarian holds that people have control over what they do and are free to choose to act other than the way they do. We are, in Sartre's view, radically free. Our ability to conceive of what is not allows us to form plans that are not determined by the past or the present. They cannot be determined because what is cannot determine what is not. Being cannot determine non-being. By this ability to pursue what is not, we make ourselves whatever we choose to be regardless of the influences of our environment or our heredity. We can tell ourselves that other forces make us do what we do, but doing this is a form of "bad faith." It is a deliberate attempt to deceive ourselves, a way of trying to avoid our radical responsibility. We choose whether we give in to our emotions and desires; we choose whether we allow our environment to influence us; we choose whether we follow the promptings of our hereditary makeup. Because we are ultimately free, Sartre holds that we are fully responsible for our behavior and actions. And this is the source of our anguish. Since we are fully responsible for what we do, we have no one and nothing to blame for what we are, other than ourselves.

> **libertarianism** in metaphysics, the view that determinism is false and that people are free to choose to act other than they do

The future, then, is not fixed. There is not just one possible path leading from the past into the future, as the determinist says. Instead, the indeterminist holds that the future branches off into many possible paths. Of course, only one of those futures will be chosen. But we could have chosen one of the other paths. We are free because we could have acted other than the way we did.

Although the indeterminist rejects the determinist's claim that all human actions are caused by antecedent events, he agrees with the determinist on one important point. The indeterminist agrees with the determinist that determinism rules out freedom and responsibility. We can summarize the view of the libertarian, then, in the following argument:

1. Humans are free and are personally responsible for what they do.

2. Human freedom and personal responsibility rule out causal determinism.

3. So human actions are not causally determined by previous events and the laws of nature.

Yet do we have the kind of absolute freedom that Sartre attributes to us? Is the criminal wholly to blame for his crimes? Are you wholly to blame for who and what are you today? And if you deny that you are free and responsible, are you really using this very denial as an excuse to escape your responsibility? Is the denial of freedom always a form of bad faith?

Other indeterminists have argued that new scientific theories, in particular quantum theory, also imply that the future is not causally determined by the past. Quantum theory holds that at least at the subatomic level, it is not possible to simultaneously determine both the position and the velocity of a par-

---

[47] Jean-Paul Sartre, *L'Etre et le Neant* [1943], trans. H. E. Barnes (London: Methuen, 1957), 433–437.

ticle, and so it is not possible to predict its position at a future moment. At the subatomic level, therefore, the future is indeterministic.

But not everyone accepts these arguments. Determinists have claimed that Sartre makes human choices mysterious and unexplainable, and that Sartre's views also fly in the face of what we know about human psychology and the extent to which we are shaped by our past. Moreover, determinists have argued that the appeals to quantum theory are beside the point, because what is at stake is human behavior at the level of ordinary objects, not the behavior of subatomic particles.

COMPATIBALISM

But perhaps indeterminism is not the only way of saving freedom and responsibility. In an effort to reconcile our notions of freedom and moral responsibility with determinism, some philosophers have advanced a view called **compatibalism.** Compatibalism rejects the view that determinism rules out freedom and responsibility. Instead, compatibalists argue, causal determinism is compatible with freedom. How is this possible?

compatibalism a view that attempts to reconcile freedom and responsibility with determinism

Compatibalism saves freedom by redefining it. According to the compatibalist, to say that a person is free is to say that the person is not impeded by external restraints or confinements. A person wearing handcuffs or in prison is not free. But a person who is free to do what her own desires or character move her to do *is* free. Still, since a person's desires and character are molded by her heredity and upbringing, they are causally determined by external factors. Ultimately, then, a person's actions are determined by the antecedent causes that formed her desires and character.

One of the first philosophers to propose a compatibalist view was the British materialist Thomas Hobbes:

> LIBERTY, or freedom, signifies properly the absence of opposition; by [this], I mean [the absence of] external impediments to motion. . . . [When] living creatures . . . are imprisoned, or restrained with walls or chains . . . we . . . say they are not at liberty. . . . [When] man . . . finds no[thing to] stop [him from] doing what he has the will, desire, or inclination to do [he is at liberty]. . . . Liberty and necessity are consistent. . . . [Like] the water that has not only liberty, but a necessity of descending by the channel; so, likewise . . . the actions which men voluntarily do . . . because they proceed [from] their will, proceed from liberty, and yet because every act of man's will and every desire and inclination proceeds from some cause, and that from another cause, in a continual chain . . . [all actions also] proceed from necessity. So that to him that could see the connexion of those causes, the necessity of all men's voluntary actions would appear manifest.[48]

Compatibalists are also able to recognize moral responsibility. To say that a person is responsible for an action is to say that the action flowed from inside the person, from what he is. So when a person's actions are caused by his inner

---

[48] Thomas Hobbes, *Leviathan*, Chapter 21 in *Hobbes Selections*, ed. Fredrick J. E. Woodbridge (New York: Scribner's, 1930), 369–371.

desires and his character, they flow from the person and from what he is, making him responsible for those actions.

The compatibalist, then, can agree with the determinist that human actions are predetermined. But he rejects the idea that determinism rules out freedom or responsibility. The compatibalist argues like this:

1. Human actions are causally determined by previous events and the laws of nature.

2. Causal determinism does not rule out freedom and personal responsibility.

3. So humans are predetermined and can also be free and personally responsible for what they do.

But whereas compatibalism appears to wed freedom with determinism, doesn't it leave the key question unanswered? If we are not free to act against our desires, then isn't there still a clear sense in which we are not free? Maybe we are "free" in the sense that we are not chained down and physically restrained from acting. But aren't we unfree in the more important sense that we do not ultimately control what we do? If a person is not free to choose her desires, and these desires determine her actions, then isn't she ultimately unfree? How can we hold a person responsible for the actions that flow from her desires when she does not control her desires?

Is it clear, then, that compatibalism has really reconciled freedom and determinism? Yet the other views on determinism that we have examined seem to be equally problematic. Because it denies freedom and moral responsibility, determinism does not accord with how we generally experience our own actions. Indeterminism seemingly preserves freedom and responsibility at the expense of scientific respectability. Compatibalism, which tries to reconcile freedom and responsibility with determinism, apparently leaves the issue unresolved in some ultimate sense. Which view of reality makes the most sense?

Some philosophers have agreed that perhaps we are both free and determined as Hobbes suggests. But they add that we do not need to redefine *freedom* to make this point. Perhaps, they suggest, we are simply stuck with two different ways of looking at human reality. Perhaps we have to see ourselves as both free and determined. This is the view of Immanuel Kant:

> Is it possible that we take one point of view when we think of ourselves as free causes, and another point of view when we see ourselves as determined effects?
> . . . Insofar as he knows himself through his senses, man must see himself as part of the world of sense. But insofar as he assumes he has a conscious active self, he must regard himself as part of the world of understanding. . . .
> So a rational being has two points of view from which he can regard himself. . . . First, to the extent that he belongs to the world of sense, he sees himself as subject to the laws of nature. Second, to the extent that he belongs to the world of understanding, he sees himself as subject only to moral rules that are based on reason. . . . As a rational being that belongs to the world of understanding, man must think of his will as free. . . .[49]

---

[49] Immanuel Kant, *Foundations of the Metaphysics of Morals*, sec. 3. Translated by Manuel Velasquez.

Here Kant is suggesting that we have two ways of understanding ourselves and our world. First, we can think of ourselves as part of the world that we observe when we use our senses, the world that science tries to explain through scientific laws. When we think of ourselves in this way, we are looking at ourselves as an object in the world. We feel that objects in this world have to be determined, and our own actions, as part of this world, also must be determined. But Kant also suggests that we can think of ourselves as conscious beings who act in the world. When we think of ourselves in this way, we have to think of ourselves as free. We have to think of ourselves as free because if we thought other forces were determining our acts, we would not feel that we ourselves were really acting. If I am to see myself as really acting, I must believe that what I am doing comes out of my own choices and is not caused by forces external to me.

Kant does not see any way of escaping these two very different ways of looking at ourselves. We sometimes have to look at ourselves as physical objects, particularly when we try to explain our actions in terms of the laws of science, such as psychology. But we sometimes also have to look at ourselves as free, conscious beings, particularly when we try to understand ourselves as beings who act in the world. Determinism, then, is not a feature of the world. It is a feature of one way of looking at ourselves and our actions. Indeterminism is also not a feature of the world. Rather, it is a feature of another way of looking at ourselves and our actions. But both are inescapable.

So are we free or determined? Are we responsible agents or passive victims? Was Darrow right? Or was Sartre right? Or were both right, as Kant suggests? What do you think?

QUESTIONS

1.   Think about a situation in which you felt intense desire. Did you feel you were free to choose whether or not to give in to your desire?

2.   Suppose that an airplane crashes. After a lengthy inquiry, investigators announce that they have ruled out every possible cause of the crash. They have concluded that the crash actually had no cause at all. It was uncaused. Would you find this conclusion acceptable? Explain why.

3.   A determinist says that when a person deliberately does anything, she must have wanted to do it. Otherwise, why did she do it? But if so, the determinist concludes, desires cause everything we do. Is this argument correct? Why or why not?

4.   Explain how you think that Sartre would explain addiction, such as an addiction to hard drugs or to smoking. Do addictions prove that Sartre is wrong? Explain why.

5.   The philosopher John Searle, author of the book *The Rediscovery of the Mind*, once said the following in conversation: "You can't think away your own freedom. Just think what it would be like. You go into a restaurant and they confront you with a menu. Now you can't say, 'Well, look, I'm a determinist, so I'll just wait and see what I order' or 'I'll just wait and see what happens.' You

have to make up your mind. . . . I can't sit back and wait for the choice to happen. . . . You have to act, and this is the way Kant put it, you have to act on the presupposition of freedom." What does Searle's statement imply about determinism and indeterminism? How close is Searle's view to Kant's? Is Searle right?

3.8 Is Time Real?

There is something that the discussions of determinism and freedom have assumed we understand. Both the determinist and the indeterminist assume we know what it is for one event or action to cause another. But causality involves time: the movement from an earlier cause toward its later effect. So they assume that we understand what time is. But do we? Let us see.

Time seems to be the most familiar of all realities. To every action, appointment, event, experience, happening, phenomenon, circumstance, situation, sensation, incident, adventure, occasion, quest, affair, occurrence, and climax we assign a time. We continuously talk about what happened "yesterday," what we are doing "today," and what will happen "tomorrow." We use the notion of time as easily as our lungs take in air. We have no trouble understanding the meaning of "past," "present," "future," "then," "now," "before," "after," "when," "whenever," "later," "earlier," "always," "never," "soon." Yet what is time? When we ask the question, the reality that seemed so familiar slips away. As Saint Augustine wrote, "If no one asks me, I know what time is; if someone asks and I want to explain it, I do not know."[50]

Yet time is an intimate aspect of who we are and how we feel. Time, in fact, makes us who we are. To find out who I am, I need to look into my memory of my past and see what I've done and where I've been, how I've acted and responded to the needs and demands of others and to the events of my life. The same is true of other people. My understanding of who they are is based on how I have experienced them in the past: what I have seen them do and how I have seen them act. For example, have I seen them act with integrity and courage, or with expedience and cowardliness? Many of our feelings, too, depend on time. Take regret, for example. I feel regret about what is in the past that I wish I had not done. I feel regret because I cannot change the past.

Time seems especially mysterious because it seems to flow or move ever onward past us or with us. Sometimes it seems like an unstoppable river continuously flowing past a bank on which we stand. An event we look forward to in

---

[50] Augustine, *Confessions*, bk. 11, ch. 14. Translated by Manuel Velasquez.

the future comes nearer to us carried in the river of time; it approaches, it is finally here, and then it passes us and recedes into the past. Sometimes it seems as if we ourselves are in the river, carried along whether we want to be or not. It moves us inexorably forward no matter what we do. We grow, mature, and age. Our bodies move on from the immaturity of childhood, through the bloom of youth, into the maturity of adulthood, and on into the gradual decay of age. We go places and do things; our actions, pleasures, and enjoyments become vivid memories, then grow dim, and finally are forgotten. All the while death, that final end of time for us, approaches ever closer. The flow of time seems to carry us inexorably toward death, like swimmers caught in a current being swept onward toward a waterfall.

What is this time, whose flow seems so familiar, so ordinary, so threatening? To many philosophers it has seemed that the flow of time we experience is so strange that in some sense it must be unreal. For example, Saint Augustine after puzzling long and hard over the nature of time, came to the conclusion that time in a sense does not exist:

> A day contains 24 hours; during the first of these hours the rest do not yet exist; during the last of these hours the first no longer exist. . . . A single hour contains minutes that vanish as they pass. Whatever minutes have passed no longer exist, and whatever still remain do not yet exist. If we can conceive of an instant of time that cannot be divided into yet shorter moments, that is the only point of time that can exist at present. And that point flies at such lightning speed from being future to being past, that it can have no duration at all. . . . Time passes from that which does not yet exist, through that which does not endure, into that which no longer exists.[51]

So the present instant is the only part of time that is real. The rest—everything in our lives that is past and everything that is future—does not exist. The past and the future have only a shadowy mental existence in our mind. Memory preserves past instants, and in anticipation we think about the future. But outside the mind, in reality, there exists only the changing point-like instant of time that makes up the present.

However, Augustine suggested an important distinction between time from the point of view of God and time as we experience it. Think of it like this. God is outside time. From God's point of view, time is like a line of events that lies stretched out before Him. Every event and every moment of our lives lies on the line, earlier ones to the left and later ones to the right. This time line of events does not flow. In fact, nothing on the line ever changes. Everything on it is fixed. This is time from God's point of view. Notice that although nothing on the line of time changes from being future to being past, events still lie "before" or "after" each other. Time from God's point of view has "before" and "after" but no "future" or "past." On the other hand, time from our point of view is very different. We are in time. We experience time as flowing by one instant at a time. Time that was future becomes present and moves on to become the past. Moreover, we experience the past as frozen while the future is not yet fixed.

---

[51] Ibid., bk. 11, chs. 15, 18, 20, 21.

We have, then, two very different ways to think about the time in which we live. The first is time as a fixed series or line of earlier and later events viewed as if from someplace outside time. The second is time as we experience it from within, as a flow from future, through present, and into the past. Let us call time as a fixed line of events the *objective* view of time. Let us call time as we experience it the *subjective* view of time.

Why should these two views of time matter? Some people have felt that peace of mind can be found only in taking the objective view of time. The subjective view of time is the source of all our pain and sorrow. It is in subjective time that we endure separations from loved ones and from everything else that we treasure. Those we love will all age and die as their youth wastes away in changing time. Our own bodies age and waste away in subjective time. Childhood departs and is gone; youth vanishes. Things we buy or make always decay, wear out, fall apart, and are lost to us. Saint Augustine put it like this:

> My life is a distraction and dispersal [in time]. . . . I am wasted and scattered on things which are to come and which pass away. . . . Time is spent in grieving. . . . I am spilled and scattered among times whose order I do not know. My thoughts, the innermost bowels of my soul, are torn apart with the crowding tumults of change, and so it will be until I die.[52]

On the other hand, if we can attain to the view of time as objective, then perhaps we will not feel the pain and sorrow of separation and loss as intensely. We can see that from outside time nothing changes: Everything that happens is still there, fixed in objective time, never lost. We can, perhaps, see that from God's point of view, nothing is lost but always remains and endures. Loss and separation exist only from our point of view in subjective time, not in objective time.

We can, perhaps, understand why many philosophers have argued that subjective time is not real and that only objective time exists. For example, the existentialist philosopher Merleu-Ponty argued that the flow of time as we experience it cannot be real. We experience time as changing and moving toward the future because of the way our mind relates to real, objective time. However, real time does not change. The flow of time we feel is an illusion produced because we experience objective time one moment at a time.

However, the philosopher who argued most vigorously that the flow of time as we experience it is unreal is the idealist British philosopher J. M. E. McTaggart (1886–1925). McTaggart argued that it makes sense to think of time as a fixed series of moments. Objective time is real. But it makes no sense, he argued, to think of time as changing and flowing, as being "future," then "present," then "past." Our subjective idea of time is inherently contradictory and so cannot be real:

> Past, present and future are incompatible determinations. Every event must be one or the other, but no event can be more than one. If I say that any event is past, that

---

[52] Ibid., bk. 11, ch. 29.

implies that it is neither present nor future, and so with the others. And this exclusiveness is essential to change, and therefore to time. For the only change we can get is from future to present, and from present to past.

The characteristics, therefore, are incompatible. But every event has them all. If M is past, it has been present and future. If it is future, it will be present and past. If it is present, it has been future and will be past. Thus all the three characteristics belong to each event. How is this consistent with their being incompatible? . . .

I believe that nothing that exists can be temporal, and that therefore time is unreal.[53]

The contemporary Australian materialist philosopher J. J. C. Smart also argues that our experience of time as passing is an illusion. If we wanted to, he argued, we could get rid of words like *past, future,* and *now,* and talk only about where things happen in objective time. For example, instead of saying the Industrial Revolution was in "the past," we could say the Industrial Revolution lies on objective time at a point *t* that is before the year 1900. Once we give up talking about past, present, and future, we will see that events don't move from being past to being future. They are all fixed in objective time and don't change at all. So the flow of time we think we experience is really an illusion. It is not real.

In some ways, the denial of subjective time is comforting. Perhaps nothing ends, nothing dies, nothing changes. Everything is there, fixed in the frozen vastness of objective time. Yet are the arguments of these philosophers correct? Suppose Smart is right and we can stop using words that refer to past, present, and future. Will this get rid of our experience of time as flowing past us and as carrying us on through youth, old age, and death? Just because we do not talk about something, does this mean that it is no longer there?

Or let us look at McTaggart's argument. McTaggart argues that since the past, present, and future are inconsistent notions, and since reality is consistent, reality can't have a past, present, and future. But can't McTaggart's argument be turned on its head? Can't we say that since reality is consistent, and since reality has a past, present, and future, these notions must be consistent notions?

Is it really possible for us to dismiss the flow of time? Aren't we like an ostrich with its head in the ground when we try to tell ourselves that subjective time—the time of anticipation and loss, of birth, growth, and decay—is not real? Yet some philosophers have gone even further. Some philosophers have argued that all time is unreal.

Kant, for example, claimed that time—both the subjective time we experience as flowing, and objective time as the fixed series of all events—is a construct of the human mind. The world that we experience, he argued, is a disordered chaotic parade of sensations that our mind tries to put into some sort of order. The basic system that the mind uses to order all sensations is what we call time. Time is like an infinitely long container in the mind into which we insert each sensation as we experience it. Kant claimed we cannot understand or comprehend the many sensations the universe throws at us unless our mind

---

[53] J. M. E. McTaggart, *The Nature of Existence*, vol. 2, bk. 5, ch. 33.

first imposes some kind of order and regularity onto them. The most basic ordering system we use is the "representation" of time:

> Time is a necessary representation, lying at the foundation of all our perceptions. With regard to phenomena in general, we cannot think away time from them, and represent them to ourselves as out of and unconnected with time. But we can quite easily represent to ourselves time empty of any phenomena. Time is therefore given *a priori*. In it alone is all reality of phenomena possible.[54]

Our mind makes up or constructs the system of time. Then, as sensations come into the mind through the senses, the mind puts each sensation at some point on this time line. The mind then goes on, Kant argues, to organize these sensations into objects and tries to relate these objects to one another in a world of space. But the key point is that all time is a construct of the mind. Even objective time is not a feature of things as they really exist in themselves, apart from our minds.

Many scientists have claimed, however, that time really exists "out there" in objects. Still, for science, they claim, the time that is really "out there" is objective time, not subjective time. Subjective time as we experience it flows from the future into the past. Moreover, the past, as we experience it cannot change, whereas the future can. So in time as we experience it, the past is radically different from the future. For science, however, there is no difference between past time and future time. In a scientific formula, scientists claim, we can calculate the future exactly as we can the past. So, for science, subjective time is not real. As Einstein himself said, "You have to accept the idea that subjective time with its emphasis on the 'now' has no objective meaning . . . the distinction between past, present and future is only an illusion, however persistent."[55] Only objective time can be real.

But don't all the attempts to convince us that the flow of time is unreal seem wrong? Isn't the flow of time something we directly and undeniably experience? When we wish that a future event were here (like the end of school, or a celebration, or a vacation), don't we feel ourselves stuck in the present and powerless to make time move faster? When we are sorry that a past event has ended that we wish had gone on (like a pleasurable event, or time spent with a friend or relative, or even a person's life), don't we feel the inexorable movement of time carrying us away from the past into the future? Doesn't the mind gradually fill with memories of the past, and only of the past? Don't we experience the flow of time that carries us past birth, through childhood, into adulthood, and on to the slow decline of age? Surely, all of this must be real.

The French philosopher Henri Bergson agrees. Bergson argues that the scientist's objective time is just a conceptual abstraction, a construct of the mind. The image of time as a line is just that: an image. The concept of objective time is just that: a concept. Neither images nor concepts, he argues, can get at the

---

[54] Kant, *Critique of Pure Reason, Transcendental Aesthetic,* quoted in *Great Treasury of Western Thought,* ed. Mortimer J. Adler and Charles Van Doren (New York: R. R. Bowker, 1977), 1247.
[55] Quoted in Paul Davies, "Time," in Daniel Kolak and Raymond Martin, *The Experience of Philosophy* (Belmont, CA: Wadsworth, 1993), 88.

reality. Only what we directly experience—what we "intuit"—is real. What we directly experience or "intuit" within ourselves is the flow of time. We directly experience ourselves as changing and as flowing through time. Bergson calls this experience the "intuition of duration":

> If I search in the depth of my being . . . I find . . . a continuous flux which is not comparable to any flux I have ever seen. There is a succession of states, each of which announces that which follows and contains that which precedes it. They can, properly speaking, only be said to form multiple states when I have already passed them and turn back to observe their track. In reality no one of them begins or ends, but all extend into each other. . . .
>
> The unrolling of our duration resembles in some of its aspects the unity of an advancing movement and in others the multiplicity of expanding states; and, clearly, no metaphor can express one of these two aspects without sacrificing the other. If I use the comparison of the spectrum with its thousand shades, I have before me a thing already made, while duration is continually in the making. If I think of an elastic which is being stretched, or of a spring which is extended or relaxed, I forget the richness of color, characteristic of duration that is lived, and see only the simple movement by which consciousness passes from one shade to another. The inner life is all this at once: variety of qualities, continuity of progress, and unity of direction. It cannot be represented by images.
>
> But it is even less possible to represent it by concepts, that is, by abstract, general or simple ideas. . . . If a man does not himself have the intuition of the constitutive duration of his own being, nothing will ever give it to him, concepts no more than images.
>
> We easily persuade ourselves that by setting concept beside concept we can reconstruct the whole of the object with its parts, thus obtaining, so to speak, its intellectual equivalent. In this way we believe that we can form a faithful representation of duration by setting in line the concepts of unity, multiplicity, continuity, finite or infinite divisibility, etc. There precisely is the illusion. . . . For . . . these concepts, laid side by side, never actually give us more than an artificial reconstruction of the object, and they can only symbolize certain general aspects. It is therefore useless to believe that with them we can seize a reality of which they present to us the shadow alone. . . .
>
> However much I manipulate the concepts . . . I never obtain anything which resembles the simple intuition that I have of duration.[56]

Real time, then, for Bergson, is subjective time, the time flow that I experience as moving from future, through present, and into the past. I directly intuit this time. On the other hand, objective time is an intellectual reconstruction and so an illusion.

Yet is Bergson correct? Do we really have this so-called "intuition" of flowing time? Many people have argued that they do not have such an intuition. Others have claimed that even if they have this intuition, it is nothing more than an illusion. Real time has to be objective time.

Who is right? Is subjective time real, or is only objective time real? Do things end? Do we and our loved ones die? Or is every life and event really

---

[56]Henri Bergson, *An Introduction to Metaphysics,* trans. T. E. Hulme (London: Macmillan, 1913), selections from pages 9, 10, 13, 15, 16, 20.

frozen in objective time? Perhaps it depends on your point of view. Perhaps we cannot get by with only one of these two ways of approaching time. Both may be necessary, and maybe we should reject neither as unreal. When we do science and perhaps when we think about God, we may have no choice but to use the idea of objective time. When we think of ourselves and our human lives, we may have no choice but to use the idea of subjective time. Perhaps both are real. Or are they?

QUESTIONS

1. Describe as carefully as you can how you experience the sensation of the flow of time. What are its qualities?

2. Suppose that you were convinced that only objective time is real. Would this reduce your anxieties about aging, dying, or losing what you love? Why or why not?

3. Suppose that subjective time is not real. What would this imply about the "obviousness" of the experience of time as flowing? Are there other areas where what seems obvious turns out on examination to be wrong?

4. Suppose that the flow of time is an illusion. Can you think of ways in which this illusion might be caused? The physicist Paul Davies has suggested that the feeling of the flow of time is an illusion exactly like the dizzy feeling we sometimes have (perhaps after having too much to drink) that the universe is spinning, which is obviously an illusion. Is this a good comparison? Why or why not?

3.9 Chapter Summary and Conclusions

We opened this chapter by noting that what we ultimately consider real reflects and influences how we see ourselves. Questions of reality, which fall in the realm of metaphysics, tell us what ultimately matters. We discussed a number of metaphysical views, including the materialism–idealism debate; the responses of pragmatism, existentialism, and analytic philosophy; and the revival of idealism in the postmodern versions of antirealism. The main points made in the chapter are the following:

1. Metaphysics is the branch of philosophy that asks what reality and being are, and questions what can ultimately matter (3.1).

2. Materialism is the position that reality is ultimately matter. Hobbes, an early materialist, argued that only physical objects are real (3.2).

3. Idealism is the position that reality is nonmatter: idea, mind, or spirit, for example. Berkeley, an idealist, argued that since all we perceive are our own ideas, only minds and their ideas are real (3.2).

4. Pragmatism, as developed in America by Peirce, James, and Dewey, rejects all absolutistic assumptions about reality, admits the pluralistic nature of reality, and refuses to consider any claims but those focused on "fruits, consequences, facts" (3.3).

5. Logical positivists, who base their views on how language works, have generally held that metaphysics is based on linguistic confusions. Logical positivists such as Alfred J. Ayer and Rudolph Carnap argue that metaphysical statements about reality are meaningless expressions of emotion and not statements of fact (3.4).

6. Postmodern antirealists say no reality exists independent of our language, our thoughts, our perceptions, and our beliefs. Different languages, thoughts, perceptions, and beliefs create different realities (3.5).

7. The concept of human existence and being plays an important part in existentialism and phenomenology, which arose out of disillusionment with past philosophies (3.6).

8. Husserl's phenomenology emphasizes that only reality as it appears to consciousness can have any meaning to us. Heidegger's phenomenology stresses being. What is ultimately real for the phenomenologist is pure consciousness, which itself has being. Existentialism stresses personal freedom, the lack of an essential human nature, and the lack of behavioral guidelines (3.6).

9. The issue of determinism has significant implications for our views on punishment and responsibility. Hard determinists hold that all human actions are caused by previous events and the laws of nature; indeterminists hold that human actions are free and so determinism is false; compatibalists hold that determinism and human freedom are compatible. Kant agreed that determinism and indeterminism arise from two different but inescapable ways of thinking about our actions (3.7).

10. Time may be thought of as objective time, which does not flow from the future into the past, or as subjective time, which we experience as flowing from the future into the past. Many philosophers and scientists have agreed that real time is objective time whereas subjective time is an illusion that does not exist. Henri Bergson has argued that subjective time is real whereas objective time is an abstraction (3.8).

Despite the diversity of metaphysical views, many metaphysicians agree on some important issues. These points of agreement suggest insights into ourselves.

First, some metaphysicians agree that something exists outside the individual self. Even the subjective idealism of Berkeley does not deny the physical world, only its independence from mind. Despite Sartre's stress on self and Husserl's emphasis on consciousness, these thinkers recognize the distinction between things that lack consciousness, such as chairs, trees, and books, and those that do not, such as humans. However, we should quickly add that many phenomenologists deplore such a dichotomy. Nonetheless, although the self may be insular—bound by the sea of its experiences—there are other human "islands," all joined by the similarity of their conditions and circumstances.

Second, some metaphysicians accept the senses and reason as primary sources of knowledge, as the tools by which the self comes to know things. True, some metaphysicians give reason a primacy that others do not; others emphasize the importance of sense experience. But these can be seen as differences of degree, not of substance. We are most likely to know ourselves and our world by using both reason and the senses.

Finally, various metaphysicians agree that there is an order or meaning in things that the senses and reason can discover. True, materialism may hold that the order is strictly mechanistic; idealism, that it is spiritual or even supernatural; existentialism and phenomenology, that it is being or the purpose that each of us imposes on experience; analytic philosophy, that it is the symbolic form in which we express things; and antirealism, that it is in the system of concepts that we use to describe our experience. But members within each school hold that some order exists. Most important, each of us is part of that order, whatever its nature. To know the self is at least partially to know that order and how we fit into it.

At the same time, there are fundamental differences among these metaphysical outlooks that reflect and reinforce different views of human nature and of self. For the materialist, we are part of the matter that composes the universe and are subject to the same laws. As a result, the self is the product of its experiences, the sum total of everything that has ever happened to it. There is little point in speaking of individual responsibility or personal will, for we cannot help doing what we do. When we speak of mind, we really mean brain; when we refer to mental states, we are really talking about brain states. The purpose of any life is to understand how the parts of the universe, including the self, fit together and work. With such knowledge we can control our environment to some degree and perhaps improve the human condition.

For many idealists, in contrast, the individual is part of a cosmic mind, spirit, idea, or perhaps life force. In this sense, individuals are alike. But each person finds a self-identity in personal understanding. Only the individual can be aware of his or her own experiences. In the last analysis, this personal awareness and these ideas make each of us unique. The purpose of each life is to understand the order at work in the universe. This order is not matter but pure idea; for some idealists it is a divine dimension, God. In understanding this cosmic order or plan, we understand our position in it and thus the self.

The pragmatist views the self as neither primarily matter nor primarily idea. Since pragmatists avoid absolutes, they choose to see the self as consisting of many dimensions, including material and ideal. The self is a complex entity consisting of experiences, which include thoughts, feelings, sensations, concepts, attitudes, and goals. Although we are tremendously influenced by environment, we can and do play a formative role in determining the nature of our experiences. Using intelligence and reason, the individual can exercise control over nature. But we shall not find personal meaning and purpose in the cosmos, because it possesses none. For personal meaning we must turn to the consequences of our actions, judging them according to the results that they produce.

Existentialism shares pragmatism's skepticism of absolutistic doctrines. But more than any of the other outlooks, it stresses personal freedom. The self is essentially something in the making that is not finished until the individual dies. The self is whatever we choose to make it. We are ultimately free to think, choose, and act however we wish. Such freedom without guidelines is frightening, often leading to uncertainty, anxiety, and despair. But this, say the existentialists, is the human condition.

For many phenomenologists, what we are is that we exist. The fundamental self is not its characteristics, properties, or the other objective qualities, but being. The self is not our idea of what we are but the immediate concrete reality of being ourselves. We move furthest from a knowledge of the self when we separate self from subjective reality, as we do when we view it as some object to be studied, quantified, and known. We are closest to the self when we strip from consciousness the experiences of objects that occupy it. Then we realize that the self is what precedes its experiences—that is, pure being.

And for the postmodern antirealists, the self is a constructed self. The many languages and systems of concepts that we use contain within them the elements out of which we construct the concept of the self. This construct is all there is to the self. Outside of our language there is no objective, "real" self.

So, although members of different metaphysical schools share some beliefs, they vary in their approach to the issue of self. These approaches may affirm or deny the self, and view it as essentially rational, divine, mechanical, existential, or nonexistent. These views have dramatically different implications for the self and its place in the world.

3.10 HISTORICAL SHOWCASE

Hobbes and Berkeley

We have suggested throughout this chapter that people's metaphysical views influence their views of human nature. Two seventeenth-century philosophers—Thomas Hobbes and George Berkeley—illustrate the profound impact a metaphysical view can have on one's view of human nature.

Hobbes, as we briefly mentioned earlier, proposed the metaphysical view that everything in the universe is material. The view led him to propose a materialistic view of human nature. Hobbes believed that humans are, in effect, complicated machines. Berkeley, on the other hand, advanced the metaphysical claim that everything in the universe is spiritual or nonmaterial. This claim then led him to hold a thoroughly spiritualistic view of human nature: To be human is to be a kind spirit.

Examining the views of Hobbes and Berkeley in some detail will help us see how metaphysics is related to the positions we take on other philosophical issues, in particular on the issue of human nature. It will become clear, also, how metaphysics can influence our views of God and society.

HOBBES

Thomas Hobbes was a thoroughgoing materialist: He held that only material objects exist. In this respect he differed considerably from his contemporary, René Descartes (whom we showcased in the last chapter). Descartes carried over from medieval philosophers like Aquinas the view that reality consists of both material and immaterial (or "spiritual") entities. Hobbes rejected this dualistic view. The recent astronomical discoveries of Copernicus, Kepler, and Galileo had all been based on the observation of moving bodies. Influenced by their approach to reality, Hobbes reasoned that perhaps all reality could be explained in terms of the motions of bodies in space.

Born prematurely in 1588 when his mother, overcome with fear at the approach of the invading Spanish navy, went into early labor, Hobbes throughout his youth had a melancholy personality that earned him the nickname of the Crow. The son of a clergyman, Hobbes was sent at the age of fourteen to study at Oxford, where, he tells us, he learned to hate philosophy. He apparently learned enough, however, so that when he graduated in 1608 he was hired by the wealthy and aristocratic Cavendish family as a tutor for their sons. He later remarked that the job left him more than enough time to read and study while his young charges were "making visits" in town. Traveling with the Cavendish family gave Hobbes the opportunity to see much of Europe and to become acquainted with the great thinkers of the period, especially the Italian astronomer Galileo, who at this time was busily tracing the motions of the heavenly bodies with the aid of geometry. At about the age of forty, probably under Galileo's influence, Hobbes came to the conclusion that everything in the universe could be explained in terms of the motions of material bodies and that geometry could provide the basic laws of their motions. He attempted to work out the details of this philosophy in a remarkable series of writings that included his masterpiece, *Leviathan*, and a trilogy bearing the titles *De Corpore (On Material Bodies)*, *De Homine (On Man)*, and *De Cive (On the Citizen)*. Hobbes's final years were relatively happy. He died in 1679, famous for his

Thomas Hobbes: "The Universe is corporeal, that is to say, body, . . . and that which is not body is no part of the Universe. And because the Universe is all, that which is no part of it is nothing, and, consequently, nowhere."

materialistic philosophy and the political theories that grew out of it.

Hobbes was unequivocal in claiming that matter is all there is in the universe:

> The Universe, that is the whole mass of things that are, is corporeal, that is to say body; and has the dimensions of magnitude, namely, length, breadth, and depth. Also every part of body is likewise body, and has the like dimensions. And, consequently, every part of the Universe is body, and that which is not body is no part of the Universe. And because the Universe is all, that which is no part of it is nothing, and, consequently, nowhere.[1]

(Hobbes's archaic spelling has been modernized in this and following quotations.)

---

[1] Thomas Hobbes, *Hobbes's Leviathan* (Oxford: Clarendon Press, 1909; original work published 1651), 524.

In Hobbes's view the characteristics and activities of all objects, including human beings, can be explained in purely mechanical terms:

> For seeing life is but a motion of limbs, the beginning whereof is in some principal part within; why may we not say, that all *automata* (engines that move themselves by springs and wheels as does a watch) have an artificial life? For what is the *heart*, but a *spring*; and the *nerves*, but so many *strings*; and the *joints*, but so many *wheels*, giving motion to the whole body, such as was intended by the artificer?[2]

Hobbes attempted to apply this mechanism to explain the mental activities of human beings. Many philosophers, Descartes in particular, believed the mental activities of perceiving, thinking, and willing were evidence that human minds are spiritual or nonmaterial. Mental activities (thinking) and mental contents (thoughts) seem to have no physical characteristics (that is, they have no color, size, or position and seem to be nonbodily). Hobbes was particularly concerned with showing that even mental activities could be entirely explained in terms of the motions of material bodies. He begins this task by first arguing that all of our thoughts originate in our sensations (or, as he writes, in "sense"). And sensations, he claims, are nothing more than motions in us that are caused by external objects. These motions in us travel through our nerves to our brains:

> Concerning the thoughts of man, I will consider them first singly, and afterwards in train or dependence upon one another. . . .
>
> The origin of them all, is that which we call SENSE [sensation], for there is no conception in a man's mind, which has not at first, totally, or by parts, been begotten upon the organs of sense. . . .
>
> The cause of sense is the external body, or object, which presses the organ proper to each sense . . ., which pressure, by the mediation of the nerves, and other strings and membranes of the body, continues inwards to the brain and heart, causes there a resistance, or counter-pressure, or endeavor [movement] of the heart . . ., which endeavor [movement], because [it is] *outward*, seems [to us]

to be some matter without. And this *seeming* or *fancy*, is that which men call *sense*. [Sense] consists, as to the eye in *light*, or *color* . . .; to the ear, in a *sound*; to the nostril, in an *odor*; to the tongue . . ., in a *savor*; and to the rest of the body, in *heat, cold, hardness, softness,* and such other qualities as we discern by *feeling*.

> All [these] qualities . . . are, in the object that causes them, but so many . . . motions of the matter, by which it presses our organs. Neither in us, that are pressed, are they anything else, but . . . motions; for motion produces nothing but motion. . . . [Just] as pressing, rubbing, or striking the eye makes us fancy a light, and pressing the ear produces a din, so do the bodies we see, or hear, produce the same [sensations] by their . . . action.[3]

Once the motion created in our senses has traveled to the brain, the brain retains this motion, much like water continues moving after the wind stops. This "decaying" motion in our brain is the residual image that we retain in our memory. Thus, our memory of an object is nothing more than the residual motion the object leaves impressed on our brain:

> When a body is once in motion, it moves, unless something else hinders it, eternally; and whatever hinders it, cannot in an instant, but [only] in time, and by degrees, quite extinguish it. And as we see in the water, though the wind cease, the waves [continue] . . . rolling for a long time after, so also it happens in that motion which is made in the internal parts of man. . . .
>
> This decaying sense, when we would express the thing itself, . . . we call *imagination*. . . . But when we would express the decay, and signify that the sense is fading, old, and past, it is called *memory*. So that imagination and memory are but one thing.[4]

But what does all of this have to do with thinking? Hobbes held that when we are thinking, we are merely linking together the decaying images (or motions) that we have retained in our memory. Our thinking activities are thus nothing more than a sequence of motions linked together, usually as they are linked together when we first experienced

[2] Ibid., 8.

[3] Ibid., 12.
[4] Ibid., 13–14.

them as sensations. Sometimes our thinking is "unguided," as when we daydream, and sometimes it is "regulated," as when we are trying to solve some problems:

> By consequence or TRAIN of thoughts, I understand that succession of one thought to another, which is called, to distinguish it from discourse in words, mental discourse.
>
> When a man thinks on anything whatsoever, his next thought after is not altogether . . . casual. . . . The reason . . . is this. All fancies [images] are motions within us, relics of those made in the sense. And those motions that immediately succeeded one another in the sense, continue also together after sense. . . .
>
> This train of thoughts, or mental discourse, is of two sorts. The first is unguided, without design, and inconstant, wherein there is not passionate thought, to govern and direct those that follow to itself, [such] as the end and scope of some desire, or other passion, in which case the thoughts are said to wander and seem impertinent one to another, as in a dream. . . .
>
> The second is more constant, as being regulated by some desire and design. . . . From desire arises the thought of some means we have seen produce the like of that which we aim at; and from the thought of that, the thought of means to that mean; and so continually, till we come to some beginning within our own power. . . . The train of regulated thoughts is of two kinds: one, when an effect imagined we seek the causes, or means that produce it. . . . The other is, when imagining anything whatsoever, we seek all the possible effects that can by it be produced.[5]

But "trains of thoughts" are not the only things produced by the motions that begin in our senses and end in the imaginations of our brains. The motions of our imaginations also produce motions in our organs of appetite (which Hobbes thought were located mainly in the heart); these are called desires. The motions called desires, in turn, are what lead us to engage in "voluntary actions":

> There be in animals, two sorts of motions peculiar to them. One [is] called vital . . . such as the course of the blood, the pulse, the breathing, the concoction, nutrition, excretion, etc. . . . The other is . . . voluntary motion, as to go, to speak, to move any of our limbs, in such manner as is first fancied in our minds. . . . And because going, speaking, and the like voluntary motions, depend always upon a precedent thought . . . it is evident that the imagination is the first internal beginning of all voluntary motion. . . . These small beginnings of motion, within the body of man, before they appear in walking, speaking, striking, and other visible actions, are commonly called ENDEAVOR.
>
> This endeavor, when it is toward something which causes it, is called APPETITE, or DESIRE. . . . And when the endeavor is from something, it is generally called AVERSION. . . . That which men desire, they are also said to LOVE, and to HATE those things for which they have aversion. . . . But whatsoever is the object of any man's appetite or desire, that . . . he . . . calls good, and the object of his hate and aversion, evil. . . .
>
> As, in sense, that which is really within us is, as I have said before, only motion, caused by the action of external objects. . . . So, when the action of the same object is continued from the eyes, ears, and other organs to the heart, the real effect there is nothing but motion or endeavor, which consists in appetite or aversion, to or from the object moving [us].
>
> When in the mind of man, appetites, and aversions, hopes, and fears, concerning one and the same thing, arise alternately; and divers good and evil consequences of the doing, or omitting the thing propounded come successively into our thoughts; so that sometimes we have an appetite to it; sometimes an aversion from it; sometimes hope to be able to do it; sometimes despair, or fear to attempt it; the whole sum of desires, aversions, hopes and fears continued till the thing be either done, or thought impossible, is that we call DELIBERATION. . . .
>
> In deliberation, the last appetite, or aversion, immediately adhering to the action, or to the omission thereof, is what we call the WILL. . . . Will, therefore, is the last appetite in deliberating.[6]

Thus, Hobbes concluded, not only can a materialist philosophy fully account for all our obviously physical characteristics, but it can also account for all of those inner, mental activities that other philosophers take as evidence of a spiritual or non-

---

material mind: sensing, remembering, thinking, desiring, loving, hating, and willing. These mental activities do not require us to say that some kind of nonmaterial reality exists in addition to the material objects in the world. There is no such thing as a nonmaterial reality: Everything consists of matter and its motions.

Hobbes felt that his materialistic philosophy also provided the foundations for a social philosophy. By examining the basic material characteristics of human individuals, he felt he could explain why our societies are structured as they are. Hobbes began by maintaining that the central desires that affect the relations between individuals inevitably lead them to quarrel with one another:

> So that in the nature of man, we find three principal causes of quarrel. First, competition; secondly, diffidence; thirdly, glory.
>
> The first makes men invade for gain; the second, for safety; and the third, for reputation. The first use violence, to make themselves masters of other men's persons, wives, children, and cattle; the second, to defend them; the third, for trifles, as a word, a smile, a different opinion, and any other sign of undervalue, either direct in their persons, or by reflection in their kindred, their friends, their nation, their profession, or their name.[7]

Because of these antagonistic drives, individuals would inevitably strive "to destroy or subdue one another" if it were not for the restraints that the "common power" of government is able to impose on them. If people were in a "state of nature"—that is, if they were in the situation they were in before any government restrained them from harming one another—they would be constantly at war, and life would be miserable:

> Hereby it is manifest, that during the time men live without a common power to keep them all in awe, they are in that condition which is called war, and such a war as is of every man against every man. . . . In such condition, there is no place for industry, because the fruit thereof is uncertain: and consequently no culture of the earth; no navigation, nor use of the commodities that may be imported by sea; no com-

modious building; no instruments of moving, and removing, such things as require much force; no knowledge of the face of the earth; no account of time; no arts; no letters; no society; and which is worst of all, continual fear, and danger of violent death; and the life of man, solitary, poor, nasty, brutish, and short.[8]

To escape the brutal state of nature into which their passions continually push them, people at last decide to form a government (or, as Hobbes calls it, a Leviathan). This government is meant to set up a "common power" possessing enough force to establish law and order and thereby put an end to fighting. We set up a government by entering into a "social contract" with one another. That is, we make an agreement (or "covenant") with one another to hand over all power to a person or a group. That person or group then becomes the "sovereign" ruler and has the authority to use the power or force of the citizens themselves to enforce the law (which the sovereign makes) and to establish peace and order. We thus emerge from the dreadful state of nature by becoming "subjects" and taking on the constraints of life in a civil society:

> The final cause, end, or design of men, who naturally love liberty and dominion over others, in the introduction of that restraint upon themselves, in which we see them live in commonwealths, is the foresight of their own preservation, and of a more contented life thereby; that is to say, of getting themselves out from that miserable condition of war, which is necessarily consequent, as has been shown, to the natural passions of men, when there is no visible power to keep them in awe, and tie them by fear of punishment to the performance of their covenants. . . .
>
> The only way to erect such a common power, as may be able to defend them from the invasion of foreigners, and the injuries of one another, and thereby to secure them in such sort, as that by their own industry, and by the fruits of the earth, they may nourish themselves and live contentedly; is, to confer all their power and strength upon one man, or upon one assembly of men, that may reduce all their wills, by plurality of voices, unto one will: which is as much as to say, to appoint one man, or assembly of men, to bear their person; and every one to own, and

---

[7]Ibid., 96.

[8]Ibid.

acknowledge himself to be the author of whatsoever he that so bears their person, shall act, or cause to be acted, in those things which concern the common peace and safety; and therein to submit their wills, every one to his will, and their judgments, to his judgment. This is more than consent or concord; it is real unity of them all, in one and the same person, made by covenant of every man with every man, in such manner, as if every man should say to every man, *I authorize and give up my right of governing myself, to this man, or to this assembly of men, on this condition, that you give up your right to him, and authorize all his actions in like manner.* . . . this is the generation of the great LEVIATHAN. . . . And he that carries this person, is called SOVEREIGN, and said to have *sovereign power*; and everyone besides, his SUBJECT.[9]

Thus, the materialist philosophy that Hobbes created also gave him the basic concepts he needed to explain the formation of governments. Governments are simply the outcome of the motions we call "desires." Desires lead people to fight with one another (for their material possessions), and this results in a continual "war of all against all." A further desire or motion, the desire for peace, then leads people to form governments.

BERKELEY

George Berkeley is perhaps the most famous of all those idealist philosophers who hold that reality is primarily spiritual and not material. To some extent Berkeley was reacting to the philosophy of materialists such as Hobbes, whose views were becoming popular in the wake of the growing influence of the new sciences. Such materialist philosophies, Berkeley felt, left no room for God and thus were inimical to religion. What better way to combat atheism than to prove that materialism was false and that all reality is spiritual!

Berkeley was born in 1685 in Kilkenney, Ireland. As a teenager he was sent to Trinity College in Dublin, where he graduated with a master's degree in 1707. Berkeley stayed on at Trinity College as a teacher for six years. There, at the age of

George Berkeley: "All of the choir of heaven and furniture of the earth, in a word all those bodies which compose the mighty frames of the world, have no substance without a mind; their being is to be perceived; consequently so long as they are not actually perceived by me or other created spirits, they must either have no existence at all or else exist in the mind of some eternal spirit."

twenty-four, he finished writing what was to become the classic exposition of an idealist philosophy, *A Treatise Concerning the Principles of Human Knowledge*. In 1713 Berkeley left Trinity College. He was by now an ordained Protestant minister, and in 1729 he and his recent bride traveled as missionaries to Newport, Rhode Island, where he planned to organize a college that would eventually be established in Bermuda. But funding for the college never materialized, and in 1731 he returned to England. In 1734 Berkeley became a bishop in the Church of England and was assigned to the diocese of Cloyne in Ireland. Sixteen years later, at the age of sixty-five, he retired to Oxford with his wife and family. There he died in 1753.

Berkeley held the view that all we know or per-

---

[9] Ibid., 128, 131–132.

ceive of the world around us are the sensations we have: the colors, sights, sounds, and tastes we experience. We commonly attribute these sensations to material objects outside us. When our eyes see a small round patch of red, for example, we might infer that outside us there exists a material object that we call an apple and that light coming from this material object causes our eyes to have the sensation of red color. However, Berkeley questioned this inference. He pointed out that we really have no reason to say that in addition to the sensations we experience within our minds, there *also* exists outside us (or, in his words, "without us") some kind of material objects. We do not even have any idea what these so-called material objects would be like since all we perceive are our sensations and these sensations are clearly not material objects since our sensations exist entirely in our minds (or, in Berkeley's words, "our spirits"). All that exists besides our minds, or "spirits," Berkeley concluded, are the sensations we perceive in our minds and the mental images we voluntarily form in them. Berkeley used the term *ideas* to refer to the contents of our minds, including both the sensations we have and the mental images we form. Thus, for Berkeley, the world consists entirely of minds ("spirits") and ideas.

Berkeley summarized his view in the Latin slogan *esse est percipi*, which means "to exist is to be perceived": The only things that exist, besides minds, are the ideas perceived within minds. As he flamboyantly asserted, "All the Choir of Heaven and the furniture of earth, in a word all those bodies which compose the mighty frame of the world, have no substance without a mind."[10] Thus, Berkeley was a complete idealist: He held the view that reality consists of nothing more than the ideas in our minds.

Berkeley's views are most clearly expounded in the short work he titled *A Treatise Concerning the Principles of Human Knowledge*. He opens the treatise with a remark expressing what many newcomers to philosophy feel: that philosophy seems to create more "doubts and difficulties" than it resolves:

> Philosophy being nothing else but the study of wisdom and truth, it may with reason be expected that those who have spent most time and pains in it should enjoy a greater calm and serenity of mind, a greater clearness and evidence of knowledge, and be less disturbed with doubts and difficulties than other men. Yet so it is, we see the illiterate bulk of mankind that walk the high road of plain common sense, and are governed by the dictates of nature, for the most part easy and undisturbed. To them nothing that is familiar appears unaccountable or difficult to comprehend. They complain not of any want of evidence in their sense, and are out of all danger of becoming skeptics. But no sooner do we depart from sense and instinct to follow the light of a superior principle, to reason, meditate, and reflect on the nature of things, but a thousand scruples spring up in our minds concerning those things which before we seemed fully to comprehend. Prejudices and errors of sense do from all parts discover themselves to our view; and, endeavoring to correct these by reason, we are insensibly drawn into uncouth paradoxes, difficulties, and inconsistencies, which multiply and grow upon us as we advance in speculation, till at length, having wandered through many intricate mazes, we find ourselves just where we were, or, which is worse, sit down in a forlorn skepticism.[11]

To resolve the "uncouth paradoxes, difficulties, and inconsistencies" that give philosophy a bad name, Berkeley undertakes to examine "the first principles of human knowledge"—that is, the primary sources from which we draw all our knowledge. He begins by pointing out that if we look into our minds, we will see that everything we know consists either of sensations ("ideas imprinted on the senses or perceived by attending to the passions") or mental images ("ideas formed by help of memory and imagination"). Consequently, each object we know in the world around us (such as an "apple, a stone, a tree, a book and the like") is really nothing more than a collection of ideas (sensations of color, touch, smell, taste, or hearing). In addition to ideas, he notes, there are also "active

[10] George Berkeley, *A Treatise Concerning the Principles of Human Knowledge*, in *The Works of George Berkeley*, vol. 1, ed. George Sampson (London: George Bell & Sons, 1897), 181–182.

[11] Ibid., 161.

beings" or "minds." In fact, ideas can exist only in minds. Since all objects consist of ideas and since ideas can exist only in the mind, it follows that the objects in the world exist only in the mind! Berkeley argues for this startling conclusion in the following passages:

It is evident to anyone who takes a survey of the *objects* of human knowledge that they are either ideas actually imprinted on the senses, or else such as are perceived by attending to the passions and operations of the mind, or lastly, ideas formed by help of memory and imagination—either compounding, dividing, or barely representing those originally perceived in the aforesaid ways. By sight I have the ideas of light and colors, with their several degrees and variations. By touch I perceive, for example, hard and soft, heat and cold, motion and resistance, and of all these more and less either as to quantity or degree. Smelling furnishes me with odors, the palate with tastes, and hearing conveys sounds to the mind in all their variety of tone and composition. As several of these are observed to accompany each other, they come to be marked by one name, and so to be reputed as one thing. Thus, for example, a certain color, taste, smell, figure, and consistency having been observed to go together are accounted one distinct thing signified by the name "apple"; other collections of ideas constitute a stone, a tree, a book, and the like sensible things—which as they are pleasing or disagreeable excite the passions of love, hatred, joy, grief, and so forth.

But, besides all that endless variety of ideas or objects of knowledge, there is likewise something which knows or perceives them and exercises divers operations, as willing, imagining, remembering, about them. This perceiving, active being is what I call "mind," "spirit," "soul," or "myself." By which words I do not denote any one of my ideas, but a thing entirely distinct from them, wherein they exist or, which is the same thing, whereby they are perceived—for the existence of an idea consists in being perceived.

That neither our thoughts, nor passions, nor ideas formed by the imagination exist without the mind is what everybody will allow. And it seems no less evident that the various sensations or ideas imprinted on the sense, however blended or combined together (that is, whatever objects they compose), cannot exist otherwise than in a mind perceiving them.—I

think an intuitive knowledge may be obtained of this by anyone that shall attend to what is meant by the term "exist" when applied to sensible things. The table I write on I say exists, that is, I see and feel it; and if I were out of my study I should say it existed—meaning thereby that if I was in my study I might perceive it, or that some other spirit actually does perceive it. There was an odor, that is, it was smelled; there was a sound, that is to say, it was heard; a color or figure, and it was perceived by sight or touch. This is all that I can understand by these and the like expressions. For as to what is said of the absolute existence of unthinking things without any relation to their being perceived, that seems perfectly unintelligible. Their *esse* is *percipi*, nor is it possible they should have any existence out of the minds or thinking things which perceive them.

It is indeed an opinion strangely prevailing amongst men that houses, mountains, rivers, and, in a word, all sensible objects have an existence, natural or real, distinct from their being perceived by the understanding. But with how great an assurance and acquiescence soever this principle may be entertained in the world, yet whoever shall find in his heart to call it in question may, if I mistake not, perceive it to involve a manifest contradiction. For what are the forementioned objects but the things we perceive by sense? And what do we perceive besides our own ideas or sensations? And is it not plainly repugnant that any one of these, or any combination of them, should exist unperceived? . . .

But, say you, though the ideas themselves do not exist without the mind, yet there may be things like them, whereof they are copies or resemblances, which things exist without the mind in an unthinking [material] substance. I answer, an idea can be like nothing but an idea; a color or figure can be like nothing but another color or figure. If we look ever so little into our thoughts, we shall find it impossible for us to conceive a likeness except only between our ideas. Again, I ask whether those supposed originals or external things, of which our ideas are the pictures or representations, be themselves perceivable or not? If they are, then they are ideas and we have gained our point; but if you say they are not, I appeal to anyone whether it be sense to assert a color is like something which is invisible; hard or soft, like something which is intangible; and so of the rest. . . .

But, [suppose] it were possible that solid, figured, movable substances may exist without the mind, corresponding to the ideas we have of bodies, yet how is it possible for us to know this? Either we must know it by sense or by reason. As for our senses, by them we have the knowledge only of our sensations, ideas, or those things that are immediately perceived by sense, call them what you will; but they do not inform us that things exist without the mind, or unperceived, like to those which are perceived. This the materialists themselves acknowledge. It remains, therefore, that if we have any knowledge at all of external things, it must be by reason, inferring their existence from what is immediately perceived by sense. But what reason can induce us to believe the existence of bodies without the mind, from what we perceive, since the very patrons of matter themselves do not pretend there is any necessary connection betwixt them and our ideas? I say it is granted on all hands (and what happens in dreams, frenzies, and the like, puts it beyond dispute) that it is possible we might be affected with all the ideas we have now, though no bodies existed without resembling them. Hence it is evident the supposition of external bodies is not necessary for the producing of our ideas; since it is granted they are produced sometimes, and might possibly be produced always in the same order we see them in at present, without their concurrence. . . .

But, say you, surely there is nothing easier than to imagine trees, for instance, in a park, or books existing in a closet, and nobody by to perceive them. I answer you may so, there is no difficulty in it; but what is all this, I beseech you, more than framing in your mind certain ideas which you call books and trees, and at the same time omitting to frame the idea of anyone that may perceive them? But do you yourself perceive or think of them all the while? This therefore is nothing to the purpose; it only shows you have the power of imagining or forming ideas in your mind; but it does not show that you can conceive it possible the objects of your thought may exist without the mind. To make out this, it is necessary that you conceive them existing unconceived or unthought of, which is a manifest repugnancy. When we do our utmost to conceive the existence of external bodies, we are all the while only contemplating our own ideas. But the mind, taking no notice of itself, is deluded to think it can and does conceive bodies existing unthought of or without the mind, though at the same time they are apprehended by or exist in itself. A little attention will discover to any-

one the truth and evidence of what is here said, and make it unnecessary to insist on any other proofs against the existence of *material substance*.[12]

Berkeley's views were naturally accused of leading to skepticism, the view that we cannot know anything about reality. For Berkeley's views are but a short step away from the view that since the ideas in our minds might be false and since all we know are the ideas in our minds, we can never know anything for sure about the real world. However, Berkeley did not intend his idealist philosophy to encourage skepticism. On the contrary, he felt that "the grounds of Skepticism, Atheism and Irreligion" lay in materialism. Those who hold that only matter exists, he felt, were inevitably led to the view that God does not exist since God is a nonmaterial spirit. The best way to combat atheism, then, was to prove that matter does not exist and that, on the contrary, only spirits and their ideas exist. If spirits and ideas are the only reality, in knowing these we know all the reality there is. Thus, skepticism, like atheism, is false.

Berkeley, in fact, took great pains in his attempt to show that God exists. God is a crucial part of his universe and plays an essential role as the source of the world we see displayed before our senses. If we examine the ideas in our minds, he argues, we will see that some of them require the existence of another "spirit" to produce them, and this is God. God produces in us the sensations that we perceive as reality and ensures that we perceive an orderly reality in which we can plan our lives and look easily toward the future. Berkeley concludes that the "surprising magnificence, beauty, and perfection" of the orderly display that God creates in our minds and that we call the world should fill us with admiration:

> I find I can excite [some] ideas in my mind at pleasure, and vary and shift the scene as oft as I think fit. It is no more than willing, and straightway this or that idea arises in my fancy [imagination]; and by the same power it is obliterated and makes way for another. . . .

---

[12] Ibid., 179, 180–182, 186–187, 189.

But whatever power I may have over my own thoughts, I find the ideas actually perceived by sense have not a like dependence on my will. When in broad daylight I open my eyes, it is not in my power to choose whether I shall see or no, or to determine what particular objects shall present themselves to my view; and so likewise as to the hearing and other senses; the ideas imprinted on them are not creatures of my will. There is therefore some *other* will or spirit that produces them.

The ideas of sense are more strong, lively, and distinct than those of the imagination; they have likewise a steadiness, order, and coherence, and are not excited at random, as those which are the effects of human wills often are, but in a regular train or series, the admirable connection whereof sufficiently testifies to the wisdom and benevolence of its Author. Now the set rules or established methods wherein the mind we depend on excites in us the ideas of sense are called "the laws of nature"; and these we learn by experience which teaches us that such and such ideas are attended with such and such other ideas in the ordinary course of things.

This gives us a sort of foresight which enables us to regulate our actions for the benefit of life. And without this we should be eternally at a loss; we could not know how to act on anything that might procure us the least pleasure or remove the least pain of sense. That food nourishes, sleep refreshes, and fire warms us; that to sow in the seedtime is the way to reap in the harvest; and in general to obtain such or such ends, such or such means are conducive—all this we know, not by discovering any necessary connection between our ideas, but only by the observation of the settled laws of nature, without which we should all be in uncertainty and confusion, and a grown man no more knows how to manage himself in the affairs of life than an infant just born. . . .

But if we attentively consider the constant regularity, order, and concatenation of natural things, the surprising magnificence, beauty, and perfection of the larger, and the exquisite contrivance of the smaller parts of the creation, together with the exact harmony and correspondence of the whole, but above all the never-enough-admired laws of pain and pleasure, and the instincts or natural inclinations, appetites, and passions of animals; I say if we consider all these things, and at the same time attend to the meaning and import of the attributes: one, eternal, infinitely wise, good, and perfect, we shall clearly perceive that they belong to the aforesaid

spirit, "who works all in all," and "by whom all things consist." . . .

It is therefore plain that nothing can be more evident to anyone that is capable of the least reflection than the existence of God, or a spirit who is intimately present to our minds, producing in them all that variety of ideas or sensations which continually affect us, on whom we have an absolute and entire dependence, in short "in whom we live, and move, and have our being." That the discovery of this great truth, which lies so near and obvious to the mind, should be attained to by the reason of so very few, is a sad instance of the stupidity and inattention of men who, though they are surrounded with such clear manifestations of the Deity, are yet so little affected by them that they seem, as it were, blinded with excess of light.[13]

Berkeley's idealist philosophy, then, provided him with what he thought was an irrefutable proof of the existence of spiritual reality, including God, and of the nonexistence of the material world on which Hobbes and other materialists insisted.

QUESTIONS

1. Carl Sagan has said that "each human being is a superbly constructed astonishingly compact, self-ambulatory computer." In what respects is this similar to Hobbes's view? In what respects does it differ?

2. As the contemporary philosopher J. J. C. Smart writes, "By 'materialism' I mean the theory that there is nothing in the world over and above those entities which are postulated by physics. Thus I do not hold materialism to be wedded to the billiard-ball physics of the nineteenth century. The less visualizable particles of modern physics count as matter [for me]." In what respects is Smart's materialism similar to Hobbes's? In what respects does it differ? Does Smart's materialism have any philosophical implications that are radically different from Hobbes's?

3. Hobbes claims that you are nothing more than your physical body (or your brain). If this is

---

[13] Ibid., 191–192, 247–248.

true, then *you* are exactly the same as *your body* (or your brain), so whatever is true of *you* must be true of *your body*. But consider the following objection to Hobbes: "Although *you* can be morally blameworthy or praiseworthy, can we say that *your body* or *your brain* is morally blameworthy or praiseworthy? Although *you* can have wishes (for example, to do math) or thoughts (for example, about philosophy), does it make sense to say that *your body* or *your brain* has these wishes or thoughts? Although *you* can love God, isn't it absurd to say *your body* or *your brain* loves God? Although it makes sense to say that *you* have a body, does it make sense to say that *your body* has a body?" Evaluate these criticisms.

4. Do you think Hobbes's description of the quarrelsomeness of human nature is an accurate description of your own self? Of others? Is Hobbes correct in claiming that without the restraints of government, you would involve yourself in a continual "war against every man" and that your life would be "solitary, poor, nasty, brutish, and short"?

5. Must a materialist philosophy like Hobbes's take a pessimistic view of human beings? Contrast Hobbes's views with those of B. F. Skinner.

6. Do you agree with Berkeley's criticism that philosophy inevitably draws us "into uncouth paradoxes, difficulties, and inconsistencies, which multiply and grow as we advance, till, at length, . . . we find ourselves just as we were, or, which is worse, sit down in a forlorn skepticism"? What assumptions about the purpose and nature of philosophy does

Berkeley make? How does this compare to Plato's conception of philosophy?

7. Do you think this is an adequate summary of Berkeley's main argument: "All the objects we perceive are only ideas; ideas exist only in minds; therefore all the objects we perceive exist only in minds"? Do you think any parts of this argument are false? Explain.

8. The English writer Dr. Samuel Johnson once said something like the following as he kicked a rock: "There! I thus refute Berkeley!" Would this show that Berkeley's idealism is false? Why?

9. To what extent do the following two verses (of unknown authorship) correctly express the role God plays in Berkeley's philosophy?

> I have always thought that God
> Must find it exceedingly odd
> To think that his tree
> Won't continue to be
> When there's no one about in the quad.

> Dear Sir:
> Your astonishment's odd.
> For I am always about in the quad.
> And so my tree will continue to be,
> Since observed by
> > Yours faithfully,
> > God.

10. Berkeley's idealism is very different from the way we usually think of the world, but does it make any *practical* difference? Would anything be different for you if Berkeley is correct? Should you do anything differently?

3.11 Readings

Is reality real? Jorge Luis Borges, a South American writer and poet who considered himself a metaphysical idealist, suggests in a haunting story that reality may be nothing more than a mental fiction that we have willed into being. Philosopher A. A. Luce explicitly argues in support of such idealism. Scientist John Gribbin claims that the contemporary scientific theory of quantum mechanics implies that at the most basic subatomic level, nothing is real until it is brought into being by our very observations. Together these essays force us to face a troubling question: What exactly is the nature of the so-called reality that surrounds us?

JORGE LUIS BORGES

The Circular Ruins

> And if he left off dreaming about you . . .
> —*Through the Looking Glass*, VI.

No one saw him disembark in the unanimous night. No one saw the bamboo canoe running aground on the sacred mud. But within a few days no one was unaware that the taciturn man had come from the South and that his home had been one of the infinity of hamlets which lie upstream, on the violent flank of the mountain, where the Zend language is uncontaminated by Greek, and where leprosy is infrequent. The certain fact is that the anonymous gray man kissed the mud, scaled the bank without pushing aside (probably without even feeling) the sharp-edged sedges lacerating his flesh, and dragged himself, bloody and sickened, up to the circular enclosure whose crown is a stone colt or tiger, formerly the color of fire and now the color of ash. This circular clearing is a temple, de-

From *A Personal Anthology* by Jorge Luis Borges, edited and translated by Anthony Kerrigan (New York: Grove Press, Castle Books, 1967). Copyright © 1967 by Grove Press. Used with permission of Grove/Atlantic, Inc.

voured by ancient conflagration, profaned by the malarial jungle, its god unhonored now of men. The stranger lay beneath a pedestal. He was awakened, much later, by the sun at its height. He was not astonished to find that his wounds had healed. He closed his pale eyes and slept, no longer from weakness of the flesh but from a determination of the will. He knew that this temple was the place required by his inflexible purpose; he knew that the incessant trees had not been able to choke the ruins of another such propitious temple down river, a temple whose gods also were burned and dead; he knew that his immediate obligation was to dream. The disconsolate shriek of a bird awoke him about midnight. The prints of bare feet, some figs, and a jug told him that the people of the region had reverently spied out his dreaming and solicited his protection or feared his magic. He felt the cold chill of fear, and sought in the dilapidated wall for a sepulchral niche where he concealed himself under some unfamiliar leaves.

The purpose which impelled him was not impossible though it was supernatural. He willed to dream a man. He wanted to dream him in minute totality and then impose him upon reality. He had spent the full resources of his soul on this magical project. If anyone had asked him his own name or about any feature of his former life, he would have been unable to answer. The shattered and deserted temple suited his ends, for it was a minimum part of the visible world, and the nearness of the peasants was also convenient, for they took it upon themselves to supply his frugal needs. The rice and fruits of the tribute were nourishment enough for his body, given over to the sole task of sleeping and dreaming.

At first his dreams were chaotic. A little later they were dialectical. The stranger dreamt he stood in the middle of a circular amphitheater which was in some measure the fired temple; clouds of taciturn students wearied the tiers; the faces of the last rows looked down from a distance of several centuries and from a stellar height, but their every feature was precise. The dreamer himself was delivering lectures on anatomy, cosmography, magic: the faces listened anxiously and strove to answer with understanding, as if they guessed the importance of that examination, which would redeem one of them from his insubstantial state and interpolate him into the real world. In dreams or in waking the man continually considered the replies of his phantoms; he did not let himself be deceived by the impostors; in certain paradoxes he sensed an expanding intelligence. He was seeking a soul worthy of participating in the universe.

At the end of nine or ten nights he realized, with a certain bitterness, that he could expect nothing from those students who accepted his teaching passively, but that he could of those who sometimes risked a reasonable contradiction. The former, though deserving of love and affection, could never rise to being individuals; the latter already existed to a somewhat greater degree. One afternoon (now even the afternoons were tributaries of the dream; now he stayed awake for only a couple of hours at daybreak) he dismissed the entire vast illusory student body for good and retained only one pupil. This pupil was a silent, sallow, sometimes obstinate boy, whose sharp features repeated those of his dreamer. The sudden elimination of his fellow students did not disconcert him for very long; his progress, at the end of a few private lessons, made his master marvel. And nevertheless, catastrophe came. One day the man emerged from sleep as from a viscous desert, stared

about at the vain light of evening, which at first he took to be dawn, and realized he had not dreamt. All that night and all the next day the intolerable lucidity of insomnia broke over him in waves. He was impelled to explore the jungle, to wear himself out; he barely managed some quick snatches of feeble sleep amid the hemlock, shot through with fugitive visions of a rudimentary type: altogether unserviceable. He strove to assemble the student body, but he had scarcely uttered a few words of exhortation before the college blurred, was erased. Tears of wrath scalded his old eyes in his almost perpetual vigil.

He realized that the effort to model the inchoate and vertiginous stuff of which dreams are made is the most arduous task a man can undertake, though he get to the bottom of all the enigmas of a superior or inferior order: much more arduous than to weave a rope of sand or mint coins of the faceless wind. He realized that an initial failure was inevitable. He vowed to forget the enormous hallucination by which he had been led astray at first, and he sought out another approach. Before essaying it, he dedicated a month to replenishing the forces he had squandered in delirium. He abandoned all premeditation concerned with dreaming, and almost at once managed to sleep through a goodly part of the day. The few times he did dream during this period he took no notice of the dreams. He waited until the disk of the moon should be perfect before taking up his task again. Then, on the eve, he purified himself in the waters of the river, worshiped the planetary gods, pronounced the lawful syllables of a powerful name and went to sleep. Almost at once he dreamt of a beating heart.

He dreamt it active, warm, secret, the size of a closed fist, garnet-colored in the half-light of a human body that boasted as yet no sex or face. He dreamt this heart with meticulous love, for fourteen lucid nights. Each night he saw it more clearly. He never touched it, but limited himself to witnessing it, to observing it or perhaps rectifying it with a glance. He watched it, lived it, from far and from near and from many angles. On the fourteenth night he ran his index finger lightly along the pulmonary artery, and then over the entire heart, inside and out. The examination satisfied him. The next night, he deliberately did not dream. He then took up the heart again, invoked the name of a planet, and set about to envision another one of the principal organs. Before the year was up he had reached the skeleton, the eyelids. The most difficult task, perhaps, proved to be the numberless hairs. He dreamt a whole man, a fine lad, but one who could not stand nor talk nor open his eyes. Night after night he dreamt him asleep.

In the Gnostic cosmogonies, demiurges fashion a red Adam who never manages to get to his feet: as clumsy and equally as crude and elemental as this dust Adam was the dream Adam forged by the nights of the wizard. One afternoon, the man almost destroyed all his work, but then changed his mind. (It would have been better for him had he destroyed it.) Having expended all the votive offerings to the numina of the earth and the river, he threw himself at the feet of the effigy, which was perhaps a tiger or perhaps a colt, and implored its unknown help. That evening, at twilight, he dreamt of the statue. He dreamt it alive, tremulous: it was no atrocious bastard of a tiger and a colt, but both these vehement creatures at once and also a bull, a rose, a tempest. This multiple god revealed to him that its terrestrial name was Fire, that in this same circular temple (and in others like it) it once had been offered sacrifices and been the object of a cult, and that now it would magically animate the phantom dreamt by the wizard in such wise that all creatures—except Fire itself and the dreamer—would believe the phantom to be a man of flesh and blood. It directed that once the phantom was instructed in the rites, he be sent to the other broken temple, whose pyramids persisted down river, so that some voice might be raised in glorification in that deserted edifice. In the dream of the man who was dreaming, the dreamt man awoke.

The wizard carried out the directives given him. He dedicated a period of time (which amounted, in the end, to two years) to revealing the mysteries of the universe and the cult of Fire to his dream creature. In his intimate being, he suffered when he was apart from his creation. And so every day, under the pretext of pedagogical necessity, he protracted the hours devoted to dreaming. He also reworked the right shoulder, which was

perhaps defective. At times, he had the uneasy impression that all this had happened before. . . . In general, though, his days were happy ones: as he closed his eyes he would think: *Now I shall be with my son.* Or, more infrequently: *The son I have engendered is waiting for me and will not exist if I do not go to him.*

Little by little he got his creature accustomed to reality. Once, he ordered him to plant a flag on a distant mountain top. The next day the flag was fluttering on the peak. He tried other analogous experiments, each one more audacious than the last. He came to realize, with a certain bitterness, that his son was ready—and perhaps impatient—to be born. That night he kissed his child for the first time, and sent him to the other temple, whose remains were whitening down river, many leagues across impassable jungle and swamp. But first, so that his son should never know he was a phantom and should think himself a man like other men, he imbued him with total forgetfulness of his apprentice years.

His triumph and his respite were sapped by tedium. In the twilight hours of dusk or dawn he would prostrate himself before the stone figure, imagining his unreal child practicing identical rites in other circular ruins downstream. At night he did not dream, or dreamt as other men do. The sounds and forms of the universe reached him wanly, pallidly: his absent son was being sustained on the diminution of the wizard's soul. His life's purpose had been achieved; the man lived on in a kind of ecstasy. After a time—which some narrators of his story prefer to compute in years and others in lustra—he was awakened one midnight by two boatmen: he could not see their faces, but they told him of a magical man at a temple in the North, who walked on fire and was not burned. The wizard suddenly recalled the words of the god. He remembered that of all the creatures composing the world, only Fire knew his son was a phantom. This recollection, comforting at first, ended by tormenting him. He feared lest his son meditate on his abnormal privilege and somehow discover his condition of mere simulacrum. Not to be a man, to be the projection of another man's dream—what incomparable humiliation, what vertigo! Every father is concerned with the children he has procreated (which he has permitted) in mere confusion or felicity: it was only natural that the wizard should fear for the future of his son, thought out entrail by entrail and feature by feature on a thousand and one secret nights.

The end of his caviling was abrupt, but not without forewarnings. First (after a long drought) a remote cloud, light as a bird, appeared over a hill. Then, toward the South, the sky turned the rosy color of a leopard's gums. Smoke began to rust the metallic nights. And then came the panic flight of the animals. And the events of several centuries before were repeated. The ruins of the fire god's sanctuary were destroyed by fire. One birdless dawn the wizard watched the concentric conflagration close around the walls: for one instant he thought of taking refuge in the river, but then he understood that death was coming to crown his old age and to absolve him of further work. He walked against the florid banners of the fire. And the fire did not bite his flesh but caressed and engulfed him without heat or combustion. With relief, with humiliation, with terror, he understood that he, too, was all appearance, that someone else was dreaming him.

A. A. LUCE

Mind Without Matter

I am . . . asking, "Does matter exist?" And I answer, "No"; but I am also asking a deeper, constructive question, viz.: "What precisely do I see and touch?" If we know precisely what we see and touch and otherwise sense, the question about matter settles itself automatically. . . .

I open my eyes and see. What precisely do I see? I stretch out my hand and touch. What precisely

do I touch? What precisely do we see and touch, when we see and touch? That is our question. We have many names in ordinary life for the myriad things we see and touch — shoes, ships, sealingwax, apples, pears and plums; those names are precise enough for action, but they are not precise enough for thought; thought is concerned with common features and resemblances, more than with differences and distinctions. Now; when I see ships and shoes and apples and so forth, what precisely do I see that is common to all those sights? I see colours and shades of colour, light and its modes, illuminated points and lines and surfaces. Those are the things I actually see, and I call them inclusively visual data; they are the elemental objects of the sense of sight. And when I touch shoes and ships and apples and so forth, what precisely do I touch that is common to all those touches? I touch hard, soft, solid, fluid, resistant, yielding, and (in the wider sense of "touch") hot, cold, warm and tepid. Those are the things I actually touch, and I call them inclusively tactual data; they are the elemental objects of the sense of touch. . . .

The theory of matter . . . requires us to hold that in every instance of sense-perception there are two factors to be recognised and distinguished, viz. the actual object of sense, the sense-data[1] actually perceived by eye or ear or hand or other sense organ, and the material substance, itself unperceived and unperceivable, that supports the sense-data. The case against the theory is, in outline, that the theory postulates an intolerable division, based on an improbable guess. It is not a theory reasonably distinguishing homogeneous parts in a thing, like shell and kernel, pea and pod. It is a theory requiring us to break up the one homogeneous thing into two heterogeneous and inconsistent parts, and, incidentally, to pin our faith to the existence of material substance, for which there is not the slightest evidence from fact.

Let us take an instance, and see how the theory of matter works out. See yonder mahogany table. Its colour is brown, in the main, though it is veined and grained in lighter colours. Its touch is hard and

From *Sense Without Matter or Direct Perception* by A. A. Luce (London: Thomas Nelson and Sons, Ltd., 1954). © 1954 by Thomas Nelson and Sons.

[1] Colors, sounds, tastes, tactile sensations, smells, etc.—actual objects of sense. —Ed.

smooth. It has a smell and a taste and a sound; but I hardly ever need to bother about them; for I know the table ordinarily by its colours and by the cut and shape of its lines of light and its shading, and if I am in doubt I can handle it, and feel it and lift it up. It is a sensible table. It is a sensible table through and through. I can bore holes in it, can plane away its surfaces, can burn it with fire and reduce it to ashes; and I shall never come on anything in it that is not an actual or possible object of sense; it is composed entirely of sense-data and *sensibilia*.[2] Now the theory of matter brings in totally different considerations; it asks me to believe that all these sense-data and *sensibilia* do not constitute the real table. I am asked to believe that beneath the table I see and touch stands another table, a supporting table, a table of a totally different nature that cannot be seen or touched or sensed in any other way, a table to be taken on trust, and yet a highly important table, because it is the real, invariable, material table, while the table I see and touch is only apparent, variable, inconstant and volatile. The visible-tangible, sensible table has colour and hardness and the other qualities by which things of sense are known and distinguished. The real table has none of these.

What an impossible duality! Yonder mahogany table proves to be two tables. It is a sensible table, and it is a material table. If I take the theory seriously, and go through with it, I am bound to believe the same of everything else around me; wherever I look, I am condemned to see double, and to grope my way through life with divided aim and reduced efficiency.

No rational account of the coexistence of the two tables has ever been given, nor could be given. Some say that the "real table" is the *cause* of the apparent table, but how the cause works is a mystery. Some say that the "real table" is the original, and the apparent table a copy; but what would be the use of a copy that is totally unlike its original? And who, or what, does the copying, and how? The two tables are left there, juxtaposed, unrelated and unexplained. They are not two aspects of the one

thing; they are not two parts of the one thing; they have nothing in common; they are not comparable; they could not stem from the one stock; they are heterogeneous; they are at opposite poles of thought; they differ as light from darkness; if the one is, the other is not. No mixing of the two is possible; they cannot be constituents of the one thing; for they are contradictories; if the table is really coloured, then it is not matter; if the table is really matter, then it is not coloured. The supposition of two heterogeneous bodies in the one thing of sense is self-contradictory, destroying the unity of the thing. . . .

Then consider the question of evidence. What evidence is there for the existence of matter? What evidence is there for non-sensible matter? Why should I believe in the matter of materialism? Set aside the misunderstanding that confuses matter with the sensible; set aside the prejudice that would identify with matter the chemical atom, or the subatomic objects of nuclear physics; set aside the legend of the constant sum-total of energy from which all springs and to which all returns; set aside mere tradition and the voice of uninformed authority. And what philosophical evidence is there for the matter of materialism? There is no evidence at all. Writers on matter appeal to prejudice and ignorance in favour of matter; they assume and take it for granted that everyone accepts the existence of matter; they never attempt to prove its existence directly. There is no direct evidence to be had. They try to establish it indirectly. There could not be an external *thing*, they say, unless there were matter; unless there were matter, they say, there would be no cause of change in the external world, nor any test for true and false. . . .

I have examined the typical case of seeing and touching, and have shown that there is no place for matter there. I have examined the normal perceptual situation, and have shown that it contains no evidence for matter, and that the forcible intrusion of matter destroys the unity of the thing perceived and of the world of sense. The onus of proof is on the materialist, and the immaterialist can fairly challenge him to produce his evidence. If there is matter, produce it. If there is evidence for matter,

---

[2] Possible sense data. —Ed.

produce it. Neither matter, nor valid evidence for matter, has ever yet been produced.

Let me clinch the argument with an appeal to observable fact in a concrete case. If matter is, I ask, *where* is it? If matter is, it is in things, and in all external things, and the type of external thing selected is neither here nor there. I will choose a homely, explorable thing that we can know through and through, a mutton chop. If matter is, it is in this mutton chop. I ask, where? Where is it in this mutton chop? Where could it be? Take away from this given chop all its sense-data, including its obtainable sense-data. Take away those of the outside and those of the inside, those of the meat and the bone, those of the fat and the lean, be it cooked or uncooked. Take away all that we do sense and all that we might sense, and what is left? There are its visual data, its browns and reds and blacks and whites, and all the other colours and hues of its surface and potential surfaces and centre. There are its tactual data, its rough and smooth, hard and soft, resistant and yielding, solid and fluid, and those varied palpables that admit my knife or hinder its easy passage. It has auditory data; its fat and lean and bone make different sounds when struck by knives and forks. Many smells and savours go to its composing, raw or cooked. Air and moisture link it to its sensible context, and show as steam and vapour under heat. The chop has sensible shapes that may concern artists and even geometricians; it has sensible contents and sensible forms that are specially the concern of chemist and physicist; they are no less sensible and no less real than those contents and forms that are of importance to the butcher and the housewife and the cook. Take them all away in thought. Take away all the *sensa* and the *sensibilia* of this mutton chop, and what is left? Nothing! Nothing is left. In taking away its *sensa* and *sensibilia* you have taken away all the mutton chop, and nothing is left, and its matter is nowhere. Its matter, other than its sense-data, is nothing at all, nothing but a little heap of powdered sentiment, nothing but the ghost of the conventional thing, nothing but the sceptic's question-mark. . . .

JOHN GRIBBIN

Nothing Is Real

Erwin Schrödinger was an Austrian scientist instrumental in the development, in the mid-1920s, of the equations of a branch of science now known as quantum mechanics. Branch of science is hardly the correct expression, however, because quantum mechanics provides the fundamental underpinning of all of modern science. The equations describe the behavior of very small objects—generally speaking, the size of atoms or smaller—and they provide the *only* understanding of the world of the very small. Without these equations, physicists would be unable to design working nuclear power stations (or bombs), build lasers, or explain how the sun stays hot. Without quantum mechanics, chemistry would still be in the Dark Ages, and there would be no science of molecular biology—no understanding of DNA, no genetic engineering—at all.

Quantum theory represents the greatest achievement of science, far more significant and of far more direct, practical use than relativity theory. And yet, it makes some very strange predictions. The world of quantum mechanics is so strange, indeed, that even Albert Einstein found it incomprehensible, and refused to accept all of the implications of the theory developed by Schrödinger and his colleagues. Einstein, and many other scientists, found it more comfortable to believe that the equations of quantum mechanics simply represent some sort of mathematical trick, which just happens to give a reasonable working guide to the behavior of atomic and subatomic particles but that conceals some deeper truth that corresponds more closely to our everyday sense of reality. For what quantum mechanics says is that nothing is real and that we cannot say anything about what things are doing when we are not looking at them. Schrödinger's mythical cat was invoked to make the differences between the quantum world and the everyday world clear.

In the world of quantum mechanics, the laws of physics that are familiar from the everyday world no longer work. Instead, events are governed by probabilities. A radioactive atom, for example, might decay, emitting an electron, say; or it might not. It is possible to set up an experiment in such a way that there is a precise fifty-fifty chance that one of the atoms in a lump of radioactive material will decay in a certain time and that a detector will register the decay if it does happen. Schrödinger, as upset as Einstein about the implications of quantum theory, tried to show the absurdity of those implications by imagining such an experiment set up in a closed room, or box, which also contains a live cat and a phial of poison, so arranged that if the radioactive decay does occur then the poison container is broken and the cat dies. In the everyday world, there is a fifty-fifty chance that the cat will be killed, and without looking inside the box we can say, quite happily, that the cat inside is either dead or alive. But now we encounter the strangeness of the quantum world. According to the theory, *neither* of the two possibilities open to the radioactive material, and therefore to the cat, has any reality unless it is observed. The atomic decay has neither happened nor not happened, the cat has neither been killed nor not killed, until we look inside the box to see what has happened. Theorists who accept the pure version of quantum mechanics say that the cat exists in some indeterminate state, neither dead nor alive, until an observer looks into the box to see how things are getting on. Nothing is real unless it is observed.

The idea was anathema to Einstein, among others. "God does not play dice," he said, referring to the theory that the world is governed by the accumulation of outcomes of essentially random "choices" of possibilities at the quantum level. As for the unreality of the state of Schrödinger's cat, he dismissed it, assuming that there must be some underlying "clockwork" that makes for a genuine fundamental reality of things. He spent many years attempting to devise tests that might reveal this

underlying reality at work but died before it became possible actually to carry out such a test. Perhaps it is as well that he did not live to see the outcome of one line of reasoning that he initiated.

In the summer of 1982, at the University of Paris-South, in France, a team headed by Alain Aspect completed a series of experiments designed to detect the underlying reality below the unreal world of the quantum. The underlying reality—the fundamental clockwork—had been given the name "hidden variables," and the experiment concerned the behavior of two photons or particles of light flying off in opposite directions from a source. . . . In essence it can be thought of as a test of reality. The two photons from the same source can be observed by two detectors, which measure a property called polarization. According to quantum theory, this property does not exist until it is measured. According to the hidden-variable idea, each photon has a "real" polarization from the moment it is created. Because the two photons are emitted together, their polarizations are correlated with one another. But the nature of the correlation that is actually measured is different according to the two views of reality.

The results of this crucial experiment are unambiguous. The kind of correlation predicted by hidden-variable theory is not found; the kind of correlation predicted by quantum mechanics is found, and what is more, again as predicted by quantum theory, the measurement that is made on one photon has an instantaneous effect on the nature of the other photon. Some interaction links the two inextricably, even though they are flying apart at the speed of light, and relativity theory tells us that no signal can travel faster than light. The experiments prove that there is no underlying reality to the world. "Reality," in the everyday sense, is not a good way to think about the behavior of the fundamental particles that make up the universe; yet at the same time those particles seem to be inseparably connected into some indivisible whole, each aware of what happens to the others.

The search for Schrödinger's cat was the search for quantum reality. From this brief outline, it may seem that the search has proved fruitless, since there is no reality in the everyday sense of the word. But this is not quite the end of the story, and the search for Schrödinger's cat may lead us to a new understanding of reality that transcends, and yet includes, the conventional interpretation of quantum mechanics.

3.12 Suggestions for Further Reading

Aune, Bruce. *Metaphysics: The Elements*. Minneapolis: University of Minnesota Press, 1985. A difficult but excellent discussion of the major issues in contemporary metaphysics.

Ayer, A. J. *Language, Truth and Logic*, 2d ed. New York: Dover, 1946. In this challenging book, Ayer sets out the basic arguments of the logical positivists.

Carter, William R. *The Elements of Metaphysics*. New York: McGraw-Hill, 1990. A very simple and readable survey of the basic questions of metaphysics.

Foster, John. *The Case for Idealism*. Boston: Routledge & Kegan Paul, 1982. An interesting contemporary discussion of a fascinating view of reality.

French, Peter A., Theodore E. Uehling, Jr., and Howard K. Wettstein, eds. *Realism and Antirealism*. Minneapolis: University of Minnesota Press, 1988. Although many of the articles in this collection are difficult, they represent some of the best thinking on the debate between realists and antirealists.

Garry, Ann, and Marilyn Pearsall. *Women, Knowledge, and Reality: Explorations in Feminist Philosophy*. Boston: Unwin Hyman, 1989. A very good collection of some of the best feminist writings on epistemology and metaphysics.

Gribbin, John. *In Search of Schrödinger's Cat*. New York: Bantam, 1984. A very clear account of quantum theory and some of its metaphysical implications.

Griffin, David Ray, ed. *Physics and the Ultimate Significance of Time*. Albany, NY: SUNY Press, 1986. A collection of interesting essays on the reality of time.

Hamlyn, D. W. *Metaphysics*. Cambridge: Cambridge University Press, 1984. A very good, concise, and readable overview of the major issues.

Harding, Sandra, and Merrill Hintikka, eds. *Discovering Reality: Feminist Perspectives on Epistemology, Metaphysics, Methodology, and Philosophy of Science*. Dordrecht, Holland: D. Reidel, 1983. A good collection of articles on metaphysics and epistemology from feminist perspectives.

Hoy, Ronald C., and L. Nathan Oaklander, eds. *Metaphysics*. Belmont, CA: Wadsworth, 1991. An excellent collection of classical and contemporary writings.

Husserl, Edmund. *Phenomenology and the Crisis of Philosophy*. Trans. Quentin Lauer. New York: Harper & Row, 1965. These two essays by the "father of phenomenology" present the framework and method of Husserlian phenomenology.

Krishnamurti, J., and David Bohm. *The Ending of Time*. New York: Harper & Row, 1985. An outstanding synthesis of Eastern and Western approaches to reality by an Eastern philosopher and a Western scientist.

Moser, Paul K., ed. *Reality in Focus*. Englewood Cliffs, NJ: Prentice-Hall, 1990. A very good collection of articles that includes discussions of the philosophical implications of contemporary science.

Pears, D. *Ludwig Wittgenstein*. New York: Viking Press, 1979. This readable paperback explains the life and thought of Wittgenstein in a lively fashion.

Salmon, Wesley. *Scientific Explanation and the Causal Structure of the World*. Princeton: Princeton University Press, 1984. A very clear account of the role that chance and causality play in contemporary scientific theories.

Smith, John E. *Purpose and Thought: The Meaning of Pragmatism*. London and New Haven: Hutchinson and Yale University Presses, 1978. Smith explains the basic ideas behind pragmatism.

Urmson, J. O. *Berkeley*. Oxford: Oxford University Press, 1982. This is an easily readable introduction to the life and thought of Berkeley.

Warnock, Mary. *Existentialism*. Oxford: Oxford University Press, 1970. One of the foremost writers on the subject, Warnock presents a succinct and trenchant analysis of the main concepts of existentialism.

CHAPTER 4

Philosophy and God

The highest that man can attain in these matters is wonder.
GOETHE

4.1 Introduction: What Is Religion?

Perhaps no other area of life is as important yet contains such excruciating uncertainties as religion. Consider "The Road," a very brief "parable" told by John Hick:

> Two men are traveling together along a road. One of them believes that it leads to the Celestial City, the other that it leads nowhere. But since this is the only road there is, both must travel it. Neither has been this way before, therefore neither is able to say what they will find around each corner. During their journey they meet with moments of refreshment and delight, and with moments of hardship and danger. All the time one of them thinks of his journey as a pilgrimage to the Celestial City. He interprets the pleasant parts as encouragements and the obstacles as trials of his purpose and lessons in endurance, prepared by the king of that city and designed to make him a worthy citizen of the place when at last he arrives. The other, however, believes none of this, and sees their journey as an unavoidable and aimless ramble. Since he has no choice in the matter, he enjoys the good and endures the bad. For him there is no Celestial City to be reached, no all-encompassing purpose ordaining their journey; there is only the road itself and the luck of the road in good weather and in bad.
>
> They do not entertain different expectations about the coming details of the road but only about its ultimate destination. Yet, when they turn the last corner, it will be apparent that one of them has been right all the time and the other wrong. . . . [T]he choice between theism [belief in God] and atheism [belief in no god] is a real and not merely an empty or verbal choice.[1]

So much depends on the choice between belief and unbelief! There is perhaps no greater influence on one's view of oneself and one's destiny than the choice between belief and unbelief. For example, the Judaic and Christian religious traditions share the belief that humans are creatures who stand midway between nature and spirit. We are on the one hand finite, bound to earth, and capable of sin. On the other, we are able to transcend nature and to achieve infinite possibilities because we possess the divine (Godlike) qualities of consciousness and the ability to love. Primarily because of Christianity, we view

If God did not exist it would be necessary to invent him.

VOLTAIRE

When I think of the incredibly rich complexity of things and the massiveness of it all, I find it impossible not to believe that it was God who brought this about.

NICHOLAS WOLTERSTORF

---

[1] J. H. Hick, *Philosophy of Religion* (Englewood Cliffs, NJ: Prentice-Hall, 1973), 91.

ourselves as beings with a supernatural destiny, as possessing a life after death, as being immortal. Shakespeare expressed this view when he wrote: "What a piece of work is a man! How noble in reason! How infinite in faculty! In form, in moving, how express and admirable! In action how like an angel! In apprehension how like a god!" (*Hamlet*, II, ii, 317).

On the other hand, those who reject all religious belief do not see themselves as transcending nature; nature, in fact, is all there is. For those who reject religion, humans are certainly not immortal, nor do they have any kind of spiritual nature. Those who reject religion do not see human life as having a supernatural destiny, nor any destiny at all beyond death. Shakespeare also expressed this sentiment when he wrote, late in his life: "Life's but a walking shadow, a poor player / That struts and frets his hour upon the stage, / And then is heard no more; it is a tale / Told by an idiot, full of sound and fury, / Signifying nothing" (*Macbeth*, V, v, 17).

PHILOSOPHY AND LIFE

Defining *Religion*

Sometimes the most ordinary things create tremendous bafflement. Everyone knows what religion is. But can you define it? Here are several attempts:

Religion is concern *about experiences which are regarded as of supreme value; devotion towards a power or powers believed to originate, increase, and conserve these values; and some suitable expression of this concern and devotion, whether through symbolic rites or through other individual and social conduct.*
Edgar S. Brightman

Any activity pursued in behalf of an ideal and against obstacles and in spite of threats of personal loss because of conviction of its general and enduring value is religious in quality.
John Dewey

Religion is the ritual cultivation of socially accepted values. J. Fischer

Religion is a propitiation of, and dependency on, superior powers which are believed to control and direct the course of nature and human life.
Sir James G. Frazer

Religion is a theory of man's relation to the universe. S. P. Haynes

Religion is a sense of the sacred. Sir Julian Huxley

Religion is (subjectively regarded) the organization of all duties as divine commands. Immanuel Kant

Religion consists in the perception of the infinite under such manifestations as are able to influence the moral character of man. Max Muller

Religion is one's attitude toward whatever he considers to be the determiner of destiny. James Bissett Pratt

The essence of religion is the feeling of utter dependence upon the infinite reality, that is, upon God.
F. Schleiermacher

Religion is man's ultimate concern for the Ultimate. Paul Tillich

Religion, as a minimum, is the belief in spiritual beings. E. B. Taylor

Religion is a belief in an ultimate meaning of the universe.
Alfred R. Wallace

A religion, on its doctrinal sides, can thus be described as a system of general truths which have the effect of transforming character when they are sincerely held and vividly apprehended.
Alfred North Whitehead

Obviously, the very definition of this pervasive phenomenon is controversial. Even today there is no widespread agreement about how to define *religion*, although everyone seems to know exactly what it is.

QUESTION

1. How would you define *religion*?

Obviously, the choice to accept or to reject religion can deeply influence our view of ourselves and of our destiny. In fact, as the example of Shakespeare suggests, our religious choices can change as we travel on our journey through life, and this in turn can transform profoundly how we look at ourselves and our final destiny. Yet, as Hick's parable of the Road implies, the choice to accept or reject religious belief will not be definitively validated or refuted until the end of our journey—if then. Which, then, should we choose? Which choice—to accept or reject religious belief—is more reasonable during the journey? That is the basic question we address in this chapter: How reasonable is religion?

Before we turn to address this question directly, however, we should briefly look at a more basic issue: What, exactly, is religion? Although *religion* is extremely difficult to define, we should attempt to get a clearer idea of what it is before we continue.

When you hear the word *religion*, what do you think of? A church? A synagogue? A belief? For many people the word *religion* refers to a belief in God that is institutionalized and incorporated in the teachings of some group such as Catholicism, Judaism, or Islam. Yet some religions do not seem to have a belief in God. Buddhism, for example, although usually considered a religion, contains no belief in a personal God like the God of the Judaic and Christian traditions. Other religions, such as the Unitarian Church, have few or no official beliefs. Some religions, such as the Episcopal Church, have highly institutionalized rituals. Others, like the Quaker Church, have little ritual. Many religions stress personal commitment based on a meaningful relationship with the sacred, which is often a Supreme Being. Other religions, like animistic religions, seem to place little importance on personal commitment. It is easier, perhaps, to note common features of religion than to define it, and that is the approach we will take, although qualifications may still be necessary.

Professor Ninian Smart suggests that religion has six dimensions.[2] Although not all dimensions are found in all religions, still every religion shares in some or all of these to a lesser or greater degree: (1) doctrine, or a set of beliefs about the universe and its relation to the supernatural such as the belief that there is a single God who created the universe, or the belief that the universe is controlled by the law of karma; (2) experience, or an emphasis on events in which the believer feels immediately and strikingly the presence of God or of a supernatural dimension; (3) myth, or a set of stories that convey sacred or special meaning, such as the story of Adam and Eve or the story of the illumination of the Buddha; (4) ritual, or acts of worship, prayer, sacraments, and readings of sacred scriptures; (5) morality, or a set of rules and precepts believers are enjoined to follow; and (6) organization, or an organized social group that preserves and perpetuates the religion.

Although religion frequently finds expression through institutionalized ritual and orthodox belief, religion is not just an institution, a collection of doctrines, or a stylized ritual. Morality, feeling, and emotion are also important features of religion. In fact, many people today feel that the emphasis on a

---

[2] Ninian Smart, *Worldviews* (New York: Charles Scribner's Sons, 1983).

symbolic object of devotion, ritualized through an organizational structure, has blurred religion's real import: a deep and personal experience with the object of one's chief loyalty. Many religious leaders have spoken in terms of personal commitment, experience, and need. In so doing they have recognized one of the roots from which religion springs: our unending search for meaning and fulfillment.

In our investigation of religion, however, we will set aside many of these prominent dimensions of religion in order to concentrate on two: religious doctrine and religious experience. Our aim, as we suggested earlier, is to look closely at the issue that should be critical for the person considering the kind of fundamental choice between belief and unbelief that Hick's parable suggests: Is religion reasonable? So we will look most closely at how reasonable it is to believe what religion asks us to believe, and how reasonable it is to trust the experiences of religion.

In this chapter we shall have numerous occasions to speak of **religious belief,** which we'll use in its most general sense: the doctrines of religion about the universe and religion's relation to the supernatural. On the other hand, when we use the term *religious experience*, we shall be referring to an experience of this supernatural order and our individual place in this order. Having found this place, people feel an intense personal relationship with the rest of creation, perhaps even with a Creator. In this respect, possibly, we all seek a religious experience; we all search for an internal peace resulting from a harmonious personal relationship with all other living things. Religious belief and experience continue to be of intense philosophical interest. They are also intimately joined with the issue of self.

> **religious belief** in its broadest sense, the belief that there is an unseen order and that we can do no better than to be in harmony with that order

Where do we find religious experience today? Some find it in the existence of a personal God. Therefore, we will begin by examining the most basic religious belief; we will look at whether it is reasonable to believe that God exists. We will then look more closely at what religious belief itself is and whether it is possible to believe even without good reasons to believe. However, many people relate to the divine without relating to a Supreme Being. They claim that religious experience is an intimately personal encounter with the basis of all being, with the source of all reality. We will therefore turn next to discussing religious experience in order to develop a clearer understanding of what it is and whether it makes sense. Finally, there are many Westerners who turn to Eastern thought—Hinduism and Buddhism, for example—in their search for a belief that is reasonable. We will therefore look briefly at some major themes in Eastern religious traditions.

In this chapter we explore these and related concerns by thinking philosophically about religion. The philosophy of religion can encompass many aspects of religion, including God, immortality, salvation, creation, and all particular religions. Here we focus on God and on the nature and varieties of religious experience, on the many ways in which individuals claim to discover their place in the cosmos.

It is important not to confuse the philosophy of religion with theology. Literally speaking, **theology** means simply the rational study of God. In practice, however, the term is usually reserved for the rational study of religious beliefs

> **theology** the rational study of God, including religious doctrines

by scholars committed to those beliefs. Theologians study God and the religious beliefs of a community with the assumption that God exists and that those religious beliefs are true. By contrast, philosophers approach God and religious beliefs without these assumptions: For the philosopher, these assumptions must themselves be proved.

QUESTIONS

1. Explain the difference between religious belief and formal theology.

2. Evaluate this statement: "For many people, belief in science has achieved the status of a religion." Can science be a religion? Explain.

3. What kinds of beliefs or behavior would someone have to adopt before you would be willing to say that the person is "religious"? What does the term mean to you?

4.2 Does God Exist?

The most common way for people of a Judeo-Christian culture to find their place in the scheme of things is through a relationship with a personal God. **Theism** is belief in a personal God who is creator of the world and present in its processes and with whom we may come into intimate contact. **Monotheism** is the belief that there is only one God. Most of us have been raised to accept a concept of God as a single, all-powerful, all-knowing, and all-good Being who, having created life, actively participates in the lives of creatures by listening to and answering prayer. This God is the basis for the view of the human as divine, as having an immortal soul and a supernatural destiny.

theism the belief in a personal God who intervenes in the lives of the creation

monotheism the belief in a single God

This theistic concept has perhaps never been under greater attack than it is today. Even theologians are asking whether the believer can any longer believe in this traditional God. They are questioning an assumption that has centuries of tradition behind it, that is a cornerstone of the lives of many people today, and that forms the basis not only for our religious beliefs and experiences but also for our perception of ourselves and the world.

CRITICAL THINKING

"I believe in God because the Bible says that God exists." Is anything wrong with this claim?

Wilbur Daniel Steele, in his short story "The Man Who Saw Through Heaven," portrays the dimensions of the problem facing the contemporary theist. In it he depicts Herbert Diana, a self-educated man who like many theists has accepted a conventional number of scientific facts as more proof of "what God can do when He puts His mind to it." Intellectually, Diana has accepted the fact of a spherical earth speeding through space, but in his heart he knows

The Ancient of Days, William Blake. Theism is a belief in a personal God who is creator of the world and with whom we may come into intimate contact. This God is the basis for the view of the human as divine, as having an immortal soul and a supernatural destiny.

"that the world lay flat from modern Illinois to ancient Palestine, and that the sky above it, blue by day and by night festooned with guiding stars for wise men, was the nether side of a floor on which the resurrected trod."[3] What will happen when a man of such simple faith looks through a powerful telescope into an ink-black sky and faces the enormous scale of the universe? How can his simple belief in a personal God stand up to the sudden realization that God must also be personally and completely involved in an infinity of galactic universes and lives? For the first time in his life, Herbert Diana's faith is tested. His simple ideas of a heaven "up there" and a hell "down there," of a God who is personally concerned with each person's immortal destiny, and of the infinite importance of a single soul and what that soul chooses to do—all these beliefs suddenly shrink in the vastness of what his eyes have seen and his mind cannot forget.

In a sense we are all Dianas, for we live in a period that pits traditional religious concepts against the growing weight of scientific fact. Can we, *should* we, believe in the God of theism, or must we modify this belief and perhaps abandon it? Consider, as Diana must, the billions of galaxies and the billions

Maybe the existence of the Earth is not part of God's plan.
PETER VAN INWAGEN

---

[3] Wilbur Daniel Steele, "The Man Who Saw Through Heaven," in *The Search for Personal Freedom,* 3d ed., ed. Neal Cross, Leslie Lindou, and Robert Lamm (Dubuque, IA: W. C. Brown, 1968), 27.

of stars in each that perhaps contain planetary systems. Imagine how many millions of satellites must have supported organic life at some time. Imagine how many millions of creatures must have existed, perhaps grotesque by our standards, but creatures nonetheless. And consider further how many generations of "these enormous and microscopic beings" may have existed—astronomers estimate that the universe is about fourteen billion years old. Do we know the God who rules over such a universe?

Today science has brought many of us, like Herbert Diana, to ask not only if we believe in a traditional God but also if there is any God at all. Nevertheless, despite the rise of science and the decay of traditional religious forms, religion thrives in this country. In other words, while rational arguments might have an impact on the beliefs of people like Herbert Diana, in general they have little effect on most people's beliefs. In fact, Diana is ultimately able to return to his "simple faith," not because he has new evidence but because he chooses to believe rather than not to believe. Believing in a personal God is his way of locating himself in the scheme of things. Such people don't believe on the basis of scientific evidence, which may or may not support their belief.

Interestingly, some philosophers also have held that God's existence is so obvious that it hardly needs proof. During the Middle Ages, Saint Anselm (whose ontological argument we will examine) held that we have within our minds a conception of God that compels us to believe that God exists. Several centuries later, the French philosopher René Descartes held that we have in our minds an idea of a perfect God that we could not have made up ourselves. The perfection of the God we have in mind, he argued, compels us to acknowledge that God must exist. In fact, Descartes held, we could not know *anything* with certitude if there were no God to guarantee that our knowledge is generally accurate. Thus, for Descartes, God is the foundation on which all our scientific knowledge is built. (For a fuller discussion of Descartes's philosophy, see the showcase at the end of this chapter.)

Others find in science a new basis for religious belief. In fact, appeals to reason and experience have figured prominently in the history of Christian theology. For example, numerous theologians have used logic to argue for the existence of a personal God, as we shall shortly see. But it is vital to recognize the purpose of these arguments: to advance the personal quest to know God. Knowledge of God was and continues to be one of the most significant topics occupying thinkers. And the arguments advanced for God's existence are one element in the centuries-long attempt to determine the extent to which humans can have rational knowledge of God and to which philosophy has a bearing on theological matters.

We begin our overview of philosophy and religion with some of these arguments for the existence of God. We present them as illustrations of a traditional way by which people have fortified their religious convictions, strengthened their relationship with a personal God, and discovered something about that God. In reading these arguments, notice their reliance on reason and sense experience, on rationalism and empiricism, and keep in mind the contrasting approach, which is essentially nonrational. We will see how this latter approach has been attempted

The very impossibility in which I find myself to prove that God is not, discloses to me His existence.

JEAN DE LA BRUYÈRE

CRITICAL THINKING

Suppose psychologists prove that belief in God originates when people are taught to believe in God from an early age. Would this show that the belief must be wrong?

Saint Anselm: "There is, then, so truly a being than which nothing greater can be conceived to exist, that it cannot even be conceived not to exist; and this being thou art, O Lord, our God."

and how for many people today it serves as the basis for religious belief and experience. In reading this chapter, then, you will begin to mine two rich veins in the development of religious thought, the rational and the nonrational.

THE ONTOLOGICAL ARGUMENT

Earlier theologians had propounded arguments that God's existence is self-evident, but Saint Anselm was the first to assert his argument in a formal, self-conscious manner. Anselm (1033–1109), who was the archbishop of Canterbury, offered an argument, known as the ontological argument, that relied on reason alone. Later arguments on this subject would be based on the experience of the things of the world, but Anselm held that the mind by itself could arrive at such a realization.

The **ontological argument** is an argument for the existence of God deduced from the nature of God's being. God, Anselm reasoned, is "that than which none greater can be conceived." Now, what if God were just an idea? If so, we could easily conceive of something greater: a God who actually existed. Therefore, Anselm concluded, if God is "that than which none greater can be conceived," then God must exist.

This is about as distilled a version of Anselm's ontological argument as one is likely to get. To appreciate it fully, you must follow its development in Anselm's most important philosophical work, the *Proslogion*. In reading the following passage, keep in mind the impulse behind it: *"Credo ut intelligam"*—"I believe

ontological argument an argument for the existence of God based on the nature of God's being

in order that I may understand." Thus, without belief, one can have no understanding of God:

> Truly there is a God, although the fool hath said in his heart, there is no God.
>
> And so, Lord, do thou, who dost give understanding to faith, give me, so far as thou knowest it to be profitable, to understand that thou art as we believe; and that thou art that which we believe. And, indeed, we believe that thou art a being than which nothing greater can be conceived. Or is there no such nature, since the fool hath said in his heart, there is no God? (Psalms xiv.1). But, at any rate, this very fool, when he hears of this being of which I speak—a being than which nothing greater can be conceived—understands what he hears, and what he understands is in his understanding; although he does not understand it to exist.
>
> For, it is one thing for an object to be in the understanding, and another to understand that the object exists. When a painter first conceives of what he will afterwards perform, he has it in his understanding, but he does not yet understand it to be, because he has not yet performed it. But after he has made the painting, he both has it in his understanding, and he understands that it exists, because he has made it.
>
> Hence, even the fool is convinced that something exists in the understanding, at least, than which nothing greater can be conceived. For, when he hears of this, he understands it. And whatever is understood, exists in the understanding. And assuredly that, than which nothing greater can be conceived, cannot exist in the understanding alone. For, suppose it exists in the understanding alone: then it can be conceived to exist in reality; which is greater.
>
> Therefore, if that, than which nothing greater can be conceived, exists in the understanding alone, the very being, than which nothing greater can be conceived, is one, than which a greater can be conceived. But obviously this is impossible. Hence, there is no doubt that there exists a being, than which nothing greater can be conceived, and it exists both in the understanding and in reality.
>
> And it assuredly exists so truly, that it cannot be conceived not to exist. For, it is possible to conceive of a being which cannot be conceived not to exist; and this is greater than one which can be conceived not to exist. Hence, if that, than which nothing greater can be conceived, can be conceived not to exist, it is not that, than which nothing is greater can be conceived. But this is an irreconcilable contradiction. There is, then, so truly a being than which nothing greater can be conceived to exist, that it cannot even be conceived not to exist; and this being thou art, O Lord, our God.
>
> So truly, therefore, dost thou exist, O Lord, my God, that thou canst not be conceived not to exist; and rightly. For, if a mind could conceive of a being better than thee, the creature would rise above the Creator; and this is most absurd. And, indeed, whatever else there is, except thee alone, can be conceived not to exist. To thee alone, therefore, it belongs to exist more truly than all other beings, and hence in a higher degree than all others. For, whatever else exists does not exist so truly, and hence in a less degree it belongs to it to exist. Why, then, has the fool said in his heart, there is no God (Psalms xiv.1), since it is so evident, to a rational mind, that thou dost exist in the highest degree of all? Why, except that he is dull and a fool?[4]

CRITICAL THINKING

Does Anselm assume that if it is impossible to think of something with the human mind, then it is impossible for that thing to exist in reality? Would this assumption be true?

Anselm has had his supporters over the years. But more people have attacked the ontological argument. The eighteenth-century German philosopher Im-

---

[4]Saint Anselm, *Saint Anselm: Basic Writings,* trans. S. N. Deane (La Salle, IL: Open Court Publishing, 1962). Reprinted by permission.

manuel Kant was one. He claimed that the concept of an absolutely necessary being is not proved by the fact that reason apparently requires it.

To understand Kant's criticism, ask yourself this: Under what conditions will a triangle have three sides? Obviously, when and where there is a triangle. In other words, *if* there is a triangle, it has three sides. But *if* is conditional— that is, what follows it may not be. "If there is a triangle" does not imply that there necessarily *is* a triangle. Likewise, "*If* there is a perfect being, then a perfect being exists" does not mean a perfect being does exist. Kant claims that Anselm is defining God into existence—that he is asking us to form a concept of a thing in such a way as to include existence within the scope of its meaning. Undoubtedly, Anselm would object that it is contradictory to posit a triangle and yet reject its three sides. Kant would agree. But he would add that there is no contradiction in rejecting the triangle *along with* its three sides: "The same holds true of the concept of an absolutely necessary being. If its existence is rejected, we reject the thing itself with all its predicates; and no question of contradiction can then arise."[5]

But a perfect being is unique. Because Anselm thought nonexistence was an imperfection and therefore inconsistent with the nature of a perfect being, he argued that a perfect being must exist. And he was right, assuming that existence adds to a thing. But imagine a perfect companion. Attribute to it all the properties that will make it perfect. Then ask yourself, "Does its existence add anything to the concept?" The point is that to assert existence is not to add a property but to assert a relationship between the thing conceived and the world. In other words, you do not add anything to the creature of your fantasy by positing its existence; you merely establish its relationship to other things. This is what Kant meant when he wrote: "When I think of a being as the supreme reality, without any defect, the question still remains whether it exists or not."[6]

THE COSMOLOGICAL ARGUMENT

After Anselm, the next important attempt to justify God's existence was made by the greatest of all the rational theologians, the thirteenth-century Christian philosopher Saint Thomas Aquinas (1225–1274). His arguments are systematically organized and borrow many ideas from Aristotle. In his monumental works, *Summa Theologica* and *Summa Contra Gentiles*, Aquinas offers a total of five proofs. The two proofs we will examine here begin with an observation about the physical universe. Thus, they are said to be a kind of **cosmological argument** because they result from a study of the cosmos. (For the other proofs and a fuller discussion of his philosophy, see the showcase on Aquinas at the end of this chapter.)

Aquinas's version of the cosmological argument—which he borrowed from Aristotle—begins with the observation that things in the universe "are moving":

The celestial order and the beauty of the universe compel me to admit that there is some excellent and eternal Being, who deserves the respect and homage of men.

CICERO

cosmological argument an argument for the existence of God that claims that there must be an ultimate causal explanation for why the universe as a totality exists

---

[5] Immanuel Kant, *Critique of Pure Reason*, trans. Norman Kemp Smith (New York: St. Martin's, 1929; original work published 1781), 502.
[6] Ibid., 505–506.

> It is evident that some things in the world around us are moving. Now if something is moving, it must have been moved by something else. But if that which moves the things we see around us is itself moving, then it too must have been moved by something else, and that by something else again. But this cannot go on to infinity because then there would be no first mover. So there must be a first mover that is not itself moved, and this is God.[7]

Aquinas's point is that if any object in the universe is moving, it must have been moved by something else that was also moving, and this second moving object must have been moved by something else that was also moving, and this must have been moved by a fourth moving object, and this by a fifth, and so on. But a chain of moving objects in which the motion of each depends on the motion of an earlier moving object has to derive its original motion from somewhere. Aquinas argues that this chain of motion cannot be just an infinite chain that never had an originating mover. For if there were nothing that first started things moving, then they would never have begun to move. So, he concludes, there must be a "First Mover"—i.e., a Being in whom all the motions of the universe originate. Is Aquinas's argument correct? Before we discuss that question, let's look at a second, more sophisticated kind of cosmological argument that Aquinas also presents.

Aquinas's second kind of cosmological argument starts by noting that things in this universe are caused: Their existence is caused by other things. Aquinas then reasons that these observed effects are the last in a chain of such effects. However, this chain must not go back endlessly, because then it would have no beginning. The chain of existence, like the chain of motion, must start somewhere. According to this cosmological argument, the chain of causes must start with a being who itself is uncaused. Such a being Aquinas terms God.

This argument is elaborated in the following passage from his *Summa Theologica*:

> [One] way [of proving God's existence] is based on the nature of efficient causes. In the world we see around us, there are ordered lines of efficient causes [in which each member of the line produces the next member]. But nothing can be its own efficient cause, since then it would have to exist prior to itself and this is impossible. Now it is not possible for a line of efficient causes to extend to infinity. For in any line of efficient causes, the first is the cause of the intermediate ones, and the intermediate ones cause the last one. Now if we remove any of the causes, we remove all the remaining effects. So if there were no first cause then there would be no last cause nor any intermediate ones. But if a line of efficient causes extended back to infinity, then we would find no first cause. Consequently, if the line of causes extended back to infinity, there would be no intermediate causes nor any last causes in existence in the universe. But we know this is false. So it is necessary to admit that there is a first efficient cause. And this we call God.[8]

CRITICAL THINKING

Does Aquinas assume that cause–effect relations really exist between things outside the mind? Could cause–effect relations be nothing more than mental constructs we make up to connect things we experience and to make predictions? If they were mental constructs, then would Aquinas's argument still stand up?

Philosophers have raised two key objections to this cosmological argument. The first concerns its contention that there can be no infinite regress in the

---

[7] Thomas Aquinas, *Summa Contra Gentiles*, bk. 1, ch. 13, translated by Manuel Velasquez.
[8] Saint Thomas Aquinas, *Summa Theologica*, I, q.2, a.3. This edited translation is by Manuel Velasquez.

causal sequences of the universe. But why not? Isn't it possible that the universe has simply existed forever and that things in it have simply been moving forever? Isn't it possible that the universe has always been around and that both motion and causality have always operated within it?

Yet supporters of the cosmological argument have been encouraged by recent scientific evidence suggesting that the universe began with a "big bang." According to astronomers, the universe is currently expanding. All the galaxies of stars in the universe are being hurled outward and away from one another, as if propelled by a terrific explosion that occurred at the heart of the universe many billions of years ago. To explain this phenomenon, astronomers have theorized that many billions of years ago, the universe began as an infinitesimal point that exploded suddenly into a huge ball of matter and that has continued exploding outward to form the gigantic universe we see around us. That explosion—the "big bang"—marked the beginning of the universe and set everything in the universe moving outward as it is still doing. Until the big bang occurred, the universe itself did not exist: There was no time, no space, no matter, no anything. With the big bang, matter, space, and time itself came into existence.

Many philosophers have asserted that the big bang is exactly the kind of starting point of the universe that the cosmological argument points toward. If the big bang theory is correct, then the universe has not existed forever. There is no infinite chain of motions and causes stretching backward in time forever. Instead, we are forced to conclude that the universe has existed for only a few billion years, and that it had a definite beginning. And only an infinitely powerful Being—God—can account for this beginning of the universe.

Yet, even if the big bang theory is correct, does it really prove that there is a God that created the universe? Couldn't something other than God have caused our universe to come into existence? Isn't it possible, for example, that the universe we know is caused by events in some other unknown universe, which in turn is caused by some other unknown universe, and so on to infinity? Or isn't it possible that our one universe has forever been contracting into a point, then exploding, then contracting again, and then exploding again in a never-ending cycle? In short, even if the universe as we know it had a beginning, can we be sure that ours is not one of an infinite series of universes that goes back forever?

Aquinas was aware, of course, of the possibility that the universe may have existed forever. Consequently, he argued that even if we assume that the universe has existed forever and that the chain of motion and causality has been occurring forever, a First Cause is still necessary. Aquinas reasoned that an infinite regress might account for the individual links in the causal chain, but not for the existence of the entire chain itself. Similarly, although the motion of each moving thing might be accounted for by the motion of an earlier moving thing, the question still arises: What is the origin of the motion of the entire chain? To explain how the entire chain of causes, or the entire chain of motion, came into existence, he claimed, we must posit a God who created them. Is he right?

Suppose that a friend visits you at college. You want to show her around the campus. So you take her to the library, the humanities building, the science

> **CRITICAL THINKING**
> Suppose we can explain all phenomena by assuming that no supernatural beings exist. Would this show that supernatural beings do not exist?

God is at liberty to create whatever initial state of the universe he wanted to.
WILLIAM CRAIG

labs, the cafeteria, and so on, until she sees the entire college. After this tour, she asks, "But where is the college?" You might find that a silly question, since you have already shown her the college by showing her its parts.

In a similar way, the eighteenth-century philosopher David Hume questioned Aquinas's argument:

> Did I show you the particular causes of each individual in a collection of twenty particles of matter, I should think it very unreasonable, should you afterwards ask me, what was the cause of the whole twenty. For this is sufficiently explained in explaining the cause of the parts.[9]

Hume is arguing that the individual links in the causal chain each find their cause in their immediate predecessors. This fact is enough to account for the chain itself. The same kind of logic might be applied to motions and to existences. In other words, if Hume's argument has merit, there is no need or any logical justification for positing a first mover or a first cause of existence.

Yet is it clear that Hume is right? Notice that Hume's objection relies on the assumption that the whole is not greater than the sum of its parts. If this assumption is rejected, then an explanation is required for both the parts and the whole. And then, perhaps, we might want to conclude that Aquinas is right after all.

The second objection to the cosmological argument is that its conclusion is contradicted by its premise. To illustrate, Aquinas insists that every event must have a cause. But if this is so, why stop with God? The notion of an uncaused cause seems to contradict the assumption that everything has a cause. And even if there is an uncaused cause, why must it be God? The nineteenth-century German philosopher Arthur Schopenhauer (1788–1860) expresses this objection succinctly when he writes that the law of universal causation "is not so accommodating as to let itself be used like a cab for hire, which we dismiss when we have reached our destination."[10]

A number of contemporary Thomists (thinkers who generally agree with Thomas Aquinas) have modified this first-cause argument. For them, the endless series that the argument dismisses is not a regress of events in time but a regress of explanations. John Hick (1922–), lecturer in divinity at Cambridge University, interprets the position as follows:

> If fact A is made intelligible by its relation to fact B, C, and D (which may be antecedent to or contemporary with A), and if each of these is in turn rendered intelligible by other facts, at the back of the complex there must be a reality which is self-explanatory, whose existence constitutes the ultimate explanation of the whole. If no such reality exists, the universe is a mere unintelligible brute fact.[11]

But how do we know that the universe is not "a mere unintelligible brute fact"? Hick's argument appears to present a dilemma: Either a first cause exists, or the

---

[9] David Hume, *Dialogues Concerning Natural Religion*, ed. N. Kemp Smith (Edinburgh: Nelson, 1947), 18.

[10] Quoted in C. J. Ducasse, *A Philosophical Scrutiny of Religion* (New York: Ronald Press, 1953), 335.

[11] John Hick, *Philosophy of Religion* (Englewood Cliffs, NJ: Prentice-Hall, 1963), 21. Reprinted by permission.

universe makes no sense. But can't the universe make sense as something that is simply there?

THE DESIGN ARGUMENT

The most popular of the arguments for God's existence has been the proof from design, often called the teleological argument. Simply put, the **argument from design** states that the order and purpose manifest in the working of things demand a God. Even when evolutionists offer a scientific explanation for such apparent order, supporters of the design argument reply, "Yes, but why did things evolve in this way and not in some other?" Traditionally a prominent argument for God's existence, the design proof is still accepted today by some biologists, such as Edmund W. Sinnot, and some theologians, such as Robert E. D. Clark. In 1802 theologian William Paley presented one of the best-known expositions of the design proof. Comparing natural organisms to the mechanism of a watch, Paley argued that just as the design of a watch implies the existence of a maker, so the design found in natural organisms implies the existence of a "Divine Agency":

argument from design argument for the existence of God which claims that the order and purpose manifest in the working of things in the universe require a God

The fundamental physical forces of the universe are exactly what they needed to be to bring us the sort of complex universe we have.
KEITH WARD

In crossing a heath, suppose I pitched my foot against a *stone*, and were asked how the stone came to be there. I might possibly answer, that for anything I knew to the contrary, it had lain there for ever: nor would it perhaps be very easy to show the absurdity of this answer. But suppose I had found a *watch* upon the ground, and it should be inquired how the watch happened to be in that place; I should hardly think of the answer which I had before given, that for anything I knew the watch might have always been there. Yet why should not this answer serve for the watch as well as for the stone? Why is it not as admissible in the second case as in the first? For this reason, and for no other, viz. that when we come to inspect the watch, we perceive (what we could not discover in the stone) that its several parts are framed and put together for a purpose, e.g., that they are so formed and adjusted as to produce motion, and that motion so regulated as to point out the hour of the day; that if the different parts had been differently shaped from what they are, of a different size from what they are, or placed after any other manner, or in any other order, than that in which they are placed, either no motion at all would have been carried on in the machine, or none which would have answered the use that is now served by it. . . . This mechanism being observed . . . the inference, we think, is inevitable, that the watch must have had a maker; that there must have existed, at some time, and at some place or other, an artificer or artificers, who formed it for the purpose which we find it actually to answer; who comprehended its construction and designed its use. . . .

[E]very indication of contrivance, every manifestation of design, which existed in the watch, exists in the works of nature; with the difference, on the side of nature, of being greater and more, and that in a degree which exceeds all computation. I mean, that the contrivances of nature surpass the contrivances of art, in the complexity, subtlety, and curiosity, of the mechanism; and still more, if possible, do they beyond them in number and variety; yet, in a multitude of cases, are not less evidently mechanical, not less evidently contrivances, not less evidently accommodated to their end, or suited to their office, than are the most perfect productions of human ingenuity. . . .

CRITICAL THINKING

Scientists say evolution and natural selection explain why the parts of living creatures are so perfectly adapted to their functions. Does this mean the design argument has to be mistaken?

We can marvel at the structure of a little flower on the desert floor and its delicacy.
MARILYN ADAMS

The more complex, over long periods of time, can come out of a fundamentally mindless process.
DANIEL DENNETT

> Every observation which was made [above] concerning the watch, may be re-
> peated with strict propriety concerning the eye, concerning animals, concerning
> plants, concerning, indeed, all the organized parts of the works of nature. . . .
>
> Were there no example in the world of contrivance, except that of the *eye*, it
> would be alone sufficient to support the conclusion which we draw from it, as to the
> necessity of an intelligent Creator. . . . If there were but one watch in the world, it
> would not be less certain that it had a maker. . . . So it is with the evidences of a
> Divine agency.[12]

As was the custom of religious thinkers of his day, Paley called on a long list
of examples from the sciences (especially biology) to demonstrate his argument.
The migration of birds, the instincts of other animals, the adaptability of species
to various environments, and the human ability to base forecasts on probable
causation all suggested a plan and a planner.

Many contemporary writers have agreed. How, they wonder, can we otherwise explain our continued safety from the two zones of high-intensity particu-
late radiation trapped in the earth's magnetic field and surrounding the planet?
As one writer says, "The ozone gas layer is mighty proof of the Creator's fore-
thought. Could anyone attribute this device to a chance evolutionary process?
A wall that prevents death to every living thing, just the right thickness, and
exactly the correct defense, gives every evidence of plan."[13]

But critics have asked, "Does the appearance of order necessitate conscious
design?" The order in the universe, they say, could have occurred by chance
through an incredibly long period of evolution. Hume argues that in an infinite
amount of time, a finite number of particles in random motion must eventually
achieve a stable order. After all, it is impossible to imagine a universe without
some design. In fact, by definition, a universe must have design.

As Charles Darwin later contended, the life around us has won in the
"struggle for survival"—the fit have survived, and the unfit have perished. Because of a process of natural selection, in which those that can adapt survive
and the rest die, all surviving organisms are perfectly adapted to their environment. Concerning our safety under an ozone umbrella, both Hume and Darwin
would point out that it is not explained by a God who made things and then
shielded them, but by an evolutionary fact: Only life that adjusted to the precise
level of ultraviolet radiation penetrating this ozone has survived. In other
words, life has adjusted itself to the ozone layer; the ozone layer was not adjusted
so that it would sustain life.

THEISTIC ALTERNATIVES
TO TRADITIONAL MONOTHEISM

We have looked at several arguments for the existence of God and seen some
of the problems that these arguments carry. But it is not just the arguments for
God that raise difficulties. Many people have argued that the very concept or

---

CRITICAL THINKING

Suppose scientists proved
that life could arise from
a "primeval soup" of non-
living chemicals. Would
this show that life on earth
was not created by God?

---

*I think if God wanted to leave
a sign that he created the universe and he existed in it, he
would have created some incredibly beautiful universe
with exceptionally good moral
human beings, rather than
this chaos where we have to
struggle to survive.*

NICK SMITH

---

[12] William Paley, *Natural Theology*, in *The Works of William Paley* (Philadelphia: Crissy & Markley,
1857), 387–485.
[13] Arthur I. Brown, *Footprints of God* (Findlay, OH: Fundamental Truth Publishers, 1943), 102.

idea of God creates problems. For example, consider the criticisms some have made of the traditional concept of God's all-knowing nature.

If God is all-knowing, God is aware of what is going on. But can God be aware of our travail without suffering with us? Some Christians say that is precisely why God became man. But how can the timeless and unchanging become incarnate in our world of change? In addition, God's knowledge of our changing world is said to be itself unchanging. How is this possible? Furthermore, traditional theism speaks of a God that transcends creation; God is said to be different from and superior to what God made. But isn't perfect knowledge contingent on knowing something "inside out"? Parents never completely know their offspring, for they can never fully know what that offspring feels, thinks, and desires. If God has perfect knowledge, then isn't God a composite of the many things that make up reality? But if this is so, how can God at the same time be separate and distinct from the creation?

These kinds of criticisms, coupled with the problems of the arguments for the existence of God, have led some reflective theists to search for alternative ways of thinking about God. The criticisms and problems, they feel, show that the concept of God in traditional monotheism is inadequate. But not being willing to abandon God completely, these thinkers have searched for alternative understandings of what God is and how God relates to the universe. Yet these alternatives to traditional monotheism have been fraught with problems. To understand some of the problems, let us very briefly consider two alternative conceptions of God: pantheism and panentheism.

Pantheism means, literally, "all God." It is the belief that everything is God and God is everything. In brief, God and the universe are identical. Pantheists see God as an immense, interconnected system of nature, in much the same way as did philosopher Baruch Spinoza (1632–1677). Spinoza reasoned that if God is all-powerful, all-knowing, and all-present, as traditionalists claim, then God must be everything. If God is everything, God can't be separate from anything. If God is all-powerful, there can be no world outside God. Hence, all of nature, everything that is and we ourselves, must be God. He summarizes his view of God in these words:

> I have now explained the nature and properties of God: that he necessarily exists, that he is one alone, that he is and acts solely from the necessity of his own nature, that he is the free cause of all things and how so, that all things are in God and are so dependent on him that they can neither exist nor be conceived without him, and lastly, that all things have been predetermined by God, not from his free will or absolute pleasure, but from the absolute nature of God, his infinite power. . . .
>
> The human mind is part of the infinite intellect of God. Therefore, when we say the human mind perceives this or that, we are saying nothing but that God, not insofar as he is infinite, but insofar as he is explained through the nature of the human mind . . . has this or that idea.[14]

But how can God be constituted of the incomplete, changing parts we see in nature? If the world around us is limited, and God is the world, then isn't God

pantheism the belief that everything is God

Has God any dwelling-place save earth and sea, the air of heaven and virtuous hearts? Why seek the Deity further? Whatever we see is God, and wherever we go.

LUCAN

---

14 Benedictus Spinoza, *The Ethics*, trans. E. Curley, in *The Collected Works of Spinoza*, V. I (Princeton, NJ: Princeton University Press, 1985), Pt. I, appendix, 439, and Pt. II, prop. 11, 456.

limited? If we are changing and perishable, and God is us, then isn't God changing and perishable? Spinoza's pantheism perceives things as necessary — that is,
as incapable of being otherwise. If this is so, what happens to free choice? What
happens to the human as an experience-confronting, choice-making entity in
a universe that is wholly dominated by God since it is God?

Peculiar to the twentieth century is a brand of theism known as **panentheism,** which attempts to merge theism and pantheism. Rather than believing
that all is God, panentheists hold that all is *in* God. God interpenetrates everything, as in pantheism, but God is also transcendent, beyond experience. Developed by G. T. Fechner, Friedrich von Schelling, and Charles Peirce, panentheism sees God as a Supreme Being whose original nature is fixed, unchanging,
and inclusive of all possibilities. But at the same time God has a historical nature that exists in time as a growing, changing, expanding dimension. Therefore, God is a unity of diversity, being and becoming, the one and the many.
God contains all contrasts.

Still, problems of logic remain. How can such a fusion of opposites occur?
Did God create God's temporal nature? What precisely is the relationship between God's finite nature and God's infinite nature? Was God "compelled" to
exist in time? Panentheism may be another alternative to traditional monotheism, but it seems to raise further complexities that require an almost mystical
grounding to be accepted.

The problems inherent in monotheism and its alternatives have led many
to disbelieve God's existence. Disbelief generally takes the form of atheism or
agnosticism, the two main nontheistic alternatives to monotheism.

> **panentheism** the belief that God is both fixed and chang-ing, inclusive of all possibilities

QUESTIONS

1. Anselm argues that a perfect being must exist because the lack of existence is an imperfection. Could you argue that, on the contrary, a perfect being
must not exist because existence is an imperfection? Explain.

2. If you believe in God, do you believe on the basis of Anselm's ontological
argument? If you do not believe in God, do you disbelieve because you consider
the ontological argument inadequate?

3. Explain the difference between these two statements: "If there is a perfect
being, then a perfect being exists" and "If there can be a perfect being, then a
perfect being exists." Which represents the ontological argument? Which is the
objection to it? With which do you agree, and why?

4. Evaluate these statements:
   a. God was the first event.
   b. God caused the first event.
   c. God is an uncaused cause.
   d. A mind without a body, God, created matter, including bodies.

5. Do you agree that if there is no first cause, the universe makes no sense? Is
an infinite regress nonsensical?

6. If you believe in God, do you believe because of the cosmological argument? If you do not believe in God, do you disbelieve because of the inadequacy of the argument?

7. Aquinas's proofs are based on analogical reasoning, in which he compares what we have experienced directly with what we have not. What is the source of his analogy in his cosmological argument? Is the analogy a good one?

8. Explain what Hume means when he says, "A universe by definition must appear designed, for it shows design."

9. In what ways would you say organic evolution is compatible with the account of creation given in Genesis? In what ways is it incompatible?

10. If you believe in God, do you believe because of the argument from design? If you do not believe in God, do you disbelieve because of the inadequacies in the argument from design?

11. Some people have claimed that the order we attribute to the universe is only apparent. We crave order and so see things as having an order even when they are random. How would these claims affect the argument from design?

12. Some people have claimed that the existence of the atmospheric ozone layer that protects life on earth is proof of God's foresight and so is more evidence of design. But it is probable that we are destroying the ozone layer by releasing chlorofluorocarbon gases, which break it down. How does this possibility affect the claim that the ozone layer is evidence of design?

13. The scientists who study thermodynamics claim that the universe as a whole is gradually becoming more and more disordered. How would this claim, if true, affect the argument from design?

14. What implications does pantheism have for the question of who you are? Do these implications attract you to or repel you from the idea of pantheism? What could count as proof for or against pantheism?

4.3 Atheism, Agnosticism, and the Problem of Evil

As we've just seen, various philosophers have pointed out what they consider to be obvious flaws in each of the traditional proofs for God's existence. Additional objections have also been raised. The objections raised to the arguments for the existence of God have led many people to the conclusion that belief in a traditional God is not reasonable. Whereas agnostics have concluded that they just don't know whether or not God exists, atheists go a step further and decide that they know that God does not exist. Let's look first at atheism.

ATHEISM

Atheism denies the major claims of all varieties of theism. In the words of atheist Ernest Nagel (1937–), "Atheism denies the existence . . . of a self-consistent, omnipotent, omniscient, righteous and benevolent being who is distinct from and independent of what has been created."[15]

atheism denial of theism

God does not know everything and never has known everything.
MAURICE MAETERLINCK

Atheists are sometimes portrayed as evil curmudgeons. But philosophical atheists tend to share a number of respectable characteristics. First, although they often differ on how to establish claims to knowledge, they agree that sense observation and public verification are instrumental and that scientific method is the measure of knowledge and truth. As Nagel states, "It is indeed this commitment to the use of an empirical method which is the final basis of the atheistic critique of theism." Thus, by means of respectable methodology, the atheist claims to explain what theists can account for only through introducing an unverifiable hypothesis about a deity. Atheists claim that the variety of things we experience in the universe can be accounted for in terms of the changes that things undergo when relating with other things. At the same time, there is no discernible unifying pattern of change. "Nature," says Nagel, "is ineradicably plural, both in respect to the individuals occurring in it as well as in respect to the processes in which things become involved." In short, "An atheistic view of things is a form of materialism."

With their emphasis on empiricism and the physical world, many atheists accept a code of ethics such as utilitarianism. *Utilitarianism* holds that the happiness or unhappiness produced by an action determines its morality. There is no code of morality apart from the results of human action. The final standard of moral evaluation is not a commandment of the gods or some divinely inspired code of conduct, but the satisfaction of the complex needs of all human creatures.

As a result of these viewpoints, many thoughtful atheists have focused on the world here and now. They have taken firm stands against authoritarianism while stressing the importance of the individual. For example, the philosopher Bertrand Russell opposed moral codes that tried to repress human impulses in favor of some otherworldly ideal. Because atheists cannot fortify their moral positions with promises of immortality, threats of damnation, or guarantees of righteous recompense, they must rely on what Nagel calls "a vigorous call to intelligent activity—activity for the sake of realizing human potentialities and for eliminating whatever stands in the way of such realization."

But the central feature of atheism is the belief that there are good reasons to believe that God does not exist. What can such reasons look like? We have seen several objections to the arguments for the existence of God. But even if these objections were correct, all they would show is that we don't have a good proof that God exists. For all we know, God might exist even though we can't prove He exists. How, then, can anyone show that God does not exist? Here we consider perhaps the major argument against the existence of God, the problem of evil.

---

[15] Quoted in *Encounter: An Introduction to Philosophy*, ed. Ramona Cormier, Ewing Chinn, and Richard Lineback (Glenview, IL: Scott, Foresman, 1970), 224.

Clearly, humans continue to be beset by all kinds of problems: sickness, poverty, suffering, and death. Yet theism insists that there is an all-good, all-powerful Creator. Is this not at least paradoxical? How is evil compatible with an all-good Creator? If God is all-powerful, surely God could destroy all evil. If God doesn't, why not? Is God really not all-powerful? Or is it that God is unwilling? But if God is unwilling, then God seems to have evil intentions, which certainly aren't consistent with the nature of an all-good God.

In his *Dialogues Concerning Natural Religion*, a three-person discussion of the chief arguments for God's existence, Hume considers this question of evil. His conclusion, in the words of one of his characters, Philo, is that one's experience in the world argues against the existence of an all-good, all-powerful being:

> My sentiments, replied Philo, are not worth being made a mystery of; and, therefore, without any ceremony, I shall deliver what occurs to me with regard to the present subject. It must, I think, be allowed that, if a very limited intelligence whom we shall

CRITICAL THINKING

Does Hume assume that if a good God could prevent evil, God would? Is this assumption correct?

PHILOSOPHY AND LIFE

Religion and Science

For many people the growth of science has made the so-called truths of religion increasingly difficult to maintain. However, some have found science not so different from religious belief. Contemporary Christian philosopher Étienne Gilson is a good example.

Gilson argues that contrary to the traditional distinction between science and religion, the language of modern science and the questions it asks are fundamentally nonscientific. For example, Gilson cites the English astronomer Sir James Jeans's description of the emergence of life as "highly improbable," of human existence as "accidental," and of the entire creation as "surprising." In Gilson's view such descriptions, strictly speaking, are not scientific. Therefore, he suggests that in facing the most basic questions, such as the origin of the universe, science, like religion, must operate on a kind of

faith or belief and not on established fact.

He then observes that in its attempt to explain the origin of things, science shows a markedly nonscientific or metaphysical bent. The reason is that such investigations imply a search for the first cause or causes of things, a subject that has traditionally been addressed by metaphysics. More to the point, in attempting to account for things, some scientists appeal to chance. Others, while assuming the operation of mechanical laws of nature, nonetheless propose a self-made, spontaneously arising universe. Such explanations, says Gilson, are essentially no different from, say, Thomas Aquinas's cosmological argument that premises a cause for every event and concludes with an uncaused cause.

In brief, then, Gilson's view is that the more scientific we become,

the more metaphysical we must be—and the more religious. In the end, he sees much of contemporary science as providing a methodological basis for demonstrating the efficacy of religious truths.

QUESTIONS

1. Do you agree that the distinction between science and metaphysics is not clear-cut?

2. Investigation of the microcosmic reality and the astrophysical macrocosm seems to produce in many scientists a humility and sense of reverence that borders on the religious. A long line of scientists, including Einstein, have seen the universe as God's "sensorium." What do you think they mean by this?

3. Are there any facts of science that make you more inclined to religious belief? Less inclined?

suppose utterly unacquainted with the universe were assured that it were the production of a very good, wise, and powerful being, however finite, he would, from his
conjectures, form *beforehand* a different notion of it from what we find it to be by
experience; nor would he ever imagine, merely from these attributes of the cause of
which he is informed, that the effect could be so full of vice and misery and disorder,.
as it appears in this life. Supposing now that this person were brought into the world,
still assured that it was the workmanship of such a sublime and benevolent being, he
might, perhaps, be surprised at the disappointment, but would never retract his former belief if founded on any very solid argument, since such a limited intelligence
must be sensible of his own blindness and ignorance, and must allow that there may
be many solutions of those phenomena which will forever escape his comprehension.
But supposing, which is the real case with regard to man, that this creature is not
antecedently convinced of a supreme intelligence, benevolent, and powerful, but is
left to gather such a belief from the appearances of things—this entirely alters the
case, nor will he ever find any reason for such a conclusion. He may be fully convinced of the narrow limits of his understanding, but this will not help him in forming an inference concerning the goodness of superior powers, since he must form
that inference from what he knows, not from what he is ignorant of. The more you
exaggerate his weakness and ignorance, the more diffident you render him, and give
him the greater suspicion that such subjects are beyond the reach of his faculties.
You are obliged, therefore, to reason with him merely from the known phenomena,
and to drop every arbitrary supposition or conjecture.[16]

Hume is saying that if we presuppose an all-good, all-powerful God, then we,
in effect, rationalize away the evil that we experience as being something beyond our ability to comprehend. But if we don't presuppose such a being, then
our experience in the world lends no support to the claim that an all-good,
all-powerful being exists. If we don't take God's existence for granted, then
the experience of "vice and misery and disorder" in fact argues against the
theist's God.

There have been a number of attempts to deal with the problem of evil.
The early Christian theologian Saint Augustine (354–430), for one, argues
that evil is a negative thing—that is, the absence of that good that is due a
creature. To be real, said Augustine, is to be good. Since only God is perfectly
good, only God is wholly real. Therefore, God's creation, being finite and limited, must contain incomplete goodness—that is, evil. But this argument seems
to dodge the issue. Call sickness lack of health, if you wish, and suffering lack
of peace—the fact remains that people experience pain and suffering, which
they commonly regard as evil. Why does an all-powerful God allow such "ab-
sences of good"?

Others argue that evil is necessary for good, that only through evil can good
be achieved. It is true that in many instances good seems to depend on evil, as
in the case of having to suffer surgical pain to rid one's body of disease. But to
say that God can bring about good in no other way than through inflicting pain
seems to deny God's omnipotence.

But the most common and serious attempt to escape the problem of evil is
to claim that human freedom is the cause of evil. Since we are free, we are free

*I see little evidence in this
world of the so-called goodness
of God. On the contrary, it
seems to me that, on the
strength of His daily acts,
He must be set down a most
stupid, cruel and villainous
fellow.*

H. L. MENCKEN

---

[16] Hume, *Dialogues Concerning Natural Religion*, pt. XI.

to do evil as well as good. Even an omnipotent God could not make us free in all other respects but not free to do evil, since this would be contradictory. Therefore, evil results from free human choice.

But there are several problems with this argument. First, it does not account for natural evils: earthquakes, droughts, and tornadoes. Humans apparently exercise no control over these. So the argument can pertain only to moral evils — that is, those perpetrated by humans on other creatures: war, murder, and torture. Undoubtedly we are free to do this evil, but why does an all-powerful God enable us to do such terrible things? After all, if God is all-powerful, God could have made us differently. Already we are vulnerable, limited creatures. Why not make us unable to do evil? Perhaps we do not really understand the nature of evil; what we perceive as evil may in God's eyes be good. But if this is so, even more complex questions arise concerning the nature and morality of the Supreme Being. We are also left puzzled about what goodness itself really is.

John Hick, the Thomist we encountered earlier in this chapter, has taken a novel approach to the problem of evil. In his *Philosophy of Religion,* Hick suggests that a world without suffering would be unsatisfactory. Consistent with the thinking of early Hellenistic fathers of the Christian church, such as Irenaeus, Hick seems to argue that while humans are made in the image of God, they have not yet been brought as free and responsible agents into the finite likeness of God as revealed in Christ. The world, then, "with all its rough edges," becomes the sphere in which this stage of the creative process takes place:

> Suppose, contrary to fact, that this world were a paradise from which all possibility of pain and suffering were excluded. The consequences would be very far-reaching. For example, no one could ever injure anyone else: the murderer's knife would turn to paper or his bullets to thin air; the bank safe, robbed of a million dollars, would miraculously become filled with another million dollars (without this device, on however large a scale, proving inflationary); fraud, deceit, conspiracy, and treason would somehow always leave the fabric of society undamaged. Again, no one would ever be injured by accident: the mountain-climber, steeplejack, or playing child falling from a height would float unharmed to the ground; the reckless driver would never meet with disaster. There would be no need to work, since no harm could result from avoiding work; there would be no call to be concerned for others in time of need or danger, for in such a world there could be no real needs or dangers.
>
> To make possible this continual series of individual adjustments, nature would have to work by "special providences" instead of running according to general laws which men must learn to respect on penalty of pain or death. The laws of nature would have to be extremely flexible: sometimes gravity would operate, sometimes not; sometimes an object would be hard and solid, sometimes soft. There could be no sciences, for there would be no enduring world structure to investigate. In eliminating the problems and hardships of an objective environment, with its own laws, life would become like a dream in which, delightfully but aimlessly, we would float and drift at ease.
>
> One can at least begin to imagine such a world. It is evident that our present ethical concepts would have no meaning in it. If, for example, the notion of harming someone is an essential element in the concept of a wrong action, in our hedonistic paradise there could be no wrong actions — nor any right actions in distinction from wrong. Courage and fortitude would have no point in an environment in which

---

Either this God doesn't exist or he's not very good. Why is he sitting there in his heaven watching the people in those box cars roll off to concentration camps in the 1940's?

NICK SMITH

Many people assume that God is basically there to make us happy.

WILLIAM CRAIG

If there's a God it's not a sentimental God.

KEITH WARD

there is, by definition, no danger or difficulty. Generosity, kindness, the *agape* aspect of love, prudence, unselfishness, and all other ethical notions which presuppose life in a stable environment, could not even be formed. Consequently, such a world, however well it might promote pleasure, would be very ill adapted for the development of the moral qualities of human personality. In relation to this purpose it would be the worst of all possible worlds.

It would seem, then, that an environment intended to make possible the growth in free beings of the finest characteristics of personal life, must have a good deal in common with our present world. It must operate according to general and dependable laws; and it must involve real dangers, difficulties, problems, obstacles, and possibilities of pain, failure, sorrow, frustration, and defeat. If it did not contain the particular trials and perils which—subtracting man's own very considerable contribution—our world contains, it would have to contain others instead.[17]

Persons of faith may be largely indifferent to evil as an issue, since they "know" their God beyond rationality and can easily say that we can't begin to fathom God's mystery. In the last analysis, evil may be a problem only for those whose tolerance of mystery is minimal. The rationalist or empiricist must explain away mystery rather than confronting it and getting intimations of the divine and the holy. But for many people, evil just isn't a problem.

Not so, however, for the atheist. For the atheist, the problem of evil is a plain and unanswerable reason for concluding that God does not exist. But most people are not so analytical. Instead, they charge atheism with abandoning humankind to its own devices and with ignoring the persistent belief in a force superior to humankind, a force that often leaves us with hope, confidence, faith, and love in the face of apparently insurmountable troubles. To strip us of these qualities is to leave us both ill equipped to cope with life and, more importantly, morally bankrupt.

Finally, consider this observation about atheism, which is more of an insight than a criticism. Atheism, to use Nagel's own term, involves a "commitment" in much the way that theism or monotheism does. In other words, empirically minded atheists erect their position as much on a commitment of faith as do those who hold religious positions. All the characteristics of atheism that Nagel cites are founded as much on a categorical commitment as are the characteristics of the religionist. The commitments obviously differ: The religionist's commitment is to nonrational, nonempirical ways of knowing; the atheist's is to empiricism. If this is so, we should ask the atheist for empirical–rational reasons for committing oneself to empirical–rational standards and subsequently to atheism. Lacking these reasons, by what criterion can we judge the empiricist–atheistic commitment of faith to be more sound than the theistic commitment?

AGNOSTICISM

Having studied the arguments for and against the existence of God, many thinkers claim that neither side is convincing. As a result, they say they just don't know whether God exists—a position known as **agnosticism.**

> **CRITICAL THINKING**
>
> Suppose that all of the arguments for the existence of God are mistaken and that it is impossible to prove that God exists. Does this show that God does not exist? Then suppose there is no way of showing that God does not exist. Is this a good reason to believe that God does exist?

agnosticism a claim of ignorance; the claim that God's existence can be neither proved nor disproved

---

[17] Hick, *Philosophy of Religion*, 45–46.

The nineteenth-century English scientist Thomas Huxley was a well-known agnostic. For Huxley, agnosticism expressed absolute faith in the validity of the principle that "it is wrong for a man to say that he is certain of the objective truth of any proposition unless he can produce evidence which logically justifies that certainty."[18] Huxley would find sympathy among contemporary linguistic analysts who go further and assert that the propositions "God exists" and "God does not exist" are meaningless because there is no possible way of verifying these claims. However, the linguistic analyst is much harsher than Huxley ever intended to be. For Huxley, the statements were at least meaningful, if insoluble. So he suspended judgment, as he did on the real nature of such ultimates as matter and mind. The agnostic position implies ignorance of the nature of such things. As Huxley put it,

> We have not the slightest objection to believe anything you like, if you will give us good grounds for belief; but, if you cannot, we must respectfully refuse, even if that refusal should wreck morality and insure our damnation several times over. We are quite content to leave the decision to the future. The course of the past has impressed us with the firm conviction that no good ever comes of falsehood, and we feel warranted in refusing even to experiment in that direction.[19]

But if it is unclear whether or not God exists, as the agnostic claims, why then do so many of us continue to believe? In his short work *The Future of an Illusion*, Sigmund Freud suggested an influential answer to that question. Freud, who was the founder of modern psychoanalysis, was hostile to religious belief. He suggested that our belief in God is an "illusion" that has its origins in "infantile" needs. In spite of having no good reason to believe in God, he claimed, people continue to believe because they have an "infantile" need to feel that someone is protecting and watching out for them. This need leads them to believe that there is a being that watches out for them, and they imagine that this being is like the father who looked after them when they were children. In a later work, *New Introductory Lectures in Psychoanalysis*, Freud wrote the following:

> The God-Creator is openly called Father. Psychoanalysis has concluded that he really is the father, clothed in the grandeur in which he first appeared to the small child. The religious man's picture of the creation of the universe is the same as his picture of his own creation. . . . He therefore looks back on the memory-image of the overrated father of his childhood, exalts it into a Deity, and brings it into the present and into reality. The emotional strength of this memory-image and the lasting nature of his need for protection are the two supports of his belief in God.[20]

Freud's suggestion is intriguing. And many people today accept it. But is it true? Is there any way of proving that it is true? Perhaps not. Freud offers even less in the way of proof than traditional believers have offered for their own belief in

CRITICAL THINKING

Does agnosticism assume that suspension of belief is possible? Is this assumption correct?

---

[18] Quoted in *Encounter: An Introduction to Philosophy*, ed. Ramona Cormier, Ewing Chinn, and Richard Lineback (Glenview, IL: Scott, Foresman, 1970), 227.
[19] Ibid., 230.
[20] From Sigmund Freud, *New Introductory Lectures in Psychoanalysis*, 1933.

God. Moreover, even if Freud is correct, and our belief in God originates in our own childhood needs, this would not show that belief in God is an "illusion." It may be that we came to believe in God out of needs that originated in childhood, yet our belief may very well still be true!

The philosopher Immanuel Kant proposed a more sympathetic explanation of why we believe in God even though we cannot prove that God exists. Kant agreed that there is evil and injustice in this world. Morally good people often suffer and end up unhappy, while many bad people prosper and live happy lives. But the fact that sometimes good people unjustly suffer while evil people unjustly prosper should not lead us to reject God. On the contrary, Kant argued, the fact that this world is unjust obliges us to pursue a world that is perfectly just, and this in turn obliges us to believe in a God who alone can bring about a perfectly just world:

> We ought to strive to bring about the supreme good [perfect justice]. Because we ought to bring about this supreme good, it must be possible for it to exist. . . . But the supreme good is possible in the world only if there exists a Supreme Being who can bring about a world in which happiness is correlated with moral goodness. Now a being that is capable of bringing about a just world as the moral law requires, is an intelligence (a rational being). And a being that acts according to the requirements of the moral law, has a will. Therefore, the supreme creator of the world, whose existence must be supposed if the *sumum bonum* is possible, is a Being who causes the world by His intelligence and will . . . that is, God. [21]

Kant is arguing that we feel an obligation to work for a world in which, we might say, "Justice prevails." This would be a world in which moral goodness is rewarded with happiness. But, claims Kant, if we have an obligation to do something, then it must be possible to do it. For we cannot have a moral obligation to do something that is impossible. So, since we have an obligation to work for a world in which justice prevails, we must believe it is possible for such a world to exist. In other words, we must believe that it is possible for a world to exist in which good people are always rewarded with happiness and in which evil people likewise get what they deserve. Such a world is possible only if there is a God who will eventually punish evil and reward the good, perhaps in some afterlife. So, since our obligation to pursue a just world forces us to believe that a just world is possible, we are also forced to believe that there exists a God who can make such a world possible.

Kant's suggestion, like Freud's, is an intriguing response to our inability to either prove or disprove that God exists. It is an alternative to agnosticism. But, again, we must ask this: Is it reasonable? Unlike Freud, of course, Kant does not claim that belief in God is an illusion. Kant claims only that even if God's existence cannot be proved, and even if evil in the world casts doubt on God's existence, we are still forced to believe that God exists. We are forced to believe

---

[21] Immanuel Kant, *Critique of Practical Reason*, trans. T. K. Abbot (London: Longmans Green, 1927), pt. 1, bk. 2, ch. 2, para. 5, pp. 220–222.

in God, that is, if we feel that we have an obligation to make this a better, more just world. However, Kant's argument leaves open the question of whether God exists. Although we must *believe* that God exists, we cannot *know* that God exists.

Perhaps, then, the existence or nonexistence of a theistic God cannot be proved. But lack of certain evidence does not make the question any less important. Even if we feel we lack sufficient evidence, we still must live our lives as if we believe or disbelieve. If we disbelieve, we will not join a church, pray, or worship. We will not feel the presence of God as we walk through a hushed forest of tall trees. If we believe, however, we will not only do these things, but we will also see ourselves as having a spiritual dimension, perhaps one that survives after death. In short, if we lack belief, then we will live our lives in one way, and if we believe, we will live in another way. The question is this: Is it possible to be an agnostic in practice? In the end, mustn't the agnostic choose to live either as a believer or as a nonbeliever? And, most often, won't the agnostic choose to live as if he or she is in fact an unbelieving atheist?

This raises the question of whether the agnostic's suspension of belief is really possible in pratice. It may be possible to say to ourselves intellectually that we do not take a position on the question of whether God exists. But in the end we must choose how we are to live. And doesn't this choice in the end commit us to a life of belief or a life of unbelief? This, perhaps, is part of what Kant meant when he claimed that our moral commitments force us to take a position on the question of God. The way we choose to live our life implies certain commitments. In light of these commitments, is it really possible to live as an agnostic?

Most intellectual people do not believe in God, but they fear him just the same.

WILHELM REICH

QUESTIONS

1. In your view, is atheism more or less rational than agnosticism? Is atheism more or less virtuous than agnosticism?

2. Explain the following statement: "The existence of evil can only show that God is either not all-knowing or not omnipotent; it cannot show that God does not exist." Is this statement correct?

3. Theists sometimes claim that God could not have denied human beings free will and still made them morally responsible for their actions and so deserving of heaven or hell in an afterlife. Explain this claim and evaluate it.

4. A playwright once wrote, "If God is good, He is not God; if God is God, He is not good." Explain.

5. The seventeenth-century French philosopher Blaise Pascal suggested that atheism is not a good bet: "Let us weigh the gain and loss in betting that God exists: if you win, you win everything; if you lose, you lose nothing. You should unhesitatingly bet that He exists!" Do you agree?

4.4 Traditional Religious Belief and Experience

RELIGIOUS BELIEF

Even if the existence of God is not an issue for a person, the question of whether or not to *believe* in a divine dimension may be. Is the cosmos far-flung matter that originated in chance and is propelled by accident? Or is it — scientific explanations notwithstanding — something sacred, something divine? How we answer these questions will greatly affect our self-concepts and consequently our lives. In this case, the belief is as important a question as the fact.

A simple example will illustrate the influence of belief in our lives. Suppose at some point in college you begin to question whether you should actually be there. You are finding it neither interesting nor manageable. Besides, you have a pretty good job that you like, and if you work full time, you can make enough money to get married. On the other hand, limiting your education might restrict your personal and professional opportunities. What should you do, stay in school or quit? You must choose; there is no escaping the issue.

Obviously, there is no certain answer. The best you can do is open-mindedly collect and weigh the data and decide. But whatever your choice, you will undoubtedly *believe* you are doing the right thing. In fact, that belief will help you make the decision, which will have important consequences for your life. Your decision might be reversible, but it will steer your life in a certain direction. That direction will be full of experiences that another direction might have lacked, experiences that will help shape you. So, in believing you should choose a particular direction, you have really decided to a degree what you will become.

Like the dilemma of whether to stay in school, the answer to the question of God's existence is inconclusive; you cannot resolve it absolutely. But the question of *belief* in a divine dimension — whether theism, pantheism, or panentheism — is not. You can decide whether to believe, and your decision, if you are true to it, will affect your life, because through it you relate yourself to the world and everything in it.

People can respond in many ways in deciding whether to believe. One response is to be so overwhelmed by the question of God's existence that we give up hope of ever believing anything. But this reaction is a decision — a decision to remain uncommitted. Another possibility is to avoid the anguish of decision making by choosing whatever belief is conventional, popular, acceptable, or fashionable — in effect, to choose to become one of the statistics that we allow to formulate our beliefs. Or we can face up to the anguish of decision making, consider the implications, choose to believe or not to believe, and then live that decision. The decision is ours to make.

Death is the true inspiring genius, or the muse of philosophy. . . . Indeed, without death men could scarcely philosophize.

ARTHUR SCHOPENHAUER

If only God would give me some clear sign! Like making a large deposit in my name at a Swiss bank.

WOODY ALLEN

There are many paths to God, my son, I hope yours will not be too difficult.

LEW WALLACE

"THE WILL TO BELIEVE"

Is there any evidence for believing in a divine dimension of any sort? Ultimately, must religious belief be based on evidence? Perhaps it can be a personal decision made with the heart. In a classic address titled "The Will to Believe," American philosopher William James confronted this issue. (After delivering the speech, he wrote that he wished he had titled it "The Right to Believe.") The thrust of James's address is captured in the following argument:

> Our passional nature not only lawfully may, but must, decide an option between propositions, whenever it is a genuine option that cannot by its nature be decided on intellectual grounds; for to say, under such circumstances, "Do not decide, but leave the question open," is itself a decision—just like deciding yes or no,—and is attended with the same risk of losing the truth.[22]

Without understanding the terms as James understands them, we can easily misconstrue what he is saying.

First, consider the word *option*. By this, James means a choice between two hypotheses, a *hypothesis* being anything that may be proposed for our belief. "There is a divine dimension to the universe" is a hypothesis; so is "There is no divine dimension to the universe." Some hypotheses are *live*; a live hypothesis "appeals as a real possibility to him to whom it is proposed." For example, the proposal that you believe in the Mahdi (the Islamic messiah) would probably not be appealing to you because of your probable Western acculturation and likely ignorance of Islam. The hypothesis would be a *dead* one. Yet, if you are an Arab, it would probably be very much live. The deadness or liveness of any hypothesis, then, is not a quality inherent in the proposal but a quality determined by the individual thinker. It is an indication of our willingness to act; a hypothesis is most live when we are willing to act irrevocably—that is, to believe.

James distinguishes several kinds of options: (1) living or dead, (2) forced or avoidable, and (3) momentous or trivial. A genuine option is living, forced, and momentous.

By a *living* option, James means one in which both hypotheses are live ones. For example, the proposal "Be a theosophist or be a Muhammadan" would probably be a dead option, because neither proposal is likely to be a live one for you. On the other hand, "Be a Christian or be an atheist" would probably be a living option, because both choices are probably live for you.

Now, suppose that someone proposed "Either love me or hate me." You could avoid a decision by remaining indifferent to the person. Likewise, if someone proposed "Either vote for me or vote for my opponent," you could avoid the decision by not voting at all. Options like these are *avoidable*. On the other hand, if someone said "Either accept this proof or go without it," you would be forced to make a choice. When there is no way to avoid a decision, the option is *forced*.

---

[22] Quoted in *Encounter: An Introduction to Philosophy*, ed. Ramona Cormier, Ewing Chinn, and Richard Lineback (Glenview, IL: Scott, Foresman, 1970), 236.

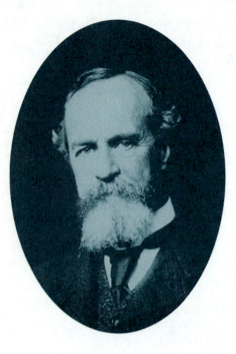

William James: "To say, 'Do not decide, but leave the question open,' is itself a decision—just like deciding yes or no,—and is attended with the same risk of losing the truth."

Finally, an option is *momentous* when the opportunity is unique, when the stakes are significant, and when the decision is irreversible. For example, a friend comes by one night with some "surefire" stock. This once-in-a-lifetime opportunity, she promises, will yield incredible riches. To accept her offer or reject it would be a momentous option. On the other hand, whether to wear jeans or slacks to school would be a *trivial* option, because it is not unique, attended by high stakes, or irreversible.

Belief is not a matter of decision.
KEITH WARD

Now, what does James mean by "our passional nature"? James forsakes objective certainty. He claims that we can never be absolutely sure of anything except that consciousness exists. But he does *not* abandon the quest for truth itself; he still believes that truth exists. This belief in the truth springs more from desire and feeling than from reason; it is more passional than rational. But the belief provides the best chance of attaining truth, "by systematically continuing to roll up experiences and think." His point is that since we can never know anything with certainty, there will inevitably be a nonintellectual, nonrational element to what we choose to believe—a passional element. As James writes, "Instinct leads, intelligence only follows."

The first two tasks of this passional element are knowing the truth and avoiding error. Deciding which of these two "commandments" is more important may have a strong impact on our lives. For example, suppose you regarded the avoidance of error as paramount and the search for truth as secondary. Since there is very little if anything for which there is incontrovertible evidence, you would probably draw no conclusions. The result would be lifelong intellectual suspension. Imagine a child who cannot choose one of thirty-one ice cream flavors for fear that he will regret his choice. James suggests that when we are more committed to avoiding error than to chasing the truth, we necessarily lose the truth, since we will never be able to find absolute supporting evidence. To make such a choice is to be "like a general informing his soldiers that it is better to keep out of battle forever than to risk a single wound. Not so are victories either over enemies or over nature found."[23] Or, we might add, over the self.

James does not say that avoiding error should always be subordinate to attaining truth, however. In options that are not momentous, James claims that we can save ourselves from believing a falsehood by not deciding until all the evidence is in. This approach would apply to most of the scientific questions and human issues that we are likely to face. In other words, in most choices the need to act is seldom so urgent that it is better to act on a false belief than on no belief at all. But he also argues that there are forced and momentous choices that we cannot ("as men who may be interested at least as much in positively gaining truth as in merely escaping dupery") always wait to make. As he put it, "In the great boardinghouse of nature, the cakes and the butter and the syrup seldom come out so even and leave the plates so clean."

Granted, for some people religious belief is not a hypothesis that could possibly be true. But for most it is a live option. To these people, James says that religious belief is a momentous option. They stand to gain much by their belief and to lose much by their nonbelief. It is also a forced option. If they choose to wait in order to avoid error, they risk losing the chance of attaining the good that religious belief promises: "It is as if a man should hesitate indefinitely to ask a certain woman to marry him because he was not perfectly sure that she would prove an angel after he brought her home. Would he not cut himself off from that particular angel-possibility as decisively as if he went and married someone else?" Or, more simply, if the ice cream shop closes while the child is debating his choice, the result will be the same as if he had chosen to have no ice cream. When a question cannot be answered on intellectual grounds, James argues that we not only can but *should* allow our "passional nature" to decide it. We must choose to chase truth, not to avoid possible error; for in fearing to be duped, we exclude the possibility of being right.

James's argument has relevance not only for those who believe in a personal God but also for those whose innermost feelings detect a divine dimension at work in the cosmos, but not necessarily a Supreme Being. Because he relies on the importance of personal experience in religious belief, James provides a philosophical basis for a personal encounter with the sacred, whatever we may perceive that to be. Just what constitutes a personal experience of the divine is a complex question, but individuals often use it as their source of or justification for religious belief.

PERSONAL EXPERIENCE OF THE DIVINE

Very few of us today believe in God because of rational proofs. Many people, perhaps most, do not need any rational proof for their religious belief, any more

CRITICAL THINKING

Does James assume that if belief in something has significant benefits, then the belief must be true? Is this assumption correct?

---

[23] William James, *The Varieties of Religious Experience* (New York: Longmans, Green, 1929), 74.

than they need proof that they feel joyful or loving. Others might point out innumerable reasons for not feeling joyful or loving, but to those experiencing these feelings, such arguments mean nothing because they have directly experienced the feelings. Similarly, many people who believe in God do so, they claim, because they have experienced an unseen reality, and they feel that this unseen reality is deeper and more real than their sense experiences.

For many people, these religious experiences are simply quiet moments in which they have "felt" a divine presence, and this calm feeling was strong enough to convince them that God exists.

Other people claim to have had extraordinary "ecstatic" experiences coupled with dramatic insights and intense religious feelings. One problem of trying to speak of such experiences is that, by nature, they defy verbalization. But consider R. M. Bucke's description of a religious experience, quoted by William James:

> All at once, without warning of any kind, I found myself wrapped in a flame-colored cloud. For an instant I thought of fire . . . the next, I knew that the fire was within myself. Directly afterward there came upon me a sense of exultation, of immense joyousness accompanied or immediately followed by an intellectual illumination impossible to describe. Among other things, I did not merely come to believe, but I saw that the universe is not composed of dead matter, but is, on the contrary, a living Presence; I became conscious in myself of eternal life. . . . I saw that all men are immortal: that the cosmic order is such that without any preadventure all things work together for the good of each and all; that the foundation principle of the world . . . is what we call love, and that the happiness of each and all is in the long run absolutely certain.[24]

Bucke is describing a mystical experience. Religious belief often originates in such mystical states of consciousness.

In his *Varieties of Religious Experience*, James suggests that all mystical experiences have two common characteristics. One is *ineffability*—that is, the state defies expression. The experiencer feels that the mystical experience cannot be adequately reported. The other is a *noetic quality*—that is, to the individual the experiences appear to be knowledge. They provide an insight into human experience that no amount of intellectualizing can plumb. They are revelations and illuminations full of meaning, truth, and importance.

Mysticism, then, is the experience of a reality that we can truly know only when we surrender our individual selves and sense a union with the divine ground of all existence. Certainly, mystical experiences vary in content, but they often involve an acute awareness of a divine presence and of a direct communion with divinity, although this divinity is more likely to be an incomprehensible entity than a theistic deity.

Like most people at some time or other, mystics have a longing to go beyond the imperfect world of which they are a part. They may feel an urge for something permanent and free that transcends sorrow and is of everlasting value. Most Westerners try to quell such feelings and desires by seeking outside them-

Mystics are very self-conscious about the possibility of self-deception.

WILLIAM WAINWRIGHT

A genuine experience of God is self-authenticating.

WILLIAM CRAIG

The brain is capable of lots and lots of illusory and hallucinatory activity.

PAT CHURCHLAND

Perceptions ought to be taken at their face value in the absence of positive reason for challenge.

RICHARD SWINBURNE

mysticism the philosophy of religion contending that reality can be known only when we surrender our individuality and experience a union with the divine ground of all existence

---

[24] R. M. Bucke, quoted in William James, *The Varieties of Religious Experience* (New York: Modern Library, 1902), 390–391.

selves, but mystics turn inward. What occurs is impossible to describe — it must be experienced. But the writings of mystics indicate that above everything else, the inner way leads to an understanding that all is one and one is all, that the self is one continuous process with God, the cosmos, or whatever term a particular culture or individual chooses to call ultimate and eternal reality.

Such an inner experience has been termed *religious experience, mystical experience,* or *cosmic consciousness,* but the philosophy of religion employs the term *numinous experience* to describe this mystical consciousness of the holy. Peter Koestenbaum lists several elements of the numinous experience.[25] One is a feeling of infinite dependence, of the experiencer and the mundane world being insignificant. The person's values change, and a new sense of reality supplants the old. For example, Thomas Aquinas, a consummate rational theologian, underwent a mystical experience after completing his major work. Afterward, he described his previous efforts as so much straw compared with what he'd experienced. He never wrote another line.

Another aspect of the numinous is mystery. Mystery is closely related to James's ineffability. Since our language is designed to handle ordinary experience in the ordinary world, a numinous experience is often described simply as a mystery or miracle. In Plato's Myth of the Cave, recall that a prisoner escapes from the cave where humankind is condemned to watch shadows on a screen, which it then takes for reality. After contemplating the real world, the prisoner returns to the cave and attempts in vain to enlighten his cavemates. Their points of reference and his are different, so he cannot convey his experience. A similar communication gap faces the mystic.

Terror is also an element of the numinous. This terror results from the total annihilation of our world of experience as we know it, the removal of all stability and substance from our existence. Numerous Old Testament passages evidence the kind of dread that accompanies the numinous. Speaking through one of the prophets, the God of the Old Testament says, "Their slain shall also be cast out, and their stink shall come up out of their carcasses and the mountains shall be melted with their blood" (Isa. 34:3) and "For the indignation of the Lord is upon all nations, and his fury upon all their armies: he hath utterly destroyed them, he hath delivered them to the slaughter" (Isa. 34:2). Literally interpreted, these references suggest that God must be capable of evil. But viewed analogically, they represent the element of terror in the numinous.

A fourth aspect of the numinous is bliss. References to heaven, paradise, salvation, and love all suggest a feeling of supreme fulfillment and satisfaction. The numinous satisfies the most profound yearnings of the human heart. Thus, Saint Catherine of Genoa writes, "If of that which my heart is feeling one drop were to fall into hell, hell itself would become life eternal."[26]

There are many other characteristics of the numinous. The key point is that religion may be approached through a numinous experience. Yet the claim

> *The ordinary man or woman in the pew or in the mosque hasn't had an experience of this kind. And probably never will.*
>
> WILLIAM WAINWRIGHT

CRITICAL THINKING

Does the mystic assume that if one feels deeply that something is real, then it must be real?

> *Reason refuses its homage to a God who can be fully understood.*
>
> M. F. TUPPER

---

[25] Peter Koestenbaum, *Philosophy: A General Introduction* (New York: Van Nostrand Reinhold, 1968), 140–147.
[26] Ibid., 146.

Ecstasy of Saint Teresa, Giovanni Lorenzo Bernini. A fourth character of the numinous is bliss. References to heaven, paradise, salvation, and love all suggest a feeling of supreme fulfillment and satisfaction. The numinous satisfies the most profound yearnings of the human heart.

that people have direct experiences of the divine can be questioned. How can a finite human being experience an infinite God? If we experience something, then mustn't we experience it through the senses that we have? And if so, then won't it have to have sensory qualities like colors, sounds, feelings, and shapes? But certainly God does not have these sensory qualities. So how can what we experience be God? At most, mustn't we say that what is experienced is something other than God, something that the believer interprets as representing God? But how can we ever be sure that our interpretation isn't mistaken? How can we be sure the experience is not an illusion or a hallucination?

In spite of these difficulties, the 1990s have seen a continued and intense interest in what we can call the transformation of consciousness, much of which springs from a sense of personal estrangement from the world. Many people feel out of touch and try to locate themselves in the scheme of things. Often, they reject traditional prescriptions for inner peace and contentment and instead follow their own vague but pressing sense of what is good for them. This pursuit takes many forms—among them the New Age movement, self-healing, consciousness expansion, the human potential movement—but all have nonrational, mystical overtones.

In the following section, we introduce three nontraditional religious movements—radical theology, feminist theology, and the study of Eastern religious thought. Although quite different in content and methodology, they are similar

Buddhist mystics don't report being aware of Christ, not to mention the Virgin Mary, and Protestants don't seem to get visited by the Virgin Mary very much.

WILLIAM ALSTON

in their attempts to gain religious understanding through a nontraditional transformation of consciousness.

QUESTIONS

1. Can you give some examples from your own life of what James means by "a live hypothesis"?

2. Have you ever had what you call a personal religious experience? What made it religious and different from other, more ordinary experiences? Could a person have religious experiences without believing in God? Explain. Could someone have a personal religious experience that was false? How would you distinguish the real from the false experience?

3. Is mysticism necessarily in conflict with institutionalized religion? Is it necessarily in conflict with rationality?

4. Can you describe the view of reality that mysticism requires? What view of human nature does mysticism require? Do you believe these views are correct? Why or why not?

5. Some varieties of mysticism emphasize feelings at the expense of reason. Is there any reason to accept feelings when they conflict with reason? Is this question self-contradictory? How would the mystic justify his or her feelings?

6. Evaluate this statement of seventeenth-century French philosopher Blaise Pascal: "If we submit everything to reason, our religion will have nothing in it mysterious or supernatural. If we violate the principles of reason, our religion will be absurd and ridiculous." Are we forced to accept this dilemma?

4.5 Nontraditional Religious Experience

RADICAL THEOLOGY

Some philosophers have responded to nagging questions about the existence and nature of a Supreme Being by developing a school of theology that deviates from traditional theism more radically than do pantheism and panentheism. The radical theologians, as these thinkers are often termed, perceive God not as a being among other beings but as an aspect of reality. As a result, they feel that our relationship with God is more experiential than rational. The modern roots of this view can be traced to such thinkers as the Danish philosopher Søren Kierkegaard (1813–1855).

Søren Kierkegaard: "If God does not exist, it would of course be impossible to prove it; and if he does exist it would be folly to attempt it."

Kierkegaard

The northern European society into which Kierkegaard was born was thoroughly Christian. Everyone shared the same dogmas, although few gave much thought to their beliefs. All attended the same Lutheran churches and church social functions and mechanically mouthed the doctrines that they were raised to espouse. While this behavior passed for Christianity, Kierkegaard believed that it was anything but that. In his view, such behavior lacked passion, and so did the Christians who displayed the behavior. Where they should have felt fear, these people were complacent; where they should have shown intensity, they were secure. To put it bluntly, Kierkegaard was revolted by these self-professed pillars of the Christian community. Appropriately enough, then, in works such as *Philosophical Fragments* and *Concluding Unscientific Postscript*, Kierkegaard expounded a view of Christianity and of being a Christian that was at once new and yet very old.

Central to Kierkegaard's religious thought is his distinction between the objective and subjective thinker, which is essentially a distinction between reason and faith. The objective thinker strikes an intellectual, dispassionate, scientific posture toward life. In effect, the objective thinker adopts the view of an observer. In contrast, the subjective thinker is passionately and intensely involved with truth. Truth for the subjective thinker is not just a matter of accumulating evidence to establish a viewpoint, but something of profound personal concern. Because questions of life and death, of the meaning of one's existence, of one's ultimate destiny, often preoccupy subjective thinkers, Kierkegaard sometimes calls them existential thinkers.

Although Kierkegaard is primarily concerned with subjective thinking, he never denies that objective thinking has its place. He simply asserts that not all of life's concerns are open to objective analysis. Indeed, from Kierkegaard's view, it would be fair to say that life's most important questions defy objective analysis. A good example, which also happens to be Kierkegaard's preoccupation as a religious thinker, is religious belief. Religious belief, says Kierkegaard, is not open to objective thinking because it involves a relationship with God. Stated more exactly, religion and religious belief are a confrontation with the unknown, not something knowable. In the following passage from *Philosophical Fragments*, Kierkegaard demonstrates what he means:

> But what is this unknown something with which the Reason collides when inspired by its paradoxical passion, with the result of unsettling even man's knowledge of himself? It is the Unknown. It is not a human being, in so far as we know what man is; nor is it any other known thing. So let us call this unknown something: *the God.* It is nothing more than a name we assign to it. The idea of demonstrating that this unknown something (the God) exists, could scarcely suggest itself to the Reason. For if the God does not exist it would of course be impossible to prove it; and if he does exist it would be folly to attempt it. For at the very outset, in beginning my proof, I would have presupposed it, not as doubtful but as certain (a presupposition is never doubtful, for the very reason that it is a presupposition), since otherwise I would not begin, readily understanding that the whole would be impossible if he did not exist. But if when I speak of proving the God's existence I mean that I propose to prove that the Unknown, which exists, is the God, then I express myself unfortunately. For in that case I do not prove anything, least of all an existence, but merely develop the content of a conception. . . .
>
> The works from which I would deduce God's existence are not directly and immediately given. The wisdom in nature, the goodness, the wisdom in the governance of the world—are all these manifest, perhaps, upon the very face of things? Are we not here confronted with the most terrible temptations to doubt, and is it not impossible finally to dispose of all these doubts? But from such an order of things I will surely not attempt to prove God's existence; and even if I began I would never finish, and would in addition have to live constantly in suspense, lest something so terrible should suddenly happen that my bit of proof would be demolished. From what works then do I propose to derive the proof? From the works as apprehended through an ideal interpretation, i.e., such as they do not immediately reveal themselves. But in that case it is not from the works that I make the proof; I merely develop the ideality I have presupposed, and because of my confidence in *this* I make so bold as to defy all objections, even those that have not yet been made. In beginning my proof I presuppose the ideal interpretation, and also that I will be successful in carrying it through; but what else is this but to presuppose that the God exists, so that I really begin by virtue of confidence in him?[27]

From this passage it is clear that Kierkegaard condemns the proofs for God's existence, as well as other attempts to "know" God. The reason is that by Kierkegaard's account, God cannot be known; God is not subject to rational,

---

[27] Søren Kierkegaard, *Philosophical Fragments,* trans. David Swenson (Princeton, NJ: Princeton University Press, 1936). Copyright © 1936, 1962 by Princeton University Press. Excerpt reprinted by permission of Princeton University Press.

objective analysis. But if the point of religion and religious faith is not to know God, then just what is their point? To *feel*, rather than to know.

In the end, rational thinking, which is the religious expression of objective thinkers, points to the existence of God but gives individuals little on which to erect a relationship with God. "I contemplate the order of nature," says Kierkegaard, "in the hope of finding God, and I see omnipotence and wisdom; but I also see much else that disturbs my mind and excites anxiety. The sum of all this is objective uncertainty."

Faced with objective uncertainty, with the inconclusiveness of objective analysis and rational debate and "proofs," we are anguished. This anguish, this suffering, is compounded by the anticipation of our own death and our feeling of smallness and insignificance in the face of the eternal order of things. The debates go on; our lives ebb away. We must make a decision.

Kierkegaard calls this decision the "leap of faith"; it consists of a commitment to a relationship with God that defies objective analysis. Of course, we may choose not to make the leap of faith; we may, instead, try to minimize our suffering through professional understanding and knowledge, through objective analysis. But for this alternative, Kierkegaard has only sarcasm. *"The two ways,"* he says: "one is to suffer; the other is to become a professor of the fact that another suffered."

Tillich

The chief exponent of radical theology in our time has been Protestant theologian Paul Tillich (1886–1965). Tillich, an existentialist, contends that traditional theism has erred in viewing God as *a being* and not as *being itself*. He believes that the proofs for God's existence, discussed earlier, have fostered this error. As a result, we have bound God to our subject-object structure of reality. He—notice the sexualization—is an object for us as subjects, becoming the target for our prayers, worship, and supplications. "He" becomes almost some *thing* to which we direct our lives. At other times we make ourselves an object for God as subject. Because theism posits an all-knowing, all-powerful God, and because we are neither, the relationship must therefore be one of superior (God) to inferior (us), controller to controlled, subject to object. An antagonistic tension results. As Tillich says, "He deprives me of my subjectivity because he is all-powerful and all-knowing. I revolt and try to make him into an object, but the revolt fails and becomes desperate. God appears as an invincible tyrant, the being in contrast with whom all other things are without freedom and subjectivity." [28] This image of God as "invincible tyrant," he feels, is a much more telling blow to theological theism than all the objections to the traditional proofs for God's existence. Tillich believes that his criticism is justified, for God as tyrant is "the deepest root of the Existentialist despair and the widespread anxiety of meaninglessness in our period." Notice that Tillich rejects

---

[28] This and all other Tillich quotations are from Paul Tillich, *The Courage to Be* (New Haven, CT: Yale University Press, 1952). Reprinted by permission.

Paul Tillich: "Depth is what the word God means, the source of your being, of your ultimate concern, of what you take seriously without any reservation. 'Life has no depth. Life is shallow. Being itself is surface only.' If you could say this in complete seriousness, you would be an atheist; but otherwise you are not. He who knows the depth knows about God."

traditional theism not on empirical but on theological grounds. For Tillich, theism is just bad theology.

If Tillich and other radical theologians reject the theistic concept of God, what do they offer as a substitute? What kind of God do they believe in? Tillich's God is a "God above God," "the ground of being." This God transcends the God of theism and so dissipates the anxiety of doubt and meaninglessness. This ground of being is not proved, because it cannot be. It is neither an object nor a subject. It is present, although hidden, in every divine–human encounter.

CRITICAL THINKING

"Everyone has an ultimate concern, so everyone believes in God." Evaluate the assumptions this argument makes.

Tillich grants that this notion is paradoxical. But he notes that biblical religion and Protestant theology are already studded with paradoxes. Consider the "paradoxical character of every prayer of speaking to somebody to whom you cannot ask anything because he gives or gives not before you ask, of saying 'thou' to somebody who is nearer to the I than the I is to itself." Indeed, it is paradoxes like these, says Tillich, that "drive the religious consciousness toward a God above the God of theism, a God that is the Ground of our very being."

The "ground of being" is only one of Tillich's many slippery concepts. "Depth" is another. "Depth is what the word God means," he writes, but, even so, the word seems to have no meaning. "If the word has not much meaning for you, translate it," advises Tillich, "and speak of the depths of your life, of the source of your being, of your ultimate concern, of what you take seriously without reservation." Atheists might reply, "That there is no God—now *that* I take seriously, without any reservation." But Tillich would say that this is impossible, for genuine atheists would have to forget everything traditional that they ever learned about God, maybe even the word itself. The only people who can rightly call themselves atheists are those who can say, "Life has no depth. Life is shallow. Being itself is surface only." Writes Tillich, "If you could say this in complete seriousness, you would be an atheist; but otherwise you are not. He who knows the depth knows about God."

Like many existentialists, Tillich is not easy to understand. But, clearly, he believes that traditional theism has erred in making God an object. It does so in its definitions of God and in its proofs of God's existence. God cannot be proved, as if God were an equation or a laboratory specimen. Such "objectivation" not only limits the deity but also raises the very kinds of inconsistencies that lead to a loss of faith. Therefore, Tillich's God defies traditional definitions and proofs. His concept of God corresponds somewhat with the mystic's but still is significantly different. Where the mystic would reject sense experience and reason when taken as ultimate, and through intuition alone move to a knowledge of God, Tillich confronts the world of experience and its nagging questions. He is no escapist, no dodger of doubt. On the contrary, he faces the concrete world of finite values and meanings and uses all its imperfections, skepticism, and meaninglessness to confront what is ultimately real: being. And in this ground of all being he experiences God. Everyone does "who knows the depth."

Besides having many elusive concepts, Tillich's theology provokes other objections. He seems to be saying that those who do not recognize his God, the ground of all being, are not ultimately concerned. Suppose you tell an unaccomplished violinist that the reason she failed to become a virtuoso is that she never practiced long enough. "Long enough!" she protests. "Are you kidding? Why, I have practiced every day of my life!" "Obviously, it wasn't long enough," you reply, "because you never became a virtuoso." Clearly, by "long enough" you mean "until one becomes a virtuoso." Your directive to the would-be virtuoso, then, is nothing more than "Practice until you become a virtuoso, and you will become a virtuoso." In logic, a statement whose predicate repeats its subject, as this one does, is called a **tautology.** When Tillich says "He who knows the depth knows about God," is he actually saying "He who knows about God knows about God"? When he argues "If one is ultimately concerned or has the courage to be, then one knows God," isn't he saying "If one knows God or knows God, then one knows God"? Tillich has been accused of arguing tautologically, of defining something into existence.

Tillich also claims to have an experience of divine presence, of a merging with some fundamental reality. No one may question Tillich's experience; it is as personal as a headache or a hunger pang. But his interpretation of his experience can be questioned. We can and should, it seems, ask for verification when he interprets that experience as resulting from contact with the ground of all being. Tillich must verify the reality of the ground of all being and establish it as the cause of his transcendent experiences.

Tillich would probably reply that the knowledge of his God is a completely different kind of knowledge from that which we customarily speak of. He would argue that his knowledge transcends empirical data and defies scientific verification. It is knowledge whose source is much closer to mystical intuition than to senses or reason, although the latter are instrumental in generating the intu-

A man's religion is the truth he lives habitually, subconsciously and consciously.
BENJAMIN C. LEEMING

tautology a statement whose predicate repeats its subject in whole or in part

itive response. This knowledge is rooted in a personal experience, traditionally induced through prayer and meditation.

FEMINIST THEOLOGY

Many feminists, too, have challenged the traditional Western concept of God and religion. Their most important objections are that God is portrayed as male and is associated with religious beliefs and practices that are oppressive to women.

For example, God has traditionally been said to have no sex, and many philosophers have been careful to emphasize this point. Yet these same philosophers, as well as the majority of people, continue to use male pronouns—*He* and *Him*—to refer to God. Both Christianity and Judaism have traditionally characterized "Him" in male roles, particularly as a male parent, a "Father." The result is that in Western people's real, practical, and lived religious experience, God is thought of as a male despite the denials of philosophers and theologians. The feminist philosopher and theologian Mary Daly, in her groundbreaking book *Beyond God the Father*, has argued that this male conception of God has had a profoundly oppressive impact on women:

> If God in "his" heaven is a father ruling his people then it is in the "nature" of things and according to divine plan and the order of the universe that society be male dominated. Within this context, a *mystification of roles* takes place: The husband dominating his wife represents God "himself." The images and values of a given society have been projected into the realm of dogmas and "Articles of Faith" and these in turn justify the social structures which have given rise to them and which sustain their plausibility.[29]

Moreover, in a surprising reversal of biological fact, Christianity and Judaism have suggested that the woman is born from the man's body and not the man from the woman's. The Old Testament story that Eve, the first female, was made out of Adam's rib implies that males are prior to females and their source. The Judeo-Christian Bible also implies that sin and evil originated with a woman—Eve—who tempted the man—Adam—into the "Fall." Subsequently, Christianity went on to hold that salvation has to come from a male person—Jesus Christ, who is the "Son of God" and whom God sent forth to be crucified as a sacrifice to save us all from sin and evil. Christianity has also given mostly to males—priests and pastors—the authority to lead Christians in their daily lives, and many of the major Christian religions—such as Roman Catholicism—still refuse to ordain women as priests or allow them to become bishops. The most orthodox segments of Judaism have also similarly allowed only males—rabbis—to play leadership roles.

Daly, perhaps the most articulate feminist critic of traditional religious beliefs, summarizes her criticisms of religion in general, and Christianity in particular, in these propositions:

---

[29] Mary Daly, *Beyond God the Father* (Boston: Beacon, 1974), 206.

There exists a planetary sexual caste system [patriarchy], essentially the same in Saudi Arabia and in New York, differing only in degree.

This system is masked by sex role segregation, by the dual identity of women, by ideologies and myths. . . .

All of the major world religions function to legitimate patriarchy. This is true also of the popular cults such as the Krisna movement and the Jesus Freaks.

The myths and symbols of Christianity are essentially sexist. Since "God" is male, the male is God. . . .

The myth of feminine evil, expressed in the story of the Fall, is reinforced by the myth of salvation/redemption by a single human being of the male sex [Jesus Christ]. The idea of a unique divine incarnation in a male, the God-man of the "hypostatic union," is inherently sexist and oppressive. Christolatry is idolatry.[30]

Daly argues that by making God male, males have been able to use God to justify and maintain their power and authority over women: It is right for males to rule since the highest "leader"—God—and the "savior"—Jesus Christ— are male. Moreover, since women are the source of evil and had their origins in man (Adam's rib), it is appropriate that they be ruled by men. Thus, the traditional male concept of God has played and continues to play a major role in keeping women oppressed and dominated by men.

Daly and other feminist thinkers have suggested that the male concept of God cannot be reformed because it has too many masculine connotations that make it oppressive to women. Maleness is an essential part of the traditional Western concept of God and cannot be separated from it. Instead, the concept must be abandoned, allowed to wither and die, and replaced with new religious symbols and concepts associated with "The Goddess":

> For some feminists concerned with the spiritual depth of the movement, the word "God" is becoming increasingly problematic, however. This by no means indicates a movement in the direction of "atheism" or "agnosticism." . . . Some reluctantly still use the word "God" while earnestly trying to divest the term of its patriarchal associations, attempting to think perhaps of the "God of the philosophers" rather than the overtly masculist and oppressive "God of the theologians." But the problem becomes increasingly troublesome, the more the "God" of the various Western philosophers is subjected to feminist analysis. "He"—"Jahweh"—still often hovers behind the abstractions, stunting our own thought, giving us a sense of contrived doublethink. The word "God" just may be inherently oppressive. . . .
>
> For an increasing minority of women—and even for some men—"Goddess" is becoming more functional, meaningful, and loaded with healing associations. . . . The use of the expression, "The Goddess," is a way . . . of exorcising the male "God," and of affirming a different myth/reality.[31]

A significant and growing number of women, Daly holds, are breaking away from the Judeo-Christian concept of God, which "legitimates patriarchy—the prevailing power structure and prevailing world view." Efforts to reform these Western religions, she claims, are useless and will "eventually come to be recognized as comparable to a Black person's trying to reform the Ku Klux Klan."

---

[30]Mary Daly, "The Qualitative Leap Beyond Patriarchal Religion," *Quest*, vol. 1, no. 4 (Spring 1975), 20.
[31]Ibid., 33.

Instead, feminists who seek a religious dimension in their lives are increasingly finding meaning in "The Goddess." They are creating a revolutionary and powerful new community, a new "sisterhood," that rejects the prevailing male view that power must be understood as power *over* people. In the consciousness of this new sisterhood, power is experienced as "power of presence to ourselves and to each other." This new movement is not hierarchical; that is, unlike male organizations, it is not based on leaders who have "power" over their followers. Thus, the notion of "The Goddess" will not lead to an oppressive female-dominated society like the male-dominated society that the notion of a male God has been used to produce:

> More than this: radical feminism means saying "Yes" to our original birth, the original movement-surge toward life. This is both a remembering and a rediscovering. Athena remembers and rediscovers her Mother. That which is generated between us is Sisterhood. We are then no longer confined by our identities as "Mother" or "Daughter." The Daughter is *not* obedient to the Mother "unto death." The Mother does not send her forth to be crucified for the sins of women or of men. Rather, they go forth as Sisters. Radical feminism releases the inherent dynamic in the Mother-Daughter relationship toward Sisterhood, which is thwarted within the Male-mastered system. The Mother does *not* demand self-sacrifice of the Daughter. Rather, both demand of each other affirmation of the self and of each other in an ongoing personal/political process which is mythic in its depths—which is both exorcising and remythologizing process.[32]

Daly is perhaps the harshest and most extreme critic of traditional religious concepts, and it is certainly difficult for men not to feel put off by her strong language and unrelenting attacks on everything that is male. Nevertheless, many of her criticisms of religion are incisive and telling blows against the often-oppressive maleness of the traditional Western concept of God and the sexism that affects much of traditional Western religious thought. It cannot be denied that these traditions have been used to justify the so-called right of men to rule over women. Thus, although one might argue with this or that element of the feminist perspective represented by Daly, much of what she says rings absolutely true.

Nevertheless, many feminists, while agreeing with much of Daly's critique, have objected to several facets of her thinking. In particular, some feminist theologians have questioned whether the male features of the traditional Western concepts of God and religion are really as necessary and essential to these as Daly claims they are. For example, as the feminist theologian Pamela Dickey Young writes,

> The maleness of God could be questioned on the grounds of intellectual credibility as well, for any God that could be either male or female could not be the kind of God whom Christians claim. Any God who is the universal, omnipresent God Christians claim is not subject to the biological definitions and limitations of human beings. . . .
>   Although for Christians it is in Jesus that they see God's presence, God's love and care exemplified, that this decisive revelation has taken place in a man is, in a very

---

[32] Ibid., 28.

real sense, accidental. . . . From God's point of view, females are as apt as males to be such representative figures. . . .

Although God's re-presentation of Godself to Christians takes a male form [Jesus Christ], this can in no way be used to argue that God could never be represented in a female form. . . .

But does this re-presentative function where a male is the re-presentative [of God] imply the maleness of God? Clearly, if I am right about how others, both male and female, might also be seen as revealing God, as re-presentations of God, then the maleness of one savior figure does not imply anything about the maleness of God. Also, as I have argued [above] . . . , as much as Christians have implied the maleness of God by what they have said, such maleness, given what Christians have understood by the concept of "God," is incredible.[33]

Young is arguing here that the male qualities attached to the concept of God and to Christianity are not necessary to either. Male qualities are "accidental" or nonessential elements that got attached to God and to Christianity when these were introduced into human societies that were already sexist and dominated by males: "Because of our long history of the oppression and degradation of women, patriarchal cultures and societies are more apt to recognize the representation of God in a male." Thus, for Young and for other feminist theologians, the traditional Western concepts of God and religion need not be male-centered. On the contrary, Young argues, it is the task of the feminist to identify the sexist, oppressive, and male elements that have infected these and to work for reform.

It is not clear whether feminists such as Young can succeed in purging the Western concepts of God and religion of their sexist leanings. Daly may be correct when she writes that "dressing up old symbols just will not work for women who are conscious of sexist religiosity." Both Daly and Young are inviting us to come with them on different journeys toward an understanding of God and religion that is neither sexist nor oppressive. But where either of those journeys will lead—or even whether they will succeed in going anywhere—is still unclear. What is clear is that each one of us has to make his or her own journey toward an understanding—or rejection—of God and religion.

EASTERN RELIGIOUS TRADITIONS

Eastern religious traditions are many and varied. It is neither our intention nor within our capabilities to mention all of them, let alone discuss them adequately. But we outline two religions to which many Westerners are turning for meaningful religious experience: Hinduism and Buddhism.

Hinduism

One of the oldest Eastern traditions is Hinduism, which has been practiced by hundreds of millions of people for about five thousand years. Hinduism has many divisions and subdivisions, and no leader or belief is accepted by every Hindu sect. In fact, Hinduism is so diversified that it is very difficult to describe

---

[33] Pamela Dickey Young, *Feminist Theology/Christian Theology* (Minneapolis: Fortress Press, 1990), 97, 98, 99, 101.

as a whole. Any attempt at description is bound to be an oversimplification. A further complication is that our language has no precise equivalents for certain Indian terms and concepts.

Aware of these limitations, let us begin with the literary source of Hindu teaching. Although many texts form the body of Hindu scripture, one has influenced Hindu thought more than any other: the Bhagavad-Gita, the Song of the Lord, which is part of the great epic Mahabharata. Reading the Gita will introduce you to the principal concepts of Hinduism, as well as to beautiful poetry.

One concept common to all expressions of Hinduism is the oneness of reality. This oneness is the absolute, or **Brahman,** which the mind can never fully grasp or words express. Only Brahman is real; everything else is an illusory manifestation of it. A correlative belief is the concept of **atman,** or no self. What we commonly call "I" or the self is an illusion, for each true self is one with Brahman. When we realize this unity with the absolute, we realize our true destiny.

Also common to all Hindu thought are four primary values. In order of increasing importance, they may be roughly translated as wealth, pleasure, duty, and enlightenment. Wealth and pleasure are worldly values, but when kept in perspective they are good and desirable. The spiritual value of duty, or righteousness, refers to patience, sincerity, fairness, love, honesty, and similar virtues. The highest spiritual value, though, is enlightenment, by which one is illuminated and liberated and, most importantly, finds release from the wheel of existence. Repeated existence is the destiny of those who do not achieve enlightenment.

To understand enlightenment you must understand the law of **karma,** the law of sowing and reaping. All of us, through what we do or do not do, supposedly determine our destiny. If we are particularly evil, we may find ourselves reborn as subhumans. If we are noble, we may be reborn as especially favored humans. This wheel of existence turns until we achieve enlightenment, after which we are released from this series of rebirths.

Sri Sarvepalli Radhakrishnan, the Hindu philosopher whom you previously met in Chapter 1, lists in *A Source Book in Indian Philosophy*[34] seven other characteristics common to all Indian thought. First is an emphasis on the spiritual. It is the spiritual that endures and is ultimately real. Second is the realization that our philosophy and our life are inextricably enmeshed. What we believe is how we live; if our beliefs are in error, our lives will be unhappy. Third is a preoccupation with the inner life. The road to enlightenment stretches not outward but inward. To understand nature and the universe, we must turn within. Fourth is an emphasis on the nonmaterial oneness of creation. There are no polarities; a single spirit provides cosmic harmony. Fifth is the acceptance of direct awareness as the only way to understand what is real. The Indian believer finds this direct perception through spiritual exercises, perhaps through the practice of yoga. Reason is of some use, but in the last analysis we know only through an inner experience of oneness with all of creation. Sixth is a healthy respect for tradition, but never a slavish commitment to it. The past can teach but never rule. Finally, Indian thought recognizes the complementary nature of

Brahman the Hindu concept of an impersonal Supreme Being; the source and goal of everything

atman the Hindu idea of the self after enlightenment; the concept of no self

karma the Hindu law of sowing and reaping; determines what form and circumstances we assume in each reincarnated state

---

[34]Sarvepalli Radhakrishnan and Charles A. Moore, eds., *A Source Book in Indian Philosophy* (Princeton, NJ: Princeton University Press, 1957), xx–xxvi.

Dancing Ganesha, India, ninth century. To understand enlightenment you must understand the law of karma, the law of sowing and reaping. The wheel of existence turns until we achieve enlightenment, after which we are released from this series of rebirths.

all systems of belief. Hinduism is not rooted in any single doctrine, nor does it claim a monopoly on truth or wisdom. It preaches tolerance of all sincere viewpoints and includes many of these within its own spiritual teachings.

Buddhism

Another major Eastern tradition is Buddhism, contained in the teachings of its founder, Siddhartha Gautama, or the Buddha. Since Gautama found no evidence for belief in a personal God, his teachings are a diagnosis of and a prescription for the "disease" of living.

The Buddha preached the Four Noble Truths. As we saw in Chapter 2, the Buddha held that everything in the universe is continually changing: Everything that lives falls into death and rises again to new life, only to fall again into death in a ceaseless round of loss and suffering. Our cravings keep us returning to this passing world through successive "rebirths." Release from this suffering, he preached, could only be gained by putting an end to this craving for pleasure, for continued life, and for power. And the key to ending this craving is following the Noble Eightfold Path:

> And this is the Noble Truth of Sorrow. Birth is sorrow, age is sorrow, disease is sorrow, death is sorrow; contact with the unpleasant is sorrow, separation from the pleasant is sorrow, every wish unfulfilled is sorrow—in short, all the five components of individuality are sorrow.
>
> And this is the Noble Truth of the Arising of Sorrow. It arises from craving, which leads to rebirth, which brings delight and passion, and seeks pleasure now here, now there—the craving for sensual pleasure, the craving for continued life, the craving for power.
>
> And this is the Noble Truth of the Stopping of Sorrow. It is the complete stopping of that craving, so that no passion remains, leaving it, being emancipated from it, being released from it, giving no place to it.
>
> And this is the Noble Truth of the Way which leads to the Stopping of Sorrow. It is the Noble Eightfold Path—[having] Right Views, Right Resolve, Right Speech, Right Conduct, Right Livelihood, Right Effort, Right Mindfulness, and Right Concentration.[35]

It might be useful to show how the Eight Noble Truths contrast with some of Tillich's ideas. The First Noble Truth, which is concerned with the suffering that we experience in living, Tillich might call existential despair, although he would attribute it to theism. The Second Noble Truth identifies the cause of this suffering or, more accurately, this frustration: clinging or grasping based on **avidya**—ignorance and unawareness. The person who lacks awareness is committed to the world of things and illusion, *maya*, and not to the concrete world of reality. The unaware person also tries to control himself and the environment. These attempts are futile; the result is self-frustration and the viciously circular pattern of life called **samsara,** the round of birth and death. Tillich might see this as the false subject–object distinction that we customarily make. The Third Noble Truth concerns the ending of samsara, called nirvana—release or liberation. We achieve nirvana when we stop grasping and clinging; then we are released from the round of incarnations and enter a state that defies definition. Tillich would call it experiencing the depth, the ground of all being. The Fourth Noble Truth describes the Eightfold Path of the Buddha's **dharma**—that is, the moral doctrine whereby self-frustration is ended. We will examine this concept more carefully in Chapter 7.

avidya in Buddhism, the cause of all suffering and frustration; ignorance or unawareness that leads to clinging

samsara in Buddhism, the round of birth and death

dharma in Buddhism, the doctrine whereby self-frustration is ended; the Eightfold Path

Zen Buddhism

Of the many forms of Buddhism practiced today, Zen Buddhism has been particularly attractive to Westerners. Japanese scholar D. T. Suzuki has rendered the philosophy of Zen Buddhism marvelously accessible to the Western mind.

---

[35] William Theodore de Bary, *Sources of Indian Tradition*, vol. 1, from *Samyutta Nikaya* (New York: Columbia University Press, 1958), 99.

In "Zen Buddhism" he shows how Zen has established itself firmly on a teaching that claims to be

> A special transmission outside the Scripture;
> No dependence on words or letters;
> Direct pointing at the Mind of Man;
> Seeing into one's Nature and the attainment of Buddhahood.[36]

These four lines, says Suzuki, describe the essentials of Zen Buddhism and provide insight into its religious impulses.

Suzuki points out that the first line does not imply the existence of an esoteric Buddhist teaching that came to be known as Zen. Quite the opposite is true. "A special transmission outside the Scripture" is understood by reference to the second line, which asserts Zen's lack of dependence on words and letters. "Words and letters" and "the Scripture" stand for conceptualism and all that the term implies. Zen abhors and avoids words and concepts, as well as the reasoning based on them. It views preoccupation with ideas and words as an empty substitute for experience.

In contrast, Zen upholds the direct experience of reality. It does not tolerate secondhand accounts or authoritative renderings of reality. Zen followers aspire to drink from the fountain of life rather than to listen to accounts of it. The ultimate truth is a state of inner experience achieved by means of wisdom. This state is beyond the realm of words and discriminations. To discriminate is to be caught in the endless cycle of birth and death with no hope of emancipation, attainment of nirvana, or realization of Buddhahood.

How, then, are we emancipated? How does Zen help one achieve nirvana or Buddhahood? In answering this, Zen reminds us that we live in a world of dualities, of contradictory opposites. To be emancipated from the world may mean to leave or to deny it. Some people have taken this to mean self-destruction, but Suzuki suggests that this is a misinterpretation of Zen teaching. It is the mere amassing of knowledge, the storing of shopworn concepts, that is self-destructive. Rather, emancipation consists of recognizing the inadequacy of explanations and discriminations, of rejecting the notion that an explanation of a thing or fact exhausts the subject. For Zen, there is no better explanation than actual experience, and actual experience is all that is needed to attain Buddhahood.

To grasp the meaning of the last two lines—"Direct pointing at the Mind of Man; / Seeing into one's Nature and the attainment of Buddhahood"—we must understand what is meant by *Mind, Nature,* and *Buddhahood.*

Mind does not refer to our ordinary functioning mind, the mind that thinks according to the laws of logic and psychological explanations. It is the mind that lies beneath all of these thoughts and feelings. For the Zen Buddhist, the Mind is also known as Nature—that is, reality. We may look on the Mind as the last point that we reach when we dig down psychologically into the depths of a thinking and feeling subject. Nature is the limit of objectivity. But the natural objective limit is the psychological subjective limit, and vice versa. When we reach the

---

[36] Daisetz T. Suzuki, "Zen Buddhism," in *The Essentials of Zen Buddhism*, ed. Bernard Phillips (New York: Dutton, 1962), 73.

one, we find ourselves in the other. True, in each case we start differently: We go out to Nature; we go in to ourselves. But in the end, the two merge. When we have the Mind, we have Nature. When we understand Nature, we understand the Mind. They are one and the same.

Now we can speak of enlightenment, of Buddhahood. The person who has a thorough understanding of the Mind and whose movements are at one with Nature is the Buddha, the enlightened one. Nature personified is the Buddha. In effect, then, Mind, Nature, and Buddha are three different points of reference for reality. The ideal of Zen, then, as expressed in the four lines, is to seize reality without the interference of any agency—intellectual, moral, or ritualistic.

The direct holding of reality is the awakening of **prajñā** transcendental wisdom. Transcendental wisdom answers all questions that we can formulate about our spiritual life. Thus, wisdom is not the intellect in the ordinary sense. It transcends dialectics of all kinds. It is not analytical reasoning but a leap over the intellectual impasse, and in this it is an act of will. At the same time, it sees into nature. There is a noetic quality about it. It is both will and intuition. Zen is associated with willpower, because avoiding the tendency to analyze and intellectualize requires an act of will, an individual effort. Outsiders can only help by reminding us that all outside help is futile.

> **prajñā** in Zen Buddhism, transcendental wisdom

The literature of Zen glitters with anecdotal reminders of this. An especially graphic story involves a Zen Buddhist monk who is asked about the depths of the Zen River while he is walking over a bridge. At once he seizes the questioner and would have hurled him into the rapids had others not frantically interceded. The monk wanted the questioner to go down to the bottom of the river to take its measure.

The basic principle of Zen is the growth or self-maturing of the inner experience. People used to intellectual exercises, moral persuasion, and devotional exercises will find Zen a disarming if not heretical teaching. But this is precisely what makes Zen unique in the history of religion. It proposes that we look within a thing to understand it. In contrast, we usually describe a thing from the outside to understand it; we speak of it in objective terms. Although this objective method has its place and value, Zen proposes a method that for millions gives the key to an effective and all-satisfying understanding.

Differences Between East and West

Obviously, there is much more to Hinduism, Buddhism, and Zen than we have outlined. Nevertheless, these sketches illustrate major differences between Eastern and Western thought. Let's consider these differences more closely.

First, the East rejects the West's "objectified" God. There is no claim of a personal, all-knowing, all-good, all-powerful, and all-loving God as there is in the Western tradition. As a result, Eastern thinkers have never debated God's existence. As a corollary, Buddhism does not share the Western view that there is a moral law, enjoined by God or by nature, that it is our duty to obey. In contrast, Western religions frequently include behavioral proscriptions that if violated may lead to eternal damnation. In short, our tradition presents a God who expects us to behave in a certain way. In contrast,

The Buddha's precepts of conduct—abstinence from taking life, taking what is not given, exploitation of the passions, lying, and intoxication—are voluntarily assumed rules of expedience, the intent of which is to remove the hindrances to clarity of awareness. Failure to observe the precepts produces bad "*karma*" not because *karma* is a law or moral retribution, but because all motivated and purposeful actions, whether conventionally good or bad, are *karma* insofar as they are directed to the grasping of life. Generally speaking, the conventionally "bad" actions are rather more grasping than the "good."[37]

Moreover, whereas the thrust of Western religion traditionally has been to align us with our divine Creator, Eastern thought (like Tillich's emphasis on being) aims to ground us in what is real. To do so, Eastern thought generally prescribes discipline, self-control, moderation, and detachment. Although these values are frequently observed in Western religious practice, they are usually practiced as means to an end: salvation and reward. Though they are ways of attaining wisdom and truth, they are also ways of avoiding damnation.

Perhaps these differences explain why there has been a growing interest in the United States in Eastern thinking and religions. Many people are turning away from traditional faiths in favor of Zen Buddhism, Yoga, transcendental meditation, Krishna Consciousness, Vedanta, and so on. Obviously, converts to Eastern religions have not stopped asking about their place in the scheme of things. On the contrary, they are asking perhaps more intensely than ever before. Apparently, the traditional concepts of self, subject–object distinction, Judeo-Christian dogma, the egocentric emphasis on one's personal relationship with a theistic God, and the dismissal of nonhuman natural objects as essentially inferior and alien are no longer meaningful for them. Many features of Eastern thought allow people to explore in new directions: the emphasis on the workings of the mind and inner growth; the importance of discipline, practice, and method; a distrust of doctrines and dogmas; and hope for integrating body and intellect, feelings and reason, through a personal philosophy. But a central feature seems to be the reevaluation and redefinition of one's traditional concept of the divine and one's relationship to it.

Yet the many differences between Eastern thought and Western outlook should not be ignored. In the end they pose the fundamental question that the Westerner must ask about Eastern religion: Is it too alien to be truly understood by us? Is it too alien to meet our standards of what is reasonable? Is it too alien to be ultimately meaningful for us?

All religions pronounce the name of God in their particular language. As a rule it is better for a man to name God in his native tongue rather than in one that is foreign to him.

SIMONE WEIL

QUESTIONS

1. In your own words, what is Tillich's objection to traditional or theological theism? Are you sympathetic to Tillich's objections? If so, cite instances to illustrate that your sympathy is grounded in experience.

2. Anglican bishop John Robinson has said, "The traditional material is all true, no doubt, and one recognizes it as something one ought to be able to respond

---

[37] Alan Watts, *The Way of Zen* (New York: Pantheon, 1957), 61. Reprinted by permission.

to, but somehow it seems to be going on around one rather than within. Yet to question it openly is to appear to let down the side, to be branded as hopelessly unspiritual, and to cause others to stumble." First interpret this statement; then explain it from the viewpoint of a church leader. Finally, ask yourself if it has any meaning for you.

3. Anselm's ontological argument claims that existence is a necessary part of the meaning of a perfect being. Is Tillich similarly claiming that God is a necessary part of the meaning of "ultimately concerned"? Is he defining God into existence?

4. Some people claim that the mere fact that Tillich interprets his own knowledge of the "depth" as an experience of God does not make it so. Neither does it guarantee the existence of God. Are such critics distinguishing between belief and knowledge? How?

5. Some people compare Tillich's claim that experience of the "ground of all being" is an experience of God to the claim "I have a toothache because some mad genius has possessed my body and is causing the pain." Evaluate this analogy.

6. Do you think that Tillich's claims need public verification, as critics say they do? Is Tillich talking about a completely different kind of knowledge, a knowledge that transcends empirical data? In what ways is this a mystical knowledge?

7. Would you say that James's two characteristics of a mystical experience would also apply to a drug-induced state of consciousness?

8. Do you agree that the Western concept of God is sexist? If not, how do you respond to Daly's criticisms? If you agree that our idea of God is sexist, then do you believe it can be changed?

9. What would you say are the main sources of attraction for Westerners in Eastern thought?

10. What obstacles would you note that many Westerners might face in adjusting to Eastern thought?

4.6 Chapter Summary and Conclusions

All religions speak of personal commitment and experience and of our need to find our place in the cosmic scheme of things. Traditionally in the West, these phenomena have been sought through a relationship to a personal, theistic God, and many arguments have been assembled for God's existence. Seeing weaknesses in the theistic position, however, many people have adopted pantheism or panentheism, others atheism or agnosticism.

Whether or not God exists, the question of religious belief persists and affects our lives. For many people, this decision involves a relationship not to a personal God but to a divine dimension to the universe, which they sense through personal experience. There has been a growing emphasis on this kind of personal experience as the basis of religious belief. In this connection we examined mysticism and movements with mystical overtones, such as radical theology and Eastern religious thought. The main points of this chapter are the following:

1. Traditionally, religion refers to a belief in God that is institutionalized and incorporated in the teachings of some religious body, such as a church or synagogue. Today, emphasis is on deep personal experience with the object of one's chief loyalty (4.1).

2. Theism is the belief in a personal God who has created the world and is immanent in its processes, and with whom we may come into intimate contact (4.2).

3. Three traditional arguments for a theistic God are the ontological argument (such as Saint Anselm's), the cosmological argument (such as Saint Thomas Aquinas's), and the argument from design (such as William Paley's). Each of these arguments has its critics (4.2).

4. Besides the traditional objections made to these arguments, critics have raised objections to the traditional concept of God: How can God be all-knowing and yet not suffer along with us? How can God be unchanging and yet have perfect knowledge of our changing world (4.2)?

5. In response, pantheism argues that everything is God and God is everything, whereas panentheism argues that everything is in God, who is both fixed and changing, unity and diversity, inclusive of all possibilities (4.2).

6. Atheism and agnosticism are responses to the difficulties in the traditional arguments for a theistic God. Atheism claims that we know God does not exist, arguing particularly that the existence of evil implies there is no all-good and all-powerful God. Agnostics claim that we know neither that God exists nor that God does not exist (4.3).

7. William James called the acquisition of religious belief a live, forced, and momentous option (4.4).

8. Many people, unable to find religious belief or experience in a theistic God, find both in a deep personal encounter with a divine dimension (4.4).

9. Mysticism claims direct and immediate awareness that is not dependent on direct sense experience or on reason. The mystical experience is inexpressible and noetic. It has the characteristics of the numinous (4.4).

10. Radical theology, as presented by Søren Kierkegaard and Paul Tillich, has mystical overtones (4.5). It appeals to deep personal experience as justification for belief. Tillich's God is being itself, the "God above God," the "ground of all being."

11. Feminist theology has argued that much in the Western concept of God and religion is sexist and that these sexist notions have been used to oppress women. Feminist theologian Mary Daly claims that these notions cannot be reformed and should be abandoned in favor of female symbolism and female religious communities. Other feminist theologians disagree and argue for reform from within (4.5).

12. Eastern religious views, such as Hinduism, Buddhism, and Zen Buddhism, are highly sympathetic to claims of personal religious experience (4.5).

Clearly, the philosophy of religion has had a long and illustrious history that continues to unfold. The concept of religious experience is inextricably linked with a psychology of self, for religious experience is one way that we can integrate our personalities and lives and thereby achieve wholeness. Perhaps this wholeness is what psychologist Abraham Maslow means when he speaks of "peak experiences," vivid moments in our lives when everything seems to fall into place, when our vision is clear, our lives meaningful, and our place in the order of things certain.[38]

The moments that Maslow describes seem linked to feelings of self-fulfillment, achievement, and creativity. Thus, they can happen to anyone. But we must allow them to happen; we must open ourselves to them. Hasn't this element of personal receptivity always been an integral part of religious teaching, of the numinous? Isn't it there even if often buried under pomp and ceremony?

Humanistic psychology has suggested ways of getting in touch with the self and thereby with religious impulses. It has spurred interest in expanding our awareness of self by increasing our creativity, improving our health, enhancing our learning and problem solving, and, most important, providing ecstatic experiences. Mind and brain investigations that attempt to see the human from all sides have led to new concepts of self that originate in a kind of religious experience, in which we experience self and reality in a new and different way.

Rather than viewing humans as a bundle of responses to stimuli, we now accept the richness and complexity of the human and the importance of each individual. Central to this emphasis on the individual is a recognition of wholeness. Can the centuries-old split between mind and body be abandoned for a *holistic* approach that recognizes the inseparability of mind and body and the influence of each on the other? Appropriately, we recognize more clearly the roles of emotions and spiritual feelings in our lives and the limitations of logic and rationality. As a rule, subjective experience is gaining respect in scientific circles, a place heretofore reserved for objective experience. The realization that science and individual experience are not incompatible is growing. In addition, whereas we once had presumed ourselves to be objects of Freud's subconscious forces, we have now found a belief in our own capacity for growth, self-transcendence, or what Maslow calls self-actualization.

The potential for what we have been calling religious experience is staggering. In the future, areas of conscious awareness that we hardly dream of today may open up. This awareness will no doubt be accompanied by a deep and reverent sensitivity to the profound mystery of life and our wondrous part in it.

---

[38] See Abraham Maslow, *Toward a Psychology of Being* (New York: D. Van Nostrand, 1968).

4.7 HISTORICAL SHOWCASE

Aquinas, Descartes, and Conway

In this chapter we have examined a broad range of philosophical issues raised by belief in God. But we have tended to treat these issues in isolation from other philosophical questions. By contrast, most major philosophers have felt that questions about God are deeply related to other important philosophical issues. For this reason, philosophers' views on God have profoundly influenced their positions on other philosophical questions.

Here we showcase three philosophers whose views about God determine their views on other important philosophical issues: Thomas Aquinas, René Descartes, and Anne Conway. By examining their work, we get an idea of how these three philosophers incorporate God into a large philosophical system. Moreover, in becoming acquainted with them, we will see how a person's position on one philosophical issue can dramatically affect and interact with that person's views on other issues in philosophy.

Thomas Aquinas: "There must be something which is the cause of the Being, Goodness, and other perfections of things, and this we call God. . . . The eternal law is the plan in God's mind in accordance with which every motion of the universe is governed."

AQUINAS

No period of history has been more preoccupied by religion than the medieval era, and the greatest of the medieval thinkers was Thomas Aquinas. Although Aquinas was influenced by the writings of Aristotle, he was also deeply affected by the events of the fifteen centuries (322 B.C. to A.D. 1225) that separated him from Aristotle, Plato, and the other Greek philosophers. Those centuries saw the Roman Empire (ca. 300 B.C. to ca. A.D. 500) rise and spread over Europe and also witnessed the birth of Christianity at the very height of the empire's power. They also saw the collapse of civilization, as barbarian tribes repeatedly invaded the empire until, after centuries of battering, it was destroyed and Europe descended into the Dark Ages.

During the Dark Ages, Christianity spread gradually, but most philosophy ceased while men and women concentrated on surviving in the barbaric world that Europe had become.

It was not until Aquinas's times that conditions in Europe once again became conducive to philosophical activities and that new centers of learning—the first universities—were established. But the Europe that emerged from the Dark Ages had become completely Christianized; consequently, philosophy tended to focus on religious concerns. It was only natural that Thomas Aquinas's thinking should focus on the philosophical problems raised by the religion that now dominated Europe.

Born in 1225 to a wealthy family of the Italian nobility, Saint Thomas Aquinas was raised to hold high office in the Roman Catholic church, a position that his family hoped would prove advantageous to their political fortunes. In preparation for this career, the family sent him at the age of five to study in a Benedictine monastery, where he remained until he entered the University of Naples at the age of fourteen. At Naples, Thomas came into contact with the Dominicans, an inspiring order of monks dedicated to poverty and to service through teaching. In spite of vigorous opposition from his family, Thomas entered the Dominican Order in 1241, dashing his family's hopes for his ecclesiastical career. Four years later the order sent him to the new University of Paris to study under Albert the Great, a scholar of towering intellect already famous for his knowledge of Aristotle's doctrines. Under Albert's influence, Thomas began to draw heavily on Aristotle's teachings, gradually producing a brilliant synthesis of Christian theology and Aristotelian philosophy. Aquinas remained a dedicated Christian scholar and teacher throughout his life, churning out a prodigious number of writings until his death in 1274. In his two greatest works, the *Summa Contra Gentiles* and the *Summa Theologica*, Thomas addresses virtually every philosophical issue raised by Christianity and resolves them in a way that many feel is philosophically sound yet true to the Christian faith. Aquinas's philosophy, in fact, often has been called the Christian philosophy and is still held by a large number of Christians.

Aquinas did not confuse religious faith with philosophy. With great care he distinguished among truths that are known by faith, truths that are known by reason, and truths that are known by both faith and reason. Philosophy, he held, consists of truths that our unaided reason can discover by reflecting on our natural experience in the world. Theology, on the other hand, begins with truths that have been revealed by God through Scripture and accepted by faith and from these revealed truths draws further religious truths. There is some overlap between philosophy and theology, however, because some truths that can be discovered by our unaided reason have also been revealed by God:

> Some truths about God exceed the capacity of our human reason. An example of this is the truth that God is three persons in one. But there are some truths that reason by its very nature is also able to discover. Examples of these are the truths that God exists, that there is only one God, and similar truths. In fact, these truths about God have been proved by several philosophers who have relied completely on the light of their natural reason.[1]

Central to Aquinas's philosophy are his famous five proofs for the existence of God (one of which is the cosmological proof), some of which were influenced by Aristotle's views on causes. Each of the proofs begins by pointing to some aspect of the world we experience: its motion, its causality, its contingency, its imperfection, or its unthinking order. Each proof then argues that this aspect of the world cannot account for itself: Each aspect depends for its existence on something—a Divine Being—that is utterly different from the objects we experience. The motion of objects demands the existence of an unmoved mover, the causality we see at work demands the existence of something that is uncaused, the contingency of objects demands the existence of something that is noncontingent, the existence of imperfect objects demands the existence of something that is perfect, and the existence of order among objects that do not think demands the existence of something that thinks and that produces that order:

> That God exists can be proved in five ways.
>
> The first and clearest way is the argument from motion. It is certain and evident to our senses that some things in the world are in motion. Now if something is moved, it must be moved by something else. . . . For nothing can change from being potentially in motion to being in a state of actual movement unless something else that is in actual movement acts on it. . . . So whatever is moving must be moved by something else. Now if that by which it is moved is itself moving, then it, too, must be moved by something else, and that by something else again. But this cannot go on to infinity because then there would be no first mover. And if there were no first mover, then nothing would move since each subsequent mover will move only to the extent that it is moved by the motion imparted by the first mover. The [other] parts of a staff, for example, will

---

[1] Saint Thomas Aquinas, *Summa Contra Gentiles*, I, q.3, a.2. This edited translation is by Manuel Velasquez.

move only to the extent that the [top of the] staff is moved by the hand. Therefore, there must be a first mover that is not moved. And this first unmoved mover is what we mean by God.

The second way is based on the nature of efficient causes. In the world we see around us, there are ordered lines of efficient causes [in which each member of the line produces the next member]. But nothing can be its own efficient cause, since then it would have to exist prior to itself and this is impossible. Now it is not possible for a line of efficient causes to extend to infinity. For in any line of efficient causes, the first is the cause of the intermediate ones, and the intermediate ones cause the last one. Now if we remove any of the causes, we remove all the remaining effects. So if there were no first cause then there would be no last cause nor any intermediate ones. But if a line of efficient causes extended back to infinity, then we would find no first cause. Consequently, if the line of causes extended back to infinity, there would be no intermediate causes nor any last causes in existence in the universe. But we know this is false. So it is necessary to admit that there is a first efficient cause. And this we call God.

The third way is based on contingency and necessity. It proceeds as follows. We find in nature things that are contingent. These are things that are generated and that can corrupt, and which therefore can exist or can cease to exist. Now it is impossible for such contingent things to exist forever. For if it is possible for something to cease existing, then eventually a moment will come when it will cease to exist. Therefore, if everything were contingent, then eventually everything would have ceased existing. If this happened, then even now nothing would exist, because something can start to exist only through the action of something that already exists. It follows that not everything is contingent, that is, some things must exist necessarily, that is, forever. Now every necessary thing is caused to exist forever either by something else or not by anything else. But as we proved above, it is impossible for a line of causes to be infinite. So there must exist something which derives its necessary existence from itself and not from something else, and which causes the existence of all other necessary beings. This is what we all mean by God.

The fourth way is based on the degrees of perfection that we find in things. Among the objects in our world some are more and some less good, true, noble, and the like. But to say that a thing has more or less of a certain perfection is to say that it resembles to a greater or lesser degree something which perfectly exemplifies that perfection. . . . So there must be something which is most perfectly true, most perfectly good, most perfectly noble, and, consequently, which most perfectly exists (since, as Aristotle shows, those things that are perfectly true also exist perfectly). Now that which most perfectly exemplifies some quality, also causes other things to have that quality to a greater or lesser degree. Fire, for example, which most perfectly exemplifies the quality of heat, is the cause of the heat in hot things. Therefore, there must be something which is the cause of the being, goodness, and every other perfection in things. And this we call God.

The fifth way of proving God's existence is based on the order in the universe. We see that things which lack knowledge, such as natural objects, act for an end. That is, their activity is always or nearly always aimed at achieving the best result. It is clear, therefore, that their activity is not produced by chance but by design. Now things which lack knowledge cannot move unerringly toward an end unless they are directed toward that end by some being that has knowledge and intelligence much like an arrow is directed toward its target by an archer. Therefore there must exist an intelligent Being Who directs all natural things toward their respective ends. This Being we call God.[2]

Aquinas says that each of the five proofs for the existence of God tells us something about God. The first proof implies that unlike anything in the universe, God imparts motion to everything without moving and therefore without being in time or being material. The second implies that unlike anything we know, God is the uncreated creator that causes everything to exist. The third tells us that—again unlike anything in our experience—God cannot cease existing because God's existence does not depend on anything else. The fourth tells us that unlike anything in the universe, God is perfect goodness, perfect truth, perfect nobility, and perfect existence. And the fifth tells us that God is the supremely wise intelligence in whom all the order in the universe originates.

---

[2] Saint Thomas Aquinas, *Summa Theologica*, I, q.2, a.3. This translation copyright © 1978 by Manuel Velasquez.

Nevertheless, Aquinas cautions, there is such a vast gulf between ourselves and God that the knowledge of God that we can glean from the five proofs is very imperfect. Each proof merely tells us that some aspect of the universe we experience requires the existence of something else that is *unlike* anything in that universe and therefore *unlike* anything in our experience. Aquinas expresses this idea by asserting that although the proofs show us *that* God is, they do not tell us *what* God is. The proofs gives us what Aquinas calls a "negative way" of knowing God. They do not give us a positive conception of God but lead us to *remove* certain ideas from our conception of God: God is *not* in motion, God is *not* created, God is *not* dependent, God is *not* imperfectly good, God is *not* guided by blind instinct.

But does this *via negativa*—this negative approach—provide us with the only knowledge we have of God? Are we doomed to know only what God is *not* and never to have any positive knowledge of God? At first sight it would seem that we could never have any positive knowledge of God, because all our positive knowledge is based on our experience of the universe, and God is unlike anything in our experience. However, Aquinas identifies an imperfect kind of positive knowledge of God that is open to us. He calls this "knowledge by analogy" or "analogical knowledge" of God.

Aquinas explains analogical knowledge as follows: He points out that there are certain words—such as *good*, *wise*, and *loving*—that we apply both to God, whom we do not experience, and to human creatures, whom we do experience. We say, for example, that God is good, wise, and loving, and we say that this or that person of our experience is good, wise, or loving. We could conceivably be applying such words to both God and humans in any of three ways.

First, the words could have a *univocal* meaning; that is, they could have exactly the same meaning when applied to God, whom we do not experience, as when applied to the humans we do experience. But this is impossible since God and humans are so unlike that the goodness, wisdom, and love of God must be different from the goodness, wisdom, and love we experience in humans:

It is impossible for a word to be applied univocally to both God and the creatures he produces. For when an effect is not equal to the power of the cause that produced it, the effect receives only an imperfect likeness of the cause: that is, the effect will be like the cause only to an imperfect degree. . . . Thus, when the word "wise" is applied to human beings, the word in a way comprehends and includes in its meaning the thing to which it refers [i.e., imperfect wisdom as we experience it and as God produced it]. But this is not so when the word is applied to God. For when the word "wise" is applied to God it refers to something [perfect wisdom] that exceeds the meaning of the word and which is not comprehended.[3]

Second, then, words applied to both God and creatures could have an *equivocal* meaning: They could mean something totally different when applied to each. But this, too, is inadequate, Aquinas insists. If the words we use changed their meaning when we applied them to God, then we could not say anything at all about God. For we would never know what our words meant when we applied them to God since their meaning derives entirely from our experience of creatures:

Neither can we say that words that are applied to God and creatures have a purely equivocal sense, although some thinkers have held this view. If words that applied to both God and creatures were purely equivocal, then our experience of creatures would not allow us to know anything about God nor to prove anything about God. For the words we used in our reasoning would always be exposed to the fallacy of equivocation. [They would have one meaning in part of our reasoning and another meaning in another part.] Now this is contrary to the procedure of some philosophers, such as Aristotle, who managed to prove many things about God. It also contradicts scripture which says "The invisible things of God are clearly seen, being understood from the things that He created."[4]

Humans, then, must reflect God's nature to some degree since they are God's creation: The goodness, wisdom, and love of humans that we experience must reflect imperfectly the perfect good-

---

[3] Ibid., I, q.13, a.5.
[4] Ibid.

ness, wisdom, and love of God, in whom they originate. So, Aquinas concludes, the third and correct way in which we apply to God certain words whose meaning is based on our experience of humans is *by analogy*. Words such as *wise, good,* and *loving* are applied both to God and humans with an *analogical* meaning: The words do not have a completely different meaning when applied to each, but their meaning is also not exactly the same:

> We have to conclude that these words are applied to both God and creatures in an *analogous* sense, that is, with a meaning that is based on a relationship. . . . For example, the word "healthy" can be applied to a medicine as well as to an animal because of the relationship the medicine has to the health of the animal: the medicine is the cause of the animal's health. In a similar way, words can be applied to both creatures and to God in an analogous and not in a purely univocal nor in a purely equivocal sense. Consider that we can apply to God only words whose meanings we draw from our experience of creatures. Consequently, when we apply a word to both God and creatures, its meaning has to be based on the relationship that creatures have to God: they are related to God as to their origin and their cause in whom all their perfections pre-exist in a way that excels their existence in creatures. Now this kind of common possession of perfections is the basis of a kind of meaning that is midway between pure univocation and pure equivocation. When a word is applied analogically in this way to two different beings its meaning does not remain completely identical as with univocal uses, nor does it have completely different meanings as in equivocal uses.[5]

Our experience of humans, then, gives us an imperfect but positive knowledge of attributes that exist in God in a perfect way. We can never fully comprehend God's own unique and perfect goodness, wisdom, and love, which are quite different from our imperfect and partial goodness, wisdom, and love. So *good, wise,* and *loving* do not have exactly the same meaning when applied to God and humans. Nevertheless, we do experience the partial goodness, wisdom, and love of humans and know that it reflects the perfect goodness, wisdom,

and love of God from whom they derive. This knowledge allows us to say that there is some similarity of meaning among *good, wise,* and *loving* when used to describe both God and humans.

The universe that God created, Aquinas holds, is governed by laws that are imposed by God. Aquinas calls these laws the eternal law, and he likens God to a ruler or a craftsman who fashions the laws of the universe:

> Before any craftsman makes something, he must have in his mind an idea of what he will make. Similarly, before a ruler governs his subjects, he must have in his mind some idea of what his subjects are to do. The craftsman's idea of what he will make constitutes a plan of the object to be made (it is also part of what we call his skill). And the ruler's idea of what his subjects are to do constitutes a kind of law. . . . Now since God is the wise creator of the universe, He is like a craftsman who makes something. And He is also like the ruler since He governs every act and motion of every single creature. Consequently, the idea in God's wise mind, according to which everything was created, can be called a plan (or an ideal model, or even a part of God's skill); and since everything is also governed according to this same idea, it can also be called a law. So the eternal law is nothing more than a plan in God's mind, in accordance with which every act and motion of the universe is directed.[6]

The laws that order the universe govern creatures through the natural forces and inclinations that were made part of their natures when they were created. As part of that universe, human beings are also subject to the eternal law of God through the natural inclinations within us that move us toward our own ends and activities. Unlike other creatures, however, human beings use their reason to direct themselves toward their ends:

> It is clear from the preceding article that the eternal law is the guide and standard for everything that is subject to God's provident direction. Clearly, therefore, the activities of all creatures are equally determined by the eternal law. Their activities are determined by the natural forces and inclinations that were made part of their natures when they were cre-

---

[5] Ibid.

[6] Ibid., I–IIae, q.93, a.1.

ated [by God]. These natural forces and inclinations cause creatures to engage in their appropriate activities and attain their appropriate ends.

Now rational creatures [such as humans] are also subject to God's provident direction, but in a way that makes them more like God than all other creatures. For God directs rational creatures by instilling in them certain natural inclinations and [reasoning] abilities that enable them to direct themselves as well as other creatures. Thus human beings also are subject to the eternal law and they too derive from that law certain natural inclinations to seek their proper ends and proper activities. These inclinations of our nature constitute what we call the "natural law" and they are the effects of the eternal law imprinted in our nature.

Thus, even scripture suggests that our natural ability to reason (by which we distinguish right from wrong) in which the natural law resides, is nothing more than the image of God's own reason imprinted on us. For Psalm Four asks, "Who will show us what is right?" and it answers, "The light of Thy Mind, O Lord, which has been imprinted upon us."[7]

Aquinas argued that morality is based on these "natural inclinations" or this "natural law" that God instilled within us. Our reason perceives as good those things toward which we are naturally inclined and perceives as evil whatever is destructive of those goods. It is morally right to pursue the goods toward which we are naturally inclined and morally wrong to pursue what is destructive of those goods. Thus, natural law is the basis of morality:

> A thing is good if it is an end that we have a natural inclination to desire; it is evil if it is destructive of what our nature is inclined to desire. Consequently, those kinds of things that our nature is inclined to desire are perceived by our reason as good for our human nature. And our reason will conclude that those kinds of things ought to be pursued in our actions. But if our reason sees a certain type of thing as destructive of what human nature is inclined to desire, it will conclude that that type of thing ought to be avoided.

We can therefore list the basic [moral] precepts of the natural law by listing the kinds of things that we naturally desire. First, like every other nature, human nature is inclined to desire its own survival. Consequently it is a natural [moral] law that we ought to preserve human life and avoid whatever is destructive of life. Secondly, like other animals, human nature is inclined to desire those things that nature teaches all animals to desire by instinct. For example, all animals have an instinctive desire to come together in a union of male and female, and an instinctive desire to care for their young. [So it is morally right to pursue these things.] Thirdly, human nature is inclined to desire those goods that satisfy our intellects. This aspect of our nature is proper to human beings. Thus, human nature is inclined to desire knowledge (for example, to know the truth about God) and to desire an orderly social life. Consequently, it is a natural [moral] law that we ought to dispel ignorance and avoid harming those among whom we live.[8]

Thus, for Aquinas, the God whose existence is implied by an imperfect universe is also the God who creates the moral laws that we come to know by reflecting on our basic human inclinations. God is not only the foundation of the existence of the universe but also the foundation of morality.

DESCARTES

The role that God plays in the philosophy of Descartes is different from the role that God plays in other philosophies, such as that of Aquinas. For Aquinas as well as for other philosophers, God's existence is a conclusion we reach by coming to know the world around us. For Descartes, however, God is the One who guarantees that we can come to know the world around us. For Descartes, God is not a Being whom we come to know *after* we know the world around us; instead, God is a Being whom we must know about *before* we can know anything for certain about the world around us. God does not come at the end of knowledge but at the beginning!

There are also many other differences between Descartes and Aquinas. Some of these differences undoubtedly reflect the changes that had taken place in Europe during the 350 years between

---

[7] Ibid., I–IIae, q.91, a.2.

[8] Ibid., I–IIae, q.94, a.2.

René Descartes: "I noticed that while I wished to think all things false, it was absolutely essential that the 'I' who thought this should be something, and remarking that this truth, 'I think, therefore I am' was so certain that all the extravagant suppositions of the skeptics were incapable of shaking it, I came to the conclusion that I could receive it as the First Principle of the philosophy I was seeking."

them. Europe was no longer dominated by a single religion: Protestantism had appeared to compete with Catholicism. The physical sciences were emerging under the impetus of the new discoveries and theories of Galileo and Copernicus. Many of the new modern nations of Europe had already established themselves with their own particular languages, governments, and cultures. The New World of the Americas was being explored. And everywhere fresh minds were bubbling with new ideas and disputing the old medieval views—including those of Aquinas—that had so long dominated European intellectual life.

René Descartes was born in 1596 in Touraine, the son of a councillor of the Parliament of Brittany. A brilliant young man, he was sent in 1604 to

study in the Jesuit college of La Fleche, where, although he was impressed by the precision of mathematics, he was deeply distressed by the disputes and doubts that surrounded all other realms of knowledge, especially philosophy. The end of school, in 1612, left him feeling unsettled and dissatisfied. As he later wrote in his *Discourse on Method,* a short philosophical work in which he described how he came to formulate his own philosophy,

> As soon as I had completed the entire course of study at the close of which one is usually received into the ranks of the learned, . . . I found myself embarrassed with so many doubts and errors that it seemed to me that the effort to instruct myself had no effect other than the increasing discovery of my own ignorance. And yet I was studying at one of the most celebrated Schools in Europe. . . . I was delighted with Mathematics because of the certainty of its demonstrations and the evidence of its reasoning. . . . On the other hand, . . . I shall not say anything about Philosophy, but that, [although] it has been cultivated for many centuries by the best minds that have ever lived, . . . nevertheless no single thing is to be found in it which is not subject to dispute, and in consequence which is not dubious. . . . [A]s to the other sciences, inasmuch as they derive their principles from Philosophy, I judged that one could have built nothing solid on foundations so far from firm.[9]

Disillusioned, Descartes joined the army at the age of seventeen and began to travel, hoping that by studying "the great book of the world" he would find more truth than he had found in school:

> This is why, as soon as age permitted me to emerge from the control of my tutors, I entirely quitted the study of letters. And resolving to seek no other knowledge than that which could be found in myself, or at least in the great book of the world, I employed the rest of my youth in travel, in seeing courts and armies, in speaking with men of diverse temperaments and conditions, in collecting varied experiences, in proving myself in the various predicaments in which I was placed by fortune, and under all circumstances bringing my mind to bear on the things

[9] René Descartes, *Discourse on Method,* in *The Philosophical Works of Descartes,* vol. 1, trans. and ed. Elizabeth S. Haldane and G. R. T. Ross (Cambridge: Cambridge University Press, 1911), 83, 85, 87.

which came before it, so that I might derive some profit from my experience.[10]

But the young Descartes found himself as dissatisfied by the many conflicting opinions he encountered on his travels with the army as he had been by his formal studies in school. This led him one fateful winter day to resolve to see whether he could reach the truth by studying his own inner being:

> [During the time] I only considered the manners of other men I found in them nothing to give me settled convictions; and I remarked in them almost as much diversity as I had formerly seen in the opinions of philosophers. . . . But after I had employed several years in thus studying the book of the world and trying to acquire some experience, I one day formed the resolution of also making myself an object of study and of employing all the strength of my mind in choosing the road I should follow. . . . I was then in Germany, . . . returning from the coronation of the Emperor to rejoin the army, [when] the setting in of winter detained me in a quarter where, since I found no society to divert me, while fortunately I had also no cares or passions to trouble me, I remained the whole day shut up alone in a stove-heated room where I had complete leisure to occupy myself with my own thoughts.[11]

There in his quiet little "stove-heated room" Descartes thought back to the careful method of reasoning that he had admired in mathematics. This method, Descartes felt, begins with "simple" truths that are so "clearly and distinctly perceived" that they cannot be doubted and proceeds to the more complex truths that rest on the simple truths. Perhaps this method of reasoning could be used in other fields to establish all truth with certitude:

> Those long chains of reasoning, simple and easy as they are, of which geometricians make use in order to arrive at the most difficult demonstrations, had caused me to imagine that all those things which fall under the cognizance of man might very likely be mutually related in the same fashion; and that, provided only that we abstain from receiving anything as true which is not so, and always retain the order which is necessary in order to deduce the one con-

clusion from the other, there can be nothing so remote that we cannot reach to it, nor so recondite that we cannot discover it. . . . Considering also that of all those who have hitherto sought for the truth in the Sciences, it has been the mathematicians alone who have been able to succeed in . . . producing reasons which are evident and certain, I did not doubt that it had been by means of a similar method that they carried on their investigations.[12]

Convinced that in mathematics he had found an instance of the only reliable method for discovering truth, Descartes summarized his new method in four rules:

> The first of these was to accept nothing as true which I did not clearly recognize to be so: that is to say, carefully to avoid precipitation and prejudice in judgments, and to accept in them nothing more than what was presented to my mind so clearly and distinctly that I could have no occasion to doubt it.
> The second was to divide up each of the difficulties which I examined into as many parts as possible, and as seemed requisite in order that it might be resolved in the best manner possible.
> The third was to carry on my reflections in due order, commencing with objects that were the most simple and easy to understand, in order to rise little by little, or by degrees, to knowledge of the most complex. . . .
> The last was in all cases to make enumerations so complete and reviews so general that I should be certain of having omitted nothing.[13]

Feeling he now had a method for pursuing the truth, Descartes left his little room and again took up his travels. Nine years passed before he felt ready to apply his method to philosophical issues:

> Inasmuch as I hoped to be able to reach my end more successfully in converse with man than in living longer shut up in the warm room where these reflections had come to me, I hardly awaited the end of winter before I once more set myself to travel. And in all the nine following years I did nothing but roam hither and thither. . . . Nine years thus passed away before I had taken any definite part in regard to the difficulties as to which the learned are in the habit of disputing, or had commenced to seek the foundation

---

[10] Ibid., 86.
[11] Ibid., 87.

[12] Ibid., 91–92.
[13] Ibid., 92.

of any philosophy. . . . [Then I] resolved to remove myself from all places where any acquaintances were possible, and to retire to this country [Holland, where] . . . I can live as solitary and retired as in deserts the most remote.[14]

Here, in solitude, Descartes began writing a long series of "meditations." Slowly he built a philosophy that, he was convinced, was as solid and certain as mathematics because it relied on the same method. He began by putting his first rule into practice by "rooting out of my mind" all opinions that were the least bit doubtful. Through this "method of doubt" Descartes came upon the basic truth that was to serve as the "simple" principle from which he would "rise to the most complex":

I do not know that I ought to tell you of the first meditations there made by me, for they are so metaphysical and so unusual that they may perhaps not be acceptable to everyone. . . . Because I wished to give myself entirely to the search after Truth, I thought that it was necessary for me to take an apparently opposite course, and to reject as absolutely false everything as to which I could imagine the least ground of doubt, in order to see if afterwards there remained anything in my belief that was entirely certain. Thus, because our senses sometimes deceive us, I wished to suppose that nothing is just as they cause us to imagine it to be; and because there are men who deceive themselves in their reasoning and fall into fallacies, even concerning the simplest matters of geometry, and judging that I was as subject to error as was any other, I rejected as false all the reasons formerly accepted by me as demonstrations. And since all the same thoughts and conceptions which we have while awake may also come to us in sleep without any of them being at that time true, I resolved to assume that everything that ever entered into my mind was no more true than the illusions of my dreams.

But immediately afterwards I noticed that while I thus wished to think all things false, it was absolutely essential that the "I" who thought this should be something, and remarking that this truth, "I think, therefore I am" was so certain and so assured that all the most extravagant suppositions brought forward by the skeptics were incapable of shaking it, I came

to the conclusion that I could receive it without scruple as the first principle of the Philosophy which I was seeking.

And then, examining attentively that which I was, I saw that I could conceive that I had no body, and that there was no world nor place where I might be; but yet that I could not for all that conceive that I was not. On the contrary, I saw from the very fact that I thought of doubting the truth of other things, it very evidently and certainly followed that I was. On the other hand if I had only ceased from thinking, even if all the rest of what I had ever imagined had really existed, I should have no reason for thinking that I had existed. From that I knew that I was a substance the whole essence or nature of which is to think, and that for its existence there is no need of any place, nor does it depend on any material thing; so that this "me," that is to say, the soul by which I am what I am, is entirely distinct from body, and is even more easy to know than is the latter; and even if body were not, the soul would not cease to be what it is.

After this I considered generally what in a proposition is requisite in order to be true and certain; for since I had just discovered one which I knew to be such, I thought that I ought also to know in what this certainty consisted. And having remarked that there was nothing at all in the statement, "I think, therefore I am" which assures me of having thereby made a true assertion, excepting that I see very clearly that to think it is necessary to be, I came to the conclusion that I might assume, as a general rule, that the things which we conceive very clearly and distinctively are all true — remembering, however, that there is some difficulty in ascertaining which are those that we distinctly conceive.

Following upon this, and reflecting on the fact that I doubted, and that consequently my existence was not quite perfect (for I saw clearly that it was a greater perfection to know than to doubt), I resolved to inquire whence I had learnt to think of Something more perfect than I myself was. And I recognized very clearly that this conception must proceed from some Nature which was really more perfect. As to the thoughts which I had of many other things outside of me, like the heavens, the earth, light, heat, and a thousand others, I had not so much difficulty in knowing whence they came, because, remarking nothing in them which seemed to render them superior to me, I could believe that, if they were true, they were dependencies upon my nature, in so far as it possessed some perfection; and if they

---

[14] Ibid., 98–100.

were not true, that I held them from nothing, that is to say, that they were in me because I had something lacking in my nature. But this could not apply to the idea of a Being more perfect than my own, for to hold it came from nought would be manifestly impossible; and because it is no less contradictory to say of the more perfect that it is what results from and depends on the less perfect, than to say that there is something which proceeds from nothing, it was equally impossible that I should hold it from myself. In this way it could not but follow that it had been placed in me by a Nature which was really more perfect than mine could be, and which even had within itself all the perfections of which I could form any idea—that is to say, to put it in a word, which was God. To which I added that since I knew some perfections which I did not possess, I was not the only being in existence; but there was necessarily some other more perfect Being on which I depended, or from which I acquired all that I had.[15]

Thus, Descartes was led by his method to realize that he existed, that he had a soul, and, most important, that God existed, for, as Descartes reasoned, God is the foundation of all truth. God is not a deceiver, and God ensures that whatever we "clearly and distinctly" understand is true. Error arises only when we pass judgment on matters that are not clearly and distinctly understood:

For, first of all, I recognize it to be impossible that He should ever deceive me; for in all fraud and deception some imperfection is to be found, and although it may appear that the power of deception is a mark of subtlety or power, yet the desire to deceive without doubt testifies to malice or feebleness, and accordingly cannot be found in God. . . .

Whence, then, come my errors? They come from the sole fact that since the will is much wider in its range and compass than the understanding, I do not restrain it within the same bounds, but extend it also to things which I do not understand. . . .

But if I abstain from giving my judgment on anything when I do not perceive it with sufficient clearness and distinctness, it is plain that I will act rightly and will not be deceived. But if I decide to deny or affirm [what is not clear and distinct], then I no longer make use as I should of my free will. . . .

So long as I restrain my will within the limits of my knowledge so that it forms no judgment except on matters which are clearly and distinctly represented to it by the understanding, I can never be deceived. For every clear and distinct perception is without doubt something and hence cannot derive its origin from what is nothing, but must of necessity have God as its author—God, I say, who, being supremely perfect, cannot be the cause of any error; and consequently we must conclude that such a perception is true.[16]

Having found the source of truth and knowledge, Descartes turned to the final major philosophical question that confronted him: Did the material world around him really exist, or was it merely a figment of his imagination?

Now that I have noted what must be done to arrive at a knowledge of the truth, my principal task is to endeavor to emerge from the state of doubt into which I have these last days fallen, and to see whether nothing certain can be known regarding material things. . . . Nothing further remains, then, but to inquire whether material things exist. . . . I find that . . . there is in me a certain passive faculty of perception, that is, of receiving and recognizing the ideas of material things. . . . But, since God is no deceiver, it is very manifest that He does not communicate to me these ideas directly and by Himself, nor yet by the intervention of some creature [different from the material objects I think I perceive]. For since He has given me no faculty to recognize that this is the case, but, on the other hand, a very great inclination to believe that they are conveyed to me by material objects, I do not see how He could be defended from the accusation of deceit if these ideas were produced by causes other than material objects. Hence we must allow that material things exist.[17]

Thus, the existence of a perfect God is our only guarantee that our knowledge about the world is accurate. If it were not for God, we could never be sure that any of our so-called knowledge of external reality is true. For earlier philosophers, God is primarily the foundation of reality, what accounts for the existence of the objects in the universe. But for

[15] Ibid., 100–102.

[16] René Descartes, *Meditations on First Philosophy*, in *Philosophical Works*, 172, 175–176, 178.
[17] Ibid., 179, 185, 191.

Descartes, God is primarily the foundation of our knowledge, what accounts for the fact that we can know the objects in our universe.

Descartes's philosophy made him famous, and within a short time at least two of the crowned heads of Europe were asking his advice. In 1649 Descartes received an invitation from Queen Christina of Sweden, who requested him to instruct her in the mysteries of philosophy. Being eager to please her, Descartes traveled north to Sweden and there began tutoring the busy queen at the only hour she had free: five o'clock in the morning. The bitter cold and the early hour combined to weaken Descartes's health, and within a few months he caught pneumonia. On February 11, 1650, Descartes died.

ANNE CONWAY

Whereas both Aquinas and Descartes give God a very prominent position in their philosophies, Anne Conway more thoroughly developed a philosophy based wholly on the nature of God. She was truly obsessed by the idea of a God who is perfect in every way, and her fascinating and visionary philosophy is an attempt to describe the consequences of this idea. Unfortunately, because Conway was a woman in a male-dominated society, her work was largely ignored, and when male philosophers took over her ideas they failed to attribute them to her.

Conway was born on December 14, 1631, into a wealthy, energetic, and intellectually talented English family headed by Elizabeth and Heneage Finch, a lawyer. Tragically, her father died just a week before her birth. Virtually nothing is known of Anne's childhood other than that she received a remarkably full education. In 1651 she married Edward Conway, a wealthy landowner with some connections to the court of Charles II. Several philosophers, including Henry More and Ralph Cudworth, were frequent guests at their house; through them, especially More, Anne came in contact with some of the major philosophical currents of the age.

Throughout her life Conway was plagued by migraine headaches. These may have been partially responsible for her death in 1679 at the age of 48. Conway died while her husband was away in Ireland, and his friends, wanting to let him see her before she was buried, had her body pickled in wine and stored in a vat in his library until he returned to bury her.

Toward the end of her life Conway wrote a short work called *The Principles of the Most Ancient and Modern Philosophy*, which was published after her death. In that work she traced the fundamentals of her philosophical views.

Conway begins her philosophy focused on God, the most perfect of all beings. From this simple beginning, she deduces in a rationalist manner the main characteristics of the universe as she sees it. Although she does not attempt to prove that God exists, she goes to great lengths to explain what God has to be like. Since God is perfect, he must possess all perfections, including unlimited ("infinite") wisdom, goodness, justice, omniscience, and omnipotence. God is also a "spirit"—that is, a being capable of thinking and awareness. Although God has no physical body (and so no shape), he is the creator of the life, the bodies, and all other goods that creatures have:

> God is a Spirit, Light, and Life, infinitely Wise, Good, Just, Mighty, Omniscient, Omnipresent, Omnipotent, Creator and Maker of all things visible and invisible. . . . He hath no manner of darkness or corporiety [physical body] in him, and so consequently no kind of Form of Figure whatsoever. . . . He is in a true and proper sense a creator of all things, who doth not only give them their Form and figure, but also being, life, body, and whatsoever else of good they have.[18]

God, Conway holds, cannot change because he is already perfect. If he were to change, he would then have to either become more perfect or less perfect. But he cannot become more perfect since he is already fully perfect, nor can he become less perfect, for then he would not be God.

Moreover, Conway argues, because God is unchanging, he is outside of time. To see what she

---

[18] Anne Conway, *The Principles of the Most Ancient and Modern Philosophy*, ed. Peter Loptson (Boston: Martinus Nijhoff, 1982; original work published 1692), 149.

means it may help to consider that when we say that time is passing, we mean that certain changes have occurred: The hands of a clock have moved across its face, or the sun above us has moved across the sky. But imagine that everything in our universe came to a complete stop so that nothing changed in any way: Absolutely nothing moved, and everything remained completely fixed in a frozen state. In such a completely frozen universe, nothing would distinguish one moment from another. Time would then be meaningless. Time requires change; without change, there is no time. Thus, Conway claimed, time itself is nothing but change. Since God is unchanging, God is not in time: He exists outside of the universe of time and change in a timeless state called "eternity," where the whole history of the universe appears before him as if in a single present, unchanging moment. By contrast, all creatures change and so are subject to time:

> In God there is neither time nor Change, nor Composition, nor Division of parts: He is wholly and universally one in himself and of himself, without any manner of variety or mixture. . . . For . . . Times . . . are nothing else but successive Motions and operations of created beings. . . . The eternity of God himself hath no times in it; nothing therein can be said to be past, or to come, but the whole is always present. . . . And the reason hereof is manifest; because time is nothing else but the successive motion or operation of creatures; which motion or operation, if it should cease, time would also cease, and the creatures themselves would cease with time. Wherefore such is the nature of every creature, that it is in motion, or hath a certain motion, by means of which it advances forward, and grows to a farther perfection. And seeing in God there is no successive motion or operation to a farther perfection; because he is most absolutely perfect. Hence there are not times in God or his eternity.[19]

Conway argues that although God is completely free to create whatever he chooses to create, he had to create us. God is free, yet he has to do what he does. How is this possible? How can God be both free and unfree? Conway explains that there is nothing greater than God that can force him to do anything: There is no external force that can make him do one thing rather than another. So God is completely free from any *external* forces. But God is perfectly good, so he cannot be "indifferent" (unconcerned) about doing good; that is, his own inner goodness forces him to do what is good. So whatever God does, he does it because it is a good thing to do. Therefore, although God is free from external forces, he is also unfree because his own inner goodness forces him to do whatever is good. Since it is good to create good things, God is forced to create good creatures:

> Although the Will of God be most free, so that whatsoever he doth in the behalf of his creatures, he doth freely without any external violence, compulsion, or any cause coming from them—whatsoever he doth, he doth of his own accord—Yet that indifference of acting, or not acting, can by no means be said to be in God. . . . Seeing his infinite wisdom, goodness, and justice is a law unto him, which he cannot transgress. . . . Hence therefore it evidently follows that it was not indifferent to God, whether he would give being to his creatures or no; but he made them out of a certain internal impulse of his divine wisdom and goodness, and so he created the world or creatures as soon as he could.[20]

In fact, Conway argues, because God has to create anything that is good, and because there are infinite numbers of good things that an all-powerful God can create, God must create infinite numbers of creatures inhabiting infinite numbers of worlds:

> These attributes duly considered, it follows that creatures were created in infinite numbers, or that there is an infinity of worlds or creatures made of God: for seeing God is infinitely powerful, there can be no number of creatures so great, that he cannot always make more: and because, as is already proved, he doth whatsoever he can do [that is good]; certainly his will, goodness, and bounty is as large and extensive as his power; whence it manifestly follows that creatures are infinite, and created in infinite manners, so that they cannot be limited or bounded with any number or measure.[21]

---

[19] Ibid., 149, 154, 155.

[20] Ibid., 157, 158.
[21] Ibid., 158–159.

Not only are there infinite numbers of worlds in the universe around us, but there are also infinite numbers of worlds within each of us, and within each of these worlds in us is another infinity of worlds, and within each of these worlds another infinity of worlds, and so on. For God can create ever-smaller good things or "monads" within each good thing he creates, and, after all, God must create whatever is good:

> Also by the like reason is proved, that not only the whole body or system of creatures considered together is infinite, or contains in itself a kind of infinity; but also that every creature even the least that we can discern with our eyes, or conceive in our minds, hath therein such an infinity of parts, or rather entire creatures, that they cannot be numbered; even as it cannot be denied that God can place one creature within another, so he can place two as well as one, and four as well as two, so also eight as well as four, so that he could multiply them without end, always placing the less within the greater. . . . This being sufficient to demonstrate that in every creature, whether the same be a spirit or a body, there is an infinity of creatures, each whereof contains an infinity and again each of these, and so *ad infinitum*.[22]

Thus, for Conway, creativity is one of God's essential attributes: For God to be God, he must create. And, Conway holds, this creativity is from all eternity, so for an infinite length of time an infinity of creatures have existed. The universe is infinite in time as it is infinite in creatures.

According to Conway, the essential difference between God and the infinite creatures he creates is changeability. God, as we have seen, does not change and is outside of time. However, the creatures he creates all change in time. Whereas God is perfect and cannot become better or worse, creatures are imperfect and so can change for the better or for the worse. But their changes into better or worse creatures are governed by God's justice.

At this point Conway reaches a breathtaking conclusion. She argues that God's justice demands that over time each creature change into a higher or lower kind of creature. Consider, Conway suggests, that all creatures have a soul or a spirit. Now what is to become of this spirit at death?

> Now I demand, unto what higher perfection and degree of goodness, the being or essence of a horse doth or may attain after he hath done good service for his master, and so performed his duty, and what is proper for such a creature? Is a horse then a mere fabrick or dead matter? Or hath he a spirit in him, having knowledge, sense, and love, and divers other faculties and properties of a spirit? If he hath, which cannot be denied, what becomes of this spirit when the horse dies?[23]

Conway's answer is simple. If a creature has done good deeds in its life, she proposes, then justice demands that at death it be changed into a better creature. On the other hand, if a creature has done evil in its life, then at death justice demands it change into a lower creature. Thus, Conway argues, since God is just, his justice requires a kind of transmigration of spirits. Men and any other creatures who do evil are changed at death by God's justice into worse creatures, whereas creatures who do good are changed by God's justice into better ones:

> Now we see how gloriously the justice of God appears in this transmutation of things out of one species into another; and that there is a certain justice which operates not only in men and angels, but in all creatures, is most certain; and he that doth not observe the same may be said to be utterly blind: for this justice appears as well in the ascension of creatures as in their descension; that is, when they are changed into the better and when into the worse; when into the better, this justice distributes to them the reward and fruit of their good deeds; when into the worse, the same punishes them with due punishments, according to the nature and degree of the transgression. . . .
>
> For example: is it not just and equitable, if a man on earth liveth a pure and holy life, like unto the heavenly angels, that he should be exalted to an angelical dignity after death, and be like unto them . . .? But if a man here on earth lives so wickedly and per-

---

[22] Ibid., 159–160.

[23] Ibid., 180–181.

versely that he is more like a devil raised from hell than any other creature, if he dies in such a state without repentance . . . shall not such deservedly become like devils . . .? But if a man hath neither lived an angelical or diabolical, but a bruthish, or at leastwise an animal or sensual life on earth; so that his spirit is more like the spirit of a beast than any other thing: shall the same justice most justly cause that as he is become a bruth, as to his spirit . . . that he also (at least as to his external form in bodily figure) should be changed into that species of beasts, to whom he was inwardly most like . . .?[24]

But Conway's greatest contribution to philosophy lies in her method of bringing the body and the spirit together. The philosopher Descartes, before her, had claimed that humans have both a body and a spirit. But the body, Descartes claimed, is utterly different from and distinct from the spirit: They are two different and separate things. So different are they that it seems that the body and the spirit cannot possibly affect each other. That set the basic problem for philosophy after Descartes: How is the body related to the spirit when they are two different and separate things?

Conway avoids Descartes's problem by proposing that body and spirit are not two different things, but rather that they are merely aspects or qualities of the same thing. Every creature, Conway claims, exhibits both bodily qualities and spiritual qualities. Even the "lowest" physical creatures such as rocks and plants have some rudimentary spiritual consciousness, some minimal levels of awareness, life, and thinking. On the other hand, even the "highest" spiritual creatures, such as angels, have some residual bodily qualities, some minimal degree of physical qualities. Everything in the universe, then, is both bodily and spiritual. So body and spirit are not to be thought of as *things*. Instead, they are merely two different kinds of qualities that all creatures possess to a greater or lesser degree.

Conway provides several arguments in support of her view that every creature—even something like a rock—has both physical and spiritual qualities. For example, she argues that whatever God creates has to have some of his qualities: God communicates something of himself to each thing he creates. Since God is a spirit, everything he creates has to have some spiritual qualities. Moreover, God creates creatures so that they can share eternal life with him. But how can they do this unless they have spiritual qualities?

> For seeing God is infinitely good and communicates his goodness in finite ways to his creatures; so that there is no creature which doth not receive something of his goodness, and that very largely: and seeing the goodness of God is a living goodness, which hath life, power, love, and knowledge in it, which he communicates to his creatures, how can it be that any dead thing should proceed from him or be created by him? . . . Has not God created all his creatures of this end, that in him they might be blessed and enjoy his divine goodness, in their several states and conditions? But how can this be without life or sense?[25]

Thus, the universe as conceived by Conway is much richer and more dynamic and orderly than other philosophers had ever suggested. Not only are there an infinity of worlds within worlds in her vision of the universe, but these infinite numbers of creatures are all living, thinking, and feeling creatures as well. Everything in the universe is alive and has some degree of awareness, from the simplest grain of dust to the highest angel. Moreover, although there is a constant churn of change as creatures continuously mutate into higher or lower creatures, this change is all regulated by God's justice, which ensures that each creature at death will be reborn into the kind of creature it deserves to be.

Perhaps because Conway was a woman and so condemned to be ignored by a world thoroughly dominated by males, her thought had very little direct impact on philosophy. However, after her death, the German philosopher Gottfried Leibnitz (1646–1716) studied her work and based his own famous views on those of Conway. Leibnitz took from Conway the idea that God creates infinitely many "monads" (without, of course, giving her

---

[24] Ibid., 184, 185.

[25] Ibid., 196.

credit for the idea). Leibnitz also took from her the idea that God's goodness compels him to create good things, as well as the idea that because God is perfectly good, the universe of creatures he creates also has to be perfectly good. Thus, through Leibnitz and other male philosophers, many of the major ideas of Conway entered the mainstream of philosophy, although the men who took over her ideas relegated her name to obscurity.

Conway's philosophy is notable not only for its unwavering focus on God, but also because of the view that it provides of human beings. Conway's views on God's justice and the transmigration of creatures, in fact, are very similar to the Hindu religious view of karma and rebirth. Hindu religious thought has traditionally held that at death all living creatures are reborn as new living creatures. The kind of creature one becomes after death depends on one's karma—that is, the totality of good or evil deeds one has performed during one's past. If one's deeds were good, then one is reborn into a higher creature; if one's deeds were evil, then one is reborn into a lower animal. Conway's philosophy comes to exactly the same conclusions, but on the basis of a conception of God that is much more familiar to Westerners.

QUESTIONS

1.   What is the difference between theology and philosophy? Between religion and philosophy? Evaluate this statement: "The God of the philosophers is not the God of religion." Can religion be rational?

2.   Evaluate each of Aquinas's proofs for the existence of God. Why do you think a believer like Aquinas would be concerned with proving God's existence? Does it make sense to believe without proof? Why or why not?

3.   Does Aquinas's theory of analogy really explain how it is possible for religious believers to speak about God? Contemporary theories of language hold that words mean whatever we, the speakers of the language, *intend* them to mean. How can we intend words to have a meaning that we do not understand when applied to God? Does

Aquinas's theory imply that God must be *like* the world that God creates?

4.   Some people have held that Aquinas's views about right and wrong are a Christianized version of Aristotle's views on virtue. Do you agree? What aspects of Aquinas's views about morality would an atheist have to reject? Which aspects would an atheist be able to retain?

5.   Compare the interests and approaches of Descartes and Aquinas. What accounts for these differences? Which seem to be more "modern"? Why?

6.   How useful are Descartes's four rules for discovering the truth? Could you use them, for example, as the basis for discovering the truth about God for yourself? Explain.

7.   Descartes criticized all philosophy prior to his because "no single thing is to be found in it which is not subject to dispute, and in consequence which is not dubious." Explain whether this criticism applies to Descartes's own philosophy and to his own views about God. Why would Descartes have felt that his philosophy was immune from his criticism?

8.   How reasonable is Descartes's "method of doubt"? Evaluate this statement: "Descartes's method of doubt shows that we cannot know for certain that there is a world around us or that any conclusions we have reached about this external world are true. Moreover, Descartes fails miserably in his attempts to show that we can know anything for certain about the external world. After Descartes, we must resign ourselves to complete skepticism about the external world and must forever remain locked up within our minds."

9.   Evaluate Descartes's proof for the existence of God. How does it compare to Anselm's ontological proof? Is Descartes's proof immune from the method of doubt?

10.   Is Descartes correct in claiming that "if I abstain from giving my judgment on anything when I do not perceive it with sufficient clearness and distinctness, it is plain that I will act rightly and will not be deceived"? Do you decide of your own free will to believe what you believe?

11. Can the existence of a good, all-powerful God be reconciled with the fact of human error?

12. Explain why Conway holds that God is "outside of time." Do you agree with Conway's view that time is change? Explain your answer.

13. Explain Conway's view that God is both free and unfree.

14. Is there a "smallest" creature in Conway's philosophy? Explain.

15. Explain why Conway believes that God's justice requires transmigration.

16. How, exactly, did Conway try to avoid Descartes's body/mind problem? Do you think she succeeded in doing so? Explain your answer.

4.8 Readings

Should the events around us influence our belief in God? Science fiction writer Arthur Clarke suggests in his short story that belief in God can be maintained even in the face of an evil so monstrous that it would suggest there is no God. Atheist Antony Flew and believer Basil Mitchell debate in their articles whether it makes sense to hold that nothing can happen that can affect one's belief in God. These readings, then, should lead you to examine your own religious beliefs and the extent to which they are or should be influenced by what happens in the world around you.

ARTHUR C. CLARKE

The Star

It is three thousand light-years to the Vatican. Once I believed that space could have no power over Faith. Just as I believed that the heavens declared the glory of God's handiwork. Now I have seen that handiwork, and my faith is sorely troubled.

I stare at the crucifix that hangs on the cabin wall above the Mark VI computer, and for the first time in my life I wonder if it is no more than an empty symbol.

I have told no one yet, but the truth cannot be concealed. The data are there for anyone to read, recorded on the countless miles of magnetic tape and the thousands of photographs we are carrying back to Earth. Other scientists can interpret them as easily as I can—more easily, in all probability. I am not one who would condone that tampering with the Truth which often gave my Order a bad name in the olden days.

The crew is already sufficiently depressed, I wonder how they will take this ultimate irony. Few of them have any religious faith, yet they will not relish using this final weapon in their campaign against me—that private, good-natured but fundamentally serious war which lasted all the way from Earth. It amused them to have a Jesuit as a chief astrophysicist: Dr. Chandler, for instance, could never get over it (why are medical men such notorious atheists?). Sometimes he would meet me on the observation deck, where the lights are always low so that the stars shine with undiminished glory. He would come up to me in the gloom and stand staring out of the great oval port, while the heavens crawled slowly round us as the ship turned end over end with the residual spin we had never bothered to correct.

"Well, Father," he would say at last. "It goes on forever and forever, and perhaps *Something* made it. But how you can believe that Something has a special interest in us and our miserable little world—that just beats me." Then the argument would start, while the stars and nebulae would swing around us in silent, endless arcs beyond the flawlessly clear plastic of the observation port.

It was, I think, the apparent incongruity of my position which . . . yes, *amused* . . . the crew. In vain I would point to my three papers in the *Astrophysical Journal*, my five in the *Monthly Notices of the*

Originally published in *Infinity Science Fiction* (November 1955). Copyright © 1955 by Royal Publications, Inc. Reprinted by permission of the author and the author's agents, Scott Meredith Literary Agency, L. P., 845 Third Ave., New York, NY 10022.

Royal Astronomical Society. I would remind them that our Order has long been famous for its scientific works. We may be few now, but ever since the eighteenth century we have made contributions to astronomy and geophysics out of all proportions to our numbers.

Will my report on the Phoenix Nebula end our thousand years of history? It will end, I fear, much more than that.

I do not know who gave the Nebula its name, which seems to me a very bad one. If it contains a prophecy, it is one which cannot be verified for several thousand million years. Even the word nebula is misleading: this is a far smaller object than those stupendous clouds of mist—the stuff of unborn stars—which are scattered throughout the length of the Milky Way. On the cosmic scale, indeed, the Phoenix Nebula is a tiny thing—a tenuous shell of gas surrounding a single star.

Or what is left of a star . . .

The Rubens engraving of Loyola seems to mock me as it hangs there above the spectrophotometer tracings. What would *you*, Father, have made of this knowledge that has come into my keeping, so far from the little world that was all the universe you knew? Would your faith have risen to the challenge as mine has failed to do?

You gaze into the distance, Father, but I have traveled a distance beyond any that you could have imagined when you founded our Order a thousand years ago. No other survey ship has been so far from Earth: we are at the very frontiers of the explored universe. We set out to reach the Phoenix Nebula, we succeeded, and we are homeward bound with our burden of knowledge. I wish I could lift that burden from my shoulders, but I call to you in vain across the centuries and the lightyears that lie between us.

On the book you are holding the words are plain to read. AD MAIOREM DEI GLORIAM the message runs, but it is a message I can no longer believe. Would you still believe it, if you could see what we have found?

We knew, of course, what the Phoenix Nebula was. Every year, in *our* galaxy alone, more than a hundred stars explode, blazing for a few hours or days with thousands of times their normal brilliance before they sink back into death and obscurity. Such are the ordinary novae—the commonplace disasters of the universe. I have recorded the spectrograms and light-curves of dozens, since I started working at the lunar observatory.

But three or four times in every thousand years occurs something beside which even a nova pales into total insignificance.

When a star becomes a *supernova*, it may for a little while outshine all the massed suns of the galaxy. The Chinese astronomers watched this happen in 1054 A.D., not knowing what it was they saw. Five centuries later, in 1572, a supernova blazed in Cassiopeia so brilliantly that it was visible in the daylight sky. There have been three more in the thousand years that have passed since then.

Our mission was to visit the remnants of such a catastrophe, to reconstruct the events that led up to it, and, if possible, to learn its cause. We came slowly in through the concentric shells of gas that had been blasted out six thousand years before, yet were expanding still. They were immensely hot, radiating still with a fierce violet light, but far too tenuous to do us any damage. When the star had exploded, its outer layers had been driven upwards with such speed that they had escaped completely from its gravitational field. Now they formed a hollow shell large enough to engulf a thousand solar systems, and at this center burned the tiny, fantastic object which the star had now become—a white dwarf, smaller than the Earth yet weighing a million times as much.

The glowing gas shells were all around us, banishing the normal night of interstellar space. We were flying into the center of a cosmic bomb that had detonated millennia ago and those incandescent fragments were still hurtling apart. The immense scale of the explosion, and the fact that the debris already covered a volume of space many billions of miles across robbed the scene of any visible movement. It would take decades before the unaided eye could detect any motion in these tortured wisps and eddies of gas, yet the sense of turbulent expansion was overwhelming.

We had checked our primary drive hours before, and were drifting slowly towards the fierce little star ahead. Once it had been a sun like our own, but it had squandered in a few hours the energy that should have kept it shining for a million years. Now it was a shrunken miser, hoarding its resources as if trying to make amends for its prodigal youth.

No one seriously expected to find planets. If there had been any before the explosion, they would have been boiled into puffs of vapor, and their substance lost in the greater wreckage of the star itself. But we made the automatic search, as always when approaching an unknown sun, and presently we found a single small world circling the star at immense distance. It must have been the Pluto of this vanished solar system, orbiting on the frontiers of the night. Too far from the central sun ever to have known life, its remoteness had saved it from the fate of all its lost companions.

The passing fires had seared its rocks and burnt away the mantle of frozen gas that must have covered it in the days before the disaster. We landed, and we found the Vault.

Its builders had made sure that we should. The monolite marker that stood above the entrance was now a fused stump, but even the first long-range photographs told us that here was the work of intelligence. A little later we detected the continent's wide pattern of radioactivity that had been buried in the rock. Even if the pylon above the Vault had been destroyed, this would have remained, an immovable and all but eternal beacon calling to the stars. Our ship fell towards this gigantic bull's-eye like an arrow into its target.

The pylon must have been a mile high when it was built, but now it looked like a candle that had melted down into a puddle of wax. It took us a week to drill through the fused rock, since we did not have the proper tools for a task like this. We were astronomers, not archaeologists, but we could improvise. Our original program was forgotten: this lonely monument, reared at such labor at the greatest possible distance from the doomed sun, could have only one meaning. A civilization which knew it was about to die had made its last bid for immortality.

It will take us generations to examine all the treasures that were placed in the Vault. *They* had plenty of time to prepare, for their sun must have given its first warnings many years before the final detonation. Everything that they wished to preserve, all the fruits of their genius, they brought here to this distant world in the days before the end, hoping that some other race would find them and that they would not be utterly forgotten.

If only they had had a little more time! They could travel freely enough between the planets of their own sun, but they had not yet learned to cross the interstellar gulfs, and the nearest solar system was a hundred light-years away.

Even if they had not been so disturbingly human as their sculpture shows, we could not have helped admiring them and grieving for their fate. The thousands of visual records and the machines for projecting them, together with elaborate pictorial instructions from which it will not be difficult to learn their written language. We have examined many of these records, and brought to life for the first time in six thousand years the warmth and beauty of a civilization which in many ways must have been superior to our own. Perhaps they only showed us the best, and one can hardly blame them. But their worlds were very lovely, and their cities were built with a grace that matches anything of ours. We have watched them at work and play, and listened to their musical speech sounding across the centuries. One scene is still before my eyes—a group of children on a beach of strange blue sand, playing in the waves as children play on Earth.

And sinking into the sea, still warm and friendly and life-giving, is the sun that will soon turn traitor and obliterate all this innocent happiness.

Perhaps if we had not been so far from home and so vulnerable to loneliness, we should not have been so deeply moved. Many of us had seen the ruins of ancient civilizations on other worlds, but they had never affected us so profoundly.

This tragedy was unique. It was one thing for a race to fail and die, as nations and cultures have done on Earth. But to be destroyed so completely in the full flower of its achievement, leaving no survivors—how could that be reconciled with the mercy of God?

My colleagues have asked me that, and I have given what answers I can. Perhaps you could have done better, Father Loyola, but I have found nothing in the *Exercitia Spiritualia* that helps me here. They were not an evil people: I do not know what gods they worshipped, if indeed they worshipped any. But I have looked back at them across the centuries, and have watched while the loveliness they used their last strength to preserve was brought forth again into the light of their shrunken sun.

I know the answers that my colleagues will give when they get back to Earth. They will say that the universe has no purpose and no plan, that since a hundred suns explode every year in our galaxy, at this very moment some race is dying in the depths of space. Whether that race had done good or evil during its lifetime will make no difference in the end: there is no divine justice, *for there is no God.*

Yet, of course, what we have seen proves nothing of the sort. Anyone who argues thus is being swayed by emotion, not logic. God has no need to justify His actions to man. He who built the universe can destroy it when He chooses. It is arrogance—it is perilously near blasphemy—for us to say what He may or may not do.

This I could have accepted, hard though it is to look upon whole worlds and peoples thrown into the furnace. But there comes a point when even the deepest faith must falter, and now, as I look at my calculations, I know I have reached that point at last.

We could not tell, before we reached the nebula, how long ago the explosion took place. Now, from the astronomical evidence and the record in the rocks of that one surviving planet, I have been able to date it very exactly. I know in what year the light of this colossal conflagration reached Earth. I know how brilliantly the supernova whose corpse now dwindles behind our speeding ship once shone in terrestrial skies. I know how it must have blazed low in the East before sunrise, like a beacon in that Oriental dawn. There can be no reasonable doubt: the ancient mystery is solved at last. Yet—O God, there were so many stars you *could* have used.

What was the need to give these people to the fire, that the symbol of their passing might shine above Bethlehem?

ANTONY FLEW AND BASIL MITCHELL

Theology and Falsification

ANTONY FLEW

Let us begin with a parable. It is a parable developed from a tale told by John Wisdom in his haunting and revelatory article 'Gods'. Once upon a time two explorers came upon a clearing in the jungle. In the clearing were growing many flowers and many weeds. One explorer says, 'Some gardener must tend this plot'. The other disagrees, 'There is no gardener'. So they pitch their tents and set a watch. No gardener is ever seen. 'But perhaps he is an invisible gardener'. So they set up a barbed-wire fence. They electrify it. They patrol with bloodhounds. (For they remember how H. G. Wells's *The Invisible Man* could be both smelt and touched though he could not be seen.) But no shrieks ever suggest that some intruder has received a shock. No movements of the wire ever betray an invisible climber. The bloodhounds never give cry. Yet still the Believer is not convinced. 'But there is a gardener, invisible, intangible, insensible to electric shocks, a gardener who has no scent and makes no sound, a gardener who comes secretly to look after the garden which he loves'. At last the Sceptic despairs, 'But what remains of your original assertion? Just how does what you call an invisible, intangible,

From *New Essays in Philosophical Theology*, ed. Antony Flew and Alasdair Macintyre (New York: Macmillan, 1955). Copyright © 1955 by Antony Flew and Alasdair Macintyre, renewed 1983. Footnotes deleted. Reprinted by permission of Simon & Schuster.

eternally elusive gardener differ from an imaginary gardener or even from no gardener at all?'

In this parable we can see how what starts as an assertion, that something exists or that there is some analogy between certain complexes of phenomena, may be reduced step by step to an altogether different status, to an expression perhaps of a 'picture preference'. The Sceptic says there is no gardener. The Believer says there is a gardener (but invisible, etc.). One man talks about sexual behaviour. Another man prefers to talk of Aphrodite (but knows that there is not really a superhuman person additional to, and somehow responsible for, all sexual phenomena). The process of qualification may be checked at any point before the original assertion is completely withdrawn and something of that first assertion will remain (Tautology). Mr. Wells's invisible man could not, admittedly, be seen, but in all other respects he was a man like the rest of us. But though the process of qualification may be, and of course usually is, checked in time, it is not always judiciously so halted. Someone may dissipate his assertion completely without noticing that he has done so. A fine brash hypothesis may thus be killed by inches, the death by a thousand qualifications.

And in this, it seems to me, lies the peculiar danger, the endemic evil, of theological utterance. Take such utterances as 'God has a plan', 'God created the world', 'God loves us as a father loves his children'. They look at first sight very much like assertions, vast cosmological assertions. Of course, this is no sure sign that they either are, or are intended to be, assertions. But let us confine ourselves to the cases where those who utter such sentences intend them to express assertions. (Merely remarking parenthetically that those who intend or interpret such utterances as crypto-commands, expressions of wishes, disguised ejaculations, concealed ethics, or as anything else but assertions, are unlikely to succeed in making them either properly orthodox or practically effective.)

Now to assert that such and such is the case is necessarily equivalent to denying that such and such is not the case. Suppose then that we are in doubt as to what someone who gives vent to an utterance is asserting, or suppose that, more radi-

cally, we are sceptical as to whether he is really asserting anything at all, one way of trying to understand (or perhaps it will be to expose) his utterance is to attempt to find what he would regard as counting against, or as being incompatible with, its truth. For if the utterance is indeed an assertion, it will necessarily be equivalent to a denial of the negation of that assertion. And anything which would count against the assertion, or which would induce the speaker to withdraw it and to admit that it had been mistaken, must be part of (or the whole of) the meaning of the negation of that assertion. And to know the meaning of the negation of an assertion, is as near as makes no matter, to know the meaning of that assertion. And if there is nothing which a putative assertion denies then there is nothing which it asserts either: and so it is not really an assertion. When the Sceptic in the parable asked the Believer, 'Just how does what you call an invisible, intangible, eternally elusive gardener differ from an imaginary gardener or even from no gardener at all?' he was suggesting that the Believer's earlier statement had been so eroded by qualification that it was no longer an assertion at all.

Now it often seems to people who are not religious as if there was no conceivable event or series of events the occurrence of which would be admitted by sophisticated religious people to be a sufficient reason for conceding 'There wasn't a God after all' or 'God does not really love us then'. Someone tells us that God loves us as a father loves his children. We are reassured. But then we see a child dying of inoperable cancer of the throat. His earthly father is driven frantic in his efforts to help, but his Heavenly Father reveals no obvious sign of concern. Some qualification is made—God's love is 'not a merely human love' or it is 'an inscrutable love', perhaps—and we realize that such sufferings are quite compatible with the truth of the assertion that 'God loves us as a father (but, of course, . . .)'. We are reassured again. But then perhaps we ask: what is this assurance of God's (appropriately qualified) love worth, what is this apparent guarantee really a guarantee against? Just what would have to happen not merely (morally and wrongly) to tempt but also (logically and rightly) to entitle us to say

'God does not love us' or even 'God does not exist'? I therefore put to the succeeding symposiasts the simple central questions, 'What would have to occur or to have occurred to constitute for you a disproof of the love of, or of the existence of, God?'

University College of North Staffordshire
ENGLAND

BASIL MITCHELL

Flew's article is searching and perceptive, but there is, I think, something odd about his conduct of the theologian's case. The theologian surely would not deny that the fact of pain counts against the assertion that God loves men. This very incompatibility generates the most intractable of theological problems—the problem of evil. So the theologian *does* recognize the fact of pain as counting against Christian doctrine. But it is true that he will not allow it—or anything—to count decisively against it; for he is committed by his faith to trust in God. His attitude is not that of the detached observer, but of the believer.

Perhaps this can be brought out by yet another parable. In time of war in an occupied country, a member of the resistance meets one night a stranger who deeply impresses him. They spend that night together in conversation. The Stranger tells the partisan that he himself is on the side of the resistance—indeed that he is in command of it, and urges the partisan to have faith in him no matter what happens. The partisan is utterly convinced at that meeting of the Stranger's sincerity and constancy and undertakes to trust him.

They never meet in conditions of intimacy again. But sometimes the Stranger is seen helping members of the resistance, and the partisan is grateful and says to his friends, 'He is on our side'.

Sometimes he is seen in the uniform of the police handing over patriots to the occupying power. On these occasions his friends murmur against him: but the partisan still says, 'He is on our side'. He still believes that, in spite of appearances, the Stranger did not deceive him. Sometimes he asks the Stranger for help and receives it. He is then thankful. Sometimes he asks and does not receive it. Then he says, 'The Stranger knows best'. Some-

times his friends, in exasperation, say 'Well, what *would* he have to do for you to admit that you were wrong and that he is not on our side?' But the partisan refuses to answer. He will not consent to put the Stranger to the test. And sometimes his friends complain, 'Well, if *that's* what you mean by his being on our side, the sooner he goes over to the other side the better'.

The partisan of the parable does not allow anything to count decisively against the proposition 'The Stranger is on our side'. This is because he has committed himself to trust the Stranger. But he of course recognizes that the Stranger's ambiguous behaviour *does* count against what he believes about him. It is precisely this situation which constitutes the trial of his faith.

When the partisan asks for help and doesn't get it, what can he do? He can (*a*) conclude that the Stranger is not on our side or; (*b*) maintain that he is on our side, but that he has reasons for withholding help.

The first he will refuse to do. How long can he uphold the second position without its becoming just silly?

I don't think one can say in advance. It will depend on the nature of the impression created by the Stranger in the first place. It will depend, too, on the manner in which he takes the Stranger's behaviour. If he blandly dismisses it as of no consequence, as having no bearing upon his belief, it will be assumed that he is thoughtless or insane. And it quite obviously won't do for him to say easily, 'Oh, when used of the Stranger the phrase "is on our side" *means* ambiguous behaviour of this sort'. In that case he would be like the religious man who says blandly of a terrible disaster 'It is God's will'. No, he will only be regarded as sane and reasonable in his belief, if he experiences in himself the full force of the conflict.

This means that I agree with Flew that theological utterances must be assertions. The partisan is making an assertion when he says, 'The Stranger is on our side'.

Do I want to say that the partisan's belief about the Stranger is, in any sense, an explanation? I think I do. It explains and makes sense of the Stranger's behaviour: it helps to explain also the resistance movement in the context of which he appears. In each case it differs from the interpretation which the others put upon the same facts.

'God loves men' resembles 'the Stranger is on our side' (and many other significant statements, e.g. historical ones) in not being conclusively falsifiable. They can both be treated in at least three different ways: (1) As provisional hypotheses to be discarded if experience tells against them; (2) As significant articles of faith; (3) As vacuous formulae (expressing, perhaps, a desire for reassurance) to

which experience makes no difference and which makes no difference to life.

The Christian, once he has committed himself, is precluded by his faith from taking up the first attitude: 'Thou shalt not tempt the Lord thy God'. He is in constant danger, as Flew has observed, of slipping into the third. But he need not; and, if he does, it is a failure in faith as well as in logic.

Keble College
OXFORD

4.9 Suggestions for Further Reading

Adams, Robert M. *The Virtue of Faith and Other Essays in Philosophical Theology*. New York: Oxford University Press, 1987. A Protestant minister and respected contemporary philosopher defends traditional Christian beliefs in these essays.

Cahn, S. M., and D. Shatz, eds. *Contemporary Philosophy of Religion*. New York: Oxford, 1982. This collection of essays provides wide-ranging discussions of many of the philosophical issues raised by religion.

Camus, Albert. *The Plague*. New York: Vintage, 1972. The theme of evil permeates this novel by a leading existentialist. Ultimately, Camus's is a humanistic posture, based on compassion for the meaningless plight that all people suffer.

Daly, Mary. *Beyond God the Father*. Boston: Beacon Press, 1974. Although difficult in places, Daly's book is already a classic work in feminist theology.

Davies, Paul. *The Mind of God*. New York: Simon & Schuster, 1992. A very readable discussion of current scientific theories of the universe and what they imply about God.

Dostoyevski, Fyodor. *The Brothers Karamazov*. New York: Signet, 1971. Especially relevant in this classic is Book 5, Chapter 4, in which Ivan's philosophical crisis over the presence of evil in the world crystallizes.

Evans, C. Stephen. *Philosophy of Religion*. Downers Grove, IL: InterVarsity Press, 1985. A very readable overview of the central issues in philosophy of religion.

Friedman, Maurice. *The Human Way: A Dialogical Approach to Religion and Human Experience*. Chambersburg, PA: Anima Books, 1982. An existentialist approach to religion.

Gaskin, J. C. A., ed. *Varieties of Unbelief*. New York: Macmillan, 1989. A very good collection of classical and contemporary writings on unbelief.

Hick, John. *Evil and the God of Love*, rev. ed. New York: Harper & Row, 1978. A terrific discussion of the problem of God and evil.

———. *Philosophy of Religion*, 3d ed. Englewood Cliffs, NJ: Prentice-Hall, 1983. An introduction to the central issues in the philosophy of religion.

Kenny, Anthony. *Descartes*. New York: Random House, 1968. This is an excellent paperback introduction to the thought of Descartes.

Kolak, Daniel, and Raymond Martin, eds. *Self, Cosmos, God*. New York: Harcourt Brace, 1993. An anthology of readings on the philosophy of religion.

Kushner, Harold S. *When Bad Things Happen to Good People*. New York: Avon Books, 1981. A very moving discussion of the problem of evil.

Mackie, J. L. *The Miracle of Theism*. Oxford: Oxford University Press, 1982. A very clear discussion of the arguments both for and against the existence of God.

Moreland, J. P., and Kai Nielsen. *Does God Exist?* Buffalo, NY: Prometheus Books, 1993. A theist and an atheist debate the existence of God.

Morris, Thomas, ed. *The Concept of God*. New York: Oxford University Press, 1987. A collection of the best recent articles on the philosophy of God.

Morris, Thomas, ed. *God and the Philosophers*. New York: Oxford University Press, 1994. Twenty well-known and highly respected contemporary philosophers explain what has led them to come to believe in God.

Penelhum, Terence, ed. *Faith*. New York: Macmillan, 1989. An outstanding anthology of classical and contemporary readings on the philosophy of religion.

Peterson, Michael L., ed. *The Problem of Evil*. South Bend, IN: University of Notre Dame Press, 1992. A very good collection of classical and contemporary writings on this important issue.

Peterson, Michael, William Hasker, Bruce Reichenbach, and David Basinger. *Philosophy of Religion*. New York: Oxford University Press, 1996. An outstanding and very complete anthology of readings from classical and contemporary authors covering the main topics in philosophy of religion.

Rolston III, Holmes. *Science and Religion*. New York: Random House, 1987. A very readable discussion of the conflict between science and religion.

Rowe, William, and William Wainwright, eds. *Philosophy of Religion: Selected Readings*. New York: Harcourt Brace, 1989. An excellent anthology of classical and contemporary readings.

Smith, Huston. *The Religions of Man*. New York: Harper & Row, 1958. This paperback contains clear accounts of the major religions of the world.

Wainwright, William J. *Philosophy of Religion*. Belmont, CA: Wadsworth, 1988. An excellent but advanced discussion of the issues.

Warren, Thomas B., and Wallace I. Matson. *The Warren–Matson Debate on the Existence of God*. Jonesboro, AR: National Christian Press, 1978. A fascinating debate between a believer and an agnostic.

PART III

Epistemology

One of the fundamental branches of philosophy is *epistemology*, the study of knowledge. Specifically, epistemology deals with the nature, sources, limitations, and validity of knowledge. Epistemological questions are basic to all other philosophical inquiries. Everything we claim to know, whether in science, history, or everyday life, amounts to little if we are unable to support our claims. Thus, neither a concept of human nature and self, a theory of the universe, nor an assertion of an ordinary event ("This lemon tastes sour" or "It is raining") escapes the need for justification. Epistemology presents us with the task of explaining how we know what we claim to know, how we can find out what we wish to know, and how we can judge someone else's claim to knowledge.

Epistemology addresses a variety of problems: the reliability, extent, and kinds of knowledge; truth; language; and science and scientific knowledge. The next two chapters deal with these major epistemological topics. The first chapter focuses on the question of *how* true knowledge is acquired, and the second examines *what* true knowledge is; that is, the first chapter asks what the *sources* or bases of true knowledge are, and the second asks what the *nature* of true knowledge is.

CHAPTER 5

The Sources
of Knowledge

A man is but what he knows.

FRANCIS BACON

All I know is what I read in the papers.

WILL ROGERS

5.1 Introduction: Why Is Knowledge a Problem?

Your ideas about who you are depend on what you think you know. In fact, nothing is more important to understanding yourself than your knowledge of your past. Your past has made you what you are. Your memories of that past—of parents, of the home you grew up in, of the friends and experiences you have had—constitute your understanding of who you now are. Yet how do you know that your memories are true? Consider the following account recently written by a young college student:

> Jana never calls. I live a long way away and she is my only sibling, but she never calls. . . .
>
> Suddenly, out of the blue, she was calling me, talking to me, sharing her life with me. . . . [But] the circumstances that finally broke down the barriers between us were catastrophic, unspeakable. Our parents, my dear sister told me, had repeatedly abused her when she had been very young.
>
> I was stunned. "This abuse was . . . sexual?"
>
> "Yes, sexual."
>
> "And they both were involved?"
>
> "Yes, they and others."
>
> "Are you sure?"
>
> "YES, OF COURSE I AM!"
>
> I was furious with my parents. I had left home a few years back under the cloud of ongoing arguments with them and, since then, I had been slowly trying to patch things up. This revelation shattered the reconciliations, shattered even the desire to make the effort. With each of the many collect phone calls I accepted from Jana, my parents became more and more strangers, less the people I remembered knowing as a child. When I commented on this fact, Jana taught me about repressed memories. I was frightened beyond description. My entire life was nothing more than my memories of it. If suddenly those are taken away, if suddenly they are found to be fiction, then what am I? I too am fiction. I am the man with amnesia who knows not even his name. I am a 24-year-old adult with no memories of what really happened to him as a child. It was in the midst of that horror of no longer knowing who the hell I was that I began to search desperately for answers. . . . Jana called every other day or so to tell me new stories of abuse that had gurgled up from the black wellspring of repressed memories in her unconscious mind. Abuse by groups. Abuse with

guns. Abuse with various crude medical instruments. Abuse by physical and psychological torture.

It was in this atmosphere of dread and disgust that I discovered I too had been sexually abused as a kid. . . . I discovered my own personal experiences with the help of a psychiatric social worker. . . . The therapist suggested that it would be odd if I had been left alone while my sister had been so harmed. . . . No wonder I couldn't remember anything about my childhood! It was too horrible to remember! Over the next couple sessions she walked me through what she called "relaxation therapy." Whatever I should see, assuming it wasn't too happy, I was to consider truth. . . .

The clarity of the new memories was striking, photographic. So much better than my old memories, those fake cover-up daydreams I'd used to help me suppress the truth; they had all been cloudy. I was beginning to feel like a survivor, like I was on to the truth and it was just a matter of time until I could feel whole again. The trouble was, the closer I came to being "whole," the worse I felt. I was flunking my college classes. I was calling in to work sick. I was smoking a lot. I didn't shave. I didn't eat well. And I didn't care. . . .

Dr. Michael Fane, a psychiatrist . . . was my lucky break. He ran the clinic where my therapist worked, and part of the deal was that I had to have one diagnostic session with him before treatment proceeded. I explained to him my situation, my recent discovery of abuse, and the things I believed had been done to me . . . [He was unsupportive.] By the next morning I would wake up to find my faith in my new memories shattered. . . . I had never heard of False Memory Syndrome at this point in my life, but I knew that I had it. [1]

Working with Dr. Fane, the college student who wrote this account eventually decided that his "recovered" memories of sexual abuse were false memories. However, his sister, Jana, remains convinced that her memories are true. She has broken off all contact with her parents, whom she now sees as monsters who turned her into a dysfunctional person. She believes that her brother, who refuses to accept her knowledge that their parents sexually abused them, is "in denial" of the truth.

Jana and her brother are not the only people who fear that the most fundamental things they thought they knew about themselves might be completely false. Today, tens of thousands of men and women believe they have recalled formerly repressed memories of being sexually abused as children by parents, siblings, relatives, and family friends. Their numbers include television star Roseanne and former Miss America Marilyn Van Derbur. Before entering therapy, they claimed, they had no knowledge of the acts but suffered from a variety of "symptoms," including depression, anxiety, eating disorders, sexual problems, and difficulty with intimacy. Sometimes the recovered memories include terrifying details of torture, participation in satanic rituals, animal sacrifices, and even murder. In some cases individuals have been convicted of murder on the basis of such newly recovered memories of the past. Consider this news story:

Last November, Eileen Franklin-Lipsker, 29, stunned authorities with her story: When she was 9, she said her father — George Franklin Sr. — sexually attacked one

As for me, all I know is that I know nothing.
SOCRATES

---

[1] Eleanor Goldstein and Kevin Farmer, *True Stories of False Memories* (Boca Raton, FL: Social Issues Resources Series, 1993), 117, 118, 199, 120, 125. Used by permission of the publisher.

of her playmates and then beat her to death. Based on her statement, Franklin, 51, was arrested and held in San Mateo County jail, south of San Francisco, in lieu of $2 million bond. Franklin-Lipsker says she had repressed the memory of what she saw 21 years ago until it flashed back as she gazed at her own 5-year-old daughter. Her memory is the focus of the trial. Her sister, Janice Franklin, will testify as to her father's character. The sisters say they were molested by their father as children. Franklin-Lipsker says the victim was Susan Nason, then 8, a neighbor of the Franklins in Foster City. She disappeared September 22, 1969, while on her way to return a pair of sneakers to a friend. Her remains were found nearly two months later in a canyon near the Crystal Springs reservoir. Franklin-Lipsker testified last May that her father picked up Susan in his van and took both girls to the reservoir, where he parked and began playing with them in the back of the van. She said he lay on top of Susan and "began moving back and forth." Then they left the van, and her father came toward Nason carrying a large rock. After killing the girl, Franklin-Lipsker alleged, he threatened to kill his daughter if she told anyone. [2]

In November 1990, George Franklin was convicted of the murder. The Franklin case is not isolated. In 1994 Steven Slutzker was indicted in Pittsburgh for the 1975 murder of John Mudd when the victim's son, who would have been five at the time, said he had a flashback memory of the murder. The same year, Paula Pfiefle of Monroe, Washington, won $1.4 million when she sued a school, alleging that she had recovered memories of a teacher there repeatedly raping and sodomizing her twenty years earlier. In Washington state, Patricia Barton won a settlement from her father after she accused him, on the basis of a recovered memory, of having sexually abused her thirty years earlier, when she was five. In all these cases the accused parties have begged authorities to recognize that the "recovered" memories of abuse are figments of the mind. What the alleged victims claim to know with such certainty the accused insist never happened at all. In some cases, baffled authorities have reluctantly agreed. For example, the Franklin decision was reversed on appeal.

The theory of "recovered memories" has stirred fierce controversy. Supporters of the theory cite studies based on clinical practice. For example, Judie Alpert, a professor of applied psychology at New York University, asserts the following:

> There is absolutely no question that some people have repressed some memories of early abuse that are just too painful to remember. In their 20s and 30s some event triggers early memories, and slowly they return. The event has been so overwhelming that the little girl who is being abused can't tolerate to be there in the moment, so she leaves her body, dissociates, as if she is up on a bookshelf looking down on the little girl who is being abused. Over time, she pushes it deep down because she can't integrate the experience. [3]

Other psychologists flatly deny that these theories are scientifically valid. Professor Elizabeth Loftus is professor of psychology at the University of Washington. She asserts that the theory that people can repress memories of repeated traumatic experiences in childhood and recall them decades later is false:

---

[2] *USA Today*, October 31, 1990, "'Flashback' Focus of Murder Trial," p. 2A.
[3] Quoted in Leon Jaroff, "Lies of the Mind," *Time*, November 29, 1993, 52.

If repression is the avoidance in your conscious awareness of unpleasant experiences that come back to you, yes, I believe in repression. But if it is a blocking out of an endless stream of traumas that occur over and over that leave a person with absolutely no awareness that these things happened, that make them behave in destructive ways and re-emerge decades later in some reliable form, I don't see any evidence for it. It flies in the face of everything we know about memory.[4]

The controversy over repressed and recovered memories is a dramatic illustration of some profound issues raised by our views of what knowledge is, how we acquire knowledge, how we establish truth, and whether science gives us the

---

[4] Ibid.

PHILOSOPHY AND LIFE

Kekulé's Dream

How do we attain knowledge? By what means? Such questions address one aspect of epistemological inquiry: the sources of knowledge.

The most obvious source is sense experience. How do you know that a book is in front of you? Because you can see and feel it. But sense experience is not our only source of knowledge. If someone asked you, "How do you know that if x is greater than y and y is greater than z, that x is greater than z?" what would you say? You don't see or feel anything, but your reasoning tells you that the relation is true. Reasoning is another source of knowledge.

But sometimes we clearly get knowledge by experiences not easily defined. "I had a flash of intuition," we say, or "My intuition tells me it is so" or "All of a sudden, in a flash of intuition, I saw things clearly." It's very difficult to define *intuition*, perhaps impossible. Nevertheless, the term does label certain kinds of experience characterized by a con-

viction of certainty that comes upon us quite suddenly.

Take, for example, a most famous scientific discovery. Friedrich Kekulé, professor of chemistry in Ghent, Belgium, discovered that carbon compounds can form rings. Kekulé's discovery did not come easily. For some time he'd been pondering the structure of benzene, but he couldn't explain it. Then, one afternoon in 1865, he turned his mind away from his work:

I turned my chair to the fire and dozed. Again the atoms were gamboling before my eyes. This time the smaller groups kept modestly in the background. My mental eye, rendered more acute by repeated visions of this kind, could now distinguish larger structures, of manifold conformations; long rows, sometimes more closely fitted together; all twining and twisting in a snakelike motion. But look! What was that? One of the snakes had seized hold of its own tail, and the form whirled mockingly before my eyes. As if by a flash of lightning I awoke and this time also I

spent the rest of the night working out the consequences of the hypothesis.

Kekulé had found his clue to the structure of benzene in his dream of the snake gripping its own tail.

QUESTIONS

1. What preceded Kekulé's discovery via the creative subconscious?

2. Does this narrative tell you anything about how intuition can lead to knowledge?

3. Before Kekulé accepted the validity of his intuitive insight, he subjected it to rigorous testing. Does this suggest anything about how intuitive claims should be handled?

4. How would you distinguish between intuitive claims such as Kekulé's and others such as "My intuition tells me it'll rain tomorrow"?

SOURCE: Quoted in Gardner Lindzey, Calvin Hall, and Richard F. Thompson, *Psychology* (New York: Worth, 1975), 320.

truth. It shows how important it is to be clear about these issues. As Jana's brother says, if a person accepts the view that recovered memories are a source of true knowledge, then his past identity was but a mere "fiction" and the parents he thought he knew are really "strangers." If, as a society, we accept that recovered memories provide true knowledge of past crimes, then countless people who are unjustly living comfortable lives should be stripped of their respectability and cast into the deepest prisons. If we accept that the studies used to establish the theory of recovered memory are valid science, then we should accept that recovered memories provide true knowledge of past crimes.

Yet are recovered memories a source of true knowledge, and is the theory of recovered memories valid science? Many critics of recovered memories remind us of the seventeenth-century Salem witch trials. During these trials many women were condemned to death because men "knew" they were witches because of their supposedly witchlike behavior and then-accepted theories of witchcraft. Indeed, how often have entire societies found themselves deluded about the valid sources of knowledge and truth? For several hundred years, European society and science believed that the earth was flat and that it lay at the center of the universe. Everyone believed that the sun, planets, and stars revolved around the earth. When Copernicus, Galileo, and others suggested that this was a mistake, they were condemned and persecuted by church authorities. Church authorities believed that Scripture is the only source of true knowledge. According to Scripture, they claimed, the earth lies at the center of the universe. Today, biologists who believe in the theory of evolution are sometimes attacked by "creationists," who believe that the Bible account of how God created the world is literally true. During the Nazi era, German society claimed that it was a "scientific fact" that the Germanic races were superior to all others, and on this basis, they rounded up Jews and Gypsies, imprisoned them, tortured them, and eventually murdered millions. Here in the United States several researchers recently claimed that scientific research shows that the white race is genetically superior to the black race, and concluded that race-based public policies are justified. And in the recent past, reputable scientists claimed that women were inferior to men and that society should treat them as such.

All these events demonstrate the critical importance—both to us personally and as a society—of looking carefully at the issues of truth and knowledge. What is knowledge? What is truth? How do you tell the difference between true scientific knowledge and doubtful pseudoscience? What are valid sources of knowledge and truth?

In this chapter we examine the question of how reliable knowledge is *acquired*. We ask what distinguishes the way in which reliable knowledge is acquired from the way in which unreliable beliefs are acquired. In the next chapter, we examine what true knowledge *is* instead of looking at how it is acquired.

How do we acquire reliable knowledge? What is the source or basis of our knowledge? Philosophers have given considerable attention to questions about the sources of knowledge. One popular way of approaching the subject, though by no means the only way, is to begin by examining two very important views about the source of knowledge: rationalism and empiricism. Rationalism is the

The False Mirror, René Magritte. Are there different kinds of knowledge? If there are, how can each be obtained? What are their source? What are their limits? Rationalists endorse reason, arguing that only rational knowledge is certain. Empiricists contend that reason can only relate the facts that are presented by the senses.

view that knowledge can be obtained by relying on reason without the aid of the senses. For example, what distinguishes real knowledge from mere opinion, in the rationalist view, is that real knowledge is based on the logic, the laws, and the methods that reason develops. The best example of real knowledge, the rationalist holds, is mathematics, a realm of knowledge that is obtained entirely by reason and that we use to understand the universe.

Empiricism, on the other hand, is the view that knowledge can be attained only through sense experience. According to the empiricist, real knowledge is based on what our sight, hearing, smell, and other senses tell us is really out there, not what people make up in their heads.

In this chapter we look more closely at these two seminal theories and also consider an alternative, termed *transcendental idealism*. In doing so, we hope to throw light on the aspect of the self that knows or claims to know about itself and the world outside it. Finally, we look at science and discuss how these theories relate to the knowledge generated by the sciences.

QUESTIONS

1. What do you mean when you say you know something is true? If you are unsure that something is true, can you *know* it is true? Does knowledge require certainty?

2. How much of your knowledge depends on trusting that others have told you the truth? Make a list of crucial facts about yourself that you learned from others or that depend on what you learned from others (for example, who your parents are, how old you are, and so on). If you learn something from others, can you really be said to know it? How much of our scientific knowledge depends on trusting that others have told us the truth?

3. Can you think of some things you came to know completely on your own? How did you come to know those things?

5.2 Is Reason the Source of Our Knowledge?

By **rationalism,** we mean the belief that reason, without the aid of sensory perception, is capable of arriving at some knowledge, some undeniable truths. **Perception** refers to the processes of seeing, hearing, smelling, touching, and tasting by which we become aware of or apprehend ordinary objects such as chairs, tables, rocks, and trees. When rationalists claim that knowledge is based on reason rather than perception, they mean that we do not rely on sensory experience for some of the fundamental knowledge we have.

In effect, rationalists contend that some of our knowledge is not a product of experience but depends solely on our mental processes. They hold that we can acquire accurate knowledge about the world around us by simply looking into our minds and without observing the world.

At first sight this may strike you as an astonishingly stupid view: How can we know anything about the world without first observing it? But before we brush aside this view of knowledge, let us think a little about how mathematicians work and how their work differs from that of other scientists. Scientists such as chemists and physicists work in laboratories, where they conduct experiments and observe the results. Astronomers use giant telescopes to observe the stars. Biologists use microscopes to determine what living organisms are like. In short, these scientists need to observe the external world to check whether their theories are true. Not so the mathematician. The mathematician typically works huddled over her desk, perhaps with the shades drawn. Nevertheless, the mathematician can discover new mathematical theorems in her windowless office by using nothing more than pencil, paper, and reason. The mathematician does not need to observe the external world to see whether her theories and theorems are true! Yet the mathematical theories that the mathematician discovers by simply reasoning in her mind can accurately describe the vast reaches of the universe outside.

rationalism the position that reason alone, without the aid of sensory information, is capable of arriving at some knowledge, at some undeniable truths

perception the act or process by which we become aware of things

No fact can be real and no statement true unless it has a sufficient reason why it should be thus and not otherwise.
GOTTFRIED WILHELM LEIBNITZ

Because such knowledge does not depend on sense experience, rationalists term it **a priori,** knowledge that is known independently of sense perception and that is necessarily true and indubitable. Moreover, the rationalist holds, this knowledge that reason discovers without making experiments or relying on the findings of sense experience underlies our understanding of the universe. When astronomers investigate black holes and stars in galaxies billions of miles away, they use the theories that the mathematician reasoned out in her head. When physicists explore the intricacies of subatomic particles or when biologists examine the chemistry of DNA, they also use the mathematical theories that the mathematician simply thought up in her head. A similar point may be made about the laws of logic. The laws of logic (such as those described in the appendix to Chapter 1) are also not established by observation. Yet they underlie all our reasoning processes. So reason, without relying on sense experience, apparently gives us knowledge of truths about the world that are so basic that all our other knowledge depends on our prior knowledge of these truths.

Rationalists do not necessarily believe that all knowledge is acquired through reason alone. Most of them agree that some of our knowledge—for example, whether the sun is shining, whether giraffes have spots, whether dinosaurs existed—is derived from what we observe with our senses. However, the rationalist characteristically holds that *some* of our knowledge—particularly our most fundamental knowledge—about reality is acquired without sense experience. Just as we discover mathematical truths by reasoning inside our minds, we can discover other basic laws of the universe without ever having to observe that universe.

Rationalists also insist that some of the knowledge we acquire by using reason alone is knowledge about the world around us. We obviously have knowledge that is not about the world and that is not based on sensory experience, such as the knowledge that all bachelors are unmarried. But such knowledge is true by definition and thus does not give us any information about the world. However, the rationalist claims that some of our knowledge about the world is acquired by the use of reason alone without sense experience. For example, some rationalists have held that the laws of logic and of mathematics tell us what the world has to be like and that these laws are established solely by reason. Other rationalists have claimed that our knowledge that "every event has a cause," that "the shortest distance between two points on a plane surface is a straight line," that "the universe follows the same laws in all of its parts," and that "the processes of the universe are regular and can be explained in terms of consistent laws" are all examples of fundamental knowledge about the world around us that cannot be established by using our senses.

The history of philosophy records the thinking of many outstanding rationalists, including Plato (ca. 428–348 B.C.), Saint Augustine (354–430), Benedict Spinoza (1632–1677), Anne Conway (1631–1679), Gottfried Wilhelm Leibnitz (1646–1716), and Georg Hegel (1770–1831). Certainly among the most noteworthy is René Descartes, the seventeenth-century scientific giant who not only invented analytic geometry but also advanced a view of knowledge that greatly influenced philosophy. We begin with Descartes because his ideas have been so influential.

a priori pertaining to knowledge that is logically prior to experience; reasoning based on such knowledge

People have a very deep desire for explanation, a requirement, almost a demand, that there be explanations, that whatever you investigate, there should be a reason to explain it.

BAS VAN FRAASSEN

René Descartes: "How do I know but that there is no earth, no heaven, no place, and that nevertheless these seem to me to exist just exactly as I now see them? How do I know that I am not deceived every time I add two and three, or count the sides of a square?"

DESCARTES: DOUBT AND REASON

Curiously, many of us today can identify with Descartes's methodological point of departure—an attitude of doubt and skepticism. Today we might call his frame of mind *disillusionment*. Some would say that Descartes suffered an epistemological "credibility gap" of sorts. He seriously wondered about what he could believe, what he could be certain of. He was driven to this point by the many intellectual, scientific, and religious upheavals that his world was undergoing.

Only a few decades before Descartes was born, Martin Luther launched the great Protestant revolution. That revolution eventually engulfed all of Europe and gave birth to the religious wars that rocked the Continent for decades. Church doctrines that everyone had accepted as unchangeable dogmas were suddenly cast into doubt. At the same time, scientists like Copernicus and Galileo challenged views that had been accepted for over two thousand years. Copernicus rejected the ancient view that the earth was at the center of the universe and that the sun revolved around it. In place of this old theory, Co-

The great intellectual invention of the seventeenth century was the invention of what we call theories.
STEPHEN TOULMIN

pernicus proposed the startling new idea that the earth and the planets revolve around the sun. Peering through the newly invented telescope, Galileo discovered that the moon had mountains, that there were spots on the sun, and that the Milky Way was composed of countless stars. All this was contrary to the ancient belief that the moon, sun, and stars are perfect crystalline bodies. Galileo also rejected ideas about motion that dated back to the ancient Greeks, such as that heavy bodies fall faster than light ones, or that moving bodies eventually must come to rest. Instead, Galileo proved, all bodies fall to earth at the same rate, and moving bodies continue in motion unless stopped by friction or another external force.

We live in an age much like that of Descartes. Ours is an era of rapid change and new discoveries, of constant sensory input, and of an information explosion. The computer, the Internet, television, e-mail, and countless other forms of electronic communications have unleashed a flood of news and information. Stock market prices fall in Asia, and minutes later they drag down the stock market in New York. Television programs aired in Los Angeles instantaneously create a stir in Europe. The flow of new discoveries in science, medicine, and technology is so fast and so massive that no one can keep up. Advances in medicine extend life in ways that create troubling new questions about when life ends. Cloning raises questions about manipulating life. Rather than adding stability to life, a fast-paced, continuous flow of new knowledge and information can leave us unsteadily wobbling between old assumptions and new discoveries.

Uncertainty isn't new. In the seventeenth century, people were racked with uncertainty about how to reconcile the new ideas of Copernicus and Galileo with their old religious, philosophical, and scientific beliefs. Scientists, mathematicians, and philosophers—Descartes foremost among them—had to accommodate the new religious and scientific ideas with the traditional dogma of the Church. This was not an easy task for those who, like Descartes, had medieval and Aristotelian roots. Indeed, the age of Descartes was marked by a profound questioning of established religious authority, traditional doctrine, and time-honored opinion. From a twentieth-century perspective, we might say that one of the crucial problems of his era was how to hold on to the new ideas of the present without letting go of the historical, cultural, and intellectual past.

Descartes seems to have felt the same anxiety and doubt that we experience. He, too, became vitally concerned with discovering something that he could hold as true beyond any doubt:

> All that up to the present time I have accepted as most true and certain I have learned either from the senses or through the senses; but it is sometimes proved to me that these senses are deceptive, and it is wiser not to trust entirely to any thing by which we have once been deceived. . . .
>
> At the same time I must remember that I am a man, and that consequently I am in the habit of sleeping, and in my dreams representing to myself the same things or sometimes even less probable things, than do those who are insane in their waking moments. How often has it happened to me that in the night I dreamt that I found myself in this particular place, that I was dressed and seated near the fire, whilst in reality I was lying undressed in bed! At this moment it does indeed seem to me that

it is with eyes awake that I am looking at this paper; that this head which I move is not asleep, that it is deliberately and of set purpose that I extend my hand and perceive it; what happens in sleep does not appear so clear nor so distinct as does all this. But in thinking over this I remind myself that on many occasions I have in sleep been deceived by similar illusions, and in dwelling carefully on this reflection I see so manifestly that there are no certain indications by which we may clearly distinguish wakefulness from sleep that I am lost in astonishment. And my astonishment is such that it is almost capable of persuading me that I now dream. . . .

I have long had fixed in my mind the belief that an all-powerful God existed by whom I have been created such as I am. But how do I know that He has not brought it to pass that there is no earth, no heaven, no extended body, no magnitude, no place, and that nevertheless [I possess the perceptions of all these things and that] they seem to me to exist just exactly as I now see them? And, besides, as I sometimes imagine that others deceive themselves in the things which they think they know best, how do I know that I am not deceived every time that I add two and three, or count the sides of a square, or judge of things yet simpler, if anything simpler can be imagined? But possibly God has not desired that I should be thus deceived, for He is said to be supremely good. If, however, it is contrary to His goodness to have made me such that I constantly deceive myself, it would also appear to be contrary to His goodness to permit me to be sometimes deceived, and nevertheless I cannot doubt that He does permit this.

I shall then suppose, not that God who is supremely good and the fountain of truth, but some evil genius not less powerful than deceitful, has employed his whole energies in deceiving me; I shall consider that the heavens, the earth, colors, figures, sound, and all other external things are nought but the illusions and dreams of which this genius has availed himself in order to lay traps for my credulity; I shall consider myself as having no hands, no eyes, no flesh, no blood, nor any senses, yet falsely believing myself to possess all these things; I shall remain obstinately attached to this idea, and if by this means it is not in my power to arrive at the knowledge of any truth, I may at least do what is in my power [i.e., suspend my judgment], and with firm purpose avoid giving credence to any false thing, or being imposed upon by this arch deceiver, however powerful and deceptive he may be.[5]

Thus, Descartes took doubt to its outer limits. Our sense perceptions, he held, may be illusions or the products of our own dreams or hallucinations. Our ideas may be nothing more than the products of an evil, all-powerful being that puts these ideas in our minds. Descartes came to doubt everything of which he could not be certain. He then asked this question: Is there anything that survives an attempt to cast doubt on absolutely everything? Is there any truth that is so certain that it cannot be doubted? Ultimately, he discovered what he felt was an indubitable truth: He could not doubt that he existed. Descartes reasoned that he could not doubt that he is a thinking thing. Thus, the self whose existence I cannot doubt is the self that doubts as well as affirms, wills, and imagines — in a word, the self that thinks.

But what is thinking? What does it mean to say that I can think and reason? This is an important question, for in answering it, Descartes lays a rationalistic

> *No man knows anything distinctly, and no man ever will.*
> XENOPHANES

---

[5] René Descartes, *Meditations on First Philosophy,* in *The Philosophical Works of Descartes,* vol. 1, trans. and ed. Elizabeth S. Haldane and G. R. T. Ross (Cambridge: Cambridge University Press, 1911).

basis for knowledge. In one of the most epistemologically important of all his writings, his *Second Meditation*, Descartes attempts to describe the nature of a thinking thing. In the selection that follows, note how he abstracts from the sensuous qualities of a piece of wax, identified by perception, to demonstrate why sense experience is not the ultimate criterion of knowledge. In this way he establishes a rationalistic foundation for knowledge:

> Let us begin by considering the commonest matters, those which we believe to be the most distinctly comprehended, to wit, the bodies which we touch and see; not indeed bodies in general, for these general ideas are usually a little more confused, but let us consider one body in particular. Let us take, for example, this piece of wax: it has been taken quite freshly from the hive, and it has not yet lost the sweetness of the honey which it contains; it still retains somewhat of the odor of the flowers from which it has been culled; its color, its figure, its size are apparent; it is hard, cold, easily handled, and if you strike it with the finger, it will emit a sound. Finally all the things which are requisite to cause us distinctly to recognize a body, are met with in it. But notice that while I speak and approach the fire what remained of the taste is exhaled, the smell evaporated, the color alters, the figure is destroyed, the size increases, it becomes liquid, it heats, scarcely can one handle it, and when one strikes it, no sound is emitted. Does the same wax remain after this change? We must confess that it remains; none would judge otherwise. What then did I know so distinctly in this piece of wax? It could certainly be nothing of all that the senses brought to my notice, since all these things which fall under taste, smell, sight, touch, and hearing, are found to be changed, and yet the same wax remains.
>
> . . . We must then grant that . . . it is my mind alone which perceives . . . this piece of wax. . . . But what is this piece of wax which cannot be understood except by the mind? It is certainly the same that I see, touch, imagine, and finally it is the same which I have always believed it to be from the beginning. But what must particularly be observed is this: it is perceived neither by an act of vision, nor of touch, nor of imagination . . . but only by an intuition of the mind.[6]

CRITICAL THINKING

Descartes says that since all the sensory qualities of the wax gradually change, it follows that his knowledge that the wax remains the same cannot be based on his senses. Does this really follow?

Descartes is pointing out that our minds know that the wax remains the same piece of wax when it melts, although to our senses all of its qualities have changed. Thus, our knowledge of what the wax is does not derive from the senses or the imagination but from the mind. If that knowledge were derived from the senses, we would have to say that when wax melts it is no longer the same wax since to our senses it changes completely when it melts. Consequently, our knowledge that the melted wax is the same wax as the unmelted wax is something that we know with the mind and not with the senses.

Thus, Descartes concludes, knowledge is grasped by the mind, not by the senses. We know what things are by an "intuition" or perception of the mind, but our perceptions or intuitions can be either confused or clear and distinct. Only the clear and distinct ideas in our minds provide genuine knowledge. We have a clear idea of something when we know its nature or essence so well that we can identify it. We have a distinct idea of something when we can distinguish it from other things. Thus, for Descartes, the mind or reason is the ultimate basis of knowledge.

---

[6] Ibid., 190–191. Reprinted by permission.

Descartes's view that reason is the ultimate basis of knowledge is an example of extreme rationalism. Not all rationalists are as thoroughgoing as Descartes. Some rationalists hold that although some of our knowledge derives completely from reason, some of it also depends on the senses. The extreme rationalist, like Descartes, holds that all our genuine knowledge derives solely from reason, without the aid of the senses.

The extreme nature of Descartes's rationalism is especially evident in the way he approaches our knowledge of God and the world. Descartes argues that an imperfect creature like himself could not make up the idea of a perfect God. He concludes that the source of such an idea must be something perfect — God. He then infers that this perfect being, God, must exist.

Notice that in these reasonings, Descartes never appeals to the testimony of his senses. His claims appeal to the mind alone; he believes that they pass the test of a clear and distinct idea. Similarly, he argues for the existence of the world and other selves. Could a perfect God, he asks, deceive me into perceiving my own body, the outer world, and other individuals, as I obviously do? Remember that Descartes knew that he himself existed only as a thinking thing. True, he did perceive his own body and the outer world, but consistent with his method of doubt, he reasoned that these might be illusions, the devilish tricks of some mad genius. But could they be? He has, after all, proved that a perfect being exists. Is such trickery and deception inherent in the nature of perfection? He concludes that it is not. Therefore, he reasons, the world and other selves do indeed exist. We know they exist not because our senses tell us they exist but because the mind has reasoned to their existence on the basis of its clear and distinct ideas.

INNATE IDEAS

But how does the mind arrive at knowledge without using its senses? Descartes and other rationalists used the notion of innate ideas to answer this question. *Innate ideas* are ideas that are present in the mind from birth. Some rationalists, like Plato, believe that we are born with certain ideas fully formed in our minds. But, at birth, these ideas are hidden away in the depths of the mind or memory, so the young infant is not yet aware of them. As the person grows up, these ideas slowly emerge into the person's awareness. Other rationalists, like Leibniz, however, believe that the mind at birth has only "inclinations, dispositions, tendencies, or natural potentials" to form these ideas. As people mature, their experiences gradually shape these tendencies and turn them into fully formed ideas.

What kind of ideas might be innate? Most rationalists feel that at least the basic principles of logic and math are innate. These include the basic axioms of geometry, like the proposition that the shortest distance between two points is a straight line. They also include the basic laws of arithmetic, such as the proposition that if equal numbers are added to equal numbers, the results are equal. Moreover, some rationalists believe that the basic rules of science are also innate. This includes, for example, the rule that every event has to have a cause. It also includes the rule that nothing comes from nothing. Some rationalists

In trying to distinguish appearance from reality and lay bare the fundamental structure of the universe, science has had to transcend the "rabble of the senses."

LINCOLN BARNETT

Descartes takes the view that the human mind is made in the image of God, adapting the teaching of Genesis.

NICHOLAS JOLLEY

believe that not only are *propositions* like these innate but that the individual *concepts* are also innate. These concepts include, for example, the concept of "point," "line," "straight," "equality," "event," and "cause."

Why would anyone think that such propositions and concepts are innate? This question is at the heart of a problem that we still struggle with today: Where else could our knowledge of these propositions and concepts come from? Many philosophers feel that we cannot come to know these propositions and concepts by observing the world around us. In other words, we cannot know these by looking at things outside the mind. The things we see around us never quite live up to these propositions and concepts in our mind. For example, in geometry, mathematicians think of a real *line* as having no thickness and a real *point* as having no size. But the lines we see in the world around us are always more or less thick. And points are always of one size or another. In arithmetic, as we conceptualize it in our minds, *equal* means perfectly identical. Yet in the world around us two objects are never perfectly identical to each other. Or consider the proposition that *every event has a cause*. In the world around us and over a lifetime we may observe perhaps a few hundred thousand or even a few million events. Yet we certainly do not observe *every event*. How, then, is it that our minds know, without observing all events, that *every* event has to have a cause?

Apparently, there are certain propositions and concepts that are in our mind, yet it seems we do not come to know these by observing things in the world around us. Where, then, does our knowledge of these come from? We must be born with this knowledge, say rationalist philosophers. The rationalist philosopher Plato often discussed this issue in his dialogues. A good example is his dialogue *Meno*.

In *Meno*, Plato tells us how Socrates once made a slave boy "remember" his knowledge of geometry by showing him some imperfect figures drawn on the ground. Socrates shows the slave boy a square that is supposed to be two feet by two feet, or four square feet in size (see Figure 1, diagram a). Socrates asks the boy to draw a second square that is exactly twice the size of the first square. At first, the boy says that if you double the length of each side of the first square, you will get a second square that is exactly twice the size of the first square. But when Socrates draws a second square that is approximately four feet by four feet (Figure 1, diagram b), the boy quickly realizes that his first answer is wrong. If you double the length of each side of a square, you will get a new square that is exactly four times as big as the first square. Yet the boy knows this without making exact measurements of the squares that Socrates draws on the ground. And even if the boy had measured the squares, they would probably not have turned out to be exactly the right sizes. So where did the boy's knowledge come from?

Socrates then repeats his original question: How do you draw a second square that is exactly twice the size of the first square? The boy hesitates. Socrates draws a diagonal line from one corner to the other in the first square (Figure 1, diagram c). Then he draws a second larger square, using this diagonal line as the side of the larger square. Socrates asks the boy how big this second square is. The boy is unsure. So Socrates draws some diagonals in the larger square,

There is a fascinating desire people have to make their own theories as elegant as possible.
STEPHEN TOULMIN

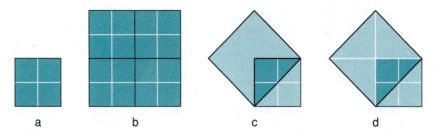

a   b   c   d

Figure 1. Socrates used similar diagrams to prove his theory of innate ideas.

dividing it into four small triangles (Figure 1, diagram d). Then Socrates invites the boy to count the triangles in the first square and the triangles in the second square. Immediately it flashes on the boy: The second square drawn on the diagonal has to be exactly twice the size of the first square! The boy "knows" this, even though, again, he does not measure Socrates' very imperfect figures. And, anyway, if he had measured the squares that Socrates drew on the ground, it would certainly have turned out that the second square was not exactly twice the size of the first square. So, again, where did the boy's knowledge come from? In a discussion with Meno, the master of the slave, Socrates answers that question as follows:

SOCRATES: What do you say of your slave, Meno? Weren't all of his answers given out of his own head?

MENO: Yes, his answers were all his own.

SOCRATES: And yet, you just told us that you never taught him geometry?

MENO: That's true.

SOCRATES: But he had these opinions somewhere inside him, didn't he?

MENO: Yes.

SOCRATES: So the person who does not know something may still have true opinions about the subject buried within himself without actually being aware of them?

MENO: He may.

SOCRATES: And just now these opinions were stirred up in the boy, as if in a dream. But if we asked him many more of these same kinds of questions, in many different forms, wouldn't he eventually come to know the subject as well as anyone else?

MENO: I think so.

SOCRATES: Without anyone telling him the answers, he can recover his knowledge from within himself, if he is only asked questions?

MENO: Yes.

SOCRATES: And this spontaneous recovery of the knowledge that is in him is a form of remembering what is already in him?

MENO: True.

SOCRATES: And this knowledge which he now remembers, he must have acquired at some earlier time?

MENO: Yes....

SOCRATES: Has anyone ever taught him these things? You should know, Meno, since he was raised in your house?

MENO: No, no one ever taught him this.

SOCRATES: Then, if he did not acquire these truths in this life, isn't it clear that he acquired and learned them during some other period?

MENO: Apparently.

SOCRATES: Before he was born with a human form?

MENO: Yes....

SOCRATES: And if the truth about reality is always in our soul, the soul must be immortal. So we must take courage and try hard to discover—that is, to remember—the knowledge within us that we are not yet aware of.[7]

In this fascinating dialogue, Plato is trying to show that there is only one way we could have come to have our knowledge of geometry. We could not have acquired our knowledge of geometry by observing things after we were born or by being told these things. We must have had this knowledge in some vague form in our minds at birth. But how did it get into our minds? Plato answers: We must have acquired this knowledge before we were born! Before we were born, Plato believes, our souls must have lived in a perfect universe where we actually observed perfectly shaped lines, squares, and triangles, along with other perfect ideas. When we are born into this imperfect world, we carry those perfect ideas within us, buried in the depths of memory.

Of course, many philosophers have rejected Plato's claim that before we were born we existed in another perfect universe. But many rationalists have accepted Plato's more basic insight: We do not acquire the basic truths of math and geometry by observing the world around us with our senses. Instead, rationalists claim, reason somehow draws the basic truths and concepts of science from within itself. Descartes, in particular, thought that it was obvious that reason contains within itself the most basic ideas on which all of our knowledge is based.

Another rationalist, Gottfried W. Leibniz (1646–1716), disagreed with Descartes. Leibniz agreed that we do not acquire our knowledge of the most basic truths about the world by observing the world around us. He also agreed that those truths must somehow be innate in us, as Plato said. But Leibniz was not willing to say that we are born with fully formed truths in our minds. Innate ideas, Leibniz claimed, are in us only as "tendencies":

If there were veins in a block of marble which marked out the shape of Hercules rather than other shapes, then that block would be more determined to that shape

In Leibniz' philosophy, the human mind is in a sense omniscient, so it really is rather God-like.

NICHOLAS JOLLEY

---

[7] Plato, Meno, 85c–86a. This translation © 1998 by Manuel Velasquez.

and Hercules would be innate in it, in a way, even though labor would be required to expose the veins and to polish them into clarity, removing everything that prevents their being seen. This is how ideas and truths are innate in us—as inclinations, dispositions, tendencies, or natural potentials, and not as acutalities.[8]

In spite of these differences, most rationalists have agreed with Plato that we have innate ideas. Nevertheless, the theory of innate ideas is difficult for other philosophers to accept. How can we have knowledge inside our minds, they ask, if we are not aware of it? To say that we "know" something is to say that we at least believe it. But how can we believe something without being aware of it? To many philosophers, it seems pointless to say that we have knowledge if we are not aware of it. But if we do not accept the theory of innate ideas, the question remains: How do we acquire our knowledge of so many basic truths that seem to lie beyond what our observations of the world around us can provide?

Let us end our discussion of rationalism by considering briefly what Descartes's view of clear and distinct ideas might suggest about the controversy over recovered memories that we discussed above. Some people with recovered memories have made the point that "the clarity of the new memories is striking, photographic." Descartes probably would object to applying his theories to memories, but the clarity, the detailed sharpness, and the convincing qualities of many recovered memories would seem to imply that they are "clear and distinct" and so can be accepted as true knowledge. That is, the inherent qualities of the recollected memories by themselves—their clarity, their distinctness, and their certitude—validate them as sources of self-evident knowledge about the past. Indeed, many lawyers have argued that the clarity and distinctness of recovered memories proves that they must be true. For example, one attorney is quoted as saying this: "I find it highly unlikely that someone who can remember what pattern was on the wallpaper and that a duck was quacking outside the bedroom window where she was molested by her father when she was four years old is making it up. Why in the hell would your mind do this?"

Juries hearing courtroom cases of childhood sexual abuse based on sharply detailed recovered memories have agreed that the clarity and distinctness of recovered memories make them self-evidently true. A follower of Descartes might even argue that since God is not a deceiver, He would not put such clear and distinct memories in our minds unless they were true. But readers should ask themselves an important question: Are we justified in claiming that memories need no external validation and that they are self-evidently true when they are clear and distinct? Does the clarity and distinctness of a memory—or of any other idea—really guarantee its truth, as rationalists like Descartes claim? On the other hand, if the inherent clarity and distinctness of recovered memories are not sufficient for us to count them as self-evident sources of knowledge of the past, then how are they to be validated?

---

[8] Gottfried W. Leibniz, "New Essays on the Human Understanding," in *Leibniz Selections*, ed. Philip P. Wiener (New York: Charles Scribner's Sons, 1951), 373.

QUESTIONS

1. What does Descartes mean by a "clear and distinct idea"?

2. In your own words, explain how Descartes concluded that a human is a thinking thing.

3. Why does Descartes believe that God exists?

4. How does Descartes use the existence of God to demonstrate that a world and other selves exist?

5. Do you agree with Descartes's view that knowledge requires certainty? If you are not certain that something is true, can you really know it is true? How much of what you believe are you certain is true?

5.3 Can the Senses Account for All Our Knowledge?

Beginning in the sixteenth century, a school of epistemology emerged that contrasted sharply with that of rationalism—empiricism. **Empiricism** is the belief that all knowledge about the world comes from or is based on the senses. Reacting sharply to rationalistic claims, empiricists claim that the human mind contains nothing except what experience has put there. Thus, all ideas originate in sense experience. Consequently, empiricism teaches that true knowledge is **a posteriori.** That is, it depends on experience; it is knowledge stated in empirically verifiable statements.

Empiricism obviously makes a lot of sense where our ordinary knowledge of the world is concerned. It is through observation with our senses that we acquire the knowledge that the sky is blue, that trees are green, that lemons taste sour, and that the seasons change in a regular cycle through winter, spring, summer, and fall. Sense observations also underlie almost all the knowledge of the natural sciences, such as the astronomer's knowledge that Halley's comet returns to earth every seventy-five years; the chemist's knowledge that when oxygen and hydrogen burn, they produce water; the physicist's knowledge that at the surface of the earth objects fall at the accelerating rate of 32 feet per second per second; and the biologist's knowledge that monkeys form social hierarchies. In all these cases our knowledge comes from and is based on sense experience.

Like rationalism, empiricism has had a long and illustrious history. Elements of empiricism can be found in the writings of Aristotle (384–322 B.C.), Saint Thomas Aquinas (1225–1274), Sir Francis Bacon (1561–1626), and Thomas Hobbes (1588–1679). In modern times the first noteworthy attack on rationalism was waged by three philosophers termed the British empiricists: John Locke (1632–1704), George Berkeley (1685–1753), and David Hume (1711–1776).

empiricism the position that knowledge has its origins in and derives all of its content from experience

a posteriori pertaining to knowledge stated in empirically verifiable statements; inductive reasoning

Is reason a truth-finding faculty all on its own? The rationalists say "Yes!" and the empiricists say, "Give us a break!"

PAUL CHURCHLAND

What can give us more sure knowledge than our senses? How else can we distinguish between the true and the false?

LUCRETIUS

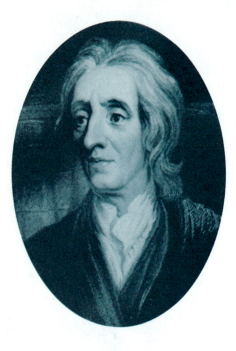

John Locke: "For since the mind, in all its thoughts and reasonings, hath no other immediate objects but its own ideas, it is evident that our knowledge is only conversant about them."

LOCKE

The English philosopher John Locke (1632–1704) was the first to launch a systematic attack on the belief that reason alone could provide us with knowledge. Locke compared the mind to a blank slate, *tabula rasa*, on which experience makes its mark. In *An Essay Concerning Human Understanding*, he stated the nature of his proposed doctrine clearly:

> Let us then suppose the mind to be, as we say, white paper, void of all characters, without any ideas:—How comes it to be furnished? Whence comes it by that vast store which the busy and boundless fancy of man has painted on it with almost endless variety? Whence has it all the *materials* of reason and knowledge? To this I answer, in one word, from *experience*. In that all our knowledge is founded.[9]

It's tempting to be lulled by the apparent simplicity and common sense of Locke's assertion. But automatic acceptance misses important philosophical implications. Consider the fact that we humans make all sorts of claims, from apparently ordinary ones such as "The lemon is sour" and "Three plus three is six" to more complex ones such as "$E = mc^2$." Yet even for the simplest claims, as Descartes demonstrated, few people could provide a sound epistemological basis. In fact, if you ask people how they know it's raining, they might tell you to go outside and see for yourself. If you ask them how they know that today is the hottest day of the year, they again might tell you to go out and *feel* it and

It is not in the power of the most exalted wit, or enlarged understanding, to invent or frame one new simple idea in the mind.

JOHN LOCKE

---

[9] John Locke, *An Essay Concerning Human Understanding*, vol. 2, ed. A. C. Fraser (Oxford: Clarendon Press, 1894), 2.

PHILOSOPHY AND LIFE

Science and the Attempt to Observe Reality

Can we ever observe the world as it is, independently of ourselves? Or do our very attempts to observe the world always *change* the world? Psychologists and sociologists often face this problem, since the very fact that people are being observed leads them to behave differently than they would if they were not being observed. The more accurately you try to determine how angry you feel, for example, the less you experience the anger you are trying to observe.

Or consider the results of a famous series of experiments called the Hawthorne studies, which tried to discover what kinds of job conditions would improve the productivity of workers. Workers were observed under various different working conditions (including noise, darkness, bright light, music, silence). The Hawthorne researchers discovered, much to their surprise, that the productivity of the workers they studied always improved no matter what the conditions. It was only much later that the researchers realized that it was the fact that the workers were being *observed* and were being rewarded with so much *attention* that led them to be more productive. Making objective observations—that is, observations that are not contaminated by the observer's activities and choices—is very difficult when observing the psychological or social world.

But surely the *physical* world can be observed objectively—that is, without it being changed by our observations. Or can it? Consider the problem of trying to measure precisely the temperature of a volume of warm water: If we insert a thermometer into the water, the temperature of the thermometer will change the original temperature of the water.

But it is when we reach the basic constituents of all matter—subatomic particles—that our attempts to observe the physical world most radically alter that world. For to observe that world, we must shoot some kind of radiation (light rays or gamma rays) at it and observe the reflected radiation. But the energy of the radiation will always disturb the subatomic particles, leaving us uncertain about what was there before the observation. In fact, modern physics explicitly holds that on principle it is impossible to observe subatomic particles without disturbing them so much that we cannot be sure where they are or how fast they are moving. Here is how a physics textbook explains the impossibility of observing the subatomic world in a way that would eliminate our uncertainty about that world:

In Newtonian mechanics, still applicable to the macroscopic world of matter, both the position and velocity of a body are easily calculable; e.g., both the position and the velocity of the earth in its orbit can be known precisely at any instant. Inside the atom this is not possible. We have already learned that electrons orbiting within atoms can absorb light energy in units proportional to the frequency of the light and that in doing so they shift energy levels. Now suppose that we could "see" an electron. You need light to see it, but when you turn on the light to see it, the electron absorbs some of the light energy and instantly moves to another energy level with a different velocity. This is implied in Heisenberg's uncertainty principle: It is impossible to obtain accurate values for the position and momentum of an electron simultaneously. In other words, observation causes a reaction on the thing observed. . . . This principle of uncertainty . . . sets fundamental limits upon our ability to describe nature.

QUESTIONS

1. What implications do the Hawthorne experiments and the uncertainty principle have for epistemology?

2. Do the Hawthorne experiments and the uncertainty principle demonstrate that we can never hope to know the world as it really is?

SOURCE: Verne H. Booth, *Elements of Physical Science: The Nature of Matter and Energy* (London: Macmillan, 1970), 327–328.

then *listen* to the weather report. If asked how they know that a lemon is sour and sugar is sweet, they might tell you to *taste* them. The question of knowledge, it seems, is bound up with what we perceive. Through perception we feel confident that we *know* how things are.

But should we be so confident? Can't there be a difference between things as they "really" are and our perception of them? Are things always necessarily what they appear to be to our senses? Suppose you are sitting in a coffee shop one morning sipping from a cup. You tell the server that it is the best cup of coffee you have ever had. But the server informs you that you are not actually drinking coffee but a new brand of tea that she gave you by mistake. "That can't be," you say. "It looks, smells, and tastes like coffee, and I know coffee when I drink it." Then the server brings the tea container over to you and lets you make a fresh cup for yourself; sure enough, it turns out to look, taste, and smell like coffee, but it is actually tea. But you continue to think that your original cup was really filled with coffee. Or take a more disturbing example: You are in a hospital recovering from an operation and are still somewhat groggy from the anesthesia when you see your long-dead great-grandfather walk into your room. You pinch yourself, you blink, you shake your head, you turn away and look back, and he is still standing there. Eventually he leaves. But you are left wondering: Was he really there as your senses said he was?

Obviously, things in reality can be different from what they appear to be to our senses. This is a fundamental epistemological problem that arises with all sensory knowledge claims. Invariably implied in such claims is one of two beliefs: Either no qualitative distinction exists between the experience and the object of the experience (for example, between my experience of coffee and the coffee itself), or experience must be distinguished from the thing itself (for example, my experience of the coffee must be distinguished from the coffee itself). In the first instance, we face serious and perhaps insurmountable difficulties in claiming that any objective reality exists because it is indistinguishable from our own experience. In other words, there's no difference between your experience of the coffee and the coffee itself, no difference between your experience of your great-grandfather and the reality itself. In the second instance, we face equally serious difficulties in trying to determine precisely how to know whether our sense perceptions square with reality. If we must distinguish our experiences of things from the things themselves, then how do we know that our experiences ever in fact correspond with the objective reality of things?

In proposing his theory of knowledge, empiricist Locke was asserting not only that knowledge originates in sense experience but also that physical objects exist outside us, that they are independent of our perceptions of them. In effect, he distinguished between entities and their appearances to us: "For since the mind, in all its thoughts and reasonings, hath no other immediate objects but its own ideas, it is evident that our knowledge is only conversant about them."[10] Thus, for Locke our knowledge of things is more accurately termed

---

[10] Locke, *An Essay*, vol. 4, 2.

our knowledge of our *ideas* of things. This is why there is a problem about the connection, if any, between those ideas and the objective world.

Locke claimed that our ideas are representative of things themselves. But the crucial question is How? According to Locke, an object has certain inherent qualities distinct from our perception of it, qualities that it would have even if it were not perceived. These he called **primary qualities.** Generally, primary qualities can be measured—for example, size, shape, and weight. These qualities, said Locke, are in things "whether we perceive them or not; and when they are of that size that we can discover them, we have by these an idea of the thing as it is in itself."[11] Thus, even if an object is not perceived, it still has a certain size, shape, and weight. For Locke, our ideas represent these primary qualities.

But Locke also believed that there are qualities that are not within an object itself. For example, a tree has color, smell, texture, and maybe even a certain taste. In the fall the tree may be one color, in the spring another—as it may be one color at dawn and another at noon. Without its leaves, the tree may be odorless; with them, it may be fragrant. What is the actual color of the tree? Its actual smell? What we term *color* and *smell* are merely powers of the tree to produce sensation in us. The color and smell are not qualities in the tree itself, but our own ideas:

> First our Senses, conversant about particular sensible objects, do convey into the mind several distinct perceptions of things, according to those various ways wherein those objects do affect them. And thus we come by those *ideas* we have of *yellow, white, heat, cold, soft, hard, bitter, sweet,* and all those which we call sensible qualities: which when I say the senses convey into the mind what produces there those perceptions; this great source of most of the ideas we have, depending wholly upon our senses and derived by them to the understanding, I call SENSATION."[12]

According to Locke, the tree has in itself no green color; it has only the power to produce in us a sensory experience or "sensation" that we call green. Such powers Locke calls **secondary qualities.**

We know how things are, therefore, because of our ideas, which represent the primary qualities of the external world. For example, if we experience the tree as being a certain height, we can trust that idea to resemble how the tree really is; if we experience it to have a certain circumference, we can trust that idea to resemble how the tree really is. Thus, we come to know the things around us by having sense experiences of their primary qualities; these experiences resemble the entities themselves.

During the early part of this century, a group of philosophers composed a book titled *Essays in Critical Realism.* Their view shows a marked Lockean flavor. Like Locke, the critical realists do not believe that the perception of entities is so direct as to be indistinguishable from the things themselves. It is not the outer object that is present in the consciousness, they argue, but **sense data.** Sense data are the images or sensory impressions—the immediate contents of

primary qualities according to Locke, qualities that inhere in an object: size, shape, weight, and so on

CRITICAL THINKING

Locke assumes that primary qualities must be real, although secondary qualities are not. Is this assumption justified?

secondary qualities according to Locke, qualities that we impose on an object: color, smell, texture, and so on

sense data images or sensory impressions

---

[11] Ibid.
[12] Ibid., 4.

sensory experience—that, according to the critical realists, indicate the presence and nature of perceived objects. Only by inference can we go beyond sense data to the object itself.

Critical realists believe that sense data provide accurate contact with entities, that they reveal what objects are and thus what the external world is like. They believe that three factors are involved in perception: (1) a perceiver, knower, or conscious mind; (2) the entity or object, consisting of primary qualities; and (3) the sense data, which serve as a bridge between the perceiver and the object.

Still, a question nags: How can we be sure that our perceptions truly represent the objects perceived? Locke tried to answer this question with his so-called copy theory. Consider the operation of the senses as so many cameras snapping pictures. The senses are "photographing" everything that comes into contact with them. The resulting photographs of our experiences are obviously not the things themselves but copies of them. These copies, claimed Locke, are so much like the actual things that through knowing and understanding them we come to comprehend the world around us:

> When our senses do actually convey into our understandings any idea, we cannot but be satisfied that there doth something *at that time* really exist without us, which doth affect our senses, and by them give notice of itself to our apprehensive faculties, and actually produce that idea which we then perceive; and we cannot so far distrust their testimony, as to doubt that such *collections* of simple ideas as we have observed by our senses to be united together, do really exist together.[13]

He is insisting that the senses can do two things: certify that things outside the self actually exist and provide an accurate picture of those things.

But no matter how representative, a photograph is not the thing itself. A difference remains between copy and thing, between our idea of something and the thing itself. If we are in touch with only our ideas of things, how do we know that they are really like the things themselves?

Furthermore, pictures are frequently distortions of reality. Perhaps the camera is malfunctioning. Are our senses perfect receivers of information? Even if they are, it is not likely that your sensory experiences are identical with mine. Whose, then, are more representative? Such unanswered questions led philosophers to propose alternatives to Locke's views.

Thus, in Locke's own time other empiricists objected that he had not fully accounted for the representative nature of our ideas. They seriously questioned whether he had fully explained how we can be sure that our sensory experiences accurately represent how things actually are. Remember that Descartes could rely on a perfect God whose existence he had derived from the clear and distinct idea of his own existence. In contrast, Locke's theory, originating in sensory experience, does not include such an epistemologically influential being. As a result, it was open to challenge from within the empirical camp. The foremost challenge was presented by the Irish bishop George Berkeley.

---

[13] Ibid., 1–2.

BERKELEY

George Berkeley agreed with Locke that ideas originate in sensory experience. Although he also accepted Locke's argument that secondary qualities are subjective, Berkeley insisted that the same could be said of primary qualities. In *A Treatise Concerning the Principles of Human Knowledge*, Berkeley says the following:

> They who assert that figure, motion, and the rest of the primary or original qualities do exist without mind in unthinking substances do at the same time acknowledge that colors, sounds, heat, cold and such like secondary qualities, do not; which they tell us are sensations, existing in the mind alone, that depend on and are occasioned by the different size, texture, and motion of the minute particles of matter. . . . Now if it be certain that those original qualities are inseparably united with other sensible qualities, and not, even in thought, capable of being abstracted from them, it plainly follows they exist only in the mind. But I desire anyone to reflect, and try whether he can, by any abstraction of thought conceive the extension and motion of a body without all other sensible qualities. For my own part, I see evidently that it is not in my power to frame an idea of a body extended and moving but I must . . . give it some color or sensible quality, which is acknowledged to exist only in the mind. In short, extension, figure and motion, abstracted from all other qualities, are inconceivable. Where therefore the other sensible qualities are, there must these be also, to wit, in the mind and nowhere else.[14]

In other words, if heat or cold is a secondary quality—a quality only of the mind, as Locke insists—then why aren't figure and extension secondary qualities as well? For example, a coin appears round from one angle and flat from another, just as a tree appears taller from the bottom of a hill than from the top. Why? Because, says Berkeley, all qualities are mind-dependent. Indeed, to think of sensible qualities as existing in outward objects is ridiculous.

For Berkeley, only minds and their ideas exist. In saying that an idea exists, Berkeley means that it is perceived by some mind. In other words, for ideas *esse est percipi:* "To be is to be perceived." On the other hand, minds are not dependent for their existence on being perceived, because they are perceivers. For Berkeley, therefore, what exists is the conscious mind or some idea or perception held by that mind. Objects do not exist independent of consciousness.

Because Berkeley claims that we know only our own ideas, he is sometimes termed a *subjectivist.* The subjectivist contends that there can be no entity without a perceiver and that everything that is real is a conscious mind or a perception by a conscious mind. When we say that an entity exists, we mean that it is perceived or at least that it could be perceived if we were to do so.

Carried to an extreme, Berkeley's thinking can become **solipsism,** the position that only I exist and that everything else is just a creation of my subjective consciousness. This position contends that the only perceiver is myself. Other persons and objects have no independent existence but exist solely to the degree that I am conscious of them.

When we do our utmost to conceive the existence of external bodies we are all the while only contemplating our own ideas.

GEORGE BERKELEY

solipsism an extreme form of subjective idealism, contending that only I exist and that everything else is a product of my subjective consciousness

---

[14] George Berkeley, *A Treatise Concerning the Principles of Human Knowledge,* in *The Works of George Berkeley,* vol. 1, ed. George Sampson (London: George Bell & Sons, 1897), 183.

But it is unfair to push Berkeley's position that far; he never did. To avoid such excesses, Berkeley relied on an outside source for his ideas: God. Things continue to exist even when no human mind is perceiving them, because God is forever perceiving them. God always has them "in mind." But now other problems arise, the chief one being this: If all that exists is a conscious mind and some perception by that mind, how do we know that God exists? If we cannot say that something material exists, how can we insist that something nonmaterial, like God, does? In one of his dialogues between Hylas (substitute "Locke") and Philonus (substitute "Berkeley"), Berkeley anticipates just such an objection:

> **CRITICAL THINKING**
>
> Berkeley assumes that since ideas exist, the minds that hold those ideas must also exist. Does this assumption hold up if we accept his view that we should not assume the external world exists because it is not perceived?

PHILOSOPHY AND LIFE

The Egocentric Predicament

In 1910 American philosopher Ralph Barton Perry published an article titled "The Ego-Centric Predicament." In it he makes a point about "objects/events" outside us— that is, real objects. Perry addresses a question that Western philosophers have long debated: What is the metaphysical status of objects/ events? What are things like outside our perception of them?

Perry reasoned that we can never observe things apart from our perception of them. This was obvious enough to Perry, because we must perceive any real object/event in order to know it. If we can't know things apart from our perception of them, then we can never know whether our perception of things changes them—thus, the egocentric predicament.

Professor of philosophy James Christian has extended Perry's point by suggesting that the egocentric predicament entails an *illusion*. This egocentric illusion lies in the fact that all our mortal lives we must occupy a physical organism—that is, we must occupy a point in space

and time. As a result, it appears to each of us that we are the center of creation. Conversely, it appears to each of us that the whole cosmos revolves around that point in the space-time that we occupy. What's more, wherever we go in space-time, this egocentric illusion pursues us, since we move our center. In a word, every living, conscious creature experiences itself as the true center of the cosmos, when in fact the cosmos has no true center.

Christian observes that when all humans take themselves as the center of things, we make *aristocentric* claims—that is, inordinate claims to superiority for ourselves or our group. Aristocentric claims arise because we fail to correct for the egocentric illusion. Taking ourselves as cosmic centers, we may claim that our existence has special meaning, that we have a special knowledge or message, or that we have special powers. Rarely, however, do we make these claims in the singular. This is not surprising, for our arrogant pride would invite scorn and ridicule. But we do make aristo-

centric claims in the plural: "*We* are something special," "*We* are favored people," or "*We* have a unique destiny." The beauty of such claims is that they're so easily reinforced by group members. Sociologists have a word for any form of aristocentrism—*ethnocentricity*, the preoccupation with and belief in the superiority of one's own culture.

When Ralph Barton Perry spoke of the egocentric predicament, he had in mind a timeless metaphysical concern. But, as so often happens, purely philosophical musings have a way of slipping into our everyday lives.

QUESTION

1. The great historian Arnold Toynbee once observed that a human self cannot be brought into harmony with absolute reality unless it rids itself of self-centeredness. Why is this so?

SOURCE: James Christian, *Philosophy: An Introduction to the Art of Wondering* (New York: Holt, Rinehart & Winston, 1973), 50–58.

HYLAS: Answer me, Philonus. Are all our ideas perfectly inert beings? Or have they any agency included in them?

PHILONUS: They are altogether passive and inert.

HYLAS: And is not God an agent, a being purely active?

PHILONUS: I acknowledge it.

HYLAS: No idea therefore can be like unto, or represent, the nature of God.

PHILONUS: It cannot.

HYLAS: Since therefore you have no idea of the mind of God, how can you conceive it possible that things should exist in His mind? Or, if you can conceive the existence of Matter, notwithstanding I have no idea of it? . . . You admit . . . that there is a spiritual Substance, although you have no idea of it; while you deny there can be such a thing as material Substance, because you have no notion or idea of it. Is this fair dealing? To act consistently, you must either admit Matter or reject Spirit.[15]

"Admit Matter or reject Spirit"—this was something Berkeley seemed unwilling to do. Some claim it was because Berkeley never intended to make such a rigorous criticism of Locke, that from the outset he disbelieved the existence of matter and tried to use the empirical method to prove this belief. When the empirical method seemed to disprove what he wanted to believe, Berkeley forsook it. In fairness to Berkeley, however, we should note the difficulty of defending the sense of the contention that there are objects that are *not* objects— objects that are unknown to subjects and that are unthought and unexperienced. Surely, Berkeley at least anticipated this problem, with which another idealist, Immanuel Kant, would subsequently deal. And, of course, Berkeley felt that he had good reasons for not applying the empirical method completely. Specifically, we have direct experience of our own conscious selves, which are not hypothetical or inferred entities on the order of God.

Finally, let us be certain about Berkeley's claims. He does not deny that there are houses, books, trees, cats, and people. But he does deny that these or any other physical objects exist independently of our minds. For Berkeley, there are not beds and then sense experiences of beds that copy or resemble beds, as Locke believed. There is only the sense experience of beds. A bed, or any other physical object, is composed of a collection of ideas.

But if we talk of our experience of a bed, we seem to be suggesting that there is a bed to be experienced. This is because our language is misleading. There simply is no appropriate way to speak of the contents of our sensory experiences without mentioning the name of the physical object that we believe is experienced. But Berkeley did not accept the existence of the physical object. Yes, for Berkeley there are beds, but *not* experiences of beds caused by beds—that is, by physical objects existing outside and independently of us. Berkeley held that *bed* and all other words for physical objects are names of "recurring patterns" of sense experiences, and no more. Physical objects are groups of sense experiences that we are constantly aware of, bundles of sense data.

We do have perceptual access to the real world and those arguments that say that we don't are bad arguments.

JOHN SEARLE

---

[15] George Berkeley, *Three Dialogues Between Hylas and Philonus*, in *The Works of George Berkeley*, vol. 1, 364–365.

Although an empiricist, Berkeley was ultimately unwilling to deny the spiritual substances whose existences he wished to prove. In short, he seems to have used empiricism to disprove what he disbelieved to begin with but to have recoiled from it when it threatened to disprove his deepest convictions. Nevertheless, he remains a critical link in understanding the dialectical development of empiricism, which Scottish philosopher David Hume extended to its logical limits.

HUME AND SKEPTICISM

It's fair to say that David Hume pushed Locke's empiricism to a thorough **skepticism**—that is, to a denial of the possibility that we can have certain knowledge about matters of fact. In other words, empirical knowledge is only probable. How Hume came to this conclusion is a long and complex affair, which we can only sketch here. (For a fuller discussion of Hume, see the showcase at the end of this chapter.)

To begin, Hume asserts that the contents of the mind can be reduced to those given by the senses and experience. He calls these *perceptions*. In Hume's view, perceptions take two forms, what he terms *impressions* and *ideas*. The distinction between them and how they relate to knowing are vital to understanding Humean thought. In *An Enquiry Concerning Human Understanding*, Hume clearly explains what he means by ideas and impressions:

> Here, therefore, we may divide all the perceptions of the mind into two classes or species, which are distinguished by their different degrees of force and vivacity. The less forcible and lively are commonly denominated *Thoughts* or *Ideas*. The other species want a name in our language, and in most others; I suppose, because it was not requisite for any, but philosophical purposes, to rank them under a general term or appellation. Let us therefore use a little freedom, and call them *Impressions*; employing that word in a sense somewhat different from the usual. By the term *impression*, then, I mean all our more lively perceptions, when we hear, or see, or feel, or love, or hate, or desire, or will. And impressions are distinguished from ideas, which are the less lively perceptions of which we are conscious, when we reflect on any of those sensations or movements above mentioned.[16]

Clearly, then, in distinguishing impressions from ideas, Hume employs an empirically observable criterion: a difference in degree of "liveliness." Thus, original perceptions are quite vivid, as are those of color or emotion. However, their vividness declines when we subsequently reflect upon them or have ideas about them. The pain you feel when you hammer your thumb is an impression; the memory of what you felt is an idea.

Consistent with this insight is the Humean belief that there can be no ideas without sense impressions. This follows from his contention that every idea is a faint impression. Thus, if there are no impressions, there are no ideas. How-

skepticism in epistemology, the view that varies between doubting all assumptions until proved and claiming that no knowledge is possible

We can never arrive at the real nature of things from the outside. However much we investigate, we can never reach anything but images and names. We are like a man who goes round a castle seeking in vain for an entrance and sometimes sketching the facades.

ARTHUR SCHOPENHAUER

---

[16] David Hume, *An Enquiry Concerning Human Understanding,* ed. L. A. Selby-Bigge (Oxford: Clarendon Press, 1894), 18.

ever, not every idea reflects an impression. We can, after all, conceive of a golden mountain or a virtuous horse, even if we've never had an impression of either. How is this possible? Hume answers that in such cases our imagination combines ideas that were acquired through impressions:

> But though our thought seems to possess this unbounded liberty, we shall find, upon a nearer examination, that it is really confined within very narrow limits, and that all this creative power of the mind amounts to no more than the faculty of compounding, transposing, augmenting, or diminishing the materials afforded us by the senses and experience. When we think of a golden mountain, we only join two consistent ideas, *gold* and *mountain*, with which we were formerly acquainted. A virtuous horse we can conceive; because, from our own feeling, we can conceive virtue; and this we may unite to the figure and shape of a horse, which is an animal familiar to us. In short, all the materials of thinking are derived either from our outward or our inward sentiments: the mixture and composition of these belong alone to the mind and will. Or, to express myself in philosophical language, all our ideas or more feeble perceptions are copies of our impressions or more lively ones.[17]

Building on this thesis, Hume then turns to the issue that concerned Locke and Berkeley, as well as Descartes: the existence of an external reality. Since there can be no ideas without prior sense impressions, Hume concludes that there is no rational justification for the belief that anything has a continued, independent existence outside us. After all, impressions are internal subjective states and thus are not proof of a continued external reality. In other words, the subjectivity of all perceptions, including ideas, plus the illegitimacy of pseudo-ideas for which there are no corresponding impressions (for example, matter, cause, and self), casts doubt on the external world.

Hume's view about the subjectivity of perceptions, then, suggests a disturbing possibility: Perhaps the external world does not exist. True, the world may appear to our senses to be consistent, regular, and predictable. Each time we look around us, the world appears more or less like it did when we last looked, so we conclude that the world is permanent and enduring. But that permanence may be an illusion. How do you know that anything continues to exist when your experience of it is interrupted? The people and chairs and books and tables around us may all appear to endure even when we are not experiencing them, but we can never be certain of that.

By what argument can it be proved that the perceptions of the mind must be caused by external objects and could not arise from the energy of the mind itself?

DAVID HUME

Hume concedes that we always act *as if* a real external world of things exists, but he asks how we can be sure of the continued existence of things when we interrupt our sensation of them. For example, before you lies this book. You're sustaining an impression of it, perhaps a tactual and visual sensation. Then you interrupt that sensation by removing your hands and closing your eyes. You may now have an idea of the book, but that idea is not enough to confirm the book's continued existence. Then why do we commonly believe the book continues to exist? Because when we open our eyes, the book sits before us. If we persisted in this exercise, the result would be the same.

---

[17] Ibid., 19.

The apparent constancy in things leads us to believe that they have an independent existence external to us. But for Hume this belief is just that, a belief, and not a rational proof. The assumption that our impressions are connected with things lacks any foundation in reasoning. What's more, even when we have an impression of the thing itself, such as this book, we have only that impression, which we can't distinguish from the book. In short, Hume believes that there is no way for the mind to reach beyond impressions and the subsequent ideas. In other words, Hume goes another step beyond questioning the permanence of the world around us. Not only do we not know whether something exists when we are not perceiving it, but we can't even be sure it exists when we are perceiving it. In short, Hume seriously doubts that there is a world external to consciousness.

This discussion may resemble Berkeley's doctrine that to be is to be perceived. But recall that Berkeley has a God who sustains things in a continued existence when no person is perceiving them. Hume does not rely on any such theological prop. He applies the doctrine of empiricism as rigorously as he can, regardless of its implications. As a result, he extends this skeptical line of reasoning beyond the existence of objects and things to questions concerning the existence of God and even of the self.

Hume's theory ends in skepticism; that is, Hume concludes that we can never know whether or not our ideas about reality are accurate. Perhaps this was inevitable. Descartes had earlier pointed out that our sensations or ideas may or may not correspond to the world outside the mind. These sensations or ideas may be generated by illusions, by our own dreams or hallucinations, or even by an evil, all-powerful being that causes these sensations or ideas to form in our minds. This possibility—that the sensations or ideas within us might not represent the real world outside—led Descartes to doubt everything. But Descartes was able to banish his doubts by reasoning that God would not lead us to think a world outside existed unless such a world really did exist.

Hume also accepted Descartes's basic premise: It is possible that the ideas in our minds may not correspond to a reality outside the mind. But unlike Descartes, Locke, or Berkeley, Hume did not rely on God to save him from skepticism. With cold logic, Hume argued that even our ideas about God may not correspond to reality. Indeed, Hume claimed, we are acquainted only with the impressions and ideas in our minds and have no access to any other reality. We have no way of knowing that the impressions and ideas in our minds represent any reality outside the mind.

Many contemporary philosophers are inclined to agree with Hume. For example, Barry Stroud argues that we have to accept Descartes's claim that since we might be dreaming, the sensations and thoughts in our minds might not correspond to any reality outside the mind. But once we accept the possibility that the sensations and thoughts within us might not represent a real world outside or independent of the mind, Humean skepticism is inevitable. We have no way of checking to see what the real world might be like except by using the sensations and thoughts within us. Real knowledge of the world is forever lost to us:

I want to reject the seventeenth century picture that sensation is essentially inside us, that when you look at something you have sensations which take place in an inner theater. I want to return to a view that's been lost as a possibility to us, which is we actually see the external world and not just an internal representation of it.

HILARY PUTNAM

If we are in the predicament Descartes finds himself in at the end of his *First Meditation* we cannot tell by means of the senses whether we are dreaming or not; all the sensory experiences we are having are compatible with our merely dreaming of a world around us while that world is in fact very different from the way we take it to be. Our knowledge is in that way confined to our sensory experiences. There seems to be no way of going beyond them to know that the world around us really is this way rather than that. . . .

What *can* we know in such a predicament? We can perhaps know what sensory experiences we are having, or how things seem to us to be. At least that much of our knowledge will not be threatened by the kind of attack Descartes makes on our knowledge of the world beyond our experiences. What we can know turns out to be a great deal less than we thought we knew before engaging in that assessment of our knowledge. Our position is much more restricted, much poorer, than we had originally supposed. We are confined at best to what Descartes calls "ideas" of things around us, representations of things or states of affairs which, for all we can know, might or might not have something corresponding to them in reality. We are in a sense imprisoned within those representations, at least with respect to our knowledge. Any attempt to go beyond them to try and tell whether the world really is as they represent it to be can yield only more representations, more deliverances of sense experience which themselves are compatible with reality's being very different from the way we take it to be on the basis of our sensory experiences. . . .

We would be in the position of someone waking up to find himself locked in a room full of television sets and trying to find out what is going on in the world outside. For all he can know, whatever is producing the patterns he can see on the screens in front of him might be something other than well-functioning cameras directed on to the passing show outside the room. The victim might switch on more of the sets in the room to try to get more information, and he might find that some of the sets show events exactly similar or coherently related to those already visible on the screens he can see. But all those pictures will be no help to him without some independent information, some knowledge which does not come to him from the pictures themselves, about how the pictures he does see before him are connected with what is going on outside the room. The problem of the external world is the problem of finding out, or knowing how we could find out, about the world around us if we were in that sort of predicament. It is perhaps enough simply to put the problem this way to convince us that it can never be given a satisfactory solution.[18]

We began this chapter with a discussion of the controversy over the theory of recovered memories. Does empiricism shed any light on that controversy? Clearly, the empiricist would deny the rationalist view that when recovered memories are clear and distinct, they must be true. An empiricist like Locke would instead say that ideas provide true knowledge only when they are based on sense experience. Hume would agree, holding that ideas should never be accepted as true unless they can be shown to have been "derived" from some "sense impression." Recovered memories, then, should not be accepted unless they can be corroborated with some kind of independent sense experience. A skeptic in the spirit of Hume might go further and hold that just as we must

---

[18]Barry Stroud, *The Significance of Philosophical Skepticism* (Oxford: Clarendon Press, 1984), 31–33. Reprinted by permission of Oxford University Press.

The Dream, Henri Rousseau. "All the sensory experiences we are having are compatible with our merely dreaming of a world around us while that world is in fact very different from the way we take it to be."

remain skeptical about our ordinary perceptions, so too we must remain skeptical about the truth of recovered memories. "The mind," Hume suggested, "is a kind of theater, where several perceptions successively make their appearance, pass, re-pass, glide away, and mingle in an infinite variety of postures and situations." When memories are "recovered" in therapy, the Humean skeptic might suggest, they simply become one more element in this jumble of ideas in the mind. It is no more possible to know whether one of them is true than it is to establish that any of our other ideas correspond to an independent reality.

But not all philosophers have accepted Hume's skepticism. In fact, it was precisely to resolve this skepticism that in the eighteenth century Immanuel Kant turned his attention to questions about the nature of knowledge. His investigations eventually resulted in a unique blend of empiricism and rationalism called *transcendental idealism.* This new approach to knowledge, Kant claimed, is the only way of resolving the skepticism of the rationalists and empiricists.

Knowledge is the knowing that we cannot know.
RALPH WALDO EMERSON

QUESTIONS

1. For Locke, shape is a primary quality and color a secondary quality. Do you agree or disagree with the following statements? Why? Consequently, would you agree or disagree with Locke's distinction?

    a. When something is not being perceived, it has shape but not color.

    b. You can experience shape with more than one sense, but not color.

    c. The shape of a thing never changes, but its color does so frequently.

    d. A thing without color can have shape.

2. Locke believed that we come into the world as a "blank slate." Ideas come after sensory experiences. Would you agree that we can have no ideas without first having sensory experiences? Or would you hold that at least some ideas (for example, "Everything must have a cause," "There is a God," "Murdering a two-year-old baby for your own pleasure is evil") do not depend on sense experience?

3. Does Berkeley's idealism deny an objective reality?

4. According to Berkeley, in what sense can we not know anything?

5. Explain this statement: "Berkeley's subjectivism originates in a physical world and ends in denying knowledge of it."

6. What evidence would you give to prove that while you were sleeping, a physical reality outside you persisted?

7. What does Hume mean by asserting that there can be no ideas without sensory impressions?

8. Explain why Hume concludes that there's no rational justification for saying that anything has a continued and independent existence outside us.

9. Describe what you consider to be the fundamental epistemological difference between Hume and Berkeley.

10. Justify the assertion that Hume pushed Locke's empiricism to its logical conclusion.

11. How does Hume push Descartes's method of doubt to its logical conclusion?

12. Do you see any way of showing that Barry Stroud is wrong when he says that we are like "someone waking up to find himself locked in a room full of television sets and trying to find out what is going on in the world outside"? Do you think there is any way of finding out what is "going on in the world outside" your mind? Do you agree with Stroud's view that we must end up as Humean skeptics?

5.4 Kant: Does the Knowing Mind Shape the World?

The question that concerned the German philosopher Immanuel Kant (1724–1804) was how to deal with Hume's wholesale skepticism. He sensed that philosophy had reached a pivotal point. Kant wanted to show that, in spite of Hume, reason can attain knowledge of reality. In doing so, he fashioned a view of knowledge, now called **transcendental idealism,** which holds that both experience and reason play a role in knowing.

In his most influential work, *The Critique of Pure Reason*, Kant accepted Hume's proposition that experience is the only basis for true knowledge of reality. Unwilling to end the debate there, however, Kant suggested that reason also contributes something to our knowledge. In *The Critique of Pure Reason* Kant stated his proposal:

> But though all our knowledge begins with experience, it does not follow that it all arises out of experience. For it may well be that even our empirical knowledge is made up of what we receive through [sense] impressions and of what our own faculty of knowledge . . . supplies from itself." [19]

Kant pointed out that our senses reveal the tastes, smells, sounds, and shapes of objects. But our senses don't reveal the relationships among objects, such as causal relationships. Reason, Kant argues, is the source of our knowledge of the relationships among objects. To understand what Kant meant, it is important to see where Kant agreed with Hume and where he disagreed.

Hume had argued that the cause-and-effect laws of science go beyond the evidence that scientists have for them. Scientists observe a few times that certain causes are followed by certain effects. They see several times, for example, that when a moving object hits another, the second object moves. They conclude that those kinds of causes will always be followed by the same effects in the future. But how do scientists know that the future will always be like the past? And how do scientists know that the phenomenon they see a few times will happen every time? Hume argued that scientists have no evidence for jumping from what they observe *some* times in the *past* to conclusions about what will happen *every* time in the *future*.

When Kant read Hume's arguments, he was stupefied. Immediately, he realized that Hume was right. Kant woke up to the fact that our unthinking acceptance of the laws of science may have no firm foundation:

> I openly confess that my recollection of David Hume was the very thing which many years ago first awoke me from my dogmatic slumber and gave my investigations in

transcendental idealism in epistemology, the view that the *form* of our knowledge of reality derives from reason but its *content* comes from our senses

Empiricists and rationalists alike are dupes of the same illusion. Both take partial notions for real parts.

HENRI BERGSON

---

[19] Immanuel Kant, *Critique of Pure Reason*, 2d ed., trans. Norman Kemp Smith (London: Macmillan, 1929; original work published 1781), 1–2.

Nude Descending a Staircase, No. 2, Marcel Duchamp. "Kant holds that the mind possesses mental 'categories.' These categories organize our perceptions into the orderly world we experience. The world as we experience it results in part from the sensations provided by our senses, and in part from the workings of the mind. The senses provide the content or stuff of experience; the mind provides its form or orderly structure."

the field of speculative philosophy a quite new direction. But I was far from following him in the conclusions at which he arrived.[20]

Kant devoted his "investigations" to showing that Hume was wrong. He granted Hume's view of the senses. All our knowledge of the world begins with sensations that come into our senses: colors, shapes, sounds, tastes, feels, smells. Hume wrote that these sensations crowd into us in a continuously changing stream:

[The sensations in our senses] succeed each other with an inconceivable rapidity and are in a perpetual flux and movement.... The mind is a kind of theater where several

---

[20] Immanuel Kant, *Prolegomena to Any Future Metaphysics*, trans. Lewis White Beck (New York: Bobbs-Merrill, 1950), 8.

perceptions successively make their appearance, pass, re-pass, glide away, and mingle in an infinite variety of postures and situations.[21]

But Kant noticed something Hume had missed. It is true that countless sensations play in our senses. Yet, strangely, we do not experience a mere display of sensations within us. When you open your eyes, for example, you do not experience changing sensations of light and colors playing in your vision. Instead, you see *objects*. When you look at the room around you, you don't see a blooming confusion of colors and lines and shapes floating and changing in front of your eyes. Instead, you see a desk, a book, a sheet of paper, and the walls of a room. Somehow the sensations that continually play in your vision get arranged by your mind into solid objects.

The same is true of your other senses. Each sense presents a stream of changing sensations. But you experience these sensations as belonging to solid objects outside you. If you listen right now, for example, you do not just sense ringing, booming, rustling sound sensations in your ears. Instead, you hear noises that seem to come from some particular place in the room. The rustling noises are from the papers on your desk. The booming sound you attribute to a truck driving past. The ringing you attribute to the telephone. Each sensation of sound, sight, touch, and smell seems to be the sound, sight, touch, or smell of an object somewhere in the space around you.

Kant argued that our mind somehow takes these many separate sensations and organizes them into objects that seem to be somewhere in the space outside ourselves. The mind is continually at work, putting order into the chaotic stream of endlessly changing sensations. It introduces order by arranging these sensations into stable enduring objects that seem to be in space outside us.

This remarkable insight of Kant—that the mind organizes its sensations into the objects we see around us—is the key to his theory. We cannot know disorganized chaos, Kant claims. The mind is a unified orderly thing and demands unity and order in what it knows. So if the mind is to know the world, it must see the world as orderly and stable. The mind cannot comprehend a chaotic confusion of disconnected sensations:

> Sensations would be nothing to us, and would not concern us in the least, if they were not received into our [orderly] consciousness. Knowledge is impossible in any other way. . . . For perceptions could not be perceptions of anything for me unless they . . . could at least be connected together into [my] one consciousness. This principle stands firm *a priori*, and may be called the "transcendental principle of unity" for all the multiplicity of our perceptions and sensations.[22]

How does the mind bring order into its sensations? Kant argued that the mind organizes its sensations into stable objects by connecting them according to twelve kinds of relationships or "categories." The most important of these is the basic law of science: that all perceived events must have a cause. The mind, according to Kant, takes earlier sensations of an object and connects them to

If man has the need of any science, then it is the one that can teach him what it means to be human.

IMMANUEL KANT

---

[21] David Hume, *A Treatise of Human Nature*, ed. L. A. Selby-Bigge (Oxford: Clarendon Press, 1894), 252–253.

[22] Immanuel Kant, *Critique of Pure Reason*, A116, trans. Manuel Velasquez.

later sensations by making the earlier ones the causes of the later ones. In this way, the mind inserts cause-and-effect relations into the world we perceive.

Suppose, for example, that you are looking at a pool table. You see a red billiard ball rolling on the green felt toward a blue ball. You see the red ball hit the blue ball, and each bounces away after the collision. What happened? According to Kant's theory, your mind had sensations of roundish red color moving across a field of green color sensations. Your mind organized these sensations into objects in space so that you saw a red billiard ball rolling across a green pool table in front of you. Then the roundish red color reached a roundish blue color lying on the green field, and the two colors moved quickly away from each other. Your mind organized these sensations into a red billiard ball colliding with a blue billiard ball on the pool table. Your mind then connected the earlier moving red sensations to the later moving blue sensations by relating them as cause and effect. As a result, you did not just see two colors moving toward each other and then moving away from each other. Instead, you saw a red ball *causing* a blue ball to move. In short, the mind connects earlier sensations to later ones by the relationship of cause and effect. In this way, we do not just see events following events, as Hume thought. Instead, we see earlier events *causing* later events. Or, more accurately, we see earlier states of objects causing later states of objects.

Hume had objected that we do not actually see causality. Causality is not one of the sensations that our senses give us. So we cannot be sure that causality is there in the world. Kant partly agreed. We do not see causality because it is a relationship between objects and is not an object itself. But we still know that causality is there in the world. It is there because the mind puts it there. Causality is a relationship that the mind uses to connect earlier sensations to later ones.

The implications of Kant's insight are astounding. First, if Kant is right, the world we see around us is a world that our own mind constructs. Sensations stream into us. But the mind organizes these into the objects that make up the world we perceive. Second, if Kant is right, then cause and effect are always part of the world as we perceive it. Hume, then, was wrong. Hume had claimed that we have no evidence that event will always be connected together by cause and effect. But if Kant is right, then events in the world *we* perceive will always be connected by cause and effect. Events will be connected by cause and effect because our mind constructs these events and always connects them by the relationship of cause and effect. Third, if Kant is right, then the world we see around us might not be the way the world really is in itself. What we see around us is a world our minds have constructed. But perhaps the world as it really is in itself is not like that. Perhaps the world as it really is in itself is quite different from the world our mind constructs.

Kant called the world that our minds construct and that we seem to see around us the "phenomenal" world. The world as it might really be apart from our mind he called the "noumenal" world. Clearly, we can never know what the noumenal world is really like. All we can ever know is the phenomenal world that we perceive after the mind has organized it by putting our sensations together. We don't know, for example, whether the noumenal world is made up

A desire of knowledge is the natural feeling of mankind.
SAMUEL JOHNSON

of objects. The very idea of an enduring object is invented by the mind to organize its sensations. Maybe the noumenal world as it is in itself has no objects in it and consists of pure field of force. We can never know. Nor can we ever know whether the noumenal world has causality in it. Maybe in the underlying noumenal world things just happen without rhyme or reason. Maybe in the noumenal world things happen without being caused to happen by earlier events. All we can be sure of is that the world *we* experience, the phenomenal world, always contains objects in causal relationships. It contains objects and causal relationships because the mind put them there.

So Kant agreed with some of what the empiricists claimed and with some of what the rationalists claimed. The empiricists are right when they claim that

> *Kant's ultimate mistake was of giving a name (noumenon) to that which he's trying to tell us cannot even be named.*
>
> STEPHEN TOULMIN

PHILOSOPHY AND LIFE

Knowledge and Gestalt Psychology

Some patterns of visual stimulation are more meaningful to us than others. Consider the following pattern. How would you describe it?

———————————
———————————
———————————

———————————

Probably you'd say that you see three sets of two horizontal lines each rather than six separate lines. This is so because you perceive items close to each other as a whole. Now consider this pattern:

o   x   o
o   x   o
o   x   o

Because we perceive items that resemble each other as units, you'd probably describe what you see as two vertical rows of circles and one of Xs rather than three horizontal rows of circles and Xs.

Why is one pattern of visual stimulation meaningful while

another is not? One answer lies in past experience: Patterns that outline shapes are meaningful if they match shapes that have been experienced and remembered. But meaningfulness also seems to be imposed by the organization of the visual system.

Some years ago a group of German psychologists, Kurt Koffka and Wolfgang Köhler among them, studied the basic principles of organization in perception. They insisted that a perception of form is an innate property of the visual system. This group of psychologists became known as Gestaltists, from the German word *Gestalt*, meaning "form."

Gestaltists focus on subjective experience and the exploration of consciousness. They see the most significant aspect of experience as its wholeness or interrelatedness. Thus, Gestaltists believe that any attempt to analyze behavior by studying its parts is futile because such an approach loses the basic characteristic of experiences: their

organization, pattern, and wholeness. For Gestaltists, no stimulus has constant significance or meaning. It all depends on the patterns surrounding events. For example, a 5′10″ basketball player looks small when seen as part of a professional basketball team but of normal size as part of a random group of individuals.

As part of their focus on subjective experience and the exploration of consciousness, Gestalt psychologists have formulated a number of descriptive principles of perceptual organization. Two are illustrated above in our two simple patterns: the principles of similarity and proximity.

QUESTIONS

1. Do Gestaltists owe anything to the theories of knowledge that preceded their investigations?

2. What connections do you see between Gestalt psychology and Kantianism?

we must use our senses to know what the world is like. The senses provide the sensations we need to know anything about the world around us. So knowledge of the world requires that we use our senses. But the rationalists are also right when they claim that we can know the basic laws that order the world without using our senses. For example, we can know that in the world that we see every event will have a cause. However, Kant argued, these laws are really just laws that the human mind uses to organize its sensations. We can come to know these laws by reasoning inside the mind because these laws are inside the mind to begin with. Yet they are also in the world we see because the mind puts them into the world when it constructs the world "out there" according to these laws.

Kant did not think that causality is the only relation that the mind puts into the world. In addition, the mind puts sensations into a world of space. The mind makes it seem to us as if there is space all around outside of us. That is, each object that the mind constructs it puts into this space that seems to be all around us. Actually, that space is all in the mind. Space is nothing more than a mental structure that the mind uses to organize its sensations. The laws of space, then, that geometry studies are really laws about the space that the mind constructs. So mathematicians can study geometry and discover new laws about space by simply reasoning in their minds. The laws they discover in their minds will apply to the world because the world is organized according to these laws.

Time, argues Kant, is also a mental construct. The mind makes it seem to us as if we and the objects around us are in time. But time is nothing more than another mental structure that the mind uses to organize its chaotic sensations. Kant claims that numbers and counting are based on time. So the laws of arithmetic and mathematics are laws that we can discover just by reasoning in our minds. The laws of mathematics that we discover in our minds will apply to the entire universe because the mind organizes the universe according to these laws.

Notice that Kant tried to resolve the same problem with which both the rationalists and the empiricists had struggled: How can we know that our ideas accurately represent the world outside of us? Descartes raised doubts about whether our ideas about the world were accurate. For all we know, what we think "in" our minds might not really be "out there" in the world. Hume concluded that we cannot be sure that our ideas accurately represent the world "outside" the mind. But Kant responded to Hume's skepticism with an answer that was simple but revolutionary. Earlier philosophers had all assumed that the world is independent of our minds. Kant rejects this fundamental assumption. Instead, he holds that the world that we see is a world that our own mind constructs. So the world has to conform to our minds:

> Hitherto it has been assumed that all our knowledge must conform to objects. But all our attempts to extend our knowledge of objects on the basis of this assumption have ended in failure. We must therefore try to see whether we may not have more success . . . if we assume instead that objects must conform to our knowledge.[23]

---

[23] Ibid., B xvi.

How do we know that the mind's ideas more or less correspond to what the world is like? We know they correspond, because the mind constructs the world in accordance with its own ideas. Because we make the world we see, we can know what it is like. Thus, skepticism is banished.

Kant's revolutionary claim that the world must conform to the mind is often referred to as the Copernican revolution in knowledge. Copernicus revolutionized astronomy by rejecting the view that the sun revolves around the earth and replacing it with the view that the earth revolves around the sun. In a similar way, Kant replaced the view that the mind must conform to the world with the view that the world must conform to the mind. Only this revolutionary view, Kant held, has the power to free us from skepticism.

The theory that Kant proposed truly revolutionized philosophy. Many philosophers, of course, rejected Kant's ideas. In particular, many rejected the central idea that the mind constructs the world that it knows. But many other philosophers who followed Kant adopted his central idea and developed it in new and excitingly different directions. Perhaps the most important of these were the so-called Romantic philosophers.

The Romantics were thinkers, poets, artists, and philosophers who were fascinated by the strange and exotic, particularly in cultures and in nature. They tended to elevate feeling and emoton above impersonal and cold reason. The romantic poet William Wordsworth, for example, inviting his sister to go with him for a walk in the woods in his poem "To My Sister," wrote the following:

> One moment now may give us more
> Than years of toiling reason:
> Our minds shall drink at every pore
> The spirit of the season. . . .
> And bring no book: for this one day
> We'll give to idleness.

Many romantics agreed with Kant that we shape and create the world we see around us. But they did not believe that the categories the mind uses to organize the world are universal and based on reason. That is, they did not believe that these categories are the same everywhere. Nor did they believe that impersonal reason is the source of those categories. Instead, many argued, a person's history, culture, and language shape the categories he uses to organize his world. And people from different cultures will use different categories to construct their worlds.

The romantic philosopher Wilhelm von Humboldt, for example, was also a linguist who had studied the various languages found in different cultures. He argued that the language of each culture contains the basic categories and structures that the people of that culture use to understand and organize their experience. We construct the world that we see according to the categories of the language that we happen to use. The world that we see around us, then, mirrors the language that our culture and our history happened to give us. If Humboldt is correct, then the members of different cultures live in different worlds. The

CRITICAL THINKING

Kant assumes that if the world as we experience it is constructed by the mind, then the ideas in our minds must correspond to that world. Is this assumption correct?

world in which a person lives and the way that the universe looks to the person depend on the language the person speaks.

Humboldt's theories have been accepted by many anthropologists and other social scientists. Perhaps the most well-known are the Americans Edward Sapir and Benjamin Lee Whorf, who together developed the "Whorf–Sapir hypothesis." The Whorf–Sapir hypothesis says that the structure of a language determines how a speaker of that language thinks. Sapir expressed this hyphothesis as follows:

> Human beings do not live in the objective world alone . . . but are very much at the mercy of the particular language which has become the medium of expression for their society. . . . The fact of the matter is that the "real world" is to a large extent unconsciously built up of the language habits of the group. . . . We see and hear and otherwise experience very largely as we do because the language habits of our community predispose certain choices of interpretation.[24]

Whorf spent many years studying the Native American Hopi language. He discovered that in the Hopi language words referring to units of time (such as *day* or *year*) differ from other words because they do not have plural forms. And they cannot be counted separately (using *one, two, three*, etc.), but only in terms of their place in a single series (*first, second, third*, etc.). Whorf concluded that the Hopi think of time as cyclic recurrences of the same units of time. Each day for the Hopi is a recurrence of the day before, rather than a completely new day. Because they see time in this way, Whorf argued, the Hopi repeat the same ceremonial acts each time period. And since it is always the same day again, they feel that the power of these acts keeps building up. The power of the ceremony of yesterday is present today because today is yesterday repeating itself. Thus, the language of the Hopi makes them see and feel time as a cyclic recurrence. By contrast, our language makes us look at time as progressing continuously into a new time that has never occurred before and, once past, will never recur again. Kant saw reason as constructing our reality, but the new Kantians believe that *language* constructs reality.

Theories like Kant's are sometimes called "constructivist" theories because they hold that reality as we know it is constructed by us. We put together the world as we know it, and for each of us there is no reality apart from the reality we build. This idea has profound implications but is easily misunderstood. For example, consider the phenomenon of recovered memories of childhood sexual abuse that we discussed earlier. What might a Kantian approach to such recovered memories say? Are such memories valid sources of knowledge? Let us think about this before we leave Kant and his followers.

The person in therapy who recovers her repressed memories gradually constructs a detailed picture of a past reality that is very different from the reality that she had previously remembered. In the spirit of Kant, we might want to say that the past world that is constructed from these memories must be as fully real as the world that we currently see around us. After all, the world that we

The striking similarities between Indian, Greek and German philosophy are easy to explain. Their languages have a common origin and a similar grammar that unconsciously dominates and directs them. These similarities bar other ways of interpreting the world.

FRIEDRICH NIETZSCHE

---

[24] Quoted in "Languages of the Americas," *Encyclopedia Britannica CD*, 1998.

see around us is also constructed by the mind and so is no more "privileged" and no more "real" than the world that our mind might gradually piece together out of its recovered memories. So for the person who comes to believe in a past world in which she was sexually abused, that awful world is every bit as real, and must be taken as seriously, as the present world that her mind similarly constructs. So Kant's theory apparently suggests that recollected memories must provide accurate knowledge of past reality because this past reality is constructed from the memories themselves. Undoubtedly, some of Kant's modern followers might accept this conclusion, especially those who think that each of us constructs his or her own world.

Kant himself, however, would object that this conclusion overlooks an important part of his theory. In his theory we can know only one real world: the world in which objects are causally related to each other. In the world we see around us, for example, bullets can cause death and fire can cause painful burns. So bullets and fires are part of the real world. Other "worlds" that our minds might construct—like the worlds of our dreams—are not real because they are not causally related to the world around us. For example, a bullet that I shoot in a dream cannot cause someone's death in the real world, and a fire that I dream cannot cause someone in the real world a painful burn. If recollected memories provide true knowledge of reality, then, the events they depict must be more than mental constructs. Real events must, then, be causally related to the actual world around us.

So Kant's theory can shed light on whether recovered memories are valid sources of knowledge. His theory implies that recollected memories can be taken as a true source of knowledge only if the events they depict had some causal effects on the world around us. People who suspect they may be survivors of childhood sexual abuse, as well as juries weighing lawsuits brought against parents accused of sexually abusing their children decades earlier, need to determine whether the world remembered by the alleged victims of sexual abuse is more than a mental construct. Kant would say they need to find independent causal effects of the abuse in the real world that indicate the abuse was actually part of the real world.

Still, not everyone has agreed with Kant's theory. Some people continue to insist that our sense experience must conform to an independent world of things if it is to give us real knowledge. We want to know if the world that we construct from our sense experience is an accurate picture of the world that is really there, independent of our sense experiences. But Kant would say that we can never know what reality is like apart from our mental construct of it. Thus, Kant's theory that we construct the world we see around us seems to leave us with a deep skepticism about our ability to know the world as it really is.

One problem with Kant's position is that in his view, the senses are our link to reality, so the question arises again whether there is a difference between reality and what we experience. If experience is the only true basis of knowledge, then it is reasonable to question the reliability of the senses as sources of that knowledge. After all, the mind can't organize our sensory experiences until it receives them. Of course, Kant claims that what the senses give us does not correspond to how things are to begin with—it is already informed by the categories. Thus, we never perceive things as they actually are. If things as such are unknowable, then we appear to be faced with thorough skepticism. We could also wonder about the mental categories themselves—whether Kant has provided a complete list and description and whether they're the same for everyone.

Despite these apparent drawbacks, Kant's views, and the view of his followers, are a serious attempt to analyze the nature of knowledge. Kant not only shows the limitations of knowledge but also validates knowledge within its proper field. More specifically, Kant is noteworthy for his portrayal of the inquisitive nature of the mind. This conception of the mind's role as a questioner of nature constitutes a new way of considering the nature of the self and its objects, and, most important, it suggests a new approach to the study of perception.

QUESTIONS

1. Kant claims that true knowledge has its basis in experience. At the same time, he states that a priori knowledge is possible. Is this a contradiction?

2. Kant concludes that we can obtain only knowledge of appearances (phenomena) and never of the way things actually are (noumena). Does this make him a skeptic? If not, what distinguishes his view from skepticism?

3. Many authors have noted that Kant's theory of the unity of consciousness changed the dispute between rationalists and empiricists. What do you think that these authors mean by this?

5.5 Does Science Give Us Knowledge?

We have examined three approaches to knowledge: the rationalist view, that some of our knowledge of reality derives from reason without the aid of the senses; the empiricist view, that our knowledge of reality must derive from our sensory experience; and the transcendentalist view, that the fundamental structures of reality (such as the fact that all events are causally related to prior causes) can be discovered by reason, whereas the particular contents of reality (such as the nature of particular events and causes) must be derived from our sensory experience.

But what can we learn from these approaches to knowledge? Can they help us distinguish knowledge from opinion? By themselves, probably not. As we shall see, there is more to distinguishing solidly based knowledge from poorly based knowledge than these approaches provide by themselves. But they do

I don't see a clear boundary between philosophy and science. I see rather gradations. It's a matter of degree.

W. V. O. QUINE

point the way to some useful and helpful insights. We now develop those insights by looking at a widely accepted and prolific source of knowledge of reality: science.

In fact, for many people today, science is the most reliable source of knowledge. Many people hold that scientific claims about the world are as close to the truth as we can get. People use the term *scientific* to suggest reliability, validity, and certainty. Thus, when someone wants to say that a certain belief is unreliable or dubious, they will say that it is "unscientific," and they will describe a claim as "scientific" to distinguish it from claims that are fraudulent or based on superstition, mere intuition, or prejudice. The methods of the sciences, many people hold, are distinctive and best calculated to yield genuine and certain knowledge of reality. But do the sciences really give us certain and valid knowledge? What methods does science use, and what justifies our reliance on them?

Perhaps the most widely accepted characteristic of science is its reliance on sensory observation. In fact, for many people a theory is scientific to the extent that it is based on sensory observations; these empiricists claim that we are justified in believing a theory if sensory observations show that it is true. But this characterization of science is inadequate because it does not tell us how scientific theories are based on sensory observations.

INDUCTIVE REASONING AND SIMPLICITY

One influential view of the relationship between scientific theories and sensory observations is known as *inductionism*. This view holds that the primary tool of the scientific method is **inductive reasoning**—that is, reasoning to general probable laws from many particular sensory observations. Inductive reasoning was suggested as the proper scientific method by Francis Bacon (1561–1626), a philosopher who (unlike many of his contemporaries) refused simply to accept without question the views of nature handed down from the ancient Greeks. Bacon insisted that instead of simply accepting ideas from the past, scientists should investigate nature by careful observation and experimentation. They should collect as many facts as possible about the phenomenon they are studying, using experiments when possible to generate additional facts. Once all the facts are collected, they should carefully sift through them and derive general conclusions from the particular facts.

inductive reasoning the process of reasoning to probable explanations or judgments

Two centuries after Bacon, another philosopher, the empiricist John Stuart Mill (1806–1873), tried to improve on Bacon by laying out what he called *canons*, or methods of induction. These were rules for determining which generalizations were supported by the many particular facts and observations the scientist collected. In the view of Bacon and Mill, scientific method is characterized by three features:

1. *The accumulation of particular observations.* Scientific method begins with the collection of as many observed facts as possible concerning the topic under investigation.

2. *Generalization from the particular observations.* Scientific method then proceeds by inferring general laws from the accumulated particular facts.

3. *Repeated confirmation.* Scientific method continues to accumulate more particular facts to see if the generalization continues to hold true. The more particular instances of a "law" that are found, the more confirmation the law has and the higher its probability.

Thus, for the inductionist empiricist, real science is distinguished from opinion, superstition, and bias by its reliance on generalization from particular sensory observations and by repeated confirmation. The pseudosciences, according to the inductionist, are not solidly based on good sensory observations and repeated confirmation.

Scientists who have used this empiricist process of compiling observations, generalizing from the observations, and repeatedly confirming the generalization are not hard to find. During the seventeenth century, Galileo Galilei (1564–1642), for example, became interested in studying the motion of falling objects. Most scientists of his time were content to accept the commonsense opinion of Aristotle, who had declared that objects fall faster the heavier they are. But Galileo decided to find out for himself. He devised a number of experiments in which he repeatedly measured how fast metal balls of different weights fell when dropped about a hundred feet. Much to his surprise, he found that every ball fell at the same rate, no matter how heavy it was. Moreover, Galileo

PHILOSOPHY AND LIFE

The Problem of Induction

All of science is based on an unproven assumption: the assumption that *the future will be like the past.* Science is based on inductive reasoning: From observations made in the past, the scientist draws conclusions about the laws and theories that will operate in the future. In fact, all our knowledge of the world around us is based on inductive reasoning that assumes the future will be like the past. We know that water will satisfy our thirst because it did so in the past, that the sun will rise tomorrow because it did so in the past, that gravity will attract objects to the ground because it did so in the past, that evolution will alter species in the future because it did so in the past, that quantum theory

will continue to predict the behavior of atomic particles in the future because it did so in the past.

But how do we know that the future will be like the past? You might be tempted to reply that you know it will because the future has always been like the past. But a moment's reflection will show you that this is circular reasoning—it assumes what it is trying to prove. For you are reasoning that since *in the past* the future was like the past, then *in the future* the future will be like the past. But this reasoning assumes that what happened *in the past* must happen *in the future,* and this is exactly what you are trying to prove.

So *past* experience does not justify our assumption that *in the future*

the future will be like the past. And if we cannot prove that this assumption is true, then doesn't all our knowledge about the world around us rest on an unproven assumption?

QUESTIONS

1. Can you think of any way of proving that the future will be like the past?

2. Is there any difference between the scientist who takes "on faith" the assumption that the future will be like the past and the believer who takes "on faith" the assumptions of religion? Does the problem of induction show that science is ultimately a kind of religion?

also found that as each ball fell, it moved faster and faster. Pressing his study, Galileo built long, smooth inclined planes and rolled balls down them. For years he worked, carefully releasing the balls and timing them. After a large number of observations, he formulated the important generalization that all objects fall to the earth at the same constantly accelerating rate. Aristotle was wrong. Countless scientists after Galileo have confirmed his law of falling bodies, making it a highly probable law.

In a similar way, Gregor Mendel (1822–1884) formulated the basic laws of heredity by growing and repeatedly cross-breeding peas, and observing the numbers of offspring with certain colors and shapes in each generation. From these observations he generalized to his laws, which say, for example, that in the second generation the ratio of a dominant genetic trait to a recessive trait is 3 : 1. Mendel's laws have been repeatedly confirmed by biologists and are now accepted as some of the fundamental laws of biology.

But inductionism has its critics. A major problem is the fact that every generalization has to go *beyond* the observations on which it is based. For example, Galileo observed that a relatively few metal balls fall relatively short distances before concluding that *every* object *always* falls to the earth at a constantly accelerating speed. Because a generalization always goes beyond the observational evidence, the evidence cannot really be said to prove the generalization. In fact, a large (potentially infinite) number of different generalizations is always compatible with any set of sensory observations and can also be said to have been confirmed by the observations of the scientist. For example, when Galileo measured his falling metal balls at several points as they dropped through, say, a hundred feet, and found that each time they were moving at an accelerating rate, he could have concluded (1) that objects fall at a gradually accelerating rate until they drop a certain distance (one hundred feet) and then fall at a uniform rate, or (2) that objects fall at an accelerating rate until they reach a certain speed and then begin to slow down, or (3) that objects fall at an accelerating rate at those points at which Galileo measured their fall but sometimes fall at a uniform rate in between those points. When so many generalizations are compatible with the observations, why should we accept one generalization rather than another?

Some inductionists have pointed to the criterion of *simplicity* as a way of deciding among competing generalizations. The scientist generally chooses the simplest generalization compatible with sensory observations. None of the generalizations suggested in the last paragraph is as simple as Galileo's.

But simplicity seems to be a rationalist criterion, not an empiricist criterion: It tells us that the world must follow simpler rather than more complex laws. And this criterion does not seem to be established by sensory observation but by reason. Thus, the inductionist method seems forced to incorporate an element of rationalism into its procedures.

But even if the inductionist can deal with this problem, there is a more serious reason that inductionism is not an adequate theory of the relation between scientific knowledge and sensory observations. The problem is that almost none of the great scientific theories are mere generalizations from a few facts. For example, Darwin's theory of evolution by natural selection claims that

Observation sentences are fundamental to scientific evidence.

W. V. O. QUINE

species evolve through time as a result of genetic changes and competition for survival and reproduction. Darwin did not establish his theory by observing a few species evolve in this way and then generalizing to the conclusion that all species evolve like this. In fact, Darwin never observed the evolution of any species because the evolution of species takes many lifetimes. So Darwin was doing something more than generalizing from a few sensory observations.

In fact, though relatively simple and low-level scientific laws are often established by induction, the great, broad, and fundamental *theories* of science that explain and relate wide arrays of phenomena and provide the bases for rich research programs are not established by induction alone. Galileo's law of falling bodies is an example of a relatively simple and low-level law that was established by induction. But this law describes the behavior of a very limited range of objects: those that fall to the surface of the earth. Isaac Newton (1642–1727) developed a broad and comprehensive theory incorporating three laws of motion and a law of universal gravitation, which together explain the motions of the moon, the planets in the solar system, and the motions of distant stars and galaxies. Yet Newton does not seem to have established his theory by merely generalizing from some sensory observations. Instead, he seems to have familiarized himself with the findings of his predecessors and then creatively fashioned a comprehensive theory that drew all of their findings together and went beyond them in a way that no one had suspected was possible. Clearly, scientific method consists of more than mere inductive generalizations.

THE HYPOTHETICAL METHOD AND FALSIFIABILITY

Because induction cannot account for broad scientific theories, many thinkers have turned in a different direction. What distinguishes scientific knowledge from pseudoscience, superstition, or bias, they claim, is the use of the *hypothetical method.* William Whewell (1794–1866), an opponent of John Stuart Mill, pointed out that advances in scientific knowledge do not depend only on the exhaustive collection of facts followed by generalization. Instead, Whewell contended, the great scientific advances occur when scientists make a creative guess or **hypothesis** about what causes or explains a particular phenomenon and then *test* this hypothesis by sensory observation and experimentation:

hypothesis in general, an assumption, statement, or theory of explanation, the truth of which is under investigation

> The conceptions by which facts are bound together are suggested by the sagacity of discoverers. This sagacity cannot be taught. It commonly succeeds by guessing; and this success seems to consist in framing several tentative hypotheses and selecting the right one. But a supply of appropriate hypotheses cannot be constructed by rule, nor without inventive talent.[25]

Darwin's theory of evolution is a good example of what Whewell probably had in mind. Darwin's theory began as a hypothesis intended to explain a large number of observations: the discovery that fossils buried in ancient layers of rock were different from but apparently related to surviving species, the

---

[25] William Whewell, *History and Philosophy of the Inductive Sciences* (1840), quoted in Stewart Richards, *Philosophy and Sociology of Science* (New York: Schocken, 1984), 529.

observation that living species occurred in groups that seemed related to each other as though they had common ancestors, the discovery that some butterfly species had gradually changed color over time in ways that made them more likely to escape being eaten by birds, the discovery that certain species had become extinct apparently as a result of competition with other species, the discovery that the fossil life forms in older rock layers are less complex than those in younger layers, and so on. All of these diverse observations could be explained, he held, by the hypothesis that species change over time by a process of natural selection, in which species that are best adapted to their environment survive and reproduce. Thus, the theory of evolution was not a generalization from observations but a creative idea advanced to explain a large number of facts. Darwin showed that all the previously unconnected varieties of animals and plants, both fossilized and living, could be put into a sequence that showed evolution over immense periods of geological time, and his theory explained why this evolution had taken place. Moreover, a broad range of biological scientists have used Darwin's theory to guide their investigations, to structure their experiments, and to decide which observations were worth making.

At the very heart of scientific method, then, is an element, a contribution, made by reason. Reason—the ability to synthesize, to relate, and to creatively formulate new conceptual structures—seems to be the source of the hypotheses that scientists come up with and use to guide their research. This is an important point. It was, in fact, a point that the transcendental idealist Kant made when he wrote that reason is the source of the basic "questions" or hypotheses that the scientist uses to explore the world of nature. As he points out, even Galileo was guided by a hypothesis when he decided to test his law of falling bodies by constructing long, smooth, inclined planes:

> When Galileo caused balls, the weights of which he had himself previously determined, to roll down an inclined plane; when Torricelli made the air carry a weight which he had calculated beforehand to be equal to that of a definite volume of water; or in more recent times when Stahl changed metals into oxides, and oxides back into metal, by withdrawing something and then restoring it, a light broke upon all students of nature. They learned that reason has insight only into that which it produces after a plan of its own, and that it must not allow itself to be kept, as it were, in nature's leading-strings, but must itself show the way with principles of judgment based upon fixed laws, constraining nature to give answers to questions of reason's own determining. Accidental observations, made in obedience to no previously thought-out plan, can never be made to yield a necessary law, which alone reason is concerned to discover. Reason, holding in one hand its principles, according to which alone concordant appearances can be admitted as equivalent to laws, and in the other hand the experiment which it has devised in conformity with these principles, must approach nature in order to be taught by it. It must not, however, do so in the character of a pupil who listens to everything that the teacher chooses to say, but of an appointed judge who compels the witnesses to answer questions which he has himself formulated.[26]

What Kant makes clear is that every scientific investigation is in the nature of an interrogation, and that it is we who have framed the questions that our observations of nature give answers to.

STEPHEN TOULMIN

---

[26] Kant, *Critique of Pure Reason*, 20.

In formulating a hypothesis, the scientist turns away from the senses to reason and attempts to create new relationships, new structures and connections, and to organize these into a theory that orders, systematizes, and explains his or her sensory observations. In formulating hypotheses, Kant might have said, the scientist also relies on other "laws of reason," such as the criterion of simplicity. Then the scientist returns to sensory observations by asking whether the theory accurately predicts new observations, whether it suggests fresh research and new experiments, or whether it points the way toward other corroborating observations. Thus, in an important way, reason lies at the heart of the hypothetical method.

Nevertheless, the most influential proponent of the hypothetical method in the twentieth century was not a rationalist or a transcendental idealist, but a modern empiricist, the philosopher Karl Popper. Popper agreed that scientific theories are not mere generalizations from experience, and he accepted the view that science progresses by formulating hypotheses that can explain many different phenomena and that guide later research. But what really distinguishes the sciences from pseudoscience and superstition, Popper claimed, is that *scientific hypotheses must be capable of being falsified through empirical observation.*

Many unscientific theories are said by their supporters to be confirmed by observation and experience. For example, astrologers will point to observed events that are consistent with some of their predictions and say that these verify their theories. Similarly, people who believe in biorhythms or extrasensory perception selectively point to observed facts that tend to confirm their theories. But any theory, Popper pointed out, can be shown to be consistent with some observed facts. Science does not proceed by trying to find facts that confirm a theory. Instead, the mark of science is that it tries to *disprove* or *falsify* proposed theories. A real scientific theory is not just one that is confirmed by some observations but one that survives repeated attempts to prove it false. Popper wrote that "there is no more rational procedure than the method of trial and error — of conjecture and refutation; of boldly proposing theories; of trying our best to show that these are erroneous; and of accepting them tentatively if our critical efforts are unsuccessful."[27]

Science has nothing to do with the quest for certainty or probability or reliability.

KARL POPPER

Popper's view that a scientific theory must be *capable of being falsified by observable events* does not mean that scientific statements are those that are actually shown to be false. Rather, a statement is scientific when some observable events or discoveries exist that *could* show the statement to be false. Science advances when the scientist formulates a hypothesis that implies that some observable event will occur and then tries to falsify the hypothesis by experiments and observations, to see whether the predicted observable event occurs as his or her hypothesis says it will. If a theory stands up to many attempts to falsify it, then we are justified in believing it. The more times we try to prove it false, and fail, the more reliable it is. For example, astronomers had noticed that the orbits of the known planets were irregular; Newton's theory of

[27] Karl Popper, *Conjectures and Refutations* (1963), quoted in Richards, *Philosophy and Sociology of Science*, 52.

motion predicted that the disturbance was caused by the gravitational attraction of an unknown planet in a certain orbit. When astronomers searched that part of the sky, they discovered the planet Neptune. Newton's theory is also regularly used to predict projectile motions and the motions of everything from trains to molecules. All these are observable events predicted by Newton's theory, which could have turned out to be false but which turned out to be true.

In a similar way, Darwin's theory of evolution predicted that under Cambrian rock formations (assumed to be 500 to 600 million years old), in older pre-Cambrian rock, scientists should be able to find fossils of organisms simpler than those in the younger Cambrian rock. The theory of evolution (in part) hypothesizes that organisms developed gradually from simple to increasingly complex forms. If evolution is a sound theory, then pre-Cambrian formations should contain simpler fossil forms. That is exactly what biologists found in 1947 in pre-Cambrian rocks in Australia.

It is important to see that the hypothetical method and the falsifiability criterion that Popper suggests imply that scientific knowledge is never more than probable; it is always open to revision based on new evidence or a new interpretation of existing evidence. A scientific hypothesis may predict certain events, and these events may occur as the hypothesis suggested. But it is always possible that other predictions of the hypothesis, not yet tested, may turn out to be wrong. A scientific hypothesis, like a generalization, always goes beyond the limited number of facts or observations that it was formulated to explain. For this reason, it is always open to refutation; it is always merely probable, never certain.

PARADIGMS AND REVOLUTIONS IN SCIENCE

Popper's view ignores the extent to which scientists are human beings who work together, who are trained to accept certain laboratory methods and research strategies, and who are deeply committed to the correctness of a core of basic theories about their subject matter. As a result, scientists tend to continue accepting a basic theory even if they run into observations that falsify the theory. In fact, in spite of Popper's claims, scientists may stubbornly cling to a theory for decades after the appearance of experimental results that are inconsistent with the theory.

The American philosopher of science Thomas Kuhn has tried to take this phenomenon into account by arguing that we should think of scientific knowledge in relation to communities of scientists who accept and work with that knowledge. Examples of these communities might include the community of biologists who accept and use Darwin's theory, the community of physicists and astronomers who accept and use Newton's and Einstein's theories, and the community of chemists who accept and use molecular theory. A person who decides to become a scientist receives a prolonged "indoctrination" into the theories and research methods of the scientific community. This research tradition or *paradigm* of science includes a way of thinking and acting; the student-scientist is taught the basic theories of the field and the appropriate methods for applying and extending those basic theories. Examples of a paradigm are the theory of

The great scientists, such as Galileo, Kepler, Newton, Einstein, and Bohr, work with bold conjectures and severe attempts at refuting their own conjectures.

KARL POPPER

the atom in chemistry, the Copernican theory that the earth and planets revolve around the sun in astronomy, and the theory of evolution in biology. In each of these cases, the community of scientists accepts the basic theory, uses it as a guide to research, and *tends to hold on to it even if some observations show up that do not fit into the theory*. According to Kuhn,

> These remarks should begin to clarify what I take a paradigm to be. It is, in the first place, a fundamental scientific achievement and one which includes both a theory and some exemplary applications to the results of experiment and observation. More important, it is an open-ended achievement, one which leaves all sorts of research still to be done. And, finally, it is an accepted achievement in the sense that it is received by a group whose members no longer try to rival it or to create alternates for it. Instead, they attempt to extend and exploit it in a variety of ways.[28]

Moreover, Kuhn argues, science does not always grow gradually, as the inductionists and the falsificationists say it does. Instead, science leaps forward through major *revolutions*. Although scientists tend to cling tenaciously to their theories, when too many observations accumulate that do not square with a theory, too many "anomalies," a "crisis" results. Some scientists start to rethink their theories, and a new theory is developed that takes the anomalies into account. A revolution occurs in the scientific community; some scientists (usually the older, established ones) continue to hold on to the old theories while other (usually younger) scientists become disciples of the new theory. New research programs and methods are developed for this new theory, and when

---

[28] Thomas Kuhn, "The Function of Dogma in Scientific Research," in *Scientific Knowledge: Basic Issues in the Philosophy of Science*, ed. Janet A. Kourany (Belmont, CA: Wadsworth, 1987), 259.

PHILOSOPHY AND LIFE

Society and Truth

In *The Art of Awareness*, J. Samuel Bois reports the following experiment:

A psychologist employed seven assistants and one genuine subject in an experiment where they were asked to judge how long was a straight line that they were shown on a screen. The seven assistants, who were the first to speak and report what they saw, had been instructed to report unanimously an evidently incorrect length. The eighth member of the group, the only naive subject in the lot, did not know that his companions had received such an instruction, and he was under the impression that what they reported was really what they saw. In one-third of the experiments, he reported the same incorrect length as they did. The pressure of the environment had influenced his own semantic reaction and had distorted his vision. When one of the assistants, under the secret direction of the experimenter, started reporting the correct length, it relieved that pressure of the environment, and the perception of the uninformed subject improved accordingly.

QUESTION

1. To what extent does our sense knowledge depend on what we *should* be seeing?

SOURCE: J. Samuel Bois, *The Art of Awareness* (Dubuque, IA: William C. Brown, 1973).

young people enter the field, they are indoctrinated into the new theory, which eventually becomes the new paradigm of science:

> Scientific revolutions are here taken to be those noncumulative developmental episodes in which an older paradigm is replaced in whole or in part by an incompatible new one. . . . Why should a change of paradigm be called a revolution? . . . Political revolutions are inaugurated by a growing sense, often restricted to a segment of the political community, that existing institutions have ceased adequately to meet the problems posed by an environment that they have in part created. In much the same way, scientific revolutions are inaugurated by a growing sense, again often restricted to a narrow subdivision of the scientific community, that an existing paradigm has ceased to function adequately in the exploration of an aspect of nature to which that paradigm itself had previously led the way. In both political and scientific development the sense of malfunction that can lead to crisis is prerequisite to revolution.[29]

The history of science is filled with examples of such scientific revolutions, Kuhn says. Some of them are the change from the medieval theory that the sun revolves around the earth to the revolutionary theory of Copernicus that the earth revolves around the sun, the change from Newton's theory that time and space are absolute and unchanging to the revolutionary theory of Einstein that time and space are relative, the change from the theory that animal and plant species do not change to Darwin's revolutionary theory of evolution. New paradigms, Kuhn insists, give us new ways of seeing the world, new ways of thinking, and new goals and methods for investigating nature.

Although Kuhn's insights into the way that science progresses are extremely valuable, they leave an important question unanswered: What is the difference between real science and superstition or pseudoscience? Kuhn seems to provide us with no way of answering this question other than to say that a theory is scientific if the community of scientists accepts it. As he wrote in one of his early works, "What better criterion could there be [of scientific knowledge] than the decision of the scientific group?"[30] This point is important because it indicates that a piece of scientific knowledge must be consistent with the knowledge prevailing among the community of scientists. Yet any group of people might claim to be a "community of scientists." For example, the International Flat Earth Research Society claims to be a group of scientists who aim "to establish as a fact that this earth is flat and plane and that it does not spin and whirl 1000 miles an hour and to expose modern astronomical science as a fraud, myth, a false religion." How, then, are we to distinguish real science from bogus science?

In his most recent research, Thomas Kuhn responded to this important question:

> What, I ask to begin with, are the characteristics of a good scientific theory? . . . First, a theory should be accurate: Within its domain, that is, consequences deducible from a theory should be in demonstrated agreement with the results of existing experiments and observations. Second, a theory should be consistent, not only internally

The deepest transition Kuhn made was to think of rationality itself as being something which is historically conditioned. That change has premeated modern culture.

IAN HACKING

CRITICAL THINKING
Kuhn assumes that the five criteria he lists will separate a good scientific theory from all bogus science. Is this assumption correct?

---

[29] Thomas Kuhn, "The Nature and Necessity of Scientific Revolutions," in *Scientific Knowledge*, 311.
[30] Thomas Kuhn, *The Structure of Scientific Revolutions* (London: Oxford University Press, 1973).

or with itself, but also with other currently accepted theories applicable to related aspects of nature. Third, it should have broad scope: In particular, a theory's consequences should extend far beyond the particular observations, laws, or subtheories it was initially designed to explain. Fourth, and closely related, it should be simple, bringing order to phenomena that in its absence would be individually isolated and, as a set, confused. Fifth—a somewhat less standard item, but one of special importance to actual scientific decisions—a theory should be fruitful of new research findings: it should, that is, disclose new phenomena or previously unnoted relationships among those already known.[31]

Many of the criteria that Kuhn suggests here are closely related to the rationalist tradition. For example, the criterion of consistency is not established by sensory observation: It is based on reason, on the idea that rationality demands consistency. The same can be said about his criterion that a good scientific theory must bring order into our sensory observations. This, as we suggested, is a function of reason: to develop a theory that, as Kant indicated, can connect and relate what the senses provide and that can provide the basis for further investigations of nature.

> *It may be that the sciences don't have some shared feature that we can hail as "the scientific method."*
>
> PHILIP KITCHER

DISTINGUISHING SCIENCE FROM PSEUDOSCIENCE

Let us attempt now to summarize what we have seen and to reach some conclusions about what scientific method is and what distinguishes science from pseudoscience.

First, scientific method incorporates elements from the views of the empiricists (in its dependence on sensory observation), the rationalists (in its appeal to simplicity, for example), and the transcendental idealists (in the creative use of reason to formulate hypotheses that can guide research into nature).

Second, particularly in the establishment of low-level laws, scientific method relies on the *inductive method of observation, generalization, and repeated confirmation by new observations*. When rival generalizations are in all other respects equal, scientists tend to accept the simplest one, the one that accounts for the facts most economically. But more important than simplicity is the number and variety of new observations that confirm a generalization.

Third, especially in the establishment of general theories but also in the establishment of some low-level laws, scientific method proceeds by the creative formulation of *hypotheses that can guide research and that can then be tested by observation*. Not all creative guesses or hypotheses are on an equal level. A scientific hypothesis must be testable by observation. It must make predictions that can be observed, and it must be capable of guiding new research and suggesting new experiments that can test the hypothesis.

Fourth, a critical element of a scientific theory is that it must be *falsifiable*: The theory must make predictions that, if it is wrong, can be shown to be false by observation. This means that science does not use a selective approach to evidence. Scientists do not pick out only the evidence and observations that

---

[31] Thomas Kuhn, *The Essential Tension: Selected Studies in Scientific Tradition and Change* (Chicago: University of Chicago Press, 1977), 321.

agree with their theories. Instead, they continually look for *disconfirming* evidence as well as confirming evidence. This contrasts with, say, the methods of psychic predictors, who point out the events that they have successfully predicted but conveniently ignore the predictions they made that never came true and the relevant events that they did not predict. Because science is always on the lookout for disconfirming evidence, scientific theories are never certain but only probable, always open to refutation by future observations.

Fifth, a scientific theory is a theory that is *widely accepted in the community of scientists;* they use the theory to guide their research but may abandon it in a scientific revolution when confronted with too many anomalies for which the theory can no longer account. This means that the evidence on which scientific theories are based must be made available to other people. Experiments or observations that confirm a theory must be capable of being replicated or repeated by others in the community of scientists. This contrasts with the methods of, say, UFO researchers, who rely on "sightings" by individuals that cannot be duplicated or repeated by others. Moreover, when confronted with sufficient phenomena that cannot be explained by their theory, scientists will abandon a theory, whereas pseudoscientific groups will not. For example, the theories of astrologers have been tenaciously clung to for centuries, no matter how much evidence has accumulated against them.

Finally, a scientific theory must meet five criteria: It must be in *accurate* agreement with observations, it must be *consistent* with other prevailing scientific theories, it must have consequences that extend *beyond the phenomena it was originally designed to explain*, it must *organize and relate phenomena* that were previously thought to be disconnected, and it must be *fruitful* by suggesting fresh research and experiments.

Clearly, these features of science are not shared by the many pseudoscientific claims that we read in newspapers and magazines and find on the Internet. They serve to distinguish genuine science from biorhythm theory, theories of extrasensory perception, parapsychology, astrology, pyramid power, and UFOs. These nonscientific theories are not in agreement with what many other people have observed, they are not consistent with science, they are used as ad hoc explanations of past events but cannot explain or predict future events, they do not help us organize and understand phenomena that were previously felt to be disconnected, and they certainly do not lead to new research programs or fresh scientific experiments. Instead, they are simply grab-bag theories: They grab at any phenomena that seem to agree with them and stuff them into their bag of "evidence."

We discussed earlier the controversy over the theory of repressed memory and of recovered memory therapy. Proponents of this theory, as we saw, claim that the theory is scientifically valid. But how does the theory fare when measured against the features that distinguish a real scientific theory from pseudoscience? On several counts, the theory of repressed memory and of recovered memory therapy measures up quite favorably. For example, the theory is widely accepted in the community of scientists composed of psychologists, particularly those belonging to the psychoanalytic school. Furthermore, the theory is in accurate agreement with observations made in clinical practice, it is consistent with certain other psychological theories, it has implications that extend beyond the phenomena of recovered memories, it is very successful at organizing and relating psychological phenomena that were previously thought to be disconnected, and it is fruitful in suggesting fresh research and experiments. Yet in other respects the theory seems to fail as a genuine scientific theory. In particular, one of the disturbing aspects of recovered memory theory is that it may not be falsifiable. In fact, efforts of critics to disprove the theory have typically been met with the response that the critics are "in denial," and patients in therapy are encouraged to believe that "the existence of profound disbelief is an indication that memories are real."

The scientific validity of the theory of repressed memory and of recovered memory therapy, then, is a complex and troubling issue. It is an issue that demonstrates the importance of having clear views on the valid sources of true knowledge and of scientific truth. And it is an issue that readers might profitably continue to pursue on their own, using the concepts and understandings they have developed in the course of this chapter.

Our review of scientific method has uncovered some important ways of separating pseudoscience from scientific knowledge. Has it helped us get closer to the truth, then? Perhaps, and perhaps not. Some people have held that science does not even deal with the truth but only with "useful fictions." Others have held that science is the best way of getting at the truth about reality. But to judge these views we must first get clear about what we mean by truth. And to that subject the next chapter is devoted.

QUESTIONS

1. Pick some theory that you believe is pseudoscientific and some theory that is widely accepted as a legitimate part of science. Use the characteristics of science enumerated in this section to explain why the first theory is not scientific and the second is. Are these characteristics adequate for distinguishing between science and pseudoscience?

2. Evaluate these statements: (a) science gives us an exact and certain knowledge of reality; (b) the primary goal of science is the accumulation of facts or data.

3. Some people argue that because scientists rely on hypotheses and accepted theories to guide their research, they approach reality with preconceptions that inevitably distort what they observe. Is this true? Would it be possible to investigate nature without preconceptions? Explain your answers.

4. What characteristics of science are present in the way that you ordinarily try to find out something about the people and the world around you? Which characteristics are absent? Does this make your knowledge more or less reliable than that of the scientist?

5. Based on the characteristics of science outlined in the chapter, can science answer the question of whether God exists?

5.6 Chapter Summary and Conclusions

The issues of who we are and how we are to live are tied to the question of knowledge. Historically, philosophers have asked this question: If there are different kinds of knowledge of reality, how can they be obtained? The most common view is that there are two types of such knowledge: rational and empirical. Among the outstanding rationalists is René Descartes, who attempted to demonstrate the validity of a priori knowledge — that is, knowledge independent of sensory perception.

In vigorous reaction to Descartes and the rationalists are the British empiricists: Locke, Berkeley, and Hume. They insist that all knowledge of reality is a posteriori — that is, it follows from experience. One crucial problem that empiricists face arises from their distinction between an objective reality and our experience of it. If these are differentiated, how do we know that our experiences correspond with how things are? Locke's answer is that our experiences represent the outside world. Berkeley says that all we ever know are our own ideas; only conscious minds and their perceptions exist. For Hume, reality is not truly knowable.

Immanuel Kant proposed his theory of transcendental idealism to demonstrate that knowledge of reality is possible. Whereas Kant argues that true knowledge of reality has its basis in sensory experience, he also claims that the mind has innate capacities to order that sensory experience and thus arrive at knowledge.

We have seen that modern science incorporates elements of all these traditions. Scientific "knowledge" is based on induction and simplicity, on the hypothetical method and creativity, on falsifiability and predictive power, on wide acceptance by the community of scientists, as well as on accuracy, consistency, explanatory power, the ability to relate what was previously disconnected, and fruitfulness. Pseudoscientific theories such as astrology do not possess these features.

The main points of this chapter, then, are as follows:

1. There are two common views regarding the sources of knowledge: rationalism and empiricism (5.1).

2. Rationalism states that some knowledge is based on reason rather than on sensory perception (5.1).

3. René Descartes was a rationalist concerned with discovering something that he could hold as true beyond any doubt. He concluded that no one could doubt that a human is a thinking being, that a thinking thing exists, that God exists, and that the world exists. All of this, he claimed, could be established by reason alone (5.2).

4. Empiricism states that all knowledge comes from or is based on sensory perception and is a posteriori (5.3).

5. John Locke held that objects have primary qualities that are distinct from our perception of them, such as size, shape, and weight. He also believed that they have secondary qualities that we impose on them, such as color, smell, and texture. We know the objective world through sensory experience, which is a copy of reality and which gives us our ideas of reality (5.3).

6. According to George Berkeley's subjectivism, we know only our own ideas. Carried to an extreme, this position can become solipsism, the position that only I exist and everything else is a creation of my subjective consciousness (5.3).

7. David Hume pushed Locke and Berkeley's empiricism to its logical conclusion. Arguing that all knowledge originates in sensory impressions, Hume distinguished between two forms of perceptions, impressions and ideas. Impressions are lively perceptions, as when we hear, see, feel, love, or hate. Ideas are less lively perceptions; they are reflections on sensations. Hume denied that there is any logical basis for concluding that things have a continued and independent existence outside us. He denied the possibility of any certain knowledge, arguing that both rationalism and empiricism are inadequate to lead to truth and knowledge. He is thus termed a *skeptic* (5.3).

8. Immanuel Kant's transcendental idealism, an alternative to empiricism and rationalism, distinguishes between our experience of things (phenomena) and the things as they are (noumena). The mind, claimed Kant, possesses the ability to sort sensory experiences and posit relationships among them. Through an awareness of these relationships, we come to knowledge (5.4).

9. Inductionism is the view that all science is based on the process of sensory observation, generalization, and repeated confirmation. This process is often used to establish scientific laws, and simplicity is one criterion for choosing among competing generalizations (5.5).

10. The hypothetical method view says that science is also based on the creative formulation of hypotheses whose predictions are then tested and used to guide research. Karl Popper argued that falsifiability is a criterion of scientific theories (5.5).

11. Thomas Kuhn argued that scientific theories are those that are widely accepted by a community of scientists. They are the basis of paradigms that guide research but that are abandoned in a scientific revolution, when too many anomalies appear that cannot be accounted for by the paradigm. Scientific theories must be accurate, consistent with other widely accepted theories, capable of explaining phenomena other than those they were developed to explain, capable of organizing phenomena that were previously thought to be unrelated, and fruitful insofar as they generate new research and new discoveries (5.5).

Knowledge, then, is not as simple as we may have thought. Neither, therefore, are our claims to know who and what we are. But the views about knowledge briefly traced in this chapter show us several important options. We may agree with the empiricists that all our knowledge ultimately derives from the senses. If so, then we must agree that the only human reality we can know is what can be sensed. To be human is to be nothing more than something that can be seen, heard, smelled, or touched. On the other hand, we may agree with the rationalists that at least some of our knowledge derives from what our reason can perceive without the aid of the senses. If we accept this view, then human reality need not be limited to what our senses reveal. Then it is possible to hold that our minds can perceive a reality that cannot be perceived by the senses, and it is possible to hold that to be human is at least in part to be a creature that transcends the senses. That, presumably, was Descartes's aim when he claimed that with the mind he could "clearly and distinctly perceive" that he was a nonextended or nonphysical thinking being. He was claiming that to be human is to be something that transcends the senses.

The history we have reviewed also presents us with another kind of option: the option between seeing ourselves as having an essentially passive mind that must conform to the world it knows or seeing ourselves as having an active mind that shapes the world it knows. From Descartes to Hume, the prevailing view was that the world exists independently of us and that we know that world only when our ideas conform to that world. In this view, our minds are passive: They are like soft lumps of clay on which the world makes its representative imprints or like mirrors that passively reflect images of the passing world. In this view, the knowing human self is essentially a passive receptacle. On the other hand, we might agree with Kant that the world we know is wholly or partly created by ourselves as knowers. Kant viewed the knowing self as active: It molds and shapes the materials provided by experience, and it introduces all or some of the order and structure we see in the world. The knowing self provides the basic categories in terms of which I see the world. As a knower, I create to a lesser or greater degree the world I know, and my own ideas shape and determine the world I experience.

Yet a third option that the theories of knowledge present is the terrifying choice between skepticism and knowledge. If we accept the skeptical view that we can never be sure whether our ideas about reality are accurate, then we must acknowledge that we cannot really know who or what we are. For each of us is part of reality, and if we have no access to reality, then we have no access to ourselves. We may agree that although we *seem* to be made of flesh and blood, we cannot be sure; we may agree that although we *seem* to be social creatures who live in a world of other selves whom we love and care for, we can never know whether this is true. Skepticism implies that we can never discover who or what we really are. On the other hand, if we conclude that skepticism is wrong and that our minds can acquire genuine knowledge about the world, then it is open to us to inquire into how much we can know about what it is to be human. It is possible for us to discover who we are. The very possibility of self-discovery requires that we reject skepticism.

5.7 HISTORICAL SHOWCASE

Hume

In this showcase we feature a British philosopher who profoundly influenced our views on human knowledge: David Hume. Hume raised profound questions about what we can know, what humans are, and whether God exists.

HUME

The man who most deeply influenced our modern perspectives on knowledge is the eighteenth-century philosopher David Hume. To a large extent, the philosophers who followed Hume either enthusiastically embraced his empiricist views or desperately sought to refute his claims. In either case, they were reacting to the radical empiricism he formulated. Everyone who follows Hume must take his arguments into account.

We showcase Hume in this chapter because of his pervasive influence on our views of knowledge. In addition, we hope that by considering Hume's work, you will appreciate how our views of knowledge can affect our views of human nature, God, and the sciences. Hume's empiricist views on knowledge led him to raise crucial questions in all of these areas.

David Hume, the "ultimate skeptic," was born in 1711 into a comfortable family who lived on a small country estate called Ninewells in Edinburgh, Scotland. Hume's father died when David was two. His mother, who took over the task of rearing him, said of the boy: "Davey is a well-meanin' critter, but uncommon weakminded." Nevertheless, a few weeks before his twelfth birthday, Hume entered Edinburgh University, where his family hoped he would be able to earn a degree in law. But university life was unpleasant for Hume, and two years later he dropped out without finishing his degree, having convinced his family that he could as easily study law at home. As Hume later wrote, "My studious disposition, my sobriety, and my industry gave my family a notion that the law was a proper profession for me. But I found an insurmountable aversion to everything but the pursuits of philosophy and general learning, and while they fancied I was poring over [the legal texts of] Voet and Vinnius, Cicero and Vergil were the authors which I was secretly devouring."[1] As a teenager, Hume sat around the house reading and complaining that he was being forced to struggle with various physical and mental ailments.

Then, in his late teens, Hume convinced himself that he had found a truly new philosophy. As he put it, "There seemed to be opened up to me a new Scene of Thought, which transported me beyond measure and made me, with an ardour natural to young men, throw up every other pleasure or business to apply entirely to it." David now spent much of his day trying to think out and express to others the "new" thoughts he felt he had discovered.

Although living at home, Hume apparently managed to get around. At the age of twenty-two he was accused by a young woman named Anne Galbraith of fathering her child, who had been conceived out of wedlock. Hume was sent away to work in the office of a Bristol merchant, but before the year was out he had quit the job he so detested and was sent to live in France on a tiny allowance. There, he spent the next three years living in "rigid frugality" while writing a book, *A Treatise of Human Nature,* in which he tried to express his new philosophy. The book was published in 1737, and by 1739 David was once again living at home in Ninewells, confident that he would soon be famous. To his bitter disappointment, when the book appeared, no one cared: "It fell dead-born from the press, without reaching such distinction as even to excite a murmur from the zealots."[2]

In 1745 Hume tried to get a position teaching ethics at Edinburgh University but was turned down. Instead he took the job of tutor to a young

---

[1] David Hume, *The Essays Moral, Political and Literary* (Oxford: Oxford University Press, 1963), 608.
[2] Ibid.

marquise who, unfortunately, turned out to be in-sane. The next several years Hume spent alter-nately working as a secretary for a general and liv-ing at home. He wrote continuously during this period, producing, among other things, a much shorter and simplified version of his *Treatise* titled *An Enquiry Concerning Human Understanding* and numerous essays on politics, literature, history, and economics. In 1752 Hume secured a position as librarian at Edinburgh University but was fired when the curators objected that his selection of books, such as *The History of Love-Making Among the French*, was obscene.

But by 1763 Hume's writings had made him fa-mous, and that year, when he traveled to France as secretary for the British ambassador, he found him-self at the center of the intellectual life of Parisian high society. There he met and had an intense love affair with the Countess de Boufflers. Three years later, having grown homesick, Hume left the countess and returned to England. After working for three years as undersecretary of state, Hume re-tired in 1769 to Edinburgh, where he lived "very opulent" and, finally, very famous, until his death in 1776.

Like Berkeley before him, Hume based his phi-losophy on the observation that all of our genuine knowledge (or "thoughts") about the world around us derives from the sensations provided by our senses. To explain this, Hume divided the con-tents of our minds into two groups, our sensations (which he called impressions) and our thoughts. All our thoughts, he held, are "copies" of our sen-sations and are derived from them. Even complex thoughts about things that do not exist, such as the thought of a golden mountain, are formed by putting together memories of simple sensations we once experienced: the sensation of gold and the sensation of mountain. Hume concluded that since genuine knowledge depends on prior sensory ex-perience, assertions that were not based on sensory experience could not be genuine knowledge:

Everyone will readily allow that there is a consider-able difference between the perceptions of the mind when a man feels the pain of excessive heat or the pleasure of moderate warmth, and when he after-

David Hume: "Here, therefore, is a proposition which might banish all metaphysical reasonings: When we entertain any suspicion that a philosophical term is employed without any meaning, we inquire, *from what impression is that supposed idea derived?* And if it be impossible to assign any, this will confirm our suspicion."

wards recalls to his memory this sensation or antici-pates it by his imagination. . . .

Here, therefore, we may divide all the perceptions of the mind into two classes or species, which are distinguished by their different degrees of force and vivacity. The less forcible and lively are commonly denominated *Thoughts* or *Ideas.* . . . Let us . . . use a little freedom and call [the other class] *Impres-sions.* . . . By the term *impression,* then, I mean all our more lively perceptions, when we hear, or see, or feel, or love, or hate, or desire, or will. . . .

Nothing, at first view, may seem more unbounded than the thought of man. . . . What never was seen or heard of, may yet be conceived. . . .

But though our thought seems to possess this un-bounded liberty, . . . all this creative power of the mind amounts to no more than the faculty of com-pounding, transposing, augmenting, or diminishing the materials afforded us by the senses and experi-ence. When we think of a golden mountain, we only join two consistent ideas, *gold* and *mountain,* with which we were formerly acquainted. . . . In short, all the materials of thinking are derived either from our outward or our inward sentiments. . . . Or, to express myself in philosophical language, all our ideas or more feeble perceptions are copies of our impressions or more lively ones.

To prove this, the two following arguments will, I hope, be sufficient. First: When we analyze our thoughts or ideas, however compounded or sublime, we always find that they resolve themselves into such simple ideas as were copied from a precedent feeling or sentiment. Even . . . the idea of GOD as meaning an infinitely intelligent, wise, and good Being, arises from reflecting on the operations of our own mind, and augmenting, without limit, those qualities. . . .

Second: If it happens, from a defect of the organ, that a man is not susceptible of [some] sensation, we always find that he is as little susceptible of the correspondent ideas. A blind man can form no notion of colors, [nor] a deaf man of sounds.

Here, therefore, is a proposition which . . . might . . . banish all that jargon which had so long taken possession of metaphysical reasonings. . . . When we entertain any suspicion that a philosophical term is employed without any meaning or idea (as is but too frequent), we need but inquire, *from what impression is that supposed idea derived?* And if it be impossible to assign any, this will serve to confirm our suspicion.[3]

Hume's "proposition"—that meaningful concepts must be "derived" from "impressions"—was a crucial step in his attempt to undermine our claims to knowledge. If a concept is not based on the sensations or "impressions" of our sense experience, he held, then it must be meaningless. Hume applied this idea ruthlessly. He argued that claims about the existence of an external world are meaningless. All we are acquainted with are the sensations we have. We have no grounds, then, for saying that an external world also exists that somehow causes us to have those sensations:

By what argument can it be proved, that the perceptions of the mind must be caused by external objects, . . . and could not arise either from the energy of the mind itself, . . . or from some other cause still more unknown to us?

It is a question of fact, whether the perceptions of the senses be produced by external objects resembling them: how shall this question be determined? By experience surely, as all other questions of a like nature. But here experience is, and must be entirely silent. The mind has never anything present to it but the perceptions, and cannot possibly reach any experience of their connection with objects. The supposition of such a connection is, therefore, without any foundation in reasoning.[4]

Not only are we unable to know whether there is an outer world; we are also unable to claim that there is any *inner self.* The very idea of a personal *me,* of the inner person called "I," has no foundation, Hume claims:

There are some philosophers who imagine we are every moment intimately conscious of what we call our SELF; that we feel its existence and its continuance in existence; and are certain, beyond the evidence of a demonstration, both of its perfect identity and simplicity. . . .

Unluckily all these positive assertions are contrary to that very experience which is pleaded for them, nor have we any idea of *self.* . . . For from what impression could this idea be derived? . . . If any impression gives rise to the idea of self, that impression must continue invariably the same, through the whole course of our lives; since self is supposed to exist after that manner. But there is no impression constant and invariable. Pain and pleasure, grief and joy, passions and sensations succeed each other, and never all exist at the same time. It cannot, therefore, be from any of these impressions, or from any other, that the idea of self is derived; and consequently there is no such idea. . . .

For my part, when I enter most intimately into what I call *myself,* I always stumble on some particular perception or other, of heat or cold, light or shade, love or hatred, pain or pleasure. I never can catch *myself* at any time without a perception, and never can observe anything but the perception. . . .

[S]etting aside some metaphysicians . . . , I may venture to affirm of the rest of mankind, that they are nothing but a bundle or collection of different perceptions, which succeed each other with an inconceivable rapidity, and are in a perpetual flux and movement. . . . The mind is a kind of theater, where

---

[3]David Hume, *An Enquiry,* 17–20.

[4]Ibid., 152–153.

several perceptions successively make their appearance, pass, re-pass, glide away, and mingle in an infinite variety of postures and situations.[5]

We cannot know whether there is any outer world beyond our sensations because all we are acquainted with are our sensations. Neither can we know whether there is an inner self because, again, all we experience is a constant flow of sensations, and we never perceive, among these sensations, an object called an inner self. All we can say, Hume claims, is that we are "a bundle or collection of different perceptions." Beyond the existence of these perceptions, we can know nothing.

What, then, is left for us to know? Perhaps a great deal. For we are at least acquainted with the perceptions our senses display before us. And from these perceptions we can reason to others. For example, if I perceive a flame, then I know that there will be heat; if I hear a voice, then I know that a person must be present. This kind of knowledge is based on our knowledge of cause and effect. I have learned that flames *cause* heat, so I reason from the flame to the heat; I have found that voices are the *effects* of people, so I reason from the voice to the person. In fact, all the natural sciences consist of laws based on our knowledge of cause and effect. On the basis of a few experiments, for example, the science of physics asserts that if an object is dropped, gravity will cause it to fall at 32 ft/sec^2. Clearly, then, from the present things we perceive, our knowledge of causes enables us to know what the future will be like. And all the natural sciences—physics, chemistry, biology—are based on this kind of causal knowledge.

But Hume, in a devastating attack on knowledge, argues that none of our knowledge of cause and effect has a rational basis. And if our causal knowledge is not rationally justified, then all the natural sciences are similarly unjustified. Hume begins by pointing out that all our knowledge of causal laws rests on our experience of the world:

All reasoning concerning matter of fact seems to be founded on the relation of *Cause and Effect*. . . .

A man, finding a watch or any other machine in a desert island, would conclude that there had once been men in that island. All our reasonings concerning fact are of the same nature. . . . The hearing of an articulate voice and rational discourse in the dark assures us of the presence of some person. Why? Because these are the effects of the human [being]. . . .

If we would satisfy ourselves, therefore, concerning the nature of that evidence which assures us of matters of fact, we must inquire how we arrive at the knowledge of cause and effect.

I shall venture to affirm, as a general proposition which admits of no exception, that the knowledge of this relation . . . arises entirely from experience, when we find that any particular objects are constantly conjoined with each other.[6]

All causal knowledge, Hume is saying, is based on our experience that in the past, events of one kind have been "constantly conjoined" with events of another kind. In the past, for example, I may have seen that when one billiard ball hits another, the second ball always rolls away. Thus, the event of one billiard ball striking another has been "constantly conjoined" in my past experience with the event of the second ball rolling away. All the causal laws of the natural sciences and all the causal knowledge of our everyday lives, then, are based on our past experience of such "constant conjunctions." But this scientific and everyday reliance on past experience, Hume points out, raises a problem. How do we know that past experience is a reliable guide to the future?

We always presume when we see like sensible qualities, . . . that effects similar to those which we have experienced will follow from them. . . . The bread which I formerly ate nourished me. . . . But does it follow that other bread must also nourish me at another time? The consequence seems nowise necessary. . . . These two propositions are far from being the same: *I have found that such an object has always been attended with such an effect*, and *I foresee, that other objects which are, in appearance similar, will be attended with similar effects*. The connection between these two propositions is not intuitive.[7]

[5] David Hume, *A Treatise of Human Nature*, ed. L. A. Selby-Bigge (Oxford: Clarendon Press, 1896), 251–253.

[6] Hume, *An Enquiry*, 26–27.
[7] Ibid., 33–34.

In this passage, Hume is suggesting that all causal reasoning is based on the *assumption* that the future will be like the past. When I see a flame and reason that it will be hot, it is because *in the past* when I perceived flame I also perceived heat. But, Hume asks, how do we know that the future will be like the past? Clearly, there is no way of *proving* that the future will be like the past:

> That there are no demonstrative arguments in the case seems evident, since it implies no contradiction that the course of nature may change, and that an object, seemingly like those which we have experienced, may be attended with different or contrary effects. May I not clearly and distinctly conceive that a body falling from the clouds, and which in all other respects resembles snow, has yet the taste of salt or feeling of fire? Is there any more intelligible proposition than to affirm that all the trees will flourish in December and January and decay in May and June? Now whatever is intelligible and can be distinctly conceived, implies no contradiction and can never be proved false by any demonstrative argument.[8]

So we cannot *prove* with "demonstrative arguments" that the future will be like the past. Perhaps, then, we know that the future will be like the past because of *past experience*? No, Hume replies, we cannot use past experience to show that the future will be like the past. For if we don't know that the future will be like the past, then we don't know that *past* experience is a reliable guide. To argue that past experience proves we can rely on past experience is to argue in a circle:

> For all inferences from experience suppose, as their foundation, that the future will resemble the past, and that similar powers will be conjoined with similar sensible qualities. If there be any suspicion that the course of nature may change, and that the past may be no rule for the future, all experience becomes useless, and can give rise to no inference or conclusion. It is impossible, therefore, that any arguments from experience can prove this resemblance of the past to the future, since all these arguments are founded on the supposition of that resemblance. Let the course of things be allowed hitherto ever so regular, that alone, without some new argument or

inference proves not that for the future it will continue so. Their secret nature and consequently all their effects and influence, may change, without any change in their sensible qualities. This happens sometimes, and with regard to some objects: why may it not happen always, and with regard to all objects? What logic, what process of argument, secures you against this supposition?[9]

Hume's conclusion is devastating: We have no way of *knowing* that causal claims are justified. All the causal laws of the sciences and our everyday causal reasonings are based on an assumption that we cannot prove or rationally justify: the assumption that the future will be like the past. But if we cannot rationally show that the future will be like the past, then why do we continually move past our experience to conclusions about the future? Because, Hume claims, we are creatures of nonrational habit:

> Suppose [a person] has lived so long in the world as to have observed similar objects or events to be constantly conjoined together. What is the consequence of this experience? He immediately infers the existence of one object from the appearance of the other. . . . There is some . . . principle which determines him to form such a conclusion.
>
> This principle is CUSTOM or HABIT. For wherever the repetition of any particular act or operation produces a propensity to renew the same act or operation, without being impelled by any reasoning or process of the understanding, we always say that this propensity is the effect of *custom.* . . .
>
> Custom, then, is the great guide of human life. It is that principle alone which renders our experience useful to us, and makes us expect, for the future, a similar train of events with those which have appeared in the past.[10]

All claims about causal connections, then, are based on our experience that, in the past, events of a certain kind have been "constantly conjoined" with events of another kind. And habit moves us from this past experience to the conclusion that, in the future, all similar events will be similarly conjoined. That is, from our past experience of the

8 Ibid., 35.

9 Ibid., 37–38.
10 Ibid., 42–44.

"constant conjunction" of events, we conclude by habit that one kind of event "causes" a second kind. But we cannot provide any rational justification for this habit of moving from the past to the future. All the causal laws of the sciences and all the causal "knowledge" of everyday life are based on nonrational "habit."

We cannot know whether an external world exists; we cannot say that the self exists; we cannot rationally justify the causal laws of any of the natural sciences or the causal reasonings of our everyday life. Can skepticism extend further? Yes. Hume went on to attack the foundations of religious belief: the claim that God exists.

Hume felt that the best arguments for God's existence were causal arguments: those that hold that God must exist because the design of the universe requires an all-powerful intelligent Creator. But all causal reasonings depend on past experience, Hume points out, and we have no past experience of other gods creating universes. Although our past experience of human beings and their products leads us to say that things like watches require intelligent human creators, we have no past experience of other universes and gods that could lead us to say that universes require intelligent gods to create them:

> In works of *human* art and contrivance, it is allowable to advance from the effect to the cause, and returning back from the cause, to form new inferences concerning the effect. . . . But what is the foundation of this method of reasoning? Plainly this: that man is a being whom we know by experience. . . . When, therefore, we find that any work has proceeded from the skill and industry of man, as we are otherwise acquainted with the nature of the animal, we can draw a hundred inferences concerning what may be expected from him; and these inferences will all be founded in experience and observation.
>
> The case is not the same with our reasonings from the works of nature. The Deity is known to us only by his productions, and is a single being in the universe, not comprehended under any species or genus, from whose experienced attributes or qualities we can, by analogy, infer any attribute or quality in him. . . .
>
> I much doubt whether it be possible for a cause to be known only by its effect . . . [when it has] no par-

allel and no similarity with any other cause or object that has ever fallen under our observation. It is only when two *species* of objects are found to be constantly conjoined, that we can infer the one from the other; and were an effect presented, which was entirely singular, and could not be comprehended under any known *species*, I do not see that we could form any conjecture or inference at all concerning its cause. If experience and observation and analogy be, indeed, the only guides which we can reasonably follow in inferences of this nature, both the effect and cause must bear a similarity and resemblance to other effects and causes which we know, and which we have found in many instances to be conjoined with each other. I leave to your own reflection to pursue the consequences of this principle.[11]

The consequence of this principle, of course, is that we cannot argue from the existence of an orderly universe to the existence of an intelligent God. Hume's skepticism, then, leaves our edifice of knowledge in shambles. The external world, the self, the causal laws of the natural sciences, our everyday causal reasoning, and our religious claims are all called into question. Can knowledge be saved? Many people think that Hume's arguments definitively destroyed all hope that it might be. But in Germany a very ordinary man, Immanuel Kant, was spurred by Hume's skepticism into constructing what many people look on as the most breathtakingly creative response that could be made to Hume. Whether that response succeeded, you must decide after reading the showcase on Kant in the next chapter.

QUESTIONS

1. How would you explain Hume's distinction between "impressions" and "ideas"? How can Hume say that all ideas are "copies" of impressions? Does Hume himself bring up any ideas that he thinks are *not* copies of impressions?

2. Hume says that philosophical terms must be tested by asking "from what impression is that supposed idea derived?" Do you think this is a good test? Are there any terms or "supposed ideas" that

---

[11] Ibid., 143–144, 148.

you would have to reject if you applied this test to your own ideas? If you applied this "test" to Hume's own philosophical terms, do you think they would all pass his test? Why?

3. How are Hume's ideas about the self similar to the Buddhist view of the self examined in Chapter 2? Do you think Hume's view of the self is a correct analysis of *your* self? Why?

4. How would you summarize Hume's criticism of the assumption that the future will resemble the past? Can you detect any weaknesses in his criticism? Explain in your own words what Hume means when he writes "It is impossible, therefore, that any arguments from experience can prove this resemblance of the past to the future, since all these arguments are founded on the supposition of that resemblance."

5. Hume asserts that all ideas are copies of impressions. Is this a generalization from his own experience? If so, then how do you think Hume would respond to this criticism: "Since Hume has shown that past experience cannot provide real knowledge of the future, he cannot claim to know that all ideas must be, now and in the future, copies of impressions"?

6. Do you see any way of showing that Hume must be mistaken in his claim that the causal laws of the sciences rest on nothing more than "habit"?

5.8 Readings

The first reading below is a short story, "Araby," by James Joyce, the renowned Irish Modernist. Driven by the illusory spell cast over him by an all-consuming romantic infatuation for a friend's sister, the young hero of Joyce's story becomes convinced that the sister has sent him on a mission to get a gift for her at a city market. Eventually, the boy realizes the illusory nature of the beliefs that his infatuation created in his mind. Joyce's story raises the question of the extent to which we ourselves have been or might be utterly deceived about the true nature of our relationships with people for whom we care deeply—lovers, friends, relatives—or deceived about who or what they really are. How can we ever know that we are not deceiving ourselves about the people around us? How can we ever know anything for sure about the world we believe we see around us? In the next article, contemporary philosopher Peter Unger argues that in fact we can never know for sure whether the beliefs we have are true or whether they are deceptions introduced into our mind by some "exotic" means or by our ordinary impulses. Unger begins by considering what he calls the "exotic and bizarre case of a deceiving scientist" who artificially implants false beliefs in our minds, and then he goes on to consider more "ordinary" cases of being deceived by our natural impulses, as is the romantic boy in "Araby." He concludes that we can never really know anything about the external world. Unger suggests that if we are to be rational and undogmatic, we should stop using the words "I know." In the last article, Thomas Nagel, also a contemporary philosopher, raises the possibility that all our knowledge about the world around us might be a giant illusion. He then examines an argument by which people have sometimes tried to prove that such skepticism is meaningless. However, Nagel concludes that this argument against skepticism fails. Yet, he suggests, we have no choice but to act as if our ordinary beliefs about the world around us are true.

JAMES JOYCE

Araby

North Richmond Street, being blind, was a quiet street except at the hour when the Christian Brothers' School set the boys free. An uninhabited house of two storeys stood at the blind end, detached from its neighbours in a square ground. The other houses of the street, conscious of decent lives within them, gazed at one another with brown imperturbable faces.

The former tenant of our house, a priest, had died in the back drawing-room. Air, musty from having been long enclosed, hung in all the rooms, and the waste room behind the kitchen was littered with old useless papers. Among these I found a few paper-covered books, the pages of which were curled and damp: *The Abbot*, by Walter Scott, *The Devout Communicant*, and *The Memoirs of Vidocq*. I liked the last best because its leaves were yellow. The wild garden behind the house contained a central apple-tree and a few straggling bushes under one of which I found the late tenant's rusty bicycle-pump. He had been a very charitable priest; in his will he had left all his money to institutions and the furniture of his house to his sister.

When the short days of winter came dusk fell before we had well eaten our dinners. When we met in the street the houses had grown sombre. The space of sky above us was the colour of ever-changing violet and towards it the lamps of the street lifted their feeble lanterns. The cold air stung us and we played till our bodies glowed. Our shouts echoed in the silent street. The career of our play brought us through the dark muddy lanes behind the houses where we ran the gauntlet of the rough tribes from the cottages, to the back doors of the dark dripping gardens where odours arose from the ashpits, to the dark odorous stables where a coach-man smoothed and combed the horse or shook music from the buckled harness. When we returned to the street light from the kitchen windows had filled the areas. If my uncle was seen turning the corner we hid in the shadow until we had seen him safely housed. Or if Mangan's sister came out on the doorstep to call her brother into his tea we watched her from our shadow peer up and down the street. We waited to see whether she would remain or go in and, if she remained, we left our shadow and walked up to Mangan's steps resignedly. She was waiting for us, her figure defined by the light from the half-opened door. Her brother always teased her before he obeyed and I stood by the railings looking at her. Her dress swung as she moved her body and the soft rope of her hair tossed from side to side.

Every morning I lay on the floor in the front parlour watching her door. The blind was pulled down to within an inch of the sash so that I could not be seen. When she came out on the doorstep my heart leaped. I ran to the hall, seized my books, and followed her. I kept her brown figure always in my eye and, when we came near the point at which our ways diverged, I quickened my pace and passed her. This happened morning after morning. I had never spoken to her, except for a few casual words, and yet her name was like a summons to all my foolish blood.

Her image accompanied me even in places the most hostile to romance. On Saturday evenings when my aunt went marketing I had to go to carry some of the parcels. We walked through the flaring streets, jostled by drunken men and bargaining women, amid the curses of labourers, the shrill litanies of shop-boys who stood on guard by the barrel of pigs' cheeks, the nasal chanting of street-singers, who sang a *come-all-you* about O'Donovan Rossa, or a ballad about the troubles in our native land. These noises converged in a single sensation of life for me: I imagined that I bore my chalice safely through a throng of foes. Her name sprang to my lips at moments in strange prayers and praises which I myself did not understand. My eyes were often full of tears (I could not tell why) and at times a flood from my heart seemed to pour itself out into my bosom. I thought little of the future. I did not know whether I would ever speak to her or not or, if I spoke to her, how I could tell her of my confused adoration. But my body was like a harp and her words and gestures were like fingers running upon the wires.

One evening I went into the back drawing-room in which the priest had died. It was a dark rainy evening and there was no sound in the house. Through one of the broken panes I heard the rain impinge upon the earth, the fine incessant needles of water playing in the sodden beds. Some distant lamp or lighted window gleamed below me. I was thankful that I could see so little. All my senses seemed to desire to veil themselves and, feeling that I was about to slip from them, I pressed the palms of my hands together until they trembled, murmuring: *"O love! O love!"* many times.

At last she spoke to me. When she addressed the first words to me I was so confused that I did not know what to answer. She asked me was I going to *Araby*. I forgot whether I answered yes or no. It would be a splended bazaar, she said she would love to go.

"And why can't you?" I asked.

While she spoke she turned a silver bracelet round and round her wrist. She could not go, she said, because there would be a retreat that week in her convent. Her brother and two other boys were fighting for their caps and I was alone at the railings. She held one of the spikes, bowing her head towards me. The light from the lamp opposite our door caught the white curve of her neck, lit up her hair and rested there and, falling, lit up the hand upon the railing. It fell over one side of her dress and caught the white border of a petticoat, just visible as she stood at ease.

"It's well for you," she said.

"If I go," I said, "I will bring you something."

What innumerable follies laid waste my waking and sleeping thoughts after that evening! I wished to annihilate the tedious intervening days. I chafed against the work of school. At night in my bedroom and by day in the classroom her image came between me and the page I strove to read. The syllables of the word *Araby* were called to me through the silence in which my soul luxuriated and cast an Eastern enchantment over me. I asked for leave to go to the bazaar on Saturday night. My aunt was surprised and hoped it was not some Freemason affair. I answered few questions in class. I watch my master's face pass from amiability to sternness; he hoped I was not beginning to idle. I could not call my wandering thoughts together. I had hardly any patience with the serious work of life which, now that it stood between me and my desire, seemed to me child's play, ugly monotonous child's play.

On Saturday morning I reminded my uncle that I wished to go to the bazaar in the evening. He was fussing at the hallstand, looking for the hatbrush, and answered me curtly:

"Yes, boy, I know."

As he was in the hall I could not go into the front parlour and lie at the window. I left the house in bad humour and walked slowly towards the school. The air was pitilessly raw and already my heart misgave me.

When I came home to dinner my uncle had not yet been home. Still it was early. I sat staring at the clock for some time and, when its ticking began to irritate me, I left the room. I mounted the staircase and gained the upper part of the house. The high cold empty gloomy rooms liberated me and I went from room to room singing. From the front window I saw my companions playing below in the street. Their cries reached me weakened and indistinct and, leaning my forehead against the cool glass, I looked over at the dark house where she lived. I may have stood there for an hour, seeing nothing but the brown-clad figure cast by my imagination, touched discreetly by the lamplight at the curved neck, at the hand upon the railings and at the border below her dress.

When I came downstairs again I found Mrs. Mercer sitting at the fire. She was an old garrulous woman, a pawnbroker's widow, who collected used stamps for some pious purpose. I had to endure the gossip of the teatable. The meal was prolonged beyond an hour and still my uncle did not come. Mrs. Mercer stood up to go: she was sorry she couldn't wait any longer, but it was after eight o'clock and she did not like to be out late, as the night air was bad for her. When she had gone I began to walk up and down the room, clenching my fists. My aunt said:

"I'm afraid you may put off your bazaar for this night of Our Lord."

At nine o'clock I heard my uncle's latchkey in the halldoor. I heard him talking to himself and heard the hallstand rocking when it had received the weight of his overcoat. I could interpret these signs. When he was midway through his dinner I asked him to give me the money to go to the bazaar. He had forgotten.

"The people are in bed and after their first sleep now," he said.

I did not smile. My aunt said to him energetically:

"Can't you give him the money and let him go? You've kept him late enough as it is."

My uncle said he was very sorry he had forgotten. He said he believed in the old saying: "All work and no play makes Jack a dull boy." He asked me where I was going and, when I had told him a second time he asked me did I know *The Arab's Farewell to his Steed*. When I left the kitchen he was about to recite the opening lines of the piece to my aunt.

I held a florin[1] tightly in my hand as I strode down Buckingham Street towards the station. The sight of the streets thronged with buyers and glaring with gas recalled to me the purpose of my journey. I took my seat in a third-class carriage of a deserted train. After an intolerable delay the train moved out of the station slowly: It crept onward among ruinous houses and over the twinkling river. At Westland Row Station a crowd of people pressed to the carriage doors; but the porters moved them back, saying that it was a special train for the bazaar. I remained alone in the bare carriage. In a few minutes the train drew up beside an improvised wooden platform. I passed out on to the road and saw by the lighted dial of a clock that it was ten minutes to ten. In front of me was a large building which displayed the magical name.

I could not find any sixpenny entrance and, fearing that the bazaar would be closed, I passed in quickly through a turnstile, handing a shilling to a weary-looking man. I found myself in a big hall girdled at half its height by a gallery. Nearly all the stalls were closed and the greater part of the hall was in darkness. I recognised a silence like that which pervades a church after a service. I walked into the centre of the bazaar timidly. A few people were gathered about the stalls which were still open. Before a curtain, over which the words *Café Chantant* were written in coloured lamps, two men were counting money on a salver. I listened to the fall of the coins.

Remembering with difficulty why I had come I went over to one of the stalls and examined porcelain vases and flowered tea-sets. At the door of the stall a young lady was talking and laughing with two young gentlemen. I remarked their English accents and listened vaguely to their conversation.

"O, I never said such a thing!"

"O, but you did!"

"O, but I didn't!"

"Didn't she say that?"

"Yes. I heard her."

"O, there's a . . . fib!"

Observing me the young lady came over and asked me did I wish to buy anything. The tone of her voice was not encouraging; she seemed to have spoken to me out of sense of duty. I looked humbly at the great jars that stood like eastern guards at either side of the dark entrance to the stall and murmured:

"No, thank you."

The young lady changed the position of one of the vases and went back to the two young men. They began to talk on the same subject. Once or twice the young lady glanced at me over her shoulder.

I lingered before her stall, though I knew my stay was useless, to make my interest in her wares seem the more real. Then I turned away slowly and walked down the middle of the bazaar. I allowed the two pennies to fall against the sixpence in my pocket. I heard a voice call from one end of the gallery that the light was out. The upper part of the hall was now completely dark.

Gazing up into the darkness I saw myself as a creature driven and derided by vanity; and my eyes burned with anguish and anger.

PETER UNGER

A Defense of Skepticism

A CLASSICAL FORM OF SKEPTICAL ARGUMENT

There are certain arguments for skepticism which conform to a familiar . . . pattern or form. These arguments rely, at least for their psychological power, on vivid descriptions of exotic *contrast cases*. The following is one such rough argument, this one in support of skepticism regarding any alleged *knowledge of an external world*. The exotic

---

[1] A silver coin worth two shillings.

Reprinted from *Ignorance* by Peter Unger. Copyright © Oxford University Press, 1975.

contrast case here concerns an evil scientist, and is described to be in line with the most up to date developments of science, or science fiction. We begin by arbitrarily choosing something concerning an external world which might conceivably, we suppose, be *known*, in one way or another, e.g., that there are rocks or, as we will understand it, that there is at least one rock.

Now, first, *if* someone, anyone *knows* that there are rocks, then the person *can know* the following quite exotic thing: There is *no* evil scientist deceiving him into *falsely* believing that there are rocks. This scientist uses electrodes to induce experiences and thus carries out his deceptions, concerning the existence of rocks or anything else. He first drills holes painlessly in the variously colored skulls, or shells, of his subjects and then implants his electrodes into the appropriate parts of their brains, or protoplasm, or systems. He sends patterns of electrical impulses into them through the electrodes, which are themselves connected by wires to a laboratory console on which he plays, punching various keys and buttons in accordance with his ideas of how the whole thing works and with his deceptive designs. The scientist's delight is intense, and it is caused not so much by his exercising his scientific and intellectual gifts as by the thought that he is deceiving various subjects about all sorts of things. Part of that delight is caused, on this supposition, by his thought that he is deceiving a certain person, perhaps yourself, into falsely believing that there are rocks. He is, then, an evil scientist, and he lives in a world which is entirely bereft of rocks.

Now, as we have agreed, [1] *if you know* that there are rocks, then you *can know* that there is no such scientist doing this to you [i.e., deceiving you to falsely believe that there are rocks]. But [2] no one *can* ever *know* that this exotic situation does *not obtain;* no one *can* ever *know* that there is *no* evil scientist who is, by means of electrodes, deceiving him into falsely believing there to be rocks. That is our second premise, and it is also very difficult to deny. So, thirdly, as a consequence of these two premises, we have our skeptical conclusion: [3] You never *know* that there are rocks. But of course we have chosen our person, and the matter of there being rocks, quite arbitrarily, and this argument, it surely seems, may be generalized to cover any external matter at all. From this, we may conclude, finally, that [4] nobody ever *knows* anything about the external world.

[A philosopher's] attempt to reverse our argument will proceed like this: [1.] According to your argument, nobody ever *knows* that there are rocks. [2.] But I *do* know that there are rocks. This is something concerning the external world, and I do know it. Hence, [3.] somebody *does know* something about the external world. . . . And so, while I might not have known *before* that there is no such scientist, at least [4.] I *now* do know that there is no evil scientist who is deceiving me into falsely believing that there are rocks. So far has the skeptical argument failed to challenge my knowledge successfully that it seems actually to have occasioned an increase in what I know about things.

While the robust character of this reply has a definite appeal, it also seems quite daring. Indeed, the more one thinks on it, the more it seems to be somewhat foolhardy and even dogmatic. One cannot help but think that for all this philosopher really can *know*, he might have all his experience artificially induced by electrodes, these being operated by a terribly evil scientist who, having an idea of what his "protege" is saying to himself, chuckles accordingly. . . .

[Suppose you were this philosopher.] Now, we may suppose that electrodes are removed, that your experiences are now brought about through your perception of actual surroundings, and you are, so to speak, forced to encounter your deceptive tormentor. Wouldn't you be made to feel quite *foolish,* even *embarrassed,* by your claims to *know*? Indeed, you would seem to be exposed quite clearly as having been, not only wrong, but rather irrational and even dogmatic. . . .

It seems much better, perhaps perfectly all right, if you are instead only *confident* that there is no such scientist. It seems perfectly all right for you to *believe* there to be no evil scientist doing this. If you say, not only that you believe it, but that you have some *reason* to believe this thing, what you say *may* seem somewhat suspect, at least on reasoned reflection, but it doesn't have any obvious tint of dogmatism or irrationality to it. . . .

ORDINARY CASES

Largely because it is so exotic and bizarre, the case of a deceiving scientist lets one feel acutely the apparent irrationality in thinking oneself to *know*. But the exotic cases have no monopoly on generating feelings of irrationality.

[For example,] you may think you *know* that a certain city is the capital of a certain state, and you may feel quite content in this thought while watching another looking the matter up in the library. You will feel quite foolish, however, if the person announces the result to be *another* city, and if subsequent experience seems to show that announcement to be right. This will occur, I suggest, even if you are just an anonymous, disinterested bystander who happens to hear the question posed and the answer later announced. This is true even if the reference was a newspaper, *The Times*, and the capital was changed only yesterday. But these feelings will be very much less apparent, or will not occur at all, if you only feel very confident, at the outset, that the city is thus-and-such, which later is not announced. You might of course feel that you shouldn't be quite so confident of such things, or that you should watch out in the future. But you probably *wouldn't* feel, I suggest, that you were *irrational* to be confident of that thing at that time. Much less would you feel that you were *dogmatic* in so being. . . .

It is hard for us to think that there is any important similarity between such common cases as these and the case of someone thinking himself to *know* that *there are rocks*. Exotic contrast cases, like the case of the evil scientist, help one to appreciate that these cases are really essentially the same. By means of contrast cases, we encourage thinking of all sorts of new sequences of experience, sequences which people would never begin to imagine in the normal course of affairs. How would you react to such developments as *these*, no matter *how* exotic or unlikely? It appears that the proper reaction is to feel as irrational about claiming knowledge of rocks as you felt before, where, e.g., one was apparently caught in thought by the library reference to the state's capital. Who would have thought so, before thinking of contrast cases? Those cases help

you see, I suggest, that in *either* case, no matter whether you are in fact right in the matter or whether wrong, thinking that you *know* manifests an attitude of dogmatism. Bizarre experiential sequences help show that there is no essential difference between any two external matters; the apparently most certain ones, like that of rocks, and the ones where thinking about *knowing* appears, even without the most exotic skeptical aids, *not* the way to think.

THOMAS NAGEL

How Do We Know Anything?

Ordinarily you have no doubts about the existence of the floor under your feet, or the tree outside the window, or your own teeth. In fact most of the time you don't even think about the mental states that make you aware of those things: you seem to be aware of them directly. But how do you know they really exist? Would things seem any different to you if in fact all these things existed *only* in your mind—if everything you took to be the real world outside was just a giant dream or hallucination, from which you will never wake up? . . .

How can you know that isn't what's going on? If all your experience were a dream with *nothing* outside, then any evidence you tried to use to prove to yourself that there was an outside world would just be part of the dream. If you knocked on the table or pinched yourself, you would hear the knock and feel the pinch, but that would be just one more thing going on inside your mind like everything else. It's no use: If you want to find out whether what's inside your mind is any guide to

From *What Does It All Mean? A Very Short Introduction to Philosophy* by Thomas Nagel. © 1987 by Thomas Nagel. Reprinted by permission of Oxford University Press, Inc.

what's outside your mind, you can't depend on how things *seem*—from inside your mind—to give you the answer.

But what else is there to depend on? All your evidence about anything has to come through your mind—whether in the form of perception, the testimony of books and other people, or memory—and it is entirely consistent with everything you're aware of that *nothing at all* exists except the inside of your mind. . . .

Some would argue that radical skepticism of the kind I have been talking about is meaningless, because the idea of an external reality that *no one* could ever discover is meaningless. The argument is that a dream, for instance, has to be something from which you *can* wake up to discover that you have been asleep; a hallucination has to be something which others (or you later) *can* see is not really there. Impressions and appearances that do not correspond to reality must be contrasted with others that *do* correspond to reality, or else the contrast between appearance and reality is meaningless.

According to this view, the idea of a dream from which you can never wake up is not the idea of a dream at all: it is the idea of *reality*—the real world in which you live. Our idea of the things that exist is just our idea of what we can observe. (This view is sometimes called verificationism.) Sometimes our observations are mistaken, but that means they can be corrected by other observations—as when you wake up from a dream or discover that what you thought was a snake was just a shadow on the grass. But without some possibility of a correct view of how things are (either yours or someone else's), the thought that your impressions of the world are not true is meaningless.

If this is right, then the skeptic is kidding himself if he thinks he can imagine that the only thing that exists is his own mind. He is kidding himself, because it couldn't be true that the physical world doesn't really exist, unless somebody could *observe* that it doesn't exist. And what the skeptic is trying to imagine is precisely that there *is* no one to observe that or anything else—except of course the skeptic himself, and all he can observe is the inside of his own mind. So solipsism is meaningless. It

tries to subtract the external world from the totality of my impressions; but it fails, because if the external world is subtracted, they stop being mere impressions, and become instead perceptions of reality.

Is this argument against solipsism and skepticism any good? Not unless reality can be defined as what we can observe. But are we really unable to understand the idea of a real world, or a fact about reality, that can't be observed by anyone, human or otherwise?

The skeptic will claim that if there is an external world, the things in it are observable because they exist, and not the other way around: that existence isn't the same thing as observability. And although we get the idea of dreams and hallucinations from cases where we think we *can* observe the contrast between our experiences and reality, it certainly seems as if the same idea can be extended to cases where the reality is not observable.

If that is right, it seems to follow that it is not meaningless to think that the world might consist of nothing but the inside of your mind, though neither you nor anyone else could find out that this was true. And if this is not meaningless, but is a possibility you must consider, there seems no way to prove that it is false, without arguing in a circle. So there may be no way out of the cage of your own mind. This is sometimes called the egocentric predicament.

And yet, after all this has been said, I have to admit it is practically impossible to believe seriously that all the things in the world around you might not really exist. Our acceptance of the external world is instinctive and powerful: we cannot just get rid of it by philosophical arguments. Not only do we go on acting *as if* other people and things exist: we *believe* that they do, even after we've gone through the arguments which appear to show we have no grounds for this belief. (We may have grounds, within the overall system of our beliefs about the world, for more particular beliefs about the existence of particular things: like a mouse in the breadbox, for example. But that is different. It assumes the existence of the external world.)

If a belief in the world outside our minds comes so naturally to us, perhaps we don't need grounds for it. We can just let it be and hope that we're right. And that in fact is what most people do after giving up the attempt to prove it: even if they can't give reasons against skepticism, they can't live with it either. But this means that we hold on to most of our ordinary beliefs about the world in face of the fact that (a) they might be completely false, and (b) we have no basis for ruling out that possibility.

We are left then with three questions:

1. Is it a meaningful possibility that the inside of your mind is the only thing that exists — or that even if there is a world outside your mind, it is totally unlike what you believe it to be?

2. If these things are possible, do you have any way of proving to yourself that they are not actually true?

3. If you can't prove that anything exists outside your own mind, is it all right to go on believing in the external world anyway?

5.9 Suggestions for Further Reading

Audi, Robert. *Belief, Justification, and Knowledge*. Belmont, CA: Wadsworth, 1988. A concise but advanced discussion of contemporary views on knowledge.

Ayer, A. J. *Hume*. New York: Hill & Wang, 1980. This paperback contains an accessible treatment of Hume by a philosopher sympathetic to his thought.

Belenky, Mary Field, et al. *Women's Ways of Knowing: The Development of Self, Voice, and Mind*. New York: Basic Books, 1986. An interesting account of the distinctive ways that women think, perceive, and discover.

Bleier, R. *Science and Gender: A Critique of Biology and Its Theories on Women*. New York: Pergamon Press, 1984. An interesting defense of the view that scientific method, at least as currently practiced in biology, is biased against women.

Delbruck, Max. *Mind from Matter? An Essay on Evolutionary Epistemology*. Palo Alto, CA: Blackwell Scientific Publications, 1986. This brilliant and all-encompassing book tries to bring together the knowledge of the sciences and the epistemological problems of philosophy.

Doney, Willis, ed. *Descartes*. New York: Doubleday Anchor, 1967. A nice group of articles on various problems in Descartes's theory of knowledge.

Dunn, John. *Locke*. Oxford: Oxford University Press, 1984. This short and easily readable book provides a good introduction to the life and thought of John Locke.

Garry, Ann, and Marilyn Pearsall. *Women, Knowledge, and Reality: Explorations in Feminist Philosophy*. Boston: Unwin Hyman, 1989. A very good collection of some of the best feminist writings on epistemology and metaphysics.

Harding, Sandra, and Merrill Hintikka, eds. *Discovering Reality: Feminist Perspectives on Epistemology, Metaphysics, Methodology, and Philosophy of Science*. Dordrecht, Holland: D. Reidel, 1983. A good collection of articles on metaphysics and epistemology from feminist perspectives.

Kempe, John. *The Philosophy of Kant*. New York: Oxford University Press, 1968. A challenging but accessible summary of Kant's central ideas.

Moser, Paul, and Arnold Vander Nat, eds. *Human Knowledge*. New York: Oxford University Press, 1987. A very complete anthology of significant writings on epistemology.

Polanyi, Michael. *Personal Knowledge: Towards a Post-Critical Philosophy*. New York: Harper & Row, 1958. Scientist-turned-philosopher Polanyi rejects scientific detachment as an ideal of knowledge. A vital component of knowledge is the passionate contribution of the person knowing what is being known. A most important alternative ideal of knowledge.

Pollock, John. *Knowledge and Justification*. Totowa, NJ: Rowman & Littlefield, 1986. A somewhat difficult but worthwhile discussion of contemporary issues in epistemology.

Urmson, J. C. *Berkeley*. Oxford: Oxford University Press, 1982. This short work presents a readable introduction to Berkeley's life and thought.

CHAPTER 6

Truth

No one is so wrong as the man who knows all the answers.

THOMAS MERTON

6.1 Introduction: Belief, Knowledge, and Truth

What you think you know about yourself depends on what you think knowledge is. For example, do you think that you can learn more about yourself from science or from religion? Your answer to this question depends on how you think we get true knowledge—through the methods of science or through the methods of religion? Or think about your experiences of self-knowledge and self-deception. Often we think of ourselves as capable, kind, and good people. Then later events reveal to us that we are actually incompetent, mean, and selfish. Our desire to feel good about ourselves led us to accept as truth what we later realized were mere self-deceptions. Perhaps this leads you to skepticism and to doubt whether you can ever know the truth about who or what you really are. Perhaps you are right. In many ways, then, both small and large, your views of who and what you are depend on your views of what knowledge is. In this chapter we examine an important aspect of knowledge: its relation to truth. To see how closely truth and knowledge are related, let us begin by getting a clearer idea about what knowledge itself is.

What do we mean when we say we know something? For instance, "I know that my car is in the parking lot." Just what do you mean when you say that? Stating the question more formally, if we let p represent any proposition, what requirements must we meet to claim that we know p?

For one thing, we believe that p is the case. If you know that your car is in the parking lot, then you believe it. You don't just have a hope, a desire, or a suspicion that the car is there. You have a positive belief. Think about that. Imagine what your friends would think if you said, "I know that my car is in the parking lot, but I don't believe it." They'd think it very peculiar, and rightly so. After all, if you're claiming to know something, how can you not believe it? Of course, we sometimes seem to dissociate belief from knowledge, as in "I know the president has been assassinated, but I don't believe it." However, this is a rhetorical utterance. We *do* believe it; otherwise, we wouldn't be shocked. Intellectually we believe it, but emotionally we're incredulous. To assert that you know p, then, is to have a certain attitude toward p—that is, to believe that it is so. Thus, "I know p" implies "I believe p."

What everybody echoes as true today, may turn out to be falsehood tomorrow, mere smoke of opinion.

HENRY DAVID THOREAU

Of course, "I believe p" does not imply "I know p." We can and do believe all sorts of things: that there's life in outer space, that we are in excellent health, that God exists, that Denver is the capital of the United States. Still that doesn't mean we know all these things. In a word, knowledge implies belief, but belief does not imply knowledge.

Knowledge also implies having evidence or justification. When you say "I know that my car is in the parking lot," you imply not only that you believe it but that you have evidence for it. So "I know p" implies "I have evidence or justification for p." Suppose someone claimed to know that the stock market will plunge next week. You'd likely ask, "How do you know that?" If the person responded "Because I believe it," you'd not take the claim seriously. Belief merely indicates an attitude toward something; it does not justify it. Only evidence does that. Another word for evidence or justification is *warrantability*. If someone claims to know that the stock market will plunge next week, he is implying a warranted belief. He has evidence or justification for what he believes.

Can we then correctly speak of knowledge as warranted belief? No. Suppose the stock market does not plunge next week. Clearly the person didn't know. Yet this doesn't mean that the belief was unwarranted. It simply suggests that knowledge implies more than warranted belief. It also implies truth. For you to know that your car is in the parking lot, your car must truly be there. You may believe it, and your belief may be warranted. Still to know it, you need more: the truth. In brief, you cannot say that you know p unless p is true.

We have now reached a useful and traditional characterization of knowledge. Knowledge is warranted, true belief. To understand knowledge fully, then, we must understand warrantability and truth, two of the topics of this chapter. Before we examine these topics, however, let us ask how adequate this traditional characterization of knowledge is. Would it be correct to say that knowledge is nothing more than warranted, true belief? Is having a warranted, true belief sufficient for having knowledge, or does knowledge involve something more?

Unfortunately, it turns out that the notion of warranted, true belief does not fully capture our notion of knowledge. Knowledge is more than warranted, true belief. But figuring out what more it involves is very difficult. To understand this difficulty, let us look at an example of a person who has a warranted, true belief but does not have knowledge. This kind of example, incidentally, is called a Gettier example, after the philosopher Edmund Gettier, who first drew people's attention to these examples and to the difficulties that they raise.

Suppose that John is a very careful person who before today has never made a mistake. Today he plans to buy some low-fat milk at the store. By mistake, however, he tells his friend Sam that he is going to buy whole milk. Later, when John goes to the store (still planning to buy low-fat milk), he accidentally picks up a container of whole milk. Not realizing his mistake, he pays for the milk and leaves the store with it. Now suppose that someone asks Sam whether he knows what kind of milk John bought at the store. Sam, of course, replies that he knows that John bought whole milk. Notice that Sam is indeed warranted in thinking that John bought whole milk, because he knows that John tells the truth and has never made a mistake. Sam also believes that John bought whole milk. And,

Truth is the object of philosophy, but not always of philosophers.

CHURTON COLLINS

CRITICAL THINKING

Gettier examples assume that people are warranted in believing things when they rely on their past experience. Is this assumption correct?

by accident, it is true that John bought whole milk. Nevertheless, we would all agree that Sam does not really know that John bought whole milk. Because Sam's belief turned out to be true entirely by accident, we are reluctant to say that his belief is genuine knowledge, even though it is a warranted, true belief.

This example shows that knowledge is more than warranted, true belief. But what more is needed to have genuine knowledge? Unfortunately, we cannot say. Many philosophers have spent a lot of time and effort trying to uncover what this "more" is. Yet no one has come up with a solution that has persuaded everyone. Nevertheless, we do know that knowledge requires at least a warranted, true belief, so these notions merit discussion.[1]

Warrantability and truth are important epistemological issues. They also affect our lives deeply, because they relate to our beliefs about ourselves and others. Which of my beliefs about myself or my friends are warranted? How can I decide what I'm justified in believing about myself and what I'm not? What can I accept as true about others? How can I learn the truth about myself? When you realize that your self-image and social interactions are tremendously affected by what you think you know, the issues of warrantability and truth become more than philosophical abstractions. In science, religion, morality, the arts, and politics, what you think you know influences how you relate and respond to the world, how you live your life, and how you respond to the people around you.

Just how sound are our beliefs? To answer this question, we must consider warrantability and truth. If our beliefs are not sound, then we should abandon them and seek alternatives. If they are sound, then we can feel secure and confident in pursuing them. Thus, the issue of knowledge as warranted, true belief is crucial both philosophically and practically.

When is a belief warranted? When do I have justification for a belief? Any answer depends on the kind of statement I'm uttering. Let's look at a variety of propositions (true or false statements) to illustrate the point:

1. X is not non-X.
2. X is either Y or non-Y.
3. All humans are vertebrates.
4. No circle is square.
5. The sum of the interior angles in a triangle is equal to two right angles.
6. The sum of the squares of the sides of a right triangle is equal to the square of the hypotenuse.
7. This is a robin.
8. Sacramento is the capital of California.
9. I am in pain.
10. It seems to me to be green.

Each of these propositions is warranted in suitable circumstances. We'd be on solid ground if we believed them. Why?

> *The greatest friend of truth is Time, her greatest enemy is Prejudice, and her constant companion is Humility.*
>
> C. C. COLTON

> *Truth is a fruit which should not be plucked until it is quite ripe.*
>
> PASCAL

---

[1] Gettier's essay and several attempts to deal with this issue can be found in *Knowledge and Belief*, ed. A. P. Griffiths (London: Oxford University Press, 1967), 144–146.

Propositions 1 and 2 are warranted in any circumstances because denying them paralyzes all thought. If they are not warranted, then we can forget ever thinking intelligently. Put another way, their denial is self-contradictory.

But what about 3 and 4? Their warrantability lies in the meaning of the terms themselves. Proposition 3 is true because the meaning of *humans* includes the meaning of *vertebrates*, and proposition 3 asserts this inclusion. Similarly, in 4, the meaning of *circle* excludes the meaning of *square*, and the proposition asserts this exclusion.

In contrast to the previous propositions, the warrantability of proposition 5 lies in its being a theorem that we can deduce from the postulates and definitions of Euclidean geometry. The same reasoning holds for 6 in its geometrical sense. In its algebraic sense, its warrantability follows from a comparable set of assumptions. The warrantability of 5 and 6, then, is furnished by the systems of which they are parts.

The remaining propositions suggest still other conditions of warrantability. Propositions 7 and 8 are hypotheses. Like all hypotheses, they must be confirmed. In other words, when you say "This is a robin," your statement entails many other statements. Some pertain to birds and animals generally, others to flight, color, and plumage. If the original statement is consistent with all the entailed statements and they themselves are warrantable propositions, then your original statement is true. "This is a robin" is confirmed. The same applies to "Sacramento is the capital of California."

On the other hand, 9 and 10 are basic statements, which don't require that kind of confirmation. Basic statements pertain to sense data; consequently, they can be false only if the speaker is lying. Their warrantability is found in the immediately experienced qualities of first-person experience.[2]

When I say that I am warranted in believing the preceding propositions, I mean that I have sufficient reason for believing them. Of course, sufficiency raises a problem. Just how much support, evidence, or justification do I need for a warranted belief? Useful here is an awareness of the modes of warranty.

Propositions 1 and 2, for example, have logical warrantability—that is, they appeal to laws of thought or logic that we consider necessarily true. Thus, proposition 1 accords with the law of identity: A is A. Everything we say presupposes that A is A. If you speak of a tree, you presuppose that the tree is a tree. If the tree were not a tree, what could you even be speaking of? Proposition 2 accords with the law of excluded middle: Everything is either A or non-A. Thus, something is either a tree or not a tree, a piece of chalk or not a piece of chalk, a desk or not a desk. Logically, there can be no middle ground. Propositions 3 and 4 represent semantic warrantability. Their warrantability can be determined merely by analyzing the meaning of the terms they use.

Propositions 5 and 6 have systemic warrantability. This means that they derive their warranty from the logical interdependence of all propositions in a deductive system.

> *All men by nature desire to know.*
> ARISTOTLE

---

[2] For a discussion of warrantability, see W. H. Werkmeister, *The Basis and Structure of Knowledge* (New York: Greenwood, 1968), especially 125–161.

Propositions 7 through 10 are cases of empirical warrantability. Their warranty stems from a confirmatory relation to specific qualities of first-person experience. Sometimes, as with 7 and 8, we must seek confirmation outside the self in the real world. Other times, as in 9 and 10, personal experience, if honestly reported, is enough.

Besides warranted, true beliefs, people can hold warranted, false beliefs and unwarranted, true beliefs. Neither case represents knowledge. These beliefs particularly arise in matters of fact, in empirical statements about the world such as propositions 7 and 8. For example, it's arguable that people in the past were warranted in believing that the earth was flat and unwarranted in believing that it was spherical. So warrantability and truth do not logically imply each other; that is, they are logically independent. *Warranty* is another word for "justification" or "evidence." It comes in degrees, as does belief, but truth does not.

We come, then, to the next concern of this chapter: truth. What is truth? More to the point, what does it mean for a belief to be true?

QUESTIONS

Which of the following can be warranted beliefs? Why?

1. This dog before me is an English shepherd.
2. I have a heart.
3. All things have qualities.
4. Hubert Humphrey once lived.
5. 3 times 2 is 6.
6. The sun will rise tomorrow.
7. A robin is a bird.
8. There's intelligent life in outer space.
9. If the battery in my car is dead, my car won't start.
10. If I release this pen and it's unsupported, it will fall.

6.2 What Is Truth?

In our everyday lives we usually get along nicely without pondering the question of truth. Since we make and affirm all sorts of statements, we seem to have little trouble dealing with truth. Thus, if someone says "Washington is the nation's capital" or "Snow is white," we say "That's true." But things are not always so clear.

Even though we distinguish between truth and falsity hundreds of times a day, we may have difficulty in expressing that distinction. What is truth?

Suppose that you have a girlfriend. You have been dating her for a long time. Although you love her passionately, you are not sure she still loves you. You are unsure about her love because she doesn't seem as interested in your company as she used to be. Sometimes she seems bored with you and more interested in others. Yet when you ask her, she says, "Yes, I still love you very much." Is she telling you the truth? The very thought that she might not be telling the truth makes you miserable. You ask her outright whether she is telling you the truth. She's offended that you should doubt her. "Of course I'm telling you the truth!" she says. "Of course I still love you!" Perhaps for several days you decide that you will take her words as true. After all, when you suspect her words are false, you feel wretched and awful. Because it makes you feel better, you decide that her words are true. At least this way you feel as you want to feel.

But then a few days later you start to think that this kind of truth is not what you need. The truth you need is more than merely accepting whatever makes you feel good. So you look for a different kind of truth. You think that maybe the truth about her love lies in what you think her actions mean. Her protestations of love just don't seem to fit with what you believe her actions mean. So you tell her that you think it's false that she loves you because to you her actions mean that her love has gone. She replies that you're mistaken. You're putting meanings on her actions that aren't there. Her actions don't mean she is bored with you, she says. It's just that she feels relaxed around you now, and feels she can be herself without needing to put up a happy front with you always. Now you are extremely perplexed. You were ready to think that her words were true only if they fit in with your beliefs about what her actions meant. Yet now you aren't sure whether these beliefs of yours about what her actions mean are themselves true.

Perhaps now you start to think that the truth you really want is the truth about what lies in her heart. What matters to you is not what makes you feel good, or what fits in with your other beliefs, but the truth about what's there inside her heart. So you ask her: "What do you really feel in your heart toward me?" Her answer leaves you even more perplexed. She says: "I'm not sure I know. I think the feelings I have for you are feelings of love. But I don't think I understand myself, or love, well enough to be sure. I think I have a lot of feelings toward you in my heart, but I'm often confused about my feelings and don't quite know what they are or what they mean. That's all I can tell you."

Now you are completely at a loss. You thought you could get at the truth if you could just get outside yourself and find out what was really there inside her heart. Yet what is in her heart is as amorphous as a cloud. You wonder now what truth itself is or even if there is such a thing as truth. Is truth just what makes us have the good feelings we want to have? Is it what fits in with our other beliefs and meanings? Is truth about what is really there outside of us? What do we mean, then, when we say that a statement is true?

The history of philosophy records several ways of looking at truth that are similar to the kinds of truth we have just been discussing. We'll consider three of them. The correspondence theory says that truth is what corresponds with what is in the real world outside us. The coherence theory says that truth is what fits in with our other beliefs and meanings. And the pragmatic theory says,

The contemplation of truth and beauty is the proper object for which we were created, which calls forth the most intense desires of the soul, and of which it never tires.

WILLIAM HAZLITT

What is truth?

PONTIUS PILATE

Truth is the highest thing that man may keep.

CHAUCER

Truth lies at the bottom of a well.

DEMOCRITUS

roughly, that truth is what gets us what we want. Each of these makes a unique contribution to understanding the nature of truth, and therefore of knowledge. As our short discussion suggests, it is important to get clear about what truth means, particularly when we are searching for the truth about ourselves and others.

CORRESPONDENCE THEORY

Undoubtedly the most popular theory of truth is the **correspondence theory,** which says that truth is an agreement between a proposition and a fact. Thus, "Water boils at 212 degrees Fahrenheit at sea level" is a true proposition because it corresponds with a fact: Water does boil at 212 degrees Fahrenheit at sea level. One example of a correspondence theorist is British empiricist John Locke.

Bertrand Russell, a modern philosopher, is also a correspondence theorist. For Russell, what we say is true if it corresponds to reality. Russell maintains that there is a realm of facts that exists independent of us. Although truth and falsehood are properties of beliefs, they depend on the relations of the beliefs to this independent realm of facts. Thus, the truth of the belief that Paris is in France depends on whether that belief corresponds to the independent fact that Paris is indeed in France. In *The Problems of Philosophy*, Russell expresses his position:

> There are three points to observe in the attempts to discover the nature of truth, three requisites which any theorist must fulfill.
>
> (1) Our theory of truth must be such as to admit of its opposite, falsehood. A good many philosophers have failed adequately to satisfy this condition: they have constructed theories according to which all our thinking ought to have been true, and have then had the greatest difficulty in finding a place for falsehood. In this respect our theory of belief must differ from our theory of acquaintance, since in the case of acquaintance it was not necessary to take account of any opposite.
>
> (2) It seems fairly evident that if there were no beliefs there could be no falsehood, and no truth either, in the sense in which truth is correlative to falsehood. If we imagine a world of mere matter, there would be no room for falsehood in such a world, and although it would contain what may be called "facts," it would not contain any truths, in the sense in which truths are things of the same kind as falsehoods. In fact, truth and falsehood are properties of beliefs and statements: hence a world of mere matter, since it would contain no beliefs or statements, would also contain no truth or falsehood.
>
> (3) But, as against what we have just said, it is to be observed that the truth or falsehood of a belief always depends upon something which lies outside the belief itself. If I believe that Charles I died on the scaffold, I believe truly, not because of any intrinsic quality of my belief, which can be discovered by merely examining the belief, but because of an historical event which happened two and a half centuries ago. If I believe that Charles I died in his bed, I believe falsely: no degree of vividness in my belief, or of care in arriving at it, prevents it from being false, again because of what happened long ago, and not because of any intrinsic property of my belief. Hence, although truth and falsehood are properties of beliefs, they are properties dependent upon the relations of the beliefs to other things, not upon any internal quality of the beliefs.

correspondence theory a theory contending that truth is an agreement between a proposition and a fact

To say of what is that it is, and of what is not that it is not, is truth.

ARISTOTLE

CRITICAL THINKING

Russell assumes that if the truth or falsehood of a belief depends on something outside the belief itself, it follows that truth and falsity must depend on facts. Does this really follow?

Bertrand Russell: "Hence, although truth and false-hood are properties of beliefs, they are properties dependent upon the relations of the beliefs to other things, not upon any internal quality of the beliefs. This leads us to the view that truth consists in some form of correspondence between belief and fact."

The third of the above requisites leads us to adopt the view—which has on the whole been commonest among philosophers—that truth consists in some form of correspondence between belief and fact.[3]

To understand Russell's version of the correspondence theory, it's necessary to see how he distinguishes a true judgment from a false one. To understand this requires familiarity with some of his language.

First, in any act of judgment, there is a mind that judges and terms about which the mind judges. Russell calls the mind the *subject* in the judgment, and the remaining terms the *objects*. Thus, when a student judges that Booth shot Lincoln, the student is the subject, and the objects are *Booth*, *shot*, and *Lincoln*. Russell calls the subject and objects together *constituents*.

Whenever we judge, we relate things—that is, we order them. This is indicated by word arrangement. The student's judgment "Booth shot Lincoln" is different from his judgment "Lincoln shot Booth," though their terms are the same. What makes one true and the other false? Correspondence with a fact. If the relationship among the terms in the judgment corresponds with the relationship among *Booth*, *shot*, and *Lincoln*, then the judgment is true:

> Thus a belief is *true* when it corresponds with a certain associated complex, and *false* when it does not. Assuming, for the sake of definiteness, that the objects of the belief are two terms and a relation, the terms being put in a certain order by the "sense" of the believing, then if the two terms in that order are united by the relation into a complex, the belief is true; if not, it is false. This constitutes the definition of truth and falsehood that we were in search of. Judging or believing is a certain complex unity of which a mind is a constituent; if the remaining constituents, taken in the order which they have in the belief, form a complex unity, then the belief is true; if not, it is false.[4]

---

[3] Bertrand Russell, *The Problems of Philosophy* (London: Oxford University Press, 1912), 283–284.
[4] Ibid., 285.

For Russell, only when a sentence expresses relations among words that mirror or correspond to the relations of a complex fact can the sentence be considered meaningful or true. For example, the sentence "The Golden Gate Bridge spans a strait in west-central California connecting the Pacific Ocean and San Francisco Bay" is meaningful and true. This sentence is true because it mirrors the relation between the bridge and the strait as described. The correspondence theory seems altogether reasonable. Yet it has significant weaknesses.

To draw out some objections to this theory and to stimulate more thinking about truth, let's have some fun by concocting an outrageous courtroom situation. The prosecution has just called Wilbur Scaife, a witness whose testimony is sure to destroy the case of nationally famous defense attorney and talk show celebrity Lamont P. Eveready. Never has Eveready had a greater challenge than to discredit witness Scaife, and he must do so fast!

BAILIFF: Do you swear to tell the truth, the whole truth, and nothing but the truth, so help you God?

SCAIFE: I do.

EVEREADY: Objection, Your Honor.

JUDGE: But the witness has not even taken his seat.

EVEREADY: Defense objects, Your Honor, on grounds that the witness has perjured himself.

JUDGE: Perjured himself? Why, he hasn't even answered a question yet.

EVEREADY: Defense humbly begs to differ, Your Honor. The witness has sworn to tell the truth, the whole truth, and nothing but the truth. Defense contends that the witness Wilbur Scaife is in no position to meet that oath, since he knows nothing of the truth of which he speaks.

JUDGE: Knows nothing of. . . .

EVEREADY: To put it simply, Your Honor, Scaife doesn't know the truth from a hole in the ground.

SCAIFE: Oh, yeah? You want to step outside and say that?

JUDGE: The witness will contain himself. Can Defense prove this contention?

EVEREADY: Defense can and will, Your Honor.

JUDGE: Then proceed.

EVEREADY: Thank you, Your Honor. Now, Mr. Scaife, you have just sworn a holy oath before God Almighty to tell the truth, the whole truth, and nothing but the truth. Is that correct?

SCAIFE: Yes.

EVEREADY: Presumably, you have sworn this oath knowing full well what it means.

SCAIFE: Yes, I have. It means I'm going to tell the truth.

EVEREADY: The whole truth and nothing but the truth.

SCAIFE: You said it.

Truth is found in the mind when it apprehends a thing as it is.

AQUINAS

EVEREADY: Now, Scaife, what in your opinion is the truth?

SCAIFE: The truth? The truth is the way things are.

EVEREADY: The way things are. All right, *American flag*—is that the truth?

SCAIFE: What about the American flag?

EVEREADY: Oh, I must say something about it?

SCAIFE: Well, sure. How else would you know if you got the truth or not?

EVEREADY: I see. So what you're really saying is that the truth refers not so much to the way things are as it does to a statement about the way things are. In other words, it would be silly to say "American flag" is true. But it would make perfect sense to say "There's a red, white, and blue American flag in this courtroom."

SCAIFE: Now you've got the truth, mister.

EVEREADY: You mean that statement is true?

SCAIFE: You bet your life it is.

EVEREADY: And tell the court, Scaife, how you know the statement "There is a red, white, and blue American flag in this courtroom" is true.

SCAIFE: Because I see that flag right over there.

EVEREADY: Because you see it. Tell me, Scaife, does everything you see lead you to make a true statement?

SCAIFE: I don't get you.

EVEREADY: Let me illustrate. You've no doubt seen a pencil resting in a glass of water.

SCAIFE: Sure.

EVEREADY: How would you describe such a pencil?

SCAIFE: You mean that it looks bent?

EVEREADY: It looks bent. Your eyes report it as bent.

SCAIFE: But it's not.

EVEREADY: No, it's not. Consequently, the statement "That pencil is bent" is not true, is it?

SCAIFE: No way.

EVEREADY: And yet your eyes report it as true, don't they?

SCAIFE: But it's different here with the flag. The flag is actually here, the way you said it was. The pencil isn't. That's the difference.

EVEREADY: The flag is actually here, the way I said it was. . . . Your Honor, the Defense wishes to call from the gallery for one question only Ms. Berth Moynier.

PROSECUTION: I object, Your Honor. Counsel's line of questioning has no purpose except to rattle, confuse, and intimidate the witness.

JUDGE: The irregularity of his request forces me to warn Defense that for his and his client's sake, the Bench hopes all this has some constructive end.

EVEREADY: I assure the Bench it has.

> *The way in which we can judge our beliefs is by testing them in experience.*
>
> PAUL CHURCHLAND

JUDGE: Will Ms. Moynier please rise?

EVEREADY: Ms. Moynier, will you please tell the court whether the following statement is true: "There is a red, white, and blue American flag in this room"?

MOYNIER: I don't know.

SCAIFE: What! She must be blind!

EVEREADY: I compliment you on your powers of deduction, Scaife. Ms. Moynier is, in fact, blind.

JUDGE: What's the meaning of this demonstration, Eveready?

EVEREADY: Your Honor, the purpose of this exercise is to show the court that what the witness, Wilbur Scaife, thinks is truth is in fact nothing but hearsay. Indeed, what the witness thinks is truth consigns truth to the very dubious area of sense data interpretation. Such interpretation must be purely subjective and need not have anything to do with the way things actually are.

> *There is no theory-independent way to reconstruct phrases like "really there."*
> THOMAS KUHN

PROSECUTION: Your Honor, I have sat here patiently while the Defense has made a mockery of this court. I submit that he has gone beyond the role of court jester and is now showing open contempt for the Bench itself!

EVEREADY: If the court will allow, the Defense would like to call from the gallery Mr. Bartholomew Peabody in order to prove the sincerity of Defense's cause.

JUDGE: With great reluctance, the Bench asks Mr. Bartholomew Peabody to rise.

EVEREADY: Thank you, Your Honor. Mr. Peabody, will you tell the court whether the following statement is true: "There is a red, white, and blue American flag in this courtroom"?

PEABODY: Well, if you want to know the truth, what you say is so and it isn't.

EVEREADY: Would you explain to the court why my statement is true and not true?

PEABODY: First, you do have a flag, all right. Any fool can see that.

SCAIFE: There! What did I tell you?

JUDGE: The former witness will restrain himself.

PEABODY: But it's not a red, white, and blue flag. It's red, white, and green.

SCAIFE: Green! He must be color-blind!

EVEREADY: Must be? Why? Because he disagrees with you?

PROSECUTION: Your Honor, how long will the Bench allow this travesty to continue?

EVEREADY: On the contrary, Your Honor, the court is hardly witnessing a travesty. Rather, in a matter of minutes, the court has heard three persons report different "truths" while supposedly observing the same object at the same time. Yet the witness Wilbur Scaife would have us believe that the truth characterizes that statement which reports an actual fact. I respectfully submit, Your Honor, that we can never know how things really are, because the only way we can come to such knowledge is through sensory experience, which I have just demonstrated to be unreliable.

JUDGE: Is Defense suggesting that in this case the testimonies of a blind person and a color-blind person are equal to that of a normally sighted one?

EVEREADY: Your Honor, may I respectfully answer with another question? Just what constitutes normal sight? Is it not a convention, a standard that the majority sets? Would the court submit the question of truth to a head count?

JUDGE: On the question of whether there is in fact a red, white, and blue American flag in this courtroom, the court might seriously entertain such a proposal.

EVEREADY: So be it, Your Honor. I submit the question to the gallery. Let a show of hands determine the truth of the statement "There is a red, white, and blue American flag in this courtroom."

JUDGE: Nobody? Not a single hand?

PROSECUTION: I object, Your Honor! The Defense has obviously stacked the gallery as a card shark would a deck of playing cards.

EVEREADY: The Prosecution's powers of deduction are as astonishing as Wilbur Scaife's, Your Honor. True, the defense has stacked the gallery, but only to demonstrate that when we insist that truth is an agreement between a statement of fact and the fact itself, we play the game of life with a stacked deck.

In effect, Eveready is asking, "Since we know only our experiences, how can we ever get outside them to verify what reality actually is?" The correspondence theory of truth seems to assume that we know not only our experiences of things but also facts about the world—that is, how the world actually is. Otherwise, how could truth be described as a correspondence between statement and fact? Of course, correspondence theorists might reply that the correspondence is between statements and reality as interpreted by us. But just who is "us"? Everyone, each individual, a consensus? And how do we ever know that our interpretation is correct to begin with? Furthermore, if truth is a correspondence between statement and fact as interpreted by us, then we say nothing at all about the world outside ourselves; we address only whether we are correctly or incorrectly representing what we believe.

Then there's the question of just what a *fact* is, a concern having profound implications outside philosophy as well. Sometimes *fact* means "true proposition," as in "It's a fact that I'm six feet tall." In other words, "The sentence 'I am six feet tall' is a true proposition." But using *fact* in this way results in circularity: A proposition is true if it corresponds to a true proposition. Or *fact* may mean the same as "actual state of affairs." In this case the correspondence theory says merely that a true proposition is one that describes a state of affairs that is actual. Nonetheless, the correspondence theory uses the word *corresponds* and not *describes*, and *corresponds* is a word that can cause confusion.

Just how does a true proposition correspond to a fact or a state of affairs? It doesn't correspond in the way that a color sample on a color chart corresponds with a color of paint on a wall. With color samples, there's a resemblance between the sample and the wall paint. Yet there's no resemblance between a proposition and a state of affairs, or even between a sentence and a state of

The greatest and highest truths have no outward image of themselves visible to man.

PLATO

La Trahison des Images, René Magritte. **Just how does a true proposition correspond to a fact or a state of affairs? There's no resemblance between a proposition and a state of affairs. Does a statement correspond to fact in the way that titles of books on library cards correspond to the books themselves? That is, is there some sort of one-to-one correspondence? If so, what is gained?**

affairs. Does a statement correspond to fact in the way that titles of books on library cards correspond to the books themselves? That is, is there some sort of one-to-one correspondence? Just as for each book there's a card, and for each card a book, so also for each statement there's a fact and for each fact a statement? If so, what have we gained? It seems at least as clear to say that a true proposition describes an actual state of affairs and thus dispose of the inherently misleading "correspondence."

COHERENCE THEORY

Exasperated by Eveready's protests, the judge has summoned him and the prosecution to the bench.

JUDGE: Now see here, Eveready, this line of interrogation can't continue. It's making a shambles of my court.

PROSECUTION: Amen!

JUDGE: Eveready, aren't you at all interested in the law?

EVEREADY: Of course I am, Your Honor. But I'm also interested in truth. Does Your Honor think the law and the truth are mutually exclusive?

JUDGE: Stop putting words in my mouth! You think I'm Scaife?

EVEREADY: I beg your pardon, Your Honor.

JUDGE: Pardon not granted. Didn't they teach you in law school the kind of truth on which much of the judicial process is based?

EVEREADY: Kind of truth? Are there kinds of truth, Your Honor?

PROSECUTION: Stop sassing the judge.

JUDGE: I'll be the judge of who's sassing me. Let me ask you something, Eveready.

EVEREADY: Proceed.

JUDGE: How are innocence and guilt determined?

EVEREADY: By a trial.

JUDGE: And what happens at a trial? I mean a normal trial, not this circus.

EVEREADY: Well, at a normal trial, lawyers present cases.

JUDGE: Exactly. And isn't it true that in theory the better case wins?

EVEREADY: In theory.

JUDGE: And what makes for the better case, Eveready?

EVEREADY: Obviously, persuading the jury.

JUDGE: Obviously. And which case, in theory, should persuade the jury?

EVEREADY: The one that hangs together better.

JUDGE: Precisely. Your job is to present the jury with pieces of a puzzle, isn't it? The jury's job is to take each piece and evaluate it. How? Well, let's see. They can't go back to the scene of the crime or to the circumstances that you describe, can they? No, they can't. So how do they figure out if a particular piece is true? I'll tell you how: usually by seeing how it fits in with all the other pieces. If it fits in, if it's consistent, if it doesn't contradict any of the other pieces, then it's true. At the very end, if you've presented a good case, all the pieces fit. The truth is right in front of their noses. "This person," they declare, "is guilty" or "not guilty."

> CRITICAL THINKING
> Does the coherence theory assume that our knowledge of reality is exactly like our knowledge of mathematics? Is this assumption correct?

Notice how the judge's theory of truth differs from the correspondence theory. According to him, a statement is true if it is consistent with other statements that we regard as true. The essential test is not correspondence between statement and fact but coherence between statement and other relevant statements. This **coherence theory** of truth, as we call it, insists that truth is a property of a related group of consistent statements. A particular statement is true if it is integrated within the framework of all the other statements already accepted as true.

Geometry is a good example of the coherence theory in operation. Geometry constructs an entire system of "truths," or theorems, by building on a few basic statements, or "axioms." In science, likewise, theories generally gain respectability when they are coherent with the body of accepted judgments. Brand Blanshard (1892–1987), a contemporary coherence theorist, illustrates the meaning of coherence in his book *The Nature of Thought*. There he arranges

coherence theory a theory contending that truth is a property of a related group of consistent statements

What makes a mathematical statement true isn't that it corresponds to something out there in the world.

D. H. MELLOR

Brand Blanshard: "A judgment of fact can be verified only by the sort of apprehension that can present us with a fact, and this must be a further judgment. And an agreement between judgments is best described not as a correspondence, but as coherence."

several familiar groups of things in a series according to how well their parts cohere:

At the bottom would be a junk heap, where we could know every item but one and still be without any clue as to what that remaining item was. Above this would come a stone-pile, for here you could at least infer that what you would find next would be a stone. A machine would be higher again, since from the remaining parts one could deduce not only the general character of a missing part, but also its special form and function. This is a high degree of coherence, but it is very far short of the highest. You could remove the engine from a motorcar while leaving the other parts intact, and replace it with any one of thousands of other engines, but the thought of such an interchange among human heads or hearts shows at once that the interdependence in a machine is far below that of the body. Do we find then in organic bodies the highest conceivable coherence? Clearly not. Though a human hand, as Aristotle said, would hardly be a hand when detached from the body, still it would be something definite enough; and we can conceive systems in which even this something would be gone. Abstract a number from the number series and it would be a mere unrecognizable x; similarly, the very thought of a straight line involves the thought of the Euclidean space in which it falls. It is perhaps in such systems as Euclidean geometry that we get the most perfect examples of coherence that have been constructed. If any proposition were lacking, it could be supplied from the rest; if any were altered, the repercussions would be felt through the length and breadth of the system. Yet even such a system as this falls short of the ideal system. Its postulates are unproved; they are independent of each other, in the sense that none of them could be derived from any other or even from all the others together; its clear necessity is bought by an abstractness so extreme as to have left out nearly everything that

Any judgment is true if it is both self-consistent and coherently connected with our system of judgments as a whole.
EDGAR S. BRIGHTMAN

belongs to the character of actual things. A completely satisfactory system would have none of these defects. No proposition would be arbitrary, every proposition would be entailed by the others jointly and even singly, no proposition would stand outside the system. The integration would be so complete that no part could be seen for what it was without seeing its relation to the whole, and the whole itself could be understood only through the contribution of every part.[5]

Blanshard is describing an ideal of coherence. Still, is the systemic coherence of propositions with one another alone a guarantee of truth? Recall that until the sixteenth century almost everyone believed that the earth was the center of the solar system. Why did everyone believe this? Because it made sense and accorded with commonsensical observation. It fit in with the widespread and naive experience of things and with religious belief. Moreover, in the second

---

[5] Brand Blanshard, *The Nature of Thought* (New York: Macmillan, 1941), 464–465. Reprinted by permission of George Allen & Unwin Ltd.

PHILOSOPHY AND LIFE

Historical Facts

What is a historical fact? Take, for example, what passes for a simple historical fact: "In the year 49 B.C. Caesar crossed the Rubicon." This is a familiar fact, and one of some importance. Yet, as the most distinguished American historian Carl L. Becker pointed out over a half century ago, this simple fact has strings tied to it. It depends on numerous other facts so that it has no meaning apart from the web of circumstances that produced it. This web of circumstances, of course, was the chain of events arising out of the relation of Caesar to Pompey, the Roman Senate, and the Roman Republic. As Becker states,

Caesar had been ordered by the Roman Senate to resign his command of the army in Gaul. He decided to disobey the Roman Senate. Instead of resigning his command, he marched on Rome, gained the mastery of the Republic, and, at last, we are told, bestrode the narrow world like a colossus. Well, the Rubicon happened to be the boundary between Gaul and Italy, so that by the act of crossing the Rubicon with his army Caesar's treason became an accomplished fact and the subsequent great events followed in due course. Apart from these great events and complicated relations, the crossing of the Rubicon means nothing, is not an historical fact properly speaking at all. . . . [It is] a symbol standing for a long series of events which have to do with the most intangible and immaterial realities, viz.: the relation between Caesar and the millions of people of the Roman world.

Clearly, for Becker "the simple historical fact" is only a symbol, an affirmation about an event. And since it's hardly worthwhile to term a symbol cold or hard, indeed dangerous to call it true or false, one might best speak of historical facts as being more or less appropriate.

QUESTIONS

1. Could Becker's analysis be applied to this statement: "The Japanese bombed Pearl Harbor on 7 December 1941"?

2. Would it be accurate to say that historians deal not with an event but with statements that affirm the fact that the event occurred? If so, what's the difference?

SOURCE: Carl L. Becker, "What Are Historical Facts?" Quoted in *Coming Age of Philosophy*, ed. Roger Eastman (San Francisco: Canfield Press, 1973), 451–452.

century A.D. the astronomer Ptolemy had elaborated and developed these observations into a complicated but consistent theory. His theory, which said that the sun revolves around the earth, could even be used to predict astronomical events successfully. In fact, the major difference between Ptolemy's theory and the theory of Copernicus, which replaced it, was that Copernicus's was simpler. (With the refinements that Kepler, Galileo, and Newton later proposed, its predictions were also much more accurate.) Yet both theories were consistent. The point is that coherence does not seem to distinguish between consistent truth and consistent error. A judgment may be true if it is consistent with other judgments, but what if the other judgments are false? If first judgments are not true, they can produce a system of consistent error.

Another objection is that a coherence theory in the last analysis seems to rely on correspondence. After all, if a judgment is coherent, it must cohere with another judgment. But what of the first judgments? With what do they cohere? If they are first, they cannot cohere with anything. Their truth, then, can be verified only by determining whether they report an actual fact. But this is the correspondence theory. However, defenders of the coherence theory insist that we can verify judgments of fact only by the coherence theory. Blanshard illustrates this point:

> Suppose we say, "the table in the next room is round"; how should we test this judgment? In the case in question, what verifies the statement of fact is the perceptual judgment that I make when I open the door and look. But then what verifies the perceptual judgment itself? . . . To which the reply is, as before, that a judgment of fact can be verified only by the sort of apprehension that can present us with a fact, and that this must be a further judgment. And an agreement between judgments is best described not as a correspondence, but as coherence.[6]

PRAGMATIC THEORY

Because of the evident weaknesses in the correspondence and coherence theories, philosophers of recent times have suggested another possibility, the pragmatic theory of truth. Let us see how it works by returning to the judge's chambers.

PROSECUTION: Well, if you want my opinion, I think the whole discussion is silly. I mean, if you want to know what's true, find out what works.

EVEREADY: What?

JUDGE: Are you saying that if something works, it's true?

PROSECUTION: What else can it be? How else can you judge what's true, except by its results? Take the theory of the sun-centered solar system, for example. What makes it true is that it works. It is true because it accurately describes a situation in such a way that people can use that description to produce desired

Looking for truth is looking for beliefs that will help you get what you want.

RICHARD RORTY

---

[6] Brand Blanshard, "The Nature of Thought," in *Philosophical Interrogation*, ed. Sidney and Beatrice Rome (New York: Holt, Rinehart & Winston, 1964), 210.

results. That theory's allowed us to plot the position of the heavenly bodies, estimate the distance between them, send satellites into space, and put men on the moon. Previous theories couldn't have produced these results. They just wouldn't have worked. That's why they were untrue, while this one is true.

EVEREADY: But if what works is true, what's stopping it from not working?

PROSECUTION: Nothing. Then it wouldn't be true any longer. The trouble with you, Eveready, is that you're hung up on the idea that truth is something absolute, something unchanging and unchangeable. Well, it's not! And you'd better get used to that. Where do you think truth comes from, anyway? It comes from you and me and the judge. And every man, woman, and child who's ever lived or will live. It doesn't grow on trees for the picking. People make it! They change it and they make it again. We make our own truth!

EVEREADY: So, according to you, if something works, it's true.

PROSECUTION: Exactly.

EVEREADY: Well, it sounds to me like you're saying that if I believe I'm Napoleon, I *am* Napoleon.

PROSECUTION: Your belief that you're Napoleon must face the test of truth: How does the belief work out in practice? Does it lead to satisfactory results? In your case, it wouldn't. People would be frightened by you, they'd avoid you, they'd probably lock you up and throw away the key. Your belief doesn't work. So it's not true.

EVEREADY: Well, what about the theory that the earth was once visited by astronaut gods? Presumably the belief worked for its author. It produced satisfactory results for him, just as you say the truth must. Now, does that make this theory true?

PROSECUTION: You make it sound as if the author were merely claiming to be happy or to have a toothache, Eveready. His claim isn't just a private one, you know. He's not just reporting his own internal state. He's making a public claim. So, as with all public claims, satisfactory results depend on more than just the results produced for a single person.

EVEREADY: But how do you know if his claim works or not?

PROSECUTION: Test it. Try it and see if it works. What else does it explain? What else does it account for? What use can we make of it? That's how to find out if it works.

The prosecution's idea of truth is different from both the correspondence theory and the coherence theory. She might admit that we can know only our experiences, so truth cannot be what corresponds with reality. She also views the coherence theory as too impractical. Instead, she wishes to introduce usefulness as the measure of truth. She insists that we can define truth only in relation to consequences. A statement is true if people can use that statement to achieve results that they need. There is no absolute or unchanging truth. To verify a belief as truth, we should see if the belief satisfies the whole of human nature over a long period of time, if it passes the tests of science, or if it aids us

We have to live today by what truth we can get today, and be ready tomorrow to call it falsehood.

WILLIAM JAMES

Begin by believing with all your heart that your belief is true, so that it will work for you; but then face the possibility that it is really false, so that you can accept the consequences of the belief.

JOHN RESECK

individually or collectively in the biological struggle for survival. In short, the prosecution argues for a pragmatic theory of truth. This position essentially states the following: If something works, it is true.

The pragmatic theory of truth is the cornerstone of pragmatism, the essentially American philosophy mentioned in Chapter 3. Recall that pragmatism has developed during the nineteenth and twentieth centuries, especially through the writings of Charles S. Peirce (1839–1914), William James (1842–1910), and John Dewey (1859–1952). The pragmatists were tired of older European outlooks, especially those that viewed humans primarily in rationalistic terms. They saw humans as needing to use the practical consequences of beliefs to decide truth and validity. Especially objectionable to pragmatists is the traditional idea of truth as something fixed and inert. Pragmatists see truth as dynamic and changing, subjective and relative. Like the correspondence and coherence theories, the pragmatic theory of truth has many forms. But the classic version was put forth by William James in *Pragmatism: A New Name for Some Old Ways of Thinking*. In it, he clearly distinguishes the pragmatic theory from other theories of truth:

> *The falseness of an opinion is not for us any objection to it. . . . The question is how far it is life-furthering, life-preserving, species-preserving, perhaps species-creating.*
>
> FRIEDRICH NIETZSCHE

> Truth, as any dictionary will tell you, is a property of certain of our ideas. It means their "agreement," as falsity means their disagreement, with "reality." Pragmatists and intellectualists both accept this definition as a matter of course. They begin to quarrel only after the question is raised as to what may precisely be meant by the term "agreement," and what by the term "reality," when reality is taken as something for our ideas to agree with.
>
> In answering these questions the pragmatists are more analytic and painstaking, the intellectualists more offhand and unreflective. The popular notion is that a true idea must copy its reality. Like other popular views, this one follows the analogy of the most usual experience. Our true ideas of sensible things do indeed copy them. Shut your eyes and think of yonder clock on the wall, and you get just such a true picture or copy of its dial. But your idea of its "works" (unless you are a clockmaker) is much less of a copy, yet it passes muster, for it in no way clashes with the reality. Even though it should shrink to the mere word "works," that word still serves you truly; and when you speak of the "time-keeping function" of the clock, or of its spring's "elasticity," it is hard to see exactly what your ideas can copy.
>
> You perceive that there is a problem here. Where our ideas cannot copy definitely their object, what does agreement with that object mean? Some idealists seem to say that they are true whenever they are what God means that we ought to think about that object. Others hold the copy-view all through, and speak as if our ideas possessed truth just in proportion as they approach to being copies of the Absolute's eternal way of thinking.
>
> These views, you see, invite pragmatistic discussion. But the great assumption of the intellectualists is that truth means essentially an inert static relation. When you've got your true idea of anything, there's an end of the matter. You're in possession; you *know*; you have fulfilled your thinking destiny. You are where you ought to be mentally; you have obeyed your categorical imperative; and nothing more need follow on that climax of your rational destiny. Epistemologically you are in stable equilibrium.
>
> Pragmatism, on the other hand, asks its usual question. "Grant an idea or belief to be true," it says, "what concrete difference will its being true make in any one's actual

life? How will the truth be realized? What experiences will be different from those which would obtain if the belief were false? What, in short, is the truth's cash-value in experiential terms?"

The moment pragmatism asks this question, it sees the answer: *True ideas are those that we can assimilate, validate, corroborate and verify. False ideas are those that we can not.* That is the practical difference it makes to us to have true ideas; that, therefore, is the meaning of truth, for it is all that truth is known as.

This thesis is what I have to defend. The truth of an idea is not a stagnant property inherent in it. Truth *happens* to an idea. It *becomes* true, is *made* true by events. Its verity *is* in fact an event, a process: the process namely of its verifying itself, its veri-*fication*. Its validity is the process of its valid-*ation*.

But what do the words *verification* and *validation* themselves pragmatically mean? They again signify certain practical consequences of the verified and validated idea. It is hard to find any one phrase that characterizes these consequences better than the ordinary agreement-formula—just such consequences being what we have in mind whenever we say that our ideas "agree" with reality. They lead us, namely, through the acts and other ideas which they instigate, into or up to, or towards, other parts of experience with which we feel all the while—such feeling being among our potentialities—that the original ideas remain in agreement. The con-nections and transitions come to us from point to point as being progressive, har-monious, satisfactory. This function of agreeable leading is what we mean by an idea's verification.[7]

CRITICAL THINKING

Does James assume that truth is a kind of event? That it can change with time? Is this plausible? Does James assume that a proposition is neither true nor false until it is veri-fied? Does his view imply that if we cannot prove something is true, then it is false?

According to James, then, we do not base truth on a comparison of a statement with some objective, external reality. Nor is truth based on coherence with other beliefs. In James's view, the essential problem with those views is that their adherents have failed to ask the right questions. They shouldn't ask how judgments correspond or relate to reality, but what difference they make. For James, the truth of an idea or judgment depends on what he calls "the practical difference it makes" in our lives.

Pragmatism continues to be one of the most vigorous living philosophies. In fact, many contemporary philosophers believe that pragmatism is the most vital and promising of all approaches to truth. Nevertheless, contemporary pragmatists approach truth differently from William James. Whereas James gave a definition of *truth*, modern pragmatists tend to argue that we should forget about trying to define this elusive idea. Instead, we should get on with the more important activity of living in open-minded, democratic communities. Richard Rorty, one of the foremost living philosophers and a staunch advocate of prag-matism, writes the following:

> We pragmatists . . . are making the purely *negative* point that we would be better off without the traditional distinctions between knowledge and opinion, construed as the distinction between truth as correspondence to reality and truth as a commen-datory term for well-justified belief. Our opponents call this negative claim "relativ-istic" because they cannot imagine that anybody would seriously deny that truth has an intrinsic nature. So when we say that there is nothing to be said about truth save that each of us will commend as true those beliefs which he or she finds good to

I admire the importance of not getting hung up on Truth with a capital "T," and realize that in ordinary life what we're concerned with is truths with a small "t."

STEPHEN TOULMIN

---

[7] William James, *Pragmatism: A New Name for Some Old Ways of Thinking* (New York: Longmans, Green, 1907), 198–199.

believe, the realist is inclined to interpret this as one more positive theory about the nature of truth: a theory according to which truth is simply the contemporary opinion of a chosen individual or group. Such a theory would, of course, be self-refuting. But we pragmatists do not have a theory of truth, much less a relativistic one.[8]

Rorty holds that the most that can be said about the notion of truth is that truth is whatever has passed society's "procedures of justification." He proposes "the ethnocentric view that there is nothing to be said about either truth or rationality apart from descriptions of the familiar procedures of justification which a given society, ours, uses in one or another area of inquiries."[9] Thus, the modern pragmatist, like William James, wants to get rid of the traditional idea that truth is correspondence with an external reality. Instead, the modern pragmatist wants us to recognize that when people say something is true, they are merely trying to "commend" it as good to believe. We commend a statement as true when it passes the tests that our community uses to distinguish what is true from what is false. Different communities, of course, have different procedures or criteria for separating true from false. Scientists use one set of procedures for deciding what they will accept as true, whereas poets, lawyers, literary critics, and movie producers use others. But no group's procedures lead to more truth about reality than any other group's. No single truth about an independent reality exists. There are only the many truths that emerge from the many different procedures that different communities use because they have found that these procedures produce worthwhile or useful results.

Pragmatism, of course, has been the subject of intense criticism. The main criticism has been that it seems to base truth on the fallible judgments of human communities. What's true may be justified for a certain community to believe, but what's justified for them to believe isn't necessarily true. Pragmatism seems to reduce epistemology to psychology.

To understand this basic criticism of pragmatism, consider a simple fact: What we were justified in believing yesterday may turn out to be false today. For example, five hundred years ago, we were justified in believing the earth is flat. Today we know it is round. Pragmatism does not seem to be able to account for this simple fact. Pragmatism says that truth is whatever a community is justified in believing after it has used its "procedures of justification." It would seem that the pragmatist would have to say that the earth really was flat five hundred years ago because we were justified in believing it was flat then. Since we are justified in believing it is round today, it is really round now! This is clearly absurd. There is a difference between truth and justified belief, but pragmatism makes them identical.

Some pragmatists have tried to deal with this objection. Truth, they say, is what an ideal community would be justified in believing if it continued its investigations indefinitely, examined all the evidence, made no mistakes, and was perfectly open to all points of view. Thus, pragmatists introduce the notion of an ideal community working in ideal circumstances to explain how we can be

Theorizing is itself another form of practice.
STEPHEN TOULMIN

The notion of one Truth is basically just the notion of one God, the powerful father-figure of monotheism.
RICHARD RORTY

Any perception of reality will always be from a point of view. But it doesn't follow that the reality perceived exists only relative to a perceiver.
JOHN SEARLE

---

[8] Richard Rorty, "Science as Solidarity," in *Dismantling Truth*, ed. Hilary Lawson and Lisa Appignanesi (New York: St. Martin's, 1989), 11.
[9] Ibid., 11.

justified in believing something that is actually false. A belief that we are justified in believing but that is false is simply a belief that an ideal community working in ideal circumstances would not be justified in believing.

However, this response seems to replace one metaphysical hang-up with another. Pragmatists have said that the idea that truth requires an external reality to which true beliefs must "correspond" is so much metaphysical garbage.

PHILOSOPHY AND LIFE

Truth and Paradox

The concept of truth has been intensively studied by logicians during the twentieth century. In fact, the vigorous attempts logicians and mathematicians have made to clarify the notion of truth have led to some of the greatest and most far-reaching mathematical discoveries of this century. Much of this work has been inspired by the realization that the very notion of truth seems to give rise to troublesome paradoxes and contradictions.

One of the earliest examples of the troublesome contradictions that the notion of truth can create is attributed to the ancient Greek philosopher Eubulides, who wrote, "A man says that he is not telling the truth. Is what he says true or false?" If what the man says is true, then the man is not telling the truth, so what he says must be false! But if what the man says is false, then it is false that he is not telling the truth, so what he says must be true! Thus, assuming what the man says is true leads us to a contradiction, and assuming what the man says is not true also leads us to a contradiction. In either case, the very notion of truth seems to generate a contradiction.

The same kinds of contradictions are generated by much simpler state-

ments, such as "This statement is not true" or

> The sentence in the box on this page is false.

But why should it matter that the very concept of truth generates contradictions? Because, unfortunately, once a single contradiction is allowed, it is easy to prove with rigorous logic that *any statement whatsoever* is true. That is, anything can be proved once you accept a contradiction. This is fairly easy to show.

Let the letter Q stand for any statement you want, such as "Unicorns exist." Now suppose that you accept as true the statement "God is good." Call this statement P. And suppose you also accept as true the contradictory statement "God is not good." Call this statement *not-P*. Now consider the following statement:

(1) Either P is true or Q is true.

You must accept that statement 1 is true, since you previously accepted that P is true. However, since you also accepted *not-P*, this means that P is not true. That is, you must also accept statement 2:

(2) P is not true.

Now you have accepted statements 1 and 2. But from statements

1 and 2, of course, it logically follows that

(3) Q is true.

And so you must accept that Q is true—that is, that unicorns exist! So by accepting the contradiction that P is true and that *not-P* is also true, we can logically prove that unicorns exist. In fact, anything at all can be proved with rigorous logic once a contradiction is accepted.

The terrible consequences that would follow should the concept of truth involve contradictions were what led twentieth-century logicians and mathematicians to invest considerable energy in trying to come up with ways to avoid contradictions. Unfortunately, this work has not yet come to any firm conclusions. The possibility that our notion of truth may be contradictory still lurks.

QUESTIONS

1. Can you conceive of some ways of avoiding the contradictions that truth seems to involve?

2. Can you conceive of some ways of avoiding the argument that once a contradiction is accepted, anything can be proved?

But to say that we have instead to believe in some kind of imaginary "ideal community" to understand the difference between truth and falsity seems also to be metaphysical garbage.

In what sense is the pragmatic theory better than the more traditional philosophies? Pragmatism maintains that it is more useful. Yet any judgment about usefulness seems to involve a large dose of subjectivity. Couldn't traditional philosophers claim that their views of truth are better in terms of their own preferences? It seems that they can. In fact, can we ask whether it is true that one view is more useful than another in a sense in which *true* does not mean "useful"?

DOES TRUTH MATTER?

The debates over the nature of truth may seem at first sight to be arid and irrelevant. What does it matter whether the correct view of truth is the correspondence theory or coherence theory or pragmatic theory? After all, whatever truth is, it seems that we will continue to believe the same truths and live the same lives. But, in fact, the parties to these debates are fighting over matters that directly affect each of us.

Consider, first, that both the coherence and the pragmatic views are opposed to the correspondence view of truth. This is only natural since the correspondence view holds that truth is objective. That is, it holds that truth depends on what the real world is like, not on what a particular person or group accepts. Both the coherence and pragmatic views, on the other hand, reject the idea that truth is objective. Instead, they hold that the truth of a claim depends on what the group that makes the claim accepts. The coherence theory says that a claim is true if it coheres with the other beliefs that a group accepts. The pragmatic theory says that a claim is true if it passes the procedures of justification that a group uses. Both theories agree that if a group accepts a claim (because it coheres with their other beliefs or because it passes their procedures of justification), then the claim is true for that group. Moreover, any conflicting claims accepted by other groups are equally true (if they meet the same criteria). One group's accepted claims are as true as the accepted claims of any other group. Ultimately, then, to reject the correspondence view of truth is to reject objectivity and to choose a relativity that sees every group's accepted claims as equally valid.

We must be careful, though, in how we use the word *relativism*. Rorty and other pragmatists say that, in a sense, they are not relativists about truth. They are not relativists, Rorty claims, if by *relativism* we mean that every belief is as good as any other and truth is whatever a group believes. Such relativism, Rorty has said, is just a "bogeyman" intended to "frighten children." However, pragmatists agree that they are relativists about truth, if by *relativism* we mean that truth is whatever a group *accepts because it passes that group's procedures of justification*. Pragmatists are relativists only in this more restricted sense.

But why does it matter that pragmatism and coherence are relativist views of truth? Consider some consequences of rejecting objectivity. If we reject objectivity, then we must agree that every group's accepted claims are equally true

I've never met a relativist. It seems to me to be a bogeyman that people think of to frighten children.

RICHARD RORTY

(as long as the group's claims are accepted because they pass their procedures of justification). We must agree that if a racist group accepts the claim that they are superior to other races, their claim is as true as our claim that no race is superior to another. We must agree that if males as a group accept the claim that they are superior to women, then their claim is as true as women's claim that males are not superior to females. It means that if one group accepts the claim that having sex with children is good, their claim is as valid as the claim that having sex with children is evil. It means that if one group accepts witchcraft and magic, then these are as valid as medicine and science are to another group. It means that if one group accepts the claim that the Holocaust never happened, then that claim is as true as historians' claim that Nazi Germans slaughtered six million Jews during World War II.

In short, if truth is what a group accepts or finds justified, then whatever one group accepts is as true as what an opposing group accepts. One group's biases, prejudices, or superstitions become as legitimate as the objections that other groups may raise to these biases, prejudices, or superstitions. If no objective truth exists, then the consequence, it seems, is that any claim accepted by a group becomes truth.

For many who hold a relativist theory of truth, these consequences are not necessarily bad. For example, some pragmatists hold that toleration is a critically important value that only relativism can preserve. Toleration is the virtue of acknowledging that we do not have a monopoly on truth and that the claims of others may be as valid as the claims we accept. Toleration is the viture that relativism prizes. Thus, defenders of relativism claim that relativism is inclusive and democratic, whereas objective views of truth are exclusive and undemocratic. Objective views of truth are exclusive and undemocratic because they hold that the views of some groups are wrong and so exclude such views.

So you see that the choice among the theories of truth is not an abstract, irrelevant exercise. A lot hangs on which theory you ultimately accept. If you opt for objectivity, you will move toward the correspondence view that truth depends on facts about the world independent of what any group happens to accept. Accepting objectivity may lead you to say that some views (like the views of the racist or the Nazi) are wrong no matter how many people accept them. On the other hand, if you opt for relativism, you will move toward the coherence or pragmatic view that truth depends on what this or that group accepts. Accepting relativism may lead you toward a more tolerant, inclusive, and democratic recognition that the views of others are equally valid. Both paths are attractive; both paths have dangerous pitfalls.

Or you may try to travel on both paths. To a certain extent, this is possible. One way to do this is to view the unique contribution that each theory makes to the realm of truth. Unquestionably, the correspondence theory fits the empirical realm. Suppose I say it's true that New York is three thousand miles from Los Angeles, it's true that a fire needs oxygen, or it's true that it's raining. Then I am probably taking *truth* to mean "correspondence." If the statements correspond to the facts, then I accept them as true.

On the other hand, coherence provides a useful way of understanding logical, necessary, or systemic truth. Thus, if I want to know whether it's true that

Truth is so obscure in these times, and falsehood so established, that, unless we love the truth, we cannot know it.

PASCAL

The attempt to find one characterization of truth that covers every kind of truth, seems to me doomed to failure.

HILARY PUTNAM

a chair cannot be a nonchair, that 56 divided by 7 is 8, or that all bachelors are unmarried, then I need only see if these statements fit in with other statements that I accept as true.

Finally, the pragmatic test seems to reveal the meaning of truth as applied to the many value judgments that we make. Thus, "Lying is wrong," "God exists," "Pleasure is the only intrinsic good," and such statements form a very important part of our lives. So do value judgments in the arts, politics, education, and other walks of life. Frequently, the best—and sometimes the only—way to verify such judgments is by applying the tests of workability. Do these beliefs pan out? The pragmatic theory thus helps us understand what truth can mean in the realm of values.

As long as we think that everything that's true or false has to be a description of some realm, we won't understand ethical truth, we won't understand logical truth, we won't understand mathematical truth.

HILARY PUTNAM

So we can see the theories of truth as complementary. Rather than viewing them as incompatible, we can use them to understand the truth of the various kinds of statements that we utter. Still, this strategy of approaching the theories of truth as complementary will take us only a certain distance, for the question still remains: How are we to evaluate the claims that others accept when we disagree with these claims and when they have an impact on the way we live? Shall we be tolerant pragmatists and say that racists or sexists are entitled to their views? What if their racism or sexism is directed against us? Or what shall we say about the adult who believes in sex with children? Shall we be tolerant relativists and say that this belief is as valid as ours? Or shall we opt for an objective view of the truth and say that this view is false and that we must not allow the person to act on it?

In short, our lives together seem to force us to choose between the objectivity of the correspondence theory and the relativism of the coherence theory or the pragmatic theory. In the end, it seems, we must opt for one or the other, and the option we choose carries significant consequences. Truth is truly significant.

QUESTIONS

1. Do you think it is ever possible to "tell the whole truth"? Explain.

2. Is describing truth as a correspondence between a statement and how things actually are an example of begging the question? In what sense does such a definition not answer the question "What is truth?" but endorse a version of that question?

3. Eveready claims, "Indeed, what the witness thinks is truth consigns truth to the very dubious area of sense data interpretation. Such interpretation must be purely subjective and need not have anything to do with the way things actually are." Cite instances or cases that illustrate Eveready's charge.

4. Do you think that there are two kinds of truth, subjective and objective—truth as an individual perceives it and truth as it actually is? Or is there just one objective truth, and everything else merely belief and opinion?

5. Show how the following statements pass the test of coherence: (a) I am a rational being; (b) I am a divine being; (c) I am a mechanical being; (d) I am an existential being; (e) I am no self.

6. Take some theory, perhaps in psychology, anthropology, economics, or history, and put it to the coherence test. Does it pass? Can you find an opposing theory that passes as well? What might you conclude about the coherence theory of truth?

7. In what sense do claims of extrasensory perception not fit in with what we claim to know? In what sense do they?

8. Demonstrate how the coherence theory of truth ultimately seems to rely on the correspondence theory. How would proponents of the coherence theory object to this claim?

9. Do you believe in God? If so, describe how this belief, working through the coherence theory of truth, influences how you see yourself, other people, the world around you, and the future of humankind.

10. Consider the fact that you are studying to enter some profession. Demonstrate how this intention is working as a truth in your life and serving as the cornerstone for a structure of other truths.

11. Take some political event from the recent past, such as the collapse of the communist nations or our own attempts to deal with the budget deficit. Show how the coherence theory of truth operated to formulate policy and direct activity. Do you think these examples are a vindication of the coherence theory of truth? An indictment? Both? Neither?

12. Cite a belief that you consider true primarily on pragmatic grounds.

13. Give an example of people creating their own truth.

14. In a sense, truth for the pragmatist is an extension of belief. Illustrate how belief can make truth. Do you detect dangers in this position? How would this position affect how you view yourself? In what sense will you be tomorrow what you decide to be today?

15. In opposition to the pragmatists and their theory of truth, critics charge, "But don't you see that you're encouraging us to see things as we would have them and not as they are?" Do you agree with this criticism?

16. Can you think of anything that, although true, does not work? Something that, although it works, is not true?

17. Make three lists of statements: (1) statements that you feel you accept mostly on pragmatic grounds, (2) statements that you feel you accept mostly because they cohere with your other beliefs, and (3) statements that you accept because you feel that they correspond to reality. What general claims can you make about the areas or fields where you tend to rely on a pragmatic theory of truth? Where you tend to rely on a coherence theory? Where you tend to rely on a correspondence theory?

18. What statements about yourself do you accept on pragmatic grounds? On the grounds of coherence? On the grounds of correspondence with reality?

6.3 Does Science Give Us Truth?

In the last chapter we discussed scientific method as a source of knowledge. We noted that it incorporates elements of empiricism, rationalism, and transcendental idealism, but we did not answer this question: Does science give us the truth? Now that we have looked closely at the question "What is truth?" let us return to the issue of whether there is truth in science. Does our discussion of the correspondence, coherence, and pragmatic theories of truth help us understand scientific truth?

Many people hold that science clearly gives us the truth about the world. After all, science has enabled us to cure hundreds of deadly diseases, to put people into space and on the moon, to send our voices and moving pictures over thousands of miles in an instant, to fly in the air faster and farther than the birds, to travel in cars and over the oceans quicker than any animal or fish, to make computers that can carry out a million calculations in a fraction of a second, and to produce steel from ore, plastic from oil, and atomic power from uranium rocks. Radio, television, rockets, telescopes, the hydrogen bomb, computers, electricity, vaccines, antibiotics, heart transplants, telephones, tape recorders, cars, airplanes, submarines, microwaves, satellites, and weather forecasting all testify to what people can create by relying on the truth of science. The success of these endeavors, many believe, is clear proof that science gives us the truth. Yet does it?

> *Science seeks only the most generally useful systems of classification; these it regards for the time being, until more useful classifications are invented, as "true."*
>
> S. I. HAYAKAWA

To focus our inquiry, we're going to have to look at some scientific theories. As we go along we'll look at three theories: the standard theory of matter, Copernicus's theory of the solar system, and the quantum theory. Some of these theories are very interesting. We will see that it's hard to know what it means to say that they are true. We'll begin with the standard theory of matter.

Since the beginning of the twentieth century, scientists have accepted the atomic theory of matter. This theory says that the objects around us are made of atoms. Each atom consists of a small, central nucleus made up of protons and neutrons and a surrounding cloud of electrons. For many years, scientists held the theory that these three kinds of particles—protons, neutrons, and electrons—are the basic building blocks from which all things are made. But experiments eventually led scientists to a new theory: The protons and neutrons are themselves made of even smaller, more basic particles. The experiments that led scientists to change their theories were done in gigantic tubes called particle accelerators or colliders, some over a mile long. From one end of one of these tubes a device shoots particles (electrons and atoms) toward the other end. At the other end, these particles smash into other particles at terrific speeds. Many of these collisions can be detected in "cloud chambers" or "bubble chambers" in which the speeding particles and collisions make tiny tracks or lines that actually can be seen and photographed (see Figure 1). Other collisions are detected using Geiger counters and other sensitive instruments that can record

> *What we're doing is setting a trap, as best we can, to trap nature and get one of her secrets.*
>
> W. V. O. QUINE

collision of
one particle
with another

Photograph of the tracks made in a bubble chamber by a tiny subatomic particle colliding and hitting another subatomic particle that broke apart when it was hit.

the collisions. In these collisions, electrons sometimes bounce off of the particles at the other end, like tiny billiard balls hitting one another. In other collisions, protons and neutrons seem to break apart into smaller things when hit by the speeding electrons.

As a result of these experiments with colliders, scientists now accept what is called the standard theory of matter. This theory says that all the ordinary material objects in the universe—from toads and trees to stars and galaxies—are made up of four kinds of basic particles: two kinds of quarks, which make up the protons and neutrons in the nuclei of atoms; electrons, which surround the nuclei; and neutrinos, which can move very fast, have virtually no mass, and are shot out of nuclear reactions. These four kinds of particles are held together and acted upon by four forces: a strong nuclear force, which holds quarks together in the atomic nucleus; a weak nuclear force, which sets off certain kinds of radioactive decay; electromagnetism, which builds atoms into molecules and molecules into the objects we see; and gravity, which holds together the planets, stars, and whole galaxies. Each of these four forces is associated with a particle: Photons carry the electromagnetic force, gluons carry the strong nuclear force, bosons carry the weak force, and gravitons carry gravity. Is this standard theory of matter true? And what does it mean to say that it is—or is not—"true"?

THE INSTRUMENTALIST VIEW

If you asked them, most scientists would say that the standard theory of matter is true. Yet is it? Well, ask yourself this: What does it mean to say that quarks, neutrinos, and electrons exist? No one has ever seen or heard or touched one of these particles, and no one ever will. They are unobservable "theoretical entities." That is, they are entities mentioned in theories, but we cannot directly observe them. In what sense do these theoretical entities exist?

Perhaps you might want to say that unobservable theoretical entities like electrons are real in this sense: The standard theory of matter, which says that electrons exist, predicts that when bits of matter hit one another at very high speeds, the dials on appropriate detectors will move and little tracks will appear in cloud chambers. Now, in fact, when scientists shoot bits of matter together at extremely high speeds in "particle colliders," the dials move and the tracks appear exactly as the theory predicts. This, you might conclude, proves that the theory is true, so electrons must exist.

Still, do successful predictions really prove that a theory is true or that its theoretical entities are real? Couldn't the theory just be a formula that works but that isn't literally true? Granted, the theory lets scientists predict what they will see when they shoot bits of matter together. But this successful prediction does not necessarily mean that the theory is true. Nor does successful prediction mean that these theoretical entities exist. In fact, many scientists and philosophers interpret the standard theory as saying something like this: "If we *assume* that matter is partly made of little electrons, we can predict that the dials on detectors will move when matter collides. But this does not mean that little electrons exist. It only means that with this assumption, we can make accurate predictions." In this view, photons, gluons, gravitons, and bosons are only imaginary things mentioned in formulas that let us accurately predict what will happen when we do certain experiments.

This view of scientific theories and of theoretical entities is the **instrumentalist view** of scientific truth. You have probably noticed that this view owes a lot to the pragmatic theory of truth. In fact, the instrumentalist view of scientific truth uses the pragmatic theory to understand truth in science.

The instrumentalist view, like the pragmatic theory, holds that when we say that a scientific theory is true, we mean only that it works. In particular, we mean that it lets us accurately predict what will happen when we do certain things. Consequently, the instrumentalist view of scientific truth says that the unobservable theoretical entities in a scientific theory are not real. They are invented or fictitious entities that serve as useful but imaginary constructs. They are useful because if we act *as if* they exist, we can make accurate scientific predictions.

The instrumentalist view has a long history. For example, in the sixteenth century, the astronomer Copernicus proposed that the earth and the planets revolve around the sun. As we noted above, everyone then believed that in reality the earth stood still and the sun and planets revolved around it. This was the theory of the astronomer Ptolemy. People believed that God, who created the universe, put humans and their earth at the center of the universe.

instrumentalist view in epistemology, the view that scientific theories can be true only in the sense that they enable us accurately to predict what will happen and that any unobservable entities postulated by the theory literally do not exist

Theologians claimed that the Bible itself declared that the sun revolved around the earth while the earth stood still. And church authorities were willing to persecute anyone who opposed these views. So, in the preface to Copernicus's book, a friend of his wrote that Copernicus was not trying to describe the real universe. Instead, Copernicus's proposal was just an imaginary model meant to "save the appearances." That is, it gave scientists a way of accurately calculating and predicting where the sun and the planets would appear in the sky. Readers, he wrote, should not take Copernicus's proposal as a description of the real structure of the universe. In reality, the sun revolves around the earth. Copernicus's proposal that the earth and planets revolve around the sun was just a useful device for calculating the positions of the planets. In short, Copernicus's theory that the earth revolves around the sun should be interpreted instrumentally.

Most scientists at the time agreed. In reality, they said, the earth stood still at the center of the universe while the sun and planets spun around it as Ptolemy said. Copernicus's assumption that the sun stood still while the earth and planets spun around it was false. But this false assumption, they felt, gives us a better way of calculating where the planets will be on any given day in the future. Here is how a book on astronomy written in 1594 put it: "Copernicus affirmeth that the earth turneth about and that the sun standeth still in the midst of the heavens, by help of which false supposition he hath made truer demonstrations of the motions and revolutions of the celestial spheres, than ever were made before."[10]

However, scientists found more and more problems with the old view of Ptolemy that the earth stands still while the sun and planets move around it. Eventually, more and more scientists began to think that Copernicus's proposal was a description of the way the universe really is. This got some of these scientists into trouble with the church. The most famous was Galileo. In 1632 he published *A Dialogue Concerning the Two Great World Systems*, in which he argued that Copernicus's view was an accurate description of the way the universe really was. For his efforts, Galileo was put on trial by the church's Inquistion, which condemned Galileo for "vehement suspicion of heresy" and sentenced him to house arrest for life. Eventually Galileo had to retract his views. Nevertheless, the future would vindicate him and his rejection of the instrumentalist interpretation of Copernicus's new theory. How, then, did Galileo interpret Copernicus? Let us see.

THE REALIST VIEW

An alternative to the instrumentalist view is the **realist view** of scientific truth, which is a version of the correspondence theory of truth. According to the realist view, scientific theories are literally true or false. The entities that a scientific theory talks about—such as the electrons, quarks, neutrinos, gluons, bosons, gravitons, and photons of the standard theory of matter—really exist

realist view in epistemology, the view that scientific theories are literally true or false and that the unobservable entities postulated in a scientific theory really exist if the theory is true

---

[10] Quoted in Michael R. Gardner, "Realism and Instrumentalism in Pre-Newtonian Astronomy," in *Scientific Knowledge*, ed. Janet A. Kourany (Belmont, CA: Wadsworth, 1987), 370.

in the world "out there." A theory—like Copernicus's, which says that the earth and planets revolve around the sun—is meant to describe the way the universe really is.

According to the realist, the world around us contains entities with definite properties. These entities have relationships to one another that are independent of us. That is, the world is made up of entities in a definite structure. The aim of science, according to the realist, is to explain this world by discovering exactly what this structure is. In other words, the aim of science is to develop theories that tell us what entities exist and how they are related to one another. A scientific theory is true if the entities it talks about really exist in the world and if these entities in reality have the relationships the theory says they have. That is, the realist says a scientific theory is true when the entities it refers to and the relationships it describes *correspond* to real entities that exist in the world and their real relationships. According to the realist, if the standard theory of matter is true, then electrons, gluons, and quarks are real and that these are related to one another in the way the theory says they are. If Copernicus's theory of the universe is true, then the planets, earth, and sun are really related to one another as his theory says they are.

Realists and instrumentalists have very different views about the aim of science. According to the instrumentalist, the aim of science is to make accurate predictions so that we can satisfy our human needs. For the realist, the aim of science is to provide true explanations of the world by telling us exactly what the structure of the world is. Notice also that the realist and the instrumentalist differ on how science proceeds. According to the instrumentalist, the scientist *invents* or makes up scientific truth. But according to the realist, scientists *discover* scientific truth. The realist believes that the truth is already there, waiting to be uncovered by the scientist. The instrumentalist believes that truth does not exist until the scientist invents it and shows that it gives us the right predictions.

Realists argue that theories give us accurate predictions simply because theories correspond to the way the world is. Theories are not true because they make accurate predictions, as the instrumentalist holds; rather, they make accurate predictions because they correspond to reality. Moreover, says the realist, most scientists will not say that they are trying to make up imaginary entities that can help them predict the future. Instead, they will say that they are trying to discover what reality is really like: They are trying to figure out what entities really exist and how those entities are really related.

THE CONCEPTUAL RELATIVIST VIEW

A third view of scientific truth, the **conceptual relativist view,** shares many characteristics of the coherence theory of truth. Conceptual relativism owes much to the philosophy of Thomas Kuhn, whom we discussed in the preceding chapter. Many people whom Kuhn has influenced have come to the conclusion that a true scientific theory is nothing more than a theory that a community of scientists accepts. A community of working scientists, they claim, has its own unique way of seeing the world. The scientists who are members of the

conceptual relativist view in epistemology, the view that a true scientific theory is nothing more than a theory that coheres with the conceptual framework accepted by a community of scientists

community have their own way of conducting research, their own research programs, their own way of interpreting what happens in their experiments, their own theories and beliefs about nature, and their own values about what counts in scientific research. These research methods, programs, theories, and values are a "conceptual framework," or system of beliefs about the world. For example, astronomers before Copernicus believed in an old theory that they found in books by Aristotle and Ptolemy. This theory said that the sun and planets revolve around the earth. They combined this theory with religious beliefs and values that said God put the earth at the center of the universe. And they looked at the sky with the naked eye to confirm these theories. These theories, methods, values, and beliefs made up the "conceptual framework" of astronomers before Copernicus. After Copernicus, scientists began to believe that they should not rely on what they found in old books and texts. Nor should they look to the church to decide scientific matters. They began to feel that, instead, they should rely on their own observations. They began to look at the sky by using the newly discovered telescope. They came to believe in Copernicus's theory that the earth and planets revolve around the sun. These new beliefs, methods, theories, and values made up a new "conceptual framework."

According to the conceptual relativist, the beliefs that make up the conceptual framework of a group are true by definition. New findings or new beliefs are true if they fit in with the accepted conceptual framework. For the conceptual relativist, then, what is true in science is what coheres with the scientific theories, beliefs, values, and research methods of a community of scientists. A particular research finding is true or false only in relation to a particular conceptual framework. The conceptual relativist believes that the standard theory of matter is true if it fits in with the beliefs, the methods, the values, and the other theories of contemporary scientists. Copernicus's theory is true if it fits in with the beliefs, methods, and other theories of contemporary astronomers.

One reason that conceptual relativists hold these views about scientific theories, they say, is that both the realist and instrumentalist views are radically flawed. Both the realist and the instrumentalist mistakenly believe that they can somehow know or observe the real world independently of their theories. Instrumentalists believe that they can independently check the world to see whether a theory's predictions are accurate. Realists believe that they can independently check the world to see whether a theory corresponds with reality. Yet these independent checks are not possible, say the conceptual relativists. Our observations and perceptions of the world are always colored and influenced by our beliefs and theories about what we should be seeing. Observations are always theory laden, say conceptual relativists. Consequently, our theories about reality influence what we think we are seeing when we observe reality.

For example, suppose that a scientist who believes in the standard theory of matter sees a little white trail in a cloud chamber. He will see the little trail as the track left behind by an electron as it moved through the chamber. He will see it this way because that is what the standard theory leads him to think he is seeing. On the other hand, suppose that you or I looked at the same vapor trail without knowing anything about the standard theory of matter. Then all we would see would be little wispy lines that appeared and then vanished inside a glass bottle. In fact, our theories and beliefs influence even our ordinary perceptions. As you read this page, for example, you do not just see black scratches on white paper, which is all that an illiterate person might see. Instead, you see words that have meaning and sense. You see meaningful words instead of black scratches because of the beliefs and theories you have about what books and writing are. These beliefs and theories affect what you see when you look at this page.

Theories, then, can never be checked against some independently observed reality because our theories have already influenced what we observe before we observe it. Consequently, we are forced to check our theories by seeing how they fit in with all our other accepted theories and beliefs, including the theory-laden observations we make of reality. We can never escape this web of belief and theory. Because theories can be checked only against other theories, we say a scientific theory is true when it fits in with our other accepted theories and beliefs.

As Kuhn pointed out, science periodically undergoes "conceptual revolutions." For example, when Copernicus's new theory replaced the old theory that the sun revolves around the earth, this was a "conceptual revolution." Kuhn suggested that when a new theory replaces an old one, there may be no rational reason for saying that the new theory is better than the old one. Many conceptual relativists who have followed Kuhn have agreed with this suggestion. They have concluded that there are no grounds for saying that one conceptual framework is better than another. That is, we cannot say that one conceptual framework corresponds to reality better than another or that one gives us better predictions. Truth is nothing more than coherence with an accepted conceptual framework. When scientists abandon one framework and replace it with another, we often must attribute the change to nonrational causes and events.

Conceptual relativists, then, do not accept the realist view that true scientific theories are supposed to explain what the universe is like. Nor do they necessarily accept the instrumentalist view that true scientific theories should let us predict what will happen. Conceptual relativists hold that true scientific theories are theories that achieve whatever values are prized in the conceptual framework of the community.

Conceptual relativists do not believe that scientific theories are true in the sense that they correspond to a real world "out there." Nor do they believe that scientific theories are true in the sense that they are useful instruments for predicting the future. Conceptual relativists believe that a scientific theory is true if it coheres or fits in with the accepted beliefs and values—the conceptual framework—of a community of working scientists. Thus, conceptual relativism is similar to the coherence theory of truth.

We saw earlier that we can interpret truth in at least three ways: as correspondence, as coherence, and as pragmatic. We have seen now that we can also interpret truth in science in three ways: according to the realist view, the instrumentalist view, and the relativist view. These three ways of understanding truth in science are similar to the three views of truth we examined earlier in this chapter. Which of these is correct? No one can answer that question for you. Scientists and philosophers themselves are divided on this question. In fact, the question itself is a paradox. For in asking which of these three views of truth is correct, aren't you asking which of them is true? Yet doesn't each view interpret the meaning of truth in a different way? Truth in science, it has turned out, is much more complicated than it first appeared to be.

QUESTIONS

1. Some realists claim that through the progress of science some so-called unobservable theoretical entities such as the atom have become observable. For example, they point to "pictures" that scientists have taken of single atoms. This proves, they say, that they were right all along when they held that the theoretical entities of true theories really exist. How would an instrumentalist or a conceptual relativist answer this claim?

2. Can you think of any statements of science that you think we accept as true because they clearly correspond to reality? Can you think of any statements of science that you think we accept as true merely because they provide accurate predictions? Can you think of any statements of science that we probably accept as true merely because they cohere with other parts of science?

3. Is it possible that the three views of scientific truth—realist, instrumentalist, and conceptual relativist—are actually complementary rather than incompatible? Explain.

4. Does it really matter whether one or the other of these views of scientific truth is correct? What difference would it make in the way you see yourself if one of these views—say, the conceptual relativist view—turned out to be correct? What difference would it make in the way you see the world around you—the planets, the stars, the plant and animal species?

5. Psychology is the scientific study of human beings. If the instrumentalist view of scientific theory turned out to be correct, how would it change what you have learned about human beings from psychology? If the conceptual relativist view of scientific theory turned out to be correct, how would it change what you have learned from psychology?

6.4 Can Interpretations Be True?

Science is not the only area of our lives where truth is important but difficult to pin down. Truth is also crucial to us when we try to interpret books, poems, movies, scripture, and even one another. Think about how often you need to interpret the words and actions of others. When someone speaks to you, you need to interpret that person's *words*: What did she mean by that? When you see someone doing something, you interpret her *actions*: Why did she do that, and what is the meaning of what she did? When you read a poem or look at a movie, you need to interpret it: What is the poem or movie trying to say? When you go to church or read the Bible, you try to interpret the words of passages in scripture. When a lawyer or a judge looks at a statute or even the Constitution, she must interpret it to determine its meaning.

But when is an interpretation true? Suppose you chance upon this passage in the Bible: "You shall not lie with a male as with a woman; it is an abomination" (Leviticus, 18:22). What does it mean? Obviously, you say, it is pointing out that homosexual activities are immoral. Yet some biblical scholars say that this "obvious" interpretation is mistaken. Homosexual relations between males, they say, were part of the ritual practices of some of the religions that opposed Judaism when this text was written. What the text is really saying, then, is to avoid the ritual practices of foreign religions. So which interpretation is true? The "obvious" one that first occurred to you or the one that some biblical scholars have proposed?

Or take, instead, a poem, like William Blake's famous "The Tyger," written in 1794:

Tyger! Tyger! burning bright
In the forests of the night,
What immortal hand or eye
Could frame thy fearful symmetry?

In what distant deeps or skies
Burnt the fire of thine eyes?
On what wings dare he aspire?
What the hand dare seize the fire?

And what shoulder, and what art,
Could twist the sinews of thy heart?
And when thy heart began to beat,
What dread hand? and what dread feet?

What the hammer? what the chain?
In what furnace was thy brain?
What the anvil? what dread grasp
Dare its deadly terrors clasp?

When the stars threw down their spears,
And watered heaven with their tears,
Did he smile his work to see?
Did he who made the Lamb make thee?

Tyger! Tyger! burning bright
In the forests of the night,
What immortal hand or eye
Could frame thy fearful symmetry?

What does this poem mean? Some literary experts have argued that the Tyger is here a symbol of the evil self who "sustains its own life at the expense of its

> *Translation is like sailing from one island to another.*
>
> PAUL RICOEUR

fellow-creatures."[11] The "forests of the night," for Blake, symbolize the "fallen world"—that is, the material world where evil reigns. The Lamb is a symbol for Jesus Christ. The answer to the question Blake asks at the end is no: The God who made the Lamb did not make the evil in the heart of the predator self. Yet other critics argue that "There can be no doubt that *The Tyger* is a poem that celebrates the holiness of tigerness."[12] The word "'*forests*' suggests tall straight forms, a world that for all its terror has the orderliness of the tiger's stripes." Blake, they say, transforms the ferocity of the tiger into the symbol of goodness. At the same time the poem tries "to satirize the singlemindedness of the Lamb." Still other critics have claimed that the tiger in Blake's poem is both good and evil, and others that it is beyond good and evil. Yet others conclude that the poem "is a maze of questions in which the reader is forced to wander confusedly."[13] What is the true interpretation of the poem? Does it have a true interpretation?

Or take a legal text. The United States Constitution states in Amendment Fourteen, which Congress ratified in 1868, that "No State shall make or enforce any law which shall . . . deny to any person . . . the equal protection of the law." What is the true interpretation of this text? Some legal scholars say it clearly means that a state cannot support a preferential treatment program. A preferential treatment program gives preference to women or minorities over white males when applying for jobs or colleges. Such programs, they argue, do not treat white males as equal to women or minorities and thus "clearly" violate the meaning of the Constitution. On the other hand, some legal scholars have argued that women and minorities have been disadvantaged in the past. Preferential programs are needed now to make them more equal to white males. So, these scholars say, the true meaning of Amendment Fourteen clearly allows preferential treatment programs. Who is right? What is the true interpretation of the Constitution? Some might want to reply that the Supreme Court decides its true interpretation. But this only pushes the problem back a step. How should the judges of the Supreme Court decide which is the true interpretation?

Hermeneutics is the study of the interpretation of words and actions. The word comes from the name of the ancient Greek god Hermes, who carried messages from the gods up in heaven to mortals down on earth. The messages were transmitted through "oracles," humans with the ability to hear and report these messages. However, the messages of the gods weren't easy to understand. For example, Croesus, an ancient king of Lydia, was planning to start a war against the Persians.[14] He consulted an oracle at a temple in the Greek city of Delphi. Croesus asked what the outcome of a war against Cyrus would be. The oracle replied, "If Croesus marches against the Persians, he will bring down a mighty empire!" The oracle's words encouraged Croesus, and he immediately attacked the Persians. But the Persian forces defeated Croesus, marched into Lydia, and

[11] Kathleen Raine, "Who Made the Tyger," *Encounter*, June 1954, 50.

[12] E. D. Hirsch, *Innocence and Experience* (New Haven, CT: Yale University Press, 1964), 247–248.

[13] L. J. Swingle, "Answers to Blake's 'Tyger': A Matter of Reason or of Choice," *Concerning Poetry*, 2 (1970), 67.

[14] This story is recounted by the ancient historian Herodotus in his history of the Persian wars, I, 53.

dismantled Croesus's empire. The defeated Croesus returned to the oracle and bitterly complained that the prophecy turned out to be false. But the oracle replied, "Croesus is wrong to complain about the Oracle's prophecy. It said that if he marched against the Persians, he would bring down a mighty empire. And he did bring down an empire: his own." The words of the oracle had at least two interpretations. Unfortunately, Croesus chose the false interpretation.

Croesus's problem is the main problem in hermeneutics. What is the true interpretation of a person's words or actions? Is a true interpretation even possible? As the Greeks' experience with oracles suggests, hermeneutics was prompted by attempts to interpret the words of a god. But it was not the Greek gods that gave interpreters their hardest problems. Hermeneutics became a major concern for those who believed in the Judaic and Christian God.

SYMBOLIC INTERPRETATION AND INTENTION

For both Christianity and Judaism, the Bible contains the words of God because God inspired the writers to write these words. But like the Greek oracles, the words of the Bible can be interpreted in many different ways. Obviously, for Christians and Jews, it is crucial to know what the true interpretation of these sacred words is. How can a believer know what he or she must do if the Bible can be interpreted in many ways? Which interpretation should he or she live by?

During the Middle Ages, philosophers and theologians developed ever-new interpretations of passages in the Bible. Many felt that besides its literal meaning, a Bible passage could have deeper symbolic meanings. For example, the thirteenth-century philosopher-theologian Thomas Aquinas (1224–1274) held that a text could have many "spiritual" interpretations. And, he claimed, they could all be true.

> The first and basic meaning of a [biblical] text is the historical or literal meaning conveyed by the words themselves. But the things and events described by the literal meaning can also have a meaning. This is the spiritual meaning of the [biblical] text. . . . Now there are three kinds of spiritual meaning. First, things and events in the Old Testament can symbolize things and events in the New Testament. This is called the allegorical sense [of the Bible]. Second, the actions of Jesus Christ described or symbolized [in the Bible] express how we ought to live. This is the moral meaning [of the Bible]. Third, the things described in the Bible can symbolize what eternal glory [after death] will be like. This is the anagogical sense. So a word in the Bible can have several meanings.[15]

In some ways Aquinas's willingness to accept many true interpretations made the problem of interpretation worse. How can a believer know when an interpretation of the Bible is true, if there can be many interpretations? Aquinas's solution was simple. The Church decides which interpretations of the Bible are true and which are false. In particular, the Church decides which symbolic interpretations are true.

But doesn't this solution create even more problems? First, how is the Church itself supposed to decide which interpretations are true? How is it to

---

[15] Aquinas, *Summa Theologica*, I, Q. 1, a. 10, trans. and abridged by Manuel Velasquez.

choose among the many literal and symbolic interpretations that human creativity can devise? Setting the Church up as an authority just pushes the problem back one step. The difficulty of trying to sift through many symbolic interpretations to find the true ones suggests a deeper problem with symbolic interpretations. Aren't symbolic interpretations really examples of seeing what you want to see? Aren't symbolic interpretations arbitrary? Symbolic interpretations seem to read into a text whatever meaning the reader would like to see.

Two hundred years after Aquinas, the Protestant reformer Martin Luther rejected the whole idea of symbolic interpretations. There was, he said, only one true meaning of scripture, and that is the literal meaning.

The nineteenth-century philosopher Friedreich Schleiermacher (1768–1834) agreed. A text is a product of the history and culture of the person who wrote it, he argued. To interpret the text, we have to know the historical situation of the author. We have to figure out, in short, what the author was thinking and intending when he wrote whatever he wrote: "The language and the history of the time the writer was living in is the context within which individual texts have to be interpreted."

Schleiermacher is not the only one who argued that there is one true and literal interpretation of a text. The philosopher Wilhelm Dilthey (1833–1911) also argued that the true interpretation of a text is the meaning that the original human author intended. To find this original meaning, he claimed, we need to put ourselves in the place and time of the historical author and try to understand what he intended by the words he wrote. To understand the actions or words of another person, we must "relive" the life of the other person. This applies, he said, not only to interpreting words but also to interpreting anything that humans produce, including art, poetry, speeches, laws, and even human history.

Schleiermacher and Dilthey, like Aquinas, obviously embraced the correspondence theory of truth. A true interpretation is one that corresponds to what the original author of a poem, law, scripture passage, or work of art intended. But while Aquinas had looked for what God intended, Schleiermacher and Dilthey insisted we must look for what the historical human authors intended.

If someone says they're in love, I have to construct this feeling within myself so that I can understand it.

I. SAFRANSKI

Many scholars accept the ideas of Schleiermacher and Dilthey. Literary critics have carefully studied what life was like at the time a poet like Blake wrote to figure out what he intended the words of his poem to mean. Legal scholars have argued that to interpret a law—such as the Fourteenth Amendment of the Constitution—we need to get back to what those who originally passed the law intended it to say. And theologians have studied life in ancient Palestine to try to determine what the authors of the Bible meant by the words they used.

But there's another way to think about interpretation. Ask yourself this: Why is interpretation even needed? Why are there many possible ways of interpreting texts? Isn't the real problem the ambiguity of language? If the language and words that we use to express our meaning were perfectly clear and unambiguous, then would there even be a problem of interpretation? What if we could develop a language that is completely clear and unambiguous? Wouldn't this eliminate the possibility of different interpretations? Wouldn't an unambiguous language eliminate the need for hermeneutics?

WITTGENSTEIN AND THE IDEAL CLEAR LANGUAGE

The idea of an unambiguous language that people could interpret in only one way was first suggested by the seventeenth-century rationalist philisopher Gottfried Leibniz (1646–1716). Leibniz argued that we should strive to develop a perfect language in which we could express our ideas with complete clarity. In this perfect language, Leibniz claimed, "there will be no equivocations or amphibolies, and everything which will be said intelligibly in that language will be said with propriety."[16] Even disagreements over interpretations could be settled "by calculating" the true meaning in this perfect language.

Leibniz never completed his ideal language. But in the early part of the twentieth century, the Austrian philosopher Ludwig Wittgenstein (1889–1951) published a seventy-five page book titled *Tractatus-Logico-Philosophicus*. His book changed the course of philosophy. Wittgenstein claimed to provide the basics of the kind of ideal language that Leibniz had only dreamed about. In his book, Wittgenstein described an ideal language that, he claimed, could express all legitimate meanings unambiguously.

Reality, he argued, consists of facts, both complex facts and simple facts. The simplest facts are "atomic facts," and complex facts are built out of these atomic facts. The propositions of an ideal language, he said, will provide "pictures" of these facts. A proposition will correctly picture a fact when it has the same kind of "structure" as the fact. That is, a proposition that expresses a fact must have words that correspond to the parts of the fact, and the arrangement of the words must correspond to the arrangement of the parts of the facts. Wittgenstein, who wrote in an oracular fashion himself, expressed these points as follows:

> *What can be said, can be said clearly.*
> LUDWIG WITTGENSTEIN

The world is the totality of facts, not of things. . . .

The object is the fixed, the existent. . . .

In the atomic fact the objects are combined in a definite way.

The way in which objects hang together in the atomic fact is the structure of the atomic fact. . . .

We make to ourselves pictures of facts. . . .

The elements of the picture stand, in the picture, for the objects.

The picture consists in the fact that its elements are combined with one another in a definite way.

---

[16] Leibniz, "Preface to the General Science," in *Leibniz Selections*, ed. Philip P. Wiener (New York: Scribner's, 1951), 16.

> That the elements of the picture are combined with one another in a definite way, represents that the things are so combined with one another.

> This connection of the elements of the picture is called its structure.[17]

In an ideal language, Wittgenstein argues, the simplest atomic facts will be expressed by simple elementary propositions. Just as complex facts are made up of atomic facts, in an ideal language complex propositions will be made up of elementary propositions. With this ideal language, Wittgenstein claimed, all facts can be expressed in a clear and unambiguous way. In fact, wrote Wittgenstein, "Everything that can be thought of at all can be thought of clearly; everything that can be said can be said clearly."[18]

Wittgenstein's theory of language was, in effect, a hermeneutic. Wittgenstein held that the only legitimate meanings were those that could be expressed in his ideal language of facts. If a meaning could not be expressed or "spoken" in his ideal language, it was not legitimate. As he put it, "Whereof one cannot speak, thereof one must be silent."[19] The only true interpretations are those that can be spoken in an ideal language that refers only to facts.

Clearly, Wittgenstein had embraced a correspondence theory of truth. Propositions are true when they correspond to the facts. Meanings are legitimate only when they can be expressed in propositions that correspond to facts.

But as Wittgenstein got older, he abandoned his search for an ideal language of facts. He also left behind his allegiance to the correspondence theory of truth. And he again changed the course of philosophy.

Wittgenstein came to feel that his whole earlier approach to language had been wrong. It was a mistake, Wittgenstein argued in his later life, to think that language can serve a single purpose and express a single meaning. His idea that a language can provide an unambiguous picture of reality was based on this mistake. We must instead acknowledge that we use language for many different purposes and in many different human activities or "games." The meaning of language or a text cannot be isolated from our human activities. The meaning of a language or a text does not depend on the "facts" it pictures. Instead, the meanings depend on how people use them in the many different activities of life:

> But how many kinds of sentences are there? You say assertion, question, and command?—There are *countless* kinds, countless different kinds of use of what we call "symbols," "words," "sentences." And this multiplicity is not something fixed, given once for all; but new types of language, new language-games, as we may say, come into existence, and others become obsolete and get forgotten. . . . Here the term "language game" is meant to bring into prominence the fact that the *speaking* of language is part of any activity, or of a form of life.[20]

What Wittgenstein was saying is that there isn't any kind of ultimate metaphysical structure to the world. What there is, is human beings engaged in all kinds of activities.

STEPHEN TOULMIN

---

[17] Ludwig Wittgenstein, *Tractatus-Logico-Philosophicus*, 1.1 and 2.026–2.1512, quoted in *The Great Treasury of Western Thought*, ed. Mortimer J. Adler and Charles Van Doren (New York: R. R. Bowker, 1977), 403, 1267.

[18] Ibid., 4.116.

[19] Ibid., 6.57.

[20] Ludwig Wittgenstein, *Philosophical Investigations*, trans. G. E. M. Anscombe, 3rd ed. (New York: Macmillan, 1953), 11e.

These later views of Wittgenstein are vitally important for hermeneutics. Wittgenstein himself did not directly discuss hermeneutics. Nevertheless, his views have clear implications for us. First, if he is right, then the dream of a clear language was just that: a dream. Second, and more important, the meaning of words is not a fixed thing. So the true interpretation of a text is also not fixed. The meaning of a text arises from the meaning that people give it as they use it in their life activities. Meaning is use. The true interpretation of a text is the interpretation that people give it as they use it.

Clearly, in these later views Wittgenstein no longer holds the correspondence theory of truth. His view of truth is now much more pragmatic. For example, an interpretation of a scripture is true for a group of people if it is an interpretation that has a use in their forms of life. The same can be said for poetry and art. A true interpretation of a poem may be one that can enrich and give significance to the life of the reader. And the true interpretation of a law, such as the Fourteenth Amendment of the U.S. Constitution, depends on the needs and concerns of those who must use the law to order their society.

While Wittgenstein was developing his new views on meaning in England, European philosophers were also developing new views on meaning. Wittgenstein had developed his new views by rejecting his own, older view that language can have only one meaning. European philosophers developed their new views by rejecting the view that there is one true interpretation of a text. For example, Dilthey and Schleiermacher had said that the one true interpretation of a text is the meaning that the original author intended. But many European philosophers now objected that we cannot ever really know the intentions of the original author, especially if the author lived centuries ago in a different culture. The most important of these new European philosophers is the German philosopher Hans-Georg Gadamer (1900–   ).

GADAMER AND PREJUDICE

Gadamer argues that when a person tries to interpret someone's words, he must rely on his own personal experience and culture. Our culture consists of the values and beliefs of our time and our society. The culture that we absorb as we grow up is a "prejudice" that influences how we interpret someone else's words. For example, suppose that because of the way I was raised in my culture I believe in angels and devils. Then when I read a Bible story about how Jesus cast devils out of a man, I may interpret the story as literally true. But suppose I grew up in a culture that does not believe in devils. Then when I read this story I may interpret it as a story that just symbolizes that Jesus can overcome evil. My prior cultural beliefs will prejudice how I interpret the story. There is no way to rid ourselves completely of these prejudices, says Gadamer. We have to interpret the words and actions of people in terms of our own historical culture. We can try to understand and correct our prejudices. But we can never completely escape them.

Because each person interprets the meaning of a text on the basis of her own personal experience and culture, people living in different times and cultures must interpret texts differently. None of these interpretations is more true than the others. As Gadamer puts it, "a text is understood only if it is understood in a different way every time."[21] A text, then, does not have a single true interpretation. Instead, the true meaning of a text depends on who is reading it and when and where they are reading it. A text can have as many true interpretations as there are people who read it in different cultures:

> An inevitable difference between the interpreter and the author [is] created by the historical distance between them. Every age has to understand a transmitted text in its own way, for the text is part of the whole of the tradition in which the age takes an objective interest and in which it seeks to understand itself. The real meaning of a text, as it speaks to the interpreter, does not depend on the contingencies of the author and whom he originally wrote for. It certainly is not identical with them for it is always partly determined also by the historical situation of the interpreter and hence by the totality of the objective course of history.[22]

However, Gadamer does not think that we can just dream up interpretations and pin them on texts. Instead, says Gadamer, interpreting a text is like talking to a person. We speak, and then the other person speaks, then with a better understanding of the person, we speak again. Then the other person also speaks again, and the process continues. In the same way, Gadamer insists, we have to carry on a dialogue with the text. First, we interpret the text in terms of the prejudices and concerns of our culture. Then we try to understand what new things the text itself is trying to say and what it might have meant in its culture. When we do this, our own cultural prejudices change and get closer to the meaning of the text. Then we use our newly informed cultural prejudices to come up with a better interpretation of the text. Then we try again to understand the text itself and its meaning in its own culture. Again our cultural prejudices change, coming closer to the meaning of the text. As we continue this dialogue, we keep developing better and more true interpretations of the text. Still, we never completely get rid of our prejudices. Our interpretations are always a combination of our own cultural prejudices and what the text was trying to say in its culture.

Gadamer, then, seems to hold to a coherence view of truth. The true interpretation is the one that best coheres with both the prejudices of our own culture and what we believe the text meant in its own culture. Truth emerges from the union of these two cultural "horizons." But there are many true interpretations, for different interpretations will fit in with the prejudices of people living in different cultures and times.

Think of the implications. A poem like Blake's "The Tyger" has no single true meaning. In particular, its true meaning is not the meaning that Blake intended. Instead it means whatever you, the reader, interpret it to mean in terms of your own cultural values and beliefs and what the poem seems to be trying to say. A law, such as the Constitution's Fourteenth Amendment, has no single true interpretation. It means whatever we, today, interpret it to mean in terms both of the current cultural values of U.S. society and what the amend-

Hermeneutics is the art of being able to listen. Learning to listen is difficult.

HANS GADAMER

A text breaks away from its author and takes on a life of its own.

PAUL RICOEUR

[21] Hans-Georg Gadamer, *Truth and Method,* trans. and ed. Garrett Barden and John Cumming (New York: Seabury Press, 1975), 275.
[22] Ibid., 274–275.

ment seems to have meant in the past. And a scripture text has no single true meaning. It means whatever the believers of each age interpret it to mean in light of their own cultural concerns and what the scripture seems to have meant when it was written.

Is Gadamer right? Is there no single true interpretation of our words and actions? Many people believe so. But not everyone. Some thinkers, like E. D. Hirsch, argue that Gadamer and his followers have confused the "meaning" of a text with its "significance."[23] The meaning of a text is what the author intended to convey literally with the words that he used. The significance of a text is the implications the text has for our actions and lives. Although the significance of a text can change from one person to another, Hirsch claims, its meaning remains the same. To find this fixed true meaning of a text, he argues, we have to do what Dilthey suggested: We have to discover what the author intended. A true interpretation is the one that corresponds with the author's intention.

We are left with a choice that in the end comes down to choosing among the theories of truth. Aquinas, Schleiermacher, and Dilthey tell us that the true interpretation is the one that corresponds with the intentions of the author, whether that author is a person or God. Wittgenstein suggests that any interpretation is true if it is one that gives pragmatic significance to our forms of life. And Gadamer tells us that a true interpretation is one that coheres with the prejudices of our culture and what we believe that a text meant in its own culture.

QUESTIONS

1. Discuss the meaning or point of a movie, novel, or poem with your friends. Which theory of interpretation do you see them using? Which theory do most of them seem to use? What is the theory of truth that they seem to be using?

2. Find an interesting novel, play, poem, or short story that scholars have interpreted in many different ways. (You might ask your English or literature instructor to recommend one, or you might try one of these: Sophocles' *Oedipus the King*, Shakespeare's *Hamlet*, Arthur Miller's *Death of a Salesman*.) Read some of the interpretations of the work you have chosen. What theory do these interpretations seem to be using? Do you think that novels, plays, poems, or short stories can have true and false interpretations? How do you tell the difference between a true interpretation and a false one?

3. Which theory of interpretation do you think is most appropriate for interpreting poetry or other works of literature? For interpreting a passage in a scripture or holy book? For interpreting a law? Why?

4. Can each of the various theories of interpretation explained above be used to interpret the *actions* of people? Explain why or why not.

5. Can the various theories of interpretation be used to interpret the meaning of a dream? Why or why not? Can dreams be true or false? Why or why not?

---

[23] E. D. Hirsch, *Validity in Interpretation* (New Haven, CT: Yale University Press, 1967).

6. Think of a dream that you had but whose meaning you could not interpret. For example, suppose that you dream that your father took you up high to the roof of a house and dropped you, and that down below your mother caught you in her arms. You go to a psychologist who tells you that your dream means that deep down you feel that your father really hated you and that only your mother really cared for you. Which theory of interpretation could she be using? Can interpretations of dreams be true or false? Why or why not?

7. Notice that when you interpret a text you have to proceed by interpreting one word or phrase or sentence at a time. Yet the meaning of the word, phrase, or sentence cannot become clear until you have interpreted the whole text. The meaning of the whole text has to influence the meaning of each of its parts. At the same time, you cannot understand the meaning of the whole text until you understand the meaning of each part. The meaning of each of the parts has to influence the meaning of the whole text. So you cannot understand the meaning of each part until you have understood the whole, and you cannot understand the whole until you have understood the parts. Does this circularity mean that it is really impossible to interpret a text? Explain why or why not.

6.5 Chapter Summary and Conclusions

We opened this chapter by noting that knowledge is at least warranted, true belief. We discussed the various modes of warrantability as they apply to various kinds of statements. We then discussed three theories of truth: the correspondence, coherence, and pragmatic theories. And we explored three related views of truth in science. The main points of this chapter are the following:

1. Knowledge is at least warranted, true belief, but Gettier examples show that something more is required for genuine knowledge (6.1).

2. *Warrantability* is another name for "justification" or "evidence" (6.1).

3. Warrantability depends on whether the statement to be analyzed is logical, semantic, or empirical (6.1).

4. The three traditional theories of truth are the correspondence, coherence, and pragmatic theories (6.2).

5. The correspondence theory of truth claims that the truth of a statement depends on its relation to the world of facts: A statement is true if and only if it corresponds to the facts. Objection: If we know only our sensory experiences, how can we ever get outside them to verify what reality actually is? What does correspondence mean? Precisely what is a fact (6.2)?

There are four sorts of men:
He who knows not and knows
*   not he knows not: he is a*
*   fool—shun him;*
He who knows not and knows
*   he knows not: he is*
*   simple—teach him;*
He who knows and knows not
*   he knows: he is asleep—*
*   wake him.*
He who knows and knows he
*   knows: he is wise—*
*   follow him.*

LADY BURTON

6. The coherence theory of truth claims that the truth of a statement depends on its relation to other statements: A statement is true if and only if it coheres or fits in with that system of statements that we already accept. Objection: Coherence is no guarantee of truth. If the first statements are false, they can produce a coherent system of consistent error. There is much disagreement even among idealists over first judgments (6.2).

7. The pragmatic theory claims that truth depends on what works. A statement is true if and only if it effectively solves a practical problem and thereby experientially satisfies us. The pragmatist sees the human as needing to use the practical consequences of beliefs to determine their truth and validity. Objection: There's no necessary connection between truth and workability. Truth is rendered a psychological, not an epistemological, concern, and it can become relative (6.2).

8. There are three views of truth in science: the instrumentalist, realist, and conceptual relativist views. The instrumentalist view is similar to the pragmatic theory, the realist view to the correspondence theory, and the conceptual relativist view to the coherence theory (6.3).

9. Truth is important for hermeneutics, which studies the interpretation of people's words and actions. For Aquinas, scripture has many true symbolic interpretations. For Schleiermacher and Dilthey, the only true interpretation is the one intended by the historical author. Wittgenstein abandoned his early ideal of a clear language of facts and proposed that the meaning of words depends on how they are used, so words can have many true interpretations. For Gadamer, an interpretation emerges from uniting our cultural "prejudices" with what the text was trying to say in its own culture, so there are many true interpretations of a text (6.4).

In the final analysis, no single theory—correspondence, coherence, or pragmatic—provides a complete solution to the problem of truth. Each has shortcomings and strengths. Equally important, each theory plays a part in the way we understand truth in the search for and discovery of self.

In everyday life, we frequently use truth as correspondence. From our earliest days in school, we are rewarded for reporting things "as they are"—Paris is the capital of France; two hydrogen atoms combine with one oxygen atom to form water. This is the primary way of gleaning information about the world. The correspondence theory also underlies what we mean by truth in relation to the quantifiable aspects of the self—height, weight, blood pressure, body temperature, and so on.

But not all aspects of self are so easily quantified. In the complex area of personal experience, for example, the correspondence theory is not so useful. How would you verify the statement "That person loves me"? You cannot verify it as you can verify "I have a temperature." You would probably evaluate it on the basis of the person's behavior toward you: "If that person loves me, would that person have said that?" In other words, you would understand truth here in terms of coherence, asking if the person's actions were consistent with loving somebody. Of course, you would be making an assumption about what loving is.

Every man seeks for truth, but God only knows who has found it.

LORD CHESTERFIELD

Our assumptions frequently distort our views of self and the world. For example, a man who is ashamed to cry publicly because it isn't manly may be acting consistently with an assumption that is warping his personality. Likewise, a woman who refuses to call a man for a date because women shouldn't be aggressive is acting consistently with an assumption that may be inhibiting her. The sources of our assumptions are less relevant here than the fact that we unconsciously measure our concepts, feelings, attitudes, and actions against them as if they were self-evident truths. Thus, we do use the coherence theory of truth, and for this reason it is crucial that our first judgments be accurate. This caution is especially applicable to judgments concerning the self or human nature.

You might use the pragmatic theory to find out whether a particular individual loves you by asking what practical difference the person's loving or not loving you makes in the person's life. Does it affect how the person feels or thinks, what the person desires, and how the person behaves? You might also ask the same questions of yourself. Suppose that even after you answer these questions you are undecided. The pragmatic theory recognizes the nonmental aspect of the self, which can and should influence decisions in cases like these. We often listen to the reasons of the heart that reason knows little about, to paraphrase the seventeenth-century French philosopher Blaise Pascal.

Thus, the correspondence, coherence, and pragmatic theories of truth can work together. Truth in many cases might be conceived as that characteristic of a statement which corresponds to a fact (correspondence), but when we cannot determine the fact, we must rely on how consistent that statement or judgment is with established truth (coherence) or how useful its consequences are (pragmatism). Again, truth might be conceived as a property of statements that have useful consequences (pragmatism), but the most useful consequence of a statement is having it turn out to correspond to the facts (correspondence) or to be consistent with other accepted truths (coherence).

Perhaps you can see even better ways of relating these three theories into a more or less satisfactory whole. Or perhaps you will conclude that only one of the theories is satisfactory and that the others must be rejected. We have seen that while the correspondence theory implies that objective truths exist, both the coherence and the pragmatic theories imply that truth is relative to what groups accept. These implications may attract us to or repel us from one or the other of the theories. The objectivity of the correspondence theory may attract you if you are concerned with holding that some claims are objectively true and others are objectively false no matter what any group accepts. The objectivity of the correspondence theory seems necessary for those who want to take a stand on the pressing social issues that confront our society. On the other hand, the relativity of the coherence and pragmatic theories will be more attractive for those who seek tolerance and open-mindedness. The relativity of the coherence and pragmatic theories of truth seems more suitable for those who believe in "live and let live," even where seemingly contemptible views are involved.

Whatever one decides about truth, however, it is clear that the theories can be the source of helpful and useful ways of understanding the truth about the self and its relationship to the world of knowledge. The theories can also clarify for us what is involved in taking a stand — or refusing to take a stand — on the issues of the day.

6.6 HISTORICAL SHOWCASE

Kant

In the last chapter we saw how Hume's empiricism led philosophy into the dead end of skepticism. If Hume's radical empiricism is accepted, then we can never hope to learn the truth about ourselves, God, or the universe.

In this chapter we showcase a philosopher who claimed to have found a way around Hume's skepticism and who, in doing so, revolutionized our views about knowledge and truth. This is the eighteenth-century philosopher Immanuel Kant.

Immanuel Kant is regarded by many as the greatest of all philosophers, especially in the field of epistemology. His unique contribution was to argue that the world of our experience is a world that our own mind constructs. Our mind can indeed know the truth about the world around us, he argued, because that world is constructed by the mind itself.

We showcase Kant in this chapter because of the radical and profound contributions he made to our conceptions of knowledge and truth. But reading Kant will also allow us to see how his revolutionary views about knowledge influenced his views on morality and God. Kant, too, exemplifies how our epistemological views affect our positions on other philosophical issues.

Although he revolutionized philosophy, Kant lived a very ordinary life. He spent all of his eighty years (1724–1804) in the small town in which he was born: Königsberg (now Kaliningrad, Russia). There he grew up, and there he went to college, supporting himself in part by his winnings from playing pool with other students. Kant remained in Königsberg after graduating, eventually becoming a teacher in the local university. As a teacher, Kant came to schedule his activities so precisely that neighbors used to set their clocks when he passed their houses on his daily afternoon walk. Although Kant remained a bachelor all of his life, he had a number of close women friends and had a reputation for being a funny, witty, and entertaining host at the dinner parties he frequently had.

Although Kant never left his birthplace, his books put him in touch with all the intellectual currents of the eighteenth century. He was well acquainted with the tremendous new discoveries in the natural sciences and was especially impressed with Newton's discoveries in physics. But when Kant came across the writings of Hume, these discoveries seemed threatened. For Hume argued that our so-called scientific knowledge is not rationally justified. In particular, he pointed out that the cause-and-effect laws of science go beyond the evidence scientists have for them. Scientists observe a *few times* that certain events have been conjoined *in the past,* and they conclude that those kinds of events *must always* cause each other *in the future.* But how do scientists know that events must always be causally connected in the future as in the past?

Kant realized that Hume's objection was devastating. If Hume was correct, then all our scientific knowledge was unjustified. Moreover, Kant soon discovered that other areas of knowledge also contained judgments that went beyond the evidence of our senses:

> I openly confess that my recollection of David Hume was the very thing which many years ago first interrupted my dogmatic slumber and gave my investigations in the field of speculative philosophy a quite new direction. I was far from following him in the conclusions at which he arrived. . . .
>
> I therefore first tried to see whether Hume's objection could not be put into a general form. I soon found that the concept of the connection of cause

and effect was by no means the only concept by which the understanding thinks the connection of things *a priori* [that is, independently of experience].[1]

Kant found three areas of knowledge in which our statements about the world go beyond the evidence provided by our sensory experience:

1. In the sciences of geometry and arithmetic. For example:

"The shortest distance between two points must always be a straight line."

"The square of the hypotenuse of a right-angle triangle must always equal the sum of the squares of the other two sides."

"The sum of 798 and 857 must always equal 1655."

2. In the natural sciences. For example:

"All events must always have a cause."

3. In philosophical metaphysics. For example:

"There must exist a God that causes the universe."

Kant termed these *synthetic* statements to indicate that each gives us genuine information about the world around us. For example, geometry tells us that the world will always obey the law that the square of the hypotenuse of right triangles equals the sum of the squares of the other two sides, while the natural sciences tell us that all events must have a cause. By contrast, Kant used the term *analytic* to refer to statements that merely give us information about the meanings of words, such as "Bachelors are unmarried males."

Kant also called the statements in the list *a priori*, pointing out two features of such statements: First, as Hume said, these statements go beyond what we can establish through our sensory experience. For example, we could never check *all* right triangles, yet geometry says the square of their hypotenuses *always* equals the sum of the squares of the other two sides. Second, we establish that these statements *must* be true by relying on our thought processes. The laws of geometry, for example, are established in the mind. A priori statements, then, are necessary and universal: They state something

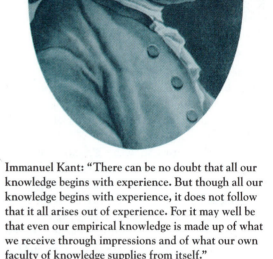

Immanuel Kant: **"There can be no doubt that all our knowledge begins with experience. But though all our knowledge begins with experience, it does not follow that it all arises out of experience. For it may well be that even our empirical knowledge is made up of what we receive through impressions and of what our own faculty of knowledge supplies from itself."**

that we know by mental processes *must* be true and that *always* holds. By contrast, Kant used the term *a posteriori* to refer to statements that can be established by sensory observations, such as "This room is empty" and "The sky above is blue." A posteriori statements are neither necessary nor universal.

But how can we know a priori propositions about the world without going outside of our minds? For example, how do we know that the outer world must always obey the laws of geometry when we can establish these laws completely within the mind? How do we know that every event must always have a cause when we have not examined every event? Is Hume correct in saying that such synthetic a priori statements are unjustified?

> Now the proper problem of pure reason is contained in the question: How are *a priori* synthetic judgments possible? . . .

---

[1] Immanuel Kant, *Prolegomena to Any Future Metaphysics*, trans. Lewis White Beck (New York: Bobbs-Merrill, 1950), 8.

Among philosophers, David Hume came nearest to envisaging this problem, but still he was very far from conceiving it with sufficient definiteness and universality. He occupied himself exclusively with the synthetic proposition regarding the connection of an effect with its cause, and he believed himself to have shown that such an *a priori* proposition is entirely impossible. . . . If he had envisaged our problem in all its universality, . . . he would then have recognized that, according to his own argument, pure mathematics, which certainly contains *a priori* synthetic propositions, would also not be possible. . . .

In the solution of our above problem, then, we are at the same time deciding as to the possibility of the employment of pure reason in establishing and developing all those sciences which contain *a priori* knowledge of objects, and have therefore to answer the questions: How is pure mathematics possible? How is pure science of nature possible? . . . How is metaphysics . . . possible?[2]

To save our knowledge from Hume's skepticism, Kant had to show that' we are justified in making statements that give us real information about the world but are established completely within the mind. To solve that problem, Kant embarked on what he called "a critique of pure reason"—an investigation of what our minds can know apart from the senses.

Kant began his investigation by granting Hume's view of our senses. Hume pointed out that all our knowledge of the world begins with sensations within us: colors, shapes, sounds, tastes, feels, smells. The senses, Hume said, provide us with a continual stream of endlessly changing

> perceptions which succeed each other with an inconceivable rapidity and are in a perpetual flux and movement. . . . The mind is a kind of theater, where several perceptions successively make their appearance, pass, re-pass, glide away, and mingle in an infinite variety of postures and situations.[3]

But Kant noticed something Hume had missed. It is true that all we receive from the senses are the sensations within us. Yet we do not *experience* a mere display of sensations within us. When I open my eyes, I do not experience changing sensations of light and colors playing in my vision. Instead, I see *objects* that appear to be *outside* of me. For example, when I look down, I see not a squarish blob of whiteness but the white page of a book a few inches away. Somehow, the sensations (colors and shapes) that continually play in my vision appear to me as objects outside of me.

The same is true of my other senses. They, too, provide only a stream of sensations within me. But I experience them as belonging to particular objects outside of me. For example, I do not merely sense ringing, booming, rustling sound sensations in my hearing. Instead, I hear noises that seem to come from some particular place in the room: perhaps a rustling noise from the pages of my book or a voice from a particular person in front of me. Each sensation of sound, feel, and smell appears to be the sound, feel, and smell of objects outside me.

Kant argued that somehow our mind takes these many separate sensations and *organizes* them into objects that appear to be outside ourselves, in space. It is as if my mind carries within it a three-dimensional representation of space, and every sensation is given a position in this mental image of space.

In fact, Kant argues, we could not experience objects as being outside of us without this three-dimensional representation of space in our minds. Even to perceive objects as outside of ourselves, we *already* have to know what outside is—that is, we have to know what space is. Moreover, although we can imagine an empty space without objects, we cannot imagine an object that is not in space. This also proves, according to Kant, that our mental representation of space has to be in our minds prior to our experience of objects:

> Space is not an empirical concept which has been derived from outer experiences. For in order that certain sensations be referred to something outside me (that is, to something in another region of space from that in which I find myself), and, similarly, in order that I may be able to represent them as outside and alongside one another, and . . . as in different places, the representation of space also must be

---

[2] Immanuel Kant, *Critique of Pure Reason*, trans. Norman Kemp Smith (New York: St. Martin's, 1929; original work published 1781), B19, B22.
[3] David Hume, *A Treatise of Human Nature*, ed. L. A. Selby-Bigge (Oxford: Clarendon Press, 1894), 252–253.

presupposed. The representation of space cannot, therefore, be . . . obtained from the relations of outer . . . [experience]. On the contrary, this outer experience is itself possible at all only through that representation.

Space is a necessary *a priori* representation which underlies all outer perceptions. We can never represent to ourselves the absence of space, though we can quite well think of it as empty of objects. It must therefore be regarded as the condition of the possibility of . . . [sensory experiences], and not as . . . [something] dependent on them.[4]

Space, then, is merely a mental representation that helps us organize our sensations so that they appear to us to be objects outside of us. There is nothing more to space than this mental image. Space does not exist independently of us outside our mind:

Space does not represent any property of things in themselves, nor does it represent them in their relation to one another. That is to say, space does not represent any determination that attaches to objects themselves and which remains even when abstraction has been made of all the subjective conditions of perception.

It is therefore solely from the human standpoint that we can speak of space, of extended objects, etc. . . . This predicate can be ascribed to things only insofar as they appear to us, that is, only to objects of sensibility [of the senses].[5]

Kant's view—that space does not exist outside the mind—may seem strange. But his view provides the key to one of his major questions: How do we know that the laws of geometry must hold true for all objects in the world even though these laws are established within the mind? Kant's solution is simple and brilliant.

First, he argues, the laws of geometry are nothing more than the laws of the mental image of space that is in our minds. That is why we can establish the laws of geometry by simply examining our inner image of space without having to examine the outer world.

Second, Kant points out, the mind puts every object we experience into this mental representation of space. All our sensations are organized by the mind into objects within its representation of space so that they appear to us as if they exist in space outside. Every object we experience will have to appear within this mental image and therefore must obey its laws. Since the laws of geometry are the laws of our mental representation, every object we experience will have to obey the laws of geometry.

Thus, Kant provided a solution to the problem that had puzzled philosophers for centuries: How do we know without going outside our minds that all objects obey the laws of geometry? The only solution, Kant held, is that we establish the laws of geometry completely a priori by simply looking within our own minds' three-dimensional image of space. We know all the objects we perceive will obey these laws because the mind places all objects within this mental image so that for us they are in space.

Using similar arguments, Kant showed that all our experience must obey the laws of arithmetic. The laws of arithmetic, he said, are the laws of time: they are laws about how units follow one after another, just like numbers follow one after another.

But where do we get our image of time? Just as we organize sensations by inserting them in space, we also organize them by inserting them in time. So time is also one of the structures of the mind. Time is like a long filing system we use to organize our sensations by placing each one at a certain point in the system. Since the image of time is within us, we can know its laws just by examining it. And since the mind makes everything we experience appear to be in time, everything must obey the laws of time. And these laws are the laws of arithmetic.

So the synthetic a priori statements of geometry and arithmetic are justified. Although these statements give us information about the structure of the world, we do not have to examine every object in the world to know these statements hold true of everything we will ever perceive. The synthetic a priori statements of geometry and arithmetic can be established by simply examining our

---

[4] Kant, *Critique*, B38, B39. (Note: The word *intuition* has been replaced here and elsewhere in the translations that follow with the much more familiar term *perception*.)
[5] Ibid., B42–B43.

inner images of time and space. Space and time are merely structures within the mind in which we position the objects our mind makes out of the sensations it receives, so that to our minds these objects exist in space and time.

But Kant also had to show that the synthetic a priori statements of the natural sciences were justified. In particular, he had to show that the causal laws of science were justified. How did he do this? Kant's solution to this problem is remarkably similar to his solution to the problem of geometry and mathematics. Kant points out that the mind organizes its sensations so that they appear to us as objects that change through time. How does the mind do this? The mind organizes its sensations into such independent objects by using twelve rules or "categories." The most important of these rules or categories turns out to be the basic law underlying the natural sciences: that all perceived events must have a cause. So just as we know that every object we experience will be organized in space and time, we can also be sure that every event we experience will be causally related to other events. How exactly did Kant prove this? Kant's argument is difficult, but with a bit of work it can be understood.

Kant first points out that our sensations appear to us to be of independent objects that last through time and that change. For example, during the time I look at this book, I feel that I am seeing the same book. My sensations appear to me to be of an object that lasts through time. And as I turn its pages, the same book appears to me to be changing.

To make my sensations appear to be changing objects, Kant says, the mind has to bring its sensations together in three ways. First, the mind has to receive or "apprehend" the many separate sensations provided by the senses. For example, each separate moment I look at the changing white book, my senses produce new and different sensations of white color. To keep perceiving the book, then, I have to keep receiving all of these separate sensations. Second, the mind has to remember the past sensations. For example, in perceiving the book, I have to keep in mind the past sensations of white, as I receive new sensations. If I continually forgot the past sensations, it would be as though a new book were continually appearing before me each moment. Third, the mind has to connect or relate the later sensations to the earlier ones. That is, the mind has to recognize that the earlier sensations and the later ones are sensations of the same object. For example, I must recognize that my later, slightly different sensations of the book are sensations of the same book I saw earlier. Otherwise, the earlier and later sensations would appear to me as many separate images of different books floating in my memory. This recognition or connection of earlier and later sensations is what finally makes me feel that I am seeing the same book but that it is changing through time:

> Each perception [of an object] is made up of a multiplicity [of sensations]. . . . In order to change this multiplicity [of separate sensations] into a single thing [an object], it is necessary first to run through and collect the multiplicity [of sensations]. This act I call the "synthesis of apprehension." . . .
>
> But if I were always to drop out of thought the earlier sensations . . . , and did not reproduce them [in my memory] while advancing to the next ones, then a complete perception [of an object] would never form. . . . The synthesis of apprehension is therefore inseparably connected with [what I will call] the "synthesis of reproduction."
>
> [Moreover,] if we were not conscious that what we are thinking of now is the same as what we thought a moment before, all reproduction in the series of perceptions would be in vain. Each perception would . . . be a new one. . . . The multiplicity could never form a whole, because it would not have that unity that [my] consciousness alone can give it [by recognizing that what I perceive now is the same as what I perceived earlier].[6]

But the mind's ability to collect sensations into unified objects that change through time would not be possible unless the mind itself also lasted through time. Suppose, for example, that I am looking at a book and receiving new sensations of white color each passing moment. If the later sensations are to be connected to the earlier ones, the

---

[6]Immanuel Kant, *Kritik Reinen Vernunft* [*Critique of Pure Reason*] (Germany: Johann Friedrich Hartknoch, 1981), A99–A103. This translation is by Manuel Velasquez.

same mind has to receive the earlier and the later ones. This means my mind has to last through time: It has to last through the earlier and later sensations. Thus, the process of receiving, remembering, and connecting sensations into objects that last through time requires a mind that also lasts through time. The unification of sensations into objects requires a "unified" mind that connects sensations:

> [But] there can be in us no kind of knowledge, no connection or unifying of one bit of knowledge with another, unless there is a unified consciousness which precedes all the data of perception. . . . This pure original unchanging consciousness I call "transcendental apperception."[7]

The mind, then, is a single consciousness that remains the same through time, contrary to Hume's claim that the mind is only a bundle of disconnected sensations. In fact, Kant argues, the mind *must* connect its sensations because it must bring all these separate sensations into itself:

> If we want to discover the internal foundation of this unifying of perceptions . . ., we must begin with pure [transcendental] apperception. Sensations would be nothing to us, and would not concern us in the least, if they were not received into our [unified] consciousness. . . . Knowledge is impossible in any other way. We are conscious *a priori* of our own enduring identity with regard to all perceptions we know. Our enduring identity is a necessary condition for us to have these perceptions. For perceptions could not be perceptions of anything for me unless they . . . could at least be connected together into [my] one consciousness. This principle stands firm *a priori,* and may be called the "transcendental principle of the unity" of all the multiplicity of our perceptions (and therefore also of sensation).[8]

What Kant is saying here is that our mind connects and unifies its sensations because it *has to.* It has to connect them together because the many sensations my senses produce must all enter one mind: my own single mind. But in order to enter into my one mind, they have to be brought together into one.

As Kant says, this point—that the mind *has to* unify its sensations—is crucial. If the mind has to unify its sensations into objects, then we know that the connections the mind imposes on objects are necessary.

What kinds of connections does the mind make between objects? Kant argues that there are twelve kinds of connections or "categories" that the mind must impose on its sensations. Only the most important of these, the relation of cause and effect, will concern us here.

Kant tries to show that the mind *must* impose causal relationships on its sensations if they are to appear as objects that change independently of us. Kant begins his argument by pointing out that changes we perceive can follow one another in an order that I can determine or in an order that is fixed. But changes whose order I determine are not changes in independent objects outside of me; they are merely changes in me. For example, if I look first at the roof of a house and then at the windows, the order of my perceptions is determined by my own will. I can change the order by simply looking first at the windows and then at the roof. So these changes in my perceptions are merely changes in *me*. They are not independent changes in the *objects* outside of me. On the other hand, changes whose order is fixed or "necessary" are changes that I see as changes in independent objects outside of me. For example, if I see a boat being carried down a river by the current, I will first perceive the boat upriver, and then I will perceive the boat downstream. The order of these perceptions cannot be determined by my own will: I cannot change the order. So I know that the changes in my perceptions of the boat are changes in the *objects* outside of me, not merely changes in *me*. And I know this only because the order of these changes is fixed by necessary causal laws and not by me. So if our sensations are to appear as objects that change independently of ourselves, they must be related by causal laws:

> The Principle of the succession of time, according to the Law of Causality: All changes take place accord-

[7] Ibid., A107.
[8] Ibid., A116.

ing to the law of connection between cause and effect.

Proof: The apprehension of the multiplicity of phenomena is always successive. The perceptions of the parts [of objects] follow one upon another. . . . Thus, for instance, the apprehension of the multiplicity in the phenomenal appearance of a house that stands before me is successive. . . . Every apprehension of an event is [similarly] . . . a perception following on another perception. But as this applies to all synthesis of apprehension, as in the phenomenal appearance of a house, that apprehension would not be different from any other.

But I observe that if in a phenomenon which contains an event I call the antecedent state of perception A, and the subsequent B, B can only follow A in my apprehension, while the perception A can never follow B, but can only precede it. I see, for instance, a ship gliding down a stream. My perception of its place below follows my perception of its place higher up in the course of the stream, and it is impossible in the apprehension of this phenomenon that the ship should be perceived first below and then higher up. We see, therefore, that the order in the succession of perceptions in our apprehension is here determined, and our apprehension regulated by that order. In the former example of a house my perceptions could begin with the apprehension of the roof and end in the basement, or begin below and end above; they could apprehend the manifold of the empirical perception from right to left or from left to right. There was therefore no determined order in the succession of these perceptions. . . . [But] in the apprehension of an event there is always a rule which makes the order of successive perceptions necessary. . . . Thus only can I be justified in saying, not only of my apprehension, but of the phenomenon itself, that there exists in it a succession, which is the same as to say that I cannot arrange the apprehension otherwise than in that very order. . . .

If therefore experience teaches us that something happens, we must always presuppose that something precedes on which it follows by rule. Otherwise I could not say of the object that it followed, because its following in my apprehension only, without being determined by rule in reference to what precedes, would not justify us in admitting an objective following. It is therefore always with reference to a rule by which phenomena as they follow, that is as they happen, are determined by an antecedent state, that I can give an objective character to my subjective syn-

thesis (of apprehension); nay, it is under this supposition only that an experience of anything that happens becomes possible.[9]

Thus, Kant proved that all events in the world we experience have to be causally connected. Let us review the steps of his argument. First, Kant showed that the mind connects ("synthesizes") its sensations into objects that last through time. It does this through apprehension, reproduction, and recognition. Second, this connecting of sensations into objects shows that our mind is unified. Third, since the mind is unified, it *must* connect its sensations together. Fourth, one of the connections the mind must impose on its sensations is the connection of cause and effect, for our sensations would not seem to us to be sensations of independently changing objects unless they were causally connected to one another.

Hume, then, was wrong. Hume said that the laws of the sciences are not well founded, in particular the laws of causality: We have no evidence that events must always be causally connected to one another. However, Kant proved that all events we experience in the world outside of us *must* be connected by causal laws. For that world is a world that the mind puts together out of its sensations by bringing these sensations together into a single mind. To bring sensations together so that they seem to be sensations of independently changing objects, the mind must connect them by causal relations. The mind, that is, *must* use the category of cause and effect to connect our sensations so that they appear to us as the independently changing world of trees, oceans, mountains, and stars that we see around us. Only by recognizing that we construct the world in our mind in this way, Kant says, can we escape Hume's skepticism about the causal laws of science.

Kant called the world as it appears in our minds the phenomenal world and distinguished it from the noumenal world. The noumenal world is the collection of things as they exist in themselves apart from our perception of them in our mind.

---

[9] Immanuel Kant, *Critique of Pure Reason*, trans. Friedrich Max Müller (New York: Macmillan, 1896), 774, 155–160.

Clearly, we can never know what the noumenal world is like: All we can know is the phenomenal world of things as they appear to us after they have been organized by the mind.

What about Hume's skepticism about God? Reluctantly, Kant agreed that we cannot *prove* that there is a God. The cosmological proofs for God, Kant pointed out, say that God must exist because God had to "cause" the universe. But the only causality in the universe is the causality our own minds put there; the concept of a cause is merely a category of the mind, nothing more. So we cannot appeal to causality to prove that God exists. Other metaphysical arguments for the existence of God, Kant held, make similar illegitimate use of concepts that are merely categories of the mind. None of these metaphysical arguments are valid proofs of the existence of God.

But Kant's views on God do not end here. Kant attempted to show that the existence of God should be accepted on the basis of our moral commitments. To understand this aspect of Kant, we must examine his views on morality.

Kant argued that a person is moral to the extent that he or she follows a principle he called the categorical imperative: "I ought never to act unless I can will my maxim to serve as a universal law." A "maxim" for Kant is the reason a person has for doing something. And a maxim "serves as a universal law" if every person consistently acts on that reason. So the categorical imperative is the moral principle that whenever I do something, my reasons for doing it must be reasons that I would (and could) be willing to have everyone act on. For example, suppose I wonder whether I should help the needy, and my reason for being reluctant to help them is simply that I do not want to take the trouble. According to Kant, I must ask myself this: Would I be willing to have everyone refrain from helping others when they did not want to take the trouble? Clearly, I would *not* be willing to have everyone do this, since I myself might need the help of others in some situations. Therefore, it would be wrong for me to refrain from helping those in need. Kant claims that sometimes it is absolutely *impossible* for everyone to act on the immoral reasons we are tempted to act on. In such

cases it is absolutely immoral to act on those reasons:

> The ordinary reason of humanity in its practical judgments agrees perfectly with this, and always has in view the principle here suggested. For example, suppose that I ask myself: Would it be morally permissible for me to make a promise I do not intend to keep when I am in trouble? . . . The shortest and most unerring way for me to discover whether a lying promise is consistent with duty is to ask myself: Could I will to have my maxim (that is, the principle, "I will get out of my difficulties with false promises") serve as a universal law, for myself as well as for others; and would I be able to say to myself, "Everyone may make a false promise when he finds himself in a difficulty that he cannot escape in any other way"? As soon as I ask myself these questions, I become aware that although I might desire to lie, I could not will to have lying become a universal law. For if lying promises became the rule, there would soon be no promises at all. There would be no promises because people would stop believing each other when they said that they intended to keep their promises; and if one person overhastily accepted the lying promise of another, that person would soon learn to do the same thing to others. So as soon as my maxim became a universal law, it would destroy itself.
>
> I do not, therefore, need any great genius to see what I have to do so that my will can be morally good. Even if I have very little experience of the world, even if I cannot prepare for all contingencies ahead of time, all I have to ask myself is this: Could you will to have your maxim serve as a universal law? If not, then you should not act on that maxim.[10]

How does Kant argue for the categorical imperative? For Kant, moral right and wrong depend on the interior motives on which the person acts. Kant argues that to the degree that a person is interiorly motivated merely by self-interest or by the pleasure he gets from an action, the action "has no moral worth." A person's behavior has moral worth only to the extent that the person is motivated by

---

[10] Immanuel Kant, *Grundlegung zur Metaphysik der Sitten* [*Groundwork of the Metaphysics of Morals*], in *Immanuel Kant Werkausgabe*, vol. 7, ed. Wilhelm Weischedel (Frankfurt, Germany: Insel Verlag Wiesbaden, 1956), 28–30. This translation copyright © 1987 by Manuel Velasquez.

"duty"—that is, by the belief that all human beings ought to act this way. Consequently, an action has moral worth only to the extent that the person is motivated by reasons that he or she feels everyone else can and ought to act on.

Kant claimed that the categorical imperative could be expressed in a second way: "Act in such a way that you always treat humanity, whether in your own person or in the person of any other, never simply as a means, but always at the same time as an end." Never treat people *only* as means but always also as ends. By this, Kant meant that we should never treat people only as tools to be manipulated or forced into serving our interests. Instead, we should always treat people as ends—that is, as free, rational persons who must be given the opportunity to decide for themselves whether or not they will go along with our plans:

> A man who is thinking of making a lying promise will realize that he would be using others merely as means because he would not be letting them participate in the goal of the actions in which he involves them. For the people I would thus be using for my own purposes would not have consented to be treated in this way and to that extent they would not have participated in the goals to be attained by the action. Such violations of the principle that our humanity must be respected as an end in itself are even clearer if we take examples of attacks on the freedom and property of others. It is obvious that the person who violates such rights is using people merely as means without considering that as rational beings they should be esteemed also as ends; that is, as beings who must be able to participate in the goals of the actions in which they are involved with him.[11]

According to Kant, this second way of expressing the categorical imperative is really equivalent to the first. The first version says that what is morally right for me must be morally right for others, or that everyone must be treated the same. The second version says that just as I give myself the opportunity to decide what I will do, I must also give others the same opportunity or, again, that everyone must be treated the same. The second version, however, unlike the first, emphasizes that morality requires us to respect the freedom of all rational persons.

Kant points out that if the categorical imperative defines morality, then morality and happiness do not necessarily coincide. For the morally good person is the one who follows the categorical imperative even when this is not in her self-interest and even when she takes no pleasure in doing so. Consequently, morally good people often suffer and fail to get what is in their self-interest. On the other hand, evil people who consistently pursue their self-interest and pleasure, even by taking advantage of others, often prosper. In this world, good people who deserve happiness often do not receive it, whereas evil people who do not deserve it do receive it.

This mismatch between morality and happiness is wrong, Kant holds, and all of us feel it ought not to be this way. In fact, we feel an obligation to seek a world where the good prosper and the evil do not, and our sense of obligation requires us to believe that such a world is possible. Such a perfect world, Kant calls a *summum bonum*, the supremely good state of affairs. But, he says, only a good God could bring such a perfect world into existence (perhaps in another life). So, if we believe such a world is possible (and we have an obligation to believe it is), we must assume that God exists. Thus, although we cannot *prove* that God exists, morality forces us to assume so:

> We ought to endeavor to promote the *summum bonum*, which, therefore must be possible. Accordingly, the existence of a cause of all nature, distinct from nature itself, and containing the principle of this connection, namely the exact harmony of happiness with morality, is also *postulated*. . . . The *summum bonum* is possible in the world only on the supposition of a Supreme Being having a causality corresponding to moral character. Now a being that is capable of acting on the conception of laws is an *intelligence* (a rational being), and the causality of such a being according to this conception of laws is his *will*; therefore the supreme cause of nature, which must be presupposed as a condition of the *summum bonum*, is a being which is the cause of nature by *intelligence* and *will*, consequently its author, that is God. . . . Now it was seen to be a duty for us to promote the *summum bonum*. Consequently it is not

---

[11] Ibid., 62.

merely allowable, but it is a necessity connected with duty as a requisite, that we should presuppose the possibility of this *summum bonum*. And as this is possible only on condition of the existence of God, it inseparably connects the supposition of this with duty; that is, it is morally necessary to assume the existence of God.[12]

Thus, Kant shifted the argument for God's existence away from metaphysics, where every other philosopher had placed it. Other philosophers had assumed that God's existence had to be proved by relying on metaphysical concepts such as the concept of causality, and such arguments had been ruthlessly demolished by the skepticism of Hume. Kant tried to show that these arguments had to fail because metaphysical concepts are merely categories in our minds; they can tell us nothing about things as they are in themselves. Instead, Kant claimed, we must believe in God on the basis of our moral commitments: Morality forces us to hold that God exists. For morality tells us that good people must be rewarded and evil ones punished, and only a God could bring about such a summum bonum. By thus placing belief in God in the realm of morality, Kant hoped, belief would be secure from the attacks of Humean skepticism.

In spite of his very ordinary life, then, Kant's philosophy was truly revolutionary. Kant taught us to believe that the world conforms to the categories of the mind, whereas we had always assumed that the mind must conform its categories to the world. He taught us that morality requires us to respect the freedom of others whether or not this pleases us and, consequently, that being moral and being happy may not coincide in this life. And he taught us to believe in God on the basis of morality instead of on the basis of metaphysical arguments. These were truly new ways of looking at the universe, new ways of thinking about ourselves and the world in which we live. It is hard to imagine a more revolutionary view of our situation.

QUESTIONS

1. In your own words, explain Kant's problem: "How are a priori synthetic judgments possible?"

2. Summarize in your own words how Kant tries to show that a priori synthetic judgments in geometry and arithmetic are possible.

3. In your own words, why does Kant say that our mind *must* connect its sensations together into objects? Why does Kant say that the mind must connect its sensations into objects that are causally connected? In your view, does Kant really answer Hume?

4. Some people have said that Kant cannot be called a rationalist or an empiricist. Why do you think they say this? Do you see any rationalist elements in Kant? Do you see any empiricist elements?

5. Is Kant's first version of the categorical imperative the same as the Golden Rule (Do unto others as you would have them do unto you)?

6. In your view, what would Kant's categorical imperative imply about the morality of suicide? About the morality of the death penalty? Explain.

7. Do you feel that Kant's argument for accepting the existence of God is correct? Why?

---

[12] Immanuel Kant, *Critique of Practical Reason*, trans. T. K. Abbott (London: Longmans Green, 1927), 220–222.

6.7 Readings

Is all truth relative? Is the truth held by one person or group as valid as the truth of any other person or group, even when those truths are incompatible? The short story by Japanese author Ryūnosuke Akutagawa suggests that there are indeed as many truths as there are persons who are witnesses to the truth. Philosopher Hugh Tomlinson agrees and goes on to argue in the second reading that the traditional realist view of truth, which holds that there is one reality and one truth corresponding to that reality, must give way to the new postmodern view that there are many truths and many realities. Feminist Anne Seller is troubled by the implications of this postmodern view and suggests a compromise between the traditional realist and the relativist views of truth; she argues that truth is found through a commitment to a group process of understanding the world through discussion and examination of one's experience with others. These readings, then, should lead us to ask whether everyone's truth is equally valid, and how it is that we personally should go about discovering truth.

RYŪNOSUKE AKUTAGAWA

In a Grove

THE TESTIMONY OF A WOODCUTTER QUESTIONED BY A HIGH POLICE COMMISSIONER

Yes, sir. Certainly, it was I who found the body. This morning, as usual, I went to cut my daily quota of cedars, when I found the body in a grove in a hollow in the mountains. The exact location? About 150 meters off the Yamashina stage road. It's an out-of-the-way grove of bamboo and cedars.

The body was lying flat on its back dressed in a bluish silk kimono and a wrinkled head-dress of the Kyoto style. A single sword-stroke had pierced the breast. The fallen bamboo-blades around it were stained with bloody blossoms. No, the blood was no longer running. The wound had dried up, I believe. And also, a gadfly was stuck fast there, hardly noticing my footsteps.

You ask me if I saw a sword or any such thing?

No, nothing, sir. I found only a rope at the root of a cedar near by. And . . . well, in addition to a rope, I found a comb. That was all. Apparently he must have made a battle of it before he was murdered, because the grass and fallen bamboo-blades had been trampled down all around.

"A horse was near by?"

No, sir. It's hard enough for a man to enter, let alone a horse.

THE TESTIMONY OF A TRAVELING BUDDHIST PRIEST QUESTIONED BY A HIGH POLICE COMMISSIONER

The time? Certainly, it was about noon yesterday, sir. The unfortunate man was on the road from Sekiyama to Yamashina. He was walking toward Sekiyama with a woman accompanying him on horseback, who I have since learned was his wife.

From *Rashomon and Other Stories* by Ryūnosuke Akutagawa. Takashi Kojima, trans. Copyright © 1952 by Liveright Publishing Corporation. Reprinted by permission.

A scarf hanging from her head hid her face from view. All I saw was the color of her clothes, a lilac-colored suit. Her horse was a sorrel with a fine mane. The lady's height? Oh, about four feet five inches. Since I am a Buddhist priest, I took little notice about her details. Well, the man was armed with a sword as well as a bow and arrows. And I remember that he carried some twenty odd arrows in his quiver.

Little did I expect that he would meet such a fate. Truly human life is as evanescent as the morning dew or a flash of lightning. My words are inadequate to express my sympathy for him.

THE TESTIMONY OF A POLICEMAN QUESTIONED BY A HIGH POLICE COMMISSIONER

The man that I arrested? He is a notorious brigand called Tajomaru. When I arrested him, he had fallen off his horse. He was groaning on the bridge at Awataguchi. The time? It was in the early hours of last night. For the record, I might say that the other day I tried to arrest him, but unfortunately he escaped. He was wearing a dark blue silk kimono and a large plain sword. And, as you see, he got a bow and arrows somewhere. You say that this bow and these arrows look like the ones owned by the dead man? Then Tajomaru must be the murderer. The bow wound with leather strips, the black lacquered quiver, the seventeen arrows with hawk feathers — these were all in his possession I believe. Yes, sir, the horse is, as you say, a sorrel with a fine mane. A little beyond the stone bridge I found the horse grazing by the roadside, with his long rein dangling. Surely there is some providence in his having been thrown by the horse.

Of all the robbers prowling around Kyoto, this Tajomaru has given the most grief to the women in town. Last autumn a wife who came to the mountain back of the Pindora of the Toribe Temple, presumably to pay a visit, was murdered, along with a girl. It has been suspected that it was his doing. If this criminal murdered the man, you cannot tell what he may have done with the man's wife. May it please your honor to look into this problem as well.

THE TESTIMONY OF AN OLD WOMAN QUESTIONED BY A HIGH POLICE COMMISSIONER

Yes, sir, the corpse is the man who married my daughter. He does not come from Kyoto. He was a samurai in the town of Kokufu in the province of Wakasa. His name was Kanazawa no Takehiko, and his age was twenty-six. He was of a gentle disposition, so I am sure he did nothing to provoke the anger of others.

My daughter? Her name is Masago, and her age is nineteen. She is a spirited, fun-loving girl, but I am sure she has never known any man except Takehiko. She has a small, oval, dark-complected face with a mole at the corner of her left eye.

Yesterday Takehiko left for Wakasa with my daughter. What bad luck it is that things should have come to such a sad end! What has become of my daughter? I am resigned to giving up my son-in-law as lost, but the fate of my daughter worries me sick. For heaven's sake leave no stone unturned to find her. I hate that robber Tajomaru, or whatever his name is. Not only my son-in-law, but my daughter . . . (Her later words were drowned in tears.)

TAJOMARU'S CONFESSION

I killed him, but not her. Where's she gone? I can't tell. Oh, wait a minute. No torture can make me confess what I don't know. Now things have come to such a head, I won't keep anything from you.

Yesterday a little past noon I met that couple. Just then a puff of wind blew, and raised her hanging scarf, so that I caught a glimpse of her face. Instantly it was again covered from my view. That may have been one reason; she looked like a Bodhisattva. At that moment I made up my mind to capture her even if I had to kill her man.

Why? To me killing isn't a matter of such great consequence as you might think. When a woman is captured, her man has to be killed anyway. In killing, I use the sword I wear at my side. Am I the only one who kills people? You, you don't use your swords. You kill people with your power, with your money. Sometimes you kill them on the pretext of working for their good. It's true they don't bleed. They are in the best of health, but all the same you've killed them. It's hard to say who is a greater sinner, you or me. (An ironical smile.)

But it would be good if I could capture a woman without killing her man. So, I made up my mind to capture her, and do my best not to kill him. But it's out of the question on the Yamashina stage road. So I managed to lure the couple into the mountains.

It was quite easy. I became their traveling companion, and I told them there was an old mound in the mountain over there, and that I had dug it open and found many mirrors and swords. I went on to tell them I'd buried the things in a grove behind the mountain, and that I'd like to sell them at a low price to anyone who would care to have them. Then . . . you see, isn't greed terrible? He was beginning to be moved by my talk before he knew it. In less than half an hour they were driving their horse toward the mountain with me.

When he came in front of the grove, I told them that the treasures were buried in it, and I asked them to come and see. The man had no objection—he was blinded by greed. The woman said she would wait on horseback. It was natural for her to say so, at the sight of a thick grove. To tell you the truth, my plan worked just as I wished, so I went into the grove with him, leaving her behind alone.

The grove is only bamboo for some distance. About fifty yards ahead there's a rather open clump of cedars. It was a convenient spot for my purpose. Pushing my way through the grove, I told him a plausible lie that the treasures were buried under the cedars. When I told him this, he pushed his laborious way toward the slender cedar visible through the grove. After a while the bamboo thinned out, and we came to where a number of cedars grew in a row. As soon as we got there, I seized him from behind. Because he was a trained, sword-bearing warrior, he was quite strong, but he was taken by surprise, so there was no help for him. I soon tied him up to the root of a cedar. Where did I get a rope? Thank heaven, being a robber, I had a rope with me, since I might have to scale a wall at any moment. Of course it was easy to stop him from calling out by gagging his mouth with fallen bamboo leaves.

When I disposed of him, I went to his woman and asked her to come and see him, because he seemed to have been suddenly taken sick. It's needless to say that this plan also worked well. The woman, her sedge hat off, came into the depths of the grove, where I led her by the hand. The instant she caught sight of her husband, she drew a small sword. I've never seen a woman of such violent temper. If I'd been off guard, I'd have got a thrust in my side. I dodged, but she kept on slashing at me. She might have wounded me deeply or killed me. But I'm Tajomaru. I managed to strike down her small sword without drawing my own. The most spirited woman is defenseless without a weapon. At least I could satisfy my desire for her without taking her husband's life.

Yes, . . . without taking his life. I had no wish to kill him. I was about to run away from the grove, leaving the woman behind in tears, when she frantically clung to my arm. In broken fragments of words, she asked that either her husband or I die. She said it was more trying than death to have her shame known to two men. She gasped out that she wanted to be the wife of whichever survived. Then a furious desire to kill him seized me. (Gloomy excitement.)

Telling you in this way, no doubt I seem a crueler man than you. But that's because you didn't see her face. Especially her burning eyes at that moment. As I saw her eye to eye, I wanted to make her my wife even if I were to be struck by lightning. I wanted to make her my wife . . . this single desire filled my mind. This was not only lust, as you might think. At that time if I'd had no other desire than lust, I'd surely not have minded knocking her down and running away. Then I wouldn't have stained my sword with his blood. But the moment I gazed at her face in the dark grove, I decided not to leave there without killing him.

But I didn't like to resort to unfair means to kill him. I untied him and told him to cross swords with me. (The rope that was found at the root of the cedar is the rope I dropped at the time.) Furious with anger, he drew his thick sword. And quick as thought, he sprang at me ferociously, without speaking a word. I needn't tell you how our fight turned out. The twenty-third stroke . . . please remember this. I'm impressed with this fact still.

Nobody under the sun has ever clashed swords with me twenty strokes. (A cheerful smile.)

When he fell, I turned toward her, lowering my blood-stained sword. But to my great astonishment she was gone. I wondered to where she had run away. I looked for her in the clump of cedars. I listened, but heard only a groaning sound from the throat of the dying man.

As soon as we started to cross swords, she may have run away through the grove to call for help. When I thought of that, I decided it was a matter of life and death to me. So, robbing him of his sword, and bow and arrows, I ran out to the mountain road. There I found her horse still grazing quietly. It would be a mere waste of words to tell you the latter details, but before I entered town I had already parted with the sword. That's all my confession. I know that my head will be hung in chains anyway, so put me down for the maximum penalty. (A defiant attitude.)

THE CONFESSION OF A WOMAN WHO HAS COME TO THE *SHIMIZU* TEMPLE

That man in the blue silk kimono, after forcing me to yield to him, laughed mockingly as he looked at my bound husband. How horrified my husband must have been! But no matter how hard he struggled in agony, the rope cut into him all the more tightly. In spite of myself I ran stumblingly toward his side. Or rather I tried to run toward him, but the man instantly knocked me down. Just at the moment I saw an indescribable light in my husband's eyes. Something beyond expression . . . his eyes make me shudder even now. That instantaneous look of my husband, who couldn't speak a word, told me all his heart. The flash in his eyes was neither anger nor sorrow . . . only a cold light, a look of loathing. More struck by the look in his eyes than by the blow of the thief, I called out in spite of myself and fell unconscious.

In the course of time I came to, and found that the man in blue silk was gone. I saw only my husband still bound to the root of the cedar. I raised myself from the bamboo-blades with difficulty, and looked into his face; but the expression in his eyes was just the same as before.

Beneath the cold contempt in his eyes, there was hatred. Shame, grief, and anger . . . I don't know how to express my heart at that time. Reeling to my feet, I went up to my husband.

"Takejiro," I said to him, "since things have come to this pass, I cannot live with you. I'm determined to die, . . . but you must die, too. You saw my shame. I can't leave you alive as you are."

This was all I could say. Still he went on gazing at me with loathing and contempt. My heart breaking, I looked for his sword. It must have been taken by the robber. Neither his sword nor his bow and arrows were to be seen in the grove. But fortunately my small sword was lying at my feet. Raising it over head, once more I said, "Now give me your life, I'll follow you right away."

When he heard these words, he moved his lips with difficulty. Since his mouth was stuffed with leaves, of course his voice could not be heard at all. But at a glance I understood his words. Despising me, his look said only, "Kill me." Neither conscious nor unconscious, I stabbed the small sword through the lilac-colored kimono into his breast.

Again at this time I must have fainted. By the time I managed to look up, he had already breathed his last — still in bonds. A streak of sinking sunlight streamed through the clump of cedars and bamboos, and shone on his pale face. Gulping down my sobs, I untied the rope from his dead body. And . . . and what has become of me since I have no more strength to tell you. Anyway I hadn't the strength to die. I stabbed my own throat with the small sword, I threw myself into a pond at the foot of the mountain, and I tried to kill myself in many ways. Unable to end my life, I am still living in dishonor. (A lonely smile.) Worthless as I am, I must have been forsaken even by the most merciful Kwannon. I killed my own husband. I was violated by the robber. Whatever can I do? Whatever can I . . . I . . . (Gradually, violent sobbing.)

THE STORY OF THE MURDERED MAN, AS TOLD THROUGH A MEDIUM

After violating my wife, the robber, sitting there, began to speak comforting words to her. Of course I couldn't speak. My whole body was tied fast to the root of a cedar. But meanwhile I winked at her many times, as much as to say "Don't believe the robber." I wanted to convey some such meaning to her. But my wife, sitting dejectedly on the bamboo leaves, was looking hard at her lap. To all appearances, she was listening to his words. I was agonized by jealousy. In the meantime the robber went on with his clever talk, from one subject to another. The robber finally made his bold, brazen proposal. "Once your virtue is stained, you won't get along well with your husband, so won't you be my wife instead? It's my love for you that made me be violent toward you."

While the criminal talked, my wife raised her face as if in a trance. She had never looked so beautiful as at that moment. What did my beautiful wife say in answer to him while I was sitting bound there? I am lost in space, but I have never thought of her answer without burning with anger and jealousy. Truly she said, . . . "Then take me away with you wherever you go."

This is not the whole of her sin. If that were all, I would not be tormented so much in the dark. When she was going out of the grove as if in a dream, her hand in the robber's, she suddenly turned pale, and pointed at me tied to the root of the cedar, and said "Kill him! I cannot marry you as long as he lives." "Kill him!" she cried many times, as if she had gone crazy. Even now these words threaten to blow me headlong into the bottomless abyss of darkness. Has such a hateful thing come out of a human mouth ever before? Have such cursed words ever struck a human ear, even once? Even once such a . . . (A sudden cry of scorn.) At these words the robber himself turned pale. "Kill him," she cried, clinging to his arms. Looking hard at her, he answered neither yes nor no . . . but hardly had I thought about his answer before she had been knocked down into the bamboo leaves. (Again a cry of scorn.) Quietly folding his arms, he looked at me and said, "What will you do with her? Kill her or save her? You have only to nod. Kill her?" For these words alone I would like to pardon his crime.

While I hesitated, she shrieked and ran into the depths of the grove. The robber instantly snatched at her, but he failed even to grasp her sleeve.

After she ran away, he took up my sword, and my bow and arrows. With a single stroke he cut one of my bonds. I remember his mumbling, "My fate is next." Then he disappeared from the grove. All was silent after that. No, I heard someone crying. Untying the rest of my bonds, I listened carefully, and I noticed that it was my own crying. (Long silence.)

I raised my exhausted body from the root of the cedar. In front of me there was shining the small sword which my wife had dropped. I took it up and stabbed it into my breast. A bloody lump rose to my mouth, but I didn't feel any pain. When my breast grew cold, everything was as silent as the dead in their graves. What profound silence! Not a single bird-note was heard in the sky over this grave in the hollow of the mountains. Only a lonely light lingered on the cedars and mountains. By and by the light gradually grew fainter, till the cedars and bamboo were lost to view. Lying there, I was enveloped in deep silence.

Then someone crept up to me. I tried to see who it was. But darkness had already been gathering round me. Someone . . . that someone drew the small sword softly out of my breast in its invisible hand. At the same time once more blood flowed into my mouth. And once and for all I sank down into the darkness of space.

HUGH TOMLINSON

After Truth: Post-Modernism and the Rhetoric of Science

INTRODUCTION

'Truth' is the basis of a powerful and persuasive apologetics — the rhetoric of science. Over the past two centuries this has swept away all rivals. It is a key part of the 'modern' perspective on the world, an unspoken assumption at the heart of our thinking. Rationality and truth have become so interwoven that any attempt to question the notion of truth seems irrational and incoherent.

'Who', asks Paul Feyerabend, 'has the fortitude, or even the insight to declare that "truth" might be unimportant, and perhaps even undesirable?'[1] This insight is a starting point of what can be called 'post-modernism'. For present purposes, this is not a cultural theory but rather an (anti-)philosophical view flowing from a 'suspension' of the notion of truth. . . .

The aim of the account that follows is to provide a sketch of the post-modernist attack on the rhetoric of truth. . . .

COMMON-SENSE REALISM

The modern notion of truth draws much of its plausibility from a set of metaphysical views which form an 'externalist' perspective on the world, what Putnam has called a 'God's Eye point of view'.[2] This perspective is now deeply embedded in our 'common-sense' attitude to the world. The 'common-sense realist' sees the world as being objectively ordered independently of all human activity. Science seeks to provide theories which 'mirror' this objective ordering, theories which are, in a word, 'true'.

The basic 'given' of common-sense realism is unobjectionable: the world is relatively independent of our dealings with it. But this is elevated into an ontological thesis that there is a single, objectively structured reality independent of human thoughts and actions. According to the realist:

> the world consists of some fixed totality of mind-independent objects. There is exactly one true and complete description of 'the way the world is'. Truth involves some sort of correspondence between words or thought-signs and external things and sets of things.[3]

It follows that the key feature of language is 'reference': bits of language are used to 'refer' to bits of

Reprinted from *Dismantling Truth: Reality in the Post-Modern World*, edited by Hilary Lawson and Lisa Appignanesi (New York: St. Martin's, 1989). Copyright © Hilary Lawson and Lisa Appignanesi. Reprinted with permission of St. Martin's Press, Inc.

the world. A statement is true if it successfully refers to the world. Whatever our subjective perceptions, the world is objectively 'out there' and the aim of our theorizing is to provide a theory which 'copies' or 'corresponds' to it.

This correspondence view of truth provides an apparently straightforward and easily applicable picture of the relation between words and world. It is a picture which fits with the way which we use simple sentences about ordinary material objects. We look to the world, to the 'thing referred to', in order to decide whether such sentences are appropriate or not: to decide whether 'there is food in the fridge', I can look in the fridge.

The common-sense realist wants to expand this picture into a general account of the relation between words and world, a general theory of truth. There are immediate difficulties with this move. What seems obvious in relation to ordinary physical objects such as cars or houses is difficult to apply in relation to the objects of the physicist or the astronomer. There is no straightforward and clear sense in which talk about quarks or quasars 'corresponds' to the world. The acceptability or utility of such talk depends on complex procedures of observation and calculation which are entirely unknown to most of us.

These problems multiply when we move outside the 'natural' sciences. The language of 'social science' often lacks clear 'objective reference': statements about the mind, social classes or historical changes have no obvious 'objects' to correspond to. The difficulties are even more formidable in areas such as religion, aesthetics or ethics. There is no uncontested way in which we can even decide on what might count as the 'objects' of such theories. On the common-sense realist view, 'true' theories about God, beauty or the good life seem impossible.

According to the realist picture 'truth' is given by a particular relationship between words and world: a sentence is true when it corresponds to the world. This involves two aspects: the items to be related and the relationship itself. From his own perspective, the realist must be in a position to give a coherent account of both.

The items to be related seem obvious and straightforward: words and objects. The common-sense realist thinks of the world as consisting, paradigmatically, of unproblematically identifiable physical objects with simple properties. From a 'God's Eye point of view' the world 'really is' divided up into objects, independently of human description and ordering.

This view of objects runs counter to the whole thrust of modern philosophy since Kant. It is ultimately dependent on the idea of the world as 'God's project', divided up according to divine categories. It was Kant's fundamental insight that 'we are giving the orders', that both concepts and experience are necessary components of knowledge. We can only have experience of a world which is already structured by our concepts; it is 'our world'. What counts as a particular object depends on the classificatory concepts which we use. We cannot 'leap outside' these concepts and directly compare them with 'unconceptualized objects'. . . .

It seems that all that words can ever be related to are objects which depend on the words used. Truth is, then, not 'objective' and unique, but 'subjective' in the sense that it depends on the particular language used. There are as many truths as there are languages and the notion of truth can no longer provide a final and objective justification for science.

RELATIVISM AND POST-MODERNISM

This account of realism can be summarized by saying that, on close examination, it collapses into relativism. This collapse has two phases. First, the insight that the world is 'our world', that what counts as a fact depends on our theories, means that there is no 'reality' for theories to correspond to. . . .

Secondly, if there are a number of incommensurable theories there are as many worlds as there are theories. In Feyerabend's words, 'we . . . cannot assume that two incommensurable theories deal with one and the same objective state of affairs . . . Hence, unless we want to assume that they deal with nothing at all we must admit that they deal

with different worlds'.[4] This view is commonly called relativism. . . .

The post-modernist story is a simple one: realism, in any of its forms, cannot be made coherent in its own terms. We have, as Putnam says, reached 'the demise of a theory that lasted for over two thousand years. That it persisted so long and in so many forms in spite of the internal contradictions and obscurities which were present from the beginning testifies to the naturalness and strength of the desire for a God's Eye View'.[5] The question is: where do we go from here?

REFERENCES

1. P. Feyerabend, *Against Method* (London, New Left Books, 1975), p. 171.

2. See Hilary Putnam, *Reason, Truth and History* (Cambridge, Cambridge Univ. Press, 1981), pp. 50ff.

3. Ibid., p. 49.

4. P. Feyerabend, *Science in a Free Society* (London, Verso, 1978), p. 70.

5. Putnam, *Reason, Truth and History*, p. 74.

ANNE SELLER

Realism Versus Relativism: Towards a Politically Adequate Epistemology

Within feminism, the argument between realism and relativism appears to be both acute and political. I shall examine this argument, primarily from a political point of view. . . .

From *Feminist Perspectives in Philosophy*, ed. Morwenna Griffiths and Margaret Whitford (Bloomington: Indiana University Press, 1988). Copyright © 1988 by Morwenna Griffiths and Margaret Whitford. Reprinted by permission.

THE APPEAL AND PROBLEMS OF REALISM

Some preliminary definitions: I characterise realism as the view that there is an objective order of reality, which can be known by the human observer. The claim that it is a fact that women's wombs do not wither if they use their brains, or that it is in multinational corporations' interests to maintain women's obsessions with food are both examples of realism. For the moment, I define relativism as the view that every woman's experience is valid, not false, illusory or mistaken, and that all ways of making sense of the world are equally valid. I shall subsequently revise this to the view that the truth of a claim is relative to the group within which that claim is made. Thus, eventually, I wish to distinguish relativism, which may be a coherent position, from subjectivism, which is certainly not.

The primary appeal of realism is political. If all views are equally valid, so are sexist ones, and relativism appears to disarm me. We also all now agree on certain truths. It is false to say that a woman's womb withers if she uses her brain, irrational to use sexual characteristics rather than economic position as the deciding factor in granting a mortgage, and patently unjust to pay less to a woman than a man for completing identical tasks. A combination of careful observation, willingness to take account of the evidence, and a commitment to consistency will reveal these truths. They are not a matter of perspective, social position or gender.

But we have to ask how these truths are known, we need an epistemology. It is here that the realist runs into difficulties. For given that it is a combination of those intellectual virtues already mentioned (consistency, careful observation etc.) which enabled us to expose the bias and falsehood of sexist views; and given that these virtues are popularly recognised as the characteristics of a scientific attitude towards the world, we might look for an epistemology based on that scientific approach. For the truth to out, feminists need only to do rigorously what men have purported to do, and indeed, we owe a great deal to feminists who have, through rigorous intellectual effort, revealed that much purportedly impartial and objective scholarship and science is grounded in male bias. We have

a better knowledge of ourselves and our past because of them.

But although this epistemology, which I call rational–scientific, is politically appealing (it enables us to say to the sexist 'you are wrong') it also raises political problems. First, it is an élitist epistemology. Only some women have the resources (time, library, etc.) to conduct such research, other women will simply have to accept it on authority. This may not be a ground for rejecting it, but it means it needs to be supplemented with an epistemology for everyday life which answers the question, 'How do I know who or what to believe?' One epistemology for the élite, another for the masses is embarrassing. Secondly, women have often experienced the scientific–rational approach as oppressive both in its process and in its findings. It has been used to make women feel foolish because they have been unable to express themselves in its terms, and it has been used to 'prove' the inferiority of women. The claim about wombs and brains came out of a scientific community that was not deliberately dishonest and was committed to certain canons of observation and rationality. Why did it take so long to discover that it was false?

THE APPEAL OF RELATIVISM

The appeal of relativism is political and epistemological, and it is often difficult to distinguish the two. Women's oppression has partly been understood in terms of the silencing of women, the denial of their experience as valid, or the treatment of it, when discovered, as neurotic. The woman who failed to find satisfaction in the fulfilment of domestic duties or who did not want to have babies was treated as a suitable case for treatment. The apprehension that such women were not sick but oppressed by a false view of what they should be came about only through women sharing these feelings and experiences with each other. The view of what they should be was seen as false, first, because it failed to tally with how they felt—women, apparently, did not become happy and fulfilled in the ways that they were supposed to, and furthermore experienced feelings of relief in being able to say this in public—and second, in the perception that the demand that they find fulfilment and happiness in these ways fitted the interests of men rather well, maintaining women's dependence upon men.

Relativism also fits with the feminist experience of finding that the world is not what it appeared to be, that instead of relying on the descriptions she grew up with, she has to create her own descriptions. [Feminist philosopher Sandra] Bartky gives a clear account of this process of confusion. She speaks of a realisation that what is really happening is quite different from what appears to be happening, and a frequent inability to tell what is really happening at all. It is not so much that we are aware of different things, but that we are aware of the same things differently, and this is an experience of anguish and confusion. Is what I say in a meeting foolish and irrelevant, or am I being ignored because I am a woman? If I refuse to compete aggressively for promotion, am I acting out of timidity and self-denial that I have been educated into seeing as proper to women, or am I demonstrating my independence of a contemptible system of values? Everyone can make her own list, but several things are clear about the kind of question or doubt that is being expressed. These are doubts about who we are, what kind of people we think that we ought to be, and hence about what we ought to do, how we ought to behave. I no longer know how to describe myself, and my relations with others, and part of the reason is my uncertainty about meanings and values. It is not that I have discovered an identity that was denied expression within a particular system of values. Rather, a feminist more commonly has the experience of changing her identity as she takes a series of decisions. . . .

To return to the feminist example: . . . My decision not to compete aggressively for promotion is a decision to see youthful fierce competitiveness as experiments in a dominant ethic which I have discovered does not suit; not as self-assertion. Or it may constitute another decision, to see myself as no longer having the energy for such self-assertion, and in this case I may find (decide?) that I am acting out of low-esteem.

Now the realist may wish to insist, but which? One of these descriptions will be correct, some decisions will be dishonest, some self-deluded, and some simply mistaken, and that suggests a standard of at least truthfulness, if not truth, and correctness, if not reality. This is a valid query. . . . So how do I find out when I am being honest, when self-deluded?

THE COMMUNITY OF RESISTANCE

The answer for me is through painstaking questioning and checking of precisely the kind that went on in women's consciousness-raising groups. For this, a commitment to listen, to care for and to support each other, and to express ourselves honestly is necessary. Only when all feel safe to speak of hidden or barely recognised experiences can knowledge of our desires and our situation emerge.

Each individual's experience, as an unconsidered given, cannot show what is going on. As an isolated individual, I often do not know what my experiences are. There can be no argument for subjectivism here, but rather for an intersubjectivism which begins in individual experiences, but instead of multiplying them (we *all* saw flashes in the sky) seeks to understand them through conversation. (Lightning or Reagan's secret weapon or group fear?)

This commitment to engage in conversation to find out what the world is like is a moral or political commitment to a community, to be with a group through growth and change. It involves me in an act of faith, not only that we will each struggle honestly for our understanding, but to a view of knowledge and politics as process, rather than achievement. In multiplying heads, we do not simply multiply intelligences and confirmations, but we produce knowledge in the exchange of views, multiple, slightly different, sometimes opposed, and in the questioning, perhaps precisely because of our differences. . . .

THE COMMUNITY AND THE PROBLEMS OF RELATIVISM

Using the community to make our decisions seems to retain the appeal of relativism without its problems (which amount to the paradox of claiming that all views are valid while aspiring to the truth).

This is seen clearly in [an] example . . . about my own past.

As I became engaged with feminism, I found myself changing in ways that are most simply and honestly described as: I used to think . . . feel . . . but I was wrong. The relativist seems either committed to saying that I was right then, and that although I now disagree with what I thought then, I am also right now, or to abandoning the use of such terms as 'right' and 'wrong'. Either of these paradoxical positions seems to commit me to denying that I have developed in a progressive way. This denies the experience I have of progress and commits the relativist to the claim that while I might *feel* as if I have developed in fact I have only changed. The relativist is then validating *all* my experiences except that which I might count as the most important in my life.

Let me briefly consider some of the ways in which I vindicate my later position, for I think that these will show the way in which appeal to community resolves the problem. I can now acknowledge and recognise feelings and experiences which I previously barely took account of or tried to rationalise as irrelevant or insane. (For example, feeling deeply insecure in the nuclear state.) I recognise that in some ways I have always thought this way but not always been able to articulate it properly. (For example, that doctors have no right to control my life.) I do not as frequently have to pretend about what I feel or like. I now find patterns of behaviour that make better sense of my life, and I also find I can honestly acknowledge inconsistencies and be prepared to live with them, while I try to work them out with others. I am no longer bullied into accepting consequences that I really do not believe. The list could be longer, and no one item on it is conclusive. Each item could be demonstrated with autobiographical details, which show how conversation, being listened to and listening, enabled me to see these things. I would summarise these vindications as a progressive release from feeling isolated, finding the world an alien and unfathomable place, into finding a community that enables me to live in the world rather than trying to escape it and, no matter how confusing these attempts are at times, to make some sense of it. This again brings out the importance of the distinction between subjectivism and relativism. I pay attention to my subjective experiences in order to find what [Hannah] Arendt called 'the world'. It is not that every individual's unexamined and undiscussed experience is true, much less her opinions, but it is only *through* examining and discussing individuals' experiences that we can do what the realist calls finding truth, what the relativist calls contributing to the construction of reality as opposed to simply being the victims of other people's constructions. . . .

CONCLUSION

> Reasonable people who are located in different parts of the social world find themselves differentially exposed to diverse realities, and this differential exposure leads each of them to come up with different— but often equally reasonable—constructions of the world. (Kristin Luker, 1984)

Quite so, and we require that our constructions fit, in a *real* way, our needs and desires, which are decided upon together with the constructions. This is neither realism nor relativism, but finding the best way to recreate our world, which can only be done through a genuinely democratic movement based on a genuinely democratic epistemology of the kind I have sketched above.

6.8 Suggestions for Further Reading

Carr, Brian, and D. J. O'Connor. *Introduction to the Theory of Knowledge*. Minneapolis, MN: University of Minnesota Press, 1982. A very readable introduction to the philosophical problems of truth and knowledge.

Castaneda, Carlos. *A Separate Reality*. New York: Simon & Schuster, 1972. The author covers the first five years of his relationship with the Yaqui Indian don Juan, whose truth and sources of knowledge defy conventional epistemological attitudes. A book sure to leave the reader asking just what truth is.

Devitt, Michael. *Realism and Truth*. Princeton: Princeton University Press, 1984. A readable but sophisticated defense of realism.

Gelven, Michael. *Truth and Existence*. University Park, PA: Pennsylvania State University Press, 1990. A highly readable and very enjoyable book on truth that takes a phenomenological approach understandable by the beginner with no background in philosophy. Gelven argues that truth is the manifestation or unfolding of what the world is like, a process that is much like the unfolding of the meaning of an insightful piece of literature.

Huxley, Aldous. *The Doors of Perception*. New York: Harper & Row, 1970. Huxley records his experiences with the drug mescaline. His account raises questions about the senses and the mind but especially about knowledge and truth.

Kirkham, Richard. *Theories of Truth: A Critical Introduction*. Cambridge: MIT Press, 1992. This is the most comprehensive treatment of theories of truth available today.

Lawson, Hilary, and Lisa Appignanesi, eds. *Dismantling Truth*. New York: St. Martin's, 1989. A collection of very readable articles on antirealist views of truth. Most of the articles support antirealism, but some argue against it.

Meiland, Jack W., and Michael Krausz. *Relativism*. Notre Dame: University of Notre Dame Press, 1982. A very good collection of articles on the debate between relativist and nonrelativist views of truth and knowledge.

Pirandello, Luigi. "It Is So If You Think So," in *Naked Masks: Five Plays*, ed. Eric Bentley. New York: Dutton, 1952. Italian novelist and playwright Pirandello's play about the mental state of a character named Ponza raises intriguing questions about the subjective/objective nature of truth. Is Ponza insane and keeping his wife and her mother from seeing each other? Or is he sane and the mother not really the mother at all but a madwoman who has never accepted the death of her daughter?

Poundstone, William. *Labyrinths of Reason*. New York: Doubleday Anchor, 1988. A fascinating discussion of the light that paradoxes and puzzles shed on knowledge and truth.

Schmitt, Frederick. *Truth: A Primer*. Boulder, CO: Westview, 1995. Although calling itself a "primer," this little book is actually a thorough treatment of the various theories of truth. Difficult but worthwhile.

Stoppard, Tom. *Jumpers*. New York: Grove, 1974. Stoppard, one of today's foremost dramatists, explores the difficulty of sustaining philosophical truth in the midst of the absurd, the comic, and the pathetic. In this play a philosopher delivers a lecture while bedlam reigns around him.

White, Alan R. *Truth*. Garden City, NY: Doubleday, 1970. This book offers a thoughtful treatment of the different meanings of truth, including three traditional and three modern concepts.

PART IV

Values

What values should we nourish in our private lives and in the public life of our communities? How should we seek solutions to our personal questions about sex, love, and abortion or to the social problems of homelessness, teenage pregnancy, racism, and sexism?

Traditionally, ethics has investigated the problem of values as they relate to human conduct—that is, questions of right and wrong, good and evil. It examines the meanings of value terms such as *obligation*, *good*, *virtue*, and *moral* to clarify our moral discourse and to understand our moral judgments. And it attempts to determine the moral principles upon which we are justified in living our lives.

Social philosophy, on the other hand, examines values as they relate to our social structures and political systems. It is concerned with understanding values such as justice, the general welfare, and human rights, on which we found our social institutions. And it attempts to determine what justifications, if any, exist for the state and its mechanisms, what our social obligations are, and what implications these have for our society.

So important are these issues that we shall devote our next two chapters to them. These chapters do not offer easy or simplistic answers; they attempt to provide a framework for understanding and developing values for yourself. In Chapter 7 we examine the public values that are critical in the decisions we make as a society: justice, human rights, law, and freedom.

CHAPTER 7

Ethics

Man is the only animal that blushes, or needs to.

MARK TWAIN

7.1 Introduction: What Is Ethics?

Moral issues are an inescapable part of who we are. For example, listen to the voices of these young men and women:

- All the other times when I did care about [birth control], when I was so afraid, I didn't get any satisfaction out of it at all, even during the whole intercourse. It seemed so one-way. Here I'm so wrapped up in being scared and he's getting the good end of it. He's not really worrying about what's going to happen to you. He's only worrying about himself. This time I think what I really thought was if you don't think about it, maybe you'll get something out of it. So I guessed it wouldn't be a hassle, I wouldn't worry about it. And I did get a lot more out of it, not worrying about it. I had thought about getting birth control pills with my boyfriend before, but that worked to where it was a one-way street for his benefit, not for mine. It would be mine because I wouldn't get pregnant, but safe for him, too, because I wouldn't put him on the spot. So I get sick of being used. I'm tired of this same old crap; forget it. I'm not getting pills for his benefit. So I never got them and I never thought I would have to 'cause I wasn't looking for anyone since I was tired of being used. Sex was a one-way street. He gets all the feelings, girls have all the hassles. She gets more emotional and falls head over heels while he could give a damn. I'm sick of it, so I thought, Hang it all [and got pregnant].[1]

- I was 26 and she was 22. . . . For her it was the second [abortion]. . . . She was 16 the previous time, and the guy had blamed her and was cruel about it. Having to go through it again traumatized her. I didn't know what to do. It numbed me out. My feelings for her and about her were pretty twisted. . . . She broke up eventually with me in a cut-and-dried, cold fashion, which I think was the result of the abortion. . . . To this day, I feel loss. I have a lack of understanding as to why it's so hard for me to accept how I feel, the pain or hurt or whatever it is. I want to derail it, but I think about it when I'm alone or when somebody brings it up. I don't really allow the feeling, even now, as I talk about it. I'm knotting in the stomach, uptight. . . . I feel guilty. Morally, in this day and age, it's not the end of the world. I don't see it as taking life away. I feel guilty in the sense that it's an unpleasant situation. You did start something, but I don't feel it's killing. If I did, I'd go nuts, I suppose.[2]

Two things fill the mind with ever new and increasing admiration and awe: the starry heavens above and the moral law within.

IMMANUEL KANT

---

[1] Quoted in Kristin Luker, *Taking Chances: Abortion and the Decision Not to Contracept* (Berkeley: University of California Press, 1975), 127–128.

[2] Quoted in Arthur B. Shostak and Gary McLouth, *Men and Abortion* (New York: Praeger, 1984), 86.

Are values objective or subjective? When I say, for example, that the *Mona Lisa* is beautiful, does the value I express originate in me or in the painting?

• [After this abortion] I'd like to get married and have a baby, but I doubt I ever will. I look too much for love and adoration, and I get them mixed up with sex. I guess I do it to get people to validate me. . . . [After the abortions] I never think about the babies at all. . . . I remember a conversation I had with a friend who'd just had an abortion. It's just an embryo, I told her, preferring to use the clinical definition. It's not a being, just a bunch of splitting cells. My friend said, "It's murder. How can you deny it's a life? It's murder, but it's justifiable homicide." . . . I agree with her, of course, but I just won't admit it. . . . Truth is hard to take, and I just don't know if I'm ready for it.[3]

These remarks remind us of the personal and moral questions we all must face: questions about the morality of sexual relationships, about the ethics of using people, about taking responsibility for the consequences of our actions, about the morality of abortion. They also remind us of the public decisions we must make as a society: whether to allow women to have abortions, whether to force unwed fathers to support their children, whether to provide sexual education in grade schools, whether to provide welfare to unwed mothers.

---

[3] Quoted in Linda Bird Franke, *The Ambivalence of Abortion* (New York: Random House, 1978), 63.

We can answer these questions only on the basis of the moral values that we believe in. Much of what we are and do, in fact, is determined by our moral values, because our values shape our thoughts, feelings, actions, and perceptions.

Yet where can we get help if we feel the need to think about our own values? In the past, perhaps because of strong family ties, we absorbed our values at the dinner table. We attended a particular church, voted for a certain party, read select magazines, and behaved in a prescribed way because our parents did. Yet for many of us today, family bonds, once strong and far-reaching, often extend no farther than the nearest freeway. Divorce, working parents, separations, and day-care centers have broken down much of family life. In fact, children today spend much more time watching television than talking with their parents. Yet the values suggested by television—acquisitiveness, selfishness, material-ism, violence—seem to be weak foundations, indeed, for building one's own values. Moreover, even when family life is intact, a blind allegiance to the val-ues proposed by parents is not necessarily commendable. To unthinkingly adopt the values proposed by your parents is to live your life according to the values others have chosen for you and not according to those you have chosen for yourself. The fundamental question is this: Will you live the life that other people want you to live and do what other people want you to do, or will you move through your life on a road you have mapped out for yourself? Will you live someone else's life, or will you live by values you have chosen?

To decide to choose your own values is to decide to philosophize. The at-tempt to examine one's values, to shape and rethink them in the light of one's own experience and reason, is a philosophical task. This philosophical task, which is the subject of this chapter, we call *ethics*.

Ethics is the study of morality. Ethics deals with morality, but it is not the same as morality. Morality is the subject matter that ethics studies. So what, exactly, is morality? **Morality** consists of the standards that an individual or a group has about what is right and wrong or good and evil. For example, suppose that you come home tired one day and for several hours you don't answer your telephone, but listen on your answering machine to people's voices when they call and leave messages. When you finally take a call, it's a friend who's upset she couldn't reach you earlier and asks whether you were home. You were home, of course, but didn't feel like answering the phone though you heard her mes-sages when she left them. You could tell the person the unvarnished truth, but you know she will feel angry and hurt. So you consider lying and saying you weren't home. However, you believe it's wrong to lie. So you tell her the truth. Here, your belief that lying is wrong is a moral standard that you follow. Moral standards are ideals that people try to live up to about what's right and wrong or good and evil.

Generally speaking, moral standards deal with matters to which we attach great importance. For example, most people in American society believe in moral standards against lying, theft, rape, enslavement, murder, child abuse, assault, slander, fraud, and lawbreaking. All these plainly deal with matters that people feel are quite serious. A person's moral standards typically come from

A cynic is a man who knows the price of everything and the value of nothing.
OSCAR WILDE

Inability to tell good from evil is the greatest worry of man's life.
CICERO

morality the standards that an individual or a group has about what is right and wrong or good and evil

many different sources and influences, including parents, church, school, television, friends, magazines, music, and associations.

So what, exactly, is ethics? Ethics begins when a person reflects on her moral standards or the moral standards of her society and asks whether these standards are reasonable or unreasonable, whether they are supported by good reasons or poor ones. So a person starts to do ethics when she takes the moral standards that she's absorbed from her family, her church, her society—and asks questions: Do these standards really make sense? What are the reasons for or against these standards? Why should I continue to believe in them? What can be said in their favor, and what can be said against them? Are they really reasonable for me to hold? Suppose, for example, that after you hang up the phone, you ask yourself whether telling your friend the truth about why you didn't answer her earlier calls was stupid. Telling the truth just hurt her feelings and made her get upset at you. Is it sometimes permissible to lie? Are some things—like people's feelings—more important than telling the truth? Why is honesty so important, anyway? What makes lying wrong? Is lying wrong because lying injures people? Then is lying right when telling the truth will hurt people more? What makes something right and wrong, and why are these so important?

When a person asks these kinds of questions about her moral standards or about the moral standards of her society, then she has started to do ethics. Therefore, ethics is the study of moral standards. It aims at developing standards that we feel are reasonable to hold, standards that we have thought about and have decided are justified.

We will begin our study of ethics by looking at an important challenge to ethics. This is the theory philosophers call *ethical relativism*. Ethical relativism holds that moral right and wrong depend on the culture a person belongs to. As we will see, this theory implies that we cannot say that one culture's moral beliefs are any better or worse than another's. But there are many problems in the theory of ethical relativism.

We will then turn to exploring several general theories of ethics. Each of these general theories proposes some general moral standards and values that it tries to defend. For most of us, ethical actions spring from general principles or values that we hold: "We should do whatever God commands us to do," "We should try to achieve the greatest happiness for the greatest number," "We should treat people only as they have consented to be treated," "We should be honest and courageous." But which principles are the most reasonable for us to adopt? We will look at the answers to this question that various philosophers have proposed. These proposals fall into three broad groups: consequentialist theories, nonconsequentialist theories, and virtue theories.

Consequentialist theories say that the morality of an action depends on its results or its consequences. For example, the theory of egoism is concerned with the best consequences for self, and utilitarianism is concerned with the best consequences for everyone. We begin our exploration of general moral theories with a look at some consequentialist theories.

We will next look at several nonconsequentialist views. Nonconsequentialist theories maintain that the morality of an action depends on factors other

He cannot long be good that knows not why he is good.
RICHARD CAREW

All wickedness is weakness.
JOHN MILTON

than consequences, such as moral rules or God's commands. For example, divine command theory is concerned with obeying the laws of God, whereas Kantian theory says that we should always treat people as ends and never use them as mere means.

Finally, we will examine virtue theories. Virtue theories say that morality depends not on rules or on the consequences of actions, but on our character. What matters in ethics is not so much what we do, but the kind of people we are. Are we generous or selfish, honest or dishonest, compassionate or mean, cowardly or courageous?

After we have looked at these three main general theories of ethics, we will see what light these theories shed on some specific moral problems. We will look at two specific moral quandaries: the issue of abortion and the issue of euthanasia.

Finally, we will end by returning to an issue that we have already explored: the issue of moral responsibility. We examined this issue briefly in Chapter 3 when we discussed the problem of determinism. Here we will look more closely at how determinism and moral responsibility are related to ethics.

QUESTIONS

1. Consider the following list of overarching values (developed by Dr. Milton Rokeach, a psychologist), and rank them in order of their importance to you: freedom, security, equality, beauty, peace, love, pleasure, salvation, excitement, comfort, self-respect, friendship, knowledge, contentment, inner harmony, wisdom, sense of accomplishment. Now consider the following personal qualities, and rank them in order of their importance to you: being logical, forgiving, clean, loving, obedient, honest, polite, responsible, ambitious, self-disciplined, open-minded, cheerful, competent. Look over both lists and ask yourself whether there are any conflicts between the personal qualities you value and the overarching values you have. What conclusions can you draw about yourself?

2. Are there other values or personal qualities that are important to you but that are not mentioned in the lists above?

3. Do you feel that you have chosen your own moral values, or have your moral values been imposed on you by your parents, school, peers, and society? To the extent that your moral values are imposed on you, can you do anything about changing them? What?

4. Explain the difference between ethics and morals.

5. Which of the following claims belong to the field of normative ethics? To descriptive ethics?

    a. Abortion is wrong.

    b. Many Americans believe that abortion is immoral.

    c. Murder means a wrongful killing.

    d. Rights are nonsense walking on stilts.

    e. The distribution of wealth in the United States is unjust.

    f. The majority of college students have engaged in sexual behavior that they feel is wrong.

7.2 Is Ethics Relative?

Ethics is not the only way to study morality. Sociology, anthropology, psychology, and other social sciences also study morality. But the social sciences study morality through a descriptive or factual investigation of moral behavior and beliefs. These sciences are concerned with how people in fact behave or what people in fact believe. Ethics asks how people should behave or what people should believe. For example, anthropologists tell us that the Inuit (Eskimos) used to abandon their elderly on the ice and allow them to die of starvation and exposure. They also inform us that some African tribes kill infant twins and require that a man marry his brother's widow. But anthropology, as such, does not try to determine whether it was right for the Inuit to abandon their elderly in this way. Nor does it try to decide whether it is right for African tribes to kill infant twins. Ethics, on the other hand, tries to answer the question of whether it is right for the Inuit, in their circumstances, to abandon their elderly. It tries to decide whether killing infant twins is right for African tribes, in their circumstances. Ethics asks how people should live, whereas the social sciences ask how people in fact live.

Although ethics and the social sciences study morality in very different ways, both have addressed one important issue. Many social scientists have been impressed by how different the moralities of different societies are. For example, many societies think that slavery is unjust, whereas others have felt slavery is permissible; some societies believe that infanticide is wrong, but other societies practice it frequently. This is also the case with differences regarding the morality of many activities, including abortion, polygamy, patricide, slavery, suicide, nepotism, sexual and ethnic discrimination, genocide, homosexuality, euthanasia, pornography, pedophilia, and the torture of animals. This diversity of moral standards has led many social scientists to embrace a view called *cultural relativism*. Cultural relativism holds that different cultures have different moralities and that what one culture believes is wrong, another culture may believe is right. In other words, cultural relativism is the view that what people believe about morality depends on the culture in which they live. Cultural relativism is undoubtedly valid. Still, many social scientists have gone a step further and embraced a view called *ethical relativism*, which is really a philosophical view and one that might be false.

To understand ethical relativism one must first be familiar with ethical absolutism. **Ethical absolutism** states that one and only one correct morality exists. Absolutists maintain that this one morality applies to everyone, everywhere, and always, although not everyone follows it or believes in it. What is a moral duty for me must also be a duty for you. What is a moral duty for an American must also be a moral duty for an Asian, African, European, or aborigine. If euthanasia is wrong, it is wrong for everyone, always, everywhere. That a society may see nothing wrong with euthanasia, lying, or cannibalism in no

ethical absolutism in ethics, the view that affirms the existence of a single correct and universally applicable moral standard

way affects the rightness or wrongness of such actions. Ethical absolutists do not necessarily claim that their own morality is the true and valid one. Yet they do insist that there is one true morality that is the same for all people in all ages and places.

Ethical relativism denies the existence of a single, universally applicable moral standard. As the name implies, ethical relativists insist that the correct morality is relative to one's society: Each society has its own morality, and an action is morally right for a person if the morality of one's society approves of the action. In short, ethical relativism holds that since there is no morality that all societies follow, each person should follow the morality of his or her own particular society.

It is important to see that ethical relativism is not cultural relativism. As we saw above, cultural relativism is the view that different societies believe in different moralities. Cultural relativism is a sociological fact: Research proves the existence of many obviously different moralities. But ethical relativists are not merely saying that what people in one part of the world *think* is right, people in a different part of the world *think* is wrong. Rather, ethical relativists assert that the same action that *is right* in one society actually *is wrong* in another. For example, anthropologists have shown that people in the jungles of New Guinea think that putting anyone over eighty years old to death is not wrong, whereas people in the United States clearly think that this is wrong. But the ethical relativist goes further and says that putting octogenarians to death *is* really right when one is a member of New Guinea society and it *is* really wrong when one is a member of United States society. In brief, ethical relativists believe that whatever the members of a society *think* is right for them to do is *in fact* what is right for them to do.

Many people have adopted the view that something is morally right if and only if their society thinks it is morally right. Yet this doctrine is very difficult to defend when we critically examine it. For example, how are we supposed to decide what "the ethical beliefs of a society" are? For example, does "U.S. society" think that abortion is right or that it is wrong? Does our society think that euthanasia is right or that it is wrong? Since our society is so deeply divided on these issues, saying what our society believes on these matters is impossible.

There is a deeper problem here. Ethical relativism says that something is morally right for a person if the person's society thinks that it is morally right. Suppose that it is a fact that all or almost all Americans believe abortion is right. Surely it doesn't follow that I myself must hold that abortion is right? Yet ethical relativism says that if my society believes that something is morally right, then it must be morally right for me also. Or suppose that everyone in my society except me believes that slavery is right. Surely it doesn't follow that I must be wrong if I think slavery is unjust? Indeed, if society's beliefs determine what the correct morality is for me, then I can never criticize my own society.

Let us look more closely at this problem. Consider that if ethical relativism were correct, then the only moral standards we could use to make moral judgments in a certain society would be the moral standards of that society. But then it wouldn't make sense to say that these moral norms are themselves morally wrong. For example, it wouldn't make sense for an American in pre–Civil

ethical relativism any view that denies the existence of a single universally applicable moral standard

*There is nothing either good or bad,
But thinking makes it so.*
WILLIAM SHAKESPEARE

Modern morality consists in accepting the standard of one's age.
OSCAR WILDE

War Southern society to say that the prevailing moral standard that permitted slavery is itself morally wrong. For what moral norms could the Southerner use other than those of his own society, which say that slavery is moral? In the same way, ethical relativism implies that I cannot criticize the moral norms of my society but must conform to them. For the ethical relativist, morality is conformity.

But the basic problem with ethical relativism is the argument that is supposed to prove it. The ethical relativist argues that the many cultural disagreements about moral matters show that no morality is valid for all societies. But isn't this a strange argument? When cultures disagree about some issue, does it follow that there is no objective universal truth about that issue? When people disagree about an issue, does it follow that all beliefs about that issue are equally acceptable? Philosopher James Rachels puts the matter quite succinctly:

> The fact that different societies have different moral codes proves nothing. There is also disagreement from society to society about scientific matters: in some cultures people believe that the earth is flat, and that evil spirits cause disease. We do not on that account conclude that there is no truth in geography or in medicine. Instead, we conclude that in some cultures people are better informed than in others. Similarly, disagreement in ethics might signal nothing more than that some people are less enlightened than others. At the very least, the fact of disagreement does not, by itself, entail that truth does not exist. Why should we assume that, if ethical truth exists, everyone must know it?[4]

There are other problems with ethical relativism. Is it really true that there are no moral standards that all societies recognize? Think about it. If a society is going to survive, don't its members have to accept some moral standards about how they should behave toward one another? Won't a society collapse if its members don't recognize the moral standard to refrain from arbitrarily murdering their neighbors? Won't the language of a society collapse if its members don't recognize the moral standard of telling the truth? Won't a society's ability to make contracts and agreements collapse if its members don't recognize the obligation to keep one's promises? Although societies may differ in many of their moral beliefs, aren't there certain basic moral standards that all societies have to accept just to survive?

Moreover, even when two societies seem to have very different moral standards, at a deeper, more fundamental level, the two societies may share the same moral values. For example, take infanticide, the practice of killing newborn infants. Some societies condemn this practice, whereas others, such as certain Inuit societies, have allowed it. What accounts for these differences? Societies that condemn infanticide do so because they value human life. Does this show that societies that practice infanticide do not value human life? Hardly. Anthropologists have noted that societies that permit infanticide exist in harsh physical environments and that they allow infanticide during times of great want. Still, they allow infanticide to ensure that their society can survive and

Right and wrong exist in the nature of things. Things are not right because they are commanded, nor wrong because they are prohibited.

R. G. INGERSOLL

---

[4]James Rachels, "Can Ethics Provide Answers?" *The Hastings Center Report*, vol. 10, no. 3 (June 1980), 34.

human life can continue.[5] So societies that permit infanticide do so because they, too, value human life. Nevertheless, to secure the survival of human life in their harsh environments, such societies must resort to the extreme measure of allowing infanticide. Societies, then, may share the same fundamental moral values. But their different circumstances or their different beliefs about the world may lead them to pursue these moral values through moral standards that, on the surface, look very different. The relativist is wrong, then, in claiming that the different moral standards found in different cultures show that there are no universal values recognized in all cultures.

Although the many objections to ethical relativism imply that it is mistaken, we should not reject the theory altogether. A fundamental point the theory is trying to make is that we should be tolerant of the moral beliefs of others. In particular, we should not assume that our own moral beliefs are the correct ones or even the best ones. The moral beliefs embedded in a culture different from our own have been fashioned over many centuries in response to the particular circumstances of that culture. For example, societies that face extreme hardships must adapt to those hardships with moralities that may look very different from ours. Yet their moralities may be trying to achieve the same basic human values for which we strive. In fact, some societies may have hit upon moral outlooks that are much better responses to the world than our own. We should, then, be tolerant and respectful of those different moral outlooks.

Yet having respect and tolerance does not mean that we cannot criticize and evaluate the moral beliefs of other cultures and those of our own culture. For example, we can ask whether the moral beliefs of our own society are reasonable, whether they are consistent, whether they look toward the true well-being of our society, whether they conform to the facts of human nature, whether they respect the dignity of persons, and whether they help produce admirable moral characters. We can ask these same questions of the moral beliefs of other cultures. Asking questions like these may lead us to conclude that our own moral beliefs are defective and that the moral beliefs of other societies are closer to adequate than are ours. Ethical relativism, which says that your society must determine your moral beliefs, would not allow you to reach this conclusion.

We will not explore ethical relativism any further. Whether we agree with the absolutist or the relativist stance, each of us still must decide what we ought to do individually and collectively. Presumably, this action requires some reasonable moral standard on which to base decisions. So whether I am an absolutist or a relativist, the question remains: What is it reasonable to hold about how I ought to behave and how my society ought to behave?

QUESTIONS

1. Explain the difference between cultural relativism and ethical relativism. Do you think that the fact that people disagree about moral right and wrong shows that ethical relativism is true? Explain.

---

[5] Glenn Hausfrater and Sarah B. Hardy, *Infanticide*, 1984.

2. During World War II, the Nazis in Germany believed that exterminating Jews and homosexuals was morally justifiable. Would an ethical relativist say that it was morally right to invade Nazi Germany to prevent the Germans from exterminating Jews and homosexuals? Explain.

3. Listen to some of your friends discussing or arguing about some moral issue — that is, some issue that involves right and wrong or good and evil. On the basis of how they argue about the issue, would you say that they are relativists or absolutists? Next ask them directly whether they are relativists or absolutists. Do any of your friends seem to be absolutists when they argue about a moral issue, yet say that they are relativists? Explain what you think is going on in such cases.

4. Explain this statement: "For the ethical relativist, morality is conformity."

5. Is the relativist or the absolutist more tolerant of people in his own society who have moral views that differ from those of the majority? Explain your answer.

7.3 Do Consequences Make an Action Right?

Consider this true story:

> Matthew Donnelly was a physicist who had worked with X-rays for thirty years. Perhaps as a result of too much exposure, he contracted cancer and lost part of his jaw, his upper lip, his nose, and his left hand, as well as two fingers from his right hand. He was also left blind. Mr. Donnelly's physicians told him that he had about a year left to live, but he decided that he did not want to go on living in such a state. He was in constant pain — one writer said that "at its worst, he could be seen lying in bed with teeth clenched and beads of perspiration standing out on his forehead." Knowing that he was going to die eventually anyway, and wanting to escape his misery, Mr. Donnelly begged his three brothers to kill him. Two refused, but one did not. The youngest brother, 36-year-old Harold Donnelly, carried a .30-caliber pistol into the hospital and shot Matthew to death.[6]

When questioned, Harold Donnelly said that he did not feel that killing his brother was immoral. It was much better for his brother to die than to suffer the terrible consequences of continuing to live. The consequences justified the killing.

Traditionally, many ethicists have contended that we should decide moral right and wrong by looking at the consequences of our actions. If the consequences are good, the act is right. If the consequences are bad, the act is wrong.

---

[6] James Rachels, *The Elements of Moral Philosophy* (New York: Random House, 1986), 82.

Thus, a **consequentialist theory** measures the morality of action by the nonmoral consequences. Consequentialists consider the ratio of good to evil that an action produces. The right action is the one that produces or will probably produce as great a ratio of good to evil as any other action. The wrong action is the one that does not.

For example, suppose that while driving down an almost deserted street one night, you momentarily take your eyes off the road and strike a parked car. You stop and cautiously look around. There's no one in sight, and no house lights are on. Using a flashlight, you estimate the damage to the parked car at about $200. You'd like to leave a note on the windshield, but you don't have insurance or the money to pay for the damage. Besides, the parked car is a new Corvette, and you assume that the owner must have insurance.

If you are a consequentialist, in determining what you should do, you'll evaluate the nonmoral consequences of the two choices. If you leave a note, you'll probably have to pay for the damage. That would greatly complicate your life: You'd have to work to pay off the debt, let other expenses slide, greatly reduce your luxuries, and possibly quit school. In contrast, if you don't leave a note, you might go unpunished while the owner foots the bill. Of course, the owner is likely to be hopping mad, perhaps even deciding to treat other motorists spitefully. Furthermore, if you are found out, you'll be in serious trouble, and even if you escape detection, you will still suffer the pangs of conscience. This is a consequentialist approach.

An obvious question arises here: In evaluating the nonmoral consequences of an action, whom do consequentialists have in mind? If you evaluate the consequences just for yourself in the preceding illustration, your judgment will be different than if you evaluate the consequences for the Corvette's owner. In deciding what to do, then, should we evaluate consequences only for ourselves, or should we consider the effects on all people involved? The answers to these questions form the bases for two consequentialist theories: egoism and utilitarianism.

consequentialist theory in ethics, the position that the morality of an action is determined by its nonmoral consequences

EGOISM

Some ethicists believe that in deciding the morality of an action, we should consider only the consequences for ourselves. These ethicists are called *egoists*. **Egoism** contends that we act morally when we act in a way that promotes our own best long-term interests. Although egoists argue about what actions will do this, they agree that once we decide such actions, we should take them. However, this notion does not imply that we should do whatever we want; often, our best immediate interests are not our best long-term ones.

Just what do egoists mean by "self-interests"? It's tempting to think that they must mean pleasure—that is, I act in my best interests when I do what will bring me the most pleasure. Holding this belief makes me a hedonist. **Hedonism** is the ethical philosophy which holds that only pleasure is worth having for its own sake. That is, hedonists view pleasure and only pleasure as having intrinsic value. Many egoists are hedonistic; for example, the ancient Greek philosopher Epicurus (341–270 B.C.) argued that people should live so

egoism a consequentialist ethical theory that contends that we act morally when we act in a way that promotes our own best long-term interests

hedonism the view that pleasure is intrinsically worthwhile and is the human's good

as to produce as much pleasure for themselves as possible. But two points need stressing. First, it's important to understand what the hedonist (or any normative theorist, for that matter) means by *pleasure*. Second, not all egoists are strict hedonists.

With respect to the first point, few popular definitions of *pleasure* would correspond with Epicurus's definition. Epicurus associated pleasure with what he termed *sober thinking* rather than sensual gratification:

> When I say that pleasure is the goal of living I do not mean the pleasures of libertines and the pleasures inherent in positive enjoyment. . . . I mean, on the contrary, the pleasure that consists in freedom from bodily pain and mental agitation. The pleasant life is not the product of one drinking party after another or of sexual intercourse. . . . On the contrary, it is the result of sober thinking—namely, investigation of the reasons for every act of choice and aversion, and elimination of those false ideas about the gods and death which are the chief source of mental disturbances.[7]

While preaching the pursuit of pleasure, Epicurus nonetheless discouraged excess. He identified simplicity and moderation in living as major goods because these carry the greatest advantages for us:

> Becoming habituated to a simple rather than a lavish way of life provides us with the full complement of health; it makes a person ready for the necessary business of life; it puts us in a position of advantage when we happen upon sumptuous fare at intervals and prepares us to be fearless in facing fortune.[8]

As for the second point above, many egoists identify the good not with pleasure but with knowledge, power, or rational self-interest. Some, in fact, associate it with self-realization, the promotion of all one's capacities. Although popularized by contemporary psychologists such as Abraham Maslow, the concept of self-realization is also evident in the works of classical philosophers. In *The Republic*, for example, Plato discusses the three active principles within each person: reason, appetite, and spirit (see Chapter 2). For Plato, each principle has a role to play, and when the principles work together, they result in personal harmony, order, and peace—self-realization. Similarly, in the first systematic examination of morality, *Nicomachean Ethics*, Aristotle stresses the life of reason, which entails the harmonious development of all functions of the human organism.

Today, self-realization as a goal of the good life continues to find philosophical expression. For example, British philosopher Francis Herbert Bradley (1846–1924) argued that satisfaction is possible only when one achieves self-realization—that is, a harmonious integration of all one's desires. Only then can a person become a self, an individual.

The point is that an egoist is not necessarily a hedonist. On the contrary, ethical egoists may hold any theory of value. However, they all agree that individuals should act in a way that advances their own best long-term interests. Ethical egoism does pose many problems. First is the issue of conflicting interests,

Morals are a personal affair; in the war of righteousness every man fights for his own hand.

ROBERT LOUIS STEVENSON

---

[7] Epicurus, "Letter to Menoeceus," in *The Philosophy of Epicurus*, ed. George K. Strodach (Evanston, IL: Northwestern University Press, 1963), 175.

[8] Ibid., 176.

which Kurt Baier (1917–   ) has expressed quite graphically. He asks us to imagine two presidential candidates, whom we will call Brown and Kory. It is in the interests of both to be elected, but only one can succeed. It follows, then, that it would be in Brown's interest but not in Kory's if Brown were elected, and vice versa. Similarly, it would be in Brown's interest but not in Kory's if Kory were liquidated, and vice versa. More important, Brown ought to do everything possible to get rid of Kory; in fact, it would be wrong for Brown not to do so. Likewise, Kory, knowing that his own liquidation is in Brown's interests, ought to take steps to foil Brown's endeavors. Indeed, it would be wrong for Kory not to do so. "It follows," writes Baier, "that if [Kory] prevents [Brown] from liquidating him, his act must be said to be wrong and not wrong—wrong because it is the prevention of what [Brown] ought to do, his duty, and wrong for [Brown] not to do it; not wrong because it is what [Kory] ought to do, his duty, and wrong for [Kory] not to do it."[9] Baier's point is that egoism seems unable to resolve conflicts of interest, which he assumes that a moral theory should do. Without that assumption, however, there are no conflicts, just a fully relativized situation in which each individual believes in his or her own best interests.

Related to this objection is a second one: Ethical egoism introduces inconsistency into moral counsel. To illustrate, let's suppose that Brown and Kory seek out the advice of Parnell. Parnell tells Brown to do whatever's necessary to prevent Kory from getting the job and to ensure that he, Brown, secures it. However, Parnell tells Kory to do whatever's necessary to prevent Brown from getting the job and to ensure that he, Kory, secures it. In her counsel, Parnell recommends two conflicting courses of action. Critics of ethical egoism fault a moral theory that allows such flagrant inconsistency in moral counsel. However, in fairness to egoism, the critics are again assuming a collective value. Egoism by definition holds no such value, so why measure it by one?

Some ethicists think that the most serious weakness of ethical egoism is that it undermines the moral point of view. By the "moral point of view," they mean the impartial attitude of one who tries to see all sides of an issue without being committed to the interests of a particular individual or group. Many ethicists maintain that the moral point of view is a necessary part of morality. One way of understanding the moral point of view is to think of it as the perspective taken by an ideal observer or judge.

An ideal observer has three key characteristics. First, the ideal observer is impartial or unbiased; that is, she does not treat herself as a special case. The ideal observer is as impartial in considering what she should do as she would be in deciding what someone unknown to her should do. Second, the ideal observer has full knowledge of the facts of the situation he must judge. Third, the ideal observer can imaginatively identify with any person involved in the situation. An individual who possessed these characteristics would be a perfect moral judge of any situation. The person can say what is morally right or wrong in any situation. Additionally, the ideal observer's view would tell the meaning of right and wrong.

---

[9] Kurt Baier, *The Moral Point of View* (Ithaca, NY: Cornell University Press, 1958), 189.

If we accept the legitimacy of this perspective, we must look for it in any proposed ethical standard. Nevertheless, ethical egoists cannot take the moral point of view. By definition, they are always influenced by their own best interest, whatever the issues, principles, circumstances, or individuals involved. Thus, Brown and Kory cannot be impartial or disinterested in determining the right courses for them to follow. What's more, if Parnell is an egoist, she can't take the moral point of view, for she must counsel each candidate with her own interest in mind.

But is the moral point of view realistic? No one can be completely impartial or disinterested. Some would even argue that approximating the perspective of the ideal observer is a surefire way to moral indecision, inaction, and passivity. Instead of engaging the issues of the day, the ideal observer is likely to withdraw from them. All moral decision making and action may involve a passional element, an essentially nonrational commitment of will that makes disinterest impossible. If this is so—and one could mount a powerful argument for it—then the most serious objection to egoism dissolves.

Obviously, the objections to egoism arise from holding a collective rather than a strictly subjective value. In fact, many consequentialists focus not on self-interest but on the interests of all involved. Such is the emphasis of the normative theory termed *utilitarianism*.

UTILITARIANISM

In contrast to egoism, utilitarianism asserts that the standard of morality is the promotion of everyone's best interest. In brief, **utilitarianism** claims that we act morally when our actions produce the greatest possible ratio of good to evil for all concerned. Again, as with all consequentialist positions, *good* and *evil* mean nonmoral good and evil.

utilitarianism in ethics, the theory that we should act in such a way that our actions produce the greatest happiness or pleasure.

As formulated and developed by Jeremy Bentham (1748–1832) and John Stuart Mill (1806–1873), utilitarianism maintains that only pleasure or happiness has intrinsic value. The opening chapter of Bentham's *Introduction to the Principles of Morals and Legislation* unequivocally states as much. Notice in the following excerpt how Bentham moves from the pleasure and pain experienced by an individual to that experienced by the group. In so doing, he lays the basis for the utilitarian moral principle that actions are right to the extent that they promote pleasure, wrong to the extent that they produce pain:

I. Nature has placed mankind under the governance of two sovereign masters, *pain* and *pleasure*. It is for them alone to point out what we ought to do, as well as to determine what we shall do. On the one hand the standard of right and wrong, on the other the chain of causes and effects, are fastened to their throne. They govern us in all we do, in all we say, in all we think: every effort we can make to throw off our subjection, will serve but to demonstrate and confirm it. In words a man may pretend to abjure their empire: but in reality he will remain subject to it all the while. The *principle of utility* recognizes this subjection, and assumes it for the foundation of that system, the object of which is to rear the fabric of felicity by the hands of reason and of law. Systems which attempt to question it, deal in sounds instead of sense, in caprice instead of reason, in darkness instead of light.

Jeremy Bentham: "Nature has placed mankind under the governance of two sovereign masters, *pain* and *pleasure*. They govern us in all we do, in all we say, in all we think. The principle of utility recognizes this subjection."

But enough of metaphor and declamation: it is not by such means that moral science is to be improved.

II. The principle of utility is the foundation of the present work: it will be proper therefore at the onset to give an explicit and determinate account of what is meant by it. By the principle of utility is meant that principle which approves or disapproves of every action whatsoever, according to the tendency which it appears to have to augment or diminish the happiness of the party whose interest is in question: or, what is the same thing in other words, to promote or to oppose that happiness; I say of every action whatsoever; and therefore not only of every action of a private individual, but of every measure of government.

III. By utility is meant the property in any object, whereby it tends to produce the benefit, advantage, pleasure, good, or happiness (all this in the present comes to the same thing) to prevent the happening of mischief, pain, evil, or unhappiness to the party whose interest is considered; if that party be the community in general, then the happiness of the community: if a particular individual, then the happiness of that individual.

IV. The interest of the community is one of the most general expressions that can occur in the phraseology of morals: no wonder that the meaning of it is often lost. When it has a meaning, it is this. The community is a fictitious *body*, composed of the individual persons who are considered as constituting as it were its *members*. The interest of the community then is, what?—the sum of the interests of the several members who compose it.

V. It is in vain to talk of the interest of the community, without understanding what is the interest of the individual. A thing is said to promote the interest, or to be *for* the interest, of an individual, when it tends to add to the sum total of his pleasures: or, what comes to the same thing, to diminish the sum total of his pains.

VI. An action then may be said to be conformable to the principle of utility or, for shortness sake, to utility (meaning with respect to the community at large), when the tendency it has to augment the happiness of the community is greater than any it has to diminish it.

VII. A measure of government (which is but a particular kind of action, performed by a particular person or persons), may be said to be conformable to or dictated by the principle of utility, when in like manner the tendency which it has to augment the happiness of the community is greater than any which it has to diminish it.[10]

In contrast to Bentham's original formulation, many modern utilitarians say that other things besides happiness or pleasure have intrinsic worth. Such things include power, knowledge, beauty, and moral qualities. Philosophers often term these views *ideal utilitarianism*. These views have attracted philosophers such as G. E. Moore[11] and Hastings Rashdall.[12] Since we'll be primarily considering classical utilitarianism, we'll use *good* to mean pleasure. However, what we'll say about classical utilitarianism applies equally to pluralistic positions if we substitute the phrase *intrinsic good* for *pleasure*.

At the outset, one may wonder whether pleasure can be calculated, as utilitarianism seems to require. Bentham thought it could. In attempting to determine how much pleasure and pain would result from a person's action, he formulated a hedonistic calculus. Bentham's hedonistic calculus determines how much pleasure an action produces based on many criteria, such as the intensity of the pleasure, how long it lasts, how certain it is to occur, and how likely it is to produce additional pleasure. Later, Mill added *quality* to Bentham's calculus, by which he meant the moral superiority that one pleasure holds over another. Although Bentham's calculus doesn't allow an exact calculation of pleasure and pain, it presents valuable criteria for evaluating actions other than immediate gratification.

In developing his calculus, Bentham seems to have had in mind a particular utilitarian theory of obligation, termed *act utilitarianism*, as distinguished from *rule utilitarianism*.

Act Utilitarianism

Act utilitarianism contends that we should act so as to produce the greatest happiness for the most people. In other words, before acting, ask yourself this: What will be the consequences of my action not only for myself but also for

> **CRITICAL THINKING**
> Bentham assumes that pleasure and happiness have a size and so can be measured and compared. Is this assumption plausible?

> **CRITICAL THINKING**
> Bentham and Mill assume that pleasure and happiness are necessarily good. Is this assumption correct? Are pleasure or happiness good for a person when acquired through evil means?

act utilitarianism in normative ethics, the position that an action is moral if it produces the greatest happiness for the most people

---

[10] Jeremy Bentham, *Introduction to the Principles of Morals and Legislation* (Oxford: Oxford University Press, 1823), 1–5.

[11] G. E. Moore, *Principia Ethica*.

[12] Hastings Rashdall, *A Theory of Good and Evil: A Treatise on Moral Philosophy*, 2 vols. (New York: Oxford University Press, 1924).

everyone else affected by my action? If the consequences are good (that is, if they will produce more happiness or pleasure than any other action I could perform in its place), the action is right; if they are bad (that is, if they will produce more unhappiness or pain than the alternatives), then the action is wrong. In effect, for act utilitarians, the end justifies the means. This can raise problems.

Suppose, for example, that you are a judge living in a small town in South Africa many years ago. The police bring a black man before you and charge him with raping a white woman the night before. The woman, who is the only

PHILOSOPHY AND LIFE

Getting to Know You: The Corporate Probe

Beth Broheimer was annoyed. "Over and over again, the same question," she thought. "What do they think I am—a thief?"

Do you think most companies take advantage of people who work for them when they can? Did you ever think about stealing money from places where you have worked? Do you believe you are too honest to steal?

At the very least, Beth decided, these were odd questions to ask someone who was applying for a job at The Gap, a chain of several hundred modern clothing outlets specializing in shirts, jackets, and Levi's jeans. But the questions went on:

If you knew that a member of your family was stealing from a place where he works, do you think you would report it to the owner of the company? Were you ever tempted to take company money without actually taking any? Do you keep out of trouble at all costs? Do you think it okay to get around the law if you don't actually break it?

Why such questions? The answer's simple: The Gap, like numerous

discount and drug stores, banks, brokerage houses, and fast-food restaurants, was subjecting Beth to a preemployment screen to determine whether she'd be likely to steal from the firm as an employee. Is such a determination possible? Yes, claim the sponsors of one such test, the Reid Report, devised by Reid and Associates, a polygraph firm based in Chicago. But the Reid Report asks other questions of the job candidate, which at best seem to relate only indirectly to the inventory's purpose:

How much money do you pay each month as a result of divorce or separate maintenance for the support of your wife and children? In the past five years about how much money, if any, have you gambled?

Before completing the Reid Report, Beth Broheimer will have answered questions about loans and debts, outside income, and personal habits (including drug and drinking habits). Indeed, by the time she's finished, she will have revealed to her prospective employer many important details of her financial

status; her criminal record, if any; her physical and mental health; and her personal life.

What will become of this information? Reid will keep the inventory dealing directly with theft. The rest of the information will be returned to her employer. And, oh yes, Reid and Associates will or will not recommend Beth Broheimer for employment at The Gap.

QUESTIONS

1. Does an employer have a right to subject a potential employee to such tests?

2. Is it proper for employers to know the details of their employees' personal lives?

3. What considerations do consequential and nonconsequential theories raise for deciding whether or not to use these tests?

SOURCE: Peter Schrag, "Confess to Your Corporate Father: Does Your Boss Know What You Do When You're Alone?" *Mother Jones* (August 1978): 56–60.

witness, has positively identified him although the rape took place in the dark of night. The rape has incensed the townspeople, and a mob of vigilantes has formed. The mob declares that if you do not sentence the black man to death, they will raid the small black settlement outside the town and kill several black women in revenge. You know that they will carry out this threat and that you have no way of stopping them. A few hours ago, though, by sheer improbable coincidence you happened to be alone at the bedside of a dying friend who—just before dying—confessed that he had committed the rape. It would be useless to bring this utterly improbable story to the mob; they would simply accuse you of trying to get the black man off the hook by making up an unlikely story. What should you do?

The implications of act utilitarianism are clear: You should sentence the black man to death although you know that he is innocent. By sentencing him to death, you would be sacrificing one innocent life to save several other innocent people; if you declare him innocent, you would be saving one life but condemning several others to death. Utilitarianism here seems to require us to condemn an innocent man to death, which seems terribly wrong.

Rule Utilitarianism

Many ethicists point out that we get into such dilemmas when we apply the "greatest happiness" principle to a *particular act* rather than to the *general rule* that the act is following. What we should be concerned with is following the rules that have the best consequences, not with carrying out the act that has the best consequences. This stance, called **rule utilitarianism,** means that we should act so that the rules governing our actions produce the greatest happiness for the most people.

For example, courts and judges should operate with the rule "We should never punish people for something they didn't do." Clearly, this rule would have the best consequences for society: People would know that the legal system would never arbitrarily punish them, and they would not suffer the fear and anxiety of never knowing how the courts will deal with them. Consequently, say the rule utilitarians, the South African judge should stick to this rule. He should not condemn the innocent man although condemning him in this instance might produce more collective happiness. In short, we should try to find the rules that will have the best consequences. We should always follow those rules no matter what might happen in a particular case.

But is it that simple? Consider, first, the problem of trying to figure out the consequences of promoting one rule over another. What research can establish with certainty that one rule will have better social consequences than another? Given our general ignorance of how societies function, it seems impossible to give definitive answers to this question.

Second, rules that allow for exceptions seem to promise more utility than rules that don't, but such rules are problematic. We have suggested, for example, that we should follow the rule "We should never punish people for something they didn't do." But wouldn't society be much better off in the long run if we promoted instead the rule "We should never punish people for something they

A good man does nothing for the sake of appearance, but for the sake of doing right.
EPICTETUS

rule utilitarianism the normative ethical position that we should act so that the rule governing our actions produces the greatest happiness for the most people

To be happy here is man's chief end,
For to be happy he must needs be good.
KIRKE WHITE

didn't do, *except in those instances where punishing them will leave everyone else better off*"? This rule will ensure that we do not punish innocent people, but it will allow for exceptions, so it should produce more utility than the first rule. Nevertheless, notice that following this second rule will again allow the judge to execute the innocent black man. Thus, rules that allow for exceptions have the most utility, but such rules allow the same injustices that act utilitarianism does. It is not clear, then, that rule utilitarianism is really an improvement over act utilitarianism.

Some Implications of Utilitarianism

In spite of these difficulties, many people believe that utilitarianism provides a very powerful analysis of ethics. To get a better understanding of utilitarianism and its difficulties, let us consider what it implies for a moral issue raised at the beginning of this chapter: our sexual behavior.

Sex is central to human life and raises a bewildering variety of moral questions. Are some forms of sexual activity—for example, incest, homosexuality, and adultery—morally deficient, or are there no limits on what is morally permissible in sex? For act utilitarianism, the answer to these questions is straightforward: Any action is morally permissible—in fact morally obligatory—if it produces a greater balance of pleasure over pain than any other available action. This seems to imply that virtually any sexual activity can be morally permissible—including incest, adultery, and homosexuality. All sexual activities would be permissible because normally they are all intensely pleasurable and sometimes at least their pleasures outweigh their harms. Many act utilitarians have reached exactly that conclusion. For example, in *Having Love Affairs* philosopher Richard Taylor offers an act utilitarian justification of adultery. He argues that since extramarital affairs based on love can often produce more good than harm for a married person, they are morally justified. Adultery based on love, Taylor argues, can provide a married person with another enriched human relationship, and these benefits justify the adultery:

> The joys of illicit and passionate love, which include but go far beyond the mere joys of sex, are incomparably good. And it is undeniable that those who never experience love affairs, and who perhaps even boast of their faultless monogamy year in and year out, have really missed something.[13]

Taylor goes on to argue that if revealing the affair to one's spouse will injure the spouse and the marriage relationship, then one should conceal the affair. Lying is justified, on act utilitarian grounds, if the net benefits of lying to one's spouse about an affair are greater than those of telling the truth. Other philosophers have used similar arguments to justify gay and lesbian sexual acts. Some have even argued that if the partners are consenting adults who take suitable contraceptive precautions, incest is morally permissible. This approach to sex would seem to rule out only those sexual acts that clearly involve harmful vio-

It is no easy task to be good.
ARISTOTLE

It is harder to fight against pleasure than against anger.
ARISTOTLE

Be sure you are right, then go ahead.
DAVID CROCKETT

---

[13] Richard Taylor, *Having Love Affairs* (Buffalo, NY: Prometheus, 1982), 12.

lence or great risks of harm. For example, this approach rules out violent rape or casual sex that risks contracting AIDS or some other venereal disease.

But is this approach to sex too permissive? Aren't some sexual acts, such as incest, intrinsically wrong? Isn't it immoral for the adulterer to break his marriage promises and then lie about it to his spouse? Perhaps even utilitarians would find Taylor's analysis too facile. Utilitarianism urges us to look beyond the immediate pleasure an action produces for oneself. It says we should also consider the beneficial and harmful consequences that our actions will produce for others now and in the future. When seen in this light, act utilitarianism might condemn many sexual activities—such as incest, adultery, and homosexuality—because of their harmful wider effects both on the individual involved and, more generally, on society.

In fact, a rule utilitarian approach to the ethics of sexuality will focus on these broader social effects explicitly. It will ask whether the long-term social consequences of moral rules that permit a certain type of sexual activity will benefit or harm society. The Ramsey Colloquium developed such an argument against various forms of sex. The Ramsey Colloquium is a group of Christian and Jewish scholars who have argued that the moral doctrines that permit adultery, divorce, and homosexuality will prove harmful to society:

> It is important to recognize the linkages among the component parts of the sexual revolution. [W]idespread adultery, easy divorce, . . . and the gay and lesbian movement have not by accident appeared at the same historical moment. They have in common a declared desire for liberation from constraint—especially constraint associated with an allegedly oppressive culture and religious tradition. They also have in common the presupposition that the body is little more than an instrument for the fulfillment of desire, and that the fulfillment of desire is the essence of the self. Finally, they all rest on a doctrine of the autonomous self. We believe it is a false doctrine that leads neither to individual flourishing nor to social well-being.
>
> Marriage and the family—husband, wife and children, joined by public recognition and legal bond—are the most effective institutions for the rearing of children, for the directing of sexual passion and for human flourishing in community. . . . Gay and lesbian "domestic partnerships" should not be socially recognized as the moral equivalent of marriage. Marriage and the family are institutions necessary for our continued social well-being. In an individualistic society that tends to liberation from all constraint, they are fragile institutions in need of careful and continuous support.[14]

The members of the Ramsey Colloquium argue that moral rules tolerant of homosexuality, adultery, and divorce are having harmful effects on family structures. These effects in turn harm society. They imply that it is wrong to accept and follow such permissive moral rules. But is this rule utilitarian argument about the morality of sexual activities correct? Is it clear to you that the acceptance of the moral permissibility of adultery, divorce, and homosexuality will have the harmful effects that critics allege? Some have argued that the reasons

---

[14]The Ramsey Colloquium, "Morality and Homosexuality," in *Today's Moral Issues*, ed. Daniel Bonevac (Mountain View, CA: Mayfield, 1996), 272–274.

for the decline of the family are many and complex, and that it is simplistic to blame this decline on permissive sexual attitudes. The problem with these rule utilitarian arguments, as with almost any utilitarian approach to ethics, is that they place such heavy burdens of information gathering on us. How are we to know exactly what the significant future consequences of our moral rules or our individual actions will be?

In spite of the questions it raises, utilitarianism identifies an important aspect of morality. It is true that future consequences are difficult to predict. Yet no one can deny that morally upright behavior, including sexual behavior, should attend to the consequences of what we do. We cannot deny that we should try to minimize the future harms that our sexual behaviors might inflict on ourselves and others. Also, we should try to do what we can to increase the well-being of our society. The problem, as we have seen, is that consequences are not all that matter in ethics. Therefore, we must turn to different approaches to ethics that can help us discern the other important elements of the moral life.

QUESTIONS

1. Some people argue that everyone is ultimately an ethical egoist. What do they mean by this? Do you agree? Would this prove that egoism is the basis for all ethics?

2. What are the connotations of the word *egoism*? Are these connotations compatible with what you know about ethical egoism?

3. With which concepts of knowledge and reality do you think ethical egoism is compatible?

4. How prevalent do you think ethical egoism is in contemporary society?

5. Below are four ethical problems. How would an act utilitarian solution differ from a rule utilitarian solution in each case?

a. An aide is conferring with the president of the United States: "Mr. President, it's imperative that you win the upcoming election. If you don't, subversives will take over the government. This could spell the end of our government as we know it. We could present the public with all the facts and let them decide, but that would only alarm and panic them. There's another way, and that is to use the enormous financial connections of this administration to manipulate and mold public opinion. This, it's true, will necessitate illegal election contributions, misrepresentation of facts, and considerable fancy footwork in the campaign. But it's an immediate, practical, and judicious solution in the best interests of the nation."

b. The daughter of a very rich and important public figure has been kidnapped. The kidnappers threaten to murder the young woman unless her father delivers $250,000 in ransom money. Authorities have told him that if he does so he'll only be encouraging future terrorist activities that will invariably involve more people, more suffering, and more deaths.

c. Taxpayer Smith decides that there are plenty of things he dislikes about the way the U.S. government is run: exorbitant defense spending, collusion between business and government, mismanaged funds, and so on. As a result, he is contemplating not paying his income taxes.

d. Jones and Brown are debating whether a person has a moral obligation to obey all laws. Jones claims that deliberately breaking a law is immoral. Brown denies this.

7.4 Do Rules Define Morality?

A **nonconsequentialist theory** maintains that the morality of an action depends on factors other than consequences. We can define the most influential nonconsequentialist theories as those that propose a single rule that governs human conduct and those that propose multiple rules. Two significant single-rule nonconsequentialist theories are the divine command theory and Immanuel Kant's categorical imperative theory. Buddhist ethics represents a kind of multiple-rule theory.

nonconsequentialist theory in ethics, the position that the morality of an action is determined by more than just its consequences

DIVINE COMMAND THEORY

The **divine command theory** is a nonconsequentialist normative theory that says we should always do the will of God. Whatever the situation, if we do what God wills, then we do the right thing; if we do not do what God wills, then, no matter what the consequences, we do wrong. There are two main types of divine command theories: those that hold that God's commands are found in sacred scriptures and those that hold that God's commands are found in human nature.

divine command theory a nonconsequentialist normative theory that says we should always do the will of God

Scriptural Divine Command Theories

A divine command theory does not state that we should obey God's laws because in so doing we will promote our own or the general good. Perhaps we will accomplish these ends, but the sole justification for obeying God's law is that God wills it. The theory also does not defend the morality of an action by promising some supernatural reward to the faithful. True, perhaps God will reward the faithful, and perhaps behaving righteously is in one's best long-term interests. But divine command theorists wouldn't justify moral actions on such egoistic grounds.

For divine command theorists, morality is independent of what any individual thinks or likes and what any society happens to sanction. God establishes moral laws; they are universally binding for all people and are eternally true, regardless of whether everyone obeys them. Such God-established laws are generally interpreted in a religious tradition and are often expressed in that religion's sacred scriptures. The Ten Commandments found in the Jewish scriptures are a good example:

> And God spoke all these words, saying, I am the Lord your God . . . you shall have no other gods before me. . . . Remember the sabbath day, to keep it holy. . . . Honor your father and your mother. . . . You shall not kill. You shall not commit adultery. You shall not steal. You shall not bear false witness against your neighbor. You shall not covet your neighbor's house. You shall not covet your neighbor's wife, or his manservant, or his maidservant, or his ox, or his mule, or anything that is your neighbor's.[15]

But contrast this Judaic view of God's commands with what many Christians today accept as the more significant expression of God's will in the Christian scriptures, the words of Jesus:

> And Jesus lifted up his eyes on his disciples, and said: . . . I say to you that hear, Love your enemies, do good to those who hate you, bless those who curse you, pray for those who abuse you. To him who strikes you on the cheek, offer the other also; and from him who takes away your cloak do not withhold your coat as well. Give to everyone who begs from you; and of him who takes away your goods, do not ask them back again. And as you wish that men should do to you, do so to them.[16]

Finally, contrast these expressions of God's commands in the Christian scriptures with what many adherents of the Islamic faith accept as the expression of God's will in the Koran, the scriptures of Islam:

> Thy Lord has decreed you shall not serve any but Him, and to be good to your parents. . . . And give the kinsman his right, and the needy, and the traveller; and never squander. . . . And keep not thy hand chained to thy neck, nor outspread it widespread altogether. . . . And slay not your children for fear of poverty. . . . And approach not fornication. . . . And do not approach the property of the orphan save in the fairest manner. . . . And fulfil the covenant. And fill up the measure when you measure, and weigh with the straight balance. . . . And pursue not what thou has not knowledge of. . . . And walk not in the earth exultantly. All of that—the wickedness of it is hateful in the sight of thy Lord.[17]

These laws, claim their adherents, apply to everybody everywhere, and their value does not depend on what produces human satisfaction, either individually or collectively. The justification of such moral laws is divine authority expressed through humans and their institutions and scriptures.

However, even a cursory look at scriptural divine command theory reveals some inherent weaknesses. First, and as the samples above make excruciatingly clear, different sacred scriptures exist. Which one expresses what God commands? It is true that there is some overlap in what each says. For example, both Judaism and Islam say that God commands us to respect our parents. But they differ in many respects about the specifics of what God commands. How

[15] Exodus 20:2–17.
[16] Luke 6:27–31.
[17] Sura 17:22–39.

are we to know which of these scriptures is right? Which one should we follow? Beyond that, how do we know that any of these writings represent the inspired word of God? Some assert that the scriptures say so. But isn't it circular reasoning to say that since a book says it's true, it must be true? And what of the fact that all these scriptures assert that they are the true, inspired word of God? Beyond that, can we be sure that God even exists? What help are these scriptural commands to the unbeliever, the agnostic, and the atheist? If morality is following what some religion says are God's commands, does it follow that the unbeliever can have no morality? And if God does exist, can we be sure that God expressed His law in one source and not in another?

Men never do evil so completely and cheerfully as when they do it from religious conviction.

BLAISE PASCAL

There is also a deeper, more fundamental problem: The scriptural divine command theory can't satisfactorily explain why God commands something. In other words, if God commands something because it is right, then the theory appears circular because it contends that something is right *because* God commands it. If something is right because God commands it, then anything that God commands must be right. Should God command cruelty, then cruelty would be right—a most difficult proposition to defend.

There is another kind of ethics that also appeals to God's command but that, paradoxically, does not require belief in God. This is natural law ethics.

Natural Law Ethics

Natural law ethics holds that humans should live according to nature. The Stoics, followers of the school of thought originally founded by Zeno around 300 B.C., held a natural law ethic. For example, they believed that there is a kind of universal natural order in the world put there by God that the human mind can discover. To the extent that humans live according to this universal order, as it is exhibited in their own human nature, they will flourish and be happy. The ancient Stoic philosopher Epictetus (c. 50–130), for example, wrote the following:

Goodness does not more certainly make men happy than happiness makes them good.

W. S. LANDOR

> The business of the wise and good man is to live conformably to nature: and as it is the nature of every soul to assent to the truth, to dissent from the false, and to remain in suspense as to that which is uncertain; so it is its nature to be moved toward the desire of the good, and to aversion from the evil; and with respect to that which is neither good nor bad it feels indifferent. . . . When the good appears, it immediately attracts to itself; the evil repels from itself.[18]

Here, Epictetus is saying that if we look at human nature we will see that it has certain natural tendencies. We have a natural tendency to believe what we discover is true, to reject what is false, and to suspend belief about matters we are unsure of. In the same way, we have a natural tendency to desire what we judge is good for us and a natural tendency to feel repelled by what we judge is bad for us. We also have a natural tendency to feel indifferent about what is neither beneficial nor harmful to us. The morally good person, he suggests, is the person who lives according to these basic natural tendencies. The

Natural law is the first principle of morality; it forbids evil and commands good.

MARTIN LUTHER

---

[18] Epictetus, *Discourses*, III, 3.

morally evil person is the one who violates these basic tendencies, perhaps by gratifying his cravings for things that his judgment says are bad for him. Moral rightness, then, is conduct that conforms to these natural tendencies.

What does this have to do with God and God's commands? The key idea is that God made human nature. So if one lives according to what human nature requires, one is living according to what God intended when He made humans. If you live according to your nature, Epictetus avers, then you can always be "conscious that you are obeying God." In short, the requirements of human nature are the commands of God. Humans can discover those commands by looking at their own nature, and in following these commands they are morally good.

Natural law ethics, then, began with the ancient Greeks. Nevertheless, the classical proponent of the idea that reason can discover God's commands by reflecting on human nature is the Christian philosopher/theologian Thomas Aquinas. Aquinas held that since God created the universe, the laws that govern it are laws that God imposed on it. In particular, God imposed on human beings certain "natural laws" through the natural inclinations that He built into human nature when He created humans. The most important of these inclinations are our reasoning abilities:

> Now rational creatures [such as humans] are also subject to God's provident direction, but in a way that makes them more like God than all other creatures. For God directs rational creatures by instilling in them certain natural inclinations and [reasoning] abilities that enable them to direct themselves as well as other creatures. Thus human beings also are subject to God's eternal law and they too derive from that law certain natural inclinations to seek their proper ends and proper activities. These inclinations of our nature constitute what we call the "natural law" and they are the effects of God's eternal law imprinted in our nature.[19]

According to Aquinas, morality arises when our reason becomes aware of the "natural inclinations" that God built into human nature. In particular, Aquinas holds, our reason tells us that we have a moral obligation to pursue those goods toward which we are naturally inclined and to refrain from destroying them:

> A thing is good if it is an end that we have a natural inclination to desire; it is evil if it is destructive of what our nature is inclined to desire. Consequently, those kinds of things that our nature is inclined to desire are perceived by our reason as good for our human nature. And our reason will conclude that those kinds of things ought to be pursued in our actions. But if our reason sees a certain type of thing as destructive of what human nature is inclined to desire, it will conclude that that type of thing ought to be avoided.
>
> We can therefore list the basic [moral] precepts of the natural law by listing the kinds of things that we naturally desire. First, like every other nature, human nature is inclined to desire its own survival. Consequently it is a natural [moral] law that we ought to preserve human life and avoid whatever is destructive of life. Secondly, like other animals, human nature is inclined to desire those things that nature teaches

Seek not the good in things external; seek it in yourselves: If you do not, you will not find it.
EPICTETUS

Nothing is evil which is according to nature.
MARCUS AURELIUS

The natural law, in its universal character, can in no way be blotted out from men's hearts.
THOMAS AQUINAS

---

[19] Saint Thomas Aquinas, *Summa Theologica*, I–II, Q. 91, a. 2. This translation copyright © 1978 by Manuel Velasquez.

all animals to desire by instinct. For example, all animals have an instinctive desire to come together in a union of male and female, and an instinctive desire to care for their young. [So it is morally right to pursue these things.] Thirdly, human nature is inclined to desire those goods that satisfy our intellects. This aspect of our nature is proper to human beings. Thus, human nature is inclined to desire knowledge (for example, to know the truth about God) and to desire an orderly society. Consequently, it is a natural [moral] law that we ought to dispel ignorance and avoid harming those among whom we live.[20]

Thus, by reflecting on our natural human inclinations we can discover the specific goods that God commands humans to pursue: human life, family, knowledge, and an orderly society. Actions are morally right when they aim at securing these goods, and they are morally wrong when they aim at destroying these goods.

Some examples might clarify what Aquinas means and might also clarify some important features of natural law ethics. Consider the issue of suicide. Aquinas held that suicide was immoral. But he did not condemn suicide merely because the Christian scriptures say that it is wrong to take one's life. Instead, Aquinas argued that human nature has a built-in inclination to desire life. For example, consider how each of us instinctively wants to stay alive and instinctively avoids life-threatening situations. Since we are naturally inclined to desire life, Aquinas held, our reason knows immediately that life is a fundamental human good that we should not destroy. And since God is the source of this inclination, the requirement that we should not destroy life is His command. Suicide, then, is wrong because it destroys what our reason knows is a fundamental human good that we should not destroy. By destroying this good, suicide violates the command of God.

> **CRITICAL THINKING**
>
> Does natural law ethics assume that what happens naturally ought to happen? Is this assumption true?

But what are we to do when there are conflicts among the goods toward which we are inclined? That is, what are we to do when we can secure one good only by destroying another? What should I do, for example, when I can save my life only by destroying another life? Is killing in self-defense always immoral? To deal with such conflicts, Aquinas proposed what we now call the "principle of double effect." Aquinas suggested that actions sometimes produce two or more effects. Killing in self-defense results in saving my life and in the destruction of the life of my attacker. When actions have such double effects, Aquinas argued, what matters is one's intention. If one's intention is aimed at saving one's own life and if one does not inflict more destruction than is absolutely necessary to save one's life, it is permissible to "allow" the destruction of life as an unavoidable side effect of preserving the good of one's life. But it would be wrong for one to deliberately intend or want the death of the other person.

Today, there are many philosophers who have adapted Aquinas's natural law theory. For example, the British philosopher John Finnis (1940–) has presented a sophisticated natural law theory in his book *Natural Law and Natural Rights*.[21] But Finnis has argued that we need to revise Aquinas's four fundamental goods and expand them to include seven basic forms of good:

---

[20] Ibid., I–II, Q. 94, a. 2.
[21] John Finnis, *Natural Law and Natural Rights* (Oxford: Oxford University Press, 1980).

Now besides life, knowledge, play, aesthetic experience, friendship, practical reasonableness, and religion, there are countless objectives and forms of good. But I suggest that these other objectives and forms of good will be found, on analysis, to be ways or combinations of ways, of pursuing (not always sensibly) and realizing (not always successfully) one of these seven basic forms of good, or some combination of them.[22]

Clearly, natural law theory does not raise all of the problems that scriptural divine command theories raise. For example, natural law theory does not have to deal with the problem that many different scriptures exist, each claiming to tell us what God commands. In fact, one of the most important advantages of natural law theory is that one does not even have to believe in God to accept the theory. For the theory claims that morality is based on living according to our human nature, and this claim does not require belief in God. All people, whether they believe in God or not, can discover what morality requires by reflecting on their own human nature. Those who believe in God, of course, will take the additional step of concluding that because God made human nature, it embodies what God intends for humans. But the unbeliever can reject this additional step and still agree that our human nature is the best guide to moral right and wrong.

Nor does natural law theory have to deal with the problem that God might command something that is bad for us. For in natural law theory whatever is good for our nature is what God commands. And what God commands when He makes our nature will be what is good for us.

Nevertheless, natural law theory has had its critics. For example, critics have asked why we should be morally obligated to pursue the goods that our natural inclinations seek. Why are our *inclinations* the measure of what is naturally good for us? Isn't it at least logically possible that we might be naturally inclined to things that are not necessarily good for us? Children often have desires for things that are bad for them. Isn't it possible for adults to similarly have inclinations toward what is evil? In addition, doesn't natural law have some damaging ambiguities? For example, natural law doesn't seem sure exactly what the fundamental goods are supposed to be. Aquinas argued that there were four, whereas modern natural law philosopher Finnis has opted for a rather different group of seven. How are we to decide not just how many there are, but exactly what they are supposed to be?

Finally, consider the problem of conflicts between fundamental goods—i.e., situations in which pursuing one good requires destroying another. Clearly, such conflicts are common in human life. Aquinas uses the principle of double effect to deal with such conflicts. He claims that we must only intend to preserve the one good and not intend to destroy the other good. But, in such cases, can we really limit our intention to the pursuit of the good? When I am forced to kill a person in self-defense, for example, don't I also really intend to destroy the life of that person? When I foresee that one of my actions will have many effects, don't I necessarily intend those effects to happen? But if the principle of

It is not by running here and there outside of itself that the soul understands morality; it learns morality from its own nature.

CICERO

---

[22] Ibid., 90.

double effect doesn't work, then won't the problem of conflicts between funda-mental goods end up destroying natural law theory?

Implications of Divine Command Ethics

Although divine command ethics has several limitations, many philosophers believe that, if used carefully, it can give us significant insights into the morality of important aspects of human life. One of the topics that divine command theorists have addressed at some length, in fact, is the topic we earlier discussed in relation to utilitarian theory: sexual activity. As we saw when we examined some of the moral code of Islam, for example, the Islamic scriptures, like the Judaic scriptures, condemn fornication. Nevertheless, such appeals to the scrip-tures of one religion mean little to those who belong to other religions or to no religion at all.

As we noted, however, natural law theory does not require belief in a par-ticular religious scripture or religious authority. For this reason it has appealed to the members of several different religious traditions and has even been per-suasive to many who believe in no religion at all. What light, then, can natural law theory shed on the morality of sex?

For natural law theory, the injunction that we should "live according to nature," when applied to sexual activity, implies that we must take seriously the basic good toward which sexual activity is naturally oriented. Some natural law ethicists have argued that it is clear that sex is naturally oriented toward the basic good of procreation. Consequently, it is immoral to engage in any sexual activity that does not remain open to this good. John Finnis argues as follows:

> [T]he choice to exclude the possibility of procreation while engaging in intercourse is always, and in an obvious and unambiguous way . . ., a choice directly and imme-diately against a basic value. . . . And if a question is raised about solitary sexual acts or sexual intercourse outside the vagina (whether homo- or heterosexual), the [natu-ral law] response . . . turns on the fact that all sexual activity . . . [must retain] . . . a sufficient openness and respect towards [this basic procreative value]. . . . [S]ome sexual acts are (as types of choice) always wrong because [they are] an inadequate response, or direct closure, to [this] basic procreative value.[23]

In this natural law approach, a sexual activity is immoral and "unnatural" if it cannot result in pregnancy or if we take steps to block the possibility of a preg-nancy. This would include all homosexual activities, as well as oral sex, anal sex, masturbation, bestiality, sex with animals, sex with dead bodies, sex with inanimate objects, and sadomasochistic sex.

For many people, the moral condemnation of such forms of sex is exactly right. They believe that natural law theory correctly identifies the fundamental purpose of sex—reproduction—and correctly evaluates sexual activities in terms of this fundamental purpose. Moreover, many people feel that, unlike utilitarianism, this approach correctly shows that there are certain forms of

---

[23] John Finnis, "Natural Law and Unnatural Acts," *The Heythrop Journal*, vol. 11, no. 4 (October 1970), 380.

sexual activity that are intrinsically immoral whatever the consequences. Consider, in fact, that many people (rightly or wrongly) describe as "unnatural" precisely those forms of sex that the natural law condemns: homosexual sex, sex with animals, sex with the dead, and so on.

But can't sex serve many purposes other than procreation, such as pleasure, intimacy, play, and communication? Why should reproduction be singled out as the only morally relevant purpose of sex? Suppose that in some sense, say a biological sense, the purpose of our sexual organs is reproduction. Still, why should this biological fact make it immoral to use them for other purposes? In an evolutionary or biological sense the purpose of teeth is to chew food and the purpose of eyes is to see. But is there anything immoral about using one's teeth to pry the top off a beer bottle or to use one's eyes to flirt? Although evolution has adapted our sexual organs for the function of procreation, they also have other functions, including that of providing pleasure. What is wrong with using them solely for the latter purpose?

However, there are other, more liberal natural law approaches to sex. For example, David Levy provides a different approach to sexual matters. He rejects the view that sexual activities are necessarily wrong when they cannot issue in reproduction. Instead, he argues, sexual activities are unnatural and immoral when they deny a basic good without necessity and do so for the sake of sexual pleasure. This understanding of natural law, Levy suggests, does not imply that, say, homosexuality is unnatural:

> [W]hat I count as the basic human goods can be rather completely listed: life, health, control of one's bodily and psychic functions, the capacity for knowledge and love. . . . I suggest that an unnatural act is one that denies a person (oneself or another) one or more of these basic human goods without necessity, that is, without having to do so in order to prevent losing some other basic human good. . . . Denying oneself or another a basic human good without some other basic human good being expected or intended to be made possible thereby is always wrong. . . .
>
> The perverted is a subclass of the unnatural. When a person denies himself or another one of the basic human goods (or the capacity for it) and no other basic human good is seen as resulting thereby, and when pleasure is the motive of the denial, the act is perverted. When the pleasure is sexual, the perversion is sexual.
>
> The child molester is a case of sexual perversion. . . . [T]he young girl sexually initiated by an older person can easily be traumatized; that there is no way of undoing the harmful effects with the ease and certainty with which they were induced establishes the correctness of classifying the case as one of sexual perversion. . . .
>
> That perversion degrades is a necessary truth . . . as I have defined perversion. . . . Although the definition of [perversion] does not, by itself, produce criteria strong enough to allow us to be decisive in the important case of homosexuality, the definition [does] seem to require rape to be included among the sexual perversions . . . [since] rape does degrade.[24]

Levy is suggesting here that the morality of a sexual act does not depend on whether the act can result in procreation. Instead, a sexual act is morally wrong only if it *destroys* a concrete instance of a basic human good. For example, child

---

[24] Donald Levy, "Perversion and the Unnatural as Moral Categories," *Ethics*, vol. 90, no. 2 (January 1980), 191–202.

molestation is wrong because it destroys the psychic functioning of the child. Rape is wrong because it destroys the psychic functioning of the adult victim. Levy's natural law approach, with its more tolerant view of homosexuality and, perhaps, of other forms of sex, seems more aligned with contemporary views of sexual morality.

Yet perhaps we should not so quickly dismiss the more conservative natural law views of philosophers like Finnis. It is true that the natural law view of Finnis has significant problems. Still, his view alerts us to an aspect of sex that is morally important, namely, the relationship of sexual intercourse to reproduction. For many people the fact that sexual intercourse can result in pregnancy raises important moral issues for anyone considering sex.

Philosophers have not been indifferent to the objections brought against natural law theory and other divine command theories. In the eighteenth century, Immanuel Kant attempted to present a nonconsequentialist theory based not on religious teaching but on reason alone.

QUESTIONS

1. Reconsider the four situations described in question 5 of Section 7.3 from the viewpoint of a divine command theorist. What decisions and actions do you think are called for? Would the judgments differ from the act utilitarian's? The rule utilitarian's?

2. Now consider the four situations from the viewpoint of a natural law theorist.

3. If you were to make a list of the fundamental human goods toward which we are "naturally inclined," what would you include in the list? What would you exclude? What criteria would you use to decide what belongs on the list and what does not?

4. Aquinas interprets the injunction that we should "live according to nature" to mean that we should respect the fundamental goods toward which reason sees we are naturally inclined. Suggest other ways of understanding the injunction that we should "live according to nature" that are different from the way that Aquinas interprets the injunction. What are the implications of your interpretation of "live according to nature" for the morality of sex?

5. Although natural law theory is usually not classified as a consequentialist theory, many people have argued that it has consequentialist elements. In what ways is natural law theory consequentialist? In what ways is it not consequentialist?

KANT'S CATEGORICAL IMPERATIVE

The eighteenth-century German philosopher Immanuel Kant was a deeply religious man. Yet he rejected divine command theories of ethics as well as utilitarian theories. Kant held that a person should decide for himself the moral laws that he will follow. He called this ability to decide for oneself "autonomy of the will." Kant contrasted this with "heteronomy." *Heteronomy* is allowing

Immanuel Kant: *"I am never to act unless I am acting on a maxim that I can will to become a universal law.* Only this principle can prevent duty from becoming a vain delusion."

someone or something else to decide the moral laws that one will follow. The trouble with divine command theories is that they say that the church or the Bible or human nature should decide for us what moral laws we will follow. Utilitarian theories are worse. Utilitarian theories say that our desires for pleasure or for happiness should decide what is right or wrong for us. So both divine command theories and utilitarian theories are heteronomous. Both hand over morality to something outside our own decision-making ability.

For Kant, autonomy or the ability to decide morality for oneself must lie at the heart of ethics. This means that ethics must study the will since our will is our ability to decide things for ourselves. Ethics must begin by looking at what a good will is.

Kant argues that nothing is good in itself except a "good will." Intelligence, judgment, and all other facets of the human personality are perhaps good and desirable, but only if the will that makes use of them is good:

> It is impossible to think of anything in the universe—or even beyond it—that is good without qualification, except a good will. Intellectual talents such as intelligence, cleverness, and good judgment are undoubtedly good and desirable in many respects; so also are character traits such as courage, determination, and perseverance. But these gifts of nature can become quite evil and harmful when they are at the service of a will that is not good. It is the same with gifts of fortune such as power, wealth, honor, and even health and that general well-being and contentment we call happiness. These will produce pride and conceit unless the person has a good will, which can correct the influence these have on the mind and ensure that it is adapted to its proper end. Moreover, an impartial rational spectator would not feel any pleasure at seeing a person without a good will enjoying continuous happiness. Thus it seems that having a good will is a necessary condition for even deserving happiness.[25]

---

[25] Immanuel Kant, *Grundlegung zur Metaphysik der Sitten [Groundwork of the Metaphysics of Morals]*, in *Immanuel Kant Werkausgabe*, vol. 7, ed. Wilhelm Weischedel (Frankfurt, Germany: Insel Verlag Wiesbaden, 1956), 18. This translation copyright © 1987 by Manuel Velasquez.

By *will*, Kant meant the uniquely human capacity to be motivated by reasons or "maxims." A "good will" is a will that is motivated to perform an act because it is a *moral duty* and not merely because the act is in one's self-interest or gives one pleasure. To be motivated by duty, according to Kant, is to be motivated to do something because one believes it is the way that all human beings ought to behave. Acting morally, then, is acting only on those maxims or reasons that you believe everyone—universally—ought to live up to. For Kant, my will is "good without qualification" only if it always has in view one principle: Can I will that my maxim be followed by everyone as a universal law? Kant expresses this idea by asking us to imagine that the laws of nature force everyone to follow the maxims that I act on. Would I still perform the actions that I plan to perform if I knew that my maxims would become laws of nature that everyone would have to follow? If not, then I should not perform the actions.

These crucial aspects of Kant's theory of ethics are presented in the following passage from Kant's masterpiece, *Groundwork of the Metaphysics of Morals*. Notice that Kant does not rely on a consideration of consequences:

> But what sort of law can this be that mere awareness of it is enough to make the absolutely good will choose to follow it regardless of the results? Since I have ruled out every motive based on the desirable results of obeying any particular law, no other motive is left for the good will to act on except the motive of obeying the [moral] law simply because it is a universal law. That is, *I am never to act unless I am acting on a maxim that I can will to become a universal law*.
>
> Thus, the basic principle that the will must follow is the principle of conforming to universal law (as distinct from a law that would require a particular action). Only this principle can prevent duty from becoming a vain delusion and a mythical notion. . . .
>
> We can express the basic principle of the categorical imperative in different words if we first note that the universal laws of cause and effect that govern the world are what we properly mean by "nature" in the most general sense of the word (these laws give nature its form). For nature is the existence of things insofar as they are structured by general laws. Consequently, the basic principle of the categorical imperative can also be expressed in the following version: *Act as if the maxims you choose to follow always became universal laws of nature*.
>
> We will now enumerate a few of the duties that follow from this version of the categorical imperative. We will adopt the usual practice of classifying duties into perfect and imperfect duties and subclassifying each of these into duties to ourselves and duties to others.
>
> 1. *Perfect duty to oneself*. Imagine a man who has been reduced to despair by a series of misfortunes. Suppose he feels tired of living, but is still able to ask himself whether it would be contrary to duty to take his own life. So he asks whether the maxim of his action could become a universal law of nature. His maxim is this: "Out of self-love I will adopt the principle that I will end my life once it contains more evils than satisfactions." Our man can then ask himself whether this principle, which is based on the feeling of self-love, can become a universal law of nature. He will see at once that a system of nature that contained a law that destroyed life by means of the very feeling whose function it is to sustain life would contradict itself. Therefore, such a law could not be part of a system of nature. Consequently, his maxim cannot become a universal law of nature so it violates the basic principle of morality.

CRITICAL THINKING

Does Kant assume that a person could never will to universalize evil or harm? Is this assumption correct?

2. *Perfect duty to others*. Imagine another person who finds himself forced to borrow some money. He knows that he will not be able to repay it, but he also knows that nobody will lend him anything unless he promises to repay it. So he is tempted to make such a promise. But he asks himself: Would such a promise be consistent with duty? If he were to make such a promise the maxim of his action would be this: "When I need money, I will borrow it and promise to repay it even if I know that I will never do so." Now I personally might be able to live according to this principle of self-interest. But the question is: Is it right? So I ask myself: What if my maxim were to become a universal law? Then I see at once that it could never even become a universal law of nature since it would contradict itself. For suppose it became a general rule that everyone started making promises he never intended to keep. Then promises themselves would become impossible as well as the purposes one might want to achieve by promising. For no one would ever believe that anything was promised to him, but would mock all "promises" as empty deceptions.

3. *Imperfect duty to oneself*. Imagine a third man who has a useful natural ability that he could develop through practice and exercise. However, he is comfortably situated and would rather indulge in pleasure than make the effort needed to develop and improve himself. But he asks himself whether his maxim of neglecting his natural gifts as he is tempted to do is consistent with his duty. He sees then that a system of nature could conceivably exist with such a universal law, even if everyone (like the South Sea islanders) were to let his talents rust and devoted his life to idleness, amusement, and sex—in a word, to pleasure. But although his maxim *could* be conceived as a universal law of nature, he could not *will* it to be a universal law of nature; that is, he could not will such a law to be implanted in us like a natural instinct. For our natural abilities enable us to achieve whatever goals we might have, so every rational person who has any goals whatever necessarily wills to have his abilities develop.

4. *Imperfect duty to others*. Imagine a fourth man who is prosperous, while he sees that others have to put up with great wretchedness. Suppose he could help them but he asks himself: What concern is it of mine? Let everyone have whatever happiness God or his own efforts can give him. For my part I will not steal from people or envy their fortune. But I do not want to add to their well-being or help them when they are in need! Undoubtedly, if such a way of thinking became universal, the human race could continue to exist; it might even be better off than if everyone were to talk about sympathy and good will and occasionally practiced it, but generally continued to cheat whenever they could and betrayed and violated the rights of others. However, although that maxim *could* be a universal law of nature, one could not *will* it to be a universal law of nature without having one's will come into conflict with itself. For we know that many situations will arise in which one will need the love and concern of others. So if one were to will such a law of nature, one would be depriving himself of that aid he knows he will need.

These are a few of the duties that can be derived from the principle we have laid down. They fall into two classes. The basic rule for evaluating the morality of our actions is this: We must be *able to will* that the maxim of our action should be a universal law. One class of duties (the perfect duties) consists of actions whose maxim cannot even be consistently *conceived* as a universal law of nature, much less could *we will* such maxims to be universal laws of nature. The second class of duties (the imperfect duties) consists of actions whose maxims *could* become universal laws of nature, but it is impossible for us to *will* that their maxims should be universal laws since such a will would be in conflict with itself. It is easy enough to see that the first class of actions violates our strict duties, while the second class violates only what it

Veracity is the heart of morality.

THOMAS HUXLEY

would be meritorious for us to do. Thus these four examples cover the main kinds of duties and show that even the strictness of the obligation can be determined by this one principle and not by reference to the purpose of the action.[26]

Kant believes, then, that there is just one command or imperative that is *categorical*—that is, presents an action as necessary of itself, without regard to any other end. He believes that from this one categorical imperative, this universal command, we can derive all commands of duty. Kant's **categorical imperative** states that we should do something only if we can will the maxim, or general rule, governing our action to become a universal law. What Kant is saying is that I should never do something unless (1) it is possible for everyone to do it and (2) 1 am willing to have everyone do it.

Some examples may make this clear. Take the first part of Kant's categorical imperative: that I should never do something *unless doing it is possible for everyone*. Consider Kant's own example of breaking a promise when it suits your purposes. Would this be morally right? Kant would say that you need to ask yourself whether everyone could make promises and then break them when it is convenient. Clearly, breaking promises like this could not become something that everyone does, because then people would stop making promises altogether. Who would accept anyone's promise, knowing that everyone breaks promises when it's convenient? Once everyone starts breaking promises, then promises are no longer possible. Since it is not possible for *everyone* to make promises and break them when is convenient, it is wrong for *you* to do so. In short, Kant's categorical imperative says that it is wrong to make exceptions of ourselves: If everyone cannot do something, then doing it is wrong for me.

Notice that Kant is not a utilitarian: He does not argue that the consequences of a universal practice would be bad and therefore the practice is bad. Instead, he claims that the practice is self-contradictory; the practice itself becomes impossible once everyone does it. His appeal is to logical consistency, not to consequences.

Take some other examples. Is it wrong for you to cheat on an exam? Kant would say this: Ask yourself whether it is possible for everyone to always cheat on exams. Clearly, if everyone always cheated on exams, the very practice of giving exams would break down. For what instructor would give an exam knowing that everyone will cheat on it? Since it is not possible for everyone to always cheat on exams, it is wrong for you to cheat on this exam. Or consider any game, such as poker or football or checkers. Is it wrong for you to secretly cheat during a game? Ask yourself whether it is possible for everyone to always cheat at games. Obviously, if everyone always cheated at games, all game activities would soon break down and cease. Since it is not possible for everyone to always cheat at games, it is wrong for you to cheat at a game. Or consider lying. Is it wrong for you to lie? Clearly, if everyone always lied, then language would break down and no one would be able to make even lying statements with it. Since everyone cannot always lie, it is wrong for you to lie.

categorical imperative
Immanuel Kant's ethical formula: Act as if the maxim (general rule) by which you act could be willed to become a universal law; the belief that what is right for one person is also right for everyone in similar circumstances

---

[26] Ibid., 28, 51–55.

But Kant also believes that there are some actions that are wrong, not because it is impossible for everyone to do them, but because *we are not willing to have everyone do them*. For example, is it wrong to refuse to help others when they are in great need? Kant suggests that it is possible for everyone to refuse to help the needy but that we would not be willing to live in a world where everyone did this. We know there may be times, Kant suggests, when we need others to help us desperately. So we would not be willing to live in a world where no one ever helped those in great need, although such a world is possible. Or consider racism and sexism. Is it wrong to discriminate based on someone's race or sex? Ask yourself whether you would be willing to have everyone discriminate by race or sex. Clearly, it is possible for a society to exist in which everyone discriminates. But would you want to live in such a world? Clearly not, for if everyone discriminates against those who are not of the same race or sex, then you will be discriminated against on some occasions. You would definitely not be willing to have everyone always discriminate against those not of the same race or sex. So discriminating against others on the basis of their race or sex is wrong for you.

Although there is only one categorical imperative, Kant felt that we could state it in various ways. Kant believed that every person has a fundamental human dignity that gives the person value "beyond all price." Thus, it is wrong to use people or to manipulate them without their consent for our own selfish desires. Kant expressed these ideas by restating his categorical imperative in these words: Act so that you always treat people as ends in themselves, and never merely use them as means. In the following passage he explains this second version of the categorical imperative:

> Now I say that man and generally any rational being exists as an end in himself. In all his actions, whether they concern himself or other rational beings, we must always regard a man as an end and not merely as a means to be arbitrarily used by this or that will. . . . Accordingly [a second version of] the categorical imperative can be formulated as follows: *So act as to treat humanity, whether in your own person or in that of any other, always also as an end and never merely as a means.* We will now inquire whether this version can be applied in practice. We will again consider our previous four examples:
>
> 1. *Strict duty to oneself.* A person who is thinking of committing suicide should ask himself whether his action is consistent with the idea that humanity is an end in itself. If he kills himself to escape his suffering, he is using a person (himself) merely as a means to maintain a tolerable existence. But a person is not a thing. That is to say, a person cannot be used merely as a means, but must always be respected as an end in himself. I cannot, therefore, dispose of my own person by mutilating, despoiling, or killing myself. . . .
>
> 2. *Strict duty to others.* A man who is thinking of making a lying promise will realize that he would be using others merely as means because he would not be letting them participate in the goal of the actions in which he involves them. For the people I would thus be using for my own purposes would not have consented to be treated in this way and to that extent they would not have participated in the goals to be attained by the action. . . .
>
> 3. *Meritorious duty to oneself.* We should not only refrain from violating our own humanity as an end in itself, but we should also try to make our actions harmonize

To do as you would be done by, is the plain, sure, and undisputed rule of morality and justice.

LORD CHESTERFIELD

Do not do unto others as you would they should do unto you. Their tastes may not be the same.

BERNARD SHAW

with the fact that our humanity is such an end. Now humanity has certain abilities that we can perfect to a greater or lesser extent. . . . When we neglect to develop these abilities we are not doing something that is destructive of humanity as an end in itself. But such neglect clearly does not advance humanity as an end in itself.

4. *Meritorious duty to others*. All men by nature want to be happy. Now humanity probably could survive even if people never helped each other achieve their happiness, but merely refrained from deliberately harming one another. But this would only be a negative way of making our actions harmonize with the idea that humanity is an end in itself. The positive way of harmonizing with this idea would be for everyone to help others achieve their goals so far as he can. The goals of every person who is an end in himself should also be my goals if my actions are really to be in full harmony with the idea that the person's humanity is an end in itself?[27]

Kant's second version of the categorical imperative implies that we should not use people as objects, as things whose only function is to satisfy our desires. Instead, he claims, morality requires that we always give others the opportunity to decide for themselves whether or not they will join us in our actions. This rules out all forms of deception, force, coercion, and manipulation. It also rules out all the ways we have of exploiting other people to satisfy our own desires without their free consent. Moreover, the second version implies that we should promote people's capacity to choose for themselves. It also implies that we should strive to develop this capacity in ourselves and in those around us (for example, through education).

Again, some examples may clarify what Kant has in mind in this second version. For Kant, to respect a person as an *end* is to respect her capacity to freely and knowingly choose for herself what she will do. To treat a person as a means is to use the person to achieve my personal interests. In effect, this second version says that we should treat people only as they freely and knowingly consent to be treated, and not merely as a means to my own goals. Kant would say that it is wrong to force or to manipulate a person into doing something, because in manipulating or forcing a person I am failing to treat the person as she has freely and knowingly consented to be treated. Is it wrong to lie or to steal from a person? Lying or stealing likewise involves doing something to a person without her free and knowing consent. What about helping those in great need? Kant would say that when people are in great need (such as the very poor), their ability to choose for themselves is compromised. Since we have a duty to promote people's capacity to choose for themselves, we should help those whose poverty prevents them from exercising their capacity to choose for themselves.

Notice that Kant is not saying that it is wrong to use people for our own ends. He is saying only that it is wrong to use people for our own ends when we have not given them a choice in the matter. For example, consider ordering a taxi driver to take you to the bus station. Clearly, you are "using" the driver as a "means" to get to the bus station. Does this make it immoral? Kant would doubtless say that it is not wrong. For when the taxidriver accepted the job of driving a taxi, he agreed to take people to the destination they ordered him to.

[27] Ibid., 68.

So when you now order him to take you to the station, you are treating him as he *previously* consented to be treated. Notice also that Kant is not saying that it is wrong to do things to people that at the moment they do not want you to do. Take, for example, a teacher who flunks a student or a judge who puts a lawbreaker in jail. Clearly, neither the student nor the lawbreaker wants to be treated this way. So is it immoral to do this to them? Kant would probably say that in reality each is being treated as he *previously* consented to be treated. The student consented to be graded by the teacher when he signed up for the course. The lawbreaker consented to be treated according to the laws of this country when he chose to live in it.

Nevertheless, Kant's theory is not airtight. First, duties frequently conflict, and Kant's theory does not seem to give us an obvious way of resolving such conflicts. If, as Kant argues, it is always wrong to tell a lie and always wrong to break a promise, then which do I choose when these duties conflict? Second, the acts that the categorical imperative says are *always* wrong do not always seem wrong. For example, Kant says that it is absolutely wrong ever to lie, no matter what good might come of telling the lie. Yet is it wrong to lie to save your life? To save someone from serious pain or injury? There is no compelling reason why certain actions should be prohibited without exception. Apparently, Kant failed to distinguish between persons making no exceptions to rules and rules having no exceptions. If a person should make no exceptions to rules, then one should never except oneself from being bound by a rule. But it does not therefore follow that the rule has no exceptions. In fairness to Kant, however, we should note that the limitations of his examples do not necessarily discredit his ethical theory.

Some Implications of Kantian Ethics

Many people today believe that Kantian ethics provides rich insights into the moral life. To see more clearly the kind of understanding of morality that Kant's ethics provides, let us consider the topic we discussed earlier: sexual behavior. Sometimes, when two people have sex, one of them might feel afterward that their partner's behavior was morally objectionable. The person might express this by saying that their partner "used" him or her or treated him or her as an "object." The philosopher Thomas Mappes has pointed out that the very idea of "using another person" and of being treated like "an object" comes from the philosophy of Immanuel Kant. It derives from Kant's principle that it is morally wrong to use a person "merely as a means." But what, exactly, does Kant's principle imply about ethics in sex? Mappes explains what it is to use a person sexually:

> The morally significant sense of "using another person" is best understood by reference to the notion of voluntary informed consent. . . . Using another person (in the morally significant sense) can arise in at least two important ways: via coercion, which is antithetical to voluntary consent, and via deception, which undermines the informed character of voluntary consent. . . . It seems clear, then, that A may sexually use B in at least two distinctive ways, (1) via coercion and (2) via deception.

There are a host of clear cases in which a [fully competent adult] person "uses" another precisely because the former employs deception. . . . Consider this example. One person, A, has decided, as a matter of personal prudence based on past experience, not to become sexually involved outside the confines of a loving relationship. Another person B, strongly desires a sexual relationship with A but does not love A. B, aware of A's unwillingness to engage in sex without love, professes love for A, thereby hoping to win A's consent to a sexual relationship. B's ploy is successful; A consents. When the smoke clears and A becomes aware of B's deception it would be both appropriate and natural for A to complain, "I've been used."

Forcible rape is the most conspicuous, and most brutal way of sexually using another person via coercion. . . . A man who rapes a woman by the employment of sheer physical force, by simply overpowering her, employs occurrent coercion. . . . When the victim of rape is treated as if she were a physical object, there we have one of the most vivid examples of the immoral using of another person.

Frequently, forcible rape involves not occurrent coercion but dispositional coercion. In dispositional coercion, the relevant factor is not physical force but the threat of harm. . . . For example, a man threatens to kill or beat a woman if she resists his sexual demands. She "consents," that is, she submits to his demands. . . . [But] it is coerced.

Although the threat of immediate and serious bodily harm stands out as the most brutal way of coercing consent to sexual interaction, we must not neglect the employment of other kinds of threats to this same end. . . . Consider . . . the following case: Mr. Supervisor makes a series of increasingly less subtle sexual overtures to Ms. Employee. These advances are consistently and firmly rejected by Ms. Employee. Eventually, Mr. Supervisor makes it clear that the granting of "sexual favors" is a condition of her continued employment. . . . [This] case [also] . . . involve[s an] attempt to sexually use another person.[28]

Kant's theory is clearly very useful for helping us see what our moral obligations are. In fact, in some respects, it sheds more light on common dilemmas in sexual matters than do other approaches to the morality of sex. For Kant's theory identifies the central importance of showing respect for the dignity of our sexual partners and the key significance of consent in morally legitimate sexual interactions.

However, some people have criticized this Kantian approach to sex since, like utilitarianism, it is too permissive. Utilitarianism approves of any sexual activity, if its pleasures and advantages are sufficiently great. Yet the Kantian approach approves of virtually any sexual activity except forced sex. This seems to include all sexual activity between informed and voluntarily consenting adults, including incest, homosexuality, and adultery, if one's spouse consents to the adultery. For many people, this is clearly a morally objectionable result.

Moreover, many have questioned whether the Kantian approach to sex makes idealistic assumptions about how real our consent can be. In the throes of sexual desire, in the sexual heat of the moment, are people really able to give their voluntary informed consent? Isn't the sometimes overwhelming power

---

[28]Thomas A. Mappes, "Sexual Morality and the Concept of Using Another Person," in *Social Ethics: Morality and Social Policy*, ed. Thomas A. Mappes and Jane S. Zembaty (New York: McGraw-Hill, 1992).

of sex incompatible with free, rational consent? Feminists have suggested that sexual roles are designed to facilitate male dominance over women and to mask from women their own real sexual desires and needs. In the context of such false consciousness, isn't the Kantian faith in informed consent unreal? For example, does the prostitute genuinely consent to her situation? Feminists ask the following: Does any woman truly consent to sex?

QUESTIONS

1. Reconsider the four situations described in question 5 of Section 7.3 from the viewpoint of a Kantian theorist, using the first version of his categorical imperative. What decisions and actions do you think are called for? Would the judgments differ from the utilitarian's? From those of natural law ethics?

2. Can the second version of the categorical imperative be applied to resolving the four situations described previously? Illustrate. Would the judgments differ from the conclusions of applying the first version?

3. Would it be possible or desirable to universalize the following maxims?
   a. "Never work unless you absolutely must."
   b. "Always do your own thing unless it hurts somebody else."
   c. "Give nothing and expect nothing in return."
   d. "Sell all you have and give to the poor."
   e. "Let your conscience be your guide."
   f. "Always stick by your friends."
   g. "Never discriminate against someone on the basis of race, religion, color, or sex."
   h. "Never punish a child physically."
   i. "Without prior approval, never take something that doesn't belong to you."

BUDDHIST ETHICS

Buddhist ethics cannot be considered a divine command theory because Buddhism does not believe in a God that issues commands. Yet Buddhism provides important insight into the moral life, and for centuries it has influenced the moral behavior of millions. Since many people in the West today are turning to it for enlightenment, we will here briefly consider its implications for ethics.

Buddhism's emphasis on ethical behavior can be generalized in two ways. First, volitional (voluntary) actions are considered supremely important, because according to the moral law of causation (karma), they determine our destiny. We will be what we have been; what we do will determine what we become. Classical Buddhism has understood this in terms of the doctrine of successive rebirths—what you are in this life is determined by what you did in your past lives. But some contemporary Buddhists have interpreted the doctrine of karma in terms of a single human life—what you are today is determined by the choices you made earlier in your present life. In either case, volitional actions are all important in determining who we are. Second, in Buddhism ethics is considered the parent of wisdom, in that reflection on the wholesomeness or

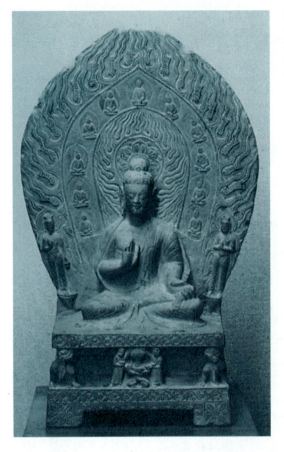

Buddha: "Morality is washed all round with wisdom, and wisdom is washed all round with morality. It is just as if one should wash one hand with the other or one foot with the other; exactly so is morality washed round with wisdom and wisdom with morality."

unwholesomeness of volitional actions leads to discipline of the mind, which eventually results in insight and enlightenment. Thus, we are always brought to the following dictum:

> Morality is washed all round with wisdom, and wisdom is washed all round with morality. Wherever there is morality, there is wisdom and wherever there is wisdom there is morality. From the observing of the moralities comes wisdom and from observing of wisdom comes morality. Morality and wisdom together reveal the height of the world. It is just as if one should wash one hand with the other or one foot with the other; exactly so is morality washed round with wisdom and wisdom with morality.[29]

Basic to the doctrines of Buddhism are the Four Noble Truths, which we have already seen (in Chapter 4) but which we should here recall so we can examine them more closely. First, from birth to death every aspect of our lives that is tied to our individuality inevitably involves suffering (although it may be temporarily avoided with youth, health and riches). Second, we suffer

---

[29] *Dighanikaya*, vol. 1, ed. T. W. Rhys Davies and J. E. Carpenter (Pali Text Society, 1947), 124.

because we desire or crave things: pleasure, life, power. The more we try to satisfy our cravings, the worse they become, making us suffer even more. Third, release from suffering can be gained only by putting an end to our craving. Finally, craving can be ended only by following the Noble Eightfold Path:

> And this is the Noble Truth of Sorrow. Birth is sorrow, age is sorrow, disease is sorrow, death is sorrow; contact with the unpleasant is sorrow, separation from the pleasant is sorrow, every wish unfulfilled is sorrow—in short, all the five components of individuality are sorrow.
>
> And this is the Noble Truth of the Arising of Sorrow. It arises from craving, which leads to rebirth, which brings delight and passion, and seeks pleasure now here, now there—the craving for sensual pleasure, the craving for continued life, the craving for power.
>
> And this is the Noble Truth of the Stopping of Sorrow. It is the complete stopping of that craving, so that no passion remains, leaving it, being emancipated from it, being released from it, giving no place to it.
>
> And this is the Noble Truth of the Way which leads to the Stopping of Sorrow. It is the Noble Eightfold Path—[having] Right Understanding, Right Thought, Right Speech, Right Conduct, Right Livelihood, Right Effort, Right Mindfulness, and Right Concentration.[30]

The Buddhist standards of morality, then, must always be conducive to the attainment of nirvana (enlightened wisdom) and the realization of the Four Noble Truths. The Buddhist ethical ideal is that of the self-reliant person, the individual who has attained personal enlightenment. Of course, as we've indicated elsewhere, enlightenment is not derived from logical deduction. But this does not mean that the individual should therefore wait for a supernatural revelation. Consider the Fourth Noble Truth, which says that the way to the cessation of suffering is to follow diligently the Eightfold Path by cultivating (1) Right Understanding, (2) Right Thought, (3) Right Speech, (4) Right Conduct, (5) Right Livelihood, (6) Right Effort, (7) Right Mindfulness, and (8) Right Concentration. These fall into three groups: Items 1 and 2 enjoin us to develop wisdom, items 3–5 urge us to practice virtue and avoid vice, and items 6–8 tell us to practice meditation. We do this essentially by following three short axioms:

> Cease to do evil.
> Learn to do good.
> Purify your own mind.[31]

In his marvelous treatment of this subject, Buddhist scholar H. Saddhatissa says that the first line, "Cease to do evil," sums up the code of Buddhist morality contained in the five precepts that invite followers to refrain from certain actions.[32] These precepts can be viewed as a "clearing away of the weeds from the soil,"[33] an ordering of the outer life before turning to the inner life, to the

---

[30] William Theodore de Bary, *Sources of Indian Tradition*, vol. 1, from *Samyutta Nikaya* (New York: Columbia University Press, 1958), 99.

[31] *Dhammapada*, ed. Suriyagoda Sumangala (Pali Text Society, 1914), 124.

[32] See H. Saddhatissa, *The Buddha's Way* (New York: George Braziller, 1971).

[33] Ibid., 32.

development and liberation of the mind, which are the goals of Buddhist teaching. These precepts represent the first steps that one can take after reading, hearing, and pondering Buddhist teaching and establishing some confidence in it. But it's important not to view these precepts as a set of rules, for Buddhism stresses the cultivation of wisdom and discernment. In other words, blind obedience to the precepts is not encouraged:

1. Refrain from harming living things.
2. Refrain from taking what is not given.
3. Refrain from a misuse of the senses.
4. Refrain from wrong speech.
5. Refrain from taking drugs or drinks which tend to cloud the mind.[34]

The first precept, to refrain from harming living things, is not just an injunction against murder or wanton killing. It suggests an abstinence from injuring or in any way harming living things and implies an awareness of the sanctity of life. If you savor the full implications of this, intriguing questions arise. For example, "the question arises whether my gastronomical pleasure should be satisfied at the expense of 'living things,' whether animals should be slaughtered so that I may disport myself in their borrowed plumes. And then the questions begin to go deeper. What of my murderous impulses when I am thwarted or humiliated? What of the secret joy I feel when someone I dislike is 'put down'?"[35] Just imagine the questions and doubts we might have on trying to implement this first precept. So much the better, for while initially disturbing us, such unrest, Buddhism teaches, ultimately results in life having a new significance and perspective. We develop a new sense of respect for self and others that permeates all our thinking.

The second precept asks us to refrain from taking what is not given. This precept invites us to develop toward the owners of inanimate objects the same respect that the first precept enjoins toward living things. Rather than merely an injunction against stealing, this second precept necessitates waiting until things are offered us. Thus, a quiet, serene patience replaces the frenzied, rapacious attitude of those living by an "I want" dictum.

The third precept, which asks us to refrain from a misuse of the senses, is often erroneously translated as a commandment against sexual misconduct. But this is only part of what the precept urges. We're advised to refrain from the misuse of the body and bodily sensations. Thus, we should avoid artificially stimulating the appetite for food as well as avoid wrongful sexual pleasures. By this precept, personal habits that lead to obesity, muscular deterioration, or any pollution of the body and its organs are to be avoided. However, Buddhism does not ask its adherents to become ascetics. It simply invites them to be ceaselessly aware of the quality and degree of their sensual activity. The senses should be enjoyed, not jaded; used, not abused.

As for the fourth precept, Buddhist literature is replete with varieties of "wrong speech." Lying, slander, gossip, malicious talk generally, violation of

---

[34] Ibid., 28.
[35] Ibid.

secrets—the list goes on. The key is self-awareness. By avoiding wrong speech, we establish a link between "right thought" and "right action." We practice right speech when we use conversation for knowing people, for understanding others and ourselves. Using a contemporary buzz word, we can translate right speech to right communication, whether it involves conversation, advertising, or political speeches.

The fifth precept takes us into the heart of Buddhist morality. Recall that the cardinal concept of Buddhist ethics is enlightenment and illumination. The central teaching is a system of meditation designed to clarify the mind so that knowledge and insight may arise in it and be reflected freely. It follows that anyone seriously interested in attaining the state of enlightened wisdom will refrain from indulgences that impair the clarity of mental vision, shroud doubts and uncertainties in a kind of euphoria, and encourage seeing things other than as they are.

As said earlier, these five precepts are summed up in the first axiom of Buddhist moral teaching, "Cease to do evil." However, these precepts are only the ground breaking and the weeding. The constructive work begins with the second axiom, "Learn to do good." This leads us to the precepts that invite followers to develop certain virtues (a topic we discuss more fully below).

Buddhist literature sparkles with various lists of "wholesome" states or "things to be encouraged," which are contrasted with "unwholesome" states or "things to be discouraged." Among the most prominent of the wholesome states is *dāna*, or giving. Unlike *caritas*, the New Testament's principle of charity, *dāna* is not aimed at encouraging philanthropy or making charitable contributions to worthy causes. Rather, *dāna* implies the gradual developing of the will to give whenever the need arises.

Another prominent Buddhist virtue, *mettā*, is often translated as "loving kindness." Whereas *dāna* is one outward manifestation of concern for the welfare of others, *mettā* embraces the whole sphere of that concern: "To develop *mettā* is to develop the state of mind wherein the joys and sorrows, the well-being and the problems of others are as important to me as my own."[36] In other words, *mettā* requires that we break down the barriers between self and others: "It has often been said that the follower of the Buddha should endeavor to feel towards all men—relations, friends, acquaintances and enemies—just as a mother feels towards her child."[37] Undoubtedly, this is a tough task. Nonetheless, according to the Buddhist code, we must do this if we're to make any spiritual progress.

But perhaps the Buddhist concept most difficult for the Western mind to grasp is the "transference of merit." We can perhaps best appreciate this by pondering the fact that a time comes when, having avoided evil and done good, we realize our inherent selfishness: We are doing good to reap for ourselves the harvest of enlightened wisdom. At this point Buddhism invites us to practice "transference of merit"—that is, to learn to will that the benefits of our good actions return not to us alone but to all humanity: "Each act of generosity, each

---

[36] Ibid., 33.
[37] Ibid.

movement of love, is no longer to be toted up in my personal account book but is to rebound to the benefit of all. Rather like a stream which feeds the ocean and which is replenished, not by means of the same water flowing back to it, but in the course of time with the falling of rains."[38]

In summary, although there are similarities between traditional Western ethics and Buddhist ethics, there are also fundamental differences. One is the Eastern interpretation of rules and commandments. Remember that the precepts of Buddhist morality should be looked on as invitations, not proscriptions. Second is the emphasis on the individual. In the last analysis, the individual avoids evil and cultivates good to facilitate personal enlightenment. Third, Buddhist morality takes root in a metaphysical outlook. Conducting our lives morally is an expeditious way to experience reality. Fourth is that Buddhism encourages practitioners to dig into their own experiences, to be open to the universe. If the path of the heart is followed, considering the consequences of action is irrelevant. If we are open to the disclosure of the world, then congruence of being and cosmos will follow.

What are the implications of Buddhism for sexual ethics? Although Buddhism suggests that there are various grades of pleasure, some of which are sexual pleasures, it takes the view that a life of pure pleasure will, by its inner nature, end up in boredom and interfere with the healthy functioning of familial and social life. The ideal, according to some Buddhist texts, is lived by those who reach a state in which "they do not indulge their sexual pleasures." Other Buddhist texts, such as the commentary on the five precepts in the *Visuddhimagga* by the Buddhist monk Buddhaghosa (c. 400), suggest that the "sexual misconduct" condemned by the Buddha includes "intercourse with men and then also with . . . women who have been betrothed, women bought with money, kept women. . . ." Thus, these Buddhist views would condemn homosexuality, adultery, and prostitution. Yet the focus of Buddhism is not on the wrongness of specific activities but on the achievement of enlightenment. Since the pursuit of sexual pleasure leads us away from this key goal, it is to be set aside.

QUESTIONS

1. Reconsider the four situations described in question 5 of Section 7.3 from the viewpoint of the five precepts of Buddhist ethics. What decisions and actions do you think are called for? Would the judgments differ from the other approaches we have seen?

2. In the play *The Victors*, Jean-Paul Sartre portrays six French Resistance fighters captured and tortured by the Nazis, who want to extract vital troop movement information from them. Just before his painful interrogation, one of the prisoners, fifteen-year-old François, informs his cellmates that he'll reveal all rather than be tortured as they have been. His cellmates have a choice: silence him, or let him speak and thus imperil the lives of sixty French soldiers.

[38] Ibid., 34.

Lucy, the boy's sister, is among the prisoners. Seeing herself bound by fidelity to the other troops, she votes to kill François. From the viewpoint of Buddhist ethics, would you say she acted wrongly? One of the other prisoners ultimately strangles François. Did he act wrongly?

3. Apply each of Buddhism's five precepts to appropriate aspects of your life. What changes would you need to make?

4. What weaknesses, if any, do you detect in Buddhist edifices?

5. What social changes might implementation of Buddhist ethics bring about? For example, how would it alter advertising or marketing generally? What impact would it have on television?

7.5 Is Ethics Based on Character?

The ethical theories that we've seen so far (with the exception of Buddhist ethics) focus on principles or rules of action. For example, utilitarianism is based on Mill's principle that "actions are right in proportion as they tend to promote happiness, wrong as they tend to produce the reverse of happiness." Kant based his ethics on the principle that one should "act so as to treat humanity . . . always as an end and never merely as a means." Modern ethics has been concerned mostly with studying such universal rules or principles, which tell us what actions are morally right or how all people ought to act.

A lot of philosophers now feel dissatisfied with this approach to ethics. One major problem, they say, is that this approach results in disagreements that cannot be resolved. Utilitarians disagree with Kantians, and both disagree with followers of natural law ethics. For example, contemporary philosopher Alasdair MacIntyre writes the following:

> The most striking feature of contemporary moral utterance is that so much of it is used to express disagreements; and the most striking feature of the debates in which these disagreements are expressed is their interminable character. I do not mean by this just that such debates go on and on—although they do—but also that they apparently can find no terminus. There seems to be no rational way of securing moral agreement in our culture.[39]

MacIntyre and others argue that with its preoccupation with conflicting rules and principles, modern ethics seems to have forgotten a part of morality that earlier ages recognized: moral virtue or character. The moral life, these philosophers suggest, is not just a matter of acting on moral rules about which

---

[39] Alasdair MacIntyre, *After Virtue* (Notre Dame, IN: University of Notre Dame Press, 1984), 3.

there are fundamental disagreements. Instead, morality is about becoming a good person and cultivating morally desirable character traits such as honesty, courage, compassion, and generosity. Instead of trying to discover universal rules about which we inevitably disagree, ethics should try to identify the character traits or "virtues" of the morally good person and explain how we can develop and acquire these traits. Ethics should not emphasize *doing* but *being*; it should not look only at how we are obligated to *act*, but also at the kind of human being we ought to *be*.

Virtue ethics, as this approach to ethics is called, is not new. We saw it when we discussed Buddhist ethics, and it is, in fact, an approach that Aristotle made the cornerstone of his moral philosophy. There is no better way of understanding virtue ethics than by examining his views. We will then turn to examine a controversial issue: whether the virtues of women should differ from those of men.

virtue ethics in ethics, the position that the moral life should be concerned with cultivating a virtuous character rather than following rules of action

ARISTOTLE'S THEORY OF VIRTUE

In his great work *Nicomachean Ethics,* Aristotle wrote that human beings can be happy only if they fulfill their basic human purpose or "function." That is, humans can be happy only if they act as humans are specifically meant to act. Since only humans can reason, Aristotle concluded that humans are meant to act with reason. That is, we humans will be happy only if we are able to act with reason in the various circumstances of our life. Since the ability to do something well is a virtue, Aristotle concludes that humans will achieve happiness only by developing their virtues:

> If in all our activities there is some end we seek for its own sake, and if everything else is a means to this same end, it obviously will be our highest and best end. Clearly there must be some such end since everything cannot be a means to something else since then there would be nothing for which we ultimately do anything and everything would be pointless. . . .
>
> Now happiness seems more than anything else to answer to this description. For happiness is something we always choose for its own sake and never as a means to something else. But fame, pleasure, . . . and so on, are chosen partly for themselves but partly also as a means to happiness, since we believe that they will bring us happiness. Only happiness, then, is never chosen for the sake of these things or as a means to any other thing. . . .
>
> So it appears that happiness is the ultimate end and completely sufficient by itself. It is the end we seek in all that we do.
>
> The reader may think that in saying that happiness is our ultimate end we are merely stating a platitude. So we must be more precise about what happiness involves.
>
> Perhaps the best approach is to ask what the specific purpose or function of man is. For the good and the excellence of all things that have a purpose—such as musicians, sculptors, or craftsmen—depend on their purpose. So if man has a purpose, his good will be related to this purpose.
>
> Our biological activities we share in common even with plants, so these activities cannot be the purpose or function of man since we are looking for something specific to man. The activities of our senses we also plainly share with other things: horses,

cattle, and other animals. So there remain only the activities that belong to the rational part of man. . . . So the specific purpose or function of man involves the activities of that part of his soul that belongs to reason, or that at least is obedient to reason. . . .

Now the function of a thing is the basis [of its goodness], but its good is something added to this function. For example, the function of a musician is to play music, and the good musician is one who not only plays music but who in addition does it well. So, the good for man would have to be something added to this function of carrying on the activities of reason; it would be carrying on the activities of reason but doing so well. But a thing carries out its proper functions well when it has the proper virtues. So the [ultimate] good for man is carrying out those activities of his soul [which involve reason] and doing so with the proper virtue or excellence.[40]

But what does it mean to have the virtue of using our reason well in our lives? Aristotle points out that where our desires, emotions, and actions are involved, both going to excess and falling short are vices. We act well when we seek the midpoint between excess and deficiency; it is, in short, being moderate in what we desire, feel and do. We acquire the virtues of living reasonably, then, when we acquire the various abilities needed to control our desires, emotions, and actions so that they neither go to excess nor fall short. Having such virtues is the key to happiness since these virtues enable us to act as humans were meant to act:

Knowledge is one thing, virtue is another.

JOHN H. NEWMAN

> Consider that the expert in any field is the one who avoids what is excessive as well as what is deficient. Instead he seeks to hit the mean and chooses it. . . . Acting well in any field is achieved by looking to the mean and bringing one's actions into line with this standard of moderation. For example, people say of a good work of art that nothing could be taken from it or added to it, implying that excellence is destroyed through excess or deficiency but achieved by observing the mean. The good artist, in fact, keeps his eyes fixed on the mean in everything he does. . . .
>
> Virtue, therefore, must also aim at the mean. For human virtue deals with our feelings and actions, and in these we can go to excess or fall short or we can hit the mean. For example, it is possible to feel fear, confidence, desire, anger, pity, plea-sure, . . . and so on, either too much or too little—both of which extremes are bad. But to feel these at the right times, and on the right occasions, and toward the right persons, and with the right object, and in the right fashion, is the mean between the extremes and is the best state, and is the mark of virtue. In the same way, our actions can also be excessive or can fall short or can hit the mean.
>
> Virtue, then, deals with those feelings and actions in which it is wrong to go too far and wrong to fall short but in which hitting the mean is praiseworthy and good. . . . It is a habit or acquired ability to choose . . . what is moderate or what hits the mean as determined by reason.
>
> But it is not enough to speak in generalities. We must also apply this to particular virtues and vices. Consider, then, the following examples.
>
> Take the feelings of fear and confidence. To be able to hit the mean [by having just enough fear and just enough confidence] is to have the virtue of courage. . . . But he who exceeds in confidence has the vice of recklessness, while he who has too much fear and not enough confidence has the vice of cowardliness.

---

[40] Aristotle, *Nicomachean Ethics*, bk. 1, chs. 2, 7. This translation copyright © 1992 by Manuel Velasquez.

The mean where pleasure . . . is concerned is achieved by the virtue of temperance. But to go to excess is to have the vice of self-indulgence, while to fall short is to have the vice of being austere. . . .

Or take the action of giving or receiving money. Here the mean is the virtue of generosity. . . . But the man who gives to excess and is deficient in receiving has the vice of prodigality, while the man who is deficient in giving and excessive in taking has the vice of stinginess. . . .

Or take one's feelings about the opinion of others. Here the mean is the virtue of proper self-respect, while the excess is the view of vanity, and the deficiency is the vice of small-mindedness. . . .

The feeling of anger can also be excessive, deficient, or moderate. The man who occupies the middle state is said to have the virtue of being even-tempered, while the one who exceeds in anger has the vice of being bad-tempered, while the one who is deficient in anger has the vice of being apathetic.[41]

For Aristotle, then, a **virtue** is the ability to be reasonable in our actions, desires, and emotions. For example, courage is the ability to deal with fear in a reasonable manner; temperance is the ability to respond to pleasures in a reasonable manner. We are not born with such abilities, he points out, but acquire them by training in our communities. In particular, we acquire them in youth by being trained repeatedly to respond to situations in a reasonable manner. As Aristotle puts it, we become virtuous by being trained to act virtuously in the appropriate situations until it becomes a habit. At first, acting virtuously is difficult, but when we have acquired the virtue, it becomes easy and pleasant:

> As is the case with any skill, we acquire the virtues by first doing virtuous acts. We acquire a skill by practicing the activities involved in the skill. For example, we become builders by building, and we learn to play the harp by playing the harp. In the same way, we become just by doing just acts, temperate by doing temperate acts, and courageous by doing acts of courage. . . .
>
> Both the moral virtues and the corresponding vices are developed or destroyed by similar kinds of actions, as is the case with all skills. It is by playing the harp that both good and bad harp players are produced [good players by repeatedly playing well, poor players by repeatedly playing poorly]. And the same is true of builders and all the rest: by building well they develop into good builders, and by building badly into bad builders. In fact, if this were not so they would not need a teacher and everyone would be born either good or bad at their trade. The same holds for the virtues. By what we do in our interactions with others we will develop into just persons or into unjust ones; and by the way we respond to danger, training ourselves to respond with fear or with confidence, we will become either cowardly or courageous. The same can be said of our appetites and feelings of anger: By responding in one way or another to these we will become either temperate and even-tempered or self-indulgent and ill-tempered. In short, acts of one kind produce character traits of the same kind. This is why we should make sure that our actions are of the proper kind: for our character will correspond to how we act. It makes no small difference, then, whether a person is trained in one way or another from his youth; it makes a very great difference, in fact, all the difference.

virtue in ethics, a morally good character trait, such as honesty, courage, or integrity

Do not talk about what a good man is, but be one.
MARCUS AURELIUS

---

[41] Ibid., bk. 2, chs. 6, 7.

Not only are character traits developed and destroyed in the same way, they also manifest themselves in similar ways. This is something we can actually see with strength. Strength is produced by taking plenty of nourishment and doing plenty of exercise, and it is the man with strength, in turn, that is best able to do these things. It is the same with the virtues. By abstaining from pleasures we develop temperance, and it is the man with temperance that is best able to abstain from them. The same holds for courage: by habituating ourselves to disregard danger and to face it, we become courageous, and it is when we have become courageous that we are best able to face danger.

A test of the presence of a certain character trait is the pleasure or pain that accompanies our actions. The person who abstains from bodily pleasures and feels pleased at this, is temperate, while the person who feels pain at having to abstain is self-indulgent. And the person who stands his ground against fearful things and takes pleasure in this or at least is not pained, is courageous, while the man for whom this is painful is a coward.[42]

One may smile, and smile, and be a villain

WILLIAM SHAKESPEARE

To understand how virtue theory can help us assess moral behavior, let us consider the issue that we discussed earlier when examining other approaches to morality: sexual behavior. As Aristotle notes, our moral character is developed through the actions that we choose, and our character in turn influences the actions we choose. Through our actions we shape the kind of person we gradually become. To assess the moral rightness or wrongness of moral behavior, then, we must look at the kind of character that the behavior produces. If the behavior tends to produce a virtuous character, then it is morally right; if it produces a vicious character, then it is morally wrong. Now consider how philosopher Janet Smith uses this approach to evaluate the moral quality of adultery:

> The very importance of the attempt to live an ethical life lies in the fact that in acting the individual forms herself or himself either for the better or for the worse. One of the foremost questions to be asked by the moral agent in the decision to do an action is: What kind of person will I become if I do this act?
>
> Let us now consider how the choice to commit adultery might reveal and affect one's moral character. . . . If it is true . . . that adulterers can be said to have undesirable moral characteristics and/or that they are forming undesirable moral characters through their choice to commit adultery, this would be taken as an indication . . . that adultery is a morally bad action. . . .
>
> For an analysis in accord with an ethics of virtue, answers to the following questions would be useful: What sort of people generally commit adultery? Are they, for instance, honest, temperate, kind, etc.? . . . Why do adulterers choose to have sex with people other than their spouses? Are their reasons selfish or unselfish ones? Do they seem to speak of their reasons for their choice honestly or do they seem to be rationalizing? What sort of lives have they been leading prior to the action that they choose; are they the sorts of lives that exhibit the characteristics we admire?
>
> Most may agree that some true generalizations could be made about adulterers that would lead us to think that in general adultery is not compatible with the moral virtues that we admire. The reaction of the American public to the extra-marital affairs of [clergyman] Jim Bakker and [politician] Gary Hart reveal well the wide-

---

[42] Ibid., bk. 2, chs. 1, 2, 3.

spread view that lying predictably accompanies the act of adultery and that adulterers are not to be trusted. Certainly, if someone told us that he or she wanted to be an honest, trustworthy, stable and kind individual with good family relationships, and wanted to know if an adulterous affair would conflict with this goal, we would have little hesitation in advising against adultery.[43]

Clearly, Aristotle's approach to ethics differs greatly from the principles approach that Mill, Kant, and others employ. The virtue approach, in fact, reminds us of several things that the rules approach neglects. First, as we have already noted, the virtue approach emphasizes the character traits of the morally good person and their development, whereas the principles approach neglects character. Yet character is undoubtedly a fundamental moral concern. Isn't each of us vitally concerned about the sort of person we are becoming? Doesn't each of us care about the sort of character we display? Isn't our character at the core of who we are, as well as at the center of how we relate to others?

Second, the virtue approach reminds us of the importance of community and early training, which the principles approach ignores. As Aristotle says, a person's character traits are generally developed by "training" within a community (such as the family, the church, the school, or other private and public associations). As a person grows and matures, his or her character is shaped by the values that these communities prize and by the traits that they encourage or discourage. Thus, the idea of community is important to virtue ethics. Virtue ethics is also concerned with the training, habituation, and inculcation of values that go on in communities such as the family, church, and school. Just as important is the inculcation of values that goes on in gangs, corporations, and prisons.

Third, this approach to ethics reminds us of the importance of personal ideals. Personal ideals are ideas we have of what the ideal person is like and the virtues that the ideal person displays. These pictures of the ideal person serve as models that we try to live up to. Often, these pictures are based on the example of real people, as described in history or stories or as seen in real life. They are our heroes and idols. The lives of exemplary people can illustrate virtue more clearly than anything else and can also inspire us to imitate them. The examples of Jesus, St. Theresa of Avila, Socrates, Joan of Arc, the Buddha, Mother Teresa, Gandhi, Florence Nightingale, Martin Luther King, Jr., Rosa Parks, Malcolm X, Harriet Tubman, Cesar Chávez, and others have inspired millions to cultivate the virtues they exhibited in their lives.

Because virtue theory provides such powerful insights into our moral lives, many philosophers today see it as better than an ethic of rules and principles, such as utilitarianism and Kantian ethics. For example, Alasdair MacIntyre has urged the adoption of virtue theory as the best way to understand our moral lives:

> If human life is understood as a progress through harms and dangers, moral and physical, which someone may encounter and overcome in better and worse ways and with

To act in conformity with virtue is nothing but acting, living, and preserving our being as reason directs.

BARUCH SPINOZA

---

[43] Janet Smith, "Moral Character and Abortion," in *Doing and Being,* ed. Janet Graf Haber (New York: Macmillan, 1993), 442–456.

a greater or lesser measure of success, the virtues will find their place as those qualities the possession and exercise of which generally tend to success in this enterprise and the vices likewise as qualities which likewise tend to failure. Each human life will then embody a story whose shape and form will depend upon what is counted as a harm and danger and upon how success and failure, progress and its opposite, are understood and evaluated.[44]

Evil destroys even itself.

ARISTOTLE

But the virtue approach is not without its difficulties. The main problem that critics have raised about virtue ethics is that it does not help answer the kinds of moral questions people most frequently ask. People seem to turn to ethics when they face situations in which they must decide what to do and the morality of the alternatives is unclear. For example, an unmarried woman finds herself pregnant and asks herself, "Should I have an abortion?" Or a woman whose injured husband has been diagnosed as "brain dead" is asked in the hospital whether she wants to have his life-support systems disconnected. In such situations people ask themselves, "What should I *do?*" not "What should I *be?*" But virtue ethics does not directly address the question of what one should *do*. Neither the woman considering an abortion nor the woman considering disconnecting her husband's life support is helped by being told that the good person has the qualities of honesty, courage, compassion, and generosity. They don't want to know what kind of character they should develop, but what they should do right now. Theirs is a question about the morality of actions not the morality of character. In situations such as these, an ethics of principle seems much more appropriate than an ethics of virtue. An ethics of principle provides rules that can help us see which actions are moral and which are not.

Nevertheless, many philosophers have continued discussing and developing virtue ethics. Some of the most important contributions have been made by philosophers exploring the differences between men and women.

MALE AND FEMALE ETHICS?

Philosophers (usually male ones) have often claimed that men and women have different ethics. Often they accompany their claim with the suggestion that the ethics of women are somehow inferior to those of men. Understandably and justifiably, these claims and suggestions have angered women.

Recently, however, several female philosophers have also begun to suggest that men and women have different moralities. Nevertheless, they have argued, the moralities of women are equal to or superior to those of men. In particular, they have suggested, men tend to focus on issues that an ethics of principles emphasizes, whereas women tend to focus on issues that an ethics of virtue emphasizes. Examining these suggestions will help us see one critical difference between the ethics of virtue and the ethics of principles.

The psychologist Carol Gilligan was one of the first women to suggest that men and women approach ethics differently. She is also one of the first to suggest that the ethics of women are not inferior to those of men. In her important

---

[44] Alasdair MacIntyre, *After Virtue*, 135.

Carol Gilligan: "Moral development for a woman is marked by progress toward more adequate ways of caring for herself and others."

book *In a Different Voice: Women's Conception of Self and Morality* (1982), Gilligan argues against the views of Lawrence Kohlberg, a psychologist whose work seems to imply that women, on average, are less morally developed than men.

Kohlberg argued that just as people's physical abilities develop through stages—a child must crawl before it walks or runs—people's moral abilities also develop through stages. He called the three main stages of moral development the preconventional, conventional, and postconventional levels. Parents and authority figures tell children at the first or preconventional level what is right and what is wrong. Children obey to avoid punishment. Consequently, at the preconventional level of moral development, morality focuses on the self. It is a matter of following authority and avoiding punishment to the self. As the child matures into adolescence, he or she develops attachments and loyalties to groups: family, friends, church, and nation. Consequently, at the conventional level, morality is based on being accepted by those in one's groups and on following their conventional moral standards and rules. If the adolescent continues to mature morally, he or she will begin to examine and question the conventional moral standards absorbed earlier in life. The adolescent may start to evaluate these standards in terms of whether they serve everyone's welfare, whether they are just, and whether they respect everyone's moral rights. For the person at this most mature or postconventional level of moral development, morality is based on universal moral principles of human welfare, justice, and rights.

Kohlberg studied numerous people and reported that in all cases people's morality develops in the same order: a preconventional focus on self, followed by a focus on conventional rules, followed by a postconventional focus on universal principles. However, not everyone develops fully through all the levels. Some people remain at the preconventional level all their lives, others make it to the conventional level and then go no further, and only a minority of people seem to make it all the way to the most advanced, postconventional level of moral development.

Significantly, more men than women seem to make it to Kohlberg's post-conventional level. Women seem to remain often at the conventional level, where attachments and loyalties to family, friends, and others are important. Whereas many men continue to move "up" to the postconventional level of impartial principles, women stay at the "lower" conventional level of personal attachments and loyalties. This implies that, by and large, women are less morally developed than men.

Enter Carol Gilligan. Gilligan pointed out a significant flaw in Kohlberg's work: He had developed his stages of moral development by studying mostly men. Consequently, Gilligan argued, his theory really describes how men's morality develops and not how women's morality develops. If women do not advance to Kohlberg's third level of male development, it is because they advance instead to a third level of female development that Kohlberg's theory ignores. Based on a study of many women, Gilligan argued that women's morality is different from men's and develops differently. Women, Gilligan argued, see themselves as persons in relationships with friends and family. When they encounter moral issues, they are concerned with maintaining these relationships and with avoiding hurt to others. For women, then, morality is mostly a matter of caring and being responsible for others with whom they are involved in personal relationships. Women end up getting shoved into Kohlberg's conventional level of morality, because that is the only level that takes relationships and personal attachments into account. But women develop by showing increasing maturity in the way they deal with relationships.

Gilligan argued that moral development for a woman is marked by progress toward more adequate ways of caring for herself and for others. Women move through three levels of development: (1) a stage in which they are overly devoted to caring for themselves, (2) a stage in which they are overly devoted to caring for others, and (3) a stage in which they achieve a balance between caring for self and caring for others.

Gilligan claimed that at the earliest or preconventional level of moral development, the female child, feeling powerless and afraid of being hurt, sees morality as taking care of herself. As the girl moves to a second or conventional level of moral development, she comes to accept the conventional standards and norms of her friends and family. These typically say that as a woman she should devote herself to caring for others even if this means neglecting her own needs. The woman at the conventional level sees morality in terms of her responsibility for maintaining the relationships within which she is enmeshed and on which others depend. If she continues to develop, she will enter a third, postconventional level of moral development. During this third stage she will begin to question the conventional standards she had earlier accepted. She will become critical of those standards that require her to sacrifice her own needs to take care of others. She will come to see herself as a self-in-relation-to-others and will see that caring for others is deeply related to and depends upon her caring for herself. At this level, she sees morality in terms of maintaining relationships through caring for herself-in-relation-to-others.

The best thing we can do is conceive a right rule of life, commit it to memory, and apply it to the particular cases that meet us in life.

BARUCH SPINOZA

According to Gilligan, then, there is a way of looking at morality that is more characteristic of women. This female perspective on morality is very different from the way men typically look at morality. When faced with moral decisions, women focus on the relationships of the people involved and see morality as a matter of taking care of the people in these relationships. When men face moral decisions, they focus on the individuals involved and see morality as a matter of following the moral rules or principles that apply to these individuals. Women focus on personal relationships; men focus on impartial rules and principles. Women are concerned with caring and maintaining personal relationships; men are concerned with justice and individual rights. In short, women tend to exhibit the personal virtues of caring and responsibility for relationships, but men tend to exhibit the more impersonal focus on moral rules and principles.

The end of all moral speculations is to teach us our duty.
DAVID HUME

But though women tend to approach ethics differently from men, Gilligan has argued, women are not inferior. Caring and responsibility for sustaining relationships, in fact, are virtues that society greatly needs. Society, she suggests, tends to disconnect people and to promote competition, individualism, separation, and independence. A male emphasis on impersonal rules and principles further encourages these tendencies. Moreover, these tendencies have broken down our communities and our networks of relationships. We need the virtues of caring and responsibility to ensure that society does not become a collection of isolated individuals who guard their individual rights and justice but who are lonely, unattached, and uncaring.

Philosopher Nel Noddings has gone further than Gilligan in arguing that the virtue of caring is superior to the focus on principles. In her book *Caring: A Feminine Approach to Ethics and Moral Education*, Noddings holds that the "feminine" virtue of caring is more fundamental than the "masculine" focus on principles:

> One might say that ethics has been discussed largely in the language of the father: in principles and propositions, in terms such as justification, fairness, justice. The mother's voice has been silent. Human caring and the memory of caring and being cared for, which I shall argue form the foundation of ethical response, have not received attention except as outcomes of ethical behavior.[45]

Noddings argues that ethics is about specific individuals in actual encounters with other specific individuals; ethics is not about abstract principles of justice and rights. The ethical person is the person who cares for another specific individual during an actual encounter with that unique person and who manifests her concern for that specific individual in concrete caring deeds. In such relationships, the caring person does not consult abstract principles or universal rules that somehow fit all humanity, nor does she reason about morality like a geometry problem. Instead, she consults her immediate "feelings, needs, impressions, and . . . sense of personal ideal" and responds to the unique individual with whom she is dealing.

---

[45] Nel Noddings, *Caring: A Feminine Approach to Ethics and Moral Education* (Berkeley: University of California Press, 1984), 1.

Noddings claims that as a person grows and acquires a "growing store of memories of both caring and being cared for," she acquires the capacity to care for others as well as for herself. Gradually, the growing person forms a picture of her ideal self as a caring person. She finds the freedom to choose whether to live up to this ideal picture of herself. Ethical behavior arises when one feels caring for another person and freely chooses to act on this feeling, motivated by the desire to live up to the ideal of being a caring person: "The source of ethical behavior is, then, in twin sentiments—one that feels directly for the other and one that feels for and with the best self, who may accept and sustain the initial feeling rather than reject it."[46]

Suppose, for example, that I meet someone I dislike but who needs my help. His need will call up in me an initial feeling of care and concern. But my dislike may tempt me to reject this initial feeling and turn away from the needy person. Yet because of my past experiences of caring and being cared for, I may also feel a desire to live up to my ideal of being a caring person. If I choose to live up to this ideal, I will accept the initial feeling of concern for the needy person and, overcoming my dislike, will act on it. The more I strive to live up to my ideal, caring self, the more I will accept and respond to my feelings of caring for others with ethical behavior. Thus, care is the basis of ethics.

Carol Gilligan and Nel Noddings have recently tempered their views. Both now agree that men as well as women are capable of approaching morality from the perspective of caring. Both also agree that women as well as men often approach morality in terms of universal moral principles. However, women see things in terms of the virtue of caring more instinctively than do men, who in turn are more likely to appeal to moral rules and principles.

But the crucial question is this: Is it good that women focus on the moral virtue of caring whereas men focus on impersonal moral rules and principles? Some philosophers have argued that it is not. Our culture has traditionally said that women are good at caring for others and has consequently relegated that job to women as mothers, wives, nurses, and schoolteachers. Our culture asks women to care for others, whatever the cost to themselves, simply because women are "by nature" good at caring. Thus, Gilligan and Noddings are indirectly encouraging this traditional view of women. Their books indirectly encourage women to serve and care for others while giving men more justification for avoiding these same tasks. On the other hand, by implying that it is natural for men to focus on impersonal principles, Gilligan and Noddings encourage men to see morality as an impersonal calculation. This subtly discourages men from becoming involved in the caring tasks that can enrich their lives and personalities. For example, the lives of fathers could be enriched by their spending more time nurturing and caring for their children. But Gilligan and Noddings imply that this is not a task for men, but for women.

Other philosophers have criticized the very idea of an ethics based on caring for specific individuals with whom we have personal relationships. Such an

---

[46] Ibid., 80.

ethics seems too narrow to encompass all our moral concerns. Clearly, we are personally related to only a few people. Through modern technology, however, our actions affect many more people than those with whom we can have personal relationships. For example, the environmental pollution that we produce with our machines and products can harm people far distant from us in time and space. Yet we will never know most of these people and never have a personal relationship with them. If ethics is only a matter of caring for those with whom we have concrete personal relationships, then ethics will have nothing to say about the wrongness of harming unknown others through environmental pollution.

This completes our overview of the main currents in ethical theory. We turn now to consider how these might apply in our own lives.

QUESTIONS

1. How, in terms of virtues, would you characterize the people in the scene from Sartre's play *The Victors* described in question 2 of the "Buddhist Ethics" section? What virtues or vices are exemplified by their actions?

2. What are the virtues or character traits that you believe are most important for the morally good person to have in today's world? Why are these important? How would you go about cultivating this kind of a character?

3. Make a list of the virtues or character traits that you feel most people would characterize as feminine and a list of those that you feel most people would characterize as masculine. In your view, is there anything sexist about these lists? Explain. Why do people see men and women in this way?

7.6 Can Ethics Resolve Moral Quandaries?

Having completed our overview of major ethical theories, we should now ask this question: Which, if any, of these theories ought we adopt as part of our own code of ethics? Unfortunately, there is no simple answer to this question. As we have seen, all the theories have flaws that limit their usefulness.

That an ethical theory lacks perfection, however, doesn't mean that it's completely useless or that the pursuit of a satisfactory theory is hopeless. Human relationships and behaviors inevitably present a tangled web of subtle, complex values. The ethical theories we've discussed are conceptual frameworks by which we can intelligently conduct investigation of the complexities of moral behaviors and relationships. What's more, ethical theories are in need of reexamination and refinement as constantly as, say, the democratic theory of government. Their imperfect state, then, is less a flaw than a challenge to humankind to constantly improve on them.

Each of these theories has an impressive range of applications. In criticizing them, philosophers invariably focus on their weaknesses. Although some people might call such activity nitpicking, it is consistent with the philosophical enterprise of pursuing truth and certainty. Philosophers raise cases that tend to break a theory down and to test its strength. Failing to grasp this aspect of the philosophical enterprise, one can easily conclude that ethical theories and moral philosophizing offer little, if anything, of worth. But this would be a gross misunderstanding that even the harshest critics would not accept. Such a view would be as indefensible as scrapping the theory of biological evolution or quantum mechanics because they are incomplete or unsatisfactory in important ways. As in the world of science, we face complex realities in the realm of human relationships and behavior that by nature challenge our best theories. And this requires cooperative attempts to test the range of theoretical applications.

Granting that these theories, though imperfect, are extremely useful, isn't the selection of one theory ultimately arbitrary? If none of them can be proved correct, does it matter which one, if any, we choose? Although this is an understandable reaction, we should reflect on the meaning of the word *arbitrary*.

It's true that it would probably be arbitrary if a person decided that it doesn't matter which code to follow. But such a position would be unsound because different codes invite us to focus on different values and aspects of morality. The thoughtful person recognizes these differences and chooses one theory or another according to the understanding of the moral life that it can provide. Such a choice, rooted in a consideration of alternatives, cannot be arbitrary. Indeed, it's based on the best available evidence. In the words of British philosopher R. M. Hare,

> To describe such ultimate decisions as arbitrary . . . would be like saying that a complete description of the universe was utterly unfounded, because no further fact could be called upon in corroboration of it. This is not how we use the words "arbitrary" and "unfounded." Far from being arbitrary, such a decision would be the most well-founded of decisions, because it would be based upon a consideration of everything upon which it could possibly be founded.[47]

Finally, we should note that the fundamental worth of studying and understanding ethical thought is not to obtain particular, definitive guides to moral conduct. If, however, our search is for reasonable, defensible ways to apply ethical values and rules in complex situations, the study of ethical theories can make us aware of the moral options available to us.

To illustrate the complexity of moral decisions and how a grasp of the normative theories can help to elucidate them, let us examine two important moral

"Tut, tut, child!" said the Duchess. "Everything's got a moral, if you only can find it."
LEWIS CARROLL

Morality is not a doctrine about how we should make ourselves happy, but how we should become worthy of happiness.
IMMANUEL KANT

---

[47] R. M. Hare, *The Language of Morals* (Oxford: Clarendon Press, 1952), 69.

issues that many of us are destined to face (or perhaps have already faced). These are the issues of abortion and euthanasia.

ABORTION

Abortion is a moral issue that is highly charged with emotion and strong opinions. It is an issue that raises questions about life and death, about what a person is and when one becomes a person, about the meaning of life, about the rights of women, and about the duties of men.

Abortion is the deliberate ending of a pregnancy before live birth. In 1973 the U.S. Supreme Court ruled in the case of *Roe v. Wade* that the Constitution guarantees each citizen a fundamental "right to privacy" and "that the right of personal privacy includes the abortion decision, but this right is qualified and must be considered against important state interests in regulation." In particular, the Supreme Court ruled, government may not make laws restricting abortions performed during the first six months of pregnancy. However, during the last three months of pregnancy, government, "in promoting its interest in the potentiality of human life, may, if it chooses, regulate, and even proscribe, abortion except where it is necessary, in appropriate medical judgment, for the preservation of the life or health of the mother."

Although the Supreme Court has settled the legal issue, the moral question still remains: When, if ever, is it moral for a person to choose to have an abortion? The issue of abortion frequently raises conflicting feelings in the person faced with the choice of abortion. Consider the real case of this mother of three anonymously named "Jane Doe" and the contradictory emotions and moral judgments that tear at her:

> We were sitting in a bar on Lexington Avenue when I told my husband I was pregnant. . . . [T]he news was greeted with shocked silence. . . . My husband talked about his plans for a career change in the next year, to stem the staleness that fourteen years with the same investment banking firm had brought him. A new baby would preclude that option. The timing wasn't right for me either. I had just taken on a full-time job. A new baby would put me right back in the nursery. . . . It was time for us, we tried to rationalize. There just wasn't room in our lives now for another baby. We both agreed. And agreed. And agreed.
>
> How could it be that I, who am so neurotic about life that I step over bugs rather than on them . . . could so arbitrarily decide that this life shouldn't be? "It's not a life," my husband had argued, more to convince himself than me. "It's a bunch of cells smaller than my fingernail." But any woman who has had children knows that certain feeling in her taut, swollen breasts, and the slight but constant ache in her uterus that signals the arrival of a life.
>
> When my name was called [at the abortion clinic], my body felt so heavy the nurse had to help me into the examining room. I waited for my husband to burst through the door and yell "stop," but of course he didn't.
>
> "You're going to feel a burning sensation now," [the doctor] said, injecting Novocaine into the neck of the womb. The pain was swift and severe, and I twisted to get away from him. He was hurting my baby, I reasoned. . . . "Stop," I cried. "Please stop." He shook his head, busy with his equipment. "It's too late to stop now," he said. "It'll just take a few more seconds."

> What good sports we women are. And how obedient. Physically the pain passed even before the hum of the machine signaled that the vacuuming of my uterus was completed, my baby sucked up like ashes after a cocktail party.[48]

Clearly, Jane Doe's decision to have an abortion was an agonizing one, filled with contradictory feelings and distressing uncertainties. We must certainly sympathize with her anguish and the anxious doubts she had about what she was doing even as she did it. But let us also ask the question that ultimately lay behind her anguish: Was this abortion morally justified?

Many moral arguments in support of the moral rightness of abortion proceed by arguing that the fetus is not a "person." Since only persons have a moral right to life, they conclude, the fetus does not have a moral right to life. For example, philosopher Mary Anne Warren asks us to imagine we encountered a new species on some far-off planet. What features would such creatures have to possess for us to decide that they had the moral rights of persons and so could not be killed and eaten like cattle? She argues that a creature is a person only if it exhibits five traits: consciousness, reasoning, self-motivated activity, the capacity to communicate, and the presence of self-concepts and self-awareness. Since fetuses do not possess these traits, she concludes, they are not persons with a full moral right to life.[49] This view is similar to the suggestion of Jane Doe's husband that the fetus is "just a bunch of cells." But critics have responded to this type of argument by pointing out that infants, retarded adults, the mentally ill, and future generations also do not have the required traits. Yet infants, retarded adults, and future generations clearly have a moral right to life. Therefore, it is unclear that we can prove that fetuses are not persons. Nor is it clear that we can prove that fetuses *are* persons. Like Jane Doe, we are left with the troubling uncertainties that the fetus may be a human "life" and "a baby," yet perhaps it might not be.

Although the arguments over the "personhood" of the fetus are inconclusive, there are other ways of approaching the morality of abortion. For example, philosopher Richard Hare argues that if we adopt a Kantian approach to morality, as summarized by the Golden Rule, we will conclude that abortion is generally immoral:

> [T]he Christian "Golden Rule," [and] the Kantian Categorical Imperative [provide the same type of argument]. . . . [But] I shall use that form of the argument which rests on the Golden Rule that we should do to others as we wish them to do to us. It is a logical extension of this form of argument to say that we should do to others what *we are glad was* done to us. Two (surely readily admissible) changes are involved here. The first is a mere difference in the two tenses which cannot be morally relevant. Instead of saying that we should do to others as we wish them (in the future) to do to us, we say that we should do to others as we wish that they had done to us (in the past). The second is a change from the hypothetical to the actual; instead of saying that we should do to others as we wish that they had done to us, we say that

Absolute good and evil are unknown to us. In this life they are blended together.

JEAN JACQUES ROUSSEAU

---

[48] Jane Doe, "There Just Wasn't Room in Our Lives Now for Another Baby," *New York Times*, May 14, 1976. Copyright © 1976 by the New York Times Co. Reprinted by permission.

[49] Mary Anne Warren, "On the Moral and Legal Status of Abortion," in *Ethics: Theory and Practice*, eds. Manuel Velasquez and Cynthia Rostankowski (Englewood Cliffs, NJ: Prentice-Hall, 1985).

we should do to others as we are glad that they did to us. I cannot see that this could make any difference to the spirit of the injunction. . . .

The application of this injunction to the problem of abortion is obvious. If we are glad that nobody terminated the pregnancy that resulted in our birth, then we are enjoined not, *ceteris paribus*, to terminate any pregnancy which will result in the birth of a person having a life like ours.[50]

This kind of Kantian approach reaches what we can call a "conservative" position on abortion. It allows aborting a mentally defective fetus that would not have a life like ours. But it would condemn having an abortion for the sake of one's career.

---

[50]R. M. Hare, "Abortion and the Golden Rule," *Philosophy & Public Affairs*, vol. 4, no. 3 (Spring 1975), 207.

PHILOSOPHY AND LIFE

Fetal Tissue Transplants

Three days after taking office, President Bill Clinton overturned a ban prohibiting spending federal funds to transplant tissue from aborted fetuses into humans. The tissues of aborted fetuses are perfect for replacing the diseased or injured tissues of patients. Research suggests that if brain cells from aborted fetuses are implanted into the brains of patients suffering from Parkinson's disease (which causes tremors, rigidity, and eventually complete paralysis), the fetus's cells will take over the functions the patient's own brain cells could no longer perform and the patient will recover fully or partially. Research also suggests that transplanting fetal pancreatic tissues into diabetics, fetal brain tissues into patients with Huntington's disease, fetal neurons into patients with spinal-cord injuries or multiple sclerosis, fetal liver cells into patients with Hurler's syndrome, and fetal cells into patients with any of more than 155 genetic disorders could produce full or partial cures of these crippling illnesses. Research has also suggested that injecting fetal tissues into muscles can accelerate healing or even enhance muscle performance, raising the possibility that athletes could take fetal tissue injections to improve their performance or that fetal cells could be used for cosmetic purposes.

Opponents of abortion argued it was wrong to lift the ban on federal funding of such fetal tissue transplants because this would ultimately encourage more abortions, which they consider immoral. A pregnant woman, they claimed, might be encouraged to abort her fetus so that its tissues could be harvested for transplants, a child might be conceived for the sole purpose of aborting it to harvest its cells for a sick relative, and women might be paid to regularly conceive and abort their fetuses to provide the raw material for transplants. Fetal tissue transplants, opponents claim, trade the life of the powerless and unconsenting unborn for the health of those already born.

QUESTIONS

1. In your view, is it moral to transplant the tissue of aborted fetuses? Would it be moral to abort a fetus intentionally in order to provide doctors with transplant material? Would it be moral to use fetal tissue for cosmetic purposes or to improve athletic performance?

2. In your judgment, was the ban on the use of federal funds for fetal tissue transplants immoral? Or was the lifting of the ban immoral?

Source: "Cures from the Womb," *Newsweek* (February 22, 1993): 48–53.

However, utilitarians propose a very different approach to abortion. Utilitarians who have supported the moral rightness of abortion have argued that any action that, on balance, has better consequences than the alternatives is morally permissible. Since abortion sometimes has better consequences than any other alterative—such as avoiding financial burdens, avoiding disgrace, or bearing a defective infant—it is sometimes morally justified. However, utilitarians are quick to point out that we should take into account all the consequences of our actions, including the effects on our future behavior. For example, philosopher Jane English argues that once the fetus comes to look like a person, killing it will lessen the respect we have for persons in general. At that point, then, it would be wrong to abort the fetus:

> Even if a fetus is not a person, abortion is not always permissible, because of the resemblance of a fetus to a person [and the bad consequences that killing such personlike creatures would have on our behaviors toward persons]. . . . [So] it would be wrong for a woman who is seven months pregnant to have an abortion just to avoid having to postpone a trip to Europe. In the early months of pregnancy when the fetus hardly resembles a baby at all, then, abortion is permissible whenever it is in the interests of the pregnant woman or her family. The reasons would only need to outweigh the pain and inconvenience of the abortion itself. In the middle months when the fetus comes to resemble a person, abortion would be justifiable only when the continuation of the pregnancy of the birth of the child would cause harm—physical, psychological, economic or social—to the woman. In the later months of pregnancy, even on our current assumption that a fetus is not a person, abortion seems to be wrong except to save a woman from significant injury or death.[51]

The utilitarian argument of Jane English comes to the conclusion that the Supreme Court was right to prohibit abortions only in the last three months of pregnancy. Moreover, her utilitarian argument would perhaps imply that the abortion decision of Jane Doe was justified. Or would it? Can we ever be certain that the consequences of abortion are better than the consequences of allowing a fetus to be born? Can we know that the future life of a fetus will produce less happiness than the happiness produced by aborting it?

One last perspective on abortion that we can examine is the approach of virtue theory. As we have seen, virtue theory can evaluate the morality of behavior by examining the kind of moral character that such behavior produces. If behavior produces virtue, then it is morally desirable; if it produces vices, then it is morally wanting. Notice how Janet Smith takes precisely this approach:

> The one characteristic that is nearly universal among women deciding to have abortions is that they are engaged in relationships that are not conducive to raising a child. . . . The relationships of women who have abortions seem characterized by instability, poor communication, and lack of true mutuality. Those involved in such relationships seem to be characterized by irresponsibility and confusion about what they really want—which results in them being dishonest both with themselves and with their partners. . . . Studies show that the women having abortions . . . display

---

[51] Jane English, "Abortion and the Concept of a Person," in *The Ethics of Abortion*, ed. R. M. Baird and S. E. Rosenbaum (Buffalo, NY: Prometheus Books, 1989), 83–92.

carelessness and indifference in their use of contraception. . . . These women seem not to have much self-knowledge, nor do they seem to be self-determining—they seem to be "letting things happen" that, were they reflective and responsible individuals, they might not accept as actions for themselves. . . . They . . . characterize abortion and indeed their own decision as taking a human life. If, then, it is a virtue to act in accord with one's principles, many of the women having abortions seem not to have this virtue and are acting in a way that will not advance their possession of it.

An ethics of virtue assesses actions by the type of character that produces and chooses these actions. Abortion, in the eyes of this interpreter, does not fare well as a moral action, according to this analysis.[52]

From the perspective of an ethics of virtue, then, abortion does not appear to be a morally upright option. Abortion is wrong because it produces a moral character characterized by carelessness, irresponsibility, dishonesty, and lack of principles. Were any of these traits evident in the characters of Jane Doe and her husband? If so, then this would tend to confirm Smith's argument. But it is important to keep in mind, as Smith herself tells us, that her argument shows only that certain vices are *usually* associated with abortion. It is always an open possibility that for some people, the traits generally associated with abortion will not for them accompany the decision to have an abortion.

The three theories of utilitarianism, Kant, and virtue, then, each provide us with insight into the ethics of abortion. None of the theories by itself is adequate, for each, as we have seen, has deficiencies and each is limited to a particular perspective on the ethics of abortion. Utilitarianism alerts us to the importance of reflecting on the consequences of choosing for or against abortion, both for ourselves and for society. Kant reminds us that it is important to ask what the significance of a fetus's future life is and whether we ourselves would value having such a life. And virtue ethics reminds us of the importance of personal responsibility and integrity in choosing for or against abortion. Taken together, then, these theories reveal several morally critical considerations that a person should keep in mind when evaluating abortion.

EUTHANASIA

Literally, *euthanasia* means "good death." However, the term today refers to any action that knowingly results in the death of a person suffering from a painful and incurable disease, as long as the action is carried out to be merciful. Often we distinguish between active and passive euthanasia. The distinction between active and passive euthanasia is based on the distinction between killing someone and allowing someone to die. In passive euthanasia, death is caused by the patient's disease, which is allowed to run its natural course without any treatment that might prolong the patient's life. In active euthanasia, the immediate cause of death is not the patient's disease but something that is done or given to the patient to cause his death, such as a lethal drug. To focus our discussion,

---

[52] Janet Smith, "Moral Character and Abortion," in *Doing and Being,* ed. Joram G. Haber (New York: Macmillan, 1993), 442–454.

consider this case, which was recounted by the journalist Stewart Alsop, who himself had cancer at the time:

> The third night that I roomed with Jack in our tiny double room in the solid-tumor ward of the cancer clinic of the National Institutes of Health in Bethesda, Md., a terrible thought occurred to me.
>
> Jack had a melanoma in his belly, a malignant solid tumor that the doctors guessed was about the size of a softball. The cancer had started a few months before with a small tumor in his left shoulder and there had been several operations since. The doctors planned to remove the softball-sized tumor, but they knew Jack would soon die. The cancer had metastasized—it had spread beyond control.
>
> Jack was good-looking, about 28, and brave. He was in constant pain, and his doctor had prescribed an intravenous shot of a synthetic opiate—a painkiller, or analgesic—every four hours. His wife spent many of the daylight hours with him, and she would sit or lie on his bed and pat him all over, as one pats a child, only more methodically, and this seemed to help control the pain. But at night, when his pretty wife had left (wives cannot stay overnight at the NIH clinic) and darkness fell, the pain would attack without pity.
>
> At the prescribed hour, a nurse would give Jack a shot of the synthetic analgesic, and this would control the pain for perhaps two hours or a bit more. Then he would begin to moan, or whimper, very low, as though he didn't want to wake me. Then he would begin to howl like a dog.
>
> When this happened, either he or I would ring for a nurse, and ask for a painkiller. She would give him some codeine or the like by mouth, but it never did any real good—it affected him no more than half an aspirin might affect a man who had just broken his arm. Always the nurse would explain as encouragingly as she could that there was not long to go before the next intravenous shot—"Only about 50 minutes now." And always poor Jack's whimpers and howls would become more loud and frequent until at last the blessed relief came.
>
> The third night of this routine, the terrible thought occurred to me. "If Jack were a dog," I thought, "what would be done with him?" The answer was obvious: the pound, and chloroform. No human being with a spark of pity could let a living thing suffer so, to no good end.[53]

Clearly, the author of this true story is not advocating passive euthanasia for Jack—that is, waiting until his disease puts him out of his misery. Instead, the author is suggesting that Jack should have been administered active euthanasia: He should have been put to death, perhaps by a doctor. At the time of this incident, it would have been illegal for a doctor to administer active euthanasia to Jack. However, in March 1996 a federal appeals court ruled that states may not prohibit doctors from helping a terminally ill person commit suicide. In effect, this ruling would make it legal for doctors to administer active euthanasia.

But even if the law allows active euthanasia, the moral question still remains: Is active euthanasia morally permissible? The conservative position on this question has been set out by many natural law ethicists, such as J. Gay-Williams:

---

[53] Stewart Alsop, "The Right to Die with Dignity," *Good Housekeeping,* August 1974, 69, 130.

Every human being has a natural inclination to continue living. Our reflexes and responses fit us to fight attackers, flee wild animals, and dodge out of the way of trucks. In our daily lives we exercise the caution and care necessary to protect ourselves. Our bodies are similarly structured for survival. . . . Euthanasia does violence to this natural goal of survival. It is literally acting against nature because all the processes of nature are bent towards the end of bodily survival. . . .

By reason alone, then, we can recognize that euthanasia sets us against our own nature. Furthermore, in doing so, euthanasia does violence to our dignity. Our dignity comes from seeking our ends. When one of our goals is survival, and actions are taken that eliminate that goal, then our natural dignity suffers. Unlike animals, we are conscious through reason of our nature and our ends. Euthanasia involves acting as if this dual nature—inclination towards survival and awareness of this as an end—did not exist. Thus, euthanasia denies our basic human character and requires that we regard ourselves or others as something less than fully human.[54]

> *To act absolutely in conformity with virtue is nothing but acting according to the laws of our own proper nature.*
>
> BARUCH SPINOZA

The natural law position, then, argues that life is a fundamental human good whose inviolable value we can uncover by reflecting on our natural inclinations. Since active euthanasia destroys this fundamental human good, it is immoral. Therefore, it would be wrong for a doctor to follow Alsop's suggestion and put Jack to death.

But we have seen that natural law reasoning has some shortcomings. In particular, natural law does not make clear why we have a moral obligation to follow our natural inclinations. Perhaps a natural law ethicist could respond that we are obligated to follow our natural inclinations because these embody God's commands. In fact, many religious traditions prohibit active euthanasia explicitly on the basis of a scriptural divine command ethic. For example, the Judeo-Christian tradition opposes euthanasia on the grounds that the commandment "Thou shall not kill" explicitly condemns active euthanasia. Yet what can such divine command approaches to euthanasia provide for the nonbeliever?

Utilitarianism provides a different approach to euthanasia. Philosopher James Rachels expresses the utilitarian argument in favor of active euthanasia as follows:

Terminal patients sometimes suffer pain so horrible that it can hardly be comprehended by those who have not actually experienced it. . . . The argument from mercy says: euthanasia is justified because it provides an end to that. . . .

I want now to present a . . . version of the argument from mercy, which is inspired by utilitarianism. I believe that the following argument is sound and proves that active euthanasia can be justified:

1. If an action promotes the best interests of everyone concerned, and violates no one's rights, then that action is morally acceptable.

2. In at least some cases, active euthanasia promotes the best interests of everyone concerned and violates no one's rights.

---

[54] J. Gay-Williams, "The Wrongfulness of Euthanasia," in *Intervention and Reflection: Basic Issues in Medical Ethics*, ed. Ronald Munson (Belmont, CA: Wadsworth, 1979).

3. Therefore, in at least some cases active euthanasia is morally acceptable.

How can it be wrong to do an action that is merciful, that benefits everyone concerned, and that violates no one's rights?[55]

It is important to notice that Rachels qualifies his argument with the proviso that "no one's rights" should be violated by an act of euthanasia. In particular, Rachels wants to rule out the possibility of involuntary euthanasia—that is, euthanasia in which the patient does not consent to being put to death. A patient has the right to refuse to be put to death, Rachels holds, and active euthanasia is not justified when it violates this right.

Obviously, Rachels disagrees with the natural law position on euthanasia. In Rachels's view, it would have been morally legitimate for a doctor to have put Jack to death. Yet is the utilitarian case for euthanasia persuasive? Doesn't the argument ignore the broader consequences of euthanasia? In many cases, won't the death of a person inflict great grief, emotional pain, distress, and even economic deprivation on those who are left behind? Moreover, once we allow physicians to put to death those who request it, will physicians gradually lose their commitment to saving life instead of destroying it? Will society move down a slippery slope toward having doctors put to death anyone whose life society deems no longer valuable (as may have happened during the Nazi era in Germany)?

However, Rachels holds that his conclusion is supported not only by utilitarianism but also by a Kantian approach to euthanasia. One problem with utilitarianism as we have seen, is that utilitarianism assumes that only consequences matter when evaluating an action, and consequences are difficult to predict. A Kantian approach does not rely on consequences:

> Kant argued that we should act only on rules that we are willing to have applied universally; that is, we should behave as we would be willing to have everyone behave. . . . If we would not be willing for the rule to be followed universally, then we should not follow it ourselves. Thus, if we are not willing for others to apply the rule to us, we ought not apply it to them.
>
> The application of all this to the question of euthanasia is fairly obvious. Each of us is going to die someday, although most of us do not know when or how. But suppose you were told that you would die in one of two ways, and you were asked to choose between them. First, you could die quietly, and without pain, from a fatal injection. Or second, you could choose to die of an affliction so painful that for several days before death you would be reduced to howling like a dog, with your family standing by helplessly, trying to comfort you, but going through its own psychological hell. It is hard to believe that any sane person, when confronted by these possibilities would choose to have a rule applied that would force upon him or her the second option. And if we would not want such a rule, which excludes euthanasia, applied to us, then we should not apply such a rule to others.[56]

This Kantian approach implies that it would have been morally permissible to put Jack to death. Although Rachels does not mention it, the Kantian approach

---

[55] James Rachels, "More Impertinent Distinctions and a Defense of Active Euthanasia," in *Biomedical Ethics*, ed. Thomas A. Mappes and Jane S. Zembaty (New York: McGraw-Hill, 1981), 355–359.
[56] Ibid.

also requires that doctors get Jack's informed consent. Yet this Kantian approach may assume a kind of ideal situation that does not obtain in a hospital situation. How realistic is it to expect a person suffering the extremities of a painful terminal illness—drugged, depressed, and perhaps subject to the subtle manipulations of an exhausted family—to be able to make choices that are free and rational?

The moral theories of natural law, utilitarianism, and Kantian ethics, then, do not agree on the subject of euthanasia. But this does not mean that the three approaches are useless. On the contrary, each approach sheds light on the factors that we must take into account to evaluate the morality of active euthanasia. Natural law reminds us of the intrinsic value of the basic good of life. It informs us that we should not take life without serious cause and without due consideration. The utilitarian argument of Rachels tells us that in some cases the evil of pain may override the value of the basic good of life. And Rachels's proviso reminds us of the key importance of securing a person's voluntary consent before administering euthanasia. Finally, the Kantian argument reminds us of our fundamental interdependence: What we may want others to do for us when we are in need, we should now be willing to do for those presently in need.

In the end we all must decide perhaps not whether abortion is right or whether euthanasia is moral, but other pressing moral issues. On what do we base these decisions that shape who and what we are and will be? If we fail to engage and resolve these questions, we run a grave risk of leaving undeveloped a significant facet of human nature and self, the moral aspect.

QUESTIONS

1. Describe some situations you have confronted that posed a moral dilemma for you. What do you feel that you *should* have done in each of those situations? What moral theories do you feel come closest to explaining why you should have done that?

2. Consider a situation that confronted you with a moral dilemma. Discuss what each of these theories of obligation would have required you to do: natural law, utilitarianism, Kant's categorical imperative, virtue ethics, Buddhist ethics. Does each of these theories provide clear guidance about what you should do? Explain.

3. Try living a day according to the utilitarian principle. What problems do you find yourself facing as you go through your day attempting to apply utilitarianism? Try the same with the other approaches to ethics that we have discussed.

4. Some philosophers hold that utilitarianism imposes extremely heavy obligations on us. Others hold that Kant's categorical imperative imposes even heavier obligations. Which of these two approaches do you think would be easier to follow? Why?

5. Write down the fundamental moral principles that you feel you should live up to. Why are these principles appropriate? How would you show someone that you are not mistaken in adopting them?

7.7 Ethics and Moral Responsibility

Suppose that you have accepted one of the normative theories according to which certain acts are right and others are wrong. Suppose further that in applying this theory, you judge that a certain action was wrong, such as Jane Doe's decision to have an abortion, or the decision to keep Jack alive with his cancer. But having made this judgment, you can always ask a further question: Should we hold Jane Doe responsible for her act? Is she at fault, and should we blame her for what she did? These questions cut to a basic issue in the study of ethics: moral responsibility. The issue of moral responsibility has far-reaching ethical implications. So, in concluding our overview of ethics, we will briefly consider this issue. We have already touched on some aspects of moral responsibility in Chapter 3 when we discussed free will and determinism.

EXCUSABILITY

A good way to enlighten the issue of moral responsibility is to connect it to the idea of **excusability.** Under certain circumstances we excuse people who have done wrong. We hold these people blameless or not morally responsible for what they did. Ethicists generally speak of four conditions under which we ordinarily excuse people: (1) excusable ignorance of the consequences or circumstances of an act, (2) the presence of a constraint that forced the person to do the act and that was so strong that no ordinary amount of willpower could overcome it, (3) the presence of circumstances beyond the person's control, and (4) the absence of either the ability or the opportunity, or both, to do the right thing in the given situation.[57]

> **excusability** the concept that under certain circumstances, people are not morally responsible for their decisions and conduct

Excusable Ignorance of Consequences

We excuse people when we don't believe they were aware of the unfavorable consequences their actions would produce or because they couldn't reasonably have known how to prevent the consequences. For example, today health professionals are cautious, or should be, about subjecting patients to X-rays because of the dangers of radiation exposure. Years ago, however, medical personnel were not aware of these dangers. Therefore, barring cases of egregiously excessive and unnecessary X-ray exposure, we generally would not hold health professionals morally responsible for damage from X-rays administered during that time. But today we would.

Not knowing how to prevent bad consequences we foresee may also excuse a person. Thus, we wouldn't hold a hospitalized patient at fault for not knowing

---

[57] Paul Taylor, *Problems of Moral Philosophy*, 2d ed. (Belmont, CA: Dickenson, 1972), 277.

The Raft of the Medusa, Théodore Géricault. Géricault's painting portrays survivors of an 1817 shipwreck who floated for weeks on a makeshift raft desperately cannibalizing one another to stay alive. Ordinarily, we excuse actions when we think that people lacked the ability to do the right act. Were the survivors of the *Medusa* morally responsible for what they did?

what to do if another patient suddenly experienced cardiac arrest. But we might blame a nurse or another health professional at the hospital if he did not take corrective action, although, of course, he could not guarantee the results.

Constraints

We usually excuse people when we think that they could not help what they did, that they had little choice in a matter. The constraints may be either external or internal. *External constraint* refers to outside factors or forces. In situations involving external constraints, we typically speak of people acting against their wills. A bank teller who turns over the bank's money to a gun-wielding robber is acting against her will. We would not condemn such behavior or blame the teller, for the act was done under coercion. In contrast, we would find fault with a teller who freely helped the robber, perhaps by telling the person beforehand the best time to rob the bank.

The compelling element of *internal constraint* comes from inside rather than from someone else. We speak of people who act in certain ways because they feel an overwhelming inner urge, desire, craving, or impulse to do so. Accordingly, we normally would not hold a kleptomaniac *morally* accountable for shoplifting a watch from a jewelry shop, or patients responsible for damage they cause during periods of postoperative psychosis. Yet we would surely blame the robber who carefully and coolly orchestrated the robbery of the jewelry shop while feeling no inner compulsion to carry out the plan. Similarly, we would blame patients who throw destructive and disruptive temper tantrums while fully in control of their actions.

Uncontrollable Circumstances

When, in our estimation, the circumstances of an act are beyond the person's control, we generally excuse the behavior. There are many circumstantial excuses that we readily accept as legitimate. Illness, accidents, and unexpected duties are typical cases. Thus, we would not hold Janet responsible for arriving late for her hospital shift if, through no fault of her own, she was involved in an automobile accident. If we learned that the accident was caused by Janet's reckless driving, however, we likely would hold her accountable for her tardiness.

Lack of Alternatives

Ordinarily, we excuse actions when we think that people lack either the ability or the opportunity to do the right act. If a man can't swim, we wouldn't blame him for not jumping into a pool to save a drowning child (although we might hold him responsible for not summoning aid or throwing the child a life preserver). Similarly, if the man could swim but failed to save the child because he saw her only when it was too late, he lacked the opportunity to save the child. Therefore, we would not consider him morally responsible.

No man voluntarily pursues evil. To prefer evil to good is not in human nature.

SOCRATES

In sketching these four conditions, philosophy professor Paul Taylor raises two important points. First, a situation that satisfies these conditions contrasts sharply with one that doesn't. Second, situations of both kinds do occur in everyday life:

> Thus, just as there are cases where a person could not have foreseen the harmful consequences of his act, there are other cases where a person does foresee such consequences and still chooses to do the act. (A man who intends to murder someone not only foresees that his victim will die but wants this to happen.) Just as there are acts done under the coercion of another person, so there are acts done when no such external constraint is present. A man who fires a shotgun at the house of a civil-rights worker in the South may have decided to do it entirely by himself and may have acted under no external compulsion. It is possible, indeed, to act in opposition to a considerable amount of external constraint. Whenever a person commits a crime he does so in spite of, rather than because of, such external constraints as threat of punishment, fear of the police, and general social disapproval. Again, consider the case in which an internal urge or drive compels a person to act against his own will. This kind of case is to be contrasted with that of a person freely choosing to do something after carefully deliberating about it. A man might be in full control of himself as he works out a plan to embezzle funds, and feel under no compulsion as

he calmly carries out his plan. In connection with the third kind of situation, just as we are sometimes prevented from doing what we ought to do by circumstances beyond our control, there are other cases where we don't do what we ought simply because we don't want to. We sometimes try to avoid our obligations when we find them onerous. Finally, although in a given situation we may lack the ability or the opportunity to do what would be right, just as often we have the capacity and the opportunity to do any number of alternatives open to our choice and yet we knowingly choose to do what is wrong. For example, the man who does not report accurately his income in order to avoid paying a tax certainly has the ability and opportunity to make out an accurate report, and knows that this would be the right thing for him to do.[58]

Thus, in everyday life there are occasions when we excuse people and occasions when we hold them responsible for their acts.

The preceding observations about moral responsibility probably seem commonsensical enough. And they remain so, until we apply the theory of determinism to human conduct. Then things tend to grow murky. Although in Chapter 3 we discussed the theory of determinism let us here briefly recall it so we can note its implications for morality.

One may go wrong in many different ways, but right only in one, which is why it is easy to fail and difficult to succeed—easy to miss the target and difficult to hit it.

ARISTOTLE

DETERMINISM

As we saw in Chapter 3, determinism is the theory that everything in the universe is totally ruled by causal laws. Accordingly, every event has a prior condition, and all events are at least theoretically predictable if all the prior conditions are known. Here we will look more closely at how ethics and moral responsibility relate to the theory of determinism.

Many people believe that moral responsibility is incompatible with determinism. They claim that when the four excusing conditions do not hold, people appear to be under no constraints and appear to have the ability and opportunity to choose any number of alternatives. Still, the deterministic argument goes, these appearances are mere illusions. If choices and actions are causally determined, then, given the causal laws operating in the situation of choice, only one course of action can possibly occur: the one that will be the effect of the previous causes that are occurring in the situation. In other words, the act that a person ultimately chooses is inevitable, since there was a set of events that, of itself, was sufficient for producing the choice; and because that sufficient condition was present, the choice of that act had to occur. In brief, the person could not have acted other than he or she did. If determinism does operate in the realm of human decision and conduct, then determinism seems incompatible with freedom and responsibility in an ethical sense.

How, then, is the so-called moral self to be understood? In response to the assertion that moral responsibility is not possible in a strictly deterministic universe, three main positions emerge: hard determinism, indeterminism, and compatibalism.

The only freedom I care about is the freedom to do right.

THOMAS HUXLEY

---

[58] Ibid., 279–280.

Hard Determinism

Hard determinism is based on the rigid causality apparent in the physical universe. Freedom is incompatible with this view, for to admit freedom is to admit an element of unpredictability in the universe. According to hard determinists, free choice amounts to little more than human ignorance. We think we are free merely because we cannot predict our own or others' future behavior. Although we cannot help engaging in the process of deliberation, the choice we make is forced on us by whichever set of motives is strongest. To insist that we are free and that we could have acted otherwise is to speak so much gibberish. After all, say hard determinists, there could never be any possible proof that we could have acted otherwise since the proof is precisely what never did occur, and never will occur. Does this mean that criminals are not morally responsible for what they do? Precisely. According to hard determinists, a criminal's genetic inheritance and environment predetermine his life of crime.

hard determinism the doctrine that every event has a cause, which entails the denial of moral freedom

Indeterminism

The opposite of hard determinism is **indeterminism,** the view that humans are exceptions to the rigid causation that occurs in nature. Like determinists, indeterminists agree that the laws of causality may apply to everything else in nature.

Yet indeterminists say humans are an exception to these causal laws. Causal laws do not apply to our free choices. Our free acts are uncaused events that are not brought about by something else. Thus, human beings are not merely personalities entirely explainable in empirical terms; we are also moral agents. When a choice between right and wrong confronts us, we consider ourselves free agents with a moral self. The moral self makes the choice and so can be held accountable for it.

indeterminism the view that some individual choices are not determined by preceding events

Compatibalism

Hard determinism and indeterminism share the assumption that determinism is incompatible with moral responsibility. In contrast, advocates of **compatibalism** attempt to reconcile freedom and responsibility with determinism. Compatibalists concede that people cannot choose to act against their individual characters. In this sense people are predetermined. But people are often free to act without any external physical restraints present to prevent them from acting. In such cases they are free agents. Yes, every act is caused, but not by something outside us. It is caused by the kind of being we are and the particular desires and habits we have. In this way, compatibalists claim that they have avoided the mistake of indeterminists, who admit of causeless acts, and that of hard determinists, who consider responsibility a fiction.

compatibalism a view that attempts to reconcile freedom and responsibility with determinism

It's apparent that none of these viewpoints presents an airtight case. Because it denies freedom and moral responsibility, hard determinism does not accord with how we generally experience our own actions. Indeterminism, in proposing the notion of uncaused acts, seemingly preserves freedom and responsibility at the expense of scientific respectability. Compatibalism, which tries to reconcile freedom and responsibility with determinism, apparently does away with something worthwhile in each. The controversy about freedom and determinism ultimately is a controversy about human nature: It cuts to the issue of what we are at the core of our being. At the same time, it has profound implications for ethics, because the position that one chooses in the controversy affects one's idea of moral responsibility.

QUESTIONS

1. Describe a situation when you were wrongly blamed for something for which you were not morally responsible. Which of the four excusing conditions were present?

2. Is there any kind of experience you could have that would prove that hard determinism is false? Explain.

3. Several years ago, three young men abducted a young woman, and, after raping her, they tortured her over several hours by mutilating her. They then buried her alive. The young men were caught and were found guilty of the murder. What do you think should have been done to them? Explain how your view regarding what should have been done to them is consistent or inconsistent with hard determinism, indeterminism, and compatibalism.

4. Political polls and projections are often said to influence the outcome of elections. What control, if any, does a forecast exercise over an event (for example, the astrological prophecies of a psychic)? If the existence of God is assumed, and if God already knows how things are going to turn out, can any of us alter that result? If we cannot alter something, are we free?

5. In *Crito*, which we read in Chapter 1, Plato shows Socrates refusing to escape from jail, even though he has been imprisoned unjustly, because such an action would violate the principles of a life dedicated to upholding the law. As a result, Socrates drinks the hemlock and dies. Was he free to choose differently? Was he a victim of his past?

6. Point to examples from your life that show you doing things for other people's reasons. Perhaps your choice to be in school or to study a particular subject would be a good place to begin. How susceptible to peer pressure do you think you are? Do you detect any pressure affecting the views you hold? In what area of life do you feel you can truly express yourself?

7. Fatalism is the belief that events are fixed, that nothing we can do will alter them—what will be, will be. Do scientific views necessitate fatalism? Is fatalism consistent with the doctrine of free will? Is it consistent with the view of the human as thinker? As existential being?

8. Can you think of any instance in which you would have no freedom at all? And if we are essentially free, how does this freedom lead to uncertainty?

7.8 Chapter Summary and Conclusions

We opened this chapter by observing that values, like so many other things today, are changing. The study of values includes debates about whether value judgments express knowledge or feeling, whether values are subjective or objective, and what is of value. One important value area is ethics. Normative ethics is the search for principles of good conduct. Broadly speaking, normative ethics can be divided into the consequentialist, nonconsequentialist, and virtue ethics schools. The consequentialist school in turn, can be subdivided into egoism, act utilitarianism, and rule utilitarianism. The nonconsequentialist school can be subdivided into single- and multiple-rule nonconsequentialism; divine command theory and Kant's categorical imperative illustrate the former, and Buddhism illustrates the latter. Virtue ethics includes Aristotle's definition of virtue as well as the theories of those who compare male and female virtues.

The main points of the chapter are as follows:

1. Ethics is the study of those values that relate to our moral conduct, including questions of good and evil, right and wrong, and moral responsibility (7.1).

2. The descriptive study of ethics, which raises the issue of ethical relativism studies ethics from a factual point of view. Normative ethics is the search for principles of moral behavior that are reasonable (7.2).

3. Consequentialist theories claim that the morality of an action depends only on its consequences (7.3).

4. Egoism is the consequentialist position that states the following: Always act in such a way that your actions promote your best long-term interests (7.3).

5. Act utilitarianism is the consequentialist position that states this: Always act so that your actions produce the greatest happiness for everyone (7.3).

6. Rule utilitarianism is the consequentialist position that states the following: Always follow those rules that tend to produce the greatest happiness for everyone (7.3).

7. Nonconsequentialist theories claim that the morality of an action depends on factors other than consequences (7.4).

8. Divine command theory is a nonconsequentialist theory that enjoins us to follow the law of God. There are scriptural and natural law versions of divine command theory (7.4).

9. Kant's categorical imperative is a nonconsequentialist position that states this: Always act in such a way that your reasons for acting are reasons you could will to have everyone act on in similar circumstances, and always treat persons as ends and not merely as means (7.4).

10. Buddhism emphasizes volition and ties morality to wisdom. Its moral code is expressed in precepts that invite followers to refrain from certain actions and to develop certain virtues (7.4).

11. Virtue ethics identifies the character traits of the morally good person; it emphasizes the kind of person we should become instead of principles of action. Some virtue theories argue that male and female virtues differ (7.5).

12. Application of the normative theories to issues such as abortion and euthanasia suggests that each theory provides important and distinctive insights into factors that should be taken into account when making moral decisions (7.6).

13. The concept of moral responsibility is associated with the concept of excusability, which holds that there are circumstances under which we should excuse people for their decisions and conduct (7.7).

14. In response to the claim that moral responsibility is not possible in a strictly deterministic universe, three main positions can be identified: hard determinism indeterminism, and compatibalism (7.7).

Whether or not we choose to acknowledge them as such, the moral values we hold and the obligations we feel constitute expressions of who we are, how we see things, and how we wish to be seen by others. In choosing a moral lifestyle, we're really defining a large part of ourselves. Yet the complexity of moral decision making persists; the choices remain murky. The question that continues to nag us is this: What moral lifestyle should I adopt to live the fullest, most rewarding life I can?

As suggested throughout this chapter, there is no single adequate answer. The nature of moral decision making disallows scientific assurance. Nevertheless, we can garner factors from our discussion that seem appropriate to a personal morality. First, any moral code that you follow must be your own. Not in the sense that you alone follow it, but in the sense that you have arrived at it through your powers of reasoning about your experience and your nature. Granted, we cannot fully escape our social, cultural, and religious backgrounds, nor would we want to. Nevertheless, if our morality is to be an expression of self, we must carefully reflect on the values that we have found to be reasonable. We must weigh their merits and liabilities in the light of our own lives, circumstances, and understanding of human nature. Such reflection places heavy emphasis on self-growth, especially on increasing our knowledge and awareness of self and the world and on being willing to adjust our moral views as we learn more. It also recognizes the dynamic, experimental value of morality.

The second factor appropriate to a personal morality is related to the first. It stems from Immanuel Kant's idea of a good will. As just suggested, to make moral decisions primarily on the basis of social or institutional influence is to surrender what most people consider a uniquely human quality: the individual capacity to make moral decisions. These outside forces should not be our primary reasons for acting morally. For the mature and thoughtful person, right intention or good will is a necessary ingredient of the true moral act. It is true that these are hazy notions, but they frequently clear up in context. For

Morality, said Jesus, is kindness to the weak; morality, said Nietzsche, is the bravery of the strong; morality, said Plato, is the effective harmony of the whole. Probably all three doctrines must be combined to find a perfect ethic; but can we doubt which of the elements is fundamental?

WILL DURANT

example, the motives of the person who gives to charity primarily for the sake of a tax write-off are different from those of the person who gives to improve the conditions of the less fortunate; the intention of the person who flatters to ingratiate is different from that of the person who speaks the truth for its own sake. The teachings of ethicists and great moral leaders have stated or implied the importance of right intention or good will in the moral act.

But these two subjective elements of a personal moral code, reasoned self-determination and right intention, are insufficient to ensure right action. After all we may be self-determining and well intentioned but still do something heinous. Therefore, the third element is an objective one, involving a consideration of the results or consequences of our actions. It seems that consequences must be a factor in any moral stance, for to be indifferent to the consequences of our actions is to act irresponsible — that is, without moral regard. As we have seen, however, determining the consequences of an action is often difficult. It requires much evidence, analysis, and reflection. Even then, we cannot be certain. But without such an examination, our action will not be, in the highest sense, moral.

No doubt there are other factors that you might wish to introduce. But these three — reasoned self-determination, right intention, and consideration of consequences — are the instruments for building a personal moral code.

7.9 HISTORICAL SHOWCASE

Nietzsche and Wollstonecraft

Many people are skeptical about the claims of morality, holding that morality is a sham of some kind. In this showcase, therefore, we discuss the views of a nineteenth-century philosopher who was completely skeptical about morality: Friedrich Nietzsche.

We then discuss the views of Mary Wollstonecraft. Wollstonecraft accepted a view of morality very much like Kant's view that morality is based on reason. Her confidence in ethics and reason is the basis of her view that women are, and should be treated as, the equals of men. Far from being skeptical of morality, she saw it as the foundation of sexual equality and built on it the first clearly articulated feminist philosophy.

By considering and contrasting the views of these philosophers, you may find it easier to make up your own mind about the future and reality of moral principles.

NIETZSCHE

The most powerful attack ever launched against morality was made by Friedrich Nietzsche. Nietzsche was born in 1844 in Roeken, Germany. His father having died when Nietzsche was four, he was raised in a household consisting of his mother, sister, grandmother, and two aunts. In 1864, Nietzsche went off to college, studying first at the University of Bonn and then transferring to the University of Leipzig. There, perhaps experiencing the first effects of his freedom, Nietzsche soon contracted syphilis, which at that time was incurable. The disease had little immediate effect on his scholarly skills, however, and he soon managed to impress his professors, particularly the widely respected Friedrich Ritschel. When Nietzsche graduated from Leipzig, Ritschel gave him an enthusiastic recommendation, and Nietzsche quickly secured a position as a professor at the University of Basel in 1869. Unfortunately, his health soon began to deteriorate because of his disease, and in 1878 poor health forced Nietzsche to resign his position. Most of the rest of his life was spent in terrible loneliness. Several times he proposed marriage to different women but was firmly rejected by each. In 1889, Nietzsche abruptly went mad. He spent much of the next eleven years in a madhouse or under the care of his doting sister. He died on August 25, 1900.

In the major writings he produced before he went mad, Nietzsche proposed the insightful view that the traditional values and ethical systems of the West were collapsing even as he wrote. The major source of their collapse, he felt, was the loss of belief in God. "God is dead," he declared, having been killed by our own modern philosophies and beliefs. Since we no longer believe in God, it is difficult for us to believe in the traditional values and ethical views that Christians and others have defended by appealing to God. The death of God has left us floating directionless in a cold, empty space. Nietzsche announced the death of God by using the highly poetic image of a madman:

The Madman.—Have you ever heard of the madman who on a bright morning lighted a lantern and ran to the market-place calling out unceasingly: "I seek God! I seek God!"—As there were many people standing about who did not believe in God, he caused a great deal of amusement. Why! is he lost? said one. Has he strayed away like a child? said another. Or does he keep himself hidden? Is he afraid of us? Has he taken a sea-voyage? Has he emigrated?—the people cried out laughingly, all in a hubbub. The insane man jumped into their midst and transfixed them with his glances. "Where is God gone?" he called out, "I mean to tell you! *We have killed him*,—you and I! We are all his murderers! But how have we done it? How were we able to drink up the sea? Who gave us the sponge to wipe away the whole horizon? What did we do when we loosened this earth from its sun? Whither does it now move? Whither do we move? Away from all suns? Do we not dash on unceasingly? Backwards, sideways, forwards, in all directions? Is there still an above and below? Do we not stray, as through infinite nothingness? Does not empty space breathe upon us? Has it not

become colder? Does not night come on continually, darker and darker? Shall we not have to light lanterns in the morning? Do we not hear the noise of the grave-diggers who are burying God? Do we not smell the divine putrefaction?—for even Gods putrefy! God is dead! God remains dead! And we have killed him! How shall we console ourselves, the most murderous of all murderers? The holiest and the mightiest that the world has hitherto possessed, has bled to death under our knife,—who will wipe the blood from us? With what water could we cleanse ourselves? What lustrums, what sacred games shall we have to devise? Is not the magnitude of this deed too great for us? Shall we not ourselves have to become Gods, merely to seem worthy of it? There never was a greater event,—and on account of it, all who are born after us belong to a higher history than any history hitherto!"—Here the madman was silent and looked again at his hearers; they also were silent and looked at him in surprise. At last he threw his lantern on the ground, so that it broke in pieces and was extinguished. "I come too early," he then said, "I am not yet at the right time. This prodigious event is still on its way, and is traveling,—it has not yet reached men's ears. Lightning and thunder need time, the light of the stars needs time, deeds need time, even after they are done, to be seen and heard. This deed is as yet further from them than the furthest star,—*and yet they have done it!*"—It is further stated that the madman made his way into different churches on the same day, and there intoned his *Requiem aeternam deo*.[1]

But the death of God, for Nietzsche, was not necessarily a bad thing. For belief in God had encouraged the illusion that there are universal and absolute truths that everyone must accept. In fact, Nietzsche maintained, there is no absolute truth. Instead, all our beliefs are nothing more than so many interpretations or "perspectives," ways we have of looking at the world. There is an indefinite number of possible interpretations of the world, all of them equally true and equally false. But some of these are more useful than others because some have the advantage of enabling us to live and

[1]Friedrich Nietzsche, *The Joyful Wisdom*, trans. Thomas Common, in *The Complete Works of Friedrich Nietzsche*, vol. 10, ed. Oscar Levy (New York: Macmillan, 1944), 167–169.

gain power over the world. Such "useful" beliefs, although as false as any others, are the ones we count as part of the "truth." As Nietzsche put it, *"Truth is that sort of error* without which a particular type of living being could not live. The value for *life* is ultimately decisive."[2]

Although Nietzsche did not believe that there is one "true" interpretation of the universe, he did think that some interpretations or ways of understanding the universe are better than others. Every event in the universe, Nietzsche maintained, can be interpreted as being produced by a force he called the "will to power." It was a useful hypothesis, he felt, to interpret events in the universe in terms of something with which we are familiar: the activity of our own wills:

> We must risk the hypothesis that everywhere we recognize "effects" there is an effect of will upon will; that all mechanical happenings, insofar as they are activated by some energy, are will-power, will-effects.—Assuming, finally, that we succeeded in explaining our entire instinctual life as the development and ramification of one basic form of will (of the will to power, as I hold); assuming that one could trace back all the organic functions to this will to power, including the solution of the problems of generation and nutrition (they are one problem)—if this were done, we should be justified in defining *all* effective energy unequivocally as *will to power*.[3]

If everything in the universe is interpreted as a result of a will to power, then all human actions must also be seen as outcomes of the will to power. The primary drives of human beings are not the pursuit of pleasure and the avoidance of pain (as Mill had argued). Instead, human beings are primarily motivated by the desire to increase their power over things and over people. As Nietzsche put it, "Life itself is essential assimilation, injury, violation of the foreign and the weaker, suppression, hardness, the forcing of one's own forms upon something else, ingestion and—at least in its mildest form—exploitation."[4] In fact, Nietzsche felt, our theories and

Friedrich Nietzsche: "God is dead! God remains dead! And we have killed him! How shall we console ourselves, the most murderous of all murderers? Shall we not ourselves have to become Gods?"

beliefs about the world should also be seen as instruments of the will to power. Interpretations of the world are instruments we use to extend our power over the world and over one another.

Just as there are no absolute truths about the world, so also there are no absolute truths about morality. Any morality, Nietzsche claimed, is also merely an interpretation of the world: "There are no moral phenomena, only moralistic interpretations of phenomena," and "There are no moral facts." Like any other kind of interpretation, a morality cannot be said to be absolutely true or false; it can only be a more-or-less useful instrument for the will to power. Moralities, then, are interpretations used as instruments to exert power over others or over the natural world. For example, Nietzsche argues that Kant, like every other moralist, proposed his moral theory in order to impose his own values:

> Apart from the value of such assertions as "there is a categorical imperative in us," one can always ask:

---

[2] Quoted in Frederick Copleston, *A History of Philosophy*, vol. 7 (Garden City, NY: Doubleday, 1963), 183.
[3] Friedrich Nietzsche, *Beyond Good and Evil*, trans. M. Cowan (Chicago: Henry Regnery, 1955), 43.
[4] Ibid., 201.

What does such an assertion indicate about him who makes it? There are systems of morals which are meant to justify their author in the eyes of other people; other systems of morals are meant to tranquilize him, and make him self-satisfied; with other systems he wants to crucify and humble himself; with others he wishes to take revenge; with others to conceal himself; with others to glorify himself and gain superiority and distinction;—this system of morals helps its author to forget, that system makes him, or something of him, forgotten; many a moralist would like to exercise power and creative arbitrariness over mankind; many another, perhaps, Kant especially, gives us to understand by his morals that "what is estimable in me, is that I know how to obey—and with you it *shall* not be otherwise than with me!"[5]

Mill's argument for utilitarianism, Nietzsche argues, was also an attempt to impose on others his personal preferences. In Mill's case these were preferences he shared with his fellow British citizens. Utilitarian arguments are merely an attempt to impose on the world the values of the English:

> Observe, for example, the indefatigable, inevitable English utilitarians. . . . In the end, they all want *English* morality to be recognized as authoritative, inasmuch as mankind, or the "general utility," or "the happiness of the greatest number,"—no! the happiness of *England* will be best served thereby. They would like, by all means, to convince themselves that the striving after *English* happiness, I mean after *comfort* and *fashion* (and in the highest instance, a seat in Parliament), is at the same time the true path of virtue; in fact, that insofar as there has been virtue in the world hitherto, it has just consisted in such striving.[6]

The ethical systems proposed by the major moral philosophers, then, are nothing more than manifestations of the will to power. The same is true of the popular moralities the masses follow. In his survey of the history of moralities, Nietzsche wrote, he had discovered two basic kinds of popular moralities. One kind was the "slave moralities" that weak people—especially the Christians—

had devised as instruments to acquire power over the strong. The other kind was the "master moralities" that had been devised by the strong to assert their power over the weak.

A master morality will normally develop in those individuals who are the strongest, those who are born with the power to dominate others. This type of morality values strength, intelligence, courage, revenge, and power seeking. In this morality a person is good to the extent that he or she has the strength to overpower others. This type of morality extols the individual.

On the other hand, a slave morality is fashioned by weak groups of people. A slave morality values whatever is useful or beneficial to the weak, such as sympathy, kindness, pity, patience, humility, and helping those in need. In a slave morality the good person is the one who helps the weak, whereas the dominating individual is seen as evil. Slave moralities are the moralities of the herd, since they extol the group and not the individual:

> In a tour through the many finer and coarser moralities which have hitherto prevailed or still prevail on the earth, I found certain traits recurring regularly together and connected with one another, until finally two primary types revealed themselves to me, and a radical distinction was brought to light. There is *master*-morality and *slave*-morality;—I would at once add, however, that in all higher and mixed civilizations, there are also attempts at the reconciliation of the two moralities; but one finds still oftener the confusion and mutual misunderstanding of them, indeed, sometimes their close juxtaposition—even in the same man, within one soul. The distinctions of moral values have either originated in a ruling caste, pleasantly conscious of being different from the ruled—or among the ruled class, the slaves and dependents of all sorts. In the first case, when it is the rulers who determine the conception "good," it is the exalted, proud disposition which is regarded as the distinguishing feature, and that which determines the order of rank. The noble type of man separates from himself the beings in whom the opposite of this exalted, proud disposition displays itself: he despises them. Let it at once be noted that in this first kind of morality the antithesis "good" and "bad" means practically the same as "noble" and "despicable";—the antithesis "good" and "*evil*" is of a different origin. The cowardly, the timid, the

[5] Friedrich Nietzsche, *Beyond Good and Evil*, trans. Helen Zimmern, in *The Complete Works of Friedrich Nietzsche*, vol. 2, 106.
[6] Ibid., 174.

insignificant, and those thinking merely of narrow utility are despised; moreover, also, the distrustful, with their constrained glances, the self-abasing, the dog-like kind of men who let themselves be abused, the mendicant flatterers, and above all the liars;—it is a fundamental belief of all aristocrats that the common people are untruthful. "We truthful ones"—the nobility in ancient Greece called themselves. It is obvious that everywhere the designations of moral value were at first applied to *men*, and were only derivatively and at a later period applied to *actions*; it is a gross mistake, therefore, when historians of morals start with questions like, "Why have sympathetic actions been praised?" The noble type of man regards himself as a determiner of values; he does not require to be approved of; he passes the judgment: "What is injurious to me is injurious in itself"; he knows that it is he himself only who confers honor on things; he is a creator of values. He honors whatever he recognizes in himself; such morality is self-glorification. In the foreground there is the feeling of plenitude, of power, which seeks to overflow, the happiness of high tension, the consciousness of a wealth which would fain give and bestow:—the noble man also helps the unfortunate, but not—or scarcely—out of pity, but rather from an impulse generated by the super-abundance of power. The noble man honors in himself the powerful one, him also who has power over himself, who knows how to speak and how to keep silence, who takes pleasure in subjecting himself to severity and hardness, and has reverence for all that is severe and hard. "Wotan placed a hard heart in my breast," says an old Scandinavian Saga: it is thus rightly expressed from the soul of a proud Viking. Such a type of man is even proud of *not* being made for sympathy; the hero of the Saga therefore adds warningly: "He who has not a hard heart when young, will never have one." The noble and brave who think thus are the furthest removed from the morality which sees precisely in sympathy, or in acting for the good of others, or in *désintéressement*, the characteristic of the moral; faith in oneself, pride in oneself, a radical enmity and irony towards "selflessness," belong as definitely to the noble morality, as do a careless scorn and precaution in presence of sympathy and the "warm heart."—It is the powerful who *know* how to honor, it is their art, their domain for invention. The profound reverence for age and for tradition—all law rests on this double reverence,—the belief and prejudice in favor of ancestors and unfavorable to newcomers, is typical in the morality of the powerful; and if, reversely, men of "mod-

ern ideas" believe almost instinctively in "progress" and the "future," and are more and more lacking in respect for old age, the ignoble origin of these "ideas" has complacently betrayed itself thereby. A morality of the ruling class, however, is more especially foreign and irritating to present-day taste in the sternness of its principle that one has duties only to one's equals; that one may act towards beings of a lower rank, toward all that is foreign, just as seems good to one, or "as the heart desires," and in any case "beyond good and evil": it is here that sympathy and similar sentiments can have a place. The ability and obligation to exercise prolonged gratitude and prolonged revenge—both only within the circle of equals,—artfulness in retaliation, *raffinement* of the idea in friendship, a certain necessity to have enemies (as outlets for the emotions of envy, quarrelsomeness, arrogance—in fact, in order to be a good *friend*): all these are typical characteristics of the noble morality, which, as has been pointed out, is not the morality of "modern ideas," and is therefore at present difficult to realize, and also to unearth and disclose.—It is otherwise with the second type of morality, *slave-morality*. Supposing that the abused, the oppressed, the suffering, the unemancipated, the weary, and those uncertain of themselves, should moralize, what will be the common element in their moral estimates? Probably a pessimistic suspicion with regard to the entire situation of man will find expression, perhaps a condemnation of man, together with his situation. The slave has an unfavorable eye for the virtues of the powerful; he has a skepticism and distrust, a *refinement* of distrust of everything "good" that is there honored—he would fain persuade himself that the very happiness there is not genuine. On the other hand, *those* qualities which serve to alleviate the existence of sufferers are brought into prominence and flooded with light; it is here that sympathy, the kind, helping hand, the warm heart, patience, diligence, humility, and friendliness attain to honor; for here these are the most useful qualities, and almost the only means of supporting the burden of existence. Slave-morality is essentially the morality of utility. Here is the seat of the origin of the famous antithesis "good" and "evil":—power and dangerousness are assumed to reside in the evil, a certain dreadfulness, subtlety, and strength, which do not admit of being despised. According to slave-morality, therefore, the "evil" man arouses fear: according to master-morality, it is precisely the "good" man who arouses fear and seeks to arouse it, while the bad man is regarded as the despicable being. The contrast attains its maximum when, in accordance with the logical consequences of slave-morality, a shade of depreciation—it may be slight and well-intentioned—at last attaches itself even to the "good" man of this morality; because, according to the servile mode of thought, the good man must in any case be the *safe* man: he is good-natured, easily deceived, perhaps a little stupid, *un bonhomme*. Everywhere that slave-morality gains the ascendancy, language shows a tendency to approximate the significations of the words "good" and "stupid."—A last fundamental difference: the desire for *freedom*, the instinct for happiness and the refinements of the feeling of liberty belong as necessarily to slave-morals and morality, as artifice and enthusiasm in reverence and devotion are the regular symptoms of an aristocratic mode of thinking and estimating.— Hence we can understand without further detail why love as a *passion*—it is our European specialty—must absolutely be of noble origin; as is well known, its invention is due to the Provençal poet-cavaliers, those brilliant ingenious men of the "gai saber" [happy science], to whom Europe owes so much, and almost owes itself.[7]

Although Nietzsche clearly favored the "master moralities" and argued that we should rid ourselves of our "slave moralities," he did not feel that one morality was more "true" than another. As there is no longer any God, there are no longer any objective moralities. Moralities are our own inventions:

What then, alone, can our teaching be?—That no one gives man his qualities, either God, society, his parents, his ancestors, nor himself (this nonsensical idea, which is at last refuted here, was taught as "intelligible freedom" by Kant, and perhaps even as early as Plato himself). No one is responsible for the fact that he exists at all, that he is constituted as he is, and that he happens to be in certain circumstances and in a particular environment. The fatality of his being cannot be divorced from the fatality of all that which has been and will be. This is not the result of an individual attention, of a will, of an aim, there is no attempt at attaining to any "ideal man," or "ideal happiness" or "ideal morality" with him— it is absurd to wish him to be careering towards some sort of purpose. *We* invented the concept "purpose"; in reality purpose is altogether lacking. One is nec-

essary, one is a piece of fate, one belongs to the whole, one is in the whole—there is nothing that could judge, measure, compare, and condemn our existence, for that would mean judging, measuring, comparing and condemning the whole. *But there is nothing outside the whole!* The fact that no one shall any longer be made responsible, that the nature of existence may not be traced to a *causa prima*, that the world is an entity neither as a sensorium nor as a spirit—*this alone is the great deliverance*—thus alone is the innocence of becoming restored. . . . The concept "God" has been the greatest objection to existence hitherto. . . . We deny God, we deny responsibility in God: thus alone do we save the world.[8]

The significance of Nietzsche's attack on morality cannot be underestimated. If Nietzsche is correct, then moral principles are nothing more than subtle or not-so-subtle tools that the weak use to secure their power over the strong. Morality is a sham. The moral principles proposed by Christians, utilitarians, or Kantians are nothing more than their attempt to impose their will on others. When I say, for example, that everyone should be charitable or that everyone should seek to maximize the happiness of everyone else, I am really trying to get you to be charitable to me or to maximize my happiness. Moral principles are thus nothing more than an expression of the will to power.

Thus, just as Hume's views had threatened epistemology, so Nietzsche's views threatened to destroy morality.

WOLLSTONECRAFT

Mary Wollstonecraft is recognized today as the first major feminist philosopher. A hard-working, independent, and enterprising woman, Wollstonecraft went against the conventions of the day. In an age when women were supposed to stay at home, Wollstonecraft left home to support herself at the age of nineteen and managed to achieve what was then unthinkable: She became an internationally known philosopher.

---

[7] Ibid., 227–232.

[8] Friedrich Nietzsche, *The Twilight of the Idols,* trans. A. M. Lucovici, in *The Complete Works of Friedrich Nietzsche,* vol. 16, 43.

The second of seven children, Mary Wollstonecraft was born on April 27, 1759. Her father, a gentleman farmer who managed to dissipate the small fortune he inherited from his own father, was subject to uncontrollable fits of rage, frustration, and drunkenness. As a nine-year-old, Mary felt she had to watch "whole nights at their chamber door" to protect her mother from her father's violence.

At the age of nineteen, seeking independence in defiance of her parents' wishes, Mary left home to work for two years as a live-in companion to a wealthy and tyrannical widow who continually reminded her of her lower status.

Mary was forced to return home in 1781 to care for her sick mother. Subjected once again to a violent family life, Mary became embittered and depressed. The death of her mother in 1782 let Mary leave home again, and she moved in with the family of her close friend Fanny Blood. Although Fanny's family was impoverished, Mary there found peace and tranquility.

In 1784, Mary, her two sisters, and Fanny opened a school in Newington Green, a town near London. Although the school prospered at first, it eventually ran up a huge debt and had to be closed. Needing money, Mary turned to writing and in 1786 published *Thoughts on the Education of Daughters*. The book attracted little attention. Later that year Mary took the job of governess to the three daughters of Lord and Lady Kingsborough. Mary hated her aristocratic employers, who constantly reminded her that she was of a lower social class. In a letter to her sister, she described Lady Kingsborough as a "haughty and disagreeable" woman whose "proud condescension added to my embarrassment."[9] After only ten months, Lady Kingsborough fired her.

Mary moved to London in 1787, where she took a job as an editor and writer for a journal. Here at last she prospered. Working at the journal was intellectually exciting, and the work allowed her to devote herself to her own writing, which now succeeded beyond her dreams. During the next few years she published numerous works, in-

Mary Wollstonecraft: "I see not the shadow of a reason to conclude that [the] virtues [of men and women] should differ in respect to their nature. In fact, how can they, if virtue has only one eternal standard?"

cluding two controversial works that made her internationally famous: *A Vindication of the Rights of Men* and *A Vindication of the Rights of Women*.

Wollstonecraft fashioned a philosophy based on a fundamental moral principle that she first set out in *A Vindication of the Rights of Men*, a work devoted to refuting the elitist philosophy of Edmund Burke. Burke held that people are fundamentally unequal and that the privileges of the upper class should be preserved. Mindful of her own unhappy experiences with upper-class women, Wollstonecraft rejected Burke's view as foolish. She argued that all human beings possess reason and that reason is the source of the equal moral rights that all human beings have. As Wollstonecraft put the matter in *A Vindication of the Rights of Men*, where she imagines herself talking to Burke:

The birthright of man, to give you, sir, a short definition of this disputed right, is such a degree of lib-

---

[9] *The Collected Letters of Mary Wollstonecraft*, ed. Ralph M. Wardle (Ithaca, NY: Cornell University Press, 1979), 164.

erty, civil and religious, as is compatible with the liberty of every other individual with whom he is united in a social compact, and the continued existence of that compact. . . .

It is necessary emphatically to repeat, that there are rights which men inherit at their birth, as rational creatures, who were raised above the brute creation by their improvable faculties; and that, in receiving these, not from their forefathers, but, from God, prescription can never undermine natural rights.[10]

According to Wollstonecraft, reason is the source of morality because it is reason that allows us to restrain our animal passions. This ability to rise above our animal nature is what sets us off from the animal world and is the source of the respect to which all humans who acquire virtue have an equal right:

> In what respect are we superior to the brute creation, if intellect is not allowed to be the guide of passion? Brutes hope and fear, love and hate; but without a capacity to improve, a power of turning these passions to good or evil, they neither acquire virtue nor wisdom—Why? Because the Creator has not given them reason.
>
> Children are born ignorant, consequently innocent; the passions are neither good nor evil dispositions, till they receive a direction. . . . If virtue is to be acquired by experience, or taught by example, reason, perfected by reflection, must be the director of the whole host of passions . . . —She must hold the rudder, or let the wind blow which way it list, the vessel will never advance smoothly to its destined port. . . . Who will venture to assert that virtue would not be promoted by the more extensive cultivation of reason?[11]

Expressing a view that she would never abandon, Wollstonecraft claimed that to the extent that women fail to develop their reason and fail therefore to rise above animal feeling and passion, they will not merit the respect that is due to a developed human being. When women fail to acquire the same "manly" virtues that males cultivate—fortitude, humanity, justice, wisdom, and truth—they give up their equality with men. Burke, she points out, claimed that women should not attempt to acquire the virtues of males but should attempt instead to make themselves pleasing to men by cultivating the virtues of littleness, weakness, and beauty. But in convincing women to pursue this path, Wollstonecraft argues, Burke has robbed them of the very thing—a developed reason—that would give them a right to moral respect:

> You may have convinced them that littleness and weakness are the very essence of beauty; and that the Supreme Being, in giving women beauty in the most supereminent degree, seemed to command them, by the powerful voice of nature, not to cultivate the moral virtues that might chance to excite respect, and interfere with the pleasing sensations they were created to inspire. Thus confining truth, fortitude, and humanity within the rigid pale of manly morals, they might justly argue that to be loved—woman's high end and great distinction—they should learn to list, to totter in their walk, and nickname God's creatures. Never, they might repeat after you, was any man, much less a woman, rendered amiable by the force of these exalted qualities, fortitude, justice, wisdom, and truth; and thus forewarned of the sacrifice they must make to these austere, unnatural virtues, they would be authorized to turn all their attention to their persons, systematically neglecting morals to secure beauty.[12]

This idea, that women are rendered inferior to men by society's insistence that they not develop their reason and by their own acquiescence in that insistence, forms the basis of Wollstonecraft's greatest work, *A Vindication of the Rights of Women*. Here, Wollstonecraft argues that society in general and men in particular keep women in an undeveloped and morally inferior state. Tragically, women themselves acquiesce in the inferior role assigned to them by men:

> The conduct and manners of women, in fact, evidently prove that their minds are not in a healthy state; for, like the flowers which are planted in too rich a soil, strength and usefulness are sacrificed to beauty; and the flaunting leaves, after having pleased

---

[10] From Mary Wollstonecraft, *A Vindication of the Rights of Men* [1790], in *A Wollstonecraft Anthology*, ed. Janet M. Todd (Bloomington: Indiana University Press, 1977), 65, 67.
[11] Ibid., 73–74.

[12] Ibid., 76–77.

a fastidious eye, fade, disregarded on the stalk, long before the season when they ought to have arrived at maturity.— One cause of this barren blooming I attribute to a false system of education, gathered from the books written on this subject by men who, considering females rather as women than human creatures, have been more anxious to make them alluring mistresses than affectionate wives and rational mothers; and the understanding of the sex has been so bubbled by this specious homage, that the civilized women of the present century, with a few exceptions, are only anxious to inspire love, when they ought to cherish a nobler ambition, and by their abilities and virtues exact respect.[13]

It is particularly through an inferior education that women are kept in a state of immaturity and dependency, she argues. They are trained to think that they must devote themselves to pleasing men and to becoming dependent on them. Women must resist these enticements:

> The education of women has, of late, been more attended to than formerly; yet they are still reckoned a frivolous sex, and ridiculed or pitied by the writers who endeavour by satire or instruction to improve them. It is acknowledged that they spend many of the first years of their lives in acquiring a smattering of accomplishments; meanwhile strength of body and mind are sacrificed to libertine notions of beauty, to the desire of establishing themselves,— the only way women can rise in the world,— by marriage. And this desire making mere animals of them, when they marry they act as such children may be expected to act:— they dress, they paint, and nickname God's creatures. . . .
>
> In the present state of society, a little learning is required to support the character of a gentleman; and boys are obliged to submit to a few years of discipline. But in the education of women, the cultivation of the understanding is always subordinate to the acquirement of some corporeal accomplishment; even while enervated by confinement and false notions of modesty, the body is prevented from attaining that grace and beauty which relaxed half-formed limbs never exhibit. Besides, in youth their faculties are not brought forward by emulation; and

having no serious scientific study, if they have natural sagacity it is turned too soon on life and manners. They dwell on effects and modifications, without tracing them back to causes; and complicated rules to adjust behavior are a weak substitute for simple principles.[14]

The popular view that women must be educated differently from men is based on the theory that the moral virtues of women are very different from those of men. Wollstonecraft argues strenuously against this popular view. Morality, she claims, is not based on gender: It is a mistake to believe that there is one morality for men and a different one for women. Women and men must be educated as equals, she argues, because both are equally endowed with reason and because a single standard of morality applies equally to men and to women. The claim that male morality is different from female morality, she argues, is what allows men to maintain a "tyranny" over women:

> To account for and excuse the tyranny of man, many ingenious arguments have been brought forward to prove that the two sexes, in the acquirement of virtue, ought to aim at attaining a very different character: or, to speak explicitly, women are not allowed to have sufficient strength of mind to acquire what really deserves the name of virtue. Yet it should seem, allowing them to have souls, that there is but one way appointed by Providence to lead mankind to either virtue or happiness. . . .
>
> I see not the shadow of a reason to conclude that their virtues should differ in respect to their nature. In fact, how can they, if virtue has only one eternal standard? I must therefore, if I reason consequentially, as strenuously maintain that they have the same simple direction, as that there is a God. . . .
>
> Women, I allow, may have different duties to fulfill; but they are human duties, and the principles that should regulate the discharge of them, I sturdily maintain, must be the same.[15]

Wollstonecraft did not deceive herself about the difficulties of overcoming the inequalities between men and women. From childhood, an unrelenting social conditioning teaches women that their place

---

[13] Mary Wollstonecraft, A Vindication of the Rights of Women, in A Wollstonecraft Anthology, 85.

[14] Ibid., 86, 89.
[15] Ibid., 87, 90, 95.

in society is to remain dependent on men and to not develop their reason as equals to men. But Wollstonecraft is confident that women will flourish as the equals of men when they are freed from the deadening influence of this conditioning:

> Novels, music, poetry, and gallantry, all tend to make women the creatures of sensation. . . . This over-stretched sensibility naturally relaxes the other powers of the mind, and prevents intellect from attaining that sovereignty which it ought to attain to render a rational creature useful to others, and content with its own station: for the exercise of the understanding, as life advances, is the only method pointed out by nature to calm the passions. . . . Yet to their senses are women made slaves, because it is by their sensibility that they obtain present power. . . .
>
> Asserting the rights which women in common with men ought to contend for, I have not attempted to extenuate their faults, but to prove them to be the natural consequence of their education and station in society. If so it is reasonable to suppose that they will change their character, and correct their vices and follies, when they are allowed to be free in a physical, moral, and civil sense.[16]

Now free of debt and a famous intellectual, Wollstonecraft traveled to France, which was then in the throes of a revolution. There, while the exhilarating madness of the French Revolution unfolded around her, Wollstonecraft met Gilbert Imlay, a dashing and liberal-thinking young American adventurer and war speculator. She fell passionately in love with him and in 1793 found herself pregnant with his child. On May 14, 1794, she gave birth to a girl, whom she named Fanny, after her friend. Imlay now withdrew his affection, and after several separations, he left her for good and went to England. In early 1795 Mary followed him, only to learn on arriving in England that he had taken up with another woman; distraught, she tried to kill herself. After her recovery, Imlay got rid of her by talking her into taking their baby and going to Scandinavia as his business representative. Mary returned from Scandinavia in late 1795, still hoping to be reconciled with Imlay, but found he had

moved in with a young actress. Again she tried to commit suicide.

Wollstonecraft now began to see a friend of many years, William Godwin. Gradually she experienced their "friendship melting into love," as he came to seem like the perfect intellectual and emotional companion. By December of 1796 she was pregnant with his child. Three months later the two were married, and Mary rejoiced that she had at last found the fulfilling and tranquil relationship for which she had always longed. Tragically, only a few months later, on August 30, 1797, Mary Wollstonecraft died of complications related to childbirth.

QUESTIONS

1. Can you explain in your own words what Nietzsche means when he says that "all mechanical happenings . . . are will-power, will-effects"?

2. Explain the differences between "slave moralities" and "master moralities." Explain how slave moralities are supposed to be expressions of the "will to power." Explain how *all* moralities are supposed to be expressions of the will to power. Do you agree? Why?

3. Explain how reason makes us "superior to the brute creation," according to Wollstonecraft, and how reason is related to virtue. Can you explain why her views cannot be classified as utilitarian? Do you see any similarities between her views and those of Kant?

4. Why, according to Wollstonecraft, are the virtues of women the same as those of men? Do you agree?

5. Explain how education affects women's reason, according to Wollstonecraft, and the effect that this has on their virtue and on the respect that is due them. What does Wollstonecraft mean when she says women become "creatures of sensation and pleasure"?

6. To what extent is Wollstonecraft's criticism of the position of women still an accurate criticism of the position of all or some women today? Explain your answer.

---

[16] Ibid., 98, 114.

7.10 Readings

The following readings focus on the implications of one of the moral theories we discussed in this chapter: utilitarianism. The first selection, "The Ones Who Walk Away from Omelas" by Ursula K. Le Guin, asks us to consider what we would think of a world in which perfect happiness for everyone is, through some mysterious arrangement, purchased at the cost of the continuous torment of a single, lonely child. Would utilitarians approve of such a world? Would you approve of it, or would you join those who walk away? In the second reading, Australian philosopher Peter Singer, who favors utilitarianism, argues that utilitarian theory implies we have an obligation to feed the starving people of foreign countries even if this means doing without luxuries. Singer believes that if we can prevent something bad from happening without sacrificing anything that is of comparable value, then we are obligated to prevent it. Because starvation is bad, we are obligated to prevent it, and since luxuries—such as more clothes or a better stereo—are not of comparable value to preventing starvation, we are obligated to spend our money on preventing starvation rather than on such luxuries. The third selection, which is also by Peter Singer, argues, again on utilitarian grounds, that our obligation not to inflict pain on animals is equal to our obligation not to inflict comparable pain on humans. To think that the suffering of animals of other species counts less than the suffering of members of our own human species is "speciesism," a wrong much like racism, which holds that the suffering of other races counts less than the suffering of members of our own race. Singer concludes that we have an obligation not to eat animals, particularly since animal flesh is not the most efficient food source, but is eaten merely because its taste is pleasing to our palate. Together, then, the selections in this chapter ask you whether utilitarianism is adequate in light of these implications.

URSULA K. LE GUIN

The Ones Who Walk Away from Omelas

With a clamor of bells that set the swallows soaring, the Festival of Summer came to the city. Omelas, bright-towered by the sea. The rigging of the boats in harbor sparkled with flags. In the streets between houses with red roofs and painted walls, between old moss-grown gardens and under avenues of trees, past great parks and public buildings, processions moved. Some were decorous: old people in long stiff robes of mauve and grey, grave master workmen, quiet, merry women carrying their babies and chatting as they walked. In other streets the music beat faster, a shimmering of gong and tambourine, and the people went dancing, the procession was a dance. Children dodged in and out, their high calls rising like the swallows' crossing flights over the music and the singing. All the processions wound towards the north side of the city, where on the great water-meadow called the Green Fields boys and girls, naked in the bright air, with mud-stained feet and ankles and long, lithe arms, exercised their restive horses before the race. The horses wore no gear at all but a halter without bit. Their manes were braided with streamers of silver, gold, and green. They flared their nostrils and pranced and boasted to one another; they were vastly excited, the horse being the only animal who has adopted our ceremonies as his own. Far off to the north and west the mountains stood up half encircling Omelas on her bay. The air of morning was so clear that the snow still crowning the Eighteen Peaks burned with white-gold fire across the miles of sunlit air, under the dark blue of the sky. There was just enough wind to make the banners that marked the racecourse snap and flutter now and then. In the silence of the broad green meadows one could hear the music winding through the city streets, farther and nearer and ever approaching, a cheerful faint sweetness of the air that from time to time trembled and gathered together and broke out into the great joyous clanging of the bells.

Joyous! How is one to tell about joy? How describe the citizens of Omelas?

They were not simple folk, you see, though they were happy. But we do not say the words of cheer much any more. All smiles have become archaic. Given a description such as this one tends to make certain assumptions. Given a description such as this one tends to look next for the King, mounted on a splendid stallion and surrounded by his noble knights, or perhaps in a golden litter borne by great-muscled slaves. But there was no king. They did not use swords, or keep slaves. They were not barbarians. I do not know the rules and laws of their society, but I suspect that they were singularly few. As they did without monarchy and slavery, so they also got on without the stock exchange, the advertisement, the secret police, and the bomb. Yet I repeat that these were not simple folk, not dulcet shepherds, noble savages, bland utopians. They were not less complex than us. The trouble is that we have a bad habit, encouraged by pedants and sophisticates, of considering happiness as something rather stupid. Only pain is intellectual, only evil interesting. This is the treason of the artist: a refusal to admit the banality of evil and the terrible boredom of pain. If you can't lick 'em, join 'em. If it hurts, repeat it. But to praise despair is to condemn delight, to embrace violence is to lose hold of everything else. We have almost lost hold; we can no longer describe a happy man, nor make any celebration of joy. How can I tell you about the people of Omelas? They were not naïve and happy children—though their children were, in fact, happy. They were mature, intelligent, passionate adults whose lives were not wretched. O miracle! but I wish I could describe it better. I wish I could convince you. Omelas sounds in my words like a city in a fairy tale, long ago and far away, once upon a time. Perhaps it would be best if you imagined it as your own fancy bids, assuming it will rise to the occasion, for certainly I cannot suit you all. For instance, how about technology? I think that there would be no cars or helicopters in and above the streets; this follows from the fact that the people of Omelas are happy people. Happiness is based on a just discrimination of what is necessary, what is neither necessary nor destructive, and what is destructive. In the middle category, however—that of the unnecessary but undestructive, that of comfort, luxury, exuberance, etc.—they could perfectly well have central heating, subway trains, washing machines, and all kinds of marvelous devices not yet invented here, floating light-sources, fuelless power, a cure for the common cold. Or they could have none of that: it doesn't matter. As you like it. I incline to think that people from towns up and down the coast have been coming in to Omelas during the last days before the Festival on very fast little trains and double-decked trams and that the train station of Omelas is actually the handsomest building in town, though plainer than the magnificent Farmers' Market. But even granted trains, I fear that Omelas so far strikes some of you as goody-goody. Smiles, bells, parades, horses, bleh. If so, please add an orgy. If an orgy would help, don't hesitate. Let us not, however, have temples from which issue beautiful nude priests and priestesses already half in ecstasy and ready to copulate with any man or woman, lover or stranger, who desires union with the deep godhead of the blood, although that was my first idea. But really it would be better not to have any temples in Omelas—at least, not manned temples. Religion yes, clergy no. Surely the beautiful nudes can just wander about, offering themselves like divine soufflés to the hunger of the needy and the rapture of the flesh. Let them join the processions. Let tambourines be struck above the copulations, and the glory of desire be proclaimed upon the gongs, and (a not unimportant point) let the offspring of these delightful rituals be beloved and looked after by all. One thing I know there is none of in Omelas is guilt. But what else should there be? I thought at first there were no drugs, but that is puritanical. For those who like it, the faint insistent sweetness of *drooz* may perfume the ways of the city, *drooz* which first brings a great lightness and brilliance to the mind and limbs, and then after some hours a dreamy languor, and wonderful visions at last of the very arcana and inmost secrets of the Universe, as well as exciting the pleasure of sex beyond all belief; and it is not habit-forming. For more modest tastes I think there ought to be beer. What else, what else belongs in the joyous city? The sense of victory, surely, the celebration of courage. But as we did without clergy, let us do without soldiers. The joy built upon successful slaughter is not the right kind of joy; it will not do; it is fearful and it is trivial. A boundless and generous contentment, a magnanimous triumph felt not against some outer enemy but in communion with the finest and fairest in the souls of all men everywhere and the splendor of the world's summer: this is what swells the hearts of the people of Omelas, and the victory they celebrate is that of life. I really don't think many of them need to take *drooz*.

Most of the processions have reached the Green Fields by now. A marvelous smell of cooking goes forth from the red and blue tents of the provisioners. The faces of small children are amiably sticky; in the benign grey beard of a man a couple of crumbs of rich pastry are entangled. The youths and girls have mounted their horses and are beginning to group around the starting line of the course. An old woman, small, fat, and laughing, is passing out flowers from a basket, and tall young men wear her flowers in their shining hair. A child of nine or ten sits at the edge of the crowd, alone, playing on a wooden flute. People pause to listen, and they smile, but they do not speak to him, for he never ceases playing and never sees them, his dark eyes wholly rapt in the sweet, thin magic of the tune.

He finishes, and slowly lowers his hands holding the wooden flute.

As if that little private silence were the signal, all at once a trumpet sounds from the pavilion near the starting line: imperious, melancholy, piercing. The horses rear on their slender legs, and some of them neigh in answer. Sober-faced, the young riders stroke the horses' necks and soothe them, whispering, "Quiet, quiet, there my beauty, my hope. . . ." They begin to form in rank along the starting line. The crowds along the racecourse are like a field of grass and flowers in the wind. The Festival of Summer has begun.

Do you believe? Do you accept the festival, the city, the joy? No? Then let me describe one more thing.

In a basement under one of the beautiful public buildings of Omelas, or perhaps in the cellar of one of its spacious private homes, there is a room. It has one locked door, and no window. A little light seeps in dustily between cracks in the boards, second-hand from a cobwebbed window somewhere across the cellar. In one corner of the little room a couple of mops, with stiff, clotted, foul-smelling heads, stand near a rusty bucket. The floor is dirt, a little damp to the touch, as cellar dirt usually is. The room is about three paces long and two wide: a mere broom closet or disused tool room. In the room a child is sitting. It could be a boy or a girl. It looks about six, but actually is nearly ten. It is feeble-minded. Perhaps it was born defective, or perhaps it has become imbecile through fear, malnutrition, and neglect. It picks its nose and occasionally fumbles vaguely with its toes or genitals, as it sits hunched in the corner farthest from the bucket and the two mops. It is afraid of the mops. It finds them horrible. It shuts it eyes, but it knows the mops are still standing there; and the door is locked; and nobody will come. The door is always locked; and nobody ever comes, except that some-times—the child has no understanding of time or interval—sometimes the door rattles terribly and opens, and a person, or several people, are there. One of them may come in and kick the child to make it stand up. The others never come close, but peer in at it with frightened, disgusted eyes. The food bowl and the water jug are hastily filled, the door is locked, the eyes disappear. The people at the door never say anything, but the child, who has not always lived in the tool room, and can re-member sunlight and its mother's voice, sometimes speaks. "I will be good," it says. "Please let me out. I will be good!" They never answer. The child used to scream for help at night, and cry a good deal, but now it only makes a kind of whining, "eh-haa, eh-haa," and it speaks less and less often. It is so thin there are no calves to its legs; its belly pro-trudes; it lives on a half-bowl of corn meal and grease a day. It is naked. Its buttocks and thighs are a mass of festered sores, as it sits in its own excre-ment continually.

They all know it is there, all the people of Omelas. Some of them have come to see it, others are content merely to know it is there. They all know that it has to be there. Some of them un-derstand why, and some do not, but they all under-stand that their happiness, the beauty of their city, the tenderness of their friendships, the health of their children, the wisdom of their scholars, the skill of their makers, even the abundance of their harvest and the kindly weathers of their skies, de-pend wholly on this child's abominable misery.

This is usually explained to children when they are between eight and twelve, whenever they seem capable of understanding; and most of those who come to see the child are young people, though of-ten enough an adult comes, or comes back, to see the child. No matter how well the matter has been explained to them, these young spectators are al-ways shocked and sickened at the sight. They feel disgust, which they had thought themselves supe-rior to. They feel anger, outrage, impotence, de-spite all the explanations. They would like to do something for the child. But there is nothing they can do. If the child were brought up into the sun-light out of that vile place, if it were cleaned and fed and comforted, that would be a good thing, in-deed; but if it were done, in that day and hour all the prosperity and beauty and delight of Omelas would wither and be destroyed. Those are the terms. To exchange all the goodness and grace of every life in Omelas for that single, small improve-ment: to throw away the happiness of thousands for the chance of the happiness of one: that would be to let guilt within the walls indeed.

The terms are strict and absolute; there may not even be a kind word spoken to the child.

Often the young people go home in tears, or in a tearless rage, when they have seen the child and faced this terrible paradox. They may brood over it for weeks or years. But as time goes on they begin to realize that even if the child could be released, it would not get much good of its freedom: a little vague pleasure of warmth and food, no doubt, but little more. It is too degraded and imbecile to know any real joy. It has been afraid too long ever to be free of fear. Its habits are too uncouth for it to re-spond to humane treatment. Indeed, after so long it would probably be wretched without walls about it to protect it, and darkness for its eyes, and its own excrement to sit in. Their tears at the bitter injustice dry when they begin to perceive the ter-rible justice of reality and to accept it. Yet it is their tears and anger, the trying of their generosity and the acceptance of their helplessness, which are perhaps the true source of the splendor of their lives. Theirs is no vapid, irresponsible happiness. They know that they, like the child, are not free. They know compassion. It is the existence of the child, and their knowledge of its existence, that makes possible the nobility of their architecture, the poignancy of their music, the profundity of their science. It is because of the child that they are so gentle with children. They know that if the wretched one were not there snivelling in the dark, the other one, the flute-player, could make no joy-ful music as the young riders line up in their beauty for the race in the sunlight of the first morning of summer.

Now do you believe in them? Are they not more credible? But there is one more thing to tell, and this is quite incredible.

At times one of the adolescent girls or boys who go to see the child does not go home to weep or rage, does not, in fact, go home at all. Sometimes also a man or woman much older falls silent for a day or two, and then leaves home. These people go out into the street, and walk down the street alone. They keep walking, and walk straight out of the city of Omelas, through the beautiful gates. They keep walking across the farmlands of Omelas. Each one goes alone, youth or girl, man or woman. Night falls; the traveler must pass down village streets, between the houses with yellow-lit windows, and on out into the darkness, and they do not come back. The place they go towards is a place even less imaginable to most of us than the city of happiness. I cannot describe it at all. It is possible that it does not exist. But they seem to know where they are going, the ones who walk away from Omelas.

PETER SINGER

Famine, Affluence, and Morality

. . . I begin with the assumption that suffering and death from lack of food, shelter, and medical care is bad. I think most people will agree about this, although one may reach the same view by different routes. I shall not argue for this view. People can hold all sorts of eccentric positions, and perhaps from some of them it would not follow

From *Philosophy and Public Affairs*, vol. 1, no. 3 (Spring 1972): 231–235, 238–240, 242–243. Copyright © 1972 by Princeton University Press. Excerpts reprinted by permission of Princeton University Press.

that death by starvation is in itself bad. It is difficult, perhaps impossible, to refute such positions, and so for brevity I will henceforth take this assumption as accepted. Those who disagree need read no further.

My next point is this: if it is in our power to prevent something bad from happening, without thereby sacrificing anything of comparable moral importance, we ought, morally, to do it. By "without sacrificing anything of comparable moral importance" I mean without causing anything else comparably bad to happen, or doing something that is wrong in itself, or failing to promote some moral good, comparable in significance to the bad thing we can prevent. This principle seems almost as uncontroversial as the last one. It requires us only to prevent what is bad, and not to promote what is good, and it requires this of us only when we can do it without sacrificing anything that is, from the moral point of view, comparably important. I could even, as far as the application of my argument to the Bengal emergency[1] is concerned, qualify the point so as to make it: if it is in our power to prevent something very bad from happening, without thereby sacrificing anything morally significant, we ought, morally, to do it. An application of this principle would be as follows: if I am walking past a shallow pond and see a child drowning in it, I ought to wade in and pull the child out. This will mean getting my clothes muddy, but this is insignificant, while the death of the child would presumably be a very bad thing.

The uncontroversial appearance of the principle just stated is deceptive. If it were acted upon, even in its qualified form, our lives, our society, and our world would be fundamentally changed. For the principle takes, firstly, no account of proximity or distance. It makes no moral difference whether the person I can help is a neighbor's child ten yards from me or a Bengali whose name I shall never know, ten thousand miles away. Secondly, the principle makes no distinction between cases in which I am the only person who could possibly do any-

[1] Bengal is an African nation that at the time of this writing was undergoing famine, its citizens migrating as refugees to other countries. [Ed.]

thing and cases in which I am just one among millions in the same position.

I do not think I need to say much in defense of the refusal to take proximity and distance into account. The fact that a person is physically near to us, so that we have personal contact with him, may make it more likely that we *shall* assist him, but this does not show that we *ought* to help him rather than another who happens to be further away. If we accept any principle of impartiality, universalizability, equality, or whatever, we cannot discriminate against someone merely because he is far away from us (or we are far away from him). Admittedly, it is possible that we are in a better position to judge what needs to be done to help a person near to us than one far away, and perhaps also to provide the assistance we judge to be necessary. If this were the case, it would be a reason for helping those near to us first. This may once have been a justification for being more concerned with the poor in one's own town than with famine victims in India. Unfortunately for those who like to keep their moral responsibilities limited, instant communication and swift transportation have changed the situation. From the moral point of view, the development of the world into a "global village" has made an important, though still unrecognized, difference to our moral situation. Expert observers and supervisors, sent out by famine relief organizations or permanently stationed in famine-prone areas, can direct our aid to a refugee in Bengal almost as effectively as we could get it to someone in our own block. There would seem, therefore, to be no possible justification for discriminating on geographical grounds.

There may be a greater need to defend the second implication of my principle — that the fact that there are millions of other people in the same position, in respect to the Bengali refugees, as I am, does not make the situation significantly different from a situation in which I am the only person who can prevent something very bad from occurring. Again, of course, I admit that there is a psychological difference between the cases; one feels less guilty about doing nothing if one can point to others, similarly placed, who have also done nothing. Yet this can make no real difference to our moral obligations. Should I consider that I am less obliged to pull the drowning child out of the pond if on looking around I see other people, no further away than I am, who have also noticed the child but are doing nothing? One has only to ask this question to see the absurdity of the view that numbers lessen obligation. It is a view that is an ideal excuse for inactivity: unfortunately most of the major evils— poverty, overpopulation, pollution—are problems in which everyone is almost equally involved.

If my argument so far has been sound, neither our distance from a preventable evil nor the number of other people who, in respect to that evil, are in the same situation as we are, lessens our obligation to mitigate or prevent that evil. I shall therefore take as established the principle I asserted earlier. As I have already said, I need to assert it only in its qualified form: if it is in our power to prevent something very bad from happening, without thereby sacrificing anything else morally significant, we ought, morally, to do it.

The outcome of this argument is that our traditional moral categories are upset. The traditional distinction between duty and charity cannot be drawn, or at least, not in the place we normally draw it. Giving money to the Bengal Relief Fund is regarded as an act of charity in our society. The bodies which collect money are known as "charities." These organizations see themselves in this way—if you send them a check, you will be thanked for your "generosity." Because giving money is regarded as an act of charity, it is not thought that there is anything wrong with not giving. The charitable man may be praised, but the man who is not charitable is not condemned. People do not feel in any way ashamed or guilty about spending money on new clothes or a new car instead of giving it to famine relief. (Indeed, the alternative does not occur to them.) This way of looking at the matter cannot be justified. When we buy new clothes not to keep ourselves warm but to look "well-dressed" we are not providing for any important need. We would not be sacrificing anything significant if we were to continue to wear our old clothes, and give the money to famine relief. By doing so, we would be preventing another person from starving. It follows from what I have said earlier that we ought to give money away, rather than spend it on clothes which we do not need to keep us warm. To do so is not charitable, or generous. Nor is it the kind of act which philosophers and theologians have called "supererogatory"—an act which it would be good to do, but not wrong not to do. On the contrary, we ought to give the money away, and it is wrong not to do so. . . .

PETER SINGER

All Animals Are Equal

Many philosophers and other writers have proposed the principle of equal consideration of interests, in some form or other, as a basic moral principle; but not many of them have recognized that this principle applies to members of other species as well as to our own. Jeremy Bentham was one of the few who did realize this. In a forward-looking passage written at a time when black slaves had been freed by the French but in the British dominions were still being treated in the way we now treat animals, Bentham wrote:

> The day *may* come when the rest of the animal creation may acquire those rights which never could have been withholden from them but by the hand of tyranny. The French have already discovered that the blackness of the skin is no reason why a human being should be abandoned without redress to the caprice of a tormentor. It may one day come to be recognized that the number of the legs, the villosity of the skin, or the termination of the *os sacrum* are reasons equally insufficient for abandoning a sensitive being to the same fate. What else is it that should trace the insuperable line? Is it the faculty of reason, or perhaps the faculty of discourse? But a full-grown horse or dog is beyond comparison a more rational, as well as a more conversable animal, than an

infant of a day or a week or even a month, old. But suppose they were otherwise, what would it avail? The question is not, Can they *reason?* nor Can they *talk?* but, *Can they suffer?*

In this passage Bentham points to the capacity for suffering as the vital characteristic that gives a being the right to equal consideration. The capacity for suffering—or more strictly, for suffering and/or enjoyment or happiness—is not just another characteristic like the capacity for language or higher mathematics. Bentham is not saying that those who try to mark "the insuperable line" that determines whether the interests of a being should be considered happen to have chosen the wrong characteristic. By saying that we must consider the interests of all beings with the capacity for suffering or enjoyment Bentham does not arbitrarily exclude from consideration any interests at all—as those who draw the line with reference to the possession of reason or language do. The capacity for suffering and enjoyment is *a prerequisite for having interests at all*, a condition that must be satisfied before we can speak of interests in a meaningful way. It would be nonsense to say that it was not in the interests of a stone to be kicked along the road by a schoolboy. A stone does not have interests because it cannot suffer. Nothing that we can do to it could possibly make any difference to its welfare. A mouse, on the other hand, does have an interest in not being kicked along the road, because it will suffer if it is.

If a being suffers there can be no moral justification for refusing to take that suffering into consideration. No matter what the nature of the being, the principle of equality requires that its suffering be counted equally with the like suffering—in so far as rough comparisons can be made—of any other being. If a being is not capable of suffering, or of experiencing enjoyment or happiness, there is nothing to be taken into account. So the limit of sentience (using the term as a convenient if not strictly accurate shorthand for the capacity to suffer and/or experience enjoyment) is the only defensible boundary of concern for the interests of others. To mark this boundary by some other characteristic like intelligence or rationality would be to mark it in an arbitrary manner. Why not choose some other characteristic, like skin color?

From Peter Singer, *Animal Liberation* (New York: Avon Books, 1977). Reprinted by author's permission. Endnotes omitted.

The racist violates the principle of equality by giving greater weight to the interests of members of his own race when there is a clash between their interests and the interests of those of another race. The sexist violates the principle of equality by favoring the interests of his own sex. Similarly the speciesist allows the interests of his own species to override the greater interests of members of other species. The pattern is identical in each case.

Most human beings are speciesists. Ordinary human beings—not a few exceptionally cruel or heartless humans, but the overwhelming majority of humans—take an active part in, acquiesce in, and allow their taxes to pay for practices that require the sacrifice of the most important interests of members of other species in order to promote the most trivial interests of our own species. . . .

For the great majority of human beings, especially in urban, industrialized societies, the most direct form of contact with members of other species is at mealtimes: We eat them. In doing so we treat them purely as means to our ends. We regard their life and well-being as subordinate to our taste for a particular kind of dish. I say "taste" deliberately—this is purely a matter of pleasing our palate. There can be no defense of eating flesh in terms of satisfying nutritional needs, since it has been established beyond doubt that we could satisfy our need for protein and other essential nutrients far more efficiently with a diet that replaced animal flesh by soy beans, or products derived from soy beans, and other high protein vegetable products.

It is not merely the act of killing that indicates what we are ready to do to other species in order to gratify our tastes. The suffering we inflict on the animals while they are alive is perhaps an even clearer indication of our speciesism than the fact that we are prepared to kill them. In order to have meat on the table at a price that people can afford, our society tolerates methods of meat production that confine sentient animals in cramped, unsuitable conditions for the entire duration of their lives. Animals are treated like machines that convert fodder into flesh, and any innovation that results in a higher "conversion ratio" is liable to be adopted. As one authority on the subject has said, "cruelty is acknowledged only when profitability ceases." So hens are crowded four or five to a cage with a floor area of twenty inches by eighteen inches, or around the size of a single page of the *New York Times*. The cages have wire floors, since this reduces cleaning costs, though wire is unsuitable for the hens' feet; the floors slope, since this makes the eggs roll down for easy collection, although this makes it difficult for the hens to rest comfortably. In these conditions all the birds' natural instincts are thwarted: They cannot stretch their wings fully, walk freely, dust-bathe, scratch the ground, or build a nest. Although they have never known other conditions, observers have noticed that the birds vainly try to perform these actions. Frustrated at their inability to do so, they often develop what farmers call "vices," and peck each other to death. To prevent this, the beaks of young birds are often cut off.

This kind of treatment is not limited to poultry. Pigs are now also being reared in cages inside sheds. These animals are comparable to dogs in intelligence, and need a varied, stimulating environment if they are not to suffer from stress and boredom. Anyone who kept a dog in the way in which pigs are frequently kept would be liable to prosecution, in England at least, but because our interest in exploiting pigs is greater than our interest in exploiting dogs, we object to cruelty to dogs while consuming the produce of cruelty to pigs. Of the other animals, the condition of veal calves is perhaps worst of all, since these animals are so closely confined that they cannot even turn around or get up and lie down freely. In this way they do not develop unpalatable muscle. They are also made anaemic and kept short of roughage, to keep their flesh pale, since white veal fetches a higher price; as a result they develop a craving for iron and roughage, and have been observed to gnaw wood off the sides of their stalls, and lick greedily at any rusty hinge that is within reach.

Since, as I have said, none of these practices cater to anything more than our pleasures of taste, our practice of rearing and killing other animals in order to eat them is a clear instance of the sacrifice of the most important interests of other beings in order to satisfy trivial interests of our own. To avoid speciesism we must stop this practice, and each of us has a moral obligation to cease supporting the practice. Our custom is all the support that the meat industry needs. The decision to cease giving it that support may be difficult, but it is no more difficult than it would have been for a white Southerner to go against the traditions of his society and free his slaves; if we do not change our dietary habits, how can we censure those slaveholders who would not change their own way of living?

7.11 Suggestions for Further Reading

Adler, Mortimer. *Six Great Ideas*. New York: Macmillan, 1981. In this interesting paperback, Adler discusses truth, goodness, beauty, liberty, equality, and justice.

Bok, Sissela. *Lying: Moral Choice in Public and Private Life*. New York: Random House, 1978. This excellent paperback provides an interesting and readable account of the ethics of deception.

Bok, Sissela. *Secrets: The Ethics of Concealment*. New York: Random House, 1983. Bok here provides an outstanding treatment of the ethical issues raised by attempts to conceal information from others.

Dennet, Daniel C. *Elbow Room*. Cambridge, MA: MIT Press, 1984. A very clear and accessible discussion of determinism and freedom. Dennet argues that freedom and determinism are compatible.

Garner, Richard. *Beyond Morality*. Philadelphia: Temple University Press, 1993. A very readable and extremely interesting defense of the view that morality has outlived its purpose.

Harris, C. E., Jr. *Applying Moral Theories*. Belmont, CA: Wadsworth, 1986. A very readable introduction to ethics.

Mackie, John. *Ethics: Inventing Right and Wrong*. Middlesex, England: Penguin Books, 1977. Mackie argues in this challenging paperback that ethical principles are not *discovered* but *invented* by human beings.

May, Bernard. *The Philosophy of Right and Wrong*. London: Routledge & Kegan Paul, 1986. This is a difficult but interesting approach to ethics written by an "analytic" philosopher.

Meilaender, D. *The Theory and Practice of Virtue*. Notre Dame, IN: University of Notre Dame Press, 1984. In this paperback, Meilaender discusses the often-overlooked topic of virtue.

Noddings, Nel. *Caring: A Feminine Approach to Ethics and Moral Education*. Berkeley: University of California Press, 1984. Noddings develops a female ethic based on the virtue of caring.

Norman, Richard. *The Moral Philosophers*. Oxford: Oxford University Press, 1983. In this introductory paperback, Norman gives a brief overview of the moral philosophies of the major ethical thinkers.

Pearsall, Marilyn. *Women and Values*, 2d ed. Belmont, CA: Wadsworth, 1993. A very good anthology of feminist writings on ethics.

Pojman, Louis, ed. *Ethical Theory*. Belmont, CA: Wadsworth, 1989. A very good anthology of writings on ethics.

Pojman, Louis. *Ethics: Discovering Right and Wrong*. Belmont, CA: Wadsworth, 1990. A very good introduction to ethics.

Rachels, James. *The Elements of Moral Philosophy*. New York: Random House, 1986. An excellent short and clearly written overview of ethics.

Scheffler, Samuel, ed. *Consequentialism and Its Critics*. New York: Oxford University Press, 1988. A very good anthology of recent articles on utilitarianism.

Schlossberger, Eugene. *Moral Responsibility and Persons*. Philadelphia: Temple University Press, 1992. Schlossberger argues for the view that we are free to choose the kind of person we will become.

Singer, Peter. *Practical Ethics*. New York: Cambridge University Press, 1979. An avowed utilitarian discusses several contemporary moral dilemmas, including euthanasia, discrimination, obligations to animals, and aid to the needy.

Sullivan, Roger J. *Immanuel Kant's Moral Theory*. New York: Cambridge University Press, 1989. The best recent discussion of Kant's ethics. Highly readable.

Thomas, William. *Mill*. New York: Oxford University Press, 1985. A very good account of John Stuart Mill's life and philosophy.

Trebilcot, Joyce, ed. *Mothering: Essays in Feminist Theory*. Totowa, NJ: Rowman & Allenheld, 1984. An interesting collection of feminist writings on ethics.

Trusted, Jennifer. *Free Will and Responsibility*. New York: Oxford University Press, 1984. A clear but sophisticated discussion of freedom and moral responsibility.

Van Wyk, Robert. *Introduction to Ethics*. New York: St. Martin's, 1990. An excellent overview.

Watson, Gary, ed. *Free Will*. Oxford: Oxford University Press, 1982. A short collection of some of the most important recent writings on freedom. Although many of the articles are difficult, some are relatively accessible.

CHAPTER 8

Social Philosophy

Freedom and bread enough for all are inconceivable together.

FYODOR DOSTOYEVSKI

8.1 Introduction: What Is Social Philosophy?

The government of the United States provides welfare for the poor, the disabled, and the unemployed. It pays for medical services for the elderly. It subsidizes the business of farmers, of fishers, and of miners. The government pays for the education of all children. It provides college students with scholarships, subsidies, and loans. It pays for low-rent public housing, for urban mass transit systems, and for highway systems. The government is the nation's largest employer. It runs a major publishing business and underwrites the Postal Service. It provides low-interest loans to exporters, farmers, house construction companies, first-time homeowners, and small businesses. In addition, innumerable government regulations touch vast areas of American life with antitrust regulations, affirmative action regulations, labor regulations, equal opportunity regulations, employee safety regulations, medical regulations, drug regulations, and even toy regulations.

Are such activities legitimate functions of government? One of the most popular conservative presidents of the twentieth century, Ronald Reagan, stated that "the taxing powers of government must be used to provide revenues for legitimate government purposes. It must not be used to regulate the economy or bring about social change." Many thinkers have agreed with him. For example, economist William E. Simon holds that "the overriding principle to be revived in American political life is that which sets individual liberty as the highest political value—that value to which all other values are subordinate and which is to be given the highest priority in policy discussions. By the same token, there must be a conscious philosophical prejudice against any intervention by the state into our lives, for by definition such intervention abridges liberty."[1]

Just as many people disagree with these conservative views, however. Almost 95 percent of Americans in a recent poll favor "the government helping people who are unable to help themselves." A 56-percent majority feel that "it is the responsibility of government to meet everyone's needs, even in the case of sickness, poverty, unemployment, and old age." And 69 percent of the public

Freedom is nothing else but the right to live as we wish.
EPICTETUS

---

[1] Quoted in *What Is the Role of American Government?* [pamphlet] (St. Paul, MI: Greenhaven Press, 1988), 81.

agrees with the statement that "our system of social services is on the right track; it provides security for the elderly, the sick, and other people in distress without depriving people of individual responsibility."[2] In fact, many critics argue that government has not gone far enough, that taxes should be used more aggressively to correct social and economic inequities.

These claims and counterclaims raise an issue that has profound implications for the way we decide to structure our society: What, exactly, should the role of government be? How big a part should government play in regulating our lives? How much should the government do for the poor and the needy among us? Which roles are appropriate for government, and which are not?

Asking how active a role the state (the highest authority in society) and its primary instrument, government, should take in the lives of its citizens leads to a broader question: What is the proper relation between individual and society? Aristotle observed that the human is a social animal. We work with, depend on, and relate to one another for our survival and prosperity. The totality of the *relationships* among people is known as society. A specific society consists of a group of human beings broadly distinguished from other groups by its interests, institutions, and culture. Because society so strongly influences our attitudes, values, loyalties, and outlooks, it is useful to examine the relationship between the individual and society in order to shed more light on the unifying theme of this text: self-identity.

In approaching this topic, we will focus on three related issues. First, we consider how the power and authority of the state may be justified. This requires a close look at contract theory, which forms the theoretical foundations for the legitimacy of our state and government. Second, determining the proper role of government inevitably raises questions of fairness and justice, so we next look at some influential theories of justice. But even if government is just, there is a third question, of the legitimacy of the means that government uses to enforce its power over citizens: law. So, third and finally, we consider the meaning of law and its relation to freedom and human rights.

> *A people that would always govern well would not need to be governed.*
>
> JEAN JOCQUES ROUSSEAU

These concepts and issues have one thing in common: They arise out of the social milieu. Although they have ethical and political implications, they do not directly involve either ethics or politics. They are not ethics, because they are not primarily concerned with establishing a norm of good conduct; they are not politics, because they are not concerned with evaluating political power and the institutions that exercise it. Rather, these concerns fall into the category of **social philosophy,** which is the application of moral principles to the problems of society, including the problems of government, justice, and freedom.

social philosophy the application of moral principles to the problems of freedom, equality, justice, and the state

QUESTIONS

1. What is a society? Draw up a list of groups that are not societies and a list of groups that you would say are societies. What are the major differences between the members of both groups?

---

[2] Dennis A. Gilbert, *Compendium of American Public Opinion* (New York: Facts on File, 1988), 212.

2.   Should small groups of experts make any of the major decisions for society, or should all major decisions be made by majority rule? Explain.

3.   Which of the following issues would you classify as personal moral issues, and which would you classify as social issues: pornography, war, nuclear weapons, abortion, premarital sex, racial discrimination, civil disobedience, labor unions, AIDS, environmentalism, drugs, homelessness, gang violence?

8.2 What Justifies the State?

The state is the highest authority in a society, with a legal power to define the public interest and enforce its definition. One clear example of the state's doing this can be seen in the graduated income tax system. The state sets priorities— that is, defines the public interest—then it taxes citizens in order to implement these priorities. In theory, Americans pay taxes proportional to their incomes: The more they make, the greater the proportion of income tax they pay. Many feel that this is fair. But with demands for and costs of goods and services rising, a sizable number of people think that this system is unfair, especially people who disagree with the programs for which taxes are spent.

Take, for example, a childless couple who live in an apartment and who both work, she as a doctor and he as a stockbroker. Since they rent and have no dependents, they can claim very few deductions on their state and federal income taxes. Because they both earn incomes, they pay hefty taxes every year. But most of their tax money goes to pay for things from which they will never benefit. This year, some of their local tax money went to pay for new school buildings, although they have no children. Some of their money went to maintain national parks, although they never plan to visit them. In addition to paying for things from which they will never benefit, some of their money pays for things with which they positively disagree. For example, some of their state taxes fund abortion clinics, although both of them feel that abortion is a form of murder. Some of their federal taxes pay for nuclear bombs, although both are pacifists and believe that it is immoral to contribute to nuclear armaments. Some of their money subsidizes the tobacco industry, although neither of them smokes—and both feel that since smoking causes cancer, it is a violation of their conscience to support a product that kills people.

Is it fair for this couple to be compelled under penalty of law to pay for programs that they cannot in good conscience support? Are they wrong to feel forced into doing things that they would not choose to do? Are they wrong to feel that the government is misusing its power?

Government is emphatically a machine: to the discontent a "taxing machine," to the contented a "machine for securing property."

THOMAS CARLYLE

But this case raises an even broader question, one that does not relate directly to any specific program, policy, or measure that the state implements in enforcing its definition of the public interest: What justifies the power of the state in the first place? What gives the state the right to tax, conscript, arm, educate, or do any of the myriad things it does? Stated another way, it is impossible to determine whether a government has misused its power until we determine the rightful limits of that power. And determining the rightful limits of authority ultimately calls for an inquiry into the legitimacy of the state's authority and power to begin with.

At different times in various societies, theories have been advanced to define the legitimacy of the state and justify its power. At times, the power of the state has been justified by appeal to divine authority. Thus, some rulers have claimed the power to rule as a divine right, as a kind of mandate from God. Other times, the state has been justified by appeal to the public interest. Accordingly, insofar as the state furthers the public interest, it is justified. But the theory that most of us today accept is that the state is justified by the consent of the governed: The legitimacy of the state stems from an agreement of the governed to be ruled by the state.

The most influential modern versions of this viewpoint are captured in the term *social contract*, which refers to a complex theory of state legitimacy that has extraordinary importance for us today. Basically, **contract theory** says that individuals agree to give up certain liberties and rights to the state, which in return guarantees such rights as life, liberty, and the pursuit of happiness. Contract theory is both an explanation of the origin of the state and a defense of its authority that philosophers have frequently used. We see versions of contract theory as far back as Plato, but its most noteworthy classical proponents were Thomas Hobbes (whom we showcased in Chapter 3), John Locke, and Jean-Jacques Rousseau. In our own century the philosopher John Rawls has proposed a new and intriguing version of social contract theory.

> *The end of democracy is freedom; of aligarchy, wealth; of aristocracy, the maintenance of education and national institutions; of tyranny, the protection of the tyrant.*
>
> ARISTOTLE

contract theory in social philosophy, the doctrine that individuals give up certain liberties and rights to the state, which in turn guarantees such rights as life, liberty, and the pursuit of happiness

HOBBES AND THE WAR OF ALL AGAINST ALL

More than any other person, Thomas Hobbes was the founder of modern political philosophy. Political theorists before him, such as Plato, Aristotle, Saint Augustine, and Thomas Aquinas, had emphasized that the state is subject to human control. In contrast, Hobbes based his political philosophy on the principles of seventeenth-century scientific materialism. According to this doctrine, the world is a mechanical system that can be explained in terms of the laws of motion. Even the behavior of humans or complex societies, it is argued, are reducible to geometric and physical explanations. From this view of reality Hobbes deduced how things must of necessity occur.

In *Leviathan*, Hobbes portrays humans as selfish, unsocial creatures driven by two needs: survival and personal gain. Therefore, human life is characterized by constant struggle, strife, and war, with individual pitted against individual in a battle for self-preservation and gain:

Thomas Hobbes: "Hereby it is manifest that during the time men live without a common power to keep them all in awe, they are in that condition which is called war; and such a war, as is of every man, against every man, and the life of man is solitary, nasty, brutish, and short."

Hereby it is manifest, that during the time men live without a common power to keep them all in awe, they are in that condition which is called war; and such a war, as is of every man, against every man. . . .

Whatsoever therefore is consequent to a time of war, where every man is enemy to every man; the same is consequent to the time, wherein men live without other security, than what their own strength, and their own invention shall furnish them withal. In such condition, there is no place for industry; because the fruit thereof is uncertain: and consequently no culture of the earth; no navigation, nor use of the commodities that may be imported by sea; no commodious building; no instruments of moving, and removing, such things as require much force; no knowledge of the face of the earth; no account of time; no arts; no letters; no society; and which is worst of all, continual fear, and danger of violent death; and the life of man, solitary, poor, nasty, brutish, and short.

The passions that incline men to peace, are fear of death; desire of such things as are necessary to commodious living; and a hope by their industry to obtain them. And reason suggesteth convenient articles of peace, upon which men may be drawn to agreement. These articles, are they, which otherwise are called the Laws of Nature.[3]

A key point for Hobbes is that the authority of the state is justified. It is justified for a simple reason: because its citizens have agreed to accept this authority. In virtue of this agreement, citizens are now bound to obey.

Notice in the final paragraph that Hobbes, while asserting that the instinct for self-preservation is the basic drive behind human behavior, states that humans have the capacity to reason. Rational concern for their own survival and

If men were angels, no government would be necessary.

ALEXANDER HAMILTON

CRITICAL THINKING

Does social contract theory assume that if there were no government, then people would be unconnected individuals? Is this assumption correct?

---

[3] Thomas Hobbes, *Leviathan* (London: J. Bohn, 1839), pt. 1, ch. 15.

for their best long-term interests impels humans to enter into a contract with one another that forms the basis for society. Because they recognize that otherwise their lives are destined to be "solitary, poor, nasty, brutish, and short," humans accept an authority outside themselves that has the power to force all to act in the best interests of the majority. For Hobbes, the agreement that establishes this authority is irrevocable. Once set up, the political body wielding this power exercises unlimited and absolute authority over its subjects and remains in power as long as it is able to compel them to do what they otherwise would not do.

The society that individuals contract for thus becomes superior to the individuals. For Hobbes, the state cannot bear any resistance to its rule. If such resistance becomes effective, the state has proven itself unable to govern—in which case the established officials no longer rule and the people are no longer their subjects. At that point the people revert to their natural state of struggle for self-preservation and gain until they form another contract.

> *Whoever desires to found a state must start with assuming that all men are bad.*
>
> NICCOLO MACHIAVELLI

LOCKE AND NATURAL MORAL LAWS

In contrast with Hobbes's pessimism, John Locke viewed humans as essentially moral beings who ought to obey natural moral rules. Where Hobbes saw warfare as the human's natural state, Locke saw our natural state as at least partly regulated by natural moral laws. As a result, Locke viewed humans as free and equal by nature, regardless of the existence of any government.

Government, he argued, doesn't decree mutual respect for the freedom and liberties of all—nature does. Humans are by nature free, rational, and social creatures. They establish governments because three things are missing in the state of nature: (1) a firm, clearly understood interpretation of natural law; (2) unbiased judges to resolve disputes; and (3) personal recourse in the face of injustices. So individuals enter into a social contract to maintain their natural rights. In one portion of his brilliant and most influential political writing, *Essay Concerning the True and Original Extent and End of Civil Government*, Locke explains the end of political society and government:

> *When we walk the streets at night in safety, it does not strike us that this might be otherwise.*
>
> GEORG F. HEGEL

> *The very idea of the power and the right of the People to establish Government, presupposes the duty of every individual to obey the established Government.*
>
> GEORGE WASHINGTON

> 123. If man in the state of Nature be so free as has been said, if he be absolute lord of his own person and possessions, equal to the greatest and subject to nobody, why will he part with his freedom, this empire, and subject himself to the dominion and control of any other power? To which it is obvious to answer, that though in the state of Nature he hath a right, yet the enjoyment of it is very uncertain and constantly exposed to the invasion of others; for all being kings as much as he, every man his equal, and the greater part no strict observers of equity and justice, the enjoyment of the property he has in this state is very unsafe, very insecure. This makes him willing to quit this condition which, however free, is full of fears and continual dangers; and it is not without reason that he seeks out and is willing to join in society with others who are already united, or have a mind to unite for the mutual preservation of their lives, liberties and estates, which I call by the general name—property.
>
> 124. The great and chief end, therefore, of men uniting into commonwealths, and putting themselves under government, is the preservation of their property; to which in the state of Nature there are many things wanting.

First, there wants an established, settled, known law, received and allowed by common consent to be the standard of right and wrong, and the common measure to decide all controversies between them. For though the law of Nature be plain and intelligible to all rational creatures, yet men, being biased by their interest, as well as ignorant for want of study of it, are not apt to allow of it as a law binding to them in the application of it to their particular cases.

125. Secondly, in the state of Nature there wants a known and indifferent judge, with authority to determine all differences according to the established law. For every one in that state being both judge and executioner of the law of Nature, men being partial to themselves, passion and revenge is very apt to carry them too far, and with too much heat in their own cases, as well as negligence and unconcernedness, make them too remiss in other men's.

126. Thirdly, in the state of Nature there often wants power to back and support the sentence when right, and to give it due execution. They who sat by any injustice offended will seldom fail where they are able by force to make good their injustice. Such resistance many times makes the punishment dangerous, and frequently destructive to those who attempt it.

127. Thus mankind, notwithstanding all the privileges of the state of Nature, being but in an ill condition while they remain in it are quickly driven into society. Hence it comes to pass, that we seldom find any number of men live any time together in this state. The inconveniences that they are therein exposed to by the irregular and uncertain exercise of the power every man has of punishing the transgressions of others, make them take sanctuary under the established laws of government, and therein seek the preservation of their property. It is this makes them so willingly give up every one his single power of punishing to be exercised by such alone as shall be appointed to it amongst them, and by such rules as the community, or those authorized by them to that purpose, shall agree on. And in this we have the original right and rise of both the legislative and executive power as well as of the governments and societies themselves.[4]

> **CRITICAL THINKING**
> Does social contract theory assume that political rights pertain only to those who can enter a social contract with others? Is this assumption correct? Does the assumption leave out any significant creatures?

In short, individuals create a political entity capable of preserving the inherent rights of "life, liberty, and estate." This contract is based on the consent of the majority, and all agree to obey the decisions of the majority. The state's authority is limited by the terms of the contract, which is continually reviewed by the citizenry. So, unlike Hobbes's absolutistic state, Locke's state is specific and limited. Most important, one of the fundamental moral rights in Locke's political state is the right to resist and to challenge authority. Hobbes believed that resistance to authority is never justified, but Locke regarded such a right as essential.

> *The only government that I recognize, is that power that establishes justice, never that which establishes injustice.*
>
> HENRY D. THOREAU

Although the contrast between Hobbes and Locke is sharp, they do agree that rationality enables humans to perceive the necessity of forming a social contract. More important, they both agree on the source of the state's authority: the consent of the governed. Locke, like Hobbes, felt that the power the state exerts is justified because it is a power that we have consented to accept. Our ancestors, Locke believed, consented to the original establishment of government. And each of us today consents again to that same government when we voluntarily choose to continue to live under that government.

---

[4]John Locke, *Essay Concerning the True and Original Extent and End of Civil Government*, vol. 4 (Oxford: Clarendon Press, 1894; original work published 1690), 4.

The Declaration of Independence, John Trumbull. Both the Declaration and Locke's contract agree that when a government infringes on the individual rights of life, liberty, and the pursuit of happiness (or property, for Locke), the people have a right to dismiss it.

Yet Locke, much more than Hobbes, also emphasized freedom. It was Locke's firm belief that government should leave people free to live and pursue whatever form of life they choose. In fact, it is the duty and purpose of government to protect the individual's freedom to pursue happiness as each sees fit.

It is difficult to exaggerate the tremendous influence that Locke's views had on political events of his time. Locke's views were adopted by several nations during what is sometimes called the "century of revolutions." In 1776, for example, the American colonies sounded a Lockean chord in these lines from the Declaration of Independence:

> We hold these truths to be self-evident. That all men are created equal. That they are endowed by their Creator with certain unalienable rights. That among these are life, liberty and the pursuit of happiness. That to secure these rights, governments are instituted among men, deriving their just powers from the consent of the governed. That whenever any Form of Government becomes destructive of these ends, it is the Right of the People to alter or to abolish it, and to institute a new Government, laying its foundation on such principles and organizing its powers in such form, as to them shall seem most likely to effect their safety and Happiness.

The similarities to Locke's position are not accidental, for the Declaration of Independence was written by Thomas Jefferson, who was an avid reader and disciple of Locke.

Democracy substitutes election by the incompetent many for appointment by the corrupt few.

GEORGE BERNARD SHAW

ROUSSEAU AND THE GENERAL WILL

Contract theory, especially as Locke developed it, led directly to the social philosophy of Jean-Jacques Rousseau (1712–1778). Some philosophers consider Rousseau the foremost philosopher of the social contract theory. However, Rousseau did not appeal to a self-evident natural moral law as Locke had. He argued that if people are to act morally, they must live under laws that they freely accept. Rousseau's emphasis, then, was on personal moral autonomy, the capacity and right of individuals to live under laws that they choose for themselves. Thus, for Rousseau the fundamental requirement of a morally acceptable government is that the governed have freely subscribed to a common body of law. In his most important work, *Of the Social Contract*, Rousseau describes his contract theory:

> The clauses of this contract are so determined by the nature of the act that the slightest modification would render them vain and ineffectual; so that, although they have never perhaps been formally enunciated, they are everywhere the same, everywhere tacitly admitted and recognized, until, the social pact being violated, each man regains his original rights and recovers his natural liberty while losing the conventional liberty for which he renounced it.
>
> These clauses, rightly understood, are reducible to one only, viz, the total alienation to the whole community of each associate with all his rights; for, in the first place, since each gives himself up entirely, the conditions are equal for all; and, the conditions being equal for all, no one has any interest in making them burdensome to others.
>
> Further, the alienation being made without reserve, the union is as perfect as it can be, and an individual associate can no longer claim anything; for, if any rights were left to individuals, since there would be no common superior who could judge between them and the public, each, being on some point his own judge, would soon claim to be so on all; the state of nature would still subsist, and the association would necessarily become tyrannical or useless.
>
> In short, each giving himself to all, gives himself to nobody; and as there is not one associate over whom we do not acquire the same rights which we concede to him over ourselves, we gain the equivalent of all that we lose, and more power to preserve what we have.
>
> If, then, we set aside what is not of the essence of the social contract, we shall find that it is reducible to the following terms: "Each of us puts in common his person and his whole power under the supreme direction of the general will; and in return we receive every member as an indivisible part of the whole."
>
> Forthwith, instead of the individual personalities of all the contracting parties, this act of association produces a moral and collective body, which is composed of as many members as the assembly has voices, and which receives from this same act its unity, its common self (*moi*), its life, and its will. This public person, which is thus formed by the union of the individual members, formerly took the name of CITY, and now takes that of REPUBLIC or BODY POLITIC, which is called by its members STATE when it is passive, SOVEREIGN when it is active, POWER when it is compared to similar bodies. With regard to the associates, they take collectively the name of PEOPLE, and are called individually CITIZENS.[5]

---

[5] Jean-Jacques Rousseau, *Of the Social Contract*, in *Ideal Empires and Republics*, ed. Oliver H. G. Leigh (London: M. Walter Dunne, Publisher, 1901), 13–14.

Jean-Jacques Rousseau: "Each of us places in common his person and all his power under the supreme direction of the general will; and as one body we all receive each member as an indivisible part of the whole."

Rousseau's reference to the "general will" deserves some elaboration, since general will is a cornerstone in his social contract. The general will should be contrasted with the "will of all," or unanimity of feeling. A group of wills is general when each member of the group aims at the common good, which is what Rousseau has in mind. True, the general will and the will of all might result in the same course, for each group member may see his or her own best interests being served. But Rousseau felt that agreement is more likely when everyone tries to determine whether a proposed action is best for the good of all, for the general good, rather than just for self.

Rousseau argues further that the general will, unlike the will of all, represents a true consensus—it's what everyone wants. Even when the minority must conform to majority will, there is no coercion or violation of personal freedom because everyone, even the minority members, seeks the general good. In other words, all parties agree on the end; they differ only in what they believe the means should be. Ultimately, they all get what they want: promotion of the common good. One glaring flaw in the whole arrangement, of course, is the assumption that the majority view accords with the general good. Such a bald appeal to head counting is, to say the least, highly questionable.

TWENTIETH-CENTURY SOCIAL CONTRACT: RAWLS

The social contract theory of Hobbes, Locke, and Rousseau was severely criticized in the eighteenth century by that most skeptical of all skeptics, David Hume. Hume struck a simple but devastating blow to social contract theory. He pointed out that there never was a social contract. Governments, he argued, are established by conquest or are handed on by the right of succession. If we go back in history, he pointed out, we will find no signs of people coming together to choose their governments. Social contract is, in short, a complete fiction:

> [Some] philosophers . . . assert . . . that government in its earliest infancy arose from consent, or rather the voluntary acquiescence of the people. . . . They affirm that all men are born equal and owe allegiance to no prince or government, unless bound by the obligation and sanction of a promise. . . .
>
> But would these reasoners look abroad into the world, they would meet with nothing that, in the least, corresponds to their ideas. . . . On the contrary, we find everywhere princes who claim their subjects as their property and assert their independent right of sovereignty, from conquest or succession. We find also, everywhere, subjects, who acknowledge this right in their prince. . . . Were you to preach, in most parts of the world, that political connections are founded altogether on voluntary consent or a mutual promise, the magistrate would soon imprison you, as seditious, for loosening the ties of obedience; if your friends did not before shut you up as delirious, for advancing such absurdities. . . . Almost all the governments which exist at present, or of which there remains any record in history, have been founded originally either on usurpation or conquest or both, without any pretense of a fair consent or voluntary subjection of the people.[6]

So devastating was Hume's attack that most philosophers gave up on social contract theory. For over a century the theory grew out of favor, and philosophers almost completely ignored it.

In the twentieth century, however, social contract theory once more resurfaced. Harvard philosopher John Rawls (1921–   ) reshaped social contract theory into a powerful new way of thinking about the nature of government and society.

Rawls agrees with Hume that the social contract is a historical fiction. People never have, and never do, come together and decide to start a government. However, Rawls argues, this does not matter. The key idea in social contract theory is that it gives us a way of thinking about what the nature and purpose of government should be. Social contract theory says that to figure out what kind of government we should have, we should imagine that we are starting our society and our government from scratch. What kind of government and society would we choose for ourselves if we were in this starting or "original" position?

Rawls proposes that if we are to determine what a just government is and, more generally, what the just principles for a society are, we must set aside everything that leads us to favor ourselves over others. A just government is one that is equally fair to everyone and shows favoritism to none. But how will we set aside the things that unjustly lead us to favor ourselves over others? Rawls suggests an ingenious answer. Imagine, he suggests, that we were about to start a new society and a new government. Suppose that by some miracle none of us

What is the end of political association? The preservation and prosperity of its members.

JEAN JACQUES ROUSSEAU

---

[6]David Hume, "Of the Original Contract," in *Essays, Literary, Moral, and Political* (New York: Ward, Lock, no date), 272–273.

knows anything about what he will be like in that new society. For example, none of us knows whether he will be male or female, black or white, rich or poor, young or old, smart or dumb, talented or untalented, needy or self-sufficient, religious or atheist. Then we would be forced to choose a government and society that is fair to everyone no matter what they happen to be like. If I do not know, for example, whether I will be black or white in this new society, then I will insist on a government that favors neither blacks nor whites. I will want a government that does not discriminate. Or suppose that I do not know whether in our new society I will be rich or poor, atheist or religious, talented or untalented. Then I will insist on a government that favors neither the rich nor the poor, neither the atheist nor the religious person, and neither the talented nor the untalented:

> Thus we are to imagine that those who engage in social cooperation choose together, in one joint act, the principles which are to assign basic rights and duties and to determine the division of social benefits. Men are to decide in advance how they are to regulate their claims against one another and what is to be the foundation charter of their society. . . .
>
> In justice as fairness the original position of equality corresponds to the state of nature in the traditional theory of the social contract. This original position is not, of course, thought of as an actual historical state of affairs, much less as a primitive condition of culture. It is understood as a purely hypothetical situation characterized so as to lead to a certain conception of justice. Among the essential features of this situation is that no one knows his place in society, his class position or social status, nor does anyone know his fortune in the distribution of natural assets and abilities, his intelligence, strength and the like. . . . Since all are similarly situated and no one is able to design principles to favor his particular condition, the principles of justice [for society and government] are the result of a fair agreement or bargain.[7]

Notice what social contract has become for Rawls. It is no longer a description of how we formed the governments that we *actually* have. Instead, it is now just an imaginary device that is supposed to tell us what kind of government we *ought to* have.

Nevertheless, the social contract for Rawls still helps explain what justifies the power and authority of government. For Rawls, the power of our government is justified if our government is the kind of government that we would choose in the original position. The authority of our government is justified not because we *actually consented* to live under our government in the state of nature. This was the view of Hobbes, Locke, and Rousseau, which Hume devastated with his criticisms. Instead, says Rawls, the authority of government is justified because we *would consent* to live under that type of government if we were in the original position.

What kind of government would we choose in the original position? Later in this chapter we will examine the principles of justice that Rawls says we would want government to live by if we were in the original position. It will suffice here to say that a just government, according to Rawls, is one that does not favor one way of life over another. It does not favor one religion over

---

[7] John Rawls, *A Theory of Justice* (Cambridge, MA: Harvard University Press, 1972), 11, 12, 13.

another. It does not favor one ethnic group over another. It does not favor one culture over another. Instead, it leaves every person free to pursue the form of life that suits her best because of her personal preferences and desires. The just government is one that provides equal political rights and equal economic opportunities for everyone without showing favoritism to any. And the just government is one that provides a suitable minimum standard of living for the least advantaged members of society.

With Rawls we have come to the most-recent major version of social contract theory. Rawls's theory has had as great an impact on thinkers today as the theories of Hobbes, Locke, and Rousseau had in their day. Yet the theory, particularly in the version of Rawls, has been subjected to intense criticisms. We will turn now to look at two major critiques of social contract theory: the communitarian critique and the feminist critique.

THE COMMUNITARIAN CRITIQUE

Communitarianism is the view that the actual community in which we live should be at the center of our analysis of society and government. Communitarians emphasize the social nature of human beings. They argue that our very identity—who we are—depends on our relationships to others in our communities. We are embedded in our community and its cultural practices. So we cannot hope to understand ourselves or our government apart from our community and its cultural traditions. Although not all would identify themselves as such, several contemporary philosophers are usually identified as communitarians, including Charles Taylor, Alasdair MacIntyre, and Michael J. Sandel. Among the classical philosophers who are sometimes identified as early communitarian thinkers are Aristotle and Hegel.

The key problem with social contract theory, argue communitarians, is that it neglects people's social nature by focusing on the individual. In making this general criticism, communitarians bring a number of more specific complaints against social contract theory.

First, some communitarians have argued, the social contract theory assumes that government or the state is an artificial construct. But the state, communitarian philosophers have argued, is natural. For example, Aristotle argued long ago that government or the state is a natural outgrowth of our natural tendency to associate with other human beings. Just as the family and the tribe are outgrowths of our natural tendencies to live with one another, so is the state:

> We get the clearest view of a thing, whether it be the state or anything else, when we see how it originates and develops. At the origins, then, we have the union of male and female, who cannot live without each other. Men and women come together so that the race may continue. Their union is not something that they decide on their own. They come together in a family because, in common with other animals and plants, humans have a natural desire to reproduce themselves. . . . From this relationship between men and women . . . comes the first association, which is the family. . . . When several families develop together, and their association aims at more than the supply of their daily needs, we have the first society, which is the village. . . . When several villages have joined together in a single complete com-

Every state is a community of some kind.

ARISTOTLE

munity, large enough to be self-sufficing, the state has come into existence. Thus, the state originates in the bare needs of life. But it continues in existence for the sake of providing its members the good life. Since the earlier forms of society are natural, so is the state. For the state is their purpose and completion, and the nature of a thing is revealed in its completion. The nature of anything, in fact, is revealed when it is fully developed, whether we are speaking of a man, a horse, or a family. . . .

In addition, we should note that the state is by nature prior to the family and to the individual, since the whole is prior to the part. For example, the foot and the hand are prior to the whole body, for if the whole body were to be destroyed, the foot and hand would die. . . . We know that the state is a creation of nature and that it is prior to the individual by the fact that the individual apart from the state is not self-sufficient. The individual is like a part that is dependent on the whole. If there were a being who could not live in society or who did not need to live in society because he was self-sufficient, then he would have to either be animal or a god. He could not be a real part of the state. A social instinct is implanted in all people by their nature.[8]

Notice that Aristotle says that the state is "prior to the individual." By this he means, first, that humans cannot develop fully unless they live in the state. In particular, Aristotle argued, our political abilities and social virtues emerge and develop only in the state. The state is nature's way of bringing these capacities out in us. Second, Aristotle also wants to say that the state is more important than an individual citizen. Just as the whole human body is more important than one of its parts, so the whole association of humans that we call the state is more important than one of its members.

Man is a political creature.
ARISTOTLE

The idea that the state is a natural outgrowth of our human nature was echoed in the nineteenth century by the German philosopher Georg Wilhelm Friedrich Hegel (1770–1831). Like Aristotle, Hegel felt that the state is the completion of all earlier human associations and more important than the individual. He agreed also with Aristotle's claim that humans can develop fully only within the state. In particular, argued Hegel, humans can develop their freedom only within the state. Moreover, the individual will develop fully only if he embraces the cultural practices of the state of which he is a member:

The State . . . is that form of reality in which the individual has and enjoys his freedom. But he can do so only if he recognizes, believes in, and wills that which is common to the Whole. And this must not be understood . . . [to mean that the state] is a means provided for his benefit. Nor [is the state a means by which] each individual . . . limits his own freedom so that [every individual] can secure a small space of liberty for himself. Rather, we affirm, that Law, Morality, Government, and they alone, are the positive reality and completion of Freedom. . . .

It must further be understood that all the worth which the human being possesses—all spiritual reality, he possesses only through the State. . . . Thus only is he fully conscious; thus only is he a partaker of morality—of a just and moral social and political life. . . .

Summing up what has been said of the State, we find that . . . its vital principle, what actuates the individuals who compose it—is Morality. The State, its laws, its arrangements, constitute the rights of its members; its natural features, its mountains, air, and waters, are their country, their fatherland, their outward material property;

---

[8] Aristotle, *Politics*, bk. I, ch. ii, translated by Manuel Velasquez.

the history of this State are their deeds; what their ancestors have produced, belongs to them and lives in their memory. All is their possession, just as they are possessed by it; for it constitutes their existence, their being.

. . . It is this matured totality which thus constitutes one Being, the spirit of one people. To it the individual members belong; each one is the Son of his Nation, and at the same time . . . the Son of his Age. None remains behind it, still less [does anyone] advance beyond it. This spiritual Being, the Spirit of his time, is his; he is a representative of it; it is that in which he originated, and in which he lives.[9]

For Hegel, freedom is more than just not interfering with the lives of others. People are free to the extent that they can do more: The more abilities they have, the freer they are. Since the state is the group in which people can most fully develop their abilities, only in the state can the range of activities open to people be expanded and widened to their fullest extent. Therefore, only in the state can people be truly free.

Already it should be clear that the communitarian views of Aristotle and Hegel directly contradict several of the assumptions of social contract theory. First, they contradict the assumption that the state is an artificial construct. Social contract theory assumes that there is no state until people come together and deliberately think it up and create it. The state does not just naturally grow and develop. However, Aristotle and Hegel reject this assumption. The state, they argue, is a natural outgrowth of our human tendencies to live together. Social contract theory is thus mistaken in its fundamental assumption that the state is an artificial construct that humans must deliberately put together.

Second, Aristotle and Hegel contradict the assumption that before the state exists, there are fully formed people who can come together to create a state. Hobbes, Locke, Rousseau, and even Rawls assume this. But Aristotle and Hegel point out that it is not possible for people to develop fully before the state exists. If there were no state, humans could not know what one is, nor would they know how to go about organizing themselves into a state. And only in the state does the individual develop the freedom required to enter an agreement. In short, before there is a state, there can be no fully formed human individuals capable of coming together to form one through some sort of agreement.

Third, and perhaps most important, communitarians agree with Hegel that the state and its cultural practices are the source of the identity of all individuals. That is, in the state we acquire the cultures and traditions that we use to define ourselves. Think, for example, of how a person growing up in the United States comes to think of himself or herself as an "American." An American thinks of himself or herself as being part of a long history that begins with the pilgrims and the thirteen colonies. An American thinks of himself or herself as part of a history that includes George Washington, Abraham Lincoln, Teddy Roosevelt, John Kennedy, and Martin Luther King. An American thinks of himself or herself as part of a nation that includes its mountains and national parks, its rebellions and wars, its music and its literature. In short, our very sense

> *Commonplace thinking has the impression that force holds the state together, but in fact its only bond is the fundamental sense of order which everybody possesses.*
>
> GEORG F. HEGEL

> *The rational end of man is life in the state.*
>
> GEORG F. HEGEL

---

[9]Georg Wilhelm Friedrich Hegel, *The Philosophy of History*, trans. J. Sibree (New York: Dover, 1956), 38, 39, 52.

of who we are depends on the cultural traditions of the state to which we belong.

Yet, as we saw, the social contract view, particularly as developed by Rawls, believes that the state must support no particular culture, but leave people free to choose their own cultural preferences. Michael J. Sandel, one of the foremost communitarian thinkers alive today, has written the following about social contract theory, particularly Rawls's version:

> Its central idea is that government should be neutral toward the moral and religious views its citizens espouse. Since people disagree about the best way to live, government should not affirm in law any particular vision of the good life. Instead, it should provide a framework of rights that respects persons as free and independent selves, capable of choosing their own values and ends.[10]

Sandel argues that it is a mistake to think that government should be neutral toward the different moral, religious, and cultural views found in a community. As Hegel argued, if an individual is to develop fully, he must live in a state that supports and nourishes a strong set of cultural traditions. Different states will support different cultural traditions, of course. For example, the state and government of Mexico will support a culture and a tradition that are very different from those that the state and government of the United States will support. But each state and its government must favor and support some set of cultural traditions. The government of each state must educate its people so that they learn about these cultural traditions and come to accept their values. For us in the United States, says Sandel, the government must support a cultural tradition that has always valued participation in the political process:

> Participating in politics . . . means deliberating with fellow citizens about the common good and helping to shape the destiny of the political community. But to deliberate well about the common good requires more than the capacity to choose one's ends and to respect others' rights to do the same. It requires a knowledge of public affairs and also a sense of belonging, a concern for the whole, a moral bond with the community whose fate is at stake. To share in self-rule requires that citizens possess, or come to acquire, [these] qualities of character, or civic virtues. But this means that [we] cannot be neutral toward the values and ends . . . citizens espouse. [We require] . . . a formative politics, a politics that cultivates in citizens the qualities of character self-government requires.[11]

Communitarians argue, then, that government must not stay away from morality and cultural values. Instead, it must strive to teach citizens the morality and cultural values that are part of their traditions.

But are the communitarians right? Consider, first, the idea that the state is natural and not an artificial construct. Is this really true? Doesn't it take a great deal of human ingenuity and effort to maintain a state? Doesn't this suggest that the state is something that human beings construct? Or take the criticism that

A state arises out of the needs of mankind.

PLATO

A government is like everything else: to preserve it we must love it.

BARON DE MONTESQUIEU

---

[10] Michael J. Sandel, *Democracy's Discontent* (Cambridge, MA: Belknap Press of Harvard University Press, 1996), 4.

[11] Ibid., 5–6.

since people need a state to develop fully, they cannot form a government in the state of nature. It is true that there are some abilities that can develop only within the political institutions of the state. But are these abilities really needed for a stateless group of people to come together and agree to form a rudimentary government?

Consider, finally, what is perhaps the most important objection of communitarians. This is the objection that government should support the cultural traditions of its people. Ask yourself this: Should all cultural traditions be supported and transmitted? Before the Civil War, many whites living in the South argued that they had developed a distinct culture and way of life on their large plantations. Slavery was a part of this Southern culture. So slavery as a cultural tradition should not be destroyed, they argued. In a similar way, many people have argued that the view that women should stay home, take care of children, and be subservient to their husbands is part of a distinct culture and way of life that should not be destroyed. Are all these cultural traditions equally valuable? If they are not, then are communitarians wrong to claim that government should support whatever traditional cultural values a nation has?

It is not clear, then, that communitarianism has made its case against the social contract tradition. However, there is a second important position that has also attacked the idea of the social contract.

SOCIAL CONTRACT AND WOMEN: THE PUBLIC AND THE PRIVATE

A significant and glaring set of problems can be raised with regard to the tradition of contract theory that Hobbes, Locke, and Rousseau represent. At the heart of contract theory is the idea that authority over adults depends on their consent. Rulers have no authority to rule unless their subjects agree or consent to that rule. For Hobbes, Locke, and Rousseau, consent alone can justify or legitimize the authority of the state. This fundamental idea is underlined in our own Declaration of Independence when it states that governments derive their just powers "from the consent of the governed." A social contract is necessary to establish the state because the contract is the means through which citizens consent to be ruled by a government.

But this fundamental idea raises an important question that many women have asked: What justifies the authority that males have traditionally exercised over females, particularly in the family? For example, Hobbes writes that a family consists of "a man and his children; or of a man and his servants; or of a man, and his children, and servants together: wherein the Father or Master is the Sovereign."[12] Locke similarly tells us that in the family "the Rule . . . naturally falls to the Man's share, as abler and stronger [than the Woman]."[13] And Rousseau writes that in the family, "when a woman complains of the unjust

---

[12] Hobbes, *Leviathan*, ed. A. D. Lindsay (New York: J. M. Dent, 1950), 172.

[13] Locke, *Two Treatises of Government*, ed. Peter Laslett (London: Cambridge University Press, 1963), 210.

inequality which man has imposed on her, she is wrong; this inequality is not a human institution, or at least it is not the work of prejudice but of reason."[14]

Hobbes, Locke, and Rousseau are merely describing the traditional view of the family, in which the man rules and the woman is ruled. But they write as if this rule of the male over the female is perfectly justified. How is this possible in view of their fundamental point that authority over adults is justified only if they consent? Do adult women, half of the human race, somehow "consent" to let men, the other half, rule over them in families? Clearly, this is not the case: Women do not enter a social contract giving men the right to rule over them. Then doesn't it follow that it is unjustified for men to exercise authority over adult women, as they have done in the traditional family?

The fact that Hobbes, Locke, and Rousseau do not apply to women the idea that ruling requires consent should alert us to another glaring problem that their theories raise. The "free" and "equal" people who enter into the social contract and who subsequently become citizens of the state are all and only men. Women are left out. Hobbes explicitly states that "commonwealths have been erected by the Fathers, not by the Mothers of families."[15] Locke, as we have seen, assumes that men are the "natural" heads of families, and it is these male heads of families that enter the social contract. And Rousseau tells us that before humanity entered the social contract, families had already been established, headed by men who subsequently formed the social contract.

Thus, social contract theory, at least as developed by Hobbes, Locke, and Rousseau, explicitly indicates that the state is created by an agreement that *males* make with each other. Since people acquire political rights only by entering such an agreement, it would seem logical to conclude that only males have political rights in the state. Hobbes, Locke, and Rousseau were males interested in writing about how males come to be governed by a state, and they simply ignored the situation of the female half of the human race. Consequently, these philosophers failed to apply their principle that adults must be ruled by consent to the situation of women in families.

Why did they fail to apply their fundamental principles to the family? These failures are perhaps related to a basic assumption we all unconsciously make: that "private" or "personal" matters, such as family matters, have nothing to do with the "public" matters of politics—what happens to women within the family is a private matter unrelated to the politics that rules our public lives. Recently, however, a number of female philosophers have pointed out that this unconscious separation of the "public" from the "private" is the source of many of the political and economic inequalities to which women are subjected. For example, political philosopher Carole Pateman writes that "the dichotomy between the public and the private . . . is, ultimately, what the feminist movement is about."[16] We must examine this claim, which has important implications for

---

[14] Rousseau, *Emile*, quoted in Susan Moller Okin, *Women in Western Political Thought* (Princeton, NJ: Princeton University Press, 1979), 11.

[15] Hobbes, *Leviathan*, 168.

[16] Carole Pateman, "Feminist Critiques of the Public/Private Dichotomy," in *Private and Public in Social Life*, ed. Stanley Benn and Gerald Gaus (London: Croom Helm, 1983), 82.

how we think about the state and which may help us see why Hobbes, Locke, and Rousseau so easily ignored half of the human race and were so willing to accept the glaringly unjustified and unequal position of women in the family.

Private life, for us, includes life within the family and the domestic and personal activities that take place within a home, such as sex, raising children, expressing intimacy, love, and affection, and doing domestic chores. Public life, on the other hand, includes the economic and political activities that take place outside the family and the home, such as paid work, buying and selling goods, voting, running for political office, and participating in legal processes. It is taken almost for granted today that the public should not interfere with the private. "A man's home is his castle," we say, implying that the world should not interfere with what goes on in the home.

But this separation of the private and the public, several female philosophers have pointed out, has kept women in an inherently unequal position. Traditionally, women have taken on the major burden of domestic work: cooking for everyone in the family, cleaning up the house, doing the laundry, and caring for the children. This gives men the time and freedom to leave the home and enter public life. Thus, the labor performed by women within the private sphere gives men the freedom to participate in the public sphere, while keeping women occupied and confined in the private.

Confining women to the private and men to the public sphere is not necessarily unfair. However, in our society, real economic and political power is available only in the public world. Men are paid for the work they perform in the public world whereas women are not paid for the work they perform in the private home, so men acquire the economic power that wealth brings and women are left economically powerless. Women may try to work for pay outside the home, but they are always disadvantaged, feminists claim, because they are still expected to do most of the housework and child care. Moreover, because women take over these domestic tasks, men are also free to run for public office and engage in those political and legal processes that are the source of political power. Women remain preoccupied at home with domestic tasks that carry no political power. Some women may become active in public affairs, but this is always difficult because domestic tasks continue to encroach on their time and because their private lives have not prepared them for engaging in the public world of politics.

In short, then, we separate the public from the private and relegate women to laboring in the private sphere, thereby freeing men to take over the public world. But since the public world is the source of economic and political power, men come to hold most of the power in our society, and women either remain wholly powerless or are greatly disadvantaged by the burdens that the private sphere puts on them. Thus, the separation of the private from the public world is the fundamental means by which women are forced into political and economic powerlessness. Moreover, because private domestic matters are assumed to have nothing to do with politics, political philosophers have ignored the private sphere of the family, even though the structure of the family (where women must labor) is the key that enables men to assume political and eco-

The power of love as the basis of a State, has never been tried.

RALPH WALDO EMERSON

nomic power. The contemporary political philosopher Susan Okin elaborates   •
on these points in her book *Justice, Gender, and the Family:*

> Thus feminists have turned their attention to the politics of what had previously
> been regarded—and . . . still is seen by most political theorists—as paradigmatically
> nonpolitical. That the personal sphere of sexuality, of housework, of child care and
> family life is political became the underpinning of most feminist thought. Feminists
> of different political leanings and in a variety of academic disciplines have revealed
> and analyzed the multiple interconnections between women's domestic roles and
> their inequality and segregation in the workplace, and between their socialization in
> gendered families and the psychological aspects of their oppression. We have strongly
> and persistently challenged the long-standing underlying assumption of almost all
> political theories: that the sphere of family and personal life is so separate and
> distinct from the rest of social life that such theories can justifiably assume but
> ignore it.
>
> The interconnections between the domestic and the nondomestic aspects of our
> lives are deep and pervasive. Given the power structures of both, women's lives are
> far more detrimentally affected by these interconnections than are men's. Consider
> two recent front-page stories that appeared on subsequent days in the *New York
> Times.* The first was about a tiny elite among women: those who work as lawyers for
> the country's top law firms. If these women have children with whom they want to
> spend any time, they find themselves off the partnership track and instead, with no
> prospects of advancement, on the "mommy track." "Nine-to-five" is considered part-
> time work in the ethos of such firms, and one mother reports that, in spite of her
> twelve-hour workdays and frequent work on weekends, she has "no chance" of mak-
> ing partner. The article fails to mention that these women's children have fathers, or
> that most of the men who work for the same prestigious law firms also have children,
> except to report that male lawyers who take parental leave are seen as "wimp-like."
> The sexual division of labor in the family, even in these cases where the women are
> extremely well qualified, successful, and potentially influential, is simply assumed.
>
> The next day's *Times* reported on a case of major significance for abortion
> rights. . . . The all-male panel of judges ruled 7 to 3 that the state may require a
> woman under eighteen years who wishes to obtain an abortion to notify both her
> parents—even in cases of divorce, separation, or desertion—or to get special ap-
> proval from a state judge. The significance of this article is amplified when it is jux-
> taposed with the previous one. For it shows us how it is that those who rise to the
> top in the highly politically influential profession of law are among those who have
> had the least experience of all in raising children. There is a high incidence of re-
> cruitment of judges from those who have risen to partnership in the most prestigious
> law firms. . . . Here we find a systematically built-in absence of mothers (and presum-
> ably of "wimp-like" participating fathers, too) from high-level political decisions
> concerning some of the most vulnerable persons in society—women, disproportion-
> ately poor and black, who become pregnant in their teens, and their future children.
> It is not hard to see here the ties between the supposedly distinct public and domestic
> spheres.
>
> This is but one example of what feminists mean by saying that "the personal is
> political," sometimes adding the corollary "the political is personal." Contemporary
> feminism poses a significant challenge to the long-standing and still-surviving as-
> sumption of political theories that the sphere of family and personal life is sharply
> distinct from the rest of social and political life, that the state can and should restrain

itself from intrusion in the domestic sphere, and that political theories can therefore legitimately ignore it.[17]

The problems that feminist thinkers have identified in political theory seem to call the whole social contract tradition into question. This tradition, and much of Western political theory, seems to be built on the assumption that our private lives and our public affairs are and should be separate. But by ignoring the private domain, the assumption ignores the most fundamental source of political and economic inequalities: the family.

Perhaps, however, it is better to see this discussion as a call to reform our ways of thinking about the family and its relationship to politics. Instead of rejecting social contract theory, perhaps we should extend its political ideals of consent, equality, and freedom into the world of the family. These political ideals, fashioned and bequeathed to us by Hobbes, Locke, and Rousseau, need not be seen as corrupt. We may say, in fact, that the reason traditional social contract theory falls short is not because of the political ideals on which it is based, but because it does not extend the political ideals of consent, equality, and freedom far enough. Our task, then, is to see how the ideals of equality, freedom, and consent can be applied to family life. Is this possible? That is a question that each of us, as we move out of the families in which we were raised and into new families of our own, will have to answer for ourselves.

QUESTIONS

1. What is the fundamental difference between Hobbes's and Locke's contract theory concepts? Between these and Rousseau's theory? Between these and Rawls's theory?

2. The contract theory contends that we should obey the state because we have contractually promised to do so. How, if at all, have you contracted to obey the state?

3. The Declaration of Independence contends that "whenever any Form of Government becomes destructive" of individual life, liberty, and the pursuit of happiness, "it is the Right of the People to alter or to abolish it." Under what circumstances, if any, would you personally exercise this right? Specifically, what conditions must prevail for you to act to alter or abolish your form of government?

4. Think of ways that your identity depends on cultural traditions. Do you think that it is the purpose of government to protect these cultural traditions? Suppose that a large, established group of people in the United States has cultural traditions brought here from another nation. Should the U.S. government protect those traditions? Why or why not?

5. Do you think that it is possible or desirable to "extend the political ideals of consent, equality, and freedom" into the family? Explain.

---

[17] Susan Okin, *Justice, Gender, and the Family* (New York: Basic Books, 1989), 125–127.

6. Feminists argue that social contract theory does not include women. Are there any other beings that the theory excludes? Is this situation good, bad, or neutral?

8.3 What Is Justice?

Whatever we believe justifies the power of government, we all agree that government must at least be just. Whether we believe that government rests on individual consent or on community values, we want government to be fair. In thinking about the nature of government, one inevitably confronts the issue and problem of justice.

But what is justice? It's common to think of justice in terms of crime and the punishments that government inflicts against criminals. Sometimes, we read of a criminal being sent to prison, and we infer that justice was meted out. Other times, we hear that someone was not punished for apparent wrongdoing, and we bemoan the miscarriage of justice. In short, we commonly think of justice in terms of *retribution*—that is, the punishment government exacts for some wrongdoing.

But we can think of justice in other terms. In fact, in a larger sense, justice deals with distribution, not merely retribution. Questions and issues arise daily about how wealth and goods should be allocated by government. Given the relative scarcity of a society's resources, how should they be distributed? Should everyone receive the same amount, should those most in need receive the lion's share, or should the resources be distributed according to the individual's potential contributions to society? If individuals belong to groups that have been unfairly discriminated against, should these persons receive special consideration and treatment? Who should have access to medical care? Only those who can afford it? Everyone who needs it? Those who are likely to benefit most?

Issues of distribution needn't be confined to wealth and goods, however. Equally important is the distribution of privilege and power. Education raises such issues. Who should have access to government-supported public education? Everyone? Everyone but immigrants? Only those who can afford to pay? Only those who promise to benefit society? Other questions of privilege and power can also be asked. Who shall be permitted to vote? To drive? To drink? Should everyone be treated the same under the law, or should certain individuals—for example, juveniles—receive special consideration?

All of these issues raise questions of distributive justice. *Distributive justice* is concerned with the fair and proper distribution of public benefits and burdens among the members of a community. Burdens include work and the costs that must be paid to develop society's productive capacities. The benefits include, of course, all the goods that people want and that society produces. Although distributive justice operates in all organizations, it applies chiefly to how government distributes benefits and burdens among its members.

Clearly, the subject of distributive justice touches many areas, from jobs to income, from taxes to medical services. Embedded in any answer to the question of how jobs should be assigned, income and taxes determined, and medical resources allocated will be a principle of distributive justice—that is, some assumption about the proper way of distributing what is available when there isn't enough for all. For example, it's commonly argued that jobs should be distributed on the basis of talent and ability. Again, it is sometimes said that large corporations should be given tax breaks so they can reinvest their savings, thus

If a ruler aims not at the common good but at his own private good, his rule is unjust.

THOMAS AQUINAS

PHILOSOPHY AND LIFE

The Purpose of Business

Business is the single most important and all-pervasive social institution of modern societies. We spend the majority of our waking hours working in a business; almost everything we eat, drink, wear, or drive is manufactured, packaged, and sold by a business; whatever money we have comes from the salary or profits that a business provides; the hospitals and doctors that provide medical care are increasingly organized as for-profit businesses; the books, magazines, and newspapers we read, the movies we watch, the television we see, and the radio we hear are all products of businesses. Businesses are the core of the economy, and our politics are almost overwhelmed by the influence of business.

But although business is such a critical social institution, we rarely pause to ask what the purpose of this all-pervasive social institution is. Is business there to serve society, or is it there to simply serve itself?

Does business have a social responsibility to make our society a better place to live, or is its only obligation to make profits? The Nobel Prize–winning economist Milton Friedman has this to say about the responsibilities of a business and of the executives who run it:

In a free-enterprise, private-property system, a corporate executive is an employee of the owners of the business. He has direct responsibility to his employers. That responsibility is to conduct the business in accordance with their desires, which generally will be to make as much money as possible while conforming to the basic rules of the society, both those embodied in law and those embodied in ethical custom. . . . There is one and only one social responsibility of business—to use its resources and engage in activities designed to increase its profits so long as it stays within the rules of the game, which is to say, engages in open and

free competition without deception or fraud.

QUESTIONS

1. Friedman argues that in a "free-enterprise, private-property" society, a business has a duty solely to "increase its profits." Why do you think he says this? Do you agree?

2. Do you think that our society really is a "free-enterprise, private-property" system? Do you believe that our system should be changed? Why?

3. Do you think that businesses have any responsibilities to society such as not using manufacturing processes that are legal but that destroy the world's environment, or not making products that are legal but that can harm or kill users?

SOURCE: Milton Friedman, "The Social Responsibility of Business Is to Increase Its Profits," *New York Times Magazine,* September 13, 1970.

increasing jobs and productivity, which in turn would benefit the whole of society. And some today claim that medical services should be provided on the basis of need. Each of these assertions implies some standard that should be considered in the distribution of certain resources: merit, social benefit, need. Whether or not these or other principles should be taken into account is one basic concern of distributive justice.

One way of approaching questions of distributive justice is to start with what is sometimes called "formal justice." Aristotle and other philosophers have argued that "formal justice" is the root meaning of *justice*. Formal justice is the requirement that we should treat similar people similarly. For example, if Jack and Jill carry the same amount of water for us, then we should pay them the same. We should not pay Jack more merely because he is a man. Nor should we pay Jill more merely because her skin is white. Formal justice, then, is a kind of consistency. Formal justice says that we should treat two cases the same when they are the same. But this raises a key question: When should we consider people to be "the same"? In many respects, Jack and Jill are not the same. We just indicated that Jack is not white but Jill is, and Jack is a man whereas Jill is a woman. But these differences are not relevant when deciding how much they each should be paid for the work they did. On the other hand, if Jill carries a bucket of water for us that is twice as big as Jack's, then this is relevant to how much each should get. The amount of work people do is a relevant difference when deciding what they should be paid for their work. The principle of formal justice, then, can be stated as follows:

> Formal justice obtains when individuals who are similar in all respects relevant to the kind of treatment in question are given similar benefits and burdens, and individuals who are dissimilar in a relevant respect are treated dissimilarly.

This formal principle of justice tells us something about what justice and injustice are. For example, if we agree that sex and race are not relevant differences when considering people for jobs, then the principle tells us that racial and sexual discrimination in hiring is unjust. On the other hand, if we agree that experience, skill, education, and ability are relevant when choosing people for a certain job, then it is just to favor those who have more experience, skills, education, and ability.

Yet the formal principle of justice does not settle all the issues. In fact, it does not settle the most pressing controversies that swirl around the issue of justice. For example, is need relevant when deciding whether it is just for government to provide welfare to people? Or take affirmative action programs, which show preference to women and minorities who have been disadvantaged in the past. Are these programs based on "relevant differences"? Are they just? What kinds of differences among people are relevant, and what kinds are not? The formal principle of justice leaves this fundamental question unanswered.

Over the centuries, society has suggested many kinds of "relevant differences" among people. For example, a simple rule that we all think is just is "first come, first served." When we are waiting to buy tickets at a movie theater or concert, for example, we stand in a line where the first to arrive is served first, and latecomers are served last. We think it is unjust when a latecomer crowds in line ahead of us. The reason, of course, is because when waiting to receive a service or good, we believe that the relevant difference among us is who took the trouble to get there first.

But no matter what principle serves as the standard for distribution, it ordinarily can be traced, and ideally should be, to a fully developed theory of justice. Thus, the person who invokes talent and ability as the principle of job distribution probably views justice itself in terms of merit. Likewise, the person who argues for special tax advantages for large corporations is viewing justice in terms of social utility. And those who think that medical resources should be equally available to all view justice chiefly in terms of equality: Everyone should be treated equally in the sense that all should get the same medical care. In fact, merit, social utility, and equality have served as focal points for various theories of justice down through the years and continue to exert profound influence on our current views of justice and the proper relationship between individual and society.

JUSTICE AS MERIT

Plato proposed the first significant theory of justice, one associated with giving to individuals what is their due. In Plato's theory, justice in the state is exactly what it is in the individual: a harmony between the various parts for the good of the whole. Social justice, then, requires cooperation among all members of a society so that society will function best. As a result, the interests of the individual must be subordinated to the larger interests and good of society.

Such a notion had significant implications for the overwhelming majority of the Greek population, who were poor and powerless. The submissive role that these people played, especially the slaves, was vital to the overall success of the society. Yet their interests and rights were kept to a minimum. Indeed, they expected reward only insofar as their actions benefited their superiors. Such an attitude could be fostered only in a rigidly structured society, whose sharply drawn class divisions left no confusion about one's place, role, or expectations in life. This is precisely the kind of society that Plato has in mind in *The Republic*: a system in which every individual has his or her place, and justice means that each person acts and is treated accordingly. In Plato's view, then, justice becomes associated with merit, in the sense that individuals are treated and expected to act according to their talents and accomplishments. People's natural talents, Plato held, make them fit for certain social roles or statuses, and what people get depends on their role or status. In the following passage from *The Republic*, Plato indicates his position quite clearly:

> Is the exclusive aim of judges in delivering judgment that no citizen should have what belongs to another or be deprived of what is his own?
> That is their aim.
> That is what we call justice?
> Yes.
> In some way then possession of one's own and the performance of one's own task could be agreed to be justice.
> That is so.

> *You have no more right to consume happiness without producing it than to consume wealth without producing it.*
>
> BERNARD SHAW

Plato: "When one who is by nature a worker attempts to enter the warrior class, or one of the soldiers tries to enter the class of guardians, this meddling brings the city to ruin. That then is injustice. But the doing of one's own job by each class is justice and makes the city just."

Consider then whether you agree with me in this: if a carpenter attempts to do the work of a cobbler, or a cobbler that of a carpenter, and they exchange their tools and the esteem that goes with the job, or the same man tries to do both, and all the other exchanges are made, do you think that this does any great harm to the city?

No.

But I think that when one who is by nature a worker or some other kind of moneymaker is puffed up by wealth, or the mob, or by his own strength, or some other such thing, and attempts to enter the warrior class, or one of the soldiers tries to enter the group of counselors and guardians, though he is unworthy of it, and these exchange their tools and the public esteem, or when the same man tries to perform all these jobs together, then I think you will agree that these exchanges and this meddling bring the city to ruin.

They certainly do.

The meddling and exchange between the three established orders [of workers, warriors, and guardian rulers] does very great harm to the city and would most correctly be called wickedness.

Very definitely.

And you would call the greatest wickedness worked against one's own city injustice?

Of course.

That then is injustice. And let us repeat that the doing of one's own job by the moneymaking, warrior, and guardian groups, when each group is performing its own task in the city, is the opposite: it is justice and makes the city just.

I agree with you that this is so.[18]

> **CRITICAL THINKING**
> Does Plato assume that it is just to sacrifice the happiness and the freedom of the individual for the sake of the larger society? Is this assumption correct?

Our object in the construction of the state is the greatest happiness of the whole, and not that of any one class.

PLATO

---

[18]Plato, *The Republic*, trans. G. M. A. Grube (Indianapolis: Hackett, 1974). Reprinted by permission.

Apparent in this selection and throughout *The Republic* is Plato's insistence not only on severe class distinctions but also on the natural *inequality* of individuals. Different people have different natural talents and abilities. These natural talents and abilities make them fit for different social roles. At the top of society are those whose talents and accomplishments make them fit to rule. Below them are those whose natural courage and aggressiveness make them fit to enter the military class. Next come those whose skills fit them to be free workers and artisans. At the bottom, almost unmentioned by Plato, are the slaves. Those with higher social status merit more than those below them, so justice requires that they get more.

Aristotle too shared the assumption that individuals are unequal and that justice is giving to unequal individuals their unequal due. Indeed, in his *Politics*, Aristotle defended slavery because he believed that those who were slaves were naturally suited for that role and would be wretched and ineffectual were they made free. Both he and Plato believed that the abilities and achievements of different people entitled them to different statuses in society. Justice means that each should act and be treated according to his or her abilities, achievements, and social status. We can summarize this notion of justice in a more general way with this statement:

> A just society is one that distributes benefits and burdens according to merit as measured by a person's talent, ability, effort, achievement, intelligence, or social status.

Notice that the principle of merit tries to put some teeth into the principle of formal justice. The principle of formal justice says that people should be treated the same except when there are relevant differences between them. Plato and Aristotle in effect hold that the main "relevant difference" among people is *merit*—i.e., what people deserve in light of their talents and achievements. This view plays an important role in many of our perceptions of justice. We feel that among athletes it is just that the highest honors should be awarded on the basis of achievement. The gold medal should go to the one who runs or swims the fastest, the one who lifts the most, or the one who throws the discus the farthest. Many college scholarships are awarded on merit: on the grades a person achieved in high school and on standardized tests. We feel it is just when jobs are awarded according to merit as indicated by a candidate's abilities and accomplishments.

On the other hand, Plato and Aristotle might question the justice of some contemporary practices. For example, it seems safe to say that both would object to heterogeneous grouping in public schools (that is, the practice of placing students of diverse abilities in the same class, as opposed to homogeneous grouping, in which only students of like ability are placed in the same class). They would object to the view that "all men are created equal" and that everyone should have equal political rights. They would certainly object to the view that everyone has an equal right to hold political office.

Many people today find Plato's and Aristotle's theory of justice objectionable because of its assumption that individuals have an unequal status. But it should be remembered that the presupposition of equality is as much an assumption as the presupposition of inequality and, as such, requires a defense.

Even though we may not all share the Greek assumption of inequality, our own conceptions of justice are in other important ways deeply indebted to both Plato and Aristotle. For example, like these two philosophers, we hold the formal principle that equals should be treated equally. The difference, of course, is that we espouse equality of status, whereas Plato and Aristotle did not endorse universal equality. Also, in his concern with the just distribution of a society's resources, Aristotle anticipated an issue that is of vital national and international concern today, in discussions of aid for the poor. Aristotle clearly recognized the importance of justice for the poorest and least powerful members of society. In his view, justice was particularly important for these people because they, unlike the rich and powerful, could not fend for themselves. Finally, much of the theorizing since the time of the Greeks has, in effect, been a response to Plato's claim that justice is giving everyone his or her due. Specifically, social philosophers since Plato have attempted to explain what an individual is due and why. Inevitably, this has called for an inspection of the relation between justice and equality.

Society never advances.
RALPH WALDO EMERSON

JUSTICE AS EQUALITY

We can readily identify with the idea of equality. After all, we have been reared in a society built on the premise that "all men are created equal." *Equal* here, of course, means "the same." Accordingly, in the United States it is widely believed that everyone is entitled to a period of roughly the same kind of education, that the sexes and races should be treated the same, that individuals should be treated the same before the law, that everyone should have the same job opportunities and the same access to medical care, that everyone should have the same right to practice religion, speak freely, travel, and so on. Similarly, we reject slavery on principle because it violates our belief that everyone is equal. We even object to snobbery, presumably because we believe that one person is not necessarily better than another because of wealth, family, intelligence, or some other source of unequal status. The point is that we needn't look far to see evidence that at least in theory, our society is erected on a commitment to egalitarianism.

Inferiors revolt in order that they may be equal, and equals that they may be superior. Such is the state of mind which creates revolutions.
ARISTOTLE

Yet what, exactly, does this commitment to equality mean? One way of trying to capture the meaning of *equality* is by taking the term quite strictly. Strict equality means exactly equal shares. We can summarize the view that justice is, strictly, giving to each an equal share, in the following statement:

> In a just society every person will be given exactly equal shares of that society's benefits and burdens.

This view is known as *strict egalitarianism*. Notice that the strict egalitarian view takes a definite position on formal justice. The strict egalitarian claims that there are *no* relevant differences among people when it comes to justice. Justice demands strict equality regardless of the differences among people.

Many philosophers have agreed that justice requires strictly equal shares. Notice that we promote strict egalitarianism in many kinds of groups and organizations. In a family, for example, we feel that children, over the course of their lives, should receive equal shares of the family's goods. When workers work in teams, some businesses pay all the members of the team exactly the same salary. This is based on research that shows that when workers in a group are paid the same, they cooperate more with one another and become more cohesive. Workers in many Asian countries also prefer to be paid close to the same as what other workers in their company receive. For this reason, wage and salary differences between top managers and lower-level employees are much smaller in Asian countries than in the United States. In fact, if we look only at economic inequalities—inequalities of income and wealth—then the United States is the most, or one of the most, unequal societies in the world.

But the view that a just society is one that promotes strict equality leads to difficult theoretical and operational problems. To get an idea of these problems, consider the practice of heterogeneous grouping in the classroom. Consistent with the belief that everyone is equal, we try to ensure that everyone has roughly the same educational opportunities, at least in the formative years. Accordingly, thirty students of widely differing abilities and capacities may be placed in the same class at the same time with the same instructor. Faced with such essential diversity, teachers often end up aiming their teaching at the nonexistent "average" class member. As likely as not, the instructional level will be too high for the slowest class members and too low for the swiftest. As a result, the slowest don't learn, and the swiftest get bored; both "turn off." Is this just?

Again, modern medical technology has made the wondrous dream of organ transplants an astonishing reality. Corneas, hearts, kidneys, bone marrow, and even livers and lungs can be transplanted with more or less success. But there's a rub: Demand exceeds supply. Who should get available organs when there aren't enough to go around? By a strict egalitarian calculation, everyone who needs a heart should have an equal chance of getting it. But suppose that two people are in need of the only available heart. One of them is an internationally renowned neurosurgeon in her forties whose survival promises to benefit countless persons. The other is a sixty-five-year-old derelict who for three decades has wantonly abused his body and whose survival promises little benefit for anyone, except possibly himself. Is it just to treat these individuals as equals in determining who will receive the heart? Or is it more just that they be treated as unequals?

The problem, of course, is that people are not equal and their inequalities seem to demand an unequal sharing in society's resources. Human beings have different needs, different abilities, different desires, and different virtues. They put forward different efforts and have different skills and different physical abilities. In fact, humans seem to be unequal in all respects. Don't we have to take these differences into account when we distribute benefits among people? Suppose that every worker is given exactly the same wage. Then better workers would have no incentive to work hard since hard work will get them exactly the same as loafing. Suppose that every needy person is given the same basket of goods. Then some will get more than they need, and others will get less than they need. On the other hand, if people are given exactly the same burdens, then some will get more than they can bear, whereas others will not get enough. Take the burdens of work. If everyone has to do exactly the same amount of

It is better that some should be unhappy, than that none should be happy, which would be the case in a general state of equality.

SAMUEL JOHNSON

work, then people who are unskilled or handicapped will have to do as much as people who are strong and skilled. This does not seem to be the best way to arrange work burdens. People's differences, then, seem to demand that they receive different shares of society's benefits and burdens.

Some egalitarians respond to these criticisms by distinguishing two kinds of equality: political equality and economic equality. People have political equality when they have an equal right to participate in our political processes. Certainly, egalitarians argue, we all agree that people should have equal political rights. Such equal rights include an equal right to vote, an equal right to run for political offices, equal civil rights, and equal rights to due process. Egalitarianism should be the rule in the political arena. But what about the economic arena? Here, say some egalitarians, we again have to make a distinction. Economic equality can mean either equality of income and wealth, or equality of opportunity. The objections that critics of egalitarianism make, they say, are problems that result if we try to make everyone's income and wealth equal. Differences among people have to be recognized when distributing income and wealth. On the other hand, they continue, there is nothing wrong with equality of opportunity. That is, everyone should have an equal opportunity to get those jobs and positions that carry higher levels of income and wealth. Society might secure equality of opportunity by giving everyone the same chance at an education and by eliminating all racial and sexual discrimination in jobs and other positions. So, egalitarians conclude, strict equality is justified in the political arena, and it is also justified in the economic arena if we are talking about equality of opportunity. Other economic benefits and burdens should be distributed according to relevant differences among people. This less-strict form of egalitarianism can be summarized as follows:

> A just society is one in which political rights and economic opportunities are distributed equally, whereas other economic benefits and burdens are distributed unequally according to the relevant differences among people.

But is even such a modified egalitarianism correct? Aren't there some differences among people that lead us to say that even political rights should not be equal? Consider the criminal. Is it wrong to say that the convicted criminal should not have the same political rights that other citizens have? Or take the person who cannot read or the person who has an IQ below 50. Should such people have the same right to vote as all others? Consider equality of opportunity. Can we really hope to achieve equality of opportunity? Won't differences among people always sabotage our attempts to achieve equality of opportunity? Suppose that we give everyone the same education. Some students will be more motivated, be smarter, and have fewer distractions than others. Such students will graduate with better qualifications than others. So not everyone will have the same opportunities when they graduate, even if everyone gets the same education. People's inequalities, then, seem to undercut the egalitarian's attempts to achieve both political equality and equality of opportunity.

For Plato and Aristotle, the natural differences among people posed no great problem, because they associated justice with unequal merit. But for modern theorists, the tension between recognizing people's differences and pursuing

Equality in society beats inequality, whether the latter be of the British-aristocratic sort or of the domestic-slavery sort.
ABRAHAM LINCOLN

equality poses an urgent problem. Indeed, it is one that British philosophers have engaged for several centuries and one that has given rise to the theory of justice associated with social utility.

JUSTICE AS SOCIAL UTILITY

One view of justice that occurs to many people today is this: Justice is what promotes the general welfare. On this view, the just society is the one that best promotes the well-being of citizens.

The theory that views justice in terms of social utility has its roots in the social and political thought of a number of British philosophers of the eighteenth and nineteenth centuries. Although British philosophers such as Thomas Hobbes, John Locke, and David Hume started from the premise that everyone is equal, they did not take this to mean that unequal treatment is never permissible. On the contrary, they associated justice with what ensures peace and security for all. In other words, justice means the public interest or social utility. What advances the good of society, or at least most of its citizens, is just. Notice that in contrast to the Greek view, no acknowledgment is made of giving individuals what befits them according to some standard of merit. Yes, individuals should get their due, but their due must be determined by appeal to the common good. The ultimate criterion of justice, then, is utility—that is, public interest or the satisfaction of the interests of at least the majority of people in society.

John Stuart Mill stated the utility view most explicitly. Mill argued that society should always try to minimize social harms and maximize social benefits. In *Utilitarianism*, Mill concedes that the notion of equality is often part of both our conception and practice of justice. But he does not believe that equality constitutes the essence of justice. Whereas the notion of justice varies in different persons, says Mill, it always conforms to the individual's idea of utility. Thus, all people believe that equality is the dictate of justice except when they feel that utility requires inequality. Then they are likely to say, for example, that the famous surgeon and the skid-row bum should not be treated as equals in determining who will get the available heart. Since preserving the life of the surgeon promises more social benefit, expediency requires inequality of treatment. The surgeon should get the organ. So we can summarize Mill's views on justice in the following statement:

> The just society is the one that distributes benefits and burdens in whatever way will produce the greatest social benefits or (when only net harms result) inflict the lowest social harms.

In Mill's view, utility or "expediency" is the ever-present criterion in determining what is just and unjust. Whatever the institution, policy, or program, its justice depends ultimately on one's opinion about expediency. Is reverse discrimination just? It may be, if it serves the public interest better than any other alternative proposed to ensure comparable opportunities. Does a fee-for-service medical system best serve society's interests? Individual answers may vary, but each of them, according to Mill, will be based on an opinion about the expe-

John Stuart Mill: "Justice remains the appropriate name for certain social utilities which are vastly more important and therefore more absolute and imperative, than any others are as a class."

diency of the practice. What is considered expedient will be considered just; what is not considered expedient will not be considered just. In the following passage from *Utilitarianism* he makes these points:

> While I dispute the pretensions of any theory which sets up an imaginary standard of justice not grounded on utility, I account the justice which is grounded on utility to be the chief part, and incomparably the most sacred and binding part, of all morality. Justice is a name for certain classes of moral rules, which concern the essentials of human well-being more nearly, and are therefore of more absolute obligation, than any other rules for the guidance of life. . . .
>
> Justice, [therefore,] is a name for certain moral requirements which, regarded collectively, stand higher in the scale of social utility. . . .
>
> It has always been evident that all cases of justice are also cases of expediency; the difference is in [a] peculiar sentiment which attaches to the former, as contradistinguished from the latter. . . . [T]his characteristic sentiment . . . is simply the natural feeling of resentment. . . .
>
> Justice [, therefore,] remains the appropriate name for certain social utilities which are vastly more important, and therefore more absolute and imperative, than any others are as a class; and which, therefore, ought to be, as well as naturally are, guarded by a sentiment [that is] . . . distinguished from the milder feeling which attaches to the mere idea of promoting human pleasure or convenience.[19]

Since Mill's utilitarian theory of justice is a logical extension of his ethical theories, it is understandable that it should invite some of the same objections. First, even if what we consider expedient we also consider just, should we do

In all that the people can individually do as well for themselves, government ought not to interfere.

ABRAHAM LINCOLN

---

[19]John Stuart Mill, *Utilitarianism* (New York: Bobbs-Merrill, 1957), 68–69. Reprinted by permission.

so? For example, most states have laws against possessing marijuana. Whether or not there ought to be such laws, or whether or not such laws are just, is another issue. To assume that merely because the laws exist that they ought to exist, or that they are necessarily just, is to commit a fallacy. Again, there are laws prohibiting active euthanasia—that is, taking direct measures to end the life, say, of someone hopelessly ill and in excruciating pain. But the question of whether there ought to be such laws is another issue. Merely because we may think of justice in terms of expediency does not necessarily mean that we ought to. Perhaps we should think of it in other terms—as, for example, the Greeks did or as strict egalitarians do.

A second, more troublesome problem with social utility arises from the inevitable clash of individual and public interests. Surely, in some cases the general utility can be served only at the expense of an individual or perhaps a small group. Take, for example, the volatile issue of nuclear waste disposal sites.

PHILOSOPHY AND LIFE

Society and the Bomb

The decision to drop the nuclear bomb that killed tens of thousands of the civilian inhabitants of the city of Hiroshima on August 6, 1945, was made while the United States was at war with Japan. Henry L. Stimson, the American Secretary of War at the time, later explained that he advised President Truman to drop the bomb on the basis of utilitarian reasoning:

I felt that to extract a genuine surrender from the [Japanese] Emperor and his military advisers, they must be administered a tremendous shock which would carry convincing proof of our power to destroy the Empire. Such an effective shock would save many times the number of lives, both American and Japanese, that it would cost. . . . Our enemy, Japan, . . . had the strength to cost us a million more [lives]. . . . Additional large losses might be expected among our allies and . . . enemy casualties would be much

larger than our own. . . . My chief purpose was to end the war in victory with the least possible cost in lives. . . . The face of war is the face of death; death is an inevitable part of every order that a wartime leader gives. The decision to use the atomic bomb was a decision that brought death to over a hundred thousand Japanese. . . . But this deliberate, premeditated destruction was our least abhorrent choice.

Objecting to this kind of utilitarian justification for killing the inhabitants of cities with nuclear weapons, philosopher-theologian John C. Ford wrote the following:

[Is] it permissible, in order to win a just war, to wipe out such an area with death or grave injury, resulting indiscriminately, to the majority of its ten million inhabitants? In my opinion the answer must be in the negative. . . . [It] is never permitted to kill directly noncombatants in wartime. Why?

Because they are innocent. That is, they are innocent of the violent and destructive action of war, or of any close participation in the violent and destructive action of war.

QUESTIONS

1. Is killing the innocent always wrong, no matter what the consequences?

2. Would you side with Stimson or Ford about the morality of dropping the bomb?

3. Do you agree that in some circumstances the use of nuclear weapons is morally permissible?

Sources: Henry L. Stimson, "The Decision to Use the Atomic Bomb," *Harper's Magazine* (February 1947), 101–102, 106, 107. John C. Ford, "The Hydrogen Bombing of Cities," *Theology Digest* (Winter 1957).

Nuclear power plants provide a sizable fraction of the electrical power that citizens use and from which many draw significant benefits. These plants also produce large amounts of radioactive wastes, which have to be stored somewhere. But many people fear that radioactive storage sites pose some level of risks to individuals living near them. Is it just for the government to insist that these individuals must bear even a negligible risk for the good of society? As another example, government spending for national defense has been declining due to political changes in the former Soviet Union and in other parts of Eastern Europe that have made the possibility of military confrontations more remote. This decline in military spending benefits all citizens, but it has also resulted in massive layoffs of individuals who worked for companies that manufactured military goods. Is it just to impose the costs of winding down military production on these few vulnerable workers? Of course, one could respond that the utility of a specific act by itself cannot give an adequate concept of justice, that what is needed is a theory of general practice along the lines of rule utilitarianism. But as we have seen (in Chapter 7), rule utilitarianism still allows the possibility of a practice that systematically increases the general utility at the expense of some individual or group. Is this just? Utility theorists would say that it is just, simply because justice ultimately has no concrete meaning apart from expediency.

JUSTICE BASED ON NEED AND ABILITY

Socialism is one of the major political philosophies of the modern world. Many countries base their social institutions on socialism, including those nations that are still "communist." Although there are many different versions of socialism, we can say, generally, that socialism holds that the wealth society produces belongs to everyone in society and so should be shared by everyone in society. Modern socialists often advocate government ownership of all factories and business enterprises. They also support government programs that distribute to everyone in society a share of the income and wealth produced by these enterprises.

There are many kinds of socialism, so it is probably not accurate to speak of "the" socialist view of justice. Still, philosophers traditionally take the dictum that Karl Marx proposed as the socialist view on distributive justice. As Marx wrote in his short work *Critique of the Gotha Program*, "From each according to his ability, to each according to his need."[20] The socialist principle can be summarized as follows:

> Work burdens should be distributed according to people's abilities, and benefits should be distributed according to people's needs.

Marx's slogan is another interpretation of what *relevant difference* means in the principle of formal justice. For Marx, the key differences that are relevant when

---

[20] Karl Marx, *Critique of the Gotha Program* (London: Lawrence and Wishart, 1938), 14, 107. This slogan was earlier stated by Louis Blanc in *L'Organization du Travail* (Paris, 1850) and later by Nikolai Lenin in his short pamphlet "Marxism on the State."

distributing things justly are people's abilities and needs. Justice requires that jobs and tasks should be assigned to people according to the skills and abilities that they have. Those with few or no abilities, of course, should have light or easy tasks, whereas those who are extremely able and talented should have heavier and more complex jobs. On the other hand, the goods that society produces—food, clothing, housing, medical care, luxuries—should be distributed according to people's needs. The greater a person's need for a specific kind of good, the more he or she should receive of that good; the less a person's need for a certain good, the less of that good he or she should receive.

We use the principle of distribution according to need and ability in many areas of our lives. In athletics, for example, the members of a team will distribute burdens according to each team member's abilities. And team members tend to stand together and help each other according to each one's need. In business, managers sometimes use this principle when they assign tasks to workers, giving the hard and complex tasks to those with commensurate abilities. And when workers seem to have special needs, many managers will try to accommodate them by giving them extra resources. In society at large, we feel that people's need should be one of the criteria that government uses to distribute benefits. This is, for example, the key idea behind government welfare programs, aid to the needy, and loans to people in disaster areas. We also feel that income taxes should be levied according to people's ability to pay: The more people earn, we feel, the more income taxes they should pay.

But the group in which use of the socialist principle is most prominent is the family. Able family members willingly work to support and help the family, whereas those who are in need are willingly supported by the family's resources. In fact, the principle of need and ability has been argued for on the notion that societies should be communities in which benefits and burdens are distributed on the model of the family.

However, Karl Marx offers a different argument. Marx argues that people should realize their human potential through productive work that exercises their particular abilities. This means that work should be distributed according to people's abilities. Second, he argues, the benefits produced through work should be used to promote human happiness and well-being. This implies that goods should be used first to meet people's basic needs and then their other, nonbasic needs.

But many people have objected to the socialist principle. First, they have argued, under the socialist principle there would be no relation between how hard a person works and the compensation he receives. Compensation, after all, would be based on need, not effort. So workers would have no incentive to work hard. Second, critics have asked, how practical is it to try to model a whole society on the family? People are self-interested and competitive. Outside the family they are not motivated by the willingness to share and help that is a natural response to life in the family. Finally, critics claim, the socialist principle can't succeed unless government forces people to live by its dictates. Under the socialist principle, people can't freely choose the job they want, but must take the job that fits their abilities. So government has to step in to decide what job best fits people's abilities and to make them take that job. Second,

Let the ruling classes tremble at a Communist revolution. The proletarians have nothing to lose but their chains. Workers of the world, unite!
KARL MARX

under socialism people can't freely choose the goods they want, but must take the goods that fit their basic needs. This means that government, again, has to step in and decide what goods best meet a person's needs. To match jobs with abilities and goods with needs, then, requires a large government bureaucracy.

JUSTICE BASED ON LIBERTY

Like socialism, liberalism is one of the major political philosophies of the modern age. Liberalism is the view that liberty is the most important value society and government can promote. In particular, liberals support freedom of conscience, freedom of speech, freedom of association, and freedom of occupation. Liberals also support equal political rights and civil liberties. During the twentieth century, liberalism divided into two camps: classical liberalism and welfare liberalism. Classical liberals favor a limited government that stays out of the free market and does not try to distribute economic goods. Welfare liberals favor a government that makes up for the harmful effects of the free market, particularly by providing economic help to the least advantaged.

We have seen that socialism has a view on justice. In a similar way, liberalism also has strong views on justice. However, since liberalism is now made up of two conflicting camps, we can expect that liberalism will have two contrasting views on justice. Let us begin with the views on justice that welfare liberals support. To get clear about these views, we will look at a philosopher whom we have already met: John Rawls.

Justice in Welfare Liberalism

As we have seen, Rawls argues that the principles of justice that govern society must be acceptable to everyone; otherwise, society will not be stable but subject to unrest. But principles that are perceived as unfair, Rawls claims, will not be acceptable to everyone. Why should people accept principles that unfairly favor others at their expense? Clearly, the principles on which a stable society is based must be principles that are fair to everyone. What principles of justice will be fair to everyone? Rawls proposes three principles: the principle of equal liberty, the principle of equal opportunity, and the difference principle.

The *principle of equal liberty* is meant to govern primarily society's political institutions (its constitution, government, courts, legislative system, and laws). The principle of equal liberty states that "each person participating in a [political] practice or affected by it has an equal right to the most extensive liberty compatible with a like liberty for all."[21] Basically, the principle of equal liberty means that everyone must have as many political rights and freedoms as possible, as long as everyone has the same ("equal") political rights and freedoms. For example, everyone must have at least the same voting rights, the same legal rights, the same right to trial by jury, the same freedom of speech, the same freedom of conscience, the same freedom of the press, and so on. In the political

---

[21] John Rawls, "Justice as Fairness," in *Philosophy, Politics, and Society*, ed. Peter Laslett and W. G. Runciman (New York: Barnes & Noble, 1962),133.

sphere, then, everyone must be equal and everyone must be granted the maximum degree of freedom compatible with everyone else having the same degree of freedom. Because the principle of equal liberty requires equality, Rawls argues, it is fair to everyone. Consequently, society's political institutions will be stable as long as they are based on this fair principle.

The *principle of equal opportunity* is supposed to govern a society's economic institutions. The principle states that desirable jobs and positions should be open to anyone who is qualified by his or her abilities. This means that job qualifications should be related to the requirements of the job and should not discriminate by race or sex. It also means that society should provide people with the training and education needed to qualify for desirable jobs.

Rawls's *difference principle* is also intended to govern primarily a society's economic institutions. Unlike the political arena, where everyone must be equal, the economic arena must allow for some inequalities. Rawls holds that inequalities are necessary in the economic arenas to serve as incentives for greater productivity. If greater economic rewards (income and wealth) are given to those who work harder and who have greater abilities, they will be motivated to be more productive, and all society will benefit.

But inequalities obviously raise the possibility of unfairness and therefore of instability. Those who are disadvantaged (those who cannot work or who have few talents and abilities) can be disfavored by principles that allow inequalities. Consequently, Rawls proposes that inequalities should be allowed only if the plight of the disadvantaged is relieved (through welfare programs, for example). The "difference" principle that he proposes to govern the inequalities in our social and economic institutions is as follows: "Social and economic inequalities are to be arranged so that they are . . . to the greatest benefit of the least advantaged."[22] Rawls calls this the difference principle because it focuses on the differences among people. Rawls's principles of justice, which we can take as the principles of justice of welfare liberalism, can be summarized as follows:

> The distribution of benefits and burdens in a society is just if
> 1. each person has the most political liberty compatible with equal liberty for all, and
> 2. economic inequalities are arranged so that
>   a. everyone has an equal opportunity to qualify for all positions, and
>   b. inequalities produce benefits for the least advantaged persons.

The second principle is fair, Rawls argues, because it is based on reciprocity, on "tit-for-tat." The principle benefits those who have talents and abilities because they have an equal opportunity to compete for the more favored jobs and positions. Their efforts thus add to the productivity of society. But the disadvantaged also benefit because the goods produced by the efforts of the talented benefit the disadvantaged through welfare programs. Thus, the advantaged "repay" the disadvantaged for the inequalities from which they benefit. This reciprocity makes the principles fair to everyone.

Although many people support the ideals of fairness that Rawls's principles embody, not everyone does so. In particular, classical liberals criticize Rawls.

> **CRITICAL THINKING**
> Rawls assumes that economic incentives are needed to get people to contribute to society. Is this assumption correct?

---

[22] John Rawls, *A Theory of Justice* (Cambridge, MA: Harvard University Press, 1972), 255.

Justice in Classical Liberalism

One of Rawls's strongest classical liberal critics is his Harvard colleague Robert Nozick (1938–   ). Nozick is not too concerned with what Rawls has to say about political liberty. Nozick also agrees that in the political arena, people should be equal and should have as much liberty as is possible. In his book *Anarchy, State, and Utopia*, however, Nozick points out that Rawls advocates a "patterned" theory of justice in economic affairs. A patterned theory is one that says goods should be distributed among the members of a society according to a certain pattern or formula. If goods are not yet distributed according to his formula, then goods must be taken from some citizens and given to others until the required distribution is achieved. Rawls's theory requires that goods be distributed according to his two principles.

Nozick objects that any patterned theory will always require the unjust use of force and coercion. People's free choices, he says, will always change any pattern that society tries to establish. Then government will unjustly have to force some individuals to give their goods to others until the required distribution is achieved again.

Nozick provides an ingenious example to illustrate his claim. He asks us to imagine a society in which goods are already distributed according to a patterned concept of justice like Rawls's. Each person then holds the goods that each should hold, no more and no less. Now suppose that a basketball star freely chooses to play several exhibition games for which he receives one dollar per ticket each game. Millions of fans freely choose to give him one dollar to watch him play. As a result of these many free choices, at the end of the season the

> *Society exists for the benefit of its members; not the members for the benefit of society.*
>
> HERBERT SPENCER

PHILOSOPHY AND LIFE

Welfare

About 13.5 percent of our population, or 33.6 million Americans, lived in poverty in 1990, 8.6 million more than in 1977, and one out of four children was poor. Also in 1990 unemployment continued to hover at 7 percent. According to a congressional subcommittee, there are perhaps 2.5 million homeless Americans. A news report described the plight of impoverished citizens:

When the last in a series of fast-food jobs expired for him, Michael An-

thony Reed, 21, started living in his Toyota [parked on Denver's streets] with his 21-year-old wife and infant daughter [Holly Reed]. Holly Reed died of hypothermia while bundled in blankets in the family car. . . .

Joe Wilkerson, 25, and his wife, Sheila, 22, are from Chicago. They are typical of the "new homeless." . . . Joe lost his $25,000-a-year job as a forklift operator. . . . So they sold all they had, left the house they rented in Chicago, and headed west with their two sons. In a month, their money—

about $500—was gone. . . . "My husband, myself, and my two sons," [said Sheila] *"were walking in the cold and the kids asked, 'Where are we going?' and we said, 'We don't know.'"*

QUESTION

1. Should the government provide welfare for families like the Reeds and the Wilkersons?

SOURCE: *Los Angeles Times*, December 26, 1982.

player holds several million dollars: He now holds more goods than he should hold. Therefore, the patterned principles will require that some of the star's goods be taken away from him and given back to others until the proper distribution is once again reestablished. Thus, patterned principles continually require that goods be taken from some and given to others in order to reestablish the distribution that people's free choices continually change. However, Nozick argues that if a distribution is changed by people's free choices, then there can be nothing wrong with it. The fans knew their money was going to the basketball star, so they can have no complaint. And the goods of those who did not see the game are unaffected. Thus, there was nothing wrong with the distribution that resulted from these free choices.

What kind of justice does Nozick propose? In keeping with his ideas about the importance of free choice, Nozick argues that justice is respecting people's free choices. Any distribution of economic benefits and burdens is just, says Nozick, if it is the result of individuals freely choosing to exchange with each other the goods each person already owns. In summary, Nozick holds the following principle, which we may take as the principle of justice of classical liberalism:

> Benefits and hardens are distributed justly when society allows every individual the freedom to do what be chooses to do for himself or for others, the freedom to keep what he makes for himself or what others choose to give him, and the freedom to keep what he has or give it to whomever he chooses.

Nozick thus raises several objections to Rawls's principles. One is that Rawls is using the better-off people in society to ensure the welfare of the worst-off. Nozick regards this ethic as fundamentally unjust. As a corollary, he claims Rawls is not impartial, for he is seeing things only through the eyes of the least advantaged. Finally, he objects to Rawls's apparent contention that when individuals have more than what his two principles allow, they are not entitled to keep what they own. A person's entitlement to what he or she owns is very much a part of Nozick's thinking, and his work is largely devoted to spelling out this concept.

But perhaps in applying Rawls's difference principle to a specific transaction, Nozick has warped it, or at least overburdened it. After all, Rawls's principle is addressing the backdrop against which public policies and decisions about redressing inequalities are to be made. It is not speaking directly to specific, small-scale instances of the sort that Nozick cites. More important, Rawls does not argue that all property should be shared. He says only that society must help the most disadvantaged members. This does not at all mean that everyone has a right to an equal share. In other words, Rawls's concept of justice does not equate fair distribution with equal distribution. Individuals have a just claim to whatever they have acquired, as long as the acquisition occurred within the context of a fair social policy.

In the following paragraph from "A Kantian Conception of Equality," Rawls makes these very points concerning his difference principle:

> In explaining this principle, several matters should be kept in mind. First of all, it applies in the first instance to the main public principles and policies that regulate

social and economic equalities. It is used to adjust the system of entitlements and rewards, and the standards and precepts that this system employs. Thus the difference principle holds, for example, for income and property taxation, for fiscal and economic policy; it does not apply to particular transactions or distributions, nor, in general, to small scale and local decisions, but rather to the background against which these take place. No observable pattern is required of actual distributions, nor even any measure of the degree of equality. . . . What is enjoined is that the inequalities make a functional contribution to those least favored. Finally, the aim is not to eliminate the various contingencies, for some such contingencies [that is, social primary goods such as (1) rights, liberties, and opportunities; (2) income and wealth; (3) the social bases of self-respect] seem inevitable. Thus even if an equal distribution of natural assets seemed more in keeping with the equality of free persons, the question of redistributing these assets (were this conceivable) does not arise, since it is incompatible with the integrity of the person. Nor need we make any specific assumptions about how great these variations are: we only suppose that, as realized in later life, they are influenced by all three contingencies. The question, then, is by what criterion a democratic society is to organize cooperation and arrange the system of entitlements that encourages and rewards productive efforts. We have a right to our natural abilities and a right to whatever we become entitled to by taking part in a fair social process. The problem is to characterize this process.[23]

In the last analysis, Rawls's welfare liberalism is most significant and controversial because it has connected justice with aiding the least advantaged. While most, if not all, of us today would agree that government should secure equal political rights, many would not have government provide material goods and social services to the disadvantaged. Indeed, in the last fifteen years there has been a concerted effort to roll back welfare programs. In claiming that justice requires a social order that respects the right of individuals to material goods and social services, Rawls puts considerable distance between himself and contemporary classical liberalism.

Justice poses a profound problem to social and political philosophers. We have surveyed philosophers over a span of more than two millennia, but no single theory of justice has received their universal endorsement. Indeed, our own society seems ambivalent, at various times giving priority to merit, social utility, equality, need, ability, and freedom. The challenge continues to be what it has always been: to effect a proper balance—whatever and wherever that may be—among these public and private values.

QUESTIONS

1.   Is it just to be taxed to fund something that you do not morally subscribe to?

2.   Can you think of a situation in which it is more just to treat people differently than to treat them equally?

3.   Is the law requiring young people to remain in school until a certain age just? Is the one that requires parents or guardians to enroll their children or charges in a school just?

---

[23] John Rawls, "A Kantian Conception of Equality," *Cambridge Review* (February 1974), 97.

4. Think of situations in your personal life where you subscribe to some of the various types of justice discussed above. What kinds of situations are appropriate for each type of justice?

5. Rawls argues for a view of justice from the position of the most disadvantaged in society. Would it be unrealistic to argue a case for a view from the position of the most advantaged in society? How might you do this?

6. Applying Rawls's difference principle to out society, which groups do you think would receive preferential economic treatment? Why?

7. What evidence indicates that Rawls's theory is already operating in our society?

8.4 Law and Civil Disobedience

Traditionally, the line of demarcation between the individual and society has been the **law,** by which we mean a rule or body of rules that tells individuals what they may and may not do.

law a rule or body of rules that tell individuals what they may and may not do

Our Western legal system inherited from the Judeo-Christian tradition, is a hierarchy of laws. For example, when a town law and a state law conflict, the state law takes precedence. Likewise, federal laws take precedence over state laws. Does anything take precedence over federal law, over the so-called law of the land? Both the Jewish and the Christian traditions maintain allegiance to a law that transcends any state, which they have historically referred to as the "law of God." We find a similar concept in ancient Greek philosophy.

The Stoics, members of the school of thought founded by Zeno around 300 B.C., believed that the world does not operate by blind chance but by reason. The universe is rational in the sense that it operates according to laws that the human mind can discover. This orderliness or world reason the Stoics termed *nature* and *logos* ("word"). Since people are happy when they act in accordance with nature—with the order of the universe—the purpose of institutions, according to the Stoics, is to enact laws that reflect this single universal law. Thus, what we today call *civic laws* have their basis in natural law. Natural law generally refers either to (1) a pattern of necessary and universal regularity holding in physical nature or to (2) a moral imperative, a description of what ought to happen in human relationships. The second definition concerns us here.

The Christian philosopher and theologian Saint Augustine presented a well-thought-out scheme of law in his *City of God*. In fact, Augustine's thought influenced Saint Thomas Aquinas, who in the Middle Ages distinguished among several kinds of law. First is divine or **eternal law**—that is, God's decrees for the governance of the universe. According to Aquinas, all things obey eternal law, and how they behave simply reflects this law. Thus, a flame rises and a stone falls. God is the lawmaker of the universe; things behave as they do because God so decrees it.

The eternal law also applies to humans, but in humans this law is merely a moral imperative that humans are free to disobey. Morality, as Aquinas conceived it, is not an arbitrary set of rules for behavior; rather, the basis of moral obligation is built into the very nature of the human in the form of various inclinations, such as the preservation of life, the propagation of the species, and the search for truth. Moral law is founded on these natural inclinations and on the ability of reason to discern the right course of conduct. The rules of conduct corresponding to these inherent human features are called **natural law.**

A good part of Aquinas's theory of natural law had already been worked through by Aristotle. In *Ethics*, Aristotle distinguished between natural and conventional justice. According to Aristotle, some forms of behavior are wrong because they violate a local law that has been passed to regulate that behavior in that particular jurisdiction. To use a contemporary example, jaywalking laws depend completely on the decisions of the local inhabitants, such laws are conventional, not natural. In contrast, Aristotle argued that some laws are based on human nature and on the nature of our societies. The behavior they prohibit is wrong under any circumstances. For example, murder and theft are wrong not because a particular group has passed laws against them but because they run counter to the social nature of human beings. Humans must live in societies, and societies cannot survive without such laws. Both Aristotle and Aquinas believed that humans can discover the natural basis for human conduct through reason. But Aquinas went further, contending that the human's existence and nature can be understood only in relation to God.

For Aquinas, then, law deals primarily with reason. Our reason uncovers the rules and standards to which human behavior should conform. Law consists of these rules and standards for human acts and is therefore based on reason. What's more, natural law is dictated by reason. Since God created everything, human nature and natural law are best comprehended as the product of God's wisdom or reason.

In summary, for Aquinas, natural law consists of that portion of the eternal law that pertains directly to humans. The basic precepts of the natural law are preservation of life, propagation and education of offspring, and the pursuit of truth and a peaceful society. These precepts reflect God's intentions for the human in creation and can be discovered and understood by reason.

Although these precepts do not vary, their enforcement does. Since different societies are influenced by different topographies, climates, cultures, and social customs, Aquinas believed that different codes of justice are needed. He called these specific codes of justice **human law.** The function of rulers is to formulate human law by informing themselves of the specific needs of their communities and then passing appropriate decrees. So, whereas natural law is general enough to govern the community of all humans, human law is specific enough to meet the requirements of a particular society.

eternal law for Aquinas, God's decrees for the governance of the universe

natural law a pattern of necessary and universal regularity; a universal moral imperative; a description of what ought to happen in all human relationships

human law for Aquinas, specific codes of justice that apply to a particular group, society, or community

The two points of difference between human law and natural law are first, that human law applies to a specific group, society, or community; and second, that human law is the expressed decrees of a human agent and not the laws operating in the universe at large. Nevertheless, a human law is a law not because it emanates from a legislator or ruler but because it implements divine law.

From Aquinas's theory of law we can draw one conclusion that has been particularly relevant to many oppressed minorities: Subjects have the right to disobey laws that are unjust or immoral. This conclusion follows from his idea that a true law must express the natural law of morality:

As Saint Augustine says, "that which is not just seems to be no law at all." Consequently, an ordinance is a valid law only to the extent that it is just. Now we say that something is just when it conforms to the [moral] principles of our reason and the basic moral principles of our reason are the natural law. So an ordinance enacted by humans is a valid law only to the extent that it conforms to the natural law. If an ordinance contradicts the natural law then it is not a valid law but a corruption of law. . . .

The ordinances human beings enact may be just or unjust. If they are just then we have a moral obligation to obey them since they ultimately derive from the eternal law of God. . . .

However, an ordinance may be unjust for one of two reasons. First, it may be contrary to the rights of humans; and second, it may be contrary to the rights of God.

A "law" can be contrary to the rights of humans in any of three ways. First, the "law" might not be aimed at achieving the common good. This would be the case, for example, if a ruler passed legislation that imposed heavy taxes that merely fed the ruler's greed and had no communal benefits. Second, the "law" might not have been enacted by a legitimate authority. This would be the case, for example, if someone tried to pass a law without having been delegated the legal authority to do so. Third, the "law" might distribute burdens unjustly. This would be the case, for example, if a law were aimed at achieving the common good, but the burdens involved in achieving that good were distributed unjustly among the citizens. Ordinances that are contrary to the rights of humans in any of these three ways are not valid laws but acts of violence. . . . We have no moral obligation to obey such ordinances except perhaps to avoid giving bad example or to prevent social disorder. . . .

Finally, a law can also be unjust when it is contrary to the rights of God. This would be the case, for example, if a tyrant were to pass a law requiring the worship of idols or any act that is against divine law. It is utterly wrong to obey such laws.[24]

As we have seen, the natural law for Aquinas is simply the moral law. So in saying that a legally enacted ordinance is a valid law only if it conforms to natural law, Aquinas is saying that a piece of legislation or a regulation is a valid law only if it conforms to the moral law. Immoral or unjust regulations, then, are not real laws at all, but just words written on a piece of paper. And since we have an obligation to obey only real laws, we do not have any obligation to obey immoral or unjust "laws." Often this point is expressed by saying that

> *All men recognize the right of revolution.*
>
> HENRY DAVID THOREAU

> *It is the duty of the people to bear any abuse of the supreme power.*
>
> IMMANUEL KANT

---

[24] Saint Thomas Aquinas, *Summa Theologica*, I–IIae, q. 95, a. 2, and q. 96, a. 4. This translation is by Manuel Velasquez.

human laws must conform to the higher law of morality, and when they do not, we must instead obey the higher law if we are to be true to our conscience.

Aquinas's view has been a point of great controversy. He is arguing that morality is part of the essential nature of law: Something is not a law unless it is moral. Although many philosophers have agreed with Aquinas, many others have strongly objected. Critics of Aquinas's view are generally called *positivists*. Positivists hold that once a piece of legislation has been passed by a legitimate authority, it is a law that we are obligated to obey regardless of whether it is immoral or unjust. A law is a law and must be obeyed.

However, the natural law view that Aquinas is advocating holds that since morality and justice must be part of any true law, unjust or immoral "laws" need not be obeyed. In particular, laws are just and must be obeyed only when (1) they serve the common good of the whole community, (2) they do not exceed the authorized power of the lawmaker, (3) they do not unjustly discriminate against some while they unfairly benefit others, and (4) they do not require citizens to violate their religious beliefs. If a law fails on any of these counts, it is no law at all.

Although positivists have criticized the natural law view of what a true law is, many political leaders have embraced the view of Aquinas, particularly those who, suffering under unjust or discriminatory laws, have advocated disobeying such laws in favor of the "higher law" of conscience. In his famous "Letter from Birmingham Jail," civil rights leader Martin Luther King, Jr., relied in part on this point to defend his civil disobedience of segregation laws:

> One may well ask, "How can you advocate breaking some laws and obeying others?" The answer is found in the fact that there are two types of laws: There are just and unjust laws. I would agree with Saint Augustine that "An unjust law is no law at all." Now what is the difference between the two? How does one determine when a law is just or unjust? A just law is a man-made code that squares with the moral law or the law of God. An unjust law is a code that is out of harmony with the moral law. To put it in the terms of Saint Thomas Aquinas, an unjust law is a human law that is not rooted in eternal and natural law. Any law that uplifts human personality is just. Any law that degrades human personality is unjust. All segregation statutes are unjust because segregation distorts the soul and damages the personality. It gives the segregator a false sense of superiority, and the segregated a false sense of inferiority. . . .
>
> I hope you can see the distinction I am trying to point out. In no sense do I advocate evading or defying the law as the rabid segregationist would do. This would lead to anarchy. One who breaks an unjust law must do it *openly*, *lovingly*, . . . and with a willingness to accept the penalty. I submit that an individual who breaks a law that conscience tells him is unjust, and willingly accepts the penalty by staying in jail to arouse the conscience of the community over its injustice, is in reality expressing the very highest respect for law.[25]

King drew on the logical consequences of the natural law view: If regulations are true laws only when they are moral and just, then people have a right to disobey an unjust or immoral "law." As King suggests in the passage above,

---

[25] Martin Luther King, Jr., "Letter from Birmingham Jail," in *Civil Disobedience: Theory and Practice*, ed. Hugo Adam Bedau (New York: Pegasus, 1969), 77–78.

Martin Luther King, Jr.: "Any law that uplifts human personality is just. Any law that degrades human personality is unjust. All segregation statutes are unjust because segregation distorts the soul and damages the personality."

he advocated nonviolent disobedience as a response to unjust laws. Civil disobedience of the kind advocated by King is the act of disobeying an unjust law openly, peacefully, and with a willingness to pay the penalty, in order to bring about a change in the law.

Of course, the very idea that an unjust law need not be obeyed makes many people very uncomfortable. Who is to decide when a law is unjust? Clearly, each individual must decide this for himself or herself. But doesn't this doctrine lead to an anarchic and chaotic situation in which each person individually decides which rules are true law and which are not?

In spite of these problems, for many minorities who have suffered discrimination under oppressive and unjust regimes, this right to disobey unjust laws has been critical; many have also advocated nonviolent resistance. The great statesman of India, Mohandas K. Gandhi, who had a profound influence on King, held that oppressed people have a moral right to disobey unjust laws; he preached this view in his campaign against the British. Moreover, like King, Gandhi also advocated nonviolent resistance to unjust laws, holding that using violence as a means to overthrow unjust laws would simply result in more violence:

> It is a superstition and ungodly thing to believe that an act of a majority binds a minority. Many examples can be given in which acts of majorities will be found to have been wrong and those of minorities to have been right. . . . So long as the

superstition that men should obey unjust laws exists, so long will their slavery exist. And a passive resister alone can remove such a superstition. To use brute-force, to use gunpowder, is contrary to passive resistance, for it means that we want our opponent to do by force that which we desire but he does not. And, if such a use of force is justifiable, surely he is entitled to do likewise by us. And so we should never come to an agreement.[26]

Still, many minority leaders have disagreed with Gandhi and King, claiming that nonviolent tactics are ineffective and that real change can be achieved only through violence. For example, Robert F. Williams, a black political thinker now living in exile in Cuba, has long advocated that blacks should use violence to do away with unjust law:

Proponents of the peaceful transition philosophy are quick to evoke the Gandhian theory of appealing to the conscience of the brutal oppressor and conquering him with the power of nonviolence and love. Gandhi's nonviolent revolution may have guaranteed the ruling powers immunity from the violence of the masses, but it most certainly left the masses exposed to the violence of the oppressors. It served to assure that only the blood of the oppressed would flow. . . . The power of nonviolence and love is a farce. Socrates was nonviolent and he, too, stressed love. He died at the hands of violent men. Christ was nonviolent and he, too, stressed love and nonviolence; be, too, died a violent death. History is replete with examples of nonviolent men as well as violent ones, who died from the power of violence either justified or unjustified.[27]

It is clear, then, that our views on the nature of law are extremely important and that these views will have significant implications for the position that we take on obedience to the law and obedience to the higher law of conscience. If morality is part of the essence of law, then unjust regulations are not real laws and need not be obeyed; nonviolent—or perhaps even violent—resistance to such "laws" is morally justified in the name of a higher law. On the other hand, if morality is not part of the essence of law, then our obligation to obey the law does not depend directly on its morality.

But when people refer to a higher law, they do not always mean a religious or God-given law. Many men who refused to fight in Vietnam, for example, were atheists who felt that fighting would violate their personal code of behavior. By higher law, then, we mean any law that an individual considers to take precedence over the body of rules that governs the activities within the state. When people appeal to a higher law, presumably they feel that the state has exceeded its rightful authority over them. But precisely when does the state exceed its authority over the individual? To what extent do the government and the public interest have authority over individuals and individual action? The answer to these questions, in part, calls for an examination of freedom and its relation to the law.

---

[26]Mohandas K. Gandhi, *Hind Swaraj or Indian Home Rule* (1909), reprinted in *Social and Political Philosophy*, ed. John Somerville and Ronald E. Santoni (Garden City, NY: Doubleday, 1963), 510.
[27]Robert F. Williams, "U.S.A.: The Potential of a Minority Revolution," *The Crusader Monthly Newsletter* ("Published in Cuba as a private publication, Robert F. Williams, publisher in exile") (May–June 1964), 1–7.

FREEDOM

If we valued only efficiency in government, then any evaluation of the rightful limits of governmental authority would be relatively simple. We would need only to determine whether or not governmental instructions as exercised through law best served the public interest. Evaluated strictly on social utility, it is entirely possible that the most authoritarian government might prove the most efficient.

But clearly our society is concerned with more than efficiency, with more than a well-oiled governmental machine. We are also concerned with justice and individual rights, issues that are not always compatible with efficiency. Contract theory regards both justice and individual rights as of paramount importance. The trouble is that contract theory is not clear about how justice and other kinds of moral considerations should be balanced against important individual rights.

One of those rights that concerns us here is political and social freedom, including the freedoms of speech, religion, and governance. History records many heroic battles fought to secure these freedoms as well as to win equality — that is, the same treatment for all citizens in a state. Freedom finds what may be its classic description in John Stuart Mill's essay *On Liberty,* in which the British social and political philosopher presents a powerful case for political individualism.

One of Mill's concerns is the freedom of the individual. He is specifically concerned with what actions individuals in society may perform. In essence, Mill claims that society may interfere with the individual in matters involving other people but not in matters involving only the individual. In effect, he distinguishes between two spheres of interest, the outer and the inner. A matter belongs to the outer sphere if it involves more than just a few individuals and to the inner if it involves only the self or a few others. The following excerpt from *On Liberty* captures the spirit of Mill's position:

> What, then, is the rightful limit to the sovereignty of the individual over himself? Where does the authority of society begin? How much of human life should be assigned to individuality, and how much to society?
>
> Each will receive its proper share, if each has that which more particularly concerns it. To individuality should belong the part of life in which it is chiefly the individual that is interested; to society, the part which chiefly interests society.
>
> Though society is not founded on a contract, and though no good purpose is answered by inventing a contract in order to deduce social obligations from it, everyone who receives the protection of society owes return for the benefit, and the fact of living in society renders it indispensable that each should be bound to observe a certain line of conduct towards the rest. This conduct consists, *first,* in not injuring the interests of one another; or rather certain interests, which, either by express legal provision or by tacit understanding, ought to be considered as rights; and *secondly,* in each person's bearing his share (to be fixed on some equitable principle) of the labors and sacrifices incurred for defending the society or its members from injury and molestation. These conditions society is justified in enforcing, at all costs to those who endeavor to withhold fulfillment. Nor is that all that society may do. The acts of an individual may be hurtful to others, or wanting in due consideration for

The less government we have the better.

RALPH WALDO EMERSON

CRITICAL THINKING

Does Mill assume that if each part of society (each person) prospers, then the whole of society will prosper? Is this correct?

their welfare, without going to the length of violating any of their constituted rights. The offender may then be justly punished by opinion, though not by law. As soon as any part of a person's conduct affects prejudicially the interests of others, society has jurisdiction over it, and the question whether the general welfare will or will not be promoted by interfering with it, becomes open to discussion. But there is no room for entertaining any such question when a person's conduct affects the interests of no persons besides himself, or need not affect them unless they like (all the persons concerned being of full age, and the ordinary amount of understanding). In all such cases, there should be perfect freedom, legal and social, to do the action and stand the consequences.[28]

Although Mill appears to have drawn some line of demarcation between society and individual, the distinction seems fuzzy. Just how many constitute "a few others"? Furthermore, Mill argues that since the individual and not society is the best judge of what advances self-interest, the individual should be free from interference in such pursuits. But it seems that we do not always know our best interests. Suppose a man who enjoys heroin "shoots up" every day. This matter might fall within the inner sphere, in which case he should be free from interference. Yet his behavior is probably not in his best interests. Therefore, it could easily be argued that his behavior should be interfered with.

The problem is that Mill's concept of freedom guarantees only noninterference, freedom from outside influence. These are the kinds of freedom guaranteed by the Bill of Rights. But perhaps some more positive guarantees are needed.

HUMAN RIGHTS

Because of the shortcomings of relying solely on freedom as a basis for determining the limits of the law, many people have felt that the law should also be judged by the respect that it shows for human rights. All people, they believe, have certain basic rights, and the law should show respect for such rights. In fact, some people have held that when a law fails to respect human rights, the law is evil and need not be obeyed.

Although the notion of a right is difficult to pin down, it has played a crucial role in our history. For example, the Declaration of Independence asserts that "all men are endowed by their Creator with certain unalienable rights . . . among these are life, liberty, and the pursuit of happiness." Several years later, the U.S. Constitution was amended to include the Bill of Rights, which was intended primarily to guarantee individuals freedom from the intrusions of government. In 1948 the United Nations published the Universal Declaration of Human Rights, stating that all human beings have "the right to own property, . . . the right to work, . . . the right to a just and favorable remuneration, . . . [and] the right to rest and leisure." And, more recently, we have witnessed an explosion of appeals to rights—gay rights, prisoners' rights, women's rights, animal rights, smokers' rights, fetal rights, and employee rights.

---

[28]John Stuart Mill, *On Liberty* (London: J. M. Dent, 1910), 77–78.

Just what is a right? The philosopher H. J. McCloskey has defined a **right** as a justified entitlement or claim on others.[29] For example, if I have a right to privacy, then I have a justified claim to be left alone by others. And if I have a right to an education, then I have a justified claim to be provided with an education by society.

The flip side of a right is a **duty,** which is an obligation imposed on individuals. That is, if someone has a right to something, then others have certain duties or obligations toward that person. If you have a right to privacy, then everyone else has a duty to leave you alone; if you have a right to an education, then society has a duty to provide you with an education. Duties are always correlated with rights.

There are two main kinds of rights, depending on the kind of justification or basis that they are given: legal rights and moral rights. *Legal rights* depend on the laws of a nation or country. For example, the laws of the United States give all citizens a legal right to equal treatment under the law. However, the laws of South Africa, throughout the eighties and into the nineties, failed to give black people the legal right to equal treatment.

Moral rights, or, as they are sometimes called, *human rights*, are rights that all people have simply because they are human beings; these right are justified or supported by moral principles that impose the same obligations on all human beings. For example, although the laws of South Africa once said that black people do not have the legal right to equal treatment, most people throughout the world agreed that the South African legal system was morally wrong and that black people everywhere, including South Africa, have a moral right to equal treatment because the moral principle of respect for human dignity requires equality of treatment.

Thus, moral or human rights are in a sense much more significant than legal rights, because we judge and evaluate legal rights in terms of people's moral rights. That is, when a country's laws violate people's moral rights, we say that the law is wrong and must be changed. The Civil War, a bloody, costly, and tragic confrontation, was fought in part because the slavery laws of the South were seen to violate the moral rights of black Americans. The civil rights movement of the sixties was a bitter struggle to change discriminatory laws that violated the moral rights of minorities and women. And we have seen bloody clashes in South Africa, Latin America, and parts of Asia over the injustice of laws that are seen to violate the moral rights of various groups. Thus, when the law violates people's moral rights, the law must be changed.

Some philosophers divide human rights into two groups: negative rights and positive rights. *Negative rights* are rights that protect freedoms of various kinds. The right to privacy, the right not to be killed, the right to travel, and the right to do what one wants with one's property are all negative rights because they all protect some form of human freedom or liberty. Negative rights impose a negative duty on other people: the duty not to interfere with a person's activities in a certain area. For example, the right of free association imposes on

right in ethics, a justified claim or entitlement to something against someone

duty in ethics, a justified obligation imposed on an individual

---

[29] H. J. McCloskey, "Rights—Some Conceptual Issues," *Australasian Journal of Philosophy* 54 (1976), 99–115.

others the duty not to prevent people from associating with whom they please. Negative rights are in fact the "freedoms-from" that Mill emphasizes in *On Liberty*. Negative rights impose minimal duties on us because they merely require us not to act.

Positive rights are rights that guarantee people certain goods: the right to an education; the right to adequate medical care, food, and housing; the right to a fair trial; the right to a job; and the right to a clean environment. Thus, positive rights impose on people a positive duty: the duty to actively help a person to have or to do something. If the poor have a right to adequate medical care, for example, then we as a society have a duty to ensure that they are provided with such care. Consequently, respecting a positive right requires more than merely not acting; positive rights impose on us the duty to act positively on behalf of others.

Without understanding the distinction between negative and positive rights, it is hard to understand many of the intense social controversies that confront our society. Many people today believe that the law should enforce only negative rights. They believe that the purpose of government is to guarantee only the freedoms-from that Mill advocated. Such people hold that government should not be involved in welfare programs, farm subsidies, or any other redistributive programs; ideally, government should only protect citizens from one another and from foreign invasion. But, as we have seen, many other Americans believe that government should do more than enforce these negative rights: It should also guarantee people's positive rights, through programs that provide the needy with a minimum level of well-being.

Both positive rights and negative rights have been defended on the basis of a variety of philosophies. But perhaps the most influential defense of human rights has been the approach advocated by the philosopher Immanuel Kant. Kant maintained that every human being has a worth or a dignity that must be respected. The individual's worth, Kant held, gives each person a value that is "beyond all price." Because of this intrinsic value or dignity, each person is an "end in himself"—that is, a being for whose sake we should all act. Consequently, Kant claimed, we each have a duty to respect every other person's freedom, as well as to help others achieve their happiness. This is the meaning of words of his that we have already seen:

> Violations of the principle that our humanity must be respected as an end in itself are even clearer if we take examples of attacks on the freedom and property of others. It is obvious that the person who violates such rights is using people merely as means without considering that as rational beings they should be esteemed also as ends; that is, as beings who must be able to participate in the goals of the actions to which they are involved with him. . . .
>
> Humanity probably could survive even if people never helped each other achieve their happiness, but merely refrained from deliberately harming one another. But this would only be a negative way of making our actions harmonize with the idea that humanity is an end in itself. The positive way of harmonizing with this idea would be for everyone to help others achieve their goals as far as he can.[30]

Civil government, so far as it is instituted for the security of property, is in reality instituted for the defence of the rich against the poor.

ADAM SMITH

---

[30] Immanuel Kant, *Grundlegung zur Metaphysik der Sitten [Groundwork of the Metaphysics of Morals]*, in *Immanuel Kant Werkausgabe*, vol. 7, ed. Wilhelm Weischedel (Frankfurt, Germany: Insel Verlag Wiesbaden, 1956). This translation copyright © 1987 by Manuel Velasquez.

Because of their fundamental human dignity, then, all persons have positive as well as negative human rights. For this reason, Kant held that government may legitimately levy taxes to care for the welfare, education, and development of persons "who are not able to support themselves."[31]

Some philosophers who agree that everyone has a basic dignity interpret the notion of human dignity differently from Kant. For example, Robert Nozick has argued that human dignity implies only that people should be free from having others interfere with their lives. In short, the only rights that humans have are negative rights to be left alone. Therefore, government should only guarantee people's negative rights and not their positive ones.

Many contemporary philosophers, however, agree with Kant's conclusions, even if they do not always accept his views about dignity. For example, Thomas Donaldson holds that people have both negative and positive human rights, even though he does not believe that these are necessarily based on human dignity. Instead, Donaldson holds that human rights are rights that should fulfill three conditions: They must protect something of very great importance to human beings, they must be subject to substantial and recurrent threats, and the obligations they impose on others must be fair and affordable. Donaldson has suggested the following list of basic human rights:

1. The right to freedom of physical movement.
2. The right to ownership of property.
3. The right to freedom from torture.
4. The right to a fair trial.
5. The right to nondiscriminatory treatment (freedom from discrimination on the basis of such characteristics as race or sex).
6. The right to physical security.
7. The right to freedom of speech and association.
8. The right to minimal education.
9. The right to political participation.
10. The right to subsistence.[32]

According to Donaldson, each of these human rights protects something of great importance to human life, each is subject to recurrent threats from governments and others around the world at the present time, and each imposes fair and affordable burdens on governments or others. Consequently, all governments of all nations should be required to live up to them. In addition, Donaldson holds, the governments of the wealthier nations should help the poorer nations provide these rights for their people.

A currently divisive issue in the United States, as we have seen, is how much the government should interfere to guarantee positive rights. Some contend that there is already too much interference, that the executive, legislative, and particularly the judicial branches of government are poking their collective noses into areas where they do not belong. In short, there are too many bad

Those who cannot remember the past are condemned to repeat it.

GEORGE SANTAYANA

---

[31] Immanuel Kant, *The Metaphysical Elements of Justice*, trans. W. Hastie (New York: Bobbs-Merrill, 1965), 93.

[32] Thomas Donaldson, *The Ethics of International Business* (New York: Oxford University Press, 1989), 81.

laws. Others claim that governmental interference is needed, that society has grown too unwieldy for individuals to fight their own battles for freedom. In short, there are too few good laws. Although these positions differ in their solutions, they are concerned with the problem that has occupied us in this chapter: how to best strike a balance between public and private interest. In other words, they are concerned with the problem of justice.

QUESTIONS

1. What laws, if any, do you regard as unjust? Why?

2. Does the state have the right to make laws concerning homosexuality, pornography, and marijuana?

3. To what extent do you feel that your own ability to live as you believe is limited by laws?

4. Do you think that every American has the right to a college education?

5. Do you think that every American has the right to medical care?

6. Do you believe that all people have the right to determine the political system under which they live? If you do, does one state have a moral obligation to assist another that is fighting to exercise that right? Is there any point at which that obligation ends?

8.5 Chapter Summary and Conclusions

We opened this chapter by keying on a recurring issue in any determination of the proper relation between individual and society: the problem of justice. Since the time of the Greeks, philosophers have proposed theories associating justice with merit, social utility, and fairness, or equality. A related issue is how the state justifies its claims to power and authority. Although there are a number of theories of the legitimacy of the state, contract theory is the view on which our own society's conception of power and governance is based. Even if the power of the state can be justified by contract theory, though, to what extent ought government be able to exercise its authority over the individual? The two extreme views on government control are anarchism and totalitarianism. Anarchism has unflinching confidence in the individual and none in the state; totalitarianism shows confidence in a strong state and government, and little if any in the individual. The consensus view in our own society falls somewhere between these extremes, with leanings toward individualism (willing individual cooperation) or paternalism (confidence in a strong authoritarian state). Whatever their leaning, contract theorists believe that the state and government

The Third of May, Francisco Goya. To what extent ought the state and its primary instrument, government, exercise its authority and power over the individual?

have the right and duty to exercise control through law, which traditionally has demarcated individual and society. Laws guarantee freedom from interference, but in a broader sense they also guarantee positive rights.

The main points of the chapter are as follows:

1. Many today accept a contractual justification for the power and authority of the state—that is, the state acquires its legitimacy through the consent of the governed (8.2).

2. Contract theory has its roots in the thought of Thomas Hobbes, John Locke, and Jean-Jacques Rousseau (8.2).

3. Contract theory was revived in the twentieth century by John Rawls, who argues that the social contract is an imaginary device for determining what a just society and government would be like (8.2).

4. Contract theory has been criticized by communitarians, who argue that it ignores the social nature of human beings, and by feminists, who argue that it assumes a nonconsensual division between the "private" realm of the family, to which women are relegated, and the "public" realm of politics and economics, in which men participate (8.2).

5. Distributive justice refers to the fairness with which a community distributes benefits and burdens among its members; the principle of formal justice says that equals should be treated equally (8.3).

6. The classical Greek view of justice, as expressed by Plato and Aristotle, associates justice with merit (8.3).

7. Egalitarians argue either for strict equality or for equality of political rights and economic opportunities (8.3).

8. The socialist principle of justice is summarized in Karl Marx's slogan: "From each according to this ability, to each according to his need" (8.3).

9. Whereas welfare liberals such as John Rawls argue that justice requires economic aid for the disadvantaged, classical liberals like Robert Nozick argue that people's free choices should be respected in all economic matters (8.3).

10. Several British philosophers of the eighteenth and nineteenth centuries, among them John Stuart Mill, associate justice with social utility, which raises the problem of balancing individual rights and interests with the common good (8.3).

11. Thomas Aquinas distinguished among divine (eternal), natural, and human law. He believed that one can break a human law if it is not consistent with a divine law or a natural law (8.4).

12. We enjoy freedom—that is, guarantees against state interference, such as the Bill of Rights (8.4).

13. Human rights are classified into negative and positive rights. Although everyone agrees that laws must be changed when they conflict with human rights, some hold that governments need only enforce people's negative rights, whereas others hold that governments are obligated to also provide for people's positive rights (8.4).

A recurrent topic in our discussion has been that of individualism. Indeed, individualism has been the most influential social philosophy of freedom in the modern West. Whether we talk of our economic, religious, or political life, the emphasis is on the individual. It will not be out of place if we end by commenting briefly on where this philosophy has led us.

The purposes of individualism seem commendable enough. As sociologist Robert Nisbet once pointed out in *The Quest for Community*, "No fault is to be found with the declared purposes of individualism. As a philosophy it has correctly emphasized the fact that the ultimate criteria of freedom lie in the greater or lesser degrees of autonomy possessed by *persons*. A conception of freedom that does not center upon the ethical primacy of the person is either naive or malevolent."[33]

---

[33] This and other Nisbet quotations are from Robert Nisbet, *The Quest for Community* (New York: Oxford University Press, 1953).

But, as Nisbet observed, the unquestioned ethical centrality of the individual does not make the philosophy of individualism valid. When the fundamental principles of individualism were being formulated in the doctrine of classical liberalism, the human was viewed as a self-sufficient, rational being who moves inexorably toward freedom and order. In short, the human was idealized as being naturally equipped with both the instincts and the reason that could make an individual autonomous. In retrospect, we can now see how thinkers regarded the individual as independent of the influences of any historically developed social organization.

Recall Hobbes. With the laws of mechanics and motions before him, Hobbes reduced society and its institutions to human atoms in motion. Just as the physical scientists of the day dealt with physical atoms in space, so Hobbes tried to build theoretical systems on human atoms alone. Like others, he strived to develop his social and political thought from the purest resources of reason, from the rigorous development of potentialities that reason taught lay everywhere in human nature. Locke and Rousseau also conceived of the individual as having powers and capacities that were not dependent on, or derived from, the social groups to which the individual belonged. Rawls, too, remains in this tradition.

As Nisbet sees it, institutions and groups were rendered secondary, "as shadows, so to speak, of the solid reality of men," to the inherent rationality and self-sufficiency of humans. Inevitably, the strategy of freedom became one of releasing individuals from institutional shackles. In short, although the philosophy of individualism began with an emphasis on the ethical primacy of the individual, it evolved into a philosophy bent on freeing individuals from traditional associations and cultures. Only in this way, it was argued, could the truly free individual unfold.

Ultimately, the price of individual freedom was detachment from the world, a defining of society in strictly objective, impersonal terms. What we have, then, is something quite remarkable—in Nisbet's words, "the conception of society as an aggregate of morally autonomous, psychologically free individuals, rather than as a collection of groups." The truth of this observation is apparent in the thinking of nineteenth-century English liberals, nearly all of whom conceived of freedom as emancipation from custom, tradition, and every kind of local group. In short, freedom lay outside association, not within. Mill is a perfect example of this thinking. In *On Liberty* he clearly implies that community or association membership is an unfortunate restriction on the individual's creative powers.

Even a cursory look at the studies in modern social psychology reveals increasing numbers of people seeking communal refuge. Numerous studies of community and family disorganization, personality disorientation, industrial alienation, and dissolution of ethnic subcultures have provided evidence for our preoccupation with social disintegration. Other studies have detailed the rise of the broken family and the decline of traditional nuclear and extended families (parents, children, and other blood relatives living in a household). "However empirical his studies of social relationships," Nisbet writes, "however bravely he rearranges the semantic elements of his terminology to support the

What experience and history teach us is this—that people and government never have learned anything from history, or acted on principles deduced from it.

G. W. F. HEGEL

In the new age, the dominant note in the corporate consciousness of communities is a sense of being parts of some larger universe, whereas, in the age which is now over the dominant note in their consciousness was an aspiration to be universes in themselves.

ARNOLD TOYNBEE

belief in his own moral detachment, and however confidently he may sometimes look to the salvational possibilities of political legislation for moral relief, it is plain that the contemporary student of human relations is haunted by perceptions of disorganization and the possibility of endemic collapse." Many years ago, Kingsley Davis, one of America's foremost sociologists, made the same point when he asked, "Can the anonymity, mobility, impersonality, specialization, and sophistication of the city become the attributes of a stable society, or will society fall apart?"[34]

Questions and observations like these indicate that the eighteenth- and nineteenth-century rationalist image of the human is inadequate. We realize today that we are not self-sufficient in social isolation and that an individual is vitally connected to social groups. We realize that these affiliations must be acknowledged. Our challenge is to create a society that allows people to live free private lives yet gives expression to their communal longings, that allows them to strike a proper balance between individual and society.

---

[34] Kingsley Davis, *Human Society* (New York: Macmillan, 1949), 342.

8.6   HISTORICAL SHOWCASE

Marx and Rawls

Two social philosophies tend to dominate much of our contemporary debate over the appropriate nature of our society: Marxism and liberalism. These two philosophies, in fact, tend to dominate much of the thinking of modern societies. The democratic and capitalist nations mainly adhere to the tenets of liberalism, whereas the socialist and communist nations continue to see themselves (even as they undergo tremendous changes) as adherents to the tenets of Marxism.

Therefore, it is appropriate for us to showcase in this chapter on society two thinkers—Karl Marx and John Rawls—who present and argue for the principles underlying these two dominant social philosophies. The writings of Marx are the origins of those social philosophies that call themselves Marxist, and John Rawls is considered by many to have articulated the central principles of modern liberalism.

MARX

Karl Marx, a seminal social philosopher of the modern age, is widely misunderstood. Marx was born in 1818 in Trier in the Rhineland to Jewish parents who, faced with anti-Semitism, turned Lutheran. After completing his studies at the gymnasium in Trier, Marx attended the universities of Bonn and Berlin.

When Marx entered the University of Berlin in 1836, the dominant intellectual influence throughout Germany and at the university was the philosophy of Georg Hegel (1770–1831). Central to Hegel's thought was the idea that reality is not fixed and static, but changing and dynamic. Life is constantly passing from one stage of being to another; the world is a place of constant change. But Hegel did not believe the change itself is arbitrary. On the contrary, he thought it proceeds according to a well-defined pattern or method, termed a *dialectic*.

The idea of the dialectic is that reality is full of contradictions. As reality unfolds, the contradictions are resolved and something new emerges. The procedure of the dialectical method can be represented as follows:

Thesis: assertion of position or affirmation

Antithesis: assertion of opposite position or negation

Synthesis: union of the two opposites

The Hegelian dialectic presumably expresses the process of development that Hegel believed pervades everything. By this account, there is only one reality: Idea. The only thing that is real is the rational; the Idea is thought itself thinking itself out. The process of thought thinking itself out is the dialectic.

In thinking itself out, thought arrives at the main antithesis to itself: inert matter. At this point Idea objectifies itself in matter: it becomes Nature or, for Hegel, the creation of the world. Life is the first sign of synthesis. Thought reappears in matter, organizing plants and displaying conscious instinct in animals. Ultimately, thought arrives at self-consciousness in human beings. The dialectic continues through human history.

To understand a society or culture, therefore, it is crucial to recognize the dialectical process that is operating. Each period in the history of a culture or society has a character of its own. This character can be viewed as a stage in the development from what preceded it to what follows it. This development proceeds by mental or spiritual laws. In effect, a culture has a personality of its own. Indeed, by Hegel's reckoning, the whole world or all of reality can be identified with a single character or personality—with what Hegel variously called *the Absolute, world self*, or *God* (taken in a pantheistic sense). All of human history, then, can be viewed as the progressive realization of this Absolute Spirit that is the synthesis of the thesis, Idea thinking itself out, with the antithesis, Idea spread out into Nature.

While at the University of Berlin, Marx read Hegel's complete works. He was drawn to a revolu-

Karl Marx: **"What constitutes the alienation of labor? First, that the work is *external* to the worker, that it is not part of his nature; and that, consequently, he does not fulfill himself in his work but denies himself, has a feeling of misery rather than well-being, does not develop freely his mental and physical energies but is physically exhausted and mentally debased."**

tionary aspect of Hegel's philosophy, namely, that history moves through a dialectical process of development. Marx also joined the Berlin Club of Young Hegelians, but soon became convinced that philosophy alone was inadequate to change the world. What was needed was social and political action.

After completing his doctoral dissertation in 1841, Marx turned to socialistic journalism, taking an editorial position in 1842 at the *Rheinische Zeitung (Rhineland Gazette)*. In this position, Marx became familiar with the social problems of the day and deepened the social orientation of his thought. Soon he became editor-in-chief of the newspaper and took it in a radical direction, conducting a campaign against Christian religion and the Christian state. As a result, the newspaper was shut down by the state censor in March 1843.

The suppression of the *Rheinische Zeitung* marked a new period in Marx's intellectual development, during which he began to formulate his materialistic concept of history and eventually became a communist. Also during this time, which he spent in Paris, Marx turned to a critical examination of Hegelian thought and in 1843 published an article on the subject: "Introduction to the Critique of Hegel's Philosophy." The article portrayed religion as an illusion resulting from the fact that the world is alienated and estranged from its real nature. Total revolution, Marx argued, is necessary to emancipate society from this condition.

Marx's critique of Hegel was significantly influenced by the work of Ludwig Feuerbach (1804–1872). In his *Essence of Christianity* (1841), Feuerbach had tried to show that Hegel's idealism was wrongheaded in that it had succeeded in eliminating physical reality. By contrast, Feuerbach held that philosophy is the science of reality, which consists of physical nature. Part of the illusion Feuerbach saw in Hegel was Hegel's belief in Absolute Spirit or God progressively realizing itself in history. In fact, according to Feuerbach, the ideas of religion are produced by human beings as a reflection of their own needs. Because individuals are dissatisfied or "alienated" in their practical lives, they need to believe in illusions such as those fostered in Hegelian philosophy. Thus, metaphysics is no more than an "esoteric psychology"; it is the expression of feelings within ourselves rather than truths about the universe. In particular, religion is the expression of alienation. Individuals can be freed from the illusions of religion only by realizing their purely human destiny in this world.

Feuerbach's influence on Marx was so great that Marx grew convinced that dialectical philosophy would avoid idealism by starting from human reality rather than from an ideal Absolute Spirit. Also, it could avoid mechanistic materialism by taking the concrete nature of the human being as its initial principle.

Although his reading of Feuerbach altered Marx's view of Hegel, Marx did preserve Hegel's notions of historical development and of alienation. These he wove into his own materialist concept of history. Like Hegel, Marx saw historical development operating in everything, but this development was material in character, not spiritual. The key to all history lay not in the individual's idea but in the economic conditions of his or her life. Again, while adopting Hegel's notion of alienation, Marx did not see it as metaphysical or religious in nature, but social and economic.

Marx's view of alienation can be found in his "Economic and Philosophic Manuscripts" (1844). His materialistic concepts of history can be found in various works of the same period: *The Holy Family* (1845), *The German Ideology* (1846), and *The Poverty of Philosophy* (1847). Until recently, Marx was best known as the author of *Das Kapital* (1867) and the *Communist Manifesto* (1848), which he wrote with friend and collaborator Friedrich Engels. Today, largely as a result of the publication of his early writings, the philosophical aspect of Marx's work has caught scholars' attention. Indeed, it is now thought that Marx's later writings cannot be fully understood and interpreted without reference to his earlier works, especially "Economic and Philosophic Manuscripts" and *The German Ideology*.

View of History

Distinctive in Marx's understanding of the world as a whole is his interpretation of history. Marx was firmly convinced that he had discovered a scientific method for studying the history of human societies, that eventually there would be a single science that combined the science of mankind with natural science. Accordingly, he held that there are universal laws behind historical change. Just as we can predict natural events like eclipses, we can predict the future large-scale course of history from a knowledge of these laws. Just as physicists aim to uncover the natural laws of the universe, so Marx believed that he was laying bare the economic laws of modern society, the material laws of capitalist production. These laws, presumably, are working with iron necessity toward inevitable results.

Like Hegel, Marx held that each period in each culture has its own character and personality.

Therefore, the only true universal laws in history are those concerned with the process by which one stage gives rise to the next. He viewed this developmental process as roughly divided into the Asiatic, the ancient, the feudal, and the "bourgeois" or capitalist phases. When conditions are right, said Marx, each stage must give way to the next. Ultimately, capitalism will give way to communism. Writing with Engels in the *Communist Manifesto*, Marx puts it this way:

> *The history of all hitherto existing society is the history of class struggles.*
>
> Freeman and slave, patrician and plebian, lord and serf, guild-master and journeyman, in a word, oppressor and oppressed, stood in constant opposition to one another, carried on an uninterrupted, now hidden, now open fight, a fight that each time ended, either in a revolutionary re-constitution of society at large, or in the common ruin of the contending classes.
>
> In the earlier epochs of history, we find almost everywhere a complicated arrangement of society into various orders, a manifold gradation of social rank. In ancient Rome we have patricians, knights, plebians, slaves; in the middle ages, feudal lords, vassals, guild-masters, journeymen, apprentices, serfs; in almost all of these classes, again, subordinate gradations.
>
> The modern bourgeois society that has sprouted from the ruins of feudal society, has not done away with class antagonisms. It has but established new classes, new conditions of oppression, new forms of struggle in place of the old ones.
>
> Our epoch, the epoch of the bourgeoisie, possesses, however, this distinctive feature; it has simplified the class antagonisms. Society as a whole is more and more splitting up into two great hostile camps, into two great classes directly facing each other: Bourgeoisie and Proletariat.[1]

Marx believed that the universal laws operating in history are economic in nature. Moreover, he saw a causal connection between the economic structure and everything in society such that the mode of production of material life determines the general character of the social, political, and spiritual processes of life. In a word, the economic structure is the real basis by which everything else about society is determined.

Based on this view of history, Marx predicted that capitalism will become increasingly unstable economically. The class struggle between the *bourgeoisie* (ownership class) and *proletariat* (working class) will increase, with the proletariat getting both poorer and larger in number. The upshot will be a social revolution: The workers will seize power and eventually institute the new communist phase of history.

View of Human Nature

Related to Marx's view of history is his view of human nature, which we alluded to in Chapter 2. Apart from some obvious biological factors, such as the need to eat, Marx denies the existence of any essential human nature — that is, something that is true of every individual at all times everywhere. He does allow, however, that humans are social beings, that to speak of human nature is really to speak about the totality of social relations. Accordingly, whatever any of us does is a social act, which presupposes the existence of other people standing in certain relations to us. In short, everything is socially learned.

The social influence is especially apparent in every activity of production. Producing what we need to survive physically is a social activity: It always requires that we interact and cooperate with others. Given Marx's account, it follows that the kind of individuals we are and the kinds of things we do are determined by the kind of society in which we live. In other words, for Marx it isn't the consciousness of individuals that defines their beings, but their social being that determines their consciousness. In commenting incisively on this point, professor of philosophy Leslie Stevenson has written the following:

> In modern terms, we can summarize this crucial point by saying that sociology is not reducible to psychology, i.e., it is not the case that everything about men can be explained in terms of facts about individuals; the kind of society they live in must be considered too. This methodological point is one of

---

[1] Karl Marx and Friedrich Engels, *Communist Manifesto*, trans. Samuel Moore (Chicago: Regnery, 1969).

Marx's most distinctive contributions, and one of the most widely accepted. For this reason alone, he must be recognized as one of the founding fathers of sociology. And the *method* can of course be accepted whether or not one agrees with the particular *conclusions* Marx came to about economics and politics.[2]

Professor Stevenson goes on to point out that despite Marx's denial of individual human nature, Marx is prepared to offer at least one generalization about human nature. It is that humans are active, productive beings who distinguish themselves from other animals by the central, overriding fact that they produce their own means of subsistence. Indeed, according to Marx, it is not only natural for humans to work for their livings but *right* as well. Thus, by Marx's account, the life of productive activity is the right one for humans.

Granted that it is proper for humans to work for their livings, what may be said about the product of that work? Like Locke before him and numerous other thinkers after him (including Rawls and Nozick), Marx thought that individuals have a legitimate claim to the product of their own labor. But Marx rejects the notion that they are entitled to own property that they have not personally produced. Neither is property ownership permissible when it enriches the already affluent at the expense of other people, thereby forcing these people to work without benefit of the products of their labor. But this, according to Marx, is precisely what capitalism encourages: the exploitation of the large working class (proletariat) at the hands of the affluent few who own the means of production (bourgeoisie). Again, here are Marx and Engels writing on this subject in the *Communist Manifesto*:

The bourgeoisie, wherever it has got the upper hand, has put an end to all feudal, patriarchal, idyllic relations. It has pitilessly torn asunder the motley feudal ties that bound man to his "natural superiors," and has left remaining no other nexus between man and man than naked self-interest, callous "cash payment." It has drowned the most heavenly ecstasies of religious fervor, of chivalrous enthusiasm, of Philis-

tine sentimentalism, in the icy water of egotistical calculation. It has resolved personal worth into exchange value, and in place of the numberless indefeasible chartered freedoms, has set up that single, unconscionable freedom—Free Trade. In one word, for exploitation, veiled by religious and political illusions, it has substituted naked, shameless, direct, brutal exploitation.

The bourgeoisie has stripped of its halo every occupation hitherto honored and looked up to with reverent awe. It has converted the physician, the lawyer, the priest, the poet, the name of science, into its paid wage-laborers.

The bourgeoisie has torn away from the family its sentimental veil, and has reduced the family relation to a mere money relation.

The bourgeoisie has disclosed how it came to pass that the brutal display of vigor in the Middle Ages, which Reactionists so much admire, found its fitting complement in the most slothful indolence. It has been the first to show what man's activity can bring about. It has accomplished wonders far surpassing Egyptian pyramids, Roman aqueducts, and Gothic cathedrals; it has conducted expeditions that put in the shade all former Exoduses of nations and crusades.

The bourgeoisie cannot exist without constantly revolutionizing the instruments of production, and thereby the relations of production, and with them the whole relations of society. Conservation of the old modes of production in unaltered form, was, on the contrary, the first condition of existence for all earlier industrial classes. Constant revolutionizing of production, uninterrupted disturbance of all social conditions, everlasting uncertainty and agitation distinguish the bourgeois epoch from all earlier ones. All fixed, fast-frozen relations, with their train of ancient and venerable prejudices and opinions, are swept away, all new-formed ones become antiquated before they can ossify. All that is solid melts into air, all that is holy is profaned, and man is at last compelled to face, with sober senses, his real conditions of life, and his relations with his kind.

The need of a constantly expanding market for its products chases the bourgeoisie over the whole surface of the globe. It must nestle everywhere, settle everywhere, establish connections everywhere.

The bourgeoisie has through its exploitation of the world-market given a cosmopolitan character to production and consumption in every country. To the great chagrin of Reactionists, it has drawn from under the feet of industry the national ground

---

[2]Leslie Stevenson, *Seven Theories of Human Nature* (London: Oxford University Press, 1974), 54.

on which it stood. All old-fashioned national industries have been destroyed and are daily being destroyed. They are dislodged by new industries, whose introduction becomes a life and death question for all civilized nations, by industries that no longer work up indigenous raw material, but raw material drawn from the remotest zones; industries whose products are consumed, not only at home, but in every quarter of the globe. In place of the old wants, satisfied by the productions of the country, we find new wants, requiring for their satisfaction the products of distant lands and climes. In place of the old local and national seclusion and self-sufficiency, we have intercourse in every direction, universal interdependence of nations. And as in material, so also in intellectual production. The intellectual creations of individual nations become common property. National one-sidedness and narrow-mindedness become more and more impossible, and from the numerous national and local literatures there arises a world-literature.

The bourgeoisie, by the rapid improvement of all instruments of production, by the immensely facilitated means of communication, draws all, even the most barbarian, nations into civilization. The cheap prices of its commodities are the heavy artillery with which it batters down all Chinese walls, with which it forces the barbarians' intensely obstinate hatred of foreigners to capitulate. It compels all nations, on pain of extinction, to adopt the bourgeois mode of production; it compels them to introduce what it calls civilization into their midst, i.e., to become bourgeois themselves. In a word, it creates a world after its own image.

The bourgeoisie has subjected the country to the rule of the towns. It has created enormous cities, has greatly increased the urban population as compared with the rural, and has thus rescued a considerable part of the population from the idiocy of rural life. Just as it has made the country dependent on the towns, so it has made barbarian and semi-barbarian countries dependent on the civilized ones, nations of peasants on nations of bourgeois, the East on the West.

The bourgeoisie keeps more and more doing away with the scattered state of the population, of the means of production, and of property. It has agglomerated population, centralized means of production, and has concentrated property in a few hands. The necessary consequence of this was political centralization. Independent, or but loosely connected provinces, with separate interests, laws, governments and systems of taxation, became lumped together in one nation, with one government, one code of laws, one national class-interest, one frontier and one customs-tariff.

The bourgeoisie, during its rule of scarce one hundred years, has created more massive and more colossal productive forces than have all preceding generations together. Subjection of Nature's forces to man, machinery, application of chemistry to industry and agriculture, steam-navigation, railways, electric telegraphs, clearing of whole continents for cultivation, canalization of rivers, whole populations conjured out of the ground—what earlier century had even a presentiment that such productive forces slumbered in the lap of social labor?[3]

According to Marx, the result of bourgeois exploitation is alienation, a key concept in his political and social philosophy.

Concept of Alienation

Marx borrowed his notion of alienation from Hegel and also from Feuerbach. For Hegel, alienation has its roots in a distinction between a subject and supposedly alien object. For Marx, the human can be considered the subject; and nature, that is, the human-created world, can be viewed as object. Humans are alienated from nature, from the world and the social relations they create. What is the cause of this alienation? Marx is rather fuzzy about this. At one point he traces its roots to the ownership of private property. Elsewhere he says that private property is not the cause but the effect of alienation. Whether private property is a cause or effect of alienation, one thing is evident: Marx associates alienation with economics, with the ownership of private property. Specifically, alienation consists of individuals not fulfilling themselves in work. Rather, because work is imposed on them as a means of satisfying the needs of others, they feel exploited and debased. What about workers who are paid handsomely for their efforts? Nevertheless, says Marx, they remain estranged. Insofar as the fruits of their labor are enjoyed by someone else, the work ultimately proves meaningless to them.

---

[3] Marx and Engels, *Communist Manifesto*.

In the following selection from his "Economic and Philosophic Manuscripts," Marx summarizes his notion of alienation as the separation of individuals from the objects they create, which in turn results in separation from other people and ultimately from oneself:

We shall begin from a *contemporary* economic fact. The worker becomes poorer the more wealth he produces and the more his production increases in power and extent. The worker becomes an ever cheaper commodity the more goods he creates. The *devaluation* of the human world increases in direct relation with the *increase in value* of the world of things. Labor does not only create goods; it also produces itself and the worker as a *commodity*, and indeed in the same proportion as it produces goods. . . .

All these consequences follow from the fact that the worker is related to the *product of his labor* as to an *alien* object. For it is clear on this presupposition that the more the worker expends himself in work the more powerful becomes the world of objects which he creates in face of himself, the poorer he becomes in his inner life, and the less he belongs to himself. It is just the same as in religion. The more of himself man attributes to God the less he has left in himself. The worker puts his life into the object, and his life then belongs no longer to himself but to the object. The greater his activity, therefore, the less he possesses. What is embodied in the product of his labor is no longer his own. The greater this product is, therefore, the more he is diminished. The *alienation* of the worker in his product means not only that his labor becomes an object, assumes an *external* existence, but that it exists independently, *outside himself*, and alien to him, and that it stands opposed to him as an autonomous power. The life which he has given to the object sets itself against him as an alien and hostile force. . . .

The worker becomes a slave of the object; first, in that he receives an *object of work*, i.e., receives *work*, and secondly, in that he receives *means of subsistence*. Thus the object enables him to exist, first as a *worker*, and secondly, as a *physical subject*. The culmination of this enslavement is that he can only maintain himself as a *physical subject* so far as he is a *worker*, and that it is only as a *physical subject* that he is a worker. . . .

What constitutes the alienation of labor? First, that the work is *external* to the worker, that it is not part of his nature; and that, consequently, he does not fulfill himself in his work but denies himself, has a feeling of misery rather than well-being, does not develop freely his mental and physical energies but is physically exhausted and mentally debased. The worker, therefore, feels himself at home only during his leisure time, whereas at work he feels homeless. His work is not voluntary but imposed, *forced labor*. It is not the satisfaction of a need, but only a *means* for satisfying other needs. Its alien character is clearly shown by the fact that as soon as there is no physical or other compulsion it is avoided like the plague. External labor, labor in which man alienates himself, is a labor of self-sacrifice, of mortification. Finally, the external character of work for the worker is shown by the fact that it is not his own work but work for someone else, that in work he does not belong to himself but to another person. . . .

We arrive at the result that man (the worker) feels himself to be freely active only in his animal functions — eating, drinking and procreating, or at most also in his dwelling and in personal adornment — while in his human functions he is reduced to an animal. The animal becomes human and the human becomes animal.

Eating, drinking and procreating are of course also genuine human functions. But abstractly considered, apart from the environment of human activities, and turned into final and sole ends, they are animal functions.

We have now considered the act of alienation of practical human activity, labor, from two aspects: (1) the relationship of the worker to the *product of labor* as an alien object which dominates him. This relationship is at the same time the relationship to the sensuous external world, to natural objects, as an alien and hostile world; (2) the relationship of labor to the *act of production* within *labor*. This is the relationship of the worker to his own activity as something alien and not belonging to him, activity as suffering (passivity), strength as powerlessness, creation as emasculation, the *personal* physical and mental energy of the worker, his personal life (for what is life but activity?), as an activity which is directed against himself; independent of him and not belonging to him. This is *self-alienation* as against the above-mentioned alienation of the *thing*.[4]

---

[4]Karl Marx, "The Economic and Philosophic Manuscripts of 1844," in *Karl Marx: Early Writings*, trans T. B. Bottomore. Copyright © T. B. Bottomore, 1963. Used with permission of McGraw-Hill Book Co.

Marx goes on to infer yet a third aspect of es-tranged labor from the preceding two: the estrange-ment of the individual from the species itself. But this needn't concern us here.

In Marx's view, when workers are alienated, they cannot be free. They may have the political and social freedoms of speech, religion, and gov-ernance that classical liberals delineate. But free-dom from government interference and persecu-tion does not necessarily guarantee freedom from economic exploitation. And it is for this kind of freedom, freedom from alienation, that Marx and Engels feel such passion.

Sense of Freedom

How can humans be free of alienation? To begin with, they must recognize that the key to freedom and the lack of it lies in economics. Therefore, hu-mans must return to a "natural" state in which they and their labor are one. This natural state is similar to Rousseau's in the sense that it recognizes the corrupting influence of society and calls for a con-ception of the state that will allow humans to be unselfish and nondestructive. But don't misunder-stand. Marx is not advocating the end of work. On the contrary, he holds that work is humanizing, en-nobling. Thus, he is urging people to liberate them-selves from alienated work. Without this kind of freedom, which is basically a freedom from material need, other freedoms are a sham.

Basically Marx prescribes a fairer distribution of wealth as a means for combating alienation and en-suring freedom. For Marx, justice requires that the means of production be owned by everyone. In un-varnished terms, in part this means no ownership of property except for those products a person makes directly. It also means an end to the worker/owner distinction, thereby making everyone a la-borer who shares in the benefits of his or her labor. Specifically, Marx calls for nationalization of land, factories, transport, and banks as a way of attaining freedom from alienation. But insofar as Marx pre-sumably believes that (1) the state is the basis of all social ills, and (2) nationalization evidently will exacerbate this by concentrating power in the hands of the state, it isn't at all clear how such in-stitutional changes could effect freedom. This ob-servation has led Leslie Stevenson to suggest that we understand Marx as saying

> at least in his early phase, that alienation consists in the lack of community. In other words, since the State is not a real community, individuals cannot see their work as contributing to a group of which they are members. It would follow that freedom from alienation would be won by decentralizing, not nationalizing, the State in genuine communities or "communes." These entities would be characterized by the abolition of money, specialization, and private property.[5]

Indeed, it may be this community element of Marx's vision that explains why Marx continues to win and hold followers. After all, it is difficult to disagree with such ideas as a decentralized society in which individuals cooperate in communities for the common good, technology is harnessed and di-rected for the interest of all, and the relationship between society and nature is harmonized. At the same time, Marx gives no good reason for assuming that the communist society will achieve any of these ideals. In fact, if the history of Russia in this century is any indication, quite the opposite seems the case.

RAWLS

A substantial part of the world's population today lives in societies that still claim to be based on the socialist views proposed by Marx. The rest of the world lives in societies that by and large follow a philosophy termed *liberalism*. Liberalism has its roots in the individualism of John Locke and John Stuart Mill. At the heart of early liberalism was the view that the best society is one in which individu-als are left free to pursue their own interests and fulfillment as each chooses. As Mill argued, the only restraints to which adult individuals should be subject are those necessary to keep one individual from harming others.

Contemporary liberalism has retained this fun-damental commitment to individual liberty but has added to it an awareness of the extent to which economic realities can indirectly limit an indi-

---

[5] Stevenson, *Seven Theories of Human Nature*, 58.

vidual's liberty. For example, the choices of a poor person are much restricted by that person's poverty, whereas wealth and property endow the rich with choices and power not available to the poor. Therefore, contemporary liberalism, has tended to incorporate the view that individuals can be constrained to provide economic support for the poor through welfare programs. Contemporary liberalism has also tended to accept the view that individuals should be given some protection against the economic power of the wealthy through laws that protect the worker. Undoubtedly, these contemporary modifications of liberalism have been greatly influenced by Marx. To a large extent, in fact, contemporary liberalism is the response that capitalist societies have made to Marx.

Perhaps the best representative of contemporary liberalism is John Rawls, a philosopher who teaches at Harvard University. In his now-classic work *A Theory of Justice,* Rawls presents a brilliant and often passionate argument in support of contemporary liberalism. Many philosophers hold, in fact, that the modern world is faced with a fundamental choice between two kinds of societies: the kind of socialist society advocated by Marx and the kind of liberal society advocated by Rawls.

Rawls was born in 1921 and received his doctorate in philosophy from Princeton University in 1950. From 1953 to 1959 he taught at Cornell University and then moved to Massachusetts Institute of Technology. Since 1962 he has been teaching philosophy at Harvard University.

For Rawls the most important question to ask about a society is this one: Is it just? The laws and institutions of a society must embody justice, or they must be reformed:

> Justice is the first virtue of social institutions, as truth is of systems of thought. A theory however elegant and economical must be rejected or revised if it is untrue; likewise laws and institutions no matter how efficient and well-arranged must be reformed or abolished if they are unjust. Each person possesses an inviolability founded on justice that even the welfare of society as a whole cannot override. For this reason justice denies that the loss of freedom for some is made right by a greater good shared by others. It does not allow that the sacrifices imposed on a few are outweighed by the larger sum of advantages enjoyed

by many. Therefore in a just society the liberties of equal citizenship are taken as settled; the rights secured by justice are not subject to political bargaining or to the calculus of social interests. The only thing that permits us to acquiesce in an erroneous theory is the lack of a better one; analogously, an injustice is tolerable only when it is necessary to avoid an even greater injustice. Being first virtues of human activities, truth and justice are uncompromising.[6]

If we are to analyze the justice of society, Rawls claims, we must look not at the particular actions of individuals, but at society's basic political, economic, and social *institutions.* Like Marx, Rawls acknowledges that social relationships have a deep and profound effect on the individual's sense of fulfillment. A society's institutions are what primarily determine what we can do and what our lives as individuals will be like. From the very beginning they favor some of us and hamper others:

> Many different kinds of things are said to be just and unjust: not only laws, institutions, and social systems, but also particular actions of many kinds, including decisions, judgments, and imputations. We also call the attitudes and dispositions of persons, and persons themselves, just and unjust. Our topic, however, is that of social justice. For us the primary subject of justice is the basic structure of society, or more exactly, the way in which the major social institutions distribute fundamental rights and duties and determine the division of advantages from social cooperation. By major institutions I understand the political constitution and the principal economic and social arrangements. Thus the legal protection of freedom of thought and liberty of conscience, competitive markets, private property in the means of production, and the monogamous family are examples of major social institutions. Taken together as one scheme, the major institutions define men's rights and duties and influence their life-prospects, what they can expect to be and how well they can hope to do. The basic structure is the primary subject of justice because its effects are so profound and present from the start. The intuitive notion here is that this structure contains various social positions and

---

[6] John Rawls, *A Theory of Justice* (Cambridge, MA: Harvard University Press, 1972), 3–4. Reprinted by permission of Harvard University Press. © 1971 by the President and Fellows of Harvard College. All rights reserved.

that men born into different positions have different expectations of life determined, in part, by the political system as well as by economic and social circumstances. In this way the institutions of society favor certain starting places over others. These are especially deep inequalities. Not only are they persuasive, but they affect men's initial chances in life; yet they cannot possibly be justified by an appeal to the notions of merit or desert. It is these inequalities, presumably inevitable in the basic structure of any society, to which the principles of social justice must in the first instance apply. These principles, then, regulate the choice of a political constitution and the main elements of the economic and social system. The justice of a social scheme depends essentially on how fundamental rights and duties are assigned and on the economic opportunities and social conditions in the various sectors of society.[7]

But what principles and rules should govern our social institutions? What guidelines and formulas should we follow when designing our institutions if those institutions are to be just? Rawls argues that to discover what just institutions should be like, we should engage in a kind of imaginary experiment. Imagine, he says, that before people formed a society, they could all gather together in a large meeting. And suppose that at this imaginary first meeting (or "original position") no one knew what place each person would have in their future society. No one knew whether he or she would turn out to be rich or poor, owner or worker, ruler or ruled. In fact, suppose that no one knew even whether he or she would turn out to be male or female, intelligent or stupid, healthy or sick, strong or weak, black or white. Suppose, that is, that everyone at this original meeting is "behind a veil of ignorance," where no one knows what each will be like in the future society.

Suppose, then, that the people at this original meeting had to choose the basic rules or principles that would govern their future society. Clearly, Rawls says, the parties in such an original position would have to be perfectly fair to everyone, since no one would know who he or she might turn out to be. In such a situation, a person would not choose principles that favor whites over blacks,

since in their future society that person might turn out to be black. Nor would a person choose principles that favor the rich over the poor since the person might turn out to be poor. In short, the "veil of ignorance" would force everyone to choose principles that would be perfectly just to everyone:

> Thus we are to imagine that those who engage in social cooperation choose together, in one joint act, the principles which are to assign basic rights and duties and to determine the division of social benefits. Men are to decide in advance how they are to regulate their claims against one another and what is to be the foundation charter of their society. Just as each person must decide by rational reflection what constitutes his good, that is, the system of ends which it is rational for him to pursue, so a group of persons must decide once and for all what is to count among them as just and unjust. The choice which rational men would make in this hypothetical situation of equal liberty, assuming for the present that this choice problem has a solution, determines the principles of justice.
>
> In justice as fairness the original position of equality corresponds to the state of nature in the traditional theory of the social contract. This original position is not, of course, thought of as an actual historical state of affairs, much less as a primitive condition of culture. It is understood as a purely hypothetical situation characterized so as to lead to a certain conception of justice. Among the essential features of this situation is that no one knows his place in society, his class position or social status, nor does any one know his fortune in the distribution of natural assets and abilities, his intelligence, strength, and the like. I shall even assume that the parties do not know their conceptions of the good or their special psychological propensities. The principles of justice are chosen behind a veil of ignorance. This ensures that no one is advantaged or disadvantaged in the choice of principles by the outcome of natural chance or the contingency of social circumstances. Since all are similarly situated and no one is able to design principles to favor his particular condition, the principles of justice are the result of a fair agreement or bargain. For given the circumstances of the original position, the symmetry of everyone's relations to each other, this initial situation is fair between individuals as moral persons, that is, as rational beings with their own ends and capable, I shall assume, of a sense of justice. The original position is,

---

[7] Ibid., 7.

one might say, the appropriate initial status quo, and thus the fundamental agreements reached in it are fair. This explains the propriety of the name "justice as fairness": it conveys the idea that the principles of justice are agreed to in an initial situation that is fair. The name does not mean that the concepts of justice and fairness are the same, any more than the phrase "poetry as metaphor" means that the concept of poetry and metaphor are the same.[8]

Rawls then argues that the imaginary parties to this original position would not choose utilitarian principles. Utilitarian principles, Rawls claims, sometimes require some people to suffer losses for the sake of maximizing society's utility. Clearly, a person in the original position would not agree to this since that person might turn out to be one of the people forced to suffer losses. Instead, Rawls claims, the parties would settle on these two principles of justice: first, that everyone in society must have equal political rights and duties, and second, that the only justifiable economic inequalities are those required to make everyone better off by serving as incentives:

> In working out the conception of justice as fairness one main task clearly is to determine which principles of justice would be chosen in the original position. To do this we must describe this situation in some detail and formulate with care the problem of choice which it presents. These matters I shall take up in the immediately succeeding chapters. It may be observed, however, that once the principles of justice are thought of as arising from an original agreement in a situation of equality, it is an open question whether the principle of utility would be acknowledged. Offhand it hardly seems likely that persons who view themselves as equals, entitled to press their claims upon one another, would agree to a principle which may require lesser life prospects for some simply for the sake of a greater sum of advantages enjoyed by others. Since each desires to protect his interests, his capacity to advance his conception of the good, no one has a reason to acquiesce in an enduring loss for himself in order to bring about a greater net balance of satisfaction. In the absence of strong and lasting benevolent impulses, a rational man would not accept a basic structure

merely because it maximized the algebraic sum of advantages irrespective of its permanent effects on his own basic rights and interests. Thus it seems that the principle of utility is incompatible with the conception of social cooperation among equals for mutual advantage. It appears to be inconsistent with the idea of reciprocity implicit in the notion of a well-ordered society. Or, at any rate, so I shall argue.

> I shall maintain instead that the persons in the initial situation would choose two rather different principles: the first requires equality in the assignment of basic rights and duties, while the second holds that social and economic inequalities, for example inequalities of wealth and authority, are just only if they result in compensating benefits for everyone, and in particular for the least advantaged members of society. These principles rule out justifying institutions on the grounds that the hardships of some are offset by a greater good in the aggregate. It may be expedient but it is not just that some should have less in order that others may prosper. But there is no injustice in the greater benefits earned by a few provided that the situation of persons not so fortunate is thereby improved. The intuitive idea is that since everyone's well-being depends upon a scheme of cooperation without which no one could have a satisfactory life, the division of advantages should be such as to draw forth the willing cooperation of everyone taking part in it, including those less well situated. Yet this can be expected only if reasonable terms are proposed. The two principles mentioned seem to be a fair agreement on the basis of which those better endowed, or more fortunate in their social position, neither of which we can be said to deserve, could expect the willing cooperation of others when some workable scheme is a necessary condition of the welfare of all. Once we decide to look for a conception of justice that nullifies the accidents of natural endowment and the contingencies of social circumstance as counters in quest for political and economic advantage, we are led to these principles. They express the result of leaving aside those aspects of the social world that seem arbitrary from a moral point of view.[9]

Rawls later elaborates his principles. The two principles of justice that would be chosen, he writes, can be formulated as follows:

---

[8] Ibid., 11–13.

[9] Ibid., 14–15.

First: each person is to have an equal right to the most extensive basic liberty compatible with a similar liberty for others. Second: social and economic inequalities are to be arranged so that they are both (a) to the greatest benefit of the least advantaged and (b) attached to offices and positions open to all under conditions of fair equality of opportunity.[10]

According to Rawls, the parties to the original position would choose the first principle, which requires equal political freedoms for everyone, because each person would want to at least be equal to everyone else in the political sphere. However, he claims, the parties would agree to allow social and *economic* inequalities if such "inequalities set up various incentives which succeed in eliciting more productive efforts" from people. For example, allowing higher wages for some people can spur them on to produce more goods, and this added productivity will work to everyone's benefit. But the parties to the original position will each want to have an equal chance at these more lucrative positions. Consequently, they will insist that these positions be "open to all under conditions of fair equality of opportunity." Moreover, the parties to the original position will want to protect themselves in case they turn out to be among the "least advantaged." So they will agree that the benefits produced by allowing inequalities should be used to protect the least advantaged.

Rawls's two principles, then, are the principles that he thought anyone—ourselves included—would choose if he or she were behind the "veil of ignorance." And since the original position requires us to be absolutely fair and just, these two principles are themselves just and express what justice requires of us.

And what does justice require of us, according to Rawls? Certainly not the kind of socialist state advocated by Marx, in which individuals are not free to own and exchange private property; in which all land, factories, transport, and banks are nationalized and controlled by the state; and in which free markets are prohibited. Nor does justice require an absolute equality. Instead, Rawls argues, justice re-

quires freedom and merely *political* equality. In particular, justice requires freedom from the interference of the state, and it allows (although it does not *require*) private property and free markets. Justice also allows *economic* inequalities, whereas it requires that the state must provide adequate welfare programs for the poor and the disadvantaged.

In short, justice requires and allows more or less what Western social, economic, and political institutions require and allow. This is perhaps not surprising, since Rawls's philosophy is intended to defend Western liberal ideals. It is, perhaps, the most powerful alternative to contemporary Marxism and the most powerful contemporary defense of liberalism.

QUESTIONS

1.   In your own words, explain what the bourgeoisie is and how it developed. Does the bourgeoisie exist today? Explain.

2.   To what extent does Marx's concept of alienation apply to modern workers? To what extent does it apply to modern college students? How would Marx analyze the contemporary trend toward careerism among today's college students (that is, the trend to see a college education as preparation for a job or a career instead of as a humanizing and liberating activity)?

3.   Explain in your own words what Rawls's "original position" is and why it is supposed to show us the meaning of justice. Do you agree that using the original position is an adequate way of determining what justice requires? Why? Do you think that Rawls's two principles of justice are adequate? Why?

4.   How do Rawls's views about society differ from Marx's? What assumptions do you think Marx and Rawls make that lead each of them to such different conclusions?

5.   What do you think Rawls would say about the justice or injustice of making pornography illegal? About making drugs such as marijuana and cocaine illegal? About nationalizing businesses? About the international problem of poverty?

[10] Ibid., 60, 83.

8.7 Readings

Is society justified in forcing people to do what they do not want to do? That is the question raised by William Carlos Williams's short story "The Use of Force," where, for her own good and for the "social necessity" of protecting others, a beautiful child is violently forced by a doctor and her parents to submit to a brutal examination that she valiantly fights against. At the end, when we see what force does to those who use it and to those on whom it is used, we are left wondering whether the use of force is ever justified. In the second reading, philosopher John Hospers, a libertarian philosopher, argues that society through its government is never justified in using force except to protect citizens against aggression by other individuals. Government has no right to force people to do what they do not want to do, either for their own good or to help others. And this implies that it is wrong for a society's government to force people not to use drugs, or to tax the unwilling rich to provide welfare for the poor. In the third reading, Malcolm X, the great American black leader, argues that the races should be in control of their own communities and that if nonviolent political methods ("the ballot") cannot secure such control, then violence and force ("the bullet") are a legitimate option. These readings, then, lead us to reflect on whether it is ever legitimate for a group to make anyone do anything against his or her will.

WILLIAM CARLOS WILLIAMS

The Use of Force

They were new patients to me, all I had was the name, Olson. Please come down as soon as you can, my daughter is very sick. When I arrived I was met by the mother, a big startled looking woman, very clean and apologetic who merely said, Is this the doctor? and let me in. In the back, she added. You must excuse us, doctor, we have her in the kitchen where it is warm. It is very damp here sometimes.

William Carlos Williams: "The Use of Force," from *The Doctor Stories*. Copyright © 1938 by William Carlos Williams. Reprinted by permission of New Directions Publishing Corporation.

The child was fully dressed and sitting on her father's lap near the kitchen table. He tried to get up, but I motioned for him not to bother, took off my overcoat and started to look things over. I could see that they were all very nervous, eyeing me up and down distrustfully. As often, in such cases, they weren't telling me more than they had to, it was up to me to tell them; that's why they were spending three dollars on me.

The child was fairly eating me up with her cold, steady eyes, and no expression to her face whatever. She did not move and seemed, inwardly, quiet; an unusually attractive little thing, and as strong as a heifer in appearance. But her face was flushed, she was breathing rapidly, and I realized that she had a high fever. She had magnificent blonde hair, in profusion. One of those picture children often reproduced in advertising leaflets and the photogravure sections of the Sunday papers.

She's had a fever for three days, began the father and we don't know what it comes from. My wife has given her things, you know, like people do, but it don't do no good. And there's been a lot of sickness around. So we tho't you'd better look her over and tell us what is the matter.

As doctors often do I took a trial shot at it as a point of departure. Has she had a sore throat?

Both parents answered me together. No . . . No, she says her throat don't hurt her.

Does your throat hurt you? added the mother to the child. But the little girl's expression didn't change nor did she move her eyes from my face.

Have you looked?

I tried to, said the mother, but I couldn't see.

As it happens we had been having a number of cases of diphtheria in the school to which this child went during that month and we were all, quite apparently, thinking of that, though no one had as yet spoken of the thing.

Well, I said, suppose we take a look at the throat first. I smiled in my best professional manner and asking for the child's first name I said, come on, Mathilda, open your mouth and let's take a look at your throat.

Nothing doing.

Aw, come on, I coaxed, just open your mouth wide and let me take a look. Look, I said opening both hands wide, I haven't anything in my hands. Just open up and let me see.

Such a nice man, put in the mother. Look how kind he is to you. Come on, do what he tells you to. He won't hurt you.

At that I ground my teeth in disgust. If only they wouldn't use the word "hurt" I might be able to get somewhere. But I did not allow myself to be hurried or disturbed but speaking quietly and slowly I approached the child again.

As I moved my chair a little nearer suddenly with one catlike movement both her hands clawed instinctively for my eyes and she almost reached them too. In fact she knocked my glasses flying and they fell, though unbroken, several feet away from me on the kitchen floor.

Both the mother and father almost turned themselves inside out in embarrassment and apology. You bad girl, said the mother, taking her and shaking her by one arm. Look what you've done. The nice man . . .

For heaven's sake, I broke in. Don't call me a nice man to her. I'm here to look at her throat on the chance that she might have diphtheria and possibly die of it. But that's nothing to her. Look here, I said to the child, we're going to look at your throat. You're old enough to understand what I'm saying. Will you open it now by yourself or shall we have to open it for you?

Not a move. Even her expression hadn't changed. Her breaths however were coming faster and faster. Then the battle began. I had to do it. I had to have a throat culture for her own protection. But first I told the parents that it was entirely up to them. I explained the danger but said that I would not insist on a throat examination so long as they would take the responsibility.

If you don't do what the doctor says you'll have to go to the hospital, the mother admonished her severely.

Oh yeah? I had to smile to myself. After all, I had already fallen in love with the savage brat, the parents were contemptible to me. In the ensuing struggle they grew more and more abject, crushed, exhausted while she surely rose to magnificent heights of insane fury of effort bred of her terror of me.

The father tried his best, and he was a big man but the fact that she was his daughter, his shame at her behavior and his dread of hurting her made him release her just at the critical times when I had almost achieved success, till I wanted to kill him. But his dread also that she might have diphtheria made him tell me to go on, go on though he himself was almost fainting, while the mother moved back and forth behind us raising and lowering her hands in an agony of apprehension.

Put her in front of you on your lap, I ordered, and hold both her wrists.

But as soon as he did the child let out a scream. Don't, you're hurting me. Let go of my hands. Let them go I tell you. Then she shrieked terrifyingly, hysterically. Stop it! Stop it! You're killing me!

Do you think she can stand it, doctor! said the mother.

You get out, said the husband to his wife. Do you want her to die of diphtheria?

Come on now, hold her, I said.

Then I grasped the child's head with my left hand and tried to get the wooden tongue depressor between her teeth. She fought, with clenched teeth, desperately! But now I also had grown furious—at a child. I tried to hold myself down but I couldn't. I know how to expose a throat for inspection. And I did my best. When finally I got the wooden spatula behind the last teeth and just the point of it into the mouth cavity, she opened up for an instant but before I could see anything she came down again and gripped the wooden blade between her molars she reduced it to splinters before I could get it out again.

Aren't you ashamed, the mother yelled at her. Aren't you ashamed to act like that in front of the doctor?

Get me a smooth-handled spoon of some sort, I told the mother. We're going through with this. The child's mouth was already bleeding. Her tongue was cut and she was screaming in wild hysterical shrieks. Perhaps I should have desisted and come back in an hour or more. No doubt it would have been better. But I have seen at least two children lying dead in bed of neglect in such cases, and feeling that I must get a diagnosis now or never I went at it again. But the worst of it was that I too had got beyond reason. I could have torn the child apart in my own fury and enjoyed it. It was a pleasure to attack her. My face was burning with it.

The damned little brat must be protected against her own idiocy, one says to one's self at such times. Others must be protected against her. It is a social necessity. And all these things are true. But a blind fury, a feeling of adult shame, bred of a longing for muscular release are the operatives. One goes on to the end.

In the final unreasoning assault I overpowered the child's neck and jaws. I forced the heavy silver spoon back of her teeth and down her throat till she gagged. And there it was—both tonsils covered with membrane. She had fought valiantly to keep me from knowing her secret. She had been hiding that sore throat for three days at least and lying to her parents in order to escape just such an outcome as this.

Now truly she was furious. She had been on the defensive before but now she attacked. Tried to get off her father's lap and fly at me while tears of defeat blinded her eyes.

JOHN HOSPERS

What Libertarianism Is

Government is the most dangerous institution known to man. Throughout history it has violated the rights of men more than any individual or group of individuals could do: it has killed people, enslaved them, sent them to forced labor and concentration camps, and regularly robbed and pillaged them of the fruits of their expended labor. Unlike individual criminals, government has the power to arrest and try; unlike individual criminals, it can surround and encompass a person totally, dominating every aspect of one's life, so that one has no recourse from it but to leave the country (and in totalitarian nations even that is prohibited). Government throughout history has a much sorrier record than any individual, even that of a ruthless mass murderer. The signs we see on bumper stickers are chillingly accurate: "Beware: the Government Is Armed and Dangerous."

The only proper role of government, according to libertarians, is that of the protector of the citizen against aggression by other individuals. The government, of course, should never initiate aggression; its proper role is as the embodiment of the *retaliatory* use of force against anyone who initiates its use. . . .

Government, then, undertakes to be the individual's protector; but historically governments have gone far beyond this function. Since they already have the physical power, they have not hesitated to use it for purposes far beyond that which was

From *The Libertarian Alternative*, ed. Tibor R. Machan (Chicago: Nelson-Hall Co., 1974), 12–20. Reprinted with permission.

entrusted to them in the first place. Undertaking initially to protect its citizens against aggression, it has often itself become an aggressor—a far greater aggressor, indeed, than the criminals against whom it was supposed to protect its citizens. Governments have done what no private citizen can do: arrest and imprison individuals without a trial and send them to slave labor camps. Government must have power in order to be effective—and yet the very means by which alone it can be effective make it vulnerable to the abuse of power, leading to managing the lives of individuals and even inflicting terror upon them.

What then should be the function of government? In a word, the *protection of human rights*.

1. *The right to life*: libertarians support all such legislation as will protect human beings against the use of force by others, for example, laws against killing, attempted killing, maiming, beating, and all kinds of physical violence.

2. *The right to liberty*: there should be no laws compromising in any way freedom of speech, of the press, and of peaceable assembly. There should be no censorship of ideas, books, films, or of anything else by government.

3. *The right to property*: libertarians support legislation that protects the property rights of individuals against confiscation, nationalization, eminent domain, robbery, trespass, fraud and misrepresentation, patent and copyright, libel and slander.

Someone has violently assaulted you. Should he be legally liable? Of course. He has violated one of your rights. He has knowingly injured you, and since he has initiated aggression against you he should be made to expiate.

Someone has negligently left his bicycle on the sidewalk where you trip over it in the dark and injure yourself. He didn't do it intentionally; he didn't mean you any harm. Should he be legally liable? Of course; he has, however unwittingly, injured you, and since the injury is caused by him and you are the victim, he should pay.

Someone across the street is unemployed. Should you be taxed extra to pay for his expenses? Not at all. You have not injured him, you are not responsible for the fact that he is unemployed (unless you are a senator or bureaucrat who agitated for further curtailing of business, which legislation passed, with the result that your neighbor was laid off by the curtailed business). You may voluntarily wish to help him out, or better still, try to get him a job to put him on his feet again; but since you have initiated no aggressive act against him, and neither purposely nor accidentally injured him in any way, you should not be legally penalized for the fact of his unemployment. (Actually, it is just such penalties that increase unemployment.) . . .

Laws may be classified into three types: (1) laws protecting individuals against themselves, such as laws against fornication and other sexual behavior, alcohol, and drugs; (2) laws protecting individuals against aggressions by other individuals, such as laws against murder, robbery, and fraud; (3) laws requiring people to help one another; for example, all laws which rob Peter to pay Paul, such as welfare.

Libertarians reject the first class of laws totally. Behavior which harms no one else is strictly the individual's own affair. Thus, there should be no laws against becoming intoxicated, since whether or not to become intoxicated is the individual's own decision; but there should be laws against driving while intoxicated, since the drunken driver is a threat to every other motorist on the highway (drunken driving falls into type 2). Similarly, there should be no laws against drugs (except the prohibition of sale of drugs to minors) as long as the taking of these drugs poses no threat to anyone else. Drug addiction is a psychological problem to which no present solution exists. Most of the social harm caused by addicts, other than to themselves, is the result of thefts which they perform in order to continue their habit—and then the *legal* crime is the theft, not the addiction. The actual cost of heroin is about ten cents a shot; if it were legalized, the enormous traffic in illegal sale and purchase of it would stop, as well as the accompanying proselytization to get new addicts (to make more money for the pusher) and the thefts performed by addicts who often require eighty dollars a day just to keep up the habit. Addiction would not stop, but the crimes would: it is estimated that 75 percent of the burglaries in New York City today are performed by addicts, and all these crimes could be wiped out at one stroke through the legalization of drugs. (Only when the taking of drugs could be shown to constitute a threat to *others*, should it be prohibited by law. It is only laws protecting people against *themselves* that libertarians oppose.)

Laws should be limited to the second class only: aggression by individuals against other individuals. These are laws whose function is to protect human beings against encroachment by others; and this, as we have seen, is (according to libertarianism) the sole function of government.

Libertarians also reject the third class of laws totally: no one should be forced by law to help others, not even to tell them the time of day if requested, and certainly not to give them a portion of one's weekly paycheck. Governments, in the guise of humanitarianism, have given to some by taking from others (charging a "handling fee" in the process, which, because of the government's waste and inefficiency, sometimes is several hundred percent). And in so doing they have decreased incentive, violated the rights of individuals, and lowered the standard of living of almost everyone. . . .

It has become fashionable to claim virtually everything that one needs or desires as one's *right*. Thus, many people claim that they have a right to a job, the right to free medical care, to free food and clothing, to a decent home, and so on. Now if one asks, apart from any specific context, whether it would be desirable if everyone had these things, one might well say yes. But there is a gimmick attached to each of them: *At whose expense?* Jobs, medical care, education, and so on, don't grow on trees. These are goods and services *produced only by men*. Who, then, is to provide them, and under what conditions?

If you have a right to a job, who is to supply it? Must an employer supply it even if he doesn't want to hire you? What if you are unemployable, or incurably lazy? (If you say "the government must supply it," does that mean that a job must be created for you which no employer needs done, and that you must be kept in it regardless of how much or little you work?) If the employer is forced to supply it at his expense even if he doesn't need you,

then isn't *he* being enslaved to that extent? What ever happened to *his* right to conduct his life and his affairs in accordance with his choices?

If you have a right to free medical care, then, since medical care doesn't exist in nature as wild apples do, some people will have to supply it to you for free: that is, they will have to spend their time and money and energy taking care of you whether they want to or not. What ever happened to *their* right to conduct their lives as they see fit? Or do you have a right to violate theirs? Can there be a right to violate rights?

All those who demand this or that as a "free service" are consciously or unconsciously evading the fact that there is in reality no such thing as free services. All man-made goods and services are the result of human expenditure of time and effort. There is no such thing as "something for nothing" in this world. If you demand something free, you are demanding that other men give their time and effort to you without compensation. If they voluntarily choose to do this, there is no problem; but if you demand that they be *forced* to do it, you are interfering with their right not to do it if they so choose. . . .

MALCOLM X

The Ballot or the Bullet

This government has failed the Negro. This so-called democracy has failed the Negro. And all these white liberals have definitely failed the Negro.

So, where do we go from here? First, we need some friends. We need some new allies. The entire civil-rights struggle needs a new interpretation, a broader interpretation. We need to look at this

From *Malcolm X Speaks*, ed. George Breitman (New York: Grove Press, 1965). Copyright © 1965, 1989 by Betty Shabazz and Pathfinder Press. Reprinted by permission.

civil-rights thing from another angle—from the inside as well as from the outside. To those of us whose philosophy is black nationalism, the only way you can get involved in the civil-rights struggle is give it a new interpretation. That old interpretation excluded us. It kept us out. So, we're giving a new interpretation to the civil-rights struggle, an interpretation that will enable us to come into it, take part in it. And these handkerchief-heads who have been dillydallying and pussyfooting and compromising—we don't intend to let them pussyfoot and dillydally and compromise any longer.

And now you're facing a situation where the young Negro's coming up. They don't want to hear that "turn-the-other-cheek" stuff, no. In Jacksonville, those were teenagers, they were throwing Molotov cocktails. Negroes have never done that before. But it shows you there's a new deal coming in. There's new thinking coming in. There's new strategy coming in. It'll be Molotov cocktails this month, hand grenades next month, and something else next month. It'll be ballots, or it'll be bullets. It'll be liberty, or it will be death. The only difference about this kind of death—it'll be reciprocal. You know what is meant by "reciprocal"? . . . I don't usually deal with those big words because I don't usually deal with big people. I deal with small people. I find you can get a whole lot of small people and whip hell out of a whole lot of big people. They haven't got anything to lose, and they've got everything to gain. And they'll let you know in a minute: "It takes two to tango; when I go, you go."

The black nationalists, those whose philosophy is black nationalism, in bringing about this new interpretation of the entire meaning of civil rights, look upon it as meaning . . . equality of opportunity. Well, we're justified in seeking civil rights, if it means equality of opportunity, because all we're doing there is trying to collect for our investment. Our mothers and fathers invested sweat and blood. Three hundred and ten years we worked in this country without a dime in return—I mean without a *dime* in return. You let the white man walk around here talking about how rich this country is, but you never stop to think how it got rich so quick. It got rich because you made it rich.

This is our investment. This is our contribution—our blood. Not only did we give of our free labor, we gave of our blood. Every time he had a call to arms, we were the first ones in uniform. We died on every battlefield the white man had. We have made a greater sacrifice than anybody who's standing up in America today. We have made a greater contribution and have collected less. Civil rights, for those of us whose philosophy is black nationalism, means: "Give it to us now. Don't wait for next year. Give it to us yesterday, and that's not fast enough."

The political philosophy of black nationalism means that the black man should control the politics and the politicians in his own community; no more. The black man in the black community has to be re-educated into the science of politics so he will know what politics is supposed to bring him in return. Don't be throwing out any ballots. A ballot is like a bullet. You don't throw your ballots until you see a target, and if that target is not within your reach, keep your ballot in your pocket. . . .

The economic philosophy of black nationalism is pure and simple. It only means that we should control the economy of our community. Why should white people be running all the stores in our community? Why should white people be running the banks of our community? Why should the economy of our community be in the hands of the white man? Why? If a black man can't move his store into a white community, you tell me why a white man should move his store into a black community. The philosophy of black nationalism involves a re-education program in the black community in regards to economics. Our people have to be made to see that any time you take your dollar out of your community and spend it in a community where you don't live, the community where you live will get poorer and poorer, and the community where you spend your money will get richer and richer. Then you wonder why where you live is always a ghetto or a slum area. And where you and I are concerned, not only do we lose it when we spend it out of the community, but the white man has got all our stores in the community tied up; so that though we spend it in the community, at sundown the man who runs the store takes it over across town somewhere. He's got us in a vise.

So the economic philosophy of black nationalism means in every church, in every civic organization, in every fraternal order, it's time now for our people to become conscious of the importance of controlling the economy of our community. If we own the stores, if we operate the businesses, if we try and establish some industry in our own community, then we're developing to the position where we are creating employment for our own kind. Once you gain control of the economy of your own community, then you don't have to picket and boycott and beg some cracker downtown for a job in his business.

Last but not least, I must say this concerning the great controversy over rifles and shotguns. The only thing that I've ever said is that in areas where the government has proven itself either unwilling or unable to defend the lives and the property of Negroes, it's time for Negroes to defend themselves. Article number two of the constitutional amendments provides you and me the right to own a rifle or a shotgun. It is constitutionally legal to own a shotgun or a rifle. This doesn't mean you're going to get a rifle and form battalions and go out looking for white folks, although you'd be within your rights—I mean, you'd be justified; but that would be illegal and we don't do anything illegal. If the white man doesn't want the black man buying rifles and shotguns, then let the government do its job. That's all. And don't let the white man come to you and ask you what you think about what Malcolm says—why, you old Uncle Tom. He would never ask you if he thought you were going to say, "Amen!" No, he is making a Tom out of you.

So, this doesn't mean forming rifle clubs and going out looking for people, but it is time, in 1964, if you are a man, to let that man know. If he's not going to do his job in running the government and providing you and me with the protection that our taxes are supposed to be for, since he spends all those billions for his defense budget, he certainly can't begrudge you and me spending $12 or $15 for a single-shot, or double-action. I hope you understand. Don't go out shooting people, but any time, brothers and sisters, and especially the men in this audience—some of you wearing Congressional Medals of Honor, with shoulders this wide, chests this big, muscles that big—any time you and I sit around and read where they bomb a church and murder in cold blood, not some grownups, but four little girls while they were praying to the same god the white man taught them to pray to, and you and I see the government go down and can't find who did it.

Why, this man—he can find Eichmann hiding down in Argentina somewhere. Let two or three American soldiers, who are minding somebody else's business way over in South Vietnam, get killed, and he'll send battleships, sticking his nose in their business. He wanted to send troops down to Cuba and make them have what he calls free elections—this old cracker who doesn't have free elections in his own country. No, if you never see me another time in your life, if I die in the morning, I'll die saying one thing: the ballot or the bullet, the ballot or the bullet.

8.8 Suggestions for Further Reading

Arthur, John, and William Shaw, eds. *Justice and Economic Distribution*, 2d ed. Englewood Cliffs, NJ: Prentice-Hall, 1991. An excellent collection of contemporary writings on justice.

Avineri, Shlomo. *The Social and Political Thought of Karl Marx*. New York: Cambridge University Press, 1968. Many people still consider this the best introduction to Marx's thought.

Dworkin, Ronald. *Taking Rights Seriously*. Cambridge, MA: Harvard University Press, 1978. This is both a challenging and interesting book on a variety of social issues by an avowed liberal.

Golding, William. *Lord of the Flies*. New York: Capricorn Books, 1959. Golding creates a "state of nature," then portrays the attitudes and behavior of a handful of innocents who find themselves a part of it. A disturbing portrayal of the darker side of human nature.

Hartman, Robert, ed. *Poverty and Economic Justice*. New York: Paulist Press, 1984. In this paperback, Hartman brings together the major ethical positions on problems of poverty.

Held, Virginia, *Property, Profits, and Economic Justice*. Belmont, CA: Wadsworth, 1980. This collection of readings from Locke and Smith down to the present examines the corporation in the light of moral principles.

Jaggar, Alison M. *Feminist Politics and Human Nature*. Totowa, NJ: Rowman & Allanheld, 1983. An important feminist contribution to political theory. This is a very readable and extremely important work.

Kipnis, Kenneth, and Diana Meyers, eds. *Economic Justice*. Totowa, NJ: Rowman & Allanheld, 1985. A very good anthology of recent writings on the topic of economic justice.

Laquer, Walter, and Barry Rubin, eds. *The Human Rights Reader*, rev. ed. New York: Meridian, 1989. An anthology of international writings and documents on human rights, including the United Nations Declarations on Human Rights.

Okin, Susan. *Justice, Gender, and the Family*. New York: Basic Books, 1989. In a book that is already regarded as a classic feminist approach to social philosophy, Okin argues that political philosophers have ignored the glaring inequalities present in the most basic institution in society: the family.

Okin, Susan. *Women in Western Political Thought*. Princeton, NJ: Princeton University Press, 1979. A very readable survey of how women have been treated by political philosophers.

Shue, Henry. *Basic Rights: Subsistence, Affluence, and U.S. Foreign Policy*. Princeton, NJ: Princeton University Press, 1980. A very good discussion of the ethical obligations of nations.

Simmons, A. John. *Moral Principles and Political Obligations*. Princeton, NJ: Princeton University Press, 1979. Exceedingly clear discussion of the major social philosophies. Simmons suggests that most of the reasons for thinking that we have political obligations are mistaken.

Walzer, Michael. *Just and Unjust Wars*. New York: Basic Books, 1977. This is a challenging book on a pressing social problem: the justice of war.

Wolff, Robert Paul. *Understanding Rawls*. Princeton, NJ: Princeton University Press, 1975. This is a difficult but useful short paperback that summarizes and criticizes the central ideas of Rawls.

CHAPTER 9

Postscript: Art and Meaning

There is both pleasure and pain in tragedy and comedy, not only on the stage, but on the greater stage of human life.

PLATO

9.1 Introduction

We have come to the end of our discussion of the main areas of philosophy: human nature, God, reality, knowledge, truth, ethics, and society. In our opening chapter, however, we noted that philosophy involves more than a discussion of these main issues. In addition, philosophy includes an examination of the basic assumptions that underlie various areas of our life. In this closing chapter we will look briefly at two of these important areas: art and the meaning of life.

These two topics are closely related. Many people find in art a key to the meaning of their lives. Their commitment to art and their immersion in art helps them find the meaning that makes life possible. Art is for them the source of meaning. On the other hand, for many people the meaning of life is a key concern of art. They see in art an attempt to express the deeper meaning and significance of life. Meaning is for them the source of art.

Not surprisingly, great artists often find themselves troubled by the question of whether life has any meaning. None has written of this more poignantly than the great Russian novelist Leo Tolstoy:

> In my writings I had advocated what to me was the only truth, that it was necessary to live in such a way as to derive the greatest comfort for oneself and one's family.
>
> Thus I proceeded to live. But five years ago something very strange began to happen with me: I was overcome by minutes at first of perplexity and then of an arrest of life, as though I did not know how to live or what to do, and I lost myself and was dejected. But that passed, and I continued to live as before. Then those minutes of perplexity were repeated oftener and oftener, and always in one and the same form. These arrests of life found their expression in ever the same questions: "Why? Well, and then?"
>
> At first I thought that those were simply aimless, inappropriate questions. . . . But the questions began to repeat themselves oftener and oftener, answers were demanded more and more persistently, and like dots that fall in the same spot, these questions, without any answers, thickened into one black blotch. . . .
>
> I felt that what I was standing on had given way, that I had no foundation to stand on, that that which I lived by no longer existed, and that I had nothing to live by. . . .
>
> All this happened to me when I was surrounded on every side by what is considered to be complete happiness. I had a good, loving, and beloved wife, good children,

Let us labor under no illusions. There are no easy solutions for problems that are at the same time intensely personal and universal, urgent and eternal.

A. J. HESCHEL

and a large estate, which grew and increased without any labor on my part. I was respected by my neighbors and friends, more than ever before, was praised by strangers, and, without any self-deception, could consider my name famous. . . . And while in such condition I arrived at the conclusion that I could not live. . . .

This mental condition expressed itself to me in this form: my life is a stupid, mean trick played on me by somebody. . . . Involuntarily I imagined that there, somewhere, there was somebody who was now having fun as he looked down upon me and saw me, who had lived for thirty or forty years, learning, developing, growing in body and mind, now that I had become strengthened in mind and had reached that summit of life from which it lay all before me, standing as a complete fool on that summit and seeing clearly that there was nothing in life and never would be. And that was fun to him. . . .

I could not ascribe any sensible meaning to a single act or to my whole life. I was only surprised that I had not understood this from the start. All this had long ago been known to everybody. Sooner or later there would come diseases and death (they had come already) to my dear ones and to me, and there would be nothing left but stench and worms. All my affairs, no matter what they might be, would sooner or later be forgotten, and I myself should not exist. So why should I worry about all these things? How could a man fail to see this and live,—that was surprising! A person could live only so long as he was drunk; but the moment he sobered up, he could not help seeing that all that was only a deception, and a stupid deception at that! . . .

"My family?" I said to myself. "But my family, my wife and children, they are also human beings. They are in precisely the same condition that I am in: they must either live in the lie or see the terrible truth. Why should they live? Why should I love them, why guard, raise, and watch them? Is it for the same despair which is in me, or for dullness of perception? Since I love them, I cannot conceal the truth from them,—every step in understanding will lead them up to this truth. And the truth is death."

"Art and Poetry?" For a long time, under the influence of the success of human praise, I tried to persuade myself that that was a thing which could be done, even though death should come and destroy everything, my deeds, as well as my memory of them; but soon I came to see that this, too was a deception. It was clear to me that art was an adornment of life, a decoy of life. But life had lost all its attractiveness for me. How, then, could I entrap others? So long as I did not live my own life, and a strange life bore me on its waves; so long as I believed that life had some sense, although I was not able to express it,—the reflections of life of every description in poetry and in the arts afforded me pleasure, and I was delighted to look at life through this little mirror of art; but when I began to look for the meaning of life, when I experienced the necessity of living myself, that little mirror became either useless, superfluous, and ridiculous, or painful to me. I could no longer console myself with what I saw in the mirror, namely, that my situation was stupid and desperate. It was all right for me to rejoice so long as I believed in the depth of my soul that life had some sense; then the play of lights—of the comical, the tragical, the touching, the beautiful, the terrible in life—afforded me amusement. But when I knew that life was meaningless and terrible, the play in the little mirror could no longer amuse me. . . .[1]

---

[1] Leo Tolstoy, *My Confession*, trans. Leo Wiener (London: J. M. Dent & Sons, 1905), reprinted in E. D. Klemke, ed., *The Meaning of Life* (New York: Oxford University Press, 1981), 9–13.

Tolstoy felt that life for him—one of the world's greatest artists—no longer had meaning. Previously, family and art had sustained him. In his love for his family he had found "the only truth," and in his art he had always advocated devotion to one's family. On the other hand, in the art of others he had found "reflections of life" that had sustained him and provided him some meaning. But now that he realized he no longer knew the meaning of life, neither his art nor his family sustained him. Finding no meaning to express in his art, and finding nothing in art that could give meaning to his life, he stopped writing. He fell into a deep depression.

We will return to Tolstoy below when we examine how he eventually answered the question of the meaning of life. Here we only need note that in his life the interplay between art and meaning is clear.

We will end this book, then, by exploring the two topics that were intertwined in the life of Tolstoy: art and the meaning of life. We begin with art, which, as we have suggested, is for many the fundamental source of meaning. Art, for many, is what gives life value. We will then discuss directly the question of whether life has meaning.

> *One ought not to talk or act as if he were asleep.*
>
> HERACLITUS

9.2 What Is Art?

Think of how art seems to surround us. In museums and galleries, of course, we can find classical paintings and statues, and in concert halls we can hear classical music being performed. But can't art be more than what's in museums and concert halls? Art can be rock music playing on the radio. It can be a television drama or a movie or a novel or a poem. Art can be the way we decorate our bodies: the clothes and jewelry we wear, the beautiful tattoos we etch into our skin, the polished metal studs we wear to decorate the piercings in our ears, nose, lips, or even tongue. Art can be the red, green, and purple colors we use to dye our hair, the stylized boots or punk paraphernalia we wear when we go out at night. Art can be the neat suit and bright tie the executive wears. It can be the sleek car, the glass building, the pleasing advertisement. Art can be the orange flames painted on the side of a car or motorcycle. Art can be the poetry on walls of bathrooms.

But is all this really art? What, exactly, is art? And what is the difference between good art and bad art? What's the difference, for example, between a good movie and a bad one? Between a good piece of rock music and a bad one? These questions, as we'll see, are connected.

Suppose that you are at a store trying to choose a knife. What's the difference between a good knife and a bad knife? A good knife is one that cuts well, as knives are meant to. On the other hand, suppose you are at a nursery trying

> *There is no surer method of evading the world than by following art, and no surer method of linking oneself to it than by art.*
>
> GOETHE

to buy an orange tree. What's the difference between a good orange tree and a bad one? Certainly, not one that cuts well. A good orange tree, instead, is one that is healthy and will produce lots of tasty fruit for many years.

These examples suggest that before we can decide what a *good* thing is, we need first to know *what* it is. The goodness of a knife is going to be different from the goodness of a plant because knives and plants are different kinds of things. So to tell the difference between good art and bad art, we need to know what kind of thing art itself is. Here, as in many other areas, the two questions "What is it?" and "How good is it?" run together.

Still, philosophers usually distinguish between these two questions. They say that you should define *art* in a way that includes both good art and bad art, since even bad art is still art. That is, your definition of *art* should be "neutral" so that you don't conclude that only "good art" is "real art." Perhaps. But, as we will see, even neutral definitions of *art* imply something about what good and bad art is.

So there are two things we want to know about art: (1) What is art? and (2) What's the difference between a good work of art and a bad one? Let's look now at some attempts to answer these questions.

ART AS IMITATION

Many people think that a work of art—such as a painting—should be looked at like a picture. In other words, a work of art presents a reproduction of something to us. For example, da Vinci's painting *Mona Lisa* represents the likeness of a person; a landscape painting can show us a view; a novel can present more or less realistic situations and events; a movie can present characters acting with more or less realistic motives. Art, then, is an imitation or representation of a reality, such as a person, a view, a set of events, or a group of characters.

If art is imitation, then, one way of separating good art from bad art is this: Art is good when it is a good imitation of reality, and bad when it is a poor imitation. Take a play, for example. We sometimes say that a play is good because it is "true to life" or bad because it "isn't true to life." We're assuming that art is imitation, and that we can judge art by how well it imitates reality.

The Greek philosopher Plato was the first to develop this view of the nature of art. But Plato did not like art, precisely because it is an imitation. Plato argued that an imitation can never be as good as the real thing. People who spend their time contemplating art, Plato held, are spending their time on a pale imitation and ignoring the real thing. For example, think of people you know who spend much of their lives watching television or reading novels. Is this as good as getting up from the couch and living real life? Moreover, in learning about real life from art, Plato suggested, people are trusting that the artist is giving an accurate picture of reality. But perhaps the picture of reality that the artist paints is distorted. Then people who believe the artist will be misled:

> We may conclude, then, that all poetry, from Homer onwards, consists in representing an imitation of its subject, whatever it may be, including any kind of human

excellence, with no grasp of the reality itself. We were speaking just now of the painter who can produce what looks like a shoemaker to the spectator who, being as ignorant of shoemaking as he is himself, judges only by form and color. In the same way the poet, knowing nothing more than how to represent appearances, can paint in words his picture of any craftsman, so as to impress an audience which is equally ignorant and judges only by the form of expression; the inherent charm of meter, rhythm and musical setting is enough to make them think he has discoursed admirably about generalship or shoemaking or any other technical subject.[2]

Aristotle, who was a student of Plato, agreed that art is imitation. But Aristotle did not condemn art. A work of art, Aristotle felt, presents a likeness of actions and events, or of objects, or even of emotions. For example, the maker of a play constructs a drama that presents before our eyes the likeness of the actions and events that befell some people or that could have befallen some people. A sculptor chisels a statue that presents to us the likeness of an animal or a person. A musician creates a melody that recreates in sound the likeness of a feeling or a mood such as bravery or calmness. From these recreations of actions, objects, and feelings, Aristotle suggests, we can draw two benefits. First, our own feelings are aroused in ways that are beneficial and satisfying. Second, the work of art can provide us with insight into human beings and their world. When we watch a play, for example, we can learn about different kinds of people and characters. We see the motives and actions that lead people to do the things they do. We learn what the consequences of people's actions can be. We discover what is valuable in human life.

The subject matter of art is life as it actually is; but its function is to make life better.

GEORGE SANTAYANA

Aristotle seems to have thought that art can represent virtually anything. Even feelings can be imitated. Music, he argued, can imitate feelings and moral qualities and can change a person's feelings and moral character:

> All men agree that music is one of the most pleasant things, whether or not it is accompanied by song. . . . Rhythm and melody can supply imitations of anger and gentleness, and also of courage and temperance, and of all the qualities contrary to these, as well as all the other qualities of character, which hardly fall short of the actual emotions. We know this from our own experience, for in listening to some strains of music our souls undergo a change. The habit of feeling pleasure or pain at mere representations is not far removed from the same feeling about the realities. . . . Even in mere melodies there is an imitation of character. . . . Some of them make men sad and grave . . . others enfeeble the mind . . . another, again, produces a moderate and settled temper. . . . Enough has been said to show that music has the power of forming the character.[3]

To see what Aristotle meant, think of the profound effect that music can have on us. For example, a rap song can imitate rage and anger at some injustice. The music may do this so well that it makes us feel angry at the same injustice. So strong can our anger be that it may lead us to change the injustice. Music can make a person feel brave; it can make a person feel fearful and cowardly; it can make a person bravely put up with pain or give in to lust and desire. And music does this by imitating these feelings or moral qualities.

---

[2] Plato, *The Republic*, trans. F. M. Cornford (London: Oxford University Press, 1941), 331.
[3] Aristotle, *Politics*, 1339b 20, translated by Manuel Velasquez.

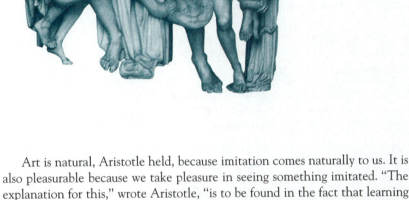

"Lacoon and His Two Sons," by Hagesandrus, Polydorus, and Athenodorus. (1st century AD). For Aristotle, art imitates a reality, arouses our feelings and teaches us the meaning of things. The statue of Lacoon shows a father desperately trying to save his two horrified sons from the strangling coils of a deadly serpent.

Art is natural, Aristotle held, because imitation comes naturally to us. It is also pleasurable because we take pleasure in seeing something imitated. "The explanation for this," wrote Aristotle, "is to be found in the fact that learning is the greatest of pleasures . . . [so we] delight in seeing an imitation because at the same time we are learning from it and gathering the meaning of things, such as what man is like."[4]

Aristotle's claim that imitation and pleasure go together may seem puzzling. How can a play, for example, with a sad or tragic ending give us pleasure? A tragedy, Aristotle suggests, imitates or recreates fearful and pitiable events, and seeing these can produce a kind of pleasure. In particular, Aristotle claims, when we witness a tragic play, we experience pity and fear, and this produces a "catharsis of these emotions." Aristotle seems to be saying that when we see a tragic play, we feel pity for the characters who suffer the tragic events, and we also feel fear at the thought that the same thing could happen to us. Having these emotions somehow purges or cleanses us of them. We get them "out of our system," and they can no longer work their destructive effects on us. The experience of tragedy, then, has a therapeutic and satisfying effect on us.

A work of art can also give pleasure because it is "beautiful." The beauty of a work of art, Aristotle said, lies in its unity: "A beautiful thing, either a living

---

[4] Aristotle, *Nicomachean Ethics*, in *Works*, trans. W. D. Ross (Oxford: Clarendon Press, 1925), vol. 60, section 1103a 17.

creature or any structure made of parts must have an orderly arrangement of those parts."[5] For example, a drama must have a beginning that connects well with the middle and an end that flows naturally from the middle and that resolves the action without leaving anything hanging. Aristotle also seems to have thought that a good work of art—in particular, a good tragedy—has to express universal truths about human nature. The behaviors of the characters, in other words, have to be plausible and motivated by psychological truths.

But many philosophers have disagreed with the idea that art should imitate reality. Shouldn't art be something more or different from a mere picture of reality? If we restrict art to presenting an accurate picture of reality, aren't we wrongly turning the artist into nothing more than a photocopy machine or a camera? In fact, wouldn't a camera do a better job?

ART AS EXPRESSION OF EMOTION

Many people see in art not a representation of reality, but an expression of emotion. When you think of rock music, for example, you might think of several songs that seem to express anger, sexual desire, excitement, or frustration; on the other hand, a sonata may express feelings of peace and calm. The view that art is an expression of feeling was nicely summarized by Leo Tolstoy:

> Art is a human activity consisting in this, that one man consciously, by means of certain external signs, hands on to others feelings he has lived through, and that other people are infected by these feelings and also experience them.[6]

Notice that for Tolstoy, art expresses feelings in two ways. First, the artist expresses his or her feelings in the work of art. Second, the work of art arouses or "ex-presses" (i.e., squeezes out) the same feelings in the audience.

During the nineteenth century, the expression theory of art became the dominant view. The development of the expression theory of art was related to Romanticism, an important movement that we mentioned in Chapter 5 when we discussed the philosophy of Immanuel Kant. Kant claims that there is more to reality than the world of nature that we see, hear, touch, and perceive with our senses. In addition, he argued, there is a deeper reality that lies behind the natural world we perceive around us. Kant calls this deeper underlying reality the "noumenal" world. He claims that it has to be the source of morality, value, and freedom. But, Kant argued, we can know nothing about the noumenal world because we can never perceive it.

Kant's idea that there is a deeper unseen reality beneath the world fascinated many philosophers. The Romantics were a group of philosophers, poets, artists, and thinkers who took this idea seriously. They felt that behind the ordinary world we experience is another more mysterious reality that is vital, portentous, and the source of deeper hidden meaning. Many of the landscape

Art is the objectification of feeling.

S. LANGER

---

[5] Aristotle, *Poetics*, ch. 7, translated by Manuel Velasquez.
[6] Leo Tolstoy, *What Is Art?* (Indianapolis: Bobbs-Merrill, 1960), 51.

paintings of the Romantic artists show scenes where light and shadows emerging from behind clouds, mountains, forests, or a far horizon hint at a mysterious reality that lies behind nature and that we cannot quite see.

Many of the Romantics came to the conclusion that although reason cannot get at this deeper reality, our feelings can. Through his feelings the artist can get in touch with this deeper, more important reality. Art came to be seen as the expression of the feelings of the artist who is in touch with the deeper, more meaningful reality that lies behind the mundane world.

Although eventually most philosophers came to reject Kant's idea that there is a noumenal world behind the ordinary world, many continued to hold the expression theory of art. Art is the expression of the feelings of the artist. And although the artist may not be in touch with the noumenal world, he is still in touch with the deeper significance of life.

The Italian philosopher Benedetto Croce (1866–1952), for example, saw art as "intuitive knowledge." To understand Croce's idea, it's important to distinguish, as he does, between two forms of knowledge: intuitive and logical. *Intuitive knowledge*, according to Croce, is knowledge you get through your imagination; it is knowledge of individual things, and it produces images. In contrast, *logical knowledge* is knowledge you get through your intellect. It is knowledge of the universal and of the relations between individual things. Rather than images, logical knowledge produces concepts. Croce identifies intuitive knowledge, or what he terms *expressive knowledge*, with art. Every true intuition is also expression. In his best-known work, *Theory of Aesthetic*, Croce makes this point:

> And yet there is a sure method of distinguishing true intuition, true representation, from that which is inferior to it: the spiritual fact from the mechanical, passive, natural fact. Every true intuition or representation is also expression. That which does not objectify itself in expression is not intuition or representation, but sensation and mere natural fact. The spirit only intuits in making, forming, expressing. He who separates intuition from expression never succeeds in reuniting them.
>
> Intuitive activity possesses intuitions to the extent that it expresses them. Should this proposition sound paradoxical, that is partly because, as a general rule, a too restricted meaning is given to the word "expression." It is generally restricted to what are called verbal expressions alone. But there exist also nonverbal expressions, such as those of line, color and sound, and to all of these must be extended our affirmation, which embraces therefore every sort of manifestation of the man, as orator, musician, painter, or anything else. But be it pictorial, or verbal, or musical, or in whatever other form it appear, to no intuition can expression in one of its forms be wanting; it is, in fact, an inseparable part of intuition. How can we really possess an intuition of a geometrical figure, unless we possess so accurate an image of it as to be able to trace it immediately upon paper or on the blackboard? How can we really have an intuition of the contour of a region, for example, of the island of Sicily, if we are not able to draw it as it is in all its meanderings? Everyone can experience the internal illumination which follows upon his success in formulating to himself his impressions and feelings, but only so fast as he is able to formulate them. Feelings or impressions, then, pass by means of words from the obscure region of the soul into the clarity of the contemplative spirit. It is impossible to distinguish intuition from

"Guernica," by Pablo Picasso. (1937). Picasso said this painting was about the Spanish Civil War. It is not like a photo of events but looking at the painting we know the feelings Picasso was expressing about the war.

expression in this cognitive process. The one appears with the other at the same instant, because they are not two, but one.[7]

Notice the difference between saying that art is an imitation of reality and that art is an expression of feelings. First, expressing feelings is different from imitating or recreating feelings. In a play, for example, we may see characters who act happy, sad, or meditative. They are trying to recreate or imitate these feelings by acting. But the feeling that the play *expresses* may be very different from the feelings that the actors are trying to *imitate*. For example, a movie might show us characters who always act cheerful, so much so that all their cheerfulness starts to look boring. The movie may be expressing a feeling of boredom with a life that is always cheerful. So the feeling the movie expresses (boredom) is different from the feelings the actors in the movie imitate (cheerfulness).

Second, an inaccurate imitation of reality can express the artist's feelings as well as an accurate one. So the view that art is an expression of feelings means that good art does not have to be an accurate copy of reality. Take modern art, such as *Guernica*, a painting by Pablo Picasso. Picasso said that this painting was about the Spanish Civil War. Yet the painting is not like a photo of events or incidents that occurred during the war. Nevertheless, when looking at the painting we know the feelings Picasso was expressing. Croce might have said that Picasso "intuited" in a deep way the horror of war and expressed this horror in a painting that evokes that same horror in us. In the expression theory, then, good art expresses feelings well, whereas bad art does not.

Art is a human activity whose purpose is the transmission of the highest and best feelings to which men have attained.

TOLSTOY

---

[7] Benedetto Croce, *Theory of Aesthetic* (New York: Macmillan, 1909), 8–9.

The expression theory of art has many important advantages. It is hard to see how some art, like music, really "imitates" anything. Yet it is easy to understand how all art, even music, can express feelings. Think, for example, of modern rock music. It is true that the lyrics of some modern rock songs tell a kind of story and so imitate reality. Yet most modern rock music seems only to express emotion. Second, the expression theory of art explains why music and art are important to us and play a big role in our lives. Music and art are important because they express emotions, and our emotions are vitally important to us. In fact, maybe there's a sense in which the Romantics were right: Our emotions put us in touch with an important aspect of reality that reason cannot reach. Perhaps the good artist can intuit and express this better than the rest of us.

But many philosophers object to the expression theory of art. What, they ask, does it really mean to say that art "expresses" feelings? When we say that a person's face expresses sadness, we usually mean that the person is feeling sad and that the outer expression on her face indicates this inner feeling she is experiencing. But this can't be what we mean when we say a work of art expresses sadness. We are surely not saying that the painting indicates the inner feeling the artist was having when he created the painting. Usually, paintings take a long time to finish. Surely the artist did not have the same sad feeling the whole time. In fact, the artist might have been having a bunch of different feelings when he created the painting, including cheerfulness, boredom, anger, and anxiety. We don't really know what the artist was feeling when he created the painting. Paintings, then, are not about the feelings of the artist. Instead, some argue, when we say a painting "expresses" sadness, we do not mean our words literally, but only metaphorically. We mean, perhaps, that the painting reminds us of sad things. Art, then, does not express the feelings of the artist. Instead, the work of art just reminds us of things that we connect with certain feelings.

These criticisms of the expression theory have led many philosophers to feel that it is a mistake to think that art is about something other than itself. For example, the imitation theory says that art is about reality and should be judged by how well it imitates reality. The expression theory says that art is about feelings and should be judged by how well it expresses feelings. But maybe art is not about something outside of itself. Maybe art should just be judged on its own terms, not by how good or bad it is at expressing or imitating other things. This is the view that art is form.

ART AS FORM

Is the Eiffel Tower a work of art? It does not represent anything, nor does it seem to express any emotion. Yet, having no purpose other than to be looked at, and with curving lines that many view as beautiful, the Eiffel Tower is seen by many as a work of art. What makes it a work of art? The critic Clive Bell said that "a work of art is an artefact that possesses significant form." What Bell was trying to say is that we should not define art in terms of its relationship to something outside the work of art, such as "reality" or "emotion." Of course,

Johnny Rotten singing. All art can express feelings. Although the lyrics of some modern rock songs tell a kind of story and so imitate reality, most modern rock music only seems to express emotion.

there must be something that all works of art have in common, something that makes us call them all "works of art":

> For either all works of visual art have some common quality, or when we speak of "works of art" we gibber. . . . What is the quality common and peculiar to all . . . [art]? There must be some one quality without which a work of art cannot exist; possessing which, in the least degree, no work is altogether worthless. What is this quality? What quality is shared by all objects that provoke our aesthetic emotions? What quality is common to St. Sophia and the windows at Chartres, Mexican sculpture, a Persian bowl, Chinese carpets, Giotto's frescoes at Padua, and the masterpieces of Poussin, Piero della Francesca, and Cézanne? Only one answer seems possible — significant form. In each, lines and colors combined in a particular way certain forms and relations of forms — stir our aesthetic emotions. These relations and combinations of lines and colors, these aesthetically moving forms, I call "Significant Form," and "Significant Form" is the one quality common to all works of visual art. . . .
>
> Let no one imagine that representation is bad in itself; a realistic form may be as significant, in its place, as part of the design, as an abstract [form]. But if a representative form has value, it is as form, not as representation. The representative element in a work of art . . . is irrelevant.[8]

Bell is arguing that something counts as a work of art simply because of the way that its parts and its materials are arranged and put together. It does not matter

The world of aesthetics is an ideal world.
WILLIAM JAMES

---

[8]Clive Bell, "The Aesthetic Hypothesis," in Alex Neill and Aaron Ridley, *The Philosophy of Art: Readings Ancient and Modern* (New York: McGraw-Hill, 1996), 100, 106.

what it is trying to imitate. For example, a painting is a work of art because of the way its colors, its shapes, and its lines are arranged. This arrangement of lines, colors, and shapes is what Bell calls the "Form" of a work of art.

For Bell, then, a work of art does not have to represent anything at all. In fact, one of the important advantages of Bell's approach is that it explains why modern abstract paintings can be real art even though they don't represent anything that we can recognize.

Notice that Bell only wrote about "visual" art—i.e., art that is meant to be seen. But other philosophers have said that Bell's views apply to all kinds of art, including music, which can only be heard. We will assume here that Bell's theory is a theory about all art, including music.

Bell thinks, then, that the form or arrangement of the parts of a work of art is what makes it count as a work of art. But not all arrangements turn a thing into a work of art. Bell claims that the parts of the work of art must be arranged in a way that will "stir our aesthetic emotions." The word *aesthetic* refers to the study of beautiful things. What, exactly, are the "aesthetic emotions"? Bell thinks that people who are sensitive to art feel a very special emotion when they see a beautiful work of art. This emotion is different from ordinary emotions, such as fear, joy, and anger. Here is how Bell tries to describe this emotion:

> All sensitive people agree that there is a peculiar emotion provoked by works of art. . . . [A]nd that this emotion is provoked by every kind of visual art, by pictures, sculptures, buildings, pots, carvings, textiles, etc., is not disputed, I think, by anyone capable of feeling it. This emotion is called the aesthetic emotion. . . .
>
> Art transports us from the world of man's activity to a world of aesthetic exaltation. For a moment we are shut off from human interests; our anticipations and memories are arrested; we are lifted above the stream of life. . . . He who contemplates a work of art, inhabit[s] a world with an intense and peculiar significance of its own; that significance is unrelated to the significance of life. In this world the emotions of life find no place. It is a world with emotions of its own.[9]

When the arrangement of colors, shapes, and lines of a painting arouse these "aesthetic emotions" in us, Bell claims, then the "Form" of the painting is "Significant" and it is a work of art. What exactly does *significant* mean? Bell admits that for many people another word for *significant* is *beautiful*. A work of art is one whose colors, shapes, and lines are arranged in a beautiful way. However, Bell cautions, we also apply the word *beautiful* to things that are not works of art. For example, we might say that a butterfly or a flower is beautiful. But a beautiful work of art, he claims, seems to move us in a way that natural beauty usually does not. Still, he admits, "some people may, occasionally, see in nature what we see in art, and feel for her an aesthetic emotion."

We need to notice a problem with Bell's view. For Bell, only a beautiful painting can be a work of art. This means that a painting or a piece of music or poetry that is not beautiful is not a work of art even if many people call it art. There seems to be something wrong here. Don't we want to say that

---

[9] Ibid., 106.

"History Lessons," by David Diao. (c. 1980). One of the advantages of Clive Bell's theory of art is that it explains why modern abstract paintings can be real art even though they don't represent anything we can recognize.

some works of art are not beautiful? Bell seems to be mixing two things together: the definition of art and the definition of good art. For Bell, only good art can be art, so there can be no such thing as bad or poor art. This seems wrong.

Yet Bell's attempt to link art to beauty seems to be on the right track. Don't we want to say that beauty is an important part of our notion of art? Even if all works of art are not beautiful, isn't beauty still an important aspect of good art?

But what is beauty? Bell suggests that something is beautiful when it arouses a special feeling in us. Bell is here following a long tradition. For example, in the thirteenth century Saint Thomas Aquinas said that beauty is "that which pleases us when we see it." He went on to add that "what is good is what all desire, . . . but the beautiful is that which requires only to be seen or known to calm the desire." [10] Aquinas is suggesting that beauty is related to a feeling in us. Moreover, he claims, it is one thing to desire to possess an object; it is another thing to see it as beautiful. When something is beautiful, I just want to contemplate it—to see it or listen to it—not to possess it. Aquinas also seems to have thought that the beauty of a thing depends on its "form." In particular, said Aquinas, a thing has beauty when its form has "[1] integrity or perfection,

---

[10] Thomas Aquinas, *Summa Theologica*, Part I, q. 5, a. 4, and Part I–II, q. 27, a. 1, translated by Manuel Velasquez.

"Spingtime," by Sandro Botticelli. (c. 1478). Aquinas held that "beauty is that which pleases when seen," and that a thing has beauty when its form has "integrity or perfection, due proportion or harmony, and brightness or clarity."

since those things which are impaired are by the very fact ugly; [2] due proportion or harmony; [3] and lastly, brightness, or clarity, which is why beautiful things have a clear color."[11]

Aquinas's idea that something is beautiful when its form arouses a special feeling in us was followed by several British philosophers in the eighteenth century. These included the third Earl of Shaftesbury (1671–1713), Francis Hutcheson (1694–1746), Edmund Burke (1728–1797), Archibald Alison (1757–1839), and David Hume (1711–1776). All of these philosophers agreed that something is beautiful when it arouses a special "aesthetic" feeling in us. All agreed, also, that this feeling is "disinterested." That is, this feeling is not the same as a desire to possess something. When I see something as beautiful, I just want to contemplate it, and this is different from wanting to acquire it. (Although when I see something is beautiful, this may create a new desire to possess it.) Finally, all agreed that this aesthetic feeling is aroused in us by the way in which the parts of the beautiful work of art are arranged. They disagreed, however, on what qualities make a work of art beautiful. For example,

Beauty in things exists in the mind which contemplates them.
DAVID HUME

---

[11] Ibid., Part I, q. 39, a. 8, translated by Manuel Velasquez.

Hutcheson thought that a beautiful work of art arouses these special feelings when its parts show a single quality: "uniformity in variety." But Hume thought many qualities can produce these special feelings, including "consistency and uniformity of the whole," "fitness to attain its end," "variety," "clearness of conception," and "exactness" of imitation.

Today, many philosophers agree with Bell that it is the form of an artwork that makes it count as a work of art, and that a good artwork is one that arouses a special "aesthetic emotion" in us. But most do not feel that only beautiful things can be art.

ART AS WHAT THE ARTWORLD SAYS IT IS

But perhaps there's another approach to defining art. Some philosophers have suggested that art should be defined as whatever people in the "artworld" say is art. The "artworld" consists of all those people who are engaged in producing art and in deciding whether it is good art or bad art.

One obvious example of an artworld consists of the painters who produce paintings, the galleries and museums that decide which paintings are good enough to exhibit, the critics who write newspaper articles saying that these paintings are good or bad, and the audiences who decide that these paintings are good enough to spend money to see them or to buy them. All these institutions and people make up the "artworld" of painting. But there are other artworlds. Think of the artworld of rock music. This artworld consists of the rock musicians who compose rock songs, the recording companies that decide which songs are good enough to make into tapes or CDs or videos, the radio and television stations that decide which tapes, CDs, or videos are good enough to put on the air, critics who write for magazines such as *Rolling Stone* about which songs are good and which are bad, and, finally, the audiences like you and me, who decide which of these songs are good enough for us to buy on tape or CD. All these people and institutions make up the artworld of rock music. Then there's the artworld of movies, the artworld of plays, the artworld of poetry, the artworld of novels, the artworld of fashion, the artworld of sculpture, etc.

One of the major proponents of this new approach to art is the American philosopher George Dickie, who writes as follows:

1. An artist is a person who participates with understanding in the making of a work of art.

2. A work of art is an artefact . . . created to be presented to an artworld public.

3. An [artworld] public is a set of persons . . . prepared to some degree to understand [a work of art] presented to them.

4. The artworld is the totality of all artworld systems.

5. An artworld system is a framework for the presentation of a work of art by an artist to an artworld public.[12]

---

[12] George Dickie, "Definition of Art," in David E. Cooper, ed., *A Companion to Aesthetics* (Oxford, UK: Blackwell, 1992), 112–113.

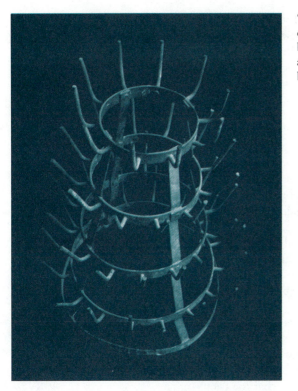

"Bottle Rack" by Marcel Duchamp. (1914). Duchamp has hung up men's urinals, wine bottle racks, bicycle wheels, snow shovels, combs, plastic boxes, and other "readymades" in museums and they have been accepted as "art" by art critics.

Notice that this way of thinking about art lets almost anything count as art. The "art" of Marcel Duchamp is a good example of how ordinary objects can become "art" when the artworld accepts them as such. Duchamp has hung up men's urinals, wine bottle racks, bicycle wheels, snow shovels, combs, plastic boxes, and other "readymades" in museums; they have been accepted as "art" by art critics.

But there are some problems with this way of looking at art. First, notice that this way of thinking sees art as having a special—almost isolated—world of its own. In earlier centuries, people used to think of art as part of everyday practical life. Art was what decorated vases or walls, or what was put up in churches or public buildings. Art was supposed to promote important aspects of everyday life like religion or morality. But in this new approach, a lot of art exists in its own little world. The artworld is an almost closed clique of artists, critics, and audiences. What does such an "artworld" have to do with ordinary life? But maybe that's the point. Maybe art is what we go to when we want to escape ordinary life. Maybe art really is completely separate from ordinary life. Take the world that people enter when they dance, or the world we enter when we close our eyes and listen to a great tune on the radio: Aren't these worlds deliberately isolated from real life? Yet many people feel that art should be more than escapism. Many people feel that art should take us deeper into reality:

show us more clearly what real life, real people, and the real world are about and show us what life means and how it should be lived.

Another set of problems is related to what brings the people in an artworld together. According to Dickie, they are joined by their "shared understandings." Take the artworld of rock music. What joins the musicians, the audience, and the critics who make up the artworld of rock music? They are joined together by their shared understanding of what rock music is about, shared understanding of what makes rock music good or bad, shared understanding of what is satisfying and pleasurable about rock music, and perhaps even a shared understanding of the history of rock music, of who the great rock musicians of the past were. But this makes the artworld of rock music static. It restricts musicians to turning out music that satisfies the shared understandings of this artworld. What about creative musicians who rebel against these shared understandings? What about musicians who want to defy the expectations of their audiences by giving them something truly new and truly different? Isn't a lot of original art the work of people who don't accept the "shared understandings" of any specific group? Does this rebellion mean that what they produce is not art? Surely not. Art is creative and continually breaks the bonds of our definitions, even of definitions like Dickie's.

But perhaps the most startling thing about this new view of art is that it completely leaves out what we have traditionally thought art is. What has happened to art as a representation of reality? What has happened to art as an expression of feeling? What has happened to the form of an artwork? What has happened to beauty in art? All that seems to be left is what the people of an "artworld" happen to like. Good art is what these people like; bad art is what they reject. Good and bad seem to be based on nothing more than a kind of majority vote.

THE END OF ART?

A lot of contemporary art in museums now seems contrived. For example, a "performance artist" may just sit naked on a chair in a museum, presenting his act of sitting as a "work of art." The French artist Duchamp, as we mentioned, became famous when he hung up an ordinary men's urinal on the wall of a museum, labeled it "Fountain," and declared it a work of art. Andy Warhol hung up paintings of soup cans.

In presenting these kinds of artworks, artists seem to be trying to push the boundaries of what we are willing to call "art." They seem almost to be thumbing their noses at earlier philosophers' attempts to provide definitions of *art*. They seem to be trying to force us to ask a question: "What is art?" It is almost as if instead of doing real art, these artists are more interested in the philosophical question we have been asking ourselves: What, exactly, is a work of art?

That is the view of the American philosopher Arthur Danto.[13] Danto argues that this new kind of art signals the end of art itself. Artists at the end of

---

[13] See Arthur Danto, *The Philosophical Disenfranchisement of Art* (New York: Columbia University Press, 1986).

the twentieth century have turned away from creating art and have started discussing philosophy. Art has now ended.

Danto claims that if we look at the history of art, we see that from the time of Plato until the nineteenth century, artists assumed that art is an imitation of reality. Throughout these many centuries artists worked at making ever-more-accurate copies of reality. But in the nineteenth century the camera was invented. The camera could create a more accurate imitation of reality than any artist could. So artists gave up the idea that art is supposed to provide a good copy of reality. They began instead to develop a new kind of art—impressionism—that does not really imitate reality. Philosophers developed a new theory for this new art: Art, they said, is an expression of emotion. Anything that expressed emotion could now be art. Art started to lose its direction. Many kinds of abstract art movements flourished and died, such as Fauvism and cubism. Philosophers came up with a fresh definition of *art* to fit this modern abstract work: Art, they said, is significant form. As artists wandered now completely without direction, they began asking themselves what art itself is. Finally, in our own time artists like Duchamp started to use their art to ask the philosophical question "What is art?" But in becoming philosophers, says Danto, artists have stopped being artists. So art has come to an end. Art had earlier understood itself as imitation of reality, then as expression of emotion, then as significant form, but now it sees itself as nothing more than an attempt by artists to understand themselves and what they are doing. But that is the end of art. The artist in our age has become something else, a philosopher. From this point, Danto suggests, art must remain pointless and directionless.

Is Danto right? In some ways, he seems to be. A lot of art today appears to be directionless. There are countless varieties of art, and new varieties are invented every day: performance art, street art, video art, computer art, etc. But there seems little real development or direction in these forms of art. Much of the contemporary art that we see in museums seems strained and seems to have little point in the traditional sense. It does not represent anything; it does not seem to express feeling; it does not have a beautiful form. Is all art dead?

Perhaps not. There is a kind of art that is very much alive. This is what we might call popular art: the art of films, of rock music, of novels. All these seem to be flourishing today, and all seem to move forward and build on their past toward something that seems to get better. The best rock music of today, for example, builds on the best of the past and goes beyond it. Rock music seems to get better, more sophisticated, more complex. The same is true of movies. Movie techniques seem to constantly improve and advance. The best of today's movies are as good or better than the movies of the past. Perhaps, then, it is only "academic" or "museum" art that has reached a dead end. Perhaps the art that continues to be a vital part of our everyday lives is still very much alive.

So what, then, is art? And what is the difference between good art and bad art? Only you can decide the answer to these questions. We've tried here to look carefully at some of the best thinking about what art is, about what it contributes to human life, and about what the difference is between good and bad art. But only you can decide which view seems to make the most sense of the art that you make part of your life. Only you can decide the meaning of *art*.

QUESTIONS

1. Explain the difference between Plato and Aristotle on the value of art.

2. Aristotle says that "a tragedy is the imitation of an action . . . with incidents that arouse pity and fear, by which the emotions undergo catharsis." Explain what Aristotle means by this.

3. Choose a movie or a popular song. Evaluate it in terms of the theory of imitation, of expression, and of form.

4. Does the definition of *art* matter? If there were no difference between what we call art and what we don't call art, would anything be different? Explain.

5. Do you agree with Danto's claim that art has ended? Explain your answer.

6. Consider different kinds of what you might call "popular art." Do these popular arts have "artworlds"? If they do, describe these artworlds. If they don't, explain why they do not have an artworld but are still art.

9.3 Does Life Have Meaning?

Perhaps the most important question in philosophy is this: Does life have meaning? Many people first turn to philosophy because they hope it will help them answer this troubling question. The philosopher and novelist Albert Camus, in fact, argued that it is the only important philosophical question:

> There is but one truly serious philosophical problem, and that is suicide. Judging whether life is or is not worth living amounts to answering the fundamental question of philosophy. All the rest—whether or not the world has three dimensions, whether the mind has nine or twelve categories—comes afterwards. These are games; one must first answer [the primary question]. . . .
>
> If I ask myself how to judge that this question is more urgent than that, I reply that one judges by the actions it entails. I have never seen anyone die for the ontological argument. Galileo, who held a scientific truth of great importance, abjured it with the greatest ease as soon as it endangered his life. In a certain sense, he did right. That truth was not worth the stake. Whether the earth or the sun revolves around the other is a matter of profound indifference. To tell the truth, it is a futile question. On the other hand, I see many people die because they judge that life is not worth living. I see others paradoxically getting killed for the ideas or illusions that give them a reason for living (what is called a reason for living is also an excellent reason for dying). I therefore conclude that the meaning of life is the most urgent of questions.[14]

It is not living that is evil, but leading a worthless life.

DIOGENES

---

[14] Albert Camus, "An Absurd Reasoning," from *The Myth of Sisyphus and Other Essays*, trans. Justin O'Brien (New York: Knopf, 1955).

People often ask about the meaning of life when death enters their lives: either the death of someone they love or their own imminent death. Death brings everything we are or ever hoped to be to a complete end. What's the point of all our striving, then? The shortness of human life, the insignificance of human life in the face of the great immensity and eternity of the universe, the apparent unconcern and uncaring impersonal coldness of the universe—all these factors can lead people to question whether human life in general, and their life in particular, has any meaning.

But for many people, the question of whether life has any meaning arises even when death is not near. Many people seem to reach a point in their lives when things seem to have no value, when the things they have spent their lives chasing begin to seem pointless. For example, Shakespeare's Macbeth killed many men and strove mightily to become king. But then, realizing that all his striving had brought him nothing that made sense of his life, he says this:

Life's but a walking shadow, a poor player
That struts and frets his hour upon the stage
And then is heard no more. It is a tale
Told by an idiot, full of sound and fury,
Signifying nothing.

Events force many people to ask whether the things they have devoted their lives to achieving have any real meaning. As we have seen, the question of whether life has meaning is one that first brings many people to philosophy.

But what, exactly, does this question mean? There are some philosophers who have claimed that the question has no meaning: It is literally meaningless. This is the position of the logical positivists, whose empiricist views we saw earlier when we discussed reality. A. J. Ayer and Rudolf Carnap, for example, argue that the only meaningful questions are factual questions whose answers can be found through sense observation. Questions about the meaning of life, they claim, cannot be resolved by sense perception, and so have no meaning.

But most people today believe that the logical positivists are mistaken. In particular, people reject the idea that questions are meaningless if they cannot be resolved through sense perception. Many of our most pressing social, religious, and moral questions seem to make perfectly good sense yet cannot be resolved through our senses. Moreover, many modern philosophers have shown—as we will see—that the question of the meaning of life can be given a perfectly understandable sense.

But if the question is not meaningless, what then does it mean? One way of understanding the question "What is the meaning of life?" is to take it as asking whether my life has a larger or more important purpose than merely living. In other words, is my individual life related to something bigger or more important that gives my life value?

This seems to be the way that Leo Tolstoy understood the question. We saw at the beginning of this chapter that at one point in his life, after he was renowned as a great novelist and artist, Tolstoy fell into a deep depression caused by his feeling that life is meaningless. Tolstoy came out of his profound funk when he reached the conclusion that his life was related to something bigger and more important than himself: God.

The question of the meaning of life, as the Buddha taught, is not edifying. One must immerse oneself in the river of life and let the question drift away.

IRVIN D. YALOM

THE THEISTIC RESPONSE TO MEANING

One way, perhaps the most common way, in which people answer the question of whether life has meaning is in terms of their relationship to God. This is an ancient response to the question. We saw earlier, for example, that Thomas Aquinas argues that everything has a purpose, including human beings:

> Now here on earth, the simplest elements exist for the sake of compound minerals; these latter exist for the sake of living bodies, among which plants exist for animals, and animals for humans. . . . Now humans naturally desire, as their ultimate purpose, to know the first cause of all things. But the first cause of all things is God. So the ultimate purpose of human beings is to know God.[15]

Aquinas's view can be called the theistic response to the question of meaning. The theistic response claims that human life has meaning because humans are part of a larger plan or order devised by God. Within that plan all things in the universe have purpose and value. The purpose of human beings, in particular, is to know God and be perfectly united with Him. Life on earth, while brief, is valuable insofar as it is a preparation for that future union with God. Human life, then, is not a tiny, insignificant, and meaningless "hour upon the stage" that ends with nothing. Human life has a meaning insofar as it has a purpose that relates me to a larger more significant whole, a whole within which I have a place.

This theistic response is the one that forced Tolstoy out of his depression. As Tolstoy wrote,

> Rational knowledge brought me to the recognition that life was meaningless—my life stopped, and I wanted to destroy myself. When I looked around at people, at all humanity, I saw that people lived and asserted that they knew the meaning of life. I looked back at myself: I lived so long as I knew the meaning of life. As to other people, so even to me, did faith give the meaning of life and the possibility of living. . . . What, then, was faith? I understood . . . that faith was the knowledge of the meaning of human life, in consequence of which man did not destroy himself, but lived. . . . If a man lives he believes in something. If he did not believe that he ought to live for some purpose, he would not live.
>
> Then I began to cultivate the acquaintance of the believers from among the poor, the simple and unlettered folk, of pilgrims, monks, dissenters, peasants. . . . I began to examine closely the lives and beliefs of these people, and the more I examined them, the more did I become convinced that they had the real faith, that their faith was necessary for them, and that it alone gave them a meaning and possibility of life. . . .
>
> I began to love these people. . . . Thus I lived for about two years, and within me took place a transformation. . . . What happened with me was that the life of our circle—of the rich and the learned—not only disgusted me, but even lost all its meaning. All our acts, reflections, sciences, arts—all that appeared to me in a new light. I saw that all that was mere pampering of the appetites, and that no meaning could be found in it; but the life of all the working masses, of all humanity, which

The striving to find meaning in one's life is the primary motivational force in man.

VIKTOR FRANKL

---

[15] Thomas Aquinas, *Summa Contra Gentiles*, Bk. III, ch. 22, para. 7, 8, ch. 25, para. 11, translated by Manuel Velasquez.

created life, presented itself to me in its real significance. I saw that that was life itself and that the meaning given to this life was truth, and I accepted it.[16]

There is, of course, not just one theist response. Each of the world's religions provides its own interpretation of the larger cosmic whole of which humans are but a part and in terms of which human life has meaning. Some, like Islam, infuse life with meaning in a way that is much like the theist response of Christianity. Other religions, like Hinduism and Buddhism, relate human life to a view of the universe that is very different from the universe of Christianity. Hinduism asserts the doctrine of rebirth and karma, and holds out the goal of absorption into Brahman after ascending the stages of consciousness. Buddhism also asserts the doctrine of rebirth and the experience of liberation from the great wheel of rebirth through the eightfold way whose goal is enlightenment. But in spite of their profound differences, all religions give meaning to life by relating the individual to a divine reality that is larger and more important than the individual.

The theist response to the search for meaning satisfies many believers, but it also raises difficult questions. First, the response obviously can depend on accepting the belief that God exists. We saw, however, when we discussed the many proofs for the existence of God, that it is very difficult to prove to ourselves that there is a god. The theist response, then, says little to the nonbeliever.

Second, some, like the American philosopher Kurt Baier, have argued that there is something "morally repugnant" about the theist response.[17] The theist view claims that humans have meaning because they have a purpose that is assigned them by God. But to see humans in this way is to see them as objects or things. Consider that tools and utensils have purposes. For example, the purpose of a knife is to cut; the purpose of a hammer is to nail. To say that humans have a purpose is to see humans as tools that are being used by God. But it is morally wrong to use humans as tools. As we saw when we discussed Kant's views on ethics, humans should be treated as ends and never used as means.

Third, some critics, such as the philosopher Kai Nielsen, have claimed that the theist response makes an illogical jump.[18] The theistic response says that since God has a purpose for my life, my life has meaning. But the second part of this statement does not follow from the first. Suppose, for example, that when you were born your father had a purpose for you: He wanted you to become a lawyer. Clearly, from the fact that your father had a purpose for you, it does not follow that your life must have meaning. In a similar way, critics claim that from the fact that God or some being out in the universe somewhere has a purpose for you, it does not follow that your life must have a meaning. If some being on a star somewhere, or even God, decides to assign you a purpose, it does not follow that this purpose gives meaning to your life. A life with meaning seems

---

[16] Leo Tolstoy, *My Confession*, 23–24.

[17] Kurt Baier, "The Meaning of Life," in Steven Sanders and David R. Cheney, eds., *The Meaning of Life* (Englewood Cliffs, NJ: Prentice-Hall, 1980), 56.

[18] Kai Nielsen, "Linguistic Philosophy and 'The Meaning of Life,'" in Sanders and Cheney, eds., *The Meaning of Life*, 129–154.

to be a life with value, and facts about other beings—even God—cannot give value to your life.

MEANING AND HUMAN PROGRESS

Many philosophers have accepted the view that the individual life has meaning only when it is related to something bigger or more important than the individual's life. But, instead of suggesting that God is the "bigger" whole that gives life meaning, they have proposed that there are other, larger realities that can infuse the individual's life with meaning. In particular, some philosophers have suggested that contributing to human progress can give meaning to human life.

Georg Hegel, for example, argued that history shows progress. "The History of the world," Hegel wrote, "is none other than the progress of the consciousness of freedom."[19] As history develops, Hegel claims, people see more clearly that humans are essentially free, and more people actually become free. In the ancient "Oriental" empires of China, India, and Egypt, Hegel claims, only one person—the emperor—was recognized as completely free. Everyone else was treated despotically. These empires were succeeded by the Greek and Roman empires, in which all citizens were recognized as free. But many people in these empires were slaves and had no freedom. The Greek and Roman empires, then, recognized only that *some* are free. These empires were eventually succeeded by the nations of the modern world. In the modern nations, which Hegel calls the "German nations," slavery is abolished and all men are finally recognized as free:

> The Orientals have not attained the knowledge that Spirit—Man as such—is free; and because they do not know this, they are not free. They only know that one is free. But on this very account, the freedom of that one is only caprice; ferocity— brutal recklessness of passion, or a mildness and tameness of the desires, which is itself only an accident of Nature—mere caprice like the former.—That one is therefore only a Despot; not a free man.
>
> The consciousness of Freedom first arose among the Greeks, and therefore they were free; but they and the Romans likewise, knew only that some are free—not man as such. Even Plato and Aristotle did not know this. The Greeks, therefore, had slaves; and their whole life and the maintenance of their splendid liberty, was implicated with the institution of slavery: a fact, moreover, which made that liberty on the one hand only an accidental, transient and limited growth; on the other hand, constituted it a rigorous thraldom of our common nature—of the human.
>
> The German nations, under the influence of Christianity, were the first to attain the consciousness that man, as man, is free: that it is the freedom of Spirit, which constitutes its essence.[20]

The progress that we see in history, Hegel holds, is not continuous. Here history moves forward, there it pauses, and there it may briefly regress. But in its overall sweep, history keeps moving toward a better and more perfect world:

---

[19] George Wilhelm Friedrich Hegel, *The Philosophy of History*, trans. J. Sibree (New York: Dover, 1956), 19.
[20] Ibid., 18.

The mutations which history presents have been long characterized in general, as an advance to something better, more perfect. . . . This peculiarity in the world of mind has indicated in the case of man . . . a real capacity for change, and that for the better—an impulse of perfectibility. . . .

Universal history—as already demonstrated—shows the development of the consciousness of Freedom on the part of Spirit, and of the consequent realization of that Freedom. This development implies a gradation—a series of increasingly adequate expressions or manifestations of Freedom.[21]

Hegel claims that if the individual person becomes a part of this progressive movement of history, his or her life will have meaning. In fact, apart from this forward sweep of history, the individual cannot find meaning. All meaning for the individual lies in entering and participating in the spirit of the age, the particular way in which freedom is evolving during the individual's lifetime.

Other philosophers have also proposed that we can see progress in history and that by taking part in this progress the individual finds meaning in life. Karl Marx, who adopted many of Hegel's ideas about how history moves from an Asiatic, through an ancient, and on to a modern society, also felt that history was progressing toward a better and more perfect world. Progress for Marx, however, is economic progress: "In broad outline, the Asiatic, ancient, feudal and modern bourgeois modes of production may be designated as epochs marking progress in the economic development of society."[22] For Marx, the more perfect future world would be a world without economic classes—the classless society: "In place of the old bourgeois society, with its classes and class antagonisms, we shall have an association in which the free development of each is the condition for the free development of all."[23] To find meaning in life, the individual must join in the struggle to overthrow the old capitalist structures, which will give way to the new, classless society.

Others have proposed different ways to contribute to human progress. Some have suggested that as scientific knowledge progresses, for the scientist life acquires meaning through the contributions that he or she makes to this progress. Others suggest that society can evolve and become better, and that by contributing to making ours a better society a person's life can have meaning. Still others believe that human life in many different ways can be made better, and so for them life has meaning when they contribute to making human life better.

But do these ideas of progress make sense today? Does history really reveal any kind of progress toward a goal? Doesn't history, on the contrary, exhibit decline, not progress? Take, for example, the state of the environment. Isn't the environment dirtier, uglier, more polluted, more crowded, and more degraded today than ever before? Or look at the state of the world. Haven't the grim experiences of two world wars in this century been enough to put an end to the traditional idea of progress and to optimistic feelings about the future? The title

Communism, like any other revealed religion, is largely made up of prophecies.

H. L. MENCKEN

[21] Ibid., 54, 63.
[22] Karl Marx, *Toward a Critique of Political Economy*, 13: 10, trans. A. Wood, quoted in *A Dictionary of Philosophical Quotations*, ed. A. J. Ayer and Jane O'Grady (Oxford, UK: Blackwell, 1992), 291.
[23] Karl Marx and Friederick Engels, *Manifesto of the Communist Party*, 6: 505, quoted in *Dictionary of Philosophical Quotations*, 288.

of a widely read book by historian Oswald Spengler that was written after the First World War seems to be a perfect description of our situation: *Decline of the West*. Critics argue that personal meaning and value cannot be based on this kind of history.

Moreover, if there is human progress in history, then it must have a goal and this goal must be valuable. But why should we accept the idea that greater freedom or a "classless society" or any other goal is worth seeking? Why should such goals matter to me? Even if such goals are valuable, how can we be sure that history is moving to achieve them? If humans have free will (which we discussed earlier), then doesn't this mean that there is no way of knowing ahead of time that humans will choose to move toward some specific goal?

The American philosopher Francis Fukuyama has recently added a startling complication to these ideas. Fukuyama has argued that history is no longer progressing toward any goal. History has already reached the goals that Hegel said history was moving toward. Fukuyama summarizes his views as follows:

> I argued that a remarkable consensus concerning the legitimacy of liberal democracy as a system of government had emerged throughout the world over the past few years, as it conquered rival ideologies like hereditary monarchy, fascism, and most recently communism. More than that, however, I argued that liberal democracy may constitute the "end point of mankind's ideological evolution" and the "final form of human government," and as such constituted the "end of history." That is, while earlier forms of government were characterized by grave defects and irrationalities that led to their eventual collapse, liberal democracy was arguably free from such fundamental internal contradictions. This was not to say that today's stable democracies, like the United States, France, or Switzerland, were not without injustice or serious social problems. But these problems were ones of incomplete implementation of the twin principles of liberty and equality on which modern democracy is founded, rather than of flaws in the principles themselves. While some present-day countries might fail to achieve stable liberal democracy, and others might lapse back into other, more primitive forms of rule like theocracy or military dictatorship, the ideal of liberal democracy could not be improved upon.[24]

History, then, has attained all its goals. So there can be no more progress: We have reached the end of historical progress.

Fukuyama's view forces us to think again about the social issues that we discussed in Chapter 8. There we discussed whether a liberal society is the best there is or whether it can be improved upon. If it is true that a government based on liberalism is the best there can be, and if all the world has accepted this view, then Fukuyama is right. We've reached our goal, and there can be no more human progress. It is foolish, then, to think that our lives can have meaning by contributing to human progress.

Yet many people today believe that humanity is in some sense still progressing. They believe that our lives can have meaning by contributing toward this progress and by "making this a better world." For example, the historian Charles Van Doren has argued that although there is little evidence for progress in economic, political, moral, or artistic matters, there is nonetheless clear

---

[24] Francis Fukuyama, *The End of History and the Last Man* (New York: Avon, 1992), xi.

"Liberty Leading the People," by Eugene Delacroix. (1830). Hegel claims that if the individual person becomes a part of the progressive movement of history toward ever greater freedom, his life will have meaning. Apart from this forward sweep of history, the individual cannot find meaning.

progress in human knowledge. We might not be becoming better people, but at least we know more now than we ever did in our earlier history.

For many people, though, the idea of contributing to human progress no longer makes sense.

THE NIHILIST RESPONSE TO MEANING

Unable to find meaning in God or human progress, many philosophers have argued that life has no meaning. The philosopher Arthur Schopenhauer argued, for example, that everything passes away and "that which in the next moment exists no more, and vanishes utterly, like a dream, can never be worth a serious effort." Schopenhauer concluded that "All good things are vanity, the world in all its ends bankrupt, and life a business which does not cover its expenses":

> A quick test of the assertion that enjoyment outweighs pain in this world, or that they are at any rate balanced, would be to compare the feelings of an animal engaged in eating another with those of the animal being eaten. . . .
>
> History shows us the life of nations and finds nothing to narrate but wars and tumults; the peaceful years appear only as occasional brief pauses and interludes. In

"The Subway" by George Tooker. (1950). Richard Taylor argues that if we look at a busy street and observe the throng doing the same things today that they did yesterday and will repeat tomorrow, we can see that life is a meaningless repetition of pointless activities.

just the same way the life of the individual is a constant struggle, and not merely a metaphorical one against want or boredom, but also an actual struggle against other people. He discovers adversaries everywhere, lives in continual conflict and dies with sword in hand. . . .

That human life must be some kind of mistake is sufficiently proved by the simple observation that man is a compound of needs which are hard to satisfy; that their satisfaction achieves nothing but a painless condition in which he is only given over to boredom; and that boredom is a direct proof that existence is in itself valueless, for boredom is nothing other than the sensation of the emptiness of existence.[25]

The contemporary American philosopher Richard Taylor also argues for the view that human life has no meaning:

We toil after goals, most of them—indeed every single one of them—of transitory significance and, having gained one of them, we immediately set forth for the next, as if that one had never been, with this next one being essentially more of the same. Look at a busy street any day, and observe the throng going hither and thither. To what? Some office or shop, where the same things will be done today as were done yesterday, and are done now so they may be repeated tomorrow . . . most such effort is directed only to the establishment and perpetuation of home and family; that is, to the begetting of others who will follow in our steps to do more of the same. . . . Our achievements, even though they are often beautiful, are mostly bubbles; and those that do last, like the sand-swept pyramids, soon become mere curiosities. . . . Nations are built upon the bones of their founders and pioneers, but only to decay

Man is abandoned by the forces that created him. Unassisted and undirected by omniscient or benevolent authority, he must fend for himself and find his way in an indifferent universe.

CARL BECKER

---

[25] Arthur Schopenhauer, *Essays and Aphorisms*, trans. R. J. Hollindale (Penguin, 1970), 41–50.

and crumble before long, their rubble then becoming the foundation for others directed to exactly the same fate.[26]

Perhaps the views of both Schopenhauer and Taylor are based on the *nihilist* view that there is now no larger whole or plan to which we can contribute. Both God and the idea of progress no longer make sense. Moreover, human life and all that humans produce is too insignificant and fleeting to be a source of meaning. Human life is just an endless repetition of the same meaningless events that came before. What then is left?

SUBJECTIVE MEANING

Some philosophers, such as R. M. Hare, have argued that the nihilist response is mistaken.[27] The key mistake of the nihilist is to fail to see that a person's life can have meaning if the person chooses goals that give direction to the person's life and the person feels that these goals matter, that they are valuable and worth pursuing. Family, country, religion, friends—all these can become my personal goals, and if these matter to me, then by choosing to pursue them, I can give my life meaning and value.

Many philosophers have argued that life can have a subjective meaning through the goals or purposes that we freely undertake to pursue. One of the earliest was Kierkegaard, for whom the starting point in life is choosing something for which I am willing to live or die:

> What I really lack is to be clear in my mind what I am to do, not what I am to know, except insofar as a certain understanding must precede every action. The thing is to understand myself, to see what God really wishes me to do; the thing is to find a truth which is true for me, to find the idea for which I can live and die.[28]

Kierkegaard described three lifestyles, which he called aesthetic, ethical, and religious. Which of these lifestyles was best for oneself, he felt, is never clear. Yet the key to living authentically is to make a decisive choice among them. And, in so choosing, one creates the meaning of one's life:

> Every human being . . . has a natural need to formulate a life-view, a conception of the meaning of life and of its purpose. The person who lives aesthetically also does that, and the popular expression heard in all ages . . . [to describe this stage of life is]: One must enjoy life. . . . We encounter [some aesthetic] life views that teach that we are to enjoy life . . . [through something] outside the individual. This is the case with every life-view in which wealth, honors, noble birth, etc., are made life's task and its content. . . . [Other] life-views teach that we are to enjoy life . . . [through something] within the individual himself . . . ordinarily defined as talent. It [may be] a talent for practical affairs, a talent for business, a talent for mathematics, a talent for writing, a talent for art, a talent for philosophy. Satisfaction in life, enjoyment, is sought in the unfolding of this talent. . . .

Make haste and enjoy life while you have it. Why care what happens when you are dead?

LIE ZI

---

[26] Richard Taylor, "The Meaning of Life," in Klemke, ed., *The Meaning of Life,* 146.

[27] See R. M. Hare, "Nothing Matters," in Klemke, ed., *The Meaning of Life,* 241–247.

[28] Søren Kierkegaard, *The Journals of Kierkegaard,* trans. and ed. A. Dru (London: Collins, 1958), 44.

In contrast to an aesthetic life-view . . . we often hear about another life-view that places the meaning of life in living for the performance of one's moral duties. This is supposed to signify an ethical view of life. . . . [But it is] a mistake to [see duty as something that is imposed] from outside the individual. . . . The truly ethical person . . . does not have duty outside himself but within himself. . . . When a person has felt the intensity of duty with all his energy, then he is ethically matured, and then duty will break forth within him. . . .

The story of Abraham [in the Bible] contains . . . a teleological suspension of the ethical. . . . [Abraham faithfully obeyed God's command to sacrifice the life of his only beloved son although human sacrifice violated his moral duty; at the last moment God stayed Abraham's hand.] Abraham represents faith. . . . He acts by virtue of the absurd. . . . By his act he transgressed the ethical altogether and had a higher telos outside, in relation to which he suspended it. . . . Why then does Abraham do it? For God's sake and—the two are wholly identical—for his own sake. He does it for God's sake because God demands this proof of his faith; he does it for his own sake so that he can prove it.[29]

Notice that for Kierkegaard, the meaning of life is subjective. It is by our personal or subjective choice of an aesthetic, ethical, or religious life that we determine the meaning of life for us. We can choose, for example, to pursue wealth or honor, or enjoyment of our talents. Then pleasure becomes the meaning of life. Such a life is limited, and the individual may eventually feel that it is not a true existence. Then he must decide whether to stay at the aesthetic stage, whose attractions he knows, or, by an act of will, to commit himself to the next stage.

The commitment to the ethical stage of life involves embracing internally the rational universal moral obligation to restrain one's desire for pleasure. Moral integrity and honesty become the meaning of life. At first, one confidently assumes that one can live up to the moral law. But eventually the individual comes to see that he cannot do what morality requires, and he experiences guilt or sin. The individual realizes that he can remain at the ethical level and keep trying to do what is right, or he can admit that he is estranged from God, whom he needs, and choose to move to the next stage.

But the move to the religious stage is filled with uncertainty, since it is a commitment not to a rational principle, but to a relationship with a person, God, who cannot be rationally understood. The move to the religious stage requires a "leap of faith" like Abraham's decision to trust God, a leap that is made alone, without any guarantee of being right, in "fear and trembling." But we must choose, and what we choose becomes the meaning of life for us.

Many years later, the French philosopher Jean-Paul Sartre took up several of these themes. Sartre was an atheist. Nevertheless, he agreed with Kierkegaard that the meaning of life is the result of a choice. Neither God nor the idea of progress can provide us with purpose and meaning unless we choose to commit ourselves to these. Then it is our choice that makes them meaningful and a source of value.

---

[29] Søren Kierkegaard, *Either/Or*, vol. II, trans. Howard V. Hong and Edna H. Hong, reprinted in Denise Peterfreund White, ed., *Great Traditions in Ethics*, 8th ed. (Belmont, CA: Wadsworth, 1996), 228, 229, 230, 232.

We met Sartre earlier when we were discussing human nature. Recall that Sartre holds that there are no fixed values to give meaning to our lives. Until we choose, life has no fixed purpose, no set values to pursue, and no objective meaning. But by choosing a cause, a religion, a life goal, I create the meaning of my life. Here is how Sartre puts this idea:

> If God does not exist, we find no values or commands to turn to which legitimize our conduct. So, in the bright realm of values, we have no excuse behind us, nor justification before us. We are alone, with no excuses. . . .
>
> To say that we invent values means nothing else but this: life has no meaning a priori. Before you come alive, life is nothing; it's up to you to give it a meaning, and value is nothing else but the meaning that you choose.[30]

But in the end, doesn't Sartre leave us without a compass as we struggle to find meaning in our lives? If Sartre is right, then before we choose, one thing has no more value than another thing. If Sartre is right, then we should be able to find meaning in our lives by choosing anything at all. But this is clearly not true. A person cannot feel that her life has meaning if she decides to devote it to making tiny little piles of sand on the beach. If we are to feel that our life has meaning, we have to devote ourselves to goals or causes that we feel, even before we choose, have value and are worth devoting ourselves to.

Sartre and Kierkegaard, then, may be right when they claim that nothing can give my life meaning unless I choose it and make it my own. But Sartre, at least, seems wrong to claim that before I choose, nothing has value. On the contrary, what I choose to devote my life to must be something that I feel ahead of time is valuable and worth pursuing. If it is not valuable apart from my choice, it cannot give my life meaning.

Does life have meaning? For many people, life does have meaning because they feel that they have a part to play in a larger whole that gives their life value, purpose, and a goal. For them, meaning might come from seeing themselves as part of a larger divine plan, or from seeing themselves as contributing to human progress. But for many, these sources of meaning are no longer useful. Some reject God; some reject the idea of human progress; still others reject both. The result is that many accept nihilism: They conclude that life has no meaning.

But Kierkegaard and Sartre reveal another possibility: the possibility of making meaning through honest and authentic choice. In a way, even those who look to God or human progress for meaning must choose to commit themselves to these. But if meaning is made through choice, then the range of meaning is wider than God and human progress. Life can have meaning through a commitment to a variety of human concerns. For one person, meaning may come through a commitment to family or to loving relationships, for another through a commitment to art, for another through a commitment to honesty and moral integrity, and for another through a commitment to religious faith.

Has all this suffering, this dying around us, a meaning? For, if not, then ultimately there is no meaning to survival; for a life whose meaning depends upon whether one escapes suffering ultimately would not be worth living at all.

VIKTOR FRANKL

---

[30] Jean-Paul Sartre, *Existentialism and Human Emotions* (New York: Philosophical Library, 1957), 23, 49.

However, the key question is the one that Sartre forces us to face: Can anything we choose make life meaningful for us? If so, then meaning is easy: We can find meaning by committing ourselves to the pursuit of money, the pursuit of pleasure, self-development, or even making little piles of sand on the ocean shore. Or, as Kierkegaard suggests, life can have meaning only if we commit ourselves to a cause that, ahead of time, we know is worth pursuing. Is finding meaning the difficult pursuit of moving through ever more authentic stages of life, finding at each stage that I need more, finding at each stage that meaning requires a commitment to what I know ahead of time will matter?

QUESTIONS

1. What meaning, if any, do you believe that life has? Explain why you believe that life has the meaning (or lack of meaning) that you describe.

2. Do you agree with Hegel that human history exhibits progress? Does human history exhibit the kind of progress that Hegel said it did? Explain your answers.

3. If you sat down to write the story of your life, do you think that your life's story would exhibit progress? Why?

4. Does it matter whether or not life has meaning? If life has no meaning but you are having a lot of fun, should you look closely at the question of whether life has meaning? If you are happy and unbothered, is it better to ignore the question, or is there some reason to look at the question closely anyway? Explain your answer.

9.4 Chapter Summary and Conclusions

We have now come to the end of our philosophical journey. If you must leave a philosophy course having learned only one thing, the prized possession might be to travel with a philosophical attitude.

A philosophical attitude does not end with a philosophy course, although it may begin with one. Rather, the philosophical attitude needs lifelong nurturing to flourish and strengthen. And it requires something else—courage—the courage to continue on the journey once begun.

The main points of this chapter are as follows:

1. The questions "What is art?" and "What is good art?" are related (9.2).

2. Plato and Aristotle proposed that art is imitation. Plato condemned art because it was only an imitation, but Aristotle held that art could provide insight into reality and a catharsis of our feelings (9.2).

3. The Romantics claimed that art is expression of feeling and that good art expresses feeling well. Benedetto Croce agreed (9.2).

4. Clive Bell argues that art is significant form, relating his theory to the aesthetic theory of beauty (9.2).

5. A recent approach to art claims that art is whatever an artworld says it is (9.2).

6. Arthur Danto has argued that art has ended because the artist has become a philosopher (9.2).

7. The theistic response to the question of the meaning of life holds that the meaning of life is to be explained in terms of the individual's relationship to a larger divine plan (9.3).

8. Hegel and Marx define the meaning of life in terms of contributing toward human progress. For Hegel, history progresses toward a fuller expansion of freedom; for Marx, history progresses toward a classless society. Fukuyama argues that the end of history has passed, so there is no longer any human progress (9.3).

9. The nihilist response to the meaning of life is the claim that life has no meaning (9.3).

10. The existentialists Søren Kierkegaard and Jean-Paul Sartre argue that the meaning of life is created by what one chooses (9.3).

9.5 Suggestions for Further Reading

Adler, Alfred. *What Life Should Mean to You*. New York: G. P. Putnam's Sons, 1958. Adler takes a psychological approach to the question of meaning in life.

Britton, Karl. *Philosophy and the Meaning of Life*. Cambridge, UK: Cambridge University Press, 1969. Britton provides a good introduction to the issues surrounding the question of the meaning of life.

Chalmers, R. C., and J. A. Irving, eds. *The Meaning of Life in Five Great Religions*. Louisville, KY: Westminster, 1965. Some good discussions of how several religions look at the question of the meaning of life.

Cooper, David, ed. *A Companion to Aesthetics*. Oxford, UK: Blackwell, 1992. Cooper's book is a kind of "dictionary" of important topics in the philosophy of art. This is an excellent resource, but not always easy reading.

Dickie, George. *Introduction to Aesthetics: An Analytic Approach*. New York: Oxford University Press, 1997. Dickie's text is a very readable and easy introduction to the philosophy of art. Dickie is one of the main supporters of the idea of an "artworld."

Frankl, Viktor. *Man's Search for Meaning*. Boston: Beacon, 1963. Frankl's reflections on the meaning of life emerged from his imprisonment in a Nazi camp for the "crime" of being a Jew. Although dated, this book is still a classic.

Klemke, E. D. *The Meaning of Life*. New York: Oxford University Press, 1981. Klemke's book includes many of the same essays contained in Sanders and Cheney (see below), but Klemke is more receptive to theistic attempts to give meaning to life.

May, Rollo. *Man's Search for Meaning*. New York: Norton, 1953. Although a bit dated, May's book is a wonderful expression of how a psychologist sees the search for meaning.

Neill, Alex, and Aaron Ridley. *The Philosophy of Art: Readings Ancient and Modern*. New York: McGraw-Hill, 1996. This anthology includes an excellent selection of readings that cover all the topics discussed in this chapter and much more. Probably the best collection of readings on philosophy and art.

Sanders, Steven, and David R. Cheney, eds. *The Meaning of Life: Questions, Answers, and Analysis*. Englewood Cliffs, NJ: Prentice-Hall, 1980. This is an excellent short collection of old and contemporary writings on the meaning of life. Although some of the articles are hard to read, many are thought-provoking and insightful.

Stern, Alfred. *The Search for Meaning: Philosophical Vistas*. Memphis, TN: Memphis State University Press, 1971. Stern discusses many of the issues covered in this chapter.

Art Acknowledgements

Art Resource   p. 300, Alinari/Art Resource (*Ecstacy of Saint Teresa* by Giovanni Lorenzo Bernini); p. 561, Louvre/Giraudon/Art Resource (*The Raft of the Medusa* by Theodore Gericault); p. 642, Prado/Scala/Art Resource (*The Third of May* by Francisco Goya); p. 671, Scala/Art Resource (*Lacoon and His Two Sons* by Hagesandrus, Polydorus and Athenodorus, 1st Century AD); p. 674, Giraudon/Art Resource (*Guernica* by Pablo Picasso, 1937); p. 679, Scala/Art Resource (*Springtime* by Sandro Botticelli, C. 1478)

The Bettmann Archive   pp. 5, 15, 19, 77, 92, 113, 145, 153, 159, 198, 199, 224, 248, 252, 275, 296, 302, 305, 320, 326, 356, 366, 406, 430, 470, 508, 524, 570, 574, 594, 599, 615, 621, 634, 646, 676, 681, 688.

The Bridgeman Art Library, Intl.   p. 681 (*Bottle Rack* by Marcel DuChamp); p. 691, Peter Willi/Bridgeman Art Library (*Liberty Leading the People* by Eugene Delacroix)

Brown Bros.   p. 135

The Computer History Museum   p. 116

Dover Books   p. 127, 495

Richard Gordon   p. 427 © Richard Gordon

Institute of Contemporary Art, Boston, Massachusetts   p. 678 (*History Lessons* by David Diao)

The Library of Congress   p. 273 (*The Ancient of Days* by William Blake)

Los Angeles County Museum of Art   p. 435, purchased with funds provided by the Mr. and Mrs. William Preston Harrison Collection. Copyright © 1984 Museum Associates, Los Angeles County Museum of Art (*La Trahison des Images* by Réne Magritte). All rights reserved.

The Metropolitan Museum of Art   p. 31, Wolfe Fund, 1931. Catharine Lorillard Wolfe Collection. All rights reserved (*The Death of Socrates* by Jacques Louis David).

The Museum of Modern Art, New York   p. 144, collection, gift of Mrs. Simon Guggenheim (*Girl Before a Mirror* by Pablo Picasso, 1932, Oil on canvas, 64″ × 51¼″); p. 179, collection, given anonymously (*The Persistence of Memory* by Salvadore Dali, 1931. Oil on canvas, 9½″ × 13″); p. 353, collection, purchase (*The False Mirror* by Réne Magritte, 1928. Oil on canvas, 21¼″ × 31⅛″); p 378, collection, gift of Nelson A. Rockefeller (*The Dream* by Henri Rousseau. 1910. Oil on canvas, 6′8½ × 9′9½″).

National Gallery of Art, Washington, D.C.   p. 87, Rosenwald Collection (*Adam and Eve* by Albrecht Dürer). By courtesy of the National Gallery of Art, Washington, D.C.

The Nelson-Atkins Museum of Art, Kansas City, Missouri   p. 312, Nelson Trust 70–45 (*Dancing Ganesha,* India, ninth century); p. 533, Nelson Trust 59–47 (*Buddha,* China, fifth century)

Philadelphia Museum of Art   p. 381, Louise and Walter Arensberg Collection (*Nude Descending a Staircase, No. 2* by Marcel Duchamp)

Richard Schultz   p. 545 (photograph of Carol Gilligan)

Whitney Museum of American Art   p. 693, Collection of the Whitney Museum of American Art, New York. Juliana Force Purchase, (*The Subway* by George Tooker, 1950, egg tempera on composition board)

Helmut Wimmer   p. 192, (*The Solar System*) © Helmut Wimmer

Yale University Art Gallery   p. 597, © Yale University Art Gallery (*The Declaration of Independence* by George Trumbull)

Yale University Library   p. 437

Glossary

Some of these terms are not used in the text but are included because they are part of the philosopher's working vocabulary. In many instances these terms carry nuances that are unmentioned here. Every attempt has been made to be concise without being misleading.

A

abstraction the mental power of separating one part of an entity from its other parts or of inferring the class from the particular instance

accidental characteristic a characteristic that is not necessary to make a thing what it is; an accompanying characteristic

act utilitarianism in normative ethics, the position that an action is moral if it produces the greatest happiness for the most people

actual duty according to William David Ross, the action one ought to perform after considering and weighing all the prima facie duties involved

aesthetics the branch of philosophy that studies beauty, especially in the arts

agnosticism a claim of ignorance; the claim that God's existence can be neither proved nor disproved

analogy a comparison; when you reason from analogy, you conclude that because two or more entities share one aspect, they share another as well

analytic philosophy the philosophical school of thought associated with Russell, Moore, Ryle, Carnap, Ayer, and Wittgenstein that emphasizes the analysis of language and meaning

anarchism the theory that all forms of government are incompatible with individual and social liberty and should be abolished

animism the belief that many spirits inhabit nature

antecedent in a hypothetical statement, the first simple sentence, usually preceded by the word *if*

anthropomorphism the attributing of human qualities to nonhuman entities, especially to God

antinomy used by Immanuel Kant to refer to contradictory conclusions arrived at through valid deduction

antirealism the doctrine that the objects of our senses do not exist independently of our perceptions, beliefs, concepts, and language

a posteriori pertaining to knowledge stated in empirically verifiable statements; inductive reasoning

a priori pertaining to knowledge that is logically prior to experience; reasoning based on such knowledge

argument a group of statements consisting of premises and conclusions of such a type that the premises are intended to prove or demonstrate the conclusion

argument from design See **design argument.**

atheism denial of theism

atman the Hindu idea of the self after enlightenment; the concept of no self

authority a common secondary source of knowledge; a source existing outside the person making the claim that the person uses as an expert source of information

autonomy the freedom of being able to decide for oneself by using one's own rationality

avidya in Buddhism, the cause of all suffering and frustration; ignorance or unawareness that leads to clinging

axiology the study of the general theory of values, including their origin, nature, and classification

axiom a proposition regarded as self-evident or true

B

behaviorism a school of psychology that restricts the study of human nature to what can be observed rather than to states of consciousness

Brahman the Hindu concept of an impersonal Supreme Being; the source and goal of everything

C

categorical imperative Immanuel Kant's ethical formula: act as if the maxim (general rule by which you act could be willed to become a universal law; the belief that what is right for one person is also right for everyone in similar circumstances

categorical statement a statement that asserts or denies that part or all of one category of things is included in part or all of another category of things

categorical syllogism an argument that consists of two premises and a conclusion, which are all categorical statements, and that contains exactly three terms

catharsis a purging or cleansing of the emotions; used by Aristotle to describe the purifying of the audience through emotional involvement in a play

causality, causation the relationship of events or of cause and effect

cause whatever is responsible for or leads to a change, motion, or condition

classification the process of grouping like things

cognition the acquiring of knowledge of something; the mental process by which we become aware of the objects of perception and thought

coherence theory a theory contending that truth is a property of a related group of consistent statements

common sense the way of looking at things apart from technical or special training

common-sense realism the epistemological position that does not distinguish between an object and an experience of it

concept a general idea, distinguished from a *percept,* which we have upon experiencing particular entities; thus, we can have a percept when we see particular citizen John Smith, but we have a concept of man, a universal unexperienced entity

conceptual relativist view in epistemology, the view that a true scientific theory is nothing more than a theory that coheres with the conceptual framework accepted by a community of scientists

conclusion the statement that an argument is intended to demonstrate or prove

conditioned genesis the Buddhist formula consisting of twelve factors that summarize the principles of conditionality, relativity, and interdependence

consequent in a hypothetical statement, the second simple sentence, usually preceded by the word *then*

consequentialist theory in ethics, the position that the morality of an action is determined by its nonmoral consequences

contingent an entity that may be and also may not be

contract theory in social philosophy, the doctrine that individuals give up certain liberties and rights to the state, which in turn guarantees such rights as life, liberty, and the pursuit of happiness

correspondence theory a theory contending that truth is an agreement between a proposition and a fact

cosmological argument an argument for the existence of God that claims that there must be an ultimate causal explanation for why the universe as a totality exists

cosmology the study of the universal world process—the process by which the world unfolds and evolves

critical philosophy the analysis and definition of basic concepts and the precise expression and criticism of basic beliefs

D

deduction the process of reasoning to logically certain conclusions

deductive argument an argument in which the premises are intended to show that the conclusion must necessarily be true

defining characteristic a characteristic in whose absence a thing would not be what it is

deism a widespread belief in the seventeenth and eighteenth centuries in a God who, having created the universe, remains apart from it and administers it through natural laws

denotation a definition that is a verbal example of what a word signifies

design argument an argument for the existence of God that claims that the order and purpose manifest in the working of things in the universe require a God

designation a definition consisting of the defining characteristics of a word

determinism the theory that everything that occurs happens in accordance with some regular pattern or law

dharma in Buddhism, the doctrine whereby self-frustration is ended; the Eightfold Path

dialectic in general, the critical analysis of ideas to determine their meanings, implications, and assumptions; as used by Hegel, a method of reasoning used to synthesize contradictions

disanalogy a difference between compared things that lessens the likelihood of an analogical conclusion

disjunct one of the alternatives of a disjunctive statement

disjunctive statement a statement that poses alternatives of the form *either X or Y (or both)*

disjunctive syllogism an argument containing two premises and a conclusion, in which one premise is a disjunctive statement, one premise affirms or denies one of the disjuncts, and the conclusion affirms or denies the other disjunct

divine command theory a single-rule, nonconsequential normative theory that says we should always do the will of God

dualism the theory that reality is composed of two different substances so that neither one can be related to the other—thus: spirit/matter, mind/body, good/evil

duty in ethics, a justified obligation imposed on an individual

duty theory in ethics, the position that the moral action is the one that con-

forms with obligations accrued in the past, such as the obligations of gratitude, fidelity, or justice

E

eclecticism the practice of choosing what is thought best from various philosophies

egoism a consequentialist ethical theory that contends that we act morally when we act in a way that promotes our own best long-term interests

emergence, emergent evolution the view that in the development of the universe, new life forms appear that cannot be explained solely through analysis of previous forms

emotivism the metaethical position that ethical statements primarily express surprise, shock, or some other emotion

empathy a psychological and aesthetic designation of the attitudes, reactions, and feelings that we experience when we identify with another person or object

empiricism the position that knowledge has its origins in and derives all of its content from experience

entelechy a nonmaterial power, vital force, or purpose that permits a form to come to realization

entitlement theory a theory of social justice contending that individuals are entitled to the holdings that they have acquired without harming anyone in the process

epiphenomenalism the view that matter is primary and that the mind is a secondary phenomenon accompanying some bodily processes

epistemology the branch of philosophy that investigates the nature, sources, limitations, and validity of knowledge

essence that which makes an entity what it is; that defining characteristic in whose absence a thing would not be itself

eternal law for Aquinas, God's decrees for the governance of the universe

ethical absolutism in ethics, the view that affirms the existence of a single correct and universally applicable moral standard

ethical relativism any view that denies the existence of a single universally applicable moral standard

ethics the branch of philosophy that tries to determine the good and right thing to do

eudaemonism the view that the goal of life is happiness—that is, a complete, long-lived kind of well-being; from the Greek *eudaimonia*, happiness

excusability the concept that under certain circumstances, people are not morally responsible for their decisions and conduct

existence actuality

existentialism a twentieth-century philosophy that denies any essential human nature; each of us creates our own essence through free action

extrasensory perception experiences outside normal sensory activity, as in telepathy

F

fallacy an incorrect way of reasoning; an argument that tries to persuade psychologically but not logically

fallacies of ambiguity fallacies that result from using words unclearly or ambiguously

fallacies of relevance fallacies of appealing to something that is not relevant to the argument

false cause the fallacy of arguing that since one event or condition was present *before* another, the earlier event or condition must be the *cause* of the later one

false dilemma an erroneous bipolarity resulting from the existence of positions between the two presented

fatalism the view that events are fixed, that humans can do nothing to alter them

finite limited

forgetful induction the fallacy of failing to take into account all the relevant evidence bearing on a conclusion

formal fallacy an argument whose form is such that the premises do not guarantee the conclusion

formalism in ethics, the view that moral acts follow from fixed moral principles and do not change because of circumstances

free will the denial that human acts are completely determined

G

Gestalt a psychological view that the whole is not just the sum of its parts

Golden Rule the ethical rule that holds: Do unto others as you would have them do unto you

H

hard determinism the doctrine that every event has a cause, which entails the denial of moral freedom

hasty generalization the fallacy of basing an inductive argument on insufficient observations or an unrepresentative sample

hedonism the view that pleasure is intrinsically worthwhile and is the human's good

humanism the view that stresses distinctly human values and ideals

human law for Aquinas, specific codes of justice that apply to a particular group, society, or community

human nature what it essentially means to be a human being; what makes us different from anything else

hypothesis in general, an assumption, statement, or theory of explanation, the truth of which is under investigation

hypothetical argument an argument containing hypothetical or conditional statements

hypothetical statement a statement of the form *if . . . , then . . .*

hypothetical syllogism a hypothetical argument consisting of two premises and a conclusion in which one of the premises is a hypothetical statement and the other premise and the conclusion consist of either the antecedent or the consequent of that hypothetical statement, or their denials

I

idealism in metaphysics, the position that reality is ultimately nonmatter; in epistemology, the position that all we know are our ideas

ideational theory the theory of word meaning that stresses the emotional impact of words

identity theory the theory that mental states are really brain states

immanent indwelling, within the process, as God is frequently thought to be in relation to the creation

immortality the belief that the self or soul survives physical death

indeterminism the view that some individual choices are not determined by preceding events

individualism the social theory that emphasizes the importance of the individual, his or her rights, and independence of action

induction the process of reasoning to probable explanations or judgments

inductive argument an argument in which the premises are intended to show that the conclusion is probably true

inductive reasoning See **induction.**

inference a conclusion arrived at inductively or deductively

infinite unlimited

infinite regress the causal or logical relationship of terms in a series that logically has no first or initiating term

informal fallacy an argument in which the premises fail to guarantee the conclusion but in which the failure is not due to the use of an invalid form; often an argument that attempts to persuade emotionally or psychologically but not logically

innate ideas ideas that, according to some philosophers such as Plato, can never be found in experience but are inborn

instrumentalism synonymous with John Dewey's pragmatism; the view that emphasizes experience and interprets concepts, beliefs, and attitudes as ways in which an organism adjusts to its environment

instrumentalist view in epistemology, the view that scientific theories can be true only in the sense that they enable us accurately to predict what will happen and that any unobservable entities postulated by the theory literally do not exist

interactionism the theory that the mind and the body interact, originally associated with Descartes

intuition a source of knowledge that does not rely on the senses or reason but on direct awareness of something

J

judgment asserting or denying something in the form of a proposition

K

karma the Hindu law of sowing and reaping; determines what form and circumstances we assume in each reincarnated state

L

laissez-faire in economics, politics, and social philosophy, the concept of government noninterference

language an aspect of human behavior that involves the use of vocal sounds and corresponding written symbols in meaningful patterns to formulate and communicate thoughts and feelings

law a rule or body of rules that tell individuals what they may and may not do

law of noncontradiction nothing can be said both to be and not to be something at the same time and in the same respect

libertarianism in metaphysics, the view that determinism is false and that people are free to choose to act other than they do; in social philosophy, the view that the right to freedom from restraint takes priority over all other rights.

linguistic analysis a contemporary form of analytic philosophy claiming that philosophical problems are partially language problems; the purpose of philosophy is to dissolve, not resolve, problems by a rigorous examination of language

logic the branch of epistemology that studies the methods and principles of correct reasoning

logical positivism the philosophical school of thought associated with Carnap and Ayer that claims only analytic and synthetic statements are meaningful and that because metaphysical and ethical statements are neither, the latter are meaningless

logos the term used by classical philosophers to describe the principle of rationality or law that they observed operating in the universe

M

materialism the metaphysical position that reality is ultimately composed of matter

maximin principle the social theory of justice that contends that inequality is allowable only insofar as it improves the lot of the worst-off in a society

maya in Buddhism, the world of illusion

mechanism the view that everything can be explained in terms of laws that govern matter and motion

meliorism from the Latin, meaning better; the view that the world is neither all good nor all bad, but can be improved through human effort

mentalism the view that mind or idea is all that exists

metaethics the study of the meanings of ethical words and of the sentences in which they appear

metaphysics the branch of philosophy that studies the nature of reality

metempsychosis the belief that upon physical death the soul can migrate into another body

monism the view that reality is reducible to one kind of thing or one explanatory principle

monotheism the belief in a single God

morality the standards that an individual or a group has about what is right and wrong or good and evil

morals the rules of conduct by which people live

mysticism the philosophy of religion contending that reality can be known only when we surrender our individuality and experience a union with the divine ground of all existence

N

naive realism the view that the world is as we perceive it to be

naturalism a view of ethics that rejects supernatural principles and maintains that morality can be explained only in terms of scientifically verifiable concepts

natural law a pattern of necessary and universal regularity; a universal moral imperative, a description of what ought to happen in all human relationships

necessary condition a way to refer to cause; for example, when B cannot occur in the absence of A, A is said to be a necessary condition of B

new realism the view that the world is as we perceive it to be

nihilism the view that nothing exists, that nothing has value; the social view that conditions are so bad that they should be destroyed and replaced by something better

nirvana in Buddhism, enlightenment that comes when the limited, clinging self is extinguished

nominalism the view that only particular entities are real and that universals represent detectable likenesses among particulars

nonconsequentialist theory in ethics, the position that the morality of an action is determined by more than just its consequences

nonnaturalism the metaethical position that ethical statements defy translation into nonethical language

nonnormative ethics the scientific or descriptive study of ethics; or the study of ethical terms, including the notion of moral justification

normative ethics the branch of ethics that makes judgments about obligation and value

O

objective a term describing an entity that has a public nature independent of us and our judgments about it

objective idealism the position that ideas exist in an objective state, associated originally with Plato

objective relativism the value theory that contends that values are relative to human satisfaction but that human needs and what satisfies them are open to empirical examination

obligation that which we must or are bound to do because of some duty, agreement, contract, promise, or law

omnipotent all-powerful

omnipresent being everywhere at once

omniscient all-knowing

ontological argument an argument for the existence of God based on the nature of God's being

ontology a subdivision of metaphysics; the theory of the nature of being and existence

ordinary language analysis the philosophical school of thought associated with the later writings of Wittgenstein and with Moore, Ryle, and others that emphasizes the analysis of the meaning of ordinary language and which attempts to correct philosophical confusions created by the misuse of ordinary language

ostensive definition a definition that consists of an instance of a word's denotation

P

panentheism the belief that God is both fixed and changing, inclusive of all possibilities

pantheism the belief that everything is God

parallelism the theory that physical and mental states do not interact but simply accompany each other

parapsychology the school of psychology that studies extrasensory powers

paternalism the view that government may legitimately decide what is in the best interests of adult citizens, just as a parent may legitimately decide what is in the best interests of the child

perception the act or process by which we become aware of things

phenomenalism the belief, associated with Kant, that we can know only appearances (phenomena) and never what is ultimately real (noumena); that the mind has the ability to sort out sense data and provide relationships that hold among them

phenomenology the philosophical school founded by Edmund Husserl, which contends that being is the underlying reality, that what is ultimately real is our consciousness, which itself is being

philosophy the love and pursuit of wisdom

pluralism the view that reality consists of many substances

polytheism belief in many gods

positivism the view that only analytic and synthetic propositions are meaningful

postulate a presupposition used as a basis for establishing a proof

pragmatism the philosophical school of thought, associated with Dewey, James, and Peirce, that tries to mediate between idealism and materialism by rejecting all absolute first principles, tests truth through workability, and views the universe as pluralistic

prajñā in Zen Buddhism, transcendental wisdom

predestination the doctrine that every aspect of our lives has been divinely determined from the beginning of time

premises the statements presented in an argument as reasons for accepting the conclusion

pre-Socratics the Greek philosophers before Socrates

prima facie duties according to William David Ross, duties that generally obligate us but may not in a particular case because of circumstances

primary qualities according to Locke, qualities that inhere in an object: size, shape, weight, and so on

principle of consistency nothing can be said both to be and not to be something at the same time and in the same respect

probability the likelihood of an event's happening or of a statement's being true

proposition a true or false statement

psychological egoism the belief that human beings are so constituted that they must always act out of self-interest

R

rationalism the position that reason alone, without the aid of sensory information, is capable of arriving at some knowledge, at some undeniable truths

realism the doctrine that the objects of our senses exist independently of their being experienced

realist view in epistemology, the view that scientific theories are literally true or false and that the unobservable entities postulated in a scientific theory really exist if the theory is true

reason the capacity for thinking relatively and making inferences; the process of following relationships from thought to thought and of ultimately drawing conclusions

referential theory a theory of word meaning that contends that words refer to things

relativism the view that human judgment is conditioned by factors such as acculturation and personal bias

religious belief in its broadest sense, the belief that there is an unseen order and that we can do no better than to be in harmony with that order

representative realism the position, associated with Locke, that distinguishes between an object and one's experience of it

right in ethics, a justified claim or entitlement to something against someone

rights those things to which we have a just claim

rule utilitarianism the normative ethical position that we should act so that the rule governing our actions produces the greatest happiness for the most people

S

samsara in Buddhism, the round of birth and life

scientific method a way of investigation based on collecting, analyzing, and interpreting sense data to determine the most probable explanation

secondary qualities according to Locke, qualities that we impose on an object: color, smell, texture, and so on

self the individual person; the ego; the knower; that which persists through changes in a person

self-determinism the view that our actions are determined, but not solely, by external forces or conditions

semantics the study of the relationship between words and reality, including their linguistic forms, symbolic nature, and effects on human behavior

sense data images or sensory impressions

situation ethics according to Joseph Fletcher, the doctrine that the moral action produces the greatest amount of Christian love (*agape*)

skepticism in epistemology, the view that varies between doubting all assumptions until proved and claiming that no knowledge is possible

social philosophy the application of moral principles to the problems of freedom, equality, justice, and the state

soft determinism a view that attempts to reconcile freedom and responsibility with determinism

solipsism an extreme form of subjective idealism, contending that only I exist and that everything else is a product of my subjective consciousness

soul the immaterial entity that is identified with consciousness, mind, or personality

subjective that which refers to the knower; that which exists in the consciousness but not apart from it

subjective idealism in epistemology, the position that all we ever know are our own ideas

substance that which is real; essence; the underlying ground in which properties inhere; that which exists in its own right and depends on nothing else

sufficient condition a way to refer to cause; A is said to be a sufficient condition of B if, without exception, whenever A occurs B occurs

T

tautology a statement whose predicate repeats its subject in whole or in part

teleology the view that maintains the reality of purpose and affirms that the universe either was consciously designed or is operating under partly conscious, partly unconscious purposes

telepathy in ESP, the name given to the phenomenon of thought transfer from one person's mind to another's without normal means of communication

terms in a categorical statement, the words that refer to the categories asserted or denied to be included in each other

theism the belief in a personal God who intervenes in the lives of the creation

theology the rational study of God, including religious doctrines

totalitarianism the political view that the state is of paramount importance

transcendental idealism in epistemology, the view that the *form* of our knowledge of reality derives from reason but its *content* comes from our senses

U

universal that which is predictive of many particular entities; thus, "woman" is a universal, since it is predictive of individual women

utilitarianism in ethics, the theory that we should act in such a way that our actions produce the greatest happiness or pleasure

V

valid in logic, having a conclusion that follows from the premises by logical necessity

validity correctness of the reasoning process; characteristic of an argument whose conclusion follows by logical necessity

value an assessment of worth

verification the proving or disproving of a proposition

virtue in ethics, a morally good character trait, such as honesty, courage, or integrity

virtue ethics in ethics, the position that the moral life should be concerned with cultivating a virtuous character rather than following rules of action

vitalism the view that there is in living organisms an entelechy, or life principle, that provides purpose or direction

Index

Time Period	Important Philosophers (placed in period of main contribution)	Political, Cultural, and Scientific Events of Period
1800 A.D.	J. G. Fichte (1762–1814) F. Schleiermacher (1768–1834) G. W. F. Hegel (1770–1831) James Mill (1773–1835) Arthur Schopenhauer (1788–1860)	Thomas Jefferson (1743–1836) president Goethe (1749–1832) publishes *Faust* (1808) Napoleon defeated at Waterloo (1815) Poe (1809–1849) publishes *Fall of the House of Usher* (1839) Revolutions in Paris, Vienna, Venice, Berlin (1848)
1850 A.D.	Ralph Waldo Emerson (1803–1882) Ludwig Feuerbach (1804–1872) John Stuart Mill (1806–1873) Søren Kierkegaard (1813–1855) Henry David Thoreau (1817–1862) Karl Marx (1818–1883) Friedrich Engels (1820–1895) Herbert Spencer (1820–1903) Friedrich Nietzsche (1844–1900)	Darwin (1809–1882) writes *Origin of Species* (1859) American Civil War (1861–1865) Lincoln's Emancipation Proclamation (1863) Huxley (1825–1895) publishes *Man's Place in Nature* (1864) Leo Tolstoy (1828–1910) publishes *War and Peace* (1863)
1900 A.D.	Charles S. Pierce (1839–1914) William James (1842–1910) Francis Bradley (1846–1924) Brand Blanshard (1892–1989) Gottlob Frege (1848–1925) Edmund Husserl (1854–1938) Henri Bergson (1859–1941) James Dewey (1859–1952) J. McTaggart (1866–1925) Mahatma Gandhi (1869–1948)	Sigmund Freud (1856–1939) publishes *The Interpretation of Dreams* (1900) Carl Jung (1875–1961) develops theory of collective unconscious and archetypes Albert Einstein (1879–1955) discovers special relativity (1905) and general relativity (1915) October revolution in Russia begins communist rule (1917) Arthur Eddington (1882–1944) publishes *Nature of the Physical World* (1928) World War I (1914–1917)
1920 A.D.	Alfred N. Whitehead (1861–1947) George Santayana (1863–1952) Bertrand Russell (1872–1970) G. E. Moore (1873–1958) Martin Buber (1878–1965) Moritz Schlick (1882–1936) Sarvepalli Radhakrishnan (1888–1975) Ludwig Wittgenstein (1889–1951) Martin Heidegger (1889–1976) Rudolf Carnap (1891–1970) H. H. Price (1899–1984)	Great Depression (1929–1939) Godel (1906–1978) discovers incompleteness theorems (1931) Margaret Mead (1901–1978) publishes *Sex and Temperament in Three Primitive Societies* (1935) Keynes publishes *General Theory* (1936)